THE YEAR'S WORK
IN ENGLISH STUDIES—1974

The Year's Work in English Studies

VOLUME 55

1974

Edited by
JAMES REDMOND

and

LAUREL BRAKE
KATHERINE DUNCAN-JONES
ELIZABETH MASLEN
A. V. C. SCHMIDT
(associate editors)

Published for
THE ENGLISH ASSOCIATION
by
JOHN MURRAY ALBEMARLE STREET LONDON

Printed in Great Britain by Cox & Wyman Ltd
London, Fakenham and Reading
0 7195 3329 5

Preface

It may help the user of this work to remember that books are sometimes published a year later in the U.S.A. than they are in the U.K. (and vice versa), that the year of publication is not always that which appears on the title page of the book, and that the inevitable omissions of one year are made good in the next; thus the search for a notice of a book or article may have to extend to the volume after the expected one and sometimes to that which precedes it. Reports of important omissions will earn our gratitude.

Offprints of articles are always welcomed, and editors of journals that are not easily available in the U.K. are urged to join the many who already send us complete sets. These should be addressed to The Editor, *The Year's Work in English Studies*, The English Association, 1, Priory Gardens, Bedford Park, London W4 1TT. We are grateful to the authors and publishers who have made our task easier by supplying books and articles for volume 55. The editors of the *M.L.A. International Bibliography, Anglo-Saxon England, The Chaucer Review, English Language Notes, Philological Quarterly,* and *Restoration and Eighteenth Century Theatre Research* have put us deeply in their debt by providing advance proofs of their bibliographies. In drawing the reader's attention at the beginning of chapters to the main bibliographical aids, we presuppose in each case a reference to the *M.L.A. International Bibliography,* and to the *Annual Bibliography of English Language and Literature* published by the Modern Humanities Research Association.

James Redmond
Westfield College
London University

Abbreviations

ABC	*American Book Collector*
ABELL	*Annual Bibliography of English Language and Literature*
ABR	*American Benedictine Review*
AI	*American Imago*
AKML	*Abhandlungen zur Kunst-, Musik-, and Literaturwissenschaft*
AL	*American Literature*
ALASH	*Acta Linguistica Academiae Scientiarum Hungaricae*
AMon	*Atlantic Monthly*
AnL	*Anthropological Linguistics*
AnM	*Annuale Medievale*
AN&Q	*American Notes and Queries*
AQ	*American Quarterly*
AR	*Antioch Review*
Archiv	*Archiv für das Studium der Neueren Sprachen und Literaturen*
AreilE	*Ariel: A Review of International English Literature*
ArL	*Archivum Linguisticum*
ArlQ	*Arlington Quarterly*
ArP	*Aryan Path*
ArQ	*Arizona Quarterly*
A.R.S.	Augustan Reprint Society
AS	*American Speech*
ASsh	*American Scholar*
ASE	*Anglo-Saxon England*
ASoc	*Arts in Society*
AUMLA	*Journal of Australasian Univs. Language and Literature Ass.*
AUPG	American University Publishers Group Ltd.
AWR	*The Anglo-Welsh Review*
BA	*Books Abroad*
BAASB	*British Association for American Studies Bulletin*
BB	*Bulletin of Bibliography*
BBSIA	*Bulletin Bibliographique de la Société Internationale Arthurienne*
BC	*Book Collector*
BDEC	*Bulletin of the Department of English* (Calcutta)
BFLS	*Bulletin de la Faculté des Lettres de Strasbourg*
BHR	*Bibliothèque d'Humanisme et Renaissance*
BI	*Books at Iowa*
BJA	*British Journal of Aesthetics*
BJDC	*British Journal of Disorders of Communication*
BJRL	*Bulletin of the John Rylands Library*
BLR	*Bodleian Library Record*
B.M.	British Museum
BMQ	*British Museum Quarterly*

ABBREVIATIONS

BNL	*Blake Newsletter*
BNYPL	*Bulletin of the New York Public Library*
BP	*Banasthali Patrika*
BRMMLA	*Bulletin of the Rocky Mountain Modern Language Association*
BS	*Blake Studies*
BSE	*Brno Studies in English*
BSLP	*Bulletin de la Société de Linguistique de Paris*
BST	*Brontë Society Transactions*
BSUF	*Ball State University Forum*
BuR	*Bucknell Review*
Carrell	*The Carrell: Journal of the Friends of the Univ. of Miami Library*
C.B.E.L.	*Cambridge Bibliography of English Literature*
CE	*College English*
CEA	*CEA Critic*
CEAAN	*Center for Editions of American Authors Newsletter*
CentR	*The Centennial Review*
ChauR	*The Chaucer Review*
ChiR	*Chicago Review*
CHum	*Computers and the Humanities*
CJ	*Classical Journal*
CJL	*Canadian Journal of Linguistics*
CL	*Comparative Literature*
CLAJ	*College Language Association Journal*
CLC	*Columbia Library Columns*
ClioW	*Clio: An Interdisciplinary Journal*
CLJ	*Cornell Library Journal*
CLQ	*Colby Library Quarterly*
CLS	*Comparative Literature Studies*
ColF	*Columbia Forum*
CollG	*Colloquia Germanica*
ColQ	*Colorado Quarterly*
CompD	*Comparative Drama*
CompL	*Comparative Literature*
ConL	*Contemporary Literature*
ConnR	*Connecticut Review*
CP	*Concerning Poetry*
CQ	*The Cambridge Quarterly*
CR	*The Critical Review*
Crit	*Critique: Studies in Modern Fiction*
Critique	*Critique* (Paris)
CritQ	*Critical Quarterly*
CritS	*Critical Survey*
CSHVB	*Computer Studies in the Humanities and Verbal Behavior*
D.A.	*Dictionary of Americanisms*
D.A.E.	*Dictionary of American English*
DHLR	*The D. H. Lawrence Review*
DiS	*Dickens Studies*
DM	*The Dublin Magazine*
D.N.B.	*Dictionary of National Biography*
Down R	*Downside Review*

ABBREVIATIONS

DR	*Dalhousie Review*
DramS	*Drama Survey* (Minneapolis)
DSN	*Dickens Studies Newsletter*
DubR	*Dublin Review*
DUJ	*Durham University Journal*
DVLG	*Deutsche Vierteljahrsschrift fur Literaturwissenschaft und Geistesgeschichte*
EA	*Études Anglaises*
EAL	*Early American Literature*
E&S	*Essays and Studies*
ECS	*Eighteenth-Century Studies*
EDH	*Essays by Divers Hands*
E.E.T.S.	Early English Text Society
EHR	*English Historical Review*
EIC	*Essays in Criticism*
EJ	*English Journal*
ELangT	*English Language Teaching*
ELH	*Journal of English Literary History*
ELN	*English Language Notes*
ELR	*English Literary Renaissance*
ELT	*English Literature in Transition*
ELWIU	*Essays in Literature* (Western Illinois U.)
EM	*English Miscellany*
E.P.N.S.	English Place-Name Society
EPS	*English Philological Studies*
ES	*English Studies*
ESA	*English Studies in Africa*
ESQ	*Emerson Society Quarterly*
ESRS	*Emporia State Research Studies*
ETJ	*Educational Theatre Journal*
EWN	*Evelyn Waugh Newsletter*
Expl	*Explicator*
FDS	Fountainwell Drama Series
FH	*Frankfurter Hefte*
FLang	*Foundations of Language*
FMLS	*Forum of Modern Language Studies*
ForumH	*Forum* (Houston)
GaR	*Georgia Review*
GRM	*Germanisch-romanische Monatsschrift*
HAB	*Humanities Association Bulletin*
HC	*The Hollins Critic*
HJ	*Hibbert Journal*
HLB	*Harvard Library Bulletin*
HLQ	*Huntington Library Quarterly*
HSE	*Hungarian Studies in English*
HSL	*Hartford Studies in Literature*
HTR	*Harvard Theological Review*
HudR	*Hudson Review*
IJES	*Indian Journal of English Studies*
IndL	*Indian Literature*

ABBREVIATIONS

IowaR	Iowa Review
IRAL	International Review of Applied Linguistics
IShav	Independent Shavian
JA	Jahrbuch für Amerikastudien
JAAC	Journal of Aesthetics and Art Criticism
JAmS	Journal of American Studies
JBS	Journal of British Studies
JCSA	Journal of the Catch Society of America
JEGP	Journal of English and Germanic Philology
JGE	Journal of General Education
JHI	Journal of the History of Ideas
JJQ	James Joyce Quarterly
JL	Journal of Linguistics
JML	Journal of Modern Literature
JMRS	Journal of Medieval and Renaissance Studies
JNT	Journal of Narrative Technique
JVLVB	Journal of Verbal Learning and Verbal Behavior
JWCI	Journal of the Warburg and Courtauld Institutes
KanQ	Kansas Quarterly
KN	Kwartalnik Neofilologiczny (Warsaw)
KR	Kenyon Review
KSJ	Keats-Shelley Journal
KSMB	Keats-Shelley Memorial Bulletin
L&P	Literature and Psychology
L&S	Language and Speech
Lang&S	Language and Style
LanM	Les Langues Modernes
LaS	Louisiana Studies
LC	Library Chronicle
LCUT	Library Chronicle of the University of Texas
LeedsSE	Leeds Studies in English
LHR	Lock Haven Review
Lib	Library
LMag	London Magazine
LWU	Literatur in Wissenschaft und Unterricht
MÆ	Medium Ævum
M&H	Medievalia et Humanistica
M&L	Music and Letters
MarkhamR	Markham Review
MASJ	Midcontinent American Studies Journal
MD	Modern Drama
M.E.D.	Middle English Dictionary
MFS	Modern Fiction Studies
MHRev	Malahat Review
MichA	Michigan Academician
MiltonN	Milton Newsletter
MiltonQ	Milton Quarterly
MiltonS	Milton Studies
MinnR	Minnesota Review
MissQ	Mississippi Quarterly

ABBREVIATIONS

MLJ	*Modern Language Journal*
MLN	*Modern Language Notes*
MLQ	*Modern Language Quarterly*
MLR	*Modern Language Review*
ModA	*Modern Age*
ModSp	*Moderne Sprachen*
MP	*Modern Philology*
MQ	*Midwest Quarterly*
MQR	*Michigan Quarterly Review*
MR	*Massachusetts Review*
MS	*Mediaeval Studies*
MSE	*Massachusetts Studies in English*
MSpr	*Moderna Språk*
NA	*Nuova Antologia*
N&Q	*Notes and Queries*
NCF	*Nineteenth-Century Fiction*
NDQ	*North Dakota Quarterly*
NegroD	*Negro Digest*
NEQ	*New England Quarterly*
NL	*Nouvelles Littéraires*
NLB	*Newberry Library Bulletin*
NLH	*New Literary History*
NM	*Neuphilologische Mitteilungen*
NMQ	*New Mexico Quarterly*
NMS	*Nottingham Medieval Studies*
Novel	*Novel: A Forum on Fiction*
NRF	*Nouvelle Revue Française*
NS	*Die Neueren Sprachen*
NTM	*New Theatre Magazine*
NWR	*Northwest Review*
NYH	*New York History*
OB	*Ord och Bild*
O.E.D.	*Oxford English Dictionary*
OL	*Orbis Litterarum*
OR	*Oxford Review*
OUR	*Ohio University Review*
PAAS	*Proceedings of the American Antiquarian Society*
PAPS	*Proceedings of the American Philosophical Society*
PBA	*Proceedings of the British Academy*
PBSA	*Papers of the Bibliographical Society of America*
PLL	*Papers on Language and Literature*
PMLA	*[Publications of the Modern Language Association of America]*
PN	*Poe Newsletter*
PP	*Philologica Pragensia*
PQ	*Philological Quarterly*
PR	*Partisan Review*
P.R.O.	Public Record Office
PULC	*Princeton University Library Chronicle*
QJS	*Quarterly Journal of Speech*
QQ	*Queen's Quarterly*

ABBREVIATIONS

QR	*Quarterly Review*
RECTR	*Restoration and Eighteenth-Century Theatre Research*
RenD	*Renaissance Drama*
RenP	*Renaissance Papers*
RenQ	*Renaissance Quarterly*
RES	*Review of English Studies*
RHL	*Revue d'Histoire Littéraire de la France*
RLC	*Revue de Littérature Comparée*
RLMC	*Rivista di Letterature Moderne e Comparate*
RLV	*Revue des Langues Vivantes*
RMS	*Renaissance and Modern Studies*
RN	*Renaissance News*
RORD	*Research Opportunities in Renaissance Drama*
RQ	*Riverside Quarterly*
RRDS	Regents Renaissance Drama Series
RRestDS	Regents Restoration Drama Series
RS	*Research Studies*
R.S.L.	Royal Society of Literature
RUO	*Revue de l'Université d'Ottawa*
SAB	*South Atlantic Bulletin*
SAQ	*South Atlantic Quarterly*
SatR	*Saturday Review*
SB	*Studies in Bibliography*
SBHT	*Studies in Burke and His Time*
SBL	*Studies in Black Literature*
SCN	*Seventeenth-Century News*
SCR	*South Carolina Review*
SDR	*South Dakota Review*
SEL	*Studies in English Literature 1500–1900* (Rice University)
SELit	*Studies in English Literature* (Japan)
SF&R	Scholars' Facsimiles and Reprints
SFQ	*Southern Folklore Quarterly*
SH	*Studia Hibernica (Dublin)*
ShakS	*Shakespeare Studies* (Cincinnati)
ShawR	*Shaw Review*
ShN	*Shakespeare Newsletter*
SHR	*Southern Humanities Review*
ShS	*Shakespeare Survey*
ShStud	*Shakespeare Studies* (Tokyo)
SIR	*Studies in Romanticism*
SJH	*Shakespeare-Jahrbuch* (Heidelberg)
SJW	*Shakespeare-Jahrbuch* (Weimar)
SL	*Studia Linguistica*
SLitI	*Studies in the Literary Imagination*
SLJ	*Southern Literary Journal*
SM	*Speech Monographs*
SMC	*Studies in Medieval Culture*
SN	*Studia Neophilologica*
SNL	*Satire Newsletter*
SNNTS	*Studies in the Novel* (North Texas State Univ.)

ABBREVIATIONS

SoQ	*The Southern Quarterly*
SoR	*Southern Review* (Louisiana)
SoRA	*Southern Review* (Adelaide)
SP	*Studies in Philology*
SQ	*Shakespeare Quarterly*
SR	*Sewanee Review*
SRen	*Studies in the Renaissance*
SRO	*Shakespearean Research Opportunities*
SSF	*Studies in Short Fiction*
SSL	*Studies in Scottish Literature*
SSMP	*Stockholm Studies in Modern Philology*
S.T.C.	*Short Title Catalogue*
SWR	*Southwest Review*
TC	*The Twentieth Century*
TCBS	*Transactions of the Cambridge Bibliographical Society*
TCL	*Twentieth Century Literature*
TDR	*The Drama Review*
TEAS	Twayne's English Authors Series
ThQ	*Theatre Quarterly*
ThR	*Theatre Research*
ThS	*Theatre Survey*
THY	*The Thomas Hardy Yearbook*
TkR	*Tamkang Review*
TLS	*Times Literary Supplement*
TN	*Theatre Notebook*
TP	*Terzo Programma*
TPS	*Transactions of the Philological Society*
TQ	*Texas Quarterly*
TriQ	*Tri-Quarterly*
TSE	*Tulane Studies in English*
TSL	*Tennessee Studies in Literature*
TSLL	*Texas Studies in Literature and Language*
TUSAS	Twayne's United States Authors Series
TWC	*The Wordsworth Circle*
TYDS	*Transactions of the Yorkshire Dialect Society*
UCTSE	*University of Cape Town Studies in English*
UDQ	*University of Denver Quarterly*
UES	*Unisa English Studies*
UMSE	*University of Mississippi Studies in English*
UR	*University Review* (Kansas City)
URev	*University Review* (Dublin)
UTQ	*University of Toronto Quarterly*
UWR	*University of Windsor Review*
VN	*Victorian Newsletter*
VP	*Victorian Poetry*
VPN	*Victorian Periodicals Newsletter*
VQR	*Virginia Quarterly Review*
VS	*Victorian Studies*
WAL	*Western American Literature*
WascanaR	*Wascana Review*

ABBREVIATIONS

WCR	*West Coast Review*
WF	*Western Folklore*
WHR	*Western Humanities Review*
WSCL	*Wisconsin Studies in Contemporary Literature*
WTW	Writers and their Work
WVUPP	*West Virginia University Bulletin: Philological Papers*
WWR	*Walt Whitman Review*
XUS	*Xavier University Studies*
YES	*Yearbook of English Studies*
YR	*Yale Review*
YULG	*Yale University Library Gazette*
YW	*The Year's Work in English Studies*
ZAA	*Zeitstchrift fár Anglistik und Amerikanistik*
ZDL	*Zeitschrift für Dialektologie und Linguistik*

Contents

CONTENTS

Note: Notices of books published in German, identified by the initials H.C.C., have been contributed by H. C. CASTEIN Dr.phil. Lecturer in Modern Languages in the University of London (Goldsmiths' College)

I

Literary History and Criticism: General Works

T.S. DORSCH

1. REFERENCE WORKS

With the publication of Volume 1, covering the period 600–1660, *The New Cambridge Bibliography of English Literature*[1] has been brought to completion, save that a fifth volume containing a detailed index is still in preparation. Since it takes in a span of more than a thousand years, the present instalment is necessarily a very substantial volume, consisting of some 2,500 closely-packed columns— not so closely packed, however, as not to be easily readable; more than fifty contributors have been responsible for its compilation. Some notion of its scope can be gained from the fact that about 190 columns are devoted to bibliographical and linguistic studies; seventy to Chaucer; about sixty to Milton; eighteen to Spenser; and 'minor' authors are treated with equal thoroughness. Shakespeare, who has perforce had to be treated in a much more rigorously selective fashion than any other English writer, receives more than 160 columns. The way in which subsidiary or background studies are covered is also very impressive—those, for example, which deal with such topics as religion, education, and manuscripts, book production and distribution in the several centuries that are represented. *New CBEL* is, after *OED*, the most valuable reference work for the student of English language and literature. Its editor, George Watson, and his many coadjutors, especially I. R. Willison, who was in charge of Volume 4 (1900–1950), are to be warmly congratulated on the care, thoroughness, and accuracy with which they have carried through a singularly exacting task. This, with perhaps a couple of supplements to bring it up to date in the 1980s and 1990s, will remain the authoritative bibliography of English literature until the end of the century.

The Oxford Companion to Canadian History and Literature, compiled by Norah Story, was published in 1967. Since that time there has been very considerable literary activity in Canada, and it has already become necessary to produce a sizeable *Supplement*[2] to the *Companion*. Three dozen scholars, under the general editorship of William Toye, have combined to bring together the several hundred entries that make up this volume. Canadian literature in French was inadequately covered in the original *Companion*; here it is given detailed attention for the first time in English. Another innovation is the inclusion of articles on children's literature, political writings, and translations; and some entries from the previous

---

1. *The New Cambridge Bibliography of English Literature: Volume 1, 600–1660*, ed. by George Watson. C.U.P. pp. xxxii+2476 columns+pp. 15 Index. £18·00. $49.50.

[2] *Supplement to the Oxford Companion to Canadian History and Literature*, ed. by William Toye. Toronto: O.U.P. pp. v+318. £5.50.

work have been reprinted with revisions that bring them up to date. Canadian readers in particular, but not they alone, will welcome the appearance of this useful *Supplement*.

Harry Blamires's *Short History of English Literature*[3] will not be of much interest to the serious student. It seldom rises above the level of narration or description. The eight pages on Chaucer tell the stories of the early poems and of a few of the *Canterbury Tales*; the criticism is negligible both in quantity and in quality, and Blamires seems all but entirely unaware that Chaucer is one of our great masters of irony. The twenty pages on Shakespeare do very little more than summarise the plots of the plays. *Paradise Lost* receives rather better treatment, but Blamires rapidly dismisses as 'remarkably superfluous' that great and glorious poem *Paradise Regained*. As a chronological account of our literature from Chaucer to Ted Hughes this volume may fitly be given a place in school libraries; it will not serve the requirements of undergraduates.

This is perhaps the point at which to mention a work entitled *Western Civilization: Recent Interpretations*,[4] which has been received. This book, the first of two projected volumes, covers the history of western man from the beginnings to 1715, arranging its material under three main headings—'The Ancient World', 'The Middle Ages', and 'Early Modern Europe'. It consists of extracts, from ten to twenty-five pages in length, from books by historians, archaeologists, and scientists, and its aim is to show how the world as we know it has

developed. Thus in the first section, to give a few examples, there are chapters from *Digging up Jericho*, by Kathleen M. Kenyon, from *The Greek Experience*, by C. M. Bowra, and from *The Problem of the Historical Jesus*, by Joachim Jeremias. The second section draws on the work of such authors as Joseph R. Strayer, R. W. Southern, and David Knowles. The third and longest section, which brings us down to post-Newtonian Europe, contains eighteen passages by, among others, Garrett Mattingly, Elizabeth L. Eisenstein (on the impact of printing), J. H. Hexter, and E. J. Hobsbawm. Clearly this can be no more than a scrappy outline history, unlikely to be used as a text book in England, although it is designed to be so used in America. Its value will depend on the degree to which it encourages its readers to seek fuller knowledge of the topics on which it touches.

2. COLLECTIONS OF ESSAYS

Essays and Studies 1974,[5] collected by Kenneth Muir, contains as usual an interesting assortment of papers. In 'Past, Present and Pinter' Nigel Alexander argues that, although Pinter's characters are 'cabinned (*sic*), cribbed, and conditioned by the past, they are never totally crushed by it. Their belief, despite all the evidence, that they can still win at the odds shows a heroic folly which may be indistinguishable from fortitude.' Philip Edwards suggests possible reasons why John Ford in *Perkin Warbeck* and Philip Massinger in *Believe As You List* should each, about the year 1630, have written a play dealing very sympathetically with a pretender to a throne who is in

[3] *A Short History of English Literature*, by Harry Blamires. Methuen. pp. viii + 536. Hardback, £2.50. Paperback, 90p.

[4] *Western Civilization: Recent Interpretations*. Vol. 1, *From Earliest Times to 1715*, ed. by Charles D. Hamilton. New York: Crowell. pp. viii + 599. Paperback.

[5] *Essays and Studies 1974*. N. S. Vol. 27, collected for the English Association by Kenneth Muir. John Murray. pp. v + 113. £1.75.

the end defeated; with copious evidence, he concludes that both plays are 'exploring the meaning of the terms "counterfeit" and "natural" in the period of perturbed and perplexed relationships between monarch and people' at this time. D. W. Jefferson analyses the complex twofold structure of *Bleak House*, and decides that in its artistry 'Dickens's achievement in *Bleak House* is surely one of the most impressive and original in the whole of narrative art'. Writing on 'Douglas and Surrey: Translators of Virgil', Priscilla Bawcutt develops the thesis that, whereas Surrey 'rivals Virgil in terseness and sometimes in elegance of phrasing, but only rarely matches the richness and suggestiveness of his language', Douglas, though he lacks Virgil's economy and can be pedantic and over-explicit, 'is far more responsive than Surrey to Virgil's linguistic subtlety ... and mysterious latencies of feeling'. Although Yeats's Crazy Jane poems and his 'Byzantium' are 'diverse, sheer opposites', Nicholas Brooke finds a relationship between them in that in both 'there is a trafficking between body and soul ... They are worlds apart; yet they are both worlds that every body and soul inhabits; and they should be celebrated.' In 'The Poem in Transmitted Text—Editor and Critic', J. E. Cross analyses passages from Old English manuscripts in order to demonstrate that 'the good critic of Old English poetry has always to concern himself with good editorial opinion and practice, and has to equip himself to test that opinion, just as he incessantly tests the opinions of lexicographers against the examples of the words used when placed back in their original contexts and may offer suggestions to them.' In the final paper, entitled 'The Essential Conrad', Norman Sherry shows that Conrad's rejection of

accepted chronological order and conventional form is quite deliberate, and helps him 'to produce "a bit of psychological document" that gives the vision of a personality by presenting faithfully the feelings and sensations connected with an event'.

Essays by Divers Hands[6] is this year edited by John Guest. The volume opens with a paper by Sir Harold Acton, 'Max Beerbohm: A Dandy among English Classics', which admirably recalls both Max's mischievous sense of fun and the lively fastidious mind which underlay all that he wrote—'The deceptively casual caricaturist becomes a Persian miniaturist in prose.' Ronald Blythe considers, in 'The Dangerous Idyll: Sweet Auburn to Akenfield', the success, or unsuccess, of a number of writers upon rural subjects, from John Clare to Richard Jefferies and Sir Henry Rider Haggard, and traces the development over the last century and a half of the whole attitude of writers to the rural in literature. Brian Fothergill's 'William Beckford, Prince of Amateurs' is an interesting, and probably still necessary, corrective to the traditional view of Beckford as a man of a scandalous, or at least dubious, way of life, justly ostracized by his contemporaries. He was in fact rather austere in temper and habits; 'in the seclusion forced on him by his social isolation and the peculiarities of his temperament, his life was devoted in its serious moments to study, collecting pictures, and the assembling of a large and important library.' Nor must we forget the writings by which he so greatly enriched the literature of his century. In 'Damn and "Blast"'! The

[6] *Essays by Divers Hands: Being the Transactions of the Royal Society of Literature.* N.S. Vol. xxxviii. Ed. by John Guest. O.U.P. pp. viii+158. £3.

Friendship of Wyndham Lewis and Augustus John', Michael Holroyd shows how the two artists 'stimulated and exasperated each other in about equal measure'. 'In retrospect, the course of their friendship seems like an endless sparring match conducted in private so as to train them for real encounters against "the enemy". For it was a common enemy they fought, and they go down fighting on the same side.' H. Montgomery Hyde provides some delightful anecdotes of 'Henry James at Home', the home being Lamb House, near Rye, where James lived in great contentment for some years, and where Hyde himself, a kinsman of James's, also later lived. William Plomer illustrates ways in which Francis Kilvert's *Diary*, 'factual, and apparently perfectly truthful, and full of well observed detail, ... gives ... an invaluable picture of day-to-day existence' in late Victorian times. 'His *Diary* gives more than a picture; it creates an atmosphere, and evokes what would now be called a life-style.' Dilys Powell displays her unsurpassed knowledge of films in discussing the kinds of plays, novels, and short stories which have shown themselves to be particularly suitable for adaptation to the techniques of the cinema. In 'Flaubert and the Art of the Short Story', A. W. Raitt demonstrates his belief that Flaubert stands supreme among those who have attained equal mastery of the genres both of the novel and of the short story. 'The *Trois Contes*, by their complexity, their density, the subtlety and power of their themes, the sense they convey of a depth and breadth of life extending far beyond their apparently restricted confines, stand alone among French and even among world short stories.' Giles St. Aubyn's very entertaining paper, 'Queen Victoria as an Author', provides some surprising information about the extent of Queen Victoria's authorship, whether in her remarkably voluminous correspondence or in her published journals, and some persuasive judgements about the quality of her writing. Finally, Constance Babington Smith, taking as her subject 'Rose Macaulay in Her Writings', reminds us that Rose Macaulay was an accomplished poet, and indeed 'wished she could be remembered as a poet'; however, whether in verse or in prose, 'in and through Rose's writings we can find the writer, the born writer, but beyond this we can find the person, the paradoxical, contradictory person, justly renowned for her clear-thinking and gaiety and humour, but also possessed of a melancholy side, an emotional melancholy side'.

Readers who are familiar with Ernst Robert Curtius's *European Literature and the Latin Middle Ages* will be glad to know that his *Essays on European Literature* are now available in an English translation.[7] These essays display a very broad range of reading and a very capacious understanding of literary tones and techniques. Curtius progresses from Virgil to the young American novelist of the 1950s, William Goyen, taking in on the way a number of German, French, Spanish, American, and English writers. Readers of *YW* will perhaps find themselves particularly interested in the essays on Emerson, Joyce, and T. S. Eliot. Curtius regarded Emerson as 'one of the most valuable legacies of the nineteenth century after the death of Goethe', and in a lively paper on Emerson's *Essays* he sets out to justify this belief. A long essay on Joyce, written in 1929, shows a remarkably close understanding of Joyce's linguistic

---

[7] *Essays on European Literature*, by E. R. Curtius. Translated by Michael Kowal. Princeton U.P. pp. xxix+508. $20. £9.60.

subtleties; Curtius sees a clear progression, in thought as well as style, from *Portrait of the Artist*, through *Dubliners* and *Exiles*, to *Ulysses*; 'it is the way from lyric to epic and dramatic expression.' Two essays on T. S. Eliot, dated 1927 and 1949, are similarly perceptive—it is worth recalling that Curtius was the first translator of *The Waste Land* into German. He disapproves of some of Eliot's critical judgements—as which of us does not?—but recognises that 'he is the discoverer of a new tone which can never be forgotten. He has heard the mermaids singing.' Other writers treated in this volume include Goethe, Schlegel, Hermann Hesse, Balzac, Cocteau, Charles Du Bos, Ortega y Gasset, Ramón Pérez de Ayala, and Jorge Guillén.

In *New Directions in Literary History*[8] Ralph Cohen has brought together a number of essays from the journal *New Literary History*, which he edits. This volume is 'the first comprehensive attempt to present the approaches to literary study that have developed from phenomenology, from stylistics and linguistics, from Marxist reconsiderations of literature, from inter-disciplinary studies, and from analyses of audience response'. It is not possible in a short notice to do justice to the essays individually; since they aim at enunciating unfamiliar critical theories, some of them are necessarily presented in somewhat abstract, even abstruse, terms. Wolfgang Iser writes interestingly on the imaginative processes involved in appreciation of a work of literature. The work must 'engage the reader's imagination in the task of working things out for himself, for reading is only a pleasure when it is active and creative'. Alastair Fowler, in 'The

Life and Death of Literary Forms', demonstrates, with copious illustration, ways in which particular genres have had their little day and died, or have been modified in such ways as to generate new genres. Robert Weimann develops further some of the views that he put forward in *New Criticism und die Entwicklung bürgerlicher Literaturwissenschaft* (1962). Michael Riffaterre examines areas of literary history in which the analysis of style is particularly helpful and significant. Other contributors to the volume include Barbara Herrnstein Smith, Hans Robert Jauss, George Garrett, and Svetlana and Paul Alpers.

Synthesis[9] contains the papers delivered at an international conference on comparative literature held in Bucharest in September 1974. Ion Zamfirescu considers the idea of comparative literature in the context of modern Romanian literature. David H. Malone's subject is 'Comparative Literature and Interdisciplinary Research'. Vera Călin provides 'A Stylistic Approach to Comparative Literature'. Mihai Novicor brings out some relationships between the comparative approach to literature and what has come to be known as the sociology of literature. A number of other aspects of comparative literature are treated in other papers. Further papers are grouped under the heading 'Lumières et Romantisme: Continuité ou Discontinuité'. Of special interest here are the contributions of Romul Monteanu on 'L'idée de génie a l'époque des Lumières et du Sturm und Drang'; Alexandru Balaci on 'Traits caractéristiques du romantisme Italien'; Eric

---

[8] *New Directions in Literary History*, ed. by Ralph Cohen. Routledge & Kegan Paul. pp. viii+263. £4.50.

[9] *Synthesis: Bulletin du Comité National de Littérature Comparée de la République Socialiste de Roumanie*, ed. by Zoe Dumitrescu–Busulenga, with assistant editors. Bucharest: Editura Academiei Republicu Socialiste România. pp. 222.

D. Tappe on 'Victorian Glimpses of Romanian Literature'; and Amita Bhose on 'The Sakuntala Epoch in European Romanticism and Indian Classicism'.

S. S. Prawer's *Comparative Literary Studies*[10] draws together the theoretical bases that underlie the papers in the work just noticed. Prawer's book 'tries to set a descriptive typology of comparative literary study which shows its significant work on the detail as well as the overall contours of the literary map'. Prawer describes, with much illustration, the different kinds of investigation carried out by scholars and critics who have found common factors in works written in various languages. He is peculiarly well fitted for his task, since he is very widely read not only in English and American, but also in a number of Continental literatures. He exemplifies the kinds of influence which different cultures may exert upon one another by means of analogy, translation, and adaptation; the metamorphoses and recurrence of themes, conventions, and literary devices of various kinds; the uses of myth; and the concepts of genre and period. While recognising that there are types of comparative studies which have little value, Prawer demonstrates how, sensibly and sympathetically applied, they are capable of 'opening up, for our emotional and intellectual enrichment, a vast storehouse of imaginative experience'.

3. FORMS AND GENRES

The only work this year specifically devoted to drama is James L. Smith's short study of melodrama[11] in the Critical Idiom series—short, but closely-packed. Melodrama came into its own as a distinctive dramatic kind in the nineteenth century, but as Smith's references to between 300 and 400 plays indicate, it has been an element in drama at all times, in Greek and Elizabethan tragedy as well as in the shockers that chilled the blood and thrilled the senses of our Victorian greatgrandfathers. Much the commonest type of recent melodrama is that which shows persecuted virtue triumphing over fiendish adversities and villainies, and Smith devotes much of his study to the century and three-quarters from Matthew Lewis's *Adelmorn the Outlaw* of 1801 down to such current television series as *Dixon of Dock Green* and *Dr. Who*. Some of the best Victorian melodramas are readily available, and readers of Smith's book will no doubt feel encouraged to seek them out.

Books on poetry are also thinner on the ground than usual, but two call for special attention, although they are not specifically devoted to English poetry. M. S. Silk's *Interaction in Poetic Imagery*[12] requires a knowledge of Greek for full understanding, since Silk draws his illustrations largely from the work of early Greek poetry, providing, however, some parallels from English poetry. Confining his treatment of imagery to metaphor, simile, and the various forms of *comparatio*—'the tropes and schemes, that is, based on analogy or similarity'—he formulates the concept of 'interaction' to bring out the different effects that may be gained by the use of imagery: amplifying, explaining, or supporting the meaning of a passage, adding aural suggestion, linking ideas, anticipating themes or

[10] *Comparative Literary Studies: An Introduction*, by S. S. Prawer. Duckworth. pp. xi + 180. £3.25.

[11] *Melodrama*, by James L. Smith. (The Critical Idiom.) Methuen. pp. 96. Hardback, £1.45. Paperback, 55p.

[12] *Interaction in Poetic Imagery: With Special Reference to Early Greek Poetry*, by M.S. Silk. C.U.P. pp. xiv + 263. £7. $21.

recalling them in retrospect. Silk's book cannot be adequately treated in a short notice; it is an important contribution to literary theory.

Many English poets have written Latin poetry, some of them a great deal of it. In an interesting volume entitled *The Latin Poetry of English Poets*[13], J. W. Binns has brought together careful studies of the Latin verse of six such poets. He himself writes on Thomas Campion; W. Hilton Kelliher on George Herbert; R. W. Condee, who is particularly impressive, on John Milton; Kenneth J. Larsen on Richard Crashaw's *Epigrammata Sacra*; Mark Storey on Vincent Bourne; and Andrea Kelly on Landor. Readers whose Latin is shaky will find it helpful that all the Latin quotations are accompanied by English translations; some will perhaps be surprised both by the quantity and by the high quality of the poetry that forms the subject of this book.

The most ambitious book on fiction this year is Harold Toliver's *Animate Illusions*.[14] With plenty of concrete illustration and analysis, Toliver 'seeks to locate the boundaries of fiction and define its art'. This involves a thoroughgoing study of many types of narrative form, from the simplicity and brevity of the parable to the various complexities of the novel and the epic, and Toliver explores also distinctions between fictional narration and historical narration. The book covers a great deal of ground and is not always easy to read; but it repays study, and is a useful contribution to literary theory.

Like Toliver, Joan Rockwell, in her *Fact in Fiction*,[15] questions how far we are likely to find realism in the novel. 'It is human relationships which count in the novel, and this distorts the concept of *work*—to take only one major human activity—almost out of existence.' Even the consciously 'proletarian' novelists who try to bring in work as subject-matter fail to do so. Miss Rockwell's main thesis in this book is 'that literature does not "reflect" or "arise from" society, but is as much a functioning part of it as any social structure, institution, or set of norms'. She develops this thesis by exploring the literary handling of Negro slavery in America, the traces of matriarchy which are part of the substance of Greek tragedy, and the shifting values of spies in English fiction. This is a stimulating book, and well written—by a sociologist who dislikes the jargon of her associates. 'I hope I have succeeded in writing in clear language,' she says. 'I have tried to avoid the cement-like opacity of regular sociologese, assuming that the eyes of other readers bounce off the page with boredom as mine do.'

In a lively book entitled *The Adventurer*,[16] Paul Zweig demonstrates how an instinctive need for adventure is in most of us to a large degree satisfied by reading about it. He gives an account of a number of works in which interest is focused upon an adventurer, who is not always the same thing as a hero. Early examples are the Homeric epics, in which Odysseus and Achilles represent in their different ways types

[13] *The Latin Poetry of English Poets*, ed. by J. W. Binns. Routledge & Kegan Paul. pp. x+198. £4.95.
[14] *Animate Illusions: Explorations of Narrative Structure*, by Harold Toliver. Nebraska U.P. pp. ix+412. $10.

[15] *Fact in Fiction: The Use of Literature in the Systematic Study of Society*, by Joan Rockwell. Routledge & Kegan Paul. pp. x+211. £3.95.
[16] *The Adventurer*, by Paul Zweig. Dent. pp. x+275. £4.50.

of the adventurer as he was conceived in the ancient world, as does Gilgamesh in the epic that bears his name. *Robinson Crusoe* might seem an obvious later example, for it is a book in which adventurous episodes abound. 'Yet *Robinson Crusoe* undermines the ethos of adventure,' for Crusoe, as Zweig sees him, is essentially 'the unadventurous hero'. Other works treated include *The History of My Life*, by Giacomo Casanova, 'the frivolous adventurer'; *The Castle of Otranto*, by Horace Walpole, together with *The Monk*, by Matthew Lewis; *The Heart of Darkness*, by Joseph Conrad; *The Narrative of Arthur Gordon Pym*, by Edgar Allan Poe; *The Seven Pillars of Wisdom*, by T. E. Lawrence; and *La Voie Royale*, by André Malraux.

Some sections of Robert A. Fothergill's *Private Chronicles*[17] are noticed elsewhere, and all that need be done here is to give a general account of the book, the sub-title of which is 'A Study of English Diaries'. Fothergill's chief aims are 'to integrate a thematic approach to the genre as a whole', to introduce the more prominent diarists by placing them in their historical settings, and to provide sustained critical discussion of at least some of them. Inevitably Pepys, Boswell, and Kilvert figure large. Other diarists who are given prominent treatment are Scott, Byron, Alice James, and Katherine Mansfield, each chosen for special qualities of style, tone, or 'self-projection' displayed by their several diaries; Benjamin Robert Haydon, Ivy Jacquier, Anaïs Nin, and W.N.P. Barbellion, as good examples of diarists whose conception and practice suggest that they are seeing their work as a form of autobiography as

much as of personal journal; and Dudley Ryder and William Windham. Many dozens of others are dealt with more briefly. It is possible to see why, within Fothergill's scheme, Evelyn receives no more than passing mention; less easy to see why Queen Victoria should be dismissed among those who lack 'the autobiographical energy and individual accent that would make them remarkable'; and Dorothy Wordsworth is also neglected, if not totally ignored, perhaps for the same reason. Still, Fothergill shows himself to be, on the whole, a judicious critic, and his book is a very worthwhile contribution to literary scholarship.

The ever-increasing interest in African writing has in recent years found expression in a number of conferences. The papers delivered at one such conference, held at Dalhousie University and Mount Saint Vincent University in 1973, are published in a special issue of the *Dalhousie Review*.[18] In 'The Limitations of Universal Critical Criteria' D. Ibe Nwoga puts the case for 'an Aesthetics of African Literature'. Now that there is a comparatively extensive body of African literature, it has become clear that fusion of the two cultures that it embodies, European and African, calls for new critical approaches. Chinua Achebe's contribution is a characteristically lively plea for individualism in the African novel; he does not want to be told that before he writes about any problem, he 'must first ensure that they have it too in New York and London and Paris'. Noting the dominance of water imagery in African poetry, Gerald Moore pays special attention to 'Oceanic and River Imagery in Two Francophone

---

[17] *Private Chronicles: A Study of English Diaries*, by Robert A. Fothergill. O.U.P. pp. x + 214. £4.50.

[18] *Dalhousie Review*, Winter 1973–4. Dalhousie University, Halifax, Canada. pp. 605–798. $2.

Poets: Tchicaya U Tam'si and J. B. Tati-Loutard'. Nadine Gordimer recalls that in the 1950s and early 1960s prose writing by black South Africans was some of the best on the continent; most of these writers are in exile and their works are banned. No fiction of real quality has, since their disappearance, been written by black writers living in South Africa. However, there are many 'people of some talent attempting to use certain conventions and unconventions associated with poetry in order to express their feelings'. Miss Gordimer quotes verse by a number of these poets (and would-be poets), singling out James Matthews as one who, though 'not a poet', at times achieves success in the medium to which he has in effect been driven by circumstances. Kofi Awoonor discusses 'Tradition and Continuity in African Literature', paying special regard to novels by Wole Soyinka and Chinua Achebe. G. D. Killam suggests that more attention should be paid in Canadian universities to the literature of Africa and of a number of other countries whose literature has much in common with that of England and North America. Gerald Moore's paper is concerned with 'The Language of Literature in East Africa'; he wonders whether a distinctive East African English idiom will be developed. Daniel P. Kunene contributes 'Towards an Aesthetic of Sesotho Prose'. Sesotho is a Bantu language spoken in Lesotho and its environs by more than three million people, and it is interesting to speculate on its literary development. Emile Snyder writes on the work, mainly the poetry, of Aimé Césaire. Finally, Claude Wauthier offers some thoughts on 'The Situation of the African Writer in Post-Colonial Africa'.

From G.–C. M. Mutiso comes a more highly specialised study, *Socio-Political Thought in African Literature: Weusi.*[19] The word *weusi* means blackness. 'Many in Africa,' says Mutiso, 'have yearned for a black ideal as the antithesis to colonial bondage', and he sets out to document 'the writers' view of *weusi* and the factors which deny it. Mutiso provides an interesting survey of African literature from the end of the second world war to 1967, showing how the writers represent a number of social types, themes, and issues in their works. He thinks it essential that the system of dominance by politics and politicians should be ended in Africa; then the future will 'present a clearer role for the literati, as distinct from the politician', and there will be hope that 'our weusi' will find its true expression.

4. BIBLIOGRAPHICAL STUDIES

The 1974 issue of *Studies in Bibliography*[20] contains, like its predecessors, a number of interesting articles on bibliographical topics. The volume opens with a long paper from Hans Walter Gabler, 'Towards a Critical Text of James Joyce's *A Portrait of the Artist As a Young Man*'. The composition of this work was extended over ten years, from 1904 to 1914, and Joyce made alterations after it had appeared in print. Gabler believes, nevertheless, that 'with our present knowledge of the publishing history and the nature of the textual transmission of the novel, a critical edition, and maybe even a definitive text, . . . is not impossible to attain'. In 'Bibliography and Science'

[19] *Socio-Political Thought in African Literature: Weusi*, by G.–C.M.Mutiso. Macmillan. pp. xiv+182. £4.95.
[20] *Studies in Bibliography*, vol. 27, ed. by Fredson Bowers. Associate editor, L. A. Beaurline. Charlottesville: Virginia U.P. for the Bibliographical Society of the University of Virginia. pp. iv+325. $15.

Thomas Tanselle tries to strike a balance between the views of those who argue that bibliography has now achieved the standing of a science and those who refuse to accept such claims. S. W. Reid notes ways in which the need to justify his lines might affect the spelling of Jaggard's Compositor B. Fredson Bowers contributes *'Beggars Bush: A Reconstructed Prompt-Book and Its Copy'*. Robert K. Turner, Jr., is also interested in bibliographical problems relating to the publication of the plays of Beaumont and Fletcher. He provides a careful study of 'The Printers and the Beaumont and Fletcher Folio of 1647: Section 1 (Thomas Warren's)'. E. F. Shields has collated the first English and the first American editions of Virginia Woolf's *Mrs. Dalloway*. The American was set from corrected, but not finally corrected, proofs of the English edition, and there are some variant readings. Both versions, Shields suggests, 'can legitimately claim to be authoritative first editions'. In 'Press-Variants and Proofreading in the First Quarto of *Othello* (1622)' Millard T. Jones lists the variants revealed by collation of the nineteen copies of Q1 *Othello*. Wayne Franklin brings forward evidence which supports the attribution to John Norton, the printer, of *An Answer to a Late Scurrilous and Scandalous Pamphlet* (London, 1642). Harold F. Brooks supplies a careful study of 'The Chief Substantive Editions of Oldham's Poems, 1679–1684: Printer, Compositors, and Publication'. Nancy and Melvin Palmer describe and tabulate the contents of 'English Editions of *Contes de Fées* Attributed to Mme. D'Aulroy'. From correspondence which passed between John Gilbert Cooper and Robert Dodsley, James E. Tierney is able to establish Cooper's authorship of at least

twenty essays in Dodsley's fortnightly *The Museum; or, Literary and Historical Register*, to which Walpole, Garrick, and Johnson were the most distinguished contributors. A. B. England finds himself able to add half a dozen poems to the 'Register of Burlesque Poems' at the end of Richmond P. Bond's *English Burlesque Poetry 1700–1750*—these in addition to those added by A. J. Sambrook in 1970. Anne Lancashire shows that there is not, as has been suggested, any relationship between Edmond Malone's list of thirty-four 'ancient plays', whose titles alone had been preserved, and the list written by John Warburton (1682–1759), Somerset Herald, of MS plays supposedly once in his possession. Very surprisingly, a fairly large number of Thomas Carlyle's books are still to be found at his homes in Chelsea and Ecclefechan. These are listed in an article by Rodger L. Tarr, who notes that the large number of non-English books reflects Carlyle's continued interest in foreign, especially German, literature. Oliver Steele prints the preliminary notes for Ellen Glasgow's novel *Virginia* which have been preserved at the University of Virginia. As an interesting 'case study in post-production censorship', Elizabeth A. Swain draws attention to the fact that an entire sixteen-page section of Owen Wister's *Roosevelt: The Story of a Friendship* was withdrawn after the production of the book had been completed, and replaced with new material in order to get rid of a potentially libellous passage. Finally, Gillian G. M. Kyles provides a note on some jottings by Stephen Crane which may be related to an unfinished early war story. The volume closes with 'A Selective Check List of Bibliographical Scholarship for 1972' compiled by Derek A. Clarke and Howell J. Heaney.

Readings in Descriptive Bibliography[21] is a collection of papers edited by John Bush Jones. In his preface Jones observes that Fredson Bowers's *Principles of Bibliographical Description*, published a quarter of a century ago, 'has never been supplanted or even significantly amended in those areas of study and methodology which are ... its primary concern'. However, there are certain topics, fields, and periods of book production for which Bowers found little or no room in his book, and Jones's purpose in the present collection is to amplify or supplement what Bowers provided. All the papers he has brought together have been published since 1953 and many of them have been noticed in previous issues of *YW*; it seems best therefore merely to list them, naming the journals in which they may be found. They are as follows: 'Purposes of Descriptive Bibliography, with Some Remarks on Methods', by Fredson Bowers (*Library*, 1953); 'Tolerances in Bibliographical Description', by G. Thomas Tanselle (*Library*, 1968); 'The Fundamentals of Music Bibliography', by Cecil Hopkinson (*Jnl. of Documentation*, 1955); 'The Bibliographical Description of Paper', by G. Thomas Tanselle (*SB*, 1971); 'Chainlines Versus Imposition in Incunabula', by Curt F. Bühler (*SB*, 1970); 'Paper as Bibliographical Evidence', by Allan Stevenson (*Library*, 1962); 'The First Edition of Ficino's *De Christiana Religione*: A Problem in Bibliographical Description', by Curt F. Bühler (*SB*, 1965); 'On the Diagnosis of Half-Sheet Impositions', by Kenneth Povey (*Library*, 1956); 'On Printing "At one Pull" and Distinguishing Impressions by Point Holes', by

David F. Foxon (*Library*, 1956); 'Bibliography and the Editorial Problem in the Eighteenth Century,' by William B. Todd (*SB*, 1951); 'The Recording of Press Figures', by G. Thomas Tanselle (*Library*, 1966); 'On the Imposition of the First Edition of Hawthorne's *The Scarlet Letter*', by Oliver L. Steele (*Library*, 1962); 'A Mirror for Bibliographers: Duplicate Plates in Modern Printing', by Matthew J. Bruccoli (*PBSA*, 1960); 'A Redefinition of "Issue" by James B. Meriwether and Joseph Katz (*Proof*, 1972). The volume closes with a 'Checklist for Further Readings'.

The English Novel,[22] edited by A. E. Dyson, is the third of the Oxford Select Bibliographical Guides to appear. Of necessity rigorously selective, it contains chapters, together with reading lists, on twenty-four major novelists, from Bunyan to Joyce. Each chapter has been contributed by an accepted authority on the novelist whom it treats. Thus, for example, Roger Sharrock writes on Bunyan, B. C. Southam on Jane Austen, Miriam Allott on the Brontës, S. Gorley Putt on James, and Malcolm Bradbury on Forster. Obviously the contributors cannot cover their ground fully, but they provide very helpful comments, adverse where necessary, on the works they describe, and the volume as a whole will prove a valuable guide to students of the novel.

Mention should be made of *The Index of Scientific Writings on Creativity*,[23] compiled by Albert Rothenberg

[21] *Readings in Descriptive Bibliography*, ed. by John Bush Jones. Kent State U.P. pp. x+208. $9.

[22] *The English Novel: Select Bibliographical Guides*, ed. by A. E. Dyson. O.U.P. pp. x+372. Hardback, £3.50. Paperback, £1.25.

[23] *The Index of Scientific Writings on Creativity: Creative Men and Women*, compiled by Albert Rothenberg and Bette Greenberg. Shoe String Press and Wm. Dawson & Sons, Ltd. pp. xiii+117. £8.

and Bette Greenberg. This is a list of writings on psychological or physical abnormalities in men and women of genius or in the characters whom they have created. Such things as insanity, drug addiction, homosexuality, and incest figure large. Shakespeare naturally provides a happy hunting-ground for the authors of the works listed. In the 350 items which appear under his name, he himself is credited with being, among other things, an insomniac, a neuropath, the possessor of a father complex, a delinquent (of what kind the title does not reveal), and a sexual psychopath; for some reason the homosexuality so often and so absurdly attributed to him is not mentioned. It is hardly necessary to say that his plays show a preoccupation with every kind of psychological horror. Ninety-three items are devoted to Van Gogh, forty-five to Mozart, thirty-one to Kafka; surprisingly, Byron and Wilde achieve scores only in the twenties. It is likely that at least some of the works listed will be of interest to students of literature, but the book as a whole will probably hold a greater appeal (and possibly even some value) for psychologists.

The latest of the Public Record Office Museum Pamphlets is *Men of Letters*.[24] This contains admirable facsimiles of letters written by Sir Philip Sidney, Francis Bacon, Ben Jonson, John Milton, Samuel Pepys, Daniel Defoe, James Boswell, Charles Dickens, and Matthew Arnold. Ann Morton provides helpful introductory notes on the writers and on the circumstances in which the letters were written.

Under the editorship of Asa Briggs, the House of Longman has published a very handsome volume of *Essays in the history of publishing*[25] to celebrate its 250th anniversary. Briggs opens the volume with a history of the firm, 'At the Sign of the Ship'; and Ian Parsons, in 'Copyright and Society', shows how the need for the protection afforded by copyright laws, felt already fairly early in the sixteenth century, grew ever more pressing, so that the Royal Charter granted to the Stationers in 1557 proved itself in time to be totally inadequate, and the first Copyright Act appeared on the Statute Book in 1709. Parsons describes later developments in the laws relating to copyright, and speculates how appropriate systems of control will be devised to secure the rights of copyright owners in our technological age with its new methods of storing and disseminating knowledge. From David Daiches comes a paper outlining the history of the publication of Shakespeare from the quartos to the editions of today. John Clive writes interestingly on the origins of the *Edinburgh Review*, on its changing character over the century and a quarter of its existence, from 1802 until 1929, and on the many famous persons associated with it as editors or contributors. In 'Disraeli's *Endymion*: A Case Study' Annabel Jones reconstructs, largely from unpublished letters, the circumstances in which Disraeli wrote his last novel and Longmans published it. The story is not only of intrinsic interest, but throws light also 'both on the relationships between author and publisher and the changing organisation of the publishing world'. Asa Briggs contributes 'The View from Badminton', an account of the admirable series of books on sports and pastimes inaugurated in 1885 under the general

[24] *Men of Letters: Facsimiles with introduction*, by Ann Morton. H.M.S.O. pp. 6 + pp. ix plates. 45p.

[25] *Essays in the history of publishing: in celebration of the 250th anniversary of the House of Longman 1724–1974*, ed. by Asa Briggs. Longman. pp. viii + 468. £5.

editorship of the Duke of Beaufort and named after his house at Badminton. In 'Latin for Yesterday' R. M. Ogilvie writes interestingly on the place of Latin in English education from Tudor times until the present day. 'Tracts, Rewards, and Fairies', by Brian Alderson, describes, with many well-chosen illustrations, the Victorian contribution to children's literature. In 'The Paperback Revolution' Hans Schmoller recalls various reprint series of the past, such as the fifty-odd 'Modern Novels' published in 1692, the competing collections in the eighteenth century of Samuel Johnson and John Bell, both called 'British Poets', a number of nineteenth-century series, some of them paper-bound, and in the present century such continental series as the Tauchnitz Books and the Albatross Library. However, the publication by Allen Lane in 1935 of the first ten Penguins was 'the event to which virtually all paperback developments in the western world during the past forty years can be traced'. Schmoller goes on to describe these developments. In 'Beyond the Book' Susan Holmes and Tim Rix consider the power of the new media of communication and the effects they are having, and conceivably in the future may have, on the production of books. Roy Yglesias takes as his subject 'Education and Publishing in Transition'; as he notes, changes in educational systems, and, too, the growing dominance of English as an international language, call for new types of text-books, especially books on the teaching of English as a foreign language. Some of the material in this paper is taken up and developed further in the final essay of this extremely interesting volume, 'Planning for Change', by Tony Becher and Brian Young.

Volume 8 of *Bookman's Price Index*,[26] compiled by Daniel F. McGrath, has as its subtitle 'A Guide to the Values of Rare and Other Out-of-Print Books'. In its 665 closely-printed pages it records the prices fetched at sales in 1973 by many hundreds of rare or comparatively rare books. Useful as such records may be to antiquarian booksellers, and perhaps to librarians, it is questionable whether they will be of much interest to many students of literature, even to those who specialize in bibliographical studies. It is not very helpful to be told that copies of the Second Folio were sold for £6,500 and £1,950 without the slightest reason being given for this great difference in the prices, or that first editions of Johnson's *Dictionary* fetched £685 and £150 without any indication being given of their condition (in this case it is evident, in fact, that in spite of the description as '1st edit.' the cheaper copy was not a first edition). However, we are told that we must not look a gift-horse in the mouth, and, a copy of *BPI* having once more been sent for notice in *YW*, it would have been churlish not to give it a mention.

5. TRANSLATIONS. ANTHOLOGIES

It is perhaps appropriate to open this section with a brief notice of a lively book which was not made available last year—*To Homer through Pope*,[27] by H. A. Mason. Mason's subtitle is 'An Introduction to Homer's *Iliad* and Pope's Translation'. His book is much more than

[26] *Bookman's Price Index: A Guide to the Values of Rare and Other Out-of-Print Books*, vol. 8. Compiled by Daniel F. McGrath. Detroit: Gale Research Co. pp. x+665. $38.50.
[27] *To Homer through Pope: An Introduction to Homer's Iliad and Pope's Translation*, by H. A. Mason. Chatto & Windus, 1972. pp. vii+216. £2.75.

this. It is, among other things, a study of many attitudes towards Homer, notably that of Matthew Arnold, who saw him essentially through Victorian eyes, and of many translators, from Chapman down to the various American translators of the 1960s. However, for the most part Mason is doing what he set out to do; that is, he is showing how greatly Pope's translations can enrich our appreciation of Homer, even if we have enough Greek to understand him in his own tongue. Mason compares many passages of the Pope not only with the original, but with other English versions as well, and from Pope's annotations, to which little attention has been paid, he can often adduce good reasons for the particular turn that Pope gave to a passage, and thus justify a rendering which has been adversely criticized. What he says of Pope's translation of the *Odyssey* in effect sums up what he feels also for the translation of the *Iliad*: 'To anyone who has acquired a taste for the poetry of Pope, to anybody with a taste for English poetry, the possibility of possessing parts at least of . . . the *Odyssey* . . . is given as immediately as to Keats a key was given through the very inferior version by Chapman. Thanks to Pope, we who search for the epics by way of translations can look beyond our noses and see that Homer has an indefinite future among us as exhibiting not only what humanity has been but what it once again might become.'

As the first instalment of a two-part study of tragedy, Brian Vickers has published a substantial volume entitled *Towards Greek Tragedy*,[28] Vickers joins issue with those critics—and they are the majority of critics—who destroy the impact of Greek

tragedy by seeing it largely in terms of its ritual origins or of distorted interpretations of Aristotle's discussion of tragedy. His first chapter opens as follows: 'Greek tragedy is about people, and what they do to each other. It deals with human relationships . . . It concerns those fundamental human passions which are reflected to a greater or lesser degree in the literature of all nations at all periods.' The thesis of the whole of the first section is that Greek tragedy is 'not a remote or metaphysical experience, but an immediate representation of human conflict and human suffering'. In the second section Vickers discusses the recurrent patterns of behaviour in Greek myth, and shows that the 'ethical narrative structure' of the myths has close links with the ethical shapes of Greek tragedy. As in the first section, there is plenty of close reference to specific plays and passages. The third and longest section consists of 'literary criticism' in the more obvious sense—close study of a number of Greek tragedies, including the *Oresteia*, *Oedipus Tyrannus*, and *Antigone*, and ending with a chapter on the Electra plays of all three playwrights, which, taken together, 'constitute a debate over revenge, guilt, and responsibility which is vigorous and at times violent'. This scholarly book promises well for its sequel, which will be of closer concern to students of English literature, since, although it will include discussion of further Greek plays, it will be concerned mainly with tragedy from Shakespeare to the present day.

Desmond Lee's translation of Plato's *Republic* was first published in 1955. Now, after sixteen reprints, it appears in a fairly substantially revised edition.[29] Without losing any

<hr />

[28] *Towards Greek Tragedy: Drama, Myth, Society*, by Brian Vickers. Longman. pp. xvi+658+viii plates. £8.95.

[29] *Plato: The Republic*, translated by Desmond Lee. Penguin Books. pp. 467. 95p. $2.95.

of the readable quality of his first version, Lee has 'tried to bring the English more severely close to the Greek', has replaced the earlier abbreviations and lapses into paraphrase with full translation, and has given the reader further help by expanding and revising notes and section headings. This is, indeed, an improved translation which will not present any difficulties to the general reader, and will be even more acceptable to the serious student than the 1955 volume.

A collection of essays on Seneca,[30] edited by C. D. N. Costa, will be generally welcomed, for few writers of the ancient world have exercised a comparable influence on both the prose and the drama of more recent literatures. In the opening essay, 'Imago Vitae Suae', Miriam T. Griffin gives an interesting account of Seneca's place in the life of his own age, but concludes that 'the literary portrait of himself as a moral teacher that Seneca has left in his essays and letters is rightly judged a more precious legacy than the historical imago vitae suae.' J. R. G. Wright discusses 'Form and Content in the Moral Essays', and D. A. Russell the 'Letters to Lucilius'. G. M. Ross writes on 'Seneca's Philosophical Influence', which was considerable not only in antiquity (pagan and Christian), but also in medieval and Renaissance Europe. The remaining three essays are devoted to the tragedies. Costa gives an admirable critical account of Seneca's own plays. G. K. Hunter discusses a number of English tragedies, mainly of the sixteenth century, in which the influence of Seneca is very evident, and in an appendix to his paper prints eight

English translations of a famous passage in the Thyestes (391–40) of which the best is that of Andrew Marvell. It might be questioned whether Hunter is right to speak of 'the pomposity of Seneca's style'; would 'pretentiousness' perhaps be a safer word? In the final essay J. W. Binns, in an attempt to help us to understand more clearly the nature of Seneca's influence on the Elizabethan drama, analyses the themes and techniques of three Senecan Latin tragedies of the period: William Alabaster's Roxana, Matthew Gwinne's Nero, and the anonymous Perfidus Hetruscus. All students of our medieval and Renaissance literature, especially Elizabethan drama, will find great interest in this book.

The History of the Franks of Gregory of Tours has had no discernible direct influence on English Literature, but indirectly, through French writers of the sixteenth and seventeenth centuries, and just possibly through Gibbon, it may have had some effect, and the translation by Lewis Thorpe in the Penguin Classics[31] therefore appropriately enough finds mention here. The translation runs easily, and Thorpe has provided an informative introduction and a descriptive index of more than a hundred pages which sets the people and places mentioned in the work against their historical background.

Sir Thomas Hoby's translation of Baldassare Castiglione's Book of the Courtier was first published in Everyman's Library in 1928. It is now published in the same series[32] with a

---

[30] Seneca, ed. by C. D. N. Costa. (Greek and Latin Studies: Classical Literature and its Influence.) Routledge & Kegan Paul. pp. ix+246. £5.75.

[31] Gregory of Tours: The History of the Franks, translated by Lewis Thorpe. Penguin Books. pp. 710. £1.

[32] Baldassare Castiglione: The Book of the Courtier, translated by Sir Thomas Hoby. Introduction by J. H. Whitfield. Dent. (Everyman's University Library). pp. xxvii+324. Hardback, £2.95. Paperback £1.50.

new introduction, 'Castiglione and the Culture of Europe', by J. H. Whitfield. This is an interesting introduction, but the student who wishes to know how profoundly Castiglione influenced English literature of conduct in the later sixteenth century will have to consult fuller literary histories of the period.

Of the Commonwealth countries Australia has developed far the most impressive literature of its own, and in particular it has produced many good, and some very good, poets. In his *Penguin Book of Australian Verse*[33] Harry Heseltine has aimed at presenting by his selection something like 'the history of articulate, personal poetry' in Australia. He has therefore chosen a few poems, sometimes only one, by more than a hundred poets rather than a larger number by, say, thirty who are accepted as being among the best. It may be felt that early poets of the stature of Charles Harpur, Henry Kendall, Mary Gilmore and Henry Lawson are badly served by this treatment; but they have been very well represented in a number of anthologies in the past, and most readers will want to know what is being done by the poets who have written in recent decades— Kenneth Slessor, R. D. Fitzgerald, A. D. Hope, and Judith Wright, for example, who have made what will undoubtedly prove to be a lasting contribution to Australian literature. Heseltine has included ten or a dozen poems by each of these poets, and he has found room for several who, being still in their twenties, have yet to make their mark. He has provided an informative introduction which will be appreciated especially by readers who are not familiar with the Australian scene.

As Geoffrey Grigson observes in his introduction to *The Faber Book of Popular Verse*[34], it is impossible to define what is meant by the term 'popular verse'; what is enjoyed in one area or environment or level of society may have no appeal elsewhere. Perhaps the only essential characteristic of popular verse is that it should not be literary. Grigson has drawn into his net a wide range of verse, from 'Legsby, Lincolnshire'— 'A thack church and a wooden steeple, A drunken parson and wicked people'—to 'Robin Hood and Allen a Dale', a number of regional versions of 'The Corpus Christi Carol', and 'The Lyke-Wake Dirge'. He has provided helpful notes which clear up the obscurities that often attend verse of this nature.

Michael Roberts's *Faber Book of Comic Verse* has been reprinted a dozen times since it was first published in 1941. Much verse has been written since the war—nonsense, parody, satire, and just plain funny verse—which qualifies for inclusion in an anthology of this kind, and Janet Adam Smith has therefore prepared a new edition[35] which, while it omits some of Roberts's later choices which have dated, includes many new poems by, to name only a few of the freshly honoured poets, W. H. Auden, John Betjeman, T. S. Eliot, Stevie Smith, Osbert Lancaster, Kingsley Amis, and Henry Reed. This is an anthology which provides much agreeable browsing.

Phyllis M. Jones's collection of *English Short Stories, 1888–1937*, first published in 1939 as *Modern English Short Stories*, has long been accepted as one of our most enjoyable antholo-

[33] *The Penguin Book of Australian Verse*, ed. with an introduction by Harry Heseltine. pp. 483. 60p.

[34] *The Faber Book of Popular Verse*, ed. by Geoffrey Grigson. Faber. pp. 376. Paperback, £1.50.

[35] *The Faber Book of Comic Verse*, ed. by Michael Roberts, with a Supplement chosen by Janet Adam Smith. Faber. pp. 400. £2.50.

gies, providing stories that vary in mood from Hardy's 'The Three Strangers' to a Lord Emsworth story by P. G. Wodehouse, and including such masters of the form as W. W. Jacobs, 'Saki', A. E. Coppard, Katherine Mansfield, and Elizabeth Bowen. It has now been made available as an Oxford Paperback.[36]

[36] *English Short Stories, 1888–1937*, selected by Phyllis M. Jones. O.U.P. (Oxford Paperbacks). pp. viii+403. 95p.

II

English Language

BARBARA M. H. STRANG and JOHN PELLOWE

This chapter is divided into two sections. The first, by Barbara Strang, deals, broadly speaking, with historical studies, but includes all lexicographical material, as well as linguistic studies bearing upon the literary use of English. The second, by John Pellowe, deals broadly speaking, with descriptive studies, but includes all bibliographical material and studies in cognate fields of enquiry relevant to the English scholar.

SECTION 1

(a) *Introductory*

The general prospect remains gloomy (cf. *YW* 54, p. 37). As last year, I have excerpted about a hundred items, and find about eighty worth mentioning; of these, five books and two articles were received through *YW* channels. The proportion of genuinely new and genuinely substantial contributions is disappointing, as will appear from the discussion below; many factors are involved, but in particular it is clear that a sad diversion of energy has resulted from the obsession, now dominant for nearly two decades, with explanation rather than description. Naturally, explanation is a loftier target than description; but it is secondary to and dependent upon description. To some extent this relationship can be concealed if one only treats of the current state of a language well known to oneself and one's readers, but it is glaringly apparent in historical studies. It would be absurd to pretend that our knowledge of the history of English is anywhere approaching descriptive adequacy.

As before, the material is arranged under sub-heads: (b) General (including wide-ranging collections); (c) Orthography/Phonology; (d) Grammar (morphology and syntax); (e) Vocabulary (including etymology, word-formation, semantic change, lexicology, lexicography, additions to the lexical record; also, on this occasion, names); (f) The linguistics of earlier periods (including both editions and studies of earlier linguists); (g) Stylistics (literary and general). Wherever appropriate within sub-sections the order is: general works, followed by work relating to particular periods in roughly chronological order. It is noticeable that a considerable number of this year's works might have been allocated to more than one place. Readers are accordingly asked to treat the chapter as a unity.

(b) *General*

Let pride of place go to a scholar long dead but too new to westerners to be treated as part of the history of the subject[1]. E. D. Polivanov (1891–1938), a pupil of Baudouin de Courtenay, mastered a huge range of languages, conducted original research on more diverse fronts than most of us today are capable of even

[1] *Selected Works. Articles on General Linguistics.* By E. D. Polivanov. Compiled by A. A. Leont'ev, Mouton. The Hague. Janua Linguarum Series Maior, 72. pp. 386. Dfl. 120 (translated from the Russian).

reading about, and while still in his thirties (1929) ventured to tell the scholarly truth about Marr. He was removed from his positions, and his work was suppressed, but not until 1937 was he put into prison where, eight months later, at the age of forty-six, he died. In the early sixties his scholarly work returned to favour in the USSR; early publications and later manuscripts began to be studied. Now Professor Leont'ev and his colleagues have collected and translated an important body of his surviving major papers, with a full bibliography and an excellent introduction outlining his life and achievements. Though most of the languages about which he wrote were non-Indo-European, the student of English will wish to concern himself with substantial parts of the work, notably Section II (five papers on the theory of language evolution); Section III (six papers on Methods of Comparative Historical Linguistics) and Section VI (three papers on Linguistics and Poetics). Through the slightly quaint English of the translation shine the majesty of his genius and the light of his integrity.

It is not clear how many English language students today feel an obligation to keep in touch with advances in our knowledge of Indo-European. Those who do will wish to read Section II (five papers on Indo-European) in the translated collection of papers by the Polish scholar Jan Safarewicz[2]. A collection of recent papers by various authors has been edited by John Anderson and Charles Jones[3]. It represents the proceedings of what is called the First Inter-

national Conference on Historical Linguistics, held in Edinburgh in 1973. There are over thirty articles in two volumes, covering a wide range of topics and representing more than one theoretical stance. The volumes are not attractive to handle or read, and they are rather carelessly produced. Among the most useful contributions are those of Eric Hamp (Vol. II, pp. 141–167—not chiefly concerned with English), and Paul Kiparsky (Vol. II, pp. 257–275—on analogical change). E. Closs Traugott claims that 'Historical linguistics has recently been revitalized' (Vol. I, p. 263) but there is little evidence of this. Many of the papers are more concerned with presenting old knowledge in a different way than with adding to knowledge. The participation is oddly selective; for instance, those (even in Edinburgh) who are doing most to advance our knowledge of the language of the past are not represented.

Joseph Greenberg has produced a work on typology[4]. This, according to a pattern of publication now all too common, represents a revision of his contribution (then still in the press!) to the eleventh volume of *Current Trends in Linguistics*[5]. He gives an

Conference on Historical Linguistics. Edinburgh, 2nd.—7th September 1973. Edited by J. M. Anderson and C. Jones. North-Holland Publishing Co. Amsterdam. North-Holland Linguistic Series Edited by S. C. Dik and J. G. Kooij. 12a, 12b pp. xvi, 415; xvi, 445. NP.

---

[2] *Linguistic Studies*. By J. Safarewicz. Translated from the Polish by L. Ter-Oganian. Mouton. The Hague. Janua Linguarum Series Maior, 76. pp. 395. Dfl. 84.

[3] *Historical Linguistics. Syntax, morphology, internal and comparative reconstruction.* Proceedings of the First International

[4] *Language Typology. A Historical and Analytic Overview*. By Joseph Greenberg. Mouton. The Hague. Janua Linguarum Series Minor, 184. pp. 82. Dfl. 10.

[5] *Current Trends in Linguistics*. Vol. 11. *Diachronic, Areal, and Typological Linguistics*. Edited by Thomas A. Sebeok. Mouton. The Hague. 1973. pp. 604. NP. The volume contains important historical and methodological contributions by Robins, Hoenigswald, Kurytowicz, Sankoff, Kiparsky, Winter, Greenberg, Labov and Gelb, but the 'case-studies' of particular languages are remote from the field of English studies.

interesting account of the term *typology*, noting that it made a late appearance in linguistics. In the nineteenth century its principal domain was morphology, until the concerns of the Neogrammarians deflected attention. However, in the present century certain sorts of structuralism have led to a revival.

Finally in this section, it is a pleasure to welcome a brief beginners' history of the language—not in English, one need hardly add.[6] In arrangement and coverage Görlach's work shows that he has thought out his task from first principles; it is simple, clear and accurate, and makes judicious use of illustrative passages. Probably no two people would carry out such a task in exactly the same way, but his is a valid way, ably followed through.

(c) *Orthography/Phonology*

The double title brings together topics that in some works can be separated, in others not. First mention must go to a good general work confined to orthography.[7] Much as there is to do in many fields of historical study, it is astonishing that there should never before have been a single outline history of English spelling. Dr. Scragg is the right man to make good the deficiency: his book is readable and nearly always accurate; the material is beautifully organized and lucidly presented; the illustrations are excellent. Chapters 4 ('Renaissance and re-formation') and 5 ('The power of the press') are particularly good. About other chapters one might quibble here and there,

and more generally one might regret the treatment of spelling in isolation from punctuation, but one must still recognize the breadth of the achievement. A paperback edition should be produced without delay.

There are further studies of particular aspects of the history of written English, all important in their way. C. J. E. Ball continues his studies of the Franks Casket ('The Franks Casket: Right Side—Again', *ES* Vol 55), showing that the symbols replacing the vowel-runes are variant forms of the consonant symbols for the last sound of the name of the vowel-rune concerned. This is highly important, not only for giving us a reading of an obscure passage, but also indirectly, for its indication of the kind of games rune-masters may like to play. Also concerned with runes is the authoritative study by D. R. Howlett in the same journal ('Three Forms in the Ruthwell Text of *The Dream of the Rood*'). It is a considerable indictment of editors that it should need to be shown at this date that two of the three problem readings which have given rise to speculation that the rune-master may have been deliberately archaising are simply not there. *bismærædu* should be *bismæradu*, and *miþ blodæ* should be *miþ blodi*; *on rodi* stands, representing analogical transfer of inflection. Moreover, iconographically the text can be linked with writings by Bede datable to 709–716; there is thus a possibility that the runic text may antedate the earliest copies of Caedmon's *Hymn*.

While these two works carry the excitement of genuinely new understanding, the same feeling, on a far larger canvas, is transmitted by two long papers from the hand of Angus McIntosh. These need to be treated together, although one did not appear until the beginning of 1975 ('Towards

---

[6] *Einführung in die englische Sprachgeschichte.* By Manfred Görlach. Uni-Taschenbücher 383. Quelbe und Meyer. Heidelberg. pp. 228. DM 17.80.

[7] *A History of English Spelling.* By D. G. Scragg. Manchester University Press. Mont Follick Series Vol. 3. pp. x, 130. £2.20.

an Inventory of Middle English Scribes', *NM* Vol. 75; 'Scribal Profiles from Middle English Texts', *NM* Vol. 76, 1975). The second to appear is logically prior in content, and appeared later as a result of the collapse of the original publishing arrangements. It arises out of the Survey of Written Middle English, which has so immensely enriched our knowledge, and has so much more to offer when its full fruits can be ripened and made available. The next stage after localization of sorts of Middle English (a task already substantially accomplished) is the identification of the profiles of individual scribes; when that has been done, we may hope to move towards the compilation of an inventory of scribes. The proposals rest on a foundation of work demanding two qualities rarely combined in an individual—the patient courage to embark on the collection and ordering of vastly complex arrays of minutiae, and the imaginative insight to read off and interpret the patterns they make. Now an even more challenging goal is envisaged, and a detailed methodology proposed for achieving it; moreover there are vivid examples of what has already been achieved. If sufficient funds and fellow-workers can be found, many fields of human endeavour far beyond the bounds of historical study of English will be enriched.

Phonological studies include three of a rather general sort. Hsin-I Hsieh ('Time as a cause of phonological irregularities', *Lingua*, Vol. 33) argues, with examples from Chinese, that exceptions to phonological change may be due to incomplete and competing sound-changes (a claim we associate with the work of W. S-Y. Wang). This is probably widely accepted in principle by historians of English, though the role of urbaniza-

tion makes the explanation differ in theoretical import for most English examples. Roger W. Westcott ('Types of Vowel Alternation in English', *Word* Vol. 26, 1970 [1974]) writes a somewhat programmatic article, proposing that systematic study of vowel alternation as a subject in itself may lead to new comparative linguistic and etymological insights. He can already suggest interesting possibilities. John Anderson and Charles Jones ('Three theses concerning phonological representation', *JL* Vol. 10) continue their exposition of dependency phonology. The presentation is in general terms, but the illustrations are drawn from the history of English. Their insistence on incorporating the syllable into the phonology is clearly right, and the particular overlapping bracketing they propose does explain an apparent anomaly in Chomsky and Halle's Main Stress Rule (but what made us take seriously work on stress which did not recognize the syllable?). However, it is the final section that particularly concerns us here. The theory is used to 'rationalise' and relate together a series of English sound-changes customarily treated in isolation from one another—i-umlaut, u-umlaut, breaking, open-syllable lengthening, the Great Vowel Shift. There is some carelessness about detail, but the work shows considerable insight.

Some of these topics continue to concern Richard M. Hogg ('Further Remarks on Breaking and Gemination', *ArL* NS. Vol. 5). He analyses the nature of breaking, showing that it can be considered independent of gemination rules, which need not be re-ordered after breaking. This continues his refutation of the O'Neil-Postal-Kiparsky myth (cf. *YW* Vol. 53, p. 46): the most influential bit of wishful thinking to emerge in the subject during recent years. Solidly traditional in method is A. S. C. Ross, who points out ('Anglo-Saxon "e" to "i" before "u"', *NQ* Vol. 219) that, *pace* Luick and Campbell, the change did occur in Anglo-Frisian in at least one word, OE *fiþer*, compositional form of *feower*.

For ME one might best record in this sub-section, despite its main title, a publication one would wish to hail as representing a major advance: the appearance, at last, of an English translation of Jordan's great handbook, now half-a-century old[8]. Unfortunately the volume calls forth mixed feelings. We are very glad to have it; but it could have been better. Jordan's original work of 1925 was revised after his death by Matthes in 1934—discreetly and respectfully; and was given a third edition with updated bibliography by Dietz in 1968. It is this which serves as basis for the translation. The translator is not prepared to efface himself to the same degree as earlier workers. He intrudes: he writes a long rambling introduction that tells us less of Jordan than of the translator's shaky grasp of the scholarly tradition of ME study. The cut-off point for the further updating of the bibliography suggests that the work has suffered considerable delay in the press. The format is quite unsuitable for a work meant to be studied in the way Jordan has always been studied.

Finally, this is one possible place for mentioning Edward Wilson's note ('The Earliest '*Tis* = "it is"', *NQ* Vol. 219). The form has been known as occurring from the fifteenth century, but it can be found in a manuscript compiled at a known date

—1372—by a known compiler—John of Grimestone. The manuscript is now in the National Library of Scotland, but analysis by the methods of McIntosh's Survey (cf. this vol., p. 37) places its composition in S.W. Norfolk, i.e., in the same county that produced the two known fifteenth-century examples, which is thus the probable locus of origin.

Cf. sub-section (f) for further material relevant to this sub-section.

(d) *Grammar*

I turn first to a group of studies relevant to the antecedents of English. W. P. Lehmann puts into practice his belief that linguistic pre-historians should turn attention to the deeper aspects of language, notably syntax. He has produced a book on the subject,[9] and an article ('Subjectivity', *Language* Vol. 50) showing in detail what can be achieved in an area generally thought too unclear to be ventured into. A little closer to our time is E. P. Hamp's demonstration that ablauting verbs are typologically but not necessarily individually old, since Germanic continued to produce them; *find, tread,* are clear examples of Germanic innovations, and we should beware of assuming that other strong verbs are old unless we have good evidence from cognates ('Two Germanic Verb Inventions', *Lingua* Vol. 34). Joseph B. Voyles, in a monograph which might be considered here or under (e), attempts a reconstruction in transformational-generative terms of part of the grammar of West Germanic, *c*200–400 AD.[10] The importance of this approach

[8] *Handbook of Middle English Grammar: Phonology.* By Richard Jordan. Translated and revised by Eugene Joseph Crook. Mouton. The Hague. Janua Linguarum Series Partica, 218. pp. xxxiv, 331. Dfl. 90.

[9] *Proto-Indo-European Syntax.* By W. P. Lehmann. Austin: University of Texas Press (not seen).
[10] *West Germanic Inflection, Derivation and Compounding.* By Joseph B. Voyles. Mouton. The Hague. Janua Linguarum Series Practica 145. pp. 204. Dfl. 52.

is that it can lead to the reconstruction of family relationships by accounting for all relevant data, unlike earlier classifications, based on very small numbers of parameters, selected on no clear basis. It is therefore essential that the remaining areas of the grammar should be worked out on a comparable plan, so that a more accurate genealogy can be reconstructed.

Haiman, though concerned with a theoretical problem indicated in his title,[11] takes as his main theme the requirement of second position for the verb in German, but also studies related patterns in the other Germanic languages, notably English, in which the constraint has suffered most. This is a highly intelligent and suggestive work.

Another crisp and competent study also appears under a broad title indicating its theoretical preoccupations,[12] but gives *en route* a close analysis of a segment of the grammar of English. Baron investigates the applicability of a case-grammar model to the history of English through tracing aspects of the development of verb-complementation from OE to the present day; it is a point of some interest that the files of the *Dictionary of Early Modern English* were made available for the study. This work, too, shows signs of having been held up in the press; good as it is, it might yet have gained from familiarity with more recent thinking about case-grammar.

Also devoted to English from the beginning to the present day is Nehls's study of the expanded form in English.[13] The first half deals with the subject in synchronic terms, and the second half historically; the book is mentioned here because this section is always the less crowded. The truth is that in both halves the work goes over well-trodden ground, and it is not clear to me that the fresh insights are sufficient to warrant full-length publication. Daisuke Nagashima has produced a further instalment of his studies of introductory *there* (cf. *YW* 53, p. 44), tracing the evolution up to the fourteenth century (excluding Chaucer, who is to be the subject of a further publication). This is a careful analysis of a corpus, but it must be said that the pattern it reveals is not entirely unfamiliar ('A Historical Study of Introductory *There*. Part II The Middle English Period', *Studies in Foreign Languages and Literatures* Vol. XXII, Osaka University College of General Education).

There is remarkably little in the way of close study of a particular period, but Dekeyser's work is an important exception.[14] He has set out to fill one part of the programme called for by F. Th. Visser (news of whose death at the age of eighty-nine, his life's work completed, reached me as I was preparing this chapter). This is not an easy book to read from cover to cover, but it is a mine of information, and will be chiefly used for 'looking it up'. It carefully analyses a pretty large corpus, half-century by

---

[11] *Targets and Syntactic Change*. By John Haiman. Mouton, The Hague. Janua Linguarum Series Minor, 186. pp. 156. Dfl. 23.

[12] *Case Grammar and Diachronic Syntax*. By Dennis E. Baron. Mouton. The Hague. Janua Linguarum Series Practica, 223. pp. Dfl. 30.

[13] *Synchron-diachrone Untersuchungen zur Expanded Form im Englischen. Eine strukturalfunktionale Analyse*. By Dietrich Nehls. Hueber. Munich. Linguistische Reihe 19. Herausgegeben von Klaus Baumgartner, Peter von Polenz und Hugo Steger. pp. 193. NP.

[14] *Number and Case Relations in 19th Century British English. A Comparative study of grammar and usage*. By Xavier Dekeyser. Uitgeverij De Nederlandsche Boekhandel. Antwerp—Amsterdam. Bibliotheca Linguistica. Editor X. Dekeyser. Series Theoretica, 1975 pp. x, 342. NP.

half-century, stylistic level by stylistic level, setting out the results with minute accuracy, and juxtaposing them to the prescriptions current in the grammars of each period. It therefore serves not only as a record of what was written and what people thought should be written, but also as a measure of the influence of the second on the first. It is pleasing to record that a useful task has been completed that will not need to be done again.

(e) *Vocabulary*

As always, there is much to report in this sub-section, most of it solid small nuggets of information. However, we may begin with a general, wide-ranging work, a collection of papers on lexicostatistics.[15] There are eleven major papers, the editor contributing a defence of the mathematical model of lexicostatistics against Chrétien's attack in 1962, which many had taken to be fatal. Though none of the papers are directly on the history of English (naturally, since the point of the method was to extend the knowledge available from Indo-European languages to the better understanding of languages not recorded in antiquity), English scholars will wish to keep abreast of developments in this field, and may find the contributions on comparative linguistics, history of linguistics, and creoles, particularly relevant. All the same, though the model may be mathematically justified, doubts must remain about it on empirical grounds; in particular, growing knowledge of the processes of re-lexicification in pidgins must raise doubts about the propriety of

<hr>

[15] *Lexicostatistics in Genetic Linguistics. Proceedings of the Yale Conference, Yale University, April 3–4, 1971.* Mouton. The Hague. Janua Linguarum Series Maior, 69. 1973. pp. 176. Dfl. 50.

using the method in relation to languages of unrecorded history—the only ones for which it is useful.

Though the material dealt with is not English, Franklin C. Southworth's 'Linguistic Masks for Power: Some Relationships between Semantic and Social Change' (*Anthropological Linguistics* Vol. 16) is of some general interest. Developments in certain Asian languages are studied, but the inference is drawn that all historians need to study semantic change in its social or linguistic context; perhaps we may hope that historians of English do not have to be given instructions on this point.

Problems in the etymology of the familiar word *hand* lead to far-reaching conclusions in an article by J. Devleeschouwer ('Le Nom Germanique de la Main', *Orbis* Tome XXIII). He demonstrates that pre-Germanic **konts* is a neologism which first appeared in a region having a Uralian substrate, and not till some centuries after the period of Indo-European conquest; it can be shown to be a pre-Germanic calque of a non-Indo-European word. Accordingly, the explanation of it must take account of ethnic duality in the origins of ancient Germanic.

Coming to studies specifically directed to aspects of English, we may make brief mention of a piece of work at a level prior to the production of historical dictionaries, namely the methodology of concordance-compilation. Sidney Berger's 'A Method for Compiling a Concordance for a Middle English Text' (*Studies in Bibliography* Vol. XXVI, 1973) expounds a well-thought out general method deriving from the author's specific experience of compiling a concordance of Laȝamon's *Brut*.

Kemp Malone offers etymologies of eleven problem words in 'Some

English Etymologies' (*Word* Vol. 26, 1970 [1974]). Old English is well and variously served. In an essay which is a pleasure to read, J. E. Cross offers much that is of value to several sorts of scholar; for the purposes of this chapter we note his requirement that the lexicographer should keep track of the source-hunter (as one might say, 'No, I don't hunt; I follow hounds'). He illustrates this by examples of lexicographical misinterpretation that can be corrected by study of sources, such as *mægðhad* in Ælfric's *Homily on St. Stephen*, which can be shown to mean virginity, not kinship ('The Literate Anglo-Saxon—on Sources and Discriminations'. Sir Israel Gollancz Memorial Lecture. *Proceedings of the British Academy*, Vol. LVIII, 1972 [1974]). Elmar Seebold starts from Latin to show how *sapiens, prudens,* and related words are rendered in OE translations ('Die ae. Entsprechungen von lat. SAPIENS und PRUDENS', *Anglia* Vol. 92). He is able to show that in early Psalters there is a preference for the *snotur* group in Mercian and the *wis* group in the south, and that the later gospels show a similar, though less clear-cut, variation between Anglian and WS. This is a fruitful approach, though one would want to know the part played by systematic instruction in Latin before concluding that the differences are genuinely dialectal. Of wider than lexical interest, but best mentioned here, is J. V. Gough's 'Some Old English Glosses' in the same volume (pp. 279–290; the Inhalt pagination is erroneous). This carefully presents what can be worked out about a series of manuscripts containing glosses, including one that is wholly new. Two notes argue (about two separate items in OE) that what has previously been taken as a single lexical unit is in origin (and meaning) really two.

A. S. C. Ross, in 'Old English "Secgan"' (*NQ*. Vol. 219), produces good evidence that, *pace* Pokorny, in addition to the familiar word 'to say' there is a homonym meaning 'to sacrifice', cognate in stem with Lat. *sacer*. In the same volume I. J. Kirby, ('Old English "FERÐ"') argues (with less complete novelty) that this item has a second self, cognate with or derived from Old Norse, meaning 'a journey', and occurring in *The Wanderer* and *The Seafarer*. Finally, Peter Bierbaumer ('AE. *Fornetes Folm*—Eine Orchideemart', *Anglia*, vol. 92) proposes an interpretation of a puzzling expression as a kind of orchid, probably O. latifolia or O. maculata.

There is also a good deal to report on the ME front. S. R. T. O. d'Ardenne('*BRATEWIL(Katherine, 1690)', *ES* Vol 55) shows that this form, accepted by *M.E.D.*, is an error for *beatewil*, meaning 'victorious, joyful'. Norman Davis also sets the record straight: under *Leopard* the *M.E.D.* records as erroneous the form *libud*; but this is merely an editor's error for scribal *libard* ('A Ghostly Middle English Form of "Leopard"', *NQ* Vol. 219). In the same volume E. J. Dobson's 'Two Notes on Early Middle English Texts' is important for both editor and lexicographer. He offers good evidence for believing in an OE *weol* 'artifice' underlying the adjective *weolie* in the *Ancrene Wisse* (interpret: 'cunning, wily, skilful, wise'; do not emend); and for interpreting *deoren* (Laʒamon's *Brut*, 28065) as 'female beast', with formative as in OE *fyxen*, NE *vixen*. Kathryn Y. Wallace produces clear, though indirect, evidence for an unrecorded item *denscot* 'danegeld' ('A French Source for an English Word not in the *O.E.D.* or *M.E.D.*' (*NQ*. Vol. 219)). D. R. Howlett ('The Meaning of Middle English "Borgener, Bur-gener"' (*NQ*. Vol. 219)) claims that *M.E.D.*'s inappropriate rendering of the word as 'Burgundian' should be replaced by one consequent upon treating it as a derivative of OF *bourgon* 'carter of ordnance'. A. S. C. Ross has two further entries relating to this period: 'Middle English "Covent"', illustrating a use of *O.E.D.*'s *Convent*, 3b, as early as *a*1428; and 'DUB', illustrating *O.E.D.*'s sense v.8 from a Latin text of 1316, and in later Anglo-Norman and English use; this may require a re-interpretation of *Cursor Mundi*, 28014 (both notes in *NQ* Vol. 219). Emeritus Professor Ross has also transmitted four notes left nearly ready for publication by his wife, the late E. S. Olszewska, all continuing her valued series of contributions on ME allitera-tive phrases with Old Norse sources (or sometimes only parallels) ('ME "Brittene & Brenne"', 'Middle Eng-lish "Tongue 7 Tothe"', 'Middle English "Trowe 7 Traist"', Middle English "Wille 7 Walde"', all *NQ* Vol. 219). Readers will be grateful for the information that her collection of material on this subject has been deposited in the library of University College, London, where it may be consulted. Finally we have a group of studies linking general vocabulary with name-elements. Nicholas Jacobs ('Middle English "Cleo" *Hill*', *NQ* Vol. 219) makes the interesting suggestion that the well-known place-name element, presumably the same as the common word of identical form used by the (probably) Glouces-tershire writer Thomas of Hales, should be derived from Lat. *clivus* via Old Welsh. Peter McClure traces the occurrence of certain plant-names in proper names ('Three Plant Names in ME. Place-Names and Surnames: "Breme", "Rounce", "Bilberry"', *NQ* Vol. 219). Karl Inge Sandred

('Two Dialect Words in the Fenland: ModE. *haff* and *stow*', *Namn och Bygd* Årgang 62) identifies *haff*, abundantly evidenced in local six-teenth-century texts, as referring to vegetation, perhaps brushwood, ob-structing a watercourse, and being a reflex of OE *haga*; *stow* refers to a dam, and appears to be from a causa-tive form of the root familiar in *stead*, *stand*.

On more recent English there is rather less. David M. Brereton pushes back the record of *theatre* from 1587 to 1548 ('Early Use of the Word "Theatre"', *NQ* Vol. 219). Moving the short distance from philosophy to early scientists (all the works analysed having been in Locke's library) Roland Hall pro-duces well over a hundred additions and antedatings for *O.E.D.* ('Ante-datings from the 1660s', *NQ* Vol. 219). About half as much is added by Mark Eccles ('Words and Phrases from Thomas Whythorne', same volume). From yet more recent periods we have A. S. C. Ross's 'Some Words from Mrs Henry Wood', and John Whitehead's rather tentative '"Whodunit" and Somerset Maugham' (both *NQ* Vol. 219). In *ES* Vol. 55, Göran Kjellmer ('On *Prestige* and *Prestigious*') traces the development and acceptation of the adjective in its modern connotation. More obliquely, dying dialect words as observed by Hardy and trans-mitted to Gosse are the subject of Douglas Wertheimer ('Some Hardy Notes on Dorset Words and Cus-toms', *NQ* Vol. 219). A very useful article, whose subject is exactly indicated in its title, is contributed by A. W. Stanforth ('Lexical Borrowing from German since 1933 as reflected in the British Press', *MLR* 69).

The dictionary situation is unusual. After the *M.E.D.* completed L in 1973 (*YW* 54, p. 44), there was an intermission until M began to appear in 1975. Likewise, the *Dictionary of the Older Scottish Tongue*, having completed M-N in 1973 (loc. cit.), did not resume with O until 1975. The *Scottish National Dictionary* has completed V. A group of related studies by the *O.E.D.* editorial staff, spanning the turn of 1973–4, were treated together last year (*YW* 54, p. 44). This leaves the very thorough 1974 revision of Hornby's dictionary[16] as the main item for notice. Foreign readers have already shown their appreciation by buying seven million copies of earlier editions, and no doubt will want to acquire the new one; it is not directed to the home market.

Some material which might have been included here is placed in subsection (f). Finally, since onomastics does not warrant a separate heading this year, I record my appreciation of the second and final volume of the *E.P.N.S.* treatment of Berkshire[17].

(f) *History of linguistics*

It has been an exciting year in this area. First mention should go to a new journal, *Historiographia Linguistica*,[18] and to two related editorial ventures. One is the series *Amsterdam Classics in Linguistics*, offering new editions of major but (usually) inaccessible nineteenth- and twentieth century works, with modern introductions, and in some cases, trans-

lations.[19] Eleven volumes were issued in 1974, bringing before the public works by such scholars as Schlegel, Rask, Bopp, Bleek, Schleicher, Lepsius, Darwin, Hehn, Delbrück, Curtius, Brugmann, Collitz, Osthoff, Pott, Jespersen and Krüszewski. The other venture is entitled *Studies in the History of Linguistics*[20]; it produced four volumes in 1974, three of them studies of earlier linguists, but the last predominantly a re-edition with new preface, etc. I regret that at the time of writing I have not seen these volumes. However, I have seen the journal, the first issue of which carried an editorial policy statement, and articles by Robins, Wunderli, Ricken and the editor on a wide range of appropriate subjects, together with a review article, four reviews, and a biographical notice about Svedelius. The second and third issues were, to an English scholar, even more interesting, with (*inter alia*) articles by Vivian Salmon on Wilkins, by Kenneth L. Miner on John Eliot of Massachusetts, and by Ilinca Constantinescu on John Wallis; they were also better produced. The editor's 'Annotated Chronological Bibliography of Western Histories of Linguistic Thought, 1822–1972' runs through the three parts. It is a sobering thought that this is about the only periodical a historian of English can pick up and read from cover to cover without finding more that is irrelevant than relevant. It is because the item is new, and because this claim can be made for it, that I have

[16] *Oxford Advanced Learner's Dictionary of Current English*. By A. S. Hornby with the assistance of A. P. Cowie and J. Windsor Lewis. Oxford University Press. pp. xxxvi, 1055. £2.50 (sic).

[17] *The Place-Names of Berkshire*. Part II. By Margaret Gelling. English Place-Name Society Vol. L. General Editor K. Cameron. English Place-Name Society. pp. 613, 7 endcover maps. NP.

[18] *Historiographia Linguistica*. International Journal for the History of Linguistics. Edited by E. F. K. Koerner assisted by John Odmark. Triannual. John Benjamins B. V. Amsterdam. Hfl. 75 for institutions, Hfl. 45 to prepaid individuals; single issues Hfl. 25.

[19] *Amsterdam Classics in Linguistics, 1800–1925*. General Editor: E. F. K. Koerner. John Benjamins B. V. Amsterdam. The 1974 issues are at prices ranging from Hfl. 28–95 for the normal edition, or Hfl. 15/20 extra for the library-bound editions.

[20] *Studies in the History of Linguistics*. Edited by E. F. K. Koerner. John Benjamins B. V. Amsterdam. The 1974 issues are at prices ranging from Hfl. 18 to Hfl. 50.

thought it proper to write at some length.

The next group of items is probably best noted here, though it might have appeared under (c). Bror Danielsson proposes, and gets to work on, a much-needed dictionary ('Proposal for DEMEP: a Dictionary of Early Modern English Pronunciation 1500–1800', *NM* Vol. 75). As General Editor he describes his policy, which includes exhaustive treatment of explicit metalinguistic evidence (but not, it seems, implicit literary evidence—hence the mention in this subsection); he also sets out the procedures to be followed by his editorial team. This is a very long-term project, and the article includes a list of desiderata and of preparatory editions being planned. One of the requirements is met by another publication from the same stable, a magnificent three-volume edition of Gill's *Logonomia Anglica*[21] (I have seen only the first two volumes, but all were promised by 1974). Part I gives a facsimile of Gill's presentation copy to the Bodleian, adding a list of transcribed words, with variants from the other six extant copies (all of which were hand-finished and corrected by the author) and from the second edition. Part II reproduces the available biographical documents, and offers an excellent Life based upon them, together with a first-rate translation of Gill's Latin text by Dr Alston. This is a faultless work of the first importance.

[21] *Alexander Gill's 'Logonomia Anglica'* (1619). Part I Facsimiles of Gill's presentation copy in the Bodleian Library (4° 930 Art.). List of Transcribed Words by Bror Danielsson and Arvid Gabrielson. Part II Biographical and Bibliographical Introduction. Notes by Bror Danielsson and Arvid Gabrielson. Translation by Robin C. Alston. Acta Universitatis Stockholmiensis. Stockholm Studies in English XXVI, XXVII. Almquist and Wiksell. Stockholm. 1972. pp. 241, 245. NP.

James A. Riddell makes two studies of early dictionaries. Logically prior (and so mentioned here despite its date) is 'The Beginning: English Dictionaries of the First Half of the Seventeenth Century' (*Leeds SE, NS* VII, 1974 for 1973 and 1974 [1975]). In a study of the sources used by Cawdrey, Bullokar and (especially) Cockeram, he corrects and amplifies the account given long ago by Starnes and Noyes, shedding, in the process, fresh light on early lexicographical method. His other study, 'The Reliability of Early English Dictionaries' (*YES* Vol. 4) points out (and it is sad that this should be necessary) that modern literary editors are unjustified in making use of unsupported early dictionary entries (or *O.E.D.* [-0] entries) as evidence of usage. A later stage in the history of lexicography concerns Kathleen M. Wales (in 'The *N.E.D.*: Letters from Dr James Murray to Dr Fitzedward Hall, 1891–1901', *NQ* Vol. 219). This is moving and illuminating material, drawn from letters in the possession of Dr C. A. Ladd.

The remaining items are rather more peripheral. There is a rather hasty monograph on the little-known eighteenth-century German linguist F. K. Fulda,[22] and an outline history of the main recent theories of sound-change, word-formation, syntax and 'textual' analysis (Winfred Nöth, 'Perspektiven der diachronen Linguistik', *Lingua* Vol. 33). More recent still in its concerns is J. Kilbury's 'The Emergence of Morphophonemics: a survey of theory and practice from 1876 to 1939' (*Lingua* Vol. 33).

(g) *Stylistics*

Here we record an article and three

[22] *The Linguistic Work of Friedrich Karl Fulda*. By Johann Vogt. Mouton. The Hague. Janua Linguarum Series Minor, 199. pp. 160. Dfl. 32.

books. Siew-Yue Killingley writes on 'Lexical, semantic and grammatical patterning in Dylan Thomas (Collected Poems 1934–1952)' (*Orbis* Vol. XXIII). The study differs in approach from many of its kind in two respects: first, it deals with a considerable body of work, not with an isolated short text; second, it insists on the desirability of relating linguistic to literary analysis—to a consideration of what the poem is about. On the other hand, it is tied in to preceding works by giving a good deal of space to discussion of recent controversies about how the linguist can approach the analysis of poetic language.

The three books are all major items, and all to be welcomed, the more so as this is a field in which customarily the available work is uneven in quality. The most general is an excellent introduction to stylistics (indeed, to language-study as a whole) by G. W. Turner.[23] He relates grammar and stylistics as complementary studies, dealing, roughly speaking, with linguistic schemes or requirements on the one hand, and with areas of choice or variation on the other. This, of course, does not confine the study of style to literature, deliberately and rightly, but many of the examples are drawn from literature, and the application to literature is never far from author's or reader's mind; moreover, the author is one of sadly few linguists who can be trusted to write about works of literature. Such a book as this has been greatly needed; at last one can recommend a beginners' text that is clear, well-written, unprovocative but challenging, rich in judgement and insight, short, cheap, and accessible. Popularization of this order is more challenging than research; the chal-

lenge is well met when, as in this case, the hardened teacher of beginners can read the book with as much enjoyment and interest as he expects his students to derive from it.

The other two books are collections. The first consists entirely of new material falling within this subsection, and is by various hands. Roger Fowler has edited with an introduction seven essays derived from papers given to a conference in 1972.[24] The contents are not even (in quality or in relevance to the student of English), but I would single out three as being of particular interest. Donald C. Freeman ('The Strategy of Fusion: Dylan Thomas's Syntax') really has something new and interesting to say about a poet whose language has been a sort of sundew for linguists—it lures them with its striking charms and then makes mincemeat of them. The editor ('Language and the Reader: Shakespeare's Sonnet 73') makes bold to hunt over even more trampled territory, and yet finds, then brings down, quarry worth catching. There is a link, through concentration on the reader and his expectations, between his paper and the last one I wish to mention ('Defining Narrative Units', by Jonathan Cullen). This is a highly interesting attempt to define the criteria by which a theory of plot can be evaluated. The topic is one intriguing to the linguist since it involves the study of information conveyed to us by language (at least in literary narrative) but completely independent of particular linguistic realizations, i.e., a study of what might be called macro-deep-structure (but do not imagine I wish to father this term on Mr. Cullen).

[23] *Stylistics*. By G. W. Turner. Pelican Books. Advisory Editor for Linguistics: David Crystal. 1973. pp. 256. 90p.

[24] *Style and Structure in Language. Essays in the New Stylistics*. Edited by Roger Fowler. Basil Blackwell. Oxford. Language and Style Series. General Editor: Stephen Ullman (another tragic loss of recent weeks). pp. vi, 262. £6.

Finally we have a collection of essays, old, revised and new, by a single hand—not all on the language of literature, but predominantly so, and best treated together as showing the diversity in unity of a single distinguished mind, that of Randolph Quirk.[25] 'Charles Dickens, Linguist' is a long study involving conflation, revision and expansion of two earlier publications: let no-one think it replaces the 1959 Inaugural Lecture *Charles Dickens and Appropriate Language*, but it does add much new material both to this and to the 1961 article, 'Some Observations on the Language of Dickens'. A brilliant study of 'Shakespeare and the English Language' is only slightly altered from a version published in 1971. 'The "Language" of Language and Literature' is completely new: it includes a very remarkable search for the canons of criticism implicit in Anglo-Saxon literature. A study of Dasent and Morris as translators can properly be included in this subsection. But with the other topics we begin to move away. There are two name-studies, three lexical studies, an analysis of our knowledge of the mother tongue, and the 1961 Inaugural Lecture, which deals extensively with the work of that nineteenth-century linguist-polymath, Latham.[26]

SECTION 2
Where relevant, the layout of this section is similar to that of its fellows in *YW* 51, 52, 53, 54. The general trends noticed in those years (1970, 1971, 1972, 1973) continue to gain momentum: the importance of ling-

uistic variation for linguistic theory, the debate on the propriety of a strict separation of semantics from syntax, and the problem of determining the extent to which semantic theory should depend upon a theory of persons transmitting and receiving meanings (pragmatics). Useful work continues to be done in syntax and phonology.

(a) *Varieties*
The fundamental technical, or academic, problem which is exercising those linguists who are attempting to determine the dependencies between linguistic variation and the non-linguistic characteristics of speech communities is that of determining the optimum way of representing such dependencies. Thus, Henrietta J. Cedergren and David Sankoff favour the expression of such relationships in the form of variable rules as outlined by William Labov in 1969. They claim firstly, that optional rules do not properly capture the nature of the systematic variation which can be found in the behaviour of a single individual, and secondly, that 'optionality' of rules is in implicit contradiction to the notion of competence itself ('Variable rules: performance as a statistical reflection of competence' *Language*). Variable rules are assigned probabilities of application whose values depend *in some way* upon the structure of the input strings. The authors provide a mathematical account of how these rules might, in general, be deemed to operate. They illustrate their views with data from English, Spanish and French, and offer some criteria for determining one best way of allowing the structure of input strings (and relevant extralinguistic information) to determine the likelihood of a rule's applying. Claire Lefebvre, on the other hand, prefers to discuss 'Discreteness and the linguistic continuum

---

[25] *The Linguist and The English Language.* By Randolph Quirk. Edward Arnold. London. pp. vi, 181. £4.00. Paperback £1.75.

[26] Unfortunately I have not been able to excerpt the journal *Language and Style* for 1974; all students working in the stylistic field will be aware that this is a journal they should watch.

in Martinique' (*AnL*) in terms of the application of implicatory relations between the occurrences of (particular values of) variables for a given lect in the speech community. (The technique is known, in linguistics, as implicational scaling. It is considered to date from work done by D. Elliott, S. Legum, & S. A. Thompson in 1969, but as a method it is formally indistinguishable from methods developed by R. Quirk in 1965.) Needless to say, there are extremely important theoretical issues which lie behind attempts such as these to determine the proper form of representation of linguistic variation. Briefly, they revolve around the question as to whether a given linguistic community has *one*, variably realized, grammar, or *many* grammars, related to each other in various ways. A method which has the (unrealized) potential to determine the answer to this question empirically is somewhat peremptorily discussed by R. B. Le Page, Pauline Christie, Baudouin Jurdant, A. J. Weekes & Andrée Tabouret-Keller in their 'Further report on the sociolinguistic survey of multilingual communities: survey of Cayo District, British Honduras' (*Language in Society*). They use one form of cluster analysis to determine the association between a small number of linguistic variants as used by 280 children in interview situations, and various kinds of socio-economic information. They express the hope that the *form* of their method is an analogue to the process of the children's search for social roles and identities. 'The deficit-difference controversy', which is related to the theoretical issues alluded to above, but which is frequently more readily comprehensible to (and misapprehended by) those responsible for educational policy, is dealt with by J. B. Pride in a full, and sensitive, manner (*ArL*). He discusses

the controversy and its relation to the logical adequacy of standard and non-standard varieties by examining a few data on negation. He insists that the importance to the problem of speech acts and speech functions has been ignored. He suggests that changes of attitude are likely to be more important than strategies to change linguistic behaviour. (He dismisses, in particular, the use of 'ghetto readers' as inept and probably counter-productive.) Jacob Ornstein and R. P. Murphy provide us with what they obviously and wrongly imagine is an exciting, synthetic, review of 'Models and approaches in sociolinguistic research on language diversity' (*AnL*). They manage to render even more opaque a loose collection of diverse research whose well-known problem of a lack of theory is not improved by superficial classifications of some of the scholars involved. W. Washabaugh ('Saussure, Durkheim, & sociolinguistic theory' *ArL*) defends Saussure's theories against attacks from those, like W. Labov and C.-J. N. Bailey, who rightly believe that grammars must be dynamic, variable, and social: he finds evidence in Saussure's work other than the posthumous *Cours*, which indicates that he was well aware of this need. David Minderhout eulogizes some sociolinguistic techniques for consumption by anthropologists ('Sociolinguistics and anthropology' *AnL*). Other writers report specific relationships between linguistic variation and extralinguistic characteristics co-occurring with it. Eddie C. Y. Kuo, for instance, examines the bilingual experience of forty seven pre-school children of Mandarin-speaking Chinese families which had immigrated to Minnesota. The difference between generations is a more powerful determinant of the language which is used than is the family status (children used Chinese to parents, English to siblings and unrelated peers). R. E. Callary discusses 'Status perception through syntax' (*L&S*). He runs an experiment in which judges are presented with material in written form which had originally been spoken by informants with known socio-economic status. The implication of the study is that judges can correctly perceive status from syntactic variation alone (variations of transposition and embedding sequencing, for example, rather than variation of morphological or grammatical form). One would be better able to evaluate the implication if one could examine the stimulus material. Franklin C. Southworth uncovers 'Linguistic masks for power: some relationships between semantic and social change' (*AnL*) and focuses our attention upon the possibility that a shift from overt to covert recognition of the distinctions in power and status within a particular language may be serving to conceal the extent of socio-economic differences between groups, rather than reflecting an actual change in social structure. Nissan Buium has undertaken 'An investigation of the word order parameter of a parent-child verbal interaction in a relatively free order language' (*L&S*) which shows that a male informant speaking Hebrew uses relatively free word order interacting with an adult, but fairly rigid (SVO) word order with his (own) two year old daughter. Such a small study is, rightly, not used to make any generalizations; it is possible to make some interesting speculations about the consequences of such facts for the facilitation by mature speakers of acquisition of language. Don. M. Taylor & Richard Clément report three experiments in 'Normative reactions to styles of Quebec French (*AnL*), and though their detailed

materials have no impact upon our understanding of English, the questions they ask also need asking for English speech communities. Do ordinary members of the speech community recognize shifts in style made by an individual in social situations which vary in their formality? Do ordinary members of the speech community have different expectations of the range of such shifts which can be made by members of different social classes? Similar kinds of experiments (using the technique of 'matched guise' due to Wallace Lambert 1967) were undertaken to determine the 'Evaluation reactions of college students to dialect differences in the English of Mexican-Americans' by B. Arthur, D. Farrar, & G. Bradford (*L&S*). They found that speech approaching the non-standard ethnic dialect of Mexican-Americans was negatively stereotyped by Anglo-American students on scales of 'success', 'ability', and 'social awareness'. Regrettably, like many other such matched guise experiments, there is a woeful lack of attention to definition of critical linguistic parameters ('non-dialect voice differences' e.g.), and an apparent blindness to the likelihood of selective listening (and selective interpretation) under any but the most aseptic of administration conditions. Hazel Francis contrasted the responses to a story reproduction task by 96 working class and 96 middle class children. She found no significant differences in the use of nominal group items or of exophoric reference. These results contradict those of P. R. Hawkins (1969). The author makes some sensible educational inferences. Though marginal to the study of English, two studies, the first by J. A. Moles ('Decisions and variability: the usage of address terms, pronouns, and languages by Quechua-Spanish bilinguals in Peru' *AnL*) and the second by Victoria R. Bricker ('Some cognitive implications of informant variability in Zinacanteco speech classification' *Language in Society*) are both of considerable importance to the methodology of sociolinguistics. The first shows how, within a close-knit speech community, variation in the choice of language or variant used seems to relate to the underlying differences of 'possible worlds' for members of that community. The second shows that the folk-linguistic taxonomies given by informants often appear incompatible, but in fact are reflections of inept elicitation procedures. Michael Agar does some 'Talking about doing: lexicon and event' (*Language in Society*). He examines the structure of some of the specialized lexicon of drug addicts in terms of case-grammatical notions and stage-process relationships in the addicts' drug taking habits. He indicates the ways in which the argot serves the function of a standardized terminology rather than as a form of concealment. Joseph E. Grimes gives a mathematical characterization of 'Dialects as optimal communication networks' (*Language*). The optimization characterizes the networks in terms of three characteristics of intelligibility tests: the typical asymmetry of intelligibility between two dialects, i, j; the sensitivity of intelligibility measures to relatively small changes in the nature (level of difficulty) of the stimulus materials; and the incompleteness of the data matrix which tabulates the inter-intelligibility measures of all possible pairs of dialects under consideration. Walt Wolfram contributes further information to the debate upon the nature of the relationship between Black English and White English (are they variants on one grammar, or are they distinct grammars?) by examin-

ing 'The relationship of White Southern speech to Vernacular Black English' (*Language*). He analysed the occurrences of copula deletion ('You hitting too hard') and invariant *be* ('He be thirteen next month'; 'He be happy if he could do it'; 'Sometimes his ears be itching') in informal interviews with 100 informants of both sexes, and in three age groups (8–10, 11–13, 16–17). He concludes that the either-or type of question posed above is quite inappropriate for the nature of the complexity of the data. Copula absence in Southern White speech was probably assimilated from a late stage of de-creolizing Black speech. The reason for the lateness of the assimilation is speculatively assigned to the syntactic disorganization which would have been concomitant upon the syntactic (functional) change in the item before its current morpho-phonological change (contraction etc.). Selective adoption of linguistic variants by one group from another is posited as being, in part, importantly dependent on the level of linguistic organization at which the variants operate. Unfortunately, the plausibility of the hypothesis does not say anything very useful about the scalar nature of this selectivity (given a fixed relationship between groups in terms of some social parameter, does group a always selectively adopt items from a particular level of organization of group b's speech patterns?). The death of Professor Harold Orton, who dedicated his lifetime to collecting, editing, and publishing the Basic Material of the Survey of English Dialects, is marked by the appearance of his and Nathalia Wright's *A word geography of England*.[27] The book includes 250 word maps, an introductory explanation of

[27] *A word geography of England* by Harold Orton and Nathalia Wright. London: Seminar Press. pp. 302. £9.80.

the editorial methods exercised upon the Basic Material and of the mapping procedures, and indexes of the notions mapped and of responses and words from the incidental material. The maps included in the book by no means exhaust what is available in the basic material. Criteria for inclusion of a notion in map form were: (a) intrinsic interest to philologists (e.g. competing lexemes before the Conquest), (b) familiarity to the general public, (c) profusion of forms (left-handed, earwig), (d) the capacity of the item to elicit foreign forms, (e) the connection between the item and characteristics of the American dialect situation. The conjoint effects of these criteria are clearly going to cause conflicts for the selectors, but these variously arbitrary criteria are not the only ones which filter the basic material for mapping. A more or less unpublic selection of the actual responses to the questionnaire items is also made, since, "it soon became clear that it was both impracticable and imprudent to try to display all the responses . . . on a single map" (p. 2). For this reason only a few words from a particular question are placed on one map for contrastive display. Unfortunately, the valid reasons which the authors use to determine *which* words shall occur on the same map, make any use of the maps for purposes other than those envisaged in the form of the 'valid reasons' absolutely infuriating. In spite of these simplificatory processes, the maps are not very easy to interpret. There is no use of colour, the symbols for variant forms are not well selected, and there are some maps which would have benefited considerably from having available different types of line to express discontinuity. At a more theoretical level, and following from earlier remarks about the criteria for inclusion of items, the

maps are almost wholly uninterpreted data. There is no attempt to draw any composite maps to show putatively significant interactions between the competing lexemes for two or more sememes (a development which the Swiss arm of the SED is putting a considerable amount of effort into). No attempt is made to determine the systematicity of the so-called incidental material in terms of interpenetrating types of 'purity'. The consideration that isoglosses might be thought of as hypotheses is nowhere in evidence. Peter Trudgill underlines the kinds of dissatisfaction I have voiced in his 'Linguistic change and diffusion: description and explanation in sociolinguistic dialect geography' (*Language in Society*). He rightly points out the apparent imperviousness of linguistic cartography to developments in sociolinguistic methodology and theoretical geography. By considering the urban lects of Norwich, England and the rural dialect area of Brunlanes, Norway, he shows how linguistic cartography can benefit immensely in terms of its explanatory power (traditionally, virtually non-existent), from a proper consideration of these disciplinary perspectives. Beat Glauser's doctoral thesis on *The Scottish-English Linguistic Border: Lexical aspects* is, empirically and methodologically, a thoroughly competent, professional, and useful monograph.[28] It is complementary to work done from the other side of the border, as it were, by Hans Speitel within the purview of the Linguistic Survey of Scotland (*ZDL* 1969). Glauser's questionnaire comprised an almost unadapted subset of that used by the Survey of English

[28] *The Scottish-English Linguistic border: lexical aspects* by Beat Glauser. Bern: Francke Verlag. pp. 288 SFr. 39.- (The Cooper Monographs Vol. 20, English Dialect Series).

Dialects (Harold Orton 1962). Items were chosen which promised, in comparison with tape-recorded material collected by his colleagues in the Borders, to yield isoglosses in that area. The questionnaire (of 106 items) was administered to eighty seven informants (of whom three were rejected), each in a different locality. Material from four other sources (SED, his colleagues, and R.Zai) provided a further twenty two informants, the whole sample having as even a distribution as could be expected, given the terrain. Background on geography, territorial history, and linguistic history occupies some 23 pages. There follows a detailed mapping of and commentary on the distribution of items (pp. 56–233), singly and compositely. The maps are very well designed and are easily interpreted. The most interesting aspect of the book is the attempt to express differentially the quantitative association between isoglosses. However, as Glauser pungently remarks, the graphical problems which crop up in an attempt to construct collective maps are direct reflections of the actual linguistic complexity of the situation (though he doesn't note that some of these complexities may be induced by the selection of localities, informants and methods of elicitation). One of the very special merits of the book is Glauser's continuous concern to keep up a confrontation between simplifications for visual comprehension and an insistence on retaining detail wherever possible.

Two very different kinds of survey from Glauser's are edited respectively by Joshua A. Fishman and by W. H. Whiteley. Both are concerned with the interdependence between national and colonial polities, on the one hand, and inter- and intra-language ecology, on the other. The Fishman volume,

Advances in language planning, is concerned with the principles of engineering the best possible interdependence.[29] The Whitely volume, *Language in Kenya*, shows, with immense scholarship and precision, the depth and breadth of knowledge about the linguistic diversity of a community which is required before planning or policy-making in linguistic matters can have the remotest chance of success.[30] This gulf, between language planning practice (as implemented by governments, industry, legislators, etc.), and language planning research, of which Fishman's volume is a collection, is alluded to, but not apologized for, in Fishman's introductory essay. A new field of applied research is often parasitic upon pre-academic practice for some time, until a sufficient number of theoretical constructs have been elaborated for the research to become self propagating. The depressing thing about language planning research, however, is that many of the theoretical developments of the last ten years have actually been in the linguistic literature for as long as forty five years. In addition, of course, language planning research is depressing because it is intimately bound up with ideological preoccupations. These ideological problems are by no means restricted to the defining ideologies of the *linguistic* groupings in the community for which some form of language planning is being proposed; they also include—indeterminately— a whole range of motivations and goals, of one political kind or another, which may have no systematic connection whatever with the linguistic situation. It is for such

[29] *Advances in language planning* ed. by Joshua A. Fishman. The Hague: Mouton. pp. 590. DFl. 28.
[30] *Language in Kenya* ed. by W. H. Whiteley. London: O.U.P. pp. 589. 4 maps. £9.25.

reasons that many linguists are dubious about the feasibility of professionally adequate language planning. Fishman sets out five characteristics of the language planning process (which he calls 'major theoretical dimensions'). They are: policy formulation and decision, codification (the establishing of patterns of langue relative to the purposes implicit in the formulation), elaboration (of the codification relative to particular environments of use), implementation ('enforcement or encouragement of the acceptance of these linguistic decisions by the target population'), and cultivation (the development of relevant stylistic varieties). The volume is divided into four sections, more or less in parallel with these distinctions. There are five papers on 'Theoretical studies', seven on 'Language policy studies' (one on Turkey, three on Africa, one on Australasia, one on the Philippines, one on Polynesia), seven on studies of 'Codification, cultivation and elaboration', and four on studies of 'Implementation, evaluation and feedback'. I am pessimistic about the good sense of anything proposed in volumes such as this, since, if the underlying assumption which motivates such work is that intergroup tensions can be minimized by some kind of language homogenization process (the most generous attribution), it is, at best, naïve to imagine that the *process* of homogenization is not itself going to contribute a whole new dimension of tensions, whose existence will exacerbate rather than alleviate those already at work in the community. This is the societal component of my pessimism, but there is a politico-ideological component as well. The totalitarian trend in governments of the world is well, and gloomily, enough documented: research of the kind presented in this book simply provides the arsenal of totalitarianism with another, and very powerful, weapon. Whiteley's volume on the other hand is very cautious about policy: each of the sixteen papers is well rooted in empirical earth. Even when judicial and educational decisions about language are discussed (notably in two papers by T. P. Gorman in Part Three, 'Language in Education'), the effective range of the decisions, and evidence for the political and linguistic elements of their rationales are carefully specified. The book contains sixteen papers, four on the 'Language situation' (W. H. Whiteley, Barbara Neale, P. A. N. Itebete, J. C. Sharman), nine on 'Language use' (four by D. J. Parkin, Janet Bujra, David Aoko, Barbara Neale, W. H. Whiteley, T. P. Gorman) and three on 'Language in Education' (two by T. P. Gorman, R. J. Hemphill). As Whiteley writes in his introduction, the first task of the Survey of Language in Kenya was to 'establish the facts'. As always, however, this also involved the research team in making methodological innovations. Both kinds of information are included in the book. The contrast between the editorial stances of Fishman's book and of Whiteley's is remarkable when one remembers that they are both addressed to the same problem. The contents are similarly distinct. In order to characterize the rational and humane tenor of this and other work of Whiteley's, it is worth quoting part of his introduction at length: 'to some extent a government may control language use: through the educational system, by passing edicts, or by setting examples, but there are limits to the extent to which this can be done, and it is clear, on the evidence of history, that if the choice of language runs counter to the prevailing patterns of language use then the language will only be used in those contexts where some degree of enforcement can be assured. This is likely to be an expensive and difficult undertaking, and one not likely to enhance the prestige of the language being enforced.' (p. 2). It is a remarkable indictment of some of the material published on 'language planning' that one should feel it necessary to quote views containing as much sound common sense as Whiteley's.

A debate similar, in many respects, to that I have just outlined about language planning in multi-lingual communities, has just been rekindled in largely monolingual, industrialized, Western societies. The debate centres upon what the relationship should be between a child's linguistic habits and the expectations of schools. The debate is often, but not necessarily, motivated (and made emotive) by appeal to the notion of 'educational failure'. Anne and Peter Doughty avoid this pitfall, and several others, by focusing on the problem through a deeper perspective of *Language and Community*.[31] Their introductory chapter stresses the importance of the situatedness of language for both its acquisition and its use ('Language'); in the second chapter ('Community') they outline certain central properties of communities and point out how the child's 'learning' to be a member of such a thing parallels his 'learning' of his language. The third chapter articulates the child's learning of his social roles with the development of his world view, his construction of reality. The fourth chapter turns from the emergence of the mental, social and linguistic development of the individual in the environment to the relationship between the school and the community, and the fifth intro-

duces the idea of a 'language climate' in the context of the family within the community. There is no index, but then the book is not that kind of book: it is intended for those who wish to re-appraise (or for those who think that there is no need to re-appraise) the relationships between learning to speak, learning to live, and learning to learn. In its length it is provocative without dogma, judicious without equivocation, and humane without permissiveness, on each of these relationships. In the same series, Geoffrey Thornton treats of the same problems, but with a closer focus on *Language, experience and the school*.[32] Thornton's approach is a good deal more pungent than that of the Doughtys. He sets out to characterize the ways in which language is used in schools (*all* the ways it is used in schools) as a complex 'message system', and at each point concentrates upon asking teachers to think carefully about the exact nature of the demands that the institution, for any piece of language behaviour required, is making upon particular children, each having a different range of experience of both language and the world. In his concluding piece, ('What is to be done?'), Thornton insists that one of the best ways of ensuring that pupils do not get condemned for not possessing knowledge and experience which they haven't been shown *how* to possess, is to provide teachers with an understanding of the nature and functions of language, especially as it affects (and effects) the learning process. This, in turn, entails other things which may need changing; school organization, methods for teaching different subjects, assessment and marking.

[31] *Language and Community* by Anne and Peter Doughty. London: Arnold. pp. 109. £1.60.

[32] *Language, experience and the school* by Geoffrey Thornton. London: Arnold. pp. 81. £1.50.

Loreto Todd has written a very useful book on *Pidgins and Creoles* as the first in a series on Language and Society launched by Routledge.[33] The series is intended for students at beginners' level, but if the quality of this first volume is maintained it will find a wide audience. Todd concentrates most of her attention upon pidgins and creoles which are English based and which have developed since the fifteenth century. She indicates the world wide distribution of the pidgin/creole phenomenon, discusses theories about the origins of such languages, shows what the creolization of a pidgin amounts to, and discusses the potential that pidgins and creoles have as media for literature and education. She concludes that the special conditions which lead to the generation of these special forms of language are important reasons why they merit special attention from linguists. There is, indeed, every reason to imagine that pidgins and creoles have critical importance for the investigation of linguistic universals and for the development of a thorough understanding of linguistic variation. The book includes a useful bibliography, but no indexes.

The social differentiation of English in Norwich is a revised form of Peter Trudgill's doctoral dissertation.[34] It is no accident that the title of the work echoes that of W. Labov's investigation of speech variation in New York City, since the basic principles of methodology and theoretical perspective are based on that earlier work. The first four chapters are given over to preliminary matters such as the geographical and historical characteristics of Norwich and East Anglia, the drawing of the sample of informants, the specification of social indices, and the design and mode of administering the questionnaire. Chapter five shows how a grammatical variable is distributed across these social indices. Chapter six specifies the phonological variables, shows their occurrence in the Survey of English Dialects material, and gives a thumbnail sketch of the history of each. Chapter seven shows in tabular and graphical form what is the covariation between speech style, social index, and rate of incidence of the variable. Apart from the details, of which there is a wealth, there are few elements of novelty in the book up to this point; chapter eight, however, is the point at which Trudgill attempts to do something new and important. He attempts to construct a diasystem for the relevant varieties of Norwich which can operate in terms of generative principles. The diasystem is constructed upon the basic unit of the syllable (as discussed by Erik Fudge) and is realized (generatively) by diasystem inventory rules, morphological alternation rules, diasystem incidence rules, phonological realization rules, phonetic mutation rules, phonetic realization rules, realization level mutation rules, and articulatory setting rules. I can find no justification for this plethora of rule categories (since, presumably, input/output costs have to be debited against the simplicity metric). In addition there appear to be insufficient conditions on input, since several outputs which the rules permit seem to me to be excessively unlikely to be represented in the Norwich speech community. Nevertheless, Trudgill's attempt in this direction deserves to be followed up, both with further East Anglian data and with contrast-

[33] *Pidgins and Creoles* by Loreto Todd. London: Routledge and Kegan Paul. pp. 106. £2.50 (paperback £1.25).
[34] *The social differentiation of English in Norwich* by Peter Trudgill. London: CUP. pp. 211. £4.90.

ive data from other environments. D. Lawrence Wieder provides some very interesting data for, and a very interesting, though difficult, theoretical perspective on, *Language and social reality*.[35] The setting for Wieder's research was a halfway house—halfway, that is, between the convict's time in prison and his release on parole. Wieder deals at some length with the rationale for such semi-corrective, semisocializing, institutions as extensions of the responsibilities of the Mental Health and Penal Correction authorities. He outlines the code, of language as well as of behaviour, as an explicitly verbalized moral order. His informants were able to specify the fundamentals of the code as a set of maxims: above all else do not snitch, do not cop out, do not take advantage of other residents, share what you have, help other residents, do not mess with other residents' interests, do not trust staff, show your loyalty to the residents. Wieder treats his material in two quite distinct ways (reflected in the two parts of the book). In part one he treats these maxims as rules which 'explain' actions. He draws up a system of norms which may be thought to lie behind these rules, and in drawing on the theory of general semiotics, and the associated sociological theories of institutions, he shows how this local norm can be interpreted as deviant in the context of the norms of the society at large. In part two, he examines the same material from the ethnomethodological viewpoint, and shows how 'telling the code' is a special case of the establishing of social reality by particular groups of members. He demonstrates the inner

coherence of the structure of this social reality and shows the ways in which it has a moral order of its own. Though the book is difficult in many respects, it is one of the very clearest of those pieces of ethnomethodological research which, as a general viewpoint, has so much to offer linguists who chafe at the interpretive constraints which their own training imposes on material truly reflecting the language behaviour of the community.

In a tradition, and with methods, directly at odds with those inherent in ethnomethodology, Donald E. Allen and Rebecca F. Guy have written on *Conversation analysis: the sociology of talk*.[36] They seek to develop and apply an extended array 'of mensural, graphic, and analytical techniques to direct dyadic conversation'. These techniques depend upon the variables of inter-syllabic intensity, definiteness of vocabulary, and various characteristics of bodily movement (eye-contact, gesture and the like). By such measures the authors hope to have provided a more exact specification of the nature of the conversational bond, and a range of measures by which the social sciences and other interested professional groups can assess the effectiveness of any particular conversational exchange. Richard Bauman and Joel Sherzer have edited an important collection of papers, *Explorations in the ethnography of speaking*.[37] The book is an outgrowth of a conference held in 1972 in Austin, Texas. Ethnographic research of the type which is epitomized in this volume is aimed at formulating descriptive theories of speaking as a

[35] *Language and social reality: the case of telling the convict code* by D. Lawrence Wieder. The Hague: Mouton. (Approaches to Semiotics, 10) pp. 236. DF1. 48.

[36] *Conversation analysis: the sociology of talk* by Donald E. Allen and Rebecca F. Guy. The Hague: Mouton pp. 284. n.p.

[37] *Explorations in the ethnography of speaking* ed. by Richard Bauman and Joel Sherzer. London: CUP. pp. 501. £9.00 (paperback £3.60).

cultural system or as part of cultural systems. As a perspective, then, it diverges rather radically from the dominant themes in present day linguistics, namely the search for rule operative grammars, and substantive universals. The book is divided into five sections, preceded by prefatory and introductory matter, and concluded by notes, references and a name index. The first section ('Communities and resources for performance') contains a very lucid account of the quantitative paradigm for the study of communicative competence, by Gillian Sankoff, and two other papers. The second section ('Community ground rules for performance') contains four papers, giving detailed accounts of the ethnography of various forms of speech in Warm Springs, Antigua, Malagasy, and Quaker meeting houses. Six papers appear in the third section ('Speech acts, events, and situations'), and five in the fourth ('The shaping of artistic structures in performance'). Three very useful and provoking papers appear in the fifth section ('Toward an ethnology of speaking'). Here we see the subject slowly moving from careful individual accounts of the sociocultural functions of various forms of speaking, to a theoretical framework for all ethnographic work. The foundations are barely laid, but this volume promises a sound building. An extremely important book for all linguists, not simply for those who feel that the heterogeneous linguistic behaviour of members of the speech community ought to be central to theory, is Charles-James N. Bailey's *Variation and Linguistic Theory*.[38] (Regrettably it was not to hand last year.) In chapter one,

Bailey shows how poorly motivated and distortive the Saussurean distinction between langue and parole, and that between synchronic and diachronic, are. Standard theory transformationalism comes in for the same treatment. (Actually, as Bailey himself hints, there is good reason for the attack upon Chomsky in these respects to be a great deal harsher than that upon Saussure, since the former had a great deal more information available which was in direct contradiction to his doctrine of homogeneity.) In chapter two Bailey introduces his 'New framework' of polylectal grammars through a consideration of what it is that the child must acquire when it is acquiring social competence (together with some sensible corrective remarks on *how* he does it). Two fundamental principles are incorporated in this account: firstly, the model must dynamically incorporate time; and secondly, the model must acknowledge the speaker-hearer's capacity to understand a wide range of distinct surface grammars and to respond appropriately to them. Chapter three discusses the notions of directionality and rate of variation in terms of the markedness of phonological segments, and chapter four brings all these arguments together in an elaboration of the wave model of the propagation of variants through a language community. For all its brevity, this is a brilliant, seminal, but nonetheless very readable book.

(b) *Psycholinguistics*

Richard L. Schiefelbusch and Lyle L. Lloyd have edited a large and generally very useful collection of material on *Language perspectives: Acquisition, Retardation and Intervention*.[39] The volume contains twenty

---

[38] *Variation and Linguistic Theory* by Charles-James N. Bailey (1973). Arlington, Va.: Center for Applied Linguistics. pp. 162. n.p.

[39] *Language perspectives: Acquisition, Retardation and Intervention* ed. by Richard L.

five contributions distributed through eight sections. The acquisition features which are dealt with include infant receptive processes, the early development of receptive language, the developmental relationship between receptive and expressive language, and the early development of concepts. These features are dealt with from the normative and from the retarded points of view. Non-verbal communicative behaviour in apes, normal and retarded humans is dealt with in three papers. Intervention strategies for the very young are discussed in three papers, and issues in the language training of the mentally retarded are raised in four papers. An important concluding paper by A. W. Staats analyses the theoretical systems in linguistic, cognitive, learning, and behavioural research, and discusses a 'neopsycholinguistics' which could embody both the cognitive and the behavioural approaches within a revised form of learning theory: Staats insists, and rightly, in my view, that the dogmatic separatism of the Chomskian and Skinnerian views is seriously impeding progress in a field of research with very fruitful possibilities. Diana Major investigates *The acquisition of modal auxiliaries in the language of children.*[40] Her major purposes were to determine the nature and status of the modal system in children of various ages, and to try to develop measures of differential exploitation and comprehension of these systems. The data were elicited by using carefully constructed verbal cues in an attempt to find out what the children *can* produce rather than what they *do*

produce. There is a chapter reviewing the literature on defining modals, and another on the formal criteria for determining modals. Eighteen modal forms were differentiated for testing (including different senses, marginals etc) and they were embodied in paradigms which distinguished progressives from perfects. The forms were administered in six different types of task (imitation, affirmative to negative conversion, Illinois psycholinguistic ability test, provision of tag questions for affirmatives, sentence completion, addressing questions to a puppet). Major's conclusions are admirably lucid and point to the need for further research on modal verb realizations within the generative framework: "further studies of the children's language should begin with the assumption that we do not yet know how to write the rules that would describe this system accurately". Eric Wanner presents experimental evidence which reflects thoughts *On remembering, forgetting, and understanding sentences.*[41] Chapter one outlines the justification for the hypothesis that the deep structure of a sentence is recovered during comprehension but not by the use of transformational rules (as parsing devices). Chapter two reports an experiment which attempts to establish the resemblance between the memory trace for sentences and their underlying propositional form. A second experiment attempted to find out why, in the light of the hypothesis, there appeared to be too much retention of superficial sentential information after comprehension. Chapter four speculates upon what the psychological processes of comprehension of sentences might be if

[40] *The acquisition of the modal auxiliaries in the language of children* by Diana Major. The Hague: Mouton. pp. 121. DFl. 14.

Schiefelbusch and Lyle L. Lloyd. London: Macmillan. pp. 670. £7.95.

[41] *On remembering, forgetting, and understanding sentences: a study of the deep structure hypothesis* by Eric Wanner. The Hague: Mouton. pp. 160 DFl. 24.

they do not depend upon transformations. The book concludes with a very tentative specification of a lexical model of sentential comprehension. Martin D. S. Braine expands 'On what might constitute learnable phonology' (*Language*). He attacks the proponents of the generative phonological view that representations are abstract. He does this from the laudable, and, in the context of this controversy, rare, point of view of some data. In addition, however, he claims that the main rationale for the 'abstractness' position—the enthroning of criteria of economy in respect of human memory and learning—is almost certainly in error. Braine considers four hypotheses as to how lexical entries are phonologically represented and argues that though the solution to which of them is closest to the truth is an empirical question, it is not an empirical question which can be answered with anything other than psychological data. Marc L. Schnitzer finds evidence in favour of the performative analysis of sentences, the actuality of discourse rules, the partial independence of syntax and semantics, the function of pronouns as pure variables, and a copula-creation rule in English, in the speech of one aphasic patient ('Aphasiological evidence for five linguistic hypotheses' *Language*). Mark Cook, Jacqueline Smith, and Mansur G. Lalljee investigate the relationship between the occurrence of filled pauses and two types of syntactic complexity ('Filled pauses and syntactic complexity' *L&S*). They found that there was no relationship between the proportion of subordinate clauses and filled pause rate, but that there was such a relationship between filled pause rate and the occurrence of longer than average clauses. However, there are clearly other, confounding, factors at work in the distribution of filled pauses. Norman C. Graham discusses 'Response strategies in the partial comprehension of sentences' (*L&S*). Children with a pre-school level of language development were asked to select one of four pictures in response to the hearing of a sentence. The sentences differed in terms of their having one of twelve different grammatical structures (the three incorrect pictures were representations of the lexical variants of the presented sentence). The results are interpreted as meaning that a limited capacity information processing model of speech perception is needed, that grammatical and lexical processing compete for the same processing capacity, and that a metric for sentence complexity is essential if progress is to be made in such a model. Ernst L. Moerk provides us with 'A design for multivariate analysis of language behaviour and language development' (*L&S*). It is a brief programmatic plea for something that many sociolinguists are already attempting (see LePage, above, & Pellowe *YW* 53). Paul A. Kolers undertakes some experiments to show the importance of 'Remembering trivia' (*L&S*). The basis for remembering trivia (features irrelevant to comprehension and interpretation) is neither pictorial memory, nor phonemic, nor articulatory memory, but appears to rest upon a suitable set towards the stimulus material in terms of a knowledge of the structure of the symbol system. Philip S. Dale found that 'Hesitations in maternal speech' were more likely to occur at sentence boundaries when mothers were talking to their younger children, than when they were talking to their older children. No differential effect appeared for the distribution with respect to three different definitions of phrase-boundary. Daniel N. Osheron and Ellen Markman investigate 'Language and the ability to evaluate contradictions and tautologies' (*Cognition*). They find that the difficulty of such sentences is not solely due to the logical words in them, that some difficulty arises from the fact that the truth value depends on linguistic form rather than the empirical facts of the matter, and that correct responses depend (necessarily) upon the ability to examine language objectively, rather than its situated function. Catherine Garvey, Alfonso Caramazza and Jack Yates discuss 'Factors influencing assignment of pronoun antecedents' (*Cognition*). They use the frame *NP1 V NP2 because Pro* ... (John telephoned Bill because he ...). The coreferentiality of *Pro* with *NP1* or *NP2* seems to depend upon a factor of direction of causality which inheres in verbs, which in turn can be manipulated by other syntactic and semantic parameters in the sentence. The authors discuss the general utility of such a test for the psycholinguistics of comprehension. Stephen Wilcox and David S. Palermo evaluate the view from '"In", "On," and "Under" revisited' (*Cognition*). They present evidence that comprehension of such locatives by small children depends as much upon strategies which interpret non-linguistic elements of context (such as the 'physical logic' of the stimulus materials) as upon any semantic features which might be deemed to underlie the linguistic stimuli. J. S. Bruner gives an incisive review of problems in research on language acquisition in the context of the question as to how the child passes from pre-speech communication to the use of language proper. He examines some of the precursors of the organizing features of language structure in terms of the mother's mode of interpreting the child's intent, the development of mutual (but possibly private) devices for reference (before deixis), the child's ways of enlisting aid for joint activities, and so on. Bruner considers whether the child's knowledge of action and interaction might not be the basis for the development of language ('From communication to language—A psychological perspective' *Cognition*). Bruner's conjecture is supported to some extent by evidence of 'Conservation accidents' noted by James McGariggle & Margaret Donaldson (*Cognition*). They conclude that characteristics of the experimenter's behaviour towards task materials can influence the children's interpretation of utterances by suggesting that the experimenter is thinking about different features of the materials than those specified linguistically; hence, traditional procedures 'may underestimate children's cognitive abilities'. A. R. Luria discusses some 'Scientific perspectives and philosophical dead ends in modern linguistics' (*Cognition*). In particular, he gives voice to the fact that he 'highly disapproves' of Chomsky's hypothesis that deep structures are innate. Luria's paper parallels Bruner's in terms of its plea for less doctrinaire and more imaginative characterizations of what can properly be done in child language acquisition studies. Ruth Clark, Sandy Hutcheson and Paul van Buren investigate 'Comprehension and production in language acquisition' (*JL*). There are many arguments, of a theoretical nature, in linguistics, which have as one of their elements the claim that, for any given type of structure, comprehension precedes production. The authors carefully distinguish two constituents of the notion 'comprehension'—firstly, appropriacy of response, secondly, understanding,—and point out the logical independency of these components. They then distinguish narrower and wider senses in which comprehension can be said to precede production, and conclude that only for the latter sense is the assertion significantly true. The conclusion rests on the notion that comprehension in the wider sense depends upon readings of the non-verbal (situational) cues which are available. Though the discussion does clarify some of the issues, it seems to introduce as many problems as it resolves.

(c) *Computational linguistics*

Hans Karlgren, in 'Categorial grammar calculus' (*Statistical methods in linguistics*), gives a very wide-ranging and general account of the false attractiveness of simple categorial grammars (attributable to (a) intractability of natural language data, (b) insufficiently general nature of such grammars). Solving these problems involves constructing two grammars, the 'solutions' of the simpler being input to the proposals of the more complex. Recognition grammars of such types, and in such relations, underline the importance of attending to equivalence and substitutability between grammars. John Lehrberger proposes extensions to traditional categorial grammars (in somewhat different ways to those of Karlgren), in his *Functor analysis of natural language*.[42] His main aim is to determine textural structure in terms of the phrasal relations between phrases which comprise that text. This he attempts to do by establishing functor phrases for a text (or a sentence) and analysing other phrases as arguments of the functor phrases. Multiple relations are permitted by

allowing a single occurrence of a phrase to be (simultaneously) the argument for more than one functor phrase. Conversely, a particular functor may have more than one set of arguments. Chapters one and two outline the historical development of categorial grammars, and discuss the view that categorial grammars are simple variants of phrase structure grammars. Chapter three is largely taken up with the development of a suitable notation for assigning structure to symbolic strings, and the representation of that structure in graph form. Chapter four discusses some formal criteria for establishing which phrases of a text may be considered as the functors, but lays great stress upon the multi-structured nature of any text, the fact that there will, as likely as not, be no unique specification of functors (and their arguments) for any given text. Chapters five, six, and seven show the importance, for a maximally sensitive 'reading' of a text, of the many-to-one and one-to-many relations between functors and arguments, the capacity of functor grammars of this kind to cope with the non-linear (i.e. co-occurrent) nature of features such as intonation, and the ways in which texts' structures may be compared in terms of the functors (and the relations between them) which occur. Richard Timon Daly examines seven arguments in empirical linguistics and psychology which make use of the theory of the mathematical structure of languages and concludes that in none of the cases has the application been successful (*Applications of the mathematical theory of linguistics*[43]). This is a rather gloomy book, and one whose basic stance is in opposition to the more positively exciting work of

---

[42] *Functor analysis of natural language* by John Lehrberger. The Hague: Mouton. pp. 155. n.p.

[43] *Applications of the mathematical theory of linguistics* by Richard Timon Daly. The Hague: Mouton. pp. 116. DFl. 24.

Montague's (see below). W. J. M. Levelt's book (*Formal grammars in linguistics and psycholinguistics* 2 vols)[44] is also rather more positive than Daly's. In volume one, Levelt provides a clear and careful account of the mathematical theory of languages and automata based largely upon the work of Chomsky. Thus, for instance, he discusses grammars as formal systems, and the way in which grammars with different defining mathematical properties can be classified hierarchically. He distinguishes amongst the properties of automata which can be taken to represent these grammars (finite automata, pushdown automata, linear-bounded automata, Turing machines). In addition, however, he provides chapters on probabilistic grammars and on a possible modelling of grammatical inference. Volume two, using the distinctions made in the first volume, surveys the most important pure and mixed models which have been applied to the solution of problems arising in the study of natural languages. Under the head of 'pure' models, are discussed varieties of phrase structure grammar; under the head of mixed models, the *Aspects* model is treated in considerable detail, and categorial, dependency, operator, and adjunction, grammars are also dealt with, though rather more summarily. Levelt not only discusses the formal structure, the mutual relations, and the linguistic peculiarities, of these grammars; he also, very clearly, points out that each has its own characteristic advantages and disadvantages. These volumes

[44] *Formal grammars in linguistics and psycholinguistics. Vol. 1 An introduction to the theory of formal languages and automata. Vol. 2 Applications in linguistic theory* by W. J. M. Levelt. The Hague: Mouton. Vol. 1 pp. 143. DFl. 16. Vol. 2 pp. 194. DFl. 26.

are a very useful addition to the literature. They provide in clear, concise, and not too painful form an introduction to a range of important problems in the theory of grammar which is ideal for the beginning postgraduate student, and useful to the professional whose central research interests lie elsewhere.

Under a different interpretation of the headline 'computational linguistics', we can consider the continuous efforts of computer scientists to write ever more general programs which will effectively model the adaptive and information processing behaviour of humans. There is a great deal of material in this field of 'machine' or 'artificial' 'intelligence', but much of it circulates in an underground fashion. I shall here only consider two items, which, between them, represent much of what is being done at the moment. Roger C. Schank discusses the relationship between 'Adverbs and belief' in terms of the capacity, which a certain class of adverbs has, to locate the sentences in which they occur in a complex conceptual, or belief, structure (*Lingua*). The class of adverbs concerned is that which includes *vengefully, mercifully, foolishly, thoughtlessly, needlessly, wrongfully, unjustly, angrily*. Schank discusses the behaviour of these adverbs within a system of conceptual dependency which he and co-workers have been developing for some years at Stanford. The internal coherence of Schank's system and its way of representing semantic and conceptual relations is, considering the lack of formalism in his approach, surprisingly good. There is not space here to illustrate properly the ways in which adverbs of the type mentioned above do give placings of sentences in overall belief structures; suffice it to say that, in better known linguistic terms, Schank characterizes dyadic presuppositions in terms of actual and imputed case relations incorporated in a time-based inferring machine. In 'John threw a hammer at Bill vengefully' we have to copy into the sentence the abstract belief structure which is associated with (conceptualized in) the notion 'revenge'. In longhand, this structure is something like 'the causal relationship between the conceptualization of person i doing something and the conceptualization that that something harms person j is caused by the causal relationship between the conceptualization that person j did something and the conceptualization that that something harmed person i.' The importance of Schank's work is that it shows that for an adequate interpretation of sentences of this type, none of the above levels of causality or of conceptualization is redundant. Donald Michie, with his usual humour, and clarity of exposition, writes *On Machine intelligence*.[45] The book comprises an introduction and fifteen papers, originally published in rather scattered sources, representing a great deal of the research which has been undertaken in the machine intelligence unit at Edinburgh between 1961 and 1973. Michie shows how a model of a machine can be developed which learns to improve its performance in noughts and crosses, and how the ability to design a machine which can do such apparently useless things is, in fact, very closely related to the skills required to solve much more obviously practical problems (such as the transfer of morse code input to written English output). He distinguishes carefully between the skills involved in one-person and two-person games (puzzles and games respectively), and claims

that 'life' is more like the latter than the former, and that learning theories based upon the 'puzzle' approach probably seriously underestimate the nature of the processes which are needed. He discusses the ways in which games can be considered to be graphs, and how playing games is equivalent to manipulating and evaluating competing graphs. Some of the reasons why games are more difficult to learn than to play are discussed. The general over-riding importance of 'looking ahead' in human activities is discussed in several places in the book, as is the need for capabilities to be suitably task-independent or general. The goals and methods of machine intelligence are compared in terms of various criteria of feasibility, assumptions, rate of progress, and commercial and financial viability, with those of other (historically earlier) fields of endeavour. The book contains a great deal of interest to linguists in the narrow sense. It is full of useful tables and diagrams, and shines with lucidity.

A third possible interpretation of computational linguistics is represented brilliantly and wittily in a book by Ben Ross Schneider Jr., *Travels in Computerland, or incompatibilities and interfaces*.[46] Schneider's book is the accumulated history of frustrations and triumphs which characterized his slow and painful attempt to put into optimal machine-readable form *The London stage, 1600–1800, a calendar of plays, entertainment and afterpieces, together with casts, box-receipts and contemporary comment, compiled from the playbills, newspapers and theatrical diaries of the period* (eleven volumes, 8026 pages). The cause and solution, of each problem, have a hallucinatory

[45] *On Machine intelligence* by Donald Michie. Edinburgh: Edinburgh U.P. pp. 199 n.p.

[46] *Travels in Computerland, or incompatibilities and interfaces* by Ben Ross Schneider Jr. London/Reading, Mass.: Addison-Wesley. pp. 244. £3.30.

hilarity about them which should educe caution from the computational optimist, and inject the literary critic with curiosity. The book should be compulsory reading in any course which deals with the computational treatment of literary materials.

(d) *Semantics, pragmatics, lexicology*

Isidore Dyen has edited the proceedings of the 1971 Yale conference on *Lexicostatistics in genetic linguistics*.[47] The volume amply demonstrates that Chrétien's critique of Swadesh's original model of the relationships between time, language divergence, and change in the word stock of particular languages, was itself largely in error (cf. remarks in *YW* 53). Chrétien's error lay in a misunderstanding of the fundamental form of statistical distributions, and their relationship to statistical inference. The book contains an introductory essay by Dyen demonstrating, with both mathematical elegance and exegetical patience, 'The validity of the mathematical model of glottochronology'. J. B. Kruskal, I. Dyen, & P. Black obtain 'Some results from the vocabulary method of reconstructing language trees' by applying a maximum likelihood method to 600 word lists (from different types of source) from four language families. They are very explicit about the reasons for, and the degree of innocuousness of, each of their statistical assumptions. It is, in fact, the reflection of the results back upon the nature and meaning of these assumptions which is perhaps of greatest interest here. By methods such as these, methodologies are baked into theories. Annette J. Dobson (in

'Estimating time separation for languages') attempts to develop a probabilistic theory of large scale language change in the context of branch set (tree) theory. David Sankoff points to a number of superficial and profound mathematical and conceptual 'Parallels between genetics and lexicostatistics'. Dyen discusses 'The impact of lexicostatistics on comparative linguistics'. Three papers discuss groupings in Hamito-Semitic, French based creoles (though there are complex theoretical arguments that a variationist (cf. C.-J. N. Bailey above) might advance against the feasibility of a glottochronological treatment of creoles), and, finally Mayan. Rulon Wells contributes a squib on the forgotten work of Thomas Young (1773–1829) who, it seems, had adumbrated, though using faulty starting values, a probabilistic theory of language relatedness. Wells' paper is complemented by Dell Hymes' account of 'Lexicostatistics and glottochronology in the nineteenth century (with notes toward a general history)', in which it is shown how long the tradition of sensible and scientific endeavour in this area of linguistic research has been.

Witold Doroszewski's *Elements of lexicology and semiotics*[48] is one of those, fortunately rare, books which hovers constantly and hauntingly between an inconsequentially romantic and a genuinely insightful conception of a difficult subject; a subject, moreover, which is in desperate need of more scholarly attention. The book abounds in undefended assumptions, the motivations for whose inclusion is often very unclear. It is frequently unclear what the thrust of a whole chapter (e.g. Chapter 4 'The dualist and monist trends in the history of

[47] *Lexicostatistics in genetic linguistics: proceedings of the Yale Conference, Yale University, April 3–4, 1971* edited by Isidore Dyen (1973). The Hague: Mouton. pp. 176. DFl. 50.

[48] *Elements of lexicology and semiotics* by Witold Doroszewski (1973). The Hague: Mouton. pp. 314. DFl. 29.

linguistic thought. Soul and Brain.') might be construed as being. Certainly, the relationship between chapters, and the function of each within the book as a whole, is not at all clear. The fact that the chapters are lectures collected from a period of ten years does not entitle their author to withhold all sense of continuity from his readers. Many sentences in the book seem to this reviewer to be literally meaningless (however much context one presses into service), for instance: "One of the corollaries of the bio-psycho-social unity of man is the desire awakening in him to be useful to his environment" (p. 7), "to meditate on something is to a certain extent to react at a given moment to a stimulus originating internally, in the memory" (p. 93), "the strengthening of the rational trend in social life is served by dictionaries" (p. 12). The book is useful for the strong reader merely as an indication of what it could have been had it eschewed romantic metaphysics and espoused refutable forms of argument. Ad de Vries has compiled a *Dictionary of symbols and imagery*.[49] It is intended to be an additional help to anyone confronted by a difficult symbol as it supplies 'associations which have been evoked by certain words . . . in Western civilization in the past'. Fine distinctions between symbols, allegories, metaphors, signs, types, images, and so on, are not made. de Vries believes that significant indefiniteness is one of the most important marks of symbols, and the dictionary is organized accordingly. As the author points out himself, "in this book truth is not of primary importance, but what was, has been, or is believed to be true'. Clearly, such an undertaking cannot satisfy all the persons who consult it,

[49] *Dictionary of symbols and imagery* by Ad de Vries. Amsterdam: North-Holland Publ. Co. pp. 515. DFl. 100.

but like one of its cousins (Brewer's *Dictionary of phrase and fable*) it answers more questions than one might expect it to, and it does so with wit and charm. Adrienne Lehrer investigates the ways in which informants are able to interpret the use of 'Extended meanings of body-part terms' (*International Journal of American Linguistics*). She points to the need to determine how productive the use of such body-part terms is (the mouth, neck, foot, bottom, lip, of pots, of houses etc.). Can hearers interpret 'the ear of the window' with any consistency? Answers to such questions will reveal important facts about semantic processes. Peter A. de Villiers shows that 'An effect of the definite article on the salience of a noun' is to make the noun in question less likely to be revised by subjects who are asked to improve semantically anomalous sentences. In addition, subject nouns are less likely to be changed in this state than object nouns in the same state, if the selectional restrictions on the verb are broken (*L&S*). Magnus Ljung makes 'Some remarks on antonymy' (*Language*), and concentrates, in particular on the notion of antonymous adjectives. He suggests, after a review of the literature, that only noun-based adjectives can be antonymous. He contrasts this class of adjectives with those derived from inalienable nouns, and shows how although it is not possible to have a feature $\pm$ inherentness (which is the source for such adjectives) indexed for each noun in the lexicon, nevertheless, inherentness within the sentence must somehow be incorporated in the grammar of English. John Haiman discusses the problematic nature of polysemy for transformational grammars with special reference to 'Concessives, conditionals and verbs of volition' (*FLang*). Using evidence from clauses and verbs of these types he outlines the ways in which polysemy in different languages might be claimed to be non-accidental: that, in fact, in many cases of polysemy, there are good structural semantic reasons why there might be a justifiable expectation that superficial morphology and syntactic behaviour would exhibit the polysemous relations which they do. Masa Muraki attempts to demonstrate the complexity but feasibility of 'Presupposition in cyclic lexical insertion' (*FLang*). The argument purports to show that lexical items having inherent or adventitious presupposition do not negate the possibility of the cyclic insertion of lexical material. E. König presents an analysis of 'The semantic structure of time prepositions in English' in terms of a logical analysis of the relations between sentences containing such items and their implications, presuppositions and so on. The author claims to reveal more of the semantic structure of such features than Leech's analysis of the same features (*FLang*). David E. Cooper asks 'Do SR's paraphrase sentences?' (see notice of P. A. M. Seuren's book below): he concludes that semantic representations cannot possibly be paraphrases since they are to include the presuppositions and the illocutionary force inherent in a sentence. By such means, the mystery as to what a SR is, is simply transferred to what kind of paraphrase such a one would be (*FLang*). Kenneth Antley discusses 'McCawley's theory of selectional restriction' (*FLang*), in a somewhat sceptical fashion. He asserts that McCawley's wish to erect selectional restrictions upon semantic, rather than syntactic, criteria creates more, and worse, problems that it solves. Eve V. Clark suggests that the idiomatic deictic use of verb pairs such as *come* and *go*, and *bring*

and *send*, comprise pairs which relate to normal-state deixis, and which in these or transferred senses have a positive member and a negative member (he came through *vs.* he went through a lot). She suggests that both forms of idiom are related to other forms of deixis, all of which derive from the basic deictic contrast between *ego* and *non-ego* ('Normal states and evaluative viewpoints' *Language*). More generally, Wallace L. Chafe discusses 'Language and consciousness' (*Language*), in terms of the relationships between the linguistic notions of *given* and *new* (of information), the distinction between such notions and contrastiveness, the relations between givenness and newness for the speaker and the addressee, the reasons why speakers may change their minds about what may properly be treated as given, the relations between givenness and memory, and givenness and egocentrism. He concludes that the given/new distinction, and its surface structure consequences ought to be a prime area of research in all languages. Ronald W. Langacker interprets 'Movement rules in functional perspective' (*Language*) by showing how raising, lowering, and fronting rules for English all conspire to increase the prominence of objective content in surface structure. The differentiation of backing rules in this respect is confirmation for the hypothesis. Peter Cole (contra Antley, above) argues that not only syntactic representations, but syntactic processes also, must have their basis in semantics. He uses, as evidence for this position, facts about the blocking of anaphoric pronominalization for indefinite antecedents from several languages. He claims that the constraint arises from the semantic properties of various classes of definite noun phrases (cf. J. A. Hawkins, below). Adrienne

Lehrer has distilled a great deal of her research and her clarity of purpose in *Semantic fields and lexical structure*.[50] She summarizes the most important research in the area, and, very properly, spends a good deal of her space discussing problems of method. Various lexical fields are used as illustrations, but that having to do with cooking is dominant. She carefully determines what a semantic field is, both in terms of linguistic practice, and in terms of folk taxonomy, and links this to a brief but clear account of the various forms of componential analysis which have been used under different theoretical perspectives. Word semantics is then related to sentential semantics in a chapter dealing with analyticity, contradiction and indeterminacy. These preliminaries are then used to discuss the problems raised by lexical gaps, belief predicates, semantic universals, restrictions upon selection, and the relationship between grammar and the lexicon. The book assumes knowledge of generative grammar, and points up the tension which exists between the desire for elegance and the desire for psychological reality in the construction of grammars; a tension that seems not only to be more obvious in the lexicon than elsewhere in language structure, but less likely to be solved by convergence. John A. Hawkins has undertaken a very careful analysis of the semantics of the articles *a, the, some*, in English. The work, as presented, is a reduction of a rather wider range of studies, whose purpose is to present conclusions, and their justifications, which are of direct relevance to the debate upon the relationship between syntax and semantics (see below P. A. M. Seuren). Hawkins'

work (*Definiteness and indefiniteness*) inclines to an agreement with, a vindication of, the semanticalness of syntax.[51] Pieter A. M. Seuren has edited an important little collection of essays on *Semantic Syntax*.[52] As we have seen in this and previous *YW* conspectuses, there is little likelihood of this debate's being resolved in any straightforward way for several years to come; indeed, it may well turn out to be one of those debates which, rather than being resoluble by appeal to principles and data already recognized within the subject, radically changes, or even splits, the subject itself. The book contains two papers by James D. McCawley, two by Seuren himself, two by George Lakoff, one by Robin Lakoff, one by C. L. Baker, and one by R. P. G. de Rijk. Two main problem areas which have bearing upon the distinction between semantics and syntax are dealt with in the collection: firstly, the way in which lexical material can be thought of as being inserted into a grammatical form; secondly, the grammatical status of logical elements in strings. The importance of the debate can hardly be overemphasized; accessibility to it, both in terms of the price of this collection, and its incisiveness, will now be universal. Arnold L. Glass & Keith J. Holyoak have conducted an experiment which, they claim, sheds light on 'Alternative conceptions of semantic theory' (*Cognition*), and favours the marker-search model of Katz to the feature-comparison model of Lakoff. The complexity of the theoretical debate seems to be such, however, that any experimental work of this kind is, almost by definition, going to incorporate over-

[51] *Definiteness and indefiniteness* by J. A. Hawkins. Cambridge: Trinity Hall. pp. 432 (mimeo) £3.00.
[52] *Semantic syntax* edited by Pieter A. M. Seuren. London: OUP. pp. 218. £1.20. paper.

[50] *Semantic fields and lexical structure* by Adrienne Lehrer. Amsterdam: North Holland Publ. Co. pp. 225. DFl. 30.

simplifications of a disastrous nature. Edwin Martin & David Woodruff Smith, in an important paper, try to account for Quine's views on the indeterminacy of translations and their relationship to his attacks on present day linguistics. This they do by contrasting Quine's views with those of C. S. Peirce, and by disentangling the indeterminacy argument from the arguments about translation and meaning ('On the nature and relevance of indeterminacy' *FLang*). The nature of presupposition comes in for some careful analysis at the hands of S.-Y. Kuroda ('Geach and Katz on presupposition' *FLang*).

Perhaps the most important single work (in this, or any, section on the state of present day English linguistic studies) to have appeared this year, is a selection of Richard Montague's papers, *Formal philosophy*, edited by Richard Thomason.[53] It is certainly not an easy book to read. There are several reasons why linguists might find it infuriating, because many of its arguments appear to omit, or ignore, facts, generalizations, and assumptions, whose relevance and utility are very widely taken to be agreed upon. But this is one of its values. Its other value is that it treats of a whole series of very complex, and related, semiotic and pragmatic issues (whose solution a great deal of general linguistic theory waits upon) with very great precision. Montague's approach depends on the adaptation of metamathematical methods and solutions to the study of syntactic, semantic and pragmatic problems in natural languages. His work thus owes a good deal to various developments in modern logic, but almost

nothing to twentieth century linguistics. There is thus a good deal of freshness in these papers, for a linguist who has some understanding of logical notation and inference (Thomason's introductory chapter provides a very useful map of Montague's main pre-occupations and methodological innovations). Montague's basic position is an extension of that of Carnap, namely, that the syntax, semantics and pragmatics of natural languages are branches of mathematics, not of psychology. Although this position is *theoretically* a radical departure from that of post-Chomskyan linguistics, it does share with the latter an unwillingness to be constrained by the statistics of the intuitions upon which it rests. Montague rejects, on the one hand, that there is an important theoretical difference between formal (mathematical, programming) languages, and natural (human) languages, and, on the other, that the formal treatments of natural language associated with MIT can ever produce a theory of truth under an arbitrary interpretation; such a theory is what Montague believed was the only serious goal in syntax and semantics. Both of these rejections are supported by various of the papers, the most important of which, in this respect, are, 'English as a formal language', and 'The proper treatment of quantification in ordinary English'. Montague also lays very important foundations, however, for precise formulations within Morris's third branch of general semiotic, namely, pragmatics ('the relations among expressions, the objects to which they refer, and the users or contexts of use of the expressions'). The book includes a bibliography of Montague's writings and a useful index. There is no doubt that Montague's pioneering work will continue to stimulate

[53] *Formal philosophy: selected papers of Richard Montague* edited, with an introduction, by Richard H. Thomason. New Haven & London: Yale Univ. Pr. pp. 369. £8.10.

important research for many years. Charles Sayward, taking nothing for granted, examines the validity of Morris's original trichotomy of semiotic (syntax, semantics, pragmatics), and the criteria it depends upon (expressions, designata of expressions, speakers of expressions), and concludes that were even 'The received distinction between pragmatics, semantics and syntax' clear, the utility of the distinctions would be uncertain (*FLang*). Harvey Sacks, Emanuel A. Schegloff & Gail Jefferson try to construct 'A simplest systematics for the organization of turn-taking for conversation' (*Language*). The model which they propose is examined in terms of the observable characteristics of conversations, and is contrasted with the form of turn-taking in other forms of speech-exchange. The model shows that conversational turn-taking is locally managed, party-administered, interactionally controlled, and sensitive to recipient design. Starkey Duncan, apparently oblivious of the research of ethnomethodology, reports 'On the structure of speaker-auditor interaction during speaking turns' (*Language in Society*). Gail Jefferson determines the nature and extent of 'Error correction as an interactional resource' (*Language in Society*). Colin Cherry has edited a collection of six papers on *Pragmatic aspects of Human communication*.[54] They are an oddly assorted collection, as Cherry himself remarks in his preface, but they each have something valuable to say. They range in content from J. C. Marshall & R. J. Wales' discussion of the relation between communicative utility and selective adaptation, through D. Dicks' 'Experiments with everyday conversation', to J. Marschak's examination

of the relationship between the theory of communication and the theory of observation. Aaron V. Cicourel, and others, have produced a disturbing, and, at times, incapacitatingly cryptic, book, about the performance of children in school, and the ineptitude of most of the ways in which this is assessed. It is based upon analyses of video- and audio-tapes of the children and their evaluators as they are actually behaving. Its most valuable feature is the data it incorporates.[55] Jerrold M. Sadock has attempted to provide an entirely linguistic account of how natural languages encode information about the intentions of speakers, and their assumptions about the speech situations which they are in. *Towards a linguistic theory of speech acts* uses a conservative version of generative semantics (or semantic syntax) to show that sentences carry a good deal more of this kind of information than had previously been thought.[56] The theory upon which the analyses are based does not survive unscathed, however. The book is clear, and very useful.

(e) *Syntax, morphology*

J. M. Anderson proposes in 'All and equi ride again' (contra Carden 1968) to analyse quantified NPs and relative constructions as partitives (*ArL*). The semantic differences between such pairs of sentences as *Everyone expects to die* and *Everyone expects everyone to die* can thus be characterized without endangering the traditional transformational nature (meaning preserving) of Equi-NP deletion. Roland Sussex shows

[54] *Pragmatic aspects of human communication* edited by Colin Cherry. Dordrecht, Holland: Reidel. pp. 178. n.p.

[55] *Language use and school performance* by Aaron V. Cicourel, K. H. Jennings, S. H. M. Jennings, K. C. W. Leiter, R. McKay, H. Mehan, & D. R. Roth. London: Academic Press. pp. 368. £6.70.

[56] *Toward a linguistic theory of speech acts* by Jerrold M. Sadock. N.Y./London: Academic Press. pp. 168 £6.25.

how there are difficulties in all the available generative or transformational-generative theories when one tries to account for 'The deep structure of adjectives in noun phrases' (*JL*). James Kilbury documents 'The emergence of morphophonemics: a survey of theory and practice from 1876 to 1939' (*Lingua*), but all too briefly. D. J. Allerton & A. Cruttenden discuss the relationship between the syntax and the intonation of 'English sentence adverbials' in British English (*Lingua*). The intonation of sentence-initial adverbials is found to depend upon syntactic class, the inherent semantics of the adverb, the attitude of the speaker, and whether the adverb modifies a sentence containing given or new information. Chisato Kitagawa examines 'Purpose expressions in English' (*Lingua*): that is, he sets out to determine the well-formedness conditions on sentences containing an *in order to* complement in co-occurrence with non-voluntative verbs. D. A. Lee discusses 'Noun phrase raising in French and English' (*Lingua*), and shows that a modification which is necessary to the Kiparskys' hypothesis about the source of infinitival complements (i.e. that infinitival complements not only arise from a verb's losing its subject in a derivation, but also from a verb's never having *acquired* a subject), favours Fillmore's account of a proper form for linguistic theory. F. J. Newmeyer documents and discusses 'The regularity of idiom behaviour' (*Lingua*). He formalizes the surprising fact that given the meaning of an idiom, and given the meaning of its literal equivalent, the syntactic behaviour of the idiom can be predicted. The formalization leads to the abandonment of the need to enter idioms as units in the lexicon. Ronald W. Langacker reviews the problem of the derivation of interro-

gatives in English in 'The question of Q' (*FLang*). His review is largely negative in terms of the specific proposals with which he deals, but he does raise the importance of distinguishing between *naturalness* and *abstractness* in syntactic explanation. Krystyna A. Wachowicz also deals with interrogatives, but with a different goal, arguing in fact, 'Against the universality of a single wh-question movement' (*FLang*). Dale E. Elliott makes some interesting observations which take one 'Toward a grammar of exclamations' (*FLang*), a barely explored sentence type in transformational treatments. George L. Dillon, complementing the work of Kitagawa (cf. above), erects 'Some postulates characterizing volitive NPs' (*JL*). Richard M. Smaby investigates the nature and extent of 'Subordinate clauses and asymmetry in English' (*JL*) and tries to show how a variety of functions is served by a unified concept. Methodology and forms of argumentation are central concerns of the paper. Ray C. Dougherty investigates 'The syntax and semantics of *Each other* constructions' (*FLang*), and concludes that two rival accounts (the conjunction reduction hypothesis, and the logical structure analysis) can both be incorporated in a modified form of his own previous proposal that such strings can be accounted for by a phrase structure analysis. Marga Reis considers, once more, problematic sentences involving change of identity, such as, *I dreamed that I was Sophia Loren and that I kissed me*; a plausible analysis for which has been given by Lakoff (in terms of a distinction between individual-counterparts and body-counterparts). She finds that it is useful to make a distinction between core-grammar and patch-up grammar, (the latter dealing with disputed or marginal cases of recoverability of intention) ('Patching up with counterparts' *FLang*). Eldon G. Lytle considers formal junctional grammars as ways of expressing the nature of the relationships between grammatical constituents in *A grammar of subordinate structures in English*[57]. According to his theory, constituents may be adjoined, conjoined, or subjoined. The rule system which emerges from this method appears to render empty the necessity for transforms to change the relations between constituents. Lytle claims that his proposals will, on the one hand, reduce the power of transformational grammars, by reducing their scope, and, on the other, make the links between transformational grammars and previous scholarship more credible (by formalizing some of the most general insights of the latter within the purview of the former).

František Daneš has edited an important collection of papers from the first international symposium on functional sentence perspective held at Marienbad in 1970, *Papers on functional sentence perspective*.[58] The volume contains nineteen papers, ten in English, four in German, and five in Russian, and although the matters discussed, and the terminology used to treat them with, are very varied, there is a strong concensus of agreement running through the volume that linguistic theories which do not have a mechanism for dealing with the informational organization within sentences and texts are badly underdetermining the data. Dieter Kastovsky has selected articles by Hans Marchand, comprising *Studies in syntax and word-formation*, to honour the latter's sixty-fifth birth-

day.[59] It need hardly be said that Marchand founded the study of word-formation on a theoretical basis virtually single-handed. This volume is an invaluable companion to Marchand's second edition of his *The categories and types of present-day English word-formation* (1969, Munich). It falls into two parts: there are six articles on the syntax of the English verb phrase, and twenty three on word-formation. It is not possible, in the space available here, to do more than refer to Marchand's wide range of interest, and his subtlety of observation: word-formation often presents untidy patterns, and it is, in part, an explanation of Marchand's pre-eminence in the field, that he does not either overemphasize or ignore this source of theoretical difficulty. Arne Juul has undertaken a careful study of *The nominal phrase and the subject-verb relation in modern English, with special reference to so-called cases of concord and discord in respect of number*.[60] The data are largely restricted to written British English. Gunnar Persson has published his doctoral dissertation on *Repetition in English*.[61] In this part (I), he examines the types of lexical repetition which occur in written and spoken (British) English. The spoken English was a corpus of approximately 94000 words drawn from the University College, London, Survey of English Usage material. The written material was composed of

---

[57] *A grammar of subordinate structures in English* by Eldon. G. Lytle. The Hague: Mouton. pp. 139. DFl. 26.

[58] *Papers on functional sentence perspective* edited by František Daneš. The Hague: Mouton. pp. 222. DGl. 28.

[59] *Studies in syntax and word-formation; selected articles by Hans Marchand; on the occasion of his 65th birthday* edited by Dieter Kastovsky. Munich: Wilhelm Fink. pp. 439. n.p.

[60] *The nominal phrase and the subject-verb relation in modern English, with special reference to so-called cases of concord and discord in respect of number* by Arne Juul. Copenhagen: Nova Mikrofilm pp. 276. DKr. 65·50.

[61] *Repetition in English; Part I Sequential repetition* by Gunnar Persson. Uppsala: Upssala Offset Center. pp. 178. n.p.

three stylistic strata (conversational, fictional, non-fictional) of approximately 500,000 words each. Persson develops a typology of repetitions (intensifying, emphatic, conjoined, mimetic, simple, and purposive) and within each type examines the syntax of the lexical items which take part. P. H. Matthews contributes the first in a new series of textbooks in linguistics from Cambridge University Press, *Morphology*.[62] It is an excellent text; well conceived, well illustrated, facing difficulties squarely without resort to facile rules of thumb, and, as one has now come to expect of CUP, splendidly printed.

(f) *Phonology*

Andreas Koutsoudas, Gerald Sanders and Craig Noll organize a great deal of evidence from different languages to support the hypothesis that all restrictions on the relative order of application of grammatical rules are determined by universal rather than by language specific principles ('The application of phonological rules' *Language*). Susan F. Schmerling undertakes 'A re-examination of "normal stress" (*Language*), and presents evidence which shows that the linguist's assumption that the stress which occurs in citation forms is the same as that which occurs on those forms sententially when no special assumptions are made by the speaker, is false. She claims that the notion of 'normal stress', even if it could be defined, would not be particularly useful in a generative framework. Geoffrey Sampson asks 'Is there a universal phonetic alphabet?' (*Language*). His answer is that not only does the hypothesis that there is a universal level of 'systematic

phonetics' (where only a fixed number of distinct values are possible for each variable) yield hardly any predictions, but that there is evidence against it. Hsin-I Hsieh cites 'Time as a cause of phonological irregularities' (*Lingua*). He solves a complex problem of irregularity by positing five successive incomplete changes.

Charles-James N. Bailey presents some arguments for 'Motivating an alternative analysis of the English inflections' (*International Journal of American Linguistics*). Ann Bodine gives 'A phonological analysis of the speech of two mongoloid (Down's syndrome) boys' (*AnL*). Her account underlines the importance of being aware of the problems of variation in the source models (parental, familial, media) and of variations in the realizations of the systems (wide range, and narrow range, vowels, are characterized). She stresses the relevance of such research for the proper determination of the biological bases of linguistic behaviour and learning, and makes contact with the universalist hypothesis of intrinsic ordering of phonological categories. John Anderson and Charles Jones present 'Three theses concerning phonological representations' (*JL*). The first is that there is reason to believe that phonological representations are more highly structured than the standard theory (of Chomsky-Halle) claims. They give evidence for this by considering how certain anomalous outcomes of the Main Stress Rule can be avoided by permitting overlapping bracketing of a syllabic kind (e.g. cluster elements can be incorporated in more than one syllable). The second thesis is that several important structural properties of syllabicity can very naturally be represented by means of modifications of, and extensions to, dependency theoretic notational devices. The third thesis is a

---

[62] *Morphology: an introduction to the theory of word-structure* by P. H. Matthews. London: C.U.P. pp. 243. £4.80 (H/Cover), £1.60. (P/Back).

virtual corollary of the first two, namely that many surface and underlying similarities and differences, in synchronically distinct and diachronically related, phonological processes, are captured naturally by a schema which at one and the same time attributes maximum structure to PRs, and expresses them in terms of both linear and non-linear ordering relations. Daniel Brink discusses important problems which arise in 'Characterizing the natural order of application of phonological rules' (*Lingua*). Whatever is to be taken as the costing index for abstract solutions to phonological problems, and however we are going to determine the priorities of relative *vs.* absolute versions of the transparency (and similar) principles, are very unclear, but Brink is certain that there can be no single principle available to close such questions. G. Knowles examines 'The Rhythm of English syllables' (*Lingua*), and points to the true but distressing fact that we do not have an adequate way of dealing with rhythm as it varies across varieties—in quite large scale ways. R. M. Allott ('Some apparent uniformities between languages in colour-naming' (*L&S*), finds, building on the pioneering work of Berlin and Kay, that there are significant constraints on phonological form of colour names in geographically and genetically unrelated languages. Sanford A. Schane, Bernard Tranel, & Harlan Lane performed an experiment whose outcome placed more rather than less weight 'On the psychological reality of a natural rule of syllable structure' (*Cognition*), the rule in question being the one which asserts that the most fundamental syllable form is CVCV. Subjects in the experiment provided such confirmation, even though the rule in question is not a particularly important one in their language.

Kerstin Hadding & Michael Studdert-Kennedy report analyses of experiments in which auditors were asked to make acoustic and linguistic judgements about stimuli whose fundamental frequencies were systematically varied, their responses enabling the authors to determine limits on the answer to the question 'Are you asking me, telling me, or talking to yourself?' (*Journal of Phonetics*). Niels Davidsen-Nielsen points to a considerable crop of difficulties associated with 'Syllabification in English words with medial *sp, st, sk*' (*Journal of Phonetics*). Harry Hollien provides a definition of vocal register as a totally laryngeal event. He posits three major registers (pulse, modal, and loft), and insists that these postulated registers must be operationally supported by perceptual, acoustic, physiological, and aerodynamic data. Such support he does in fact discover ('On vocal registers' *Journal of Phonetics*). Andrew Butcher investigates '"Brightness", "Darkness" and the dimensionality of vowel perception' (*Journal of Phonetics*) and concludes from tests on naive judges, that there is a correspondence between "brightness" and the degree of separation of first and second formants. William J. Barry in 'Language background and the perception of foreign accent' (*Journal of Phonetics*) finds that the correlation between judgements about the Englishness or Germanness of the pronunciation of English/German word pairs, and acoustic properties of those pronunciations, varies in terms of the language and dialect of the stimuli and of the judges. Olle Gunnilstam proposes a new theory of speech production which accounts for vowels and consonants in terms of two parameters: horizontality (place) for consonants, verticality (constriction) for vowels ('The theory of local linearity' *Journal of Phonetics*). A. N. Goës provides us with his preliminary report on British (R.P.) stress patterns in *The stress system of English*.[63] The book is characterized throughout by a breezy enthusiasm which, whilst it has its charms, (a) becomes tedious, (b) obscures some interesting insights. Goës's claims (to be providing a set of performance rules, which make it possible to operate the stress assignment mechanism with a high degree of reliability) are unconvincing. The 'rules' he gives are schematic at best. The incoherence of the abstract is a satisfactory diagnosis of the contents. Stephen R. Anderson's *The organization of Phonology* is a very useful, but in some ways disappointing, book.[64] It is disappointing simply because one would have liked to have had Anderson's views on the vexed and complex questions of abstractness, naturalness, and markedness, in phonological accounts of languages. It is a very useful book both for its clarity of presentation, its wealth of illustrative material, and its conscientious attempt to integrate current generative views about the nature and form of phonology with much of the pre-Chomskyan scholarship on 'classical' phonological theory. The book is devoted to the search for a formal system that allows for the adequate description of natural languages. It is primarily concerned with determining what is a problem in phonological theory, what evidence is relevant to the solution of such problems, and what sorts of things count as solutions. It accepts much of the Chomsky-Halle approach.

(g) *General*

Yorick Wilks discusses various more or less confusing ways in which linguists (and others) persist in using the terms 'theory' and 'model', and indicates how some of the confusions are pernicious, and how one can return to a 'natural' use of the distinction within linguistics by espousing the methods and rationale of computational linguistics (in particular, that branch of it sometimes known as machine intelligence) ('One small head—models and theories in linguistics' *FLang*). George Bedell denies that 'The arguments about deep structure', especially those presented by Chomsky in 'Some empirical issues in the theory of transformational grammar', have any force. He concludes that the existence of deep structure is not an empirical question. Susan Curtiss, Victoria Fromkin, Stephen Krashen, David Rigler, and Marilyn Rigler outline the horrifying biography and 'The linguistic development of Genie' (*Language*). They provide very interesting material from this child who did not begin to vocalize, let alone acquire language, until she was thirteen years seven months old. Their material throws light on hypotheses of several kinds in linguistic theory, particularly that which asserts a critical upper age for the acquisition of language. Roger C. Schank & Yorick Wilks make a spirited plea for a return to well-defined goals in linguistic theory, rejecting the avoidance of a model for performance, insisting that grammars must incorporate features for understanding and inference, and casting doubt upon the utility of importing techniques from logic to fulfil these goals ('The goals of linguistic theory revisited' *Lingua*). Arnold M. Zwicky examines several analytic procedures from phonological and syntactic studies, together with forms of argumentation. He concludes that the kinds of heuristic procedures which

[63] *The stress system of English* by A. N. Goës. Stockholm: Beckmans. pp. 189. n.p.
[64] *The organisation of phonology* by Stephen R. Anderson. N.Y./London: Academic Press. pp. 317. £9.

are implicit in much of such work argue for the remoteness of representations (the distance between the facts which make the puzzle a puzzle, and the solution which makes the solution a solution), but he warns that there is a relationship between the adequacy of representation and the extent & quality of data ('Homing-in: on arguing for remote representations' *JL*). Ray L. Birdwhistell has published a collection of his important work, spread over many years, on *Kinesics and context*.[65] Maurice Merleau-Ponty's selected essays on *Phenomenology, language and sociology* have been edited by John O'Neill.[66] They range in content from a consideration of the phenomenology of signs, through a historical interpretation of anthropology, a consideration of the metaphysics of the novel, politics in a phenomenological framework, to a consideration of visual perception; they range in style from the schematic and colloquial to the formal analysis. Don D. Roberts has performed a painstaking and very useful service for the scholarly linguistic community by describing and discussing the utility of *The existential graphs of Charles S. Peirce*.[67] Peirce's interest in and research upon a diagrammatic theory of logic is little known: it is excellent to have it available in such a lucid form. Ton van der Geest provides an *Evaluation of theories on child grammars*.[68] He develops a set of linguistic criteria which, he claims, should be satisfied by any account of language acquisition. He then applies these criteria to three types of research: the pivot-open approach, the transformational approach, and the telegraphic speech approach (Brown & others). He concludes that the most powerful form of approach would be a synthesis of the transformational and the telegraphic methods. Nathan Stemmer presents a completely different, and much more thought provoking, light upon the matter in his *An empiricist theory of language acquisition*.[69] He is concerned with the acquisition of comprehension, and he deals with it under three broad processes: isolated ostensive processes, contextual ostensive processes, and contextual verbal processes. He contrasts his position with that of nativists on the one hand, and of instrumental conditioning theorists on the order. This is an important book, and deserves a close reading. Harley C. Shands and James D. Meltzer present a conjunction of *Language and Psychiatry*, but their effort is disappointingly thin. There are no major syntheses, the bibliography is very partial (and much of what is there is peculiar): neither linguistics nor psychiatry is advanced.[70] Uhlan von Slagle attempts to solve the problems of referential meaning and semantic universals within the context of 'an adequate theory of mind' (*Language, thought, and perception*).[71] P. Beresford Ellis gives an excellent account of *The Cornish Language and its Literature*, in eight chapters, which

[65] *Kinesics and context: essays on body-motion communication* by Ray L. Birdwhistell (1973). London: Penguin. pp. 338. £1.50.

[66] *Phenomenology, language, & sociology, selected essays of Maurice Merleau-Ponty* edited by John O'Neill. London: Heinemann. pp. 352. £2.90.

[67] *The existential graphs of Charles S. Peirce* by Don D. Roberts (1973). The Hague: Mouton. pp. 168. n.p.

[68] *Evaluation of theories on child grammars* by Ton van der Geest. The Hague: Mouton. pp. 98. n.p.

[69] *An empirical theory of language acquisition* by Nathan Stemmer. The Hague: Mouton. pp. 147. DFl. 29.

[70] *Language & Psychiatry* by Harley C. Shands & James D. Meltzer (1973). The Hague: Mouton. pp. 85. DFl. 15.

[71] *Language, thought, & perception* by Uhlan von Slagle. The Hague: Mouton. pp. 60. DFl. 15.

unfold the language from Old Cornish to its death at the end of the eighteenth century and deal, finally, with the revivalist movement.[72] The argument at all points rests upon a careful consideration of documentary evidence. Ruth M. Brend has edited an important collection of papers which represent *Advances in Tagmemics*.[73] The volume is a much needed complement to the early work of K. L. Pike, B. F. Elson & V. B. Pickett, & R. E. Longacre. It comprises seven sections. There are five papers on general theory; three on phonology; three on morphology; four on sub-sentential syntax; one on sentential syntax; six on supra-sentential syntax; and one on the analysis of society. The widespread concern, on the part of contributors, to establish proper units, and to leave open questions of formalization which have no unique solution, is very refreshing. Philip L. Peterson does some careful dissection of *Concepts and Language*,[74] and recommends that the phenomenon of cognition be conceived to be similar to, and as complicated as, the phenomenon of possessing and using the conceptual structures underlying competence in a natural language. Ferruccio Rossi-Landi gives a schematic, interdisciplinary view, of the thesis of linguistic relativity, and sketches how its periodic revival is a result of its

being not a self-contained thesis in the neo-positivistic form, but a neo-idealistic thesis, with all that that implies (*Ideologies of linguistic relativity*).[75] Under the title of *Optimization of the linguistic message*, Olga Akhmanova and Tatjana Perekalskaja have edited a collection of research by members of the English Department of Moscow State University upon various theoretical and descriptive problems of discourse analysis; the papers incorporate a good deal of programmatic material, and some careful but occasionally obscure terminological innovations.[76] There are many interesting points of contact with papers in the volume edited by F. Daneš (see above[58]). Maurice Gross, Morris Halle, & Marcel-Paul Schutzenberger have edited the first international conference proceedings on *The formal analysis of natural languages*.[77] The volume consists of six parts. There are four papers on phonology (Halle, Lightner, McCawley, Schane); four on English syntax (Emonds, Moore, Postal, Ross); three on syntax of other languages (Browne, Lees, Ruwet); three on semantics (Dixon, Rohrer, Thom); four on general and psycholinguistics (Gross, Kiefer, Stefanini, Mehler); and three on formal properties of languages (Joshi, Kuroda, Peters).

[72] *The Cornish Language and its Literature* by P. Beresford Ellis. London: Routledge & Kegan Paul. pp. 230. £4.50.

[73] *Advances in Tagmemics* edited by Ruth M. Brend. Amsterdam: North Holland Publ. Co. pp. 458. DFl. 45.

[74] *Concepts and Language; an essay in generative semantics and the philosophy of language* by Philip L. Peterson. (1973) The Hague: Mouton. pp. 184. DFl. 30.

[75] *Ideologies of linguistic relativity* by Ferruccio Rossi-Landi. (1973). The Hague: Mouton. pp. 101. n.p.

[76] *Optimization of the linguistic message* edited by Olga Akhmanova & Tatjana Perekalskaja. Moscow: MGU. pp. 227. n.p.

[77] *The formal analysis of natural languages: proceedings of the first international conference* edited by Maurice Gross, Morris Halle, & Marcel-Paul Schutzenberger (1973). The Hague: Mouton. pp. 388. DFl. 80.

III

Old English Literature

D. G. SCRAGG

Comprehensive bibliographies of Anglo-Saxon studies appear annually in *ASE*, and in *Old English Newsletter* (published for the Modern Language Association of America by the Center for Medieval and Renaissance Studies, The Ohio State University). The latter also contains a review of the year's work in Old English studies. A list of Old English research work in progress compiled by Alan K. Brown appears annually in *NM*.

This chapter is based broadly on the Old English Literature section of the *ASE* bibliography, and the reviewer is grateful to its chief editor for making available advance proofs.

1. SOCIAL, CULTURAL AND INTELLECTUAL BACKGROUND

Stanley Rubin's clinical description in *Medieval English Medicine*[1] of the Anglo-Saxon, an inch or so shorter than his modern descendant, blessedly free from dental decay but racked by arthritis and a variety of eye diseases—as often exacerbated as alleviated by the attentions of his physician —is not recommended to the squeamish reader. Although the survey ends with the fourteenth century, it is largely a study of Anglo-Saxon medical tradition and practice, which remained almost unchanged, the author claims, until the Arabic (ultimately Greek) system of medicine became widely available in England during the thirteenth century. Since

the material for the survey is derived from reports 'distributed over a wide area of literature: medical, historical and archaeological', 'assembling of the evidence into a systematically arranged body of information' was not easy; and in fact the book is of mixed quality, partly for this reason, partly because it includes a good deal of fruitless speculation, for example on the specific diseases cured by the miracles described in hagiographical literature. But at its best it is a useful summary of documentary and archaeological evidence, subjected to the scrutiny of a medical mind. Though full of patronizing references to folklore and superstition, it does stress the considerable achievement of Anglo-Saxon medicine in compiling a body of vernacular literature unique in its day, described as a 'serious and not ignoble attempt of an early population to alleviate suffering and distress'.

The revised edition of Hoops's *Reallexikon der germanischen Altertumskunde*[2] now enters its second volume with parts 1–3 which take us from *Bake* to *Bewaffnung*. The entries dealing directly with Old English literature (which, without disrespect to their authors, may be said to be those which readers of this chapter will refer to least) are brief summaries of critical reviews on *Maldon* and

[1] *Medieval English Medicine* by Stanley Rubin. Newton Abbot, Devon: David & Charles. pp. 232. 8 plates. £6.50.

[2] *Reallexikon der germanischen Altertumskunde* ed. by Johannes Hoops. Second edition ed. by Heinrich Beck, Herbert Jankuhn, Kurt Rank, and Reinhard Wenskus. Vol. II Parts 1–3. Berlin: de Gruyter.

Brunanburh by K. Weimann, and on *Beowulf* by Th. Finkenstaedt, R. T. Farrell, and R. J. Cramp.

H. M. Taylor discusses 'The architectural interest of Æthelwulf's *De Abbatibus*' (*ASE*), an early ninth century Latin poem by a member of a Northumbrian abbey which 'describes in some detail two churches of the abbey'. Some valuable improvements on Campbell's translation of the poem are made possible by the author's specialist architectural knowledge. Bruce Harbert suggests that 'King Alfred's *æstel*' (*ASE*) may be a fragment of the true cross, set in fifty mancuses of gold, and fixed to the binding of each copy of the *Pastoral Care* that the king distributed. H. R. Loyn presents a readable survey of 'Kinship in Anglo-Saxon England' (*ASE*) as revealed by legal documents of the tenth and eleventh centuries, and Nicholas Brooks's review of 'Anglo-Saxon charters: the work of the last twenty years' (*ASE*) performs a most valuable service in reminding students of Old English language and literature of the achievements of historians in fields that relate closely to their own. In particular, it emphasizes how much current work is revealing about the activities of local monastic and episcopal scriptoria in the last century of Anglo-Saxon England (the period when virtually all the surviving literature was recorded) and about where the charters were written (especially important in the light of the use of such material for dialect study and for tracing the dissemination of late West Saxon).

A full examination of a minor Latin text which is often referred to but has never been properly reviewed is provided by L. G. Whitbread in 'The *Liber Monstrorum* and *Beowulf*' (*MS*). The scope and arrangement of the work, its literary sources and its origin are considered in turn, and the

possibility of a connection with Aldhelm played with. Finally, *Beowulf* as a source for the Latin work, rather than the more commonly accepted reverse view, is proposed, and supported by echoes (though very general ones) of Grendel's characteristics in the Latin text's monsters. Helmut Gneuss's 'Latin Hymns in Medieval England: Future Research'[3] traces the growth of the 'New Hymnal' and its replacement of earlier hymnals in England and on the continent during the ninth and tenth centuries, but concludes that much more work needs to be done before we can have any reliable information about knowledge and use of hymns in this and later periods, and suggests that scarcity of manuscripts may make the task of obtaining such information for Anglo-Saxon England impossible. Earl R. Anderson's discussion of 'Social idealism in Ælfric's *Colloquy*' (*ASE*) states something of the traditions to which the work is indebted (e.g. that of the school debate) and illustrates the analogies between the *Colloquy* and the Benedictine Rule, showing Ælfric's concern to inculcate in the monastic schools not just a fuller understanding of Latin but of the Benedictine ethos too. Paul Szarmach looks at the influence of the Benedictine Revival on 'Anglo-Saxon Letters in the Eleventh Century' (*Acta*), and bemoans the lack of investigation of the relationship between vernacular and Latin traditions of the period.

A galaxy of stars appear this year in a volume of studies in honour of John C. Pope[4] and the harmony they

[3] *Chaucer and Middle English Studies in Honour of Rossell Hope Robbins* ed. by Beryl Rowland. London: Allen & Unwin. pp. 424. 1 Plate. (abbreviated as *Robbins Studies*).

[4] *Old English Studies in Honour of John C. Pope* ed. by Robert B. Burlin and Edward B. Irving Jr. U. of Toronto. pp. x+330. 4 Plates. $15. (abbreviated as *Pope Studies*).

produce will surely give him pleasure. The pieces accord happily with his own interests, most being concerned with poetry, and one making an important advance in the textual study of Ælfric. All but one of the essays are reviewed below in appropriate places, the exception being Theodore M. Andersson's 'The discovery of darkness in northern literature' which sees the incidence of night-time activities in Germanic (mainly Scandinavian) literature as a reflection of the Germanic tribes' predilection for fighting at night. Michael Hunter's survey of 'Germanic and Roman antiquity and the sense of the past in Anglo-Saxon England' (*ASE*) clarifies for us the Anglo-Saxons' awareness of Germanic and Roman history and suggests that, conscious as they were of both, they failed to discriminate between the two, and that they therefore 'copied both without conceiving them as separate'.

2. MANUSCRIPT STUDIES

The recent discovery of batches of unbound sheets of certain of the collotype plates used in the Exeter Book facsimile has enabled Exeter University English Department to issue *Pages from the Exeter Book*,[5] a series of good quality reproductions of parts of *Christ* and the last batch of Riddles, together with a transcription. The final plates show the burn marks on sheets at the end of the Exeter Book which John C. Pope makes use of in 'An Unsuspected Lacuna in the Exeter Book: Divorce Proceedings for an Ill-matched Couple in the Old English Riddles' (*Speculum*). He shows that if one turns back the concluding leaves of the manuscript,

the burn marks gradually diminish, but that a failure of 'match' in the marks reveals that a leaf is missing from the codex between the beginning and the end of the problematic *Riddle 70*. Now its last two lines may be read as a regular first-person Riddle conclusion (to a description of a lighthouse?) while the opening lines though still enigmatic, are the third-person beginning of a different one.

The most glamorous publication this year is the facsimile of *The Old English Illustrated Hexateuch*[6] surviving in the eleventh-century Canterbury manuscript B.M. Cotton Claudius B. iv. It is rightly described in the introduction as 'a fascinating example of late Anglo-Saxon book production' which, because it is unfinished, exemplifies 'every stage of the creation of Anglo-Saxon illumination'. The careful scrutiny of the manuscript undertaken by the editors has revealed a good deal about the compilation of the book: separate parts of the Old Testament narrative translated by Ælfric were brought together by an anonymous compiler who added extensive passages of his own translation, some of which appear to be based on a preexisting Ælfrician summary. Other manuscripts show that the text was in circulation without illustration before the present sequence of pictures was designed for it; and the originality of the sequence is displayed by the fact that the artist on occasion follows the idiosyncratic readings of the translation, though it is felt unlikely that the illuminations were composed for the

[5] *Pages from the Exeter Book* with an introductory note by M. J. Swanton. pp. 18. 14 Plates.

[6] *The Old English Illustrated Hexateuch: British Museum Cotton Claudius B. iv* ed. by C. R. Dodwell and Peter Clemoes. Early English Manuscripts in Facsimile vol. 18. Copenhagen: Rosenkilde and Bagger. pp. 74. 5 Colour Plates and 321 pp. in collotype.

first time in this particular manuscript. Rather it looks as if this is a copy of an illustrated manuscript, perhaps made as part of 'an enterprise at St Augustine's intended to provide more than one copy of this ambitiously created design', in response to lay needs rather than monastic ones. Peter Clemoes's study of the text isolates afresh the Ælfrician and non-Ælfrician sections of the translation and finds remarkable similarities in the language of the non-Ælfrician parts to that of Byrhtferth in his *Manual*, a discovery which could open up new opportunities for the study of the work of a known writer from the late Old English period. C. R. Dodwell's survey of the paintings and their background shows how remarkably free from external influence the illuminator was, and demonstrates that he was portraying his own life and times by comparing details with the Bayeux Tapestry, some panels of which are also reproduced. The plates, in their accuracy of colour reproduction and clarity of text, do full justice to the immaculate scholarship of the editors.

Raymond J. S. Grant's meticulous collation of 'Laurence Nowell's transcript of B.M. Cotton Otho B. xi' (*ASE*) with what can be read of the Bede translation in the manuscript (burnt in the Cotton fire) shows that Nowell's text 'is of no use to the student of spellings, phonology or inflections and no dialect indications can be drawn from it', but on the other hand 'very few words are omitted, homoeoteleuta are very rare and changes of word-order are few'. Consequently the transcript of texts which do not survive elsewhere, such as the poem *Seasons for Fasting*, may be relied upon within the limitations specified. G. Kotzor's 'St Patrick in the Old English "Martyrology": On a Lost Leaf of MS. C.C.C.C. 196'

(*N&Q*) gives evidence of the contents of the lost leaf, derived from Joscelyn's sixteenth-century transcription. R. I. Page adds a footnote ('The Lost Leaf of MS. C.C.C.C. 196', (*N&Q*) suggesting the likelihood that the leaf had already disappeared by 1593. An important account of the compilation of 'British Museum MS. Cotton Vespasian D. xiv' (*N&Q*) by Rima Handley examines its make-up in terms of foliation and hands (what are now the opening quires are early additions to the original collection, and the concluding quires may be too), and of content (Ælfrician and other late Old English prose). The author shows that little light may be thrown on the manuscript's origin by its language (cf. the inferior study of this matter reviewed last year, *YW* 54, 70), but maintains that the collection it contains ('possibly a teaching manual for young religious') seems likely to have been made at Christ Church, Canterbury. She concludes with a survey of the influence of Anselm at Canterbury and the possibility of his interests being reflected in this and other vernacular manuscripts of the period.

3. VOCABULARY

Helmut Gneuss's outline of plans for the Dictionary of Old English, 'Vorarbeiten und Vorüberlegungen zu einen neuen Wörterbuch des Altenglischen',[7] has now been overtaken by the events it foretells, but a number of lexicographical studies reviewed this year should make us grateful for the fact that the Dictionary is now properly under way; for when it is finished, it will considerably

[7] *Festschrift Prof. Dr. Herbert Koziol zum siebzigsten Geburtstag* ed. by Gero Bauer, Franz K. Stanzel, and Franz Zaic. Wiener Beiträge zur englischen Philologie vol. 75. Vienna: Braumüller. pp. viii+338. 3 Plates. (abbreviated as *Koziol Studies*).

simplify the sort of painstaking industry that they reflect. For example, Hans Schabram has produced 'Das altenglische *superbia*-Wortgut. Eine Nachlese' (*Koziol Studies*), bringing his model lexicographical study up to date by adding examples of words for *superbia* in texts which have been edited since 1965. In a study clearly based on Schabram's, Elmar Seebold reviews the dialectal distribution of words of the *wisdom* and *snyttro* group in 'Die ae. Entsprechungen von lat. *sapiens* und *prudens*' (*Anglia*). An even more complex and discerning study, Nigel F. Barley's 'Old English colour classification' (*ASE*), reinterprets words that have provided many problems for readers of Old English literature. This article argues that, unlike its Modern English counterpart which is biased towards hue, the Old English colour system is 'concerned chiefly with the differentiation of light and dark' and 'contained many words of specialized sub-sets that were collocationally restricted', for instance to animals and metals, or to fabrics and dyes. Among many splashes of light that the author throws onto his difficult canvas is the fact that their red is in part our yellow, and that speculation on the copper content of 'red gold' is consequently pointless.

Allan A. Metcalf's *Poetic Diction in the Old English Meters of Boethius*[8] is a study of the words added to the prose translation of Boethius in its transformation into verse. It reveals that more than a quarter of the vocabulary of the *Meters* does not occur in the prose version, or, put another way, that metrical and syntactic demands encouraged the

versifier to use a specifically 'poetic' word on average every two and a half lines. The book identifies these and shows, by comparison with the prose source and with other Old English poems, how the poet used his specialized vocabulary and how far his practice coincides with that of other poets. Fred C. Robinson's 'Old English Awindan, Of, and Sinhere' (*Koziol Studies*) offers valuable notes on three instances of rare words or usages, the first in anonymous homiletic material (probably an error for *aþindan*), the second a gloss used to mark grammatical rather than referential meaning of the word glossed, and the third the unique compound in *Beowulf* for which a case is made for the meaning being 'standing army' (the suggestion that the prefix *sin* means 'permanent' having been made by the author in passing in an earlier article (*YW* 51, 65)). I. J. Kirby asserts that 'Old English "ferð"' (*N&Q*) is not one word but two, 'the less common one cognate with, or perhaps derived from, Old Norse *ferð* "a journey"'; it is this word, the author maintains, which is used twice in *The Seafarer* (alliterating with *feran*, lines 26 and 37) and which is again associated with movement in *The Wanderer* line 50. Finally, as a footnote to vocabulary studies, one should note the botanical pirouettes performed by Peter Bierbaumer over the meaning of the medical term 'Ae. *fornetes folm*—eine Orchideenart' (*Anglia*).

4. POETRY: GENERAL

In 'The Poem in Transmitted Text —Editor and Critic' (*E&S*), J. E. Cross illustrates his belief that a good editor of Old English literature needs to be a good critic (with 'a feeling for *what* the Anglo-Saxons are saying' and not just for the way in which they say it) with discussion of passages

---

[8] *Poetic Diction in the Old English Meters of Boethius* by Allan A. Metcalf. De Proprietatibus Litterarum Series Practica 50. The Hague: Mouton, 1973. pp. x+166. Fl. 28.

from *The Phoenix* (the Earthly Paradise at the opening of the poem, which is revealed here as 'a real place to medieval people' but apparently less well known to modern editors) and *Resignation* (which uses *bycgan* in the sense of 'pay for a sea passage'). Kathryn Hume's 'The concept of the hall in Old English poetry' (*ASE*) offers first a review of the sociological importance of the hall, with evidence drawn from archaeology, the laws and literature, and then turns to the poets to see how they adapted the basic metaphor of the hall representing safety and comfort: the ruined hall denoting transience and the 'anti-hall' negation. Dwelling on this 'idea-complex' leads, she feels, to a better perspective than earlier critics have achieved: '*The Wanderer* does not exhibit the extreme form of Christian allegorisis which Smithers postulates' and 'the validity of several heavily moralistic readings of *Beowulf* is called into question'. But it is all very impressionistic. James H. Wilson's study of *Christian Theology and Old English Poetry*[8a] is largely concerned with the allegorical interpretation of *The Wanderer* and *The Seafarer*. After an introductory survey of the foundation of the allegorical tradition on the continent, plus some evidence for its early use in England, he offers a detailed explication of the Christian theme as revealed by allegory in the two poems. Further chapters do much the same for *Exodus* and for *Christ* (the three parts of which are seen as a unity). Throughout, the author's commitment to his own theme blinds him to other possibilities, and some of the general statements he makes on Old English literature come perilously close to falsification. The

bibliography has significant omissions, such as the Leslie and Dunning/Bliss editions of *The Wanderer*, and articles by Pope, Henry, and Clemoes. Virginia Day discusses 'The influence of the catechetical *narratio* on Old English and some other medieval literature' (*ASE*), describing in particular the Latin antecedents of such Old English examples of the use of the *narratio* as Caedmon's *Hymn* and the openings of *Genesis* and *Christ and Satan*, as well as three homilies, Vercelli XIX, Ælfric's *De Initio Creaturae*, and Wulfstan's reworking of the latter. Thomas Rendall examines the theological implications of 'Bondage and Freeing from Bondage in Old English Religious Poetry' (*JEGP*) with a brief summary of patristic views of Christ's releasing of the damned and a longer survey of the theme in vernacular poetry.

As an offshoot of his work on the *O.E.D.* Supplement, R. W. Burchfield has produced an account of 'The prosodic terminology of Anglo-Saxon scholars' (*Pope Studies*) as 'one of a series of articles in which the terminology of scholarly writings on Anglo-Saxon language and literature will be presented in a historical manner after the style of the *OED*'. The terms included here, with citations from the eighteenth century to the present, are largely unrecorded in the dictionary. Thomas Cable's study of *The Meter and Melody of 'Beowulf'*[9] is the culmination of a series of articles that have been summarized in these columns in the last few years. It begins with the view that inquiring about the metrical patterns which do not occur is nearly as important as describing those that do, a point earlier commentators have overlooked. The approach

---

[8a] *Christian Theology and Old English Poetry* by James H. Wilson. Studies in English Literature vol. 71. The Hague: Mouton. pp. 196. Fl. 38.

[9] *The Meter and Melody of 'Beowulf'* by Thomas Cable. Illinois Studies in Language and Literature 64. Urbana: U. of Illinois. pp. x+122.

is based on Sievers's five types, rejecting Pope in that 'it does not follow that Old English verses, which obviously have unequal numbers of syllables, must therefore have equal measures', and rejecting also Bliss's light verses in favour of seeing all verses as having a minimum of two metrical stresses. Study of the constraints surrounding anacrusis in an A-verse and comparison with Wulfstan's prose make clear that poetic metre excludes the possibility of a 'five-position pattern', with unstressed syllables before, between and after two stresses. The problems of intermediate and clashing stress and those of some minor types are confronted, to support the author's view that a single general principle may be stated to simplify Sievers's classification into five types: 'a verse must consist of exactly four *Glieder*'; this principle may then be extended by describing the constraints that produce the types, i.e. describing 'how the four abstract entities are realized as syllables' gives you Sievers's classification. Final chapters consider the relationship of the stated principle and Sievers's five types, and press on to 'explain the aesthetic and psychological reality' of the metrical theory. Whether the views expressed in this book find general favour or not, its reader may be grateful for the fact that they are expressed lucidly and printed handsomely, so that he is given every advantage in his pursuit of them.

Amongst minor studies of metre, the most detailed is E. G. Stanley's 'Some observations on the A3 lines in *Beowulf*' (*Pope Studies*), observations which spring from the catalogue that he presents of lines of that type; the most significant of them is that 'A3 lines come very often at the beginning of sentences, and usually lead straight on to the second half-line', exceptions

occurring only when the A3 line contains a verb. Constance B. Hieatt's analysis of 'Alliterative Patterns in the Hypermetric Lines of Old English Verse' (*MP*) concludes that 'while single alliteration in the on-verse is common in normal lines, it is so rare as to be suspect in hypermetric lines, while, on the other hand, significant triple alliteration occurs only in hypermetric lines'. She is thus confirmed in her view of hypermetric lines having triple rhythm. 'On the Composition of Hypermetric Verses in Old English' (*MP* 1973), by E. Clemons Kyte, re-examines the make-up of hypermetric verses, views critically some examples which have been regarded as problematic, and concludes that no development in the use of such verses may be traced during the Old English period. Louise Rarick has counted the number of syllables per line in the better known Old English poems and concludes that 'Ten-syllable Lines in English Poetry' (*NM*) are a feature which began in Anglo-Saxon times.

5. BEOWULF AND THE FIGHT AT FINNSBURH

W. F. Bolton has compared 'The Conybeare Copy of Thorkelin' (*ES*), a heavily annotated copy of Thorkelin's 1815 edition of *Beowulf*, with Conybeare's posthumous *Illustrations of Anglo-Saxon Poetry* (1826) to show that some of Kemp Malone's criticism of Conybeare as an editor (*ES* 1968) ought to have been levelled at his literary executor.

David R. Howlett's 'Form and Genre in *Beowulf*' (*SN*) defines two types of heroic poetry, *spell*, which was a tale of treasure or supernatural creatures and events, and *gyd*, which could be a boasting speech, a tragic tale of heroes, or an elegy. Examples of these in Old English poetry are listed, and those in *Beowulf* formalized into a structure which sees the numbered fitts as the 'systematic arrangement' of the author. It follows that the writer sees *Beowulf* as a written rather than an oral composition, as does Thomas Gardner, whose 'How Free Was the *Beowulf* Poet?' (*MP* 1973) makes some welcome positive statements about the poet's skill: tracing the occurrence of specific words or word-groups in the poem, he believes, provides the critic with ample evidence of the poet's supreme competence in handling diction to achieve ironic, humorous, and other effects, and indeed shows him manipulating 'his formulaic materials in such a way that they achieved conspicuous variety', even such as might lead us to believe that 'he was capable of "looking back" in constructing his poem'. On the other hand, G. Storms feels that 'The Author of *Beowulf* '(*NM*) was a court poet rather than a monk, the poem containing natural breaks for the serving of beer, political instruction for the witan, and no allegory. The article, which offers a very personal view of the poem and its critics gathered over the many years that its author has been studying both, is valuable for its review of the Christian apologists' work and the extent to which their ideas are actually supported by the text.

The 'Three aspects of Wyrd in *Beowulf*' (*Pope Studies*) which F. Anne Payne discusses in a lively philosophical study are, in her own words, 'the basic similarities between the *Beowulf* poet's and King Alfred's use of "Wyrd" in his version of Boethius' *Consolation of Philosophy*, the relation of Wyrd to Beowulf's three battles with the monsters, and finally the nature of the error that eventually triggers Wyrd's retaliative force against the kings of the poem'. Besides revealing something of the

nature of Wyrd (as 'the force that hovers at the outer edge of man's imaginative space', for instance), the study offers novel interpretation of a number of aspects of the poem, in particular the 'error' committed by Hrothgar (in distributing democratically 'gold which ought to be reserved for the ritualistic distribution of the gift-giving') and by Beowulf (in protecting his followers too completely by not forcing them to fight the dragon with him) that brings them 'into the realm of Wyrd'. On a rather different intellectual level, William C. Johnson Jr's ' "Deep Structure" and Old English Poetry: Notes toward a Critical Model'[10] presents his belief that 'some of the original meaning of our earliest poetry' and indeed 'a theory of the Old English mind' may be arrived at by an analysis of the etymology and philosophical meaning of *ongitan* in instances of its use in the 'mere' episode of *Beowulf*.

Eric John comes to *Beowulf* as a historian rather than a literary critic and consequently should perhaps be forgiven for adopting in '*Beowulf* and the Margins of Literacy' (*BJRL*) dogmatic assumptions which the critic has learnt to reject, for example the notion that the poet is a man with 'plenty of experience of actual fighting'. However, the historian's view of the poet as 'brutally frank about the economic basis of his age's heroism' and of the poem as 'simply a series of feuds working themselves out' (put these two together and you have 'the beginning of the ideology of feudalism') is hardly worthy of more serious consideration either. More fruitful is Robert W. Hanning's '*Beowulf* as

---

[10] *In Geardagum: Essays on Old English Language and Literature* ed. by Loren C. Gruber and Dean Loganbill. Denver: The Society for New Language Study. pp. ii+42. $3.25. (abbreviated as *In Geardagum*).

Heroic History' (*M&H*), which seeks through an analysis of passages of the poem to understand the relation between literature and history in the early medieval period. It finds a Christian poet commenting upon pre-conversion heroic history through narrative structure and imagery, and exploring 'the meaning and limits of heroism, of history in a heroic age, and of the interaction between hero and history'; for example, treasure, undoubtedly important to heroic society, is used by the poet in passages heavy with irony as 'an image of flawed achievement and human limitation'. Harry Berger Jr. and H. Marshall Leicester Jr. believe that the *Beowulf* poet was concerned to present the 'fundamental conditions of social structure' in the heroic age, including the inevitability of heroic society creating 'enemies and victims as well as the heroes that thrive on them'. In 'Social structure as doom: the limits of heroism in *Beowulf*' (*Pope Studies*), they 'explore some aspects of the doom created by heroic institutions' by looking in detail at the careers of Hrothgar and Beowulf.

Detailed analysis of specific passages has produced the familiar mixed crop of studies. Fred C. Robinson, delighting the reader of 'Elements of the marvellous in the characterization of Beowulf: a reconsideration of the textual evidence' (*Pope Studies*) with his proof that old-fashioned philology may still enlarge our understanding of such a well-thumbed poem as *Beowulf*, removes supernatural characteristics usually attributed to the hero by simple recourse to the text: the descent into the mere did not occupy the space of a day for *hwil daeges* means 'daylight'; he did not swim back from Frisia with thirty suits of armour but crossed the ocean with battlegear; and the fantastic feats of the Breca episode are made

dubious by their association in the poem with Unferth, whose lack of 'high seriousness' is demonstrated. Loren C. Gruber, in 'Motion, Perception, and *oþþæt* in *Beowulf*' (*In Geardagum*), sees the conjunction as signalling not just a movement from one place to another but from one condition to another, and supports her view with analysis of three instances in *Beowulf*. J. B. Bessinger Jr's 'Homage to Cædmon and others: a Beowulfian praise song' (*Pope Studies*) draws an analogy between the creation of earth in Cædmon's *Hymn* and the creation of Heorot in *Beowulf*, and maintains it with an extended study of linguistic and thematic parallels.

Two writers this year see Hrothgar as the *he* who cannot approach his *gifstol*: Stanley B. Greenfield in '"Gifstol" and goldhoard in *Beowulf*' (*Pope Studies*) who draws a parallel between the Danish king's situation and Beowulf's when he saw the dragon's gold as a replacement for his own burnt *gifstol* (further 'positive and negative meanings for the goldhoard within the heroic ethos' are subsequently considered); and David Clipsham in '*Beowulf* 168–169' (*In Geardagum*) who considers the *gifstol* crux without being much hampered by the extensive literature on the subject. Two more articles consider Grendel's attack on Heorot, again offering the reviewer the opportunity to contrast pieces of very different quality. 'What Grendel found: Heardran Hæle' (*NM*), according to James L. Rosier, is more likely to have been *hæle* 'prosperity' than *hæle* 'man', but, as he stresses, it is the investigation which is more important than the conclusion in illustrating 'a problem of some delicacy in Old English textual criticism': discrimination between two words 'of identical form for a given context'. Raymond P. Tripp Jr, taking 'A New Look at Grendel's Attack: *Beowulf* 804a–815a' (*In Geardagum*), produces convenient new interpretations: *ac* as a concessive conjunction (with no supporting evidence other than the general desirability of seeing it so), *fag* as an otherwise unrecorded form of *feon*, and *gehwæþer* as having the meaning of *hwæþere* 'however'. In 'Inner weather and interlace: a note on the semantic value of structure in *Beowulf*' (*Pope Studies*), Robert B. Burlin examines the description of the coming of spring in the Finn episode in 'a flat, trite clause padded with a gnomic expression' and finds it typical of the poet's vision of the way things are: the coming of revenge is as inevitable as the change of season. George Hardin Brown accepts 'Beowulf 1278b: *sunu þeod wrecan*' (*MP*) in its manuscript form, with *sunu* as a genitive and *þeod* as a rare accusative; thus Grendel's mother's vengeance for her son is taken on behalf of the clan. Ronald E. Buckalew's '*Beowulf*, Lines 1766–1767: *oððe* for *seoððan*?' (*NM*) raises a new possibility of scribal error in the poem, the recognition of which solves a problem which has puzzled editors and critics: the relationship of an instance of *oððe* in Hrothgar's sermon with five examples of the same word in lines immediately preceding it. John F. Vickrey, convinced that Heremod slew his retainers for their gold and that the avaricious king mentioned later by Hrothgar in his sermon was equally rapacious, concludes in '*Egesan Ne Gymeð* and the Crime of Heremod' (*MP*) that the successor to the avaricious king gave rings *unmurnlice* 'not sorrowfully', i.e. 'gladly', the following verse *egesan ne gymeð* thus being satisfactorily explained as meaning, 'he [the successor] has no liking for terror'

(as his predecessor had). Earl R. Anderson argues for the acceptance of Holthausen's *hond* [*maððum nam*] in '*Beowulf* 2216b–2217: A Restoration' (*ELN*) but rejects his proposal for the following line in favour of *he þæt syððan* [*onfand*].

The Finnsburh Fragment has usually been edited as a postscript to *Beowulf*. Donald K. Fry has rectified the balance somewhat in his edition of *Finnsburh: Fragment and Episode*,[11] where the independent but fragmentary poem and the scop's song on the same subject in *Beowulf* are given equal treatment. The two texts appear to fit together well since, in terms of plot, the Episode begins where the Fragment ends. But understanding of the events at Finnsburh has never been as simple as that statement implies, and this edition is all the more welcome for its lengthy discussion of 'The Story'. The editor gives details of critical views expressed during the present century, and adds his own contribution (repeated, quite unnecessarily it would seem, in '*Finnsburh*: A New Interpretation', *ChauR*) by scotching the view that Hengest was unable to return home during the winter, replacing it with a picture of him 'waiting for his chance to avenge Hnæf' and manipulating his followers into their encouragement of him to take vengeance by calling a *torngemot* (which is identified as a 'Danish war-council which would result in a battle'). The introduction concludes with a useful comparison of the style of Fragment and Episode. Two features of the editing worthy of note are the inclusion in the glossary of emendations adopted by earlier editors and the addition of references to the editor's own *Beowulf and the Fight at Finnsburh: A Bibliography*

[11] *Finnsburh: Fragment and Episode* ed. by Donald K. Fry. London: Methuen. pp. xvi+84. 1 Plate. £3.

(1969) to all bibliographical entries. Both features are slightly self-indulgent, for the glossary is encumbered with miscellaneous information in support of outmoded readings, and footnotes such as 'Ker [1000]' and 'Sedgefield [1894]' are less immediately intelligible than conventional references. Also, the contractions adopted in footnotes are perverse (e.g. Chb = Chambers, Cmb = Campbell, Klb = Klaeber). But these are minor inconveniences in a useful addition to the Methuen series.

6. THE JUNIUS MANUSCRIPT

A closely argued rejoinder to those who would have us read allegorical levels into Old English poetry comes in Bennett A. Brockman's ' "Heroic" and "Christian" in *Genesis A*: The Evidence of the Cain and Abel Episode' (*MLQ*), which maintains that 'the poet's treatment of the Cain and Abel story shows that his interests differ at almost every point from those of the Fathers' and that 'the primary focus of this episode is on the human rather than the theological dimensions of the story'. Christopher Clausen's 'A Suggested Emendation in *Genesis B*' (*ELN*) involves reading the scribe's *woruld* as *werod* in line 319 in order to provide a subject for the verb *fylde* which is otherwise without one. W. F. Bolton finds 'A Further Echo of the Old English *Genesis* in Milton's *Paradise Lost*' (*RES*) in an unusual use by Milton of the phrase 'strength and art' which he feels may translate *cræft* in line 1674 of the Old English poem.

Edward B. Irving Jr., unable to revise his edition of *Exodus* when it was reprinted recently, presents in '*Exodus* retraced' (*Pope Studies*) supplementary remarks to his introduction of 1953, which involve some healthy recantation (e.g. of his decision to rearrange lines at the conclusion of the poem), but reaffirmation too (e.g. of his rejection of extensive allegorical interpretation of the poem). He supports the latter view with an extended look at the heroic aspects of the poem. Reversing the coin, we find Thomas D. Hill proposing Adam in 'The "Fyrst Ferhðbana"': Old English "Exodus", 399' (*N&Q*) as the solution to critics' difficulty in identifying the first murderer, the case being supported by quotation from patristic commentary and cited as one more example of the preoccupation of the poet with 'the typological structure of Old Testament history'.

R. T. Farrell's edition of *Daniel* and the related Exeter Book *Azarias*[12] is disappointing. Most of the introduction deals with *Daniel* (*Azarias* being included in the edition only because of its relationship with the longer poem), and the greater part of the argument concerns the structure of the poem, in particular whether or not it is complete in the form in which we have it. The case that it is complete, made here on stylistic grounds, is acceptable only if supported by evidence from the manuscript foliation; and though the latter is considered at length, in language which could have been much more technical, exact, and economical, the author appears to have overlooked N. R. Ker's view that the final gathering of the manuscript is unusually large because it is a normal eight-leaf quire inserted into the outer sheet of an older quire, the rest of which is now lost (cf. *Catalogue*, p. 408). The section on language is unhelpful; the long précis of Sisam's poetic dialect theory is not necessary, and a fuller reading of the Junius Manuscript would have shown that the editor's

[12] *Daniel and Azarias* ed. by R. T. Farrell. London: Methuen. pp. x+140. £4.50.

many non-West Saxon forms are likely to be Kentish and scribal rather than, as he maintains, Northumbrian and authorial. The textual notes are expansive and repetitive, references are frequently erroneous or incomplete (there are, indeed, a great many proof-reading errors of many sorts), and mistakes appear in all sections of the work (e.g. Kemp Malone's article is renamed 'When did Middle English really begin?', and the glossary entry *herewosa* is surrounded by unexplained question marks, a footnote to the line in which the word occurs referring the reader to an appendix which does not contain it). For all this, the book is potentially valuable, and it is a great pity that the author was not advised to take time to reconsider and to condense. The general editors of the Methuen series must thus take some of the blame for its shortcomings. Indeed one wonders what the general editors now see as their function, since the referencing and glossary entries in this book differ greatly from those in the *Finnsburh* volume published simultaneously (and reviewed above, p. 85).

Two writers locate minor sources for the final poem in the manuscript: Robert Emmett Finnegan, in 'Three Notes on the Junius XI *Christ and Satan*: Lines 78–79; Lines 236–42; Lines 435–38' (*MP*), discusses the *Visio Pauli* as a source for details of the description of hell, proposes a minor emendation to improve a reading, and justifies Eve as the sole pleader for release from bondage of the occupants of hell; and Hugh T. Keenan, in 'Satan Speaks in Sparks: "Christ and Satan" 78–79a, 161b–162b, and the "Life of St. Antony"' (*N&Q*), considers the influence of the popular life of St Antony on Satan's fiery speech and also the more general influence it might have had on the Old English poet.

7. OTHER POETRY

The arrangement of this section follows that of Volumes II, III, and VI of *The Anglo-Saxon Poetic Records*.

John C. Unrue, in '*Andreas*: An Internal Perspective' (*In Geardagum*), sees the heroic style of the poem as inevitable since it is the only means the poet has of expressing his admiration for his hero. John Casteen finds typological narration in details of the poem (in '*Andreas*: Mermedonian Cannibalism and Figural Narration' (*NM*)); biblical parallels make clear, he suggests, how the Anglo-Saxon audience was expected to view cannibalism as God's curse for the nation's sins. Constance B. Hieatt's 'The Fates of the Apostles: Imagery, Structure, and Meaning' (*PLL*) exhorts us to believe, after presenting a catalogue of the poem's images and structural features, that it 'is obviously far more meaningful and rich than it has been given credit for being'. P. B. Taylor's 'Text and Texture of *The Dream of the Rood*' (*NM*) seeks to establish ambiguity in the phraseology of the poem, and advocates the preservation of manuscript readings in lines frequently emended; as far as one can judge, since he makes little use of bibliographical references, the author is not aware of the most recent edition of the poem (Swanton, *YW* 51, 71) which makes all his points for him. Equally conservative with the text is Carl T. Berkhout, who argues (in 'The Problem of OE *Holmwudu*' (*MS*)) for the retention of the manuscript reading of this compound with the meaning 'sea-wood, ship', supporting this by reference to Augustine's use of a similar image for the Cross. Eugene R. Kintgen's examination of 'Echoic Repetition in Old English Poetry, especially *The Dream of the Rood*' (*NM*) leads him to the view that Old English poetry is 'characterized by the frequent repetition' of significant words as much as by other types of repetition such as alliteration and variation; his statistics are illuminated by a review of words for sight and seeing in *The Dream of the Rood* and their effect on the reader. Earl R. Anderson, making the somewhat surprising claim that 'the structure of *Elene* has never received any detailed attention', begins an examination of the subject in 'Cynewulf's *Elene*: Manuscript Divisions and Structural Symmetry' (*MP*) by mapping the fitts, which he sees as essential to the structural design of the poem. Interestingly, he arrives at a tripartite structure rather different from the one presented by Jackson J. Campbell (*YW* 53, 80). Comparison of the two pieces shows what a remarkable achievement Cynewulf's poem is.

Colin Chase presents 'God's presence through grace as the theme of Cynewulf's *Christ II* and the relationship of this theme to *Christ I* and *Christ III*' (*ASE*), tracing through detailed examples the way in which Cynewulf alters the theme of his source for *Christ II* (Gregory's Ascension Day homily), so that it is possible to 'establish an implicit relationship between the three *Christ* poems, each of which develops one mode of Christ's presence with man, incarnation, grace and judgment'. The link thus contrived between the three poems leads the author to speculate on the possibility that Cynewulf altered his source in order to fashion a poem which would join together two existing poems. George Hardin Brown examines the patristic background of 'The Descent-Ascent Motif in *Christ II* of Cynewulf' (*JEGP*), and shows how effectively it is used in the Old English poem where a typological contrast of such 'profound theological importance'

fits well into 'the Old English poetic technique of contrast and variation'. Bruce Mitchell argues for the plurality of 'The "fuglas scyne" of *The Phoenix*, line 591' (*Pope Studies*) by maintaining that a comparison earlier in the poem of soul and bird becomes for the moment '*identification* of the souls of the blessed following Christ with so many bright phoenixes following the sun'. Rolf Breuer's 'Vermittelte Unmittelbarkeit: Zur Struktur des altenglischen *Wanderer*' (*NM*) examines the tensions between pagan and Christian elements found throughout the poem and sees them as structural, the result of tensions in the mind of the speaker, the Wanderer. Marijane Osborn thinks that 'The Vanishing Seabirds in *The Wanderer*' (*Folklore*) are the pivotal point in the poem, for 'by recognizing an analogy between the vanishing birds and the death of men' (which she identifies as a folklore motif), the Wanderer 'begins to find a direction to his mental journey'. Douglas D. Short resolves a crux in 'The Old English *Gifts of Men*, Line 13' (*MP*) by replacing the manuscript *oþþe* with *ond*.

In 'The Modern Reader and the Old English *Seafarer*' (*PLL*), W. A. Davenport urges us to put the flesh back on to the figure of the Seafarer, emaciated by scholars obsessed by source studies; but he nevertheless seeks a source himself, that of the pleasure which the poem continues to give. His close reading of the poem, informed of course by the critical studies he feels the need to counter, reminds us that this is an evocative and lyrical poem with a message much richer than the simple didacticism of its sources, concluding that it is 'a poem in two minds, which a homily could hardly afford to be'. John C. Pope's 'Second thoughts on the interpretation of *The Seafarer*'

(*ASE*) involves a retraction of his argument for both *The Wanderer* and *The Seafarer* having two speakers rather than one. In his reexamination of difficult passages in the latter poem, he sees its first half not as an allegory but as a description of 'actual voyaging, past and prospective', which then moves, by means of the figurative meaning of some of its terms, to 'the broader idea of allegorical pilgrimage'. Friedrich Schubel, in 'Der ags. "klagende" Kuckuck' (*Koziol Studies*), considers recent critical views of a number of Old English elegies, in particular those of *The Seafarer* and *The Husband's Message* in which the cuckoo is mentioned, and sets against them an extensive survey of the use of the cuckoo-image in early literature. He concludes that the cuckoo as a symbol can only be fully understood within the total allegory of the poem in which it occurs. D. R. Howlett looks at 'Form and Genre in *Widsith*' (*ES*) and finds that 'the structure of *Widsith* as we have it is so literary as to imply the author's familiarity with the rigid shapes of Latin hymns and pattern poems'. In the division he proposes of the central section of the poem into three fitts, two of which are *gyd* and the third a *spell*, the author makes use of terminology more fully expounded in a parallel article on *Beowulf* (reviewed above, p. 82). Kemp Malone's contribution to the Pope Festschrift is a consideration of 'The rhythm of *Deor*' which begins with a classification of half-lines, continues with comment on the more recalcitrant ones, and concludes with a frequency count. It provides a useful postscript to his edition. Norman E. Eliason's 'On *Wulf and Eadwacer*' (*Pope Studies*) faces the metrical and textual complexities of the poem by seeing it as a hastily written private communication from one poet to another lamenting the separation of their joint poems. Of the two essays on the Riddles published this year, the more formidable is Nigel F. Barley's 'Structural Aspects of the Anglo-Saxon Riddle' (*Semiotica*), which supplies a detailed analysis of the Exeter Book Riddles in terms of generative linguistics, distinguishing types and illuminating the ambiguity and paradox that the genre makes use of. In a rather more relaxed paper, 'The Rhetoric of the Exeter Book Riddles' (*Speculum*), Marie Nelson argues that study of the Riddles underlines the fusion of two cultures in Anglo-Saxon literature, Germanic-heroic and patristic, and emphasizes that just as the Anglo-Saxons needed more than one frame of reference to understand their literature, so do we. She shows the knowledge of classical rhetoric displayed in the Riddles and proceeds to exemplify the artistic success of some of them in the use of such rhetoric. Richard J. Daniels, ('Bibliographical Notes on the Old English Poem *Judgment Day I*' (*PBSA*)), points to a number of errors among references to the poem by writers on Old English literature. In 'The Speaker in "Resignation": A Biblical Note' (*N&Q*), Carl T. Berkhout sees the use of the Book of Job in lines 105–8 of the poem. James E. Anderson, 'Die Deutungsmöglichkeiten des altenglischen Gedichtes *The Husband's Message*' (*NM*), reorders the runes of the poem to read *sweard* 'skin', and sees this not as a husband's message from the other world to his widow but as the vehicle for its transmission.

J. E. Cross's 'Mainly on philology and the interpretative criticism of *Maldon*' (*Pope Studies*) is a careful reexamination of the range of meaning of *lytegian* and *ofermod*, which demonstrates once again that we have no real evidence on which to base the suggestion that Byrhtnoth was 'a wholly admirable tactician' undeceived by his enemy's cunning. Furthermore, it is also made clear that the continuing attempts of the commentators to set aside the poet's criticism of his hero are unnecessary if it is accepted that the aim of the poem is to illustrate the loyalty of retainers to a leader who made a fatal tactical error. Carl T. Berkhout turns to '*The Battle of Brunanburh*'s '*Feld Dennade*—Again' (*ELN*) to maintain that the verb *dennade* may be seen as meaning 'resounded (with blood)' in the light of Biblical examples of the *vox sanguinis*. Donald K. Fry explains Cædmon's miracle (in 'Cædmon as a formulaic poet' (*FMLS*)) as the poet suddenly finding the courage to recite publicly verses with which he had been 'mentally doodling'. The resultant *Hymn*, described by Fry as oral but not extempore, is then analysed in terms of a new system of tabulating traditional poetic formulae to show how the poet might have arrived at his verses from existing models.

8. PROSE

An examination of the language and structure of 'The Hæsten Episode in 894 *Anglo-Saxon Chronicle*' (*SN*) reveals for Ruth Waterhouse the annalist's skilful presentation of different periods of time past in such a way as to contrast Hæsten's actions with those of Alfred and to pass moral judgment upon the former. Mechthild Gretsch's 'Æthelwold's translation of the *Regula Sancti Benedicti* and its Latin exemplar' (*ASE*) draws some general conclusions from the evidence presented in her doctoral thesis (reviewed last year, *YW* 54, 82). The appearance of the material in a more accessible publication (and in English) is welcomed. Dorothy Whitelock uses a detailed study of 'The list of chapter-headings in the Old English Bede' (*Pope Studies*) to consider the relationship of surviving manuscripts of the text. She speculates that 'the work was provided with a list of chapters at the place of production', possibly, though not certainly, by the translator; and even more tentatively she suggests that discrepancies in the list of chapter headings in the version of the text in CCCC 41 associate it (as do some agreements in error) with other later tenth and eleventh century manuscripts rather than with the earlier Tanner text with which Miller linked it. In 'The common origin of Ælfric fragments at New Haven, Oxford, Cambridge and Bloomington' (*Pope Studies*), Rowland L. Collins and Peter Clemoes have identified seven fragments containing excerpts from the *Catholic Homilies* and *Lives of Saints*, which have come to light in recent years, as being almost certainly from a single sizeable manuscript written very early in the eleventh century in a scriptorium which followed the old insular custom of arranging folios in quires with the hair side invariably facing outwards. The text they contain, which the authors present, reveals that the manuscript they are taken from is unique among surviving Ælfrician manuscripts in the ordering of its elements, an arrangement achieved not in Ælfric's own scriptorium but possibly in the one which produced this book. Hildegard L. C. Tristram describes an extended lamp metaphor in anonymous homilies in 'Die *Leohtfæt*-metaphor in den altenglischen anonymen Bittagspredigten' (*NM*) and shows it to derive from Biblical sources.

9. INSCRIPTIONS AND GLOSSES

D. R. Howlett's study of 'Three Forms in the Ruthwell Text of *The*

Dream of the Rood' (*ES*) maintains that two of them have frequently been misread, *bismærædu* instead of the *bismæradu* which actually occurs, and *miþ blodæ* for the correct *miþ blodi*. Putting these readings right removes the faulty archaisms which some critics have seen in the inscription, so that the text may properly be looked upon as 'the oldest copy of a Northumbrian poem'. C. J. E. Ball ('The Franks Casket: Right Side—Again' (*ES*)) adds to his earlier discussion of the subject (*YW* 67, 71) the suggestion that 'the principle which governs the selection of the irregular vowel-runes is that a variant form of the final (consonantal) rune of the name of the vowel-runes is used in place of the normal vowel-runes'. Marijane Osborn suggests a disguised connection between inscription and picture in 'The Picture-Poem on the Front of the Franks Casket' (*NM*), comprehension of which involves decoding the inscription in a manner similar to that which has been used for its right side, but different in that on the front panel the association between words and pictures is through iconographic rather than grammatical manipulation.

A comprehensive edition of the *Old English Glosses in the Épinal-Erfurt Glossary*[13] by J. D. Pheifer 'attempts no radical innovations, but tries to make the glosses more intelligible by placing them in the context of their sources and related material in other glossaries, in the light of which some new interpretations are offered'. More than fifty glosses are thus reassessed in textual notes which deal with each gloss in admirable detail. The two glossaries are presented in parallel columns, with collations from other glossaries in footnotes; indices of

both lemmata and interpretations conclude the volume. The introduction gives the manuscript background of the two principal texts and of other Old English glossaries, and a general summary of the sources; but more than half of it is concerned, appropriately enough, with language, the author describing the 'settled spelling-system' of the manuscripts and its phonological implications in depth, though he offers no revision of the traditional dating of the texts and admits that the origin of the archetype cannot be determined by linguistic evidence. Not surprisingly, in a work of this complexity, there are a number of proof-reading errors, some of which are corrected in an erratum sheet. But this is mere cavilling, as all students of Old English have reason for gratitude to the author and his press for an edition which gives pleasure not only by its scholarship but also by its presentation. In two briefer studies of glosses, J. Richard Stracke reviews the patristic background of 'Eight Lambeth Psalter-Glosses' (*PQ*) to produce more precise definitions for a number of rare Old English words; and J. V. Gough (in 'Some Old English Glosses' (*Anglia*)) prints, with extensive commentary, late glosses from four manuscripts: Ashmole 1431 (misnumbered in the article 1931), St. John's College, Oxford, 17, Cotton Vitellius C. iii, and the newly discovered British Library Additional 57337.

Finally, Angus F. Cameron's 'Middle English in Old English Manuscripts' (*Robbins Studies*), an examination of annotations recorded from the thirteenth to the fifteenth century, has led him to the happy thought that 'the ability to read Old English never died out completely in England'. Let us hope that it never will.

[13] *Old English Glosses in the Épinal-Erfurt Glossary* ed. by J. D. Pheifer. Oxford: Clarendon. pp. xcii + 166. £6.

IV

Middle English: Excluding Chaucer

R. W. McTURK and D. J. WILLIAMS

1. GENERAL AND MISCELLANEOUS ITEMS

Poetry of the Age of Chaucer,[1] edited by A. C. and J. E. Spearing, is another interesting attempt to enlarge the audience for Middle English poetry. It is an anthology, designed for sixth-formers and beginning undergraduates, containing *Sir Orfeo*, a little of the first section of *Sir Gawain*, the account of the whale from *Patience*, the Deadly Sins from *Piers Plowman*, some short poems, and Chaucer's *Friar's Tale*. A gloss and commentary face the text on the opposite page. How the attempt will work remains to be seen. Considering that few of the texts are complete works, there seems to be too much critical interpretation, especially if the book is for use in class. A beginner working on his own, on the other hand, might find it hard to learn much about the language from glosses which give meanings rather than close translation or explanation.

The Disease of the Soul,[2] by Saul Nathaniel Brody, investigates the traditional association of leprosy with moral defilement in the Middle Ages, in particular with lechery. He begins from modern description and diagnosis, partly because the disease itself seems to have changed over the years, and partly to establish a standard, since medieval writers tend to describe what they feel they ought to see. Despite the availability of cases, a heavy reliance on authority and tradition is characteristic of medical treatises on the subject. Such treatises complicate the issue with psychological symptoms and by associating cause and transmission with sexual activity. But medieval observers seem to have been faced with a disease which even now is not easy to diagnose. Brody gives an account of the leper in medieval society, his treatment by the law, the church, and his neighbours, finding considerable variation, even paradox: leprosy is a sign both of punishment and of grace. The leper's world was one of 'contradiction and inconsistency'. This seems odd when the 'ecclesiastical tradition', as retailed by the author, unequivocally presents the leper as immoral, corrupt, and terrifying. This is the tradition inherited by the poets. The book is disappointing in its treatment of leprosy in literature (Gower, Henryson, and *Amis and Amiloun* are considered, with a look at later writers), but its value is in its readable account of the context of that literature.

Medieval attitudes to leprosy are paralleled in many ways by medieval attitudes to madness. Penelope Doob's *Nebuchadnezzar's Children*[3] is

---

[1] *Poetry of the Age of Chaucer*, ed. by A. C. and J. E. Spearing. London: Edward Arnold. pp. vi+222. Cloth £3.20. Paper £1.20.

[2] *The Disease of the Soul: Leprosy in Medieval Literature* by Saul Nathaniel Brody. Ithaca and London: Cornell U.P. pp. 224. 12 Plates. £4.75.

[3] *Nebuchadnezzar's Children: Conventions of Madness in Middle English Literature*, by Penelope B. R. Doob. New Haven and London: Yale U. P. pp. xviii+248. 16 plates. £5.25.

a study of another sickness with powerful moral and spiritual associations. A study of the background to the literary treatments shows madness as an emblem of sin and a punishment, sin itself being a form of madness. The disorder is related to certain passions, especially wrath, and cures involve spiritual remedies. However, the case of Charles VI indicates some controversy about the causes, natural or moral. Doob divides literary madmen into three conventional types, Mad Sinner, Unholy Wild Man, and Holy Wild Man, using Nebuchadnezzar as an example of all three. But, although she calls him 'father of most literary madmen', she appears uncertain how far to press the suggestion that he himself is actually the source of the similar motifs. Herod is the most notable of the mad sinners, and the biblical commentaries elaborate with extraordinary detail a tradition of his mental disease. Special English contributions are added by *Cursor Mundi*, Lydgate, and of course the drama, with an increasing stress on extremes of pride and wrath. Pagan kings reveal a similar pattern, and an association with heresy (which Brody found symbolized by leprosy too). A reading of *Ywain and Gawain*, with its hero as Unholy Wild Man, shows the English poet, as distinct from Chrétien, concerned with the moral reasons for the madness. Ywain's self-mastery or otherwise is defined in relation to the herdsman, the hermit, and especially the lion. A reading of the *Vita Merlini* relates it to the Fall. Holy Wild Men are distinguished by voluntary wildness. The main example is *Sir Orfeo*, where a similarity of the structure to the Christian pattern of Fall, Redemption, and Judgment, leads to an unhappy account of the poem in which Orfeo is Christ, and his queen is guilty of sloth. Doob defends her

allegory by saying that an educated medieval reader could have worked it out. Whether the poet encouraged him is a question needing more careful scrutiny. The concluding chapter focuses on Hoccleve, whose picture of his own state is related to the conventions already examined. He is concerned with 'physical and mental disease as the consequences of moral failure', and the resulting self-portrait, Doob argues, is a fiction or might as well be.

The preface to an anthology of *Readings in Medieval Rhetoric*[4] allows some truth to the notion that the Middle Ages did nothing to develop the art of rhetoric, except that in preserving it they added to it by bringing the tradition to bear in new practical areas. Three factors are important: the hostility of Christian scholars to a pagan art, the spread of monasticism, and the increasing tendency to view rhetoric as an administrative tool rather than as a means of persuasion. The volume aims to bring together as many previously unavailable writings on rhetoric as possible. The Period covered runs from the death of Augustine to the rediscovery of Quintilian. Each piece (in an English translation) has a brief introduction. John of Garland's *Parisiana Poetria*[5] is edited by Traugott Lawler with a useful facing translation. The introduction contains an account of what is known of John's life, a date for the work, and a brief account of its contents and main sources and influences, seeing it not as a new departure but rather a new synthesis attempting (and often failing) to unite *dictamen*, poetic, and

[4] *Readings in Medieval Rhetoric*, ed. by J. Miller, M. H. Prosser, and T. W. Benson. Indiana U. P. $4.50.
[5] *The 'Parisiana Poetria' of John of Garland*, ed. by Traugott Lawler. Yale Studies in English 182. New Haven and London: Yale U.P. pp. xxv+352. £6.25.

rhythmic under one system. Lawler suggests that the text was conceived as notes for a teacher. Susan Gallick examines 'Medieval Rhetorical Arts in England and the Manuscript Traditions' (*Manuscripta*), to try to discover which rhetoricians, if any, were widely used and who the readers were, and 'to define more closely the limits of the rhetorical arts in England'. In discussing her methods of using library catalogues she points out how they can affect the results, producing in her own case an argument rather different from James J. Murphy's. Neither Matthew of Vendôme nor John of Garland can be counted writers of major influence. Geoffrey of Vinsauf, Cicero's *De Inventione*, and the *Ad Herennium* are the popular texts, with a wide audience of poets, students, friars, and preachers. Geoffrey might have been used in grammar schools, and some evidence suggests that the other two were not confined to university level.

Glending Olson traces the history of 'The Medieval Theory of Literature for Refreshment and its Use in the Fabliau Tradition' (*SP*). Some opinions saw such literature (or theatre, dance, and song) as useless where others considered it useful precisely because it relaxed and refreshed the user. John M. Hill, 'Middle English Poets and the Word: Notes Towards an Appraisal of Linguistic Consciousness' (*Criticism*), says that *Piers Plowman, Pearl, Sir Gawain and the Green Knight*, and *Everyman* share 'a thematic elaboration of the ways in which language—the word—can fail us'. His argument concentrates mainly on *Pearl* and its concern with the limitations of language in the face of divine truth, but contains also the intriguing suggestion that Gawain's adventures are the result of a misunderstanding and that he need not

have beheaded the Green Knight in the first place. 'The Appreciation of Handmade Literature' (*ChauR*), by Richard A. Dwyer, takes its theme from the revealing participation of scribes in the texts of Langland, Chaucer, and medieval lyrics. He studies scribal participations in French versions of Boethius, discovering some sense of popular medieval understanding of the *Consolatio* in their modifications and humanizations of its original rigour. In 'Middle English Styles in Action' (*ES*), H. H. Meier studies the stylistic means employed in reporting vigorous scenic action as a general impression. Authors considered include the Gawain-poet, Henryson, and Laȝamon.

Angus McIntosh (*NM*) advocates a cooperative enterprise 'Towards an Inventory of Middle English Scribes', dependent on characterizing them by linguistic and 'graphetic' profiles. In 'Chaucer, Sir John Mandeville, and the Alliterative Revival: A Hypothesis Concerning Relationships' (*MP*), C. W. R. D. Moseley suggests a connexion between three things: the popular Mandeville (an author from the Hertfordshire/Essex area); the confinement of his literary influence to Chaucer and alliterative poets; and what Moseley sees as Chaucer's simultaneous use of Mandeville and *Sir Gawain and the Green Knight*. The link is patronage, connecting the Bohuns with Mandeville and with the Lancasters. But the connexion between Chaucer and the alliterative poets is scarcely established, let alone explained. Maureen Fries gives the briefest of summary notes on 'Images of Women in Middle English Literature' (*CE*). Bengt Lindström (*SN*) provides interpretative notes on 'Four Middle English Passages', including *Aȝenbite of Inwit* and the *Gospel of Nicodemus*. Angus Cameron surveys occurrences of 'Middle English in Old English Manuscripts'[6] and finds 'clear signs that Old English MSS were being read and understood from the beginning of the thirteenth through to the early sixteenth century'. The same volume contains an article on 'Latin Hymns in Medieval England' by H. Gneuss, and many other contributions which will be noticed in the appropriate sections below.

Sheila Delany's 'Substructure and Superstructure: The Politics of Allegory in the Fourteenth Century' (*Science and Society*) was seen too late for comment this year.

2. ALLITERATIVE POETRY

Constance B. Hieatt proposes a method of scansion for 'The Rhythm of the Alliterative Long Line'[7] more like that used by Pope for Old English. She finds in the extended lines patterns analogous to Old English D and E types, although authorities usually agree that these are not found in Middle English. Such lines are not, she argues, derived from Old English hypermetrics, although their manner of alliteration may be somehow affected by them.

Thomas H. Bestul's *Satire and Allegory in 'Wynnere and Wastoure'*[8] is the first long study of the poem. While not denying its topicality he emphasizes the largely traditional character of the work, which means collecting sources and analogues for its content and form. He traces ideas about prodigality and liberality from

Aristotle and Aquinas to popular moral teaching, and in Alain de Lille and the *Architrenius*. The topic of the poem is the use of riches argued between representatives of avarice and prodigality, traditional aspects of the same vice putting up traditional defences. Apart from dream and debate, Bestul finds the form most indebted to Old French religious allegories, except that it lacks 'an obvious moral and logical purpose', and his society as well as the individual as its concern. This leads to a consideration of the poem as satire, its 'informing principle'. It is a two-fold attack on Edward III, and one of a number of works about that king's reign, but the monarch is meant to represent all rulers who misuse wealth. Bestul emphasizes the conventional nature of its targets and the universality of its message. The ironies of the description of the antagonists and their banners depends on the audience's knowledge of the abuses traditionally associated with them. The account of Waster's array is short because prodigality lacks a well-developed satiric tradition. Of the idea that Edward's inconclusive decision is not criticism of him but a picture of economic necessity, Bestul suggests that such economic realism would cast doubt on the king's moral condition. The heart of the poem is a dramatization of such advice on the use of wealth offered to kings in John of Salisbury's *Policraticus* or the *De Regimine Principum*. A final chapter on the work as an alliterative poem relates it more to the protest poems of Harley 2253 than to later satire. The book presents much valuable material, but its method of arguing by defining genres and identifying analogues creates the impression of a poem much more fragmented and heterogeneous in its whole effect than Bestul himself seems to intend. The

---

[6] *In Chaucer and Middle English Studies in Honour of Rossell Hope Robbins*, ed. by Beryl Rowland. London: George Allen & Unwin. pp. 424, £7.95.

[7] In *Chaucer and Middle English Studies*, see above, note 6.

[8] *Satire and Allegory in 'Wynnere and Wastoure'*, by Thomas H. Bestul. Lincoln: U. of Nebraska P. pp. xiv+122. $6·50.

Prologue is 'best seen as a complaint against the times' and as 'political prophecy, a well-defined medieval genre', while the fallacies of argument in the debate depend for their effect on an audience's acquaintance with Cicero and Aristotle. Such identifications may be useful and even necessary for us, but they surely belie the author's method of composition and the way an audience may be expected to respond.

Anne Kernan (*NM*) considers problems of unity in 'Theme and Structure in the *Parlement of the Thre Ages*'. The 'bracketing' or explicit labelling by its author of the content of certain passages indicates consciousness of purpose. The article seeks unstated relationships, to identify associations between the apparently unconnected parts. In the hunt Kernan rejects symbolic values for the stag and other features. The focus is on technical detail and correct procedure. The ritual is seen as associating death and pride of life in the noble animals, which connects this part with the dreamer's own mortality and the content of his dream. Problems of disproportion have to be admitted in the description of the Worthies, but in general the structure of the dream is deliberately different to distinguish symbolic from natural worlds. The theme of mortality is pursued in a pattern which Kernan relates to the Three Living and Three Dead. But a closer analogue is found in Ecclesiastes, the medieval commentaries on which reinforce the similarity. The structure and unity are thematic rather than narrative.

George R. Kaiser's 'Narrative Structure in the Alliterative *Morte Arthure* 26–720' (*ChauR*) relates to his earlier article (*YW* 54) denying that the poem contains specific historical reference. Here he considers the initial portrait of Arthur, not a specific king but an image of the heroic especially comprehensible to a fourteenth-century audience. Comparing those lines with the corresponding part of Wace's *Brut*, he finds a figure of greater complexity, made by the English poet with concrete rational detail and 'by drawing from the same stock of narrative convention as authors of contemporary romances and chronicles'. This argues against associating this Arthur with one particular source such as Alexander. Analogues are found for Arthur's ferocity, for the vows of the nobles, for the dismissal of the ambassadors and Lucius' response, for the commission of the kingdom to Mordred, and for the leavetaking. All are in some way conventional, but the result is an Arthur with depths designed for the poem's tragic theme. Charles L. Regan looks at 'The Paternity of Mordred in the Alliterative *Morte Arthure*' (*BBSIA*), arguing against J. L. N. O'Loughlin that there is no evidence that Mordred's parentage is connected with Arthur's fall, or that Mordred is Arthur's son.

W. R. J. Barron provides a valuable analysis of an unjustly neglected poem in '*Golagrus and Gawain*: A Creative Redaction' (*BBSIA*). The French source in the First Continuation of *Perceval* is 'a conventional chapter in the hagiology of Gawain'. The English retains the theme and episodic form but amputates elements belonging with other episodes so as to focus on the siege. Removal of the hunting in particular involves the poet in explaining the motives of Gawain and Golagrus in what follows. This is done through a concentration on character rather than knightly codes for their own sake. Barron relates the poet's tendencies to those of the *Morte Arthure* and *Sir Gawain*, and comments on his skill with the demanding alliterative-stanzaic medium, which suggests that his concern was poetic rather than merely with retailing a story.

Thorlac Turville-Petre discusses 'Summer Sunday, De Tribus Regibus Mortuis, and The Awntyrs off Arthure: Three Poems in the Thirteen-Line Stanza' (RES). He sees the stanza as evidence of an actual 'school' of poets, and relates it to some of the poems in Harley 2253. His aim is to discover relationships between the three poems named, mainly in matters of theme and style. An appendix lists works using the stanza. The same writer examines a connexion between 'Humphrey de Bohun and William of Palerne' (NM), suggesting that the poem was composed for Humphrey's retinue at his two manors south of Gloucester, at Haresfield and Wheatenhurst.

One of E. J. Dobson's 'Two Notes on Early Middle English Texts' (N&Q) is an interpretation of deoren in Laȝamon's Brut (Madden, 28064–71) as meaning a female animal. This leads to an emendation resulting in a line which certainly sounds very characteristic Laȝamon. C. David Benson writes of 'A Chaucerian Allusion and the Date of the Alliterative Destruction of Troy' (N&Q). He sees the poet as not only referring to Chaucer's Troilus, but also revealing his knowledge of it in other ways. It seems he expected his readers to supplement his account from Chaucer's book. Bearing in mind Mabel Day's view of its relation to the Siege of Jerusalem, Benson suggests 1400 as a 'reasonable' date.

3. THE GAWAIN-POET

W. R. J. Barron begins a welcome new series of bilingual medieval texts with an edition of Sir Gawain and the Green Knight [9] with an excellent prose

translation facing the original and an Introduction, Select Bibliography, and Notes. After placing the poem in the romance tradition, the Introduction devotes four sections—one for each Fitt—to a stimulating and detailed discussion of how the plot's conformity to the conventions of romance is superficial and deceptive. The translation is very accurate and readable owing much, naturally, to earlier editions of the poem, a debt acknowledged in the Notes, which are chiefly interesting for their discussion of ambiguities in the text. Barron on lines 237, 1237 and 1265 partly conflicts with Manfred Markus, who finds here and in lines 955 and 968, 'Some Examples of Ambiguity in Sir Gawain and the Green Knight' (NM), the recognition of which necessitates correction of the standard interpretations. John W. Martin suggests that sum of line 247 neither means 'some' nor is adverbial; it retains here its Old English meaning of 'one' and refers to Gawain, 'The Knight who Stayed Silent through Courtesy' (Archiv, 1973), thus preparing us for the entry of the hero into the action. Thomas L. Wright suggests that, as well as meaning 'in truth', the bob referring to 'Sir Gawain in vayres' (PQ) at line 1015 may invoke the vair design in heraldry, and thus exemplify the patterned pairing of companions at table, particularly Gawain and the lady.

Brian Stone's second edition of his Sir Gawain and the Green Knight [10] (YW 40. 68) has many changes in the verse translation itself, three essays, and fuller notes than some in the first

[10] Sir Gawain and the Green Knight. Second Edition. Trans. with an Introduction by Brian Stone. Harmondsworth: Penguin Books. pp. 185. 35p.

[9] Sir Gawain and the Green Knight, ed., with an introduction, prose translation and notes, by W. R. J. Barron. Manchester Medieval Classics, General Editor G. L. Brook. Manchester University Press. pp. x+179. Paperback £1.50.

edition. The translation reads extremely well, with a general tautening of certain lines, and its accuracy should satisfy the general reader without seriously disturbing the specialist. The first essay likens the Green Knight to the kind of Devil who tempts 'within the system' on behalf of God; his axe and his colour are seen as symbolic of truth, though his greenness also associates him with the green man and the wild man of medieval tradition, who are opposed to Christianity and feudal order respectively. The second essay asserts that Gawain's abandonment of truth consists only in his acceptance of the girdle, which involves breaking faith with his host; not in his treatment of the lady, which involves a rejection of the sensual element in courtly love. The third essay describes a Christmas production of the poem as a play in Stone's translation. Theodore Silverstein's verse translation of *Sir Gawain and the Green Knight*[11] has no introduction or notes, and hence no explanation of its sub-title, 'A Comedy for Christmas', apart from an indication at the end of the volume that the translation was completed in Christmas 1974. The translation is certainly comic enough, often in places where it is by no means certain that comedy was intended by the author; a comparison of lines 413–16 in Silverstein's translation with the same passage in Barron's and in Stone's will provide an example of this. '*Sir Gawain and the Green Knight* as a Christmas Poem' was discussed in *Comitatus* (1970) by Jean Louise Carrière, in an article noted, but not reviewed, in *YW* 51. 85–6. One of the poet's major accomplish-

[11] *Sir Gawain and the Green Knight. A Comedy for Christmas*. Translated from the Middle English by Theodore Silverstein. Illustrated by Virgil Burnett. Chicago and. London: University of Chicago Press. pp. vi+121. 11 illustrations. $10.

ments, it was claimed, is to demonstrate to his audience the meaning of Christmas—Christ's preservation of mankind from the effects of Original Sin—by initiating into a knowledge of its meaning the members of the Round Table who appear in the poem.

Richard Waswo sees *GGK* and *The Tempest* as 'Parables of Civilization' (*Genre*, 1973) insofar as the heroes of both works triumph over and compromise with the forces which threaten their respective societies. Gawain is Christlike in his morality, but his acceptance of the life-preserving girdle is a slip, since the human knight cannot imitate the resurrection of Christ; Prospero is Godlike in his awareness, but is not aware of everything, as is shown by what he regards as his total failure with Caliban, who is nevertheless accessible to civilizing influences. Both works thus meet D. H. Lawrence's criterion that a genuine work of art 'must contain the essential criticism of the morality to which it adheres'. J. M. Leighton, noting that green is the colour of vestments used at Epiphany, as well as of fertility, and that the Green Knight's castle is a civilized, Christian one, finds 'Christian and Pagan Symbolism and Ritual in "Sir Gawain and the Green Knight"' (*Theoria*). In re-forming his story from its sources to include an interdependent test, the poet has reorganized his material to realize a more sophisticated moral intention than simply a test of courage. Gawain must learn the true meaning of Christian values in the lands of Sir Bercilack of the high desert (*sic*), a waste land far away from the comfortable familiarity of Arthur's court. Just as the old fertility cults have been altered to conform with Christian precept, so the source stories have been re-created to serve a Christian purpose. The

1975 English number of *SELit* summarizes an article in Japanese from 1974 on 'Catholicism in *Sir Gawain and the Green Knight*', by Takero Oiji, who points out first that Gawain is an ideal Catholic knight, who resists temptation by the Lady, but finally commits a failure without knowing it; secondly, that Gawain's rising again through penance shows that the poet's view of man is typically Catholic; and thirdly, that the sacrament of penance, correct use of which was a dominant literary theme in the thirteenth and fourteenth centuries, plays a very important part in the latter half of *GGK*.

A number of articles are concerned with the blameworthiness, or otherwise, of Gawain's character. W. O. Evans, in 'The Case for Sir Gawain re-opened' (*MLR*, 1973) produces evidence that in the later Middle Ages belief in the magical efficacy of physical objects such as the girdle was not as incompatible with Christian belief as is often supposed, and argues that while it is thus no sin for Gawain to want the girdle, he is at fault insofar as he is unaware of the incipient falseness within himself which his acceptance of it implies, until he is made aware of it at the Green Chapel. The fact that he can make a perfect confession because he fails to recognize the serious implications of accepting the girdle is perhaps to be taken as an indication that the Church provides only general guidelines for the individual, who must work out details of conscience for himself; and Gawain's accusation against himself of *covetyse* is to be seen in relation to the three rules of conduct, analogous to those of the religious life, which are required of the hero of a Grail romance. For reasons of *cortaysye*, Gawain preserves his *clannes*, or chastity; but in accepting the girdle he is guilty of *covetyse*, thus breaking the knightly equivalent of the vow of poverty; and this leads him to break what is roughly the equivalent of the vow of obedience, *leute*, in his dealings with Bertilak de Hautdesert. A view rather less complimentary to Gawain is offered by Laila Gross, who produces evidence from a letter from Thomas, Duke of Gloucester, to Richard II to show that a knight in single combat was forbidden to have any magical object on his person. Thus 'Gawain's Acceptance of the Girdle' (*AN&Q*) involved breaking the chivalric as well as the moral code. Michael M. Foley, on the other hand, finds, with 'Gawain's Two Confessions Reconsidered' (*ChauR*) that Gawain's retention of the girdle is a minor offence against the knightly code more appropriately confessed to the Green Knight than the priest at Bertilak's castle. Gawain has been charged with the mortal sins of superstition, covetousness, and infidelity; but he is no more superstitious than is acceptable by the standards of medieval romance; he does not covet the girdle for its material value; and the fact that 'sware' (1108) probably means 'answer' rather than 'swear' shows that in retaining the girdle he is not guilty of forswearing an oath, but rather of cheating in a game. This slight error, motivated by fear for his life, means that in his attempt to live by two parallel moral codes, the Christian and the knightly, he falls slightly short of perfection in the latter. The two codes are represented structurally by Gawain's two confessions, which form part of the elaborate, symmetrical structure of the whole poem. Ina Rae Hark claims that a hero who supposedly trusts completely in God and Mary should not require a talisman such as the girdle. His acceptance of it is the one decisive action in 'Gawain's Passive

Quest' (*Comitatus*), and almost nullifies his otherwise successful adherence to that quest. The tension between the traditional quest form and the goals of the contemplative, rather than active, life throughout the poem points up a disparity between what Gawain considers himself to be and what he is, and the contradictions inherent in the poem from the beginning anticipate and predetermine Gawain's failure, which is the culmination of the poem's message and of Gawain's self-education. The poet does not indict Gawain for failing to be a saint, only for thinking that an arbitrary set of rules would make him one, and the quest becomes a journey to self-discovery in which Gawain must learn that he is not the perfect knight of the Pentangle but simply a worthy knight and a human being. The poem joyfully affirms humanity, but also prefigures disaster with its hints that Gawain will not accept its lesson. P. B. Taylor, in 'Gawain's Garland of Girdle and Name' (*ES*) points out that the Lady's words to Gawain in the course of her three visits to him involve an attack on his name; the girdle thus becomes 'Gawain's specious indemnity for the loss of his name as the Knight of Courtesy'. Furthermore, the Green Knight attacks Gawain's heroic character at the Green Chapel in the same way as the Lady had attacked his courtesy at the castle. But the Green Knight, in addressing Gawain ceremoniously by name after Gawain has humbled himself, is reinvesting him with a name which, now having been tested, is a true one; and the new-found name is reinforced by substitution of the girdle for the pentangle as an emblem of Gawain's worth. With new name and fame Gawain returns to Camelot only to find his sensitivity to fault in ill-accord with the heedless jollity of the court. Thus, while the

skeleton of the plot differs little from stock romance comedy, the Gawain-poet adds an ironic twist to his story, allowing Gawain to conclude his adventures unenlightened, and Camelot to take too lightly the fault he takes too seriously. A quite different view is offered by Peter Christmas, who first sets out in 'A Reading of *Sir Gawain and the Green Knight*' (*Neophilologus*) to exculpate Gawain from major failure anywhere in the poem. In Christmas's view, Gawain does emerge, for all the reservations which can be made, as the embodiment of knightly virtues, and the tone of the Green Knight's words to him at the end of the poem is one of congratulation at success, rather than of reproach over a failure. What is puzzling about the end of the poem is that Gawain remains obstinately in earnest in the face of the Green Knight's laughter and that of the court. A comparison with Chaucer's *Knight's Tale* indicates that *GGK* implies that the chivalric code will do for all the uses of this life, provided one takes it seriously. Gawain is right not to join in the laughter, because he understands that laughter is a fatal solvent of the chivalric code which gives meaning to his life. The lateness of the poem, written at a time when its values no longer enjoyed ready acceptance, adds significance to this view.

Two articles deal with rather more technical matters. Hans Kasmann gives a balanced examination of 'Numerical Structure in Fitt III of *Sir Gawain and the Green Knight*',[12] providing evidence of numerological patterns as a method of composition, apparently without any symbolic significance. The Fitt begins and ends with a seven-line bridge-passage, and each of the three days it describes

---

[12] In *Chaucer and Middle English Studies,* see above, note 6.

divides into four scenes or sections: hunt, castle, hunt, castle. In the first day, the third section has exactly the same number of lines as the first, while the total number of lines in the first and second sections is exactly twice that in the third and fourth; in the second day, there is a difference of only one line between the first and third sections, while the total number of lines in the first, third and fourth sections is exactly twice that in the second. The third day remains a problem, though even here there are clues that point to the presence of numerical relations as a structural principle; perhaps an examination of the other Fitts will provide new vantage-points from which a pattern may be discerned. Ralph W. V. Elliott distinguishes between two types of landscape description in *GGK*: the 'romantic', which includes the castle in the forest in Fitt II, and the ascent to the hill near the beginning of Fitt IV; and the 'realistic', which includes the journey to and through the Wirral in Fitt II, the terrain of the boar hunt in Fitt III, and the guide's directions to the Green Chapel, and the locality of the Chapel itself, in Fitt IV. Elliott notes 'Some Northern Landscape Features in *Sir Gawain and the Green Knight*'[13] in that Norse words are used in both these types of description. Some of them, like *felle* or *flat* or *myre*, fit readily into the alliterative patterns and the 'romantic' passages; others, however, such as *forlondes, forz, kerre, knot, scowtes* and *strothe* show that in the 'realistic' passages, des-cribing a landscape apparently famil-iar to the poet and his readers, he uses many words of Scandinavian origin.

Finally, '*Sir Gawain and the Green Knight*: An Annotated Bibliography 1950–1972', is provided by Roger A. Hambridge (*Comitatus*, 1973), who, without systematically searched foreign language periodicals, yet feels confident that no major article or book has been omitted. The annotation following each entry is intended to present its major thesis as succinctly and objectively as possible.

The most provocative contribu-tions to the study of *Pearl* are two articles by Clifford J. Peterson in *RES*. In '*Pearl* and *St Erkenwald*: Some Evidence for Authorship', he discovers the name 'I. d. Masse' spelled anagrammatically in *St. Erkenwald* in the alliterating letters of the lines corresponding in number to those at which Barbara Nolan in 1971 (*YW* 52. 86) had discovered the name 'I. Massi' concealed anagrammatically in *Pearl*. The *St Erkenwald* anagram is spelled in the same way as one of the names found in the margins of its manuscript, and the laws of probabil-ity, together with certain other features of the text, indicate that its occurrence is no accident. This dis-covery, it is suggested, confirms the validity of the *Pearl* anagram, and at the same time makes most plausible the conclusion that the two poems stem from one poet. 'The *Pearl*-Poet and John Massey of Cotton, Chesh-ire' shows that this John Massey meets all the essential requirements for identification with Hoccleve's 'maister Massy', whose name corres-ponds to the one in the anagrams in *Pearl* and *St Erkenwald*. The Hoccleve reference comes in an envoy to his *Regiment* (*sic*) *of Princes*, a copy of which, containing the envoy, was apparently sent to John of Lancaster, son of Henry IV. Massey of Cotton

[13] In *Iceland and the Mediaeval World. Studies in Honour of Ian Maxwell*, ed. by Gabriel Turville-Petre and John Stanley Martin. Published by the Organising Com-mittee for Publishing a Volume in Honour of Professor Maxwell and printed by Wilke and Company Limited, Clayton, Victoria, Australia. pp. x+176, frontispiece. $10. (Australian).

was alive during 1411–14, which fits the context of Hoccleve's reference to him; he was very probably in his maturity during the fourth quarter of the fourteenth century, the period to which *Pearl* and *St Erkenwald* are usually assigned; and his association with Prince John of Lancaster is shown by documents found in the household accounts of Henry Prince of Wales, for whom the *Regiment* was composed. Thomas A. Reisner, on the other hand, suggests that the 'pyonys powdered' of '*Pearl*, 44' (*Explicator*, 1973) may strengthen the case for John Prat as author of the poem, first proposed by Cargill and Schlauch in 1928 (*YW* 9. 101–2). 'Powdered' was a heraldic term, and the various fourteenth-century families named Prat had arms with fields either powered or charged with a variety of floral devices.

In an article on 'Color Symbolism and Mystical Contemplation in *Pearl*' (*NMS*, 1973) Robert J. Blanch shows how the author of *Pearl* uses colour symbolism, with its roots in the lapidary and exegetical traditions, to suggest aspects of the complete virtue whereby the poet-dreamer may attain spiritual peace. At each stage of contemplation in *Pearl*—the 'erber', the external world of creation; the Edenic jewel-garden, the internal world of the mind; and the New Jerusalem, the eternal world of God—colour symbolism, it is true, underscores the nature of each realm; but the poet's use of it in the descriptions of the 'erber' and the earthly paradise also prefigures the dreamer's vision of transcendence, the supernal brightness of *visio pacis*. Colour symbolism in *Pearl* finally enables the dreamer and the reader to illuminate the dark mysteries of God by piercing the veil of the supernatural, and to recognize the need for Christ's saving blood. Blanch touches on the problem that

Pearl 1007 substitutes ruby as the sixth foundation stone of the New Jerusalem for sardius in the Apocalypse. The ruby is linked with Christ's brightness, as the sardius is with His blood. Dorothee M. Finkelstein, in 'The *Pearl*-Poet as Bezalel' (*MS*, 1973) suggests that the imagery and structure at the core of *Pearl* are drawn from the Biblical account in *Exodus* of the twelve stones of Aaron's breastplate, which came to be regarded as the foundation stones of the New Jerusalem in the Apocalypse, and that the poet-as-jeweller derives from the jeweller-craftsman Bezalel in *Exodus*, a concept which, owing to the influence of Rashi, the eleventh-century Rabbi of Troyes, acquired a special significance in Victorine religious thought, to which the idea of the pearl enclosed in a coffer (lines 259, 271) is analogous. The use of ruby for sardius, and the emphasis on the order of their births in the names of the 'Israel barnes' (line 1040), suggest that the poet made use of the Biblical exegesis of Rashi and his followers; and a solution to the problem of the fifteenth section of *Pearl*, with its explicit mention of God's name and its six stanzas rather than five, is sought in the Hebrew Tetragrammaton, or four-lettered cryptograph of the divine name, the numerical value of which was known to Christian scholars. John Finlayson, in '*Pearl*: Landscape and Vision' (*SP*) finds that much recent work on *Pearl* and its background has obscured the fact that the three *loci operandi* of the poem—the 'erber', the Earthly Paradise, and the Heavenly City—are not independent descriptions presented objectively by the poet, but are all created through the eyes of the Dreamer. The *loci* are very closely related to the poem's purpose—the dramatic creation of the progress of an individual soul from darkness to illumination—and are powerful instruments in its method—the gradual development of symbolic significance through the figure of the Dreamer.

W. A. Davenport, in 'Desolation, not Consolation: *Pearl* 19–22' (*ES*) suggests full stops at the ends of lines 20 and 21, and the translation: 'Never yet did a song seem to me to have such sweetness as a moment of peace let steal over me. In truth there used to come fleetingly to me many (such moments). To think of her colour clad, as now, in mud!' Here 'moment of peace' is *any* such moment in the narrator's happy past. In '*Maskeles, Makeles*: Poet and Dreamer in the *Pearl*', (*AN&Q*, 1973) Joseph L. Baird supports Gordon's retention of *MS makeles* at 733 and 757, even though earlier editors' emendation of it to *maskeles* brought this stanza-group into line with the remainder of the poem, in which stanzas in each group are mostly linked together by repetition of the same word or phrase. Retention of *makeles* allows the view (supported at the beginning of the next stanza-group) that in 780, 'a makeles may and maskelles' the dreamer is mistakenly combining the two words as modifiers of *his* Pearl, whereas the 'may' herself has applied 'makeles' only to the Lamb and to the Pearl of Great Price.

D. S. Brewer has reprinted Gollancz's edition of *Cleanness* (*YW* 3. 40)[14] adding a prose translation to face the text; the original pagination remains. Brewer's claim that 'the translation is as literal as possible, consonant with being in

reasonably modern English; or is in as modern English as possible, consonant with being reasonably literal' is largely justified, though modern colloquialisms occasionally mar some rather poetic passages of translation (e.g. line 530). Brewer translates Gollancz's text, and the dozen or so variations from his interpretations are noted at appropriate points, as are the three occasions on which Brewer has drawn on Menner's edition of 1920 (*YW* 3. 40) for interpretations of extremely difficult lines. The lack of further commentary and bibliography at least has the advantage of drawing attention to problematic passages. The increased accessibility of the poem which this edition brings will no doubt be especially welcome to T. D. Kelly and John T. Irwin, who refer to Gollancz on the first page of their long article 'The Meaning of *Cleanness*: Parable as Effective Sign' (*MS*, 1973) and state their intention of opening up new areas for criticism of *Cleanness*, particularly its sacramental structure and parable form. There is a mirror-like symmetry in the arrangement of its four parts: it begins and ends with a feast, and between these two episodes are two destructions in which God saves a chosen few. Each is parabolic: a New Testament parable (the marriage feast) is followed by three parabolic stories from the Old Testament (the Flood, the Destruction of Sodom and Gomorrah, and Belshazzar's Feast). The marriage feast is symbolic of, among other things, the union of man and God achieved in the Eucharist, and the poet attributes his composite account of it to Matthew, rather than to Luke, not least because he wishes to evoke its context of authority in Matthew. A realization of this context aids understanding of the father-child authority motif which connects the

[14] *Cleanness. An Alliterative Tripartite Poem on the Deluge, the Destruction of Sodom, and the Death of Belshazzar, by the Poet of Pearl*, ed. by Sir Israel Gollancz, Litt. D., F.B.A. With new English translation by D. S. Brewer. Cambridge: D. S. Brewer Ltd. pp. xxxii (with one facing page) +102 (with 67 facing pages). £5.25.

three Old Testament stories in the poem. All four sections, moreover, are linked by the motifs of the body as vessel and of purification by water, and the theological cohesiveness of the poem's structure is evident in the balancing of the warning given in the destruction episodes by the sacramental framework of Baptism, Penance, Matrimony and the Eucharist as the principal means of avoiding destruction. This framework is twice reinforced by the symbolic interaction of the beryl and the pearl, with their sacramental associations. The structure balances the eschatological and hortatory impulses in Matthew's parable of the marriage feast; and a parable is linguistically an effective sign in doing what it says as far as the eschatological moral is concerned: it separates the few who understand it from the many who do not, thus acting out its moral that, on the last day, many are called, but few are chosen.

In a note on 'Jonah and Christ in *Patience*' (*MP*, 1973), Malcolm Andrew points out that Christian teaching sees Jonah as a type of Christ, since both were prophets, both spent three days and nights in a hell of one kind or another, and Jonah's descent to Joppa, according to Petrus Chrystologus and the *Glossa Ordinaria*, symbolizes the Incarnation. In *Patience* the poet sustains a series of simultaneous parallels and contrasts between Jonah and Christ, prophets who brought about the repentance of many sinners. Christ is implied as a measure of perfect man, the standard against which Jonah must be set and inevitably found wanting; Jonah is characterized as a representatively imperfect human being, able briefly to emulate Christ, though utterly incapable of doing so consistently. Thus the poet emphasizes the greatness of Christ and the feebleness by comparison of even the most worthy of men. In 'Jonah and *Patience*; the Psychology of a Prophet' (*ES*), F. N. M. Diekstra raises the question of the originality of the paraphrase in *Patience* of the biblical Book of Jonah. The poet sees Jonah's character through the eyes of a medieval moralist, and is inspired by the latent possibilities for characterization in the biblical Jonah. The theme of patience is developed in terms of Jonah's failure to submit to God's providence, his lack of stability under adverse as well as prosperous conditions, his quick anger, and his lack of mercy and consideration compared with God. Thus the poem is essentially about the opposite of patience, and the dangers of not having it; this has helped to obscure the fact that the poet's interpretation of his source is firmly embedded in the tradition of the commentaries. Diekstra finds that patristic commentary is harder on Jonah than Anderson suggests in his 1969 edition of *Patience* (*YW* 50. 92), and that Pierre Bersuire's remarks on Jonah's false pursuits, and on the moral significance of the sea, his sleep, and the woodbine, seem to conform, in their general purport, to the moral of the poem. Without insisting on Bersuire in particular, Diekstra suggests that commentaries such as his help readers of *Patience* to ask the right sort of questions by making them aware of symbolic significances more alive in the fourteenth century than now. John T. Irwin and T. D. Kelly in 'The Way and the End are One: *Patience* as a parable of the Contemplative Life' (*ABR*), claim that when the story of Jonah is seen as a symbolic representation of a meaning concealed on the surface but revealed at a deeper level as a linking of the first and eighth beatitudes, the relationship of the poem's prologue to the Jonah story becomes clear: the story is then understood to be a parable of the contemplative life. Medieval contemplative writers in trying to describe the direct perception of God use images such as the kingdom of heaven, the sight of God, the journey to a city, a servant running an errand at his master's will, the sharing in the passion of Christ, and the participation in Christ's death, entombment and resurrection. These appear in *Patience* in the story of Jonah, whose development consists in his transformation from an unwilling to a willing figure of Christ. In the woodbine episode, God makes Jonah act out a parable which He then personally explicates, and Jonah's understanding of the parable's meaning is a direct perception of God's nature. The contemplative life and the parable form connect in that the theme of Christ's parables is: 'Many are called, but few are chosen', and the relationship of contemplatives to the rest of the Church has traditionally been regarded as that of the chosen few to the many.

4. PIERS PLOWMAN

'Haukyn's Coat: Some Observations on *Piers Plowman* B XIV. 22–7' (*MÆ*) is John A. Alford's cautious title for an illuminating study. In the coat Langland seems to be describing Haukyn himself, but the relationship is more complicated. As well as being 'of Christendom', and also Haukyn's carnal nature, it carries another meaning in Conscience's advice about cleaning it, and in the mysterious promise about its future cleanness. The problems are to explain the list of strange enemies of the coat, the reference to Haukyn's wife, and the promise of his sinless future. The lines paraphrase the Sermon on the Mount, but Langland has replaced the original rust, which attacks treasure, by 'mist' as a more appropriate

enemy for a coat. The coat is given a shifting meaning as a complex image of a man's spiritual history. In Conscience's promise it is Haukyn's treasure in heaven. The wife is a reference to Haukyn's own flesh by a common exegetical formula. Conscience is describing the way not to a perfect life but to salvation. Haukyn will continue to stain his coat, but penance will enable him to put on the coat of salvation and share in the plan of redemption.

R. E. Kaske sees a relationship between 'Holy Church's Speech and the Structure of *Piers Plowman*'.[15] One of the poem's many structural patterns is based on a fourfold division of the speech in Passus I. Holy Church first discusses *bona temporalia*, divided into natural and worldly goods, and next the supreme spiritual values of truth and love. The whole speech considers the problems of natural and of Christian man in 'a symmetry of arrangement as unmistakable as it is unusual in *Piers Plowman*'. The first topic is developed in the *Visio*, with worldly goods in Passus II-IV and natural in Passus VI, and the second topic in the *Vita* where the quest for Truth (identified with the search for Dowel etc.) merges at some point with a quest for charity. Kaske suggests the turning point is Patience's riddling speech in Passus XIII. This leaves the Confession and Pilgrimage in the *Visio* to be explained as a forerunner of that later quest, while the reversal of order in the topics is explained as an exigency of a chronological narrative about attempted reform. This has to begin with sins easier to reform because further from man's basic appetites, but following too a descending order of the seriousness of those sins.

[15] In *Chaucer and Middle English Studies*, see above, note 6.

Edward C. Schweitzer tackles '"Half a Laumpe Lyne in Latyne" and Patience's Riddle in *Piers Plowman*' (*JEGP*), on the principle that all riddles present a perspective from which the solution is impossible. The search for 'a perspective not immediately obvious' leads to a number of related suggestions. *Ex vi transicionis* is a punning reference to the passion and resurrection, pre-figured in the Red Sea crossing and the sacrifice of the paschal lamb. 'Laumpe lyne' refers to the injunctions of the baptismal liturgy where a candle is presented to symbolize illumination through charity. A school-book text from Plautus may connect with this the grammatical aspect of the pun. 'A signe of the Saturday etc.' is a reference to confirmation in an apocalyptic context, and the Wednesday of Easter Week also looks forward to the Second Coming. The solution requires recognition of a continuous allusion to the mystery of Easter and the individual's sacramental participation. Its difficulty, designed to prevent automatic response to the familiar, is a rebuke to Will's expectation of an easy definition of charity.

Thomas D. Hill provides 'Two Notes on Exegetical Allusion in Langland: *Piers Plowman* B I. 115–24 and XI. 161–67' (*NM*). Holy Church's account of the rebel angels distinguishes those who believed in Lucifer from those who merely 'hoped it miȝte be so'. *The Voyage of St Brendan* is used to support the suggestion that the latter are neutral angels. The reference to God's one finger in the introduction to Trajan's second speech is explained as a name for the Holy Ghost. A relationship established here between love and law is glossed in a related passage where Spes shows Will a text written on rock.

5. ROMANCES

In the first five chapters of his book, *The Creation of the First Arthurian Romance: A Quest*, Claude Luttrell[16] seeks to show how *Erec et Enide*, the first extant Arthurian romance, was influenced by the Latin allegories of Alain de Lille. The influence is to be seen in Chrétien's treatment of the Nature topos in his portrayal of Enide; in the description of the Quadrivium on Erec's coronation robe; in his making a man's attitude to love as crucial an aspect of his conduct as in *De planctu Naturae*, and in his borrowing of a master-plan from *Anticlaudianus* in forming the mirror of marriage which *Erec* represents. The positing of Alain's influence involves re-dating *Erec* from 1170 to c. 1185, the implications of which are discussed in chapter 3, while the dating of Alain's allegories is discussed in Appendix A. Luttrell goes on, in chapter 6, to reject the theory of a common source for *Erec* and the Welsh *Gereint*, and to examine the relations between *Erec* and the Fair Unknown type of story, which survives in five principal versions, including the fourteenth century English *Lybeaus Desconus*. For the episodes of the Fair Unknown Story, *Erec* has equivalents in an order which is found to be that of this story in its original form, which is seen as identical with the *conte Erec*, the lost *conte d'aventure* from which Chrétien says that he has drawn a *conjointure*. The *conjointure* of *Erec*, as narrative structure, is then examined in chapters 9–10, where it is shown convincingly, by a comparison of *Erec* with texts more or less directly indebted to the lost *conte Erec*, that this latter was indeed Chrétien's source, which he follows both closely and individually.

16 *The Creation of the First Arthurian Romance: A Quest*, by Claude Luttrell. London: Edward Arnold. pp. viii+284. £6.

Luttrell then discusses Chrétien's transformation of his *conte d'aventure* into a *conte sentimental* in his portrayal of Enide, and in conclusion emphasizes that the approach adopted allows more originality to Chrétien than that represented by Loomis had done. In chapter 7, it may be added, he shows that Malory's Tale of Sir Gareth contains elements deriving from a *conte d'aventure* close to the *conte Erec*, but not identical with it, and in Appendix B, in a comparison between this Tale of Malory's and the second part of Hue de Rotelande's non-Arthurian romance of *Ipomedon*, that the former derives from a source close to, and perhaps descending from, the latter. This is an important book, which will undoubtedly give rise to lively and profitable debate.

William B. Holland, in 'Formulaic Diction and the Descent of a Middle English Romance' (*Speculum* 1973), criticizes the stemma for the manuscript tradition of *Arthour and Merlin* proposed by Kölbing in his edition of 1890, and suggests that of the four principal manuscripts, the three later ones, L, P, and D, preserve the results of oral transmission of the original romance. 500 lines of the earliest extant manuscript, the Auchinleck MS (A), and 500 lines of D are then compared in content with the corresponding lines of L, and are classified as identical, nearly identical, sharing sense but too different in wording to involve copying errors, and unrelated. Between A and L there are 10 lines which are identical, 48 more which are nearly so, and 164 which are similar in meaning but not close enough in wording to involve copying errors; and between D and L there are 50 identical lines, 118 nearly identical, and 205 related in meaning but not apparently copied from the same source. It is hard to make any

coherent scheme of written transmission from these statistics. On the other hand, when the first 100 lines of P and L are compared, it is found that 53 are identical, 30 nearly so, and the remaining seventeen related. P is not copied from L, but seems to have descended through written transmission from a source not very different from it. The variation of diction between the manuscripts, which differ little on a larger scale, does not indicate redactorial originality between the stages represented by the earlier and later manuscripts, as Kölbing had thought, but formulaic conventionality, the general extent of which is illustrated by a comparison of two passages from *Arthour and Merlin* with other metrical romances, which latter are documented in a lengthy Appendix. The first English text was probably a written translation from the French, not greatly different from Auchinleck, but apart from the link through written transmission of P with L it seems unlikely that any unbroken chain of written texts connects the existing manuscripts.

John and Rose Marie Beston discuss 'The Parting of Lancelot and Guinevere in the Stanzaic "Le Morte Arthur"' (*AUMLA*, 1973), a scene which is found in Malory as well as in this poem, but not in the *textus receptus* of their common source, the Old French prose *Mort Artu*. The authors set out to demonstrate that this scene is original to the poet of the stanzaic *Morte Arthur*, claiming that its genesis can be traced in the earlier scenes in this poem involving Lancelot's interview with the queen at court after the tournament, and the Maid of Ascalot's letter. The Bestons' remarks contribute usefully to a study of the poem's structure, but their discussion of the farewell scene, found in the Palatinus Latinus 1967 MS of the

Mort Artu, and printed as an appendix in Frappier's edition of the latter, fails to take account of the likelihood that this text represents a variant tradition including a final interview scene which was known to the author of the stanzaic *Morte Arthur*. Michael Twomey, in 'A Note on Detachment in the Stanzaic "Morte Arthur"' (*BBSIA*) criticizes George Kane's view (*YW* 32. 86–7) that at line 1001 of the poem Gawain is typically lacking in emotional involvement with the poem's events when he calls death *unhende* for taking the Maid of Ascalot's life. It is not Gawain, but Arthur, who is speaking, and the statement does not indicate detachment since Arthur does not know the girl, or that she has died for love of Lancelot. A measure of detachment is necessary in this poem for the realization of its subject—the death of Arthur and all that he represents; but this does not mean that the poem is emotionless, as Kane would have it. Larry D. Benson's edition, *King Arthur's Death: The Middle English Alliterative 'Morte Arthure' and Stanzaic 'Morte Arthur'* was not seen.

Raymond H. Thompson in 'Gawain against Arthur' (*Folklore*), finds the impact of a mythological pattern on Arthurian tradition in the three romances preserving the story of Gawain's birth, two in French and one in Latin. The mutual hostility of Gawain and Arthur in the *De Ortu Waluuanii* indicates a tradition at variance with the regular presentation of their relationship as warm and affectionate.

In 'The Formal Nature of Middle English Romance' Kathryn Hume (*PQ*) attempts to provide a construct of Middle English romance form which takes into account modern perspectives on the genre, and, at the same time, to recover the notion of its form implied by Middle English references to romances. A spectrum is generated by varying the relation of hero to background. At one end (Type A) are the romances in which the hero is all, and the locale unimportant; at the other (Type C) come the histories, whose events overshadow any hero the story may possess. At mid-point (Type B) both variables are significant. The story pattern of Type A is found to involve, firstly, the separation of the hero from a peaceful and ordered existence; secondly, his attempts to prove himself; thirdly, the resolving of the discord into harmonies. Type B is less uniform than Type A, but shows at least a rudimentary perception that history is not a series of disjunct events of interest only for showing off the hero to good effect; and Type C romances are the 'histories', only some of which have nominal heroes and which are characterized by the assumption that a 'chunk' of history can be presented as a closed, complete unit. The three types are exemplified respectively by, among other works, *GGK*, the alliterative *Morte Arthure* and *Melusine*. The indebtedness of the genre to French secular narrative means that much of the latter's variety was lost in the process of translation and adaptation, and the shift in the style of romances produced between 1300 and 1500 is found to be more apparent than real. The second half of the article offers a comparison of the romances with other Middle English narrative types. Romances differ from folk-tales in displaying heroes as patterns of ennobling virtues; from saints' lives in idealizing qualities different from those idealized in that genre; and from historiography in their underlying assumption that a historical movement can be dealt with finitely. Finally, English romances are distinguished from their continental counterparts by their essential morality, and their preference for action over situation.

M. Mills and D. Huws print with an introduction and Notes a fragmentary early fourteenth-century text of *Guy of Warwick*[17] preserved as part of the bindings of MSS British Museum Add. 14408 and National Library of Wales 572 (the latter fragment not previously noticed). These two manuscripts, and the one in which their bindings were originally contained, are described, and the latter's text of *Guy* is shown to go back to a source whose author tried to reduce the daunting length of the Anglo-Norman *Gui* in a manner very largely his own. His version of *Guy* was not as creative, however, as the redaction of *Gui* in his source; though he omitted much, he added little, and had an acute consciousness of the scale of his undertaking, and a growing impatience with expendable detail likely to slow down his progress through it. The Notes, despite limitations of space, give much helpful information, particularly on the relationship of this version of *Guy* to its Anglo-Norman source. Nothing of quite this kind is offered in '*Guy of Warwick*: A Medieval Thriller', by Velma Bourgeois Richmond (*SAQ*), who finds the thriller superior to the mere detective story in that its hero's own peril adds a philosophic dimension to the latter's characteristic suspense. It is not accidental that thrillers are a particularly British genre, and the heightened concern with moral values in Middle English romances, as contrasted with French originals, is an early manifestation of this concern with orthodox values.

Horst G. Ruthof, in 'The Dialectic of Aggression and Reconciliation in *The Tale of Gamelyn*, Thomas Lodge's *Rosalynde*, and Shakespeare's *As You Like it*' (*UCTSE*, 1973) finds what he calls a dialectic of events in *The Tale of Gamelyn*, which moves from an initial situation of justice to an eventual re-establishment of justice through a series of antitheses which widen from situations of family conflict to ones of social conflict, and which include, in the early stages, two syntheses or reconciliations which are more apparent than real. The purpose of correction implied by this process is lost in Lodge's *Rosalynde*, which, however, retains elements of aggression and violence. Shakespeare reintroduces the idea of correction, modified and on a higher plane, eliminates violence and gives his comedy a new homogeneous spirit.

In '*Le Bone Florence of Rome*: A Middle English Adaptation of a French Romance', Anne Thompson Lee[18] illustrates the radical alterations in descriptive technique, narrative order and dramatic focus which distinguish this romance from its early thirteenth-century French source, *Florence de Rome*. The English adaptation is some 4,000 lines shorter, and while its speed of movement sometimes creates confusion, it seldom affects the story's overall dramatic coherence. The French poem is dry and humourless, though subtle in its portrayal of character; the English poem is lively, but has little scope for more than stereotypes of character. From a study of some half-dozen episodes it emerges that, without pretending to a complex or sophisticated style, the

[17] *Fragments of an Early Fourteenth-Century 'Guy of Warwick'*, ed. by Maldwyn Mills and Danial Huws. Medium Aevum Monographs, New Series IV. Oxford: Basil Blackwell. pp. iv +110. 4 plates. £1.

[18] In *The Learned and the Lewed: Studies in Chaucer and Medieval Literature* (for Bartlett Jere Whiting), ed. by Larry D. Benson. Harvard English Studies 5. Cambridge Mass.: Harvard U.P. pp. xii+406. Frontispiece. Paper £2.75.

English adapter has achieved a tight narrative structure and a dramatic realism almost completely lacking in his French source.

Albert C. Baugh's 'The Making of *Beves of Hampton*'[19] was not available.

Two articles deal in general terms with the Middle English poems known as Breton lays. John B. Beston raises the question of 'How Much was Known of the Breton Lai in Fourteenth Century England?'[18] (i.e. of the French lai, since there is no evidence of Bretons presenting their lais in England at that time). The French lais were revived in England with the French romances during the fashion for translation then current, which suggests that the inspiration for the Middle English lais came from French sources. Eight of the nine surviving poems divide into two groups: the couplet romances of the early fourteenth century, *Sir Landevale, Lai le Freine, Sir Orfeo,* and *Sir Degaré,* and the tail-rhyme ones from the end of the century, *Sir Gowther, Sir Launfal, The Erle of Tolous,* and *Emaré.* Chaucer's *Franklin's Tale,* being part of a dramatic framework, is an anomaly. There is a regional and social difference between the two groups, the earlier coming from London and the South Midlands, the later from East Anglia; and the former group was composed in a courtly tradition, while the latter belongs to a regional school of poetry. In the earlier group, *Orfeo* is probably a rendering of the lost *Lai d'Orfée,* and *Degaré* perhaps a composite imitation of a French lai; the other two are translations from Marie de France. The authors of the later group must have known

some couplet lays, but there is no convincing evidence that they knew the French lais. The descriptions of lais in the prologue common to *le Freine* and *Orfeo,* and in the Franklin's prologue, show a limited and at times inaccurate knowledge of the French lais; and a survey of the English lays suggests that little prestige attached to a poem's calling itself a lay. The concept of the lay changed in fourteenth-century England; little is made of the genre's association with Brittany, or of commemorating an 'aventure', important concepts in the French lais. Graham Johnston, in 'The Breton Lays in Middle English'[20] points out that the 'literary Breton *lai*', as represented by Marie de France, her French and possibly her English successors, needs to be distinguished from her sources, the oral and musical Breton lais. Of their lyric and narrative elements it is the latter which she reproduces. A further distinction must be made between material in her *lais* of ultimate Celtic origin, and non-Celtic material transmitted by the Bretons. *Landevale* and *Launfal* correspond to the former category, *Lai le Freine* to the latter; *Orfeo,* which combines the Greek legend of Orpheus and Eurydice with Celtic motifs, may inherit this combination from a lost Old French *Lai d'Orphey*; and *Sir Degaré* also shows dependence on Celtic sources. These lays are warranted as specimens of the genre, and apart from *Launfal* (which depends on *Landevale*) date from early in the fourteenth century. The later *Emaré, Sir Gowther,* and *Erl of Tolous,* however, appear to be Breton lays in name only; and while there is nothing specifically Celtic about the Franklin's Tale, it is given a Breton colouring because Chaucer found the

---

[19] In *Bibliographical Studies in Honour of Rudolf Hirsch,* ed. by William E. Miller and Thomas G. Waldman. Philadelphia: U. of Pennsylvania.

[20] In *Iceland and the Medieval World,* see above, note 13.

genre of the Breton lay appropriate to the Franklin's old-fashioned romantic tastes. Chaucer's influence caused the writers of *Emaré, Erl of Tolous* and *Gowther* to associate material of widely different origin with the genre, and the author of *Sir Launfal* to re-write an early lay.

Peter J. Lucas in 'An Interpretation of *Sir Orfeo*' (*LeedsSE*, 1972) draws attention to the unifying motif of the harp, and emphasizes that *Orfeo* reflects the original Greek version of the story, which lacks the second loss of Eurydice, and which survives in three eleventh-century poems composed in France, the probable home of *Orfeo's* immediate source. No close association between the poem and the Virgilian versions of the stay is admissible. Lucas also argues convincingly against basing an interpretation of *Sir Orfeo* on a notion of the Other World as a world of the dead. The strength of the mutual love of Orfeo and Heurodis is conveyed by what they communicate to each other and by their actions; corresponding to their private love is the public loyalty Orfeo has from his subjects, especially the Steward. The bonds of private love and public loyalty are tested, the first by the unmotivated intervention of the fairies, the second by Orfeo's return to Winchester in disguise. The fairy world shares with the human world the *ympe-tre* and castles, towers, rivers, forests, etc., but differs in being menacing and cruel; those who are taken there are kept in a state of arrested mobility, from which they are only occasionally allowed respite. As a poem about tests, *Orfeo* may be compared with *GGK*, though the comparison should not be pressed too far; and it may be regarded as a psychological tonic insofar as the private and public bonds survive the tests triumphantly. Christina J. Murphy's '*Sir Orfeo*. The

Self and the Nature of Art' (*UMSE*, 1972) was not seen. Her summary of it in *MLA* abstracts for 1973 records her claim that Orfeo's recovery of Heurodis represents a significant change in the Orpheus myth made by the author of the poem, and that other such changes are the presentation of Orfeo as a non-supernatural being, the diminution of the quest-motif, and Orfeo's survival to rule his kingdom. Another article seen only in summary (in *BBSIA*, 1975) is J. Frappier's 'Orphée et Proserpine ou la lyre et la harpe' (*MLG*) which detects the influence of a tradition differing from the Latin one in Raoul Lefèvre's substitution of Proserpine for Eurydice as the wife of Orpheus in his *Recueil des hystoires troyennes* (1464.) *Sir Orfeo*, with its infusion of Celtic elements, and particularly the *aithed* theme involving the abduction of Heurodis by the king of the Other World, suggests the existence of a lost French lai of *Orphée* remembered by Lefèvre. Alice E. Lasater, in 'Under the Ympe-Tre, or: Where the Action is in *Sir Orfeo*' (*SoQ*), regards the Latin versions as the primary sources and enumerates the medieval references to the lost French 'lai d' Orphey'. She sees the *ympe-tre* as a tree with grafted branches easily associated with imps or fairy people, and finds examples in Celtic stories of trees connected with the abduction of a mortal in which a mere branch or an apple from the tree is involved. A connection between the *ympe-tre* and the branches of the tree of Elysium in the Celtic otherworld would account for Heurodis' being abducted as a result of sleeping under an *ympe-tre*, just as a similar situation occurs in the *Lay de Tydorel*. In *Sir Gowther*, *Thomas of Erceldoune*, and *Tam Lane*, sleeping under a tree in an orchard precipitates abduction to the otherworld. The *ympe-tre*, like the golden bough of Virgil, is a universal token for admission to (and often return from) the otherworld. Edward E. Foster, writing on 'Fantasy and Reality in *Sir Orfeo*' (*BSUF*, 1973) sees the world of the fairies not so much as a dead world, as one which holds the natural law in abeyance. While the story of Orfeo and Heurodis in the poem 'is literally the triumph of mutual love', the contrasting situations and world views, and the reader's consistently larger perspective on the action, make possible judgements of ulterior significance beyond the psychology of the characters. In Michael Masi's 'The Christian Music of *Sir Orfeo*' Orfeo is seen as a specifically Christian hero and his music is said to produce ecstasy. The effect he has on the animals in the wilderness is a new power resulting from penance. It is said also to bring 'order to a realm filled with menace', in the otherworld.

Mortimer J. Donovan, in 'Middle English *Emare* and the Cloth Worthily Wrought' (see footnote 18), describes the relationship to Emaré of the Sicilian monarch's gift of a cloth to her father. The description of the cloth follows a pattern observable in certain lays of Marie de France whereby a specific concrete object is chosen as the centre of the *lai* to develop new varieties of symbolic content within the poem. The cloth remains prominent from line 181 to the end, when the power of the human experience it represents is completed in clear, vivid terms.

Daryl Lane suggests that 'Conflict in *Sir Launfal*' (*NM*, 1973) can be perceived if the reader stands back from the tale so as to 'feel' the narrative as a primitive archetypal opposition of good and evil, harmony and discord. Launfal's generosity establishes him as unequivocally good; Queen Gwenere is the evil instrument of discord that clashes with this goodness; and Triamoure, Launfal's fairy lover, is established as a power of goodness both by the way she is described and by her exposure of Gwenere's mendacities, which results in justice being served and order maintained.

Ronald M. Spensley, in 'The Courtly Lady in *Partonope of Blois*' (*NM*, 1973) shows that while closely following the plot structure of his Old French source, the author carefully modifies the presentation of the three courtly ladies. In a number of scenes relating to her love for Partonope, the English Melior seems far more concerned with her reputation than her French counterpart. The author adds explanations which emphasize this concern, alters certain passages in the French which do not, and tones down or omits certain of the French Melior's impulsive words and thoughts. He also attributes to Uraque and Persowis, who harbour an unrealized love for Partonope, an exemplary restraint which is not apparent in his source, and gives a cautious, qualified recommendation of love's virtues in place of his French counterpart's blunt criticism of the lady who rejects love. A tentative explanation of these changes is found in the suggestion that the social framework in which the courtly ladies of twelfth-century romance evolve is much less rigid than that of the fifteenth-century literary stereotype of 'the courtly lady'.

J. B. Goedhals discusses 'The Romance and Prophecies of *Thomas of Erceldoune*' (*UES*, 1972), accepting the date of c. 1400 on the grounds that the prophecies in the second and third Fitts of this three-Fitt poem are historically accurate only up to that date, reached in the third Fitt. Goedhals's discussion, as much descriptive as analytical, is based on the

Thornton manuscript, though he refers to the Lansdowne version of the poem which is unique in rationalizing the Queen of Faery's recovery of her beauty after the loss of it occasioned by her acceptance of Thomas's advances. This relatively late version provides evidence that the Queen's simulated ugliness was intended as a test for Thomas, comparable to Bercilak's testing of Gawain in *GGK*. Goedhals refers to the myth of Orpheus, but not to *Sir Orfeo*, in this connection, and finally compares *Thomas of Erceldoune* with Sir Walter Scott's version of the ballad of *Thomas Rymer*, showing that while the latter retains certain features of the romance elements in *Thomas of Erceldoune*, such as Thomas's mistaking of the Elf-Queen for Mary, it is generally more direct, and the displaced sequence of the journey into Elf-land is more powerful and evocative, though the ballad's narrative strength weakens towards its end.

Two articles on *Havelok* deal with kingship from rather different points of view. Dayton Haskin, in 'Food, Clothing and Kingship in *Havelok the Dane*' (*ABR* 1973), stresses the importance of generosity in the poet's picture of the good ruler, beginning with the description of Aethelwold's reign. He outlines a series of situations in which cruelty and kindness are contrasted in cases of need for food and clothing, especially Havelok's own experiences of generosity which later inform his administration of justice as king. Haskins sees a parallel, perhaps a deliberate one, with the depiction of the Last Judgement in *Matthew* xxv. 31–46, and relates the whole theme of a king identifying himself with the poor to traditional preaching. The 'bourgeois romance' is designed, like the sermons, to pacify the poor and warn the rich. But despite its assumption of a

Christian view of history and final justice, the poem is firmly about earthly matters. In 'Theocratic and Contractual Kingship in *Havelok the Dane*' (*ZAA*), Sheila Delany and Vahan Ishkanian also see the theme as political, the nature of kingship. A résumé of the historical background aims to show how a balance achieved between the power of king, barons, and wealthy bourgeoisie is reflected in the poem in Havelok himself. The romance has something of the hagiography in its portrayal of Aethelwold, and the establishment of Havelok as miracle-working saviour-figure. But Aethelwold's reign is also defined in political terms, and there is a theme of 'consensus among all social classes'. Havelok represents a work ethic, the ideal worker seen from the employer's point of view. His social rise acquaints him with the needs of his future subjects. The absence of a religious ceremony at his accession 'serves to emphasize the rights of *regnum* over *sacerdotium*'. It is a notion of kingship away from the theocratic extreme, and Delany and Ishkanian emphasize the realistic feasibility, rather than the element of fantasy, in the social mobility indicated among Havelok's rewarded supporters.

Die anglonormanische und die englischen Fassungen des Hornstoffes, by Walter Arens, was not seen.

6. GOWER, LYDGATE, HOCCLEVE

Götz Schmitz, taking his cue from Gower's concept of 'the middle weie'[21] between 'lust' and 'lore', sets out to study the integrating function of Gower's notions of rhetoric and poetics in the *Confessio Amantis*. The

[21] *the middle weie: Stil- und Aufbauformen in John Gowers 'Confessio Amantis'*, by Götz Schmitz. Studien zur englischen Literatur, ed. by Johannes Kleinstück, Vol. 11. Bonn: Bouvier Verlag Herbert Grundmann. pp. 218. DM. 36.

short first chapter is purely introductory; the most important chapters are IV, V and VI. Chapter III foreshadows its companion corner-piece, chapter VIII, in discussing Brunetto Latini's *Livres dou Tresor*, which provided Gower with an Aristotelian notion of rhetoric—especially marked in Book VII of the *Confessio Amantis* —and hence with the desired middle way between practical and poetic purposes. In this respect Gower differs from Chaucer and other contemporaries whose notions of rhetoric descended from Geoffroi de Vinsauf. There is moreover a personal element in Gower's conception of rhetoric in that he sees the gift of speech as a mark of man's creation in God's likeness, and hence attributes to man a high degree of responsibility in relation to language. In chapter IV, where Schmitz discusses the outer framework of the *Confessio*, the passages of 'lore' in the seventh book and elsewhere which are treatise-like in character, a consideration of Gower's insistence here on the element of human responsibility—which shows itself in his recourse to the Aristotelian theory of *mesotes*, or the mean—enables Schmitz to point to stylistic and thematic links between these passages and other parts of the work. In chapter V, he discusses the framing device of the confession itself, showing how, in the dialogue between Genius and Amans, the characters of these two are skilfully differentiated—the former being presented as a fatherly admonisher, tempering his eloquence with proverbs and generalizations, and the latter being presented, with his exaggerations and contradictions, as a caricature of the courtly lover. Finally, in chapter VI, the author discusses the element of 'lust' in the *Confessio Amantis*, the exemplary tales, emphasizing the style of delicate

persuasion which they inherit from the *exemplum*-tradition, and showing how Gower takes care to reveal in them the responsibility of man as a being endowed with reason. This means, among other things, that Gower gives only as much scope in the tales to the forces of destiny as is necessary to keep the action going and to bring his characters to the making of decisions; and the decision which Amans himself has to make between 'will' and 'resoun' is linked with the occurrence in some of the tales of the 'wo-to-wel' or 'wel-to-wo' pattern, which Gower found in the legendary and tragic forms of medieval love-literature, forms in which his middle style—comparable to styles regarded as Classical or Augustan in later centuries—shows itself to greatest advantage. Of these three main chapters, the 'middle' one, placed as it is between those which deal with 'lore' and 'lust' respectively, deserves special attention, as the author himself points out. In 'The Art of High Prosaic Seriousness: John Gower as Didactic Raconteur' Anthony E. Farnham[22] traces the didactic success of the first exemplary tale in the *Confessio Amantis*, that of Acteon and Diana, to Gower's ability to create in the person of Genius a character whose moral imagination is almost as prosaically deficient as the literary imagination of Chaucer's narrator of the tale of *Sir Thopas*, and that each of the tales in the *Confessio Amantis* is a comparable achievement. Both Amans and Genius are creatures of the narrator's deficient imagination—the former a projection of his fantasies (not always impure) about love and lust, the latter of his beliefs (not always foolish) about 'wisdom' and 'lore'. In this view, the lesson of the poem as a whole is that

[22] In *The Learned and the Lewed*, see above, note 18.

only by laughter can we come to recognize our moral beliefs and intellectual assumptions for what they are. The author also suggests, in two of his footnotes, that much of the humour of the work is contained in its Latin marginalia and elegiacs.

'In Lydgate's Laughter: "Horse, Goose and Sheep" as Social Satire' (*AnM*), David Lampe suggests that, in this poem, in which each of these three animals (the third represented by a ram) pleads for individual supremacy before 'The hardy Leoun' and 'Themperiall Egle', each is made to appear ridiculous, and guilty in one way or another of pride, by its own arguments. The horse represents the warrior-nobility, while the goose and the ram represent the commons and the Lords Spiritual respectively, and the final verdict of the lion and eagle, emphasizing as it does the necessary interdependence of each animal-estate, would seem to be Lydgate's reminder to Henry VI of the rôle he should take in matters of the state. Lydgate's originality here lies in his combination of estates philosophy, and a *debat* pattern and beast-fable parliament fiction, and in the rhetorically skilful double argument he gives each debater. James I. Miller, Jr., in 'Lydgate the Hagiographer as Literary Artist'[22] shows that the arrangement and articulation of the miracles in the second half of the third book of Lydgate's *St. Edmund and St. Fremund* reveal an interest in artistic balance. Of the seven miracles the first and seventh are linked by subject-matter, the second and sixth by theme, and the third, fourth and fifth by subject-matter. This overall structure is reinforced with patterns of common rhyme in the first and seventh miracles on the one hand and the second and sixth on the other, and rhyme and verbal recurrence link one miracle to the next. Furthermore, the longer miracles show internal patterns of rhyme and phrasing. It is clear that, in this unit of his poem, Lydgate took special pains to combine parallels in word and position with modifications in content or context which would advance the presentation, and it is to be hoped that this article will stimulate a search for the same skill in design and control in other poems of Lydgate's. Elizabeth Walsh, RSCJ, gives in the same collection an enjoyable account of 'John Lydgate and the Proverbial Tiger', suggesting convincingly that Lydgate crystallized in English literature the simple and realistic understanding of the tiger as a fierce beast which is found in classical literature. An examination of tiger images shows that in works dealing with classical subjects the figure of the tiger seems to have been largely Lydgate's own contribution, conveying some unpleasant aspects of human nature, but nevertheless being used to describe pagan heroes as well as villains. In the religious poems, on the other hand, it is always used to characterize the enemies of God, and in 'Horns Away' it is used with reference to women. Susan Schibanoff, in a note on 'Avarice and Cerberus in Coluccio Salutati's *De Laboribus Herculis* and Lydgate's *Fall of Princes*' (*MP*), suggests that borrowing by the latter work from the former may explain Lydgate's representation in this poem of the three heads of Cerberus as three different aspects of Avarice, while the adoption of Cerberus, whom Lydgate calls a 'werm', as a symbol of Avarice, may have been suggested by the mention of a 'serpente' in connection with Avarice in Laurent de Premierfait's translation of Boccaccio's *De Casibus Virorum Illustrium*. The medievals connected Avarice with Cerberus through confusing Pluto with Plutus, the Roman god of wealth.

J. E. van der Westhuizen in his edition of Lydgate's *Life of Saint Alban and Saint Amphibal*[23] has in his Introduction a chapter on 'Literary Style' which illustrates certain rhetorical devices used in this poem, and complains of its prolixity and repetitiveness; but the question of whether or not there is a system in the repetitiveness, or a structure in the whole, or parts, of the poem does not seem to have been seriously asked; and the Explanatory Notes are startlingly slight: some 4,500 lines of verse are covered in five pages of Notes. One of these (for line 1559) relates to Cerberus, and consists of a passage from *The Oxford Companion to Classical Literature* quoted in a manner which does ill justice to the thought processes of its compiler, Sir Paul Harvey, as does the information that the *Companion* was published in 1947, and revised in 1940. Furthermore, van der Westhuizen's criticism, in the Introduction, of Lydgate's nature descriptions of lines 1850–81 might perhaps have been less harsh if he had not omitted from consideration the twelve lines describing the pagans which include one of the tiger images discussed by Walsh, and which suggest, albeit faintly, that an effect of contrast may be intended in this passage. Helpful features of the edition are a summary of the poem's contents indicating the sources used by Lydgate at various stages of the work, and the printing of these sources, as far as is practicable, below the relevant stanzas of the text.

A. Compton Reeves writes on 'Thomas Hoccleve, Bureaucrat' (*M & H*), showing how Hoccleve's poetry is a source of insights into his occupation, attitudes, and the general course of his life. An examination of his treatment of political subjects reveals that his political thinking was moralistic and dogmatic rather than practical, but significant in showing that he rejected his bureaucratic experience when he approached political problems.

7. MIDDLE SCOTS POETRY

Bernice W. Kliman identifies 'The Idea of Chivalry in Barbour's *Bruce*' (*MS* 1973) as Barbour's concept of the ideal knight, and discusses under various headings the way in which Barbour reconciles historical actuality with the abstract ideal of chivalry as his audience probably knew it from French romance, and with the concrete ideal of nationalism, democracy and freedom which informs his poem. The same author shows, in 'The Significance of Barbour's Naming of Commoners' (*SSL*, 1973), that certain of the latter have names associated with Aberdeen, where Barbour was Archdeacon. This suggests a possible source for his information on these commoners, and shows how, in his concern for freedom and nationalism, he names and gives prominence to commoners as well as nobles. In 'Alliteration in Barbour's *Bruce*'[24] the same author also describes a computer study which, when complete, will answer questions about the distribution and rhythm of alliteration in the poem. These questions are justified by the fact that Barbour's *Bruce* links the poems of the alliterative revival and French-inspired poems in octosyllabic couplets.

John Balaban, noting in his 'Blind Harry and *The Wallace*' (*ChauR*), that the author of this poem nowhere describes himself as blind, argues that the name 'Blind Harry' derives

[23] *John Lydgate: The Life of Saint Alban and Saint Amphibal*, ed. by J. E. van der Westhuizen. Leiden: E. J. Brill. pp. viii+319. Fl. 68.

[24] In *The Computer and Literary Studies*, ed. by A. J. Aitken, R. W. Bailey, and N. Hamilton Smith. Edinburgh U.P. 1973. pp. xi+369. £7.

ultimately from that of Garaidh, a figure of Celtic mythology whose father was blind, and that it later became a nickname or alias for the author of *The Wallace*, who flourished between 1470 and 1500, and was neither blind nor the 'burel man' he calls himself. *The Wallace*, which contrasts with Barbour's *Bruce* in being fantastically inaccurate historically, is to be seen as a conscious blending of folk-myth and Chaucerian literary conventions, and the purpose of the blending is to make Wallace seem a greater hero than he really was.

Robin Fulton discusses the structure of *The Thre Prestis of Peblis* (*SSL*, 1973), showing that in this symmetrical poem in which each of three priests tells a three-part tale, the third tale is related to the first and second in such a way as to make the reader see them in a different light.

Lois A. Ebin in 'Boethius, Chaucer and *The Kingis Quair*' (*PQ*), suggests that the latter work is more of a response to, than an imitation of, its Boethian and Chaucerian models. Like Chaucer in *Troilus* and the *Knight's Tale*, James I uses the plight of lovers—a subject largely ignored by Boethius—to examine questions raised in the *Consolation of Philosophy* about man's position in a universe which he only partly understands. Unlike Chaucer's characters, however, James's narrator learns to overcome Fortune while he remains in this world through his journey from youth to maturity, a journey which includes love as man's first guide, as is shown by the rôle which James assigns to Venus. James demonstrates by the rôle he assigns to Minerva that man's full recognition of Fortune's rôle comes from the 'wit' or 'lore' with which he meets all kinds of experience, including writing.

A second edition of Charles Elliott's selection from the poems of Robert Henryson[25] improves on the first (*YW* 44, 119) in several ways. The Introduction is fuller, the Biographical and Textual Note more tentatively phrased, and a Select Bibliography replaces the extracted 'Appreciations' of the earlier edition. *Orpheus and Erudices* is now included in full, and the Notes and Glossary have been revised and expanded. Daniel M. Murtagh discusses 'Henryson's Animals' (*TSLL*, 1972) in 'The Preiching of the Swallow', 'The Uponlandis Mous and the Burges Mous' and 'The Paddok and the Mous', claiming that these three fables resemble each other in showing up the inadequacy of convention as a defence against a reality too hard to bear. The first of the three tales does this against a background of tragic amplitude, and the second and third against a background of comedy, and for this reason these two are more frightening than the first. Nicolai von Kreisler (*TSLL*, 1973) points out more usefully that 'Henryson's Visionary Fable: ... *The Lyoun and the Mous*' is unique as a fable with both its dream framework and its Aesopic narration of the fable proper. These devices provide Henryson with an authority and an objectivity which enable him to instruct James III in the art of kingship through the character of the lion, the king of beasts, by developing the old fable which had asserted that pity is always rewarded.

Florence H. Ridley makes 'A Plea for the Middle Scots',[26] taking exception to the categorization of Henryson, Douglas and Dunbar as

[25] *Robert Henryson: Poems*, ed. by Charles Elliott. Second Edition. Clarendon Medieval and Tudor Series. Oxford U.P. pp. xxx + 203. Frontispiece. Paper £1.95.
[26] In *The Learned and the Lewed*, see above, note 18.

'Scots Chaucerians', and finding evidence of these poets' indebtedness to Chaucer surprisingly slim. More specifically, she investigates Henryson's *Testament of Cresseid*, claiming that this poem achieves its dramatic force by contrast with rather than resemblance to Chaucer's *Troilus*. J. A. W. Bennett in the new *Scottish Literary Journal* finds 'Henryson's *Testament*: a Flawed Masterpiece' and does not find the contrasts of the *Testament* with *Troilus* as pointed or as successful as Ridley does. There is no question of Henryson's ability to create arresting scenes, or of his irony, though neither of these gifts depends exclusively on Chaucer for its effects, as Bennett shows in a number of examples; to treat scenes in Henryson as ironic variations on scenes in Chaucer is to praise the right things for the wrong reason. Henryson's verisimilitude is sometimes imperfect and some of his best effects are marred by excessive alliteration, schoolmasterly pedantry, uncertain syntax and his favourite *moralitas* device. Bennett finds Cresseid's apostasy ill-grounded while sharing the poet's feeling that the gods' final judgement on her is not divinely fair. John McNamara in 'Divine Justice in Henryson's *Testament of Cresseid*' (*SSL*, 1973) suggests that since in the *Testament*, a poem set in pre-Christian times, Henryson is suggesting that divine justice has been vindicated in the actions of the pagan gods, the Christian God whom they represent must, by implication, also be just; and whatever God may choose as the ultimate resting-place for Cresseid's soul will therefore be just also. Cresseid's punishment leads to her moral regeneration and, while never confirming it, the poem never denies the possibility that she may be saved. The same question is discussed and well documented by Ralph Hanna III, who examines 'Cresseid's Dream and Henryson's *Testament*'[27] against the background of Macrobius's Commentary on the *Sommium Scipionis*. Cresseid sees in her dream mainly what she wants to see, a kind of cosmic conspiracy devoted to reducing her, through her disfigurement, to causeless ruin; but insofar as her dream is prophetic at all, it reflects only her own prior choices and their natural results. Eleanor R. Long (*Comitatus*, 1972) proposes that 'Robert Henryson's 'Uther Quair'', in which he claimed to have found 'the fatall destinee of fair Cresseid' recounted, was an anonymous fifteenth-century Latin treatise on the evils of sex based partly on Guido delle Colonne's *Historia Destructionis Troiae*, and that this treatise was not only translated into Scots by G. Myll as *The Spektakle of Luf*, but was also read in the original by Henryson, who composed the *Testament* in extenuation of the sexual promiscuity connoted in the treatise by its use of Guido's phrase, *communi nominis*, with reference to Cresseid.

Priscilla Bawcutt illustrates 'Aspects of Dunbar's Imagery,'[27] concentrating, in his more colloquial, humorous or satirical poems, on how the images work, rather than whence they derive. Some of his most arresting images employ homely objects, and sometimes an ironical twist is given to a trite simile. Dunbar delights in recording movement, and in tactile as well as visual images; he favours the succinct combination of two nouns, in which the first noun carries the metaphor; and he achieves economy by exploiting ambiguities in everyday speech. Sometimes a single image serves as the organizing princ-

[27] In *Chaucer and Middle English Studies*, see above, note 6.

iple of a whole poem, and frequent use is made of image-clusters, which may sometimes inform a whole poem.

In 'William Dunbar's Beast Fable', R. J. Lyall (*Scottish Literary Journal*) finds that Dunbar's 'This hindir nicht in Dumfermeling' belongs primarily to the genre of beast-fable, and suggests that the conjunction of Dunfermline and fable in the poem may mean that we are intended to keep Henryson in mind as we read it. It also includes elements of beast-epic and, furthermore, omits a *moralitas* and uses a lyric rather than narrative form with a refrain which in some ways replaces the *moralitas*, pointing up the strangeness of the events described, and at times intruding the poet's reactions. Bryan S. Hay claims that in the two dream-visions about 'William Dunbar's Flying Abbot: Apocalypse Made to Order' (*SSL*), Dunbar is not merely indulging in personal satire at the expense of Damian, Abbot of Tungland. In 'The Birth of Antichrist', he presents himself as ignoring the oracular significance of his dream that a flying abbot will beget the Antichrist, and accepting it merely as a direct preview of the future; his preoccupation with his benefice rather than with the impending empire of Antichrist implies a joke at the poet-dreamer's expense as well as Damian's. In 'The Fenyeit Freir of Tungland' Damian is a representative of a sinful way of life with its inevitable consequences, rather than the strictly private target of Dunbar's vituperation.

An interesting article on 'The Alliterative Ancestry of Dunbar's "The Tretis of the Tua Mariit Women and the Wedo"' comes from Catherine Singh (*LeedsSE*), who notes the coincidence of stress and alliteration in Dunbar's poem 'Sanct Salvatour!', and points out that 'The Tretis' is virtually the only example of

the sustained use in Scots of the alliterative long line without rhyme. She produces evidence that the anonymous Scots lyric 'Quhen Tayis bank wes blumyt brycht' was partly inspired by *Pearl*; that 'The Tretis' was influenced by 'Tayis bank'; and that something of Dunbar's method of describing natural settings goes back to *Pearl*. The effect achieved in 'The Tretis' is one of parody of the alliterative romances, as is shown in particular by certain archaisms borrowed from such romances. In 'Line 124 of William Dunbar's "The Tretis of the Tua Mariit Wemen and the Wedo"' (*N&Q*) the same author emends 'trawe' to 'traine' to provide the much-needed meaning of 'trick' or 'stratagem'.

R. J. Lyall, writing on 'Moral Allegory in Dunbar's "Goldyn Targe"' (*SSL*, 1973) argues that Dunbar is here concerned with the evils of an immoderate concern with the pleasures of the senses. The overthrow of Resoun signifies the setting loose of the senses, and it is appropriate that Perilouse Presence, or physical proximity, should bring about Resoun's blinding, which affects the dreamer's own vision, making his paradise appear to him as a hell. The crucial position of Resoun, the traditional opponent of Sensuality, gives added significance to the brilliant sensuousness of the opening stanzas describing the actual garden in which the poet wanders at dawn. The garden of the dream is also one of sensuous delight, but those who venture there are liable to be attacked, and if their reason fails them, the garden can become a wilderness. The language of the poem suggests that the dreamer has, in the end, learnt from his experience, and now sees his natural environment as an expression of temperate virtue rather than of sensuality.

Finally, J. Swart finds, 'On re-reading William Dunbar'[27] that the poetry of the so-called 'Chaucerians' differs from the later poetry of Wyatt, Surrey and Sackville in showing an inclination towards aureate diction, a mixture of styles and forms within the same poem, and an almost pervasive sense of moral religious connotation; while it differs from the earlier poetry of Gower and Chaucer in seeming to take for granted the culture represented by the great art of the past.

8. LYRICS AND MISCELLANEOUS VERSE

A new anthology arranges a large number of *Middle English Lyrics*[28] according to subject, with rather more detailed categories than the usual death, love, or devotion. These are accompanied by extracts from published critical work by various authors, divided into a section on 'backgrounds' and one of 'Perspectives on Six Poems'. The text is a normalized one aiming to please the non-specialist, a common practice nowadays, although we might still question how much of a real help to readers is a change from medieval to modern inconsistencies of spelling. Glosses are in the margin with annoying circles in the text as cues. Dating is relegated to a table at the end. The aim of presenting the poems as poems is well achieved, and the criticisms exemplify a variety of lively approaches, although some of the items might puzzle a new reader as much as the poems he seeks to understand. Such a reader might need considerable guidance in making the best of the rather sporadic relationship between the poems and the prose.

But the size and the intelligence of the selection of the lyrics themselves make it an inviting and useful book.

Richard Leighton Greene edits *The Lyrics of the Red Book of Ossory*,[29] a collection of Latin poems made for Ossory cathedral in the fourteenth century. Many of the poems are accompanied by lines in French and Middle English which are not intended to indicate their tunes, but which provide precious and tantalizing fragments of the profane song which the Latin texts aimed to replace. This context for aversion of 'Maiden in the Moor' justifies Greene in arguing strongly against D. W. Robertson Jr and others who believe in its concealed Christian meaning. Greene derives valuable insight from many of the other vernacular fragments too. It is a welcome edition. In the course of his argument the editor refers to Siegfried Wenzel's article, 'The Moor Maiden—A Contemporary View' (*Speculum*), which also argues for the lyric's essentially secular content, quoting a delightfully imaginative use of the poem by a preacher who incorporates it into his sermon by making it refer to mankind in a state of Golden-Age innocence. In 'The Meaning of *grein* in "Wynter wakeneþ al my care"' (*PQ*), Ann Shannon denies the relevance of *John* xii. 24–5 to the poem, which is a *memento mori* and not about resurrection. Jeffrey A. Helterman complicates the usual view by finding 'The Antagonistic Voices of *Sumer Is Icumen In*' (*TSL*). The cuckoo in the song is not part of the general rejoicing. After the celebratory description, the invocation to the cuckoo stems from the speaker's sense of isolation from the scene of regenera-

---

[28] *Middle English Lyrics: Authoritative Texts, Critical and Historical Backgrounds, Perspectives on Six Poems*, ed. by Maxwell S. Luria and Richard L. Hoffman. New York: W. W. Norton. pp. xiv+360. $10.

[29] *The Lyrics of the Red Book of Ossory*, ed. by Richard Leighton Greene. Medium Aevum Monographs, New Series V. Oxford: Basil Blackwell. pp. xxxi+87. £1.

tion. His imperative is an attempt to perpetuate summer (to keep off death), an appeal rendered ironic by its being made to a bird of so doubtful a reputation. James Travis argues for 'The Celtic Derivation of *Somer is icumen in*' (*Lochlann*), claiming that nothing in Anglo-Saxon literature anticipates either the substance or the form of this lyric, and that the music of the Reading Rota was composed neither to it nor to the Latin lyric written beneath it in the manuscript. The English lyric is evidently the translation of a Celtic original whose substance, structure and ornament are reflected in it, and the Latin lyric is modelled on the structure of the English one. The latter's quatrain pattern coincides with the pattern termed *sedrad bacach* in old Irish metrical tracts, and this pattern matches perfectly the corresponding sections of the Rota. The original could have been Welsh at least as easily as Irish; the dialect of the English lyric suggests a place of origin close to Welsh-speaking areas, and the music of the Rota exemplifies the Welsh part-singing described by Giraldus Cambrensis at a date roughly contemporaneous with the manuscript.

M. Gibinska discusses 'The Early Middle English Lyrics as Compared to the Provençal and Latin Lyrics' (*KN*), and finds that the differences between them are neither many nor radical. One reason for this is the prevalent convention of courtly love —a term which Gibinska uses cautiously, though without referring to Peter Dronke's amplification of it in his *Medieval Latin and the Rise of the European Love-Lyric*; other reasons are found in the attitudes of medieval poets and readers to poetry, attitudes which involved a strong awareness of rules and patterns to be imitated. What differences there are in the English lyric—for instance the introduction of animals into the conventional setting of the courtly *reverdie*, and the more extensive descriptions of beloved ladies—are partly to be explained by the lapse of time; some of them, however, such as one instance of a lyric using the Old English four-stress line, are to be explained by different cultural backgrounds and literary traditions. The joy of happy love—a frequent theme of the troubadours—is not expressed so directly by the English poets, whose taste was generally less sophisticated and less courtly than that of the continental writers.

William D. Paden, Jr., writing on 'Pastoral and Pastourelle' (*KRQ*) points out first that the pastourelle came to light in an urban rather than a pastoral milieu; Provence and Languedoc retained in the twelfth century the urban quality of classical civilization, and in northern France the development of the pastourelle in the thirteenth century was accompanied by that of the small cities, which produced a spiritual urbanization of the peasantry. Paden goes on to particularize Empson's notion of pastoral in the latter's *Some Versions of Pastoral,* by taking the vehicle of pastoral to be rustic nature and its designate the ethos of simplicity. The pastoral of Tibullus is more erotic than that of Virgil, and erotic pastoral attains an extreme form in the Song of Songs, from which descends, through a tradition of medieval Latin lyric, the Old French paraphrase of the Solomonic text, which comes very close to the pastourelle. The deep relationship between the pastourelle and the *canso* of courtly love, which becomes explicit in the latter's characteristic spring setting, derives from the two modes of encountering experience which inform the genres, the one a receptive simplicity of spirit, the other an earnest striving for the heights.

Peter Dronke compares 'Two Thirteenth-Century Religious Lyrics',[30] *Furibundi* and *Somer is comen ond winter gon*, seeing in each a poet 'working towards a new mode of organizing lyrical poetry'. Not all the looseness of construction in the English poem can be due to scribal transmission. The opening implies a woman longing for delivery by her knight. This is followed by paradoxical contrasts with the romance world. Dronke interprets the problematic sixth stanza as a return to that chivalric world through images of the chase with Christ as the deer. In both poems Dronke stresses the importance of the texture and sound of the verse in determining the meaning.

Several other articles in the same volume deal with lyrics and short poems. Theo Stemmler offers 'An Interpretation of *Alysoun*', suggesting Continental influence to account for the unusual rhyme-scheme, and finding pattern in the apparent metrical irregularity. Stemmler presents an intricate verbal structure which anglicizes some Continental commonplaces. Albert B. Friedman, in 'A Carol in Tradition', discusses the relationships between carol texts and possible oral versions, and prints two late versions of a carol 'to illustrate the conservativeness of folk carol transmission as a result of its control by writing and print'. Richard Leighton Greene also looks at the later records of the form in 'Carols in Tudor Drama'. Douglas Gray contributes 'Notes on Some Middle English Charms', stressing the serious importance of such pseudo-magic to people in Chaucer's day, and suggesting ways in which an understanding of

these curious texts can be of use to literary critics. A. I. Doyle's 'The Shaping of the Vernon and Simeon Manuscripts' is part of a larger enterprise in the study of the circumstances of production of all Middle English manuscripts of verse and prose. This is an important article whose discussion of the make-up and relationship of these two manuscripts is too detailed to summarize here. Finally Siegfried Wenzel examines 'The English Verses in the *Fasciculus Morum*' with a view to discovering their relation to their Latin context in the manuscripts of this fourteenth-century handbook for preachers. He distinguishes between verses which translate the preceding Latin passage, which is either in verse or prose; verses which are suggested by the preceding Latin passage; and verses which are neither translated nor suggested. This last category is subdivided into verses which are expendable, insofar as they are 'tagged on', and those which are indispensable, insofar as they are an integral part of the context. The function of the various verses seems to have been partly mnemonic, but chiefly rhetorical; and while many of them belong to a tradition of proverbial sayings, it is probable that the compiler of the handbook had a talent for making up verses of his own as well as casting current sayings in a new form.

Wenzel also prints some hundred 'Unrecorded Middle-English Verses' (*Anglia*) which are not recorded in Brown and Robbins' *Index* or its *Supplement*. Most of them occur in Latin manuscripts of the thirteenth to the fifteenth centuries, and most are integral parts of Latin works— sermons, *exempla*, or didactic passages. Excluded from this collection are unrecorded verses from Friar John Grimestone's common-place book and material from the *Fasciculus*

---

[30] In *Chaucer and Middle English Studies*, see above, note 6.

morum. Also excluded are divisions (*partitiones*) of sermon themes, and, for the most part, verses which translate biblical quotations without expansion. The list consists mainly of 'preachers' tags', versified prayers, translations of liturgical pieces, and citations of English songs, including 'Maiden in the mor lay'. The vernacular tags used by preachers, in particular, offer opportunities for further research. In 'Some Unpublished Verses in Lambeth Palace MS 559' (*RES*), S. Ogilvie-Thomson prints as six separate poems what has hitherto been treated in the Robbins *Index* as a single work, Item 2451. He suggests they are all the work of one author experimenting with well-known themes. One of the pieces, although related to known poems, is a previously unrecognized lyric.

John E. Hallwas finds that 'The Identity of the Speaker in "I am a fol, i can no god"' (*PLL*) is Satan, rather than Foolish Love, as the title *Amor Fatuus*, given by the compiler of MS Harley 7322, implies. The lyric can be understood as a boast on the part of the devil, and the first line may be taken as an instance of purposeful self-mockery, implying that anyone who loves Satan is similarly foolish and can do no good. 'I can no god' may also be read as 'I do not know God'. This, then, is the only Satanic monologue among the Middle English lyrics. Hallwas also points out that 'I am Iesu, that cum to fith' (*Expl*) is not mere didacticism, as Rosemary Woolf suggests (*YW* 49. 92); it is an identification speech delivered by Christ as the lover-knight in which He asks to undertake a personal spiritual battle for His beloved, who is at once the purpose, the opponent, and the battleground for the fight. This is the aesthetic basis for the poem, which is underlined by the fact that its odd lines

begin with letters which spell the name IESV.

Albert B. Friedman examines '"When Adam Delved" . . . Contexts of an Historic Proverb'[31] arguing that John Ball's famous couplet was an adaptation of a folk-saying, a Latin version of which descended in a manuscript tradition in England parallel to the oral, vernacular tradition. A closely related proverb is the one asserting that we all descend from Adam and Eve, which was widely current in medieval Europe. The notion of a common origin for all men, which forms the background to the view that nobility is not a matter of social position but stems from a God-given impulse towards virtue, was a theme with which all the great medieval poets were obsessed; and John Ball's couplet, though now labelled a 'democratic proverb', did not always have subversive connotations, for all the cynical nature of some of the medieval theories as to how social differences arose.

Jay Schleusener, in '*The Owl and the Nightingale*: A Matter of Judgment' (*MP*, 1973) argues on the basis of lines 659–836 of this poem that the debate between the two birds is not merely an exercise in dialectics but also 'the real confrontation of real characters in a real world' who deny the possibility of common ground yet argue with great plausibility on both sides of the question. In this passage, the narrator makes two proverbial statements which are practically, if not logically, contradictory: that it is easy for talk to go astray when the mouth speaks against the heart; and that wit is sharpest when the situation is at its worst. Despite this contradiction, the Nightingale goes on to satisfy the conditions of both proverbs, maintaining two contradictory

[31] In *The Learned and the Lewed*, see above, note 18.

positions herself: that she is not very clever, but sings sweetly enough to charm men into heaven; and that she is very clever indeed, her cleverness being superior to the Owl's strength. The narrator's remarks and the Nightingale's argument can only be understood by recognizing the middle ground—the Nightingale's plight—which both of them try so hard to obscure. Thus the author's dialectical sleight of hand draws attention to the positions assumed by the debaters; but the poem is a lesson in judgment rather than in logic, and a wise judge would concentrate as much on the birds themselves as on their arguments. John C. Hirsh, in 'Classical Tradition and *The Owl and the Nightingale*' (*ChauR*) points out the incongruity of the Owl's moralizing when set against this bird's ignoble reputation in the medieval period. Evidence for the owl's base reputation is sought in the works of classical writers, notably Ovid and Pliny; in patristic writings, especially Ambrose's *De Philosophia* as reflected in Augustine's *Contra Iulianum Pelagianum*; and in medieval literary texts, particularly Walter Map's 'Epistle of Valerius to Ruffinus' and the Roxburgh Bestiary. These and other works support the notion of the Owl's reputation as a bird of ill-omen, and associated with lechery and vice. Certain of the Nightingale's charges against the Owl may thus be seen as springing from a classical background, and while they do not guarantee the Nightingale's victory in the debate, they should at least prevent a hasty resolution in favour of the Owl.

Michael G. Sargent edits 'The McGill University Fragment of the "Southern Assumption"' (*MS*), arguing that this is a fragment not, as was earlier thought, of the *Cursor Mundi*, but of the Southern poem which Brown and Robbins term 'The

Assumption of Our Lady'. This poem, which exists in several manuscripts, would seem to be identical with the poem to which the author of the *Cursor Mundi* attributed his Assumption section, and which he believed was the work of St Edmund of Canterbury. The McGill text itself indicates a connection with the 'Southern Assumption' in that the poem's dialect is definitely Southern, its text differs considerably from the Assumption section of the *Cursor Mundi*, and the size of the McGill MS shows that it cannot have contained a poem of the length of the *Cursor Mundi*. Identification of this fragment as part of the 'Southern Assumption' seems more reasonable than the postulation of another poem, hitherto unknown, of which the McGill MS is the only reflex.

Gillis Kristensson edits, with Introduction, Notes and Glossary, John Mirk's *Instructions for Parish Priests*,[32] from MS Cotton Claudius A II and other manuscripts. Four of the latter were unknown to Edward Peacock, the previous editor of the *Instructions*, whose EETS edition of 1868 was revised by F. J. Furnivall in 1902. Kristensson summarizes in chapter I of his Introduction the little that is known of Mirk's life and works and the state of knowledge about the sources of the *Instructions*; the main one seems to have been William de Pagula's *Oculus Sacerdotis*. The manuscripts and their relationship are discussed in the next two chapters, and the general accuracy of the stemma established by Pothmann in 1914, on the basis of six out of the seven principal manuscripts which are now known, is confirmed. The remaining four chapters deal

---

[32] *John Mirk's Instructions for Parish Priests*, ed. by Gillis Kristensson. Lund Studies in English 49. Lund: C. W. K. Gleerup. pp. 287. 7 Plates. Sw. Kr. 76.

respectively with language, metre, dialects of the manuscripts, and editorial principles; the final one includes a list of transcription errors in Peacock's edition. While one might have wished for a fuller discussion of the relationship of the *Instructions* to its sources, and for more treatment of its structure and style, this book admirably fulfils its stated purpose of providing an emended text based on a study of all the known manuscripts.

Rachel Hands discusses 'Sir Tristram's "Boke of Huntyng": the Case for the Rawlinson manuscript' (*Archiv*, 1973), calling this verse treatise on hunting the 'Tristram treatise' from the attribution of its content to Tristram in its opening couplet. It forms the second section of the fifteenth-century printed *Boke of St. Albans*, and exists in two fifteenth-century manuscripts, Bodleian MS Rawlinson Poet. 143, and Lambeth Palace Library MS 491. The Lambeth text is incomplete; each of the other two texts seems to represent a conflation of two separate treatises, only one of which is represented in what survives of the Lambeth text. An examination of the relationship of the texts, under the headings of 'Omissions', 'Verbal variation' and 'Evidence of Northern origin' leads Hands to reject some recent modifications of the view that the three texts provide independent versions of the Tristram treatise, and to suggest that the Rawlinson manuscript, though less well known than the *Boke of St. Albans*, deserves to be considered at least on equal terms with the printed text.

J. B. Bessinger, Jr., with '*The Gest of Robin* Revisited'[33] finds that 'age has not withered it nor custom staled its somewhat limited variety'. He suggests that its religious or ecclesi-

astical elements, its folklore motifs, and its status as a transitional text between oral and written stages of transmission, all deserve closer study. He finds it 'heroic' rather than 'epic', though it has affinities not only with ballad and epic, but also, and most importantly, with romance, particularly *Havelok* and *Gamelyn*. Suggesting that it may be legitimately grouped with the romances through theme and content, Bessinger goes on to compare the *Gest* structurally with Malory's *Arthuriad*, seeing it as an interlaced structure in nine episodes with three plots and an epilogue. This he finds, resembles the blocking and interlocking of some of Malory's sources; thus its structure is conservative and French in orientation, of a type that Malory strove with increasing skill to remove from his narrative.

In the same volume, in 'F. J. Child and the Ballad', James Reppert attempts to reconstruct Child's ballad theory from remarks in his *English and Scottish Popular Ballads* (1882–98). For him, a ballad was only as good as its story, and the closer it was to the earliest form of its story, the better it was. The criterion of probability was important for him in recognizing the oldest forms of a story, as was the occurrence of ancient traits, by which he meant story elements drawn from material of a kind found only in popular literature. His emphasis on the aristocratic aspects of the ballads is not wholly consistent with his statements about ballad transmission which are in any case vague and unsatisfactory. He never solved the problem of classification to his own satisfaction, but a reconstruction by Reppert of the outline around which *ESPB* was organized, with descriptive headings derived from letters which Child never intended for publication, gives an increased

---

[33] In *The Learned and the Lewed*, see above, note 18.

understanding of what was in his mind as he progressed from one part of it to another.

In the Introduction to *The Border Ballads*,[34] James Reed describes his book as 'an attempt to understand Borderers and the Border, up to the union of the crowns, through their ballads seen not merely as folksong, nor simply as poetry, but as a unique record of the life, in all its joy, superstition, savagery and grief, of a remote and precarious frontier community'. His first chapter, 'The Borders and the Ballads', deals with the topography of the Border, and with its laws, customs, administration and architecture, since the ballads are to be seen as the products of a particular environment at a particular period of history. The distinction implied in Reed's statement that 'We have lost much in seeing these ballads as literature, rather than hearing them as songs', is neither developed nor qualified, and there is virtually no discussion of the complex question of 'How Oral is Oral Literature?' (which has been discussed this year by Ruth Finnegan in the *Bulletin of the School of Oriental and African Studies* in an article showing, among other things, that in the English and Scottish ballads there is a long history of mutual influence between oral and written forms). The remaining four chapters of Reed's book deal, largely descriptively and through quotation, with 'Ballads of the Middle Marches', these latter taking up two chapters, and 'Ballads of the Supernatural'. With a Select Bibliography, including a short discographical section, it provides in general a readable survey and, with plates well suited to its approach,

and Bewick woodcuts at the end of each chapter, is attractively produced.

Manfred Görlach's impressive study of *The Textual Tradition of the South English Legendary*[35] begins by facing the problems of the need to understand the nature and purpose of the whole work in its original form. He considers the unreliability of current approaches both from a general standpoint and from studies of individual legends, and introduces, from his own collation of forty items, a method in which results from both general and particular approaches can be used to control each other. The attempted reconstruction of the growth of the *Legendary* starts with an examination of the Prologues, whose two main versions suggest rather different audiences as well as different contents for the collection. It is likely that neither is original, and Görlach goes on to suggest an original collection, metrically irregular, composed in calendar order. Some relationship is suggested between the Laud manuscript and the Sarum Use for the short legends, while for the longer ones the *Legenda Aurea*, despite many divergences, must have been a source for part of the revision if not for the original. Reconstruction of that original and its early development is virtually impossible, but Görlach makes interesting conjectures about the possible management of an original compilation by a man working from a liturgical collection close to the Use of Sarum itself. Despite the Gloucester provenance of one manuscript tradition, he argues for Worcester as the home of the original, leaving open the question of which religious order was responsible because of the multiplicity of possible

---

[34] *The Border Ballads*, by James Reed. London: U. of London, Athlone Press. 1973. pp. x+218. Frontispiece. 16 plates. Maps and woodcuts. £3.50.

[35] *The Textual Tradition of the 'South English Legendary'*, by Manfred Görlach. Leeds Texts and Monographs, New Series 6. U. of Leeds School of English. pp. xii+317.

influences at various stages in its growth. The reconstruction of the textual transmission makes a cautious use of genealogical recension. There is a description of the manuscripts and a survey containing all the detailed evidence for the general conclusions and hypotheses. This is followed by a synoptic table of affiliations and another of the contents of the major manuscripts, together with a map of the early distribution of the *Legendary*.

Philip G. Buehler, in *The Middle English 'Genesis and Exodus'*,[36] gives a summary of scholarship and a bibliography of all significant contributions to the study of the poem, and provides a commentary on the text, covering questions of meaning and intention as well as observations on the peculiarities of language and scribal practice. This is a valuable supplement to Arngart's own commentary in his edition. Venetia Nelson's 'Introduction to the *Speculum Vitae*' (*Essays in Literature*) is a useful summary and analysis of what she calls 'at once the most straightforward in content and the most elaborate in structure' of the doctrinal and moral treatises of the fourteenth and fifteenth centuries.

Klaus P. Jankovsky, in 'A View into the Grave: 'A Disputacion betwyx þe Body and Wormes'' in British Museum MS Add 37049' (*TAIUS*), distinguishes the poem from the Body-Soul debates. Instead of that simple dualism, the Body is here shown as standing for the whole personality, while the worms play a role of similar complexity. The optimistic outlook of the debate is also distinctive. Jankovsky uses the manuscript illustrations in his reading, and goes on to discuss the double meaning of medieval double-decker tombs, not only as reminders of decay but as an expression of appropriate dignity and of the hope of eternity. His further exploration of fifteenth-century verbal treatments of death discovers complications in what has been commonly seen as one-sidedly horrific.

John C. Hirsh prints 'A Middle English Metrical Version of *The Fifteen Oes* from Bodleian Library MS Add B 66' (*NM*). The version is translated from an unknown Latin source and has possible echoes of Rolle. Hirsh describes the method of this devotion with its juxtaposition of the divine and human characteristics of Christ. Fred R. MacFadden considers '"Sir Penny" in England During the Middle Ages: Some Literary Records of an Early Attempt at Institutional Change from Within' (*Franciscan Studies*). In England several factions within the Franciscan order were in unusually close concord and, unlike the French, their writings against avarice do not see money as a deterministic ruling force. Sir Penny is an abstract character to be reflected on, and is used to criticize the church itself with a view to internal reform.

'*The Land of Cokaygne*' (*SH*, 1972) is a discussion of the poem by P. L. Henry accompanying the text borrowed from Bennett and Smithers with marginal glosses added. He considers the Franciscan affiliations of the manuscript, and the origins of the name, Cokaygne. He discusses the question of a specific target for the satire, especially particular religious communities, concluding that the white and grey monks referred to are Cistercians. Further consideration of the historical background leads to a

---

[36] *The Middle English 'Genesis and Exodus': A Running Commentary on the Text of the Poem*, by Philip G. Buehler. De Proprietatibus Literarum. Series Practica 74. The Hague: Mouton & Co. pp. 88. Fl. 24.

suggestion that the community concerned is Inislounaght, the Holm of Sweet Milk, on the River Suir, near Waterford, Ross and Kildare.

Dennis Casling and V. J. Scattergood discuss 'One Aspect of Stanza-Linking' (*NM*). They are concerned with the breaks that occur in such patterns of linked stanzas, and suggest that some of them at least are deliberate, serving, by breaking the normative pattern, to draw attention to particular parts of the poem. In 'A Wayle Whyt ase Whalles Bon' the break marks an emphatic personal interjection by the poet. In 'An Old Man's Prayer' it is occasioned by a shift of meaning and a change of addressee. Similar occasions are possible in the poems of Minot and in romances. Casling and Scattergood add support to the idea that the break in *Pearl* is similarly significant. In non-linked poems, for example, *The Avowing of Arthur*, an isolated link may have a similar intention.

9. MALORY AND CAXTON

Robert R. Hellenga shows that 'The Tournaments in Malory's *Morte Darthur*' (*FMLS*) do not reflect the practices of Malory's own day but those of the period in tournament history between the pitched battles of the twelfth century and the pageants of the fifteenth. They are held in clearly limited areas with grandstands provided for the spectators, though the rôle of the latter, and of ladies in particular, is minimal; the fighting comes first and there is little pageantry. Jousting has become very important—so much so, in fact, that Malory seems at times to blur the distinction between jousting and the tournament proper; and while the sense of opposing sides is still strong, the main emphasis is on individual prowess. The custom of taking prisoners is mentioned but is not

important; and the actual fighting, though seldom inhibited, is mollified somewhat by tournament etiquette and a sense of fair play.

Toshiyuki Takamiya, in '"Wade", "Dryvande", and "Gotelake"—Three Notes on the Order of Composition in the *Morte Darthur*,' (*SELit*) uses these three words to suggest that Malory wrote the Tale of Gareth, the fourth Tale in the sequence of the Winchester MS and of Caxton's edition of Malory, soon after he had turned into prose the northern alliterative poem, *Morte Arthure*, in writing the Tale of King Arthur and the Emperor Lucius, the second Tale in the sequence. Even though the reference to Wade in the fourth Tale occurs in Caxton's edition and not in the Winchester MS, its alliterative character makes it much more likely that Malory, rather than Caxton, derived it from the *Morte Arthure*; its disappearance from the Winchester MS must be due to intentional omission by a scribe. The form 'dryvande', unique in the fourth Tale, has a northern participial ending frequent in the second Tale; and the name 'Gotelake' in the fourth Tale seems to have been suggested by its use in the second, where it occurs most probably as a result of a misunderstanding of the passage in the *Morte Arthure* from which it derives. This suggests that Tales II and IV were composed within a short time of each other, and that Malory wrote the first four Tales in the order in which they are found in the Winchester MS and in Caxton, rather than in the sequence II, I, III, IV proposed by Vinaver. As the author himself admits, however, more internal evidence than this is needed to establish his hypothesis.

M. A. Whitaker finds 'Allegorical Imagery in Malory's "Tale of the Noble King Arthur and the Emperor

Lucius"', (*NM*, 1973), chiefly in the descriptions of Arthur's encounters with the giant of St Michael's Mount and with the Romans. The story of his Roman expedition reveals most clearly Arthur's stature as a mythic hero, which also shows itself at the beginning and end of Arthur's career. Structurally, the Roman expedition follows the quest pattern of departure from the familiar world of the court into an unknown environment where episodic confrontations with enemies eventually lead to a climactic victory before a return to the familiar world. Linked with this pattern is the fact that, in this Tale, the seasonal cycle produces a symbolic time scheme which seems to encompass the events of the seven-year quest within a single year. The struggle between good and evil implicit in the two main combats of the Tale enables it to be interpreted allegorically: Arthur is an idealized hero, a *Christianissimus rex*, who performs symbolic deeds in a setting that is only intermittently realistic. A different view of the same Tale is offered by Michael Stroud in 'Malory and the Chivalric Ethos: the Hero of *Arthur and the Emperor Lucius*' (*MS*); this Tale, he suggests, in which the society portrayed is violent and unforgiving, seems to contradict the view that *Le Morte Darthur* is a work of morality—a view which has itself been thought to accord ill with the fact that its author was a Newgate prisoner. Malory's understanding of chivalry was confused, and, lacking the vantage-point of a modern historian, he saw no discontinuity between what he experienced and what he read. Fifteenth-century feudalism did not recognize itself as contemptible, and in fact retained something of the ancient idea of the loyalty of warband to chief; and Malory, seeking to idealize such a system, turned naturally to the alliterative *Morte Arthure*,

a poem of ruthless, unremitting war, and sought to emphasize the parallels between Arthur and Henry V. Malory did not set out to memorialize a fictional past; he saw a direct relation between the deeds of Arthur's heroes and the actions of himself and other fifteenth-century knights— actions which contrasted, in his view, with the business interests which developed in England under Henry VI and Edward IV. He is to be acknowledged as an authentic and immensely successful spokesman for a discredited social standard.

Kirkland C. Jones describes 'The Relationship between the Versions of Arthur's Last Battle as they Appear in Malory and in the *Libro de las Generaciones*' (*BBSIA*) as intimate, insofar as this Navarrese prose chronicle departs from its principal source, Wace's *Brut*, in its account of Arthur's last battle, just as the stanzaic *Morte Arthur* departs here from its principal source, the Old French prose *Mort Artu*; and in using the stanzaic *Morte Arthur* to supplement the *Mort Artu* in his own account of Arthur's last battle, Malory keeps most of the details of the battle as recounted in the former, the main difference in his treatment being one of emphasis. If the stanzaic *Morte Arthur* dates from c. 1400, it cannot have been the source of the Navarrese *Libro de las Generaciones*, which was in existence more than half a century before that date; but the basic parallelism between these two works in the situation involving a serpent in their accounts of the peace conversations between Arthur and Mordred shows that both have drawn on a common body of materials, and that this particular situation is not purely the invention of the author of the stanzaic *Morte Arthur*.

Mention may be made of a modern English translation of the Old French

Mort Artu by J. Neale Carman,[37] who points out in his Preface that the merits of this work and Malory's are not the same, since Malory did more than translate it. The modern English translation is offered 'in part as an aid in studying the English author; in great part, though, because, despite shortcomings, the *Mort Artu* is important ideologically in ways not always perceptible in Malory's product.' This latter point may be followed up in two articles on the *Mort Artu* by R. Howard Bloch: 'The Death of King Arthur and the Waning of the Feudal Age' (*OL*) and 'From Grail Quest to Inquest: the Death of King Arthur and the Birth of France' (*MLR*). Joan M. Ferrante does not include Malory's version of the Tristan story in her comparative study *The Conflict of Love and Honour*,[38] which deals with the treatment of this story in the poems of Béroul, Eilhart, Thomas, and Gottfried, and the prose *Tavola Ritunda*; but she indicates in her Preface the importance of the story for Malory in drawing attention to the central position he gives it in his narrative. Robert L. Snyder's 'Malory and "Historial" Adaptation' (*ELWIU*) was not seen.

Barry Gaines discusses 'The Editions of Malory in the Early Nineteenth Century' (*PBSA*), quoting the correspondence between Walter Scott and Robert Southey in 1807 in which Scott allowed his plans for an edition of Malory to be superseded by those of

Southey, whose edition, however, did not appear until 1817. By then Scott had planned and failed, in 1810–11, to reprint Caxton's edition, and two editions reprinting William Stansby's 1634 edition had appeared, both in 1816. Southey was responsible only for the Preface and the Notes of his own edition; the text was prepared from Caxton's edition by William Upcott, who skilfully and mysteriously supplied the eleven leaves lacking in his copy of Caxton. Tennyson seems to have known both the 1816 editions, and Keats and Wordsworth one of them; while Southey's influenced in different ways Charlotte Yonge, Burne-Jones, Morris, Maddox Brown, Rossetti and Swinburne. The three editions combined to reintroduce Malory to the English reading public after a hiatus of almost two hundred years. Malory is also discussed in a nineteenth-century context in 'Tennyson's "The Holy Grail"': the Tragedy of Percivale', by David Staines (*MLR*), who shows that in this part of the *Idylls of the King* Tennyson employs Malory's account to create a version of the Grail story specifically suited to the nineteenth century. Tennyson makes Percivale, rather than Galahad, the focus of the poem, and allows Percivale to take over from Lancelot the rôle of the most worthy of the unworthy who receives only a partial glimpse of the Grail. The Grail quest instils humility in Percivale, yet removes him from the practical affairs of this world, and his new self-awareness lacks proper perspective; he becomes a victim of his own vision, and hence a tragic hero.

Robert L. Montgomery, discussing 'William Caxton and the Beginnings of Tudor Critical Thought' (*HLQ*, 1973), shows that Caxton deserves a place in the history of criticism for

---

[37] *From Camelot to Joyous Gard. The Old French La Mort le Roi Artu*, trans. by J. Neale Carman; ed. with an introduction by Norris J. Lacy. Lawrence, Manhattan, Wichita: The University Press of Kansas. pp. xxii + 173, frontispiece. $7.50.

[38] *The Conflict of Love and Honor. The Medieval Tristan Legend in France, Germany and Italy*, by Joan M. Ferrante. De Proprietatibus Litterarum. Series Practica 78. The Hague and Paris: Mouton, 1973. pp. 173. Paper Fl. 32. F. 49.

more than his few remarks on style or his admiration of Chaucer, insofar as the attitudes he reflects derive from concerns which continued to inform the criticism of the English Renaissance, and his unpublished translation of Ovid's *Metamorphoses* is prefaced by a genuine, though brief, poetics. His various writings show that he regards chivalric romance as almost identical with epic, and epic as identical with history, and seems to prefer history to other forms of narrative, arguing that the actuality of event and character is more likely to offer a convincing lesson to the reader. For Sidney the poetic image is more compelling than history because the poet's imagination (which does not concern Caxton) can fashion images which are not only vivid but ideal. Caxton exemplifies the Renaissance view that history is both true and useful, and places history above poetry, whose power to affect the emotions he readily acknowledges. Apparent in the preface to his translation of the *Metamorphoses* is his belief that fables are justified only by their capacity to deliver useful truth and are suspect insofar as they record extreme or painful emotions, and he is less successful than his partial model, Boccaccio, in arguing that what may seem a frivolous or impious departure from the truth is really a metaphorical construct which may be translated into sober and useful verity.

Caxton's Own Prose[39] is a collection, virtually complete, of the prologues, epilogues, colophons, and interpolations, designed by N. F. Blake as a companion volume to his *Caxton and His World* (*YW* 50), and superseding it in some matters, for example dating, which is discussed in the introduction. The introduction also deals with Caxton's reading, and several aspects of his language, such as his innovations in English vocabulary, both when influenced by French models as in the *Polychronicon*, and when introducing into his own prose words 'of more mundane quality'. There is also an examination of his sentence structure and a summary of the themes he treats and the critical vocabulary he uses.

Donald B. Sands discusses 'Reynard the Fox and the Manipulation of the Popular Proverb'[40] in the anonymous Middle Dutch poem *Reinaerts Historie*, a prose version of which was the original of Caxton's translation of *The History of Reynard the Fox*.

10. OTHER PROSE

Norman F. Blake attempts to schematize the 'Varieties of Middle English Religious Prose',[41] distinguishing five main groups: works designed for instruction, works of a historical and legendary character, affective works, spiritual autobiographies, and polemical literature. The instruction of the first group may be called primary, when an author has a particular audience in mind, and secondary, when he has to make his material interesting for a whole range of people, often by a variety of tone and approach, as in *Hali Meidenhad*. The works of primary instruction are subdivided into explanations of the tenets of Christian belief; translations of biblical texts and commentaries; expositions of the services of the Church; and rules of conduct for a particular way of life. The external form of the works of a historical and legendary character enables them to be

---

[39] *Caxton's Own Prose*, ed. by N. F. Blake. London: Andre Deutsch. 1973. pp. 188. £2.95.

[40] In *The Learned and the Lewed*, see above, note 18.

[41] In *Chaucer and Middle English Studies*, see above, note 6.

subdivided into Saints' Lives, longer historical works, historical romances (which some, as Blake points out, might not wish to include as religious prose) and apocryphal works, such as the *Gospel of Nicodemus*. The affective works are subdivided according to the purposes for which the works were written: in this case to frighten the listener, to entice the listener, to emphasize the listener's emotional affinity for Christ or Mary, and to assist the listener's devotions. Blake has fulfilled at least part of his purpose underlining the need for an index of prose to match Brown and Robbins' *Index of Middle English Verse* P. S. Jolliffe's *Check-list of Middle English Prose Writings of Spiritual Guidance*[42] goes part of the way towards meeting this need, the urgency of which is emphasized by Joliffe himself in his admirably clear and systematic introductory chapter, 'Preparing the Check-list'. His purpose is to provide a *preliminary* check-list; and among various limitations imposed on this one is the exclusion of sermons some Wycliffite writings, lists used for Christian teaching; expositions of the Decalogue, Pater Noster and Creed; writings intended for use in affective prayer; collections of formal prayers; formal Rules for religious orders; certain widely known treatises on the spiritual life which have been or are being edited; and tracts which appeared originally in early printed books. Furthermore, the list is limited primarily to manuscripts now in Trinity College Dublin or in public and semi-public depositories in the United Kingdom. The works included have been listed by their *incipits* and

classified under fifteen different headings. There is a list of manuscripts cited in the check-list, an alphabetical list of titles and authors mentioned in it, and a list of the few acephalous items included, as well as an extensive Selected Bibliography, including a supplementary list of manuscript catalogues. Despite its limitations, this book will surely encourage further systematic investigation of the teaching and literary value of prose tracts of pastoral intention concerned with confession and spiritual guidance, and is very much to be welcomed.

S. R. T. O. d'Ardenne, in '*Bratewil* (*Katerine*, 1690)' (*ES*) argues that the correct reading is *beatewil*, and this is an adjective derived from the verb *bēaten*, 'to beat', meaning primarily 'with a desire to strike, to vanquish', and hence: 'marked by victory, victorious, joyful'.

In her Introduction to *Structure and Imagery in Ancrene Wisse*, Janet Grayson[43] sets out to study 'the structural affinities of image, method of elaboration, and transition', and to show 'how by artful selection and positioning of figures the author of *AW* is able to animate the fundamental concept of "outer and inner" in order to create the kind of vibrating upward movement within the images and (in a larger sense) the chapters that gives "a curious spiral quality to the structure of the *Ancrene Wisse*"'. The 'outer rule', (Parts I and VIII) is the handmaid to *þe leafdi riwle*, the inner Rule (Parts II–VII). The bird images of Part III, for instance, show that the interaction of outer and inner aspects of experience is built into the fabric of the

---

[42] *A Check-List of Middle English Prose Writings of Spiritual Guidance*, by P. S. Jolliffe. Subsidia Medievalia II. Toronto: Pontifical Institute of Medieval Studies. pp. 253. $11.50.

[43] *Structure and Imagery in Ancrene Wisse*, by Janet Grayson. Hanover, New Hampshire: The University Press of New England for the University of New Hampshire. pp. viii+243. $10.

whole work; and 'the collective inner Rule', as reflected in Parts II–VII, 'undergoes conversion from concern with the physical world to the spiritual', the point of ultimate convergence of image 'spirals' being reached in Part VII, when Christ and anchoress confront each other and strike a bargain: His life for her love. Grayson examines the author's re-use of themes and motifs through his control of spirals, 'certainly one of the unique structural achievements of *AW*'. This argument is then pursued through eight chapters, each one of which corresponds to a Part of *AW*, and summed up in a Conclusion. Grayson's use of diagrams to assist her argument perhaps makes clearest the use of spirals in *AW* in footnote 3 of chapter Four, where the arrangement of wind and wound imagery is shown, and in the illustration of 'the spiraling attitude of the symbols' of the ladder, the wheel, and the sword, in chapter Six. Grayson's study is based on Tolkien's edition of the text of *AW* in Corpus Christi College Cambridge MS 402, which, together with the French version of *AW* found in British Museum MS Cotton Vitellius F VII, forms the basis of Berta Grattan Lee's monograph,[44] an examination of Parts II, IV and VIII of *AW*, and of every tenth page throughout the rest of the Corpus text, in relation to the corresponding parts of the Vitellius text. The purpose of choosing only these sections is to avoid duplication with Cecily Clark's study of the language of Parts VI and

VII (*YW* 49. 97). while at the same time taking a cross-section of the whole work; and the purpose of the study as a whole is to establish primarily linguistic criteria for determining the question of the originality of the French or the English version. The examination of Vocabulary, Proper Names, Negation, Morphology, and Word Order, is offered as unassailable proof that the work represented in these two manuscripts was first written in French. As the author herself admits, however, this is a study of only two texts of the *AW*, and further analysis must determine whether the other manuscripts fit the same patterns; and her suggestion on p. 78 that E. J. Dobson is not familiar with the text of *AW* seems a dangerous one in view of his weighty work on the subject (*YW* 43. 66; 48. 84; 53. 98). Barbara Raw shows that 'The Prayers and Devotions in the *Ancrene Wisse*'[45] bear witness to the strength of the Anglo-Saxon tradition in the south-west Midlands in the early Middle English period. With one or two exceptions, the texts are ones which had long been used in the official liturgy and in the private prayers of Anglo-Saxon monastic houses. The form of the devotions resembles that found in a number of eleventh-century English manuscripts; and the alternation of English and Latin texts is also characteristic of late Anglo-Saxon devotions. The brief introduction to the Aves in *AW* is its only trace of such emotional, individual prayers as those contained in *On god ureisun of ure Lefdi* or *On lofsong of ure Louerde* which are found in the Nero manuscript of the *Ancrene Riwle*. In this respect, the prayers provide a great contrast to the rest of *AW*, with its many borrowings

[44] *Linguistic Evidence for the Priority of the French Text of the Ancrene Wisse. Based on the Corpus Christi College Cambridge 402 and the British Museum Cotton Vitellius F. VII Versions of the Ancrene Wisse*, by Berta Grattan Lee. Janua Linguarum Studia Memoriae Nicolai van Wijk dedicata, edenda curat. C. H. van Schooneveld, Indiana University. Series Practica 242. The Hague and Paris. Mouton. pp. 90.

[45] In *Chaucer and Middle English Studies*, see above, note 6.

from the writings of Anselm of Canterbury, Bernard of Clairvaux, and their followers. E. J. Dobson, in the first of 'Two Notes on Early Middle English Texts' (*N&Q*) illustrates by his discussion of two words from *AW* the principle of textual criticism that readings shown by recension to have been archetypal are not to be rejected in favour of superficially 'easier' versions produced by scribal innovation. The first of the two words is *weolie* (in Corpus MS. f. 107b/7–10), which Dobson accepts as an archetypal and probably authorial reading, taking it to mean 'wily' by reference to its connection with Old Norse *vél*, 'artifice'; and the second is the word *bodi* (Corpus MS. f. 108a/11), which he also accepts as archetypal and takes to mean 'person', 'incarnate being'. A footnote points out the ambiguity intended by the lady in her use of the word *cors* at line 1237 of *GGK* (cf. Markus's view in section 3 above). In 'The Date of "Ancrene Wisse": A Corroborative Note', T. P. Dolan (*N&Q*) claims that the author's explanation of the technical term 'circumstances' in his discussion of the sacrament of Confession in Part V of *AW* shows an up-to-date awareness of the revival of interest in Confession reflected in the early thirteenth-century *Summae Confessorum* and in the greater frequency of Confession required by the Lateran Council of 1215. This helps to corroborate Dobson's view (*YW* 48. 84) that *AW* was written in or shortly before the period 1215–22.

Lowrie J. Daly, S. J. reviews 'Wyclif's Political Theory: A Century of Study' (*M&H*, 1973), suggesting that recent lack of interest in this aspect of Wyclif may be due to the declining percentage of younger medievalists able to use Latin easily. It has become evident that Wyclif's influence depended much more on his authority as a theologian than on any political skill. Research has placed Wyclif within the context of the political, philosophical and theological trends of his time, and his position within the Augustinian school has been clarified. Further research possibilities remain, however, in the large number of fourteenth and fifteenth-century scholastic writings still to be edited. The theory of dominion is central to Wyclif's political philosophy, and the Erastianism in his approach is mitigated when placed within the context of the medieval concept of the *ecclesia* with its two powers, the spiritual and the temporal. He was probably tolerated as brilliant, erratic and sarcastically critical until he openly advocated what was considered a heretical doctrine regarding the Eucharist. The questions of how far his earlier and later views as a political theorist are reconcilable, and how far his anti-papalism actually affected his overall traditional concept of the medieval *ecclesia*, still need to be answered. Sven L. Fristedt, in 'A Note on Some Obscurities in the History of the Lollard Bible' (*SSMP*, 1972) points out and corrects certain flaws in his *The Wycliffe Bible. Part II* of 1969 (*YW* 50. 106), defends his work on this subject against misleading impressions of it given by Lindberg in his article of 1970 (*YW* 51. 103), and hints at conclusions reached in his *The Wycliffe Bible. Part III* (1973) reviewed in *YW* 54. 102. Henry Hargreaves, in 'Sir John Oldcastle and Wycliffite Views on Clerical Marriage' (*MÆ*, 1973) prints from a fifteenth-century commonplace book, MS 123 in Aberdeen University Library, a Latin poem about Oldcastle which among other things raises the question of how far approval of clerical marriage was characteristic of Wycliffite circles. Hargreaves shows that Wyclif recognized the practice of the early church (I Timothy iii) without insisting at length on its imitation by the contemporary church. It may be that this point was later given greater attention by some of his followers and thus came to be regarded as a test of Lollardry by the authorities.

N. F. Blake's 'The Form of Living in Prose and Poetry' (Archiv) may be included in this section as a discussion of a poetic text composed from a prose original, Rolle's The Form of Living. The poetic text is much shorter than its prose counterpart; all that is specifically concerned with mystical devotion and practices in the prose text is omitted. The poet has tried to keep as close as he can to the prose, and there is a paradox in the fact that while the verse seems more straightforward than the prose because of its stereotyped vocabulary and repetition, meaning is often more difficult to grasp because of the inverted word order and the clumsiness of some constructions. The adaptor had to go beyond the prose to complete his couplets, and to make changes to achieve rhyme; both these features detract from the individuality of Rolle's personal style. While the verse retains many of the polysyllabic words of the prose, usually of Latin origin, it tends to simplify the doublets characteristic of Middle English prose. The verse, finally, is often more involved and wordy than the prose. These alterations spring from an attempt to make the text a moral treatise suitable for a wide audience, which suggests that poetry was still regarded as the most suitable medium for the instruction of the laity and the lesser clergy. Myrc's use of poetry in his Instructions for Parish Priests, for instance, should be regarded as normal and not an archaic survival.

S. S. Hussey, in 'Latin and English in the Scale of Perfection' (MS, 1973) discusses Thomas Fishlake's Latin translation of Hilton's Scale of Perfection in relation to its original, confining himself to Book II. It is found that York Cathedral Chapter MS XVI K 5 is the manuscript which should form the basis of an edition of the Latin text of Book II, and its text is used with the English text of British Museum MS Harley 6579 as a basis for comparison. It is clear that the translator was a careful worker and used a good English manuscript; what appear to be misreadings on his part may often be conscious 'improvements' which lessen the value of his text as a guide to the English of his original. The translation has some thirty-two omissions, mostly of passages which are unnecessary to the sense, and six cases of expansion, none of which is remarkable. Even the additions of 'Christo-centric' glosses, characteristic of Book I, are few and slight in Book II (cf. those in Hilton's English translation of the Stimulus Amoris). The Latin translation contains many doublets, thus developing a feature already well marked in The Scale; but the expansions of the Latin are somewhat offset by several phrases where the Latin is more concise than the English. The translation is not without value editorially, as it was made early enough to affect the correction of some English manuscripts of The Scale, and is a fascinating example of the treatment of a late fourteenth-century English work by a contemporary translator.

Bengt Lindström, in 'Two Notes on Dives and Pauper' (SN), draws attention to some errors of quotation from this early fifteenth-century exposition of the Decalogue in an article by Roland B. Dickison in SFQ (1960–61), and shows that the belief reflected in *Dives and Pauper* that if New Year's day and Christmas fall on a Sunday all will be well in the following year goes back at least as far as the Old English period. This belief, and the practice of predicting the year's events according to the month in which it thunders (also discussed by Dives and Pauper), are treated in Old English passages in British Museum Cottonian MS Vespasian D. XIV. Lindström also shows that in the passage about the nature and mission of angels in Book I, chapter VIII, of *Dives and Pauper*, the writer, while relying here on Bartholomew the Englishman's heavily derivative encyclopedia, nevertheless treats his source with the characteristic freedom of the medieval adapter.

James Hogg edits a thesis written some twenty years ago by Elizabeth Salter on Nicholas Love's *Myrrour of the Blessed Lyf of Jesu Christ*,[46] an early fifteenth-century translation of the pseudo-Bonaventuran *Meditationes Vitae Christi*. The relationship of the translation to its original, the manuscripts and editions of the *Myrrour* and the life of Nicholas Love are discussed. It is found that the general differences between the *Meditationes* and the *Myrrour* are due to the latter's wider audience and special polemical purpose, to provide a corrective to Lollard teaching of the early fifteenth century. The *Myrrour* is usefully placed in the tradition of Medieval Lives of Christ as one consisting of Biblical paraphrase, with didactic and meditative additions. It is concluded that the Meditation on the Sacred Humanity belongs to a tradition of affective Meditation

deriving ultimately from the Eastern church and much later influencing St Ignatius of Loyola's *Spiritual Exercises*. Love concentrates on the affective and moral uses of the Meditation rather than on its function as a preliminary to contemplation. The *Myrrour* is placed in the English tradition of prose translation, and special emphasis is laid on the importance of Latin as a stimulus to the development of English prose. Love's prose style and methods of translation are discussed on the basis of the Die Veneris section of the *Myrrour*.

T. A. Halligan follows up an article by N. F. Blake (*YW* 54. 103) in 'The Revelations of St Matilda in English: "The Booke of Gostlye Grace"' (*N&Q*), drawing attention to five surviving fifteenth-century copies of the Revelations, three in Latin and two in English, and finding in them no decisive proof of a Brigittine or Carthusian provenance for the English translation of this Latin work, the *Liber Spiritualis Gracie*, which was compiled in Germany in the thirteenth century. Of the three Latin copies of the *Liber*, the one preserved in MS Cambridge Ff 1. 19, conforms most closely to the source for the translation, but cannot actually have been its source, since it dates from later than 1450, by which time the initial translation had been made. The revelations enjoyed a respectable readership during the fifteenth century, and their dissemination in England at that time was largely due to the Carthusians.

P. S. Jolliffe, in a somewhat repetitive article on 'Middle English Translations of *De Exterioris et Interioris Hominis Compositione*', (*MS*), shows that the two Middle English texts of a long treatise in three books in Queens' College Cambridge MS 31 and University Library Cambridge

---

[46] *Nicholas Love's Myrrour of the Blessed Lyf of Jesu Christ'*, by Elizabeth Salter. Analecta Cartusiana, ed. by Dr James Hogg. Volume 10. Salzburg: Institut für englische Sprache und Literatur, Universität Salzburg. pp. iv+339.

MS Dd. 2. 33 represent two different translations of that thirteenth-century work attributed to David of Augsburg. British Museum Arundel MS 197 contains a Middle English abstract of what is found to be a version of the translation represented in the Queens' College text. Book One deals with the externals of the Religious Life, Two with the reformation of the soul which the Religious must undergo once he has grasped these externals, and Three with the processes by which the spiritual life of the Religious is brought to perfection. It is not known for certain from which Latin text either translation was made, but the Queens' College text seems a closer and more literal translation than the U.L.C. one. The former is addressed to all Religious, while the latter, 'by the hond of Thomas Prestius brother of Syon', is addressed specifically to sisters. The Queens' text differs from Syon in concluding its preface with some remarks which show that, by the fifteenth century, this treatise for Religious had been acknowledged to be of value to devout lay men and women. That such a readership for such literature was growing at that time is illustrated by a number of quotations from other manuscripts.

Bengt Lindström edits *A Late Middle English Version of the Gospel of Nicodemus*[47] from British Museum MS Harley 149. In chapter I of the Introduction, he points out the importance of this apocryphal Gospel as a source for the Harrowing-of-Hell scenes in medieval drama, and as a factor contributing to the development of the Grail legend. In chapter II he shows that the A-version, the Middle English version in BM MS Harley 149, is a composite text, based on two French sources, B and C; that the English translator had these two versions of the Gospel before him as he wrote, rather than a single text in which they were conflated; that MS Harley 149, written c. 1475–1500, or even later, is a holograph and not a copy; and that in the early part of the Gospel the translator relies more heavily on B than on C, though more on C as he progresses. In chapter III the editor discusses departures in A from the French exemplars, the most notable of which are the English translator's emphasis on Judas's treason and suicide, his representation of Pilate's wife's dream as inspired by the devil, his removal of the incident of the soldier's stabbing of Jesus's side to where it belongs in St John's Gospel, and the insertion of a version of the Creed spoken piecemeal and severally by the apostles. The remaining three chapters deal respectively with the language of A – what Samuels has called Chancery standard, 'the basis of modern written English' (*YW* 44. 84); with descriptions of the A-manuscript and of those manuscripts, designated as B1-3 and C1-2, in which the B and C versions are reflected; and with editorial matters. The texts of B1 and C1 are printed below the text of A, and are followed by explanatory Notes, a Glossary, an Index of Proper Names, and a Bibliography.

The predominance of religious literature is well illustrated by the ratio of this year's studies of religious prose to those of secular prose. In a long article on 'The Metamorphoses of Sir John Mandeville', C. W. R. D. Moseley (*YES*) discusses some of the 're-presentations' of *Mandeville's Travels* appearing in England between the second half of the fourteenth century and the eighteenth century.

---

[47] *A Late Middle English Version of The Gospel of Nicodemus*, ed. by Bengt Lindström. Acta Universitatis Upsaliensis, Studia Anglistica Upsaliensia 18. pp. 184. Frontispiece. Sw. Kr. 45.

After briefly discussing the sophistic-ated nature of the Egerton and Cotton versions, which manifests itself chiefly in the attractive *persona* of the narra-tor and in rather little being made of the element of wonder in the travels, Moseley goes on to discuss the 'Travels' as represented in compendia, particularly Hakluyt's first edition of the *Principall Navigations* (1589). He then discusses the Bodley version of Mandeville (in Bodleian MS e musaeo 116), which tends to prefer the fabu-lous to the theological or factual elements in the *Travels*; the epitome of the *Travels* in BM MS Addit. 37049, of which the opposite is true; the version in Bodleian MS Ashmole 751, which is exclusively concerned with Christian matters; and the verse item based on the *Travels* in Bodley MS e musaeo 160, which is character-ized by its vigorous piety and prob-ably appealed to an audience accus-tomed to the bluff verse of the popular romances. Moseley devotes a separate section to the Metrical Version found in Coventry Public Record Office MS Acc 325, stressing that the writer of this version placed the *Travels* in the same category as romance. The remainder of the article deals with interpretations of Mandeville in the sixteenth, seven-teenth and eighteenth centuries. M. C. Seymour edits 'A Letter from "Sir John Mandeville"' (*N&Q*), preserved fragmentarily in Latin and dateable to c. 1400. It is of interest in providing further evidence of the reputation of 'Mandeville' in late medieval Eng-land. In 'The Scribe of Huntington Library MS HM 114' Seymour (*MÆ*) shows, largely by quotation, that while the text of *Mandeville's Travels* in this manuscript belongs to the important sub-group B from which derive the majority of manuscripts of the English text, it nevertheless shows a marked divergence from the com-mon text and phrasing of its affiliates. Since the remaining contents of the manuscript yield no other solution, Seymour conjectures that the scribe 'copied paragraph by paragraph of his exemplar as it were by memory', retained the general sense and some-times the original phrasing, but more often paraphrased. Such a method would be faster than conventional transcription, and could not be applied to verse; perhaps closer inspection of other allegedly 'differ-ent' versions of prose items still in manuscript will reveal other examples of this medieval rapid-copy device. A. C. Cawley, in 'Down Under: A Possible New Source for *Mandeville's Travels*'[48] suggests that in the passage arguing that the inhabitants of the Antipodes are unlikely to fall off the earth into the firmament, the author of the *Travels* may have been influ-enced by a comparable passage in Book 2, chapter 5 of Macrobius's *Commentary on the 'Somnium Scipi-onis'*. Perhaps Mandeville, who claimed to have reached a latitude corresponding roughly to that of Sydney, sailed as close to Australia in his author's imagination as it was possible to do in the medieval period.

Rachel Hands, in '"Dancus Rex" in English' (*MS*, 1973) adds to the number of parallels already pointed out between this early Latin treatise on the management of hawks and the late fifteenth-century *Boke of St Albans*, and also draws attention to further English parallels in *Prince Edward's Book* and British Museum MS Harley 2340, both of the mid-fifteenth century. Some show signs of borrowing while a few are best attributed to a common oral tradi-tion. It is concluded that the Latin treatise, together with the one attrib-

48 In *Iceland and the Medieval World*, see above, note 13.

uted to 'Guillelmus falconarius', with which it survives in most manuscripts, was known in England, at least in part, probably through a French version of Albertus Magnus.

Ann S. Haskell, in 'The Paston Women on Marriage in Fifteenth-Century England', (*Viator*, 1973) uses the Paston letters to show that, while Margaret Paston conformed to the supportive rôle assigned to women by the chivalric ideal in being married, obedient, and chaste, she was relatively free to do what she wished otherwise. For all the handicaps she suffered, her successful management of the family estate shows that a woman could earn considerable liberty within marriage by conforming to the ideal. For women less ready to conform, however, the ideal worked less well, as is shown by Elizabeth Paston, who was severely punished for refusing a match arranged in her teens, and by Margery Paston, who was ostracized for binding herself clandestinely to the family bailiff. As in medieval Iceland, a girl's honour was regarded by her family as a precious commodity, and there was a double standard of marriage choice in that men had complete freedom in this respect while women ran the risk of ostracism in exercising their ultimate right to reject a prospective spouse or to marry independently. Alison Hanham, in '"Make a Careful Examination": Some Fraudulent Accounts in the Cely Papers' (*Speculum*, 1973), uses the Cely correspondence as evidence that the fabricated accounts relating to sales of wool and fells compiled by George Cely and preserved in a copy made from one of his account-books were motivated by a somewhat naïve wish to disguise the fact that the Celys were receiving payment from a foreign customer in London rather than at Calais, which must have been against the rules of

the Staple Company of which they were members.

J. A. F. Thomson discusses the question of 'The Continuation of "Gregory's Chronicle"—A Possible Author?' (*BMQ*, 1971–72), pointing out that the concluding section of this Chronicle—onwards from 1452, the year of the cessation of Gregory's mayoralty of the city of London—is especially concerned with ecclesiastical affairs. If Gregory's connection with the earlier part of the text is accepted, evidence for an association with him would enhance the claims of any individual to have been the author of the continuation. Thomas Eborall, Rector of All Hallows, Honey Lane, died c. 1472, was connected with Gregory as well as being a prominent London Churchman who might well have been involved in events recorded in the Chronicle. The tentative claim that Eborall was the author of the continuation seems well worth consideration. D. R. Howlett discusses 'The Meaning of Middle English "Borgener, Burgener"' (*N&Q*); both of these forms of the same word are found in the continuation of Gregory's chronicle in the account of the weapons arrayed at the second battle of St Albans in 1461. The words may refer to Burgundians, or may derive from the Old French masculine noun *bourgon*, the sense of which, both in Old French and Middle English, would have been 'carter of ordinance'.

Alexander R. Brodie discusses 'Anwykyll's *Vulgaria*: A Pre-Erasmian Textbook' (*NM*), which dates from 1483 and was originally conceived as an appendix to John Anwykyll's *Compendium totius Grammaticae*, based on Nicolaus Perottus's *Rudimenta Grammatices* of 1474. It consists of some 530 phrases taken or adapted from the plays of Terence and translated into English to illustrate, initially by oral means, points of Latin grammar, syntax and rhetoric. It is of interest in being the first English–Latin phrasebook and may be compared linguistically with later translations of the same texts.

Margaret S. Blayney has edited *Fifteenth-Century English Translations of Alain Chartier's Le Traité de L'Esperance and Le Quadrilogue Invectif*[49] from Bodl. MS Rawlinson A. 338, in which translations by one author of both these works are best preserved; and from University College, Oxford, MS 85, which preserves another translator's version of *The Quadrilogue Invective* and is the only known manuscript of this version, which is printed opposite the Rawlinson text of *The Quadrilogue* in this edition. Variants are given from the four other manuscripts in which the translations contained in the Rawlinson MS are preserved, and reference is made in the critical apparatus to the French reading when the manuscripts differ in readings or when an emendation may be briefly supported. Summaries of the two translated works are given in some Notes on the Manuscripts which precede the edited texts, and according to the editor 'The Introduction, Explanatory Notes, and Glossary of these editions will follow in another volume', as will fuller discussion of the relationship of the translations to the French texts. She is currently editing the translation of Chartier's *Dialogus familiaris amici et sodalis*, for which the translator whose work is represented in the Rawlinson MS was also responsible.

11. DRAMA
Editions and General Studies

A new edition of the *Chester Mystery Cycle*[50] by R. M. Lumiansky and David Mills replaces the old one by Deimling and Matthews. There is no attempt to construct an original text, of course, and the difficult choice of a base text, where in effect the manuscripts present two different main versions of the cycle, has been made on the justifiable grounds of simplicity of presentation and the reader's convenience. That is to say that the major variations of the late Harley manuscript appear in an appendix, while the Huntington was chosen as the best of the remaining 'Group' for the main text, with the missing Play I supplied from Harley 2013. The latter's variants of Play XVIII also appear in the appendix. The text is arranged in numbered stanzas with a norm of eight lines, a little modernization of spelling, and a minimum of emendations. A second volume of commentary is to follow.

A quantity of general studies of the drama appears all at once but they take very different lines of approach. The range of material covered in Glynne Wickham's *The Medieval Theatre*[51] resembles that of Chambers's *Medieval Stage*. But he views the development of the drama from the tenth to the sixteenth century not chronologically but under the headings of three influences on it: religion, recreation, and commerce. His justification of this approach involves some uneasy, question-begging insistence that the subject is 'a living art', and a rejection of historical and literary analysis. The Introduc-

[49] *Fifteenth-Century English Translations of Alain Chartier's Le Traité de L'Esperance and Le Quadrilogue Invectif*, Vol I, Text, ed. by Margaret S. Blayney. Early English Text Society, Original Series, 270. London, New York, Toronto: OUP for E.E.T.S. pp xvi + 247. 2 plates. £2.50 net.

[50] *The Chester Mystery Cycle*, ed. by R. M. Lumiansky and David Mills. Vol. I: Text. London: O.U.P. for E.E.T.S. Supplementary Series 3. pp. xliv + 624. 2 plates. £5.50.

[51] *The Medieval Theatre*, by Glynne Wickham. London: Weidenfeld and Nicholson. pp. xiv + 246. 44 plates. £6.

tion continues with some imprecise suggestions about the legacy inherited by the medieval drama from earlier cultures, and some generalizations about the quality of life in the tenth century rather surprisingly supported from Huizinga's *Waning of the Middle Ages*. The rest of the book is a comprehensive and entertaining survey in three sections. 'Theatres of Worship' covers religious drama in all senses from the liturgy itself, its music, iconography, and architectural context, to saints' plays and the Corpus Christi cycles about whose origin he agrees with Kolve. 'Theatres of Recreation' is about non-Christian folk customs and the Mummer's Play, and about tournaments and courtly entertainments, interludes, and civic pageantry. 'Theatres and Commerce' deals with censorship and interference under church and state, and the growth of professional exploitation of the recreational and religious theatres 'just as gradual and natural as the evolution of dramatic art itself out of the Christian liturgy and the varied social *ludi*'.

Richard Axton's main interest[52] is the 'unrecognized importance of the secular traditions', so that his study of origins and traditions devotes only a small space to church ceremony, and most to three kinds of secular performance. These are the mimicry of professional entertainers, the pagan folk drama of combat, and the 'dancing-game' or dramatic amusement of courtly society. The mimic concept in *Dame Sirith, Interludium de Clerico et Puella*, and French farces, is compared with Terence, and the practical possibilities are considered of production according to the medieval idea of Roman theatre. Axton is sceptical about the fertility origins of folk

[52] In *European Drama of the Early Middle Ages*, by Richard Axton. London: Hutchinson. pp. 228. Cloth £3.75. Paper £2.45.

ceremonies, but is more impressed by their long continuance for social reasons. He finds similarity of detail between nineteenth-century texts for such performances and early religious drama, and makes an interesting examination of a 'plough play' which is picked up later in his analysis of the Towneley Death of Abel. The *Carmina Burana* Passion is an instance of Axton's main theme, the church taking over existing secular forms. In the second part of the book he continues the theme by examining Latin, Anglo-Norman, and French plays, relating them to those traditions, especially the secular. The third part considers examples of English drama in the same way. The early plays are religious attempts to create popular drama, alongside the preaching work of the friars, but are quite distinct from liturgical influence. Coming to the cycle plays, Axton suggests that the Corpus Christi feast is not their source but 'a symptom and a regulating focus of a wider movement'. He sees provocation of the audience and the conjunction of death with comic presentation as evidence of popular tradition. 'The patterned structure of the slaying' of Chester's Innocents is festive parody. He directs attention to the tradition associating the religious plays in Chester with the civic Midsummer Watch. It is in the nature of things that the evidence for popular and secular contributions is often difficult to identify, even without going on to interpret it. In the case of the shepherds' plays the evidence is simply the manner of playing. Despite the air of insubstantiality in some of the arguments, the book has helpful insights. The reading of *Mankind* fits well with Neville Denny's, reported below. Axton sees it as the conversion of a popular element of 'game' by joining it to sermon, and therefore as 'belonging to the tradition of early pre-cycle plays'.

Stanley J. Kahrl's *Traditions of Medieval English Drama*[53] is concerned with critical methods. He presents a number of 'model approaches' to different kinds of drama. He distinguishes two main traditions of theatrical presentation: the place and scaffold of Continental theatre, and the pageant stages derived from processional tableaux. He connects each tradition with a particular area of the country, the first kind belonging mainly to the East Midlands and the second to the North. An evaluation of any play must take into account the particular tradition of presentation relevant to it. The difficulty of this line of argument is that the 'evidence' often comes from how a modern director thinks to interpret a text in performance. But Kahrl is able to characterize quite convincingly from a modern viewpoint at least what can be well done and ill done on the two kinds of stage. He adopts a functional approach to character and verisimilitude, seeing the necessity of the brutal portrayal of humanity in the Wakefield *Coliphizacio*, emphasizing its closeness to a source which he suggests is a Gospel Harmony, rather than the *Northern Passion*. The Crucifixion plays are analysed with reference to the traditional nature of the shocking details. The morality plays also create problems of evidence. Arguing against their derivation from Paternoster Plays, Kahrl seeks in them a common pattern, and evidence of a native comic tradition. His examples are *Mundus et Infans* and *Mankind*. Finally he argues the continuity in renaissance theatre both of the forms of medieval drama and of its 'basic

ideas of what constituted reality and the nature of the universe'.

The method that Kahrl exemplifies and advocates is one variety of the kind of 'formal criticism' that Alan H. Nelson rejects in favour of 'historical inquiry' in *The Medieval English Stage: Corpus Christi Pageants and Plays*.[54] This combative and stimulating book is reviewed by Kahrl himself in *CompD*. Nelson's field of inquiry is scarcely ever the text of the plays, but instead the documents of civic authorities and private witnesses about dramatic performances in all the major towns of England and Scotland. Most of the book is a city-by-city account and interpretation of these documents, following the principle that evidence from one location should not be assumed valid for what went on in another. The author cannot resist, however, occasional cross-references advantageous to his thesis. The main contentions are that the cycles of the fifteenth century developed out of the processions of the fourteenth, that the doctrinal connexion of the play to the feast of Corpus Christi is 'almost entirely incidental' and, most far-reaching of all in its implications, that in York and many other places the full plays were not performed publicly but indoors before a select audience of civic and ecclesiastical dignitaries. Nelson's views on the impossibility of true processional staging at York are well known, but this new reading of the evidence is an effective surprise. The stations referred to in the documents are viewing-points for the procession. The important people, having watched this from their station, went off (in York) to the Chamber at Common Hall to drink wine and see

[53] *Traditions of Medieval English Drama*, by Stanley J. Kahrl. London: Hutchinson. pp. 162. Cloth £3.30. Paper £2.20.

[54] *The Medieval English Stage: Corpus Christi Pageants and Plays*, by Alan H. Nelson. Chicago and London: U. of Chicago P. pp. xiv+274. Illustrated. £6·25.

the play as we know it. Nelson does admit that the smallness of the playing area might present problems, especially where a cloud machine is needed, but argues on the other hand that the Doomsday pageant waggon (*YW* 53. 103) is too cluttered to be a stage for drama. Much of Nelson's material is unpublished or difficult of access, so that it may be some time before other interpreters can effectively take up the challenge. Meanwhile we have a provocative stimulus to research, and a compendium of incidental detail about the context of medieval theatrical performance.

Robert A. Brewer's study of 'The Middle English Resurrection Play and its Dramatic Antecedents' (*CompD*) explores analogies between the liturgical and cycle traditions through an episode which in York, Towneley, and Chester forms 'a discrete dramatic unit', sharing with the liturgical versions the 'dramatic peripety' from sorrow to joy. Using the Fleury play, he argues that the way it sets the resurrection in a larger framework of redemptive history makes it a forerunner of the cycles. The Anglo-Norman *Resurreccion* and the plays from Klosterneuberg and Tours combine a 'Christ-action' and a 'Pilate-action' in ways which are also found in cycle plays. Current methods of distinguishing between liturgical and cycle traditions are limited and misleading. Jo Anna Dutka continues her investigation of music in the cycles in 'Mysteries, Minstrels, and Music' (*CompD*) by surveying the evidence for the use of instrumental music. It could be an integral part of the plays it was used in, and involved great flexibility in the placing of musicians in relation to the rest of the spectacle. These two articles, and another by Alan H. Nelson, noted later, are part of an issue of *CompD* in honour of William L.

Smoldon, which also contains articles on liturgical and Continental drama.

Clifford Davidson argues the significance of a connexion between 'Thomas Aquinas, the Feast of Corpus Christi, and the English Cycle Plays' (*MichA*). Robert Edwards's 'Techniques of Transcendence in Medieval Drama' (*CompD*) is an attack on Aristotelian critical approaches, questioning the exclusively mimetic and reconsidering the place of spectacle 'along the lines suggested by both phenomenology and structuralism'. A cycle presents an action which cannot be repeated. The audience dissociates itself from the fate of Adam in the play. The aim is transcendence rather than mimesis. Thomas P. Campbell discusses 'The Prophets' Pageant in the English Mystery Cycles: Its Origin and Function' (*RORD*). It fits with difficulty into the cycle, having no set form, and being outside the historical framework. Its origin is liturgical and so is its function in a context of historical anticipation and fulfilment. Scholars have usually concentrated on the prophecies themselves from the *Sermo de Symbolo* instead of on their original context and on the 'substitute context' provided for them in later versions. The same periodical contains reports on a conference, studies, and a performance of medieval drama.

David L. Wee's 'The Temptation of Christ and the Motif of Divine Duplicity in the Corpus Christi Cycle' (*MP*) is about the 'abuse of power theory' and the idea of a divinity who deceives the devil. He considers the importance of Gregory as a source for the conception of the devil in the plays, and compares the plays for the way each incorporates the idea of deception. Thomas N. Grove's title tells what he is about:

'Light in Darkness: The Comedy of the York *Harrowing of Hell* as Seen Against the Backdrop of the Chester *Harrowing of Hell*' (*NM*). The play is the first true comedy of the cycle. The comparison shows York allowing the audience a superior perception of Adam's limited view, so that its devil can put up a more worthwhile show of resistance. The article concludes with fanciful interpretations of the stanza patterns as an echo of the argument of the York play. In 'Community Theatre in Late Medieval East Anglia' (*TN*), Robert Wright presents material on the rural production of Corpus Christi plays, primarily from the Great Dunmow Churchwarden's Book. There is evidence of the determination of the church to persist with the Corpus Christi feast in the face of official opposition. Maps show the 'play centres and supporting communities'.

Towneley

Martin Stevens gives an account of 'The Manuscript of the *Towneley Plays*: Its History and Editions' (*PBSA*) 'to take stock of the book as a historical artifact'. Jean Forrester announces *A New Discovery*.[55] Her pamphlet looks at the evidence connecting the Towneley Plays with Wakefield, presenting new material and noting discrepancies that seem to need further investigation. The search for the original Burgess Court Rolls continues. The approach of D. W. Robertson Jr. to 'The Question of "Typology" and the Wakefield *Mactacio Abel*' (*ABR*) stems from his conviction that we tend to think of spiritual meanings in medieval works in too theoretical terms. He uses the play to demonstrate the practical

implications for the audience's everyday conduct which it elaborates to an unusual degree. Structuralism gets its ears boxed on the way for being 'not only "mystical" in its assumptions, but ... operationally inconsequential, a fact that may account for its academic popularity'. Bennett A. Brockman's reading, in 'The Law of Man and the Peace of God: Judicial Process as Satiric Theme in the Wakefield *Mactacio Abel*' (*Speculum*), may be theoretical in Robertson's terms, since it is about irony in the way that familiar processes of law are used to apply to Cain's damnation. But his citation of documents underlines the local and contemporary focus of the play's interests, which was part of Robertson's theme. Brockman demonstrates well the familiarity of such things as the terms of pardons to the inhabitants of fifteenth-century Wakefield. Cynthia H. Tyson raises an awkward question about 'Noah's Flood, the River Jordan, the Red Sea: Staging the Towneley Cycle' (*CompD*). She argues that in the four plays requiring water a mere painted cloth would not have done, which means that somehow real water was present in the acting area. If so then some of the production at least must have been static (but presumably not indoors).

York

Martin Stevens and Margaret Dorrell print a full transcription of 'The *Ordo Paginarum* Gathering of the York *A/Y Memorandum Book*' (*MP*). They also supply a translation and annotation of this important document. They have reinterpreted some of the craft names, and draw special attention to the grouping of the entries and the proximity of the two pageant lists. Clifford Davidson sets the work of the York Realist in the context of other products of civic

55 *Wakefield Mystery Plays and the Burgess Court Records: A New Discovery*, by Jean Forrester. Ossett, Yorkshire: H. Speak and J. Forrester.

munificence such as glass-painting in 'Civic Concern and Iconography in the York Passion' (*AnM*).

Chester

'The Staging of the Medieval Plays of Chester: A Response' (*TN*) by Lawrence M. Clopper is a plea for greater respect for the extant evidence, including the Rogers descriptions. Such evidence supports only four or five stops for processional staging, thus making it even more feasible than Ruth Brant Davis has argued (*YW* 54). David Mills compares 'The Two Versions of Chester Play V: *Balaam and Balak*',[56] one from the late Harley manuscript and the other from the remaining 'Group'. The latter makes it the conclusion of the Old Testament series where the former seems to be linking it with the Nativity. These differences are reflected in differences of action and the use of structure. Bennett A. Brockman approaches 'Cain and Abel in the Chester *Creation*' (*M&H*) in the context of medieval doctrine and legend. The playwright consciously tackles the problem of fitting Cain's story in with the Fall without really solving it. Even so this is the best version apart from Wakefield, succeeding through its 'human realities' in the person of Cain himself. Peter W. Travis expounds 'The Dramatic Strategies of Chester's Passion Pagina' (*CompD*), which are different in their view of Christ's mission from those of other cycles. There is in Chester's version a compassionate control of emotion, but above all an impersonal characterization of evil and a stylization of action designed to bring order and understanding, instead of heightening the audience's anxiety and guilt.

Hegge

Claude Gauvin's handsome book *Un cycle du théâtre religieux anglais du moyen âge*[57] might better be considered under general studies since, although it is about the N-town cycle, it takes that one as representative of all, or rather as coming closest to a kind of ideal cycle of which all fall more or less short. This approach, begging so many questions, is unfortunate. Gauvin also insists on Lincoln as the home of the play but, despite an impressively vast bibliography, takes no account of recent dialectal evidence that it may belong in East Anglia. The commentary on the various episodes of the play makes helpful points, and the book draws together much useful information about sources. But despite an initial rigour in the treatment of the primary material of the manuscript, the argument about the nature of the play and its production seems both speculative and unsurprising. Daniel P. Poteet II relates 'Time, Eternity, and Dramatic Form in *Ludus Coventriae* "Passion Play I"' (*CompD*), arguing that the idea of time as an imperfect image of the reality of eternity informs the structure of the play, where sacramental presentation 'undermines the priority of narrative and development'. David Mills's note 'Concerning a Stage Direction in the *Ludus Coventriae* (*ELN*) suggests that the word *bemys* in the play of the Salutation and Conception means blasts on the trumpet. There would be three trumpet blasts for the descent of each person of the Trinity to the Virgin. Mills also attempts to explain the reference to all three persons entering Mary's bosom.

[57] *Un cycle du théâtre religieux anglais du moyen âge: Le jeu de la ville de 'N'*, by Claude Gauvin. Paris: Editions du Centre National de la Recherche Scientifique. 1973. pp. 412. 12 plates. F90.

[56] In *Chaucer and Middle English Studies*, see above, note 6.

Moralities and Non-Cycle Plays

Merle Fifield's *Rhetoric of Free Will*[58] is an analysis starting from the premise that the English moralities work as drama. To identify form with materials (sources) rather than with the function of materials in a structure is wrong, and leads to a view of the play as a struggle between Vices and Virtues over a passive victim. Fifield argues that the free will of that supposed victim, Man, is the most important characteristic of the moralities, and one not available to a *Psychomachia*. That and other analogues for the moralities are reviewed so as to stress the essential difference provided by the element of choice. Each choice made by Man between his representatives and those of his enemies marks a section in the rhetorical structure. Such structures are far more complex 'than the currently approved "innocence/fall/redemption" recipe'. Fifield then discusses the moralities according to their individual variations on a structure of five actions. Especially in the fourth and fifth actions the variations seem to take precedence over any possible generalized pattern, but Fifield insists that there remains a typical form. Renaissance plays preserve the structure in many cases despite the introduction of new and complex arrangements, but new demands cause an eventual disintegration into episodic narratives.

Neville Denny speculates about 'Aspects of the Staging of *Mankind*' (*MÆ*), starting from the relationship between its Shrovetide occasion and the subtlety of its staging. The elements of the Mummer's Play and 'ancient British ritual drama' are not

borrowings so much as the result, perhaps, of an improvised method of creation among players who also appeared in those very folk plays. Conjectures follow about the costumes, stage, or rather acting area, the number and status of the performers and audience. Lawrence M. Clopper's approach to '*Mankind* and its Audience' (*CompD*) is rather different. Perhaps some of the ways we arrive at the nature of an audience from the work are based on mistaken assumptions. The Latin in the play is such that it often needs to be understood by the audience, and the farcical treatment of the fall of Mankind constitutes a kind of theatrical and social satire which 'challenges our traditional attribution of the play to the popular canon'. Catherine Belsey argues that Southern is more nearly right about 'The Stage Plan of the *Castle of Perseverance*' (*TN*) than recent rejections of theatre in the round. The plan 'precisely reflects the conception of the relationship between man and the world which underlies the moral lesson of the play'. Alan H. Nelson prints and comments on '"Of the seuen ages": An Unknown Analogue of *The Castle of Perseverance*' (*CompD*). Two reproductions show how the poem is illustrated in the manuscript. Nelson believes that the playwright might have been as much indebted to visual iconography as to literary traditions. Milton McC. Gatch makes his 'Mysticism and Satire in the Morality of *Wisdom*' (*PQ*) a plea for a better deal for the play from its critics. Stressing the importance to the play of an understanding of mystical psychology, and locating direct sources in the *Scale of Perfection*, Gatch also wants to connect the play with the household of the bishops of Ely. The continued interest shown in it after its first appearance

---

[58] *The Rhetoric of Free Will: The Five-Action Structure of the English Morality Play*, by Merle Fifield. Leeds Texts and Monographs New Series 5. University of Leeds School of English. pp. iv+52. £2.70.

was assisted by the circle of More and a later Bishop of Ely, John Morton.

An analysis of the 'Meaning and Art in the Croxton *Play of the Sacrament*' by Sister Nicholas Maltman is also a plea for greater critical respect for a misunderstood play. The grotesqueness and comedy are part of the whole purpose. There is a basically liturgical element, and the treatment of the host is not parody but a re-enactment of the Crucifixion.

V

Middle English: Chaucer

JOYCE BAZIRE and DAVID MILLS

1. GENERAL

A bibliography for the current year will be found in 'Chaucer Research, 1974. Report No. 35' by Thomas A. Kirby (*ChauR*).

Writers and their Background: Geoffrey Chaucer[1] consists of twelve original essays by outstanding medievalists which provide for the general reader some account of Chaucer's personal life and his historical and cultural context, together with an evaluation of their significance for the understanding of his work and achievement. By way of introduction, Derek Brewer's 'Gothic Chaucer' sees Chaucer as the product of 'a culture which favoured pluralism', working from the inconsistencies which signal his Gothic poetic to the competing centres of contemporary culture, especially ecclesiastical Latin and courtly cultures. Chaucer's poetry combines 'anatomy' and romance in sustaining its ironic mode, suitable for the accommodation of oppositions and inconsistencies.

F. R. H. du Boulay's account of 'The Historical Chaucer'—described by Brewer as the first consideration by a medieval historian of Chaucer's life as an historical fact—relates some aspects of Chaucer's career to his historical circumstances. It emphasizes the extent to which personal and public lives were interconnected in a small, mobile, and politically violent

society, and questions a number of assumptions about the effect of political events on the life of one whose career was modestly successful and prosperous but devoid of high ambition or power.

Editorial and linguistic matters are covered in two chapters. In 'Chaucer and Fourteenth-Century English', Norman Davis looks at the metrical and rhyming functions of dialect-variants and inflectional changes in Chaucer, before urging an assessment of Chaucer's Romance vocabulary in relation to frequency and function and the need for more work on his use of native vocabulary, to which the essay makes a number of contributions. E. T. Donaldson's 'The Manuscripts of Chaucer's Works and Their Use' reviews the problems of editorial decision in relation to the manuscripts and treatment of Chaucer's works.

Four chapters consider foreign influence on Chaucer, each presenting some introductory comment on the problems of establishing the influence and the dangers of its use in critical assessment. In 'Chaucer and French poetry', James I. Wimsatt discusses the influence of de Lorris, de Machaut and de Meun on Chaucer, concluding that Muscatine's view of French influence in Chaucer is too simplistic —a more significant hypothesis would be 'an interplay between English and Gallic elements'. Bruce Harbert's 'Chaucer and the Latin Classics' looks at the use Chaucer made of classical authors. The chapter on

---

[1] *Writers and their Background: Geoffrey Chaucer*, ed. by Derek Brewer. London: G. Bell & Sons. Athens: Ohio U.P. (1975). pp. xiv+401. £6.20 and $12; pa. $3.75.

'Chaucer and the Medieval Latin Poets' combines a discussion by Peter Dronke of Chaucer's use of the cosmological poetry of Bernard Silvestris, of Alan of Lille, and of versions of the Trojan story and a claim by Jill Mann that the imaginative quality in Chaucer's writing may have been 'stimulated by the linguistic playfulness of the Latin poets'. In an extensive and interesting study of 'Transformations: Chaucer's Use of Italian', Howard Schless proposes that Chaucer may have been led to learn Italian through his connexion 'with the customs and trade that had long been deeply involved with Italians', instancing the Bardi of Florence. Starting with the temple-description in the *Parlement*, he considers Chaucer's transformations of Italian works; in *Troilus* Boccaccio's juxtaposition of rhetorical units is replaced by characterization—Troilus manifesting character-development, Pandarus character-revelation and Criseyde 'a creative ambiguity'. Dante's influence is briefly discussed, with particular attention to the Ugolino passage in the *Monk's Tale*.

Three further chapters deal with Chaucer's relation to medieval thought. M. Manzalaoui's 'Chaucer and Science' looks particularly at astrology under its three heads of the verifiable, the pseudo-science, and the occult. Geoffrey Shepherd's 'Religion and Philosophy in Chaucer' sets Chaucer against the ecclesiastical and political ferment of his age, arguing that, despite the lack of overtly religious subject-matter or commitment in Chaucer, his recurring preoccupation with 'How does a succession of events make any sense?' may relate to contemporary concerns with freewill, foreknowledge and grace. The nature of Chaucer's essentially visual imagination is the subject of

V. A. Kolve's 'Chaucer and the Visual Arts', which stresses the close link of memory and imagination and urges that images be seen in context, with full weight given to their literal reference. In concluding chapters, L. D. Benson provides a summary of past trends, forthcoming projects, and future needs in Chaucer studies in 'A Reader's Guide to Writings on Chaucer', and a useful annotated 'Select Bibliography'.

In a collection of independently conceived essays of limited length on extensive subjects, the result is inevitably uneven, but all essays are useful and suggestive of further development, and the best contain original theses and insights. Chaucerians will welcome the book. (Reviewed by Derek Pearsall, *MLR*, 1975, pp. 846–8.)

Another major contribution by Derek Brewer is his exploration of the tension in Chaucer's poetry, 'Towards a Chaucerian Poetic', which formed the 1974 Sir Israel Gollancz Memorial Lecture (*PBA*). Chaucer's dominant poetic is the self-enclosed and self-referring poem, often with a traditional story at its base; the art of the poet is re-interpreting the narrative, demonstrated in the interaction of the often non-naturalistic sequence of events with multiple reference to traditional *topoi*, which may produce naturalistic confusion. Similar tension is generated by Chaucer's alternative poetic of credibility and motivation, an appeal to a non-literary experience —real life or the poet's own feelings —evidenced particularly in the Chaucerian narrator and anticipating Neoclassical poetic; Chaucer's 'Retraction' should be located within this alternative.

Throughout *Geoffrey Chaucer*[2]

[2] *Geoffrey Chaucer*, by John Norton-Smith. London and Boston: Routledge & Kegan Paul. pp. xiv+275. £4.95 and $15.50.

John Norton-Smith explores his belief that in Chaucer 'the mimetic process is minutely concerned with artistic means and ends'; the book is selective, avoids the usual rehearsal of accepted opinions, and points many compatibilities of style and effect with, as well as direct influence from, classical authors. An excellent example of the critical method is the discussion of *Troilus*, where Norton-Smith suggests that dramatic form, known to Chaucer from classical drama and from Trivet's commentaries, combines with the time-scale. 'The mimetic basis of the last book shows the gradual authorial conversion of the balance of narrative and dramatic elements from the dominantly narrative into the basically tragic and dramatic'. As the author withdraws from his work, the reader becomes more acutely aware of the alternation of Christian consolation and emotional bitterness. The compatibility of this tragedy of pity and fear with Senecan tragedy is illustrated—with Troilus as example, the ethical type of tragic history—and the relationship of the work to fourteenth-century conventions is indicated. Among other chapters, *The Legend of Good Women* is presented as the transfiguration of a real experience centred on Anne of Bohemia, whose removal from the G-version weakens the poem; and from the *Canterbury Tales*—here seen presenting incompleteness and imperfection in a variety of ways—particular mention may be made of the importance of Theseus's concluding Neoplatonism for the meaning of the *Knight's Tale*, the conflicting comic rhythms of the *Miller's Tale*, and the unChaucerian character of the pilgrim-Chaucer's contributions. There are revealing studies of the *Book of the Duchess* and the *House of Fame*, and revaluations of Chaucer's achievements within the usually amorphous genre of complaint, and of *Scogan* and *Bukton* with their Horatian manner. (Reviewed by R. M. Wilson, *MLR*, 1975, p. 390.)

Stephen Knight directs his attention to the way Chaucer creates meaning 'by the nature and the modulation of the poetry', though he accepts that some of the poetry serves simply as straightforward narration. *Rhyming Craftily*[3] studies certain of Chaucer's works in depth, different in kind and written at different stages. An examination of *Anelida* and the *Parlement* in juxtaposition suggests that the former is mainly unsatisfactory, while the latter is highly to be commended. With regard to *Troilus*, Knight goes further into the subject of character and style (cf. Muscatine, *YW* 38. 93–4) and examines the minor characters and the narrator himself. In the *Knight's Tale* there are four main areas of discussion: the two lovers, Theseus, the narrator, and the major set-pieces. Then the tales of the Manciple and Franklin are set side by side, followed by a commentary on the 'mechanics' of the *Nun's Priest's Tale*; and the work concludes with an Appendix on 'The Figures of Style: the "Easy Ornaments"', with illustrative quotations.

Who's Who in Chaucer,[4] by A. F. Scott, falls into two parts, the first covering the *Tales* and the second five major poems. A typographical distinction is made between the names of historical and fictitious or legendary characters, and each part includes a section for animals.

A. C. and J. E. Spearing are the editors of *Poetry of the Age of*

[3] *Rhyming Craftily*, by Stephen Knight. London, Sydney etc.: Angus & Robertson (U.K.) Ltd. 1973. pp. xviii+247. £4.95.
[4] *Who's Who in Chaucer*, by A. F. Scott. London: Hamish Hamilton, Elm Tree Books. pp. xii+145. £2.50.

Chaucer,[5] intended mainly for A-level students, which contains much excellent introductory background material, as well as presenting the *Friar's Tale* and two of Chaucer's *balades* among the selection of Middle English works.

John Leyerle gives a straightforward exposition of 'The Heart and the Chain'[6] as poetic nuclei in some of Chaucer's major poems, the one representing love and its mutability, the other order and its confinement. In the *Book of the Duchess*, where the Black Knight is specifically identified with John of Gaunt, the nucleus is *hert-huntyng*, as has been argued elsewhere. Both the literal sense of bonds and the metaphorical—the *faire cheyne of love*—are to be discerned in the *Knight's Tale*. The *Miller's Tale* and the *Parlement* are dealt with briefly, the one with its nucleus of holes, the other of place. But *Troilus* is discussed in detail, with its 'extremely simple and pervasive nucleus, the heart', and the paper concludes with the relation of Chaucer's use of the heart and chain as nucleus-metaphors to long-existing literary traditions.

In 'Chaucer's Courtly Love' (*L and L*), Edmund Reiss finds that courtly love, realized with ironic scorn despite the lovers' nobility, is the love found in the three works of Chaucer where love is central to the narrative. In the *Book of the Duchess* love is a destructive force, allied to fortune, to be expelled from both knight and narrator; the *Knight's Tale* places love in

an ironic frame with the emphasis on woe; and in *Troilus* the double sorrow is Troilus's loving and Criseyde's desertion, and love is circumscribed by contexts of sorrow and mutability.

Romances implied to Chaucer the conflicting clerkly rôles of moralist and authority in love, argues R. T. Lenaghan in 'The Clerk of Venus; Chaucer and Medieval Romance' (*L and L*), and, tracing this thesis through the disconnected episodes of marvel and sentiment of the *Squire's Tale* to the Franklin's enthusiastic response and to his tale (with its traditional opposition of *gentilesse* in clerk and knight), he considers the effect on the narrator-Chaucer and on the sculptured narrative of the *Knight's Tale* and *Troilus*.

Christopher Brookhouse's 'In Search of Chaucer: The Needed Narrative' (*L and L*) sees Chaucer's art arising from the poet's own pain and uncertainty, dealing in themes of loneliness and loss, deriving artistic order from human chaos, and in the *Tales* combining 'a fundamental interest in the power of words' with a realistic and metaphorical journey.

Thomas J. Garbáty maintains in 'The Degradation of Chaucer's "Geffrey"' (*PMLA*) that in the early poems the narrator represents the 'reasonable' man (in the legal sense) and appears dull-witted only because placed in situations with dominant individuals such as the Black Knight and the Eagle. But in the *Tales* Harry Bailley occupies that position and pilgrim-Chaucer, particularly in the *Sir Thopas*-episode, is represented as an 'uncomprehending caricature'.

F. N. M. Diekstra illustrates *Chaucer's Quizzical Mode of Exemplification*,[7] that is his use of incongruous

---

[5] *Poetry of the Age of Chaucer*, ed. by A. C. and J. E. Spearing. London: Edward Arnold. pp. vi+221. £3.20; pa. £1.20. Readings of the poems are available on tape or cassettes.

[6] In *The Learned and the Lewed*, ed. by Larry D. Benson. Harvard English Studies 5. Cambridge, Mass.: Harvard U.P. pp. xii+ 405. £9.90; pa. £2.75. (Abbreviated: *L and L*).

[7] *Chaucer's Quizzical Mode of Exemplification*, by F. N. M. Diekstra. Nijmegen: Dekker & Van De Vegt. pp. 24.

examples which eschew simple moralities and convey a sense of the absurd and chaotic.

Theodore A. Stroud's review article, 'Genres and Themes: A Reaction to Two Views of Chaucer' (*MP*), comments on the trends in modern criticism revealed in books by Eliason (*YW* 53. 108) and Steadman (*YW* 53. 117).

The summary of Irena Varnaite's 'Problems of the Analysis of Chaucer's Poems' (*Literatūra*, 1973) suggests that it is concerned with the evolution of Chaucer's art in the five poems preceding the *Tales*, stressing the extension of existing genres, the growth of realism and motivation, and the rôle of the narrator.

Tauno F. Mustanoja's study of 'Verbal Rhyming in Chaucer'[8] suggests that, in using verbs as rhyme words, Chaucer was merely conforming with established practice.

A computer-study correlating four levels of metrical stress with six iambic patterns for a selection of passages from Chaucer's poems, Merle Fifield and James Modena's 'Stress as a Component of Metrical Variety in Chaucer's Prosody—A Computer Aided Analysis' (*Siglash Newsletter*), points out that most of Chaucer's verses are regular iambic pentameter and the minority variants can mostly be comprehended under four types of variation. Some development of Chaucer's prosody can be traced, in the number of variations and in the distribution of stress-contrasts among the feet.

Ralph W. V. Elliott's *Chaucer's English*[9] gives a striking impression of

the range of registers on which Chaucer drew to create his unique style. After a clear discussion of the English of Chaucer's time in all its complexity, Elliott places the extremes of Chaucer's registers as the colloquial and the formally rhetorical and proceeds to explore the colloquial and technical registers, with a chapter on Chaucer's oaths. Concentrating on vocabulary and meaning, Elliott is happiest when linking linguistic data to stylistic effect, as in the thematic implications of Christian oaths in *Troilus* or the scientific terminology of the *Canon's Yeoman's Tale*, 'Chaucer's most daring experiment in sustained technical diction'. A final chapter studies the creation of the individual voices of fifteen characters in the *Tales* from a mixture of registers. Outstanding is Elliot's study of Chaucer's prose, in which he defends the *Astrolabe* as 'no mean achievement' and praises *Boece* for its passages of controlled and inventive prose which, as 'an invaluable linguistic practice ground', directly influenced Chaucer's linguistic development; by his high valuation of the prose works, including the *Parson's Tale*, Elliott can convincingly argue the burlesque function of *Melibee*'s 'mock didactic style'.

In 'Chaucer and Chrétien and Arthurian Romance' (*Robbins*), Derek Brewer proposes that references to Chrétien's works may underlie *Tales* VII, 3211–3, and the reference to *the book of the Leoun* in the 'Retraction'; Chaucer's generally derisory attitude towards Arthurian romance perhaps suggests an earlier attraction to Chrétien's stories and, given that he did know them, suggests further points of comparison.

In 'Chaucer, Sir John Mandeville, and the Alliterative Revival: A Hypothesis concerning Relationships' (*MP*), C. W. D. R. Moseley suggests

[8] In *Chaucer and Middle English Studies*. In honour of Rossell Hope Robbins, ed. by Beryl Rowland. London: George Allen & Unwin Ltd. pp. 424. £7.95. (Abbreviated: *Robbins*).

[9] *Chaucer's English*, by Ralph W. V. Elliott. London: Andre Deutsch. pp. 447. £4.95.

that Chaucer and the northern poets of the alliterative revival may have had access to Mandeville's *Travels* because the work was possibly written by a dependant of the Bohuns, whose circle included John of Gaunt's household and the alliterative poets. Sumner Ferris traces the connexion between 'Chaucer, Richard II, Henry IV, and 13 October' (*Robbins*) in terms of the devotion to the Confessor by Richard, continued by Henry and recognized by Chaucer—hence the grant to the poet of a tun of wine in letters patent on that date (the feast of Edward's translation) in 1398 and 1399. Lois A. Ebin's discussion of 'Boethius, Chaucer, and *The Kingis Quair*' (*PQ*) develops a critical view of James's poem with occasional contrasts with Chaucer.

Morton W. Bloomfield, who is concerned with 'Chaucer and Reason' (*Unisa English Studies*, 1973), cites examples to illustrate that theme from many of the poet's works, and notes *inter alia* the 'rationality of Chaucer's wives'.

Chaucer, as 'an example of a true author whose work bears a complex relationship to oral literature', is cited by Robert Kellogg in 'Oral Literature' (*NLH*, 1973). Among others, some examples from Chaucer are used in the course of Richard A. Dwyer's article, 'The Appreciation of Handmade Literature' (*ChauR*), which is concerned with both scribal and authorial collections and revisions of various works.

N. E. Osselton's 'Bilderdijk and Chaucer'[10] examines the four Chaucerian translations (one via Voltaire) made by the Dutch poet

Bilderdijk, pointing to the use of Speght's 1687 edition and the reliance on Chaucer's rather than Dryden's version of the *Nun's Priest's Tale*.

Peter M. Vermeer's review article on Ian Robinson's *Chaucer and the English Tradition* (*YW* 53. 107), 'Chaucer and Literary Criticism' (*Dutch Quarterly Review of Anglo-American Letters*), while acknowledging its critical insights, draws attention to the serious shortcomings of this and other books by Robinson.

Roger Hart has written an amply illustrated account of *English Life in Chaucer's Day*.[11] Useful background information for Chaucer studies is provided by Paul Piehler's *The Visionary Landscape: A Study in Medieval Allegory*,[12] Marcelle Thiébaux's *The Stag of Love: The Chase in Medieval Literature*,[13] Penelope B. R. Doob's *Nebuchadnezzar's Children: Conventions of Madness in Middle English Literature*,[14] William Calin's *A Poet at the Fountain: Essays on the Narrative Verse of Guillaume de Machaut;*[15] and also *Landscapes and Seasons of the Medieval World*[16] by Derek Pearsall and Elizabeth Salter, which contains

[10] In *Ten Studies in Anglo-Dutch Relations*, ed. by Jan van Dorsten. Publications of the Sir Thomas Browne Institute, Leiden General Series No. 5. Leiden: Leiden U.P. London: O.U.P. pp. x+271.

[11] *English Life in Chaucer's Day*, by Roger Hart. London: Wayland Publishers. New York: G. P. Putnam's Sons. pp. 128.

[12] *The Visionary Landscape: A Study in Medieval Allegory*, by Paul Piehler. London: Edward Arnold. 1971. pp. viii+170.

[13] *The Stag of Love: The Chase in Medieval Literature*, by Marcelle Thiébaux. Ithaca and London: Cornell U.P. pp. 249. £7.40.

[14] *Nebuchadnezzar's Children: Conventions of Madness in Middle English Literature*, by Penelope B. R. Doob. New Haven and London: Yale U.P. pp. xviii+247. £6.25.

[15] *A Poet at the Fountain: Essays on the Narrative Verse of Guillaume de Machaut*, by William Calin. Lexington: U. P. of Kentucky. pp. 263.

[16] *Landscapes and Seasons of the Medieval World*, by Derek Pearsall and Elizabeth Salter. London: Paul Elek. 1973. pp. xvi+ 252. Plates VIII+66.

very brief sections devoted to Chaucer.

2. CANTERBURY TALES

Chaucer. The Canterbury Tales,[17] edited by J. J. Anderson, contains 'Part One: Early Appreciations' (from Caxton to Arnold) and 'Part Two: Twentieth-century Criticism', a selection of eleven articles, all of which have previously appeared in print. (Reviewed by R. M. Wilson, *MLR* 1975, p. 390.)

Dora Maček's 'A Draft for the Analysis of Verbal Periphrases in the "Canterbury Tales"' (*Studia Romanica et Anglia Zagrebiensia*, 1972–3) is a preliminary study of the nature and function of compound verb-forms employing specified auxiliaries in the first 835 lines of the *Tales*, which points problems for future studies using a larger sample.

In his discussion of 'Some Fifteenth-Century Manuscripts of the *Canterbury Tales*' (*Robbins*), Daniel S. Silvia divides them into three groups and concludes that 'roughly sixty' manuscripts now extant contain, or once contained, complete fifteenth-century texts of the *Tales*. Of the remainder, sixteen are anthologies, and three never had the complete *Tales*. Some of the anthologies contain 'courtly' works, the others 'moral pieces'; two Huntington Manuscripts, 144 and 140 (one secular, one religious), are studied carefully by Silvia.

'The Language of Some Fifteenth-Century Chaucerians: A Study of Manuscript Variants in the *Canterbury Tales*' (*SMC*), by Sherman M. Kuhn, is illustrated by examples which show 'different types of vocabulary and as many different textual

problems as possible', and concludes with an examination of an extract from the *Nun's Priest's Tale*.

'The Interludes of the Marriage Group in the *Canterbury Tales*' (*Robbins*) aid the emotional as well as the intellectual climax of the Group in the opinion of Clair C. Olson. The effect of the first climax—the tales of the Friar and Summoner—is produced with 'atmospheric appropriateness', while the second—the strongly contradictory tales of the Merchant and the Squire—though leading from the *Clerk's Envoy* to the *Franklin's Tale*, prevents the basic plan from appearing too schematic. Olson touches also on the contribution made to the Marriage Group by the Host's comments on his own marriage. In 'The Sequence of the *Canterbury Tales*' (*ChauR*) Edward S. Cohen proposes a new order for the tales and a timetable for the journey, pointing out examples of inconsistent revision.

A. A. Prins's 'The Dating in the *Canterbury Tales*' (*Robbins*) seeks to reconcile the apparent problem of date suggested by the start of the *Prologue* and the introduction to the *Man of Law's Tale* by relating the latter to the stellar zodiac and the precession of the equinoxes, both of which Chaucer can be shown to have known.

In the course of a discussion of folk-lore study in literary criticism, 'Boccaccio, Chaucer and the International Popular Tale' (*WF*), Francis Lee Utley draws attention to the common folk-tale background of Chaucer and Boccaccio and examines folk-versions of the *Friar's Tale* and the 'Enchanted Pear Tree' of the *Merchant's Tale*.

A. V. C. Schmidt has provided an edition[18] combining the *General Pro-*

---

[17] *Chaucer. The Canterbury Tales*, ed. by J. J. Anderson. Casebook Series. Macmillan. pp. 255. £2.50; pa. £1.

[18] *Geoffrey Chaucer: The General Prologue; The Canon's Yeoman's Tale*, ed. by

logue and the *Canon's Yeoman's Tale*, each with its own section of introduction and extensive commentary. It is intended for sixth-formers and undergraduates.

Greater space is devoted to the Squire in Thomas J. Hatton's useful discussion of 'Thematic Relationships Between Chaucer's Squire's Portrait and Tale and the Knight's Portrait and Tale' (*SMC*), since Hatton is pointing out—using the Knight and his tale for comparative purposes—that the Squire's portrait is consistent with newer readings of his tale which note its false values. Chaucer by this means may have been suggesting to the court that there should be a return to the values exemplified in the *Knight's Tale*. George F. Reinecke's 'Speculation, Intention, and the Teaching of Chaucer' (*L and L*) speculates on the significance of seven references in the *Tales* which the author feels can properly be the subject of conjecture in teaching students.

In a lengthy article, 'The Lay Pilgrims of the *Canterbury Tales*: a study in Ethology' (*MS*), George J. Engelhardt uses of necessity technical language, but also resorts to uncommon terms to express plain facts. He discusses the ethos of *contemptus mundi* and of *dignitas humanae naturae*, the former descriptive and the latter prescriptive, both being represented in the *Prologue*. Engelhardt then proceeds to study not only the pilgrims themselves, but also their tales with some consideration of the relationships between them all. John McKee comments on the organization of the portraits in 'Chaucer's *Canterbury Tales*, General Prologue' (*Ex*).

By a detailed examination of

'Chaucer's Art of Portraiture' (*SMC*) in three of the *Prologue*-portraits, Roger P. Parr illustrates how Chaucer, while still using rhetorical features, exemplifies the change from poetic convention to poetic creation.

Richard L. Hoffman suggests that 'The Wife of Bath's Uncharitable Offerings' (*ELN*) may be a further example of her spiritual deafness to the words of Christ.

'Plot and characters, particularly the contrast of Theseus to everyone else, express a vision of a receptive, suffering universe; this vision is hauntingly reaffirmed in the poem's texture, in such patterns as the festal-mourning cycles, prison and entrapment images and metaphors, and animal references.' Thus Georgia Ronan Crampton considers *The Condition of Creatures*[19] with particular reference to the *Knight's Tale*, claiming that the poem has a satisfying aesthetic structure whereby Theseus's Boethian consolation provides a fitting end to the sequence which begins with the intercession of the Theban women and reaches a climax in Arcite's death. But this structure conceals an underlying philosophical confusion, that man lives in an irrational universe which denies his power of action, so that Theseus finally voices only a hope, not a reassurance. Chaucer here, as elsewhere and in contrast to Spenser, celebrates sufferance, not action, a concern reflected also in the recurring theme of the bargain, a freely relinquished freedom.

The *Knight's Tale* embodies in both matter and form a dual vision in its criticism as well as its celebration of chivalric life. Thus Ronald B. Herzman in 'The Paradox of Form:

A. V. C. Schmidt. London: U. of London P. Ltd. pp. viii+175. pa. £1.50.

[19] *The Condition of Creatures: Suffering and Action in Chaucer and Spenser*, by Georgia Ronan Crampton. New Haven and London: Yale U.P. pp. x+207. $10.

The Knight's Tale and Chaucerian Aesthetics' (*PLL*). The tale calls attention to its own form, its possibilities, and its limitations, and also to wider issues, such as the nature of Chaucer's narrative art. The whole tale demonstrates the rules which not only regulate the private affair of the lovers, but also link it to the community; it is with the working out of this thesis that Herzman concerns himself in the article, showing that the lovers' celebration is also related to their inability to achieve perfection. Alan T. Gaylord turns to 'The Role of Saturn in the *Knight's Tale*' (*ChauR*) allowing it less importance than it is usually given. Saturn, who is pre-eminently the planet, is Chaucer's own addition to his source. The way in which the tale works out the theme, 'the wise man rules the stars', is examined in its complexity by Gaylord. Saturn proves to be 'a kind of baleful summary of the implications in the infatuate desires of the lovers', and eventually Theseus's speech affirms that the benevolent guidance of the world is that of Jupiter. Frederick Turner undertakes 'A Structuralist Analysis of the *Knight's Tale*' (*ChauR*) and finds binary oppositions, first in the description of the lists, 'the most geometrical and diagrammatic part of the poem'. Further examples of this are shown in the context of 'triadic, quadratic, and circular structures'. From this background emerge the theme of marriage and incest and that of 'brotherhood, sibling harmony, and conflict between siblings'. Turner concludes by drawing parallels with the *Miller's Tale*.

In the course of a review of 'The Medieval Theory of Literature for Refreshment and its Use in the Fabliau Tradition' (*SP*), Glending Olson, after examining the statements of various writers, such as

Hugh of St Victor and Bonaventura, concludes that literature sometimes was held to refresh and relax its audience. The last section discusses fabliaux in this connexion.

Chaucer at Oxford and Cambridge,[20] by J. A. W. Bennett, concerns the rôles of his clerks from both places. The first chapter demonstrates the value of evidence in 'rolls and records' for reconstructing the background knowledge, not only for individual points in other works, but also for the tales of the Miller and Reeve; and in the latter 'not a detail . . . can be faulted'. Bennett wonders whether, because of the close parallels and contrasts, the two tales were meant to be read as one. 'Town and Gown' discusses in detail the situation produced by the absence of the collegiate system and institutions which made possible the tricks of Nicholas. The intellectual development of Merton is traced through the careers of its alumni and the records of its library, which indicate the learning of men who were Chaucer's contemporaries. 'A Jolly Miller' relates details of the *Reeve's Tale* to actual facts. Bennett's book—representing the Alexander Lectures delivered at Toronto—is most informative and sustains the reader's interest throughout.

J. Burke Severs continues his informative study of 'Chaucer's Clerks' (*Robbins*), paying most attention to those in the tales of the Miller and Reeve. He points out details in their lives as students (though it is not certain that Absolon was one) which are of significance for the tales, such as Nicholas's skill in astrology or the fact that Alan and John are fellows of a college. In both

[20] *Chaucer at Oxford and Cambridge*, by J. A. W. Bennett. Oxford: Clarendon P. Toronto and Buffalo: U. Toronto P. pp. ix + 131. £4.50 and $7.50.

tales the opposition of educated versus uneducated is of importance in the plot. Finally Severs considers the Clerk of Oxenford (particularly his age), Jankyn and his book, and details about the University of Orleans in connexion with the Franklin's clerk.

Although Alvin W. Bowker acknowledges the farcical side of the tale, he concentrates more on the darker aspects, the seeds of which are early discernible in the character-mixtures of the protagonists, of whom the least complicated is John. In 'Comic Illusion and Dark Reality in The Miller's Tale' (*Modern Language Studies*) he shows how the darker colouring of the world gradually appears and how the world is primed for catastrophe 'by the very people who have added to [the] gaiety and brilliance'. In the tale Chaucer shows the fabliau as 'an appropriate mode for the expression of a serious commentary on man and his world'.

Beryl Rowland's 'Chaucer's Blasphemous Churl: A New Interpretation of the *Miller's Tale*' (*Robbins*) re-examines the mixing of sacred and obscene in the tale and illustrates its medieval humour—'not only verbal blasphemy but blasphemy of situation and action'. She pays most attention to the connexions with the Virgin and with the mystery plays. Certain terms, for example in the *Knight's Tale*, must be accepted at their face value, even though attempts are made to read bawdy meanings into them, but '*Double-entendre* in The Miller's Tale' (*EIC*) is demonstrated by Paula Neuss through reference to the language which can be read on one level for the *cherles'* kind of *solaas*, though it also contains *doubles entendres* which may then provide *sentence*.

In the discussion of 'The Parody of Medieval Music in the *Miller's Tale*'

(*JEGP*), which adds much depth of meaning to the tale, Jesse M. Gellrich shows in detail how 'the profane intentions of the characters juxtapose the profound meanings of the music for the purpose of creating comic incongruity', and how, by using musical images Chaucer may have added to the tone of comic irony. Not only are there echoes of divine songs, but the psaltery itself has relevance for this parodic purpose. A. Leyland sees further significance in the reference in the '"Miller's Tale" [I (A) 3449]' (*N&Q*) to St Frideswide.

In considering 'The *Reeve's Tale* as a Fabliau' (*MLQ*), Glending Olson draws not only on specific analogues, but also on characteristics of the genre, of which two aspects in particular are dealt with: 'the social pride of the Symkyn family and the atmosphere of game and contest [rather than revenge] which permeates the tale'. Olson stresses that the tale is not merely using fabliau motifs, but is in itself a rich fabliau.

'An Analogue (?) to the *Reeve's Tale*' (*Robbins*) that Thomas A. Kirby presents is a modern story with certain elements found also in Chaucer's tale. John W. Conlee comments on 'John Barth's Version of *The Reeve's Tale*' (*AN&Q*) in The *Sot-Weed Factor*. Although the name is mentioned only once, Timothy J. O'Keefe points out that the 'Meanings of "Malyne" in The *Reeve's Tale*' (*AN&Q*, 1973) are such that they reinforce the moral of the tale in several ways.

Sheila Delany, in 'Womanliness in the *Man of Law's Tale*' (*ChauR*), first studies three passages concerned with Constance's relation to a man or men, passages which are incongrous and emphasize how her rôle is to be interpreted. The contrast of Constance with the Sultaness and

Donegild in behaviour and character is stressed by the references to the antithesis between May and Eve. The article concludes with apposite references to the 1381 rebellion and to modern literature. In support of his argument in 'Chaucer's Man of Law and the Tale of Constance' (*PMLA*) that the tale is intended as 'an encomium upon the teller's profession', Walter Scheps analyses the *Prologue* portrait and the several parts of the tale, dwelling on elements of the teller's character that are reflected in the tale. Finally he compares the tale with others written in rhyme royal, and notes that Trivet's version contains little legal rhetoric and few references to law; Chaucer draws on *Rhetorica ad Herennium* for much of the legal colouring. William C. Johnson, Jr, concludes at the end of 'Miracles in *The Man of Law's Tale*' (*BRMMLA*), in which he closely compares Chaucer's version of three miracles with those of Trivet, that, unlike Trivet's concern, Chaucer's is 'not theological, but aesthetic in a humanistic sense' for 'theology becomes the handmaiden of art'. Margaret Schlauch discusses *Historia o Cesarzu Otone*, 'A Polish Analogue of the *Man of Law's Tale*' (*Robbins*), which is a prose text of the sixteenth century derived from a French romance. Michael R. Peed notes 'An Analogue of the "Man of Law's Tale"' (*AN&Q*), the Old French *Berta aus Grans Pies*. In 'Chaucer's "Phislyas": A Problem in Paleography and Linguistics' (*ChauR*), Philip D. Ortego supports a sense of 'medicine' for 'phislyas' at B 1189.

A fairly wide field is covered by Anne Kernan's 'The Archwife and the Eunuch' (*ELH*). The Pardoner does more than interrupt her prologue; he emphasizes the division in it, playing a rôle in the shift from defence of marriage to the means by which the Wife dominated her husbands. Although the two pilgrims may seem to be at opposite poles, yet they 'form a counterpoint of minor antitheses and likenesses' and both go on to reveal in practice the evils against which they preach initially; and in their tales each is really represented by a character associated with the motif of regeneration and renewal. Finally, the fact that the characters and their relationship can be illuminated by the concept of *cupiditas* is considered in the light of the writings of Augustine and others of the fathers. After an introductory section dealing with the attitude to old age in medieval and earlier days, the greater part of 'The Wife of Bath and All her Sect' (*Viator*) is devoted to a long and informative account of 'the literary tradition of the randy old woman', going back to classical times. In this way William Matthews illuminates the portrait of the Wife, but he points out that, in creating her, Chaucer may also have been much influenced by fabliaux. In a discussion of 'The *Traductio* on *Honde* in the *Wife of Bath's Prologue*' (*Notre Dame English Journal*, 1973) Allan B. Fox comments on the significance of the word's occurrence in a variety of rhyme forms and also of the 'progress' of these repetitions in relation to the Wife's ultimate 'victory' over Jankyn. In 'Astrology and the Wife of Bath: A Reinterpretation' (*ChauR*) B. F. Hamlin pursues the significance of astrological allusions in the Wife's prologue, and supports Pratt's assertion concerning the 'theme of unification' for her character afforded by these. Thomas Andrew Reisner's note, 'The Wife of Bath's Dower: A Legal Interpretation' (*MP*), suggests that the Wife was a 'venal adventuress'. The use of *quoniam* in 'Chaucer's *Wife of Bath's Prologue*, D. 608' (*Ex*) on stylistic grounds is explained by Dennis Biggins.

He also reviews possible evidence concerning the Wife of Bath's marital status—whether she is wife or widow —and then suggests in '"O Jankyn, be ye there?"' (*Robbins*) that its inconclusive nature is not unfitting in view of the contradictory impressions Chaucer gives of the Wife. Barry Sanders argues for 'Chaucer's Dependence on Sermon Structure in the Wife of Bath's "Prologue" and "Tale"' (*SMC*), in which the Wife satirizes the clergy and shows why woman has to have the upper hand.

'Letter and Gloss in the Friar's and Summoner's Tales' (*JNT*, 1973), by Mary Carruthers, deals with the most expanded treatment of glossing in Chaucer's work. The Friar's summoner is wedded to the letter, and, in his inability to understand his own tale, the Friar's glossing rebounds against himself; while the Summoner operates on the literal level throughout his tale, revealing himself as one who considers spiritual meaning empty show. The aim of Penn R. Szittya's 'The Friar as False Apostle: Antifraternal Exegesis and the *Summoner's Tale*' (*SP*) is to show that the tale's comedy is 'theological as well as scatological, learned as well as obscene', and this is achieved by concentration on the pattern of allusion to the apostles. Such a pattern is closely linked with the antifraternalism of the day and the exegesis of certain biblical verses.

Though a pedagogical rejoinder to the Wife's argument, the Clerk's tale is addressed rather to her audience. Accepting her view of marriage as a contest of wills, he teaches a moral lesson, showing how Griselda, in suppressing her desires, demonstrates a more disciplined *maistrie* than Walter. As well as seeing 'Chaucer's Clerk as Teacher' (*L and L*), Robert Longsworth is also concerned with the Clerk's pedagogical manner.

In considering 'The Image of Paradise in the *Merchant's Tale*' (*L and L*) Kenneth A. Bleeth notes that analogues contain the basic 'ingredients'. He explores the way in which Chaucer has emphasized certain aspects of the Fruit Tree story and also, in detail that raises some interesting possibilities, shows how the framework of the fabliau plot 'brings into relief its latent religious elements'. In 'Chaucer's *The Merchant's Tale*: Tender Youth and Stooping Age' (*AI*), Robert J. Kloss scrutinizes the effects of Chaucer's focus on the male rather than the female, and of his ageing that protagonist so much in comparison with the analogues. He sees in January's behaviour 'a series of representative infantile fantasies', putting May in the mother-relationship for satisfying his needs; and then along with Damien is introduced an oedipal situation. The subject of 'Biblical Women in the Merchant's Tale: Feminism, Antifeminism, and Beyond' (*Viator*) is thoroughly investigated and annotated by Emerson Brown, Jr. Starting with the biblical examples of *good conseil* that women can offer men (1362–74)—found also in *Melibee*, though they have been debased by the Merchant—Brown proceeds to examine them, both from the Merchant's unsympathetic point of view, and also against the background of the medieval moral and typological interpretations given them. Through this review, the Merchant's approach is seen to be a 'cynical literalism', a spiritual blindness. From Chaucer's 'wryly humorous continuation' of Claudian's *De raptu Proserpinae*, where the devil has met his match, Brown passes to the Christian view in human history of the 'triumph of a woman over the ruler of the underworld', together with the levels on which the pear-tree episode can be used. The interpretations assigned by medieval mythographers to the legend of Pluto and Proserpine indicate 'the deep spiritual alienation from God' that is both cause and result of January's marriage. Marcia A. Dalbey, in 'The Devil in the Garden: Pluto and Proserpine in Chaucer's "Merchant's Tale"' (NM), develops this argument by citing Ovide moralisé in some detail for comparison. In entering the garden the three protagonists put themselves under the rule of the deities and ultimately of the devil.

John F. Adams considers the significance of 'The Janus Symbolism in "The Merchant's Tale"' (SMC), a tale which is both fabliau and romance.

Discussing the limited knowledge of the Breton lay in England in 'How Much Was Known of the Breton Lai in Fourteenth-Century England?' (L and L), John B. Beston points out that Chaucer's prologue to the Franklin's Tale is vague and inaccurate, that there is no evidence that Chaucer knew Breton lays, and that the poem, though the only great Middle English lay, is not a Breton lay. As Gertrude M. White points out in 'The Franklin's Tale: Chaucer or the Critics' (PMLA), the tale and its teller have given rise to differing opinions, but for light on the tale one must turn to Chaucer's own writings. Although the Merchant's Tale provides a striking and dramatic foil— and this point is demonstrated in some detail—the fact that the values found there are 'dramatized and explored throughout The Canterbury Tales and stated in several lyrics' is shown to be also of great significance. Commenting 'On the Franklin's Prologue, 716–721, Persius, and the

Continuity of the Mannerist Style' (PQ), Constance S. Wright traces the development up to Chaucer of the 'affected modesty topos'. The association between the Franklin and the Man of Law reflects a real-life association, as D. W. Robertson, Jr, indicates in 'Chaucer's Franklin and his Tale' (Costerus). He continues by looking at Chaucer's presentation of the character of the former, and supports his interpretation of this in his subsequent discussion of the tale. The message of the tale and its characters are well shown to be not what the Franklin himself thought they were. Robertson concludes that Chaucer's interest lay in the Franklin as a dispenser of justice rather than as a person.

E. R. Amoils explores the significance of linking the Physician's and Pardoner's tales in terms of the themes of 'Fruitfulness and Sterility in the "Physician's" and "Pardoner's Tales"' (ESA), drawing upon both the Roman de la Rose and the Parson's Tale for supporting evidence. The Physician and Pardoner, nominally opponents of death, actually seek only money; the Pardoner contrasts with Virginia in his hypocrisy and his spiritual and physical sterility.

For David M. Andersen, 'The Pardoner's True Profession' (NM) is seen in his adaptation of the cult of relics to pagan magical practices to meet the needs of his usual audience, the peasantry. In 'Chaucer's Pardoner's Tale and the Irony of Misinterpretation' (JNT, 1973), A. Leigh DeNeef finds the unity of introduction, Prologue, Tale, and invitation in 'the myopic confusion of literal and extra-literal meanings'. Joseph R. Millichap discusses the thematic reversal in images of transformation and 'Transubstantiation in the Pardoner's Tale' (BRMMLA). The

Pardoner seeks the pilgrims' approval on aesthetic grounds for his performance as an actor, and, to sharpen their appreciation, he deliberately projects an image of lechery (of which he is incapable) and avarice (which is unconfirmed). But, argues Edward I. Condren in 'The Pardoner's Bid for Existence' (*Viator*, 1973), the self-conscious irony of the tale's performance is undercut by an unconscious irony, seen in the contradiction of substance and accident in the opening homily, and in the twin reflections of the Pardoner's private and public lives, the death-loving Old Man, and the death-hating rioters. Despite an audacious attempt finally to bring the two extremes of his performance together, the Pardoner is denied his applause by the Host's inability to accept his aesthetic vision; the failure which the Pardoner, in his preoccupation with death, already knew, is publicly confirmed. In 'Chaucer's Pardoner: Sex and Non-Sex' (*SAB*) Stephen Manning claims to see a pattern of oral imagery with a strongly aggressive element in the Pardoner's Prologue and Tale. The Pardoner seeks a communion of laughter from the pilgrims but undergoes oral castration from the Host. The episode ends with a kiss of peace which 'suggests the possibility of ultimate reconciliation through Christ's pardon'.

After comparing the tale with its analogues, in 'Source and Theme in the Shipman's Tale' (*University of Dayton Review*), Joseph R. Millichap concludes that variations between them 'show Chaucer's complex and ironic treatment of morality in a traditional framework'. The *Pardoner's Tale* realizes the distinction between intellectual and emotional awareness of death via a fusion of realistic and symbolic modes, argues Malcolm Pittock in '*The Pardoner's*

Tale and the Quest for Death' (*EIC*). The literal-minded rioters cannot understand the warnings given them, but their psychology is revealed by the symbolic overtones of their words and deeds (e.g. the quest as a parody of Redemption). The tale suits the Pardoner, who acknowledges the fact of sin but cultivates evil, an abuse licensed by the Church which serves to blur moral distinctions.

Pittock's commentary on *The Prioress's Tale. The Wife of Bath's Tale*,[21] designed for students, contains inter alia useful sections on anti-Semitism in the attitudes of the Prioress and of Chaucer, the medieval church's view of marriage, anti-feminism, and the articulation of the Wife's tale and her prologue. Albert B. Friedman discusses 'The *Prioress's Tale* and Chaucer's Anti-Semitism' (*ChauR*), for which latter many writers have tried to exculpate the poet; this Friedman considers misconceived since Chaucer was a man of his age. Nor is Chaucer satirizing the Prioress as a bigot. Instead, Friedman contends that the tale is a simple one of pathos without particular emphasis on brutality or anti-Semitism. 'The Prioress's Avowal of Ineptitude' (*ChauR*) concerns her assertion of her inability to praise the Virgin fittingly. Donald W. Fritz gives examples through the ages of avowals of the ineffable nature of things divine. In examining the meaning of the miracle he draws parallels between the tale and the Demeter-myth and comments on the significance of the grain. Audrey Davidson discusses '*Alma Redemptoris Mater*: the little clergeon's song' (*SMC*), identifying it as a marian antiphon, and produces a reconstructed chant for it. She also

[21] *The Prioress's Tale. The Wife of Bath's Tale*, ed. by Malcolm Pittock. Notes on English Literature. Oxford: Basil Blackwell. 1973. pp. iv+99. 75p.

considers why Chaucer used this particular antiphon here.

Dolores L. Cullen examines the significance of *drasty* as applied to 'Chaucer's *The Tale of Sir Thopas*' (*Ex*). Two articles treat *Melibee*, the first accepting it as a serious work. After recognizing the apparent dullness of the tale, Richard L. Hoffman takes up in 'Chaucer's Melibee and Tales of Sundry Folk' (*Classica et Mediaevalia*, 1974 for 1969) the interpretation placed on it by Robertson and Huppé. He contends that medieval readers would have associated Prudence and her counsels with the first of the cardinal virtues and also understood that they as well as Melibee were being admonished to remember that Christ defeated the World, the Flesh, and the Devil in the Crucifixion. Citing specific examples, Hoffman relates the axiomatic *sentences* of *Melibee* to the *sentences* of other tales, and concludes that 'if the *General Prologue* and the *Parson's Tale* are the pillars' of the *Tales, Melibee* is the keystone. Dolores Palomo looks at 'What Chaucer Really Did to *Le Livre de Mellibee*' (*PQ*). A close comparison with its original reveals that Chaucer's translation has by its style inflated a 'pretentious and undistinguished piece of bourgeois moralizing just to the point of ridiculousness but not to the point of obvious risibility'. She first suggests—developing several points—that *Melibee*, as well as *Thopas*, may have been intended 'as a kind of literary criticism by example', and that they both express perspectives of the male/female relationship. The final comments, on the tale's context, lend support to the main argument.

Richard Zacharias comments on the two analogies contained in 'Chaucer's *Nun's Priest's Tale*, B². 4552–63' (*Ex*).

J. Kieran Kealy considers the significance for the tale of 'Chaucer's Nun's Priest's Tale, VII, 3160–71' (*Ex*).

Paul E. Beichner, in 'Confrontation, Contempt of Court, and Chaucer's Cecilia' (*ChauR*), compares Chaucer's presentation of the confrontation between Cecilia and Amalchius with the Latin legend to show the heightened dramatic effect which Chaucer achieves.

Lawrence V. Ryan's 'The Canon's Yeoman's Desperate Confession' (*ChauR*) discusses 'Chaucer's unusual adaptation of the ritual outlined in the confessional manuals as a means of depicting the psychological predicament of the Yeoman'.

Roy J. Pearcy poses the question, 'Does the Manciple's Prologue Contain a Reference to Hell's Mouth?' (*ELN*), referring to 1.38 ('The devel of helle . . .'). He then considers medieval representations of Hell's Mouth and suggests that there may be a link between this prologue and the Parson's.

3. TROILUS AND CRISEYDE

A detailed application of her views on 'Action and Passion in Chaucer's *Troilus*' (*MÆ*) (see p. 155) leads Georgia Ronan Crampton to a number of interesting conclusions. The three characters 'approach life in distinct psychological modes related to the *topos* of action and suffering'— Troilus as a man of passion, sympathetic, and Pandarus as the doer, 'worldly but never worldly-weary'. Criseyde both suffers and acts; she is generally receptive to a variety of experiences and is presented and perceives through filters—other people, various conventions etc.—but she acts decisively at Deiphebus's house, gaining a new freedom which Fortune will deny.

An intelligent discussion of the

rhetorical function of 'The Audience of Chaucer's *Troilus and Criseyde*' (*Robbins*) by Dieter Mehl stresses that, whatever the 'real' audience, the poem creates its own audience, variously characterized, to pass judgements, note narrative gaps and artificialities, and be alert to a range of responses, thus enabling the poet to encourage the right questioning and go some way towards preventing the wrong sort of question or response from his reader.

Considering 'Processes of characterization in Chaucer's *Troilus and Criseyde*',[22] Ida L. Gordon claims that Chaucer manipulates his characters so that they are at once vehicles of a theme and also the more psychologically credible and complex. Boccaccio's story has been seen as a series of situations in which the characters' responses reveal different aspects of the problem of love, and specifically of the relationship of sexual and universal love, and realism is rarely sacrificed to theme. Characters' responses are linked to the situation by a number of oblique devices, especially by the narrator and consistency here is rarely sacrificed to theme. The characters themselves do not develop, but the reader's evaluation of them does.

William Provost's *The Structure of Chaucer's Troilus and Criseyde*[23] is a description—as opposed to interpretation—of the poem by reference to the distribution of a number of different devices whose occurrences are listed in Appendix-tables. Within

'time-units' Provost distinguishes 'objective' and 'subjective' time, tracing the occurrence of and tensions between the two, while 'narrative units' are marked out by transitions among five narrative modes. The relationship between different kinds of unit consist primarily of a chronological-sequential arrangement, tellingly varied in the later books, and secondarily of patterns distinguishable in terms of form and content. A final chapter discusses structural devices—proems, lyrics, rhetorically elaborated temporal references, dreams, letters, the epilogue—which occur only sporadically at certain points in the narrative.

In considering Chaucer's changes from Boccaccio, Jeffrey Helterman's 'The Masks of Love In *Troilus and Criseyde*' (*CL*) suggests that Chaucer's Troilus undergoes a progression in love from seeing Criseyde as simulacrum, through ascribing a metaphysical value to his love, until, with her departure, he loses her as herself—a progression similar to that in Dante's *Vita Nuova*. To this structure Chaucer brings a Petrarchan style, seen first in Troilus's use of Petrarchan language which prevents him from seeing the value of love; and finally, like Petrarch after Laura's death, Troilus comes to a true understanding of love's worth and sorrow. Examining 'Chaucer's Troilus and Self-Renunciation in Love' (*PLL*), F. Xavier Baron concludes that Troilus's self-renunciation is dominated at first by vanity but later by fatalism, correlating with his progress from shallow lover to one of heroic stature; in achieving this ideal, in contrast to Diomede, Pandarus, and Criseyde, Troilus exemplifies a noble, divine ideal of self-denial.

Daniel Cook prefers Root's text, based on the *beta*-version of *Troilus*

[22] *Studies in Medieval Literature and Languages: in memory of Frederick Whitehead* ed. by W. Rothwell et al. Manchester: Manchester U.P. New York: Barnes & Noble Books. 1973. pp. viii+403.

[23] *The Structure of Chaucer's Troilus and Criseyde*, by William Provost. *Anglistica* XX. Copenhagen: Rosenkilde & Bagger. pp. 120. Dan. krs. 60 (without subscription), krs. 50 (to subscribers).

to that of Robinson and his followers, based on the *gamma*-version, and his discussion of 'The Revision of Chaucer's *Troilus*: The *Beta* Text' (*ChauR*) justifies this preference by a series of comparisons between significantly variant passages from the two versions. After considering the 'Minor Changes in Chaucer's *Troilus and Criseyde*' (*Robbins*) which constitute improvements in language or rhythm, Charles A. Owen Jr discusses the artistic justifications for three instances of cancelled or shifted stanzas in the poem.

Two critics have independently reviewed the evidence for clandestine marriage in the Middle Ages and reached the same conclusion—that Chaucer expected his audience to recognize the relationship between Troilus and Criseyde as one of clandestine marriage rather than of illicit, non-marital love. John B. Maguire's 'The Clandestine Marriage of Troilus and Criseyde' (*ChauR*) draws attention to telling references in the poem, particularly those without Boccaccian counterpart, while Henry Ansgar Kelly's 'Clandestine Marriage and Chaucer's "Troilus"' (*Viator*, 1973) additionally points out other Chaucerian examples.

C. David Benson's 'A Chaucerian Allusion and the Date of the Alliterative "Destruction of Troy"' (*N&Q*) suggests a date of c1400, rather than the more usual c1350–1400, for the *Destruction* on the basis of the reference to and echoes of *Troilus* in the poem. Allen D. Lackey comments on John Hagopian's interpretation (*YW* 36.85) of the comparison with Oedipus in 'Chaucer's *Troilus and Criseyde*, IV, 295–301' (*Ex*, 1973).

In 'Troilus and Oedipus: The Genealogy of an Image' (*ES*) Julia Ebel suggests that Statius's *Thebaid* is the source of an image-pattern of blindness and light culminating in the

analogy of Troilus and Oedipus at IV, 300.

Francis Lee Utley explores 'Chaucer's Troilus and St Paul's Charity' (*Robbins*) by examining the compatibility of Troilus's virtues, attested at six major points in the poem, with the heads of *The Sixtene Poyntis of Charite*, a fifteenth-century poem.

John Warrington's student edition of *Troilus and Criseyde*[24] (*YW* 34.59) now appears in a revised version with introduction by Maldwyn Mills, briefly comparing Chaucer's treatment with that of Boccaccio.

Florence H. Ridley makes 'A Plea for the Middle Scots' (*L and L*), and takes issue with those who compare the Scots poets with Chaucer to the former's detriment; by her own comparison of *Troilus* and Henryson's continuation, she shows that the latter did not imitate, but developed seminal ideas in Chaucer.

4. OTHER WORKS

Writing on 'Now (This), Now (That) and *BD* 646' (*L and L*), Leger Brosnahan comments on the phrase's proverbial origin and its grammatical reference. Robert M. Jordan examines 'The Compositional Structure of the *Book of the Duchess*' (*ChauR*) for an elegy that is 'extraordinarily indirect'. Jordan demonstrates in tabular form that the poem consists of clearly defined sections, which he examines in detail, showing their differing conventions of style and content. He holds that the narrator's dramatic function and characterization were of less importance than his rôle as link between the several parts. In his consideration of 'The *Book of the Duchess*, Melancholy, and that

---

[24] *Geoffrey Chaucer: Troilus and Criseyde*, ed. by John Warrington; revised by Maldwyn Mills. London: Dent. New York: Dutton. pp. xvi+337. £2.50; pa. £1.25.

Eight-year Sickness' (*ChauR*), John M. Hill asserts that the narrator is suffering from head melancholy, supporting this statement by an examination of the symptoms. Such an illness would explain his attitude to the story of Alcioune, and for this sickness the *phisicien* would be sleep. An appendix discusses the re-dating of the poem as a commemorative rather than occasional work. The dating is also the subject of John N. Palmer's 'The Historical Context of the *Book of the Duchess*: a revision' (*ChauR*), citing a letter written by the Count of Flanders, which leads him to date Blanche's death in 1368. Palmer believes as well that the poem was completed by November of that year. Allen D. Lackey comments on the allusion to Jason and Medea found in 'Chaucer's *Book of the Duchess*, 330' (*Ex*). In '*Troilus and Criseide*: The Narrator and the "Olde Bokes"' (*AN&Q*), Michael R. Peed seeks to identify 'the various masks behind which the poet speaks'.

Reginald Berry suggests in 'Chaucer's Eagle and the Element Air' (*UTQ*) another possible iconographic source; air would provide a link between the Eagle and the medium of sound upon which he expounds, as that element was represented by an eagle according to medieval natural science and used in the iconography of the Four Elements. After establishing the characteristics of the genre, Michael R. Kelley looks at 'Chaucer's *House of Fame*: England's Earliest Science Fiction' (*Extrapolation*). The main scientific explanation —which is based on the findings of medieval science—is to be found in the Eagle's words in Book II, and the rest of the narrative depends on this for its plausibility; the other Books also show connexions with the current beliefs. 'A Borrowing from Tibullus in Chaucer's *House of Fame*' (*ChauR*)

is suggested by John W. Carr who believes that the line was derived from a manuscript owned by Salutati. In a group of manuscripts containing an interpolation of the *Roman de la Rose*, Marsyas undergoes a grammatical sex transformation and this was probably Chaucer's source for the story. Such is Alfred David's proposal in 'How Marcia Lost Her Skin: A Note on Chaucer's Mythology' (*L and L*), and he ends with justified warnings against crediting Chaucer and his audience with knowing a great amount of 'learned Christian exegesis of classical mythology' and against overlooking the qualities of humour in Chaucer's versions of the myths. The terms used for various kinds of dream mentioned in 11.7–11 are discussed in 'Una *crux* chauceriana: i sogni nella *House of Fame*' (*Rivista di Letteratura Moderna e Comparate*) by Enrico Giaccherini, who sees in the six terms three contrasted pairs. [M.D.]

H. M. Leicester, Jr's 'The Harmony of Chaucer's *Parlement*: A Dissonant Voice' (*ChauR*) suggests that in seeking the meaning of his personal problem, Chaucer was led into fragmentation rather than unity because the various authoritative traditions to which he appealed were by then so specialized that they pointed in different directions and encouraged the rhetorical flourishes, erudite display, and misplaced emphasis which draw attention to the narrator. The parliament itself stresses individuality against the traditionally unifying and rational figure of Nature, here helpless; and the sense of unity reauthorized by the roundel is sustained only by 'self-conscious self-limitation'. Here problems and techniques of the later works are emerging.

Amant's sleeve-basting, at 95–99 and 104–6 of Chaucer's version, is 'An Iconographic Detail in the *Roman de la Rose* and the Middle English *Romaunt'* discussed by Graham D. Caie (*ChauR*).

In 'The Textual Reliability of Chaucer's Lyrics: *A Complaint to his Lady'* (*M&H*), Paul M. Clogan objects to modern editorial emendations of Chaucer's *Complaint to his Lady* because they destroy the experimental and unfinished quality of 'an exercise in different keys on the conventional theme of unrequited love'.

J. D. North gives a detailed description and explanation of the workings of 'The Astrolabe' (*Scientific American*).

VI

The Earlier Sixteenth Century

WILLIAM TYDEMAN

1. GENERAL

Philip Lee Ralph's unpretentious and helpful guide, *The Renaissance in Perspective*,[1] attempts to 'give concisely both a broad description and an interpretation of its essential character and its relevance for succeeding ages', viewing the Renaissance as a product of the Middle Ages 'not simply in the retention of vestiges of belief and behavior patterns, but in its most striking and triumphant achievements'. A general discussion of conflicting theses concerning the notion of 'rebirth' leads into surveys of the actuality and the ideals of Renaissance Politics, while 'The Condition of Society' involves examination of economic and social forces at work during the period and of the Church, where the peculiar nature of the Renaissance papacy and its relationship to the currents of the age is described. 'Letters and Learning' treats of humanism and the revival of learning, Petrarch and Boccaccio being selected for most detailed treatment; 'The Uses of History' deals with Machiavelli and Guicciardini, education and the printing press. The longest and perhaps best chapter is devoted to the fine arts; 'Views of Man and the Cosmos' presents the Renaissance in the context of the history of ideas, and its surprising deficiency in the two key areas of philosophy and science, although this is regarded as far from negating the value of the thought of

the age. The final chapter, 'Descent from the Summit', views the Renaissance as a turning-point in the course of Western civilization, the culmination of a long and irregular evolution as much as a period when new forces and ideas were coming into being; indeed, 'rather than a rebirth or a new birth, it was the final testament of an exhausted age—less the dawn of a new day than the magnificent sunset of one that was dying'. 'A discerning backward glance sees in the Renaissance a proving ground both for liberating forces that have carried man forward and for disruptive tendencies that have threatened him with the loss of his humanity'.

The Meaning of the Renaissance and the Reformation[2] represents the kind of highly professional general survey which American scholars produce with such skill and regularity: eight specially written chapters by leading experts contribute to a discussion of what the editor sees as predominantly an intellectual revolution. All the essays are followed by excellent selective bibliographies of varying lengths, and there are some pleasing illustrations and two useful maps. Richard DeMolen's stimulating introduction speaks of a movement 'evolutionary in its origins but revolutionary in its effects', tracing its origins to long-term economic causes leading to the medieval commercial

---

[1] *The Renaissance in Perspective*, by Philip Lee Ralph. Bell. pp. xiii+273. £3.

[2] *The Meaning of the Renaissance and the Reformation*, ed. by Richard L. DeMolen. Boston: Houghton Mifflin. pp. xii+385. $5.95.

revolution in Italy, and to social and economic conditions able to support the cultural and artistic phenomenon of the Renaissance. The Protestant Reformation is viewed as 'a reaction against the inconsistency in the ideals of Christianity and in the actual organization of the church and the practices of its members'. Lauro Martines's very factual chapter focuses on the city and the urban environment, concerning itself with 'innovation and the ensemble of innovation' in the Burckhardt tradition: Margaret Aston centres her discussion of the Northern Renaissance on Erasmus, the first European to become the spokesman of a whole generation, and on the influences shaping those northern humanists who by 1520 held the intellectual initiative of the Renaissance. John Headley next provides the longest contribution, an excellent account of the causes, course, and effects of the Continental Reformation, seeing its origin as a 'new apprehension of reality' which raised the issue of authority in the church, and 'thus called into question the whole system of scholastic theology, papal government, and monastic piety'. Professor Headley sees the church failing to respond to 'the impending dissolution of the Christian community caused by the growing territorial states ... the religious needs of an increasingly articulate laity, and a dangerous loss of focus in religious experience'; the resolution lay in a fundamental reinterpretation of authority. Arthur Slavin's survey of the English Reformation lays more emphasis on the Reformation as 'a conscious effort to restore the past', attaching significance to the antecedents of Henry's resistance to the Papacy: 'as Henry VIII slowly abandoned his assent to Rome's power in England, he gave scope to the native desire for reform.

The king's own rebellion was the occasion of the Reformation in England, but not its cause.' John Olin's brief essay on the Counter-Reformation looks at the way the lively awareness of the need for reform in Christian life and society and for more extended spiritual renewal made itself manifest within the framework of the Catholic Church. Richard Reed is less concerned to survey those voyages of discovery leading to the expansion of Europe than to consider some of the basic implications of that expansion, and to examine its effect on the European consciousness, while De Lamar Jensen in 'Power Politics and Diplomacy: 1500–1650' treats of the period as one which saw 'great change and innovation in the purposes and conduct of European affairs', and demonstrates the impact of modern notions of diplomacy on negotiations between nations, notably 'the gradual elaboration of a new concept of international relations and law, based on the larger community of diversity among sovereign nation-states, each with its own national laws within the framework of a common body of laws governing the relationship among them'.

Hester Chapman's latest historical biography *Anne Boleyn*[3] is, like its many predecessors, colourful yet objective, all that is known of Anne's career and personality being set forth with clarity and a minimum of digression. No attempt is made at a radical re-interpretation of the facts or a revolutionary new reading of Anne's character; indeed the writer rarely indulges in speculative psychological probings, an authorial trait which is more than welcome. If Miss Chapman is occasionally beguiled into asserting where more cautious

[3] *Anne Boleyn*, by Hester Chapman. Cape. pp. 244. £3.25.

historians might conjecture, this remains a generally accurate biography which, if rarely startling or revealing, will only occasionally raise scholarly eye-brows. One of Hester Chapman's earlier biographies, *The Sisters of Henry VIII*,[4] has recently been reissued; this study is important in reminding us of the personal qualities and varying fortunes of two further members of the extraordinary Tudor family.

Jasper Ridley's biography of Mary Tudor[5] is competent, straightforward, and unremarkable. The presentation is predominantly factual and a degree of over-simplification is to be expected, but the tone occasionally veers towards that of a school textbook, a persistent danger when a skilled professional historian writes for a popular market. With its wealth of illustrative matter, this study will provide the layman with a reliable general portrait of an intriguing and isolated woman. Fortuitously, an excellent companion-piece is provided by Edward Grierson's animated account of Mary's husband, Philip II of Spain, in *King of Two Worlds*.[6] This consistently illuminating and well-illustrated biography of 'one of the most intriguing and enigmatic men who ever sat on a throne' skilfully portrays the man who in 1554 married Mary in Winchester Cathedral, and Philip emerges as a far more human and sympathetic figure than English tradition usually allows.

Despite its flamboyant main title and its clumsy secondary one, *Statesman and Schemer: William, First Lord Paget, Tudor Minister*[7] by Samuel Rhea Gammon, proves to be a sober and factual chronicle of the career of a born survivor in the hazardous world of Tudor politics, who served five sixteenth-century sovereigns without incurring serious personal danger. Professor Gammon sets out every stage in Paget's progress and every aspect of his official duties with commendable clarity, so that an admirably detailed picture forms of the way in which Tudor government business and diplomatic negotiations were conducted; if the man himself remains a shadowy figure to the end, it is perhaps the inevitable fate of one who seems to have specialized in the art of dogged self-advancement by discreet self-effacement.

An equally thorough but more controversial study of the known facts is Barrett L. Beer's *Northumberland: The Political Career of John Dudley, Earl of Warwick and Duke of Northumberland*,[8] the first scholarly biography of Dudley to be published. Professor Beer offers a radical re-examination of Northumberland's career, viewing as a totality a life often regarded as one of intrigue and selfish ambition, and setting in perspective the traditional legend of 'the wicked duke' who not only tried to divert the royal succession from Mary Tudor in 1553 but who must also be held responsible for the domestic failures of Edward VI's reign. The writer does not regard Northumberland as fundamentally an ambitious man: emerging as the dominant

---

[4] *The Sisters of Henry VIII*, by Hester Chapman. Cape. 1969. Reissued, Bath: Cedric Chivers. pp. 223. £2.80.

[5] *The Life and Times of Mary Tudor*, by Jasper Ridley. Weidenfeld and Nicolson. pp. 224. £2.65.

[6] *King of Two Worlds: Philip II of Spain*, by Edward Grierson. Collins. pp. 240. £4.50.

[7] *Statesman and Schemer: William, First Lord Paget, Tudor Minister*, by Samuel Rhea Gammon. Newton Abbot: David & Charles. 1973. pp. 296. £5.25.

[8] *Northumberland: The Political Career of John Dudley, Earl of Warwick and Duke of Northumberland*, by Barrett L. Beer. Kent, Ohio: Kent State U.P. 1973. pp. xi+235. $10.

figure in English politics as a result of conciliar rejection of Somerset's policies, he was faced with responsibilities for which he was poorly prepared, and struggled with challenges which called for political genius of the highest order. It seems clear that Northumberland assiduously attempted to restore England to health and stability, but whatever the truth, this thought-provoking study will repay careful perusal and judicious consideration.

William E. Wilkie's *The Cardinal Protectors of England: Rome and the Tudors before the Reformation*[9] is an intriguing scholarly survey of Anglo-papal relations between 1485 and 1539, whose chief aim is to examine the personal links between Guilio de' Medici (later Clement VII) and Cardinal Campeggio, and Henry VIII and Wolsey. There is much in this admirable study to interest the general reader as well as the specialist: it brings a great deal of fresh evidence to bear on the much discussed topics of Henry's divorce and the 'breach with Rome'.

The Reformation of Images: Destruction of Art in England, 1535–1660[10] is John Phillips's thoughtful account of the way in which the history of iconoclasm reflected 'the broad social, political, economic and religious revolution that was taking place in Reformation England', and how it 'revealed the full range of human response and motivation as to why images were either preserved, mutilated or destroyed'. Mr Phillips shrewdly observes that 'iconoclasm has been as intense a religious phenomenon as iconolatry: the prohibition and destruction of images is as much a part of religion as the shaping and venerating of them', and proceeds to examine 'the very special role these tangible signs played in medieval life and thought' before discussing the growth of gainful iconoclasm dictated by political and economic motives under Henry VIII, and of its more doctrinaire counterpart under Edward VI. Subsequent chapters concern the restoration of images under Mary, compromise under Elizabeth, a period of transition under James I, and the advent of the 'new Anglicanism' under Charles I. The book ends with the Puritan reaction to Laud's changes, and a summary epilogue where the author contends that 'the reformation of images in England was defined by the larger needs of church and state as institutions and by some profound changes in human consciousness rather than by any genuine intellectual discretion concerning the properties of images'. This is a lively and stimulating study, with some excellent illustrations of the work of both mutilation and restoration.

Michael Foss's *Undreamed Shores: England's Wasted Empire in America*[11] traces Britain's share in opening up the New World, from John Cabot's Newfoundland expedition of 1497 and 'the modest tapestry of English exploration in the reign of Henry VII' to the more grandiose enterprises of Thomas Stukeley, Humphrey Gilbert, and Raleigh. As the author demonstrates from his several examples 'the temper of mind of the Elizabethan adventurer was quite unsuitable for the quiet, patient work of establishing a colony' and *Undreamed Shores* shows how the

[9] *The Cardinal Protectors of England: Rome and the Tudors before the Reformation*, by William E. Wilkie. Cambridge U.P. pp. ix+262. £4.50. $14.50.

[10] *The Reformation of Images: Destruction of Art in England, 1535–1660*, by John Phillips. Berkeley: U of California P. 1973. pp. xiii+228. $11.

[11] *Undreamed Shores: England's Wasted Empire in America*, by Michael Foss. Harrap. pp. 186. £3.75.

would-be colonizers were striving to reconcile impossible opposites. The illustrations, which include a generous selection of John White's delicate water-colours, have been expertly chosen to complement the text, but the lack of a bibliography is a serious omission, especially since there are no footnotes or any acknowledgements of the sources from which Michael Foss has compiled his most readable outline.

I have not seen the collection of essays by various hands grouped together by Robert S. Kinsman under the title *The Darker Vision of the Renaissance: Beyond the Fields of Reason*, and Paul O. Kristeller's *Medieval Aspects of Renaissance Learning* was not available for review.

2. ERASMUS AND MORE

The long-awaited first volume of the University of Toronto's Collected Works of Erasmus in English translation fully justifies many of the superlatives bestowed on it; as Literary Editors of the whole project and editors of the first specimen of a series which will run to some forty-seven volumes, R. A. B. Mynors and D. F. S. Thomson must have felt expectations weighing heavily upon them at times. But *The Correspondence of Erasmus 1484 to 1500*[12] in most respects launches the enterprise worthily on its way: the format is generous and dignified, the text set out with wide margins on good paper, although it is inconvenient to have the verso pages numbered on the inside corners. The letters themselves appear on the same page as the un-

fussy annotations by Wallace K. Ferguson, and are arranged in chronological order as far as it can be ascertained; the translations are based on Allen's texts in the authoritative *Opus epistolarum*. Allen's numbering has also been followed, thus facilitating cross-references, and in the majority of cases Allen's ascriptions of date have been adhered to. Each letter has a brief introduction and notes, often based on Allen's edition but supplemented from more recent scholarship; there is a separate note on coinage and currency from John H. Munro, along with other useful editorial material. Biographical notes are brief but adequate, and there is apparently a Biographical Register in active preparation. The index seems meagre, but we are assured that a fuller index is planned when the correspondence is completed, and that this will list topics and references rather than merely people, places, and titles. The translations themselves have the virtue of readability, although they sometimes err in attempting to render Erasmus's more vivid turns of phrase by rather threadbare modern idioms which considerably weaken the force of the originals. Although one aim of the series is obviously to cater for the non-specialist reader, there is no excuse for omitting in the notes the sources where previous translations may be found for the purposes of comparison, nor for failing to provide details of the present whereabouts of any surviving holographs.

Perhaps the most disappointing feature of the present volume however is Wallace K. Ferguson's introduction, which is little more than a general survey. Professor Ferguson scarcely develops his argument that while Erasmus's letters up to August 1514 form a relatively minor contribution to the intellectual history of

---

[12] *The Correspondence of Erasmus*, Vol. 1: *Letters 1 to 141, 1484 to 1500*, trans. by R. A. B. Mynors and D. F. S. Thomson, annotated by Wallace K. Ferguson. Collected Works of Erasmus. Toronto and Buffalo: U of Toronto P. pp. xxvii + 370. $25. £12.

his age, they none the less cast a particularly revealing light on their author's personality and character. As his essay develops, one realizes with a sense of shock that instead of an introduction to the letters in the first volume, Professor Ferguson is proposing in the course of a mere dozen pages to discuss the whole of Erasmus's epistolary experience. One is not demanding the copious, almost over-conscientious introductory essays which are such a feature of the Yale edition of More for example, but in an edition of this importance and authority, one is entitled to ask for something a little less bland and generalized, and more relevant to those letters actually before the reader. As it is, the present essay is not a satisfactory prologue to the letters of 1484 to 1500, nor a sufficiently comprehensive survey of the correspondence as a whole, and it must unfortunately lead one to qualify one's praise for what is otherwise a most commendable opening performance.

Sister Geraldine Thompson's *Under Pretext of Praise: Satiric Mode in Erasmus' Fiction*[13] concerns a relatively neglected aspect of his work, 'and what it contains of instruction and delight', chiefly treating of *The Praise of Folly*, the colloquies, and the two long dialogues *Julius Exclusus* and *Ciceronianus*, in the light of the view that 'the fictional works are the *exempla* that give life and specificity to the great theories of a great man'. The introduction stresses the three focal points in Professor Thompson's analysis: Erasmus's belief in the teachability of man and in the educator's rôle in bringing him to

humane learning and goodness; the moralistic emphasis of Erasmus's writings and his concern for man as a moral creature; his admirable use of irony (along with other techniques) to point his meaning. But the actual treatment of the fiction is wider-ranging and more richly suggestive than these opening remarks predict: the initial chapter on the general principles of Erasmian satire is a masterly handling of its subject, essaying accurate description while avoiding dogmatic definition, and while offering many insights into the satiric genre in general, demonstrating by discussion and illustration what is uniquely characteristic of Erasmus's art. Part of the author's conclusion is that 'he established and made popular the ironic way of writing, showing irony to be the most flexible and adaptable of figures, and the only figure capable of conveying a satiric message of complexity and even profundity', and her succeeding analyses explore the subtle nature of Erasmus's achievements in the field of satiric fiction and in the colloquies, not all of which are satirical. *The Praise of Folly* is viewed as primarily a satire in which parody, eulogy, and paradox are geared to a serious didactic purpose, that of 'an incisive and serious moral indictment of European society in all its aspects . . . a thoroughly human dramatic monologue, having as its satirical and allegorical device a woman', and an oration pointing to the heavenly Jerusalem. Professor Thompson brings out the multiple nature of the figure of Folly, and is particularly sensitive to the change in tone at the work's conclusion. While the *Praise* is given high commendation, the writer does not underplay what she sees as the weaknesses of the *Julius Exclusus* or the *Querela Pacis*, and she finds the irony of the colloquies

[13] *Under Pretext of Praise: Satiric Mode in Erasmus' Fiction*, by Sister Geraldine Thompson. Erasmus Studies 1. Toronto and Buffalo: U of Toronto P. 1973. pp. xvi+200. $12.50.

less satisfying than that of the *Praise* 'largely because the characters are too knowing . . . the reader rarely has to flex a cerebral muscle of his own'. Above all, this scholarly and penetrating study never forgets the fundamental importance of Erasmus's Christian humanist position, and that even in the less satisfying satires 'there is still some recognition of, and appeal to, the many-sided, complex heart and mind of man'.

In 'The Metamorphoses of Moria: Structure and Meaning in *The Praise of Folly*' (*PMLA*) Wayne A. Rebhorn urges that a satisfactory interpretation of the work must be based on all three sections, and argues that the unity and meaning of *The Praise of Folly* are identical with the metamorphoses of Folly, who in her opening sentences defines her essential power as the power of transformation. Thus while Stultitia in the long first part mingles sympathy and tolerance with witty mockery and occasional annoyance, the middle section is marked by scorn, outrage, and unmitigated invective, which reveals 'the idolatry and futility involved in worshipping this mutable goddess'.

In the final section Folly is once again serious and unironic, and her vision of Christian folly 'adds a new perspective to the *Praise* which transcends the illusory hope of the first section and the horrifying "reality" of the second . . . the spiritual life of heaven . . . is the true reality for man'.

Clarence H. Miller's 'Some Medieval Elements and Structural Unity in Erasmus' *The Praise of Folly*' (*RenQ*) draws attention to the medieval aspects of the *Moria*, suggesting that the work has 'suffered from a too thorough-going victory of the humanist campaign against medieval theology, hagiography, and literature', reminding readers that 'for all its

brilliant rhetorical fanfare, Folly's proem is a reworking of a thoroughly medieval topos, the revival of nature and man in the springtime', and that Erasmus made use of his knowledge of scholastic theology to dispatch his enemies. Conservative theologians found the book infuriating not only for its wit but for its accuracy. However not all the medieval ideas in *Moria* are exposed to ridicule: some of Erasmus's more reactionary views, notably his conservative attitude to the merchant classes, rely significantly on medieval techniques such as the complaint or the satire of estates, and a sense remains that medieval satire and Renaissance paradox have not quite coalesced. P. G. Bietenholz in 'Ambiguity and Consistency in the Work of Erasmus of Rotterdam' (*WascanaR*) challenges the commonly accepted view of the ambiguity in Erasmus's writings, seeing it as 'the humanist's precision instrument for mastering verbal expression in the Latin language', but also as a weapon of self-defence, and as a register of his exceptional awareness of the individual quality implied in the passing of words between two human beings. However, 'he never quite brought himself to be inconsistent . . . for Erasmus ambiguous words were a means of doing justice to the complexity of impressions and situations, but where he really stood on an issue was hardly ever in doubt'.

John F. Fleischauer draws attention to 'A New Sixteenth-Century Translation of Erasmus' (*PBSA*) located in the Charles Patterson Van Pelt library of the University of Pennsylvania, but temporarily misplaced; it is an imperfect copy of an edition of the Latin text of *De Civilitate Morum Puerilium* followed by an English translation of unknown authorship completed with Robert Whittinton's version as it appeared in de Worde's edition of 1532. The evidence leads Fleischauer confidently to attribute publication to John Walley, but dating still remains a problem, although c. 1550 is likely. No guess as to the translator is as yet possible.

The latest volume in the Yale edition of the Complete Works of St Thomas More consists of his Latin translations from Lucian, the 'first fruits' of his Greek studies, splendidly edited by Craig R. Thompson.[14] It represents the first scholarly edition of material which includes Lucian's Greek originals in facsimiles taken from the Aldine edition of 1503 probably used by More, More's versions of the *Cynicus, Menippus, Philopseudes*, and *Tyrannicida*, with English translations supplied from the Loeb versions in an Appendix, and More's dedicatory letter to Thomas Ruthall, with his declamation in reply to the *Tyrannicida*, both with English versions provided by the present editor. Comparison between Lucian's Greek and More's Latin is facilitated by having them printed on facing pages, but anyone requiring help in reading More's work will find constant reference to the Appendix somewhat inconvenient. Opinion will inevitably be divided as to the wisdom of giving preference to the needs of readers wishing to compare More's translation with its source rather than to those in that surely larger group (acknowledged by Professor Thompson as those with 'small Latin and no Greek') who want to read and comprehend what More wrote; at least the problem does not arise with the letter to Ruthall and the reply to Lucian, where the English lies hap-

pily opposite the Latin. Thompson's introduction sets More's translations into the context of the humanists' re-discovery of Greek writers, among whom Lucian became something of a favourite with translators and imitators. Whether Erasmus or More knew Lucian first, and which of them suggested the joint project of translating some of his dialogues is unknown, but not only are the translations and the reply virtually More's earliest surviving Latin writings, they are probably the first of his prose compositions to be published, and apart from a few epigrams, his first writings of any kind to appear in print. In More's lifetime they seem to have been printed more frequently than any other of his works, including *Utopia*. Of especial interest is More's reply to the *Tyrannicida* written in competition with Erasmus and the only surviving example of such a contest between the two friends. By Tudor standards 'More was a careful, conscientious translator, accurate and resourceful: a man who respected his text and wanted to render it correctly'. A large part of Lucian's appeal was due to his varied range, but it was the satirical prose dialogue which proved the ideal medium in which to express his gifts for irony, social criticism, and dramatized conversation, and it was for his cleverness, wit, and entertainment value that More largely admired him. Wisely Professor Thompson is inclined to minimize More's direct debts to Lucian in later writings, preferring to regard any influence as general and pervasive rather than specific, consisting as it does of resemblances of conception, tone, approach, and invention, most notably in the rhetorical use of irony. More never seems to have forgotten the Lucianic dialogues, but there is evidence to suggest that he eventually

[14] Thomas More: *Translations of Lucian*, ed. by Craig R. Thompson. The Complete Works of St Thomas More. Vol. 3. Part I. pp lxxii+218. New Haven and London: Yale U.P. $15.

repudiated his one-time literary favourite, whose works he was the first Englishman to translate into Latin.

One of the most potentially promising books on Thomas More to appear during the year is Sister Mary Edith Willow's study, *An Analysis of the English Poems of St Thomas More*,[15] but despite its disciplined scholarly approach, it is ultimately a disappointment. Originating as a doctoral dissertation, it unfortunately still bears too many marks of its genesis. More wrote twelve poems in English, totalling less than 1,500 lines, and while some readers may not feel that to devote nearly three hundred pages to such a small if important proportion of More's literary output is a further indictment of excessive scholarly specialization, the method of Dr Willow's painstaking analyses, which proceed by accumulating observations rather than by selecting salient features and illuminating them, is far from reassuring. She never fears to state the obvious, and to state it several times if necessary, while too often her commentary seems laboured and without critical point. If the aim was to 'entice' readers to give More's poems 'a fair chance', a rather less prolix method of communicating pleasure should have been found. Unfortunately this is not the end of the matter: as the author remarks 'Thomas More's poetry has not been looked into carefully by the majority of Morean scholars; consequently, it has not been appreciated impartially and criticized objectively', but however true these words may be, the study of early Tudor prosody and rhetoric has not stood still since 1956, the date of the last work cited in the bibliography, and one suspects that the work has not been revised for publication in the light of recent scholarship. Indeed, even judged in the context of twenty years ago, this book has a slightly old-fashioned air, fanciful hypotheses, romantic generalizations, and out-dated concepts marring the thoroughness and precision of the actual analyses themselves. All that is achieved here might have been accomplished in a narrower compass, and given her lack of critical sophistication but undoubted admiration for More's poems, Dr Willow might have been more happily employed in providing us with a well-annotated edition of them.

The first issue of *Moreana* for 1974 is mainly an index for Volumes I to X spanning the years 1963 to 1973. Ten separate indices cover articles in English; articles in French; those in other tongues; reviews in English; those in French; poems; photographs of authors and *amici*; Iconographia (which takes in portraits, cartoons, autographs, facsimiles, etc.); allusions to the Scriptures; a general index of persons and things, in which More's literary works appear under his name, but are listed in chronological order of composition rather than alphabetically. The whole issue is a careful guide to the contents of its thirty-nine predecessors. No 41 begins with an article by John Headley 'On More and the Papacy', criticizing Richard C. Marius's somewhat simplistic view of More's attitude to the papacy as expressed in the Yale edition of the *Confutation of Tyndale's Answer* (*YW* 54. 133–4), and his misconstruction of Headley's own treatment in the *Responsio ad Lutherum* of 1969 (*YW* 50. 139–40). On the basis of a passage in the *Responsio* Marius claims More as a conciliarist, but Headley argues that 'whatever conciliarist strains may lurk in the

[15] *An Analysis of the English Poems of St Thomas More*, by Sister Mary Willow. Bibliotheca Humanistica & Reformatorica. VIII. Nieuwkoop: De Graaf. pp. 285. Hfl. 80.

Responsio, the full weight of More's ecclesiological view lies elsewhere', More maintaining 'that *consensus* is not enough, for if the church is to know itself and to maintain that community and universality, it must have a recognizable touchstone in the papal primacy, divinely founded'. More was never able to expand his affirmation of papal primacy, but 'there persists in a muted undertone the vital adherence to Rome', and from 1523 to his death 'the fact of papal primacy runs as a continuing thread through More's thinking on the church'. Charles Clay Doyle gathers together some Moreana from the period 1604 to 1660; Andrew M. McLean contributes 'A Note on Thomas More and Thomas Starkey' in which he points out affinities and correspondences between More's works and Starkey's *Dialogue between Reginald Pole and Thomas Lupset*, seeing the humanistic emphasis in the latter work as in the tradition of Erasmus and More. However, Starkey's continual concern is with the feasible and the immediate, not with the ideal commonwealth or the perfect courtier; *Utopia* by contrast is an idealistic programme or model for the reform of society, brilliantly characterizing its foibles, yet failing as a practical document for reform. 'The practical aim of Starkey is in sharp contrast to More's poetic vision.' The remainder of the issue is mainly composed of reviews and ephemera, although Richard S. Sylvester's annual newsletter from Yale contains the latest information on the progress of the Yale edition, and André Blanchard prints some interesting 'Poèmes du XVIe Siècle à la mémoire de Thomas More et de John Fisher', complete with French prose translations.

The June issue includes Emile V. Telle's reprint of the 'Eloge de Thomas More par Richard Dinot', the writer being a Protestant pastor who died c. 1590; appropriately Johanna M. Butler's brief 'More in Sixteenth Century France' follows, drawing attention to an allusion to More's death in Maurice Scève's *Délie* (1544), and the connexion is more fully explored in Kenneth Lloyd-Jones's 'Thomas More and Maurice Scève's *Délie*', which addresses itself to the 'background, circumstances and implications' of Scève's reference. In 'Some Reflections on the "Vision" Attributed to Thomas More' Joseph Butkie, Sabita Sankaran, and Donald Vecchiolla advance interpretations of a number of aspects of a 'Vision' poem attributed to More, featured in *Moreana* 37 (*YW* 54. 136). Allusions to Wolsey, More and Fisher, Henry VIII and other figures are detected; the semi-dramatic structure is seen as an original contribution to the genre of vision sonnets. G. P. Garavaglia writes on 'Cresacre and Thomas More during the English Revolution, 1640–1660', while Robert P. Sorlien has successfully tracked down a reference in the work of Lord Henry Howard concerning a remark made by Thomas Cromwell to More ('Howard on Cromwell on More'). Karl Schroeder in 'George Gilbert and the More Fresco of 1583' comments on the issue's cover illustration of the executions of More, Fisher, and Margaret Pole by tracing the career of Gilbert (1555–1583), founder and organizer of the Catholic Association, who financed a secret press in England, and paid for Pomerancio's paintings of English confessors and martyrs in the English College chapel at Rome. Raymond Himelick discusses 'Walter Ralegh and Thomas More: the Uses of Decapitation' and finds More anticipating Ralegh's image of decapitation in 'The Passionate Man's Pilgrimage' in *A Dialogue of Comfort Against Tribulation*: 'Ralegh is graphic and circumstantial where More . . . is laconic; but the conceit is the same. The Catholic martyr must be given credit for precedence; whether for anything more can be only a matter of tentative speculation.' Jacques Gury's '*Sequentia Utopica*', on the relation between the 1516 and 1518 maps of Utopia, the similarity of Utopian cities, and an eighteenth-century account of a Christian Utopia, is of some interest.

The double issue for November starts with Howard Baker's article on 'Thomas More at Oxford', a careful consideration of the evidence for More's Oxford years (probably 1492–4), chiefly in connexion with his collegiate affiliations. In 'Aesthetic Distance in the *Utopia*' Irma Ned Stevens explores the way in which More employs ironic handling of the main characters, paradoxical names, juxtaposition, implication or indirection, and the attribution of explicit criticism of England to the Utopians, to achieve aesthetic distance in his satire. More is able to detach himself further by the fact that 'on the occasions when the direct criticism is not expressed by the Utopians, it is not the author or the character *More* but Hythloday who speaks . . . *More* has merely recorded verbatim Hythloday's "careless simplicity" of speech'. While Hythloday often seems to represent More's own viewpoint, he also serves to distance his creator's sincerely held beliefs: 'just as Hythloday is often a foil for More's presentation of the Utopian view (the norm), so the character *More* sometimes serves as foil for Hythloday's expression of admirable ideas'. Judith Doolin Spikes discusses 'The Book of Thomas More: Structure and Meaning', arguing that the plot is more than a succession of episodes, but a series of variations on the theme of responsibility, upon some aspect of which 'all of the episodic material, major and minor, is designed to reflect or to elaborate'. Timothy J. McCann provides information on 'Catherine Bentley, Great Grand-Daughter of St Thomas More, and her Catholic Connections in Sussex', but an article of more general interest is Louis A. Schuster's 'Reformation Polemic and Renaissance Values' which reflects on the controversy between More and Tyndale after 'four intervening centuries of increasing secularization of religious values' during which 'we have become immunized against the experience of passionate intensity over differences in creed such as fired Reformation Europe'. Schuster reveals Tyndale and More divided by dissimilar temperaments and sensibilities, differences in conditioning and experience, divergent concepts of faith, and opposed anthropologies, and how the 'polemical mode in which the sundering and fragmentation of Christendom was conducted' operates by 'a series of either/or propositions, or mutually exclusive alternatives'. Thus 'the more each side tries to counterbalance the other, the more entrenched either becomes in defending a position representing only a partial truth'. Andrew M. McLean introduces 'Another English Translation of Erasmus' *Coniugium*: Snawsel's Looking Glasse for Maried Folkes (1610)', providing an extract from Snawsel's version together with Erasmus's Latin original. Jacques Gury contributes a brief essay on 'The Abolition of the Rural World in Utopia', which draws our attention to More's remarkable termination of country life in the second half of the first chapter of Book II: 'uprooting the country people, doing away with the professional farmer, obliterating totally the rural world was a revolution never dreamed of before, and which, even nowadays, no one would dare to advocate openly'. But the reason is clear: 'More realized that to break away from the evils of his day, to bring about a true commonwealth, mankind had to tear down the whole fabric of the feudal world even if it meant destroying the rural world first. Henri Gibaud's 'Thomas Morus en Icarie' is primarily concerned with the role assigned to More in Etienne Dolet's *Voyage en Icarie*; Helena Frecker writes of a World Congress in Washington to commemorate the 600th anniversary of Petrarch's death; Richard Sylvester writes again of the St Thomas More Project. The remainder of the issue comprises a large number of reviews, notes, and almost forty pages of *Ephemerides Moreanae*.

Stressing that *Utopia* is in some respects a dream, Michèle Le Doeuff in 'La rêverie dans "Utopia"' (*Revue de Métaphysique et de Morale*, 1973) analyses the imaginary materials which More employs in Book II where features of the island's geography are just as important as the study of its institutions. Le Doeuff emphasizes the enclosed and insulated nature of the island, with its inland gulf like a mirror forming a theatrical stage, and argues that this imaginary geography affirms that the Utopian state, while aware of its own internal harmony and stability, is blind to all else, and contemplates only itself, like Narcissus in the myth. But if More's work is a dream centred on a conception of happiness that excludes the outside world, it becomes a political work simply because the individual cannot be totally self-sufficient, and institutions are unjust; thus More moves on to express his political concern in Book I. Arno Löffler in discussing 'Die Figur des Hythlodaeus in Thomas Mores

"Utopia"' (*GRM*) insists that the Utopian polity is not to be regarded as the blueprint for a perfect state, as Hythloday conceives it, but as a faulty example of human endeavour concerning the ordering of the state and society. He points out that Erasmus regarded More's book as a bright amusing work, not primarily as the model of an ideal state, but as a discussion of the sources of political and social grievances. In this interpretation Hythloday's name, profession, and account of Utopia should alert us to his paradoxical function in the book, and the ideal reader who recognizes the contradictions in the Utopian polity, and is able to distance himself sufficiently to understand the satire and the jokes, and enjoy them, will find that the key to such a stance lies in the figure of Raphael Hythloday.

An Italian edition of *More's Fancies Sports and Merry Tales*[16] is now available, preceded by an excellent if lengthy introductory essay on More's humour and its literary antecedents by Vittorio Gabrieli. I have been unable to see Martin Haley's selection of examples of *Thomas More as Poet*, and C. L. Mee Jr's *Erasmus: The Eye of the Hurricane* was not made available for review.

3. PROSE

Kalyan K. Chatterjee's *In Praise of Learning: John Colet and Literary Humanism in Education*[17] sets out to develop 'a historical study of Colet's intellectual life' and to define his place as the pioneer of a humanist programme of education, using the

---

[16] *Thomas More: Fancies Sports and Merry Tales*, ed. by Vittorio Gabrieli. Bibliotheca Italiana di testi inglesi. 22. Bari: Adriatica Editrice. pp. 261. 4.000 Lire.

[17] *In Praise of Learning: John Colet and Literary Humanism in Education*, by Kalyan K. Chatterjee. New Delhi: Affiliated East-West P. pp. vii+121. Rs. 25.

term 'humanist' to indicate an interest in the study of Greek and Latin writers, including the Church Fathers. The early chapters explore Colet's own education and the evolution of his thought, culminating in his advocacy of the value of a humanist education, the background, origin, and development of which are then discussed. The final chapters deal with his educational notions, his status as a humanist, and with the climax of his educational policy in the founding of St Paul's School where his influential theories were put into practice. Professor Chatterjee brings out the formative influence of English and continental scholarship on Colet, and the impact of Platonic concepts and expressions, many of which he borrowed to elucidate points of Christian theology. He also employed the scholarly methods of the humanists in interpreting the Scriptures, in which exercise he was careful not to depart from his scriptural text, and his exegetical style is clearly affected by the humanist orientation of his scholarship. Colet sought to base Christian theology on the new learning of his age, and as he developed from theologian and exegete to humanist educator, he argued like Erasmus that a complete understanding of the scriptures required an understanding of language itself. Thus he shared the renewed humanistic emphasis on grammar and rhetoric studied in conjunction with classical literature, while his 'intellectual partnership' with Erasmus led to an educational programme which emphasized 'eloquence' and 'good literature' as its twin goals, a programme in which both humanists found 'an answer to the intellectual and moral degradation of Christendom that they detected as a result of the submerging of the old learning . . . Virtuous learning was their alternative to both scholasticism and monasticism'. To Colet literature was not merely an exercise in rhetoric, but also something to be valued for its content, its moral and philosophical aspects as well as its rhetorical structures. Colet's school seems to have been deliberately planned to remedy the state of learning in England by creating an establishment where his unorthodox policies could be developed, and he relied on Erasmus's aid to define and elaborate the programme to be followed there: 'the *raison d'être* of Colet's new school was the introduction of a curriculum that emphasized the new humanistic conception of the value of language and literature in education'. '"Good literature" to Colet represented not only "clene and chast Laten", not only expulsion of "blotterature", but also training in wisdom, good manners and principles, which he considered essential for the propagation of the true notion of the Christian religion . . . His educational aim came to be a humanistic one, not through outright secularism but through his belief that the moral wisdom and intellectual brilliance of the classics was an aid to the conduct of a virtuous and enlightened life.'

Newly reprinted is Henry R. Plomer's study of *Wynkyn de Worde & His Contemporaries from the Death of Caxton to 1535*,[18] first published in 1925 (*YW* 6. 117); among the best-known of this very active group of printers are Richard Pynson, Julian Notary, Robert Copland, John and William Rastell, John Skot, and Thomas Berthelet. Plomer's approach is predominantly factual and descriptive, and to those who are not bibliographical enthusiasts, his book may

[18] *Wynkyn de Worde & His Contemporaries from the Death of Caxton to 1535*, by Henry R. Plomer. Grafton. 1925. Reissued, Folkestone: Dawson. pp. 264. £6.50.

initially appear somewhat dry fare, but in the event Plomer contrives to give a cogent and even engrossing account of the English printing and book trades between 1491 and the death of de Worde in 1535, which has not been superseded by any work since published, although inevitably some points of detail now require modification. Beginning with a picture of the book trade at Caxton's death and the rivalry between native booksellers and their foreign competitors, Plomer proceeds to devote chapters to de Worde's early career, his relations with Caxton whose business he inherited, and to the characteristics of the books he produced in Westminster until he moved his printing-office to Fleet Street in 1500. His output between 1501 and 1520, his rivalry with Pynson and collaboration with Copland, his educational and theological publications, his will, his work as a printer, bookseller, and binder, the nature of his printing devices are all discussed in some detail. From the point of craftsmanship Plomer regards Richard Pynson as the best printer that had appeared in England, and two chapters are devoted to Pynson's productions both before and after he removed to Fleet Street following an affray. Among printers subsequently discussed perhaps the most interesting is John Rastell, not merely for his links with the circle of Thomas More, but for the varied range of his achievements and the vicissitudes of his career: his son William published many of More's writings and several of the plays of John Heywood. The majority of the printers whose work is described were based in London, but a final chapter is concerned with provincial and Scottish presses, among which Oxford, Cambridge, York, and Edinburgh are the leading examples. There was room for a con-

cluding summary to this work, the generous supply of details being more than sufficient to obscure the broad overall picture of printing activity which Plomer was so well qualified to provide, and which non-specialist readers would surely have welcomed.

In the University of Exeter's Medieval English Texts series comes a pleasant facsimile edition of Wynkyn de Worde's *Gesta Romanorum*,[19] printed in about 1510; in a rather terse prefatory note Ronald Tamplin points out that de Worde's edition of forty-three of the stories from the whole 'has the virtue of being an authentic late medieval story-collection of manageable size, rather than a modern selection of stories from a larger body made in response to a modern sensibility. It indicates medieval allegorical method and romance preoccupations, holding story-material and moralization in an impressive balance.' The text is printed from the unique copy in the possession of St John's College, Cambridge, with pagination added, and is an excellent and inexpensive reminder of the nature of the early English printed book. However, the reproduction of illegible words (pp. 33, 75, 84, 134, 142) and even the occasional passage (pp. 82, 98, 149) is a reminder of one occasional drawback with cheap facsimiles which lack textual apparatus: editorial assistance is sometimes necessary if we are to read them without frustration. Also available is a reproduction of a 1595 version of the *Gesta Romanorum* 'newly persued by Richard Robinson.'[20]

[19] *Wynkyn de Worde's Gesta Romanorum*, ed. by Ronald Tamplin. Exeter Medieval English Texts. U of Exeter. pp. viii+162. £1.
[20] *Gesta Romanorum: a record of auncient histories newly perused by Richard Robinson* (1595). Introduction by John Weld. New York: Scholars' Facsimiles and Reprints. 1973. pp. ix+159. $25.

George L. Scheper in 'Reformation Attitudes toward Allegory and the Song of Songs' (*PMLA*) reveals that while traditional allegorization rested secure during the Reformation, fundamental differences between medieval and Protestant spirituality are manifested in commentaries on the Song of Songs, the *locus classicus* of the allegorical interpretation of Scripture, and that they stem from basically different interpretations of the nuptial metaphor. The attitudes towards allegory do not differ fundamentally: most Protestants continued the traditional reading that viewed the Song as a dialogue between Christ and the Church or the faithful soul. However, at the Reformation 'the aptness of the nuptial metaphor in terms of the moral, domestic virtues of Christian marriage' is developed; 'the sexual interpretation of the allegory is only hinted at' so that in the Protestant commentaries we witness 'the supplanting of a mystical, sacramental spirituality by a more rationalistic and moralistic Christian spirit'.

Patricia S. Barry in 'The Four Elements and *The Governour*' (*Wascana R*) demonstrates how popular social theory became involved with symbolism and allegory in sixteenth-century England; seeing its English origins in the interlude of *The Nature of the Four Elements* which is 'largely an illustrated lecture and dramatized sermon in verse' in which earth, air, fire, and water are given a life of their own, she goes on to point out how Elyot in the first four pages of *The Governour* accomplishes an identification of the Four Elements with living beings, expanding on the notion enough to demonstrate what kinds of creatures an Englishman might have had in mind when using the elements as their symbols. The Four Elements seem to have possessed for Elyot a

graduated social value, and his identification of them with the strata of the social order squeezed from the old Three Estates of the Realm the appearance of four new degrees of men. The new estate, the gentry of governors and magistrates, was now shown to share the semi-divine authority of the king, and Elyot's 'sanctification of a class of humdrum civic officials through whom celestial influences could reach the earth-bound English' allowed some of his countrymen 'a glorious, if fictitious, prospect of the universe in keeping with Renaissance values and modes of thought'.

Alvin Vos in discussing 'The Formation of Roger Ascham's Prose Style' (*SP*) is inclined to dispute that Isocrates is the model for 'Ascham's rhetorical periods', Ascham's known admiration of the Greek orator and the apparent similarity of their styles notwithstanding. Vos believes that 'the force of Cicero in the development of Ascham's prose, and thus of Renaissance prose generally, is underestimated' and he proceeds to demonstrate that 'Ascham's chief model is his favorite author Cicero, as mediated by his mentor John Sturm', who valued the early Cicero for his *concinnitas* ('neatness' or 'symmetry') and bequeathed his predilection to Ascham. In Vos's opinion 'in Ascham's admiration for the early, more Gorgian Cicero ... lies the most obvious and convincing rationale for the style of his rhetorical periods ... All the Isocratean elements of his style can be found in Cicero, who is, after all, Ascham's first love.'

Pamela M. Black in 'Matthew Parker's Search for Cranmer's "great notable written books"' (*Library*) provides an interesting account of Parker's success in 1563 in enlisting the help of the Privy Council in recovering two books of Cranmer's writings from Dr Stephen Nevinson, then Ecclesiastical Commissioner for Canterbury, the two books now styled as British Museum MSS Royal 7 B xi and xii. She then proceeds to trace how the books might have come into Nevinson's hands, exploring the relationship between the printer Reyner Wolfe, and Cranmer and Nevinson respectively. Wolfe as printer of several of Cranmer's works may have enjoyed his special protection and patronage, and as a keen collector of manuscripts Wolfe may have taken custody of Cranmer's two commonplace books. Nevinson was Wolfe's son-in-law, and it would have been natural for him to have received the books from his father-in-law, especially as he was an authority on ecclesiastical history and canon law. Thus his claim to the books was a valid one.

4 POETRY

S. K. Heninger Jr's learned and lively study, *Touches of Sweet Harmony: Pythagorean Cosmology and Renaissance Poetics*,[21] seeks to reconstruct in all its ramifications 'a doctrine which was prominent in the renaissance', most notably in its cosmological notion of a divinely ordered universe, and to throw light on the modes of thought which it induced, particularly the nature of a poetics derived from such a doctrine. 'Many renaissance authors, including some of the best, were eager proponents of the prevailing cosmology. With extraordinary optimism, they conceived of their works as autonomous art objects that imaged the perfection of the cosmos. They reproduced the infinite variety of the

universe in their subject matter and the natural processes of the universe in their poetic techniques. They sought to create literary microcosmoi.' Starting with the Pythagorean commonplace of the music of the spheres and the Renaissance notion that 'art was intended to reflect and reveal these touches of sweet harmony which infuse our universe', the author's introductory chapter deals with the inter-relationship between cosmological assumptions and theories of art, and argues that we must decide 'what cosmology is operative for any theory of art before we begin constructing its esthetics and applying it to individual works . . . determining an author's cosmology is prerequisite to understanding his work'. The main body of the book begins with a summary of the state of Renaissance knowledge of Pythagoras, and a survey of the chief available materials purveying Pythagorean beliefs. In Part II under such headings as 'Numbers', 'Cosmos', 'Concepts of Deity and of Time', 'Occult Sciences', and 'Moral Philosophy' the nature of the Pythagorean tenets on those topics is reconstructed, although the doctrine was of course transmitted as a complete and self-consistent body of thought. Part III examines a few of the aesthetic assumptions arising from Pythagorean cosmology: 'Poet as Maker' considers the view that the poet is a creator acting in the likeness of the godhead; 'Metaphor as Cosmic Correspondence' treats of the notion of metaphor as dependent upon correspondences between the various levels of creation, while 'Poem as Literary Microcosm' studies the idea that the poem serves as a microcosm in literary form. The whole work is written with enviable ease and lucidity, and ranges widely in the fields of Renaissance literature and learning; its illustrations both graphic and

[21] *Touches of Sweet Harmony: Pythagorean Cosmology and Renaissance Poetics*, by S. K. Heninger Jr. San Marino: The Huntington Library. pp. xvii+446. $19.50.

literary are excellently chosen, and *Touches of Sweet Harmony* can be recommended as a most valuable and enlightening addition to the study of Renaissance poetry and ideas.

Forty-six years after the appearance of W. E. Mead's E.E.T.S. edition of Stephen Hawes's *The Pastime of Pleasure* (*YW* 9. 116–7) comes its companion volume, *The Minor Poems* edited by Florence W. Gluck and Alice B. Morgan,[22] which brings together Hawes's shorter poems for the first time. Indeed it is also the first occasion on which the four poems in the present volume have ever been edited, three of them having been reprinted only once since the original sixteenth-century editions appeared, and the fourth existing only in a unique print of 1515 housed in a private collection until 1938. Thus many readers are likely to be encountering some or all of Hawes's shorter pieces for the first time, and they could hardly hope for a more scholarly presentation than that offered by the present edition. The four poems are *The Example of Vertu*, 'the first chivalric allegory in English'; a versified sermon *The Conuercyon of Swerers*; *A Ioyfull Medytacyon* written for the coronation of Henry VIII; *The Conforte of Louers*, a visionary consolation, at least in form. A biographical note outlines all that is known of Hawes's apparently short life, and bibliographical notes list the various printed editions and manuscript extracts which are extant, together with two further attributions to Hawes; the illustrations, textual notes, and glossary are first-rate. A sympathetic and judicious introduction begins with a frank appraisal of Hawes's metrical usage,

[22] Stephen Hawes: *The Minor Poems*, ed. by Florence W. Gluck and Alice B. Morgan. Early English Text Society. 271. Oxford U.P. pp. xlviii+178. £2.50.

admitting that 'it is not the variations from a norm which offend, so much as the absence, in general, of any norm at all', and that 'any attempt to classify Hawes's metre seems doomed to failure', concluding with engaging honesty that after all the rehabilitatory theories have been examined, 'the verse of Hawes and his contemporaries will continue to appear metrically deficient'. Hawes allowed the low metrical standards of his day to make him careless: 'in his handling of metre, as in his use of syntax or his treatment of allegory, Hawes was willing to do only enough to place himself in the already accepted tradition'. In matters of grammar and syntax Hawes was of his age: 'in the poetry we are considering, grammatical disorder is sufficient to make the reader uncertain where he is in the progression of thought', although, as with his use of metre, Hawes can occasionally reveal a degree of competence too often negated elsewhere. His lack of technical strength as a stylist is further undermined by the weakness and conventionality of his poetic figures: his images are generally trite, his adjectives vague and imprecise, while 'tags and fillers' are employed to excess. His general carelessness over such matters of technical organization contrasts with his evident concern for aureation, which at least 'provides relief from nebulosity'. The editors prefer however to regard Hawes as a traditional poet occasionally stumbling into novelty, rather than as a pioneer, 'consciously altering his verse to meet new challenges and to attract new audiences': 'in the larger area of genre he is persistently medieval ... In matters of poetic technique he is further allied with the fifteenth century: at the same time, it is possible to find portents of the future in most of Hawes's poems'. Of these the editors find the use of the knight engaged in a symbolic but secular quest the most important, but suggest that when he wished to exploit a new theme, Hawes was hampered by conventions he was content to employ on other occasions. Thus in the allegorical poems he yoked together 'two traditions which were moving in opposite directions', the dying romance and the changing allegory, which was now developing along secular, political, and realistic lines. 'Despite his conscious stance of looking backward, Hawes was inevitably moving forward, urged on by pressures to which he responded, it would seem, quite unconsciously', and although he emerges as 'a literary conservative, content with the traditional forms of his art', yet he also exemplifies trends which would ultimately alter those forms. 'He is a splendid representative of the transitional quality of the early Tudor period: his work displays the insufficiencies of the medieval conventions and the unconscious attitudes which led to the innovations of the Renaissance.'

Penelope Schott Starkey in 'Gavin Douglas's *Eneados*: Dilemmas in the Nature Prologues' (*SSL* 1973), describing how in the thirteen original prologues and four concluding sections Douglas speaks with an individual voice, offers a re-reading of the three so-called nature prologues in order to show that the nature paintings of winter, spring, and summer exist not merely for their own sake but to lead into issues with which the poet is preoccupied. Literary conventions and vignettes of the outside world are a preliminary to a presentation of the inner world of the poet's mind as it grapples with the conflict of vocation and the desire for literary fame, a dilemma experienced by many 'clerkis' of the Middle Ages.

Thus it is the 'relationship of the man to his work which shapes these nature prologues ... they provide a conventional framework in which Douglas reveals and attempts to work out his own conflicts and goals'. Denna Delmar Evans's 'Gavin Douglas and the Selden B 24 Manuscript' (*SSL* 1973) suggests the likelihood of Douglas's knowledge of Chaucer having stemmed from the Selden manuscript once belonging to Lord Henry of Sinclair, who may possibly have been the cousin 'Sanct Clair' who urged Douglas to translate the *Aeneid*. Among its Chaucerian items the manuscript contains the *Legend of Good Women*, which was first published in 1532, but which Douglas alludes to in 1512 or 1513, a factor increasing the probability that he was familiar with the Selden B 24 text. A. S. G. Edwards notes a verbal resemblance between 'Douglas's "Palice of Honour" and Lydgate's "Fall of Princes"' (*N&Q*), Douglas's lines 1673–4 seemingly deriving from lines 811–2 of Book V of Lydgate's poem.

Felicity Riddy's '*Squyer Meldrum* and the Romance of Chivalry' (*YES*) studies the manner in which Lindsay distances the Squyer from the romance tradition, thus rendering the poem more than an exercise in nostalgia, and Meldrum's life not simply an expression of chivalry in action but a commentary on it. Lindsay creates within the decorum of a received style a manner flexible enough to encompass a whole range of perspectives on romance; 'the variations of tone in the *Historie* ... are the necessary outcome of Lindsay's attempt to maintain an equilibrium between a poetic vision of life and life itself; during the course of the poem the vision is obliterated and something more prosaic but no less honourable offered in its place'. The *Historie* presupposes an audience thoroughly familiar with romance as a genre and alert to the poem's allusiveness, but in turning Meldrum into a romance hero, 'Lindsay reveals the simplifications of that poetry for what they are . . . as the poem proceeds we are made more and more clearly aware that romance is an imperfect paradigm of ife . . . The way in which the *Historie* honours, laughs at, and in the end discards romance is an acknowledgement of the growth in the sixteenth century of new evaluations of the nature of the good life that render the old fictions obsolete'.

In 'Skelton's *Collyn Clout*: Visions of Perfectibility' (*PQ*) Kenneth John Atchity contends that the 'various levels of human awareness' in the poem 'can be placed in perspective by considering the Latin epigraphs which Skelton set before and after his poem'. Careful notice of the epigraphs can reconcile the tensions in *Collyn Clout* and illuminate its structure, the final example in particular suggesting that the poem's tensions are conceived by Skelton as 'ephemeral manifestations' of the central antithesis between perfection and imperfection, and that 'the reconciliation of the imperfect and the perfect is in the poet's recognition that there are *three* levels of perfection', a delineation given body by reference to Psalm 94. 'The parallels between the psalm and *Collyn Clout* are so impressive that to neglect them is to miss what may well be the most profound expression of Skelton's satirical vision'. V. J. Scattergood in 'Skelton's "Ryotte": "A Rusty Gallande"' (*N&Q*) points out affinities between Ryotte in *The Bowge of Courte* and the many impecunious but extravagantly dressed gallants frequently mocked in late medieval satire. Almost all Ryotte's characteristics are those of the traditional gallant: his fashionably short gown, his dagger, his empty purse, his drinking and dicing, his lechery, his Francophile tastes.

By comparison with other works in the Critical Heritage series, Patricia Thomson's volume on Sir Thomas Wyatt[23] appears disappointingly slight; although one rapidly realizes that she has reproduced much of the relevant criticism that exists prior to 1954, the point at which she terminates her selection with an extract from C. S. Lewis's *Oxford History*, one cannot avoid wishing for more. Of course there is practically no criticism available from the period of Wyatt's lifetime, and thereafter all too little of value until almost the late nineteenth century; even in the present century it may be said that only in the last thirty years has Wyatt's work been discussed at all extensively. The editor's brief introduction traces Wyatt's critical fortunes and sets her extracts in a context of sorts, but merely sketches the post-war expansion of interest in the verse and prose which has produced the work of Otto Hietsch, D. W. Harding, Kenneth Muir, H. A. Mason, Raymond Southall, and Patricia Thomson herself. The earliest passages reprinted are from the preface to Wyatt's translation *The Quyete of Mynde*, and from Leland's *Naeniae* which might surely have been reproduced in its entirety; Surrey's tributes are followed by those of Tottel, and Sackville in *A Myrroure for Magistrates*; the scattered references contained in Puttenham's *Arte of English Poesie* are usefully gathered together, but Ascham's remarks in *The Scholemaster* (1570) might have been worth more than an allusion in the introduction. The most serious gap in the

[23] *Wyatt: The Critical Heritage*, ed. by Patricia Thomson. The Critical Heritage Series. Routledge & Kegan Paul. pp. ix+186. £4.50.

collection occurs between Drayton's tribute of 1627 and Thomas Warton in 1781; if Thomas Fuller and David Lloyd are unreliable witnesses, Cibber's *Lives of the Poets* (1753) and Horace Walpole's *Miscellaneous Antiquities* II (1772) could have supplied two sufficiently interesting extracts. G. F. Nott and Robert Bell are rightly featured as the best of the earlier nineteenth-century critics, but space might have been found for parts of Alexander Chalmers's essay of 1810, printed in an edition of *The Works of the English Poets*, and for Gilfillan (1858), the excellence of whose brief comments is tantalizingly referred to, while Palsgrave's notes on the Aldine Wyatt might have been set out fully. J. Churton Collins's introduction to *The English Poets* (1880) is ignored, and W. E. Simonds perhaps deserves a fuller hearing; although none would quarrel with the selection of W. J. Courthope as the leading late Victorian, one might argue that the observations of Ten Brink, J. J. Jusserand, or Harold Child in the *Cambridge History* were at least as valuable as Agnes K. Foxwell's highly subjective, biography-ridden, even fanciful remarks of 1913. No-one would dispute the remainder of the choices of J. M. Berdan, Tillyard, the *T.L.S.* review of the latter, and lastly Lewis, but it seems strange to have omitted E. K. Chambers's fine essay of 1933, and if the terminal point is to be 1954, then surely it is even more peculiar to have left out H. Hallett Smith's splendid piece on 'The Art of Thomas Wyatt' (*HLQ*) and D. W. Harding's sensitive 'The Rhythmical Intention of Wyatt's Poetry' (*Scrutiny*) both published in 1946, and praised in the editor's introduction? Kenneth Muir's 1949 introduction to his Muses' Library edition was presumably also available for inclusion.

The editor of a collection such as the present one is faced with a difficult task of selection, and where modern criticism is involved, costly royalties can sometimes become an intrusive factor in the final choice. But in a series which has generally been notable for its relatively comprehensive coverage of the available material, this volume on Wyatt, thin as it must inevitably be, might have included more and still avoided obesity. The bibliography which over-scrupulously cites only two works as 'of use in determining extremes of recent criticism' is sadly inadequate.

Thomas A. Hannen's 'The Humanism of Sir Thomas Wyatt' forms the second chapter of Thomas O. Sloan and Raymond B. Waddington's collection of excellent unpublished essays entitled *The Rhetoric of Renaissance Poetry from Wyatt to Milton*,[24] each of which seeks to examine some aspect of English Renaissance poetry in the context of rhetorical technique. Hannen devotes twenty pages to modifying H. A. Mason's view that Wyatt's humanism is chiefly manifested in his interest in translation, which 'carries across' basic human values from one culture to another, continually renewing the tradition: he emphasizes instead the poet's concern for the problem of bringing to public life the wisdom and stability usually found only in philosophy, and this is seen as more effectively defining his humanism. Regarding the true humanist's goal as 'an eloquence that would combine wisdom with rhetorical skill so as to produce virtuous action in both speaker and audience', and the ideal of eloquence as becoming harder to achieve once a humanist

[24] *The Rhetoric of Renaissance Poetry from Wyatt to Milton*, ed. by Thomas O. Sloan and Raymond B. Waddington. Berkeley: U of California P. pp. vi+247. $10.

feels impelled to a more direct involvement in practical affairs, Hannen sees Wyatt's agony resulting from his attempts to 'find a way to maintain his integrity while he continues to be fully involved in the ever-changing patterns of court intrigue'. 'Wyatt is not a saint reluctantly dealing with the world; he is an active courtier trying to remain a decent man, and a poet trying to find an honest and appropriate stance towards his experience.' Analyses of 'Ys yt possible' and 'It may be good, like it who list' suggest that for Wyatt 'rhetoric could never have meant only the art of *belles-lettres* or a dusty subject for schoolbooks. It was a subject for deep moral concern and sometimes, at the dangerous court, the science of self-preservation'. Furthermore, 'by restricting the term 'Humanism' to translation, Mason obscured an important continuity in Wyatt's work—his attempt, which he shared with all the important humanists, to find an eloquence that would reconcile thought and action so as to create a human society in which a man could participate without losing his self-respect'.

Wyatt's verse also features in Robert H. Deming's complex if stimulating discussion of 'Love and Knowledge in the Renaissance Lyric' (*TSLL*) which examines the concept of the self in English Renaissance lyrics and the relationship between self-conscious lyricism and an acceptable kind of knowledge, seeing lyric poetry which figures forth the consciousness of self in acts of loving and knowing as becoming poetry of self-knowledge. 'For the "object" that the love-poet desires to love and to know is his own "inner capacity" and his own "inner reality", defined in time and the world but especially in the wholeness of his mind ... if we wish to learn "why and how" Renaissance poets made their poems, we must consider poetry as a means of knowing (an epistemological structure) rather than as an object of knowledge. We must further consider the poetry as models of self-discovery and self-knowing and as models descriptive of the process of gaining self-knowledge.' It is in love poetry especially that the Renaissance poet attempts to harmonize the essential dilemma of the duality of his existence, to resolve the warfare between man's rational part and the 'passionate nature'.

In 'A Sonnet of Anne Boleyn by Wyatt' (*RES*) Richard Leighton Greene discusses 'Grudge on who liste, this ys my lott', 'a first-person lyric in the verse-form of the medieval carol which has a young woman as its speaker', observing that the first line of its burden is 'an unmistakable translation' of the motto or device used on the livery of Anne Boleyn's servants in 1530: 'Ainsi sera, groigne qui groigne'. 'The use of this motto as the burden of the carol can hardly be coincidental': the speaker represents Anne, but there is no reason to suppose that she was the actual author. The carol probably refers to Anne's love for Henry VIII at the time, and 'thus understood, becomes a striking example of the Tudor lyric which is not a general or fictitious and conventional love song, but which is connected with a real social situation'. 'Wyatt and Petrarch: A Puzzle in Prosody' (*JEGP*) by Robert B. Ogle returns to the baffling question of the so-called metrical and rhythmical roughness of Wyatt's translations from Petrarch, and suggests that the Italian in his sonnets and Wyatt in his versions of them were often imitating 'a classical rhythm which they knew well ... the rhythmic patterns called *logaoedic* because they seemed to combine effects of poetry and prose'. Since Wyatt was capable of 'smooth' versification and not infrequently fails to achieve it in the Petrarchan sonnets, it is at least arguable that 'he was here trying for other poetic effects', and in this context the influence of Italian and classical prosodic modes is at least plausible. Ogle proceeds to demonstrate the recurrent metrical similarity between Petrarch's sonnets and Wyatt's versions, generally explicable in the common prosody of the ancient logaoedic rhythms, and that Wyatt was apparently 'primarily interested in conveying accurately in English both Petrarch's meaning and his verse-patterns. Raymond Southall's 'Wyatt and Kytson' (N&Q) explains the ironic advice given in Wyatt's third satire, not to lend 'Onles it be as to a dogge a chese', as having reference to the emetic effect of a cheese on a dog who 'returns' it with interest! Southall supports Nott's opinion that Sir Thomas Kytson is alluded to in the poem: as a Freeman of the Mercers' Company and of the Merchant Adventurers, Sheriff of London and a Knight in 1533, he represents just the kind of notable upstart the poet refers to in the satire.

Walter R. Davis's discussion of 'Contexts in Surrey's Poetry' (ELR) explores the poet's pursuit of wholeness and singleness of effect, bringing out Surrey's concern for the total effect of a poem rather than for sharp detail, and for the interrelation of the individual human being with his natural context. For Thomas Warton Surrey was 'the first English classical poet', and his attempt to relate the classical past to the present, both in his translations from Virgil and in his original poems, is part of his classicism. In the elegiac poems in particular 'we find an impressive fusion of broad objectivity with intense personal feeling', and Davis concludes that 'the richness of his poetic output

depends, not on the delineation of intense feeling detached from context in order to be fully explored, but rather upon the evocation of context in order to examine feelings in their fullest light ... it reaches out to include in its scope past times both distant and near, the world of nature, and the nature of poetic traditions'. Priscilla Bawcutt in 'Douglas and Surrey: Translators of Virgil' (E&S) considers some of the stylistic differences between these earliest and most successful sixteenth-century translators, and 'the relation between their styles and their aims and methods as translators'. Both based their versions directly on the Latin original as it appeared in sixteenth-century editions, which often accounts for apparent blunders in translating, but while Surrey is terse and economical, striving for Virgilian brevity and an innovative style, Douglas is leisurely and ample, assimilating Virgil to already existing narrative modes. What appears as diffuseness is often an attempt to catch the fullness of Virgil's meaning, his poem giving the impression of being translation and running commentary all in one, and he is more responsive than Surrey to Virgil's linguistic subtlety. 'At his best Surrey mirrors in his own work the polished surface of Virgil. Douglas, at his best, penetrates beneath the surface and conveys something of Virgil's mysterious latencies of feeling.'

A. S. G. Edwards has three articles on Cavendish's *Metrical Visions*. 'The Date of George Cavendish's *Metrical Visions*' (PQ) challenges the assumption that the *Visions* were composed in the late 1550s, and argues from a re-examination of the available evidence that the poems antedate *A Myrroure for Magistrates*, the two 1554 editions of the *Fall of Princes*, and Cavendish's *Life of Wolsey*. The

Metrical Visions seem to have been begun no earlier than June 1552 or 1553, and not to have been worked on between the middle of 1554 and the end of Mary's reign, a fair copy being completed by 24 June 1558, to which additions were made after 17 November 1558. Thus Cavendish emerges as the precursor rather than the imitator of *A Myrroure for Magistrates*. In 'The Dugdale Manuscript of George Cavendish's *Metrical Visions*' (*PBSA*) Edwards discusses the copy of *Metrical Visions* in Bodleian Library MS Dugdale 28, a manuscript which has unaccountably escaped the notice of all editors of Cavendish's poems. It is clear that the Dugdale version was copied from that in the British Museum Library MS Egerton 2402, the autograph manuscript, but textually Dugdale contains a number of changes, which 'do seem to impose a firmer syntactical and grammatical control . . . reducing the redundancies and confusions of Cavendish's style', and a number of readings introduced into Dugdale seem to confirm the apparent evidence of scribal intervention for these changes. In 'The Author as Scribe: Cavendish's Metrical Visions and MS Egerton 2402' (*Library*) Edwards argues that the version of the *Visions* in the Egerton manuscript is a fair copy embodying final authorial intention. The careful presentation and attention to physical detail suggests a finalized text, while the frequent corrections are of initial transcriptional errors rather than revisions. The majority of other alterations involve corrections to the rhyme scheme. The Egerton text 'points up the clear necessity for an editor to recognize the potential for authorial fallibility even in an autograph manuscript'.

David Scott Kastan in 'An Early English Metrical Psalm: Elizabeth's or John Bale's?' (*N&Q*) queries the ascription of a metaphrase of Psalm 13 (A. V. 14) appearing at the end of Elizabeth I's translation *A Godly Medytacyon of the Christen Sowle*, published in Wesel in 1548. Bale appears to have seen the work into print, contributing an extended dedication and conclusion, and not only did he write Psalm metaphrases, but the metaphrase of Psalm 13 appears in Bale's *Expostulation or Compleynte Agaynste the Blasphemyes of a Franticke Papyst of Hamshyre* of 1552: there seems little doubt of Bale's authorship therefore.

Normand Berlin's workmanlike study of Thomas Sackville[25] is divided into seven chapters, four of which deal with the *Mirror for Magistrates* and Sackville's contributions to it, the *Induction* and the *Complaint of Henry, Duke of Buckingham*. There is a brief survey of Sackville's career, an account of the genesis, history, and purpose of the *Mirror*, and a discussion of Sackville's borrowings, but the central chapters are devoted to a detailed examination of the two poems which, although never arresting or especially rigorous as criticism, does succeed in conveying something of the quality of the verse and in illuminating its techniques. In addition the author shrewdly diagnoses the most important distinction between the poems: 'the *Induction* states the didactic intent and presents what is essentially a descriptive mood piece; but the *Complaint* states its didactic intent again and again, and never forgets it. For this reason, the second poem contains more maxims, more lesson-teaching, aphorisms, more exempla, and has less description, less color, less variety . . . But it is perfectly suited to its author's intent, and has its own dimension of

[25] *Thomas Sackville*, by Normand Berlin. Twayne's English Authors. 165. New York: Twayne. pp. 140. $6.95.

worth.' This is generally a sensible and careful study, but it is strange that Virgil's epic should appear as the 'Aeniad' on no less than six occasions.

The *Induction* is among those 'Mirrors of Mutability: Winter Landscapes in Tudor Poetry' (*ELR*) discussed by Alan Bradford, who sees the winter landscape as invariably emblematic of 'that aspect of the human condition that so preoccupied the Renaissance imagination', and he highlights the astonishing extent of parallel developments within the framework of a narrow and well-defined convention by citing an anonymous parodic moralization of a Surrey poem from the Arundel Harington manuscript, and Shakespeare's sonnet 73. Sackville's poem, adjudged to be 'one of the first truly great Elizabethan poems', is found to be indebted to the Arundel Harington piece, though other sources including Douglas's seventh prologue and Lindsay's *Dreme* are indicated as part of the poem's background tradition. 'Sackville described his winter setting in terms of a poetic diction and a system of imagery that were the common currency of pre-Spenserian Tudor verse.' However Sackville's is the most important of all winter landscapes in Tudor poetry, because 'without being profoundly original, it nevertheless subsumes its analogues by virtue of its definitive eclecticism'.

5. DRAMA

J. A. B. Somerset has made a useful selection of *Four Tudor Interludes*[26] for the Athlone Renaissance Library, although the principle on which *Mankind*, Heywood's *Play of Love, Lusty Juventus*, and *Like Will to Like* were chosen in preference to

[26] *Four Tudor Interludes*, ed. by J. A. B. Somerset. Athlone P. pp viii+184. £4. £1.75 paperback.

other plays is not revealed. Somerset remarks that the choice was not easy, 'since so many other early interludes remain relatively inaccessible to students and readers'; however an extract from *Mankind* and the whole of *Like Will to Like* appear in Peter Happé's Penguin edition of *Tudor Interludes* (*YW* 53. 142–3), albeit in unmodernized texts. There is luckily no overlap with Schell and Shuchter's anthology (*YW* 50. 115), although David Bevington's promised *Medieval Drama* will include the whole of *Mankind*.

These reservations aside, *Four Tudor Interludes* is a very satisfactory piece of editing: the copy-texts are the earliest original versions supplied by the Macro manuscript, Rastell's 1534 folio of *A Play of Love*, Vele's quarto of *Lusty Juventus* (c. 1550), and Allde's quarto of *Like Will to Like*. The texts are generally modernized, although archaic forms are preserved where a word is obsolete or where rhyme or metre dictates it. The editor adds a few indications of exits and entrances, and gaps in the text of *Lusty Juventus* are supplied from the second quarto. The plays themselves are set out generously, although all annotation appears at the back of the volume and there is no separate glossary. The helpful but non-technical introduction sets out to argue the vitality and versatility of the interlude form, demonstrating how the devices of allegory are capable of modification to suit many dramatic requirements, from theological debate to social satire. 'The plays strive for relevance to the issues of the day, and present moral and ethical problems vividly through polarized clashes of argument and combat'; at the same time they are popular theatre, 'highly conventional works which repeat well-known comic and other motifs.'

Mankind is defended for its serious moral aspects as well as its lively humour, while Heywood's *Love* is seen as reconciling seemingly impossible opposites in the tradition of Lucianic dialogue. *Lusty Juventus* and *Like Will to Like*, both concerned with religious polemic and social satire, none the less exhibit strongly contrasted structures, 'evidence of experimentation in diverse ways of writing plays for a small company'. But while *Lusty Juventus* advocates the importance of providing the young with careful training, *Like Will to Like* admits that it is too late to redeem the unregenerate.

Gordon Kipling in 'The Early Tudor Disguising: New Research Opportunities' (*RORD*) highlights the court disguisings of Henry VII, which involved professionals rather than noble amateurs, a fact frequently ignored. The essence of the Tudor disguising was the costumed dance, often introduced by an elaborate prologue which defined and 'set' the dance and was usually bound to it thematically. In Henry's reign the fruitful association of the disguising with the Chapel Royal was the most important innovation, the Chapel supplying a reliable and continuously available group of talented actors. Presentation grows more spectacular towards the end of the reign, when 'dramatic pageantry becomes the soul of the show' under the supervision of William Cornish. Serious as are the textual and conceptual problems involved, Kipling believes that a new history of the disguising as a distinctive form of dramatic art is now possible, and that it may reveal 'that the essential inspiration for the brilliance of the Stuart masque comes not from Italy, but from the native genius and thoroughly professional work of men like William Cornish at the court of . . . Henry VII'.

Bruce R. Smith in 'Sir Amorous Knight and the Indecorous Romans' (*Ren D* 1973), commenting that classical comedies appear among Henry VIII's courtly revels at an impressively early date, asks how Plautus and Terence fitted in 'with men and manners a thousand miles and seventeen-hundred years away'. 'How were these new and strange Romans accommodated within the more usual disports of an evening? Did their appearance at the court of Henry VIII have any lasting influence on English court dramatists?' Smith's answer is that the Roman dramatists were required to fit in with the variety traditional in court revelry: 'Henry VIII and his courtiers looked at Plautus and Terence with their own eyes, not with the eyes of literary historians conscious of cultural contexts' while their English imitators perforce let 'more immediate objects divert their eyes from distant classical models'.

Under the title 'Dangerous Sport: The Audience's Engagement with Vice in the Moral Interludes' (*RenD* 1973) Robert C. Jones comments that recent studies and performances of the moralities have made us aware that 'what engages the spectators is the representation of the very vices that it is the play's business to make them reject', and his essay concerns the ways in which the morality dramatists worked to resolve that conflict. Throughout the plays, confrontations in which our theatrical response defines our relationship to the Vice or vices are constant, and 'the very theatricality through which the vices engage the audience gives the satire its special effect'. We are repeatedly made conscious of our theatrical reactions and their implications, particularly 'that our very responses to the play are actual manifestations in ourselves of the better and worse impulses in man that are being represented on-stage; and we can accordingly place our delight in the vices as something in us to be guarded against. This technique is perhaps the fullest theatrical realization of the possibilities of instruction through entertainment in the moral plays.'

Ian Lancashire in 'Robert Wyer's Alleged Edition of Heywood's *Play of the Weather*: The Source of the Error' (*Library*) traces the erroneous attribution partly to a Cambridge librarian who between 1750 and 1778, in classifying a volume of early black-letter editions, treated Wyer's colophon for another book as part of Middleton's quarto of the *Weather* which lacked its colophon page, and thus misdirected future bibliographers consulting his catalogue. A similar error had been made earlier in the century by Thomas Tanner, and was repeated from that source by Thomas Warton in the third volume of his *History of English poetry* (1781).

David M. Bergeron draws attention to an 'Early Use of the Word "Theatre"', (*N&Q*) in Hall's *Union of the Two Noble and Illustre Famelies of Lancastre and Yorke* (1548), where it appears with the meaning assigned to it under '4' by the *O.E.D.*: 'temporary platform, dais, or raised stage, for public ceremony', Hall's use predating the Holinshed reference cited by *O.E.D.* as its earliest instance.

Finally, two chapters in Normand Berlin's *Thomas Sackville* noticed above (pp. 189–90) discuss *Gorboduc* and Sackville's contribution to Elizabethan tragedy. The writer attempts to investigate the intrinsic worth of the play as well as its importance to English dramatic history, and sets about establishing its early theatrical and publishing fortunes, its authorship, its political intentions, its literary origins in chronicle, Seneca, and the morality play, and its use of blank verse. Sensibly Berlin argues that many critics' tendency 'to stress only the immediate political issues has caused them to slur the play's artistic worth and to narrow the play's political range'. He also deals with *Gorboduc's* general as well as topical relevance but perhaps the question of the degree to which the play relies on Seneca provokes the most useful and judicious discussion. Elsewhere the arguments that the dumb-shows are quite likely to be of native origin and that the blank-verse displays an unexpected degree of variation are not developed sufficiently to enable readers to judge these matters for themselves. The succeeding commentary on *Gordobuc* is lucid and sound, though far from original, yet, while not indulging in indiscriminate praise, it makes a good case for the play's stageworthiness and artistic unity. However the frequent assertion that it is the first chronicle play in English would seem to ignore the existence of Bale's *King Johan*.

VII

Shakespeare

DAVID DANIELL, ANGUS EASSON
ELIZABETH MASLEN and ANDREW SANDERS

As in previous issues the survey below must inevitably be selective and is not intended to duplicate the annual bibliographies and surveys in *PMLA, SEL, ShS, SJH, SJW, SRO* and *SQ*.

1. EDITIONS

The Macmillan edition of *Richard III*[1] is 'designed essentially for schools' and the text (in main, the Folio) faces the notes, allowing plenty of room for the annotation, which is both explanatory and discreetly critical. The introduction begins with the Tudor myth, rather crudely seeing Shakespeare as part of the 'Tudor machine', but pointing well to Richmond's final speech as an ordinary Englishman's prayer for peace and safety. The sources are handled well, as is also Shakespeare's development of themes and dramatic imagination in shaping Thomas More's contribution to the chronicle. On Richard as Machiavel and tragic figure, Adams is brief but useful, but there is no link with *Henry VI* and little about verse, dramatic convention or technique (though some of this is covered in the notes).

2. TEXTUAL MATTERS

There are interesting ideas for editors in Neil Carson's survey of 'Some Textual Implications of Tyrone Guthrie's 1953 Production of *All's Well That Ends Well*' (*SQ*), since despite the savaging of the text, not

least in Lavatch's omission, Guthrie had to find practical solutions of the Folio's difficulties, and behind changes Carson sees a rigorous dramatic logic, challenging generally held assumptions about staging certain scenes and even the nature of the text itself. Various scenes are considered in detail, including Parolles's mute presence in III. iii, and the staging of II.i and IV.i (which relates interestingly to Jörg Hasler's view in his book noted below); while Guthrie also faced the problems of Violanta and Lords E and G. However high-handed the director's tactics, 'they clarify relationships ... and solve some inconsistencies which existing texts leave unsatisfactorily explained'. Millard T. Jones surveys 'Press-Variants and Proofreading in the First Quarto of *Othello*' (*SB*), so that by presenting a list of press-variants revealed by collation of Barlett and Pollard's nineteen copies of the first Quarto, a scholar using one may know how his text differs from the others. In the process Jones concludes that it would be unwise without more evidence to accept corrections as proof that the Quarto's errors derived from the manuscript, and even less wise to accept substantive variants between Quarto and Folio as Shakespeare's first and second thoughts. Shakespeare's spelling will need further consideration after S. W. Reid's carefully argued 'Justification and Spelling in Jaggard's Compositor B' (*SB*), the theory of which, if confirmed, would require examinations

[1] *Richard III*, ed. by Richard Adams (The Macmillan Shakespeare). London: Macmillan. pp. 322.

of spellings in lines of verse and of single lines of prose ending within two ems of the measure and would rescue from virtual oblivion and uselessness a large number of other spellings. 'An Unknown Shakespearian Commonplace Book', of about 1660, noted by Gunnar Sorelius (*Lib* 1973), shows Shakespeare amongst the top three favourites, and is indicative of the taste of the period. The importance of the British Museum's acquisition of uncut sheets, on which the title page and first eight pages of the text of *The Tempest* have been imposed in octavo, is recorded by R. J. Roberts in 'Rowe's Shakespeare: An Experiment of 1708' (*Lib* 1973). Anne Lancashire in 'Warburton's List and Edmond Malone: A Non-Existent Relationship' (*SB*), demolishes the idea that the list (in Malone's 1778 essay on the chronology of Shakespeare) of thirty-four lost plays was derived from the list compiled by Warburton of those destroyed by his cook.

3. BIOGRAPHY AND BACKGROUND

Shakespeare's connexion with the Queen's Men (1583–92) and the shortlived Pembroke's Men (1592–93) is argued by G. M. Pinciss in 'Shakespeare, Her Majesty's Players and Pembroke's Men' (*ShS*). The evidence begins with Greene's attack, which might be prompted by loss of income from a company preferring to take plays from their 'Shake-scene', and continues with Shakespeare's familiarity with plays in the repertory: echoes from the *Famous Victories* may be not the result of Shakespeare's authorship but of his constant exposure to the play, if he were an actor in a company that also owned the *Troublesome Rayne, True Tragedy of Richard III,* and *King Leir.* The argument is well conducted and

concludes with the speculation that the Pembroke's Company was a branching from the Queen's. A challenge to Alfred Harbage's contention that the majority of Shakespeare's audience were working-class people comes in Ann Jennalie Cook's 'The Audience of Shakespeare's Plays: A Reconsideration' (*ShakS*), which has little difficulty in showing the shakiness of the term 'working-class', and questions whether the working-class did have leisure and opportunity for theatregoing. All indications are that the Elizabethan worker was an occasional rather than habitual frequenter of the theatre, and a brisk, efficient piece concludes with analysis of Harbage's contemporary descriptions, doubting whether they support the claim of a composite picture which is a true indication of Shakespeare's audience.

Two documents are investigated by John Doebler's 'A Lost Paragraph in the Revels Constitution' (*SQ*), which prints the whole document from two manuscripts in the Folger Library (Chambers having printed from the defective transcript of Alfred Kemper (1835) (see *Elizabethan Stage*, i, 74)); and by Jarold Ramsey's 'The Importance of Manningham's Diary' (*ShakS*), which restores some of the deletions of the Camden Society edition (1868). Ramsey favours Curle as informant for the Burbage and 'William the Conqueror' story; but his proposed emendation of Malvolio's 'gesture in smiling' to 'gesture in suiting', already suggested by Hotson, is challenged by T. W. Craik in the New Arden (1975, p. xxvii fn. I) from his direct examination of the manuscript. Other details in this article show Manningham's interest in sermons, and an unsophisticated if charming collection of bawdry.

Russell Fraser's *The Dark Ages and*

the Age of Gold[2] sets out to do something of interest and value: 'to describe and interpret the breaking away of the present from the mediaeval past'. He locates this break 'in England in the sixteenth century, on the Continent two hundred years before'. The reason why a much later time is named The Age of Reason is 'the gigantic and atavistic presence ... of Shakespeare ... the last and greatest of mediaeval artists ... With the death of Shakespeare,' he suggests, the capacity 'to entertain concurrent truths which may be contradictory' disappears, to be recovered in the nineteenth century; it becomes 'more powerfully emergent in the literature and psychology of our own time.'

Professor Fraser hopes 'to engage the interest of the commuter as he journeys to work on the train.' But with its twenty-page selective bibliography and constant allusion across all boundaries, this is not, in fact, a book to take up lightly. It is a clever book which too frequently trips the reader up with undifferentiated erudition (symptomatically, the last reference is to Eldridge Cleaver; and sentences are likely to include allusions to a tenth century cleric, Chairman Mao, a nineteenth century minor scientist, and a hippy leader). There is a serious lack of critical edge, that rigour of thought which knows what to exclude. This is a great pity, for the analyses of various artistic situations, generally pointed in the direction of Shakespeare, are often stimulating. Certainly the explorations of the state and nature of poetry and its functions, in all aspects, in the sixteenth century, are accurate and alert; but the lack of focus is fatal.

What might have been in Shakespeare's mind and how it may control or colour what he writes is the concern of W. Gordon Zeeveld's *The Temper of Shakespeare's Thought*.[3] This is difficult ground, and Zeeveld is properly cautious, claiming that 'the aspects of Shakespeare's thought here dealt with are indicative, not definitive'. Four main concepts are considered: Ceremony, Commonwealth, Equity, and Civility. Under Ceremony, for instance, the idea of honour is discussed (though not much is said about the thought of the time) and ceremony's relationship to the Reformation and controversy about forms and ritual, the chapter naturally being closely linked to the Histories. Again, the permutations and shifts in meaning of words like *kind/gentle/civility/polity/policy* are investigated under Civility and linked to the Comedies and Romances: Robin Hood, for instance, is seen as a flouter of Civil order who yet served scrupulously the law within himself and so provided a popular image of innate nobility. Some of the intellectual milieu presented seem remote from Shakespeare, yet it is argued well that Hooker's rôle of reconciliation in the Church led to his stress on the values inherent in customary observances of tradition, whether ecclesiastical or political, so that through the concept of ceremony Zeeveld can link the tensions of religious settlement to the tensions of earlier Civil Wars, the material of Shakespeare's Histories. The doubts that arise do not concern the historical evidence; rather they arise again and again over points of detail in the critical evidence, which inevitably call in question the rightness of the material presented. It may be a minor detail that Elizabeth is

[2] *The Dark Ages and the Age of Gold*, by Russell Fraser. Princeton University Press. pp. xi & 425. £10.20.

[3] *The Temper of Shakespeare's Thought*, by W. Gordon Zeeveld. New Haven & London: Yale U.P. pp. xv & 266. £6.

made *publicly* to say 'Know ye not that I am Richard II?' (it was to William Lambarde in her Privy Chamber, and Zeeveld misquotes: see New Arden, p. lix), but such details are cumulative and sow doubts —Hotspur and Sir Walter Blunt may be food for worms but they are not food for powder; Ovid among the Goths scarcely saw himself as part of a vogue for the primitive; Richard's soldier-audience on his return from Ireland, far from being unable 'to conceal their scorn of his perform-ance', are conspicuous by their silence; and what is the meaning of 'Robin's ale flowed freely, whetted no doubt by rustic Maid Marians'? We may gain '*a* meaning consistent with Shakespeare's temperament and with that of the audience for which he wrote', but in an area always very difficult to characterize, doubt about this study will remain.

4. GENERAL CRITICISM

A useful guide, edited by Stanley Wells,[4] provides the essential basis for beginning Shakespeare studies. The seventeen chapters deal with the study of Shakespeare, the text, the theatre, the plays and poems by categories concluding with *Henry VIII*, *The Two Noble Kinsmen* and apocrypha. Each chapter has an essay followed by appropriate bibliography, divided (on the plays) as Texts, Critical Studies and Commentary, the Plays, which allow the contributor to provide both information and critical guidance. It is not always easy to locate certain items (which exactly are the Early Comedies and which the Middle?) though a run through the biblio-graphy of the appropriate chapter or its first section shows this (the Con-

tents page might have been specific, though). There are odd divisions, *Coriolanus* being grouped with *Timon of Athens*, not with the other Roman plays; and *Sir Thomas More* is dealt with under apocrypha, which is fair enough but makes the entry difficult to find without other indication (an index might be useful) or reading through Norman Sanders on 'Shakespeare's Text'. There are some omissions: Sanders refers to 'The Passionate Pilgrim', directing us to James Nosworthy on the poems, where it is not to be found by name in discussion or bibliography. Again, Sanders refers to McKerrow's biblio-graphical work, and the *Prolegomena* is named—but the proposed Oxford Old Spelling Shakespeare not itself mentioned; other concordances are listed, but not T. H. Howard-Hill's. In spite of minor blemishes, then, this is a basic working-manual.

A generous addition to the Critical Heritage series[5] offers material under four kinds: literary criticism; adapta-tions of plays; theatrical criticism; and textual criticism. As Vickers points out in his useful introduction, it is the last which is most important for this period which runs from Rymer's *Short View of Tragedy* to Warburton's notes (in Theobald's edition), which prepare us for Warburton's edition of 1747. Vickers hopes the volume will 'permit the reinstatement of Theobald as one of the three or four major figures in the development of our understanding and appreciation of Shakespeare'. Even Pope's badness (wishing to interpolate 'Sir Francis Drake' to fill up a blank in *Henry VI*) serves a purpose when it rouses up a great

---

[4] *Shakespeare: Select Bibliographical Guides*, ed. by Stanley Wells. London: Oxford U.P., 1973. pp. 300. £3.25. Paperback £1.

[5] *Shakespeare: The Critical Heritage* (vol. 2) *1693–1733*, ed. by Brian Vickers. London and Boston: Routledge and Kegan Paul. pp. xi & 549. £8.95.

editor: Vickers feels that Theobald's notes 'show a judgment superior to almost all critics this side of Dr Johnson' and praises Theobald's excellence as scholar and critic. Theobald's fault was too much respect for Warburton, the saddest fact about the two men's relationship being 'that Warburton learned nothing from it'. New light is thrown on Shakespeare when we find Theobald's favourite play was *Coriolanus* (though he wanted more pathos and less sublime) or see the sense he made of Duncan's gold-laced skin (some reference might have been made to *Double Falsehood*). Many items in the volume seem feeble or fretfully repetitious of neo-classical canons, but Vickers urges us to think ourselves back to the age. Adaptations include extracts from Cibber's *Richard III*, Gildon's *Measure for Measure* ('Think not I've changed my Ducal Robes for these/ Because I love.—No, 'tis a cause more wrinkl'd') Granville's *The Merchant of Venice*, Dennis's *Merry Wives* and *Coriolanus*, Theobald's *Richard II* and Hill's *Henry V*. Useful juxtapositions are Oldmixon on the mangling of Shakespeare and Gildon's version, with Sewell on the same topic followed by Dennis's *Coriolanus*.

The most exciting and brilliant critical contribution this year is undoubtedly James Smith's *Shakespearian and Other Essays*,[6] tactfully edited by E. M. Wilson. Smith published an essay on *As You Like It* in 1940 and was working on a book on Shakespearean Comedy when he died in 1972; sections on *Twelfth Night* and *The Merry Wives of Windsor*, known to have existed, are lost, and of the other essays (on

6 *Shakespearian and Other Essays*, by James Smith. Ed. by E. M. Wilson. Cambridge: Cambridge U.P. pp. vii & 351. £5.50.

Much Ado, The Merchant of Venice, All's Well, Measure for Measure, The Winter's Tale, and *The Tempest*) only that on *Much Ado* has appeared in print, though other work goes back to the 1940s and much was being revised at the time of his death. Indeed, the piece on *Measure for Measure* breaks off in mid-sentence, and with the others there is often that sense produced by Michelangelo's Slaves of a line or form emerging only to lose itself again in the original block; the fragments of essays and book are as provocative as criticism as those sculptures are as art. There are oddities, often Puckish in nature: scorn for the humanists ('cadaverists, rather'), assumption of ignorance on topics where one suspects great erudition, and doubt whether Smith ever actually saw any of these plays or thought of them dramatically (an aside on *Much Ado* notes that 'the scenes are said to be successful on the stage'), the usual reference being to the *reader*. What Smith above all offers is close readings of the text and close awareness of their local meaning, and the implications of these for the whole play. The interplay between these foci is part of his mastery, while his sense of argument, the placing of points, the return along trails that he seems to have worked to the end, a questioning of himself—these all suggest the cunning and insight of a subtle, delighted mind. Smith's use and reading of a remark in *All's Well* ('The web of our life is of a mingled yarn, good and ill together') demonstrates that subtlety and his use of it to bore deep into the heart of the play, while never losing sight of its human meaning. The leading idea of the book, we may surmise, was the nature of comedy and its relationship to tragedy, which Smith sees as different in degree not kind: 'In comedy the materials for tragedy are procured . . .

but they are not, so to speak, attended to, certainly not closely examined. And so what might have caused grief causes only a smile, or at worst a grimace.' What might seem almost dismissive of comedy is belied by the essays themselves and by that connexion in 'degree' with tragedy; for whether in *As You Like It*, where Smith maintains that a 'tragic note or undertone is thus inseparable from pastoral, and if subdued is only the more insistent', or in *Much Ado*, where the serious play of Beatrice and Benedick shows a violent handling of the vapid cynicism of the society around them 'until a gust of tragedy should blow through the air of Messina, dispelling vapidities for a while', there is always a sense of the importance of what is being investigated and of the challenge Shakespeare throws down, as in the defence of Dogberry and his kind, who 'are necessary in the background to reduce the figures in the foreground to the required proportions—to the proportions of apes . . . for whom no tricks are too ferocious, too fantastic'. *The Merchant of Venice* essay disputes the fairness of the caskets and of Shylock's defeat (a splendid passage describes how Shylock is made to turn his weapons against himself) and its gnomic ending suggests a struggle to make the play yield meaning, the essay having suggested the struggle to be worthwhile: Shylock 'makes of the play a mirror of the human struggle with what is too opaque to allow a shape, or at times anything, to be seen; too hard to allow the imposition of a shape. The struggle is the more impressive.' The essay on *All's Well* champions Parolles as the play's centre, 'one of the most tragic, if not the most significant, figures in it', tragic because 'he is old in rashness, and in itself this implies grave sin'. The fragment on *Measure for Meas-*

ure sees the Duke not as Divine Providence but as one who has come to knowledge of how to use Authority; but it also sees Angelo as right to refuse Isabella's demand, stressing the deputy's 'For then I pity those I do not know'. *The Winter's Tale* is pursued partly in relation to *King Lear*, both in relation to the grotesque (tragic here as it is comic in *Lear*) and the viewpoint (as in baroque art) which is necessary if the whole is not to be a meaningless jumble. The longest piece, on *The Tempest*, explores the dream, and fruitfully pursues its progenitors in De Eslava and Strachey's account of the Bermuda voyage. Caliban is elevated to the 'verge of concluding that no other character in the play is human in the like degree', while Prospero is closely questioned and found to be a 'man who knows the truth, but who is humanly imperfect in the interpretations he produces in the light of it: not a sensitive nature'. The essay ends enigmatically yet jovially as Smith urges the reader to enjoy the play as he enjoys life: 'No desperation, no complacency; be cheerful. Tragicomedia?'

A memorial volume of Peter Ure's writings on Elizabethan and Jacobean Drama,[7] scrupulously edited by J. C. Maxwell, includes three Shakespearian essays: 'Shakespeare and the Inward Self of the Tragic Hero' (Ure's inaugural lecture published in 1961); 'Character and Role from *Richard III* to *Hamlet*' (published in Stratford upon Avon Studies: V); and the previously unpublished '*Macbeth*'. The three, as Maxwell observes, suggest that Ure was working towards a book hinging on the metaphor of inner and outer being, an awareness

[7] *Elizabethan and Jacobean Drama: Critical Essays*, by Peter Ure. Ed. by J. C. Maxwell. Liverpool: Liverpool U.P. pp. viii & 258. £5.

of the individual self and of the part or rôle performed, together with (as a third element) the continual traffic between them, transforming the substance of both. On *Macbeth*, Ure develops earlier points about characters who nerve themselves to complete their rôles, the ritual always faltering on the edge of 'ordinary wishes or sympathies.' So Macbeth is seen as creator of a rôle in order to perform a task 'which he invented for himself in the first place' and much of the 'traffic' between inner and outer consists of attempts to imagine and be that rôle; thus in his Tarquin soliloquy he can just 'sufficiently narrow the gap between assumption and enactment of the rôle, adequately prick the sides of his intent, by using this spur and raising himself on these stilts of art.' It is part of his tragedy (why we regard him as pitiable, not execrable) that the 'monster of evil that MacDuff and Malcolm need to see . . . is in the end simply not there; Macbeth never quite succeeded in imagining him.'

Research work on specialized topics is represented by four studies[8] of varying usefulness. Tommy Ruth Waldo's study makes large claims

[8] Salzburg Studies in English Literature: Jacobean Drama Studies Vol. 45. *Musical Terms as Rhetoric: The Complexity of Shakespeare's Dramatic Style*, by Tommy Ruth Waldo. Salzburg: Universität Salzburg. pp. 174.
Commentary and Control in Shakespeare's Plays, by Peter Bilton. Oslo, Bergen, Tromsö: Universitetsforlaget/New York: Humanities Press. pp. 247.
Salzburg Studies in English Literature: Elizabethan and Renaissance Studies Vol. 39. *The Words of Mercury: Shakespeare and English Mythography of the Renaissance*, by Noel Purdon. Salzburg: Universität Salzburg. pp. 246.
The Cooper Monographs on English and American Language and Literature, Vol. 21. *Shakespeare's Theatrical Notation: The Comedies*, by Jörg Hasler. Berne: Francke Verlag. pp. 244. Sfr. 45.

that it 'is an analysis of Shakespeare's use of musical terms as they illustrate his control of words and style. It demonstrates that by acting with extraordinary versatility upon the admonitions of the rhetoricians with which he and his contemporaries were familiar, Shakespeare developed a style which was a unique thing.' The study does nothing so large; it is narrowed down to passages in selected plays, the terms being handled under various categories such as 'Simultaneous Meanings' and 'Two Chains of Meanings'. The study is thorough (within its limits) and written without zest or punch. More satisfactory is Peter Bilton's study of *Commentary and Control*, though this is defeated by including all the plays (except *Henry VIII*), so that space is not available for full or exploratory readings. Again, Bilton claims to be doing something new, 'to reflect a struggle to break out' from the problem that reality is changed by one's very attempt to pin it down and that Shakespeare's plays come veiled in interpretation. The relation between this and the idea of the spectator's experience, particularly of those characters who seem to be reliable commentators on the action and so control the spectator's judgement, is not inevitable. Given the space available, there seems too much re-telling of the plots and the conclusions, if acceptable, are scarcely surprising: that Exeter and Lucy in *I Henry VI* guide our responses; that in the later Histories the commentary 'becomes increasingly concerned with' problems like deposing the King, the qualities of the good king, and 'with the individuals caught in their toils'; and so on. Noel Purdon's study of English mythography is altogether a different matter: it has its faults and crudities—occasionally too much bounce and carelessnesses (Bottom, as

Puck's use of 'bum' reminds us, did not mean 'arse'); and the illustrations are poorly reproduced. But it is often genuinely witty, clearly good-humoured and the result of a great deal of work. The relationship between mythology and poetry, 'nowhere more profound, and nowhere less fathomed, than in the poetry of the English Renaissance', leads Purdon, 'before succumbing to any preconceptions about Shakespeare's actual use of myth in his plays', to become acquainted 'with the sources of myth which he himself knew, with that score or so of books which formed the Renaissance sensibility.' This investigation takes account of the different kinds of books (the illustrations are handy here) and of their knowledge and popularity, arguing for instance that neither Batman's *Golden Booke of the Leaden Goddes* nor Linche's version of Cartari (*The Fountain of Ancient Fiction*) show much sign of being widely used by poets, while annotated editions of poets (e.g. translations of Ovid) presenting gods who are unclassical and bizarre, render the confident assumptions of previous critics about the use of English manuals no longer tenable. After considering the Poetics and Rhetoric of Myth, Purdon turns to Shakespeare and the Climate of Myth, stressing the excitement of the antic and grotesque, now a lost tradition because the later seventeenth century (quoting St Evremonde, 1678) loved 'plain truth'. Myth was used as Icon and served rhetoric as a quarry for speech-building, but also, Purdon argues, was used as a method of dramatic structure. He ends with the Mythological Psychomachia of *A Midsummer Night's Dream*. As with Waldo, we may wonder how much of this is not discernible from close examination of the play, though it is undoubtedly a subtler and fuller

reading than could be attempted without the spade-work of the earlier sections, and anyone who directs us away from historical meanings of the Vestal throned in the West and back to the play itself is to be welcomed. Jörg Hasler's work on *Shakespeare's Theatrical Notation* concerns Shakespeare's 'producing hand' in the text itself, the indications of what the actors are to do through gesture and placing on the stage, and the methods by which the dramatist 'can organize and control the gestic, mimic and scenic form of the play-in-performance'. He takes the Comedies from *The Comedy of Errors* to *Twelfth Night* and considers amongst other things the interaction of verbal against specifically dramatic (stage) imagery, the dramaturgy of Peter Quince, eavesdropping, and finales (that is, the problems of removing people from the stage). He is illuminating on the closing exeunt in *The Merchant of Venice* and his final chapter ('Word-Scenery') is excellent on that play's last act. Francis Berry's 'Shakespeare's Stage Geometry' (*SJH*) looks at the use of a third *vertical* dimension on stage, the throne on the dais or the raised platform, implying the pre-eminence of those raised up, and in discussing *Richard III, Romeo and Juliet*, and *Coriolanus* he links them to 'a geometry of speech which puts heaven, worldly success and joy above, while hell, failure and misery are put below.' A. B. Kernan points to a stage of the mind, in 'This Goodly Frame, the Stage: The Interior Theatre of Imagination in English Renaissance Drama' (*SQ*), relating the arrangements of space in the physical theatre to the model of the conservative world view, a world in which by imaginative creation Shakespeare can seem to manipulate reality though always calling us back to the full scene of theatre and audience. In what is largely a survey of contemporary criticism, Robert P. Adams looks at 'Transformations in the late Elizabethan Tragic Sense of Life: New Critical Approaches' (*MLQ*) and finds they took place in the work of playwrights between 1596 and 1603; he sees a gap between *Henry V* and *Hamlet*, as Granville-Barker did in his British Academy lecture of 1925. Anne Paolucci's 'Shakespeare and the Genius of the Absurd' (*CompD* 1973) suggests states of mind and representation through dramatic techniques used in common by Shakespeare and dramatists like Albee, Beckett, Camus and Ionesco. Richard Levin cries ineffectually in the wilderness against a practice he detects in 'On Fluellen's Figures, Christ Figures, and James Figures' (*PMLA*), arguing that the attempt to parallel Shakespeare's characters with Christ or other heroes is something already ridiculed by Fluellen's parallels between Henry V and Alexander. Tagore's interest in and criticism of Shakespeare is reviewed by Visvanath Chatterjee (*Tagore Studies*). R. A. Foakes's survey ('What's New in Shakespeare Criticism' (*English*)) of critical works over the last decade, sees the English as amateurs, the Americans as professionals, and argues (though his praise of particular works qualifies this) that the most significant movements in recent criticism are American. Francis Hayes, in 'The Great Dismal Swamp of Amateur Freudian Literary Criticism' (*MLJ*), pleads for 'concern for linguistic pollution', attacking 'a foolish movement which is in reality a marauding raid on sanity, a trend that is strangling the judicious use of speech by substituting graceless hypothetical jargon.' This is cheering stuff; Hayes wields a pick-handle rather than a foil, but his brief

encounter is essential reading for all critics. He shows clearly the distinctive clarity both of Shakespeare and of a fine Shakespearean, Robert Heilman. In 'Echoes of *1 Henry IV*, *King Lear*, and *Macbeth* in *Wit's Triumvirate* (1635)' (*SQ*), Cathryn A. Nelson, who is preparing yet another edition of the play, notes an echo from each work plus two other possibles.

Articles dealing with Shakespeare's language include Peter J. Gillett's 'Me, U and Non-U: Class Connotations of Two Shakespeare Idioms' (*SQ*), which looks at the ethic dative 'me' and the Renaissance English 'your' (= 'the typical' or simply 'the'), suggesting that certain occurrences in Shakespeare have social connotations: Gillett argues that many uses of 'me' suggest a tone of amazement or incredulity at an act of effrontery or piece of presumption, the high rate of occurrence in *1 Henry IV*, pre-eminently treating of honour, enforcing this. There are interesting suggestions about Mercutio's (wrong) conception of Tybalt's character and about 'me' implying superiority of speaker, with its use by Non-U speakers in an attempt to prove U-ness. Class distinctions are also the concern of Carol Replogle in 'Shakespeare's Salutations: A Study in Stylistic Etiquette' (*SP* 1973): the need to distinguish fitting and proper respect from what might be felt as obsequiousness—so that Shakespeare and his audience for instance, unlike us and Joan La Pucelle, would have taken seriously the listing of Talbot's titles. *Richard II*, *Henry IV*, and *King Lear* are looked at and Replogle concludes that titles are manipulated 'with careful discrimination for a wide variety of dramatic purposes.' Gerald A. Smith's '"Good-brother" in *King Lear* and *Antony and Cleopatra*' (*SQ*) points to the meaning 'brother-in-law' when the two words are hyphenated, certain in the first play (IV.ii) and possible in the latter (II.viii). More marginal to Shakespeare, but interesting, is an account by Mimi Chan and Helen Kwok, 'Figuratively Speaking: a Study of the Cantonese-Speaking Undergraduate's Response to Figures of Speech in Shakespeare' (*SQ*), which demonstrates from their experience in Hong Kong that many figurative expressions in Shakespeare and English are almost paralleled in Chinese: a section on those not paralleled would have been interesting. Other articles in the same issue, which was devoted to pedagogy, include Peter Milward on 'Teaching Shakespeare in Japan', a pleasing and personal view indicating Shakespeare's popularity and the freshness and immediacy of his students' response; William A. Jamison's account of teaching all the plays in chronological order (37 in two semesters) appears in 'The Case for a Compleat Shakespeare'; Deborah A. Williams writes on 'Shakespeare in the High School Classroom'; Eliza Alling's 'Dear Will' is epistolary facetiousness about *Hamlet*; and Edward Partridge's 'Re-presenting Shakespeare' takes a healthy stand against the workshop conception if it includes work of a theatre course rather than literature—though Partridge seems to accept the premise of many committed writers on Shakespeare as drama: that literary critics *never* treat the plays as though they were drama.

Robert Y. Turner treads again a well-worn path in *Shakespeare's Apprenticeship*,[9] with the special handicap of a joyless, over-weighty, flat-footed erudition. 'As I see the continuum of Shakespeare's appren-

[9] *Shakespeare's Apprenticeship*, by Robert Y. Turner. Chicago and London: U. of Chicago P. pp. 293. £7.45.

tice plays' he writes, 'they recapitulate phylogenetically the main historical movement in drama of the sixteenth century from the generalized didactic morality play to the relatively literal drama as a distinctive art form'. Early errors do not inspire confidence: Shakespeare, even in legend, did not poach deer from 'Chalchote', nor did Greene refer to a 'Shakes-scene'. The first chapters, on 'The Problem of Dialogue', 'Confrontations' and 'Persuasions', tie the idea of the tyro playwright to flat statements about the plays in a way which is seldom illuminating and often quite wrong: 'With regard to the topic of apprenticeship—to state roughly the contrast between earlier and later persuasions—the young Shakespeare emphasized moral clarity in the earliest chronicles and verisimilitude in the later plays'. Mr Turner is as sprightly a companion as a Government sociological survey, and about as sympathetic to his subject: 'Whatever the cause', he writes 'unsuccessful persuasions begin to occur in Shakespeare's works . . . about 1592, while scenes of successful persuasions grow less frequent. Probably only the accidentals of his stories cause the change, but it is worth noting that full dramatization of the unsuccessful persuasion exhibits an emphasis similar to the later confrontations upon the defeated rather than the triumphant'. Later chapters include the inevitable 'Moral Equations' and 'Speeches of Emotion', 'Neo-Classical Stipulations', 'Comic Characterization', 'Comic Uses of Language' and 'The Powers of Rhetoric and Mimesis.'

R. E. Burkhart, in 'Obedience and Rebellion in Shakespeare's Early History Plays' (*ES*), follows Michael Manheim's *The Weak King Dilemma* (*YW* 73) to show 'that the pre-Tudor kings in the plays are portrayed by

Shakespeare as deserving rebellion rather than as meriting obedience. Rebellion itself, though evil in many ways while it is happening, will be seen as a necessary means to the eventual good of the Tudor dynasty'. He briefly surveys the *Homilies* tradition, and modern critical comment on the plays, before turning to *King John*. Burkhart uses the Bastard to illustrate the point that 'the resolution of the conflict has little to do with the morality of rebellion'. Brief analyses of the *Henry VI* plays and *Richard III* lead to the conclusion that 'we are concerned, not with a rigid doctrine, but with portrayal of kings who are either suited or unsuited for kingship'. 'Richard Plantagenet and Henry Tudor, although they were rebels, were not condemned for it'.

A. L. French, in 'The Mills of God and Shakespeare's Early History Plays' (*ES*), starts from Moulton's point made in 1885 about the plays being concerned not so much with the punishment for the ancient specific crimes on Richard II, as with a pattern of crime and punishment worked out within the plays themselves. French goes on, interestingly, to question 'whether the text of the first tetralogy does, in fact, support notions of order, justice and moral equity'. What follows, however, is disappointing. A simple account of the deaths in the plays, under the question 'whether it is really proper to see divine justice in all of them', turns into the forcing of large academic notions ('our normal moral terminology') on to the plays, and dismay at the discovery that they do not fit. The piece is suddenly refreshed by a quotation from A. P. Rossiter at the end; but most of it is the wordy rehearsing of the obvious, by the way of a basic misquotation of Longfellow.

Marjorie B. Garber, in *Dream in Shakespeare: from Metaphor to Metamorphosis*,[10] attempts 'a study of Shakespeare's developing use of dream'. A simple account of the origin of some ideas about dreams in the English Renaissance leads to a brief treatment of Clarence's dream in *Richard III*, which allows no reference to the single most important fact about dreams in this play—that they are the culmination of a system, which includes oaths and portents, set up right at the beginning of *1 Henry VI*, and clearly to be seen in that light. Her theory that there are 'structural affinities between the dream world and the fictive world of art' leads her to put excessive weight on the experience of Sly in *The Taming of the Shrew*. On *Romeo*, Garber interestingly says, 'Two doctrines of dreams are expounded ... that of Romeo looking backward to the old tradition of omen and portent; that of Mercutio looks forward to dream as fantasy, the significant product of the shaping imagination'. But the total subjection of a critical stance to some ideas about dreams vitiates much of what is said about Shakespeare. The section on *Julius Caesar* makes it clear that the author is riding a thesis into wonderland. A long account of *A Midsummer Night's Dream* disappointingly reveals nothing new. The Tragedies are seen, perversely, as dream vehicles. Everything is controlled by the magic formula—'dream reveals character, permits speculation, insight, and self-delusion'. The Romances, not surprisingly, are all dream. Freud's crude list of dream symbols dominates; having in five lines disposed of the symbol of 'the storm or tempest'

[10] *Dream in Shakespeare: from Metaphor to Metamorphosis*, by Marjorie B. Garber. New Haven and London: Yale U.P. pp. 226. £4.50.

in the Romances, she says 'castration and consequent infertility are associated with the cutting of hair . . .' as a comment on *Pericles*. Freud, in fact, becomes the excuse for a distressing mixture of high-flown speculations in cloudy sentences, and such crunching banalities as 'Boxes and chests appear prominently in both *Pericles* and *Cymbeline*.'

From time to time there appears a low-key, modest, unassuming book which both demonstrates, and calls out, love for Shakespeare. Such a volume is Alexander Leggatt's *Shakespeare's Comedy of Love*,[11] which manages to give a close reading of the comedies from *The Comedy of Errors* to *Twelfth Night* without ever inducing the sinking feeling which such a phrase usually implies. The book affirms the qualities of the comedies themselves, and by being fresh in every line conveys a sense of new encounter—a rare enough quality. The intention of the book is 'to reverse one of criticism's normal interests, to seek not the internal unity of each play but its internal variety'. Least good on *The Two Gentlemen of Verona* (he is in good company, there) he is balanced and shrewd on *The Taming of the Shrew* ('Petruchio, in his "taming-school" really does teach Kate, and teaches her that inner order of which the music and mathematics offered to Bianca are only a reflection'.) He is excellent on *Love's Labour's Lost*, and brilliant from then on. Illuminating the Caskets scenes in *The Merchant of Venice*, he writes 'if we think of Portia as being wooed first by Othello and then by Coriolanus, we may be closer to the comic effect Shakespeare is aiming at'. Mr Leggatt says of *Much Ado About Nothing* that 'the

[11] *Shakespeare's Comedy of Love*, by Alexander Leggatt. London: Methuen. pp. xiii & 272. £3.95. Paperback £1.50.

play asserts more confidently than its predecessor the idea of human reality at the heart of convention; and in that way, besides being a notable achievement in its own right, it prepares for the triumphs of *As You Like It*'. The chapter which then follows is one of the best pieces of sustained criticism of *As You Like It* that has appeared for a long time. The final chapter points to the different world again of *Twelfth Night*, and then briefly beyond.

Robert F. Willson's 'The Plays within *A Midsummer Night's Dream* and *The Tempest*' (*SJW*) suggests that plays within plays communicate in stylized form the playwright's sense of the materials of his art, and distinguishes harmony (with the philosophical vision affirmed by such pieces in the Romances) from cacophony with comic overtones (which characterizes the manner of the early plays-within).

A persuasive and challenging argument is mounted by David Scott Kastan (in 'The Shape of Time: Form and Value in the Shakespearean History Plays' (*CompD*)), who suggests that the History genre, contrary to Irving Ribner's argument, 'can only be defined on the basis of dramatic form'—not by claims of an emerging Elizabethan sense of genre, by legitimate claims to historicity, or by authorial intention. He questions the origin of the genre in Morality structures (more properly the sacred prototypes of secular romance), the History play dealing with a fallen world of politics, firmly orientated in time with no supra-historical perspective; so that in *Richard II*, for example, the action of the ending is not, 'as with the action of tragedy, a movement toward self-consummation' and even *Henry VIII*, an unusually self-contained historical action, 'is embedded in a larger temporal context that the play is unable to enclose.'

A stimulating and exciting study of the Roman plays is presented in J. L. Simmons's *Shakespeare's Pagan World*,[12] which deals with the three major Roman plays and has an interesting appendix on the Moral Environment in Shakespeare's English History Plays. Simmons's thesis is that Shakespeare's 'conception of the Roman world and its place in universal history generated a particular and distinctive kind of tragedy in the three major Roman plays'. He shows how their historical character creates a special kind of tragedy that distinguishes them from Bradley's Great Four, the most important factor being the 'historically pagan environment out of which each tragedy arises'. Instead of the moral certainty found in the Great Tragedies, there is difficulty in deciding what is good and what is evil. For Simmons it is interesting that *Coriolanus* (which most clearly isolates these distinct features) is so perverse and ironic not only because it is Shakespeare's last tragedy but also because it logically extends fundamental aspects of those tragedies that preceded it, since the pre-Christian world of Rome's tragic plight (more genuinely Roman than is usually recognized) is one where all 'attempts to rise above the restrictions of man and his imperfect society, are tragically affected by the absence of revelation and the real hope of glory.' St Augustine's visions of Rome and of the City of God are used appositely and the echo of Revelation in Antony's 'Then must thou needs find out new heaven, new earth' is tragically impossible, rather than wrong. Simmons is excellent on Coriolanus, a protagon-

ist whose moral vision is unblinkingly the moral vision of Rome, and on Shakespeare's use of Plutarch (in particular the mocking of self and the people when Coriolanus asks for the voices). On *Antony and Cleopatra* he brings out well the comic pattern and its relation to English Histories like *Henry IV*, sees the absurdity in Antony's death and (rather like Anne Barton on the play, noted below) stresses that the nature of Antony's tragedy is still contingent upon Cleopatra's enigma: 'Even at his death Antony's view is only fragmentary; but Cleopatra will put all of the fragments of his great vision together.' Enobarbus is part of this comic suggestiveness, though in a comic world he would never have been forced into an unreasonable choice, made to deny 'the spiritual reality of the heart's affections'; and Cleopatra is allowed what is essentially a comic victory, closely tied up with our involvement in her choice of action: 'This comic victory ironically emerges while we fear that her desire for life will ruin everything. Instead, it glorifies everything.' A fruitful, provocative book.

Lawrence Danson's *Tragic Alphabet*[13] examines aspects of the language of eight Shakespearean Tragedies by assessing the appropriateness of the way in which characters express themselves or the manner in which Shakespeare has expressed his play. The book deals with the four major tragedies, together with *Titus Andronicus*, *Troilus and Cressida*, *Julius Caesar* and *Coriolanus*. The subject is treated thoughtfully and carefully though there are points at which Danson appears to be playing with terms or ideas which suit his

---

[12] *Shakespeare's Pagan World: The Roman Tragedies*, by J. L. Simmons. Hassocks: The Harvester Press. pp. viii & 202. £6.

[13] *Tragic Alphabet: Shakespeare's Drama of Language*, by Lawrence Danson. New York and London: Yale U.P. pp. xi, 200. £5.50.

argument more than the play in question. He is at his most persuasive in his studies of *Othello* and *Macbeth* and in his final chapter on *King Lear* which valuably discusses the problem of communication and expression.

An interesting verbal link between two plays is provided by Roger Warren (in 'Prospero's Renunciation and Coriolanus's Capitulation' (*N&Q*)), who points out that Ovid's Medea supplies details to Coriolanus when he yields to his mother, as well as the model of Prospero's speech (V.i.), and suggests that since Shakespeare has given Prospero the power to cause violent confusion which he specifically reserves to the gods in Coriolanus, 'he uses similar language to make a similar point about a would-be superman coming to terms with his humanity'.

Howard Felperin seeks in *Shakespearean Romance*[14] to provide a working theory of romance so as to tackle the plays, since the genre presents problems to modern criticism that tragedy or comedy does not. In his choice of plays he treats *Pericles* and *Henry VIII* as though entirely by Shakespeare and excludes *The Two Noble Kinsmen*; an appendix surveys the critical and theatrical history of the plays. Though his investigation of romance is not so fundamental to the plays as he suggests, it is concise and clear, giving in small space most of what is needed (contrast Hallett Smith's book reviewed last year) and he argues well for the seriousness of the form (the kind of seriousness we feel in Milton). Shakespeare's Romances impose strict limits on the open-ended nature of romance; so that the created rival world is controlled by Hermione's wrinkles and the collapse of

[14] *Shakespearean Romance*, by Howard Felperin. Princeton, New Jersey: Princeton U.P., 1973. pp. xi & 319. £6.40.

Prospero's masque when he thinks of Caliban, Shakespeare's form being stubborn in its 'refusal to accept and repeat the conventions of romance without revaluating them.' In looking at the relationship between the earlier comedies and the late Romances, Felperin insists that, despite common motifs, plays like *A Midsummer Night's Dream* and *The Tempest* are fundamentally different and he finds the latter structurally impossible without the tragedies preceding it. He links the Christian echoes of *Antony and Cleopatra* with the world of *Cymbeline* (a play hovering between the pagan and Christian worlds), so seeing a growing towards the Last Plays, with the lovers breaking 'into the apocalyptic order of romance, the order proclaimed at the end of *Cymbeline*, where the power of faith and love makes the relations of men and gods more than that of thieves to keepers'. Yet he finds *Cymbeline* ultimately unsatisfactory, too topical, though English history there takes on the formal pattern of romantic comedy, as it does also in *Henry VIII* (see Kastan's opposite view, above), where instead of the earlier historical pattern of falls that are good for England (e.g. Richard III's), the falls of Buckingham, Katherine and Wolsey are fortunate from their own point of view. The integration of imagination and reality is pursued in *The Winter's Tale*, where Shakespeare has to solve the problem of Job's daughters, of bringing everyone to final happiness, yet bringing home the 'abiding sense of sorrow and loss'.

Kenneth J. Semon's 'Fantasy and Wonder in Shakespeare's Last Plays' (*SQ*) ranges more widely than his article on *The Tempest* noticed last year, but is not so sprightly, though making good points. Wonder in these plays 'arises from the restoration of order to a world engulphed in chaos', and people, not understanding, believe and embrace that mystery; on *The Winter's Tale* he is interestingly near to James Smith (see above) on the difficulty of language, particularly in the narration of Perdita's recognition; while he finds that in suggesting alternative causes for Mamilius's death, Shakespeare, in leaving the matter open, suggests causes more profound than those graspable by human sense through a language based on logical propositions. *The Tempest*'s world is 'the most fantastic and profound. Only here does a conspiracy seem comic, and only here does man control his world'. His stress on Prospero's interruption of the masque in the previous article, which made the play's conclusion harder to attain, is absent here.

5. SHAKESPEARE IN THE THEATRE

Attention is drawn by several items this year to the vexed issue of Shakespeare as drama, and to the opposition of script (on the page) and play (in performance). The opening of Peter Thomson's review of the 1973 Royal Shakespeare Company's Stratford season in *Shakespeare Survey 27* is boldly polemical in its concern not with the company and the stage, but with the audience and the academics. Thomson seems to qualify last year's welcome of John Russell Brown's essay 'Free Shakespeare' (reviewed in book form below) in recalling with approval Meyerhold's plans for a new *Othello*, suggesting that it would have 'offended, even outraged, Shakespearian scholars', and that if amongst British directors only Peter Brook has comparable vision and authority, he has amply demonstrated his ability to offend scholars (Brown's argument partly is

that we are dominated by directors' theatre). Thomson's experience of reviewing for *ShS* has increased an awareness 'of the breach between universities and the theatre' and he urges that, as Shakespeare belonged to an excitable and unpretentious audience, he should be restored to one. The problem of performance is the answer to a theatrical question ('how can we make this script into a play?') which academics are unlikely ever to have to ask and to which they should be sympathetic. Thomson is too sensitive not to allow that, while Shakespeare's work does not play itself, 'inspiration has become compulsory for all directors, and those who don't have it must be severely tempted to cultivate the appearance of having it.' Maintaining that where the director's theatre addresses serious attention to the actor's art, it is the highest development of western theatrical method so far, he begins to view the season in terms of 'straight' and 'crooked' productions, taking up the academics' cry for 'straighter' productions but using the term to his own end. There was no master-plan as with the previous year's 'Romans'. David Jones's *Love's Labour's Lost* was the 'straightest': the design successfully enclosed the play in its rural setting, much of its attractiveness being due to Ian Richardson's Berowne, relishing the verbal challenge; while Derek Smith's Holofernes provoked laughter if he successfully explained his comic lines 'and if he didn't, we laughed in appreciation of his faith in us'. Marcade's entrance (see Harbage, below) 'was as unobtrusive as his exit, but it provided the necessary deepening of the lovers' experience'. *As You Like It* bid fair to be the 'crookedest' production; confused and jolly, it showed the characteristic of 'crooked' Shakespeare in pursuing 'relevance' at all costs. The main plot in general was allowed to speak for itself; a well-known professional wrestler played Charles, Eileen Atkins's Rosalind seemed disturbed by a taller Celia; Richard Pasco's Jacques is praised. Thomson makes no bones about his dislike of Terry Hands's *Romeo and Juliet*, an apparent rush job, where the director 'had tried to save time by telling the actors what to do instead of letting them discover their own style'. The set confined the action largely to centre stage and the gang warfare, with Tybalt a skinhead bully and Mercutio perhaps a muscular advocate of gay liberation, suggested that *West Side Story* was returning an influence to its original. Apart from the meretriciousness (however effective a theatrical moment was gained) of Bolingbroke playing the groom, John Barton's *Richard II*, with Pasco and Richardson alternating as King and Bolingbroke, is highly praised, 'the passionately sensed and consistently argued presentation of a vision', an outstanding attempt through stress on rôles and on a child's view 'to give the text life not merely *in* but *of* the theatre'.

Reporting on Shakespeare in Britain 1974 in *Shakespeare Quarterly*, Robert Speaight castigates poor planning at Stratford. *King John* was a pastiche version of John Barton's, interpolating material from the sources and hopelessly obscuring its design. Emrys James played the king as a jittery buffoon, while Pasco, excellent casting in an honest production, seemed unhappy as a Faulconbridge become a semi-relevant accessory. The current production space, the square, black, box-like enclosure used also for *King John* and *Richard II*, was unhelpful to *Cymbeline*, together with the inadequacy of the costumes and the mis-staging of the bedroom scene. Despite shortcomings, the production made sense of a strange and sometimes silly play; Jupiter's descent was a spectacular theophany and the political issues clearly stated and resolved. Barton's *Richard II* was revived, gaining from the actors' long acquaintance with the lines, and the production only faltered towards the end, 'with Northumberland suddenly on stilts, Aumerle's conspiracy pushed dangerously close to farce'—isn't it? See Sheldon P. Zitner, below—and Bolingbroke as groom. The bridge for Flint Castle had gone. Narcissus was the focal point for Peter Gill's *Twelfth Night*, his picture the only pictorial element in a bleak décor; Jane Lapotaire and Mary Rutherford as Viola and Olivia were good if rather lost in the vast area of the stage, Sir Toby preserved breeding with the belching, and Speaight praises Nicol Williamson's Malvolio (though the present reviewer found him in the London transfer unsure of accent and often nearly inaudible). *Measure for Measure*, though Maria Bjornson's imaginative décor promised at least serious treatment of a serious theme, was an 'impertinent travesty of a difficult play'. The Duke was a conjurer, who descended at the end with a placard proclaiming 'Deus ex machina' and Speaight saw the influence of Edward Bond. In London, Peter Hall's *The Tempest* at the National Theatre, despite venial faults, showed the play wonderfully understood, with an unmistakable tempest at the beginning, Prospero's cave and Caliban's cell placed in opposition on the stage, while in Gielgud's Prospero renunciation, like forgiveness, came hard and we realized 'that Ariel is stronger than Prospero.' Stratford's *Cymbeline* was also visited by Frank Kermode (*TLS*), whose heart went out to those faced with the problems of staging a work which is one of the less obviously major items of a classic writer's canon. The production stressed the Vision of Jupiter and its political significance, invited giggles 'where we ought to be disturbed', and cut heavily: 'should our Shakespearians not at least consider playing all the notes? There would still be room for interpretation.'

North American Shakespeare festivals of 1974 are reported in detail in *Shakespeare Quarterly*. Berners W. Jackson at Stratford, Ontario, saw *Love's Labour's Lost, King John*, and a revival of last year's *Pericles*, with only small cast changes, the Simonides austere rather than avuncular, and a Dickensian rather than Hogarthian Boult. *Love's Labour's Lost* favoured the comics, Berowne being played as 'a bright young man on a verbal ego trip'; the setting was nineteenth century and Marcade's entrance stunning. Peter Dew's *King John* was blessedly honest and straightforward, working excellently when staged by someone whose understanding 'derived from a rigorous and sensitive reading of the text.' As last year, the review of Stratford, Connecticut (by Peter Saccio) finds an object lesson in the dominance of set, two unchanging architectural units which imposed upon the audience by scale, a considerable success in *Romeo and Juliet*, and a disaster in *Twelfth Night*. Audience objection, probably due to the influence of Zeffirelli's film, was heard to the age of a Romeo who looked under twenty-five; the Chorus recited two of the sonnets at the end of the first half and at the close. The indoor (Lincoln Center) and outdoor (Central Park) seasons of the New York Shakespeare Festival are reported by M. E. Comtois and Jack J. Jorgens: indoors, *Troilus and Cressida* was

fallaciously linked to Vietnam, *The Tempest* seemed to reject urban life, and *Macbeth* was Watergate. The productions were played in a 'black box' auditorium, with exposed lighting and the downstage exits through aisles which dissect audience space. *Troilus* was the most eccentric—at Hector's slaughter the entablative space at the back, filled by a sheet of flexiglass, was backlit and hosed from behind with 'blood'. Costumes were outrageous and incoherent, Diomedes in a black negligée and Achilles in bikini with matching green feather boa. *Macbeth* showed the impossibility of presenting Shakespeare's tragedies as 'black satirical commentaries'. The same company outdoors played a limp *The Merry Wives of Windsor* and an overwhelmingly successful *Pericles* as put on by a troupe of travelling players. At San Diego, the first two scenes of *Twelfth Night* were played simultaneously and Feste's songs given to Viola and Fabian; in Oregon, the words of Ovid bedecked the stage and were chanted (in Latin or English?) to strike the keynote of *Titus Andronicus*; while the offer to Proteus by Valentine was conveyed by dumbshow to the audience as a ruse devised by him and Silvia. At Colorado, an alcoholic Macbeth was provided with six witches (seeing double?), attractive to boot; *Timon of Athens* was played at nineteen lines per minute. Another *Macbeth*, at the Odessa Globe, a crude cash-in on *The Exorcist*, had three young demons that possess Lady Macbeth, who dies of 'overwhelming tension' during the added exorcism scene. Maine interestingly offered a Shylock who did indeed begin by playing the bond as a merry jest. Champlain compounded its omission of the prison scene *in toto* from *Cymbeline* by having the lovers in *The Tempest* paw each other, Ferdinand inserting a log between

Miranda's legs. Perhaps academics do sometimes have justice on their side.

A fascinating and valuable study of *The Royal Shakespeare Company: The Peter Hall Years*[15] is provided by David Addenbrooke, who after a brief survey of the Memorial Theatre's growth and development and of Hall's career, looks at the organization of the Company (particularly useful here are the appendices showing administrative and artistic responsibility; attendance figures and takings; the form of long-term contract introduced by Hall; listings of productions and tours—though not Theatregoround; staff lists; statements of policy; and awards) during the Crucial Years (1960–63) when the first subsidy was granted and Brook and St Denis were brought in; then during the period as the *Royal Shakespeare Company* (1963–68). As Hall says in his introduction, 'It is pleasing that a theatre company's organization and growth rather than its productions, should be thought worthy of this amount of study', though these latter are not neglected, with chapters on New Concepts and Major Productions (including the Wars of the Roses, Brook's *Lear* and Hall's *Macbeth*). The study is rounded off by interviews (selected from a much larger number drawn on by Addenbrooke throughout the book).

John Russell Brown's ideas about Shakespeare in the Theatre, already current (see *YW* 52 & 53), are gathered in *Free Shakespeare*,[16] an imperative or question as much as a description. The book does not hold together well, its 'occasional' development appearing in, for instance, the (interesting) surveys of design style at Stratford over ten years and of certain Shakespeare productions: though both argue that the designer and director have taken over from the actor, it is not always clear when Brown is approving what he vividly describes, and when he is condemning. His central concerns—with coming freshly to Shakespeare; defending our own creative response and strengthening it; seeing no absolute division between reading, teaching, performing, watching or working on Shakespeare; and urging an actors' theatre—all put him on the side of the angels, but his plans are more nebulous ('tentative' might be a fairer term). He points to the nature of performance in the Elizabethan theatre and suggests, though not wanting any kind of archaeological reconstruction, that here may be the freer models we need—where 'an actor caught a new reality in the ever-changing performance and achieved its expression from his position of prepared, inner power'. Brown would make great demands upon his actors and he suggests, experimentally, the establishment of a company of twelve or so, to give a fluid group situation: they would have no scripts, only cues, and would take rôles of varying importance, the most vital features being 'the primary control by the actors themselves and the ability to change from performance to performance'. The Actors' Theatre Company is clearly attempting something like this, and the currency of Brown's ideas is shown both by Thomson's remarks reviewed above (on actor/audience relationship) and by contributions in *Shakespeare Quarterly* on the workshop and Shakespeare. In this periodical, Jackson G. Barry's 'Shakespeare with Words: The Script and the

[15] *The Royal Shakespeare Company: The Peter Hall Years*, by David Addenbrooke. London: William Kimber. pp. xviii & 334.
[16] *Free Shakespeare*, by John Russell Brown. London: Heinemann Educational Books. pp. vi & 113. Paperback 75p.

Medium of Drama' acknowledges Brown (and Granville-Barker) and is critical of the idea of 'the play itself', a single entity, though he confuses the issue by admitting that there may be productions called 'wrong' (therefore, presumably, others can be 'right': the problem is perhaps only one of terms, but it is there too in Peter Thomson's 'straight' and 'crooked'). Indeed, Brook's *A Midsummer Night's Dream* is called 'incorrect' on what seem legitimate academic grounds. Still, his stress on play (in performance) as against script is valuable, and more relevant to Brown's concerns than Patricia K. Meszaros's 'Notes on a Workshop Approach to Shakespeare' (not uninteresting, but more workshop than Shakespeare: 'trust walks' may be useful to the actor as a preliminary to Gloucester's leap, but they don't solve the problem of making the script into a play). J. L. Styan's 'Direct Method Shakespeare' is lightweight, dealing with matters covered more interestingly by the two previous writers; while in 'Viva Voce: On Speaking and Hearing Shakespeare's Sentences', Warren J. MacIsaac stresses the need for openness and variety of experience, linking back to Addenbrooke's account of Peter Hall's stress on verse-speaking.

Two more volumes of *In Shakespeare's Playhouse,*[17] by Ronald Watkins and Jeremy Lemmon have appeared, devoted to *A Midsummer Night's Dream* and *Hamlet*. As proposed in their earlier *The Poet's Method*, a 'detailed and analytical

account' is given of each, 'as if in continuous performance in Shakespeare's playhouse': 'The question we have constantly proposed to ourselves is "What did the Chamberlain's Men do?"' As historical reconstruction these are useless: the frontispiece represents misleadingly the proportions of the theatre described, and the authors never clearly define the limits of the 'discovery' space and the 'chamber' or balcony—though given that their tiring house space has a depth of only ten feet, neither could extend much behind the tiring-house wall. Yet in *A Midsummer Night's Dream*, Titania's bank *and* the hawthorn brake, together with a good deal of action are in the discovery space; while in *Hamlet*, the whole of the first scene (guards, Horatio, and ghost) is played in the chamber, while the opening of scene two has all the court in the discovery space for sixty lines. There is no sense given of a distinctive Elizabethan style of acting: when Theseus warns Hermia she is 'but as a form of wax', the actor's 'eloquent hands illustrate the modelling image of his comparison', and Burbage is to undertake some kind of expressive mime during 'O that this too too solid flesh', but the authors' silence on its form suggests they boggled at what it might be. No hint is given about possible Elizabethan rhetorical style in language or gesture. There are more particular sillinesses: why should either guard at Elsinore have a pack (they are in a castle, not on a battlefield)? What is this council table for scene two, round which we have the bustle of Polonius and at which Hamlet is seated? These all go against our sense of the speed of Elizabethan playing and no evidence is adduced for this elaborate use of impedimenta. The mechanicals' daily occupations are marked by visible

[17] *In Shakespeare's Playhouse: A Midsummer Night's Dream;* and *In Shakespeare's Playhouse: Hamlet*, by Ronald Watkins and Jeremy Lemmon. Newton Abbott: David and Charles. pp. 150 each. £3.95 each. *In Shakespeare's Playhouse: The Poet's Method*, by Ronald Watkins and Jeremy Lemmon. Newton Abbott: David and Charles. pp. 207. £4.50.

properties: 'Flute uses a pair of bellows, which he is mending, to blow down the neck of Snug, whose strident saw is drowning Quince's attempt' to get attention. This is *bad* school production, not Chamberlain's Men's, and it is a relief to turn from this archaeological fustian to the latest collection of *Prefaces to Shakespeare* by Harley Granville-Barker.[18] Two prefaces (to *Macbeth* and *A Midsummer Night's Dream*, 1924) have not been previously reprinted, while the Introduction to *The Player's Shakespeare* is the original version of 1923; three other prefaces and the British Academy lecture of 1925 are included. Edward M. Moore provides a useful introduction, outlining Granville-Barker's career, though his notes fail to distinguish Byron the poet from Byron the burlesque writer. Granville-Barker's strengths are his sensitivity to the text (script?) and his practical involvement as man of the theatre; even when chatty and exclamatory he can illumine, for instance, 'the perfect sufficiency of Hermione's eight lines (oh, how a lesser dramatist might have overdone it with Noble Forgiveness and what not!)'. Above all, he is concerned with the practical realization of the plays while being true to Shakespeare: 'Gain Shakespeare's effects by Shakespeare's means when you can. But gain Shakespeare's effects; it is your business to discern them.' In discussing *Macbeth*, he is excellent on casting and therefore on the nature of the characters, quoting an excellent insight of Bradley's on Banquo, and demonstrating thereby the fruitful interplay of criticism and experience. To look at the closing paragraphs of the British Academy

lecture is to see how John Russell Brown and Peter Thomson and the academic can contribute each to other: 'To transport Shakespeare from the world of theatre into a vacuum of scholarship is folly. Must we say (I will not admit it) that in the theatre scholarship cannot find a place?'

Interesting light is thrown on Shakespeare in the nineteenth century by W. W. Appleton's *Madame Vestris and the London Stage*,[19] including Shakespeare 'opera-tized' in 1823–4, *The Tempest* having Vestris as Ariel and Macready as Prospero; while in 1827 amateur performances in Lord Normanby's private theatre at Florence included Charles Mathews in *Much Ado*, *Merchant* and *I Henry IV*, and a *Romeo and Juliet* of archaeological exactness; later, in *A Midsummer Night's Dream* (1840–41), reverting to the original text, Vestris played Oberon. Louis D. Mitchell's 'Command Performances during the Reign of George I' (*ECS*), though mainly recording operas, farces and pantomimes, includes *Julius Caesar, Merry Wives, The Tempest* and *Henry VIII*; and Billy J. Harbin's 'John Hodgkinson in the English Provinces, 1765–1792' (*TN*) includes ten plays in the repertoire, amongst them two of Garrick's adaptations. Designs for an eighteenth-century *The Tempest* are the concern of Rüdiger Joppien's 'Philippe Jacques de Loutherbourg und Shakespeares *Sturm*' (*SJH*); and other articles on design in the same publication include Russell Jackson's 'Designer and Director: E. W. Godwin and Wilson Barrett's *Hamlet* of 1884'; Sybil Rosenfeld's 'Alma-Tadema's Designs for Irving's *Coriolanus*', the artist's first work for the

---

[18] *Prefaces to Shakespeare: VI*, by Harley Granville-Barker, intro. by Edward M. Moore. London: Batsford. pp. 167. £2.50. Paperback £1.20.

[19] *Madame Vestris and the London Stage*, by W. W. Appleton. New York/London: Columbia U.P. pp. x & 231.

stage, projected in 1879 but not presented until 1901 as Irving's twelfth and last Shakespeare production, with its Etruscan setting and ten scenes, plates (wrongly numbered in text) helping the reconstruction; Peter Loeffler's 'Gordon Craig und der Moskauer Hamlet von 1922'; and Edmund Stadler's 'Regieskizzen von Adolph Appia zu Shakespeares *Hamlet*'; and Rolf Badenhausen's 'Caspar Nehers Bühnenbauten und Kostüme für *Hamlet* (1926) unter Leopold Jessner'. Details of rôles Kean was to have played are in 'Aut Caesar Aut Nullus: Edmund Kean's Articles of Agreement, 1825' by Alfred L. Nelson and B. Gilbert Cross (*Nineteenth Century Theatre Research*); and the same journal has an account of Poole's 1828 travesty of *Hamlet* playing in 1840 with great success, in David L. Rinear's 'Burlesque Comes to New York: William Mitchell's First Season at the Olympic'; while in 'Two Notes on William Poel's Sources', Stephen C. Schultz suggests, in speaking and speed, the influence of Samuel Brandram the reciter, and on Poel's notions of 'tunes' and 'keywords', that of the Comédie Française. A mildly entertaining footnote is J. W. Robinson's 'An Amateur among Professionals: "When I performed Othello"', a street ballad of 1836, companion to one on Richard III, ludicrously describing an amateur's performance of the rôle.

More directly theatrical, Arthur Colby Sprague considers when Marcade's entrance was first seen as essential to a change of mood in *Love's Labour's Lost*, and 'Monsieur Marcade' (*TN*), noting that a 1918 Old Vic producer hoped the audience would be 'lightly amused by it', refers to Granville-Barker's preface and an Oxford production of the same year (1924) as first giving emphasis to the entrance. Two modern productions are considered by Wolf-Rainer Wilberg's 'Ein "Zersplitterter" *Hamlet*: Bemerkungen zur Kollage von Charles Marowitz' (*SJW*), and by Günther Jarfe's examination of the 1972 National Theatre production in 'Das Bühnenbild in *Macbeth*' (*SJH*). In the same journal Timothy O'Brien describes 'Designing a Shakespeare Play: *Richard II*', which takes account of general company policy and gives details of the upper level for Flint Castle (done away with in the 1974 revival). The seasons in Germany are described (for the East) by Armin-Gerd Kuckhoff's 'Shakespeare auf den Bühnen der DDR im Jahre 1972': listing casts, theatres, and plays (fourteen in all); and (for the West) by Christian Janslin's 'Bühnen bericht 1973', a survey and list of productions, twenty plays in all, the Last Plays and *Henry IV* being notably absent. A pleasant but unchallenging chat, 'Judi Dench talks to Gareth Lloyd Evans' (*ShS*), includes comments on Zeffirelli's Old Vic *Romeo and Juliet*, Trevor Nunn's *The Winter's Tale*, and a West African tour of *Macbeth* (though Dench misremembers that she *did* play Lady Macbeth in England—at Nottingham in 1962, and very good she was). Particularly interesting is her account of a sense of rhythm she has learnt for Shakespeare, so that she feels an absence, even pain, when something is cut.

6. INDIVIDUAL PLAYS AND POEMS

All's Well That Ends Well

The most important article is that by W. L. Godshalk, '*All's Well That Ends Well* and the Morality Play' (*SQ*), which has the double advantage of a critically alert background and something useful to say. Taking up recent suggestions about the possible modifications of the Morality tradition, Godshalk argues that we must be more alert to the alterations in that tradition, the biggest change being that made by Shakespeare in this play. 'Ostensibly the play is a refutation of the Morality ethic, since Helena gains her desired end through questionable means'. But 'the play does not truly end "well" for either Helena or Bertram. From this stance, the play may be seen as an ironic or even comic confirmation of Morality ethics, where we are shown what happens when bad means achieve their proper ends *without metaphysical intervention*'. 'The characters,' he concludes, 'are not kept morally distinct . . . the King, like the other characters, retains a moral obtuseness which will lead by moral causality to recurring cycles of deception. For the sophisticated audience, the effect is darkly humorous—a comic Morality Play'. Neil Carson suggests 'Some Textual Implications of Tyrone Guthrie's 1953 Production of *All's Well That Ends Well*' (*SQ*). He enters the thorny wood of the Folio stage directions, and zestfully hacks a way through. His method is one too often neglected in strictly editorial discussions—analysis of the possibilities of stage production. The piece is especially valuable on what can loosely be called the E. and G. problem (the confused designations of some minor characters), and Guthrie's solution of 'carefully introducing distinctions among the characters generally lumped together' is usefully explored. Frances M. Pearce contributes 'In Quest of Unity: A Study of Failure and Redemption in *All's Well That Ends Well*' (*SQ*). She writes: 'Through the simultaneous development of romantic and realistic viewpoints in the play we are made aware of a paradox about the power . . . and the powerlessness of love', a

paradox growing from 'the basic organizing and unifying pattern . . . failure redeemed by grace.' Though the analysis is perhaps over-long there are good insights on the way.

Antony and Cleopatra

Anne Barton's inaugural lecture[20] begins by pointing to certain plays by Sophocles that reach their tragic climax, then without warning press on beyond it, a feature she terms a 'divided catastrophe'. She suggests that 'a dramatist is likely to experiment with a divided catastrophe when he wants and needs, for some reason, to alter the way his audience has been responding to the experience of the play'. She looks at the way Antony in Act IV seems to move towards reconciliation within himself between the warring values of Rome and Egypt; and she argues that we want terribly to believe it, since our sympathies are all with Antony, even the interchange of male and female between the protagonists holding something of the search for unity and wholeness. With Antony's death comes a feeling that the conclusion is at hand; that Cleopatra will follow without delay —yet there remains the whole of Act V. Barton here surveys earlier plays on Cleopatra, only Daniel's offering a significant link: 'I think myself that his reading of Daniel's play impelled him towards the one use, in all his tragedies, of the divided catastrophe.' (Barton apparently agrees with Arthur M. Z. Norman's belief (1958) that Daniel's version served as precedent for 'Shakespeare's daring use of two climaxes.') We want Cleopatra to die and she is able by her decision to define their love, which people throughout the play have tried to pin

[20] '*Nature's piece 'gainst fancy': the divided catastrophe in 'Antony and Cleopatra*', by Anne Barton. London: Bedford College, U of London, 1973. pp. 20.

down without any sense of progression in their attempts. In the end Cleopatra 'not only redeems the bungled and clumsy nature of Antony's death . . . by catching it up and transforming it within her own, flawless farewell; she crystallizes and stills all the earlier and more ambiguous tableaux of the play'.

Peter Meredith usefully reopens the problem of '"That Pannelled Me at Heels": *Antony and Cleopatra* IV.x.34' (*ES*), rejecting Hilda Hulme's 'parnel/pernel' ('a priest's concubine; a harlot') on linguistic, semantic and paleographic grounds, as also 'spaniel'd'. His own candidate is 'pantled', diminutive of 'pant', for which he gives evidence of existence, use, and transition to Folio's 'pannelled'; and he links it to the imagery sequence of the passage. John Shaw's '"In Every Corner of the Stage": *Antony and Cleopatra*, IV.iii.' (*ShakS*) argues interestingly if not entirely convincingly that the setting of the soldiers, related emblematically to the world/ stage equation, shows that Shakespeare wished to signify that the stage did indeed represent the world at that moment and not just Alexandria; so that Hercules (changed from Plutarch's Bacchus) is not simply going from the city and to Caesar's camp, but is leaving the earth altogether, the dramatization of the departure of a certain kind of virtue heralding the demise of Antony and of greatness on earth. Though not directly concerned with Shakespeare, Mary Morrison's survey, 'Some Aspects of the Treatment of the Theme of Antony and Cleopatra in Tragedies of the Sixteenth Century' (*Journal of European Studies*), includes amongst nine plays Garnier's *Marc Antoine*, the Countess of Pembroke's translation, Daniel's *Cleopatra*, and Samuel Brandon's Tragicomoedia of the *Vertuous Octavia*.

As You Like It.

In a brief but useful note, Winifried Schleiner ('"'Tis like the howling of Irish Wolves against the Moone": A Note on *As You Like It* V. ii. 109' (*ELN*) persuasively suggests that critics from Malone on have been barking up the wrong tree, making a simple combination of topical ideas (the Irish veneration of wolves, and the supposed moon idolatry of the "wild Irish") into an unnecessarily complicated matter, with all the paraphernalia of a supposed lost allusion.

Coriolanus

Joseph Weixlmann's 'How the Romans were beat Back to their Trenches: An Historical Note on *Coriolanus*, I.iv' (*N&Q*) offers conjectures as to the staging of the scene, drawing on earlier suggestions.

Cymbeline

John Scott Colley's 'Disguise and New Guise in *Cymbeline*' (*ShakS*) fails to provide the answer he hoped for to the unsatisfactory nature of Posthumus but is interesting. Colley's approach is through the Elizabethan understanding of this raging, jealous husband, and his discussion throws up interesting ideas about Posthumus's emblematic rôle, 'not a moving psychological portrait, but . . . rather a pictorial one', and about moral states suggested through costume and costume changes. It may be doubted, as Colley claims, whether the Elizabethans saw in Posthumus's 'guises' sufficient indication of moral growth for the comic conclusion of his personal drama to be artistically convincing; but there are insights into the presentation through report and Posthumus's 'determination to die an emblem of truth': his great deeds are performed while wearing humble weeds, and presumably he will once again adopt the prince's garb, 'that will not belie his true nature.' Imogen is also discussed and her 'blindness' linked to that of Posthumus.

Hamlet

D. K. C. Todd's *I am not Prince Hamlet*[21] does not really constitute a study of the play; rather it uses the play as a base from which the author bounces off often disparate ideas about Shakespeare, the teaching of English in Universities, and himself. Todd plays on paradoxes and rhetorical questions, but he also hazards questions on the treatment of incest, fratricide and madness in *Hamlet*. The book is whimsical and uneven in its approach, but it manages to be stimulating about some important problems.

Harold Skulsky's article '"I know my course": Hamlet's confidence' (*PMLA*) treats the tradition of *notatio*, or the remarking of inward character from outward nature, in the play. Skulsky argues that, whereas Hamlet taunts Polonius and Claudius with the defects in their observation, the Prince himself is a failure in his *notatio*, and this failure is due to the 'same hubristic optimism as his successes'.

More hazardously, Keith Brown ('Polonius, and Fortinbras [and Hamlet?]' (*E.S.*)) suggests a link between Polonius and the Danish statesman Henrik Ramel (Ramelius). He also argues for an active Jacobean interest in Denmark, due not only to historic familiarity but also to the presence of a Danish Queen familiar with Ramel. Brown concludes with the suggestion that the figure of Hamlet may be related to contemporary contradictory impressions of

Denmark. More trenchantly, in 'Hamlet and the "Moriae Encomium"' (*ShS*), Frank McCombie points to Shakespeare's probable knowledge of Erasmus's *Moriae Encomium*, and demonstrates its likely influence on the humanistic values of the play.

Most rewarding is Juliet McLauchlan's 'The Prince of Denmark and Claudius's Court' (*ShS*), which argues the connexion between Claudius's violation of natural order before the beginning of the play and the importance of his assuming the title of 'Denmark'. Consequently, in his contact with Elsinore, Hamlet's view of the world has degenerated, and his own personality shows a disintegration of the Renaissance ideal. At the end of the play, Juliet McLauchlan argues, we observe the tragic waste of potential, for Hamlet neither achieves a higher understanding nor has he regained 'wholeness'.

Henry IV

Alan C. Dessen's 'The Intemperate Knight and the Politic Prince: Late Morality Structure in *I Henry IV*' (*ShakS*) is complementary to Norman Council's discussion of the play ('Prince Hal: Mirror of Success' (*ShakS*)). Council's article is essentially a chapter from his *When Honour's at the Stake*, noticed last year, and relates interestingly to David Scott Kastan's article on the Histories discussed above. Dessen re-examines the assumptions as to what constitutes a morality play, to show that to accept the idea of Falstaff as Vice and Hal as 'Every Prince' is 'to simplify and distort Shakespeare's carefully wrought dramatic structure', since in many moralities the *Humanum Genus* figure is absent; and patterns of corrupted figures set against a homilectic virtue, as well as dramatic structures built upon dual protagonists and consecutive scenes of their

[21] *I am not Prince Hamlet*, by D. K. C. Todd (Shakespeare Criticism Schools of English). University of London Press. pp. 199. £2.95.

way of life, show that '"Unification in a central character" is decidedly *not* the sole means by which the morality . . . achieved its goals.' Hal is not *Humanum Genus* since Riot (if this is Falstaff) is not in charge but rather tolerated and enjoyed, while Hal's control is demonstrated by his 'I know you all' soliloquy. An interesting analysis of the dual structure follows, and at Shrewsbury 'Hal's erect posture over such recumbent figures is therefore a visual summary of his total triumph, not only as a warrior who has won honour but more important as a controller rather than one of the controlled'. Hal's control of the situation (though most readings of the play unhampered by a theory of dramatic tradition have long accepted the idea) is emphasized by Paul A. Gottschalk's 'Hal and the "Play Extempore" in *I Henry IV*' (*TSLL*), which begins by denying that the dramatic rôle-playing in the Boar's Head is a play within a play and so cannot lead to a 'discovery of self through pretense'. Since Hal is in the same mind as in his II.i soliloquy, he cannot be said to reject Falstaff as such in the play episode (he has already done so); rather Shakespeare copes with the problem of moving towards an inevitable conclusion by providing Hal with three analogous episodes of promise (soliloquy, play, interview with Henry IV) that seem to build to the fulfilment of Shrewsbury, but do little to bring it about. Each episode is followed by an apparent moral lapse to maintain suspense. In the play scene, Hal 'is speaking first as player-King and then in his actual rôle of future king, and we see that the two rôles are continuous, that, in fact, Hal hasn't been acting at all', but transforms play back into reality, a device marking a shift not in Hal's character but in the point of view of

the play itself. Gottschalk's idea does not entirely account for Hal's gilding with a lie Falstaff's claim to Hotspur, since there ought to be no suspense through apparent moral lapse if the play is completed at Shrewsbury; but it is useful on structure and play. Paul N. Siegel's 'Falstaff and his Social Milieu' (*SJW*) suggests the knight is very much from the London of Shakespeare's time, comparing him with Samuel Rowland's 'melancholy knight', 'in his disdain for the commercialism and the degeneracy of the age, in his pride in his lineage', which leads not to condemnation but the rather unexpected praise of the knight as a 'representative of the enduring spirit of ordinary humanity coping through the ages with the knocks of a rough world'. Myra Hinman contributes 'Teaching *I Henry IV* to Beginning College Students' (*SQ*) to a pedagogical symposium; and though to say of Henry's opening speech that the 'broken phrases are themselves panting and "shortwinded"' is useless impressionism, she is right in stressing for these students comedy, not history. Christopher R. Reaske's 'A Shakespearean Back Drop for Dryden's *Mac Flecknoe*?' (*SQ*) links Flecknoe's props as king with those of the play scene in *I Henry IV*.

Henry V

Investigating the echoes of Tamburlaine in the play, Roy Battenhouse suggests, in 'The Relation of Henry V to Tamburlaine' (*ShS*), that previously these have been noted rather than probed. His enquiry rejects the idea of Henry V as a Christian hero, opposed to Tamburlaine; he sees likenesses in their scope of ambition and the proven hollowness of their triumphs (though surely that sense is hardly enforced in *Tamburlaine* as the Chorus enforces the loss of France in

Henry V; and the parallels of the queens seems a confusion between plays and history). Objections crop up again as Battenhouse compares the killing of Calyphas with the rejection of Falstaff, a parallel in action but hardly in tone. Again while Pistol's Tamburlaine vein may parody Henry, do parodies work only one way? Good points include his stress on the humorous element. Though the essay is provocative, the accepted complexity of Henry's image is not substantially altered.

Henry VI

Gwyn Williams' 'Suffolk and Margaret: a Study of Some Sections of Shakespeare's *Henry VI*' (*SQ*) analyses the 'illicit . . . unhistorical' love-affair in a detailed commentary, raising the most interesting question of Shakespeare's purpose in the invention, and then saying that it is no more than an essay in tragic relationships. In the present climate of rediscovery of the *Henry VI* plays, one hoped for more. Hanspeter Born very usefully rehearses at length a familiar problem in 'The date of *2, 3 Henry VI*' (*SQ*), collecting, and lucidly treating, all the evidence, and coming firmly to the conclusion that Shakespeare wrote the plays between March and August 1592.

Julius Caesar

The meaning and implication of 'Stoic' are raised first by Giles Monsarrat's 'Le Stoïcisme dans *Julius Caesar*, Ou les préjugés de la critique' (*EA*). Noting that, despite Harbage's caveat of 1952, critics have not limited use of the word 'stoicism', he looks more closely at Plutarch's references and concludes we should not equate the term 'Stoic' with constancy or fortitude. A second article offers a scathing, well-directed assault on Brutus's reputation (Marvin L. Vawter's '"Division 'tween Our Souls": Shakespeare's Stoic Brutus' (*ShakS*)), rightly claiming the deciphering of Brutus as the beginning of unravelling the play's complexity. Starting from the observation that most critical discussion implies that the character must be salvaged from outright condemnation, Vawter denies that Brutus is either hero or pathetic victim. He shows what Shakespeare might know of Brutus's Stoicism, chiefly from Cicero's polemic (which fundamentally argues that 'the Stoics simply do not understand the true nature of human beings') and contends that Brutus ironically demonstrates the insufficiency of virtue-reason, so that 'his inflated mind tyrannizes over his body and the emotional feeling within the body. That is, his mind is the tyrant and his heart is the bondslave.' There are weaknesses in verbal interpretation, and we surely are not to see Portia as bleeding at the moment she talks of her self-inflicted wound; but the idea is persuasive that 'Brutus commits, not a sacrificial ritual of cultural salvation, but a savage felony of cultural assassination.' Emile Gasquet examines the politics of the play in 'Le Machiavelisme d'Antoine dans *Julius Caesar*' (*EA*), linking it to modern concerns as a play which, 'like *Les mains sales* of Sartre, is a reflection on the ways and means of politics, on the connexion between politics and morals, not . . . an abstract reflection, but one translated at the human level in a conflict that troubles the soul and wounds the heart.' A lighter note is introduced by E. L. Dachslager, whose '"The Most Unkindest Cut": A Note on *Julius Caesar* III.ii. 187' (*ELN*) suggests (from Plutarch) that Brutus's one wound given to Caesar was 'about his privities', and that Antony alludes to this in his oration.

King Lear

S. L. Goldberg's *An Essay on King Lear*[22] opens appropriately with the quotation bidding us to 'speak what we feel, not what we ought to say'. It is a dense and acute study which weighs and rejects much recent interpretation that has tended to seek formulable philosophies in the play. Goldberg starts with Johnson's disquiet, and develops it through Bradley's observations into a careful and searching argument, continually stressing neither a confident sense of affirmation nor one of negation. The book points to themes of love and forgiveness together with the horrors of blinding as the 'positive and negative poles of the one moral force'. Questions are forced on characters by the play's world, but neither the play, nor the audience's study of it, offers reasoned answers to them.

An opposite position is confidently taken by Hugh L. Hennedy in his essay '*King Lear*: Recognizing the Ending' (*SP*). Hennedy traces the idea of 'recognition' through the play, and holds that the ending affirms hope rather than despair.

Donna B. Hamilton argues that Shakespeare may have drawn from both the legend of Robert of Sicily and Lodge's *Robert the Devil* ('Some Romance Sources for *King Lear*' (*SP*)); and in his 'Comparative Reception of *King Lear*: An Experiment in International Education' (*SQ*), P. J. Mroczkowski reports the results of a poll of response to the play by British, French and Polish students. Mroczkowski finds that his groups reacted similarly, and concludes that thus literature informs basic scales of value.

[22] *An Essay on King Lear*, by S. L. Goldberg. Cambridge U.P. pp. 192.

Love's Labour's Lost

S. K. Heninger, Jr., in 'The Pattern of *Love's Labour's Lost*' (*ShakS*), contributes a long piece of heavy and very erudite critical analysis of the songs, as illuminating the 'esthetic and thematic problems raised by the play's ending. The play's structure and its poetic theme depend upon the integration of drama and song, two disparate orders of poetic endeavour'. Robert G. Hunter's 'The Function of the Songs at the end of *Love's Labour's Lost*' (*ShakS*) develops a strongly personal account of an attempt to reconcile 'linear, Lenten time with circular, Carnival time' in the play (with special reference to the songs) and a postscript supporting the Shakespearean ascription of the poem recently noticed in Cambridge University Library MS Dd.5.75. Folio 46, by a singularly inept association with his reading of *Love's Labour's Lost*. Neal L. Goldstein writes '*Love's Labour's Lost* and the Renaissance Vision of Love' (*SQ*) to counter some of the more unbalanced American criticisms of the play in the sixties, whereby all its elements were subjugated to its language.'In the present study,' he writes, 'I address myself to an analysis of the play in terms of the Renaissance vision of love, specifically to Shakespeare's satirizing of Florentine Neoplatonism and Petrarchanism, the major components of that vision.' He maintains that the play is 'a uniquely English treatment of the vision of love born in Renaissance Italy', the Englishness being mockery in the best sixteenth-century tradition. Though this very long article has some interesting material to offer, and rightly concludes that the play, in presenting the tension between spirit and sense, does not 'ever fully make up its mind', the comedy Shakespeare wrote somehow slips through the critical net.

Macbeth

In his thorough but conventional reading, *The Primrose Way*,[23] Clifford Davidson sees the play as treating a disturbance of natural order. He stresses scriptural and historical parallels for the play's imagery and theme, and examines *Macbeth* in the light of Elizabethan and Jacobean reasoning on the cosmos and the commonwealth. Davidson justifies his reading by quoting an interesting range of contemporary theorists and theologians.

In his article 'Macbeth's Genial Porter' (*ELR*), Michael J. B. Allen suggests a 'chain of connexion' resultant from the entry for '*genius*' in Calepine's *Dictionarium* (1516). Allen seeks to show a relation between the porter's rôle of '*genius loci*' and the play as a whole, and more tenuously considers the porter as an '*alter ego*' for Macbeth. More conventionally, Fernand Lagarde ('Rowe's Temple Haunting Martlet Re-examined', *Caliban* (Annales Publiées par L'Université de Toulouse le Mirail) Tome X) argues that Rowe's emendment of 'barlet' to 'martlet' (I.vi.3) correctly reflects Shakespeare's heraldic reference to the line of Edward the Confessor.

Measure for Measure

The reader should not be put off by Joanne Altieri's second sentence in 'Style and Social Disorder in *Measure for Measure*' (*SQ*): 'Both the management of standard stock characters and his manipulation of the *Stiltrennung* move the playworld into discord—away from the formal and thematic harmonies of the romantic comedies into a world where the variety of social images is not resolved but left

in friction at the play's close'. A comparison of Dull (compared with Dogberry—'It is surprising how many effects Shakespeare could derive from a few bald devices') leads to a contrast of low comic speech with heavily patterned prose speeches, especially those between Isabella and the Duke in III.i, and the observation that the only character who can use both styles is Escalus. The 'discontinuous speech styles' mirror the 'fragmented society' of Vienna: 'No longer can closing marriages constitute harmonic symbols'. 'Mode and Character in *Measure for Measure*' by Lucy Owen (*SQ*) tackles the problem of dramatizing a state of mind—in this case forgiveness—complicated by the absence of direct presentation of the divine and by the increased realism of the characters. Some illuminating illustrations support the first part of the analysis, before she explores 'the two major types of change represented in the play, one of which expresses sin, the other its forgiveness and redemption'. She follows A. P. Rossiter in calling the first 'shiftingness,' and herself explores the second, as 'change of heart,' penetratingly, focusing on Isabella's dilemma. Her final account of the states of intention and actuality in the characters is especially fine. Harold Fisch, in 'Shakespeare and the Puritan Dynamic' (*ShS*) tackles three Puritans, (Shylock, Malvolio, and Angelo) as demonstrating the use of abuse of power. Insisting that Shakespeare took Puritanism very seriously, Fisch relates his characters, especially Angelo, to Ramist dialectic and to current Puritan concerns.

The Merchant of Venice

This play has inspired two striking articles which place it in larger contexts. 'The Elizabethan Stage Jew and Christian Example:

[23] *The Primrose Way: A Study of Shakespeare's 'Macbeth'*, by Clifford Davidson. Conesville, Iowa. John Westbury & Associates. pp. 105.

Gerontus, Barabas, and Shylock' (*MLQ*) is Alan C. Dessen's slightly over-sensitive analysis of an apparently persecuted Jewishness in a Christian society (beginning 'There is no final solution to the Shylock problem'). With useful relation to Robert Wilson and Marlowe, and by way of G. K. Hunter's exposition of sixteenth-century views of Jewishness as a state of mind rather than a matter of race or religion, he gives a demonstration of Shylock's 'function as a theatrical device . . . to anatomize the inner reality of a society Christian in name but not necessarily in deed.' The method is not new, but Dessen makes a more illuminating comparison than is commonly found. More surprising, more academically rigorous, and more stimulating, is W. Nicholas Knight's long account of 'Equity, *The Merchant of Venice* and William Lambarde' (*ShS*), which is clearly going to prove seminal in *Merchant* studies. The good Lambarde has been haunting the battlements of the Shakespearean world for some time: so many of his interests seem oddly to have the same colour-range as Shakespeare's, without ever quite making shapes that would fit. Now Professor Knight fits a piece of him in, just where he is needed, in Shakespeare's precise treatment of specialized branches of the law: and he does two other things as well—he makes the best case yet to appear for the value of the accumulating knowledge of Shakespeare's life as comment on the work, and he opens new territory of response to the intricacies of Shylock *v.* Antonio. By both illuminating for us the contemporary conflict between law and equity, and at the same time firmly linking the play to the personality and viewpoint of Lambarde, Professor Knight gives the student of *Merchant* something both stimulating and

beyond mere speculation. For Lambarde was Master of Chancery, and writing a book about it too, and a Chancery case of Shakespeare's was one of a group which caused much legal concern. Lambarde went to plays in Surrey Bankside. In *The Merchant of Venice*, Shakespeare 'is presenting Chancery procedure and advocating that it be used precisely along its theoretical lines of a superior court with its accompanying appellate function and humane spirit, so as not to abrogate the common law of Queen's Bench and Common Pleas, and thus become merely a rival court.' No wonder a book of Lambarde's carries Shakespeare's signature.

John K. Hale's '*The Merchant of Venice* and *Il Pecorone*' (*AUMLA*, 1973) discusses the relationship between play and source.

The Merry Wives of Windsor

In *PMLA*, J. A. Bryant, Jr., writes 'Falstaff and the Renewal of Windsor'. He quotes only two critics later than Frye in 1948, both of them of the fifties. He seems not to know of H. J. Oliver's fine Arden edition. He does not seem aware of the play's great success on the stage, or indeed of any serious criticism. Yet he writes that 'over the years surprisingly few' have challenged Dennis's and Rowe's 'contention that Shakespeare wrote it in response to the Queen's expressed wish to see Falstaff in love'. What follows is an attempt to what one can only term mythify Falstaff (yet again) by means of the *Golden Bough* and the rituals of 'Carrying out Death'. Bryant solemnly observes: 'Frazer records no observance in which laundry, as such, is used as part of a ceremony' but he draws his supposed Shakespearean parallels from Debschwitz in Thuringia and mid-lent observances in parts of

Silesia—only to point out that the parallels do not fit at all. The bulk of the article is an attempt to equate Falstaff with scapegoat rituals, by means of illustrations from Frazer and generalizations about the play. The result is a conspicuous lack of assistance in understanding *Merry Wives*.

A Midsummer-Night's Dream

Richard Henze ('*A Midsummer Night's Dream*: Analogous Image' (*ShS*)) sets out to show that 'while Shakespeare's dramatized theory of the imagination resembles somewhat that of Sidney and his colleagues, it reveals itself finally to be a theory of the creative imagination unfettered by Platonic frenzy or Aristotelian ideal imitation as it demonstrates the selective imitation that will proceed from observation of life, experience with common images, and awareness of the nature of the audience's relationship to a play.' N. D. Isaacs and J. E. Reese write a brief piece ('Dithyramb and Paean in *A Midsummer Night's Dream*' (*ES*)) to suggest 'very broadly, many ways in which . . . it . . . seems to be patterned on a Dionysian celebration', described as 'a periodic suspension of Apollonian order.' After listing several elementary characteristics of the play, and describing their own list as 'so large a number of suggestions, correspondences, parallels, and allusions' they then disarmingly, but possibly unwittingly, state that their attempt 'to render meaningful' the Dionysian-celebration pattern of *A Midsummer Night's Dream* fails. This is an overblown account of a supposed function of an imposed pattern which doesn't fit: it quite fails to throw any useful light on the play whatever. Yet Thomas Clayton achieves yet worse: ' "Fie What a Question's That If Thou Wert Near

a Lewd Interpreter": The Wall Scene in *A Midsummer-Night's Dream*' (*ShakS*) can only be described as preposterous. Clayton writes an inflated, long, arch article, in the style of chic/lavatorial *graffiti*, to suggest that the lovers' dialogue was supposed to take place between Wall's parted legs, thus affording 'a line in wry . . . equivocation and a spectacle of kinetic grotesquerie.' Clayton seems quite ignorant of the ancient European two-finger gesture, which is perfectly adequate, needs no further gloss, and is obvious from 'let him hold his fingers thus.'

Much Ado about Nothing

Robert F. Fleissner makes the best case yet for the identification of Meres' mysterious 'Love's Labour's Won' with *Much Ado*, and neatly points out that in spite of all the recent fun with 'noting' and 'nothing' Meres' title is a better one. ' "Love's Labour's Won" and the Occasion of *Much Ado*' (*ShS*) reviews with economy and grace the cases for other identifications, and in supporting his good case for *Much Ado* becomes only mildly fanciful (the registering of the play 'in the century-year 1600 lent itself easily to another titular pun: 'A doo' and 'a Doo' stand as puns on 1600 *Anno Domini*' —but what about Won/One?) He is safer on Won/Nothing ground, though still increasingly speculative.

Othello

Gino J. Matteo's *Shakespeare's Othello: The Study and the Stage 1604–1904*[25] attempts to bring together three centuries of theatrical and literary interpretation of the play. Matteo deals with the critical response to textual variants and dedi-

[25] *Shakespeare's Othello: The Study and the Stage 1604–1904*, by Gino J. Matteo. Salzburg Studies in English, Salzburg. pp. 286.

cates subsequent chapters to the results of *Othello*'s consistent popularity. The volume is a comprehensive and useful conflation of sources, charting often familiar territory, but offering a sound general commentary. Matteo ends his survey with a brief discussion of Bradley, concluding that interpretation has most frequently been dependent upon contemporary taste.

Doris Adler's article, 'The Rhetoric of Black and White in *Othello*' (*SQ*), concerns itself with the problem of teaching the play to black students and studies the rhetorical values and the overtones of the word 'black' and 'white' within the play.

Pericles

The use of myth to provide structure is considered by Peggy Ann Knapp in 'The Orphic Vision of *Pericles*' (*TSLL*), which claims that the 'narrative that reveals the real structure of *Pericles* is the myth of Orpheus'; but as she has then to find a romance version of the story, it is not clear how a parallel of the play with 'Sir Orfeo' really helps, since the connection takes us as easily back to Gower; and other romances by their very nature (e.g. 'Sir Gawain and the Green Knight') have the 'distinguishing' elements of narrator, incident, wandering, striving—and finding. Neatly written though it is, the article's parallels are not functional but casual, except insofar as both are romances and Knapp wants an Orpheus parallel. James O. Wood seeks to restore more of the play to the bard in 'Shakespeare's Hand in *Pericles*' (*N&Q*), arguing for Shakespearean usage in I.i (Antiochus's description of his daughter). He also suggests that much of the vocabulary and imagery in the first part is indigenous to Shakespeare's early work, and the

whole play is perhaps apprentice work to which later touches were added in the last three acts. John P. Cutts's long title hides a short and modestly useful note: 'Pericles in Rusty Armour, and the Matachine Dance of the Competitive Knights at the Court of Simonides' (*YES*) suggests the influence of Sidney's *Arcadia* on the presentation of the tournament of knights, who dance a matachine, 'which supposedly first demonstrates their military prowess and then supposedly underscores their manly prowess in bed.'

The Phoenix and the Turtle

This lively study[26] is often illuminated by wit and a sense of humour, no mean achievement given some of the searches for meaning provoked by the poem. Underwood draws heavily on Rollins's *Variorum* edition (properly acknowledged) for work up to 1936 and, though the main study finishes in early 1970, there is an appendix of later work. He starts first with the text and its authenticity (Underwood believes Shakespeare wrote it), the categories here including 'Bemused Acknowledgement of Authenticity' and 'Armed Assertion of Authenticity'. He notes that it is now so generally accepted in the canon that Prince, in the New Arden, never raises the question of authenticity. Then he looks at allegorical interpretation, both related to Chester's *Love's Martyr* and *in vacuo*; he surveys the Classical and Source studies; and he concludes with Critical and Dramatic Interpretations, which embrace the poem's relationship to its intellectual environment (e.g. Platonism), to the

[26] *Shakespeare's 'The Phoenix and Turtle': A Survey of Scholarship*, by Richard Allan Underwood. (Salzburg Studies in English Literature: Elizabethan Studies, vol. 15) Salzburg: Universität Salzburg. pp. 366. £4.80.

metaphysical style, and to similar concerns in the plays. Underwood is prepared to be downright, and to defend what seems unjustly neglected, as between Bates and Bradbrook: 'In general, I do not think Bradbrook has thought about the poem a great deal; and in spite of the few excesses of his article, I think that Bates has'. There is no index, and, though not directly on the poem, R. L. Green's 'The Phoenix and the Tree' (*English* 7: 1948) might have been in the bibliography.

The Rape of Lucrece

G. W. Majors, in 'Shakespeare's First Brutus: his Role in *Lucrece*' (*MLQ*), comments on the original, carefully ambivalent treatment of L. Junius Brutus, 'the mysterious pragmatist who gets the last word and the last seven stanzas'. Majors suggests that we might read Brutus as capitalizing on the woe of Collatine and Lucretius, rather than assuaging it, and follows that line most interestingly. He notes shrewdly that 'The conclusion ... is noisy with source echoes, most of them traceable to one or both of the Augustans [Ovid and Livy]'; and he opens up this strange, political figure in one of the best short critical comments on the poem for a long time.

Richard II

Lois Potter may attach undue importance to the Christ-figure idea of Richard when she begins 'The Antic Disposition of Richard II' (*ShS*) by arguing 'that Richard is in fact rather less virtuous than has often been thought and, just for that reason, a '"better" dramatic character', and the *dramatic* nature of the character she gives may not be self-evident, but she offers many insights into the seriousness of Richard, a man who believes in himself and the importance of his rôle even when he is

acting. She notices a disparity between Richard's silence or deflationary responses in the first part of the play and his eloquence in the second (related to Emrys Jones's 'scenic structure', perhaps?), but is not satisfied with the idea that an actor should interpret one part according to how the other is played. Taking Nicholas Brooke's idea that Richard confuses our response to the cosmic and political themes he embodies and expresses, she argues that the 'interest of Richard's character lies in his ability to *use*, and not simply to embody, the emotional associations of these themes. This use only gradually becomes conscious and ... co-exists with a capacity for emotional involvement.' She sees Richard at Barkloughly as still believing effective action possible, but caught in the contradictory rôles of King and Christian, between which he oscillates yet each of which he plays sincerely. Cut off from effective action, Richard begins to make use of the two rôles for his own purpose (the most exciting point in Potter's argument), so that in the Deposition scene he can outweigh Bolingbroke and his peers and by words opens the way for 'just such a conspiracy as we see taking shape', and in his coffin Richard 'dominates the scene in his silence as he had dominated it before with words'.

Despite the brashness of its beginning, including an apparent readiness to cut Gloucester's 'suicide', Sheldon P. Zitner's 'Aumerle's Conspiracy' (*SEL*) argues well for inclusion of the conspiracy in performance, seeing it as fully intended farce (as in the Prospect Theatre's production), and speaks of York's putting on of his boots and the Duchess's exit as 'harsh geriatric slapstick'. More doubtful is his corollary that Shakespeare in this was exhibiting a clear disaffection with the mode of historical tragedy.

Richard III

An important critical analysis is William B. Toole's 'The Motif of Psychic Division in "Richard III" ' (*ShS*). The aim is to show how Shakespeare's treatment of the motif of division, acting as 'a dramaturgical and thematic principle', is worked out through Richard's character. A sensible account of the relationship between internecine divisions, in the individual and in the state, setting the play in its proper place with the *Henry VI* plays, leads to a long and valuable commentary on Richard's split nature, showing that the two selves shift into different selves as the play proceeds, as he suffers at the same time 'psychological attrition'. Admirable observation shows why Richard's final encounter with conscience lacks stature, but 'succeeds in moving the drama at least a few steps away from fascinating melodrama toward the profundity of tragedy.' Two other pieces on *Richard III* are less helpful, to say the least. Bettie Anne Doebler, writing '"Dispaire and Dye": The Ultimate Temptation of Richard III' (*ShakS*), induces the same ultimate temptation in the reader. Any material that illuminates Richard wisely and understandingly is welcome, and her aim—to demonstrate 'Shakespeare's use of the popular symbolic tradition of the *ars moriendi* to dramatize the example of a wicked king who has lived badly and must be shown to die badly'—is not unpromising. But what follows is heavily obfuscating. *Richard III*, V.iii. 'moves closer to the theological dimension than much of Shakespeare' and 'is not sensitive to the iconographical implications of both staging and language'. One is tempted to prescribe a hearty dose of G. B. Shaw on Richard's end. Yet there is worse. John B. Harcourt, in '"Odde old Ends, Stolne . . .": King Richard and Saint Paul' (*ShakS*), breaks the butterfly of dramatic genius upon the wheel of *lumpen* erudition, and succeeds, in one revealing paragraph, in giving a summary of 'most twentieth-century conceptions of Saint Paul' as 'a disturbed fanatic morbidly concerned with women's hair' and more, and worse.

Romeo and Juliet

James C. Bryant, in 'The Problematic Friar in *Romeo and Juliet*' (*ES*), is rightly dissatisfied with an over-simple view of Friar Lawrence as 'grave, wise, patient'. But instead, Bryant solemnly tricks him out with subtle and damning complexities, some of them derived from mediaeval comic stage friars, seeing him 'seemingly deprived of those qualities one expects either in an admirable man or a dedicated clergyman'.

See also under *Titus Andronicus*.

The Sonnets

John Bayley initiated some three months of correspondence with his article 'Who was the "man right fair" of the Sonnets?' (*TLS*). The article, written in response to Rowse's book, warns against close biographical identification, but suggests that the early sonnets indicate a non-sexual relationship between homosexual patron (Southampton) and flattering poet. Most contentiously, Bayley suggests that the 'friend' of Sonnets 133, 134 and 144 should be identified as Shakespeare's punning reference to his own male member.

An opposite view is taken by Purvis E. Boyette in his 'Shakespeare's Sonnets: Homosexuality and the critics' (*TSE*). Boyette examines whether or not criticism of homosexual themes in the Sonnets reflects what he terms a 'homophobic bias', and ends by strongly attacking those critics who seem to him to exhibit such a prejudice.

More mildly, J. Bunselmeyer in his 'Appearance and Verbal Paradox: Sonnets 129 and 138' (*SQ*) notes that the element of falseness in personal relationships is aptly expressed by Shakespeare through the use of verbal paradox. Bunselmeyer considers the 'irresolvable paradox' at the end of Sonnet 129, and the use of language in Sonnet 138, and points through it to the poet's more general interest in appearance and reality. Equally interesting is Michael West's 'The Internal Dialogue of Shakespeare's Sonnet 146' (*SQ*). West weighs the conflicting views of the sonnet as either explicitly Christian or explicitly Platonic, and examines it in terms of the tradition of a debate between body and soul. He concludes by suggesting that the poem be best viewed as a struggle to balance two competing Christian traditions with 'a more acute consciousness of the need for grace'. In 'Sonnet 130 and the *Aeneid*' (*SQ*), A. W. Trueman points to a comparison between the Sonnet and *Aeneid* I 402–5.

The Taming of the Shrew

Michael West, in 'The Folk Background of Petruchio's Wooing Dance: Male Supremacy in *The Taming of the Shrew*' (*ShakS*) notes the play's popularity in performance, its unpopularity with critics (who intellectualize and so misconstrue the play's treatment of women's rights) and the further conflicting responses among critics themselves. So far so doubtful. But Mr West further suggests that the ambivalent responses are caused not by ignorance (such as, one might offer, the notion that the play is about women's rights, as if it was an invention from America in the seventies) but by the effect of 'the real sources of the play's imaginative appeal' which is the Elizabethan dance pattern, detectable in the vocabulary of I.ii. 53–82. The idea is possibly a useful one, but its application is unhappy. Mr West's method includes a far-fetched, derivative and erroneous gloss on Ind. i.83–5, referring to the plays 'of the village like Barton-on-the-Heath and Wilnecote' (sic): an inability to weigh the value of evidence ('It has been conjectured that like many other Stratfordites Shakespeare once kept doves'—we are referred to Emma Phipson, *The Animal-Lore of Shakespeare's time* (*1883*)) and some singularly savage remarks about G. B. Shaw. The play, he concludes, is not about women's rights after all, but sexual rights: Katherine's last speech is 'a token of Kate's acquiescence to the demands and joys of sex.'

The Tempest

D'Orsay W. Pearson's '"Unless I Be Reliev'd by Prayer": *The Tempest* in Perspective' (*ShakS*) is provocative. Its faults are clear: too absolute an idea of Prospero's character as benevolent and omniscient is set up as the current critical image and hence easily thrown down; and an insistence upon interpretations of episodes and passages (indeed, of the whole nature of romance) without allowing for other possibilities. Pearson, through a well-written and persuasively argued essay, seems to throw out a strong challenge. The first part disputes that we in Prospero Shakespeare's positive glorification of the theurgist's art, all magic, whether black or white, being condemned, no theory of beneficient magic ever becoming part of general learning in Elizabethan England, much less accepted as lawful; so that recognizing Prospero 'as a type of the potentially damned sorcerer is essential to any realization of the full scope of *The Tempest*.' The second part develops this idea, denying that Prospero is properly in control until after Ariel's description of the nobles' condition, the spirit acting as a medium of grace—since only Prospero's 'recognition of his error and of its relationship to his planned revenge against those who have injured him (an obvious attempt to gratify his self-love) prevents the play from becoming an exposition of Prospero's tragedy.' Despite Pearson, many contemporary critics argue strongly for the humanity of Prospero (the obvious embarrassment at the confession of failure to Miranda during the revelation of scene two; the forgetfulness of the conspiracy during the masque), while the fact that Prospero never changes anyone's nature directly by his power—Pearson stresses the failure with Caliban's education—is rather evidence of the difficulty of being human than evidence of the failure of magic. And further, there is the curious question, never touched on by Pearson, as to whether *The Tempest* is a Christian play. Is it governed by the laws of Shakespeare's own society or is the magic, like the gods of the other Romances, strictly false but benevolent in its dramatic context? Further, Prospero's repentance does not (as Pearson contends) bring about his daughter's marriage, which was certain (as is the whole action of the play) before he renounced his magic. Yet the notion of Prospero as Shakespeare's poetic testament is usefully questioned once more, and there are many insights. A brief note by Jacqueline E. M. Latham ('"Standing Water" in *The Tempest* and Joseph Hall's "Characters"' (*N&Q*)) suggests a link between Hall's 'Of the Slothful' and Sebastian's ascribing his ebbing to 'Hereditary sloth'.

Titus Andronicus

This tragedy now attracts a good deal of attention. Clifford Chalmers Huffman, in 'Bassiano and British History in *Titus Andronicus*' (*ELN*), usefully injects into the debate about the conflicting principles of succession at the opening of the play the suggestion that we are to read, rather than Roman history, British "history"—the "matter of Britain" in fact. This is a valuable article, which could have done with much fuller development; but Huffman demonstrates clearly something that is being increasingly understood about the play—that the young playwright is the master of a new kind of dramatic control. In 'The Aesthetics of Mutilation in *Titus Andronicus*' (*ShS*), Albert H. Tricomi most interestingly charts 'the ways in which the figurative language imitates the literal events of the plot', thus making the play 'a significant dramatic experiment'. Metaphor, unusually, 'draws its images directly from the narrower events of plot'; and 'the oddly alluring relationship between language and event ... the chasm between the spoken word and the actual fact' produce, further, a refusal to allow metaphor as euphemism. By means of 'the most profound impulse ... to make the word become flesh', Shakespeare is able to make several literal meanings, so that 'this tragedy leaps with an inextinguishable wittiness toward the multiple perceptions that ordinarily belong to the world of intellectual comedy.' Two good illustrations clarify the argument: Aaron's literal *machinations* of plot create 'an act of synecdoche'—when he does 'engineer the return of Titus' sons ... he returns the part for the whole'; and Lavinia's 'lips do speak; her handless hands, indeed, do write'. This excellent piece finally shows well how Shakespeare seeks to outdo both Seneca and Ovid.

Not quite so impressive is R. Stamm, who writes 'The Alphabet of Speechless Complaint: A Study of the mangled daughter in *Titus Andronicus*' (*ES*). Stamm examines Lavinia in a close and subtle line-by-line analysis; but the excellent aim—of demonstrating Shakespeare training himself 'in the art of expressing emotion and meaning ... through gesture and the other visual elements' is not quite achieved. (See also Lawrence Danson: *Tragic Alphabet*[13])

A. L. & M. K. Kistner, in 'The Senecan Background of Despair in *The Spanish Tragedy* and *Titus Andronicus*' (*ShakS*), state that the protagonist in Senecan drama 'discovers that whatever means most to him, his absolute, is irrevocably taken from him', a state leading to madness, or a desire for suicide or revenge or a selected combination of these. One wonders why this needed pointing out.

By contrast, G. K. Hunter's comparison of similarities in two plays is refreshingly original and stimulating. In 'Shakespeare's Earliest Tragedies: *Titus Andronicus* and *Romeo and Juliet*' (*ShS*), he calls *Romeo and Juliet* 'well-loved' and *Titus Andronicus* 'much disliked', but shows a formal relationship between them 'in terms of the polar characteristics of tragedy they exhibit'. Professor Hunter is wise about our post-Enlightenment delusion about 'unbloody' tragedy, and while demonstrating the parallels between *Titus* and *King Lear*, and *Romeo* and *Antony and Cleopatra*, shows that throughout Shakespeare's mature tragedies the principle holds that 'the ritual of *Titus* is complemented by the domesticity of *Romeo*'. Professor Hunter is excellent on the structural similarities of the openings in the exposition of the two households, while alert to the very different ways in which the conflicts are handled.

Uniquely in Shakespeare's tragedies, 'the two plays are ... tales whose significance is expressed in terms of single ... well-chosen ... cities'. Concentrating on *Titus*, this subtle, balanced and helpful analysis of the rôle of locality shows a most interesting development of the implications of the specifically family situations, especially on the question of the tombs.

Troilus and Cressida.

N. T. Jones-Davies, in 'Discord in Shakespeare's *Troilus and Cressida*; or, The conflict between "Angry Mars and Venus Queen of Love"' (*SQ*) tries an interesting gods' eye view of the play, showing that 'the ancient deities—Mars, Venus, Jupiter, Mercury, Apollo—preside over the destinies of both Greeks and Trojans.' It is a useful approach, showing that 'the play expresses the inconclusive discord that results from the failure to keep constancy in war and love. Jupiter has failed to preserve *discordia concors*.' Camille Slights, in 'The Parallel Structure of *Troilus and Cressida*' (*SQ*) examines briefly the obvious parallelism. She gives a straightforward account, somewhat unsubtle, and overwritten in its conclusion about seeing 'Man stripped naked and lashed by the satirist's whip'. Charles R. Forker contributes a brief note 'Milton and Shakespeare: the first Sonnet on Blindness in relation to a speech from *Troilus and Cressida*' (*ELN*) which, though primarily about Milton, illustrates simply the 'expansion of context' as an aim of Ulysses' speech in I.iii; the piece is useful as itself being an expansion of context, tactfully controlled.

Tetsuo Kishi in 'Dryden and Shakespeare' (*ShStud*), seeing that neither the style nor characterization of the original play satisfied Dryden, finds that despite his belief that the end was not properly tragic, to keep Cressida faithful to Troilus makes the play not more tragic, only less ambiguous. Emil Roy takes the original text in 'War and Manliness in Shakespeare's *Troilus and Cressida*' (*CompD* 1973) and subjects it to psychoanalysis, an interpretation in which Oedipal issues are tinged with the unresolved issues of earlier phases of childhood development, the characters working out in adulthood and middle-age the issues of the anal stage of infancy, namely the problem of autonomy. This is a fascinating reading of the situation, but it breaks down on a close reading of the text, since however much the Greeks 'try to penetrate, to poke into' Troy, the city's feminised gates 'with massy staples/And corresponsive and fulfilling bolts' surely symbolize, cry out another meaning than 'a woman's ability to resist penetration'.

Twelfth Night

James F. Forrest contributes a short but overwritten gloss ('Malvolio and Puritan "Singularity"' *ELN*) on some Puritan connotations of the word, which does add sharpness to Malvolio's intention 'to read politic authors'. R. Chris. Hassel Jr. (*SQ*), in quest of an answer to Malvolio's M.O.A.I. riddle, pursues the obvious into the remoter complexities of that journal's debate with itself.

The Two Gentlemen of Verona

Thomas E. Scheye in 'Two Gentlemen of Milan' (*ShakS*) calls this 'such a thin play that one can almost see through it'. Nevertheless, he recounts the plot, calling his method one by which 'we can approach a paradigm to describe what happens in the green world'.

Venus and Adonis

William E. Sheidley in '"Unless it

be a boar": Love and Wisdom in Shakespeare's *Venus and Adonis*' (*MLQ*), wisely does not concentrate on 'the analogy to the gloss on Ovid', but looks elsewhere for the poem's meaning. With controlled reference to other sixteenth-century poetry, he shows helpfully that Shakespeare raises his reader 'to a viewpoint from which love is revealed not to present ... a dreary choice between lust and chastity, but to offer a welcome alternative in the "warme effects" of charity to the self-defeating paralysis of pride'. It is difficult to see quite what is the point of 'Shakespeare's Venus: an Experiment in Tragedy' (*SQ*) in which James H. Lake, after deploring a lack of serious critical attention, while in footnotes calling attention to many treatments of the poem far, far better than his own, then proceeds to put matters right by simply telling the story.

The Winter's Tale

The main repetitions between the two parts of the play as cited by James Edward Siemon in '"But It Appears She Lives": Iteration in *The Winter's Tale*' (*PMLA*) are nothing new, though there is an awareness that if Florizel and Perdita are surrogates for Hermione and Leontes, they are also alternatives. The argument's most interesting point is about Hermione's death (though Siemon too readily accepts that the report of the revelation of Perdita's identity suggests that it and Hermione's restoration 'are of potentially equivalent dramatic force': whatever their potential, Shakespeare emphasizes Hermione by showing, not reporting). Hermione, as is clear from the evidence in Act III, is truly dead, since 'for our sense of providential munificence to be complete, our experience of irrevocable loss must also be real. Hermione's restoration is a gift of the gods, even though men must through their actions earn such gifts'; no real attention however is given to the implications, dramatic or psychological, of this assertion. Raymond J. Rundus contributes an uncertain note on 'Time and his "Glass" in *The Winter's Tale*' (*SQ*), where he suggests that the 'glass' might be a mirror, not an hourglass, yet lamely adds, this is a 'much less likely possibility' suggesting no purpose it would serve nor what Time 'turning' his glass could mean. Potentially more interesting is the observation that some pictures of Time denote Youth or Age according to which part of the glass is full of sand.

VIII

English Drama 1550–1660: Excluding Shakespeare

BERNARD HARRIS and BRIAN GIBBONS

1. EDITIONS

Irving Ribner's death in 1972 was a loss to the specialist criticism of drama in this period, as his volume on *Tamburlane* reminds us.[1] It provides a text of the play together with a case-book of some useful recent criticism; the essays collected are by Una Ellis-Fermor, Ethel Seaton, Roy Battenhouse, Helen Gardner, G. I. Duthie, Eugene Waith, Clifford Leech, Robert Kimbrough, Susan Richards, David Daiches and Kenneth Friedenreich, who prepared this book for press with the help of other colleagues. Well conceived, admirably chosen, and balanced, it makes a good tribute to its editor. Alvin B. Kernan has provided *The Alchemist* in a notable series.[2] His introduction, though brief, as is customary in this series, deals with essentials; of the language of Sir Epicure Mammon he observes: 'The poetry contains perfectly the impulses behind it: as the appetite calls out continually for novel satisfactions, the imagination obliges with rapidly intensifying images of power and pleasure, and the rhetoric soars upward to create, in words at least, the joys which appetite has desired and imagination has envisioned.' Ultimately, Kernan observes, 'alchemy contains the play's only judgment on the meaning and the practicality of the Renaissance desire to break at once the shackles of things as they are and to make the world over into gold. Along with the alchemists, the characters of the play seem to believe that nature—the world, that is, as created and given to man, not made by him—is infinitely plastic and will accept any shape that man desires.' In the discussion of alchemy in Act II Kernan sees Jonson advancing 'a conservative conception of the inescapable slowness and limits on the possibility of change and the dependence of any change in man on improvement of his moral nature.' There is a brief appendix on Jonson's use of alchemy and a convenient glossary of alchemical terms; but the appendix on text, sources and, particularly, stage history, is too abbreviated to do more than refer us elsewhere. A group of Elizabethan tragedies essential for the student of this period has been made available in an edition which replaces Ashley Thorndike's collection of 1910. Freshly presented by T. W. Craik, with modern apparatus, the plays are *Gorboduc, Cambyses, The Spanish Tragedy* and *Arden of Feversham*.[3] A second volume has been published in

---

[1] Christopher Marlowe's *Tamburlaine, part one and part two; text and major criticism*, ed. by Irving Ribner. New York, Bobbs Merrill: Methuen. pp. xi+356. £1.10.

[2] The Yale Ben Jonson. General edds. Alvin B. Kernan and Richard B. Young. *The Alchemist*, ed. by Alvin B. Kernan. pp. ix 246. $2.95.

[3] Everyman's University Library. *Minor Elizabethan Tragedies*, ed. by T. W. Craik.

a most welcome series.[4] J. P. Cutts has edited the manuscript play *Loves Changelinges Change*, which is based on Sidney's *Arcadia*. The introduction, much of which has appeared in other critical forms, contains an account of the manuscript, corrective of earlier scholars, comments on the stage problems and some comparison of the text with that of Sidney. The editor asks for forbearance concerning his text, because of the extreme difficulty of the handwriting, and this will be readily given by anyone with even modest acquaintance with such matters; the difficulties are clear in the typescript, and one must be grateful that despite them an edition made of the play has been made available at all.

2. STAGE STUDIES

Richard Southern has produced a volume of enormous size in response to his theme of the gradual evolution of staging in England to this period.[5] It is impossible to summarize such a book, which a leisurely progress might seem an apt simile for, covering the ground as it does from the mid-fifteenth century to the time of the production of Shakespeare's first play around 1590. The Third and Fourth Parts of this immense study are of most immediate concern in this chapter. They contain sections on 'Diversions from Interlude Tradition 1553–1560', a brief series of analyses of a dozen plays between 1560–1566, 'Interludes into Drama 1566–1576', and studies of four plays performed after the building of The Theatre in

1576—they are *The Marriage of Wit and Wisdom, The Three Ladies of London, The Three Lords and Three Ladies of London,* and *The Coblers Prophesie.* Naturally terms of reference which concentrate on methods of stage presentation mean that plays get unequal treatment depending on their degree of interest or difficulty in such staging matters; however, there is some correlation between interest in this drama and the ambition of its staging; of the earlier plays, *Pacient Grissill* and *Horestes* reveal such complexities and are treated at appropriate length, while of the later plays the discussion of *The Three Ladies of London* and *The Three Lords and Three Ladies of London* is particularly fruitful. Other plays which might seem to deserve fuller treatment have been denied it because of existing full accounts in the work of other critics; this is a modest decision but one which makes the rhythm of the book occasionally erratic. Southern has too much knowledge to come to a single conclusion at the end of such an account; but from several conclusions he offers two may be selected. Despite all qualifications 'there does seem to be a thread of development running from a medieval formalism through to a sophisticated humanism in the space of these significant seventy-five years. I do not wish to be concerned with the profitless question whether the plays themselves became any *better* in quality—there are brilliant moments even in the earliest of them as well as tedious passages in the latest—but there does seem to be a broadening, with experience, of the capacity to sense what situations, and what method of presenting those situations, will seize most aptly on the attention of an audience and will allow the essence of the entertainment to be communicated to them with the most striking effect. In other words a

---

[4] *Loves Changelinges Change*: an anonymous play based on Sidney's *Arcadia*, ed. by John P. Cutts. North American Mentor Texts and Studies series, No. 2. General edds, Clifford Davidson and Nancy Cutbirth. Fennimore, Wisconsin: John Westburg. pp. xix + 82. $10.

[5] *The Staging of plays before Shakespeare*, by Richard Southern. Faber and Faber. pp. 603. £12.

development of theatrical technique.' And for a final conclusion: 'every specialist who has written on the subject would be glad to know what James Burbage must have had in mind when he planned The Theatre. Many of them have argued backwards—from, for instance, the Swan drawing of De Witt and Van Buchell. My present book belongs with the minority who argue forwards from the basis of what preceded, that is to say of what Burbage as a player is likely to have been used to in his acting experience up to the date of his planning The Theatre.' The view that 'the conventions and presentation-tradition worked out in the Tudor halls formed the basis for the acting-conventions and the form of playwriting developed on the Elizabethan public-playhouse stage—and subsequently on the indoor 'private house' stages' is literally illustrated and supported in the text by numerous plates and figures.

Ahmad Ramez Kutriech, in 'The doubling of parts in *Enough Is as Good as a Feast*' (*ELN*) argues for 'four instances of cleared stage' which 'actually divide the play into five scenes which divide the good characters' camp from that of the evil characters.' A chart indicates the relationship of cleared stage to the play's lines, and the assumption is that four players can perform this interlude, even if '*Enough* was possibly written with a quick-change versatile player in mind to play many smaller rôles.' Richard De Molin has a note on 'Richard Mulcaster and Elizabethan Pageantry' (*SEL*). He discusses Mulcaster's summary of the pageant performed before the coronation in 1559, which gave a careful account of the content and emblematic significance of that event. He notes that Mulcaster worked on the Lord Mayor's pageant in 1568 and

that he wrote some speeches for the 1561 pageant, which he quotes. Jackson I. Cope, in 'Marlowe's *Dido* and the titillating children' (*ELR*), believes we have made miscalculations about the play, 'Marlowe's only text written not for the public theater, but for the Queen's Children of the Chapel. Having listened too intently to the siren song of its sweet verse, we have shipwrecked its fine farce.' With their 'rhetorical training, the sweet-singing boys were ideally prepared to declaim complex verse.' To this ability Marlowe directed his serious adaptation of Virgil, adding to poetic declamation 'a framing induction, a comic nurse, and multiple suicide at the close.' These additions, it is claimed, 'are interpolated to exploit the self-conscious theatrical situation, vectored by sexually romantic love matter, a literate audience, and the little boy players.' John Scott Colley surveys the scholarly debate on the subject of 'Music in the Elizabethan Private Theatres' (*YES*) and considers it an exaggeration to claim that the place of music was especially important among the boy actors' performances. Though pre-performance and between-the-acts music was important, he argues that music in the plays at the Private Theatres was not more frequent or unusually important; some dramatists did exploit the musical talent of the boys, but equally some did not. In the same way the acting style was not of one kind and various styles were originated or evolved by dramatists; Colley offers discussion of the work in this context of Marston, Chapman and Middleton. This is a careful and sensible account, and a fair analysis of the subject. Mary Edmond sheds some light on 'Pembroke's Men' (*RES*) by adding Simon Jewell's name to the list of actors in the shadowy company of 1592. She quotes Jewell's will, which gives clues to the operations of this travelling company, with a common stock of costumes, properties and playbooks: they divided profits at intervals during the tour. Various people named in the will are conjecturally identified, including the 'Mr Iohnson' possibly Ben Jonson, who was owed £13.6.8d, and might have begun playing and writing at this date, five years before he is mentioned in Henslowe in 1597—a possibility supported by Aubrey's note on his early career in Shoreditch. Miss Edmond notes that the sum owed to Jonson is a large one, probably for more than acting, and most likely for rewriting several plays. Jonson was in the reformed Pembroke's Men in 1597, which might help to support the conjecture that he was with them in 1592. It is also argued that Jonson became a freeman of the Tylers and Bricklayers Company not by apprenticeship but by patrimony (his father was a freeman), which would have been much quicker and would have enabled him to begin an acting and writing career earlier than is usually supposed, so that he could indeed have been with Pembroke's Men in 1592.

In a short but important note on 'Early cast lists for two Beaumont and Fletcher plays' (*TN*) David George describes the implications of a scrapbook in the Folger Shakespeare Library: 'It is a rich collection of pre-Restoration stage materials, and among these riches are two items relating to performances of *Philaster* and *The Maid's Tragedy*'. It is the author's hope to show that they date from *c.* 1640 and *c.* 1660. He believes the first item 'seems to me to reveal a real cast for *Philaster*, dating from the years 1638 to 1642, and probably does not differ much from the cast that played *Philaster* at court, 21 February 1636/7.' The second item relates to

early casts of *The Maid's Tragedy* (1610?). George notes that the Folger document's information has been taken from the 1650 quarto of this play,' the real date of which is probably 1660'; parts are printed on the verso, including 'Hart opposite Amintor, Wintersal opposite Evadne, and Cartwrite opposite Calinax'. George observes that when these 'Old Actors' joined the King's Company under Killigrew in November 1660, women actors were recruited to the troupe. Wintershall would hardly have played Evadne after that— although in point of fact we do not know how long men continued to play women's rôles after the advent of actresses.'

3. BIOGRAPHICAL, TEXTUAL and SOURCE STUDIES

Mark Eccles observes (*N&Q*) that R. Prior's article on Antony Munday (*YW* 1973, p. 194) in *N&Q* repeats information in an essay by Eccles published in 1959; Eccles adds some further points. David McPherson has compiled 'An annotated catalogue of Ben Jonson's library and marginalia' (*SP*), which offers thirty three new titles and corrects various errors, with an introduction giving biographical facts. (See below, p. 269.) Mary Hobbs contributes notes on 'Robert and Thomas Ellice, friends of Ford and Davenant' (*N&Q*). Ford dedicated *The Lover's Melancholy* and the second printing of *'Tis Pity* to these two gentlemen. She writes that it seems likely that about 1628–9 literary circles of lawyers and others centring on the Inns of Court included Ford, himself a member of the Middle Temple, his kinsman John Ford Esquire of Gray's Inn, William Davenant who in 1628 was lodging with Edward Hyde, later Earl of Clarendon, in the Middle Temple, Henry Blount and the brothers

Ellice. This may have some bearing on the disputed date of composition of *'Tis Pity*. Though not printed until 1633 the verse by Thomas Ellice may suggest that it derives from this earlier period when association between Ford and Ellice seems certain. Herman Doh indicates 'Compositorial responsibility in *Fortune by Land and Sea* 1655' (*Lib*). He distinguishes two compositors, noticing their habits of justifying which provide clear evidence of respective responsibility, and is possibly a more widely useful method of distinguishing between the work of one compositor and another in many Renaissance dramatic texts, especially when they are shoddily and hurriedly produced, as is the case with the text he is analysing. Doh uses evidence of spelling and punctuation to show that the compositors were influenced in their choice of variants by considerations of justifying lines. D. J. Lake considers 'The integrity of the *Parnassus* trilogy' (*N&Q*). He refutes the view of J. B. Leishman and G. C. Moore Smith that the case for two authors rests on the assertion of the author of Part III that he has a 'ruder quill'. Leishman declared that he would not have supposed, but for this, that there was more than one author, since the three plays share stylistic peculiarities. Lake thinks this the decisive fact, noting that 'ruder' may mean 'more satiric' not 'less skilful', while it may not even be a comparative at all, necessarily. He also offers statistical evidence of stylistic features to support the claim that there was only one author.

Suzanne Gossett writes on 'The term "masque" in Shakespeare, Fletcher and *The Coxcomb*' (*SEL*). She considers the question of whether a masque was cut from the text of *The Coxcomb*, since the line in the play

'Come, where's this masque' suggests that one was intended, though it is not there. The word 'masque' in Shakespeare appears to refer always to a show of a formal spectacular kind, but in Beaumont and Fletcher Miss Gossett believes it becomes 'any symbolic representation for an idea or situation', even the mere presentation of a person disguised or misrepresented, or an apparition. Hence, characters in the plays use the word loosely to mean any form of show; in the case of *The Coxcomb* it is a dance that is referred to, and there is no reason to suppose anything has been cut from the text. In *The Elizabethan Theatre IV*[6] J. W. Lever's '*The Wasp*: a trial flight' discusses the history of the play's fortunes since it was discovered among MSS in Alnwick Castle in 1872; it was not considered of much interest by G. E. Bentley, who did not record the unpublished edition by J. J. Gourlay in the University of Newcastle upon Tyne. The conjectural date is 1634–6. Lever considers the play 'a shrewd comment on Stuart politics disguised, like the Wasp himself, in a "fantastick & ridiculous habit".' Buckingham is identified as the concealed villain. The essay then discusses the MS, with a two-page badly reduced illustration from it, and considers the actors named in it, the casting, and questions of staging which suggest that the play was written for performance at Salisbury Court, by a cast including King's Revels actors, either shortly before the closing of the theatres in 1636 or after re-opening in 1637. Donald K. Anderson Jr explains Tamburlaine's declaration 'Here at Damascus will I make the point That shall begin the perpendicular' in a note on 'Tamburlaine's Perpendicular

6 *The Elizabethan Theatre IV*. University of Waterloo: Macmillan Canada. pp. xvii + 148. £4.50.

and the T-in-O maps' (*N&Q*). A common kind of medieval and Renaissance map represented the rough shape of a T, being the bodies of waters dividing the continents: the vertical bar of the T being the Mediterranean Sea, its base the strait of Gibraltar; the right-hand horizontal bar the river Nile, the left-hand the Tanais. At the junction of the T, the centre of the world, lies Jerusalem. So 'perpendicular' refers to this 'T', with Damascus replacing Jerusalem as the centre. Donald Edge contributes a note on 'Salamints in John Lyly's *Love's Metamorphosis*' (*N&Q*), suggesting that the word combines the property of 'calamints', the Eurasian aromatic plant with purple flowers which do *not* change colour during the day, and 'calamanco', a herb which destroys a man's 'talent', associated by Lyly with the idea of Niobe's inconstancy. J. C. Maxwell notes (*N&Q*) that in Chapman, *The Widow's Tears* V.iv.39 'paces' is a possible emendation of 'pace is'. Robert T. Guerrein, 'A mistaken attribution in Parrott's edition of Chapman' (*N&Q*), identifies the source for III.i.10-24 of *The Tragedy of Byron* as Suetonius, *De Vita Caesarum*, Bk VII. 1. Peter Walls, in 'Jonson's borrowing' (*TN*) relates the masque of *Pleasure Reconciled to Virtue*, in respect of its antimasque, to the antimasque in Robert White's *Cupid's Banishment*, performed eight months earlier at Greenwich before the Queen. J. R. Mulryne describes French 'Sources for the sub-plot of *Women Beware Women*' (*RES*), noting Langbaine's suggestion in 1691— *True History of the Tragicke Love of Hipolito and Isabella Neapolitans* (1628)—but raising the problem that Middleton died in 1627, while *Women Beware Women* was written in 1622; so that he must have worked from one or both of the French versions, one

in the Arsenal Library in Paris, one in the Bodleian. Mulryne concludes, after a meticulous analysis, that the source is the 1597 Rouen text in the Arsenal Library (*L'Histoire Veritable des Infortunes et Tragiques Amours D'Hypolite et d'Isabelle Neapolitains*).

4. BOOKS AND ARTICLES

Elizabethan and Jacobean Drama[7] is a collection of essays by the late Peter Ure. All but one have been previously published but deserve this new form. The essays show over many years Ure's preoccupations with the drama of this period, including, of course, that of Shakespeare; and whether the essays are early work or late they show scholarship of a scrupulous kind, and criticism of range, tact, and wit. Ure's interest in this drama has an uncommon consistency which gives the book itself a coherence of attention quite different from a sense of a miscellany. Greville, Marston, Chapman, Heywood and Ford are the playwrights regularly considered, more than Marlowe, Jonson and Webster; and it is not difficult to see why when reading the early piece on *Sophonisba*, or the learned article on 'The Widow of Ephesus: some reflections on an international comic theme', or the later study of Chapman's tragedies, for the focus is on varieties of Stoicism, that 'emphasis on the inward rather than the outward man', which he traces across Marston (in the Roman tragedy of *Sophonisba*) Greville and Chapman. This is more than a collection of essays, it is a new book. About twenty-five volumes of reproduced dissertations have come from Salzburg on matters related to

[7] *Elizabethan and Jacobean Drama: critical essays by Peter Ure*, ed. by J. C. Maxwell. Liverpool University Press. pp. viii+258. £5.

the drama of this period.[8] It is perhaps more a testimony to the enormous industry devoted to this drama in the past quarter century (some of the theses seem that old) than any sign of the state of present vitality. Three series are involved, Elizabethan & Renaissance Studies, Elizabethan Studies, and Jacobean Drama Studies. (They will be referred to hereafter as Salzburg Studies). On the whole some substantial documentary theses read better than much of the literary criticism. A recent German doctoral thesis, for instance, Hans-Joachim Hermes' *Die Lieder im anonymen Englischen Renaissance-Drama 1580–1603*, makes an extremely effective survey of its material. E. D. Pendry's *Elizabethan Prisons and Prison Scenes* is a substantial account of an historical reality, a social institution, and its dramatic representation. The thesis, then, is both a work of history and social criticism, and a work of literary criticism; it is based on considerable research under all headings, and is written with exceptional point and pertinence; like the numerous effective illustrations, it lets the facts speak for themselves. Arthur F. Kinney has provided in *Markets of Bawdrie: the dramatic criticism of Stephen Gosson*, a thorough edition of *The Schoole of Abuse, An Apologie for the Schoole of Abuse,* and *Plays Confuted in Fiue Actions*, each work well introduced, supported by reference to other criticism, and provided with a bibliographical and explanatory account. This is a model edition of a writer whose work it will help to make more accurately available, and its importance to be more clearly recognized. Some general studies in this series may be noted here, before turning to

accounts of particular dramatists, where works in this series will recur. Robert E. Morsberger writes a brief study of *Swordplay and the Elizabethan and Jacobean Stage*; its dedication to Ronald Colman, Douglas Fairbanks Jr., Errol Flynn, and so on sufficiently indicates the prevailing tone. The assertion that 'the motion picture audience far more closely approximates the audiences of the Globe and Curtain playhouses than does the legitimate stage audience, which more nearly resembles those of the Tudor and Stuart court productions or of Blackfriars' is amusing, but fails to discriminate between an illiterate audience sophisticated in an oral tradition, and a literate audience unsophisticated in a visual tradition. Stephen C. Young's *The Frame Structure in Tudor and Stuart Drama* argues that 'A dramatic frame is a complete dramatic action within which the presentation of a full length play occurs as an event.' He discusses the 'supernatural frame', ranging from the purely abstract connection to the play as in *Love and Fortune* to a close narrative connection in Marlowe's *Dido* (one notes the inclusion of this play with pleasure, though the discussion of it is rather brief). Then comes the 'narrative frame' and *The Old Wives Tale*, a discussion of the '*Shrew* plays' which has the observation that, though the frame structure is never explicitly used again by Shakespeare, its use was the beginning of a long investigation of the nature and function of dramatic illusion. The thesis continues by examining Jonson's Comicall Satyres and Beaumont's *Knight of the Burning Pestle*, where 'the frame threatens to swallow up the original play until 'the London Merchant' begins to seem only a thin excuse, an occasion for the antics of the frame characters and their ludicrous

[8] Salzburg studies in English literature, under the direction of Professor Erwin A. Stürzl: Institut für Englische Sprache und Literatur, Universität Salzburg.

inventions. This leads in turn to the problem of the relationship between the two plays inside the frame.' There is also a discussion of the 'dotage' plays of Jonson, and the suggestion that Jonson in the induction to *The Magnetic Lady* repeats the material used in *Every Man Out* because in the Caroline period, romances, pastorals, and tragicomedies were more numerous on the stage than they had ever been, and Jonson's critical principles and reformist aims needed repeating, and needed the device of the frame to make that repetition not unironically clear. The thesis is well-written, and had it been compressed and rewritten would have surely made a good longish article. James T. Henke's *Renaissance Dramatic Bawdy (exclusive of Shakespeare) an annotated glossary and critical essays* is useful both for its basic information and for its system of cross-references, to plays quoted and to potential synonyms: a good guide. Joseph Henry Stodder's *Satire in Jacobean Tragedy* isolates a particular dramatic strain and draws widely but briefly on many playwrights, Marston, Jonson, Chapman, Tourneur, Webster, Middleton and Massinger; despite the range attempted this is a successfully succinct account. Martha Hester Fleischer's *The Iconography of the English History Play* is deservedly made available. This is a rich study. The author humbly observes 'my chief regret is the lack of illustrations', but the enlargement of sensibility which her scholarship ensures means that those who have eyes to see, see better. She remarks of the popular English history play in the age of Shakespeare 'I mean to demonstrate that these plays convey significance by means of visual conventions and commonplaces, and that the nonverbal images so employed actually constitute a visual vocabulary current at least in

this dramatic genre.' This is only one of the aims of her endeavour, but it is of the utmost importance because she puts her considerable knowledge of the Renaissance behind her general intention to alert us to the iconography of a particular dramatic form, the history play; her central chapters on the state, the garden, and the battle are exemplary criticism. Charlotte N. Clay's *The role of anxiety in English tragedy: 1580–1642*, is a study of the drama of this period reviewed under the gaze of subsequent observation; it is none the less valid for being so viewed. Two chapters, 'Concepts of anxiety' and 'The tragic view', establish her personal viewpoint and relate it to more general concepts of the age; this is a highly individual study, but one which individual readers may profit from; it has a conclusion—'When tragedy presents despair and defiance in place of courage and transcendence, the end of great tragic art is at hand.' It is a work written out of conviction and is compelling in its belief; a notable study of a theme not examined before in this precise manner.

Little has been published on the drama of this period outside the traditional field demarcated by the university wits. J. M. R. Margeson analyses 'Dramatic form: the Huntington plays' (*SEL*), arguing that the real control in a romantic play of this kind is exercised through the familiarity of certain story patterns and the conventions belonging to them. Because the audience knows these patterns, the playwright can allow the links between the episodes to be filled in by their imagination and concentrate on the dramatic moments he wishes to highlight. Confrontation and the emotional and moral reactions of characters count for more than the how and why of intrigue.

Margeson concludes that the moral, idealizing quality of chronicle romance made history and legend into something local, human, and individual. In Salzburg Studies Virginia Mason Carr's *The drama as propaganda; a study of The Troublesome Raigne of King John* inevitably tangles with the controversy over authorship and text, but it is her main concern to discuss the play as one which 'could be considered the best history play of those that have come down to us, besides Shakespeare's own, and Marlowe's *Edward II*.' But the discussion of the play is so hindered by references to *King John* that it never provides a clear account of *The Troublesome Raigne*, and the conclusion that 'in its didacticism the *TR* is closer to the Elizabethan idea than *KJ* is. It is less the product of a poetic genius and more the representative of its culture' is very confused both in syntax and argument. Sallie Bond has a discussion of 'John Lyly's *Endymion*' (*SEL*) which is concerned with its topical allusions to personalities in the court. She describes the play as a game of court life, applicable to all the nobles and to the queen herself. She sketches possible allusions and notices the degree of distancing which keeps identifications uncertain. Real courtiers are incorporated into the play world, details carefully confused: 'romantically enough they have remained in the texture of *Endymion* like flies in amber'. Kyd has occasioned serious and sustained response. Scott McMillin writes on 'The Book of Seneca in *The Spanish Tragedy*' (*SEL*) This is a good intelligent essay, asking the simple question, why do Hieronimo's quotations from Seneca seem to imply that he does not understand them very well? He notes that Empson drew attention to the fact, and argued that it was part of Kyd's

design. So McMillan offers an ingenious explanation. These speeches from Agamemnon, Clytemnestra, Andromache and Oedipus 'have nothing to do with revenge, and wrenching them to prove the case for vengeance seems to be a piece of desperate logic'. We are not to see this as evidence that 'the impromptu scholarship of a madman is liable to error.' If they are not about revenge they are, in a sense, about safety, and in each safety is ironically converted into loss: 'The meaning shared among the Senecan examples is insistently ironic: preservation and loss, at moments of extremity, are figures of each other.' All the Senecan characters are caught by this irony, and perhaps, McMillin comments, we might think Hieronimo is caught in the simple ironic position of missing this moral point; in an extreme action like the revenge he is planning, he is bound to ensure his own self-destruction. This must, however, be rejected, since from the moment he discovers his son's corpse Hieronimo has understood the depths of the Senecan truth: his remaining life will serve only to give meaning to self-loss—'his heart is dead, his life is his dead son—' from the discovery of his son's corpse to the final accomplishment of revenge Hieronimo's life is 'a lively form of death'. So the safety spoken of in the Senecan quotations must refer to playing for time until this revenge can be accomplished. Also, he has so mastered the irony of the situation of the Senecan characters that he accepts it as the 'only valid ground of action': 'he knows the situation better than they and means to enact it'. Literally, the quotations are wrenched from their original meaning, for they do not bear upon revenge; beneath the language, however, lies a radical similarity to Hieronimo's own situation; it is this which matters to him. The final play-book text is incomprehensible since it is translated into four foreign tongues, but the situation, under this cloak of incomprehensibility, is made real, obvious, a lively form of death. This is a discussion of the play which explores some of Kyd's central dramatic concerns, even if the search for symmetry in explaining the quotations seems strained. In '*The Spanish Tragedy*: a speaking picture' (*ELR*) Donna B. Hamilton writes eloquently about this most eloquent of plays: she observes 'man's compulsive search for order and meaning' in face of life's destructive or incomprehensible forces, that 'Discerning a pattern, or even creating one by establishing a ceremony, simplifies, makes concrete, and provides direction for the variously complex and contradictory aspects of experience—and with this human impulse Kyd seems sympathetic.' Further, 'Alongside the ceremonies, strategies, and loyalties of family and state, Kyd places the artistic response as another variety of man's attempts to come to terms with experience through ritual and pattern. But he suggests that the artistic response can be superior to those other attempts by being honest and by admitting that man's grief is man-made, while at the same time furnishing him with a means of making his own relief.' Thus, Hieronimo is Kyd's vehicle for exploring the process and the validity of this artistic response. Through Hieronimo's involvement as an artist 'we realize how very intimately the play is bound to Renaissance ideas of the means and purposes of art. As Hieronimo's distrust of authority grows, his inclination to impose his own order increases.' In doing so he behaves as an artist. 'Just as a poem or a painting or a play gains in quality when it is informed with a profound

truth, so too are Hieronimo's artistic experiences more valuable as he moves further and further away from the reiteration of his experiences and closer to an interpretation, or, in other words, as he acts less like the historian and more like the poet.' Sidney's doctrine could not be better expounded. Kyd also crops up as a suitor to Mary Herbert, Countess of Pembroke, for his version of *Cornelia* is part of the complex context of Elizabethan closet drama which Russell E. Leavenworth provides for his study of Daniel's *Cleopatra* in the Salzburg Studies. Robert H. West's 'The impatient magic of Dr Faustus' (*ELR*) is both a valuable review article of recent critical interpretations of 'a perennial question of *Faustus* criticism'—that of 'whether the obvious Christian context of the play is a believing one or an ironic one'—and a contribution to further discussion. The tone of the review is admirably fair-minded, and the learning in demonology is used for clarification, in detail and in generalization, of the play's difficult arguments. West has past support for his claim that in assessing Faustus's condition from a basis of this critic's interest in demonology 'I am concerned at last not with lore but with dramatic effect, which must be the conclusive guide to the play's meaning.' The article provides indices from demonology to chart 'the course of the conflict in Dr Faustus 'as a struggle 'conventionally with hell, not with heaven.' Demonology confirms that Faustus was 'neither worthy nor wise', but he was both 'energetic and accomplished' and certainly 'bold'. Thus 'Faustus' judgement is faulty, but at the beginning his impetuosity and insistence are awesome, and later his rhetoric remains often equal to his plight. Grant that Faustus acts for appetite, not for mankind or cosmic justice. Grant that he defies neither God nor Lucifer more than he has to and cringes at the payment of his final end. Still his decisions for magic and for witchcraft are of utmost daring, long sustained by no common means, and at infinite cost. Demonology does not suggest anything morally redemptive in those decisions or in Faustus' precarious faithfulness to hell. But it does suggest that in them Faustus was a man of stature and that his fate is dramatically moving.' Two works in the Salzburg Studies series may be mentioned here; Claude J. Summers in *Christopher Marlowe and the politics of power* makes a clearly charted way through all the plays and is particularly effective on the two parts of *Tamburlaine*; Adrianne Roberts Baytop's *Dido, Queen of Infinite Literary Variety* is disappointing in view of the potential of the subject—she includes a translation of only part of William Gager's Latin tragedy of 1583, and her discussion of Marlowe's play is as sketchy and inadequate as the rest of her comment on Renaissance dramatic attention to Dido. After Marlowe, Marston, Chapman, Jonson and Webster continue to dominate critical attention. John Colley has a very successful account of *John Marston's theatrical drama* in the Salzburg Studies: well written and comprehensive in treatment it lacks, perhaps, only recognition of the actual performances of Marston on the stage. His techniques in theatre do work, and can be demonstrated in fact, not merely defended in theory. David J. Houser discusses 'Marston's disguised dukes and *A Knack to Know a Knave*' (*PMLA*) in such a way that the earlier play presents a helpfully simple instance of a pattern treated with varying complexity, subtlety and seriousness by Marston. Houser

asserts that in his view insufficient attention has been paid to the importance of *A Knack to Know a Knave* in relation to Marston, but although his discussion of Marston is clear it is also entirely uncontentious and adds nothing new, which possibly suggests that the attention given in the past to *A Knack* by Marston scholars was about right. In '*The Malcontent* and "Dreams, Visions, Fantasies"' (*EIC*) T. F. Wharton counters some recent critical opinions as over-cunning misinterpretations of the play's ironic mode. *The Malcontent*'s 'successes have nothing to do with irony, and its ultimate failure is due to a reluctance to exploit irony.' Some very pertinent relationships are shown between the theme of rôle-playing, Marston's fascination by 'impersonation' and 'wish-fulfilment' and the presentation of the court of Genoa, peopled by characters who delude themselves by fantasies and 'habitually conceive self-glorifying visions.' There are studies of Mendoza, Pietro and Malevole/Altofronto, and a strong claim that the latter is a test case for the presentation of high-mindedness and moral recovery. The use of religion is successful only when Marston's 'characters' appeal to it, or when it is 'tied to the intermittent theme of transience.' But, in *The Malcontent*, 'Marston's fundamental convictions are satiric.' Brownell Salomon considers 'The theological basis of imagery and structure in *The Malcontent*' (*SEL*). This discussion takes a predictable, and culpably partial direction. Finding 'Calvinistic pessimism' in *The Scourge of Villanie* leads to the detection of passages in *The Malcontent*, which are likened to passages or ideas in Calvin. We are to see this 'pessimism' opposed by a 'humanistic optimism' which is 'mediated in accordance with God's providence'. The article ignores important shaping forces in *The Malcontent* which the best modern criticism has brought out, and treats the religious ideas without integrating them with the rest of the 'ideas' in order to establish their full context, dramatic emphasis, and place in the full theatrical meaning of the play. There are two long, thorough, and extremely worthwhile studies of Chapman in the Salzburg Studies series. Peter Bement discusses 'action' and 'contemplation' in his study of *George Chapman: action and contemplation in his tragedies*; he surveys the comedies and poems, and then devotes a chapter to *Bussy*, another to *Byron*, and a third to *The Revenge of Bussy*, before discussing the final plays under the title 'The tragedy of Public Man'. Derek Crawley, on the other hand, in his *Character in relation to action in the tragedies of George Chapman* has a shorter prefatory chapter on the background, dating of the plays, a survey of critical opinion and an account of stoicism, which he follows with a separate chapter for each of Chapman's tragedies. Both books are worth consulting. Crawley concludes 'it is, then, with *Caesar and Pompey* that Chapman succeeds most completely in relating in an organic and artistic way his didacticism to the requirements of dramatic form. And it is with the character of Pompey—whose tensions engage both our hearts and our minds—that he reaches his high-water mark of character portrayal in tragedy'. He agrees with Jacquot who sees a grandeur in this play which the others do not possess, disagrees with Peter Ure who finds it the 'dullest' of Chapman's tragedies. Bement considers that it is in *The Revenge of Bussy* that, in Clermont's perfect stoic manliness, we see the 'real

victory of virtue and goodness over fortune and the spiritual vulgarity of "greatness". Stoicism may truly be said to crown the ethical quest of Chapman's tragedies: Clermont leads a supremely virtuous life of action because his stoic principles not only render him impervious to the assaults of fortune and external evils but also ally him directly with an ultimate rational law in nature against random and evil forces.' He continues 'the fact that in *Caesar and Pompey* Chapman comes close to admitting the failure of Stoicism to answer the real problems of virtuous action in a morally intractable environment shows the increasing importance of Christianity in his work . . . *Chabot* completes this process: Cabot's faith in a stern and stoic-derived Justice fails because of the frailty he shares with all mankind . . . in *Chabot* we see the courageous admission that there exists a tragic gap between learning and life'. Bement concludes that the plays 'are not melodramas marred by pedantry and didacticism, but philosophic dramas burning with Chapman's "strangely intellectual fire".' In *Elizabethan Theatre IV* S. Schoenbaum offers a cheerful journalistic survey of current attitudes to Ben Jonson in 'The Humorous Jonson'; after the preliminary caution that anniversary conferences such as that for Shakespeare in 1964 or this for Jonson in Waterloo Ontario in 1972 produce occasions where the writer 'has to say something, but he has nothing to say'. Alexander W. Lyle writes on 'Volpone's two worlds' (*YES*) and notices that in his bedchamber, where his art rules, Volpone has complete control, we respond to him as a player in a play world. When he emerges from his bedchamber, however, into the piazza and then other parts of the real world of Venice (Lyle's distinction here seems very suspect) we are to see Volpone's control weaken and then collapse because his art cannot draw the 'natural world into his fictive power'. Lyle notes the remark of C. G. Thayer that if *Volpone* 'has a flaw, it lies in the fact that, unlike most of Jonson's comic figures, Volpone almost becomes a human being. He is vicious enough, to be sure, but his surface is so clever, witty and engaging that his harsh sentence seems to be inflicted on a *person*, rather than a comic character'. On the whole, this article seems to beg too many crucial questions to carry much conviction. C. J. Gianakaras in 'Jonson's use of "Avocatori" in *Volpone*' (*ELN*) makes a firm defence of Jonson's accuracy in following historical fact rather than using dramatic effect. Two problems are identified in 'the shifting meaning of the term "avocatore" through time'. Reliance on Contarini alone as Jonson's presumed source for Venetian procedures is insufficient. For one moment in the history of Venice 'the Avocatori *did* exercise judicial powers as well as those of investigation'. Jonson realized this and his 'seemingly idiosyncratic employment of the title "avocatore" shows that awareness.' Jonson possessed 'a sophisticated grasp of Venetian justice as it existed during the republican period of that city. His use of "Avocatori" as agents of justice coincides with their actual responsibilities at that precise moment in history'. A. Richard Dutton considers 'The significance of Jonson's revision of *Every Man In*' (*MLR*) and takes the occasion to dissent from the idea that after *Volpone* Jonson became more indulgent and tolerant, that, in Harry Levin's words, he 'gradually relinquished his loudly proclaimed moral purposes'. Dutton oddly omits *Eastward Ho* from consideration when

arguing that *Epicoene* is Jonson's first play to be set in London. He discusses the proposition that after 1609 Jonson set plays in London and 'deliberately appointed himself playwright to the city, just as he had effectively become masque-maker to the Court'. Considering the revised *Every Man In*, Dutton finds the play is not effectively changed so as to bring it closer to the mature London plays. In the early plays the audience remained essentially outside the dramatic illusion, passing judgement on it; the relationship between play and audience being essentially static. The self-conscious and largely explicit playing with the dramatic illusion, which is a crucial feature of the best plays, helps to break down this formal barrier, and the strong contemporary flavour and the London settings after 1609 help further to break down the barrier, implicating the audience in the process of recognizing and exposing folly. The audience is no longer a passive judge, and the early plays with their 'bland finality' of ending, and their 'bland morality' are succeeded by more complex endings with more complex moral insights. This is a readable, straightforward and commonsense discussion. William Blissett writes on the significance of certain aspects of *Bartholomew Fair*, which a performance before James I must have emphasized: the play was performed at Court on All Saints Day 1614. This article— 'Your Majesty is Welcome to a Fair'—in *Elizabethan Theatre IV*, explores the tone and presentation of the episodes and speeches dealing with justice, abuses, pork and tobacco, and other matters known to be of personal interest or abomination to the king, but finds that Jonson has taken care to leave the king's withers unwrung. Blissett notices also that *The Gypsies Metamorphosed*, with its swirl of low-life, cony-catching, purse-taking impudency, its flood of demotic speech, its extravagant attack on tobacco, and its 'applications' that it would be absurd to take offence at, is the likest to *Bartholomew Fair* among the masques'. This is a cheerful, dispensable essay. Dale B. Randall's *Jonson's Gypsies Unmasked*[9] is a finely produced, well-illustrated and well-printed book which evolves a flexible and discursive manner with which to tackle the awkward problem of assembling pertinent information about political and Court issues and personalities, about the background of Tudor and Stuart gypsies, the evolving form and conventions of the masque, Ben Jonson as a Court poet, dramatist and maker of masques, and the particular circumstances in which this particular masque, *The Gypsies Metamorphosed* (arguably his best) was written and performed. This is a scholarly and dense piece of work, full of interest in the actualities of Court Life, in the difference between the experience of reading a masque in a great university library today and seeing it for the first time at Court in James' presence: even if there is one respect in which the scholar can recapture the courtier's perspective— as Randall observes, 'one need not suppose that the King and his court sat down to the evening's entertainment unfortified by drink'. Here is one of a number of instances in which Randall implies that the performance of this masque had certain elements in common with the presentation of 'The murder of Gonzago' to Claudius at Elsinore, except that, as Randall says, 'there is no indication that Jonson succeeded in catching the conscience of the King' and 'all we may say for sure . . . is that the wisest

fool in Christendom called for his bowl and his gypsies two more times, and Buckingham, the star, continued to dance.' Randall's main point is persuasive. He puts it succinctly: it is that 'Jonson is using these gypsies to display Thievish Opportunism and Fraud (or some such traits—we should not be narrowly specific) *as they are embodied* in Buckingham, his family, and his friends.' Randall gives so much useful detailed information that his essay is a valuable handbook in the complex craft of reading a masque rightly, and of illustrating a characteristic mode of making social and political comment in the Elizabethan, Jacobean and Caroline theatre. Perhaps it is proper to notice that the book is distinguished by a tone and manner that attractively, courteously, and considerately strive for clarity as well as accuracy and detail, and treat the reader as an intelligent serious adult. There seems to have been little attention paid elsewhere in this drama other than to Webster. Marilyn L. Johnson has a study of *Images of Women in the works of Thomas Heywood* in the Salzburg Studies series, which is commendable in many ways, though Vives is strangely absent; and Carolyn Asp has published, in the same series, *A Study of Thomas Middleton's tragicomedies*, which are *A Fair Quarrel, The Old Law* and *The Witch*. '*A Fair Quarrel* investigates the opposing claims of conscience and reputation; *The Old Law* presents the conflict between man's law and great creating nature; *The Witch* illustrates the absurdity of private revenge and the sacredness of solemn oaths'; this is a careful study of a group of plays deserving such scrutiny. From the same series comes Daniel Jacobsen's *The Language of The Revenger's Tragedy*, a long, careful consideration of irony,

---

[9] *Jonson's Gypsies Unmasked*, by Dale B. J. Randall. Duke University Press: Durham, North Carolina. pp. xi+200. $9.50.

wordplay, imagery, metaphorical and metonymical figures, exhibiting 'the stylistic coherence of the play.' The detailed discussion of the poetry, exploring meaning, texture, syntax and movement, with an alertness to the dramatic situation and theatrical effect, is well handled and straight-forward in a way that seems to be becoming all too rare in discussions of Renaissance drama today; rare enough too is the sense of how to use the tools of linguistics in the service of literary appreciation, and how to keep the terminology and the tropes of Renaissance rhetoric in their deservedly modest place in a dis-cussion of poetry. This is a study which is always interesting even when going over ground already well-mapped; Jacobsen is quick to ack-nowledge debts to other scholars; the study develops towards its focus in the final chapter (a discussion of the metonymical basis of imagery in the play) with well-planned momentum. Jacobsen writes with clarity and with-out jargon, for instance, noting the combination of metonymy and meta-phor in 'Is the day out o' th' socket/ That it is noon at midnight?' he comments 'day' is a metonymy for 'sun', while 'out o' th' socket' evokes both the image of the fixed place of the sun in its orbit and of a wall socket which would hold a torch— thus combining the imagery of the artificial light of the night with the natural one of day. And perhaps it is not out of the question, given the commonplace image of the sun as the 'eye of heaven' on the one hand and this author's predilection for the image of empty eye-sockets on the other (cf. the 'unsightly rings' of I.i. 20, and the 'hollows' of III.v. 149) that this grotesque image is also involved. Later Jacobsen sums up by citing the phrase 'gather him into boldness', unfolds the layered com-plexity of meaning and suggestion in it, and concludes 'the image is characteristic of the figurative langu-age of the play, in that rather than being strictly metaphorical, the lang-uage suggests varying levels of mean-ing through ambiguous syntax and the employment of idioms in unex-pected ways'. Another important point is made about metalepsis ('a technique for condensing and en-capsulating a complex sequence of ideas in simple, precise and vivid images of beginning and ending') when Jacobsen writes 'its condensa-tion often yields the effect of bold metaphor where in fact there is no metaphor at all' and cites the line 'Melt all his patrimony in a kiss' where the 'coalescing of the two images brings forth a third image which rests upon the ambiguity of 'in'; the kiss becomes the solvent in which the patrimony melts (one thinks of a sweet dissolving on the tongue), while the idea of melting something rich and precious in a solvent recalls to Muriel Bradbrook the legend of Cleopatra melting a pearl in a cup of wine as well as the union pearl which Claudius drops into Gertrude's cup in the last act of *Hamlet*. In addition to suggesting these multiple levels of imagery the line also resumes two of the main themes of the play: the transforma-tion of property, amassed through labour and wise husbandry over a long time into vain pleasures that last but a moment, and the 'vicious minute' of lust that signals the betrayal of innocence and the triumph of sin. This is a useful piece of work, very thorough but not at all pedes-trian, using knowledge of linguistics and rhetoric to bring out freshly the nature and quality of the poetry's life. It suggests that practical criticism ought to be done more often; to write on this plan, (to echo Dr Johnson) it is at least necessary to read and think. Anne Lancashire explores a wide and interesting range of non-dramatic literature in support of her argument that we extend a play-title to 'The Second Maiden's Tragedy: A Jacobean Saint's Life' (RES). She proposes that two versions of the life of Sophronia be recognized as the source of Act III of the play. The sensationalism and emphatic lack of realism correspond to many detailed generic elements in the lives of saints and martyrs; the play appears in this context as a highly religious drama, its specific didactic religious sources carefully combined with traditional elements to present a Jacobean saint's life directed in reproof of the immoral Court of James I. There has been considerable work on Webster; three studies in the Salzburg Studies attest the diverse attractions of his work; Joseph Henry Stodder's *Moral perspectives in Webster's major tragedies* is a reasoned enquiry into the possibilities of moral order in Webster's handling of his two main tragedies, Muriel West's *The Devil and John Webster* is a remarkable handbook of demonology in the two main tragedies (why is *The Devil's Law Case* so rarely considered?), an index to images and actions well worth the attention of Webster's readers, and Eloise K. Goreau's *Integrity of life: allegorical imagery in the plays of John Webster*, an extremely well-written account of its subject enhanced by reference to other literature—recalling Webster, as it were, from the isolation in which so many critics place him. S. W. Sullivan considers 'The tendency to rationalize in *The White Devil* and *The Duchess of Malfi*' (YES), and finds that Webster explores the theme of attempted evasion of responsibility; in *The White Devil* Webster offers an 'acute, often satirical, and sometimes moving de-lineation of ways in which people seek to evade awareness of guilt'; this process has a structural function; the theme of the play is seen in relation to that of *The Duchess of Malfi*, where Bosola constantly seeks and fails to escape moral responsibility, as his adoption of the manner and rôle of malcontent shows.

Anders Dallby has a most interesting survey of the history, dramatic structure and stage effectiveness of *The White Devil* in *The Anatomy of Evil*.[10] It is worth quoting from his conclusions: 'The problem which Webster's tragedy poses and only partly solves, even within the limitations of the Jacobean view (as distinct from the slightly less sceptical Elizabethan attitude), is the problem of man's confrontation with evil, and of the evil element in man himself. As far as we can judge, Webster's reading of this problem results in a profoundly pessimistic view of the state into which man has fallen, and of the society of his time, particularly its higher layers; but a basically optimistic view of the possibilities open to man'. Three further volumes in the Salzburg Studies series deserve consideration; Bertha Hensman's *The shares of Fletcher, Field and Massinger in twelve plays of the Beaumont and Fletcher canon* is the fruit of much close reading and wide knowledge— it will be an additional benefit if it secures the early completion of an edition, but meanwhile it is to be read for its own qualities; Tucker Orbison's *The tragic vision of John Ford* is a contemplation of *'Tis Pity, Love's Sacrifice, The Broken Heart* and *Perkin Warbeck*, relating Ford's concepts of tragedy to contemporary and later insights; Florence Ali's

[10] Lund Studies in English 48. *The Anatomy of Evil, a study of John Webster's 'The White Devil'*, by Anders Dallby. Lund: CWK Gleerup. pp. 236.

Opposing absolutes: conviction and convention in John Ford's plays makes an incidentally convincing criticism of *The Fancies, Chaste and Noble*. She subscribes to current orthodoxy that *Perkin Warbeck* is 'the most profound of Ford's plays'. Philip Edwards has written a remarkably fresh comment on 'The royal pretenders in Massinger and Ford' (*E&S*); his purpose is 'to suggest some possible reasons why two of England's leading dramatists, about the year 1630, should each have been moved to write a play dealing very sympathetically with the appearance of a pretender to the throne, who is in the end defeated.' The plays are *Perkin Warbeck* and *Believe As You List*, the latter 'is a play on recent European history gone over with a paint-brush to make it look like ancient history.' Both men, Ford and Massinger, 'took the true story of a pretender to a European throne, a pretender whom events and history had discredited, and invested that pretender with dignity and credibility in his conflict with the established ruler.' The reference to history is meticulous: 'It is of the utmost importance to stress that nostalgia and reaction were basic elements in the opposition to Charles at the time that *Perkin Warbeck* and *Believe As You List* were written.' Moreover,

'The complaint was not that Charles was a feudal incubus, hampering progress and the advancement of freedom, but that, in his autocracy and would-be absolutism, he was a dangerous innovator.' Edwards' main proposition is that 'both Perkin Warbeck and Antiochus represent a luminous figure appearing from the mists announcing that he is the dead past, newly come alive in order to bring succour to an ailing nation. He has a kind of beauty of being, he is the guardian of the idealized, authentic, undivided life, when truth and government were not separated.' Edwards is rightly insistent that 'we must renounce two things completely if we are to make sense of the conflict of the two 'competitors for kingdoms' (Ford's phrase) in each play. The first is the temptation to read the plays allegorically, and the second is the nineteenth-century view o Charles I as the pale figure of an obsolete Divine Right theorist holding up the cause of economic liberty.' Rather, 'We are invited to see in each play a spiritual hollowness in the established government, and to share a conviction that the ethics of success on which it builds are bound to suppress the qualities of truth represented by the saintly king beckoned up from the past.'

IX

The Later Sixteenth Century: Excluding Drama

JOHN ROE

This chapter is arranged as follows:
1. General; 2. Sidney; 3. Spenser;
4. Chapman; 5. Ralegh; 6. Poetry;
7. Prose.

1. GENERAL

It seems appropriate to open with a book as wide in scope and purpose as S. K. Heninger's *Touches of Sweet Harmony*.[1] Professor Heninger's aim is to show that the concerns of a Renaissance poet are limitless and that the poem itself reflects not only its own creation but also the divine. In his chapter on 'Metaphor as Cosmic Correspondence' he argues accordingly, 'The job of "making" then becomes not so much a creation of something new, but rather a discovery of something already prescribed in God's book of nature'. What has inspired Professor Heninger to undertake this large inquiry, the fruits of which are exemplified in the rich documentation of the history of Pythagoreanism in the sixteenth century, is something fundamentally simple: the concern for students whose critical education had unfitted them to read the long epic poems of the Renaissance. 'Quite early in my reading of renaissance literature I became aware that not only certain passages but whole works would not submit to the terms of analysis then

in vogue. *Paradise Lost* was openly denounced, while *The Faerie Queene* was relegated to a definitive edition, and no one even mentioned Sidney's *Arcadia*'. The rehabilitation of Spenser is now complete, and Professor Heninger's task has been further to enlarge and explain the vistas that have opened. He does his job thoroughly, showing, for example, in the central section of his book, how Renaissance philosophers evolved finite structures (like the tetrad which formed itself from the four elements) which could represent the infinite. These chapters, on numbers, the cosmos, the occult sciences, time, and eternity, are fascinatingly illustrated with maps, charts, diagrams, emblems, and figures. Such scholarship amply repays the reader's time, but a niggling doubt remains. The student of faltering faith who feels that, before embarking on the adventures of Red Crosse and company, he must first master the involutions of Renaissance mathematics, may decide that Spenser's book is too heavy to hold.

The editors of *The Rhetoric of Renaissance Poetry*[2] address themselves to another large question: how far the arguments over the various manifestations of rhetoric in the

[1] *Touches of Sweet Harmony: Pythagorean Cosmology and Renaissance Poetics*, by S. K. Heninger. Folkestone: Dawson & Sons, Ltd. Illustrated, pp. xxvii+446. £9.50.

[2] *The Rhetoric of Renaissance Poetry: From Wyatt to Milton*, edited by Thomas O. Sloan and Raymond B. Waddington. Berkeley and Los Angeles and London: University of California Press. Plate, pp. vi+247. £5.50.

poetry of the period can be resolved. Of the several essays present those of the editors themselves keep this problem most in mind. Thomas O. Sloan gives a history of examples of rhetoric from Wyatt to Milton and notes a major disagreement among modern critics: the emphasis on logic by Ong and Tuve, and that on meditation by Martz. His attempt at reconciling the two would appear so successful as to make one wonder whether there is any further point in distinguishing rhetoric as a special activity in poetry. (This book may signal the revenge of the New Criticism). The essays tend to divide between those who look for signs of contemporary rhetorical or oratorical practice in the poetry and those who are unwilling to differentiate. This can make for amusing contrasts— between, for example, John T. Shawcross, who shows a movement of the private into the public sphere, and Professor Sloan, who shows how the public becomes private. Anthony LaBranche's essay has a precise end which is to rescue Daniel's reputation from the jagged contradiction opened in it by Ben Jonson. He suggests that the rival claims of honesty and poetic skill are met and resolved by Daniel's 'rhetoric of thoughtfulness'. Leonard Nathan, again precisely, distinguishes Tudor and Renaissance structural habits to show the superiority of Gascoigne's 'Lullabie' over its earlier models. Michael Murrin asks naïve questions in an attempt to display the sophistication of Spenser's narrative art in 'The Rhetoric of Fairyland'. And Raymond B. Waddington maintains an overall view when discussing Shakespeare's fifteenth sonnet in terms of the art of memory. (The book includes essays on Wyatt, Donne, Herbert, and Crashaw).

Ursula Kuhn's *English Literary Terms in Poetological Texts of the* *Sixteenth Century*[3] is a desirable reference work. She takes as her 'texts' works by fifteen authors whom she considers (allowing that her choice must to some extent be arbitrary) most central. Her fifteen includes Puttenham, Harvey, Sidney, Ascham, and Elyot, but also Gosson, E. K., and Richard Wills. The book divides into two sections: one a list of topics (e.g. Bible, eclogue, decorum, English literature, imitation) and the other of ancient and modern authors. The thoughts of Miss Kuhn's fifteen authorities appear at the appropriate places in the lists, often finding themselves usefully adjacent to each other (Sidney and Gosson under 'theatre', for example). What distinguishes her work from other recent good handbooks is her intricate but efficient system of cross-reference which allows a particular topic (e.g. 'wantonness') to be pursued easily and considered from all the angles furnished by her texts. The acid test of her fifteen choices is whether they seem to sum it all up between them, and it is this reader's impression that they do. The size of the 'dictionary', however, and its present division into three separate volumes make it physically awkward to manage.

In *Angell Fayre or Strumpet Lewd*[4] Esther Yael Beith-Halahmi covers the legend of Jane Shore, comparing treatments of this royal mistress from Thomas More's account of her to Heywood's play *Edward IV* (and includes Rowe's *The Fair Penitent* for

[3] *English Literary Terms in Poetological Texts of the Sixteenth Century*, edited by Ursula Kuhn. Salzburg: Institut für Englische Sprache und Literatur. 3 vols., pp. xxxiii+1038. £4.80 per volume.
[4] *Angell Fayre or Strumpet Lewd: Jane Shore as an Example of Erring Beauty in Sixteenth-Century Literature*, by Esther Yael Beith-Halahmi. Salzburg: Institut für Englische Sprache und Literatur. 2 vols., pp. iv+361. £4.80 per volume.

good measure). She announces at the beginning an interest in the changes in sixteenth-century opinion on the degree of responsibility attaching to someone who, though passively, is nonetheless at the centre of important political events. Accordingly, she reveals a constant swing between treatments that reflect moral disapproval and others that encourage sensual appreciation. In this latter area she contrasts a clumsy poem by Anthony Chute, which is confused about its aims, with Drayton's accomplished blend of the immoral and the insouciant in *England's Heroicall Epistles*. Marriage enters as a sub-theme giving rise to speculations on the difference between courtly and domestic notions of ethics. This useful, illuminating study concludes: 'In spite of individual differences of emphasis, the awareness of the ethical implications of sensuality is evident in all the Elizabethan works'. The author adds that the distinction between courtly and popular ballad treatment of Jane lies in the former's more delicate balance of moral and sensual.

Three essays appear on education. Boyd M. Berry, in 'The First English Pediatricians' (JHI), looks at the work of Thomas Phaire and particularly John Jones, whose *The Arte and Science of preserving Bodie and soule in all healthe, Wisedom, and Catholike Religion* (1579) he subjects to a quite individual, psychoanalytical study. Emphasizing the paranoia in Jones's images of bodily disintegration, Mr Berry questions afresh the positive emphasis on micro-macrocosmic correspondence of the Tillyardian World Picture. However, he admits that while he thinks Jones's dissonant voice should be heard he does not think it undermines belief in the achievement of Tudor humanism. Richard L. DeMolen continues to

round out his picture of Mulcaster as a progressive educator in 'Richard Mulcaster and the Profession of Teaching in Sixteenth-Century England' (JHI). Similarly regarding the twin progress of humanism and education, Lisa Jardine demonstrates from the curriculum, in 'The Place of Dialectic Teaching in Sixteenth-Century Cambridge' (SRen), that this university moved nearer to, not away from, the main intellectual and poetic concerns of the years 1560–90.

2. SIDNEY

J. G. Nichols has written a very good introduction called *The Poetry of Sir Philip Sidney*.[5] His book addresses itself through *Astrophil and Stella* (to which it is mostly devoted) to the wider problem of reading poetry, especially Elizabethan poetry. Mr Nichols covers all the ground this necessarily entails and clearly enjoys discussing the tricky questions set by the sonnet sequence. Dealing judiciously with various modern attempts at solving these, he seems to place his own faith in a 'dramatic' reading and demonstrates his reasons for doing so convincingly. But his promising attempt at relating Sidney's poetry to his poetic theory does not get very far. A reader, unless he is himself new to Sidney, will not find Mr Nichols's book full of novel arguments; but he will find in it a wise, balanced, sensitive set of appraisals.

A Comparison of Sidney's Old and New Arcadia,[6] by Robert Eril Levine, attempts to make sense of the relationship between the two. Mr Levine defies those who would see in the *New*

[5] *The Poetry of Sir Philip Sidney: An Interpretation in the Context of his Life and Times*, by J. G. Nichols. Liverpool: Liverpool University Press. Plate, pp. x+171. £4.

[6] *A Comparison of Sidney's Old and New Arcadia*, by Robert Eril Levine. Salzburg: Institut für Englische Sprache und Literatur. pp. 122. £4.80.

Arcadia a move towards epic, arguing that the real difference between the two versions is the deeper irony of the later one. The point is made by a few well-chosen episodes in which the action comically undercuts what the heroes and heroines say of themselves and their intentions. Mr Levine successfully refutes those 'who talk about Sidney's *Arcadia* as a "builded ideal" or a "mature and practised philosophy"'. But it would still seem possible, to take his first point, to speak of a serious version of epic which did not preclude irony, even comic irony.

Looking at the problem of 'Rebellion in the *New Arcadia*' (PQ), Martin Bergbusch finds 'specific influence of Huguenot thought about insurrection' to be 'clear and unmistakable'. (The Huguenot position is that insurrection is only justified when it will bring about a reformation of the state, i.e. when the deposed ruler is 'absolutely bad'). Lest the idea of such conjectures in Sidney's mind should cause alarm, he adds defusingly: 'Undoubtedly, when he wrote of rebellion in the *New Arcadia*, he was more concerned with the circumstances on the Continent than with the situation in England'.

In 'Philosophy, History, and Sidney's *Old Arcadia*' (CL), P. Jeffrey Ford selects two of the contestants from the *Apology for Poetry* and considers how the *Old Arcadia* might reconcile them. The possibility is suggested by Tasso's harmonious achievement in the *Gerusalemme Liberata*. Mr Ford argues accordingly, and plausibly, that Sidney's romance remains true to the varied nature of experience (history) and yet, through devices of symmetry, repetition, and analogy manages a unity of a moral kind (philosophy). Presumably, in bringing her enemies into this alliance, poetry only demonstrates her control over them rather than doubling the force of their threat to her.

The poetry receives its fair share of erotic and spiritual interpretation. Alan Sinfield, in '*Sexual Puns in Astrophil and Stella*' (EIC) calls for recognition of such wordplay at an early stage of the sequence—long before the voluptuous suggestions of sonnet sixty-eight onwards. This reading would render Astrophil from the start more knowing and witty than his 'traditional image of the elegant but naïve courtier'. Whether the balance needs to be redressed is open to question; at any rate Astrophil is coarsened in the attempt. Dorothy Jones goes much further in 'Sidney's Erotic Pen: An Interpretation of one of the *Arcadia* Poems' (JEGP). Nothing 'slips' by, and while her response to the tone of 'What tongue can her perfections tell' is unobjectionable and even accurate, her Freudian-Partridge identification of some of its 'parts' is quite obscene.

Completely unrelated to these concerns, Russell M. Brown, in 'Sidney's *Astrophil and Stella*, I' (*Expl*, vol. xxxii), explains 'sunne-burn'd' from a description in Wilson's *The Arte of Rhetorique*.

In a more earnest vein, Robert H. Deming's 'Love and Knowledge in the Renaissance Lyric' (*TSLL*) examines the problem of the self and self-knowledge as manifested by such poetry. Taking his cue from Cassirer's *The Individual and the Cosmos in the Renaissance*, he inspects lyrics from Wyatt to Donne, but focuses his argument through *Astrophil and Stella*. 'Sidney', he says, 'has engaged in that self-conscious dialectical examination of his own consciousness, has in poetry turned himself into an object for his own contemplation'. The consequences of taking this step are explored fully, if somewhat humourlessly, and the poem's function as a means ('organon') of knowing elaborately explained; but the ironies attendant on the quest (as far as concerns Sidney) are rather passed by.

One of the darkest of recent readings of *Astrophil and Stella* is Andrew D. Weiner's 'Structure and "Fore Conceit" in *Astrophil and Stella*' (*TSLL*). This essay replaces the normally accepted tripartite structure of the sequence with one of five sections or movements. Each of the movements registers a change in the identity of Astrophil who by the fourth movement is 'revelling in sin.' The argument presses home unrelentingly, helped by a quotation from Bruno's dedication to *De gli eroici furori* attacking profane love and by a merciless couplet from the Calvinist Greville (although Astrophil's continuing love for Stella in the last movement is allowed to have 'something pathetically ennobling').

As if to put these things in perspective, G. F. Waller conducts a balanced examination of the psalms (brother's and sister's) in '"This Matching of Contraries": Calvinism and Courtly Philosophy in the Sidney Psalms' (*ES*). Mr Waller judges that the psalms 'reveal a fascinating and hitherto unexplored complexity in the intellectual history of the Sidney circle, a tension between Courtier and Christian, between Castiglione and Calvin'.

In more general terms, Sidney is twice related to his contemporaries. John P. Cutts, in 'Pericles in Rusty Armour, and the Matachine Dance of the Competitive Knights at the Court of Simonides' (*YES*), examines tournament and dance episodes in the *New Arcadia* and *Pericles* and decides that Sidney 'may well have provided Shakespeare with basic material'. Victor Skretkowicz, Jr. cites

Christopher Clifford's *The School of Horsemanship* (1585) and the correspondence and *Journal* of Walsingham, in 'Greville and Sidney: Bibliographical Addenda' (N&Q), to suggest that the literary friendship of Sidney and Spenser continued into the 1580s via Lodowick Bryskett. (He also speculates on Greville's possible continental adventures in 1587–88).

Finally, Katherine Duncan-Jones remarks and resolves an interesting puzzle in 'Sidney in Samothea: A Forgotten National Myth' (*RES*). Why was Samothea, the birthplace of Philisides, not used by other Elizabethan poets to evoke a British Golden Age? The answer, well documented by the essay, is that John Stow firmly discredited the myth in 1580. Annius of Viterbo had originally perpetrated the 'error' which Holinshed maintained.

3. SPENSER

This year several studies appear that include a consideration of Spenser and one other major poet. Georgia Ronan Crampton compares suffering and action in Spenser and Chaucer in *The Condition of Creatures*.[7] Despite some of the passive situations and inactive moods of heroes like Red Crosse and Guyon, Spenser's knights are agents rather than patients. Chaucer's, by contrast, endure rather than perform. Mrs Crampton analyses at length action in the Knight's Tale and the first four books of *The Faerie Queene* showing how in places *agere* and *pati* appear to merge into each other, the Medieval Spenser encountering the Renaissance Chaucer. Notwithstanding, 'Spenser's heroes face the ruck of events and strive to order them so as

---

[7] *The Condition of Creatures: Suffering and Action in Chaucer and Spenser*, by Georgia Ronan Crampton. New Haven and London: Yale University Press. pp. x+207. £5.

to bring about a better world; and though that world, gallantly new and golden, cannot be imagined as ever achieved, the doing. ... is always under way. Chaucer's people, few of whom are heroes, are not making up a new world or restoring a golden one but for the most part coping with one another within the same old world, leaden, but dear and engaging'. If this conclusion is unsurprising, the book's usefulness may be said to lie not in its main but its subordinate distinctions particularly its illustration of them.

While similarly looking back to the Middle Ages, Patrick Cullen's *Infernal Triad*[8] also intends a comparison of Spenser with Milton. The infernal triad of the World, the Flesh, and the Devil, old though it be, has its part to play in the allegory of both poets. Professor Cullen acknowledges in his introduction that he is aware of the dangers of scheme-hunting, but insists that the triad can be discerned repeatedly in the epic situations of Milton and Spenser. He begins by tracing backwards and his chapter 'The Pilgrimage of Christian Life' makes some scholarly connexions between Spenser and earlier 'pilgrim' works such as Stephen Hawes's *Pastime of Pleasure* and Jean Cartigny's *The Wandering Knight* (both interested in 'man's war against the Flesh, the World, and the Devil'). The value of applying the triad to the adventures of Spenser's knights is that it demonstrates ably the nature of the various traps they get caught in. The triad apart, much of Professor Cullen's analysis proceeds in the manner of Paul Alpers; but he remarks an important difference between them: 'Alpers' insistence that

we are not encouraged to sit in judgment on the knight is at best a misleading truth. To be sure, we are not to judge the knight self-righteously or complacently ... But judge we must; otherwise we will also duplicate his errors'. His argument, at least as far as it concerns Spenser, carries authority but despite his wish not to constrict the poem with his triadic reading, *The Faerie Queene* is diminished by it. One prefers the more conventional trust placed in Renaissance heroes by Mrs Crampton.

A Japanese scholar, Haruhiko Fujii, brings Spenser and Milton together under pastoral in his work *Time, Landscape and the Ideal Life*.[9] His study opens on *The Shepheardes Calender*, progresses to Calidore's book in *The Faerie Queene* (via such figures as Colin Clout and Astrophel) and closes on *Lycidas*. In writing about Spenser, Mr Fujii traces the fascinating, overall development of mood from melancholic to heroic, while keeping a strict sense of the divisions between and within works. Spenser's pastoral is carefully distinguished from that of Theocritus and Virgil, and *The Shepheardes Calender* itself shown to have three phases: recreative, moral, and plaintive. Using Panofsky's book on Dürer (which has helped him to study the woodcuts at the head of the eclogues), the author finds in Colin Clout a peculiarly Renaissance kind of melancholy according to which Colin's deepening sadness heralds a depth of maturity. All important is a process of 'inner time' which will bring about first love's mystery (as in *Astrophel*) and last heroic action (Calidore). The book expresses effortlessly, and in a pleasingly evocative way, how

[8] *Infernal Triad: The Flesh, the World, and the Devil in Spenser and Milton,* by Patrick Cullen. Princeton: Princeton University Press. pp. xxxvi+267. $13.50.

[9] *Time, Landscape and the Ideal Life: Studies in the Pastoral Poetry of Spenser and Milton,* by Haruhiko Fujii. Kyoto: Apollonsha. pp. vi+272. Yen 3,000.

seemingly separate moods belong to the same design.

The broad subject of Spenser's depiction of history and geography, fabulous and real, attracts Michael O'Connell's attention in 'History and the Poet's Golden World: The Epic Catalogues in *The Faerie Queene*' (*ELR*). Sidney's discrimination between the truths of history and poetry has inspired this essay (which in many ways is uninspired) to say that differences in the chronicles read by Arthur and Guyon in the Chamber of Eumnestes suggest that 'Spenser intends ... to use our consciousness of history as a foil for the specifically idealized terrains of his poetic world, to contrast our sense of the past to his created ideal'. In Book IV, Mr O'Connell claims, Spenser exchanges this distinction between poetry and history for a more straightforward celebration of the poet and poetry-making ('mythopoeia').

Structuralism keeps its guns trained on the epic, witness Rawdon Wilson's 'Images and "Allegoremes" of Time in the Poetry of Spenser' (*ELR*). 'The allegoreme should be thought of as a self-contained unit of compound imagery which shows, typically, a narrative construction in interrelated events within a "block" of time'. Understanding this enables us to recognize more clearly that 'Spenser's vision is an inherently moral one that sees the chief problem of human existence as that of engaging in right action with time—or through it—against the awesome standards of eternity'. All the same, the discovery of a structural characteristic that made better sense of acknowledged difficulties such as the relationship of time to the Garden of Adonis would seem more useful.

Also taking something of a structuralist approach, Stan Hinton raises the question of identity in 'The Poet and his Narrator: Spenser's Epic Voice' (*ELH*). Analysing the relationship of the poet's voice to the voice narrating the various episodes, he rather frighteningly finds that the latter 'is an immensely complex being who appears in many guises and at many levels'. Sometimes an episode (for example, the battle of Artegall with Radigund) will act as 'a structural analogue of the narrator's conflicting comments'.

Judith Dundas imposes architectonic shape on the poem in order to predict what its unwritten part would have been in '*The Faerie Queene*: The Incomplete Poem and the Whole Meaning' (*MP*). Citing all the available evidence (including the prefatory letter) to the effect that Spenser's contemporary readership would have been sure of the end, she finally summons Alberti (perhaps a bit wilfully) as a witness on design to argue that once the principle of 'enclosed space and containing form' is understood the remaining part of the poem can be imagined from what is there.

Andrew D. Weiner draws on his interest in Sidney (*The Defence of Poetry*) to defend a related point in '"Fierce Warres and Faithful Loves": Pattern as Structure in Book I of *The Faerie Queene*' (*HLQ*). Like Judith Dundas, he feels that Paul Alpers is wrong to object that an interest in structure is too much at odds with the way we naturally read the poem. But unlike her, he must have the end in order to make sense of the parts. Reading is a waiting game and only at last can we know how much we have been 'moved' (in Sidney's sense). In addition, he checks up on Spenser's Protestant credentials finding them to be comfortably nonpartisan.

On a more philosophical front, Dwight J. Sims detects a refinement of Neo-Platonism in 'The Syncretic Myth of Venus in Spenser's Legend of Chastity' (SP). Pico is more congenial to Spenser than Ficino because he is not exclusively spiritual. Spenser in turn develops Pico's physical allowances to a 'more pragmatically human approach to love, still highly moral, but much more clearly secular and realistic'. A valid iconographic interpretation of Venus and Diana in Book III of *The Faerie Queene* strengthens the case for the difference between Spenser and the Italians.

Paul D. Green examines contemporary history in 'Spenser and the Masses: Social Commentary in *The Faerie Queene*' (*JHI*). He finds nothing but reinforcement of the view that Spenser despised the lower orders and illustrates his argument, disappointingly, from all the old, familiar places.

Robert L. Entzminger, on the other hand, belongs to a different school in 'Courtesy: the Cultural Imperative' (*PQ*). Courtesy, as depicted in Book VI, reflects a unifying principle necessary to the survival of civilization.

Two critics have tackled the question of the varying character or usage of a single personification or figure. Walter M. Kendrick, in 'Earth of Flesh, Flesh of Earth: Mother Earth in *The Faerie Queene*' (*RenQ*), suggests that 'Mother Earth exists in *The Faerie Queene* as a kind of vast amoral potential, a barely sentient but powerfully living source of flesh'. Amoral in nature, and not given extended allegorization herself, she can lend her weight (literally) to good or evil. Some vivid examples follow. The knights, themselves of flesh, bring out one meaning of earthliness. Their main quest, Mr Kendrick stirringly and dramatically observes, is to free their souls from their mortal frame before their bodies revert

finally to earth. Elizabeth Story Donno takes on the daintier figure of Cupid in 'The Triumph of Cupid: Spenser's Legend of Chastity' (*YES*). Like Mother Earth, Cupid himself is neither one thing nor the other, neither true nor false. Epithets such as 'false archer', therefore, 'serve not to characterize the god himself but to characterize the perspective of a victim or the quality of a response elicited'. The argument nicely delineates Cupid's function 'within the providential scheme': many characters fall in love but those of a better nature fare better.

Lloyd A. Wright conducts an orthodox defence of Spenser's way of dealing with (and in) temptation in 'Guyon's Heroism in the Bower of Bliss' (*TSLL*). The poetry sympathetically underscores the reader's dissatisfaction with arguments for destroying the Bower, but good reasons —connected with Salvation—are nonetheless given why he should resist the place's sensuous appeal.

'The Moralized Song: Some Renaissance Themes in Pope' (*ELH*) is a fluent, enjoyable essay by the late Kathleen Williams which makes positive use of Spenser to disclose unsuspected generosity in Pope's satiric vision.

Patsy Scherer Cornelius devotes a full-length study to *E. K.'s Commentary on The Shepheardes Calender*.[10] A firm advocate of E. K., Miss Cornelius subjects his commentary to some scrutiny and finds much to say on behalf of its accuracy and usefulness. Although die-hard critics of E. K. are unlikely to be converted by her skilful defence of his merits, she may have convinced them that his purpose at least was genuinely to

[10] *E. K.'s Commentary on The Shepheardes Calender*, by Patsy Scherer Cornelius. Salzburg: Institut für Englische Sprache und Literatur. pp. 111. £4.80.

elucidate and otherwise flatter Spenser's text rather than to use it as an occasion for self-display.

On a smaller scale, C. R. B. Combellack argues from metre in an attempt to explicate the riddle of the lines 'For what might be in earthlie mould/ That did her buried body hould', in 'Spenser's *Shepheardes Calender* (*November*), 158–162' (*Expl*). And in an unenthralling contribution to the subject of 'Spenser and Symbolic Witchcraft in *The Shepheardes Calender*' (*SEL*), D. Douglas Waters analyses various eclogues from the perspective of Anglican and Puritan attitudes towards church vestments concluding that Spenser was 'within conforming range of the Elizabethan Settlement'.

The marriage poetry receives some attention. James McAuley warms to the theme of Protestantism in 'The Form of Una's Marriage Ceremony in *The Faerie Queene*' (*N&Q*). Observing that this ceremony is neither Christian nor 'Roman-Classical' in usage, he declares that it reflects rather the recovery of the primordial tradition by Spenser's England. The bride represents the Protestant faith, and so 'Una's marriage to St. George of England by a rite which is antecedent to Christian or Roman usage and administered by her father Adam seals the authenticity of the Elizabethan religious establishment'.

Within the confines of the shorter marriage poems, Michael West is in a mood for comparisons in 'Prothalamia in Propertius and Spenser' (*CL*). Remarking distinct echoes of Propertius III. 20 in *Epithalamion*, he speculates that the latter and *Prothalamion* (with its accent on betrothal) recall the Roman poet's concern for contract. Being aware of the danger of associating the sort of love Propertius knew with the nuptial poetry of the Elizabethan, Mr West

forestalls objection by an appeal to 'the syncretistic spirit of the Renaissance'. But Frank B. Young, in 'Medusa and the *Epithalamion*: A Problem in Spenserian Imagery' (*ELN*), hardly gets away with his argument, that the image of Medusa in stanza eleven shatters with its ugliness the previous stanza's image of physical beauty, only to make way for an eventual image of spiritual beauty.

William C. Johnson exposes the craftiness of the craftsmanship in 'Spenser's *Amoretti* and the Art of the Liturgy' (*SEL*). Comparing Lenten days and dates in the *New Testament* and the *Book of Common Prayer* with the Lenten sonnets, he demonstrates triumphantly how 'almost unnoticed Spenser put aside the laws of courtly love and put, in their stead, a Christian outlook'.

Helen Cooper's wide-ranging investigation into the false etymology of 'eclogue' ('goat-talk'), in 'The Goat and the Eclogue' (*PQ*), ends with examples from Spenser and Edward Fairfax (*Hermes and Lycaon*). She shows interestingly how the goat, rather than the gentle sheep, became the pastoral associate of satire. Possible analogues of a stanza on pilgrimage are reported by Joan Heiges Blythe in 'Spenser's *The Faerie Queene*, IV, i, 20' (*Expl*. vol. xxxii).

4. CHAPMAN

Chapman warrants a section to himself on the strength of Raymond B. Waddington's tribute in *The Mind's Empire*.[11] This intricate, interesting analysis of the forces at play in Chapman's poetic personality signals its direction by distinguishing be-

[11] *The Mind's Empire: Myth and Form in George Chapman's Narrative Poems*, by Raymond B. Waddington. Baltimore and London: Johns Hopkins University Press. pp. xii+221. £6.60.

tween Elizabethan and Metaphysical religious verse: 'The meditative voice did not affect (Chapman); *Good Friday, 1613. Riding Westward* can cast little light on *A Hymn to Our Saviour*. His religious poems are private only in the sense that the actions of the hierophant at the altar are, while fully displayed, inscrutable and isolated. Chapman's most private poems are his translations of Petrarch's *Penitential Psalms*'. Ceremony, myth, sacred ritual; the poet as priest or *vates*; such are the accentuations or character Professor Waddington discerns. The poetry above, the myth below: the relationship of myth to form, as the title indicates, is a chief concern. Interpreting according to both ancient and contemporary understandings of myth, Professor Waddington produces such absorbing accounts as that of the three identities of the moon-goddess in *The Shadow of Night*: 'an elaborate thematic structure—allocating to Luna the "natural" or "philosophic" meaning, to Diana the political and military, to Hecate the poetic, metamorphosing each and subsuming all within the controlling image of Cynthia'. The book pursues these lines with the help of Wind, Gombrich, Yates, and Panofsky, and invokes Brooks Otis's discussion of the *Metamorphoses* of Ovid to support its view of a consistently epic intention in the conclusion to *Hero and Leander*. Professor Waddington's exegesis is engrossing, and more often than not valuable, but one is reminded how much Chapman is his own exegete and one still looks (perhaps foolishly) to free him from his own clutterings. On occasion Professor Waddington goes straight to the centre, as when he shows how the poet performed a propagandist service for Elizabeth helping her to assume the rôle, in her own way and

for her own purposes, 'of a now-forbidden Blessed Virgin'.

In 'Chapman's Missing Couplet' (*ELN*) Leon Krisak disagrees with the argument of Phyllis Brooks Bartlett (expressed in her edition) that a couplet is to be assumed missing between lines 321 and 322 of *The Teares of Peace*.

5. RALEGH

John Racin contributes a thorough, substantial survey of Ralegh's historiography in *Sir Walter Ralegh as Historian*.[12] First he traces the rise and fall of *The History of the World* from its zenith in the seventeenth century (owing to a misreading of it as a work of Republicanism) to its nadir in Matthew Arnold's inaugural lecture at Oxford in 1857, and afterwards to its recovery in our own day. Then he declares the irresolvable paradox of Ralegh's aims: to explain history according to providence (theology looking to the *Old Testament*) and to tell it according to human record (the secular-classical tradition). Mr Racin considers Ralegh to have been among the more ambitious of historians, making syntheses (e.g. history, theology, and philosophy) where others were content to allow divisions. But his very enterprise isolated him. Noting the implicit quarrel between Ralegh and the Sidney of *The Defence of Poetry*, Mr Racin says that, notwithstanding, Sidney, Amyot, and Bacon were all aligned against Ralegh in 'the limitation of historiography to second causes'. From paradox to pessimism: the author convincingly rounds off his essay with a demonstration that Ralegh's belief in human capacity to learn from history is matched point for point with his

[12] *Sir Walter Ralegh as Historian: An Analysis of The History of the World*, by John Racin. Salzburg: Institut für Englische Sprache und Literatur. pp. v+216. £4.80.

despair at the hopelessness of man (and not divinity) to shape his own ends.

Philip Edwards pursues an enjoyable lucid line of argument in 'Who Wrote *The Passionate Man's Pilgrimage*?' (*ELR*). Whoever it was, he says, it was not Ralegh. Following Robert Southey, he makes an interesting case for Catholic authorship, but cannot feel very strongly about the candidacy of either Southwell or the semi-Catholic William Alabaster. But to make up for this indecisiveness, he offers the plausible speculation that the poem's metrical oddness resulted from the printer's excision of images of Catholic sentiment.

A similar interest governs Michael L. Johnson in 'Some Problems of Unity in Sir Walter Ralegh's *The Ocean's Love to Cynthia*' (*SEL*). He picks his way through image after image in an attempt to understand the relationship of myth (especially pastoral) to structure, but to no avail. Suggesting that the problem of unity would not have occurred if Ralegh had attempted a sonnet sequence like Sidney's, he daringly concludes that the poem was in fact composed 'as a collage of incomplete sonnets'.

6. POETRY

The shadows about the tomb of Everard Guilpin have begun to disperse as a result of D. Allen Carroll's welcome edition of *Skialethia*.[13] This is a critical, old-spelling edition (though slightly modernized) which happily makes more generally available these seventy epigrams and seven satires. *Skialethia* was entered in the *Stationer's Register* on 15 September 1598 and published anonymously,

but on 1 to 4 June 1599 it was burnt by the Archbishop's order. 'In accounts of the rise of formal satire in England', states the informative introduction, 'it belongs just after Donne, Hall, and Marston, and in studies of the influence of Martial, after Davies and Harington'. The introduction also considers how the classical and contemporary manner fit each other in Guilpin. Idiom, topical reference, the constantly shifting quality of the satires all require a full commentary. This edition's, about one and a half the length of the text, is very serviceable. As well as explicating basic problems of meaning, it catches echoes of Nash, Davies, Hall, and Marston (to whom the satirist was connected by family). In 'Donne and Gilpin (sic): Another Conjecture' (*N&Q*) Heather Dubrow Ousby traces a purely literary relationship in hazarding the thought that two of Guilpin's epigrams owe something to Donne's 'Phryne' in their images of female make·up.

Another edition, this time an anthology, is *Sonnets of the English Renaissance* which was prepared by the late J. W. Lever.[14] In his introduction, which takes its bearings from his earlier study of Elizabethan love sonnets, Professor Lever says that his aim was 'to show something of that diversity in unity by making comparison more easy between sonnets that are readily available in anthologies and others which are only accessible in scholarly editions devoted to individual poets'. Undergraduates are likely to find Professor Lever's concise, suggestive notes very useful. The selection itself describes a plausible (if debatable) alteration in outlook from Wyatt's humanist self-confidence to the deepening religious

[13] *Everard Guilpin: Skialethia or A Shadow of Truth, in Certain Epigrams and Satyres*, edited by D. Allen Carroll. North Carolina and London: University of North Carolina Press and Oxford University Press. pp. vii + 246. £7.25.

[14] *Sonnets of the English Renaissance*, edited by J. W. Lever. London: Athlone Press. pp. 186. £4. (paperback £1.50).

anxiety of the Holy Sonnets. Greville, Drummond of Hawthornden, and William Alabaster help Donne to close the age. By far the largest sections go to Shakespeare (fifty-four sonnets), Sidney (forty-two from *Astrophil and Stella* plus 'Thou Blind Man's Mark' and 'Leave Me, O Love'), and Spenser (thirty-four *Amoretti*). The compilation and balance of the whole (while making sense in the terms proposed by the editor) will almost certainly attract disagreement, as will the modernization of texts. But the overall endeavour can be saluted.

Drayton's sonnets have drawn a full-length study from Louise Hutchings Westling—*The Evolution of Michael Drayton's Idea.*[15] Miss Westling shows keen interest in the 'libertine' pose of the 1599 edition, especially in terms of how it developed. Smarting from contemporary sonnet satire, Drayton responded by giving his speaker a voice that sounded like the voices of his critics, hence the appearance of 'rough and sinewy new sonnets ... added at significant points'. The author acknowledges that the work she has undertaken on the revisions of *Idea* has in part been done by others, but she contends that insufficient notice has been taken 'of the changes in shape and purpose of the sonnet sequence'. The 1594 Tottel had brought Wyatt freshly to mind and Drayton's aim was now twofold: both to introduce roughness (of Wyatt's kind) and to expel it (when it meant awkwardness). Drayton, consequently, became innovative while remaining conservative. Tottel himself had of course smoothed out Wyatt metrically, and Miss Westling

is not clear whether she thinks Drayton looked back through Tottel to the real thing or whether she thinks the changes in metre did not affect significantly Wyatt's attitudes. She sums up the advantages of creating a 'libertine' speaker in the following useful phrase: 'This persona allowed him to introduce colloquialism, dramatically energetic rhetorical devices and a much hardier language and frame of reference into his sonnets'.

Daniel's sonnets receive their due from Joseph Kau in '*Delia's* Gentle Lover and the Eternizing Conceit in Elizabethan Sonnets' (*Anglia*). The poet's unassuming voice, not very audible beside the more confident proclamations of his contemporaries, has made his powers to immortalize his lady seem less than they are. Mr Kau extols the properties of this voice, particularly its 'unaffected ease and good taste in handling the conceit'.

In 'Gascoigne's Fable of the Artist as a Young Man' (*JEGP*), M. R. Rohr Philmus takes the poems of *The Adventures of Master F. I.* more seriously than usual declaring that they focus the artistic enterprise (being 'arranged, carefully and critically, to trace the ideal story of F. I.'s growth as a poet'). Significance lies here and not in *The Adventures* as a proto-novel. What we are getting from the story is a glimpse into 'the process of art and an awareness of technique as self-discovery'.

Alan T. Bradford begins his large survey of 'Mirrors of Mutability: Winter Landscapes in Tudor Poetry' (*ELR*) by presenting winter as a *topos*, the obverse of the *locus amoenus* in Medieval and Renaissance poems. Sackville's *Induction* to the *Mirror for Magistrates* established the terms of winter that were to appear in *The Shepheardes Calender*, Shakespeare's seventy-third sonnet, and Richard

---

[15] *The Evolution of Michael Drayton's Idea*, by Louise Hutchings Westling. Salzburg: Institut für Englische Sprache und Literatur. pp. viii+187. £4.80.

Niccols's poem 'A Winter Night's Vision' (unfortunately the discussion excludes Campion's 'Now Winter Nights'). Mr Bradford's promising conclusion is that in internalizing winter (making it into a mirror of men's minds) Sackville created a *topos* that became able to embrace passionately the theme of mortality and deliver its *carpe diem* message, in contrast to its Medieval *de casibus* warning.

The question of authorship excites Thomas Clayton in ' "Sir Henry Lee's Farewell to the Court": The Texts and Authorship of "His Golden Locks Time Hath to Silver Turned" ' (ELR). Mr Clayton brings impressive circumstantial and textual evidence for attributing "His Golden Locks", which appears on the last page of Peele's *Polyhymnia* (1590), to Lee himself. Hennig Cohen (*Expl*, vol. xxxi) looks at 'Nashe's *The Song* ("Adieu, Farewell Earth's Bliss")' and compares the two opening words: '*Adieu* literally links with the liturgical refrain and ... contrasts with the secularity of *farewell*'.

Norman K. Farmer, Jr. has consulted the Warwick manuscript for 'Holograph Revisions in Two Poems by Fulke Greville' (*ELR*). The changes in *Caelica* seventy-seven and seventy-eight appear to concern thought or ideas rather than metre, and he concludes that they reflect a desire to relate each poem to the whole. Consequently, he disagrees with Bullough and proposes that *Caelica* be read as a sequence, despite its multiple voices, like Sidney's or Spenser's.

The relation of parts to the whole exercises J. R. Brink, in 'The Rhetorical Structure of Sir John Davies's *Nosce Teipsum*' (YES), who alludes to principles of rhetorical organization to explain the confusing, disorganized appearance of the second

elegy. The latter is so formed in order to answer fully and in every aspect the questions posed by the first elegy (according to classical practice). What Davies most achieves in the second elegy is the 'effortless justification of original sin by analogies between God's law and the common law'. Mr Brink considers another problem about the poem in 'The Composition Date of Sir John Davies' *Nosce Teipsum*' (HLQ). Among the various sorts of textual and biographical evidence brought forward to refute Grosart's theory that it was composed in a penitential mood in 1598 are two salient facts: Nashe's reference in *Strange Newes* (1592 or 1593) to 'John Davies soule' and a humorous aside at the poem in the Middle Temple Christmas revels on 27 December 1597—both prior to the quarrel with Martin and expulsion. Mr Brink favours 1592 as the date of composition adding, 'There is no evidence that Davies "progressed" from light to solemn works; nor is there justification for assuming that he was a social climber who wrote *Nosce Teipsum* for mercenary reasons and actually revealed himself in the *Epigrammes* and *Gulling Sonnets*'.

James L. Saunderson reports on 'Recent Studies in Sir John Davies' and Margaret B. Bryan does the same for 'Recent Studies in Campion' (both in *ELR*).

Finally, in the course of an elegant, informative treatment of the underside of Theodore Beza's reputation, Anne Lake Prescott studies the repercussions of his *Juvenilia* on this side of the channel in 'English Writers and Beza's Latin Epigrams: The Uses and Abuses of Poetry' (*SRen*).

7. PROSE

R. D. (Sir Robert Dallington?) published his translation of Francesco

Colonna's *Hypnerotomachia* as *The Strife of Love in a Dreame* in 1592.[16] It is now available in a facsimile edition. Lucy Gent, whose interest in the visual arts makes for a pertinent, lively introduction, comments on the inferiority of the English woodcuts (also reproduced) to those of the original. Within England she remarks the influence of the translation on Chapman, Drayton, and Ovidian romances, and describes effectively its main features: its schemes of alchemy and numbers; its 'imaginative sensitivity to precious stones'; its dream-like atmosphere; and its peculiar insistence on the proximity of life and art.

Charles Howard Larson performs a service in presenting his edition of Robert Greene's *Ciceronis Amor.*[17] His useful introduction, which notes how Greene reversed Plutarch's description of Cicero's shrewish wife Terentia (whom the orator eventually divorced) by making her into a romance heroine, remarks: 'Greene is breaking new ground in English prose fiction: William Painter and Barnabe Rich had earlier told short historical tales, adapted from the Italian *novelle*, but no one had worked with an extended narrative based on a historical figure'. The introduction also prepares the reader to receive *Tullies Love* in her appropriate genre, making some helpful observations on the romance and friendship. On style Mr Larson is less successful, distinguishing the book's partly Ciceronian, partly Euphuistic elements, but no

more. The footnotes identify classical and mythological names and, with a few exceptions, elucidate difficult words and phrases. Greene's other character gets a note from David Parker in 'Robert Greene and *The Defence of Conny Catching*' (*N&Q*). Mr Parker believes (unlike I. A. Shapiro) that Greene is the author, on the basis of the work's success in terms of the complex tradition of double irony in rogue literature: 'A tension between conventional judgment of criminals and radical judgment of social ills is typical of the moral pattern of all the Conny-catching pamphlets'.

Nashe is variously championed by Alexander Leggatt and Kenneth Friedenreich. The former takes pains to demonstrate 'Artistic Coherence in *The Unfortunate Traveller*' (*SEL*), pointing to the recurrence of the 'frailty of flesh' motif and claiming a more than usually acknowledged coherence of tale and hero in the Italian episodes (the whole anticipating 'the now familiar theme of the education of the hero'). The latter, in 'Nashe's *Strange Newes* and the Case for Professional Writers' (*SP*), takes Harvey's attack on Greene in *Foure Letters* and compares Nashe's reply on behalf of paid authors. Harvey is cleverly lampooned in exactly the style he attempts to discredit. The effect of the exchanges in Mr Friedenreich's opinion (endorsing Maurice Croll's) is to advance prose along anti-Ciceronian lines.

Paul A. Jorgensen has looked widely and illuminatingly at prayers, tracts, and sermons in 'Elizabethan Religious Literature for Time of War' (*HLQ*). Much of this material was published in the year of the Armada or just afterwards, and while its originality as literature is expectedly slight ('a topical situation encourages much humble talent to

---

[16] *Hypnerotomachia, The Strife of Love in a Dream (1592)*, by Francesco Colonna, translated by R. D., a facsimile reproduction with an introduction by Lucy Gent. Delmar, New York: Scholars' Facsimiles and Reprints. 1973. pp. xx+100. $20.

[17] *Robert Greene's Ciceronis Amor: Tullies Love*, a critical edition by Charles Howard Larson. Salzburg: Institut für Englische Sprache und Literatur. pp. lxi+156. £4.80.

express its concern') it achieves a surprising degree of introspection— more than outward circumstances might encourage.

In conclusion, T. R. Howlett reminds the compilers of the new *S.T.C.* of errors and omissions in 'Nicholas Breton: A Note on Revised *Wing*', and Merrill H. Goldwyn assures Roger Geimer that Churchyard was receiving his money before 1597, in 'A Note on Thomas Churchyard's Pension' (both in N&Q).

The Earlier Seventeenth Century, Excluding Drama

ROBIN ROBBINS

The chapter is arranged as follows: 1. General; 2. Poetry; 3. Prose. A selective review of books may be found in *SEL*.

1. GENERAL

The Intellectual Revolution of the Seventeenth Century[1] offers twenty-nine contributions by nineteen authors teasing out the connections between political and scientific developments on the one hand and utopianism, millenarianism, and religious attitudes on the other. The result, as well summarized in Charles Webster's introduction, is not to replace one simple orthodoxy with another, but to qualify, enrich, and diversify extant interpretations, revealing new problems and directions of enquiry. S. F. Mason shows how advances in astronomy, mathematics, the physical sciences, and technology were stimulated by navigation, industry and war. So far as religion was concerned, Calvin's predestined universe promoted a mechanistic view excluding miracles and supernatural agencies, though the idea of a world created perfect led to reactionary rigidity, whereas progress was facilitated by belief in present imperfection and future perfectibility. Against Christopher Hill's correlation of the rise of science with the English

revolution, H. F. Kearney argues that the former was neither particularly English nor particularly revolutionary, but rather a European evolution: 'English politics are irrelevant, partly because they are politics but even more because they are English.' Christopher Hill counters that the exemplary and necessary skills of clockmaking were centred in Protestant parts of Europe, but Theodore K. Rabb points out that the scientific centre of Europe before 1640 was Catholic Italy. Copernicus, Galileo and Descartes were believing Catholics; Kepler relied on the Jesuits for astronomical information; he and Brahe were patronized by the Catholic Rudolf II, and Copernicus flourished in Catholic Poland, while Luther and Calvin were anti-Copernicans. Christopher Hill rejoins that nevertheless 'a protestant environment was more favourable to the spread of scientific ideas than a post-Counter-Reformation Roman Catholic environment.' Barbara J. Shapiro takes the ground that most scientists, continental or English, were indifferent to theological quibbles, unsympathetic to dogmatism, and opposed to religious strife, finding in the contemplation of nature a refuge and respite from dispute. Finding no strongly committed Puritans among the scientific leaders in Oxford and Cambridge in the 1650s, she sees Wilkins as an especially significant figure—an intruded Puritan

[1] *The Intellectual Revolution of the Seventeenth Century*, ed. by Charles Webster. Routledge & Kegan Paul. pp. x+445. £5.95.

head of house who harboured Anglicans, then a bishop who protected Dissenters. It was the Latitudinarians who most notably favoured the new philosophy; the positive contribution of religion lay not in definite doctrines but in an emphasis on the need for a humble sense of one's own fallibility, both as a Christian and as a scientist. With its other essays on Harrington, the Levellers, Diggers and other millenarians, and on Harvey and Baxter, this volume substantially stimulates and increases our understanding of seventeenth-century English minds.

The military side of the English revolution is amply and ably dealt with by Brigadier Peter Young and Richard Holmes in *The English Civil War*.[2] After a brief account of the political, economic and religious issues and events preceding the outbreak of war in 1642, they describe the composition, tactics, equipment and organization of the armies. Within the broader scales of time each of the three distinct wars is then analysed theatre by theatre or campaign by campaign, to make sense of the many engagements which though simultaneous were detached in their immediate causes and effects. Only the non-soldier thinks that wars consist of battles: it is clear that many an engagement was decided as much by questions of supply, training, and morale as by strategy and numbers. Yet despite Parliament's initial command of the sea, the arsenals, and London's money, much of the fighting here described in detail could have gone either way. Thus suspenseful narrative coexists with hard information, and both evoke the

ferocity and foulness of cavalry charge and cannonade, musketry and push of pike. After a brief survey of law and order under the Protectorate, especially of the 'iron puritanism of the major-generals' which instilled in the English an enduring hate of military rule, the authors conclude with a discussion of the war's effects on the constitution, land ownership, trade, industry, and the craft of war. The book is well supplied with chronological tables, maps, glossary and bibliography.

Of all primary sources, personal letters often provide the most intimate insight into fears, hopes, and motives. In *King Charles, Prince Rupert, and the Civil War*[3] Sir Charles Petrie presents in a narrative setting a collection of letters written by and about some of the war's chief figures. The breach between Charles and Rupert after the latter's surrender of Bristol, Charles's relationship with his queen, and the characters of Fairfax, Montrose, and others, are illuminated, if only partially, by this rather random gathering, in which lurks no hitherto unsuspected master of epistolary style. The linking passages are necessarily simplified but unnecessarily tendentious. Given the various and disconnected nature of the letters, a calendar of them would have been helpful.

Our understanding of the rise of English lexicography is advanced in two articles by James A. Riddell: in 'The Beginning: English Dictionaries of the First Half of the Seventeenth Century' (*LStE*) he extends and corrects Starnes and Noyes's work by establishing seven or possibly eight further sources for Robert Cawdrey's *Table Alphabeticall*, the reuse of

[2] *The English Civil War: A Military History of the Three Civil Wars, 1642–1651*, by Brigadier Peter Young and Richard Holmes. Eyre Methuen. pp. 366. £6.25. Paperback £2.50.

[3] *King Charles, Prince Rupert, and the Civil War, from original letters*, ed. by Sir Charles Petrie. Routledge & Kegan Paul. pp. viii+136. £2.95.

some of these as well as the finding of two new ones by John Bullokar for his *English Expositor*, and the similar process of compilation by Henry Cockeram for his *English Dictionarie*, ending with a glance at lexicographers' changing attitudes to their craft as the century went on. Mr Riddell's 'The Reliability of Early English Dictionaries' (*YES*) is a short caution against the uncritical use of such as Bullokar, Cockeram and Blount to gloss seventeenth-century usages.

2. POETRY

John Broadbent's popular anthology *Signet Classic Poets of the 17th Century* [4] divides into two volumes by design as well as bulk. The first presents on average nearly twenty poems or extracts each from Jonson, Donne, Herbert, Herrick, Milton, Crashaw, Vaughan, Marvell and Dryden; the second about two-and-a-half from a hundred others. The distinction thus made is usually reasonable, though it is questionable whether Herrick deserves five times as much space as Rochester. A biographical sketch precedes the sample of each poet; explanation and comment follow each piece. In the first volume each poet is also accorded a critical introduction (in Jonson's case uncritical in its regurgitation of Freud's overextended figment, anality) in which the reader is told how to read the verse, and what to read of the critics. The provocative critical *mots*, here and in the broader commentaries of Volume Two, are so knottily compressed and polysyllabic as sometimes to seem beyond their presumed readers; occasionally, they are just badly written. One wonders,

too, just who is supposed to be listening when in Commentary 3 of Volume Two Mr Broadbent announces that he 'would recommend Quarles for major independent work on almost any line': the anthology is hardly a guide for potential major, independent scholar-critics, though a tantalizing browse for pre-university and general arts students, and, one hopes, so divinely dissatisfying that they will range further.

The Norton Critical Edition of *Ben Jonson and the Cavalier Poets*,[5] selected and edited by Hugh Maclean, is not a critical edition but an anthology culled from the first editions of Jonson, Corbett, Herrick, Carew, Shirley, Fane, Randolph, Habington, Waller, Suckling, Godolphin, Cartwright, Montrose, Denham, Lovelace, Cowley, Vaughan and Stanley, emended in the light of information taken from nineteenth and twentieth-century editors. The poems are furnished with sound explanatory footnotes (which do not, however, point out the classical echoes and allusions which these poets, especially, expected their readers to appreciate); relatively important variants are listed in a section of textual notes. The last third of the volume comprises an interesting collection of critical opinions from those of Jonson himself onwards, and an extensive bibliography of modern scholarship and criticism. This well-produced book offers something more than a sample, if somewhat less than a thorough knowledge, of the Tribe of Ben.

Waller, Vaughan, Denham, Crashaw and Cowley are more substantially represented in *Silver Poets of the Seventeenth Century*,[6] a col-

[4] *Signet Classic Poets of the 17th Century* ed. by John Broadbent. New York, Ontario and London: New American Library, New American Library of Canada, New English Library. 2 vols. pp. xix+377, xxviii+483. Paperback $2.25 per vol.

[5] *Ben Jonson and the Cavalier Poets*, sel. and ed. by Hugh Maclean. New York: Norton. pp. xxii+591. $12.50. Paperback $4.95.

[6] *Silver Poets of the Seventeenth Century*,

lection designed to give inexpensive but annotated texts of less available poets, and, in the case of Waller, Denham and Cowley, to revive interest in their kind of public poetry. The editor in his introduction characterizes the talents of each poet (rather palely for Crashaw and Vaughan), and in his notes at the end provides occasional elucidation of the poems—too occasional, for example, in regard of Crashaw's 'New Year's Day', in which the references to phoenixes and the Magi need to be pointed out if the lines in which they occur are to do more than decorate. Notes that are both inadequate and hidden towards the end of the book are doubly frustrating, open to criticism by the informed, and neglect by the ignorant. The modernized texts are generally acceptable, though at times metrically insensitive, as in 'lingering' for 'ling'ring'. The bibliography does not suggest familiarity with the latest and best critical scholarship. Since the poems are worth having, it is a pity that the ancillary matter could not have been made more useful to more readers.

Patrick Grant's *The Transformation of Sin*[7] studies the ideological background of Donne's *Holy Sonnets*, Herbert's *Temple*, Vaughan's *Silex Scintillans*, and Traherne's poems and meditations. The basic hypothesis of the book posits a movement from Augustinian guilt to rationalist enlightenment, and sees the four poets as a group distinguished not by stylistic norms but by their particular theological concern to work out a middle way. Donne's preoccupations

---

[7] *The Transformation of Sin: Studies in Donne, Herbert, Vaughan, and Traherne*, by Patrick Grant. Montreal, London and Amherst: McGill-Queen's and U. of Massachusetts P. pp. xiii+240. $15.

ed. by G. A. E. Parfitt. London: Dent; Totowa, N.J.: Rowman & Littlefield. pp. xxi+266. £2.95. Paperback £1.25.

with original sin and punishment, the cross and atonement, repentance and the last things, are shown to be emphatically rooted in the doctrines of Augustine as promoted and elaborated by the Franciscans, and in conflict with an assertive self which is stiffened by newer ideals of latitude. It is seen to be significant that most of the earlier medieval lyrics with which Herbert's verse has obvious affinities were by Franciscans, as also, it appears, the influential *Biblia Pauperum*; an extended account of the analogous thought of Juan de Valdés and his relation to Little Gidding illuminates Herbert's harmonious modification of traditional Augustinianism by seemingly Calvinist doctrines of justification by faith, election and predestination. There is a discrepancy between the doctrines expressed by Vaughan in his orthodox prose (and in his more prosaic verse) and the beliefs implicit in his most vital poetry; Mr Grant demonstrates the antecedents in Platonist and Hermetic philosophy of a view of the Fall as rather deprivation than depravity, to make up for which man should trust rather to the light of his own reason than merely to faithful dependence on the grace of God: though Vaughan nowhere goes to this latter extreme, his feelings that man is an exile on a lower plane of being, and that God is immanent in a shining natural order, have to strive against a hard-line, Augustinian/Reformation ethos of guilt. Traherne shared the theological problems of his predecessors, but presented a new resolution, which Mr Grant derives from Irenaeus. Though concerned with content and background, the book does not ploddingly match poem after poem to source after source: the explanations are related discriminatingly to the finest poems, and by revealing more fully the basic tension which was their *raison d'être* lead us to a deeper understanding of their artistry. Not so Philip C. McGuire, who, in 'Private Prayer and English Poetry in the Early Seventeenth Century' (*SEL*), assembles from manuals of devotion, Catholic and Puritan alike, statements of the principal elements of conference with God—confession, invocation, and thanksgiving—, and, not surprisingly, detects them in poems by Donne, Jonson and Herbert. Such analogues as are adduced are biblical commonplaces, and despite the assertion that Jonson's 'Hymne to God the Father' is thoroughly indebted to manuals of prayer it remains likely that both organization and content derived from the tens of thousands of prayers heard and read by any Christian in daily life.

A. J. Smith's paperback edition of Donne, *The Complete English Poems* (*YW* 52.218), has been reissued in hard covers with minor revisions (which do not include a bibliography updated to guide us through the numerous quatercentenary publications of 1972).[8] With explanatory notes that fill more pages than the poems, this remains the most convenient edition for students. Murray Roston opens his critical study, *The Soul of Wit*,[9] by arguing that Donne does not in his poetry merely amalgamate the factual world with the emotional, but transmutes the actual through perception of its spiritual significance. The fulcrum of the book is a discussion of mannerist perspective in religious painting, its startling viewpoints and disregard of the dynamics of reality contrasting with the serene realism of earlier Renais-

sance painting, and with the assertive solidity of the baroque. Mr Roston contends that such 'disturbance' expresses not mere doubt or indirection but a faith in the miraculous supremacy of religious power over natural laws which possessed Donne as it did Tintoretto and El Greco. Donne's control of hyperbole is contrasted, however, with Crashaw's habitual collapse into indulgence, and his technique of salvation through urgent personal experience compared with Milton's reliance on the baroque might of his God-ordered universe. The urbane fallacies of Donne's pseudo-logical poems are seen to express a contempt for the rationalism of the mind, setting it beneath a supposed logic of the spirit, attacking reason with paradox in the Judaeo-Christian tradition. Thus the amatory and the devotional poems are a continuity: in both, the anxious self struggles with the here and now to find reassurance and illumination. Mr Roston detects in the Counter-Reformation spirit of renewed mystical fervour the roots both of the religious mannerist painters' striving for emotional shock, and of the surprising openings and profoundly witty inversions by which Donne establishes an ascendancy of spiritual over material, whether at lovers' partings or in the face of death, paying court to women or to God. This is a well argued and illuminating book.

In 'Donne through French Eyes', a paper first given in Oxford in 1953 and now printed in *Aspects du XVIIᵉ Siècle*,[10] Pierre Legouis surveys Donne's reputation in France, extending—and in two postscripts bringing up to date—the argument as to whether 'The Extasie' is a poem of

[8] *John Donne: The Complete English Poems*, ed. by A. J. Smith. Allen Lane. pp. 679. £4.
[9] *The Soul of Wit: A Study of John Donne*, by Murray Roston. Oxford: Clarendon Press. pp. ix+236, 12 plates. £5.

[10] *Aspects du XVIIᵉ Siècle*, by Pierre Legouis. Paris, Montreal and Brussels: Didier, 1973. pp. xiv+263. 70 fr.

rationalized seduction or a Platonic triumph of modesty and high philosophy, cynical casuistry or serious argument for its own sake. In 'La Thème du Rêve dans le "Clitandre" de Pierre Corneille et dans "The Dreame" de John Donne' he notes the similar situation in the play as revised between 1657 and 1660 and the poem—a dream interrupted by its subject—, and suggests a link in the author's common acquaintance, Constantin Huyghens, who published translations from Donne in 1658. Josephine Miles's *Poetry and Change*[11] has two chapters on Donne: 'Ifs, Ands, and Buts for the Reader of Donne' is an attempt to clarify his dialectic with himself by extracting and characterizing his connective words; 'Twentieth-Century Donne' seeks in modern poets the concern with and countering of concepts, the effortful articulation of exploring thought, found from Wyatt to Cowley. L. C. Knights draws attention to the gulf between Donne's extreme self-deprecation and his huge aspirations in 'All or Nothing: A Theme in John Donne', a contribution to *William Empson: The Man and His Work*.[12]

In 'John Donne's Changing Attitudes to Time' (*SEL*) G. F. Waller charts the modulation in his preoccupation with the passage of time between early poems and late sermons, from youthful defiance to terrified orthodoxy. On the basis of the allusion to Ronsard in the *Paradoxes and Problems*, Clayton D. Lein's 'Donne and Ronsard' (*N&Q*) infers a possible familiarity with the French poet's works not limited to the *Amours*, and sees in

Ronsard a zest for amatory exploration and simultaneity of various attitudes to love which suggest more than merely parallel temperaments. M. R. Woodhead notes 'A Mid-Seventeenth-Century Allusion to "The Extasie"' (*N&Q*) by William Shipton in *Dia, a Poem*, published in 1659 while he was an undergraduate at Cambridge. Marvin Morillo argues in 'Donne's "The Relique" as Satire' (*TSE*) that the poem is consistently ironic, with the openly cynical eroticism of the first stanza continued implicitly through the third by the presentation of fidelity and ignorance of sex as miraculous 'by a voice still echoing with sexual innuendo, ... disingenuous beyond the credulity of any but those whom a foolish idolatry has rendered utterly gullible.' Heather Dubrow Ousby offers 'Donne and Gilpin: Another Conjecture' (*N&Q*) regarding parallels between the former's 'Phryne' and the latter's *Skialetheia*. The way in which the poet plays with his persona in tensely balanced uncertainties in the first three satires, and his acceptance in the fourth of the satiric character, and in the fifth of the persistence of corruption and the moralist's task, are brought out by Richard C. Newton in 'Donne the Satirist' (*TSLL*). Leonard D. Tourney puzzlingly claims depth of feeling as well as original wit and insight for what are admitted to be theatricalized Renaissance commonplaces in 'Convention and Wit in Donne's *Elegie* on Prince Henry' (*SP*). John J. Pollock's 'Note on Donne's "Elegie on the L. C."' (*N&Q*) rejects the interpretation of sweet briar and tree as images of pride and ambition, preferring to see them as emphasizing the theme of dependence. Michael Gregory in 'A Theory for Stylistics— Exemplified: Donne's Holy Sonnet XIV' (*Lang&S*) demonstrates the

---

[11] *Poetry and Change*, by Josephine Miles. Berkeley, Los Angeles and London: U. of California P. pp. [v]+243. £10.75.

[12] *William Empson: The Man and His Work*, ed. by Roma Gill. Routledge & Kegan Paul. pp. x+244. £4.95.

pedestrian application of a jargonized process (as productive for bad poems as for good) which, while offering 'a closer look at the lexis, both situationally and collocationally', and detecting high verbality and lexical diversity (which last 'is linguistically dynamic because, formally, it opens up the range of acceptable collocational probabilities and, contextually, it involves the verbalization of a range of diverse experiences'), is most memorable for reminding us solemnly that the father of the author of 'Batter my heart' was an ironmonger. In 'Donne's "Lamentations of Jeremy" and the Geneva Bible' (*ES*) John J. Pollock proves by careful collation of the poem with various versions of the Bible that in translating Tremellius Donne turned for suggestions of word and phrase to the Geneva Bible much more often than to the King James version; such knowledge of his practice helps in establishing the text.

Introducing *Ben Jonson*,[13] a selection in the Poet to Poet series, Thom Gunn stresses the varieties and contrasts, going on to discuss and distinguish types of occasional poem, the classical and the baroque, Jonson's public and private selves, and his interwoven patterns of statement and feeling. The choice of poems is not idiosyncratic—it includes all the best-known—, and offers a useful introduction to Jonson the poet for the common reader. Brief explanatory notes appear at the end. *A Celebration of Ben Jonson*[14] contains two essays mainly concerned with the poems: in '"A More Secret Cause";

The Wit of Jonson's Poetry' Hugh Maclean distinguishes the poet's more positive concept of his function from the playwright's, and brings out the order and propriety of some of the complimentary poems; L. C. Knights, who also starts from a distinction between the stances adopted in the plays and the poems, in 'Ben Jonson: Public Attitudes and Social Poetry', sees the apparently miscellaneous poetic corpus as unified in its firm, graceful and vital expression of social values. T. J. B. Spencer's contribution to *The Elizabethan Theatre, IV*,[15] 'Ben Jonson on his beloved, The Author Mr. William Shakespeare', attempts to find some grounds for Dryden's implicit characterization of the eulogy prefixed to the First Folio as 'An Insolent, Sparing, and Invidious Panegyrick' detecting a lack of sympathy, in its obvious hyperbole. S. P. Zitner's 'The Revenge on Charis' in the same volume strains learnedly to find in 'Her Triumph' the retribution threatened in 'What He Suffered'. Herford and Simpson's two lists of Jonson's books are superseded by David McPherson's 'Ben Jonson's Library and Marginalia: An Annotated Catalogue' (*SP*), which records more marginalia, adds twenty-five titles genuinely supposed to have belonged to Jonson (bringing the total up to 207), and updates details of location for forty-one of them. The introduction discusses the apparent composition of the collection, with its unusual emphasis on literature and literary criticism (though English is thinly represented by Chaucer, Puttenham, Spenser, Fulke, Greville, Daniel, Drayton,

[13] *Ben Jonson*, sel. by Thom Gunn. Penguin. pp. 208. Paperback 30p. or $1.25.

[14] *A Celebration of Ben Jonson: Papers presented at the University of Toronto in October 1972*, ed. by William Blissett, Julian Patrick and R. W. Van Fossen. Toronto and Buffalo: U. of Toronto P., 1973. pp. xiii + 196. $8.50.

[15] *The Elizabethan Theatre, IV: Papers given at the Fourth International Conference on Elizabethan Theatre held at the University of Waterloo, Ontario, in July, 1972*, ed. with an introduction by G. R. Hibbard. Macmillan. pp. xv + 175. £4.95.

King James and Marston), and the nature of Jonson's annotations—'those of a scholar of strong but sporadic interests, not the rough notes of a working dramatist and poet'. One of these strong interests is suggested by six annotations on Martial referring to oral sexual intercourse. It hardly needs saying that Mr McPherson's catalogue (though necessarily incomplete because of the fire of 1623: it is pointed out that Jonson may be presumed to have owned at least twice as many books as are known) is indispensable to further scholarly work on poet or playwright. Gail Kern Paster shows in 'Ben Jonson and the Uses of Architecture' (*RenQ*) how he expressed his theories of literature in terms shared with the humanist architects including Inigo Jones, and accorded to architecture a place alongside poetry, history and sculpture, denouncing Jones only because of his preoccupation with the trivial and transitory illusions of painting and carpentry for the masques. Such was Jonson's esteem for the dignity of architecture, both functional and monumental, that, endowed with moral values, it appears as a paradigm of human excellence in his poems, in *The Masque of Queens*, and in *Prince Henry's Barriers*— where, ironically, it is made immune to time. In 'Ben Jonson's *Epigrammes*: Portrait-Gallery, Theater, Commonwealth' (*SEL*) Bruce R. Smith compares him with other imitators of Martial, showing his relative success in combining brevity, precision and rhetorical point with variety of subject and tone. Mr Smith goes on to elucidate Jonson's conception of the epigrams as monumental inscriptions, as portraits of virtue and vice, as *Bartholomew Fair*-type drama played before a select audience, and as the feigning of a commonwealth,

and in conclusion suggests that 'On the Famous Voyage' parodies the narrative prolixity of rival epigrammatist (and coprologist) Sir John Harington. Less substantial contributions are T. J. Kelly's 'Jonson's "Celebration of Charis"' (*CR*), a eulogistic commentary, and Hugh Maclean's brief note, 'Ben Jonson's *Timber*, 1046–1115, and Falstaff' (*PLL*), whose adduction of parallels is utterly unconvincing.

The first thirteen chapters of *Robert Herrick* by George Walton Scott[16] are, unfortunately enough, a staccato recitation of the known facts of the poet's life, padded out with contemporary and local colour. The account is lucid, but sloppily written, spattered with minor inaccuracies, and larded with unsupported conjectures (occasionally betrayed by the introductory phrase 'No doubt . . .'). From the poems, Mr Scott half-heartedly attempts to deduce Herrick's personality and their degree of sincerity, dodging the conclusion which must be prompted by intrinsic confessions of a life chaste in act, and by the fact that Herrick's only known sexual success was with a fourteen-year-old in Westminster, that the erotic poems are verbalized masturbation fantasies, the voyeurist products not only of rural isolation but of that personal hideousness evinced by Marshall's frontispiece. The subsequent enumeration of classical influences is useless in its superficiality: Mr Scott is obviously far out of his depth; nor does he regain it in flatly stating that 'Herrick's view of nature was animistic'. Chapters on the most anthologized poems labour to document commonplaces, to produce such critical insights as 'Somewhere in the back of his mind . . . he seems

16 *Robert Herrick, 1591–1674*, by George Walton Scott. Sidgwick & Jackson. pp. 200. £4.50.

to have felt something inexplicable and distant', to label favourite lines as 'exquisite', and to offer explication that is less of an unfolding than a dismemberment. Those who have left higher education for more respected occupations may smile when reminded of the drearier sort of student essay by the chapter which begins 'Herrick was of course fortunate in being born when the English language was moving from strength to strength. Jacobean English, almost identical to Elizabethan, reached its heights in the Authorized Version of the Bible.' The chronicle of admirers and detractors through the ages is no more than a scissors-and-paste job. Of some use are the listing of musical settings and the chronological table, though why the latter should mention the murder of Rizzio, a quarter of a century before Herrick's birth, yet not the births of Donne or Burton, is mysterious. For a work which reproaches Moorman as 'inaccurate and at times false', and Marchette Chute as 'lacking in judgement', Mr Scott's book is shallow and careless. The shoddy proof-reading and discontinuities of sense and syntax imply a rush to cash in on the tercentenary of Herrick's death: *si monumentum requiris—quaere ultra*.

Ceremony as an 'imaginative means of celebrating life through art' is the governing concept of Robert H. Deming's attempt in *Ceremony and Art*[17] 'to discover the understanding consciousness of Robert Herrick's aesthetic vision'. He shows how a spirit of grave playfulness integrates such opposites as the so-called pagan classical and the Christian, Nature and Art, lust and chastity, in balanced tensions—'orderly disorder', 'wild civility' and 'cleanly wantonness'—

[17] *Ceremony and Art: Robert Herrick's Poetry*, by Robert H. Deming. The Hague and Paris: Mouton. pp. 176. dFl. 32.

just as 'To the Virgins to make much of Time' and 'Corinna's going a Maying' accommodate desire and chastity, *carpe diem* and Christianity, in marriage. Mr Deming's examination of the ceremonies of Herrick's created cosmos moves through poems with Roman gods, the unambiguously Christian *Noble Numbers* and the fairy poems to a group of love poems in which actual ceremonies occur. In the pieces on death there is likewise a concern with 'the proper performance of sacred ceremonies as the right and just enactment of the law, and the power of these ceremonies to form a bond which links the mortal with the immortal life', well exemplified in 'To the reverend shade of his religious Father' in which the poem, after expounding the rites duly though belatedly performed, becomes itself an enactment bestowing immortal life. Against those who see in Herrick a wilful pagan, Mr Deming argues that the Roman rites of sacrifice, funeral and wedding are not reconstructed entire for their own sake, but that selected aspects are incorporated and subordinated in new poetic constructs to fit the occasions celebrated. Classical ideals, High Anglican liturgy and country custom are fused in an imaginative attempt to preserve the old, much loved order against the destroying Puritans. Sometimes an anxiety to document the origins of Herrick's ideas leads Mr Deming into solemn absurdities of redundant scholarship on commonplaces: Herrick's association of cypress with funerals, and awareness that Puritans considered Christmas Day popish need not the authority of Shakespeare or John Taylor the Water Poet. Nor do the conventional images in 'The Star-song' have to be echoes of Crashaw (probably not yet published when it was written). Yet though over heavy in places, this is a substantial and interesting book. In its unregenerate form as a dissertation it was a principal begetter of A. Leigh DeNeef's 'This Poetick Liturgie',[18] which sees that 'Herrick's artistic process . . . is controlled by a conscious *poetic* ceremonial'. This is not merely the use of rituals as material but a mode of poetic expression ritualizing even that which is not literally rite, and extracting deeper significance from that which is; sacramentalizing life in public celebration, and imparting to 'what is transient, mutable, dying', transcendence, immutability and eternality. Despite a professed resistance to over-schematization, Mr Deneef dispenses with selective criteria of quality, attempting instead to master the entire corpus by dividing and subdividing it into a ramshackle taxonomy of 'voices', 'types', 'forms', 'groups', 'classes' and 'personae', fleshing out the skeleton principally with thematic summary, in the mass of which one is lost without the wall-chart presumably used to construct the book (with it, we should probably not need the book). In attempting to see the Hesperidean orchard for the Herrickal trees, Mr DeNeef entangles us in wearisome thickets of expository prose. Shonosuke Ishii offers in The Poetry of Robert Herrick[19] a digest of the life and letters, and comment on the poems that is more conventionally pious than originally analytical—a survey of Herrick's fondness for small things (not mentioning the girl in Westminster), his supposed mistresses (ditto), his imagery (explaining Eliot's 'direct sensuous apprehension of thought' as 'an intellectuality which sustains undulating sentiment'), his celebratory verse, 'aromatic humour', attitudes to time and death, his epithalamia, and the interest of his short poems for the Japanese reader. Appended are ambiguously prudish comments on the epigrams as weeds in the garden of the *Hesperides* (prettiness and 'healthy, merry cleanliness' are Mr Ishii's chief critical criteria), and some vague observations on Renaissance and Baroque painters. Despite much counting of lines and word-uses, an impression is left of not really coming to grips with Herrick as a craftsman or as a real man. The bibliography 'Herrick in Japan' will be useful; the 'Select Bibliography', however, is not so select as to exclude Emily Easton, Oliver Elton, or Rose Macaulay's historical novel. There is more solid scholarship in Paul Merchant's note on 'A Jonson Source for Herrick's "Upon Julia's Clothes"' (*N&Q*), which points out several close similarities to the second stanza of the song in *Epicoene*.

The English Poems of George Herbert, edited by C. A. Patrides,[20] gives the text of the first edition of 1633, adding the six poems peculiar to the Williams manuscript, and the three in Walton's *Life*. Two further appendixes set out the two versions of 'The Elixer' in the Williams manuscript, and give five poems supposedly parodied by Herbert. In his substantial introduction Dr Patrides examines the 'complexity dormant within apparent simplicity' of Herbert's poems, their relationship to wisdom literature, parables and the psalter, their imagery, their preoccupation with the eucharist, and their diverse

[18] 'This Poetick Liturgie': Robert Herrick's Ceremonial Mode, by A. Leigh DeNeef. Durham, N.C.: Duke U.P. pp. vii+200. $7.50.

[19] The Poetry of Robert Herrick, by Shonosuke Ishii. Tokyo: Renaissance Institute, Sophia University. pp. v+188. $5. £1.80. Yen 1300.

[20] The English Poems of George Herbert, ed. by C. A. Patrides. London: Dent; Totowa, N.J.: Rowman & Littlefield. pp. vii +247. £2.25. Paperback £1.

voices. Subjoined is an indispensable note on typology, and, at the end of the book, a bibliography of over 400 titles (including those not numbered). The annotation at the foot of each page is designed to increase understanding rather than to bludgeon with scholarship. This is altogether an exemplary edition for students (and their teachers), setting a new standard for Everyman's University Library texts of the period.

Mark Taylor's brief study, *The Soul in Paraphrase*,[21] examines the coincidence between Herbert's views and those of Augustine on rhetorical eloquence, forming as they do the basis for Herbert's vision of divine poetry as 'the human image of the all-encompassing word of God'. After analysing his concepts of a poem's existence in time and eternity, Mr Taylor expounds his use of synaesthesia, especially as it involves light. Sister Thekla treats *The Temple* as 'the positive, living, day-to-day balance and resolution of a theology' in *George Herbert: Idea and Image*.[22] The bulk of her book is consequently of an expository, paraphrastic nature, taking one by one the doctrinal items which engaged the poet's attention, and weaving from his verse a sort of *De Doctrina Herbertiana*. Refreshing as it is to read a book innocent of footnotes, in which there is no significant mention of any other writer, ancient or modern, there is hardly anything in the expansions and rhetorical questions of its first three parts which would not be obvious to any sympathetic reader capable of understanding Herbert's language on a literal level. Part IV, a 'Synopsis of

the Imagery' with seven complex diagrams linking various categories of words, promises 'a practical visual demonstration ... of the complex relationships of words'. The connexions and connotations thus displayed, however, are either obvious while reading the poems, or in fact need the poems to explain them. Sister Thekla concludes with a plea for Christians to use literature as a common ground of understanding on which they may unite against 'militant atheism'. W. Hilton Kelliher gives an informed and informative account in *The Latin Poetry of English Poets*[23] of Herbert's Latin poetry, without shedding much light on the English poems. Robert Higbie examines in detail 'Images of Enclosure in George Herbert's *The Temple*' (*TSLL*), finding a progression from a preoccupation with defence against and control over sin through a sense of the self as a prison to a longing to enter God's 'ideal home' (*sic*), a temple that is not earthly, raised in the heart. Marvin Morillo points out in 'Herbert's Chairs: Notes to *The Temple*' (*ELN*) that the chairs in 'Mortification' and 'The Pilgrimage' are not the static hearthside furniture emblematic of old age but conveyances, as in *Othello*, V.i.82–3, 98–9.

Lesser poets received this year perhaps disproportionately less attention. From an examination of the only manuscript known to survive, Theresa G. Hoar shows in 'A Note on Sir John Beaumont's "Crowne of Thornes" in BM. Add. MS. 33,392' (*N&Q*) that the scribe transposed about fifty-seven lines of Book IX, dislocating the elaborate scheme of apostles, gates of the Heavenly Jersualem, months, signs of the zodiac, and events and places.

[21] *The Soul in Paraphrase: George Herbert's Poetics*, by Mark Taylor. The Hague and Paris: Mouton. pp. ix+127. $9.50.

[22] *George Herbert, Idea and Image: A Study of* The Temple, by Sister Thekla. Filgrave, Bucks: Greek Orthodox Monastery of the Assumption. pp. 308. Paperback £2.85.

[23] *The Latin Poetry of English Poets*, ed. by J. W. Binns. Routledge & Kegan Paul. pp. x+198. £4.95.

In 'George Wither: Origins and Consequences of a Loose Poetics' (*TSLL*) Thomas O. Calhoun traces the development from the various personae in the satires, elegies and pastorals of the solipsistic voice and style of *Britain's Remembrancer*, which, while collapsing as art, nevertheless embodies an important innovation in the fitting of method to matter—in this case in its random observations of the chaotic corruption of the plague. Charles Larson provides exegetical comment on 'The Somerset House Poems of Cowley and Waller' (*PLL*): both celebrate order and grace, though Waller does so with characteristic fulsomeness and a less certain dignity. In answering the problem 'Why Was Man Created in the Evening? On Waller's "An Apologie for Having Loved Before"' (*MLR*) Karl Josef Höltgen addresses himself not to God's reasons but to the origin of the legend, which he finds in the Talmud. He further notes the similarity of the picture of Adam's successive wonderment to an Arabic anecdote about Abraham, without establishing for either idea the particular work to which the poet was indebted. On 'Cleveland's "Square-Cap": Some Questions of Structure and Date' (*DUJ*) Margaret Forey shows from an unpublished poem by William Strode that the name 'Calot-Leather-cap' refers not to a lawyer, whose skull-cap was of velvet, but to a new court fashion. Taking this into account, Cleveland's choice of suitors is analysed; Monmouth-cap's 'plush' is glossed as 'his wealth'. From the dates of Cleveland's model, the ballad 'Blew Cap for me' (1633), of Jonson's mention of the leather calot as a ridiculous court fashion in *The Magnetick Lady* (1632), and of Cleveland's similar situation to that of Square-cap—a young graduate

without a fellowship—(1631–4), the date of composition is narrowed down plausibly to 1633–4. Kenneth J. Larsen's essay on Crashaw's *Epigrammata Sacra* in *The Latin Poetry of English Poets*[23] shows how their close relationship to the Anglican liturgy enables them to be dated, and thus facilitates the tracing of a change in Crashaw's religious allegiance between 1631 and 1635 from a Puritan belief in salvation by faith alone (and anti-papal zeal) towards a Laudian elevation of love and good works. Charles Clay Doyle in 'An Unhonored English Anacreon; Sir John Birkenhead' (*SP*) compares three translations and an imitation of Anacreon (made for Henry Lawes) favourably for wit and vividness with those by Herrick, Stanley and Cowley. 'Some Versions, Texts and Readings of "To Althea, from Prison"' (*PBSA*) by Thomas Clayton lists and discusses the variations in six manuscripts, without threatening the authority of *Lucasta*—which was, of course, seen through the press by Lovelace himself—and incidentally further contaminating the tradition by attributing the word 'swell' to BM. MS. Harleian 6918's 1.31, at one point in the discussion. In 'Sir John Denham at Law' (*MP*) Herbert Berry charts the cavalier's progress through the lawyers' kingdom from prodigious wastrel to large-scale property speculator.

Andrew Marvell: The Complete English Poems, first published as a paperback in 1972 (*YW* 53.233), has now appeared in hard covers with minor revisions.[24] The preface to George R. Guffey's *Concordance to the English Poems of Andrew Marvell*[25]

[24] *Andrew Marvell: The Complete English Poems*, ed. by Elizabeth Story Donno. Allen Lane. pp. 314. £2.50.
[25] *A Concordance to the English Poems of Andrew Marvell*, comp. and ed. by George R.

claims with a hopeful air that the work is based on the second rather than the third edition of Margoliouth's Oxford text because the second seemed well established, and the third made few significant changes (ten are listed in a footnote). This is shown to be rationalizing nonsense when, as in line 4 of 'The Statue at Charing Cross', an obvious misprint in Margoliouth is solemnly recorded, given a frequency of 1 and a relative frequency of 0.0000. The page references to the second edition will become more annoying as time goes on to those interested in looking up the poems themselves. As a compromise, however, the Marvell canon is accepted to be that delivered by Legouis. Numerous but relatively insignificant words which have been counted and assigned a frequency index but not given in context lines are listed in the preface, and an index of words in order of frequency is appended. This concordance makes possible whatever is possible with a concordance (subject to the strictures above and the shakiness of the canon as regards the satires): we may see straightaway, for instance, that *he* is recorded as occurring exactly four times as often as *she*. An intelligent reading of 'Marvell's "Unfortunate Lover" as Device' (*MLQ*) is offered by Peter T. Schwenger, who argues that the last line—'In a Field *Sable* a Lover *Gules*'—should be taken not generally as a coat of arms but more specifically as that personal form of heraldry, a device, carried by Love's banneret, for which ll. 55–6, 'a Lover drest/In his own Blood does relish best', provide a motto in which the words *drest* and *relish* have the gastronomic meanings 'sauced' and 'savour'. Mr Schwenger also speculates that the love that never had a

Guffey. Chapel Hill: U. of North Carolina P. pp. xv + 623. $30.

chance of this poem and 'The Definition of Love' might have been homosexual. In 'Theme and Counterthemes in "Damon the Mower"' (*CL*) Elaine Hoffman Baruch asserts that Marvell extends and replies to both Stanley's 'Acanthus Complaint' and its original, Tristan L'Hermite's 'Les Plaintes d'Acante', examining Marvell's interweaving of pastoral and biblical themes, and seeing, for example, triple meanings, literal, sexual and religious, in *hay* and *mow*. Dale Herron tries 'to discover how Marvell develops his meditative experience to include the noblest aspirations and mysteries of Christian poetry yet controls the central paradox of man's dual nature within the created universe' in 'Marvell's "Garden" and the Landscape of Poetry' (*JEGP*), analysing the threefold withdrawal of the speaker into the garden, of his mind from physical pleasure, and of the soul from his body, and the cyclical attainment of and descent from 'the mystical heights of visionary inspiration'. R. I. V. Hodge puts forward the possibility in 'Marvell's Fairfax Poems: Some Considerations concerning Dates' (*MP*) that 'Upon the Hill and Grove at Bill-borow' was written after the death of Lady Fairfax in 1665. More plausible and interesting is the idea that the 'Epigramma in Duos montes Amosclivum Et Bilboreum' might have been written to celebrate the marriage of Mary Fairfax to Buckingham in 1657, the two hills emblematizing the qualities of the two peers, once on opposite sides in the Civil War but now united. In 'Andrew Marvell's "The First Anniversary of the Government under Oliver Cromwell": The Poem and Its frame of Reference' (*MLR*) A. J. N. Wilson gives a detailed reading which takes into account both the political context and the background of religious and classical values and allusions. A note on 'Marvell and the Two Learned Brothers of St. Marthe' by Pierre Legouis (*PQ* 1959), shedding some hypothetical as well as factual light on a passage in the second part of *The Rehearsal Transpros'd*, is reprinted in *Aspects du XVII*e *Siècle*[10] along with 'Marvell and the New Critics' (*RES* 1957). In the four pages between these essays, M. Legouis rejects the claim by Raymond A. Anselment (*MP* 1970) that *The Rehearsal Transpros'd* is carefully constructed, and furthermore sees Parker portrayed not as a sincere zealot but as an ambitious timeserver. On the same work, he finds in 'Marvell and Julian' (*N&Q*) that the enigmatic 'Son' of Constantine whom Marvell offers from the *Caesares Juliani* as a precedent for Parker in proclaiming toleration for debauchery derived from a mistake in Marvell's Greek text for Jesus himself—an irony the satirist might not have wished to adopt from his author, Julian.

On Henry Vaughan as a poet, Melissa Cynthia Wanamaker in '*Discordia Concors:* The Metaphysical Wit of Henry Vaughan's *Silex Scintillans*' (*TSLL*) applies Dr Johnson's definition to the Silurist's paradoxical patterns of contrariety: inner reality and outer appearance, heavenly and earthly, true light and false, spiritual day in physical night. These oppositions are also explicable in the philosophical terms elucidated by Alan Rudrum, who, in 'An Aspect of Henry Vaughan's Hermeticism: The Doctrine of Cosmic Sympathy' (*SEL*) distinguishes the rôles of hermetic philosophy in the earlier and later poems, in the former as a vocabulary of conceits, in the latter 'a complete and subtle expression of a life-attitude' entailing belief in the total

involvement of nature, God and man. It is argued that in order to create his finest poems Vaughan needed a given system of ideas which embraced his personal feeling for nature as well as for God; which provided, as did hermeticism, a network of analogical relationships and metaphorical correspondences between earth and heaven, the visible and invisible, physical and spiritual. In accordance with this analysis is Florence Sandler's view of the poet's brand of Christianity in 'The Ascents of the Spirit: Henry Vaughan on the Atonement' (*JEGP*) seeing him as an old-fashioned Neoplatonist rather than a Christian Humanist, and furthermore close to Cudworth in an emphasis on the Johannine rather than the Pauline view of the Crucifixion. Robert Wilcher examines Vaughan's allusions to the contemporary political situation in '"Daphnis: An Elegiac Eclogue" by Henry Vaughan' (*DUJ*), and proceeds interestingly to read 'Daphnis' as an elegy written in the first place for Charles I, which was only later adapted for Thomas Vaughan. Especially cogent are the allusions revealed to the *Eikon Basilike*.

3. PROSE

Bacon's *Advancement of Learning* and *New Atlantis* have been re-edited and reprinted from Wright's and Spedding's editions respectively by Arthur Johnston,[26] for the Oxford Paperback English Text series, the former work obviously inviting comparison with the Everyman reprint of Kitchin's edition for which Mr Johnston provided an introduction a year earlier (*YW* 54.233). Wright's text is the more respectable (Kitchin, for example, modernizes *deficience*

---

[26] *Francis Bacon: The Advancement of Learning, and New Atlantis*, ed. by Arthur Johnston. Oxford: Clarendon P. pp. xxvi + 297. £3.50. Paperback £1.50.

to *deficiency* in xxv. 6), and in place of the inadequate glossary at the end of the Everyman all glosses, explanations and translations immediately necessary for comprehension are here given at the foot of the page, lengthier comment appearing at the end. Mr Johnston also indicates when the use of a word is the first recorded in the *O.E.D.*, or antedates the first entry there. The reading list in the Oxford edition includes a dozen or so articles not cited in the earlier bibliography. In addition the new volume provides a chronological table and, of course, *New Atlantis*. The new introduction manages not to repeat its predecessor, but goes considerably wider and deeper, outlining the personal, intellectual and historical contexts of Bacon's learned enterprise, his crusade against words and systems, the Solomonic ideal and the vision of progress. In conception and execution this is a most useful edition.

A Concordance to the Essays of Francis Bacon by David W. Davies and Elizabeth S. Wrigley[27] is announced as the first instalment of a project which may cover the entire works. The main body of the concordance lists words in the contexts of the lines in which they occur in the Spedding, Ellis and Heath edition, with volume, title, page and line references thereto. Appended are separate lists in alphabetical and frequency order of words included in and omitted from the concordance. The use of the nineteenth-century collected works leads the editors into various sillinesses, such as 'the word *honey-suckle* has been key punched as one word, because Bacon writes it only once in hyphenated form, all other times as one word': in the 1625 edition the word is printed all four times with a hyphen (and the accidentals even of this edition cannot be proved to be Bacon's). Likewise, 1625 has *Pine-Apples* and *Pine-Apple-Trees*, but Davies and Wrigley give *Pine Apples* and *Pineapple Trees*, and so on throughout, to the misleading of the tyro, and despair of the initiate. The banausic idiocy of a computer whose supposed controllers are content to be the mere mechanicals of literary studies solemnly lists in alphabetical position in the concordance and index, and tabulates as a unique usage, the form *maintian*—not Bacon's at all, but a nineteenth-century misprint. It is to be hoped that the funds of producers and purchasers alike will not be further squandered on work so thoughtlessly conceived and carried out.

Lisa Jardine sets out in *Francis Bacon: Discovery and the Art of Discourse*[28] to give 'a consistent rather than a revolutionary reading' of Bacon's methodology as propounded and implemented in his works. This she does by discussing them against a dialectical background, showing that Bacon's rejection of dialectical method (as reformed for teaching purposes by the humanists) as a tool of discovery resulted not from deep scholarly expertise or familiarity with sophisticated continental discussions of processes of acquiring knowledge, but as a development from and partial reaction against the dialectic handbooks in use during his undergraduate years at Cambridge. As a means of presenting knowledge, on the other hand, the traditional methods were in his writings rather supplemented than

[27] *A Concordance to the Essays of Francis Bacon*, ed. by David W. Davies and Elizabeth S. Wrigley. Detroit: Gale Research Co., 1973. pp. xi+392. $24.

[28] *Francis Bacon: Discovery and the Art of Discourse*, by Lisa Jardine. Cambridge U.P. pp. viii+267. £4.90.

replaced by new forms. The history of dialectical theory and method in the fifteenth and sixteenth centuries shows how, from the medieval concept of a key to all disciplines, dialectic was reduced to a means of teaching, of ordering discourse so as to be effective and acceptable—a shift in functional emphasis from judgement to composition, from the metaphysical to the literary, from Aristotle to Cicero and Quintilian, from pure dialectic to a blending with rhetoric. In equating the laws of dialectic with those of reasoning, and claiming universality for his divisive method, Ramus, like his predecessors, failed to distinguish the ordering of discourse from the method of investigating fundamental principles, a distinction strongly made in a Cambridge controversy of the 1580s presumably known to Bacon. Nevertheless, the latter is still essentially Aristotelian in his assumption that science must be based rather on a knowledge of fundamental causes and principles defined in terms of essential qualities than on the best predictive hypotheses available from quantitative analysis. Dr Jardine summarizes the doctrine of the 'Idols' (retaining that misleading translation); Bacon's largely traditional faculty psychology, assigning to the rational soul memory, imagination and reason; his classification of knowledge, which stood out from previous schemes in not initially separating theoretical and practical but bracketing them together for each branch of knowledge; and his *philosophia prima* of universal principles, on which even the inductive investigator is expected to proceed. Succeeding chapters expound his theory of forms, the detailed procedure of his interpretative method, and the use of working generalizations and analogies as interim guides to experiment in natural history, and as principal techniques for deriving precepts in ethics and civics (exemplified in the *History of Henry VII*, which attempts not accurate, objective documentation but an understanding of public events in general by interpretation of a particular sequence of causes and motives). The last third of the book examines Bacon's ideas and practices concerning the methods of communicating knowledge, previously divided between dialectic and rhetoric, but set up by him as an autonomous field of study to be distinguished from procedures of discovery. These methods include parable (for example, the philosophical, political and ethical significations of myths in *De Sapientia Veterum*), smaller-scale comparisons, apophthegms, proverbs and examples, and the responsible use of rhetoric's persuasive colouring, its evocative illustrations and *sententiae*. The concluding discussion of the method of the *Essays* demonstrates their strategy of persuasion by non-rational, 'insinuative' devices. The light shed by this scholarly book on Bacon as philosopher and writer is undeniably dry, yet all the more Baconian for that.

James Stephens is concerned in 'Bacon's Fable-making: A Strategy of Style' (*SEL*) not so much with his making of fables as with his reinterpretation of them in *The Wisdom of the Ancients* to serve his philosophical purposes, and rashly asserts 'Bacon's belief in the hieroglyph as an ideal form for the communication of knowledge' (also, even less helpfully, that Book I of the *Novum Organum* is 'hypnotic'). The images in *The Advancement of Learning* of the scientist as farmer, doctor, and so on are first of all said to be developed, but six lines later to be 'never the subject of discussion or elaborate expansion'. The account of the *Novum Organum* (relying on the standard translation) denigrates Bacon's argument by characterizing it as 'dependent on the force of pictures', whereas these contribute rather memorability than persuasive force. In 'Francis Bacon and Alchemy: The Reformation of Vulcan' (*JHI*) Stanton J. Linden contrasts the satirical literary tradition with Bacon's objective attitude to alchemy, which deplores the admixture of superstition but envisages its restoration and reformation through applied reason, which, with the aid of experiment, would rescue it from credulity, fantasy and mystifying jargon. The *Sylva Sylvarum* shows, however, that in practice Bacon's physical science remained animistic and semi-occult, positing spirits, sympathies, antipathies and correspondences, and that he preserved a belief in the possibility if not probability of transmuting silver into gold, at least by reasoned and controlled processes. In 'The Non-Political Past in Bacon's Theory of History' (*JBS*) Arthur B. Ferguson examines Bacon's promotion and use of intellectual history, which he saw not only as matter of record but as a search for understanding of the generation of ideas in their cultural contexts, though he saw these as separate layers of the universal experience rather than elements in a connected historical process.

Donne's interest in and attitude to death are reduced in prominence and absolved of morbidity by Bettie Anne Doebler, who in *The Quickening Seed*[29] sets them in the context of his whole sermonic output and seventeenth-century eschatology. The first

third of her thesis comprises an account of Judaic, Graeco-Roman and Christian attitudes to death, including brief surveys of *ars moriendi* and meditational literature. The doctrines and devotional practice of Donne's time are illustrated primarily from Hooker, Andrewes and Perkins, and examined as they are concentrated artistically in 'Goodfriday, 1613', which is fruitfully related both to the writings of others and to Donne's own sermons. His reworking of various conventional themes of Christian tradition is shown by close consideration of the funeral sermons on King James and Sir William Cockayne (unfortunately misnamed 'Sir William Knight'). For Ms Doebler, Donne's treatment of particular themes, such as warning, consolation, preparation and physical dying itself, express 'the constant effort to balance and to synthesize material and spiritual reality'. While recognizing the relationships of sermons to external events, she likes to think of them as also the record of inner development, a long learning of the craft of dying. Her study continues with an examination of the other last things, judgement, hell and heaven, showing Donne's emphasis rather on the damned man's estrangement from God than on the physical pains of hell, from the contemplation of which he constantly leads his congregation on via the way of repentance to a beatific vision of God in heaven. This lucidly written book concludes with an account of Donne's teaching on and commitment to divine mercy as the ultimate means of triumph over death. In 'Post Seventeenth-Century Texts of John Donne's *Biathanatos*' (*PBSA*) Ernest W. Sullivan II turns unnecessarily heavy artillery on twentieth-century selections, but damningly exposes the doctoring of Hebel's facsimile, and

[29] *The Quickening Seed: Death in the Sermons of John Donne*, by Bettie Anne Doebler. Salzburg: Institut für Englische Sprache und Literatur. pp. v+vii+297. Paperback £4.80, $12.50.

with excoriating *odium philologicum* anatomizes the false principles and disastrous procedure of a professedly critical text recently accepted as a doctoral dissertation at Princeton.

Other prose writers of the period have received scantier attention. Richard L. Nochimson's 'Studies in the Life of Robert Burton' (*YES*) sift with judicious rigour the myths and facts regarding his birth, childhood, education, character, habit of life, career, possessions, bequests and death. Raman Selden distinguishes the successive stages of Hobbes's conceptions of wit, fancy, judgement and imagination, and his changing attitudes to unguided association and purposive thought, in 'Hobbes and Late Metaphysical Poetry' (*JHI*), arguing that his shift during the 1640s from mechanico-materialism to neoclassical rationalism corresponds to a change in poetic language from the spontaneous, fragmented fancifulness of the late metaphysicals such as Cleveland to the neoclassicism of such as Davenant. In 'Holland and the Seventeenth-Century Translations of Sir Thomas Browne's *Religio Medici*', a contribution to *Ten Studies in Anglo-Dutch Relations*,[30] C. W. Schoneveld closely analyses the rhetorical patterns of section i.9 of the original to show the different manners and degrees in which the Latin, French and two Dutch versions depart therefrom.

Astrologers and tellers of jokes are usually confined to the stage: it is not often that real ones speak to us directly. William Lilly, as Katharine M. Briggs says in the introduction to her edition of his autobiography, *The Last of the Astrologers*,[31] 'seems really

not to have known what a rogue he was.' His ingenuous account of a disingenuous career—which included impersonation, theft, forgery, subornation and perjury—, the financial details, his matter-of-fact dismissal of his wives' deaths, and his talent for survival, anticipate the tone and content of Defoe's novels. The autobiography, though judiciously reticent on occasion about Lilly's anti-royalist activities, is rich in fragments of social and political history, details of the shady world of quacks and astrologers, and of grubby dealings in parliament. There are, too, flashes of Aubreyan characterization, as of the 'profound Divine' who 'was so given over to Tobacco and Drink, that when he had no Tobacco, he would cut the Bell-ropes and smoke them.' The introduction gives a summary of Lilly's life, and an explanation of astrology and astrological terms. Concise explanatory notes (not consistently relevant, and Lilly's schoolmaster, John Brinsley, deserves a note) follow each chapter, but—regrettably in a book teeming with names—there is no index. The '*Merry Passages and Jeasts*': *A Manuscript Jestbook of Sir Nicholas Le Strange (1603–1655)*[32] now edited in full for the first time from British Library MS. Harley 6395 by H. F. Lippincott is no laughing matter but rather, as the editor claims in his preface, it gives an unusually informal picture of town and country life and attitudes for all classes of people in the first half of the seventeenth century. Some of the anecdotes

[30] *Ten Studies in Anglo-Dutch Relations*, ed. by J. van Dorsten. Leiden: Leiden U.P.; London: Oxford U.P. pp. x+271. £9.50.

[31] *The Last of the Astrologers: Mr. William Lilly's History of His Life and Times from*

[32] '*Merry Passages and Jeasts*': *A Manuscript Jestbook of Sir Nicholas Le Strange (1603–1655)*, ed. by H. F. Lippincott. Salzburg: Institut für Englische Sprache. pp. viii+258. Paperback £4.80, $12.50.

the year 1602 to 1681, reprinted from the second ed. of 1715, with notes and introduction by Katharine M. Briggs. Folklore Society. pp. xix+108. £3.

involve literary men such as Shakespeare, Jonson, Corbett and Bacon. The introduction describes the manuscript and its handwriting, and discusses its authorship and date, the L'Estrange family (throughout spelt Le Strange), other manuscripts of Sir Nicholas, his character, and the truthfulness, content, style and diction of the jestbook. Editorial principles of modernization, expansion, addition and correction are fully and fairly stated. The text is followed by explanatory notes, and lists of persons, places, expanded forms, and references.

Milton

C. A. PATRIDES

1. GENERAL

The year's most spectacular opinion is ventured by John T. Shawcross, who affirms that the significance of Milton's *Apology against a Pamphlet* (1642) resides, *inter alia*, in 'the anal personality, both expulsive and retentive' (below, p. 295). The rest of the year's work is, by comparison, utterly dull.

The inordinate labours of the Milton industry have elicited much adverse comment. For the record only, however, the bibliography on Milton compiled by C. A. Patrides for *The New Cambridge Bibliography of English Literature* contains nearly sixty columns of entries, compared with over seventy for Chaucer and twice as many for Shakespeare.

The tercentenary of Milton's death was marked by several conferences as well as by an exhibition of books, manuscripts, portraits, illustrations, and associated items, held at the King's Library of the British Museum (reported in *TLS* 15 November under the title 'The Living Milton'). The occasion was also observed by a special issue of *Etudes anglais* devoted entirely to his poetry and prose (No. 4: Oct.–Dec.). The diverse essays are listed below, but notice should here be taken of a general study, Kenneth Muir's 'Personal Involvement and Appropriate Form in Milton's Poetry', which attractively expounds some of the recurring themes in Milton's work.

John M. Steadman's *The Lamb and the Elephant*[1] is an embarrassment. For what can be said of a great scholar—certainly one of our foremost authorities on the intellectual dimension of the Renaissance—that has not been said before? He has read very widely and reflected very deeply, yet also manages to write very lucidly —precisely when so many other scholars terrorize us with their turgid prose, their emaciated thoughts, and their constricted range. It is patently obvious where Steadman should be sought in the river 'wherein the little lamb may wade, and the great elephant freely swim'! But I misapply a statement which in his latest study he borrows from Boccaccio's description of poetry in *The Life of Dante* and uses it generally to suggest the varieties of poetic experience, and particularly to measure the distance between *invisibilia* and *visibilia*, idea and sense, abstraction and embodiment, theory and practice. To understand what is involved, however, it is necessary first to regard the classical and medieval traditions through Renaissance spectacles, thereby to perceive both the continuities and discontinuities, and thence ideal imitation no less than actual execution. Milton's presence in these aspirations is of paramount importance; but incapable as Steadman is to discourse on one figure to the exclusion of

[1] *The Lamb and the Elephant: Ideal Imitation and the Context of Renaissance Allegory*, by John M. Steadman. San Marino, Calif.: The Huntington Library. pp. xlvi+254. $17.50.

another, and both at the expense of the wider context, the frame of reference expands until it becomes an exhilarating venture into the infinitely variegated mind of the Renaissance. The book, utterly lucid as already stated, is nevertheless extremely complex, all the more because it endeavours with boundless ambition to touch roots. But patient readers will be amply rewarded, while others will simply be content with the footnotes, themselves of such range as to be veritable bibliographical guides over terrains both familiar and unfamiliar.

Earl Miner completes, with *The Restoration Mode from Milton to Dryden*,[2] the ambitious trilogy on which he had embarked with *The Metaphysical Mode from Donne to Cowley* (1969) and *The Cavalier Mode from Jonson to Cotton* (1971). The latest study, no less magisterial than the other two, surveys Milton's major poems within the context of the age at large, emphasising 'modes within the whole': the nature of 'the public mode' which aligns Milton with Dryden, the nature of narrative, the nature of values. Given the size of the subject, order constantly threatens to collapse into disorder, and thoroughness into superficiality. But the lucid style advances lucidly, covering the apparent vices as well as the unapparent virtues.

William Kerrigan in *The Prophetic Milton*[3] aspires to defend the poet 'against his friends'; and his polemical introduction protests the critical tendency 'to neutralize [Milton's] constant identification with the prophets of God'. So prophecy—'a

mode of intimate action'—is asserted here with appropriate zeal, and indeed 'enthusiasm'. Yet the argument is not nearly so novel as we are led to believe, in that it mirrors interests present at least since Sir Herbert Grierson's *Milton and Wordsworth: Poets and Prophets* (1937)—here inadvertently bypassed in silence. Nor is it entirely unique, given the ever-increasing emphases now current, whether on Milton's Biblical burden, his interest in time and history as apocalyptic of the divine purpose, and even his sympathetic response to 'radical' thought. The first half of Kerrigan's study is devoted to a survey of theories of prophecy and inspiration up to and including Milton's age, without necessarily advancing our understanding of, say, typology or the impact of Joachimism (Helen Gardner's perceptive remarks on the one in *The Limits of Criticism*, and Marjorie Reeves's magnificent investigation of the other in *The Influence of Prophecy in the Later Middle Ages*, are alike bypassed with unbecoming silence). The second half of the study, however, provides in three chapters sustained celebrations of the prophetic dimension in Milton's prose and poetry. Detailed and lucidly articulated, the three chapters can be profitably read without the context of the gratuitous introduction or the incomplete surveys of the background.

Kerrigan's approach is removed from Donald F. Bouchard's—in *Milton: A Structural Reading*[4]— thrice as far as is the centre from th' utmost pole. 'Enthusiasm' now yields to a sustained search for 'form' and, ultimately, 'truth'. Bouchard embarks on his pilgrimage armed with a

---

[2] *The Restoration Mode from Milton to Dryden*, by Earl Miner. Princeton, N.J.: Princeton University Press. pp. xxiv+587. Cloth £10.50, paperback £5.10.

[3] *The Prophetic Milton*, by William Kerrigan. Charlottesville, Va.: University Press of Virginia. pp. x+285. $12.50.

[4] *Milton: A Structural Reading*, by Donald F. Bouchard. London: Edward Arnold. pp. 180. £4.95.

terminology which, cryptic enough to have taxed the resources of medieval scholasticism, must often be accepted on faith. The Biblical texts are, *inter alia*, drawn from Lévi-Strauss ('Truth lies rather in the progressive expansion of meaning: but an expansion conducted inwards from without and pushed home to explosion-point') and from Ronald Barthes ('form, it has been said, is what keeps the contiguity of units from appearing as a pure effect of chance: the work of art is what a man wrests from chance'). But the maze—to borrow the metaphor from its context in Bouchard's introduction and beyond—is intentional. We are invited to follow Milton's oscillations as he merges composition with decomposition, i.e. the construction of one edifice involving reconstruction in the next. Thus myth which in *Comus* had served to purge ambiguities, in *Lycidas* compounds them— and so calls for reappraisal. Similarly, the ideal community espoused in the prose works propels Milton to a recomposition in *Paradise Lost* (see below, p. 290), terminating only in the literalness of *Paradise Regained* which literally abrogates man as he was understood and praised by Renaissance humanists inclusive of Milton. Bouchard's thesis, then, pertains to a cumulative process where every step involves the destruction of an idol. One would have wished that he himself had exercised the idol of cryptic phrasing and pompous terminology; but the argument, as argument, commands respect, not least because it is one of the most impressive of recent efforts to see Milton in total terms.

Christopher Hill's singular view of Milton in *The World Turned Upside Down* was noticed last year (*YW* 54.250). It is now made more explicit in his lecture 'Milton the Radical' (*TLS*) where we are confronted by a

Milton thoroughly conversant with the non-Laudian, non-Puritan 'third culture' of his time. Indeed 'most of his ideas', Hill claims, should be sought in the radical circles of Familists, Ranters, Fifth Monarchists, Muggletonians, and the rest. A typical assertion suggestive of the radicals' influence reads: 'Milton laid little stress on the Incarnation, the Crucifixion or the Atonement (or indeed on miracles generally: his is a rationalizing theology). All men can attain to oneness with God through Christ, to sonship'. But the description applies to a host of Milton's contemporaries, for instance the Cambridge Platonists, who are not likely to be charged with radical thought even if they were in fact distinctly radical (but not in Hill's particular sense of the word). 'Milton the Radical', as Paul Helm and James M. Lewis remark in the same journal, is an overstated thesis where apparent similarities have been transmuted into precise equations.

Hugh M. Richmond's exposition of Milton as *The Christian Revolutionary*[5] is likely to elicit the enthusiastic response of the very young, and drive the rest to madness. The first dozen pages sketch, with stunning rapidity, the presence in Occidental experience of 'two polarized types of personality': on the one hand, 'the truly Erotic radical, mystical and revolutionary'; and on the other, of course, its opposite. One of the guiding lights here is Anders Nygren's *Agape and Eros*; and as Richmond appears not to be cognizant of the numerous criticisms and corrections of Nygren's outrageously simplistic thesis (*vide* M. C. D'Arcy, Frederick C. Grant, A. H. Armstrong, *et al.*), it is inevit-

[5] *The Christian Revolutionary: John Milton*, by Hugh M. Richmond. Berkeley and London: University of California Press. pp. xi+204. $7.50; £4.40.

able that he should proceed in the way he does. And the way involves, alas, the hapless Milton—now seen as trapped between two mutually exclusive frames of reference, the intellectual (approximately Greek but more particularly Platonic) and the 'intuitive' (generally Protestant). Initially, it appears, Milton was prey to 'stilted orthodoxy'; but eventually—more or less when he wrote *Lycidas*—he is supposed to have journeyed by way of an ever-increasing 'ambivalence' to the intuitive spirit that informs his last three poems. The details are often illuminating, and consistently challenging; and the attractive style is throughout lucid in the extreme. But the overall thesis, grounded as it is on a naïvely conceived dichotomy, severs the intuitive which Richmond admires from the platonic which he deplores, in order to see conflict where there was patently a valiant effort to re-create (in both senses of the word) the one as much as the other. The experiences of 'agape' and 'eros' are indeed diametrically opposed, in theory; but in practice they have yielded the inclusiveness represented by the passionate cry of Ignatius, 'My Love [*eros*] was crucified' (*Epistola ad Romanos*, VII, 7, *apud* Pseudo-Dionysius, *De divinis nominibus*, IV, 12). Richmond's thesis, in other words, shows precisely what he asserts of Milton on one occasion: 'a kind of provocative self-confidence that positively invites disaster'.

Milton Studies VI contains fourteen essays.[6] Most are noticed below, but mention should here be made of two. The first is by Leonora L. Brodwin who in 'Milton and the Renaissance Circe' outlines the myth's traditional dimensions before applying them to Milton's poems, notably *Comus*, *Paradise Lost* and *Samson Agonistes*. The second is by Anne B. Long who in '"She May Have More Shapes than One": Milton and the Modern Idea that Truth Changes' suggests that Milton's system of 'progressive revelations of accommodated truths' invites the individual freely to exercise his creative impulse.

Of the three essays in Edward LeComte's *Milton's Unchanging Mind*,[7] the first—entitled 'Milton versus Time'—surveys the poet's total output to demonstrate the extent to which he was 'obsessed with time'. The other two essays are noticed below (pp. 294 and 295). William B. Hunter, Jr., in 'John Milton: Autobiographer' (*MiltonQ*) proposes that the arrangement of the 1673 edition of the *Poems* was intended as 'part of the record of his spiritual development'. D. Douglas Waters attends to 'Milton's Use of the Sorcerer-Rhetorician' in *Comus*, the polemical prose, and the major poems (*MiltonQ*). Michael Lieb in 'Milton and the Metaphysics of Form' (*SP*) argues that the poet's 'fundamental outlook as a writer' resides in the imaginative confluence of Platonic vision and Aristotelian categories. Samuel S. Stollman in 'Milton's Dichotomy of "Judaism" and "Hebraism"' (*PMLA*) comments on Milton's endorsement of the Hebraic or universal, at the expense of the Judaic or particular.

The Everyman edition of Milton's *Poems*, first published in 1956, is now available in a reprint.[8] It carries the same textual introduction by the editor, B. A. Wright; a bibliography

[7] *Milton's Unchanging Mind: Three Essays*, by Edward LeComte. Foreword by Douglas Bush. Port Washington, N.Y.: Kennikat Press, 1973. $7.95; £5.60.
[8] *Milton: Poems*, edited by B. A. Wright. Everyman's Library. London: Dent; New York: Dutton. 1956; reprinted 1973. pp. xlii+501. Paperback 65p.

[6] *Milton Studies VI*, edited by James D. Simmonds. Pittsburgh, Pa.: University of Pittsburgh Press. pp. 306. $16.95.

selectively brought up to date; and a glossary by W. H. D. Rouse. There is no annotation.

Background studies include *The Rhetoric of Renaissance Poetry: From Wyatt to Milton*, edited by Thomas O. Sloan and Raymond B. Waddington (California). John Wain's *Johnson as Critic* reprints selections from Dr Johnson's *Life of Milton* together with three essays from the *Rambler*—two on Milton's versification, the third on *Samson Agonistes*.[9] Barbara K. Lewalski in 'On Looking into Pope's Milton' studies in profuse detail Milton's impact on Pope, while Lois Bonnerot examines critically the labours of 'Chateaubriand traducteur de Milton' (both in *EA*). Nancy M. Goslee considers Keats's understanding of Milton's technique in '"Under a Cloud in Prospect": Keats, Milton, and Stationing' (*PQ*). Horst Meller's sustained study *Das Gedicht als Einübung* places William Empson's *Milton's God* (1961, rev. ed. 1965) within a comprehensive context.[10] Wide-ranging reviews of the year's work include in particular the survey by Joseph A. Wittreich, Jr. (*MiltonQ*).

Students of Milton and his illustrators will be interested in Nigel Gosling's *Gustave Doré*.[11] A generously illustrated critical biography of the artist, it provides a context for Doré's fifty illustrations of *Paradise Lost* (1866). As usual, we are told, 'Doré proved much less at home with virtuous and peaceable characters, especially when one of them was a

naked girl'. Only Satan came alive, 'as a kind of proto-Batman'.

It is worth noting that the covers of *Milton Quarterly* continue to reproduce diverse, and frequently most valuable, illustrations. The year's issues include the portrait of Milton at the age of ten (reproduced in colour), two relatively unknown illustrations by William Hogarth (on the councils in Hell and Heaven respectively), and an engraving by John Martin from the 1850 edition of *Paradise Lost* (on Satan *en route* to Eden).

2. THE MINOR POEMS

Sharon Cumberland and Lynn V. Sadler in 'Phantasia: A Pattern in Milton's Early Poems' (*MiltonQ*) study the term's moral implications from the *Nativity Ode* to *Comus*. Gayle E. Wilson remarks on the presence of decorum in the epitaph on the Marchioness of Winchester (*MiltonQ*). R. W. Condee surveys 'The Latin Poetry of John Milton',[12] emphasizing in particular the importance of *Epitaphium Damonis*. In a humbler contribution, C. Harold Hurley proposes that the 'key' to *L'Allegro*, lines 45–6, is the cheerful man's determination to partake of mirth's pleasantries (*ELN*).

Last year's edition of *Comus* is decidedly indispensable. Edited by S. E. Sprott and handsomely produced by the University of Toronto Press,[13] it contains transcripts of the three earliest and most dissimilar versions of the masque, here printed in parallel columns: the Trinity College MS, the Bridgewater MS, and the first edition of 1637. In two appendices, moreover, the editor

---

[9] In *Johnson as Critic*, edited by John Wain. London and Boston: Routledge and Kegan Paul, 1973. pp. x +472. £6.95.

[10] In Chapter III of *Das Gedicht als Einübung: Zum Dichtungsverständnis William Empsons*, by Horst Meller. Heidelberg: Carl Winter—Universitätsverlag.

[11] *Gustave Doré*, by Nigel Gosling. Newton Abbot: David and Charles, 1973; New York: Praeger, 1974. pp. 112. £3.95; $12.50.

[12] In *The Latin Poetry of English Poets*, edited by J. W. Binns. London: Routledge and Kegan Paul.

[13] *A Maske: The Earlier Versions*, edited by S. E. Sprott. Toronto: University of Toronto Press, 1973. pp. 230. £11.90.

provides the words of the songs in music manuscripts, and a reconstructed text. The usefulness of the edition can hardly be overestimated.

Richard Kell in 'Thesis and Action in Milton's *Comus*' (*EIC*) accepts the poem's psychological truth but in seeing a discrepancy between its thesis and its action proclaims it 'a damaged work of art'. Armand Himy usefully juxtaposes 'Bacchus et Comus' (*EA*) in pursuit of Milton's 'technique of degradation'. *Milton Studies VI* (above, p. 285) contains three essays on *Comus*. First, Alice-Lyle Scoufos in 'The Mysteries of Milton's *Masque*' reads the poem in the unlikely light of the apocalyptic preoccupations of medieval and Reformation playwrights, among them Thomas Kirchmayer whose *Pammachius* (1538) is here quoted to demonstrate its 'voluptuous vulgarity'! Next, Terry K. Kohn in 'Landscape in the Transcendent Masque' examines the symbolic Wood, the emblematic worlds of Neptune and Sabrina, and the realistic landscape in the foreground, to present with acumen a persuasive case for their interpenetration. Finally, Thomas O. Calhoun advances from a general title ('On John Milton's *A Mask at Ludlow*') to a most particular thesis, that the poem's children and adults represent a 'dramatic collusion' at the expense of 'the erotic dilemma' of the adolescents. The first study is clearly irrelevant; the second, engagingly direct; and the third, the figment of an overactive imagination.

The title of Haruhiko Fujii's *Time, Landscape and the Ideal Life* specifies the common elements he detects in the pastoral poetry of Spenser and Milton.[14] Two chapters are devoted

to Milton: the first, 'The Changing Landscape of *Lycidas*', traces the movement from the disturbance of the natural order to its rejuvenation; while the second, 'Thomas Warton's Romantic Interpretation of *Lycidas*', studies Warton's views (1785) in order to understand the extent to which the Renaissance pastoral was eventually prey to dramatically different sensibilities. Fujii's style, it may be added, eschews the barbarous dissonance so common—alas!—to native speakers of English.

Inwrought with Figures Dim, David S. Berkeley's full-length study of 'the key to *Lycidas*', argues that 'the most subtle and fundamental complexity of *Lycidas* inheres in its typology'.[15] The evidence is presented in over two hundred pages exploding with references to a host of primary sources, all pressed to the service of an approach heretofore applied only to the major poems. The dead Lycidas is now claimed to be on a pilgrim's progress from the earthly Paradise to Heaven, typological stages such as Cambridge confirming the historical reality of the one and anticipating the eventual advent to the other. Far more controversial, however, is the extended commentary on 'that fatall and perfidious Bark/Built in th' eclipse, and rigg'd with curses dark' (ll. 100–1), now said to involve a condemnation of the Laudian establishment's rampant Satanic forces. Such an apocalyptic reading, on the other hand, naturally leads to the last chapter where the experience of Lycidas, it is explained at length, 'serves as the reality of which Christian baptism is a similitude, inverts the salvation of Noah,

[14] *Time, Landscape and the Ideal Life: Studies in the Pastoral Poetry of Spenser and Milton*, by Haruhiko Fujii. Kyoto: Apollonsha. pp. iv+272. Yen 3000.

[15] *Inwrought with Figures Dim: A Reading of Milton's 'Lycidas'*, by David Shelley Berkeley. De Proprietatibus Litterarum, Series Didactica, 2. The Hague and Paris: Mouton. pp. 233. Dutch guilders 20.

adumbrates the Last Judgement, and fulfils the typological Red Sea experience and pagan intimations of the Harrowing of Hell'.

Two minor items on *Lycidas* may also be recorded. First, Charlotte F. Otten argues that the myrtles (l. 2) are 'brown' for reasons of botanic accuracy: no poetic precedents need be sought (*EIC*). Lastly, James F. Forrest annotates at length the 'mantle blue' near the end of the poem (*MiltonQ*).

Sonnet XIX ('When I consider how my light is spent') gained some notoriety when John Sparrow proposed that the 'talent' refers neither to Milton's failing eyesight nor to his literary activities but to his procreative powers: 'Milton was as a young man extremely susceptible to feminine allurements' etc. (*TLS*). The patently frivolous argument did not amuse. As Helen Gardner protested, 'It is one thing to make jokes by finding unintended sexual references in poems in the common-room. It is another thing to put them in print' (*ib.*). Alastair Smart, more severely, enrolled Sparrow's effort among the 'unworthy readings' of Milton's poetry. Sparrow himself finally acknowledged that he was not 'serious' even if his interpretation was 'seriously meant'. His aim was evidently to discredit the excessive search for sexual innuendo in Shakespeare by pointing to its absurdity when the same methods are applied to Milton.

Charles R. Forker relates the same sonnet to the speech on cosmic order in *Troilus and Cressida* (*ELN*), while Dixon Fiske claims that its Dantesque 'Ere half my days' argues a critical period in the speaker's life, finally overcome in the sonnet's sestet (*ELH*). Charles Larson in 'An Architectural Pun in Milton' (*AN&Q*) focuses on 'orb' in Sonnet XXII ('Cyriack, this three years day'). John

C. Ulreich annotates the 'Typological Symbolism in Milton's Sonnet XXIII' (*MiltonQ*)—also the concern of John J. Colaccio's discriminating study '"A Death like Sleep": The Christology of Milton's Twenty-Third Sonnet' (*MiltonS*), where Christian typology is wedded to Neoplatonic thought to present a persuasive case for the dramatic representation of the persona's fallen nature in conflict with Christian precepts.

W. K. Wimsatt's *Literary Criticism: Idea and Art* (California) reprints C. L. Barber's 'A Mask presented at Ludlow Castle: The Masque as a Masque' and Louis L. Martz's 'The Rising Poet, 1645' (both from *The Lyric and Dramatic Milton*, edited by Joseph H. Summers, 1965). Josephine Miles's 'Words and Themes in Milton's *Lycidas*' (in her *Poetry and Change*, California) is a reprint of 'The Language of *Lycidas*' (from *Milton's Lycidas': The Tradition and the Poem*, edited by C. A. Patrides, 1961).

3. 'PARADISE LOST'

The two editions of Milton's poetry now in progress (*YW* 53.243–4) have gained one more volume each: in *The Macmillan Milton*, an edition of Book IV by T. M. Gang;[16] and in *The Cambridge Milton*, an edition of Books VII–VIII by David Aers and Mary Ann Radzinowicz.[17] Gang provides an adequate introduction, and equally adequate notes conveniently printed immediately opposite the text; there are moreover the usual appendices on the Miltonic universe, the poem's sources, and a graded

[16] *The Macmillan Milton* (general editor, C. A. Patrides): *Paradise Lost, Book IV*, edited by T. M. Gang. pp. 136. Paperback 65p.
[17] *The Cambridge Milton* (general editor, John Broadbent): *Paradise Lost, Books VII-VIII*, edited by David Aers and Mary Ann Radzinowicz. pp. 146. Paperback £1.00.

reading list. Aers and Radzinowicz, on the other hand, allot themselves separate introductions for each Book, the one aspiring to emulate the well-attested thrusts of the general editor (John Broadbent), the other providing a sustained if brief reading of Book VIII. An appendix by Lesley Aers gathers passages from Isaiah, Plato, Lucretius, Karl Barth, the Diggers, Wallace Stevens, *et al.*, in the earnest hope that someone will discern patterns not otherwise readily apparent.

Centred on *Paradise Lost*, A. G. George's study of *Milton and the Nature of Man*[18] is an energetic survey of several clusters of ideas inclusive of the interdependence of body and soul, the reflection of the divine 'image' in man's rational faculty, and the relations between man and woman considered as an analogue of the relations between God and man. The survey, as a survey, is rather eclectic; nor is it distinguished by originality. Moreover, as A. G. George is not fully conversant with the whole range of Miltonic criticism and scholarship, he simplifies all too often and in consequence displaces sombre sophistication by an endearing naïvety. But the zest is unmistakable. Whether the discourse concerns the delineation of the Fall or the nature of the poem's 'myth'—'the circumambient myth of *Paradise Lost*'—the tendency is to invoke unexpected allies (Barth or Toynbee) in order to provide a commonsensical vision of Milton's achievement. It should be added, emphatically, that the study is extremely readable. The lucidity is palpable; and since the author is an Indian, one may only reiterate what was earlier observed of another foreign scholar, Haruhiko Fujii (p. 287).

Thomas Wheeler's *'Paradise Lost' and the Modern Reader*[19] is modest in length and naïve in its stated thesis. But the modesty and the naïvety are apparent, not real; for the argument will most likely generate a number of studies several times the length of Wheeler's. The vast ambition here, after all, is to redirect our attention from the background to the foreground, to the poem itself, now measured by a 'modern reader' not in the light of an obsolete Christian humanism but 'against his own experience'. A parallel ambition nearly three decades ago, A. J. A. Waldock's *'Paradise Lost' and its Critics* (1947), had terminated in largely negative conclusions, especially because Adam's disobedience through his selfless love for Eve appeared to destroy the poem's stated objectives. Yet Wheeler—no less a 'modern reader' than Waldock was—firmly concludes that the motivation in Adam's disobedience is in fact 'utterly selfish'. It is tempting to maintain that the diametrically opposed claims of Waldock and Wheeler simply cancel each other out, were it not that Wheeler advances to a persuasive exposition of the relations between Adam and Eve ('the chief glory of the poem, the portion which speaks most directly and profoundly to the modern reader'). To the extent that the exposition convinces, this slim but elegant study may be recommended for articulating, with commendable lucidity, a dimension of experience central to any reader—even if he is obsolete enough to be a Christian humanist.

The special issue of *Etudes anglaises*

---

[18] *Milton and the Nature of Man: A Descriptive Study of 'Paradise Lost' in Terms of the Concept of Man as the Image of God*, by A. G. George. London: Asia Publishing House. pp. ix + 161. £3.00.

[19] *'Paradise Lost' and the Modern Reader*, by Thomas Wheeler. Athens, Ga.: University of Georgia Press. pp. xi + 132. $7.50.

(above, p. 282) contains four essays on *Paradise Lost*. Two are surveys, Jacques Blondel's 'Aspects de la critique miltonienne d'aujourd'houi' and Roy Flannagan's 'Milton Criticism, Present and Future'; a third, by Micheline Hugues, is concerned with 'Le Myth de Babel dans *Paradise Lost*'; while the last, by Lois Potter, examines 'Paradise and Utopia: Human Interest in *Paradise Lost*'. *Milton Studies VI* (above, p. 285) also contains four essays on the poem. The first is Barbara K. Lewalski's 'Milton on Women—Yet Once More', which argues that Eve is not the submissive creature we are often led to believe but demonstrably a participant 'in the full range of human activities and achievements'. The second essay is Virginia R. Mollenkott's 'Milton's Technique of Multiple Choice', which includes among the reasons for the poet's deliberate ambiguities an emphatic inclination to uphold the mysteries of the creation and a desire to superimpose Hebraic exclusiveness on the richly poetic Greek myths. The third essay is Dustin H. Griffin's 'Milton's Evening', which focuses on the poem's description of the evening (IV, 598–609) as a starting point for an engaging examination of the implications, for the entire poem, of its diurnal rhythms. The last essay is Peter Lindenbaum's 'Lovemaking in Milton's Paradise', which terminates its journey through traditional observations on sexual intercourse before the Fall with the ringing declaration that Milton's Eden is 'both like our present life and unlike it'; but the expedition meanders as much as the author's style does, especially his interminable sentences.

Michael Lieb in '"Holy Name": A Reading of *Paradise Lost*' (*HTR*) sagely emphasizes the sense of mystery pervading Milton's vision, and exhaustively studies traditional efforts to maintain that mystery. Judith A. Kates in 'The Revaluation of the Classic Heroic in Tasso and Milton' (*CompL*) perceptively studies the reconsiderations of 'heroism' in *Gerusalemme Liberata* and *Paradise Lost*. William P. Shaw in 'Milton's Choice of the Epic for *Paradise Lost*' (*ELN*) argues the obvious point that Milton favoured the epic form because of its inclusiveness. Sanford Budick's chapter on 'Milton's Epic Reclamations' in his *Poetry of Civilization*[20] maintains that *Paradise Lost* and *Samson Agonistes* provide models 'for the supremacy of logos over mythos, of reason over Satanic idol-making'. The core of Bouchard's impressive study (above, p. 283) is also devoted to *Paradise Lost*; and while the argument remains within the circle of the rearing and demolition of several idols as stated before, it encompasses singularly suggestive observations on the poem's language and structure.

Lolette Kuby in 'The World is Half the Devil's: Cold-Warmth Imagery in *Paradise Lost*' (*ELH*) believes that the indicated images constitute evidence of Milton's dualistic tendencies. Jun Harada in 'The Archetype and Ectypes of Belial in Milton's Epic Poems' (*SELit* 1973) studies the self-destructiveness of evil through the prototypical Belial, here said to be 'ontologically an externality-conditioned evil and functionally a secondary vice to be activated by some other evil agent'—whatever *that* means. Baldwin Peter in 'Milton's Hell Hounds and the Children of God' (*MiltonQ*) glances at the Cerberean dogs within the context of the poem's trinitarian parody. Frank S. Kastor's

[20] *Poetry of Civilization: Mythopoeic Displacement in the Verse of Milton, Dryden, Pope, and Johnson*, by Sanford Budick. New Haven and London: Yale University Press. £4.90.

Milton and the Literary Satan[21] presents schematically Satan's appearances in literature, sub-literature, and non-literature. The aim is to provide a background against which Milton's conception of Satan can be judged. In the event, however, the precedents are chosen with casual abandon, even as Milton's synthesis is never perceptively articulated. The style is frequently infelicitous, and sometimes rather vulgar.

Hannah D. Demaray in 'Milton's "Perfect" Paradise and the Landscapes of Italy' (*MiltonQ*) persuasively attributes the alleged flaws in Milton's prelapsarian Eden to the 'controlled irregularities and artificial elements' habitually present in Italian painting and landscape conventions. The essay is necessarily centred not only on a reconsideration of Milton's visit to Italy but on the visual interpretations of the Edenic landscape by Bassano, Tintoretto, Titian, and Jan Brueghel. S. A. Fisher defends Raphael ('this healthy, friendly angel') against anyone who dares think he shouldn't have blushed in *Paradise Lost* VIII 618–9 (*Expl*), and Francis C. Blessington in 'Maia's Son and Raphael Once More' examines the angel's descent to earth in the light of the *Aeneid* IV 219–80 (*MiltonQ*). William McQueen considers some of the implications of the War in Heaven (SP). So does Stella P. Revard, who in 'The Warring Saints and the Dragon: A Commentary upon Revelation 12.7–9 and Milton's War in Heaven' (*PQ*) examines the allusion's apocalyptic dimensions in relation to seventeenth-century attitudes. Revard further argues, in 'Vision and Revision: A Study of *Paradise Lost* XI and *Paradise Regained*' (*PLL*), that the

[21] *Milton and the Literary Satan*, by Frank S. Kastor. Amsterdam: Rodopi N.V. pp. 119. Dutch guilders 20.

penultimate book of the major epic is important to its 'sequel' in that Michael's descent in the one presages the dove's descent on Christ in the other, and thereby completes the process earlier seen dimly and distantly.

Boyd M. Berry in 'Puritan Soldiers in *Paradise Lost*' (*MLQ*) advances from Puritan sermons on 'spiritual soldiering' to the conception of several characters in the poem; but the equation is much too forced to be convincing. Naseeb Shaheen in 'Milton's Muse and the *De Doctrina*' (*MiltonQ*) claims that the poem's five invocations are alike addressed to the Holy Spirit. James Hoyle in '"If Sion Hill Delight Thee More": The Muse's Choice in *Paradise Lost*' (*ELN*) examines the antecedents and purpose in Milton's invocation of the Muse rather from Mount Sion than from Mount Sinai (I, 6–12). W. F. Bolton detects the 'influence' of the Old English *Genesis* 413–7 and 1671–8 on *Paradise Lost* I 692–9 and II 404–13 (*RES*). S. Viswanathan annotates VIII 253–5 (*MiltonQ*). Denis Donoghue's 'God without Thunder' in his *Thieves of Fire* (Faber, 1973) is a reprint of the essay on Milton noticed in 1972 (*YW* 53.245).

Joseph A. Wittreich, Jr., studies the three designs of Milton's first illustrator (*SCN*)—not indeed John Baptist Medina (*pace* Helen Gardner's claim in *A Reading of Paradise Lost*, 1965) but Dr Henry Aldrich (*pace* Suzanne Boorsch as noted in *YW* 53.247). J. H. Tisch studies two eighteenth-century German versions of the poem in '*Paradise Lost* "in der vollen Pracht der deutschen Hexameters"': Observations on the Milton Translations by F. W. Zachariä and Simon Grynäus' (*Seminar* 1973); he also covers the same ground, albeit more briefly, in 'Between Translation and Adaptation: *Paradise Lost* in German 1682–

1760'.[22] Along the same lines, Janifer G. Stackhouse attends to 'Early Critical Response to Milton in Germany: The *Dialogi* of Martin Zeiller' (*JEGP*). Edna Newmeyer, finally, defends Milton against Wordsworth's charge that the passage on Abel's sacrifice (X, 429–43) is 'inelegant and reminds one too strongly of a Butchers stall' (*MiltonQ*)

4. 'PARADISE REGAINED' AND 'SAMSON AGONISTES'

The first part of Patrick Cullen's *Infernal Triad* is devoted to Spenser, and the second to Milton;[23] yet the argument—'that in Milton allegorical schematizing is much more prominent than we are accustomed to expect'— depends on an explication of the Spenserian approach which, it is here maintained, the later poet adapted to his purposes. Milton's vast respect for Spenser is hardly unknown; but to propose that he also derived from Spenser an allegorically disposed triadic pattern not only for the major epic but for *Paradise Regained* and *Samson Agonistes*, is to invite a charge of gross over-simplification and, indeed, superficiality. Cullen's ambition is to sharpen our awareness of the complexity of the composite nature of the temptations in *Paradise Regained*, of the transformation of tragedy as genre in *Samson Agonistes*, and of the indebtedness of both poems to Spenserian schemes beyond the immediate context. Such aspirations are commendable. But hyperbole often mounts to the point of incredul-

ity, as in the unwarranted speculation that in *Paradise Regained* 'the triadic structure is the tetradic division', according to which the three temptations unfold in four books so as to reflect the nature of the God-Man himself: '*three* (*deus*, the spiritual) and *four* (*homo*, the corporal, the mental)'! Stylistically, too, the book is distinguished by a certain languor —made worse by several monstrous footnotes which threaten to displace the text, and sometimes do.

The year produced four other studies of Milton's shorter epic: Jean-François Camé's examination of 'La structure mythique de *Paradise Regained*' (*EA*); Emory Elliott's investigation of 'Milton's Biblical Style in *Paradise Regained*' (*MiltonS*) which studies in generous detail the poem's numerous Scriptural allusions so as to demonstrate how they provide 'essential details of the encircling framework of Christ's total career and teachings'; Elaine B. Safer's concern with 'The Socratic Dialogue and "Knowledge in the Making" in *Paradise Regained*' (*MiltonS*) which invokes a well-attested dimension to restate the mental process involved in the rejection of the mock set of values espoused by Satan; and Ira Clark's study of 'Christ on the Tower in *Paradise Regained*' (*MiltonQ*) which focuses on the implications of the poem's climactic temptation.

An edition by Ann Phillips of *Samson Agonistes*,[24] intended strictly for sixth-formers, provides a general introduction on Milton's life, his poetic style ('not intimate'), and his critics, as well as a particular introduction on the poem's plot, characters, etc. The edition could not be accused of sophistication.

Anthony Low's several essays on

---

[22] In *Expression, Communication and Experience in Literature and Language*, edited by R. G. Popperwell. London: Proceedings of the XIIth Congress of the International Federation for Modern Languages and Literatures, 1973.

[23] *Infernal Triad: The Flesh, the World, and the Devil in Spenser and Milton*, by Patrick Cullen. Princeton, N.J.: Princeton University Press. pp. xxxvi+267. $13.50.

[24] *Samson Agonistes*, edited by Ann Phillips. London: University Tutorial Press. pp. 139. 90p.

Samson Agonistes, all noticed in these pages over the last few years, have now yielded a major study of the play in *The Blaze of Noon*.[25] A comprehensive survey of recent discussions, the study also aspires to extend our understanding of *Samson Agonistes* as regards its patterns of thought, its characters, its verse, and its irony. Spectacular pyrotechnics should not be sought in this book for they will not be found. Low's voice is deliberately irenic, and his pace relaxed—perhaps too relaxed. The advantages, however, are obvious; for eschewing polemics, he is given to a well-advised caution, as when the larger claims on Milton's irony by others are properly reduced to the sage observation that 'one might claim that Milton approaches even Sophocles in this respect'. Thus, too, John F. Huntley's important essay on the role of the Chorus (*MP* 1966) is welcomed as 'judicious', even as the excesses of other readers are censured without passion but firmly. The weakest part of the study is the unaccountably brief chapter on aspects of the verse; but there are on the other hand several chapters which redress the balance, especially in connection with the enlightening discussion of the play's sustained deployment of irony.

The chapter on *Samson Agonistes* in Bouchard's study (above, p. 283) is adapted from 'Samson as Medicine Man' (noticed in *YW* 53.248). Five shorter studies of the play may also be recorded: Michael Cohen's survey of the implications of 'Rhyme in *Samson Agonistes*' (*MiltonQ*); Jeanne K. Welcher's brief discussion of 'The Significance of Manoa' (*MiltonQ*); Jack Goldman's essay on the back-

ground to 'The Name and Function of Harapha in *Samson Agonistes*' (*ELN*); John M. Steadman's defence of the play's moral and emotional unity in 'Milton's *Summa Epitasis*: The End of the Middle of *Samson Agonistes*' (*MLR*); and Carole S. Kessner's view of 'Milton's Hebraic Herculean Hero' (*MiltonS*) which grants that the 'outlines' of Milton's Samson are borrowed from the Hebraic myth but argues that the poem's 'substance and spirit' should be sought in Euripides's *Heracles*. Notes include Jackson C. Boswell's examination of the play's serpentine imagery, especially the reference to Dalila in l. 763 (*MiltonQ*); and the comments by J. J. M. Tobin on Samson's simile of hornets in ll. 19–20 (*Expl*), and by Douglas P. Collins on the Chorus's comparison of Dalila to a ship in ll. 710–18 (*N&Q*).

5. PROSE

Milton's *Selected Prose*, edited by C. A. Patrides,[26] provides the annotated text of five prose works in full (*Of Education, Areopagitica, The Tenure of Kings and Magistrates, A Treatise of Civil Power, The Readie and Easie Way*) and abridged versions of two more (*Of Reformation* and *The Doctrine and Discipline of Divorce*). There are in addition several extracts, mainly on literature, and the biographies by John Aubrey and Edward Phillips. The editor provides an introduction ('Milton in the Seventeenth Century') and an extensive bibliography subdivided into sections.

An essay not earlier noticed, John Illo's 'The Misreading of Milton',[27]

---

[25] *The Blaze of Noon: A Reading of 'Samson Agonistes'*, by Anthony Low. New York and London: Columbia University Press. pp. xi+236. £6.00.

[26] *John Milton: Selected Prose*, ed. C. A. Patrides. The Penguin English Library, Penguin Books. pp. 426. Paperback 50p; $1.95.

[27] In *Radical Perspectives in the Arts*, edited by Lee Baxandall. Penguin Books, 1972.

argues with revolutionary zeal that *Areopagitica* is 'a militant and exclusivist revolutionary pamphlet', concerned with 'a conditional, not absolute, freedom of expression'. As the author protests that he was unduly neglected by 'Milton circles', he may wish to mark that his essay is also mentioned in the edition cited in the previous paragraph, and in the volume cited in the next.

Achievements of the Left Hand, a collection of ten essays on Milton's prose,[28] carries a vulgar jacket showing an improbable left hand where Blake's left-handed Ancient of Days might have done better. The ten contributors, at any rate, write with their *right* hands. Joseph A. Wittreich, Jr., in '"The Crown of Eloquence": The Figure of the Orator in Milton's Prose Works', authoritatively demonstrates Milton's advance through an imaginative deployment of the classical and Christian oratorical traditions to an idealistic vision entirely his own. Michael Lieb, in 'Milton's *Of Reformation* and the Dynamics of Controversy', attends with thoroughness to the tract's thematic and structural dimensions in an effort to establish the salient issues behind the polemics. John F. Huntley, in a wide-ranging study of 'The Images of Poet and Poetry in Milton's *The Reason of Church-Government*', perceptively argues the affinities between the tract's discourse on poetry and its polemical intent, and unhesitatingly proclaims that the discourse bears 'little direct relation' to the concept of poetry underlying *Paradise Lost*. Edward S. LeComte, in 'Areopagitica as a Scenario for *Paradise Lost*' (also available in his

book, as above, p. 285), invokes numerous details from the treatise and the poem to confirm their close relationship. John T. Shawcross, in 'The Higher Wisdom of *The Tenure of Kings and Magistrates*', locates the tract's 'philosophical and enduring significance' in its radical idealism which 'clearly agree[s] with the so-called radical views of the youth of our last decade ... well short, however, of Jesus-freaks'. Florence Sadler, in 'Icon and Iconoclast', studies—with considerable impatience, it may be noted—the Biblical framework of Milton's efforts to shatter the royal 'image' in his *Eikonoklastes*. Austin Woolrych, in 'Milton and Cromwell: "A Short but Scandalous Night of Interruption"?', examines in great detail the fluctuations in Milton's complex attitude to Cromwell, and asserts that the quoted phrase (in *The Likeliest Means to Remove Hirelings*, 1659) alludes to the Rump's six-year lapse of power. Harry Smallenburg, in 'Government of the Spirit: Style, Structure and Theme in *Treatise of Civil Power*', convincingly demonstrates that the tract's argument is sustained by its style. Walter J. Ong, in 'Logic and the Epic Muse: Reflections on Noetic Structures in Milton's Milieu', dwells on the historical and immediate contexts of Ramist logic and Milton's 'addiction' to it in *The Art of Logic* and elsewhere. Finally, William B. Hunter, Jr., in 'The Metaphysical Context of Milton's *Christian Doctrine*', sketches the treatise's historical and theological background in order to demonstrate 'the highly eclectic system of a man who has read widely but who has refused to be dominated by any single school'. *Achievements of the Left Hand* also carries a ninety-page appendix, 'A Survey of Milton's Prose Works' by John T. Shawcross. Authoritative as regards dates of

---

[28] *Achievements of the Left Hand: Essays on the Prose of John Milton*, edited by Michael Lieb and John T. Shawcross. Amherst, Mass.: University of Massachusetts Press. pp. viii+396. $12.50.

composition, editions, select further studies, and the like, it also includes the judgement quoted earlier (p. 282). Surprisingly enough, the collection has no contribution by Donald M. Rosenberg; worse still, none of his excellent studies of Milton's prose are even once referred to.[29]

Of Education is studied within its French context by Olivier Lutaud in 'Le "Savant Instituteur" et les "Labour'd Studies of the French"' (*EA*), while a phrase from the same treatise—'laborious ascent'—is endowed by Charles R. Geisst with distinctly Platonic implications (*N&Q*). Edward S. LeComte reprints in his book (above, p. 285) an essay on Milton as 'Satirist and Wit' first published in *Th' Upright Heart and Pure* (edited by Amadeus P. Fiore, 1967). Claud A. Thompson unravels the bibliographical tangle of the four seventeenth-century editions of *The Doctrine and Discipline of Divorce* (*PBSA*); Roger Lejosne examines the patterns of 'Nature humaine et loi divine dans le *Tetrachordon*' (*EA*); and Theodore L. Huguelet in 'The Rule of Charity in Milton's Divorce Tracts' (*MiltonS*) considers the Rule as Milton's 'master rule of exegesis', traces some of its antecedents, and confirms its importance for the tracts. Leo Miller in 'Milton, Fichlau, Bensen and Conring' (*PBSA*) looks at some of Milton's enemies after the publication of the *Defensio pro populo anglicano*; he also notes two relevant letters from Heinsius (*N&Q*). Austin Woolrych in 'Milton and Richard Heath' (*PQ*) identifies the recipient of a letter from Milton in 1652. Robert W. Ayers studies the

context of 'The Editions of Milton's *Readie & Easie Way*', now said to have been published in February 1660 (*RES*). The seventh volume of the Yale edition of the *Complete Prose Works*, covering the years 1659–60, was issued to reviewers[30] only to be withdrawn. It will be reviewed when it is made available again.

Maurice Kelley's edition of *De Doctrina christiana*, noticed last year (*YW* 54.251), is now the recipient of further adverse comments. For instance, Joseph A. Wittreich, Jr., warns against 'the narrowness of its perspective' (*MiltonQ*), while William B. Hunter, Jr., lists its shortcomings in considerable detail, notably the absence of theological sophistication and editorial responsibility in dealing with the background to Milton's treatise (*SCN*). Hunter also observes that John Carey's translation of the Latin text is unreliable because it is neither accurate nor discriminating enough in its rendering of Milton's carefully deployed terminology.

John Milton among the Polygamophiles elicits on sight the stall-reader's cry in Sonnet XI: 'bless us! what a word on/A title page is this!' Yet the subject, as a subject, is far from frivolous, since *De doctrina christiana* encompasses polygamy among its manifold burdens, and a scholarly study of its context was bound to be undertaken sooner or later. The year has in fact yielded two such studies, with equally intriguing titles: *After Polygamy was made a Sin*, by John Cairncross,[31] who devotes a few superficial pages to Milton; and the

---

[29] For the record, they include: 'Theme and Structure in Milton's Autobiographies', *Genre* for 1969; 'Parody of Style in Milton's Polemics', *MiltonS* for 1970; and 'Satirical Techniques in Milton's Polemical Prose', *Satire Newsletter* for 1971.

[30] *Complete Prose Works of John Milton* (general editor, Don M. Wolfe): Volume VII, edited by Robert W. Ayers. New Haven and London: Yale University Press. pp. xiii+538. £12.50.

[31] *After Polygamy was made a Sin: The Social History of Christian Polygamy*, by John Cairncross. London: Routledge and Kegan Paul. pp. vi+236. £4.25.

more ambitious *John Milton among the Polygamophiles*, by Leo Miller,[32] who breathlessly points to every polygamous-minded man from the Reformers themselves to veritable quacks, then extends his search beyond the seventeenth century, and expires at last with a series of quotations from *The New York Times* (up to 1969) to demonstrate the reprehensible morals of latter-day polygamophiles—not to mention such prospects as 'megafamilies'.

Milton is misplaced *en route*.

[32] *John Milton among the Polygamophiles*, by Leo Miller. New York: Lowenthal Press, P.O. Box 1107, New York 10009. pp. xii + 378. $15.

XI

The Later Seventeenth Century

JAMES OGDEN

This chapter has four sections: 1. General bibliography, anthologies, literary history and criticism; 2. Dryden; 3. Other poets, dramatists and prosateurs, considered in rough chronological order in each subsection; 4. Background studies. The treatment of philosophy in section 3 and of art and music in section 4 is highly selective and depends partly on what was readily available for review.

1. GENERAL

The major current bibliographies continue to appear in *PQ* and *RECTR*, though my eagerly awaited Fall 1974 *PQ* did not arrive till autumn 1975. It lists significant books, articles and reviews published during 1973 on English, American and European bibliography, history, thought, fine arts and literature, 1660–1800. The sections on history and the fine arts are selective, but the work still runs to some 370 pages not counting the index. A high standard of accuracy and comprehensiveness is attained. Comments on articles tend to be brief and noncommittal, while reviews of books tend to be detailed and fierce. George Hammerbacher's 'Restoration and Eighteenth Century Theatre Research Bibliography for 1973' (*RECTR*) is as usual pretty comprehensive, annotated, and indexed. Users of *Restoration and Eighteenth Century Theatre Research: A Bibliographical Guide, 1900–1968* (*YW* 52.245) will find remarks on its shortcomings and lists of omissions in a review by D. F. McKenzie in *N&Q*.

A number of general articles can be recommended. Paul C. Davies and Arthur J. Weitzman pursue their controversy (*YW* 53.252, 54.253) on 'Who were the Restoration Liberals?' (*EIC*). Davies still believes the Restoration wits were liberal in the sense of not being conservative, referring to drama and satire. Weitzman still believes Restoration drama and satire, when not merely frivolous, was an essentially illiberal defence of aristocracy. (Davies writes from Bangor, Wales, and Weitzman from Boston, Massachusetts.) H. James Jensen's 'Note on Restoration Aesthetics' (*SEL*) stresses that Restoration critics, while they were disposed to think art they merely enjoyed was inferior to art which appealed to their understanding, did appreciate the *élan vital* of great works. When Dryden defines a good play as 'a just and lively image of human nature' he is not simply calling for regularity and verisimilitude; he is saying that the play's motion, spirit or life must be felt. Such qualities could be found above all in Shakespeare, 'and it is the recognition of an *élan vital* in Shakespeare's works which, probably as much as anything else, accounts for the difference between French and English theory, appreciation, and practice of poesy' in our period and later. Jensen has a point, but it seems worth asking how the French came to supply his phrase for the qualities they were apparently slow to appreciate. George L. Dillon, in 'Complexity and Change of Character in Neo-Classical Criticism' (*JHI*), argues that neo-classical critics were inclined to emphasize simplicity and consistency of characterization, but awareness of complexity and change is strikingly apparent in the historiographical work of a Frenchman living in England, Saint-Évremond, and that near the end of the seventeenth century these subtler ideas began to make their way in literary criticism.

(a) Drama

A. Norman Jeffares edited an anthology of *Restoration Comedy* for the Folio Society in four splendid volumes.[1] It comprises twenty-four plays produced between 1664 and 1722. The texts are based on the first editions, except that of *The Constant Couple*, where the third edition, revised by Farquhar, is preferred. Hence it is surprising that Vanbrugh's revised scenes for *The Provoked Wife* are not given, even as an appendix. A textual note on *The Beaux Stratagem* remarks on the difficulties of deciding on the copy-text and refers us to Jeffares's own FDS edition; similar cautionary notes and references might have been given in other cases, notably *The Way of the World* (see section 3 (*b*) below). Spelling and typography have been modernized, and some small changes have been made for the sake of consistency, but the original punctuation has been largely retained, as an indication of how the lines were meant to be spoken. A general note on the text explains these matters, and textual notes at the end of each play record departures from the copy-texts. The general introduction deals briskly with theatre history, the effects of

actresses and sliding scenery, the audiences, the sources and development of the plays, their typical subject-matter, and the complaints of such as Collier. Short introductions to each play give biographical information about the dramatists, sketches of stage history, and critical comments. Most obscure words and allusions in the texts are briefly explained in footnotes, as are some (Salop; Bridewell; Aristotle) which are not particularly obscure. There are twenty-four illustrations: portraits of dramatists and leading players, and early engravings of scenes from the plays. Jeffares aims at representing the best dramatists, showing the variety and development of Restoration comedy, and selecting plays that are amusing in themselves. Farquhar is represented by three plays; Dryden, Wycherley, Etherege, Mrs Behn, Congreve, Cibber and Vanbrugh by two each; and Killigrew the elder, Sedley, Durfey, Ravenscroft, Crowne, Shadwell and Steele by one each. While no two experts would agree on how best to achieve Jeffares's aims, arguably his selection is rather odd. Asked which writer of Restoration comedies would come most often in the top twenty-four, one would not immediately fix on Farquhar. It is hard to think of a definition of Restoration comedy which would make room for Steele's *Conscious Lovers*, as Jeffares seems to admit in his comments on that play. And Dryden's *Marriage à la Mode* should surely have been preferred to either *Sir Martin Mar-all* or *The Kind Keeper*, if not to both. But in general this is an excellent anthology, providing good texts of plays by minor dramatists which are not readily available, and thus perhaps inspiring critics to take a more comprehensive view of comedy through our period.

Most of the well-known contem-

---

[1] *Restoration Comedy*, ed. by A. Norman Jeffares. Folio Press. 4 vols., pp. xxvii + 624, xiii + 651, xiii + 656, xiii + 593. £32.50 the set.

porary criticism of Restoration drama is included in *The English Stage: Attack and Defence, 1577–1730*,[2] a series of photo-facsimile reprints illustrating, the publishers explain, legal, moral and critical attacks on and defences of the English stage, during its great era. Rymer, Langbaine, Dennis, Gildon, Collier, Congreve, Settle, Vanbrugh and Oldmixon are among the authors represented. They are now joined by Donald Bruce, whose object in *Topics of Restoration Comedy*[3] is 'to present Restoration Comedy as a debating comedy, and as morally purposeful within its debates'. He begins by emphasizing that after the Restoration 'London became a licentious capital', and the comic dramatists set up 'as informal judges of their audience's conduct'. A chapter of briskly potted biographies of Etherege, Shadwell, Mrs Behn, Wycherley, Congreve, Vanbrugh and Farquhar follows; so brisk in the case of Farquhar that *The Recruiting Officer* is not even mentioned, and so potted in that of Shadwell that he and Dryden are said to have together 'created a small literature of abuse which does credit to neither of them'. There are four chapters on the topics debated: the country and the city, genuine honour and modishness, reason and passion, Epicureanism, the roles of the sexes, constancy and inconstancy. These are considered with examples from all the well-known plays and from Shadwell and Mrs Behn. Mr Bruce's style is more lively and less censorious, and Restoration comedy emerges as more entertaining and less morally purpose-

ful, than we might have expected. The book makes a good short introduction for students. Two books that I have not yet seen should be mentioned here: Terence Tobin's *Plays by Scots, 1660–1800* (University of Iowa Press) and Joan C. Grace's *Tragic Theory in the Critical Works of Thomas Rymer, John Dennis, and John Dryden* (Fairleigh Dickinson University Press).

Several articles in *RECTR* and *TN* dealt with the minutiae of theatre history. Of these Oscar L. Brownstein's 'The Duke's Company in 1667' (*TN*) is of some interest. Brownstein reports on a survey of St Bride's parish at that time, which gives an impression of 'a theatrical community whose pillars were quite middle class in their habitation and life-style, an image too easily concealed behind the flash and colour of the lives of a few actresses and playwrights'. A more general study is Alois M. Nagler's 'Courtiers, Beaux, Wits and Cits',[4] a lively account of the Restoration theatre audience, well illustrated from contemporary sources. The playgoers did not necessarily go to see the plays, but the playwrights tolerated them all, except perhaps the 'criticks'.

(b) Poetry

An anthology of *Poems on the Reign of William III* was edited and introduced by Earl Miner.[5] The poems are *An Epistle to Dorset* by Charles Montagu; an anonymous

---

[2] *The English Stage: Attack and Defense, 1577–1730*, ed. by Arthur Freeman. New York: Garland Publishing Inc.; London: George Prior Associated Publishers Ltd. 50 vols. £500; individual volumes £11.90.

[3] *Topics of Restoration Comedy*, by Donald Bruce. Gollancz. pp. 189. £3.75.

[4] pp. 108–28 in *Essays on Drama and Theatre Presented to Professor Dr B. Hunningher*, ed. by Mrs Erica Hunningher-Schilling. Amsterdam/Baarn: Moussault's Uitgeverij; Antwerp: Standaard Uitgeverij, 1973. Paperback, no price stated.

[5] *Poems on the Reign of William III* (*1690, 1696, 1699, 1702*), ed. by Earl Miner. Augustan Reprint Society No. 166. Los Angeles: William Andrews Clark Memorial Library. pp. 41. By subscription.

Poem Occasion'd by the Happy Discovery of the Horrid and Barbarous Conspiracy to Assassinate His Most Sacred Majesty; *On the Happy Accession of King William and Queen Mary* by John Guy; and *The House of Nassau* by John Hughes.

Professor Miner, who has already published substantial books on Dryden, 'the metaphysical mode' and 'the Cavalier mode' (*YW* 48.233; 50.213–14; 52.216, 246), completed his heroic exploration of seventeenth-century poetry with *The Restoration Mode from Milton to Dryden*.[6] By 'mode' he means the poet's way of seeing himself, others, and the world; the metaphysical mode was predominantly private, the Cavalier social, and the Restoration public. The change to the public mode involved a re-ordering of genres, lyrical being supplanted by narrative poetry. Miner does not quite avoid pitfalls of his own making: the re-ordering of genres begins some twenty years before the Restoration, the book's title is also misleading because there is neither chronological nor logical progress 'from Milton to Dryden', and the Restoration lyric might have been more aptly and fully treated in relation to the Cavalier or social mode. But the scheme's defects are offset by its advantages. The concept of mode helps Miner occupy the middle ground between the old 'historical' and the new 'critical' approaches to literature. Minor works, such as Kynaston's *Leoline and Sydanis*, Cowley's *Book of Plants*, and especially Chamberlayne's *Pharonnida*, are enthusiastically revalued, and the three major poets are seen more closely in relation to each other than has been usual. Milton, Dryden and Butler turned to the public mode and to narrative forms almost contemporaneously, Milton to reward us with 'simple magnificence', Dryden to give us a feeling for 'vital reality, or, to use one of his favorite words, harmony', and Butler to induce 'a lasting fear that at the center of our hopes we shall discover degradation'. Miner is obviously happier when praising the grand conceptions of Milton and Dryden, but does not fail to convey his wonder at 'that great beast, *Hudibras*'. And in general he avoids the customary pedantries and controversies of academe, seeking always to point out 'those excellencies which should dedelight a reasonable reader'. *The Restoration Mode* is engagingly written and, I must say, beautifully printed; few critical works of its length are so consistently readable.

Another critical book on Commonwealth and Restoration poetry, David Farley-Hills's *The Benevolence of Laughter*,[7] is more limited in scope. Dr Farley-Hills remarks that despite the theoretical prestige of epic and tragedy, the period was strongest in satire and comedy, and he seeks to revalue its non-dramatic comic poetry. He distinguishes celebratory comedy, the typical Elizabethan kind; the mixture of celebratory and satirical comedy, forming burlesque, the typical Commonwealth kind; satirical comedy, the typical Restoration kind; and dispassionate, balanced comedy, found especially in Rochester. The transition from celebratory to satirical comedy is seen in the 'drolleries' or anthologies of comic poetry of the Commonwealth period, and in *Hudibras*. *Last Instructions to a Painter* is accepted as Marvell's and as the first great comic satire of the Restoration, 'arguably . . . Marvell's finest poetic achieve-

---

[6] *The Restoration Mode from Milton to Dryden*, by Earl Miner. Princeton U.P. pp. xxiv + 587. £10.50; paperback £5.10.

[7] *The Benevolence of Laughter*, by David Farley-Hills. Macmillan. pp. viii + 212. £5.95.

ment'. Dryden 'tends to think of the bad in terms of the ludicrous and the ludicrous in terms of the bad. He is therefore supremely successful at comic satire, but much less so at both non-satirical comedy and non-comic satire.' Rochester is the most original and best comic poet of the time, especially in 'Timon', 'Tunbridge Wells', 'A Satyr against Mankind', and 'Artemisia to Chloe'. He judges the world, not like Marvell and Dryden by the standards of an idealized past, 'but by the less dogmatic, more relativistic standards of a kind of sceptical rationality'. In the next century laughter became less and less permissible in serious poetry, and even now we have not quite thrown off the solemnity of Romanticism. Dr Farley-Hills's book has not fully emerged from its thesis-cocoon, but in general he is right, and he has fresh and illuminating things to say about particular poems.

(c) Prose

Two highly specialized articles come under this heading. Audrey Eccles, in 'The Reading Public, The Medical Profession, and the Use of English for Medical Books in the 16th and 17th Centuries' (*NM*), reports that early medical texts were usually in Latin and meant for University-educated physicians. The spread of literacy in English led to the translation of medical texts for use by surgeons and midwives, whose education was inferior. The physicians objected, claiming people would resort to dangerous self-medication, and quacks would multiply. The translators accused them of special pleading, and argued that their work would benefit everyone by spreading medical knowledge. By the end of the seventeenth century English was established as the medium for general medical books, but for another

century Latin remained in use for papers addressed to scholars. C. John Sommerville, 'On the Distribution of Religious and Occult Literature in Seventeenth-Century England' (*The Library*), argues that although almanacs were extremely popular in the seventeenth century as sources of astrological lore, by the time the Society for Promoting Christian Knowledge was founded in 1699 'the majority of English families, and surely all literate families, must have owned some religious books'.

2. DRYDEN

(a) General

Drydeniana is part of a series of facsimiles of scattered and rather inaccessible books, pamphlets and broadsides which can help us to understand the context of Restoration and eighteenth-century literature.[8] The publishers claim to have reprinted 'virtually all contemporary pamphlets which deal with Dryden in a substantial way'. There are 73 items, including works by Charles Blount, Settle, Shadwell and Luke Milbourne.

General essays dealt with Dryden's ideas of reason and of heroism. In recent years Philip Harth and others have tended to explain Dryden's conversion to Roman Catholicism by reference to his political views. In 'The Importance of Right Reason in Dryden's Conversion' (*Mosaic*) R. W. McHenry argues that the crucial change was not in his political views at all, but in his perhaps unconscious abandonment of the belief in 'right reason', which had been emphasized by Anglican apologists from Hooker

[8] *The Life and Times of Seven Major British Writers: Drydeniana.* New York: Garland Publishing Inc.; London: George Prior Associated Publishers Ltd. 14 vols. £151.90; individual volumes £10.85.

onwards as a source of authority independent of either private illumination or church tradition. There are signs of scepticism about this idea in *Religio Laici*; in *The Hind and the Panther* it is scarcely invoked at all. Bredvold was after all right in thinking Dryden's conversion largely the result of a change of view about reason. In 'Shifting Concepts of Heroism in Dryden's Panegyrics' (*PLL*), Michael West pursues his studies in Dryden's idea of heroism (*YW* 54.257–8; section 2 (*c*) below). Referring to a selection of panegyrical poetry and prose from *Heroique Stanzas* to the dedication to the *Fables*, West argues that 'his encomia move from hero-worship to a profounder mistrust of the hero, and a consequent effort to redefine heroic standards in Christian terms'.

(b) Poetry

Fables (1700) was added to the Scolar Press's series of Dryden facsimiles.[9] It is reproduced in the original size with a short introduction by Professor James Kinsley. Volume IV of the California *Dryden*[10] appeared, and includes *A Discourse Concerning Satire*; the translations of Juvenal and Persius; a large part of Dryden's Ovid and a foretaste of his Virgil; the epistles to Congreve and Kneller; and the ode on the death of Purcell. The translations of Juvenal and Persius are printed opposite Latin texts based on the editions of Prateus (London, 1691) and Casaubon (London, 1647) respectively. The headnotes by Frost to the *Discourse* and by Chambers to the translations

of Juvenal and Persius, especially the former, are full-scale critical essays. The commentary and textual notes are as usual in this edition extremely thorough; indeed the former in its fullness occasionally achieves comic effects, for example on 'Where the Rank Matrons, Dancing to the Pipe,/ Gig with their Bums, and are for Action ripe' (Juvenal VI 432–3): '*Gig*. "To move to and fro" (*OED*, citing this line)'. A point of special interest is that the seventeen additional and variant lines in Juvenal VI, surviving only as manuscript notes, are here printed as footnotes. The editors believe them to have been written and suppressed by Dryden himself, Dearing somewhat implausibly suggesting revision rather than censorship. Their suppression renders the text much less obscene but rather more obscure. W. B. Carnochan's 'Some suppressed verses in Dryden's translation of Juvenal VI' and a letter from Kenneth Monkman (*TLS* 21 and 28 January 1972) supplement the California editors' commentary here. *Absalom and Achitophel and Other Poems* were edited by Philip Roberts.[11] The other poems are *Mac Flecknoe, The Medal*, lines 310–509 of *The Second Part of Absalom and Achitophel*, and *Religio Laici*. The prefaces to *Absalom and Achitophel, The Medal* and *Religio Laici* are included. The texts are based on the earliest editions, 'modernised as regards punctuation, spelling and capitalisation'. To encourage readers to go straight to the texts there is no editorial introduction, though a brief preface gives us some idea of what to expect, and there is a full list of 'Principal Dates in Dryden's Life'. At the back we find extensive com-

[9] *Fables Ancient and Modern*. Menston: Scolar Press, 1973. pp. [vi]+[xlii]+646. £15.00.

[10] *The Works of John Dryden. Vol. IV: Poems 1693–1696*, ed. by A. B. Chambers and William Frost; textual editor Vinton A. Dearing. Berkeley, Los Angeles and London: U. of California P. pp. ix+824. £16.50.

[11] *Absalom and Achitophel and Other Poems*, ed. by Philip Roberts. Collins Annotated Student Texts, 1973. pp. 189. Paperback £1.25.

mentaries, critical extracts, and a bibliography; the commentaries give the necessary factual information and draw attention to characteristics of Dryden's technique, especially his use of contrast and ambiguity. Donald Thomas's *Selection from John Dryden* (*YW* 54.256) gives a rather better idea of Dryden's variety and of the background to his work, but Dr Roberts's commentary is undoubtedly more critical and sophisticated.

Several critical books considered Dryden in relation to other poets. Sanford Budick's *Poetry of Civilization*,[12] subtitled 'Mythopoeic Displacement in the Verse of Milton, Dryden, Pope and Johnson', has a complex argument which is obscured by jargon. Plato first exemplified 'mythopoeic displacement' or 'the antimythic reversion to an antecedent myth', and such 'dialectically controlled mythmaking' can be seen in Horace, Juvenal, Milton and the English Augustan poets. The chapter on Dryden emphasizes the parallels with *Paradise Lost* in *Absalom and Achitophel*, which is destructively critical of 'Whiggish myths of pastoral perfectionism' but amplifies the Tory myth of covenantal renewal. An interesting suggestion is that Dryden's hatred of Whig intrigues so affected his idea of 'plot' that the poem avoids the more obvious kinds of narrative continuity. Earl Miner's *The Restoration Mode*[6] has a chapter on 'Dryden's Heroic Idea' and a section on 'Dryden's Esteem of Merit, Man, and Love'. Miner is mainly concerned with Dryden's narrative poems; in the former, with *Annus Mirabilis, The Hind and the*

Panther and the *Aeneis*, and in the latter with the *Fables*. David Farley-Hills's *The Benevolence of Laughter*[7] has a chapter on Dryden as a writer of comedy and comic poetry, mainly about *Absalom and Achitophel*, and concluding that 'it is typical of Dryden that his finest comic poem should be devoted to the solemn purpose of expelling the comic spirit'.

Of this year's critical essays, Thomas H. Fujimura's 'The Personal Element in Dryden's Poetry' (*PMLA*) was one of the most ambitious. Fujimura argues that since 'the triumph of Romanticism' the personal element in Dryden has been 'de-emphasized'; at least, Miner and other authorities have overemphasized the idea that Dryden is a 'public poet'. Dryden's best poetry after 1685 is strongly personal, says Fujimura, though 'the literary strategies available to a neoclassical poet facilitated the generalization of the private theme' and so tended to obscure it. From the satirist's apologia in the Oldham elegy, through the self-questioning of the Roman Catholic convert in the Anne Killigrew ode and the bitterness of the deposed laureate in the epistle to Congreve, and finally in the triumphant dramatization of his powers as a poet in *Alexander's Feast*, 'we can see the progress of Dryden's mind and spirit'. Some details in the argument are questionable: surely the Oldham elegy is more than a satirist's apologia, since Dryden implies Oldham was merely a satirist, and could not have written, say, a fine elegy? The general line of argument is acceptable, but will probably not seriously disturb Miner and the rest: one can see what they mean when the Oldham elegy is compared with *Lycidas*. And in a debate between these two sides critical points could easily be neglected; public or private,

[12] *Poetry of Civilization. Mythopoeic Displacement in the Verse of Milton, Dryden, Pope, and Johnson*, by Sanford Budick. New Haven and London: Yale U.P. pp. xv + 179. £4.90.

the Congreve poem still seems a splendidly ridiculous engine for hoisting Congreve's bust onto Shakespeare's pedestal.

There were rather fewer essays than usual on Dryden's original poetry. James Black, in 'Dryden on Shadwell's Theatre of Violence' (*DR*), sees *Mac Flecknoe* as less a lampoon on Shadwell and more a satire on bad plays generally. The violence of language and action in Shadwell's comedies, particularly *The Libertine*, is a major target, but the poem also expresses Dryden's growing disillusionment with the heroic drama. The essay includes helpful explanations of various allusions. Christopher R. Reaske, in 'A Shakespearean Backdrop for Dryden's *Mac Flecknoe*?' (*SQ*), notes similarities between Shadwell and Falstaff. Thomas E. Maresca's discussion of 'The Context of Dryden's *Absalom and Achitophel*' (*ELH*) is difficult to follow and impossible to summarize. The 'context' is not something outside the poem, but the effect obtained by setting the story 'in pious times' before the establishment of the Levitical priesthood, so that David 'lives under the dominion of grace, in a kind of golden world where what nature prompts is after God's own heart'. The opening lines also establish 'a subsidiary dialectic of grace, law and nature', and the poem contains 'an image cluster which sums up fully all the ramifications of this dialectic', since 'the relations of fathers and sons, the metaphors of paternity and sonship, offer the key to the totality of the poem'. David exercises authority in his kingdom as does a father in his family or God in the universe; with Professor Maresca, apparently, as a loyal subject. Margaret Duggan, in 'Mythic Components in Dryden's *Hind and Panther*' (*CL*), argues that the

Panther represents Latitudinarianism, and allusions to many characters in Ovid's *Metamorphoses* associate her with 'a multiplicity of archetypal wrongdoings'. The Hind of course represents Roman Catholicism, and Ovidian allusions associate her with good characters who are misunderstood and victimized; but in her case some allusions, particularly those to Io, create difficulties. For example, the Hind is like Io in being hunted, but unlike her in not being an adultress; Dryden while underlining the one parallel cannot entirely erase the other. Ms. Duggan concludes that seeing the Hind 'as an evocation of the Church as Spouse of Christ explains and interprets the subliminal elements of the Io myth in Dryden's poem'. This conclusion is ingenious, and the essay as a whole is illuminating, though like most discussions of allusion in poetry it assumes a superbly fit audience of people who can simultaneously remember and forget.

Among essays on or relating to Dryden's translations, Eric A. Havelock's 'The *Aeneid* and its Translators' (*HudR*) should not be missed. It is exceptionally well written and challenging, and if its arguments are accepted it must revolutionize our thinking on Virgil. According to Havelock, the *Aeneid* has traditionally been seen as in essence a civilized, 'proto-Christian' heroic narrative, so translators have aimed at a smoothly flowing style, with effects of grandeur and elegance, and have done less than justice to the poem's psychological complexity and emotional turbulence. A tendency to confine the poem 'in a rhetorical strait-jacket' is seen 'at its most extreme' in Dryden, who thus occupies a central place in a tradition of misunderstanding from Dante to T. S. Eliot. Dryden enthusiasts should also find time for 'Wordsworth's *Aeneid*' by Willard Spiegel-man (*CL*). Comparisons between Dryden's and Wordsworth's versions show that Dryden is relatively good where pomp and energy are wanted, and relatively weak at rendering the *lacrimae rerum* (a phrase Dryden omits entirely). William Frost's 'Dryden's Versions of Ovid' (*CL*) is a discursive essay, well illustrated, seeking to show that 'Ovid's inventive-ness as a psychologist of ordinary life, a poet-social-scientist treating a galaxy of moral dilemmas arising out of human sexuality . . . endeared him to Dryden', and inspired translations which remain 'unsurpassed'. D. W. Hopkins had two notes on Dryden and Ovid in *N&Q*: 'Two Hitherto Unrecorded Sources for Dryden's Ovid Translations' are translations of Ovid by Charles Hopkins and Peter Ker, and 'Dryden and Sandys's Ovid: A Note' concerns a hitherto unremarked quotation from Sandys's Ovid in *An Essay of Dramatic Poesy*.

Having commended H. James Jensen's 'Comparing the Arts in the Age of Baroque' (*ECS* 1973; *YW* 53.262) I must draw attention to W. John Rempel's 'The Sound of Trum-pets' (*ECS*). Rempel corrects and supplements Jensen: baroque trum-pets had a softer sound than Jensen supposes, and Dryden's stanza on violins in *A Song for St Cecilia's Day* refers to the tone and character of music for violins compared with that for viols. While Rempel may be right about baroque trumpets, Jensen cannot be wholly wrong about what Dryden expects when '*The* TRUM-PET *shall be heard on high* . . . *And* MUSICK *shall untune the Sky*': that must surely be an awful sound. William A. McIntosh considers Handel's settings of *A Song for St Cecilia's Day* and *Alexander's Feast* in 'Handel and the Muse' (*Cithara*, 1973).

(c) *Drama*

Dryden's Rhymed Heroic Tragedies,[13] by Michael W. Alssid, is based on a dissertation completed in 1959. The work's origin has not been disguised, though the biblio-graphy and footnotes have been updated. Alssid reviews criticism of the heroic plays down to about 1970, somewhat allusively for the last ten years; explains Dryden's explanation of 'The Idea of Heroic Tragedy'; analyses *The Indian Emperor, Tyrannic Love, The Conquest of Granada* and *Aureng-Zebe*; discusses their 'language' or style; and finally explores some relations between them and Dryden's other poetry. Dryden tried to unite epic and tragedy, and at times Alssid seems to be trying to unite heroic tragedy and dissertation; the work is inordinately long, divided into five chapters, and written in stilted prose which keeps lapsing into absurdity (for instance where he explains how Dryden's characters differ from those of an unnamed 'dramatist like Shakespeare'). The analytical chapter compels most ad-miration, and parts of it have already appeared as articles (*YW* 43.191, 46.220).

I have noted only two articles on Dryden's plays, one of them omitted last year. Michael West, in 'Dryden and the Disintegration of Renaissance Heroic Ideals' (*Costerus*, 1973), argues that 'the entire progression of Dryden's dramas is perhaps best explained as the final stage in the decay of Renaissance ideals of Christian heroism'. Susan Staves, in 'Why Was Dryden's Mr. Limberham Banned?' (*RECTR*), reopens that

[13] *Dryden's Rhymed Heroic Tragedies: A Critical Study of the Plays and of their Place in Dryden's Poetry*, by Michael W. Alssid. (Salzburg Studies in English Literature: Poetic Drama, 7). Salzburg: Institut für Englische Sprache und Literatur. 2 vols., pp. [viii]+429.

question and after a thorough examination of the evidence concludes that 'we do not know'. It was not banned because it was too obscene or too effective as a satire on keeping mistresses; nor because Limberham was taken to represent Shaftesbury or any of his party; nor because he was meant to represent the Earl of Lauderdale, Charles II, or James Duke of York. Possibly some of the audience 'decided to apply the character of Limberham to the Earl', and Charles as Lauderdale's protector decided to ban the play.

(d) Prose

Dryden's translation of Louis Maimbourg's *Histoire de la Ligue* was edited by Alan Roper for the California *Dryden*.[14] *The History of the League* was the only work of Dryden's which had not been reprinted in its entirety since it was first published. It is now reprinted 'almost *literatim*' from the first edition. Roper says 'Drydenians', as distinct from 'lovers of literature' generally, should perhaps be able to read it, 'if not with pleasure, at least with interest', because it 'bears upon some of the more important questions we have come to ask about Dryden. These are questions about his sense of history and translation; his conversion—the obscure pathway from *Religio Laici* to *The Hind and the Panther;* his prose style and the mind it reveals'. These points are elaborated in a long learned introduction and detailed explanatory notes, though the light thrown on that obscure pathway is dim as the borrowed beams of moon and stars. Roper returns to the definition of 'Characteristics of Dryden's Prose' in an essay in *ELH*. He

analyses the translations of Maimbourg and the first book of the *Annales* of Tacitus. 'Dryden's adventures with succinct Tacitus and copious Maimbourg show us how to identify important features of Dryden's original prose, so different from theirs'. We note some faults, but we become aware of his 'confident movement through time, space, or the points of an argument', his tendency to subsume analysis under drama or narrative, his 'emphasis upon human actors, upon people doing things', his genius for 'the word not merely apt, but striking, the word not merely just, but lively'. Whatever those who argue about Dryden's real or apparent scepticism may say, his exploratory syntax expresses 'a mind naturally diffident or sceptical', while his diction expresses sometimes authority and always confidence. This Dryden is at his best in the preface to the *Fables*. Roper's own style here has something of his master's eloquence. In another detailed analysis of Dryden's prose, 'Ease and Control in Dryden's Prose Style' (*SHR*), Gary Stringer argues that 'Dryden's prose style is best described as a blending of restraint and freedom', and that in 'the interplay between the abstract and the concrete' Dryden 'comes very near the ideal'.

Dryden's criticism received attention in C. H. Salter's trenchantly written and well-illustrated essay on 'Dryden and Addison' (*MLR*). But Salter is mainly out to prove Addison a much less intelligent and original critic than Dryden; I would not have thought many people needed convincing of that. Poor Addison emerges as a plagiarizing student of the worst sort, concealing his sources or affecting to disagree with them, if necessary by misrepresentation. Who would not weep, if Atticus were he!

[14] *The Works of John Dryden. Vol. XVIII: Prose: The History of the League 1684*, ed. by Alan Roper; textual editor Vinton A. Dearing. Berkeley, Los Angeles and London: U. of California P. pp. ix + 577.

3. OTHER AUTHORS
(a) Poets

There were valuable critiques of Samuel Butler in two of the general books noticed above, and highly specialized articles in two of the learned journals. Earl Miner[6] has a chapter on 'Butler: Hating Our Physician' and a subsection on 'The Return of Justice in *Hudibras*'. The former is particularly good, seeing *Hudibras* as a whole and stressing the 'central role of the Lady, and of her prototype, Trulla'. The latter comes to the conclusion that '*das ewig weibliche* sets things right in a way other than that imagined by Goethe'; in the enthusiasm of his peroration Miner nods over his German, but the contrast is certainly striking. David Farley-Hills[7] quotes the poem's nineteenth-century editor, the Revd. George Gilfillan, in support of his view that Butler in the end laughed himself into sympathy with his hero, so *Hudibras* should be seen not as a satire but as a farce obscured by satirical passages. Sv. Brunn, in 'The Date of Samuel Butler's *The Elephant in the Moon*' (*ES*), argues that this satire was finished somewhere between November 1675 and August 1676. There is an allusion to it in La Fontaine's *Un animal dans la lune*. Ann Kline Kelly notes 'A Rowlands–Butler–Swift Parallel' (*N&Q*).

Rochester's life and work continue to stir the imagination and were this year subjects of two books and a number of critical articles. John Adlard's *The Debt to Pleasure*[15] is an anthology of accounts of Rochester by his contemporaries, and of his own

poetry and prose, so arranged as to form 'a composite biography' and to 'present a man who broke through the cold crust of conventional behaviour to explore freely pleasure, violence, and love'. The texts are reliably reproduced so far as I can judge (though 'tear' for 'tears' in 'Absent from thee, I languish still' is debatable), and spelling, punctuation and capitalization have been sensibly modernized. Among items which are previously unpublished or not easily obtainable are extracts from *Sodom, or The Quintessence of Debauchery*, a work which may not be Rochester's but which evidently includes spirited and funny passages as Adlard says. Graham Greene's *Lord Rochester's Monkey*[16] is less enthusiastic. This life of the poet was written around 1931 to 1934 and was turned down by Heinemann, presumably because of the danger of prosecution for obscenity. To please an age more gallant than the last it has now been issued in coffee-table format with many well-chosen and finely reproduced illustrations, including Lely's naked Nelly. The text has been but little revised in the light of recent research. Greene knows scholars now believe Rochester was not responsible for the Rose Alley attack on Dryden, but not that they think a speech on the Exclusion Bill formerly attributed to Rochester was actually by Lawrence Hyde, as he could have discovered by reading David Vieth's annotated bibliography in his edition of the *Complete Poems*. And Greene might have taken more seriously Vieth's findings on the canon and text of the poems. Yet the book as a whole is more scholarly than it may at first seem. Greene has 'tried hard' and successfully 'to

[15] *The Debt to Pleasure. John Wilmot, Earl of Rochester, in the eyes of his contemporaries and in his own poetry and prose*, ed. by John Adlard. Cheadle Hulme, Cheshire: Carcanet Press Ltd. pp. 141. £2.20; paperback 95p.

[16] *Lord Rochester's Monkey*, by Graham Greene. Bodley Head. pp. 231. 221 illustrations, 22 in colour. £5.

avoid any unacknowledged use of the imagination', but has used his novelist's gifts in interpreting the rather limited sources and filling in the background. He thinks Rochester may have inherited his habits of dissipation from his aristocratic father, and his awareness of Puritan values from his Puritan mother. He associates the bad habits with London and the moral awareness with the regular visits to the country estates. Rochester's satirical poetry was the work of a 'spoiled Puritan . . . who hated immorality in others'. Burnet's account of his conversations with Rochester is accordingly found 'convincing', but there is no mention at all of the influence of the freethinker Charles Blount, which Adlard believes could have been healthier than Burnet's had it been more sustained. As Greene almost admits, while Rochester's deathbed repentance was genuine enough in its way, it is doubtful if he was fully convinced of the truth of religion; more probably he retained his belief that the right use of reason was to teach men to enjoy life, and repented only that he had not restrained his excesses. This is more than a coffee-table book; it is a serious, sympathetic, but unrevised study of Rochester as a burnt-out case.

Among critical studies David Farley-Hills's[7] is the most detailed and comprehensive. His book includes two chapters on Rochester, dealing with the lyrical and burlesque poetry but emphasizing the major satires, especially 'Artemisia' and 'A Satyr against Mankind'. He concludes: 'In Rochester's satires man is seen on his own. Unable to rely on a god-given order, he uses his rational faculties not to solve the problem of his being, for that is insoluble, but to come to terms with the fact of its insolubility.' Rochester's rejection of Christian eschatology is the theme of Reba Wilcoxon's 'Rochester's Philosophical Premises: A Case for Consistency' (ECS). That there is no place for rewards and punishments other than this life is stated in his translations of passages from Lucretius ('The gods, by right of nature, must possess') and Seneca ('After death, nothing is, and nothing, death'), and implied in 'Upon Nothing' and 'A Satyr against Mankind'. Rochester distrusted *a priori* reasoning and favoured a theory of knowledge based on sense perception. He believed pleasure was the greatest good, but knew that some pleasures were better than others, as can be seen in 'Upon Nothing', 'A Satyr against Mankind', and even such an apparently simple song as 'Love and Life'. These philosophical premises are self-consistent and help to explain the prevalence of obscenity, parody and paradox in his poetry. From the premises we descend or, according to the point of view, ascend to the conclusions. Carole Fabricant, in the normally chaste pages of *JEGP*, gives a detailed account of 'Rochester's World of Imperfect Enjoyment'. Despite the poet's reputation as libertine and sensualist, his poems are obsessively concerned with the failure of sex; ideal sexual experience is invoked only for its remoteness from ordinary experience to be stressed. Other Restoration poets often enough describe sexual experience in unattractive terms, but do not go as far as Rochester 'in showing how a world of dynamic potency can turn abruptly into a universe of irreparable decay'. Among the many poems about impotence, Rochester's 'The Imperfect Enjoyment' is remarkable for its bitterness, compared with the more calmly ironic or resigned tone of the others. Etherege, in his 'Imperfect Enjoyment', actually blames his mistress, and others suggest that the failure is only temporary, but Rochester's violent curse on his member suggests the end of all physical pleasure. So Rochester is at his most eloquent when expressing his disgust with sex. We are reminded not so much of Donne's *Songs and Sonets* as of his *Devotions*, where there is a similar sense of bodily failure as characteristic of human life. This remarkable essay does much to explain the horrid fascination of Rochester, though Ms. Fabricant suggests something she presumably does not mean when she says that in 'Could I but make my wishes insolent' the fop 'quite literally' suffers from 'sex in the head'. Finally, two essays omitted from *YW* 54 may be noted: in '"An Allusion to Horace"'; The Politics of John Wilmot, Earl of Rochester' (*DUJ*, 1973) Joseph A. Johnson Jr. argues that Rochester should be seen as a serious poet and critic, and in 'Rochester's "The Maim'd Debauchee"': A Poem to Rival Marvell' (*EnlE*, 1973) Stuart Silverman offers a highly personal interpretation of Rochester's poem.

Two articles of more specialized interest deserve mention. In 'Rochester and Defoe: A Study in Influence' (*SEL*), John McVeagh claims that 'as man and poet, Rochester captured Defoe's imagination'. Throughout Defoe's work Rochester is named or quoted more than any other author. Defoe wrote mainly in support of Enlightenment orthodoxy, but nihilistic ideas fascinated him and were associated by him with Rochester, who had given them witty and memorable expression. Rochester is partly responsible for those glimpses Defoe gives us of man's darker side. In 'Rochester's "Impromptu on Louis XIV"' (*N&Q*) A. S. G. Edwards quotes a Latin version of the couplet, from a commonplace book dating probably from the late 1670s, tending to confirm Vieth in attributing the couplet to the poet. This commonplace book also includes, incidentally, the play *Sodom*.

John Oldham is the subject of a brief critical account by Earl Miner in *The Restoration Mode*.[6] Miner confesses that 'those of us who think our own lives have moved from a poverty like Oldham's to a small estate with books and friends can have a fondness for Oldham', but 'truth requires me to say that by the standards I have tried to exercise Oldham is a poet of shreds and patches and occasional flights'. He somewhat despairingly suggests that 'if we knew the man better, we might find greater coherence in his poetry'. Scholars are labouring to supply such knowledge. In two articles in *N&Q* K. E. Robinson gives new facts about 'The Family of John Oldham' and identifies a borrowing from Oldham in *The Art of Sinking in Poetry*. Harold F. Brooks gives detailed attention to 'The Chief Substantive Editions of Oldham's Poems, 1679–1684: Printers, Compositors, and Publication' (*SB*). Bibliographical evidence confirms that, apart from 'A Satyr Against Vertue' in *Satyrs Against the Jesuits*, all the authorized first editions were almost certainly printed from autograph copy, and apart from *Satyrs Against The Jesuits* all may very well have been set up by the same compositor. Yet Brooks ends with a warning for bibliographers in other fields: in the absence of the author's manuscripts, proceeding on the evidence of compositor analysis alone, he would have adopted for his forthcoming edition certain spellings which are not Oldham's.

Since the death of Samuel Garth 'little attempt has been made to evaluate the poetic quality of *The*

Dispensary', John F. Sena reports. His essay on 'Samuel Garth's *The Dispensary*' (*TSLL*) supplies this want. He considers that the poem's most effective satire is found in the character sketches and in some digressions on the vanities of the beau monde; it also contains good descriptions, especially in the night-pieces. But as a whole it is limited by its subject, the quarrel between the physicians and the apothecaries, in which Garth was too heavily committed to the physicians' side. Sena thus reaches a conclusion which was more pithily stated by a critic he does not mention: since *The Dispensary* has ceased to be 'supported by accidental and extrinsick popularity, it has been scarcely able to support itself' (Johnson). In a modest way it continues to support scholarship. In 'The Birthplace of Samuel Garth' (*AN&Q*), Sena shows that Garth was born at Bolam, Co. Durham, not in Yorkshire as his biographers have supposed, and presumably went to school at the neighbouring village of Ingleton.

Finally, one article about a very minor poet and two about anonymous poems. Sir Geoffrey Keynes introduces and prints in full 'An Unrecorded Poem by Sir William Petty' (*BC*, pp. 179–86 and 575–6). It is an elegy on the Earl of Ossory, of which another printed copy, with a manuscript attribution to Petty, was found recently after an I.R.A. bomb had damaged the library at Caledon Castle, Co. Tyrone. Petty's poem is admittedly terrible, so Keynes might have pointed out that the Earl's death also inspired some rather bombastic lines in *Absalom and Achitophel*. Robert Willman, in 'A Note on the Date of "Popish Politics Unmasked"' (*N&Q*), argues that this satirical broadside is incorrectly dated in the recent edition of *Poems on Affairs*

of State. It belongs to the summer of 1680 rather than the winter of 1680–1. Hence perhaps 'illegal organization and armed risings were more seriously considered by the Whigs in the summer of 1680, before the failure of parliamentary Exclusion, than historians have hitherto believed'. Gillian Fansler Brown in '"The Session of Poets to the Tune of Cook Lawrel": Playhouse Evidence for Composition Date of 1664' (*RECTR*), argues that this satire too is incorrectly dated in *Poems on Affairs of State*.

(b) Dramatists

Charlene M. Taylor's edition of Etherege's *She Would if She Could*[17] was briefly noticed in *YW* 52, but as the book is now available in Britain it deserves further comment. The editing is competent, though I noted an error at I.i.28: for 'bring' read 'bringing'. In her introduction Professor Taylor seeks to show that this play, described by Pepys as 'mighty insipid', never more than moderately successful on the stage, and no longer in the professional repertoire, nonetheless has great historical importance. If 'Restoration comedy gains its distinctive nature ... from its fusion of social, romantic, artificial, and intellectual strains', then *She Would if She Could* has a strong claim to being considered the first play of the new kind. The strongest satire is directed against Lady Cockwood, the forerunner of such amorous ladies as Loveit, Fidget and Wishfort. Courtall and Freeman are true Restoration gallants: witty, perceptive and not altogether dishonourable libertines. The witty heroines Gatty and Ariana are still more of an influential innovation. The play works

---

[17] *She Would if She Could*, by Sir George Etherege, ed. by Charlene M. Taylor. (RRestDS). Arnold, 1973. pp. xxix+132. £1·80; paperback 90p.

round to a typically tentative and ironic resolution, and uses several devices to insist on its own artificiality and so make the audience think about what is presented. But it is debatable whether some devices which Professor Taylor says create 'alienation', such as asides, are not just evidence of clumsy writing.

Etherege is the only Restoration dramatist whose personal correspondence survives in any quantity. It nearly all belongs to the years 1685–88 when Etherege was English Resident to the Diet of the Holy Roman Empire at Ratisbon. Since the last edition more letters and better texts have become available, and a new selection has now been edited by Frederick Bracher.[18] He lists more than 400 letters, but has printed only what he thinks should be most interesting to students of Etherege and English literature, though he has 'interpreted this principle broadly' for letters not previously published. Hence about 230 letters are printed in whole or part, of which about half appear for the first time. Bracher supplies a useful and up-to-date sketch of Etherege's life, helpful notes, and a good index. Etherege emerges as a satirical observer of the diplomatic scene and, more surprisingly, a fanatical supporter of King James II.

Two articles emphasized the political bias of Dryden's enemies. In 'Political Satire in *The Rehearsall*' (*YEB*) George McFadden does not deny that Dryden's heroic plays are ridiculed by Buckingham, but argues that the burlesque was meant to 'set up a barrier of English common sense between all-too-human royalty and the kind of divinizing public adulation which Louis XIV received in

France'. McFadden refers to Dryden's claim that 'my betters were more concerned than I was in that satire', and brings forward evidence to suggest that the 'Two Kings of Brentford' were Charles II and James Duke of York, and that Bayes was Henry Bennet, Earl of Arlington, who was Buckingham's chief enemy among Charles's ministers at the time. In 'The Significance of Thomas Shadwell' (*SP*), Alan S. Fisher argues that 'Shadwell more than any other writer of his time, was Laureate of Whiggery'. Whiggery must be taken to mean a self-confident literal-mindedness and a determination to make explicit what more sceptical Tory writers were generally content only to suggest. Shadwell's comedies tend to show, perhaps most explicitly in *The Scowrers*, that gentlemen rakes can do no wrong, whether they reform or not; and in his adaptation of *Timon of Athens*, the Duke of Buckingham 'becomes the hero ... in the role of Alcibiades', restoring liberty to the city.

There were no major contributions to Wycherley studies this year. In '"Where are your Maskers?" Queries about the finale in Wycherley's *The Country Wife*' (*Archiv*) H. M. Klein wonders whether Horner's question near the end of the play, 'Doctor, where are your maskers?' should have been a request for musicians addressed to Sir Jasper Fidget. As Klein sees evidence of either hasty writing or textual corruption, it may be worth noting that the problem seems to disappear in the theatre. An exchange of views between Ben R. Schneider Jr. and Ian Donaldson (*N&Q*), arising from Donaldson's adverse review of *The Ethos of Restoration Comedy* (see also *YW* 52.255–6), bears interestingly on the interpretation of *The Plain Dealer*. George Weales's 'William

---

[18] *Letters of Sir George Etherege*, ed. by Frederick Bracher. U. of California P. pp. xxv+324. £15.

Wycherley' (*MQR* 1973, not mentioned in *YW* 54) is a good general survey of Wycherley's life and work.

The standard biographical work on Otway and Lee was reprinted.[19] A study of Otway's tragedies, *From Heroics to Sentimentalism* by Hazel M. Batzer Pollard,[20] is essentially a doctoral dissertation of 1956. Footnotes and bibliography have been thoroughly updated, but arguments and conclusions are little changed. The main influences on Otway in rough chronological order were heroic drama, Racine, and Shakespeare. In *Alcibiades* and *Don Carlos* he is already showing signs of emancipation from heroic drama; in his adaptation of *Bérénice* he looks to Racine for an excuse for his own inclination to focus on the sufferings of a sympathetic hero and heroine; in *Caius Marius, The Orphan* and *Venice Preserved* he develops his own creative powers more surely and freely under the influence of Shakespeare. In his last three tragedies he has abandoned heroic drama for 'the drama of sensibility'—he has also abandoned rhyme for blank verse, a point which deserved greater prominence. This development is judged to be mainly for the better; *The Orphan* is excessively sentimental but the extravagances of both heroics and sentimentalism are avoided in *Caius Marius* to some extent, and in *Venice Preserved* almost entirely. It seems to follow that 'the drama of sensibility' needed tempering with realism, satire

and farce, though that is not one of Dr Batzer's conclusions, and the 'Nicky-Nacky' scenes of *Venice Preserved* are left in the decent obscurity of a learned footnote. Dr Batzer undoubtedly deserved her Ph.D., but I think that even in 1956 her views were rather less startlingly original than she and her husband, who contributes a panegyrical prologue, would have us believe. A not dissimilar view of *Venice Preserved* is taken by Jack D. Durant in '"Honor's Toughest Task": Family and State in *Venice Preserved*' (*SP*). He argues that the play is not fundamentally pessimistic. The tranquillity of Jaffeir and Belvidera at the end of Act I, the reformation of Priuli, and the criticism of the doctrines of heroic friendship affirm 'the sacramental integrity of marriage and family relationships'. Domestic tranquillity is analogous to political stability: 'Through the tragic sufferings of Jaffeir, Belvidera, and Priuli, and through the flawed sexual and social ethics of Pierre, Antonio, and Aquilena, Otway points the way to political ruin: the abandonment of family covenants for the sake of appetites, petty sentiments, heroic posturings, and vain republican dreams'. But the total effect is surely more complex than Durant's phrase 'Tory affirmation' allows, since Antonio, whose sexual and social ethics may well be thought flawed, is not a republican plotter but a member of the establishment.

With Congreve 'the present Age of Wit obscures the past', according to Dryden, because in *The Double Dealer* he successfully mixes Jonsonian and Fletcherian elements. Audiences have generally found the mixture unpalatable, however, and in '"The Mixed Way of Comedy": Congreve's *The Double Dealer*' (*MP*) Brian Corman nicely articulates our

---

[19] *Otway and Lee: Biography from a Baroque Age*, by Roswell Gray Ham. Greenwood Press Reprints, Westport Publications Ltd. pp. xiv+250. £8.
[20] *From Heroics to Sentimentalism: A Study of Thomas Otway's Tragedies*, by Hazel M. Batzer Pollard. (Salzburg Studies in English Literature: Poetic Drama, 10). Salzburg: Institut für Englische Sprache und Literatur. pp. iv+301.

critical reactions. Congreve sought to combine the Jonsonian form of comedy, showing the punishment of villainy, with the Fletcherian or typical Restoration form, showing the triumph of sympathetic heroes and heroines. Lady Touchwood and Maskwell are villains in the tradition of Volpone and Mosca, but in the interests of comedy are less threatening and attractive; Mellefont and Cynthia are innocent victims in the tradition of Bonario and Celia, but at times are more like the usual witty lovers of Restoration comedy. So the audience does not always know how to respond; the balance of serious main plot and frivolous sub-plot is upset; and the ending is unsatisfactory. Corman concludes that 'it took Sheridan, who further reduced the power of his rogues and thus diluted greatly the punitive nature of his comedy, to produce a more satisfying ending from similar materials in *The School for Scandal*'. Another interesting Congreve item was D. F. McKenzie's review for *N&Q* of John Barnard's edition of *The Way of the World* (*YW* 53.265). McKenzie strongly objects to the use of the first quarto as copy-text. Since the text of the collected *Works* of 1710 and 1719–20 was clearly what Congreve wanted posterity to read, 'the only possible procedure' for a modern editor is to choose one of those and then eliminate errors.

Vanbrugh's *Provoked Wife* was edited for the New Mermaids by James L. Smith.[21] The fully modernized text is based on the first edition, with the revised scenes in an appendix. In his critical introduction Mr Smith argues for the play's coherence as a sort of Shavian marriage debate,

but he is well aware of its farcical side, and of Vanbrugh's 'ultimate affection' for his characters. This awareness comes partly from a thorough study of the stage history, of which we are given a lively sketch. The revised scenes, where Sir John Brute is disguised as a woman, are rightly considered even funnier and better than the original ones, where he is disguised as a parson. The woman-hater's impersonation of his own wife is psychologically interesting, and reflects ironically on Lady Fancyfull as well as Lady Brute. Mr. Smith's annotations are helpful and unobtrusive; altogether this is an excellent and reasonably priced edition of this strangely neglected masterpiece. *The Relapse*, which is far more often performed, has now been added to the Davis-Poynter playscripts series.[22] *The Provoked Husband*, Colley Cibber's completed and revised version of Vanbrugh's *A Journey to London*, was edited by Peter Dixon for the Regents Restoration Drama series.[23] In his introduction Mr Dixon shows that Cibber has so changed the direction of Vanbrugh's original, and so 'taken the edge off Vanbrugh's forcefulness', that although about a third of *The Provoked Husband* derives from Vanbrugh it is essentially Cibber's play. Cibber's further changes after the first performance were meant to make the play more acceptable to the contemporary audience, and affected his own work as well as Vanbrugh's, so Mr Dixon has justifiably used the first version of the first edition as copy-text. He has investigated these difficult textual problems with great

[21] *The Provoked Wife*, by Sir John Vanbrugh, ed. by James L. Smith. (New Mermaids Series). Benn. pp. xxxii+128. Paperback, 90p.

[22] *The Relapse*. A Davis–Poynter Playscript. pp. [x]+145. Paperback £1.50.
[23] *The Provoked Husband*, by Sir John Vanbrugh and Colley Cibber, ed. by Peter Dixon. (RRestDS.) U. of Nebraska P., 1974. Arnold, 1975. pp. xxvii+176. £4; paperback, £1.95.

thoroughness, and has produced the best modern edition of the play.

A new biography of Vanbrugh, *Masks and Façades* by Madeleine Bingham,[24] will please those who like good-humoured lives of famous people. Its general style is gossipy, though in Vanbrugh's case there does not seem to be very much to gossip about. He was a successful playwright who suddenly took to architecture, and a confirmed bachelor who suddenly took to marriage. He apparently succeeded at everything in great style, offending nobody except the impossible Sarah Duchess of Marlborough, who insisted on thinking that an Englishman's home need not literally be his castle. There are many apt quotations from Vanbrugh's letters. The book does not throw much new light on the genius that is evident enough in the plays and still more at Castle Howard, Blenheim and Seaton Delavel. Among the many excellent illustrations, however, are engravings of these and other buildings from *Vitruvius Britannicus*. Miss Bingham can be added to Lincoln B. Faller's list of those who have given Vanbrugh less than due credit for 'subtlety and seriousness' in *The Relapse* and *The Provoked Wife*. Faller knows these plays are very funny, but in 'Between Jest and Earnest: The Comedy of Sir John Vanbrugh' (*MP*) he rightly says that Lord Foppington's wit, aplomb and genuine decency save him from becoming merely a comic butt, and we laugh at Sir John Brute's beastliness 'because we are at a loss to respond any other way'. The plays end conventionally with betrothals or marriages, but are more deeply concerned with marriages in the process

of collapse. In *The Relapse*, Tom Fashion is dubiously rewarded with Miss Hoyden, while Vanbrugh poses the problem of Amanda, bewildered at the discovery of her husband's faithlessness; in *The Provoked Wife*, marriage for Belinda and Heartfree is 'a great leap in the dark', while Vanbrugh explores the dilemma of Lady Brute, unable either to love or to deceive her vicious husband. He is distinguished from earlier Restoration dramatists by a sympathetic insight into such human problems, and from later eighteenth-century ones by an unwillingness to dispose of them by sentimental and unrealistic means. This is a stimulating critical article; others on Vanbrugh this year are of less general interest. In 'Vanbrugh: Additions to the Correspondence' (*PQ*) Arthur R. Huseboe considers two letters and a memorandum which were not included in Webb's edition of Vanbrugh's letters, and which relate to his work as opera manager and as architect. In '"Lead Out" in Vanbrugh's *The Provoked Wife*' (*N&Q*) Huseboe explains this phrase in IV.ii as a reference to gentlemanly customs of ceremonious attendance on ladies. In 'The Original and "Improved" Comedies of Sir John Vanbrugh: Their Nineteenth-Century London Stage History' (*RECTR*; corrigenda, vol. xiii no. 2, p. 62) Barry N. Olshen considers *The Confederacy, The Relapse* and Sheridan's adaptation, *A Trip to Scarborough*, and *The Provoked Husband*. The so-called improvements were prompted at least as much by concern for decency and decorum as by theatrical requirements.

Articles on Farquhar dealt with his army career, the interpretation of *The Constant Couple*, and the stage history of *The Beaux Stratagem*. In 'George Farquhar's Military Career' (*HLQ*)

---

[24] *Masks and Façades*, by Madeleine Bingham. George Allen & Unwin Ltd. pp. 376. 24 plates and 3 line illustrations. £6.95.

Robert John Jordan showed that Farquhar was more involved in the Earl of Orrery's Regiment than has been thought. The army seemed to promise security, but led to financial embarrassment; yet Farquhar's army experiences aided his development as a writer, and his widow's military pension was perhaps an oblique reward for his literary achievements. Jordan's statement that 'Whitchurch in Lancashire' was the regiment's 'point of embarkation for Ireland' in 1704 cannot be correct, since Whitchurch is in Shropshire and is not a port; presumably he means Whitehaven, Cumberland. In '*The Constant Couple*: Farquhar's Four Plays in One' (*ELH*), Jackson I. Cope contends that the play is 'a comedy of wit; a burlesque; a scandalous *roman-à-clef*; and a problem play'. It has various standard characters and situations of Restoration comedy, but in its revised version especially it is a pointed burlesque on Lee's *Rival Queens* and heroic drama generally, a scandalous comment on the relationship in real life between two of the leading players, and hence a reminder to the audience of the difference between heroic posturing and everyday cynicism. If Cope's interpretation is accepted it must considerably raise our respect for Farquhar as a playwright, though the effectiveness of the play evidently depended on knowledge beyond the reach of a modern audience. In '*The Beaux' Stratagem* on the Nineteenth Century London Stage' (*TN*) Barry N. Olshen shows that the play continued to be revived often enough early last century, and despite cuts there were no radical changes in its plot, characters, and general spirit. But by 1856 much bowdlerization was needed; all references to beds, for instance, had to go.

Finally some articles on minor figures. Anthony Hammond's 'John Wilson and the Andronicus Plays: A Reconsideration' (*YES*) looks at three plays about the Byzantine usurper, Andronicus Comnenius. Hammond agrees with an inscription in the British Museum copy of the anonymous *Andronicus* (1661): 'Verry Badd'; *The Unfortunate Usurper* (1663), also anonymous, is hackwork; Wilson's *Andronicus Comnenius* (1664), though faulty, has its good points, notably the rather Shakespearean blank verse. All three use Thomas Fuller's account of Andronicus's life as a source, and draw or hint at a parallel between Andronicus and Cromwell. Robert M. Otten's 'Son of Ben, Son of Brugis: A New Source for John Wilson's *The Projectors*' (*RECTR*) shows that Wilson was indebted to Thomas Brugis's *The Discovery of a Projector* (1641). Charles L. Batten Jr., in 'The Source of Aphra Behn's *The Widow Ranter*' (*RECTR*), says she may have known the pamphlet *Strange News from Virginia*, as has been assumed, but she must also have used the Report of the King's Commission on the Virginian rebellion, or an account closely derived from it. R. J. Jordan throws light on 'Thomas Southerne's Marriage' (*N&Q*). He married Agnes, daughter of Sir Richard Atkins, sometime sheriff of Buckinghamshire; she was a widow with two children, but she probably brought him an income of around £400 a year. James F. Forrest's article on 'Clarendon on the Stage' (*MLR*) is noted in the next section.

(*c*) *Prose Authors*

New editions of two very different Restoration autobiographies, William Lilly's and Richard Baxter's, appeared this year. *The Last of the Astrologers* reprints Lilly's *History of his Life and Times*, from the 1715 edition, with notes and an introduction by Katharine M. Briggs.[25] Dr Briggs gives a helpful explanation of astrology and remarks on Lilly's portraits of his fellow astrologers, a 'gallery of quacks and imposters who make Ben Jonson's Face and Subtle look comparatively respectable'; she might also have noted that the character of Sidrophel in *Hudibras* was based partly on Lilly himself. The autobiography is full of fascinating if rather unreliable detail about life in England during the interregnum. Lilly was an amiable rogue with a talent for survival. When he prophesied the end of the Rump in one of his almanacs he was arrested, but he contrived to see 'Mr. Speaker *Lenthall*, ever my Friend', who showed him the offending passages. Lilly 'presently sent for Mr. *Warren* the Printer, an assured Cavalier' and had six amended copies run off. When the parliamentary committee, 'being 36 in Number that Day, whereas it was observed, at other Times, it was very difficult to get Five of them together', showed him his almanac he disowned it, and pulling the amended copies from his pocket said, 'These I own, the others are Counterfeits, published purposely to ruin me'. The committee 'look'd upon one another like distracted men' and Lilly was soon released. The Folklore Society can be congratulated on making this lively book available, though an index would have improved its usefulness to scholars. The new edition of J. M. Lloyd Thomas's abridgment of the *Reliquiae Baxterianae*[26] is also welcome. Scarcely

any alteration has been made to Lloyd Thomas's text, but the editor, N. H. Keeble, has supplied a good scholarly introduction, has updated the bibliography and notes, and has revised the index. Baxter's autobiography, Keeble maintains, does not focus on the author as an individual, but 'as one of those who strove, not to promote any dogma or church polity, but to lead sincere, charitable and conscientious lives following the commandments of God'; it is not the work of an eccentric, but 'a vindication of the Puritan spirit'.

Roger Sharrock contributed the Bunyan chapter to *The English Novel: Select Bibliographical Guides*:[27] it is just what anyone embarking on a serious study of Bunyan wants. Among this year's articles in learned journals Elizabeth Adeney's 'Bunyan: A Unified Vision?' (*CR*) is especially good. Ms. Adeney argues that Bunyan is most himself in the comic passages of the first part of *Pilgrim's Progress*. Despite his intellectual approval of Christian, as the pilgrimage progresses a gap appears between the imaginative writer and the Puritan dogmatist; Bunyan's feeling for life proves stronger than his creed. This is an unpretentious and stimulating critical essay. Elmo Howell's 'Bunyan's Two Valleys: A Note on the Ecumenic Element in *Pilgrim's Progress*' (*TSL*) is about the valleys of Humiliation and the Shadow of Death as representations of religious experiences which are not confined to Puritans. Howell thinks the former represents coming to

[25] *The Last of the Astrologers. Mr William Lilly's History of his Life and Times from the year 1602 to 1681*, ed. by Katharine M. Briggs. (Mistletoe Books No. 1). Folklore Society. pp. [xix]+108. £2.25; paperback, £1.50.
[26] *The Autobiography of Richard Baxter*, abridged by J. M. Lloyd Thomas, ed. with

[27] *The English Novel: Select Bibliographical Guides*, ed. by A. E. Dyson. O.U.P. £4.25; paperback, £1.75.

an introduction by N. H. Keeble. (Everyman's University Library). London: Dent, Totowa, N.J.: Rowman & Littlefield. pp. xxx+314. £3; paperback, £1.50.

erms with the flesh and the latter a phase of 'spiritual aridity', seeing parallels with the first and second dark nights of the soul of St John of the Cross. Clifford Johnson's 'A Biblical Source for Bunyan's "Wide Field Full of Dark Mountains"' *N&Q*) is Jeremiah 13:15–16 in the Authorized Version, where Johnson thinks Bunyan misunderstood 'mountains' as referring to mounds 'about the size of a prairie-dog hill'. Or in Bunyan's terms, where Bunyan makes a molehill out of a mountain. It seems far more likely that Bunyan understood the word 'field' to mean a large area, in fact a sort of plain, as in the case of Langland's 'field full of folk' for example. Finally, students of Bunyan should not miss Vincent Newey's 'Wordsworth, Bunyan and the Puritan Mind' *ELH*), where suggestive comparisons are made between *The Prelude*, Resolution and Independence' and other poems of Wordsworth's, and *Grace Abounding* and *Pilgrim's Progress*. Newey's assertion that Part II of *Pilgrim's Progress* is to Part I what *The Excursion* is to *The Prelude*, though nicely phrased, is surely unfair to Part II, which could never be dismissed in the way Francis Jeffrey dismissed *The Excursion*.

There were two interesting articles on Clarendon. George Watson, in The Reader in Clarendon's *History of the Rebellion*' (*RES*), asks for whom Clarendon originally designed his work: for Charles I, for contemporary Englishmen, for posterity? No single purpose is likely to have been constant, but the echo of Hooker's *Laws of Ecclesiastical Polity* in the opening sentence, and especially the reference to 'posterity', suggest that 'the reader envisaged by Hooker . Clarendon's too'. Both wrote 'to ensure that posterity, viewing from a distance the victory of the Puritan

cause, should not suppose it to represent God's final purpose'. A letter to Gilbert Sheldon suggests Clarendon wanted to justify not Charles I in particular, but monarchy in general, and there are signs that he addressed himself to a fit audience though few of future statesmen. But he was perhaps too angry to read the lessons of history clearly; and his implied moral, that in politics pragmatism is always best, is unconvincing in relation to the events he had to record. James F. Forrest, in 'Clarendon on the Stage' (*MLR*), draws attention to Clarendon's 'Dialogue concerning Education', probably written about 1668, in which the theatre is deplored by the Country Gentleman and the Lawyer, and defended by the Alderman, the Courtier, the Colonel and, with reservations, the Bishop. They debate the question of men and women wearing each other's clothes, a practice forbidden in Deuteronomy but increasingly popular on the stage with the advent of actresses. The dialogue exhibits Clarendon's own talent for drama.

Clarendon's fall from power in 1667 is one of the major events recorded in the eighth volume of Latham and Matthews's edition of Pepys's *Diary*.[28] This volume maintains the high standards of its predecessors; the editors' contribution to the delight of reading it no more needs my commendation than does Pepys's own. A phrase on p. 400, 'at the Swan I did besar Frank', was for a pretty while mighty puzzling, but on p. 456 Pepys 'did fling down the fille' at the Swan 'upon the chair and did

[28] *The Diary of Samuel Pepys: Volume VIII*, ed. by Robert Latham and William Matthews (contributing editors: William A. Armstrong, Macdonald Emslie, Oliver Millar, the late W. F. Reddaway). Bell. pp. xiv+626. 6 plates. £6.

tocar her thigh with my hand', and a footnote explains that the girl was Frances ('Frank') Udall. Presumably slight difficulties of this sort will disappear with the publication of the index volume. Meanwhile new books on Pepys continue to be brought out. Richard Ollard's *Pepys*[29] is more compact and in some ways more accurate than Sir Arthur Bryant's three-volume biography, but in places seems overshadowed by its predecessor and by the *Diary* itself. For example Ollard is obliged to forgo the story of how Pepys unravelled the monstrous tangle of red tape that in 1660 stood between him and his clerkship in the Navy Office, which 'has been so well told by Sir Arthur Bryant' and in the diary 'that no further account is necessary'. And readers expecting new light on Pepys's friendships with Newton, Wren, Dryden or Kneller (all featured on the blurb) will be disappointed. They will get more satisfaction from the three chapters which discuss, with judicious selections from the diary, Pepys's style of life, morality, tastes and interests. Ollard is at his best in his account of Pepys's work at the Navy Office. He shows us a man dedicated to the very well-paid but essentially thankless task of creating order out of chaos and old night; in fact it is one of his major themes that 'Pepys's deepest springs of action were artistic'. By setting down his experience in the diary he had enabled himself to make sense of it, and 'by preserving everything he could lay hands on in the way of nautical archives, he ... equipped himself to reduce the naval universe to harmonious rationality', thus laying a foundation for some three centuries of British sea power. Pepys's extra-ordinary zest for life and work is certainly captured in this stylish and nicely organized narrative. Ollard also writes on 'Who was Pepys's Deborah Egmont' (*TLS*): the Mrs Egmont who wrote to Pepys from The Hague in 1689 was certainly not the former Deborah Willett, who had been his mistress, but was the lady who helped him to refute the charge of treason against him at the time of the Popish Plot.

Pepys's *Diary* is inevitably a major topic in Robert A. Fothergill's *Private Chronicles*,[30] a study of English diaries which were composed more or less deliberately as serial autobiographies and can be considered to have literary importance. Fothergill remarks that Pepys's style, which is certainly not artless, seems so 'natural' as to provide a touchstone of excellence in the genre. This impression is partly owing to familiarity and partly genuine; Pepys's diary 'displays less affectation, less posturing, less verbal self-dramatization than any other diary of comparable density'. Pepys's needs and responses also seem 'natural', as it seems 'everyone, whether or not he is capable of acknowledging it, has experienced life in the same way'. But this naturalness may be seen as 'the persistence into adult life of a child's habit of confiding everything to God'. Fothergill grimly concludes that while growing out of this habit entails loss, 'to persist in casting one's experience in that oddly simplistic fashion, to become as a little child in one's periods of self-encounter, seems like a kind of suspended development'.

The Marquess of Halifax's 'pregnant wit and piercing thought' remain a source of controversy. In

---

[29] *Pepys: A Biography*, by Richard Ollard. Hodder & Stoughton. pp. 368. 24 plates, 9 line-drawings, maps as endpapers. £3.95.

[30] *Private Chronicles: A Study of English Diaries*, by Robert A. Fothergill. O.U.P. pp. viii+214. £4.50.

'Halifax's *Character of a Trimmer* and L'Estrange's Attack on Trimmers in *The Observator*' (*HLQ*, 1973; not mentioned in *YW* 54), Thomas C. Faulkner criticizes J. P. Kenyon (*YW* 51.258) and Mark N. Brown (*YW* 53.269–70) for denying that Halifax's pamphlet was prompted by attacks on moderates in L'Estrange's political journal. L'Estrange would call anyone a 'Trimmer' who was not a high Tory, including Halifax; he was therefore 'probably instrumental' in provoking the pamphlet, which implicitly attacks L'Estrange. In 'Trimmers and Moderates in the Reign of Charles II' (*HLQ*) Brown replies vigorously. L'Estrange's idea was to discredit moderation by imputing it to base motives, and the term 'Trimmer' acquired strong pejorative overtones. Halifax's pamphlet took the form of a character of a Trimmer as 'a literary device, rather than a political confession'. Halifax was not and would not want to be generally known as a Trimmer; if he had been, the literary device would have compromised the pamphlet's anonymity. What Faulkner takes as allusions to L'Estrange could equally well be allusions to other authors, and Halifax's pamphlet is not merely a response to personal attacks but a complex and important political work, 'a solitary voice of moderate opinion in the prevailing atmosphere of Tory reaction'. Brown also identifies 'Bishop Cartwright's Answer to Halifax's "Letter to a Dissenter" (1687)' (*N&Q*): it is probably *A Modest Censure of the Immodest Letter to a Dissenter* (1687).

In conclusion, a glance at some of the year's work on the philosophers. *The Locke Newsletter*[31] includes two previously unpublished manuscripts of Locke's writings on morality, introduced by Thomas Sargentich; an essay on Locke's movements in 1686–7 by E. S. de Beer; 'Are Locke's Ideas of Relation Complex?' by J. Douglas Rabb; 'Hume's Use of Locke on Identity' by Roland Hall; a list of additions to Christensen's bibliography of work on Locke before 1929; and a progress report on the forthcoming Clarendon Edition of Locke, by P. H. Nidditch. Of more general interest are Frank E. Manuel's 1973 Fremantle Lectures, which were published as *The Religion of Isaac Newton*.[32] Professor Manuel argues that Newton's religion was primarily historical and scriptural, and that 'the metaphysical disputations in which he was sometimes enmeshed ranked quite low in his esteem'. He believes that 'the fervour of Newton's quest for a knowledge of God was related to a psychic quest for his own father', and Newton's religious feelings are therefore traced to his early experiences. The 'uneasy' relationship between his religion and his scientific work, and his attacks on ancient and modern corrupters of the simple purity of the primitive church, are examined. His work on the language of prophecy and his method of scriptural interpretation reveal the search for unity and simplicity that also marked his scientific system. The lectures draw on manuscripts which have only recently become available, two of which are published for the first time as appendices. *JHI* as usual includes a number of essays which may well be of interest to specialists in Restoration literature. George L. Dillon's on literary criticism has been mentioned above (section 1). J. A. Redwood's 'Charles

[31] *The Locke Newsletter*, No. 5, ed. by Roland Hall. York: Dept. of Philosophy, U. of York. pp. 90. Free to Locke scholars.

[32] *The Religion of Isaac Newton*, by Frank E. Manuel. Clarendon Press: O.U.P. pp. vii + 141. £3.50.

Blount (1654–93), Deism, and English Free Thought' deals with an important figure in the development of free thought in England. Redwood reviews what is known of Blount's life and work, mentioning his admiration for Dryden but not his friendship with Rochester.

4. BACKGROUND STUDIES

Literary students wanting to get the feel of this period could do worse than invest in Daphne Foskett's up-to-date and comprehensive study of one of the finest English portrait painters, Samuel Cooper.[33] Although he was friendly with Pepys, Butler, Aubrey, Evelyn and other famous writers, disappointingly little is known of Cooper's life, and the biographical part of Miss Foskett's study is necessarily a survey of facts and problems. This tentativeness is unfortunately carried over into her assessment of Cooper as an artist, but thirteen portraits are reproduced in colour, and seventy-four in monochrome, so we can judge for ourselves. What seems typically English about them is a certain inspired amateurism in the execution, and an unmistakable honesty of characterization. Here we have Cromwell with his warts; a determined and formidable Charles II; his mistresses, the ambitious Barbara Villiers and the relatively easy-going Frances Teresa Stuart; and a splendidly sardonic Gilbert Sheldon, Archbishop of Canterbury. The book includes an appendix on the painter's technique by V. J. Murrell.

Ian Spink's *English Song: Dowland to Purcell*[34] demands and eventually repays more sustained reading. It is the first comprehensive and critical survey of this great period of English song, remembered for what Milton calls 'airs and madrigals that whisper softness in chambers', but remarkable too for the growth of ambitious vocal forms more suited to the stage. The achievements of Dowland and perhaps also of Henry Lawes are already quite widely appreciated, so Mr Spink's sections on the catches and glees of the interregnum, on the songs of the Restoration court and theatre, and on Purcell, are especially valuable as well as especially interesting to students of our period. The decline in the popularity of the declamatory air coincided with the Restoration taste for lighter songs in dance rhythms. Purcell began with such songs and never entirely renounced them; but around 1683, in settings of Cowley and other writers with Pindarick tendencies, he began to aim at something more elaborate and serious. He resolved the problem of large-scale vocal form by means of the ground bass till about 1688, and then turned more to Italianate binary and *da capo* forms. His songs are 'arguably ... his finest works'. Mr Spink's main concern is quite properly with the music itself; there are hundreds of musical examples, many of complete songs, much accompanying analysis, valuable bibliographies of seventeenth-century song-books and major secondary sources, and a list of the principal manuscript song-books, 1600–1660. Music students will find this book indispensable, and it should lead to more of this splendid music being performed. Literary students, given a liking for the music and some technical knowledge, will be able to keep going. They will be encouraged at finding accounts of musical settings of more or less familiar lyrics, and

[33] *Samuel Cooper 1609–1672*, by Daphne Foskett. Faber & Faber. pp. 151. 87 illustrations, 13 in colour, 74 in monochrome. £6.50.

[34] *English Song: Dowland to Purcell*, by Ian Spink. Batsford. pp. 312. 14 illustrations. £5.50.

if they find themselves regretting the absence of biographical and background information they will ponder the illustrations, for instance that of young Henry Lawes, the future Attendant Spirit in *Comus*, surely already too portly for the part.

XII

The Eighteenth Century

K. E. ROBINSON

This chapter is in five sections: 1. General; 2. Poetry; 3. Prose; 4. Drama; 5. The Novel.

1. GENERAL

The period is again well served by the *PQ* bibliography, the selective notices and reviews in *The Scriblerian* and the annual review article in *SEL* (this year by Winton Calhoun). 1974 produced a good crop of studies of and pertaining to the background. Two books of very different approach deal with madness, the eighteenth-century mind and literature. Max Byrd's *Visits to Bedlam*[1] takes as its starting point the opposition between the traditional view of madness as divine inspiration and the distrust of it as an evil, characteristic first of the middle ages and then of the eighteenth century—more precisely of the period 1660 to 1759 when Young could quote approvingly Cicero's 'Nemo igitur vir magnus sine aliquo adflatu divino umquam fuit'. *King Lear* furnishes a complex focus for Byrd's exploration of 'reason in madness': whereas its 'themes of madness and wisdom, madness and blindness, madness and misery' exist in a perfect suspension, in the age of Pope and Swift 'they reappear in altered and dogmatic form'. In *The Dunciad* dunces replace fools and Pope 'persistently chooses unprophetic madness as the external representa-

tion of the Dunces' immoral nature because his audience understands madness only in that way, ... as wilful evil'. In the chapters which follow (on Swift, Johnson, melancholy and the sublime in the mid-century, and Cowper and Blake) Byrd is both more expansive and more limited. He is inevitably led to ask about fears of madness in Swift and Johnson, but he tends to work in a spirit of sociological and psycho-analytic hypothesis which jars even when he is advancing in reasonable ways. 'The sociological principle of the identity of opposites suggests,' he asserts, 'that, like all great writers, Pope, Swift and Johnson speak from painful psychic intuitions ... of what human beings may become.' No-one would deny that the earlier eighteenth century was profoundly anxious about irrationalism; it is merely that Byrd's approach makes him insensitive to nuances. On the other hand Michael V. DePorte's modest study of Augustan ideas of madness, *Nightmares and Hobbyhorses*,[2] seems to me one of the best books of the year. DePorte investigates the 'dark side of the Enlightenment' by describing the theories of mental disorder and the criteria for sanity advanced by English thinkers in the hundred years following the Restoration. He surveys the complex material before him with

---

[1] *Visits to Bedlam: Madness and Literature in the Eighteenth Century*, by Max Byrd. University of South Carolina Press. pp. xvii +200. $9.95.

[2] *Nightmares and Hobbyhorses: Swift, Sterne, and Augustan Ideas of Madness*, by Michael V. DePorte. The Huntington Library. pp. xi+164. $10.00.

ease and careful scholarship, distinguishing between the various mechanistic pathologies which had superseded the humoural explanation of madness, demonstrating how Hobbes and Locke removed the examination of insanity from a theological, or even conventionally moral, context and indicating how Hobbes's identification of fancy and madness precipitated uneasiness about the imagination in the eighteenth century. A section entitled 'Madness and Subjectivity' shows DePorte at his most incisive. Here he argues that Cartesian rationalism brought its own peculiar fears of irrationalism, that eighteenth-century man was alarmed that just as secondary qualities had been shown not to be inherent but an imposition of the mind, other mental constructs hitherto taken to be trustworthy might also be delusory. Both Hobbes and Locke (the latter particularly) intensified the fears: 'by drawing attention to the almost limitless possibilities for error they made men both more conscious of human singularities and more distrustful of them'. Against this background DePorte considers Swift and Sterne. In Swift's case he is most concerned with the battle between his desire to hold to absolute values and his empiricist contempt for the visionary and theoretical. On the one hand Swift preached that man should have faith in 'the Evidence of Things not seen', on the other he believed that seeing things invisible spelt madness. Sterne is presented as the first important eighteenth-century writer to escape the fear of subjectivity. 'The style of *Tristram Shandy* is an empirical demonstration of the value of singular and idiosyncratic perception' because it casts aside rules, customs and expectations in the spirit of letting 'people tell their own stories in their own way'.

By comparison Pat Rogers' *The Augustan Vision*[3] is disappointing. It lacks the particularity and incisive knowledge which yield such important general insights in *Nightmares and Hobbyhorses*. Moreover, Rogers seems peculiarly insensitive to language, often striving more for brash effect than precision: 'In the popular image of Sam Johnson, there is a component of easy-going Fleet Street irreverence, as of Lunchtime O'Booze interbred with a television pundit. The picture is travestied, of course, but it is not absolutely without foundation'. Rogers' own 'easy-going Fleet Street irreverence' leaves one unsure of the implications of his arguments. As the chapter headings tend to suggest—'Roles and Identities', 'Men, Women and Sex', 'Communication'—the opening section of Rogers' book defines the Augustan 'vision' by a series of rather crude contrasts with the present. Although the discussions of the literature which form the latter part of the book are on the whole more palatable, they do suffer from the overwriting so characteristic of criticism and reviews in today's mass media. Fielding's plays show, for example, a 'dancing continuity between events and ideas. . . . Fielding uses the play-within-the-play to create a shimmering, evanescent effect in which fiction and reality become blurred'! It is a pity that such an opportunity to provide a general background book much needed by students should have been so wasted.

Two well-known writers on the eighteenth century set out to challenge the drift of modern criticism. Martin C. Battestin[4] brings an

[3] *The Augustan Vision*, by Pat Rogers. Weidenfeld & Nicolson. pp. 318. £4.50.
[4] *The Providence of Wit: Aspects of Form in Augustan Literature and the Arts*, by Martin C. Battestin. Oxford: The Clarendon Press. pp. xv + 331. £10.00.

extensive knowledge of the period's theology to his argument that 'the delight in form and artifice that we have long associated with this period was a function of the Augustan faith in a world orderly in all its parts, from Newton's universe to the microcosm, man'. The basic assumption of Battestin's book is that since theology and aesthetics so interpenetrate in the period from 1660 to 1750, and since form in art is dictated by the age's and the writer's intellectual tenets, works of art express formally a vision of order. He finds an informing principle of order in Gay, Pope, Fielding and Goldsmith and much the same principle realized ironically in Swift. Sterne's form on the other hand seems to him to embody a profound scepticism about the possibility of objective coherence, a view of Sterne not unlike DePorte's. There is no doubt that Battestin issues a timely reminder that modern criticism has tended to lose sight of rational order in eighteenth-century literature, but he overstates the case. DePorte's study is an ample rejoinder: Hobbes and Locke prompted severe anxiety about objectivity and the irrational in minds and writers before Sterne, even if that anxiety did not reach the extreme of Sterne's solipsism. Battestin fails to strike a balance between responsiveness to the intellectual background and responsiveness to individual texts. He reads the eighteenth-century writers as, one suspects, they would have liked to be read rather than in the works they produced. But despite its pitfalls—perhaps because of them—this is a useful work. Irvin Ehrenpreis's uneasiness about modern criticism centres upon its attachment to the symbolist virtues of suggestion, allusion and organic form. He argues that the preference (entertained by Eliot *et al.*) of oblique to

direct poetry which led to the eighteenth century appearing limited has precipitated later critics into a search for implicit meaning. In *Literary Meaning and Augustan Values*[5] Ehrenpreis himself puts his trust in the Augustans' 'faith in explicit meaning, a desire for clarity'. There is undoubtedly sense and justice in his attack on the effort 'to distill peculiarly modern features from Augustan literature'—his debunking of the modern obsession with personae is still mordant although, like most of the book, it has already seen publication—but in returning us to the explicit in eighteenth-century literature he does nothing to resolve Eliot's (or Leavis's) view of its limitations. Thus, quoting a passage from Halifax he praises roughly those qualities remarked upon by L. C. Knights in his famous essay on Restoration comedy, but he nowhere attempts to describe his attitude towards the limiting context in which he places them. Versed in the byways of periodical literature Ehrenpreis often seems oddly unaware of major critical achievements related to his theme. Despite its apparent honesty and undaunted forthrightness this is a work which seems to issue from a mind aggressively convinced of its professorial rightness. One feels at many points that there is much more to be taken into account.

Several figures of historical interest have received attention. *Newcastle. A Duke without Money: Thomas Pelham-Holles 1693–1768* by Ray Kelch[6] is not the biography it might be

---

[5] *Literary Meaning and Augustan Values*, by Irvin Ehrenpreis. University of Virginia Press. pp. vii+119. $6.75.

[6] *Newcastle. A Duke without Money: Thomas Pelham-Holles 1693–1768*, by Ray A. Kelch. University of California Press. pp. x+222. $12.00.

expected to be but a detailed study of Newcastle's finances to substantiate the idea that it was not political expenses which thrust him into difficulty. Brian Fothergill's *The Mitred Earl: An Eighteenth-Century Eccentric*[7] is a biography of the 'more brilliant than solid' Frederick Hervey, Earl of Bristol and Bishop of Derry, who oscillated between politician and scholar, collector and lover, annoying George III as well as attracting the censure of Horace Walpole. Although Hervey's political intrigues were considered by some to be dangerous, they were nothing in comparison with the reforming zeal of Louis Kronenberger's *The Extraordinary Mr. Wilkes.*[8] Johnson, Boswell, Reynolds, Sterne and Garrick all have their place in Wilkes's biography, but it is interesting not least for Wilkes himself. Kronenberger charts the life in the belief that 'there is no reason to try to whitewash Wilkes, if only because his faults were glaring, but also because they were colourful and human enough to make him, simply as John Wilkes, a subject of interest'. It is not the role of exemplary hero which makes Marlborough a subject of interest for Correlli Barnett in his *Marlborough*[9] but the private man 'sensitive, emotional, highly strung even . . . a tragic figure, whose gradual descent from greatness to dismissal is deeply moving'. It is odd that little of this man finally emerges from Barnett's portrait. There is a companion book in David Green's *Blenheim*.[10] Turn-

ing from the martial to the domestic and pastoral, there is a most sensitive account of William Paley, *Paley: Evidences for the Man.*[11] Paley is represented not only as very much a man of the eighteenth century, rational and optimistic, but as a man of rich humanity, an understanding and caring father and husband, good-humoured, alive to simple pleasures and deeply curious about men and nature. Samuel Palmer, whose domestic life was rarely the fructifying experience which Paley understood, must be the most enigmatic figure to have been honoured with a biography in 1974. Raymond Lister's *Samuel Palmer*[12] belongs properly to the chapter on the nineteenth century, but it ought to be mentioned here because of Palmer's association with Blake. It sometimes seems that Lister's work on the letters has bred a little contempt, but his biography is none the less welcome. Firmly in the period, Ronald Paulson's *Hogarth: His Life, Art and Times*[13] is now available in an abridged, single volume edition. The abridgement is designed to provide a reliable introduction to the career: it omits much of the detail of the two volume edition and the analysis of Hogarth's art.

Amongst the books of a broader historical interest is E. Royston Pike's *Human Documents of Adam Smith's Time,*[14] a useful selection of snippets arranged thematically and

[7] *The Mitred Earl: An Eighteenth-Century Eccentric*, by Brian Fothergill. Faber & Faber. pp. 254. £3.75.
[8] *The Extraordinary Mr. Wilkes*, by Louis Kronenberger. New English Library. pp. 269. £3.25.
[9] *Marlborough*, by Correlli Barnett. Eyre Methuen. pp. 288. £5.50.
[10] *Blenheim*, by David Green. Collins. pp. 162. £3.95.

[11] *Paley: Evidences for the Man*, by M. L. Clarke. S.P.C.K. pp. 161. £2.95.
[12] *Samuel Palmer: A Biography*, by Raymond Lister. Faber & Faber. pp. 299. £6.25.
[13] *Hogarth: His Life, Art, and Times*, by Ronald Paulson (abridged by Anne Wilde). Yale University Press. pp. xiii+461. Paperback $8.95.
[14] *Human Documents of Adam Smith's Time*, by E. Royston Pike. George Allen & Unwin. pp. 253. £5.50, paperback £2.95.

supplemented with Hogarth plates and a brief introduction to Smith's life. *The Provincial Towns of Georgian England* by C. W. Chalklin[15] is a very detailed study of the residential development of various towns from 1740 to 1820. Divided into four parts, the first deals with the extent of urban growth, the second with land promoters, the third with the builders and the final part with the relationship between local and national building patterns. In addition there are many fine plates. Sixteen very varied contributions make up *The City and Society* edited by Paul Fritz and David Williams.[16] James Clifford offers an urbane glimpse into some of the less well-researched aspects of eighteenth-century urban life: toilet arrangements, chamber pots, sewage disposal, night-men, street lighting, scavengers and street robbery. In a wide-ranging paper Nicholas Phillipson explains why Edinburgh should have become such a rich centre of culture in the eighteenth century, particularly between the 1750s and 1780s. He focuses upon the anxieties aroused by a deterministic ideology and the difficulties which faced those trying to allay them in the context of the 'ruthless intellectual honesty' of Adam Smith and David Hume. Another paper concerned with Edinburgh as well as other intellectual centres in the same period is Roger Emerson's 'The Enlightment and Social Structures'. Emerson investigates 'how their size and institutional complexity affected their intellectual milieu, how in fact their enlightenments were limited and skewed by

social determinants'. Finally, P. H. Lang contributes a leisurely piece on music in the European Courts.

Those stirred by the exhibition of Fuseli might like to purchase Carolyn Keay's representative selection of his sketches and paintings, available in a sturdy and very reasonably priced paperback.[17] Miss Keay provides a brief and sensible introduction and her selection is interesting not least for its theatrical subjects. The facsimiles of William Gilpin's *Observations Relative Chiefly to Picturesque Beauty* for Cumberland and Westmorland[18] and the River Wye[19] issued by The Richmond Publishing Company serve as a useful reminder that at his best Gilpin deserves a place in the prose section of this chapter. The ending of the Cumberland and Westmorland volume has, despite its clumsy punctuation, a freshness and particularity worthy of note: 'After this, the country is gone. London comes on apace, and all those disgusting ideas, with which its great avenues abound—brick-kilns streaming with offensive smoke—sewers and ditches sweating with filth—heaps of collected soil, and stinks of every denomination—clouds of dust, rising and vanishing, from agitated wheels, pursuing each other in rapid motion . . .'. The Wye volume contains a general introduction by Sutherland Lyall. If we move from the picturesque to the Gothic, there are two items to report: a paperback edition of Kenneth Clark's *The Gothic*

[15] *The Provincial Towns of Georgian England: A Study of the Building Process 1740–1820*, by C. W. Chalklin. Edward Arnold. pp. xxii+367. £10.00.

[16] *City & Society in the Eighteenth Century*, edited by Paul Fritz and David Williams. Hakkert, Toronto. pp. xii+301. $12.00.

[17] *Henry Fuseli*, by Carolyn Keay. Academy Editions. pp. 88. £5.95, paperback £2.95.

[18] *Observations on the Mountains and Lakes of Cumberland and Westmorland*, by William Gilpin, with an introduction by Sutherland Lyall. The Richmond Publishing Company. pp. 1+268+xvi. £7.50.

[19] *Observations on the River Wye*, by William Gilpin, with an introduction by Sutherland Lyall. The Richmond Publishing Company. pp. xviii+99. £5.00.

Revival[20] and a coffee-table book, *The Gothick Taste* by Terence Davis,[21] useful for its illustrations. Another lavishly illustrated book is *English Decoration in the Eighteenth Century* by John Fowler and John Cornforth'.[22] Its authors distinguish and explore four phases of style, each influenced by the French: the first is characterized by an imitation of the style associated with the reign of Louis XIV; the second by a magnificent dressing of the concept of parade in Palladian costume; the third by a growing interest in the villa in which privacy, convenience and elegance were to be more important than parade and magnificence; and the final stage, beginning about 1770, by a gathering decline in taste and vitality. There is much of related interest in the first volume of Rudolf Wittkower's minor writings, *Palladio and English Palladianism*,[23] particularly in 'Classical Theory and Eighteenth-Century Sensibility'. Herbert M. Atherton's *Political Prints in the Age of Hogarth*[24] is concerned with prints from 1727 to 1763, ranging its material by topic under the following heads: printshops, the emblematic tradition and the caricature, governmental attitudes, allegories of patriotism, the country party, the city, Walpole and Bute and the Pictorial Characters. Atherton's volume is in some ways complementary to the only anthology relevant to this section, H. T. Dickinson's *Politics and Literature in the Eighteenth Century*.[25] Dickinson offers his selection as a contribution to remedying the insufficiencies of the Namierite approach which 'while undeniably offering valuable insights into the nature of the eighteenth-century political system, neglects the political climate which influences or restricts what politicians do'. I have been unable to consult a copy of James S. Malek's *The Arts Compared: An Aspect of Eighteenth-Century British Aesthetics*.[26]

Amongst the articles of general interest, A. J. Kuhn (*ELH*) examines Warburton's attacks on Methodism in *The Doctrine of Grace* in contrast to the works of William Law and John Byrom. He is especially concerned with Law's conviction of 'the precedence of mysticism over physico-mathematics in the eternal truth of things', a conviction influenced by Boehme. Kuhn's article concludes with an account of Wesley's relations with Law, Wesley's rejection of Boehme and Law and fascination with Hutchinson. John T. Ogden (*JHI*) considers the term 'distance' in eighteenth-century aesthetics. Working from a statement by Kant ('space and time as the necessary conditions of all outer and inner experiences are merely the subjective conditions of all our intuitions'), he argues that as the century progresses 'distance' becomes more than a simple objective measurement and expresses the relationship between the object perceived and the perceiving consciousness. According to Ogden, investigation of this relationship provided a means of

---

[20] *The Gothic Revival. An Essay in the History of Taste*, by Kenneth Clark. John Murray. pp. xii+236. Paperback £2.00.

[21] *The Gothick Taste*, by Terence Davis. David and Charles. pp. 168. £12.00.

[22] *English Decoration in the Eighteenth Century*, by John Fowler and John Cornforth. Barrie & Jenkins. pp. 288. £10.00.

[23] *Palladio and English Palladianism*, by Rudolf Wittkower. Thames & Hudson. pp. 224. £8.50.

[24] *Political Prints in the Age of Hogarth*, by Herbert M. Atherton. Oxford: The Clarendon Press. pp. viii+294. £10.00.

[25] *Politics and Literature in the Eighteenth Century*, by H. T. Dickinson. Dent. pp. xxiv+234. £2.50, paperback £1.50.

[26] *The Arts Compared: An Aspect of Eighteenth-Century British Aesthetics*, by James S. Malek. Wayne State University Press. pp. 175. $10.95.

grappling with the problems posed by Cartesian dualism and a path towards the reintegration of subjective and objective. Although marred by jargon, Stephen K. Land's article on universalism and relativism in eighteenth-century translation (*JHI*) is not without interest. Land bases his discussion on the opposed views of Locke and Hume: 'where Hume suggests a necessary semantic equivalence between languages, Locke indicates actual semantic discrepancies'. At the root of their disagreement lie different notions of the ways in which simple ideas are compounded into complex. Having established the distinction, Land considers the opinions of other eighteenth-century thinkers, notably David Hartley and Priestley.

In a less theoretical vein there is a paper by Howard D. Weinbrot (*ECS*) carefully documenting the reactions against Augustus Caesar and Horace in the eighteenth century. Weinbrot discovers that 'throughout the Restoration and eighteenth century there existed a substantial and articulate voice which denied the poetic myth of the virtues of Augustus'. This voice is heard not only in a writer like Fielding but in Pope too. P. J. Korshin's description of types of eighteenth-century literary patronage (*ECS*) is also very much involved with realities. He sketches in the trend which removed patronage from the hands of the privileged few to the public and government and concludes with a review of Johnson's attitude towards patronage. In accepting his pension in 1762, Johnson was 'reaping the rewards of a system which allowed him to profit without sacrificing his independence'.

2. POETRY

There are two anthologies of verse, one of the *Augustan Lyric* edited by

Donald Davie,[27] the other of English *Poetry 1700–1780*, edited by David W. Lindsay.[28] Davie's anthology is most welcome. Together with its introduction it demonstrates the existence of a lyric tradition often overlooked by focusing on the most intense and passionate writers of the century (Pope, Swift, Johnson and Goldsmith). All four were of a 'profoundly radical and reactionary imagination'—'Tories in a world of Whigs'—and the natural mode for them was the critical. At the heart of Davie's lyric tradition is Prior, who restored the urbanity of Carew and Marvell to a bourgeois society. Davie sketches in the significance of Prior's influence, finding his exhortation to 'e'en talk a little like the folks of this world' fulfilled by most of the poets whom he prints: Anne, Countess of Winchilsea, Isaac Watts, Addison, Gay, Wesley, Thomson, Collins, Duddridge, Smart, Garrick, Cunningham, Toplady, Newton, Cowper, Mulgrave and Blake. David W. Lindsay's introduction suffers by comparison. Where Davie's is forthright, challenging and full of a sense that its argument matters to him, Lindsay's is a dense and plodding scholarly rehearsal of the received literary history. The anthology itself may, however, be useful. It does contain the whole of *Trivia* and *The Rosciad* which are difficult for students to obtain outside expensive editions.

The works of Battestin and Ehrenpreis noticed above obviously bear heavily on the poetry, and there is a study of the elegy by Donald C. Mell, *A Poetics of the Augustan*

[27] *Augustan Lyric*, edited with an introduction by Donald Davie. Heinemann. pp. viii+181. £2.50.

[28] *English Poetry 1700–1780: Contemporaries of Swift and Johnson*, edited with an introduction by David W. Lindsay. Dent. pp. xxviii+239. £3.25, paperback £1.65.

Elegy: Studies of Poems, by Dryden, Pope, Prior, Swift, Gray, and Johnson.[29] Mell holds that the poetics of the elegy have to do with "a tension of conflicting opposites", with, fundamentally, a conflict between the order and artistry of the elegy itself and the flux and disorder of life. Mell's definition is both too broad and too limiting; it finds little place, for example, for the consolation. If the book is valuable at all, it is for its discussion of individual poems. Mell devotes separate chapters to the explication of Dryden's elegy on Oldham, Pope's 'Unfortunate Lady', Prior's 'An Epitaph', Swift's 'Death of Dr. Swift', Gray's 'Death of West' and Johnson's poem on the death of Levet. Still on a general note, A. B. England (*SB*) reports addenda to Bond's register of burlesque poems.

Two hitherto unpublished letters from Prior to Edward Southwell (dated 1703 and 1703/4) appear in *The Scriblerian* transcribed and described by Richard B. Kline, narrowing the gap in the record of Matthew Prior's life in London during the years 1701 to 1705. In the same number H. Bunker Wright reviews the three twentieth-century biographies of Prior. The letters of Samuel Garth are also the subject of a paper. John F. Sena (*BNYPL*) provides texts of the thirty-one extant letters (twenty-eight of which are published for the first time) together with a prefatory life. *The Dispensary* is examined by the same writer (*TSLL*) in an attempt to establish its value. Sena discovers a concern with the quality of contemporary morals beneath its particular satiric urge, and he praises the enduring quality of Garth's rhetorical ability in the satiric

sketch; but neither these merits nor Garth's wide-ranging interests prevent the poem being 'more self-consciously didactic than imaginative, ... more circumscribed than universal, and replete with intrusions of the author's personal prejudices, predilections, and passions'.

Apart from Battestin's interesting discussion of *Trivia* in *The Providence of Wit*, denying the charge of shallowness and arguing that the neatness of the couplets is a defense against the difficulties of urban existence ('patting everything into place, smoothing things over, rendering them, as it were, harmless'), there is little of interest on Gay. Pat Rogers includes a section on Gay in his *Augustan Vision*, but it is by and large confined to the accepted notion of the verse as easy and journalistic. He is more specifically engaged in 'Satiric Allusions in John Gay's Welcome to Mr. Pope' (*PLL*), where he argues that the 'Welcome' is an ironic account of George's arrival in England and progress to Greenwich in 1714 and return from Hanover in 1720. Swift's verse portraits are studied by Alan S. Fisher (*SEL*) on the basis of two assumptions: first, that to 'study portraits is to study the way an author transforms the facts of the world he inhabits into the patterns of his imagination', and second, that satiric power speaks of, and is the outcome of, deep pessimism. The opposed readings of 'A Description of a City Shower' by Ehrenpreis on one side and O Hehir and Savage on the other are synthesized by John I. Fischer (*TSL*). In Fischer's opinion both views are acceptable; the poem represents a 'cheerful acceptance of the urban scene' and the 'ludicrous attempt of an imperfect, trivial London to live up to classical dialects and situations'. Swift's 'esteem and gratitude' to Stella is the subject of James L. Tyne's examination of the

---

[29] *A Poetics of the Augustan Elegy: Studies of Poems by Dryden, Pope, Prior, Swift, Gray, and Johnson*, by Donald C. Mell. Amsterdam: Rodope N.V. pp. 116. Hfl. 25.

'love' poems (*TSL*). Tyne believes that Swift responded to Stella's good sense and good humour on the one hand and to her gentleness, tenderness and patience on the other, with a love which ought properly to be described as '*amor benevolentiae*'. In a second paper Tyne (*PLL*) reveals Swift pointedly mimicking the stylistic idiosyncrasies, over-hyperbole and 'crude classicism' of the Laureates Eusden and Cibber in 'On Poetry. A Rhapsody' so as to contrast Hanoverian England and classical Rome. John M. Aden's contribution to *Quick Springs of Sense: Studies in the Eighteenth Century*, edited by Larry S. Champion,[30] continues his exploration of the 'Unprintables'. 'The Lady's Dressing Room', 'The Progress of Beauty', 'Strephon and Chloe' and 'Cassinus and Peter' all use shock tactics to replace delusion with reality; and all seek 'to say something corrective of human psychology, conduct and morality'.

The Penguin 'Poet to Poet' series now boasts a selection of Pope's verse from the hand of Peter Levi.[31] Levi's introduction is generous, perhaps a little too generous: 'after Shakespeare . . . Pope is probably the funniest, the most sinuous and all-including, and morally the strongest English poet'. He seems to feel it unnecessary either to defend this opening judgment or define its terms, with the result that one is left unsure about the precise implications of his assessment. This can be annoying when he appears to be on the brink of making a point of some importance. as, for example, in the following: 'His poetry as it developed was full of contradictions and within the limits

of the brilliance of surface and sharpness of form which so delighted him he took all the contradictory elements as far as they would go, extending the limits of his form and the capabilities of his surface by the same process in which he explored their apparent narrowness'. The most notable feature of the selection itself is its inclusion of a large number of minor poems. A belief that the visual is very important in Pope's verse lies behind Clarence Tracy's illustrated edition of *The Rape of the Lock, The RAPE Observed*.[32] De Guernier's illustrations seem to Tracy to smack of studio cliché far removed from the particularity of Pope's canvas; his own illustrations consist of photographs of objects and engravings which, he hopes, will restore that particularity and enable the modern reader to enjoy the visual. In fact the illustrations do not seem to shed any new light. Tracy takes his text from the Twickenham edition. The Twickenham edition of the complete poetry forms the base for *A Concordance to the Poems of Alexander Pope*, edited by Emmett G. Bedford and Robert J. Dilligan,[33] which supersedes the Abbott concordance. Advanced computer technology has made it possible for the new concordance to reproduce 'virtually all the typographical distinctions of the original'; each entry contains a reference to the number of the relevant Twickenham volume, an abbreviated title, the line number and the page number. Despite its pretensions to reclaim Pope from historicists and formalists, Frederick M. Keener's *An Essay on*

[30] *Quick Springs of Sense: Studies in the Eighteenth Century*, ed. by Larry S. Champion. University of Georgia Press. pp. vii + 254. $9.00.

[31] *Pope*, selected with an introduction by Peter Levi, S.J. Penguin, pp. 192. 0.60p.

[32] *The RAPE Observ'd: An Edition of Alexander Pope's Poem 'The Rape of the Lock'*, by Clarence Tracy. University of Toronto Press. pp. xxv + 101. £6.25.

[33] *A Concordance to the Poems of Alexander Pope*, ed. by Emmett G. Bedford and Robert J. Dilligan. Gale Research. 2 vols. pp. lxxxviii + 819; viii + 741. $85.00.

Pope[34] is a naïve affair. He hopes to effect the reparation by exploring the man and the work in inter-relation to reveal the essential modernity of his poet; but far from understanding modernity in a properly Arnoldian way, Keener simply projects fashionable concerns onto Pope, making him, amongst other things, pacifist and troubled with guilt about possessing private property. Keener's critical procedure often typifies the sort of unthinking reading which Ehrenpreis's *Literary Meaning and Augustan Values* attacks—his account of *The Rape* is openly novelistic; but the most annoying characteristic of the book must certainly be its delight in fatuous questions. There can be few who will ask seriously with Keener how the lock rises to the sky.

Most of the attention given to Pope in articles is directed towards *The Rape of the Lock* and *The Dunciad*. William F. Cunningham Jr.[35] concerns himself with the 'narrator' of *The Rape* whose subtly modulated voice presents 'the complexity of the truth' in such a way that Belinda and Clarissa are reconciled. Pat Rogers (*RES*) makes the most out of 'native faery lore' so that the central battle becomes that between the sylphs, who represent 'frivolity, heedlessness, the lighter impulses of women', and the gnomes, who represent 'what might be briefly termed biology'. The prize for the most tactless paper on Pope goes to Wolfgang E. H. Rudat (*TSL*) who attempts to 'sexualize' Belinda's 'painted vessel' by ingenious explication of allusions. Barry M. Kroll (*Thoth*) considers Belinda in relation to humoural

[34] *An Essay on Pope*, by Frederick M. Keener. Columbia University Press. pp. 196. $9.00.
[35] *Literary Studies: Essays in Memory of Francis A. Drumm*, ed. by John M. Dorenkamp. Worcester: Holy Cross College. pp. 284. $9.50.

doctrine, and Clarissa's speech engages the attention of John Trimble (*TSLL*). Trimble finds her a complex prude: she makes sense, but she espouses virtue in the spirit of an opportunist, 'less for its own sake than for its practical advantages'. Elias F. Mengel's assumption (*ECS*) that Pope was responsible for all the *Dunciad* prints leads him to regard them as just as integral to the poem as its apparatus. They are, he claims, mock-emblems which reflect the wit of the poem. Mengel's argument meets with approval from William Kupersmith (*ECS*) and James Sambrook (*ECS*) who both suggest further readings. In an excessively long article Pat Rogers (*Anglia*) demonstrates how Pope characteristically exploits a penumbra of doubt which surrounds proper nouns used idiosyncratically. Pope's technique is viewed against the background of the writings of contemporary grammarians to illustrate the paradox that 'Dulness who literally is not real and whose title is allegorical, exists within the poem' as real people named within the poem do not. Two papers are concerned with parody in *The Dunciad*. C. R. Kropf (*PLL*) opines that the miscreation of 'a new cosmic order' by Dulness parodies the vision of the third day of creation in *Paradise Lost* so that the goddess becomes an 'inverted godhead'; whilst the focus of Traugott Lawler's efforts (*SEL*) is on the pastoral spilling over into *The Dunciad* in parody of Virgil's *Eclogues* especially the Fourth and Sixth. In his contribution to *Quick Springs of Sense*, B. L. Reid looks at Pope's verbal artistry and the unity of *The Dunciad*. He insists, as many before him, on the importance of 'images of movement appropriate to the nature of Dulness' and concludes that 'the unifying movement is that of common cause, of energy, of passion, of intellectual outrage that emerges in visions that have the insistent recurrence of nightmare and merge finally into a single vision, sufficiently apocalyptic'.

Evelyn Hoover (*EIC*) lays bare similarities between Racine's *Phèdre* and *Eloisa to Abelard*. Both Pope and Racine create 'a world in which virtually nothing is simultaneously desirable and possible'; and both celebrate 'the quality of endurance, the capacity of the consciousness besieged by intolerable contradiction, passionate strife, extreme perplexity, to ensure its own actions'. The 'Epistle to Bathurst' is served by two notes from Graham Nicholls (*N&Q*). The first deals with a debt to *Volpone*; the second demonstrates that the tale of Sir Balaam is similar at some points to Ned Ward's *The Wealthy Shop-keeper, or the Charitable Citizen*. More generally, Hugh Kenner (*ELH*) writes on 'Pope's Reasonable Rhymes', defining two types of rhyme: 'normal' and 'incongruous'. 'Normal' rhymes deal in received pairs of rhyme words—Kenner instances must/dust and high/sky—whilst the 'incongruous' are such pairs as mankind/behind or built/gilt. Each type has a characteristic use: the 'normal' for truisms or the sentientious and the 'incongruous' for deflation. Kenner also argues that there may be a connection between Pope's sense that 'normal' rhyme represents order and Bishop Wilkins' outline for a new ordered language in *An Essay Towards a Real Character and a Philosophical Language*. Finally, there is an assortment of notes. *The Scriblerian* prints and describes a new Pope letter and a portrait after Kneller; H. A. Mason (*N&Q*) treats of a connection between Dryden's *Georgics* and *An Essay on Criticism*; and K. E. Robinson (*N&Q*) indicates a parody of lines from John Oldham

in *The Art of Sinking*. James King's 'Pope and Erasmus' "Great Injur'd Name"' (*ES*) explores the controversy precipitated, particularly amongst Pope's Roman Catholic neighbours, by *An Essay on Criticism*. According to King, Pope saw Erasmus as 'a prototype of the Roman Catholic who strongly objects to his faith and yet remains within the fold'.

Some fourteen years after her collation of the first sixteen editions of Isaac Watts's *Hymns and Spiritual Songs*, Selma L. Bishop has now produced '*Hymns and Spiritual Songs*' (*1707*), *A Publishing History and a Bibliography*,[36] covering the period 1707 to 1962. Miss Bishop's study is most useful for its illustration of the popularity enjoyed by the *Hymns* in the eighteenth and nineteenth centuries, a popularity which does not pass unnoticed in David Fountain's tercentenary tribute to Watts, *Isaac Watts Remembered*.[37] Fountain is 'one in the long line of Dissenters' and well suited to his task, but his sympathies push him into unobjective eulogy. Nevertheless, this ought to prove a very palatable (and inexpensive) introduction to the life.

The only piece to record on Thomson is a bibliography by Hilbert H. Campbell (*BB*) of twentieth-century criticism and commentary with selected eighteenth- and nineteenth-century items. Collins, however, fares rather better, as the subject of the 1973 Warton Lecture by Arthur Johnston (*PBA*). This is a rather disappointing life and letters excursion, which examines Collins' range of reading in sixteenth-century literature of England, Italy, France

[36] *Isaac Watts's 'Hymns and Spiritual Songs' (1707). A Publishing History and a Bibliography*, ed. by Selma L. Bishop. Ann Arbor: Pierian. pp. xxiv+479. $19.95.
[37] *Isaac Watts Remembered*, by David Fountain. Worthing: Henry E. Walter. pp. 112. 0.75p.

and Spain and remembers Warton's high hopes of the projected history of the revival of learning under Leo X, of which only the introduction was finished. Collins was a 'bookish young man, likely to be excited by someone else's poem or novel or article, or by talk about such things'. Johnston looks too at Collins' experiments with structure and sound patterning. Goldsmith is represented by George S. Rousseau's Critical Heritage volume[38] which includes sections of material relevant to 'The Deserted Village' and 'Retaliation', as well as more general comments in the section 'On Goldsmith's Life and Works'. Gray receives massive attention in a collection of papers from the Bicentenary Conference at Carleton University, edited by James Downey and Ben Jones.[39] Jean Hagstrum's contribution leads the way with an exploration of Gray's sensibility, a term which is used to link the realms of taste and the deep passions, the public and the private worlds of Gray. Hagstrum finds these worlds at variance because the torturing passions which welled beneath Gray's friendships could not receive open expression, resolution or fulfilment, despite artistic control. The diffident Gray of Ian Jack's leisurely 'Gray in his Letters' is much more conventional; but Arthur Johnston's account of the poetry is at pains to stress the boldness, the fashionableness, the linguistic daring and the concentrated melancholia of the *Elegy*. As a complement to this restoration of Johnson's view (without its judgments), there is Roger Lonsdale's

sifting of the data of the relationship between Johnson and Gray. Unlike Johnston, Donald Greene remains unimpressed by the poetic language of most of Gray's work. In a refreshingly sensible and intelligent piece he sets Gray beside Johnson and Wordsworth who by contrast understood the proper language of poetry. The dialectic continues with El. Mandel's complex defence through a consideration of the implications of Gray's and Smart's 'metaphoric identification of music and poetry'. In the words of Donald Davie's 'Afterword', Mandel tends to elevate Smart so as to rescue Gray 'clinging as it were to Smart's coat-tails'. The patterns of critical response in the eighteenth and nineteenth-centuries, including the Johnson-Gray controversy, are traced by Alastair MacDonald. Like all the papers (even Jack's) it presents a Gray slightly out of key with his age. This isolation is given a fresh inflection by George Whalley's 'Thomas Gray: A Quiet Hellenist'. Whalley insists on Gray's 'courage in facing a Latin world in a Greek spirit'. Of the remaining papers those by Irene Taylor and Ben Jones, both on illustrations, are particularly worthy of mention, not least because they are accompanied by twenty-five finely produced plates from Bentley and Blake. The rest of the year's work on Gray can be noticed briefly. Thomas R. Carper (*N&Q*) contributes a note on the dating of Gray's translations from the Greek Anthology, whilst Richard Eversole (*N&Q*) argues that the assumption that the narrator of the *Elegy* reflects upon rustic memorials made of stone is historically implausible. Judith K. Moore (*TSL*) writes briefly on the circumstances and diction of the 'Sonnet on the Death of Richard West'.

From Gray's 'Sonnet' we move to

[38] *Goldsmith. The Critical Heritage*, ed. by George S. Rousseau. Routledge & Kegan Paul. pp. xxvi+385. £7.50.

[39] *Fearful Joy: Papers from the Thomas Gray Bicentenary Conference at Carleton University*, ed. by James Downey and Ben Jones. McGill-Queen's University Press. pp. xvii+266. $11.50.

Thomas Edwards, 'the real father of the eighteenth-century sonnet', as he is described by his most recent editor. That editor is Dennis Donovan who is responsible for the Augustan Reprint Society facsimile of *The Sonnets of Thomas Edwards* (*1765, 1780*).[40] The sonnets are most interesting for their satires on Warburton. It is odd that J. D. Fleeman's name appears neither on the cover nor title-page of the second edition of the Nichol Smith and McAdam *Poems of Samuel Johnson*.[41] He has not merely corrected but re-edited and reordered the works in strictly chronological sequence. Apart from one or two unfortunate printing errors, the absence of just recognition for the reviser is the only thing which mars this impeccable edition. Critically, the poetry receives scant attention. In an often heavy-handed paper, George T. Amis (*MLQ*) considers that 'The Vanity of Human Wishes' reproduces the basic pattern of Juvenal's *Tenth*: a proposition followed by illustrative examples and 'a "conclusion" which assumes the proposition'. This pattern allows the poem to seem episodic and discontinuous when in fact it is unified by a firm controlling personality, 'a speaker consciously being literary, holding things at a distance, dealing formally and generally with matters of personal importance'.

It is as well that Robert Fergusson was not in charge of the kitchens when Johnson was afforded his 'superb treat' by the University of St Andrews. Fergusson did not take at all kindly to 'what Sam, the lying loun!/Has in his Dictionar laid

down' and might have been sufficiently outraged to have had his guest fed on 'gudely hamel gear'. In their fine edition of *Poems by Allan Ramsay and Robert Fergusson*,[42] A. M. Kinghorn and Alexander Law remind us that a poem such as 'To the Principal and Professors of the University of St Andrews, on their superb treat to Dr Samuel Johnson' 'has a style and character ... quite different from any convention that Johnson could have recognised' (here the old Scots flyting tradition). They emphasize that it would be inadequate and unfair to discuss Ramsay and Fergusson in the same terms as English poets of the same century. The text of this selection is based on the Scottish Text Society's editions. Burns is represented by Donald Low's unexceptional Critical Heritage volume.[42a] For those interested in Cowper, the most significant piece is the chapter on Cowper and Blake in Max Byrd's *Visits to Bedlam*.[1] Byrd shows himself sensitive to Cowper's 'helplessness and ... blind terror at the forces set against him'. As Byrd recognizes, Cowper was far more severe on his madness than his contemporaries were. On a different tack David Boyd (*PLL*) explores the interpenetration of pastoral and satire in *The Task*.

Blake is no less attractive to critics than in previous years. D. G. Gillham's *William Blake*,[43] which concentrates on the *Songs*, is based on three assumptions: that the *Songs of*

---

[40] *The Sonnets of Thomas Edwards* (*1765, 1780*), ed. by Dennis Donovan. Augustan Reprint Society 164. University of California Press. pp. 58. By subscription.

[41] *The Poems of Samuel Johnson*, ed. by David Nichol Smith and Edward L. McAdam. Second edition. Oxford: The Clarendon Press. pp. xxviii+496. £7.00

[42] *Poems by Allan Ramsay and Robert Fergusson*, ed. by Alexander Manson Kinghorn and Alexander Law. The Association for Scottish Literary Studies. Scottish Academic Press. pp. xxxiv+225. £3.75.

[42a] *Robert Burns. The Critical Heritage*, ed. by Donald Low. Routledge & Kegan Paul. pp. 447.

[43] *William Blake*, by D. G. Gillham. Cambridge University Press. pp. 216. £3.70, paperback £1.30.

Innocence and *Songs of Experience* were conceived as an artistic whole, that the poems are dramatic (that is, Blake does not speak in his own voice or through a character) and that Blake's later works do not help us in the interpretation of the *Songs*. No doubt this is a book which will annoy because it demotes the later works; but it is stimulating to have a stout defence of the inherent freshness of the lyrics in the face of a tendency to assume a 'fixed symbolic significance'. Gillham's study is intended as introductory, but Thomas R. Frosch's *The Awakening of Albion: The Renovation of the Body in the Poetry of William Blake*[44] is much more a book for the initiated. Frosch is exercised by the concerns which fan out from Blake's pressing awareness of the body, its strengths, weaknesses and potentialities. One of these concerns is with a sense of identity in some way at odds with the physical, another with freedom as it relates to man's capacity for perception and his ability to harness his own energies. In describing how Blake conceived of the reorganization of human perception necessary to the reawakening to, and reachievement of, freedom, Frosch draws freely on Wordsworth, Shelley and Rilke and Lawrence. The failure to grasp this imaginative freedom is represented in the Prophetic Books by the pale imitations of the Zoas, literally and metaphorically in the dark until the reawakening. It is impossible to do full justice to the complexity of Frosch's subject and treatment in a small space; suffice it to say that this is a challenging book, written with an acute sense of the difficulties of getting onto terms with Blake. Anne Kostelanetz Mellor's

Blake's Human Form Divine[45] focuses upon the development of form in Blake's work, 'both as a philosophical concept and as a stylistic principle', in a way that relates her work to Frosch's. She attempts to show that in 1795 there was a contradiction between Blake's simultaneous rejection of the tyranny of the outline or 'bound or outward circumference' which reason and the human body impose upon man's potential divinity and his commitment to a visual art characterized by outline. This conflict became for Blake 'a profound philosophical issue, the dilemma of personal salvation itself,' for it begged the question of how the individual can attain to divinity whilst contained within a mortal form. Miss Mellor charts Blake's efforts to resolve the conflict through his 'visual-verbal art', as he moves from the benevolently closed world of the *Songs of Innocence* which 'realises the fusion of God and man', through 'the malevolently closed world of hierarchism' to the celebration of the human form divine in *Jerusalem*. Her book as a whole tends towards the schematic, but there are many interesting points by the way.

Amongst the periodical essays there are review essays by Dewey Faulkner (*YR*), Morris Eaves (*ECS*) and John E. Grant (*WC*), together with a reply to Grant from Wagenecht (*WC*). There are several papers of biographical interest. Gerald E. Bentley Jr. (*MP*) explains how a newly discovered letter from Cromek to the poet James Montgomery casts new light on Cromek's relationship with Blake, making the latter seem more patient and tolerant than has hitherto been judged to be the case on the evidence of the vitriolic verses on

[44] *The Awakening of Albion: The Renovation of the Body in the Poetry of William Blake*, by Thomas R. Frosch. Cornell University Press. pp. 211. £3.75.

[45] *Blake's Human Form Divine*, by Anne Kostelanetz Mellor. University of California Press. pp. xxiii+354. £7.50.

Cromek which Blake inscribed in his *Notebook*. Judith Wardle (*SIR*) examines the relationship between Blake and Hayley, and E. D. Mackerness writes on Blake and the Malkins (*DUJ*). As usual the illustrations attract a lot of attention. Robert N. Essick and Andrew Wilton comment respectively on a newly unearthed engraving and a most interesting fan design (*BN*); and at slightly greater length John E. Grant and Robert E. Brown (*BN*) anatomize Blake's vision of Spenser's *Faerie Queene*. Arnold Fawcus (*TLS*) takes up the worries about the authenticity of the so-called New Zealand set of *Illustrations for the Book of Job*. After careful consideration of the known sets (including those described recently by John E. Grant [*TLS*, 1973]), he backs the opinion of Keynes and Binyon that the watercolours were the final reduced studies for the engravings, with some reservations about the title-page and the unevenness of quality, particularly in the colouring. His conclusions are challenged by David Bindman (*TLS*), who argues that the New Zealand set 'bear all the marks of careful and uninspired copies'. As publisher to the Blake Trust, Arnold Fawcus is very much involved in the reproduction of Blake's work; his efforts at the Trianon Press together with similar efforts are evaluated by G. E. Bentley Jr. (*BN*). On a bibliographical note, Peter Roberts has produced 'A Blake Music Review & Checklist' (*BN*).

Amongst the general studies of the works and their underlying principles is a piece by Roger Murray (*SIR*) which investigates the ideal of simplicity in relation to ideas of the sublime in the eighteenth century, especially those of Blair and especially in the context of *Jerusalem*. Barbara F. Lefcowitz (*PMLA*) fears that the heavy emphasis on the inward vision of Blake's personal myth has reached a point where the poetry might seem to be lacking in objective content. She attempts to redress the balance by examining Blake's 'diverse responses to the object world' under five heads: nature as energy; nature seen in humanized terms; nature as an element in the landscape of human experience; the relationship between man and nature as it is changed by vision; and the transmutation of energy into art. Miss Lefcowitz concludes that 'the self can only push to full being against a rich and external reality'. Mary Lynn Johnson explores the borderland between emblem and symbol, stressing the unique position of Blake as poet and designer working simultaneously in the symbolic mode and the emblem tradition. Blake's wing-clipper, rose, sunflower and lily can be recognized as emblematic figures, but, according to Miss Johnson, they are emblems with all the power of new-forged symbols. The relation of Blake to an earlier tradition is also the subject of an enquiry by Richard G. Green (*CL*) who compares Blake and Dante on paradise.

The *Songs* receive mixed treatment. Roy J. Pearcy explains the possible connection between Blake's 'Tyger' and Crashaw's paraphrase of Thomas of Celano's *Dies Irae*; whilst Porter Williams Jr. (*ELN*) tries to establish the precise way in which the idea of 'duty' hovers uneasily between the spiritual and the sweeper's unquestioning acceptance of the duty of cruel labour. According to Williams, Blake presents the sweeper as performing a spiritual duty by showing compassion towards Tom; but a practical aspect of that compassion lies in the sweeper's realistic advice that Tom and others had better perform the duties inflicted upon them by their hard task-masters. Gary J. Taylor (*SIR*) speculates that the form of *The Marriage*, although unique, might have been suggested by the primer. For Taylor *The Marriage* is 'a primer, a rich mosaic of parables, emblems, un-commandment, history and credo'. He concentrates his examination of the primer itself on John Newberry's *A Little Pretty Pocket-Book*. Where Taylor tries to reinstate a familiarity we have lost, Nancy M. Goslee (*SIR*) argues that familiarity with the Jerusalem stanzas has obscured our understanding of their imaginative complexity. She believes that the stanzas are the model for the narrative visions of Blake's two final prophetic books. They assert in public symbols the private inspiration which the figures of Milton and Blake struggle to confirm; and *Jerusalem* retains and expands these symbols in order to reclaim the fallen Albion for his emanation, Jerusalem. Randel Helms's reading of *Ezekiel* and *Jerusalem* (*SIR*) leads him to believe that Blake used *Ezekiel* more as a 'sounding-board' than a source. Helms discovers recast allusions to *Ezekiel* and postulates that Blake worked from his memory of its structure, making startling changes but ending up with 'a prophetic structure that is at once new and strangely traditional'. Finally, for items not mentioned here (and for those which are), there is the *ELN* annual bibliography for the Romantics.

3. PROSE

Three writers are concerned bibliographically with the periodical. David Fairer (*RES*) attacks the authorship problems in *The Adventurer*, whilst Robert B. White, contributing to *Quick Springs of Sense*, tries to sort out the details of the piracy of the *Female Tatlers*. James E. Tierney (*SB*) examines *Museum* attributions in the unpublished correspondence of John Cooper. Addison, too, is the subject of bibliographical attention. Samuel J. Rogal's checklist of Addison's works and the major scholarship devoted to him (*BNYPL*) should be used with some circumspection: it is not always so accurate as it ought to be. C. H. Salter (*MLR*) links Addison's critical tenets with Dryden's. In Slater's opinion, Addison popularizes Dryden without properly acknowledging his debt; moreover, 'it was Dryden, not Addison, who broke with the formal canons of neo-classical criticism, laid the foundations of Romantic aesthetics, and did for criticism what Descartes did for philosophy'. Salter's elevation of Dryden to the status of proto-Romantic is almost as fatuous as Robert C. Hinman's similar elevation of Bacon: Addison has little to fear.

Pat Rogers (*BNYPL*) has added the memoirs of Warton (1715) and Somers (1716) to the John Oldmixon canon on reasonable external and internal grounds; and John C. Riely (*RES*) looks into the background to the publication of Bolingbroke's *Works*. Riely deals particularly with the difficulties experienced by Bolingbroke's literary executor, Mallet, who felt it necessary to consult Chesterfield about how he might obviate political and ecclesiastical opposition to the publication. The major interest of those writing on Defoe's prose has also been the bibliography. Paula Backscheider's edition of *A Short Narrative of the Life and Actions of his Grace John, Duke of Marlborough* (*1711*) for The Augustan Reprint Society[46] is notable

[46] *A Short Narrative of the Life and Actions of His Grace John, Duke of Marlborough* (*1711*), ed. by Paula R. Backscheider. Augustan Reprint Society 168. University of California Press. pp. 51. By subscription.

mainly for its discussion of the attribution; and Rodney M. Baine's paper 'Daniel Defoe and *Robert Drury's Journal*' (*TSLL*) is solely concerned to prove both that there 'is not an iota of external evidence to connect Defoe with the *Journal* and that the internal evidence points away from Defoe even as editor or "Transcriber"'. Frank H. Ellis (*N&Q*) corrects the disinformation of an earlier note to do with *The Vision* and a broadside entitled 'She put her Hand upon his Scull'. He denies firmly on internal evidence that the latter could possibly have been by Defoe. But by far the longest study of attribution is Stieg Hargevik's *The Disputed Assignment of Memoirs of an English Officer to Daniel Defoe*, published in two parts in the Stockholm Studies in English series.[47] Part I offers a quantitative study of Defoe's prose as a basis for attribution. Hargevik establishes 'a list of words and of collocations of individuality-limited linguistic elements characteristic of Defoe on the basis of a one-million-word sample'. This list, together with a list 'of items found to have a smaller relative frequency in Defoe than in a comparative . . . sample from contemporary writers', is then applied to the *Memoirs* and reveals that it is very unlikely that Defoe was the author. Part II is concerned with Captain George Carleton as a historical character and examines the veracity and authenticity of the *Memoirs*. Reviewing previous opinion, Hargevik inclines to believe that the *Memoirs* stem from an authentic document which, with omissions and some encrustations from the pen of a ghost

[47] *The Disputed Assignment of Memoirs of an English Officer to Daniel Defoe*, Parts I and II, by Stieg Hargevik. Acta Universitatis Stockholmiensis. Almquist and Wiskell International. pp. 110+lxxiii and 107. By subscription.

writer (*not* Defoe), forms the backbone of the book. Indeed, Hargevik discovers a 'deeply felt personal' disappointment which 'increases the authenticity of the *Memoirs*'. In order to emphasize the unlikelihood of Defoe's authorship, Part II concludes with a demonstration of differences in both opinion and the representation of facts in Carleton and Defoe. In the introduction to his study Hargevik remarks that he came to centre upon the *Memoirs* because 'its unusual freshness and vivacity could not be the product of the repetitive Daniel Defoe'; such an attitude towards Defoe's style is the subject of G. A. Starr's 'Defoe's Prose Style: 1. The Language of Interpretation' (*MP*). Starr makes a plea for looking beyond the orthodox view of the prose as characterized by plainness and loose and sprawling syntax. John McVeagh (*SEL*) examines Rochester's influence on the apparently antipathetic Defoe. Working from Defoe's 'deep love of Rochester's poems', McVeagh argues that Rochester impressed himself as man and poet upon Defoe's imagination, so much so that his philosophy penetrated into Defoe's mind where it could never be properly assimilated. McVeagh focuses upon *Jure Divino* as manifesting certain inconsistencies in Defoe's theory of man and society, as a result, in part, of Rochester's influence. It is unfortunate that the paper as a whole rests upon a rather crudely systematic reading of Rochester. Miriam Leranbaum (*HLQ*) seeks to dispel the notion that *The Shortest Way* is a satire and to suggest that a more apt description is Defoe's own, that it is a 'banter' or 'hoax'. Miss Leranbaum finds *The Shortest Way* an excellent imitation of militant High-Church propaganda of the sort that Dissenters and moderate Churchmen saw as divisive and dangerous.

Defoe, she believes, wished to expose the dangers and to rally moderate support. Benjamin Boyce treats *The Shortest Way* as 'characteristic Defoe fiction' in *Quick Springs of Sense*.

Mandeville's response to the charge that he had sought 'to debauch the Nation' was *A Modest Defence of Publick Stews* (1724) which argued ostensibly that the authorities ought to contain what they could not legislate out of existence. Richard I. Cook has now edited *A Modest Defence* for the Augustan Reprint Society.[48] In his introduction, Cook animadverts upon Mandeville's ambivalent attitude towards the world of 'happy whores and contented customers' which the *Defence* seems to recommend; but it is a shame he could not be more precise about Mandeville's complex irony in the *Moriae Encomium* tradition. For all that, Cook's chapter on *A Modest Defence* in his introductory excursion into Mandeville in the Twayne's English Authors series[49] is the best part of his book. Cook's study is head and shoulders above the normal run of books in the series; it moves chronologically through the works, placing greater emphasis upon the lesser known, and includes a descriptive checklist of studies of Mandeville.

Interest in Swift seems unabated. The *Journal to Stella*, edited by Harold Williams, has appeared as volumes 15 and 16 of *The Prose Works*;[50] but, since this is simply a reprinting of the 1948 edition, there is nothing to comment upon here.

Gulliveriana IV[51] and *V*,[52] edited by Jeanne K. Welcher and George E. Bush, contain respectively longer and shorter imitations of *Gulliver's Travels*. In the fifth volume the editors claim that the imitations 'illustrate what readers and writers . . . retained from their reading of *Gulliver*, what understanding they had of its theme and intentions'; but one often has to search very hard for evidence of anything approaching real understanding. Robert C. Elliott (*ELH*) is exercised by modern misreadings of Swift's works which see Swift as nihilistic and his readers as guilt-ridden. He opposes to these attitudes his own belief that Swift always provides positives, even if it is not directly. Moreover, it is clear to Elliott from the 'formal ordering' of Swift's work and from the 'paths he leaves open' that he dismisses the possibility that reason or religion 'may be mere projections of our minds'. Although one can understand and sympathize with Elliott's reaction against some modern criticism, the tormented Swift of DePorte's study of madness[2] seems much closer to the truth. Indeed, DePorte's chapter on Swift is undoubtedly the most important piece on that writer to appear in 1974. Swift's hatred of Descartes, the 'mad introvert', and his influence, was idiosyncratic; but, as Michael R. G. Spiller (*RES*) shows, it may have been a hatred Swift shared with Meric Casaubon, who, like Swift, saw Descartes as an enthusiast and connected his name with experimental philosophy, mystical theology and religious fanaticism.

[48] *A Modest Defence of Publick Stews* (*1724*), by Bernard Mandevile, ed. by Richard I. Cook. Augustan Reprint Society 162. University of California Press. pp. v + 78. By subscription.

[49] *Bernard Mandeville*, by Richard I. Cook. Twayne's English Authors Series. Twayne. pp. 174. $7.95.

[50] *Journal to Stella* by Jonathan Swift, ed. by Harold Williams. 2 vols. Basil Blackwell. pp. 801. £11.50.

[51] *Gulliveriana IV*, ed. by Jeanne K. Welcher and George E. Bush, Jr. Scholars' Facsimiles and Reprints. pp. xxx + 384. $35.00.

[52] *Gulliveriana V: Shorter Imitations of Gulliver's Travels*, ed. by Jeanne K. Welcher and George E. Bush, Jr. Scholars' Facsimiles and Reprints. pp. xlvi + 382. $35.00

In a model essay, Clive R. Probyn (*Medical History*) investigates Swift's attitude towards physicians. He demonstrates that Swift shares the traditional sense that the medical profession was satirically vulnerable; but he opines that its claim to be able to repair the human condition intensified both Swift's satire and his awareness of 'depths of corruption stretching far beyond surgical reparation'. On a more pedestrian note, Anne Kline Kelly (*N&Q*) reports on 'A Rowlands–Butler–Swift Parallel'; whilst Emily H. Patterson (*Anglia*) provides evidence that Swift was convinced of Atterbury's innocence, in the form of marginalia inscribed in his copy of Clarendon's *History* and Burnet's *History of His Own Time*. Frank H. Ellis and David Wooley disagree in consecutive issues of the *TLS* about the identity of 'Swift's Seventh Penny Paper'. Sarah, Duchess of Marlborough, commented sarcastically on Swift's appointment as Dean of St Patrick's; now Elizabeth G. Riely comments on the Duchess (*Scriblerian*) in a note describing a series of unpublished letters by the Duchess recently acquired by the Osborn Collection at Yale.

When Swift praised Marvell's *Rehearsal Transpros'd* in the 'Apology' to *A Tale of a Tub*, the Marvell was little read. Raymond A. Anselment (*HLQ*) thinks that the taste which Swift's appreciation implies is central to the vision of *A Tale*. According to Anselment, both Marvell and Swift felt that to be lacking in taste was not merely to be lacking in social grace but to be in violation of propriety; and this violation was tantamount to an 'assertion of self-sufficiency' and hence enthusiasm and modernity. In the opinion of Alan S. Fisher (*HLQ*) *A Tale of a Tub* is the expression of a 'rueful joy' which may be understood by ascertaining Swift's attitudes towards Erasmus and Hobbes. Swift wished ruefully to share 'the surefooted perceptions' of Erasmus, but recognized that he inhabited a world committed to measurable truth. Galileo had 'reduced the universe to matter and motion' and Hobbes had impressed the reduction on the English mind; but, Fisher argues, faced with this restraint Swift could still be joyful, simply because he was anachronistically committed to 'integrity and right reason' in a solitary and subversive act of defiance. Two notes by Clive T. Probyn complete the papers on *A Tale*. Both are in the nature of a gloss: the first supplies contexts for the phrase 'An Iliad in a Nut-Shell' (*N&Q*), and the second (*N&Q*) a context for the description of the brain as a 'Crowd of little Animals . . .', which is an unacknowledged borrowing from Wotton's *Reflections upon Ancient and Modern Learning*. The only piece I have come across on *The Battle of the Books* is a tendentious note by Robert Folkenflik (*RLV*) on allusions to Dryden; and *A Modest Proposal* fares little better with Thomas Lockwood (*PLL*), who attempts to direct attention away from the 'voice' to what it says. *Gulliver's Travels*, on the other hand, is predictably popular. It is difficult to see what, apart from its sections devoted to early and early-modern comment, the new Casebook for *Gulliver's Travels* (edited by Richard Gravil)[53] has to recommend it in preference to similar collections. As is usual with the series, there are no new pieces. Nor is there anything fresh about James L. Clifford's contribution to *Quick Springs of Sense*: it adopts the same critical focus and the same

[53] *Swift—Gulliver's Travels: A Casebook*, ed. by Richard Gravil. Macmillan. pp. 256. £2.50, paperback £1.50.

critical frame as the earlier *MLQ* essay. For Robert P. Fitzgerald (*SP*), the structure of *Gulliver's Travels* is defined by the 'analogous intertwining' of two ideas: that social order frustrates the individual's need to adapt to society and that, although man desires to comprehend his condition, he cannot be confident about the truth or value of what he knows. Fitzgerald finds Gulliver capable of irony, but Everett Zimmerman (*PMLA*) considers him a 'false prophet, only capable of simulating moral insight'. Invective seems to Zimmerman a cloak for guilt and the *Travels* both a satire and a 'psychological analysis of Gulliver as satirist'. Zimmerman believes that Gulliver's attitudes at the end of Book IV are preferable to his earlier 'determination to see no evil'. Margaret Bryan (*ConnR*) sees a development in Gulliver embodied in his use of a looking-glass on four separate occasions. In fact, Gulliver, on this view, suffers a decline rather than development, from self-awareness to self-delusion and pride. In his introduction to the Casebook, Richard Gravil writes of the 'hard' view of Book IV as almost a thing of the past; but it is not so to Gordon Beauchamp (*MichA*) who bases his paper on R. S. Crane's use of Plato's allegory of the cave to propose that the Houyhnhnms are a Platonic society and Gulliver deserving of satire because he shirks enlightenment. It almost comes as a surprise to stumble on an essay which deals at any length with Book III. Anne Patterson supplies the surprise in a consideration of 'Swift's Irony and Cartesian Man' (*MQ*). Miss Patterson not only lays bare the purpose behind Swift's scientific satire but asserts the essential modernity of his concerns: the Cartesian world, materialist and mechanistic, low in

'responsibility for active moral choice', is fundamentally our own as well as Book III's. The *Discourse Concerning the Mechanical Operation of the Spirit* is also a valuable source of material for Miss Patterson's argument. Still on Book III, Clive T. Probyn (*Neophilologus*) suggests that the background for the linguistic satire may be found in the work of John Wilkins. Finally, parallels between Book II and Harrington's *Oceana* lead Myrddin Jones (*PQ*) to speculate that the King's wisdom mirrors Harrington's ideals and that Brobdingnag represents an ideal society which England ought to emulate. The eulogist of 'Verses on the Death of Dr. Swift' is, according to Peter J. Schakel (*MLQ*), of the Opposition party; and the eulogy is 'an idealized portrait of Swift as the embodiment of the values the eulogist associates with the Opposition'.

Following their *Samuel Johnson's Early Biographers*, O. M. Brack Jr. and Robert E. Kelley have now collected fourteen short biographical notices of Johnson, written between 1762 and 1786, into *The Early Biographies of Samuel Johnson*.[54] These are of very mixed quality, but they do demonstrate forcefully that Johnson's stature as a great figure of pious benevolence was recognized in his own lifetime. The editors supply tactful annotations as well as cross-references to Boswell, Piozzi and Hawkins. A similarly conceived volume is to be found in Arthur Sherbo's edition of Shaw's *Memoirs of the Life and Writings* and Hester Piozzi's *Anecdotes of the Late Samuel Johnson* in the Oxford English Memoirs and Travels series.[55] As memoirs

[54] *The Early Biographies of Samuel Johnson*, ed. by O. M. Brack Jr. and Robert E. Kelley. University of Iowa Press. pp. 367. $15.00
[55] *Memoirs of the Life and Writings of the Late Samuel Johnson and Anecdotes of the*

valuable for the earlier and later Johnson respectively, these lives make a complementary pair. Sherbo's introduction is unexceptional, but his explanatory notes are useful, not least for their careful correction of error. John Wain's new biography of Johnson[56] is certainly the most important work to have appeared on Johnson this year. The popular conception of Johnson has always been Boswell's; one hopes that Wain's biography will release the real man. He recognizes that Boswell's monumental Great Cham allows insufficient room for 'the deeply humanitarian Johnson, the man who from first to last rooted his life among the poor and outcast', and his biography attempts to right the perspective. Boswell takes his place amongst Johnson's other literary friends and acquaintances and they in their turn take their place alongside Mrs. Desmoulins, Frank Barber, Levet and Anna Williams, who are as much a part of Johnson's life as the great. Johnson becomes in Wain's hands less the conversationalist and personality and more the deeply self-conscious man of letters capable of rare humanity. More scholarly than he cares to admit, Wain has enriched the orthodox view with more recently discovered facts which often emphasize Johnson's humanity and his capacity for exuberant enjoyment of life. Boswell could admit Johnson's failings but always artfully extenuated them; John Wain finds little need to explain away, for his conception of what it is to be human is richer than Boswell's could ever have been. The

most intimate details of Johnson's complex character are laid open to view with a respectful but never idolatrous sympathy, a sympathy which is in the end the hallmark of the book. Of the articles of a biographical nature, 'Johnson's Struggle with his Personality as Presented in His Prayers' by John D. Cormican (*BSUF*) supplements Wain's account of Johnson's internal conflicts. When Johnson visited Braidwood's Academy in Edinburgh he asked one young woman to resolve a multiplication problem and was much impressed by the outcome. That young lady is now identified by Ralph E. Jenkins (*N&Q*) who draws on the evidence of an apparently reliable eighteenth-century annotation to the *Journey*. She was Miss Dashwood, niece to Sir Francis Dashwood, the organizer of the Hellfire Club. Donald Greene, whose review of John Wain's book involved him in a disagreement with David Pole (*TLS*), is also in debate with John D. Ramage (*SBHT*) about Johnson's politics.

I have been unable to consult a copy of R. D. Stock's anthology of Johnson's criticism, *Samuel Johnson's Literary Criticism*, in the Regents Critics series,[57] but I understand that it contains unmodernized texts of the prefaces to the *Dictionary* and to Shakespeare, pieces from the *Adventurer*, *Idler* and *Rambler*, the tenth chapter of *Rasselas* and a scanty selection from the *Lives*. Although Dustin Griffin's study of Johnson's funeral writings (*ELH*) is primarily concerned with the poetry, it pays careful attention to his theoretic statements about epitaph and elegy. Moreover, it is Griffin's view that to understand Johnson's work in these

[56] *Samuel Johnson*, by John Wain. Macmillan. pp. 388. £4.95.

Late Samuel Johnson, LL.D. During the Last Twenty Years of his Life, by William Shaw and Hester L. Piozzi respectively, ed. by Arthur Sherbo. Oxford English Memoirs and Travels. O.U.P. pp. 201. £4.00.

[57] *Samuel Johnson's Literary Criticism*, ed. by R. D. Stock. Regents Critics Series. University of Nebraska Press. pp. 269. $12.50, paperback $3.50.

two genres is to go a long way towards understanding the total oeuvre, for death clearly occupies a central place in Johnson's mind. Examining the *Essay on Epitaphs* which Johnson contributed to the *Gentleman's Magazine* in 1740, Griffin rehearses the belief that Sherbo's attribution of *An Essay on Elegies* to Johnson is mistaken. Robert Folkenflik (*BNYPL*) renews the debate about its attribution, still opposed to Sherbo; but Sherbo himself (*BNYPL*) not only finds crucial inaccuracies in Folkenflik's argument but turns it to his own service. Something of the background to the *Dictionary* is illuminated by Paul J. Korshin (*JHI*), who speculates on Johnson's knowledge of Renaissance lexicography and its methodological similarities with Johnson's own work. The *Sale Catalogue* (1785) of his library includes 'important monuments of Renaissance lexicography, often very rare editions'; and Johnson's hand in the compilation of the massive *Catalogues Bibliothecae Harleianae* must have brought him into contact with a reasonable number of its 345 dictionaries. The most important ways in which the *Dictionary* is related more to the Renaissance than to the English tradition lie for Korshin in 'his mixture of copious illustrations and terse explanations, his conception of the dictionary as both a word-list and an intellectual history of an entire culture and his evoking the prefatorial theme of monumental and solitary labours'. Charles L. Batten Jr., (*MP*) goes in search of 'Johnson's Sources of "The Life of Roscommon"' and finds them not in Fenton's *Waller* but in a version of Fenton's note on Roscommon's life and a 'Memoir' by George Sewell, both contained in the 1731 revised *Works of the Earls of Rochester, Roscommon and Dorset* (reissued in

1739). Imlac's reliability is stoutly defended by Donald T. Siebert Jr. (*ECS*) against an attack from Arthur Scouten. Scouten (*ECS* [1973]) had argued that Imlac's language in Chapter X betrays his wrongheadedness; Siebert counters with the objection that 'the point is not that Imlac is wrong but that his grandiose language has betrayed him into a state of solipsistic rapture'. Johnson's interest in second sight and the relationship between Martin Martin's 'An Account of Second Sight' (a section of his *Description of the Western Islands of Scotland*), a pseudonymous *Treatise on the Second Sight* (1763) and Johnson's account of the phenomenon in the *Journey* is described by Thomas Jemeliety (*SEL*). Although, as Johnson remarked, 'the state of the mountains, and the islands, is equally unknown with that of Borneo or Sumatra', there were those besides Johnson who explored the Highlands in the eighteenth century. Three records of such explorations, two of them predating Johnson's, are now available in *Beyond the Highland Line*, edited by A. L. Youngson.[58]

As son of the Edinburgh lawyer who aided Lt.-Col. Ralph H. Isham in the purchase of the Boswell papers, David Buchanan is well suited to tell the story of that purchase in *The Treasure of Auchinleck: The Story of the Boswell Papers*;[59] but for those who prefer to read Boswell, there is the third volume of the Yale *Correspondence*[60] which includes correspondence with Goldsmith and

[58] *Beyond the Highland Line: Three Journals of Travel in Eighteenth-Century Scotland*, ed. by A. L. Youngson. Collins. pp. 252. £4.00.

[59] *The Treasure of Auchinleck: The Story of the Boswell Papers*, by David Buchanan. McGraw-Hill. pp. 371. $14.95.

[60] *The Correspondence of James Boswell*, Volume III, ed. by Charles N. Fifer. Yale Edition of the Private Papers of James Boswell. McGraw-Hill. $20.00.

Reynolds. Irma S. Lustig is very much concerned with Boswell the man, particularly with his response to the Jews, in her 'Boswell and the Descendants of Venerable Abraham' (*SEL*). Miss Lustig places his sympathetic response in the wider context of his openness to other denominations, which stemmed from curiosity and doctrinal uncertainty prompted by a repulsion from 'the bleakness of Presbyterian worship' and the theory of predestination. In a paper on Mickle's unfinished 'Prospects of Liberty and Slavery' (which is seen as a part of the process by which *The Lusiad* developed), Monica Letzring (*MLR*) suggests that Boswell approved of it so enthusiastically because it was to include homage to the House of Auchinleck as well as a paean to General Paoli and the Corsican struggle for independence. Donald Greene's review (*TLS*) of the John Wain biography of Johnson comments very unfavourably upon the unreliability of Boswell as biographer, but the Boswell of W. K. Wimsatt's 'Images of Samuel Johnson' (*ELH*) is a very different creature. Wimsatt contrasts Boswell's portrait of the monumental Johnson and Boswell's 'way of responding to mere facts so as to invest them with a kind of hyperactuality and heightened import' with the lesser portraits of other, particularly female, biographers. Felicity A. Nussbaum (*SEL*) writes in praise of Boswell's attempts to order the contradictory qualities of Johnson's character by attributing them to an 'energetic vitality of . . . mind', so subordinating his less attractive traits (his 'apparently rigid piety, gloomy melancholy, and argumentative spirit') to his extraordinary and admirable virtues. This sensitive frankness about Johnson's faults is summed up for Miss Nussbaum in Boswell's own comparison of Johnson to 'a warm West-Indian climate, where you have a bright sun, quick vegetation, luxuriant foliage, luscious fruits, but where the same heat sometimes produces thunder, lightning, and earthquakes in a terrible degree'.

Horace Walpole was not sympathetic to Boswell or Johnson. In the latest volumes to mark the inexorable progress of the Yale edition of the *Correspondence* (volumes 37 to 39, containing the correspondence with his cousin Henry Seymour Conway and his family),[61] Walpole remarks on Boswell's *Journal of a Tour to the Hebrides* as a 'most absurd enormous book' in which 'the more one learns of Johnson, the more preposterous assemblage he appears of strong sense, of the lowest bigotry and prejudices, of pride, brutality, fretfulness, and vanity —and Boswell is the ape of most of his faults, without a grain of his sense. It is the story of a mountebank and his zany'. Apart from this comment, there is little of direct literary interest. I have been unable to consult a copy of *A Bibliography of the Strawberry Hill Press*.[62] edited by A. T. Hazen and J. P. Kirby. It is a pity that Gibbon attracts so little serious attention. This year Roger J. Porter (*ECS*) looks at *The Autobiography* and Grant L. Voth (*SEL*) comments on a part of *The Decline and Fall*. Porter argues that the six versions of 'Memoirs of My Life' normally referred to as *The Autobiography* suggest that Gibbon was of two minds

[61] *Horace Walpole's Correspondence with Henry Seymour Conway*, ed. by Wilmarth S. Lewis *et al.* Yale Edition of Horace Walpole's Correspondence, Volumes 37–39. O.U.P. pp. 584, 578 and 557.

[62] *A Bibliography of the Strawberry Hill Press . . . Including a New Supplement. Together with a Bibliography and Census of the Detached Pieces*, ed. by A. T. Hazen and J. P. Kirby. Dawsons. pp. xxxiv+300.

regarding the nature of the self and his role as autobiographer. In the act of describing his past actions in the present, however, Gibbon implicitly recognizes what autobiography means for him. It becomes 'a way of realizing and defining the self not in retrospect but at the very moment he writes the final pages, when a crisis of selfhood is revealed'. The end constitutes 'a new stage of self-knowledge'. In attempting to amend the view that there is a simple controlling tone for chapter XV of *The Decline and Fall*, Voth points to the substantive and rhetorical complexity of Gibbon's attack on Christianity: Gibbon manipulates tone not only to attack but to indicate the basis of that attack.

The only piece of interest on Burke is by William Christian, 'James Mackintosh, Burke, and the Cause of Reform' (*ECS*). Christian opines that Burke was not the cause of Mackintosh's shift away from the principles supposed to lie behind *Vindiciae Gallicae*. Although there was some change of heart in Mackintosh about parliamentary reform, his early beliefs were by no means so radical as they have been taken to be and he had substantially given ground before his interview with Burke in late 1796.

4. DRAMA

The *RECTR* continues to fill a need for the critic and historian of the theatre, and the annual *SEL* review article by Winton Calhoun is also of interest. For primary material there is Terence Tobin's *Plays by Scots 1660–1800*,[63] a detailed survey of more than a hundred plays by Scottish dramatists at home and abroad. Tobin includes a useful list of plays and entertainments. Samuel J. Rogal (*RECTR*) prints a list of

plays appended to Thomas Lowndes' 1777 edition of Cibber, and Edward Quinn et al., include references for eighteenth-century criticism in their critical bibliography of the major Shakespearean tragedies.[64] The value of A. Norman Jeffares' four volume anthology, *Restoration Comedy*[65] is, as its title suggests, mainly for the Restoration, but it does provide adequate texts, tactfully annotated and with a minimum of textual apparatus, of *The Conscious Lovers, The Careless Husband* and *Love's Last Shift*. Elegantly produced, these are volumes for the general reader rather than the scholar. The eighteenth-century editors (Rowe, Pope, Theobald, Hanmer, Warburton, Johnson and Capell) are the subject at one remove in Robert F. Willson's summary of McKerrow's 1933 lecture on the early editors of Shakespeare (*Shakespeare Newsletter*). The critical perceptions of many of these writers, together with those of Addison, Steele, Welsted and others, are represented in the second volume of Brian Vickers' remarkably interesting Critical Heritage work on Shakespeare.[66] Representative works of less well-known critics, participants in the theatre controversy, are reprinted in facsimile by Garland, prefaced with introductory notes by Arthur Freeman. *Mr. Law's Unlawfulness of the State Entertainment Examin'd*, by S. Philomusus, George Anderson's *The Entertainment of the Stage* and Allan Ramsay's *Some Few Hints in Defence of Dramatical Entertainments* form

---

[63] *Plays by Scots 1660–1800*, by Terence Tobin. University of Iowa Press. pp. 242. $12.95.

[64] *The Major Shakespearean Tragedies: A Critical Bibliography*, by Edward Quinn, James Ruoff and Joseph Grennen. New York: Free Press. pp. 293. $8.95.

[65] *Restoration Comedy*, ed. by A. Norman Jeffares. 4 volumes. The Folio Press. pp. 2524. £32.50.

[66] *Shakespeare: The Critical Heritage, Volume II*, by Brian Vickers. Routledge & Kegan Paul. pp. 549. £8.50.

one volume,[67] and a second contains three pieces by Arthur Bedford; *Serious Reflections on the Scandalous Abuse and Effects of the Stage, A Second Advertisement Concerning the Profaneness of the Play-House* and *A Sermon Preached in the Parish-Church of St Butolph's Aldgate*.[68]

There is more in the way of theatre history from Louis Mitchell (*ECS*) who discusses George I's renewal of the royal interest in, and patronage of, the stage, dealing particularly with command performances. L. W. Conolly (*SQ*) draws attention to the fact that *The Merchant of Venice*, so much a part of the eighteenth-century theatre's Shakespeare repertoire, was not performed during the parliamentary debate upon the Naturalization Act in 1753 for fear of exciting prejudice. De Louterbourg's stage designs are treated by Ralph G. Allen (*TSL*) and Rudiger Joppien (*SJH*). Allen comments on his first important Drury Lane design, for *A Christmas Tale*, remarking upon de Louterbourg's 'ability for making tame fancies seem unpredictable and strange'; and Joppien studies the work for *The Tempest*, a play which lent itself rather more obviously to de Louterbourg's histrionic temperament. Amongst those concerned with the plays themselves, Eve R. Meyer (*ECS*) investigates Turkish elements, especially in the opera, whilst David Mayer (*TQ*) makes some interesting remarks in passing about eighteenth-century pantomime in a wider study of the sexuality of pantomime. More important is Winton Calhoun's contribution to *Quick Springs of Sense*. Calhoun attempts to lay bare some

of the complications beneath the received theatrical history, questioning the assumptions that someone advocating reform was in favour of sentimentalism and that the exhortations of Collier and societies for the reform of manners effectively purged the English stage. Appeals for reform continued for many decades after Collier; and there were also those who, like Adam Ferguson, Samuel Richardson, Thomas Jefferson and Diderot, believed that the drama could augment or even replace the church 'in the capacity of moral instructor'. Several dusty corners of knowledge about the performers have been explored. There is a comprehensive account of Dibdin's role in his miniature theatre by Robert Fahrner (*TN*), and Marion H. Winter (*TN*) furnishes information on the Price family, who together have represented almost every branch of the entertainment profession: equestrians, actors, musicians, dancers, acrobats, mimics and rope-walkers. The career of 'the provincial Garrick', John Hodgkinson, between 1765 and 1792 is described by Billy J. Harbin (*TN*). A better known performer is Mrs. Clive, who is once more allowed to plead her case against Fleetwood and Rich in The Augustan Reprint Society's facsimile of *The Case of Mrs. Clive*, edited by Richard C. Frushell.[69] Garrick, who was, unlike Kitty Clive, re-engaged in 1744, receives meagre attention this year. James E. Tierney (*PBSA*) corrects the dating of a letter to Robert Dodsley in the Little and Kahrl edition; and Betty Rizzo's discovery of a new prologue by Christopher Smart (*PBSA*) serves as a reminder of both a 'forgotten skirmish' in the theatre war and the

---

[67] *Mr. Law's Unlawfulness of the Stage Entertainment Examin'd*, by S. Philomusus, ed. by Arthur Freeman. Garland. $25.00

[68] *Serious Reflections on the Scandalous Abuse and Effects of the Stage*, by Arthur Bedford, ed. by Arthur Freeman. Garland. $25.00.

[69] *Catherine Clive—The Case of Mrs. Clive*, ed. by Richard C. Frushell. Augustan Reprint Society 159. University of California Press. pp. 22. By subscription.

alliance of Smart, Fielding, Garrick and Woodward against Dr. John Hill. John Philip Kemble, on the other hand, is honoured with an edition of the *Promptbooks*[70]—judging from the first volume (the only volume made available to this reviewer), a very fine edition. Each facsimile promptbook is prefaced with a discussion of (i) the history of Kemble's use of the play, (ii) Kemble's own performance or that of other leading actors, (iii) the publication of Kemble's acting version, (iv) distinctive features of the acting version, (v) the significance of the promptbook reproduced and the location and significance of related promptbooks and (vi) the staging. In his 'General Introduction' in the first volume, Charles H. Shattuck supplies a background to the promptbooks as well as necessary information about staging techniques.

Turning to works on the individual dramatists, there are two works on Rowe to report: an edition of *The Tragedy of Jane Shore*, edited by Harry William Pedicord,[71] and a full-length exploration of the tragedies by Landon C. Burns.[72] For his copytext Pedicord favours the first edition rather than the second, corrected edition used by the play's last editors (Nettleton and Case), and he provides a tactfully modernized text. Some of his glosses on the text are too literal and miss the sense of the passage—'mincing minions' (III, 72)

is scarcely explained by 'dainty favourites'—but this is a minor, if annoying, defect. The introduction is a workmanlike affair, treating of the play's sources and theatrical history. Pedicord suggests that Heywood's *Edward IV, Part II* ought to be regarded as a more important source than heretofore and concludes that in reshaping Heywood, Rowe was 'returning to the methods he had pursued in adapting Massinger, compressing a sprawling canvas of action and dialogue into a well-articulated form determined by the dramatic rules of his age'. Landon C. Burns's study comes in the Salzburg Studies in English Literature series. He demonstrates in detail (sometimes pedestrian detail) how the successful sentimental-heroic form of *Jane Shore*, in which tears are more desirable than tragic catharsis, emerged in the course of Rowe's development. Burns is ready to concede that Rowe's tragic vision was, like his century's, severely limited: 'He either failed to realize the larger scope and meaning that attend truly great dramas, or he deliberately ignored them in favour of a more immediate surface appeal'. At the same time he seems ill-at-ease at having to admit that Rowe's significance is only historical, and he argues, against the drift of the book, that the better plays are 'inspiring and memorable', sharing transcendent qualities with *King Lear* and *Oedipus Rex*. This is a critically unsure book, but its historical business might be of some use.

Cibber has prompted no more than a couple of notes. Duncan Eaves and Ben D. Kimpel (*N&Q*) point out that letters from Young and Cibber to Richardson reveal their contrasting personalities; and there is a half-hearted suggestion from Sean Shesgreen (*AN&Q*) that

[70] *The Kemble Promptbooks*, ed. by Charles Shattuck. 11 vols. Folger Facsimiles. University Press of Virginia. $220.00

[71] *The Tragedy of Jane Shore*, by Nicholas Rowe, ed. by Harry W. Pedicord. Regents Restoration Drama Series. University of Nebraska Press. pp. 97. $8.95, paperback $1.85.

[72] *Pity and Tears: The Tragedies of Nicholas Rowe*, by Landon C. Burns. Institut für Englische Sprache und Literatur. University of Salzburg. pp. 256. £4.80 or by subscription.

Cibber is satirized in the 1754 revised edition of *Jonathan Wild*. It is only to be expected that most of the interest in Gay should centre upon *The Beggar's Opera*. Joseph Haslag[73] carefully separates it from Brecht's *Threepenny Opera*, insisting on the necessity of reading it against the background of the contemporary poetics which it burlesques. William McIntosh (*ECS*) tries to explode the critical commonplace that the ostensible intention behind *The Beggar's Opera* was 'the dissolution of Handelian opera' and the unseating of Walpole. Just as McIntosh finds modern criticism wanting, Harold G. Moss (*N&Q*) is dissatisfied with the editors, who are insufficiently alive to Gay's debts to earlier writers in *The Beggar's Opera*—Moss is particularly interested in D'Urfey. It is a shame that Haslag did not deal with the moral significance of Gay's divergence from the classical; but Joan H. Owen (*BNYPL*) is directly concerned with Gay's moral attitudes. In her opinion, *Polly* was intended as a burlesque of *All for Love*, to expose the absurdity of heroic conventions and values in the real world.

The *Grub Street Opera* seems to Harold G. Moss (*TS*) to offer pointed satire beneath a slight musical grace. Moss believes that Fielding deliberately tried to offset the fierceness of his attack with musical settings. Peter Lewis (*N&Q*) provides three notes on the plays: one on the subject of the influence of *The British Stage* (1724) in Fielding's satire, another on a reference to Merlin's cave in *Pasquin* and the third on caricature in *The Historical Register*. There are also two more general

papers on Fielding's work which touch upon the drama. Anthony J. Hassall (*PQ*) finds the image of puppet and puppeteer neatly expressive of the relationship between the author and his work; whilst C. R. Kropf (*PMLA*) investigates the relationship between educational theory and human nature in *The Fathers, or The Good-Natur'd Man*. The Fathers seems to Kropf to be underpinned by one of the three attitudes towards education and man distinguishable in Fielding's works: that man is originally a blank paper and that education alone determines his character. As well as appearing as a critic in *Shakespeare. The Critical Heritage*,[66] Steele is represented by a reprinting of John Loftis's *Steele at Drury Lane*,[74] G. S. Rousseau's Critical Heritage volume for Goldsmith[38] provides texts of early reviews of the plays as well as many snippets relevant to Goldsmith's position in the theatre. It is particularly useful to have sizeable pieces from Thomas Davies' *Memoirs of Garrick* to support Davies' belief that Goldsmith was 'an inexplicable existence in creation'; and it is good, too, to have some of Cumberland's warm account of Goldsmith's later years, especially his relation of the complex (and comic) arrangements made by Johnson, the Burkes, Reynolds, Fitzherbert, Caleb Whiteford 'and a phalanx of North-British pre-determined applauders, under the banner of Major Mills, all good men and true' to ensure the good reception of *She Stoops to Conquer*. According to Oliver W. Ferguson in *Quick Springs of Sense*, Goldsmith's doubt that 'the exhibition of human distress [would] afford the mind more entertainment than that of human absurdity' brought a response in the form of the

---

[73] *Studien zur englischen und amerikanischen Sprache und Literatur: Festschrift fur Helmut Papajewski*, ed. by Paul Buchloh, Inge Leimberg, and Herbert Rauter. Neumunster. pp. 256. n.p.

[74] *Steele at Drury Lane*, by John C. Loftis. Greenwood Press. pp. 260. $13.25.

'Dedication to Distraction' from Sir Fretful himself, Richard Cumberland. The success story of George Lillo's *The London Merchant* is investigated by Harry W. Pedicord (*PQ*) who finds reasons for it in the 'tradition, teachings, and active support of the Ancient Order of Free and Accepted Masons'.

It is always surprising to find someone taking Johnson's *Irene* seriously. Philip T. Clayton (*TSL*) argues with more energy than tact that Johnson's close obedience to neoclassical rules indicates that its heroine is Irene not Aspasia—the play remains, the play remains the same. Sheridan is meagrely represented, especially after the attention he received last year. Sheridan's moral values, as they appear in *School for Scandal* and his 1788 Westminster Hall Speech, are explored by Jack D. Durant (*SBT*); and Philip K. Jason (*TS*) contends that Sheridan's concern with the relation of the fictional world of the play to the actual world of human affairs constitutes a major part of his attraction for the modern audience.

5. THE NOVEL

The one book of a general nature worth mentioning is an important one, R. F. Brissenden's *Virtue in Distress: Studies in the Novel of Sentiment from Richardson to Sade*.[75] Brissenden defines sentimentalism as informed at root by the belief that the spontaneous moral responses of the individual, despite their subjectivity, are reasonable. As such it represents 'both an idealistic and freshly empirical and pragmatic approach to life ... which clearly enabled people ... to explore human problems in a new and illuminating manner'. At the same time it could easily degenerate

into sentimentality. The theme of virtue in distress arises from a recognition of the gap between moral idealism and the practical or social world. It seemed impossible for individual acts of benevolence to effect any change in the larger and harsh reality of an inequitable society, and there was a gathering suspicion that there was perhaps something unwholesome about deriving pleasure from charitable behaviour which was bound to be ineffective. The emphasis upon feeling itself (pity, according to a minor novelist, is 'the greatest luxury the soul of sensibility is capable of relishing') coexists with uneasiness that, as Sade's Dubourg puts it, 'charity's pleasures are nothing but sops thrown to pride'. Brissenden is largely concerned with the novelistic heroes who represent an awareness of the gap mentioned above, and the dangers of sentimentality. Parson Yorick is for him typical of such heroes, 'at once admirable and pathetic'. He is admirable for his sensitivity, generosity, candour and benevolence, and pathetic (and comic) because these virtues fail to impact themselves upon the world. Brissenden argues that the reader as well as Yorick has constantly to ask himself whether the feelings precipitated by situations within *A Sentimental Journey* are 'genuinely altruistic and appropriate' or whether they are in some way egotistic. Yorick is seen as typical, too, in finding difficulties in contexts which involve poverty or the opposite sex. The contact with poverty necessarily poses questions about sincerity or complacency in the face of an unalterable society, and the sexual business not only involves a searching interest in the grounds of Yorick's affections but points to a real dilemma in sentimentalist thought. If man was to be ultra-sensitive, his body could not

[75] *Virtue in Distress: Studies in the Novel of Sentiment from Richardson to Sade*, by R. F. Brissenden. Macmillan. pp. 306. £5.95.

but be involved: that is, heightened sexual responsiveness was a logical corollary of heightened moral responsiveness. These heroes are placed in novels where the subject is not moral action but moral discrimination: 'the important thing is not the doing of good deeds, but the right analysis of morally intricate and perplexing situations'. This is very much the bare bones of Brissenden's argument: the demands of space do not allow a proper account of his fine responsiveness to the nuances, ramifications and sense of the modernity of his topic—the sixth chapter deals in some detail with related thought in later literature—but this is certainly a book to be warmly recommended.

The second part of the book is concerned with individual authors and novels. According to Brissenden, Richardson provides us in *Clarissa* with a story which is both 'a comment on the facile assumption that man is naturally a rational and benevolent creature' and, in Lovelace ('the pitiable, perverted and impotent villain'), an upholding of the value of the sentimental optimism that man can release his capacity for altruism. *Clarissa* is a great novel for Brissenden because of 'the unremitting thoroughness and the compassion' with which it tests the sentimental ideal against the reality of man's nature. In his very different way, Sterne demonstrates that he is aware of the fallibility of pure feeling whilst placing his trust in it as the root of all that is good in human relations. The combination of satiric wit and sentimentality in *Tristram Shandy* constitutes, in Brissenden's opinion, the recognition and evaluation of feeling. The profoundly comic optimism of Sterne is here presented as very different from the mood of *The Vicar of Wakefield*. Ostensibly a sentimental comedy, *The Vicar* is at

base as pessimistic and elegiac as *A Deserted Village* and *The Traveller*. It seems to Brissenden that Goldsmith conceived of society as so irrational and unjust as to make well-nigh fatuous the efforts of the morally responsible to live a good life. To survive, Primrose needs 'the magical assistance' of Thornhill. When the focus moves to Mackenzie and Melmoth, they exhibit nothing of the qualities of these writers. Mackenzie's sentimentalism is 'narcissistic and self-indulgent', and Melmoth is a 'sanctimonious fraud' keen to appeal to the better feelings of his audience. Peacock, Austen and Sade were, on the other hand, anti-sentimentalists. There is a paper of related interests in Cynthia G. Wolff's discussion of some of the problems surrounding presentations of secular heroinism in the eighteenth century (*MLS*). Irène Simon (*EA*) writes in a general mood on 'Le roman feminin en Angleterre au XVIIIe siècle'.

Dirk Barth's unrevised doctoral dissertation, *Prudence im Werke Daniel Defoe*,[76] makes rather plodding reading. Barth is heavily committed to a very technical, quasi-scientific terminology derived from contemporary stylistics and semantics and he often dresses up the most obvious points with undue complexity. Anyone with a reasonable critical sensitivity would expect the meaning of a term, such as 'prudence', to vary in inflection from context to context; but Barth substitutes for this sensitivity a cumbersome methodology based upon Wittgenstein's notion that 'the meaning of a word is its use in context'. Barth considers Defoe's 'prudence' in terms of 'honesty', 'self-interest' and 'safety', 'sense',

[76] *Prudence im Werke Daniel Defoe*, by Dirk Barth. Europaische Hochschulschriften ser. XIV: Angelsachsische Sprache und Literatur, 13. Bern: H. Lang. pp. viii+173.

'passion', 'moderation' and 'religion sobriety and duty'. J. A. Michie's contribution on 'The Unity of *Moll Flanders*' to *Knaves and Swindlers: Essays on the Picaresque Novel in Europe*[77] is much more alert to the problems and intricacies facing the reader, even if it does tend to make a silk purse out of Defoe's novel. Reviewing the various attitudes towards the unity of *Moll*, Michie argues that 'there is a strong structural unity, involving theme, character and action'. This unity, he believes, cannot be discussed meaningfully by considering either 'the surface logic of outward action' or the 'logic of spiritual change within Moll'; what is required is a reconciliation of these approaches, 'the union of the story of Moll's aspirations to middle-class gentility with the moral fable of what became of her in the process of striving towards that end'. For Michie the unity is rooted in the tensions between the social and economic aspirations of the protagonist and her moral and religious scruples, the difficulties of being good in the process of 'making good'. In Moll's progress necessity is replaced by greed and our attitude towards Moll's repentance in relation to the retaining of her ill-gotten gains is affected by an awareness of this distinction. Michie's answer to those who, like this reader, would want to object that Defoe's silence on the distinction is at odds with the tone and professions of the Preface, is simply that this is a reflection of an ambiguity inherent in the mercantile society of Defoe's day. For those not familiar with the critical debate to which Michie addresses his discussion, Edward Kelley's edition of *Moll*

Flanders: An Authoritative Text, Backgrounds and Sources[78] includes critical essays by McKillop, Watt, Booth, Price, Novak and Starr. For his text Kelley has preferred the first to the second (and corrected) edition, but he has adopted readings from the second in a few cases on the grounds that 'it appears that the corrector of the second edition had access to Defoe's manuscript'.

Of those concerned with *Robinson Crusoe*, Maximillian E. Novak is interested in the work's imaginative genesis whilst Sally D. Siegel (*Thoth*) discusses paradox and unity. The best essay is from Pat Rogers (*EIC*) who argues that Crusoe is *homo domesticus* and his story one of home-making and housekeeping. Rogers feels that attention has been paid to Crusoe's 'productive, quasi-economic way of living' at the expense of due recognition for his domesticity: finding a home is Crusoe's first aim. Rogers works steadily through the book, selecting passages which define Crusoe's motives as providing for his domestic comfort and well-being. He concludes that the evidence suggests that the real subject has little to do with quasi-primitive man or with the capitalist ethic: the story is one of 'a Caribbean nabob' who makes 'a little England' in foreign surroundings. The papers by McVeagh (*SEL*) and Starr (*MP*), mentioned in the prose section of this chapter, also touch upon the novels.

Elizabeth Bergen Brophy's *Samuel Richardson: The Triumph of Craft*[79] is an attempt to demonstrate that Richardson was a very self-conscious artist and not a novelist 'by accident'

[77] *Knaves and Swindlers: Essays on the Picaresque Novel in Europe*, ed. by Christine J. Whitbourn. Oxford University Press for the University of Hull. pp. 145. £3.50.

[78] *Moll Flanders: An Authoritative Text. Backgrounds and Sources, Criticism*, ed. by Edward Kelley. Norton Critical Edition. Norton. pp. ix+444. $3.45.

[79] *Samuel Richardson: The Triumph of Craft*, by Elizabeth B. Brophy. University of Tennessee Press. pp. 131. $7.25.

or 'despite himself'. She holds that the critic should concern himself with Richardson's 'deliberate aims' which constitute 'the most important factor in the success of the novels'; she is suspicious of those who deal with his unconscious, which is 'at best a subject of informed speculation'. The book is written to a very simple recipe: first, Miss Brophy formulates Richardson's artistic precepts, and then she matches them with the practice of the novels. Because of Richardson's diffidence as an artist, the precepts emerge rather more from statements made in the personal correspondence than from the more formal prefaces and postscripts to the novels; but there is no doubt for Miss Brophy that beneath this diffidence Richardson saw himself as an innovator, that he 'began writing fiction with the deliberate design of creating a new and different "course of reading"'. Yet she is forced to admit that Richardson was neither an original nor a deep thinker; and this want is felt in her description of his commitment to a didactic art, teaching by engaging the emotions in 'the moral trial of exemplary characters' through a form conspicuous for its verisimilitude. Commenting upon the success and failure of Richardson's works in relation to his precepts, Miss Brophy finds *Pamela* to be a novel which permits strong emotional identification, but one which also suffers from a one-sided point of view. *Pamela II* and *Sir Charles Grandison* fail because Richardson substitutes trifling questions of propriety for moral dilemma; but *Clarissa* is supremely successful, according to Miss Brophy's criteria. The reader is involved both emotionally and intellectually in Clarissa's moral conflict. What Miss Brophy has to say warrants a paper, perhaps, but not a book; the formula

for her study and the rather intentionalist criteria which underpin it are critically limited—especially when we consider Richardson's own uneasiness about his craft (as shown, for example, in his revisions of *Clarissa*). It is precisely this uneasiness which is the subject of an interesting paper by Shirley van Marter ('Hidden Virtue: An Unsolved Problem in *Clarissa*' (*YES*)). Miss van Marter explores Richardson's difficulties in integrating pleasure with instruction in the face of the troublesome success of Lovelace and mixed reception given to Clarissa. By collating the four editions published in Richardson's lifetime, Miss van Marter has unearthed eight revisions affecting the presentation of Hickman's character to support Richardson's discussion of Hickman both in letters and the Postscript printed for the third edition (1751). Richardson's defence against the charge that Hickman was too stiff and sober to be likeable was simply that he intended to polarize Lovelace and Hickman; but in the revisions we find him attempting to alleviate the over-formality. They include two new letters (21 and 22 of Book II in the third edition) which furnish 'our only sustained glimpse of his inner thoughts' and the deletion of lines from Anna to Clarissa which refer directly to Hickman as 'a man of that antiquated cut. . . . A great deal too much upon the formal . . .'. This essay should be read with another modestly scholarly piece by Miss van Marter ('Richardson's Revisions of *Clarissa* in the Second Edition' (*SB*)), which passed unnoticed in last year's reviews. Here Miss van Marter argues that many of the substantive changes are not merely a response to the readers' difficulties but a deliberate attempt to heighten the tragedy. Leo Braudy's contribution to

New Approaches to Eighteenth-Century Literature (edited by Philip Harth)[80] is a relentlessly psychological study of the 'identity of the self' in *Clarissa*. On *Pamela* there is Roy Roussel (*ELH*) who accounts for Richardson's reconciliation of distance and presence in and through the letter. Margaret A. Doody's *A Natural Passion: A Study of Samuel Richardson*[81] was reviewed in error in *YWES* 1973.

From the author of *Pamela* we move to the creator of an anti-Pamela in John Cleland, who is the subject of a critical biography by William H. Epstein, *John Cleland: Images of a Life*.[82] Epstein's researches into the life seem to have been painstaking: Cleland emerges as an oddly able man who never realized his talents, thwarted by circumstances which he took insufficient care to control. *Fanny Hill*, produced in a bid to extricate himself from debtors' prison, only involved him in pornography charges; but in later life he courted respectability to such an extent that the antisentimentalist becomes the sentimentalist in *Memoirs of a Coxcomb* (1751) and *The Woman of Honour* (1778). Epstein is openly unsympathetic to the later man: 'his shrill calls for natural simplicity—tolerable perhaps in a younger man tinged with idealism and searching for an identity—seem merely immature and irritating in an older man'. Critically, Epstein doesn't offer much beyond placing *Memoirs of a Woman of Pleasure* in its artistic and his-

torical context: those interested in the value of *Fanny Hill* would still do better to turn to Malcolm Bradbury's *CQ* article. It is to be regretted that Epstein should resort to such a gratuitous style.

In *Marriage: Fielding's Mirror of Morality*,[83] Murial Brittain Williams argues that Fielding's eighteenth-century context represents an important moment in the changing attitudes towards marriage. Fielding, she opines, is particularly exercised by questions such as: should marriage be based on romantic love or on prudential considerations? and should the parent or the child have the right to select the mate? The Restoration flippancy towards the institution of marriage may have inspired the corrective impulse of the sentimental drama, but, according to Miss Williams, the first important focus for 'the marriage debate' was the novel. *Pamela* 'served as the literary outlet and the new form evolved primarily to accommodate the new ideas and aspirations of the middle class, specifically new attitudes towards marriage'. Miss Williams discusses Fielding's development from an apprenticeship in drama (closely related to the Restoration dramatic tradition) to the novel, in which he defined the foundations of morality (and, therefore, of love and marriage) as humane feeling, right reason on a purely secular plane and charity on the Christian. She describes a maturing and sobering progress from a tolerant and genial acceptance of imperfect nature to a troubled and earnest anxiety for the harmony at the centre of his concept of order. Dealt with only incidentally in *Joseph Andrews* and *Jonathan Wild*, courtship and marriage are centrally

---

[80] *New Approaches to Eighteenth-Century Literature*, ed. by Philip Harth. Columbia University Press. pp. 185. $7.50.

[81] *A Natural Passion: A Study of the Novels of Samuel Richardson*, by Margaret A. Doody. Oxford: The Clarendon Press. pp. 410. £8.00.

[82] *John Cleland: Images of Life*, by William H. Epstein. Columbia University Press. pp. 284. $9.95.

[83] *Marriage: Fielding's Mirror of Reality*, by Murial Brittain Williams. University of Alabama Press. pp. vi+168. n.p.

involved in *Tom Jones* and *Amelia*, respectively. It is clear from the array of ill-matched marriages that Fielding was not blind to the difficulties of finding an ideal marriage inspired by mutual trust, sufficient means and the wife's subordination—hence the disbelief in Tom's reformation and Booth's conversion. Claude Rawson's Penguin *Critical Anthology* for Fielding[84] is of most interest for the novel, but it ought to be consulted, too, by those interested in the prose and the drama. Rawson's selection falls into three unequal sections (criticism up to 1755; 1756–1938; and 1939 to the present), each prefaced with a guide to the contours of the views it produced. Rawson has preferred to err on the side of being over-comprehensive: there is little to justify, for example, the inclusion of the following lines from Denis Diderot, as they stand; 'I shall not be pleased with you or myself if I do not bring you to appreciate the truth of *Pamela, Tom Jones*, or *Clarissa* and of *Grandison*'; but Rawson does have an eye for exactly how much quotation is required to represent faithfully. This capacity is particularly useful in the final section where he is often dealing with lengthy studies. The omission of most significance is Rawson's own work. This modestly presented volume should prove most welcome not only to those interested in Fielding but to those more generally curious about the history of taste. It is supplemented with a selected bibliography.

There is also a selection of criticism (including Battestin, Booth, Crane, Empson and Hilles) appended to Sheridan Baker's Norton Critical Edition of *Tom Jones*[85]. Baker includes, too, a map of Tom's route to London, as well as more conventional annotations. The text is a faithful reproduction of the fourth edition except for typographical idiosyncrasies and errors. Adaptations of *Tom Jones* are the province of Raymond J. Rundus (*BNYPL*) who supplies a history and criticism of works inspired by, and derived from, *Tom Jones* as an addenda to Cross (III, 189–366). *Quick Springs of Sense*, edited by Larry S. Champion, contains several pieces on Fielding. A. S. Knowles, Jr., treats the Mr. Wilson episode of *Joseph Andrews* and the Old Man of the Hill episode of *Tom Jones* as contributions to the theme of retirement; whilst C. J. Rawson considers language, dialogue and point of view in Fielding generally and J. Paul Hunter explores the lesson of *Amelia*. Battestin's paper on *Amelia* in *ELH* is in much the same mood as his *Providence of Wit*. He believes that the qualities which make *Amelia* Fielding's most troublesome novel are precisely those which render it his most intellectually ambitious, 'the product of his maturest thinking about human nature and ... the grounds of order in society'. In Battestin's view, *Amelia* was written to substantiate the Christian humanist vision which provided the foundations for the meaning and coherence of Fielding's world, a vision profoundly threatened by a new scepticism in religion and empiricism in morality whose powerful proponent was David Hume. The clash is dramatized in Booth. In *Amelia* Fielding articulates a view hitherto discernible in only inchoate form in his writing, that passion alone is the spring of human behaviour. Amelia is the embodiment of Field-

[84] *Henry Fielding: A Critical Anthology*, ed. by Claude Rawson. Penguin. £1.80.
[85] *Tom Jones: An Authoritative Text, Contemporary Reactions, Criticism*, ed. by Sheridan Baker. Norton Critical Edition. Norton. pp. viii+934. $3.95.

ing's ethical system that 'only religion by appealing to our hopes and fears with the promise of future rewards and punishments, can prevent anarchy in the moral order'. C. R. Kropf (*PMLA*) is concerned generally with the question of whether Fielding presents a consistent or unified view of human nature. He attempts to synthesize two opposed views: that Fielding held to a latitudinarian position and that he studiously refused to subsume nature under any theory or system. Kropf approaches his compromise by way of Fielding's references to education and educational theory. He distinguishes three attitudes: first, that man is originally a blank paper and that education alone determines character; second, that man is originally a blank paper but that early habits so dictate the character that later change through education is impossible; and third, that man's character is determined by innate qualities beyond the reach of education. According to Kropf, Fielding shifts between these theories; but *Amelia* represents an extension of them. As Booth's development shows, a man's character, though predetermined and incapable of transformation, can be mended and repaired.

To move to the work of Francis Coventry is not to move far away from Fielding: Coventry, a disciple of Fielding, wrote only one novel, *The History of Pompey the Little or the Life and Adventures of a Lap-Dog*, which is now edited by Robert Adams Day in the Oxford English Novels series.[86] In his introduction Day gives the necessary details of the biography and publishing history as well as placing Coventry's efforts in the tradition of Swift, Pope and Fielding. Coventry alludes constantly to these three and 'continually quotes or perhaps merely lifts passages from them'. Day feels that the work is best approached critically as though it were an offshoot 'in narrative prose of the formal poetic satire in the tradition of Juvenal', in which 'the problem of handling the Juvenalian protagonist as a believable human being are solved by making him non-human', a pivot for Coventry's satire on the decay of values symptomized by the elevation of lap-dogs above humans. The problems facing the editor of *Pompey* are here sensibly overcome. For the third and final edition Coventry dropped some chapters and added others as well as making slight changes of wording; but in Day's opinion the changes were for the worst. He has, therefore, retained basically the text of the first edition and supplemented it with the new chapters from the third. There are also some incidental alterations to the first, necessary in dove-tailing the best from both versions.

Richard A. Lanham takes the opposition between the Victorian and modern views of the Sterne of *Tristram Shandy* as his starting point for *Tristram Shandy: The Games of Pleasure*.[87] Lanham argues that the Victorians were in a sense correct to find Sterne unserious where the modern critic finds him comically serious about an absurd world. He is convinced that Sterne believed that man naturally seeks (and should seek) pleasure rather than truth, that the grand systems of truth are largely irrelevant to his personal interests. Even the sentiment which some critics take as bridging the gap

[86] *The History of Pompey the Little or the Life and Adventures of a Lap-Dog*, by Francis Coventry. Edited by Robert Adams Day. Oxford English Novels. O.U.P. pp. 221. £4.00.

[87] *Tristram Shandy: The Games of Pleasure*, by Richard A. Lanham. University of California Press. pp. x + 174.

between the characters' solipsistic worlds is the result of intensely personal interests: 'one of the lessons Tristram teaches us is that when we feel for others, we do so largely for the pleasure of the feeling'. The contrast between the traditional world of public values and Sterne's world of deeply private ones is summed up by Sterne's application of the 'older public oratorical and narrative modes to the novel's new private life'. Lanham's book is both perceptive in flashes and a critical cock-and-bull story; the latter because it is founded on the rigid thesis that Sterne's characters are acutely self-aware about their relationship with the larger world, as persons 'self-conscious about language and literary form, making of language a *ludus*, a knowing public display of rhetoric, a game'. *Tristram Shandy* is the subject, too, of a chapter in A. D. Nuttall's fine book about the rise of solipsistic fear as a 'fertile source of disquiet' in literature, *A Common Sky: Philosophy and the Literary Imagination.*[88] Nuttall is concerned with Sterne's refusal to distort reality in the interests of formal coherence and with the zest which followed from Sterne's perception of the world before him as unmanageable, zest which manifests itself in a genuinely moral exploration of the relationship between the writer and reality. Behind the unsystematic progress of Sterne's novel lies a formal norm: *Tristram Shandy* is 'an ingeniously sustained description of the norm of linear narrative'. Further, the norm for Sterne's intellectual extravagance is 'the rock-hard scientific world-picture which Locke had codified'. Sterne's attitude towards Locke was

[88] *A Common Sky: Philosophy and the Literary Imagination*, by A. D. Nuttall. Chatto & Windus for Sussex University Press. pp. 298. £3.95.

ambivalent: when Tristram speaks of Locke's *Essay* as 'a history-book of what passes in a man's own mind', Sterne shows an 'affectionate vigilance'. His reading of Locke was not frivolous, but he did recognize his comic potential. Nuttall concludes that *Tristram Shandy* is not 'the destroyer of the fashionable world-picture, but, with its chaotic determinism, its biological psychology and its microscopic observation, its one adequate literary monument'. Along with Michael V. DePorte's treatment of Sterne in *Nightmares and Hobbyhorses*,[2] Nuttall's chapter represents the best work to appear on Sterne this year: if anything it has the edge over DePorte's contribution in catching much more of the exuberance and fulness of Sterne's thoughtful playfulness. Chinmoy Banerjee (*TSLL*) is also interested in Sterne and Locke. Banerjee argues that Sterne's train of ideas is better illuminated in the context of Renaissance learning and contemporary thinking than in the light of Locke's *Essay*. The psychological aspects of the train of ideas were of little concern for Locke, but the principle behind the succession of ideas in the mind had been a subject of interest since Aristotle; Hume and his associationist followers provided the contemporary theoretical context. Banerjee is particularly interested in Alexander Gerard's *Essay on Genius*. As the title of F. Doherty's paper might suggest ('Bayle and *Tristram Shandy*: "Stage-Loads of Chymical Nostrums and Peripatetic Lumber"' [*Neophil.*]), his article is largely an addition to our knowledge of Sterne's place in the tradition of learned wit. Doherty investigates Sterne's reading of Bayle's *An Historical and Critical Dictionary* which Sterne borrowed whilst a Prebend of York Minster for a total of ten months in 1752–53.

Sterne 'saw and enjoyed the joke of using scurrilous or obscene anecdotes or snippets of anecdotes from the *Dictionary* to complicate his own telling of a tale in *Tristram Shandy*'. He looked on the vast work as another monument to man's absurdity, and saw the parade of learning as a worthy counterpart to Burton's *Anatomy*.

Alan B. Howes' *Critical Heritage* volume on Sterne[89] contains material on Sterne up to the 1830s, largely devoted, where the comment is particular, to *Tristram Shandy*. It is especially good to have extensive representation of Sterne's reception in Europe (although this does sometimes become repetitive), but it seems unnecessary, as it does in Rawson's Penguin *Critical Anthology* for Fielding,[84] to print passages from the creative works. It would have been sufficient to supply page references, and the space saved could have been used fruitfully to extend the discussion of post 1830s criticism in Howe's introduction. Howes notes that 'recent criticism has managed to explore new territory', but he allows himself only one short paragraph of elucidation.

Goldsmith, the novelist, is represented in George Rousseau's *Critical Heritage* volume[38] by early remarks on *The Vicar of Wakefield* and some more general remarks from later writers up to the late nineteenth century. In addition the Oxford English Novels series celebrated the 200th anniversary of Goldsmith's death to the day (4 April) with an edition of *The Vicar*, edited by Arthur Friedman.[90] The text is sub-

[89] *Sterne: The Critical Heritage*, ed. by Alan B. Howes. Routledge & Kegan Paul. pp. 488. £7.25.

[90] *The Vicar of Wakefield: A Tale Supposed to be Written by Himself*, ed. by Arthur Friedman. Oxford English Novels. O.U.P. pp. 207. £3.00.

stantially that established by Friedman for his *Collected Works of Oliver Goldsmith*: that is, the text of the first edition with revisions from the second edition, for which Goldsmith seems to have been responsible. In his introduction Friedman urges that 'the most important thing to say about *The Vicar* is not that it has a sentimental plot but that it is a rather special kind of comic novel'; and he distinguishes it from the tragic novel with a sentimental plot (*Clarissa*) and the serious novel with a sentimental plot (*Pamela*). In discussing the narrator (a 'fallible paragon'), Friedman is impatient with the more recent criticism which has dwelt on his untrustworthiness, hypocrisy and worldliness. He puts his trust in Goldsmith's own description of the 'hero of this piece' who 'unites in himself the three greatest characters upon earth; he is a priest, an husbandman, and the father of a family. He is drawn as ready to reach, and ready to obey, as simple in affluence and majestic in adversity'.

Robin Fabel's interest in Smollett (*ECS*) is mainly in the man, particularly in his patriotism and relation to English politics between 1756 and 1771; but the focus of attention for the majority of the essays on Smollett is *Humphry Clinker*. Linda Pannill (*Thoth*) concentrates on patterns of imagery, whilst Edward Copeland (*TSLL*) goes in search of a genre and finds it in the 'comic pastoral poem in prose'. Copeland insists on the general widening of the concept of pastoral during the eighteenth century before looking at Smollett's own experiments with the tradition in an effort to place *Humphry Clinker*. Even if, as the tone of the essay suggests, the classification is doomed to failure, there is much of value by the way. Copeland examines carefully Smollett's farce *The Reprisal* which he finds full of the dialectic structure of country versus city and nature versus art, and as such characteristic of all worthwhile pastoral. *The Reprisal* is offered as a significant key to *Humphry Clinker*, which shares with it a 'benign, comic and sentimental world of pastoral'. Robert Folkenflik (*PQ*) sees *Humphry Clinker* as an exploration of human relationships presented through the medium of individual voices. Each perspective is partial, at the mercy of the ironies of the larger view enjoyed by the reader. According to Folkenflik, although we sympathize with Matt Bramble, our movement in and out of the various consciousnesses enables us to recognize their selfhood to be comically limited: we encompass all their views in a tolerant and embracing vision which prepares us for the social vision of the good life at the novel's end. In short, *Humphry Clinker* is for Folkenflik not a farewell to but a transcendence of the picaresque.

Finally, in 'Ev'ry Woman is at Heart a Rake', Patricia M. Spacks (*ECS*) is exercised by the portrayal of women in the eighteenth century, especially in the work of Fanny Burney. From Lady Wishfort to Geraldine, woman was represented as mysteriously sexual: not all, but most, supported Pope's dictum. Miss Spacks finds that in fiction and autobiography by women in the eighteenth century, the attitude towards sexuality displays itself in an obsession with innocence, a concern for the dangers of imagination and passion, anger at men (even a longing to be a man) and the longing to be a child. The list, according to Miss Spacks, emphasizes the woman's lack of freedom.

XIII

The Nineteenth Century

LAUREL BRAKE, J. A. V. CHAPPLE and J. R. WATSON

The chapter has five sections: 1. Romantic Verse and Drama is by J. R. Watson; 2. Victorian: General and 3. Victorian Verse and Drama are by Laurel Brake; 4. Nineteenth-Century Prose Fiction and 5. Selected Prose Writers are by J. A. V. Chapple.

1. ROMANTIC VERSE AND DRAMA

The most useful bibliographical aids to the romantic period are the *MLA* bibliography and the annotated 'Selective and Critical Bibliography' edited by David V. Erdman and others in *ELN*. The summer number of *TWC* reviews books on the period, and provides a very useful 'Annual Register' of Wordsworth scholarship (by Thomas M. McLaughlin) and Coleridge scholarship (by Jane Matsinger). Similarly a Bibliography of Theatre Research is compiled by L. W. Conolly and J. P. Wearing in *Nineteenth Century Theatre Research*. William S. Ward submits additions to his earlier published work in 'Index and Finding List of Serials Published in the British Isles, 1789–1832: A Supplementary List' (*BNYPL*). Also in *BNYPL*, Robert J. Gemmett gives an account of 'The Beckford Book Sale of 1804', with a transcription of the catalogue; and Phillips G. Davies provides 'A Check List of Poems, 1595 to 1833, Entirely or Partly Written in the Spenserian Stanza', which includes many items from the romantic period. Of particular concern to bibliographical scholars is Volume 9 of the series *Sale Catalogues of Libraries of Eminent Per-*sons.[1] It deals with the libraries of Southey, Wordsworth, Thomas Moore, Haydon and Bernard Barton. The most impressive is Southey's marvellous collection; the best of Wordsworth's library was picked out by his family before the sale, and Bernard Barton's library was small. But the Moore catalogue lists a great number of autograph letters, and the Haydon sale (at his bankruptcy in 1823) has a pathetic interest.

An extensive review article, George Whalley's 'Some Studies of Wordsworth and Coleridge' (*QQ*) is a retrospective survey, dealing chiefly with the bicentenary volumes of 1970 and 1972.

In *The Permanent Pleasure: Essays on Classics of Romanticism*,[2] Richard Harter Fogle has reprinted fifteen of his essays, including some on Coleridge, Shelley and Keats. Fogle is a fine critic, and he has provided some strong orthodox readings of major romantic poems such as 'Kubla Khan', the 'Ode on a Grecian Urn', and the 'Ode to the West Wind'. Much less conventional, indeed marvellous and extraordinary, is Harold Bloom's *The Anxiety of Influence*.[3]

---

[1] *Sale Catalogues of Libraries of Eminent Persons.* Volume 9: Poets and Men of Letters, ed. by Roy Park. Mansell with Sotheby Parke Bernet. pp. vi + 558. £13.50.

[2] *The Permanent Pleasure: Essays on Classics of Romanticism,* by Richard Harter Fogle. Athens, Ga.: U. of Georgia P. pp. xiii + 225. $8.50.

[3] *The Anxiety of Influence,* by Harold Bloom. New York: O.U.P. 1973. pp. viii + 157. £2.70.

It touches the romantic poets specific-ally at certain points, with brief discussions of Wordsworth, Blake, Shelley and Keats; but its whole argument (that 'strong poets' fight their way out of the influence of their predecessors and 'clear imaginative space for themselves') is very important for the period. Milton, as Bloom points out, was the most dominating of all poets, and the anxiety caused by his shadow is a major force in the work of the romantics. But such a summary does not convey anything of the excitement of Bloom's book: it is remarkably complex, and at the same time powerfully illuminating, not least about the practice of reading and criticism.

Less astonishing than this, but also very enjoyable, is Hubert F. Babinski's *The Mazeppa Legend in European Romanticism.*[4] This is a crisp and informative book, one of those which really does add something to the store of knowledge. It deals naturally with Byron's poem, where it stoutly rejects archetypal and symbolic interpretations; but this occupies one chapter only, and the book also discusses Byron's predecessors and the French romantics, and the later development of the legend in Eastern Europe. Not so helpful (though this is not the author's fault) is Frank J. Messmann's biography of the influential connoisseur, Richard Payne Knight.[5] Subtitled 'The Twilight of Virtuosity', the book shows the twilight to have been almost total darkness and the virtuosity the excesses of a feeble dilettante. Messmann works hard at his subject, but the more he describes

Knight the more tasteless and boring he seems to have been.

In 'Natural Supernaturalism's New Clothes: A Recurrent Problem in Romantic Studies' (*TWC*), Dennis Taylor considers some central questions of romanticism in relation to the concept of a fixed and permanent work of art. By dividing his article into various questions and supplying brief, suggestive answers, Taylor manages to cover a great deal of ground without becoming gnomic or superficial. I have not been able to see Max F. Schulz's 'The Perseverance of Romanticism: From Organism to Artifact' (*Clio.*).

The most notable event of Wordsworth scholarship has been the publication of the *Prose Works* [6] edited by W. J. B. Owen and Jane Worthington Smyser. Each section is prefaced by an introduction and there are elaborate textual and explanatory notes. The contents are predictable except in the case of the *Guide to the Lakes*, where some interesting additional material is provided. The volumes provide a necessary and badly-needed standard text; a shorter and handier selection of the critical prose is found in Owen's selection, *Wordsworth's Literary Criticism.*[7] The texts are taken from the *Prose Works*, and the selection is sensible, though the notes do not seem entirely appropriate, containing as they do some textual information and some rather heavy-handed attempts at liveliness. The *Prose Works* are used by Patrick Holland, in 'Wordsworth and the Sublime: Some Further Considerations' (*TWC*), who questions the

---

[4] *The Mazeppa Legend in European Romanticism*, by Hubert F. Babinski. New York and London: Columbia U.P. pp. x + 164. £5.85.

[5] *Richard Payne Knight*, by Frank J. Messmann. The Hague: Mouton. pp. 178. D.Fl. 34.

[6] *The Prose Works of William Wordsworth*, ed. by W. J. B. Owen and Jane Worthington Smyser. Oxford: Clarendon P. Vol. I, pp. xxiv + 415; Vol. II, pp. viii + 465; Vol. III, pp. viii + 475. £22.00.

[7] *Wordsworth's Literary Criticism*, ed. by W. J. B. Owen. Routledge & Kegan Paul. pp. xii + 236. £4.95.

ideas of Albert O. Wlecke (see *YW* 54. 309) and affirms Wordsworth's establishment of a similitude between imagination and nature.

An important bibliographical aid is David H. Stam's *Wordsworthian Criticism 1964–1973*.[8] This is a checklist of books and articles, sensibly and quietly annotated. Published by the New York Public Library, it is an addition to that library's 1965 publication, *Wordsworthian Criticism 1945–1964*. The present volume includes additions to the former, and a comprehensive index to both volumes.

Robert Marchant's *Principles of Wordsworth's Poetry*[9] is a strange book, though not, I found, strange in a very helpful way. Marchant's argument, if I have understood it correctly through the convoluted and messy sentences of the first chapter, is that Wordsworth's poetry is a particularly 'pure' phenomenon: the poetry is the poetry, and nothing else. It is not its ideas, but something deeper, a fusion of sense and expression, Shelley's 'sort of thought in sense'. The criticism which follows this theory necessarily has to eschew ideas and themes: it becomes a matter of paraphrase and quotation, an 'indexical' criticism which draws attention to the particular essence of different poems, since Marchant sees the language as the created form of the poet's inner experience. Wordsworth's language is also the subject of Bowman G. Wiley's *The Clear Synthesis*,[10] a more conventional and limited study published in

the *Romantic Reassessment* series. Wiley examines the style of Wordsworth's descriptive poetry by comparing the account of the alpine tour in *Descriptive Sketches* with the same tour in Book VI of *The Prelude*. Wiley takes the unhappiness of *Descriptive Sketches* too seriously, and in some respects the examination of both poems is ponderous even before the stylistic analysis begins; but the book will have a definite usefulness for the student of descriptive language. Another stylistic by-way is explored in *TWC*, where Anne Marie Cavaglia's 'lying still' pun (*YW*. 54. 312) brought forth a number of other suggestions, most of which seem even more unlikely, from W. S. Minot, John I. Ades, and Gordon K. Thomas.

Other studies of Wordsworth's language include Eric R. Birdsall's 'Wordsworth's Revisions to *Descriptive Sketches*: The Wellesley Copy' (*TWC*), which describes alterations to the poem dating probably from 1814 or later; and James E. Swearingen's 'Wordsworth on Gray' (*SEL*), which discusses Wordsworth's relationship to eighteenth-century diction.

Monica Davies's *Wordsworth: a Selection*[11] is probably intended as a school text, though many undergraduates would find the notes, which are both factual and critical, very helpful. The introduction is brisk, simple and straightforward, and the selection is good, though there is nothing (except 'There was a Boy') from *The Prelude*. An interesting general article by Vincent Newey, 'Wordsworth, Bunyan and the Puritan Mind' (*ELH*), makes some significant comparisons between Wordsworth, Cowper and Bunyan: *The Prelude* is seen as close to *Grace*

[8] *Wordsworthian Criticism 1964–1973*, by David H. Stam. New York: The New York Public Library and Readex Books. pp. 116. $10.00.

[9] *Principles of Wordsworth's Poetry*, by. Robert Marchant. Swansea: Brynmill P. pp. 112. £2.70.

[10] *The Clear Synthesis: A Study of William Wordsworth's Stylistic Development as a Descriptive Poet from 1793 to 1808*, by Bowman G. Wiley. Salzburg: Romantic Reassessment, 16. pp. viii+338. £4.80.

[11] *Wordsworth: A Selection*, ed. by Monica Davies. University Tutorial P. pp. viii+206. 70p, paperback 40p.

Abounding and *The Pilgrim's Progress*, and 'Resolution and Independence' as expressing the tensions which affect the Puritan mind. Other studies of comparison and influence are Willard Spiegelman's 'Wordsworth's *Aeneid*' (*CL*) which discusses Wordsworth's translations of Virgil, and discovers him looking uneasily over his shoulder at Dryden; James L. Hill's 'The Frame for the Mind: Landscape in "Lines Composed a Few Miles Above Tintern Abbey", "Dover Beach" and "Sunday Morning"' (*CentR*); Alice V. Stuart's brief 'Scott and Wordsworth: A Comparison' (*Contemporary Review*), which deals with 'Fidelity' and Scott's 'Helvellyn'; and Robert Brainard Pearsall's note of a recurring metaphor in 'Wordsworth, Housman, and the Metaphor of Hand Upon Heart' (*AN&Q*).

A sociological approach to Wordsworth is used by J. P. Ward in 'Wordsworth and the Sociological Idea' (*CQ*). This is a wide-ranging and stimulating article, which stresses the social and cultural worlds of Wordsworth's poetry, the 'functional relationship', 'the constraining culture', and Wordsworth's interest in 'the marginal man'.

The influence of Godwin on *The Borderers* is the subject of Donald G. Priestman's '*The Borderers*: Wordsworth's Addenda to Godwin' (*UTQ*), which is a careful assessment of Wordsworth's use of, and dissatisfaction with, Godwinian ideas of reason. The influence of Rousseau on Godwin is the subject of Jean de Palacio's 'Godwin et la Tentation de l'Autobiographie' (*EA*); and Joseph Kestner suggests that Rousseau's influence lies behind 'We Are Seven' and 'The Tables Turned' in 'Rousseau and Wordsworth: *La Nouvelle Héloïse* and Two *Lyrical Ballads*' (*Iowa English Bulletin*).

Maurice Kirkham highlights the interaction of youth and age, and their symbolic development in the poem, in 'Innocence and Experience in Wordsworth's "The Thorn"' (*ArielE*). Brief articles on short poems include Walter S. Minot's 'Wordsworth's Use of *diurnal* in "A Slumber Did My Spirit Seal"' (*PLL*, 1973), and a note (*TLS*, Sept 13) by Donald H. Reiman, which suggests that powerful feelings for Dorothy lie behind ''Tis said that some have died for love'. Wordsworth's best-known short poem is the subject of Harvey Peter Sucksmith's 'Orchestra and the Golden Flower: A Critical Interpretation of the Two Versions of Wordsworth's "I Wandered Lonely as a Cloud"' (*YES*): with a skilful reference to Sir John Davies, Sucksmith shows Wordsworth orchestrating daffodils, stars and waves in a cosmic rhythm, and relates the 1815 version of the poem to Wordsworth's theories of poetry.

Two brief notes on 'Tintern Abbey' appear in *TWC*. Peter A. Brier, in 'Reflections on Tintern Abbey' suggests that the enveloping of the ruin by nature is something which Wordsworth saw and used 'at the edge of the poem' to symbolize natural religion. James D. Wilson, in 'Tennyson's Emendations to Wordsworth's "Tintern Abbey"', shows Tennyson trying to shorten some of the great passages of the poem in a surprisingly insensitive way. In 'The Integrity of Wordsworth's "Tintern Abbey"' (*JEGP*) John R. Nabholtz considers the thematic unity of the poem in a very effective manner, though his emphasis on the final section leads him to an awkward view of the central part as transition rather than climax.

In a superb account of '*Peter Bell* the First' (*EIC*), Mary Jacobus relates the poem to Methodist conversion reports, and goes on to suggest that the poem is an act of 'literary self-definition' for Wordsworth which is a remarkable challenge to 'The Ancient Mariner'. In 'Belief and Death in Wordsworth's *Peter Bell*' (*BNYPL*), Donald M. Hassler emphasizes the stark realism of the poem, its facing of death, and its implied transcendentalism.

Frank D. McConnell's reading of *The Prelude*, *The Confessional Imagination*,[12] is sensitive, probing, balanced, generous and humane. It sees the poem as shaped by the tradition of Augustinian confession, modified by the English Protestant movements of the seventeenth and eighteenth centuries, with their emphasis on justification and on the kingdom of God in this world. This, in turn, leads to a rejection of the daemonic and, in this book, to a study of image and language, particularly the language of confession. But this summary of the argument does not convey enough of the book's sensitive yet definite placing of the poem in these traditions, and the unobtrusive awareness of the best recent criticism of Wordsworth. Some of the comparisons are very illuminating, especially the analogy between the Simplon Pass episode and the Pendle Hill vision in George Fox's journal. McConnell is also very good on the trigonometry of the boat-stealing episode, on the blind beggar, and on the language of the Snowdon passage.

More work on the manuscripts is the foundation of Michael C. Jaye's 'Wordsworth at Work: MS.RV Book II of *The Prelude*' (*PBSA*). Jaye deals with a manuscript, probably of 1799–1800, which contains the second part of a 'two-part poem'. The text of the two-part *Prelude* of 1798–99 has been reprinted in the new edition of the *Norton Anthology of English Literature*,[13] which I have not been able to see.

In 'Wordsworth's Ontology of Love in *The Prelude*' (*CQ*), Richard Gravil finds parallels in the poem between Wordsworth and Buber, Spinoza and Kierkegaard, and emphasizes the link between imagination and love. A number of articles on *The Prelude* deal with specific books or episodes. Jim Springer Borck, in 'Wordsworth's *The Prelude* and the Failure of Language' (*SEL*, 1973), suggests that Wordsworth was uncomfortable with mature poetic language when dealing with childhood experience. In 'Wordsworth's Shell of Poetry' (*PQ*), Melvyn New suggests that the shell in Book V is the shell of the tortoise, out of which the lyre was first made. David V. Boyd writes on the techniques of satire in 'Wordsworth as Satirist: Book VII of *The Prelude*' (*SEL*, 1973). One of the 'spots of time' receives attention in Richard E. Brantley's 'Spiritual Maturity and Wordsworth's 1783 Christmas Vacation' (*SEL*); and in '"The Prelude", Book XIV and the Problem of Concluding' (*Criticism*), Jeffrey Robinson discusses the conflict between assurance and uncertainty, and the relationship between individual growth and community life, in the last book of the poem.

Karl Kroeber's '"Home at Grasmere": Ecological Holiness' (*PMLA*) suggests that the poem is alert to the continuity of existence, and that it is not a celebration of a retreat but a vision of the wholeness of life in nature. In 'The Development of Imagery in "Home at Grasmere"' (*TWC*), Muriel J. Mellown notes the passing from external and literal levels

---

[12] *The Confessional Imagination*, by Frank D. McConnell. Baltimore and London: The Johns Hopkins U.P. pp. x+212. £5.50.

[13] *The Norton Anthology of English Literature*, 3rd Ed., 2 Vols. New York: Norton. pp. 5036. $9.25 per vol, paperback $7.45.

to internal and figurative ones in the descriptions of harmony and paradise.

C. E. Pulos clarifies Wordsworth's different uses of light in the Immortality Ode, in a skilful argument for 'The Unity of Wordsworth's Immortality Ode' (*SIR*). The Ode also features in Joseph M. Griska Jr's 'Wordsworth's Mood Disturbance: A Psychoanalytic Approach to Three Poems' (*L&P*): Griska suggests that Wordsworth 'exhibited the symptoms of neurotic depression', and studies the tension which is found in the Ode, in 'Resolution and Independence', and in 'Elegiac Stanzas'.

In 'New Light on *The Excursion*' (*ArielE*), Alan G. Hill offers an important new approach to the poem by showing its affinities to a Latin dialogue known to Wordsworth, the *Octavius* of Minucius Felix. In 'Wordsworth and Ordinary Sorrow: "The Ruined Cottage"' (*CR*, 1973), Ros Eason gives a sensitive reading of the poem and asks some awkward questions about the relationship between man and nature, and man and the community in the poem.

Two short studies dealing with the later Wordsworth combine in one volume of the *Romantic Reassessment* series. In 'The Quest for Maturity: A Study of William Wordsworth's *The Prelude*',[14] Penelope June Stokes emphasizes the maturing of thought, especially with regard to nature and religion, revealed in Wordsworth's alterations to the poem between 1805 and 1850. Dorothea Steiner's 'The Essential Voice in the Later Wordsworth' sees that voice as appearing in the Duddon sonnets and the Evening Voluntaries.

Paul Kaufman prints four letters from John Peace, City Librarian of Bristol from 1839 to 1845 in 'John Peace to William Wordsworth: Four Unpublished Letters' (*ELN*). An unpublished letter of Wordsworth's, dated 1829 and concerning fire insurance, is published by Jeffrey Robinson in *The Wordsworth Circle*. A member of the Wordsworth and Coleridge circle is the subject of Jane Worthington Smyser's 'The Trial and Imprisonment of Joseph Johnson, Bookseller' (*BNYPL*), which deals with Johnson's publication of Gilbert Wakefield's *Reply* to the Bishop of Llandaff.

Volume 3 of the Coleridge *Notebooks*[15] covers the years from 1808 to 1819. It is full of fascinating material, and, as the editor points out, it is probably the most complex of the five volumes anticipated. Coleridge was restless, unsettled and directionless for much of the time, and yet some of the years, especially 1810 and 1811, show a remarkable intellectual and enquiring energy. Some of the entries in this volume have the particular interest of showing the germination of ideas which later appeared in *Biographia Literaria* and the *Lay Sermons*. Kathleen Coburn and her assistants have, as usual, done an amazing amount of tracing of obscure references and reading of strange books. If all this seems too formidable, Professor Coburn gives a modest, short and lucid account of the notebooks in *The Self Conscious Imagination*.[16] The title is an ingenious lever into the central theme of the

[14] *The Quest for Maturity*, by Penelope June Stokes; *The Essential Voice in the Later Wordsworth*, by Dorothea Steiner. Salzburg: Romantic Reassessment, 44. pp. 113. £4.80.

[15] *The Notebooks of Samuel Taylor Coleridge*, Vol 3: 1808–19, ed. by Kathleen Coburn. Routledge & Kegan Paul, 1973. Text, pp. xxii+692; notes, pp. xxxv+960. £18.00.

[16] *The Self Conscious Imagination*, by Kathleen Coburn. O.U.P., published for the University of Newcastle-upon-Tyne. pp. viii +77. £1.75.

first chapter, or lecture (the book is a printing of the Riddell Memorial Lectures at Newcastle), which concerns Coleridge's awareness of self and also his awkwardness and self-doubt. The second treats of the interaction between the self and others, and the third with the natural and spiritual worlds. Together these themes make a good introduction to the abundance and complexity of the notebooks, and present a Coleridge who is more impressive than some recent books have suggested.

On a smaller scale, a similar introduction to the letters is found in Earl Leslie Griggs's 'Coleridge as Revealed in his Letters' in *Coleridge's Variety*,[17] a collection of bicentenary lectures and essays edited by John Beer. Throughout this is a remarkable book: not only are the contributions distinguished, but they also have a notable quality of affection, even love, about them, so that the reader finishes the book with an almost palpable sense of the power which Coleridge's mind continues to exercise over his readers. In a brief introduction to the volume, L. C. Knights draws attention to the particular virtue of Coleridge's literary criticism and its concern for life as a whole. Among the essays and lectures, George Whalley's 'Coleridge's Poetic Sensibility' is masterly: beginning with the poet's awareness of delicate sense-impressions, it traces their growth towards symbol, and the energizing and unifying nature of Coleridge's perception. J. B. Beer's 'Ice and Spring: Coleridge's Imaginative Education' is also very illuminating, beginning with Coleridge's schooldays and proceeding to images of fountains and ice in his poetry. In 'Coleridge: A Bridge between

Science and Poetry', Kathleen Coburn (in a lecture given appropriately at the Royal Institution) discusses the relationship between Coleridge and Humphry Davy, and refutes any suggestion that Coleridge was a theorizer, uninterested in the practical. M. H. Abrams, in 'Coleridge and the Romantic Vision of the World', discusses *Biographia Literaria* as a spiritual autobiography which contains a new world-view, a conversion to transcendentalism: he is particularly good on the union of Coleridge's religious concern with the nature philosophy, and has a moving conclusion about the need for such a vision 'to salvage our world while it is still fit to live in.' Thomas McFarland's contribution entitled 'Coleridge's Anxiety', sees anxiety in a Freudian way as the fundamental cause of Coleridge's illnesses and hypochondria; McFarland traces this back to the poet's childhood, and suggests that in his fight against anxiety, Coleridge becomes existentially heroic. In 'Coleridge on Powers in Mind and Nature', Dorothy Emmet writes of Coleridge seeking an analogue in nature for something in the mind, and connects this with a daemonic creative power that can be good or evil. D. M. MacKinnon's 'Coleridge and Kant' begins with the charges of plagiarism, and then moves into a subtle and profound discussion of two contrary and intertwined movements in Coleridge's thought: the poetic, prophetic and transcendental, and the analytical and logical. Owen Barfield, in a very enjoyable though slighter piece, 'Coleridge's Enjoyment of Words', deals mainly with the prose, and with Coleridge's inventiveness. Finally J. B. Beer, in 'A Stream by Glimpses: Coleridge's Later Imagination', discusses Coleridge's interest in animal magnetism, his own magnetic

---

[17] *Coleridge's Variety: Bicentenary Studies*, ed. by John Beer. Macmillan. pp. xxiv+264. £8.00.

qualities, and his sense of the attraction between man and man, and man and nature.

A. J. Harding's *Coleridge and the Idea of Love*[18] is subtitled 'Aspects of relationship in Coleridge's thought and writing', and it examines this theme both in individual friendship and in social thinking. Without over-simplifying, Harding provides a clear guide to individuality and relationship in Coleridge: his account of 'The Eolian Harp' as myth-making is good, and so is the examination of relationships in the other poems. In fact, the section on the poems could well have been longer, though in its present form it fits neatly into an account which takes in Coleridge's life, his writings on religion, and his political and social thinking. Molly Lefebure's *Samuel Taylor Coleridge: A Bondage of Opium*[19] is not a book for scholars, though its general idea (the study of the effect of addiction on Coleridge's life and writings) is a fruitful one. The danger of such a subject is that, lacking evidence about cause and effect, it will become a matter of assertion rather than fact, and this is exactly what happens. In his years as a 'junkie', before he was taken in by Gillman and became, eventually, 'the guru of Highgate', the addiction, it is argued, ruined his marriage and caused him to be deceitful about his poetry and his plagiarisms. As the author reminds us from time to time, the testimony of an addict is unreliable, and she accepts the charges of plagiarism and regards 'Kubla Khan' as a fascinating and beautiful confidence trick. She also accepts with enthusiasm the idea of Wordsworth's love for his sister,

which leaps about in flames of passion.

The Everyman *Poems*[20] of Coleridge has been reprinted with a new and enlarged introduction by John Beer. This traces the main features of Coleridge's developing art, and is especially interesting about the images of light and radiance. The text is the best for student use, since it contains both the 'Letter to Sara Hutchinson' and 'Dejection: an Ode', as well as a straightforward text of 'The Ancient Mariner'. Each of the major poems is preceded by a brief but informative introduction. Paul Magnuson's *Coleridge's Nightmare Poetry*[21] has not been available for review; and I have not seen Michael Cooke's 'De Quincey, Coleridge, and the Formal Uses of Intoxication' (*Yale French Studies*).

In 'The Fixed Crime of *The Ancient Mariner*' (*EIC*), George Bellis discriminates neatly between various interpretations of the poem, arguing that the mariner is fated to kill the albatross, and that he comes to know the full value of love after the destruction of it. Charles E. May's 'Objectifying the Nightmare: Cain and the *Mariner*' (*BSUF*, 1973) suggests that the mariner's act is an 'act of separation' like that of man from God. Abe Delson sensibly returns to natural symbolism, and to different views of nature in 'The Symbolism of the Sun and Moon in *The Rime of the Ancient Mariner*' (*TSLL*), and Sarah Dyck, in 'Perspective in "The Rime of the Ancient Mariner"' (*SEL*, 1973) finds Coleridge using contrasting points of view to challenge and involve the reader. I have not been able to see 'A Reading of "The Ancient Mar-

[18] *Coleridge and the Idea of Love*, by A. J. Harding. Cambridge: Cambridge U.P. pp. xii+281. £7.25.

[19] *Samuel Taylor Coleridge: A Bondage of Opium*, by Molly Lefebure. Gollancz. pp. 537. £6.00.

[20] *Samuel Taylor Coleridge: Poems*, ed. by John Beer. Dent. pp. xxxvi+371. £1.10.

[21] *Coleridge's Nightmare Poetry*, by Paul Magnuson. Charlottesville U.P. of Virginia. pp. xv+133. $9.50.

iner"' (*Costerus*, 1973) by Edwin Moses.

Analogues and possible sources for 'Kubla Khan' are the special concern of Robert F. Fleissner. He suggests *A History and Description of Africa* by Leo Africanus as one source (*Negro American Literature Forum*); and in '*Hwaet! Wē Gardēna*: "Kubla Khan" and Those Anglo-Saxon Words' (*The Wordsworth Circle*) he links Coleridge with *Beowulf*. This certainly seems a whole world away from a previous Fleissner analogue for the poem, Squire Allworthy's estate in *Tom Jones*; a footnote to this is provided by Susan Miller Passler, in 'Coleridge, Fielding and Arthur Murphy' (*The Wordsworth Circle*), which finds a parallel with Murphy's 'Essay on the Life and Genius of Henry Fielding, Esq' (1762) with reference to the river image of the poem. I have not seen another analogue study, Michael Greer's 'Coleridge and Dante: Kinship in Xanadu' (*University of Dayton Review*). In 'The Daemonic in *Kubla Khan*: Toward Interpretation' (*PMLA*), Charles I. Patterson Jr. sees the daemonic forces of the poem as powerful but not evil.

In 'Dramatic Reconciliation in Coleridge's Conversation Poems' (*PLL*, 1973) Ronald C. Wendling argues that Coleridge's tentative beliefs, his sense of failure, and his unassertive vision are important constituents of these poems.

Several articles deal with Coleridge's criticism. In 'Coleridge's "Philocrisy" and His Theory of Fancy and Secondary Imagination' (*SIR*), S. V. Pradhan discusses Coleridge's use of Reason, Understanding and Sense (taken from Kant) and links this to his critical distinctions between Fancy and Imagination. His critical approaches are neatly described and defended by Peter

Hoheisel in 'Coleridge on Shakespeare: Method Amid the Rhetoric' (*SIR*), which emphasizes Coleridge's ability to see the plays as 'romantic dramas, imaginative incarnations of moral ideas', with a particular stress on poetry and character. In 'A Nineteenth - Century Touchstone: Chapter XV of *Biographia Literaria*' (in *Nineteenth-Century Literary Perspectives, Essays in Honor of Lionel Stevenson*),[22] U. C. Knoepflmacher argues that the Shakespearian criticism of Chapter XV is an integral part of Coleridge's assessment of Wordsworth, especially the Wordsworth of *The Excursion*; Coleridge is here urging Wordsworth towards a Miltonic and philosophical position, and setting up a Milton–Shakespeare antithesis which became central to nineteenth-century criticism. In 'Coleridge's Political "Sermons": Discursive Language and the Voice of God' (*MP*, 1973) David R. Sanderson argues that Coleridge's prose begins with his own discursive language, struggling to express his complex ideas, and later turned towards the language of scripture, especially in the *Lay Sermons*.

In 'Samuel Taylor Coleridge as Abolitionist' (*ArielE*), Barbara Taylor Paul-Emile discusses the change in Coleridge's attitudes to slavery, from liberalism to paternalism and a concern for civilizing the emancipated. An exposition of Coleridge's views on race, taken from unpublished manuscript fragments, is given by J. H. Haeger in 'Coleridge's Speculations on Race' (*SIR*).

Coleridge's influence is traced by Richard A. Hocks, who finds *Walden* a Coleridgean work of art in 'Thoreau, Coleridge, and Barfield: Reflections

[22] *Nineteenth-Century Literary Perspectives, Essays in Honor of Lionel Stevenson*, ed. by Clyde de L. Ryals. Durham, N.C.: Duke U.P. pp. xxiv+294. £5.90.

on the Imagination and the Law of Polarity' (*CentR*, 1973); by Burton R. Pollin who finds echoes of Coleridge in Oscar Wilde, both in diction and rhythm, in 'The Influence of "The Ancient Mariner" upon "The Ballad of Reading Gaol"' (*Levende Talen*)—something which is also briefly noted in Bloom's *The Anxiety of Influence*; and by Michael Munday, who shows how John Wilson, although writing a hostile review of *Biographia Literaria* in 1817, used Coleridge's terms in his later criticism, in 'John Wilson and the Distinction between Fancy and Imagination' (*SIR*).

One number of *TWC* is devoted entirely to a catalogue by H. O. Dendurent of The Coleridge Collection in Victoria College Library, Toronto; it is a full check-list of this great collection of books, manuscripts, letters and miscellanea relating to the poet, second only to the collection in the British Museum. One of the British Museum manuscripts is the subject of Fran Carlock Stephens's 'Cottle, Wise and "Ms. Ashley 408"' (*PBSA*), which deals with each section of a problematical manuscript and points out T. J. Wise's errors in his *Catalogue of the Ashley Library*.

Norman Fruman's remarkable book continues to cause trouble. R. A. Foakes has a review article in *EIC*, entitled 'Repairing the Damaged Archangel', and Thomas McFarland, in 'Coleridge's Plagiarisms Once More: A Review Essay' (*YR*), engages in fierce controversy with Fruman and points out some of Wordsworth's debts to Coleridge.

Peter Mann prints two interesting autograph letters of Coleridge, one to Joseph Cottle (hitherto published in an abbreviated form) and the other to the comic actor George Bartley (*RES*). Thomas L. Fenner prints a newspaper account in '"The Tra-

veller" Reports on Coleridge's 1811 Lectures' (*N&Q*); while in *AN&Q* Hartmut Breitkreuz contributes a short note on 'Coleridge at Göttingen in 1799' including an account of his *Harz-Reise*.

Continuing his series 'The Cool World of Samuel Taylor Coleridge' with 'Bawdy Books and Obscene Ballads' (*The Wordsworth Circle*), P. M. Zall traces the great change that took place in the period in attitudes towards obscenity, from eighteenth-century levity to nineteenth-century severity. In another of the series, 'Implacable Christian', Zall gives an account of Edward Christian, judge and upholder of the rights of copyright libraries.

Basil Willey describes a friendship in 'Charles Lamb and S. T. Coleridge' in the New Series of *The Charles Lamb Bulletin* (1973). Other articles related to romantic poetry are Hugh Sykes Davies's 'Charles Lamb and the Romantic Style' (January 1974), and Richard Madden's 'The Old Familiar Faces', which relates to Coleridge and Wordsworth; others in the 1974 *Bulletin* refer to Southey and Hood, and there is a very enjoyable essay on Lamb as poet, 'Satire and Humor in Lamb's Verse', by Howard O. Brogan. James T. Willis examines a poem and its painting in 'New Lamb Material in the Aders Album: Jacob Götzenberger and Two Versions of "Angel Help"' (*HLB*).

A Southey number of *TWC* includes the following articles: 'Portraits of Southey', by Kenneth Curry; 'Southey: A Critical Spectrum', by Peter F. Morgan, which discusses Southey's views on history and literary criticism, and his dislike of philosophy and metaphysics; 'Zukovskij and Southey's Ballads: The Translator as Rival', by Warren U. Ober and Kenneth H. Ober, a discussion of three of Southey's ballads translated into Russian; 'The Rochester Southey Collection', by Robert Volz and James Rieger, describing the library holdings at Rochester; and 'Four New Southey Letters', by Andy P. Antippas. A more extensive article in the same number, by Ernest Bernhardt-Kabisch, is entitled 'Southey in the Tropics: *A Tale of Paraguay* and the Problem of Romantic Faith'; acknowledging the deadness of Southey's poetry, it seeks to show some central concerns of romanticism appearing in his poems. Charles L. Proudfit's 'Southey and Landor: A Literary Friendship' points out some generous and fruitful connections between the two writers; while Michael N. Stanton (the guest editor of this number of *TWC*) writes on 'Southey and the Art of Autobiography'. Finally P. M. Zall, in 'The Gothic Voice of Father Bear', discusses Southey's possible authorship, concluding that he never claimed to be the originator of 'The Three Bears' but may have been the first to write it down; the tale itself is then printed with all its original type (Father Bear in 24-point Black Letter Gothic).

Romantic Criticism is well represented in *Robert Burns, the Critical Heritage*.[23] The period covered is from 1786 to 1837, and it contains major contributions from Wordsworth, Scott, Jeffrey, Hazlitt, Carlyle and De Quincey. Smaller notices come from Coleridge, Byron, Keats, Dorothy Wordsworth and Jane Austen. Burns is an interesting case, the local working-class poet whose work really does transcend the limits of place and social class. As such it was not only original, but alarming: as the editor, Donald A. Low observes, the first reviewers 'paid

tribute, and then took fright'. Low's selection allows the reader to observe the passion behind Wordsworth's praise compared with the judicial balance of Scott's account, and Low rightly draws attention to the sharpness of Byron's comments. He concludes his introduction with a brief survey of Burns criticism since 1837, with particular reference to Stevenson, MacDiarmid and Edwin Muir. In 'Robert Burns's Satire' (*Scottish Literary Journal*), John C. Weston emphasizes the savagery and bite behind the comic and ironic voice in Burns.

The third volume of the new edition of Byron's letters and journals is entitled *Alas! The Love of Women*,[24] and it is certainly dominated by women. It shows Byron at his busiest in high society: perplexed by Lady Caroline Lamb, confiding in Lady Melbourne, enjoying the company of Lady Oxford, and beginning to correspond with Annabella Milbanke. In poetry it was the year of *The Giaour* and *The Bride of Abydos*. The journal covers the months from November 1813 to April 1814, including the publication of *The Corsair* and the celebrated poetry pyramid with Scott at the apex.

Women also figure largely in some other books about Byron. Margot Strickland writes about eight of them in *The Byron Women*,[25] with a romantic preface which reminds us that 'confronted with a Byron, women do not behave logically but biologically'. Fortunately the rest of the book is not like this, though it is not a serious contribution to Byron scholarship and it is often too vaguely and indiscriminately charitable. Both Ms Strickland

[23] *Robert Burns, the Critical Heritage*, ed. by Donald A. Low. Routledge & Kegan Paul. pp. xvi+447. £8.25.

[24] *Alas! The Love of Women*. Byron's Letters and Journals, Vol. 3, ed. by Leslie A. Marchand. John Murray. pp. xiv+285. £4.75.

[25] *The Byron Women*, by Margot Strickland. Peter Owen. pp. 224. £3.60.

and Catherine Turney, in *Byron's Daughter*,[26] have no hesitation about the parentage of Medora. These are muddy waters indeed, but Ms Turney insists that Medora inherited from her father 'fierce pride, temper, and a liking for money'; Augusta, it seems, was 'caught up in a tempest of passion' and found herself 'in the family way'. Such expressions throughout spoil what could have been an interesting life, though hardly one which deserves such full-length treatment. It is a relief to turn to the severity of Malcolm Elwin's *Lord Byron's Wife*,[27] which has been reprinted, and to H. O. Brogan's astringent 'Lady Byron: "The Moral Clytemnestra of Her Lord"' (*DUJ*) which shows Annabella as devious and crafty in her self-justification. Complementary to this is Brogan's '"Byron So Full of Fun, Frolic, Whit, and Whim"' (*HLQ*), which is a defence of Byron's character against charges varying from bad manners to cruelty. Yet another of the poet's acquaintances is the subject of Cecily Lambert's 'Most Gorgeous Lady Blessington' (*KSMB*), which gives a lively account of the author of *The Conversations of Lord Byron*.

Light is also thrown on the Byron marriage by Doris Langley Moore in *Lord Byron, Accounts Rendered*,[28] especially in an important appendix on 'Byron's Sexual Ambivalence' which convincingly discusses Byron's homosexual relationships and refutes suggestions of perverted sexual practices as the cause of the breakdown. The book is, of course, much more than this: it is a financial biography, though with none of the nightmare

pointlessness that a study of laundry bills might imply. It shows Byron in many lights, being profligate, generous, loyal and warm-hearted; two figures also emerge from the shadows, John Hanson, his solicitor, and Lega Zambelli, his Italian steward. Above all, the book shows the part played by money in the day-to-day decisions of Byron's life—not least during the period of his marriage.

As part of the commemoration of the 150th anniversary of Byron's death, two great New York libraries put on a Memorial Exhibition, *Byron on the Continent*.[29] In it there were some unusual items, including a copy of the first printing of 'Fare Thee Well' and the anti-Byronic *Lord Byron's New Poems* of 1816. The limited edition catalogue is an attractive volume, full of information. Douglas Dunn's *A Choice of Byron's Verse*[30] contains some of the best of the shorter poems and melodies, *Beppo*, *The Vision of Judgment*, and extracts from *Don Juan*; the 'Byronic Byron' is poorly represented.

M. Roxana Klapper's *The German Literary Influence on Byron*[31] is an original and useful study, which draws attention to the strong affinities between Byron's work and some German literature. *Manfred* and *Faust* are obviously related, but Klapper finds the influence of *Faust* in other places; she also finds *Werther* in *Childe Harold's Pilgrimage* and Gessner's *Der Tod Abels* in *Cain*. This is one of the *Romantic Reassessment* series, which also prints two

[26] *Byron's Daughter*, by Catherine Turney. Peter Davies. pp. xvi+320. £3.75.

[27] *Lord Byron's Wife*, by Malcolm Elwin. John Murray. pp. 556. £7.50.

[28] *Lord Byron, Accounts Rendered*, by Doris Langley Moore. John Murray. pp. 512. £6.75.

[29] *Byron on the Continent: A Memorial Exhibition, 1824–1974*, by Donald H. Reiman and Doucet D. Fisher. New York: The New York Public Library and the Carl H. Pforzheimer Library. pp. 85. $5.00.

[30] *A Choice of Byron's Verse*, ed. by Douglas Dunn. Faber. pp. 164. £1.10.

[31] *The German Literary Influence on Byron*, by M. Roxana Klapper. Salzburg: Romantic Reassessment, 42. pp. iv+206. £4.80.

very inferior studies by Charles J. Clancy. One is a *Review of Don Juan Criticism: 1900 to 1973*,[32] which is supposed 'to marshall useful critical perceptions' and which turns out to be rather a pointless exercise. Clancy's other work, *Lava, Hock and Soda-Water: Byron's Don Juan*,[33] does not boil, intoxicate, or sparkle: it is a heavy-handed dissection of the elements of epic, comedy and farce in the poem. With the first of these two numbers there is a defence of the series as a whole by the editor, Dr James Hogg, which sets new standards in childishness and vulgarity. Some volumes in the series have been useful, and better than one might have expected; others have been worse. But a defence like this does the series no good.

Peter Brent's *Lord Byron*[34] is a pictorial biography for the general reader, but it contains some fine illustrations of Byron and his contemporaries, and is particularly rich in contemporary cartoons. *The Byron Journal*, now in its second year, begins with a characteristically sane lecture by Andrew Rutherford, 'Byron: A Pilgrim's Progress', which discriminates nicely between the sterile isolation of his romantic poetry and the honourable convictions of the later years. Juliusz Zulawski traces 'Byron's Influence in Poland', and Keith Train traces Byron's antecedents back to the Norman Conquest in 'The Byron Family'. Margaret J. Howell describes an elaborate production of *Sardanapalus*

[32] *Salzburg Studies in English Literature and the Critics*, by Dr James Hogg; *Review of Don Juan Criticism: 1900 to 1973*, by Charles J. Clancy. Salzburg: Romantic Reassessment, 40. pp. 94. £4.80.

[33] *Lava, Hock and Soda-Water: Byron's Don Juan*, by Charles J. Clancy. Salzburg: Romantic Reassessment, 41. pp. iv+273. £4.80.

[34] *Lord Byron*, by Peter Brent. Weidenfeld & Nicolson. pp. 232. £3.25.

by Charles Kean in 1853; and Eric Singer, in a tiresome wisecracking style, contributes 'Some thoughts on Canto II of Byron's *Don Juan*'. The thoughts, fortunately, are more sensible than the language.

In 'Byron and the Levels of Landscape' (*ArielE*), Bernard Blackstone provides some fascinating insights into the human and the natural in Byron: he emphasizes the tender-toughness of nature, the fusion of the sensual and spiritual, and above all, the passion for the sea which anticipates Swinburne. Edward E. Bostetter's 'Masses and Solids: Byron's View of the External World' (*MLQ*) is concerned with the poet's empiricism, demonstrating various attitudes to the world which is seen as deteriorating, as benign, as active and sometimes hostile, and as indifferent.

Milton Wilson's 'Traveller's Venice: Some Images for Byron and Shelley' (*UTQ*) is scholarly and delightful: it traces images of Venice (gondolas, coffins, the virgin city, queen, mirror) in travel writing and topographical description, from the Renaissance to the romantic period. K. G. Churchill's 'Byron and Italy' (*The Literary Half-Yearly*) emphasizes Byron's active response to the world around him, and the individuality of his approach to Italy, ruined yet attractive.

Bernard Blackstone writes of Canto II of *Childe Harold's Pilgrimage* in 'Byron's Greek Canto: The Anatomy of Freedom' (*YES*), pointing out the richness and complexity of the multiple layers of meaning in the verse: it involves a pilgrimage in the steps of St Paul and also an awareness of the wisdom and power of the Greek Gods. In 'The Narrator of *Don Juan*' (*ArielE*), David Parker shows how Byron exploited his habit of posturing, and links *Don Juan* with the rogue tradition in literature.

Byron's plays continue to receive attention. Stuart M. Sperry's 'Byron and the Meaning of "Manfred"' (*Criticism*) examines the structure of the drama and its relationship to a 'catharsis' at its centre. David Eggenschwiler considers its aesthetic effects in 'The Tragic and Comic Rhythms of *Manfred*' (*SIR*). In '"The New Prometheus of New Men": Byron's 1816 Poems and *Manfred*' (in *Nineteenth-Century Literary Perspectives, Essays in Honor of Lionel Stevenson*), John Clubbe considers the influence of Aeschylus's *Prometheus Bound* and the Prometheus myth generally on *Childe Harold's Pilgrimage* III, *Manfred*, and the other poems of 1816. Accepting the political origins of *Marino Faliero*, Thomas L. Ashton examines its transformation to drama in '*Marino Faliero*: Byron's "*Poetry* of Politics"' (*SIR*). In 'The Moral Ambiguity of *Marino Faliero*' (*AUMLA*), G. W. Spence discusses the motivation of the Doge and of Faliero, demonstrating the honesty with which Byron presents their positions.

Jerome J. McGann's 'Milton and Byron' (*KSMB*) discusses the influence of Milton on Byron's Satanism, and the presence of Milton himself in Byron's poetry, especially in *Childe Harold's Pilgrimage* IV. The literary friendship is traced in detail in John Clubbe's 'Byron and Scott' (*TSLL*, 1973); and in 'Arnold, Byron and Taine' (*ES*), J. P. Farrell considers the influence of Taine in improving Arnold's opinion of Byron. Molly Tatchell prints a savage lampoon on the Prince Regent in 'Byron's *Windsor Poetics*' (*KSMB*), and a brief account of 'Byron and the Luddites' is given by William Whitlock (*KSMB*).

Jack Stillinger's *The Texts of Keats's Poems*[35] is a rigorous exam-

ination of the currently used texts. It discusses the holographs and their relationship with early copies or printed forms, and argues strongly for the adherence to a single text. It also takes into account new discoveries of manuscripts and copies which have not been incorporated into recent editions. It provides the necessary groundwork for an entirely new edition: according to Stillinger, in the two best modern texts 'approximately one-third of the poems have one or more wrong word in them'. Stillinger's book will be necessary, pending an edition based upon it, for all scholars of Keats. Christopher Ricks's *Keats and Embarrassment*[36] is an unusual and brilliant book, which illuminates a whole area of Keats's poetry which has often been dismissed as immature and sensuous. Ricks is often able to show that a dismissal of a Keats passage as poetically tactless can be based on an incomplete or inattentive reading. Like Empson, Ricks is particularly good at using parody, as well as comparison, to make his point: his thesis is that Keats's special goodness as man and as poet lies in his awareness of embarrassment and his embracing of human awkwardness. This gives the book a sympathy and tenderness which blends with its wide reading and close study of lines and images.

François Matthey's *The Evolution of Keats's Structural Imagery*[37] traces a pattern in romantic poetry of downward journeying followed by an ascent. Matthey suggests that Keats

[36] *Keats and Embarrassment*, by Christopher Ricks. Oxford: Clarendon P. pp. vi + 224. £3.75.
[37] *The Evolution of Keats's Structural Imagery*, by François Matthey. Schweizer Anglistische Arbeiten, Band 78. Berne: Francke Verlag. pp. vi+278. S.Fr. 38.00.

[35] *The Texts of Keats's Poems*, by Jack Stillinger. Cambridge, Mass.: Harvard U.P. pp. xviii+297. $12.95.

broke with this tendency and produced instead a pyramidal structure, which is the foundation of his greatest poems. Matthey discovers some interesting symmetrical patterns in Keats's poems, and points to syntactical similarities: but there is a certain heavy mechanical application about it which sorts oddly with the sense of organic growth which is felt in Keats's poetry. One result is that Matthey prefers, for instance, the *Indicator* version of 'La Belle Dame', which is less magical and dreamlike than the latter one or the transcripts. I have not been able to see a book devoted to 'La Belle Dame' in the context of romanticism, Barbara Fass's *La Belle Dame sans Merci and the Aesthetics of Romanticism.*[38]

In *From Innocence through Experience: Keats's Myth of the Poet,*[39] Priscilla Weston Tate studies the poetry of Keats as mythopoeic, and is particularly concerned with Keats's developing myth of the poet. She sees the early Keats's imagination as Innocence, reaching for knowledge and Experience; the later poems, written out of Experience, struggle towards a higher Innocence, a world in which the imagination can survive. Another wide-ranging general study is Nancy M. Goslee's '"Under a Cloud in Prospect": Keats, Milton and Stationing' (*PQ*), a stimulating article on the different meanings and implications of 'stationing', particularly in relation to the poet's stance as visionary and the statuesque qualities of *Hyperion*. Other articles which link Keats to his predecessors are Ronald Primeau's 'Chaucer's *Troilus and Criseyde* and the Rhythm of

Experience in Keats's "What can I do to drive away"' (*KSJ*), which has a wider reference than the title suggests, and considers Keats's reading and use of Chaucer in several places; and Mario L. D'Avanzo's '"Ode on a Grecian Urn" and *The Excursion*' (*KSJ*), which discusses the influence on Keats of Book IV of Wordsworth's poem, with its discussion of the relation between art and life, permanence and impermanence.

An interesting revaluation of *Isabella* is implied by Louise Z. Smith in 'The Material Sublime: Keats and *Isabella*' (*SIR*), which sees the poem as balancing romantic involvement and a detachment, in the acceptance of the fierce destruction of love. In 'Spectral Symbolism and the Authorial Self: An Approach to Keats's *Hyperion*' (*EIC*), Geoffrey H. Hartman considers the relationship between the poet's quest for identity and the presentation of the gods: his argument is too complex for summary, but it is extraordinarily suggestive about Keats's relationship to the myth and his reasons for abandoning *Hyperion*. Richard Harter Fogle, in 'Keats's *Lamia* as Dramatic Illusion' (*Nineteenth-Century Literary Perspectives, Essays in Honor of Lionel Stevenson*), argues for a Coleridgean 'suspension of disbelief' in the poem, which leads to an approach to both Lamia and *Lamia* from different distances and perspectives, each beyond the rational analysis or paraphrase of the poem. In 'The Occasion of Keats's "Ode to a Nightingale"' (*DUJ*), R. L. Smallwood supports Brown's description of the poem's composition, and examines the poem in relation to the physical setting. Arthur H. Bell's '"The Depth of Things": Keats and Human Space' (*KSJ*) deals with the use of space, especially in 'The Eve of St Agnes' and the 'Ode to a Nightingale'.

---

[38] *La Belle Dame sans Merci and the Aesthetics of Romanticism,* by Barbara Fass. Detroit: Wayne State U.P. pp. 311. $15.95.

[39] *From Innocence through Experience: Keats's Myth of the Poet,* by Priscilla Weston Tate. Salzburg: Romantic Reassessment, 34. pp. ii+147. £4.80.

In '"*The Cap and Bells*, or . . . The Jealousies"?' (*BNYPL*) Howard O. Brogan traces allusions to the Prince Regent, and imitations of Byron, but prefers a more personal interpretation, with Keats as Elfinan and Fanny Brawne as Bellanaine. In 'Edward Holmes and Keats' (*KSJ*), Leonidas M. Jones identifies Holmes, Keats's schoolfellow, as the author of a long obituary letter in the *Morning Chronicle*. Norman A. Anderson provides 'Corrections to Amy Lowell's Reading of Keats's Marginalia' (*KSJ*) from books in the Houghton Library at Harvard. John U. Peters examines the methods and theories behind Jeffrey's 1820 review of Keats in 'Jeffrey's Keats Criticism' (*Studies in Scottish Literature*, 1973); and David H. Stam gives an account of Leigh Hunt's work as a reviewer between 1833 and 1834 in 'Leigh Hunt and The True Sun' (*BNYPL*).

The fifth and sixth volumes of the Carl H. Pforzheimer Library's *Shelley and his Circle*[40] appeared in 1973. They continue the work of their magnificent predecessors, displaying the lives of Shelley and his friends through the manuscripts in the collection. In these volumes there is much useful and interesting material from Leigh Hunt, and concerning Trelawny, Williams and others. The former editor, Kenneth Neill Cameron, is the author of a major biographical and critical study, *Shelley, The Golden Years*.[41] After a brief biographical section dealing with the years 1814–22, the full weight of the book is concentrated in the second

and third sections, on the prose and the poetry. Here, as one might expect, Cameron's chief virtue is his exemplary clarity: he is outstanding at laying out the major themes and disentangling confusions. The Shelley who emerges is almost startlingly clear: a precise, powerful revolutionary thinker and poet, not a Platonist complicating his ideas with vitally metaphorical language.

Richard Holmes's *Shelley, the Pursuit*[42] is for those who would see Shelley very plain. It is determinedly anti-romantic, since Holmes sees Shelley-lovers for the most part as sweet old people bemused by an Ariel figure. The book's energies and faults spring from this: it is readable, thorough, exciting, yet one cannot escape the feeling that Holmes is somehow trying too hard. He dislikes the big scene, and dismisses the burning of the bodies at Viareggio in a few curt sentences; his interpretation of the Tan-yr-Allt attack is rigorously circumstantial, with the famous drawing 'supposedly' made by Shelley as 'a myth in the making'. The result of all this is that Shelley appears as a restless, immature intellectual, bothered about money, with a crusader's disregard for others and yet also an extraordinary charm. The facts, of course, speak for themselves, without Holmes's frequent reference to the 'idealizers' and his modern expressions such as 'Byron desperately needed the break' and Williams 'had done time at Eton'. In the interpretation of certain difficult episodes, such as the death of Clara or the 'Neapolitan child' affair, Cameron is less ready than Holmes to impute blame to Shelley, and in general is more convincing.

Kathleen Raine's preface to her

---

[40] *Shelley and His Circle, 1773–1822*, Vols V and VI, ed. by Donald H. Reiman. Cambridge, Mass.: Harvard U.P., 1973. pp. xliv+1196. £30.00.

[41] *Shelley, The Golden Years*, by Kenneth Neill Cameron. Cambridge, Mass.: Harvard U.P. pp. 669. £10.00.

[42] *Shelley, the Pursuit*, by Richard Holmes. Weidenfeld & Nicolson. pp. 829. £7.95.

selection of Shelley[43] in the Penguin 'Poet to Poet' series is, I believe, just about the best introduction to Shelley there is. It is tough-minded and discriminating, yet also enthusiastic and, at times, very moving. It places the poet in the Platonist tradition, and without being specious about relevance, links him with the revolutionaries of our own day. The selection is also very good: *Julian and Maddalo* is included, and the whole of *Prometheus Unbound*, as well as most of the shorter poems one would wish to see. But the book's usefulness for students is not so great as it might have been because of the stupid decision not to print line-numbers.

In *Shelley's Polar Paradise: A Reading of Prometheus Unbound*,[44] William H. Hildebrand interprets the poem as psycho-drama, not as political or platonic. Hildebrand sees Jupiter and Prometheus as opposites contending within a single being, agents in the drama who act out hidden psychic experiences. Certain elements in this reading, such as the recalled curse, take on a considerable importance; the relationship between the self and others becomes the saving union, and the myth of Hope suggested in the poem's final lines is explained. James R. Bennett prefers to emphasize the realism of the early part of the drama in 'Prometheus Unbound, Act I, "The play's the thing"' (*KSJ*), adding a final sharp comparison with Bertrand Russell. The symbolic motif of the 'multitudinous orb' in *Prometheus Unbound* is the subject of Thomas A. Reisner's 'Some Scientific Models for Shelley's Multitudinous Orb' (*KSJ*); Reisner

detects Shelley's source in the work of the Swiss physicist and astronomer Euler, combined with an idea from Laplace.

Martin J. Svaglic's 'Shelley and *King Lear*' (in *Nineteenth-Century Literary Perspectives, Essays in Honor of Lionel Stevenson*) notes the particular appeal of *King Lear* for Shelley; it is a play which is moral without being didactic, and it is concerned with regeneration as *Prometheus Unbound* is. Svaglic also points out borrowings from *King Lear* in the drama. Another general article, by Robert A. Hartley, considers the figure of the circling serpent in 'The Uroboros in Shelley's Poetry' (*JEGP*), finding it symbolic of goodness, change and liberty.

A Variorum edition of *A Defence of Poetry*[45] is provided by Fanny DeLisle in two volumes of the *Romantic Reassessment* series. She chooses MS D as a base text, and supplies notes of all textual variants; critical notes include summaries of previous criticism, and discussion of sources and analogues. DeLisle's own contributions involve a wide knowledge of Shelley's own work, and of his readings in such eighteenth-century figures as Monboddo and Hume.

Four stages of the poet's dream-voyage in *Alastor* are discussed by John C. Bean in 'The Poet Borne Darkly: The Dream-Voyage Allegory in Shelley's *Alastor*' (*KSJ*). A stimulating pictorial comparison, 'Experience as History: Shelley's Venice, Turner's Carthage' (*ELH*), Karl Kroeber deals with the interaction of past, present and future in both artists. Burton R. Pollin finds the source of the phrase 'intellectual

---

[43] *Shelley*, selected by Kathleen Raine. Harmondsworth: Penguin, 1973. pp. 380. 50p.

[44] *Shelley's Polar Paradise: A Reading of Prometheus Unbound*, by William E. Hildebrand. Salzburg: Romantic Reassessment, 18. pp. v+300. £4.80.

[45] *A Study of Shelley's A Defence of Poetry: A Textual and Critical Evaluation*, by Fanny DeLisle. Salzburg: Romantic Reassessment, 27 & 28. pp. xiv+633. £4.80 per vol.

beauty' not in Plato but in Godwin, in 'Godwin's *Memoirs* as a Source of Shelley's Phrase "Intellectual Beauty"'(*KSJ*). In 'Henry Buxton Forman and his Shelley Reprints' (*BC*), John Collins discusses, in particular, Forman's publication of offprints and his connections with T. J. Wise.

Two books by Trelawny have been reprinted. David Wright's edition of *Records of Shelley, Byron and the Author*[46] contains a lively and discriminating introduction to Trelawny's spectacular account. It is clear that Trelawny, though often untruthful, was not simply a liar and a cad: Wright instances his kindness to Mary Shelley and Jane Williams after the deaths of their husbands. Fiction, though, was what Trelawny did best: and *Adventures of a Younger Son*[47] is now formally acknowledged as such by being published in the Oxford English Novels series. As William St Clair, who introduces it, says, Trelawny would probably have objected; yet it was originally published as a three-volume novel, and certainly has its share of excitement and romance. It is fact blended with fiction, and with an admixture of brutality which is not found in the *Records*. For this edition the printer's errors have been corrected, and the deleted material restored from the original manuscript at Harvard. A fine portrait, now in Montreal, is reproduced by Marcia Allentuck in 'An Unremarked Drawing of Edward Trelawny' (*KSJ*).

Mark Storey's *Clare, the Critical Heritage*[48] is a generous selection of reactions to Clare from 1820 to 1964. More than most volumes of the series, it is concerned with a reputation that is still developing, and much of the fascination of the volume is in the incompleteness of even the most recent criticism. There is, as Storey says, 'the sense of a series of gropings towards some kind of critical truth', but no definitive account of Clare's elusive and inconsistent charm. Storey's own book, *The Poetry of John Clare*,[49] comes pat on its cue, since it is the first complete attempt to study Clare's poetry as a whole. As such it is a very good, well-balanced and informative book: it modestly but quite truthfully calls itself a 'Critical Introduction', and Storey writes so competently that the reader wishes for more detail on occasion. This is particularly the case over a poem like 'The Parish', which illustrates Clare's little-known power as a satirist, and over the great lyrics of 1844. Storey is particularly good at charting the various constituents of Clare's poetry, the lyricism, the detail, the inherited tradition of nature poetry: though again the reader wishes for more extended discussion of *The Shepherd's Calendar*, perhaps with less of Grahame, Cole and Hurdis.

J. W. and Anne Tibble's selection of Clare[50] has been reprinted. It is a useful and inexpensive book, though one would like to have seen 'The Flitting' and 'Decay' included. Barbara Lupini takes a phrase from a Van Gogh letter of 1874 and uses it to illuminate a comparison between poet and painter in '"An Open and

[46] *Records of Shelley, Byron and the Author*, by Edward John Trelawny, ed. by David Wright. pp. 324. Harmondsworth: Penguin, 1973. 40p.

[47] *Adventures of a Younger Son*, by Edward John Trelawny, ed. by William St Clair. O.U.P. pp. xxiv+480. £5.50.

[48] *Clare, the Critical Heritage*, ed. by

[49] *The Poetry of John Clare*, by Mark Storey. Macmillan. pp. xii+228. £5.95.

[50] *John Clare, Selected Poems*, ed. by J. W. and Anne Tibble. Dent. pp. xxxvi+361. 75p.

Mark Storey. Routledge & Kegan Paul, 1973. pp. xviii+453. £7.50.

Simple Eye": The Influence of Landscape in the work of John Clare and Vincent van Gogh' (*English*). In '"Very copys of nature": John Clare's Descriptive Poetry' (*PQ*), Janet M. Todd argues that Clare's persistence in the descriptive (as opposed to a 'romantic' mode) was one reason for his decline in popularity; though she argues that Clare does have a philosophy of nature and man. A minor problem concerning a Thomas Clare has been cleared up by G. D. Crossan (*TLS*, March 1), who also describes a presentation copy of *The Shepherd's Calendar* to the painter William Hilton. Another painter, Rippingille, is one of the recipients of some unpublished letters from Clare (now in the Bodleian Library) printed by Mark Storey (*RES*).

Joseph Kestner, in 'The Genre of Landor's *Gebir*: "Eminences Excessively Bright"' (*The Wordsworth Circle*) provides a detailed examination of *Gebir* in relation to the Latin epyllion, with particular reference to the style. In 'The Silent Years of George Crabbe' (*MSpr*), Hans Östman discusses the poet's reading and development between 1785 and 1807.

Two volumes in a new Salzburg series, *Poetic Drama and Poetic Theory*, deal with Byron and the romantic drama. Boleslaw Taborski's *Byron and the Theatre*,[51] though written in a jerky and uncomfortable English, is a pleasing study because it considers the plays as living theatre. Taborski gives an account of Byron's own interest in the theatre, and of performances of his plays in his lifetime, both in London and the provinces; and he ends with suggestions for Byron's plays as radio drama, or as subjects for experimental theatre.

Allen Perry Whitmore's *The Major Characters of Lord Byron's Dramas*[52] is less successful. It is a pedestrian affair, which does not convince the reader that the plays are remarkable or memorable because of their characters.

A lesser-known romantic verse drama is the subject of Parks C. Hunter Jr's 'William Godwin's Lengthy Preoccupation with *Antonio*' (*KSJ*), which discusses Godwin's revisions. Kean's conditions of employment and his agreements with R. W. Elliston are the subject of '*Aut Caesar Aut Nullus*: Edmund Kean's Articles of Agreement, 1825' (*Nineteenth-Century Theatre Research*) by Alfred L. Nelson and B. Gilbert Cross.

2. VICTORIAN: GENERAL

The most inclusive bibliography for this period is the MLA list, but the June 1975 number of *VS* includes a fairly comprehensive Victorian Bibliography for 1974, edited by Ronald E. Freeman, which lists reviews under book entries. Stuart Curran surveys the year's work in the nineteenth century in the Autumn 1975 number of *SEL*. Several more specialist bibliographies are available: in *VP* by Tobias Rich, in *VPN* by J. Don Vann and K. Mews, in *ELT*, and in *NCTR*.

Edward Alexander seeks to illuminate 'the modern temper' in his comparative study of Matthew Arnold and John Ruskin between 1848 and 1867.[1] Both men shared the feeling that their moves from art to society involved alienation from themselves,

[51] *Byron and the Theatre*, by Boleslaw Taborski. Salzburg: Poetic Drama and Poetic Theory, 1. 1973. pp. vi+395. £4.60.

[52] *The Major Characters of Lord Byron's Dramas*, by Allen Perry Whitmore. Salzburg: Poetic Drama and Poetic Theory, 6. pp. 145. £4.80.

[1] *Matthew Arnold, John Ruskin, and the Modern Temper*, by Edward Alexander. pp. xviii+310. Columbus: Ohio State U.P. 1973. $11.

but Arnold's detachment—classical and Victorian—distinguished him from Ruskin's Romantic immersion and commitment. These respective patterns reveal themselves in the two critics' personal and intellectual histories which Alexander traces from choice of profession (neither committing himself to any one vocation, but both finding their nascent aesthetic propensities undermined by the events of 1848) to their mature strategy regarding 'the darkness of the modern world' (Arnold's detachment and resultant sanity and Ruskin's commitment and madness). Chapters on their attitudes towards the past and the present, the modern element in literature, and the threat of anarchy involve close reading of passages from the major texts of both authors. The success of this study derives primarily from the usefulness of the comparison since Alexander's interpretations of his authors' lives as individuals are not new. Throughout Alexander finds stimulating perspectives in the comparison: on the one hand the contrast of Ruskin's selection of specific political doctrines from Homer with Arnold's adoption of the general spirit of Homeric nobility is shown to leave Ruskin free and Arnold unable to admire modern writers; while Ruskin's view of anarchy as coextensive with industrialism seems partial in light of Arnold's feeling that anarchy is only one manifestation of a deeper moral and spiritual anarchy to be remedied by culture, rather than merely new economic arrangements. If this book did nothing more than introduce readers of Arnold to Ruskin it would be welcome, but it provides an apposite context for Arnold's thought and development, if not anything as abstract as 'the modern temper'.

Chadwyck-Healey have made the archives of George Allen & Co.

(1893-1915),[2] Kegan Paul, Trench, Trübner & Henry S. King (1858-1912),[3] and the Cambridge University Press (1696-1902)[4] available on microfilm, and accompanying each of these is a guide and/or index. Among the recipients of letters listed in the George Allen index are Dickens, Elizabeth Gaskell, and John Ruskin. The Kegan Paul index is of authors and titles in the production ledgers, accounts, and contracts, and Mark Rutherford and Richard Chenevix Trench, the Apostle and later Archbishop, are to be found there. Both of these lists begin with a curious and defensive Publisher's Note which warns that since the list should be looked upon as a finding list to the microfilm rather than a work of significant scholarship, it will be a negligent researcher who relies too heavily on the index and fails to make his own checks. Although one note insists this is 'intended as a warning and not an apology' one may feel an apology is due for the high price of such indices whose limitations 'stem from the method and circumstances of their compilation'. Leedham-Green's and D. F. McKenzie's *Guide* to the Cambridge archives is altogether more professional though it is restricted to an introduction and summary, due to D. F. McKenzie's *A Bibliographical Study* of the Cambridge University Press (1966). The

[2] *Index to the Archives of George Allen & Co. 1839-1915.* pp. 128 (unnumbered). Bishops Stortford and Teaneck, N.J.: Chadwyck Healey and Somerset House. £15. 27 reels and index £310/$775.

[3] *Index of Authors and Titles. Kegan Paul, Trench, Trübner and Henry S. King. 1858-1912,* by Sandy Merritt. pp. 130 (unnumbered). Bishops Stortford and Teaneck, N.J.: Chadwyck-Healey and Somerset House. £15. 27 reels and index £285/$715.

[4] *A Guide to the Archives of the Cambridge University Press,* by E. S. Leedham-Green with an introd. by D. F. McKenzie. pp. 34. Bishops Stortford: Chadwyck-Healey. 80p. 11 reels and index £112/$280.

project of microfilm publication of publishers' archives is welcome however. Readers may now travel to the few libraries that can afford them rather than to the publishers themselves.

E. V. Neale (1810–1892) and the Co-operative movement is the subject of *Christian Socialism and Co-operation in Victorian England* by Philip N. Backstrom.[5] Neale, an Evangelical gentleman turned socialist, envisaged the Co-operative movement as an effective force (but a panacea, paternalistic not Marxist) in combatting capitalism and changing the mode of production. Backstrom sees the failure of his ideas to prevail as indicative of real doubts whether the overall efforts of the movement constitute a 'working class movement'. Backstrom's biography (drawn partly from Neale's recently discovered Journal) also takes issue with Beatrice Webb's understanding of Neale and Co-operation in 1891: Neale is in the first rank of those who built Co-operation as an organized movement of self-help.

In *Authors, Publishers and Politicians*[6] James L. Barnes examines the quest and failure to reach an Anglo-American copyright agreement between 1815 and 1854. In the main this book focuses on the American publishing scene, rooting the growth of the cheap and pirate press in the devastating American depression of 1837–43 (during which time Dickens made his first visit). But chapters on the impact of foreign reprints on the British book trade, the discussions of international copyright occasioned by Parliamentary legislation between 1838–44, and the British attempt to

compensate for absence of international copyright through the Law Courts illuminate the position of the British author at home as well as abroad. Barnes notes that piracy thrived in Britain as well as in the Republic, with Routledge and Bohn pirating many of their cheaper editions; he also documents the strong advocacy of copyright by Bulwer and Dickens, and their failed attempt to arrange 'funds' (bribery) for the American campaign for Senate legislation between 1851 and 1853. Full notes accompany this well-written and interesting account.

The recovery of letters and other manuscript material of Hurrell Froude's has resulted in a first full-scale study, *Hurrell Froude and the Oxford Movement*, by Piers Brendon.[7] The author corrects the impression of Froude's childhood given by Anthony, his younger brother, in *The Nemesis of Faith*, assesses in subsequent chapters Froude's romanticism, his relationships with Keble, with Newman, the Tracts, and the Movement. Brendon convincingly denies that the crisis of 1826/27 was homosexual rather than more generally spiritual, and concludes with a highly interesting chapter on the publication of Froude's *Remains* (1838) by Newman and Keble, whose Imprimatur made the *Remains* the official apologia for the movement, turning it irrevocably to the right. Froude's intensity and hard-won saintliness won him the trust, friendship, and dependence of Keble and Newman, beside whom he is shown to take his place, though dying at 32, as an architect of the Oxford Movement.

Truth to Life[8] is a study of the art

[5] *Christian Socialism and Co-operation in Victorian England*, by Philip N. Backstrom. pp. viii+238. Croom Helm. £5.95.
[6] *Authors, Publishers and Politicians*, by James L. Barnes. pp. xvi+311. Routledge. £5.75.

[7] *Hurrell Froude and the Oxford Movement*, by Piers Brendon. pp. xix+235. Elek. £6.80.
[8] *Truth to Life*, by A. O. J. Cockshut. pp. 220. Collins. £3.

of biography in the nineteenth century. The first four essays consider its form, tradition, and certain constituent elements—the death scene and the reassessment of the past. A last essay on the milieu precedes Cockshut's discussions of six biographers and their biographies—Stanley's Arnold, Smiles, Trevelyan's Macaulay, Froude's Carlyle, Morley's Gladstone, and Ward's Newman. With the exception of the full and suggestive 'Sketch of a Tradition' Cockshut's general chapters are thin or mainly functional; in the more substantial chapters on specific works Cockshut does raise and consider interesting general questions concerning the genre as well as specific points, and the range of the texts suggests that variety and representativeness as well as quality figured in their selection. But still in these elegant thoughtful essays, one regrets the sacrifice of anything approaching completeness for the leisurely cultivated insight. There is no conclusion and while *Truth to Life* has much to recommend it, *the* book on nineteenth-century biography for our time has yet to be written.

Marcus Cunliffe's *The Age of Expansion, 1848–1917*[9] is a world history with emphasis on Europe for the intelligent layman, with many illustrations from contemporary sources that will interest the scholar as well. The three chapters of the Second Part, 'Europe and the World', provide an overview of European Imperialism in America, Asia, and Africa. For the student of Victorian literature the European perspective is instructive, and although the book lacks notes, the bibliography is wide-ranging and interesting.

John Foster's central concern in *Class Struggle and the Industrial Revolution*[10] is the development and decline of a revolutionary class-consciousness in the second quarter of the nineteenth century. But he also addresses himself to the larger question of the nature of the change which English capitalism underwent at the same time. Three towns—Northampton, South Shields, and Oldham—serve as models of different phases of the country's development. Foster concludes that in Oldham ('by no means unique') the changes associated with liberalization were part of a process by which capitalist authority was reimposed and the working class vanguard isolated; and that an earlier development of mass class-consciousness made this necessary. This lucid study provides an illuminating context for the thought of Carlyle, Ruskin, Arnold, and Morris.

In 1878 the Vicar of Akenham, a hamlet in Suffolk, refused to say or allow a Christian burial service for a two-year-old Baptist child because he was unbaptized; the rural populace, as yet without nonsectarian cemetaries, were still forced to bury their dead in the burial ground of the parish Church which treated all non-Anglicans in this way. Ronald Fletcher[11] reconstructs the event and its ramifications (it resulted in the passage of a law rectifying the situation) through contemporary documents—a plethora of letters in three local papers, the report of the trial in a Westminster court, contemporary articles on the outcome, and discussion concerning the Burial Amendment Act of 1880. Dr Fletcher's refusal to tell the story himself may

[9] *The Age of Expansion, 1848–1917*, by Marcus Cunliffe. pp. 336. Weidenfeld & Nicolson. £4.95.

[10] *Class Struggle and the Industrial Revolution*, by John Foster. pp. xvi+346. Weidenfeld & Nicolson. £6.00.

[11] *The Akenham Burial Case*, by Ronald Fletcher. pp. 280. London: Wildwood House. £3.95.

frustrate the reader who wants potted history, but for those sufficiently interested in the issues raised by Jo's graveyard in *Bleak House* and the status and feeling of Dissenters in the late nineteenth century, the testament of the colloquial, journalistic, and legal response is eloquent.

Cruel Habitations by Enid Gauldie[12] is a history of working-class housing between 1780 and 1918. While the subject of this book must remain 'background' for the reader of Victorian literature, it brings to mind many literary depictions of interiors and streets, and the reader tempted to dismiss the documentation element in *Mary Barton* or *Bleak House* as 'unimportant' or secondary will be encouraged to think again by this full, informative, and illustrated book. The literary commonplace of the Pre-industrial idyll is also questioned: pre-industrial rural housing, it is argued, was so inadequate that it contributed to the movement to the cities when opportunities for city factory work arose. The author examines the creators of legislation on housing to discover in them the inadequacies of their legislation, and also how fear of the mob determined the attitudes of the middle class electorate toward housing. *Cruel Habitations* is both descriptive sociologically and historical in its treatment of the poverty and public health aspects; of private housing such as Company Towns, Building Societies, and Philanthropic Housing and Freehold Land Associations; and of legislation and public responsibility in, for example, the provision for lodging houses and the Royal Commission. She concludes that a failure of imagination, not of purpose, delayed real housing reform. Like Steven Marcus on Engels she suggests that Victorian writing

reported but did not convey experience.

In *The Victorian School Manager*[13] Peter Gordon traces in great detail the emergence of the school manager from the undefined and varied body of men formerly responsible for the establishment of schools. In the course of chapters on the voluntary school manager, school board administration and management, and how it operates locally, the appointment of school managers, innovation by the Voluntary School Association, and the 1902 Act, he examines relationships between school board, town council, ratepayer, clergyman, land owner, subscriber, and teacher which bring Jane Eyre, Phillotson, and Bradley Headstone as well as Matthew Arnold to mind. This book fails to handle a great mass of facts gracefully, but some of the primary source material (letters, journals, records) which builds (and obscures) the argument is uniquely informative. Gordon treats the history of nineteenth-century education as social history; the anatomy of complex and diverse interest groups is divulged and a sense of the day-to-day workings of the society emerges.

Pressure from Without[17] is a collection of twelve original essays on sources of external pressure on legislation from groups (i.e. the Philosophical Radicals or those concerned with single issues such as anti-slavery, suffrage, foreign affairs, the separation of church and state, and administrative, land, or moral reform) and individuals (William Lovett, Shaftesbury, Edward Baines), with parliamentary reform, free trade, and dissent the main foci. In her introductory

[12] *Cruel Habitations*, by Enid Gauldie. pp. 363. Allen & Unwin. £5.75 and £3.00.

[13] *The Victorian School Manager*, by Peter Gordon. pp. xiv+337. Woburn P. £6.00.

[14] *Pressure From Without*, ed. by Patricia Hollis. pp. xi+334. Edward Arnold. £5.50.

essay Patricia Hollis suggests that pressure groups indirectly co-opted working men into political activity, and that the politics of deference declined accordingly; but she assesses their clear effectiveness in Parliamentary Reform as mainly negative in that they prevented reactive laws rather than achieved Reform. But pressure groups did contribute significantly to arousing and directing public opinion which did influence legislation positively. Brian Harrison's piece on 'State Intervention and Moral Reform' seems particularly useful to readers of Dickens, Thackeray, Hardy, and Elizabeth Gaskell. But because the essays as a whole define the dangers of the society detected and resisted by the voluntary groups, they compare interestingly with the emphases and preoccupations of the literature; guides to further reading accompany each essay. *Pressure from Without* concerns the issues, legislation, and social consciousness which informs nineteenth-century literature—some of which is itself pressure from without.

In *The Victorian Country Child*[13] Pamela Horn traces the day-to-day experiences of average rural children (mainly of farm workers) at home, school, and in work on the land, in cottage industry, or in domestic service. Chapters on church and chapel, holidays, sickness, and crime, and a variety of documents make this a work which will interest readers of Dickens, Arnold, and Hardy.

Steven Marcus[16] undertakes a critical examination of Engels's *The Condition of the Working Class in England in 1844* as an exploration of problems of method in a literary

criticism which must 'sustain the claim to cognitive status'. In close reading of passages from Dickens, Disraeli, de Tocqueville, and other contemporary responses to Manchester, Marcus argues that the newness of the situation in the 30s and 40s consisted not only of conditions but the struggle of the human consciousness to make (and often to resist) the necessary accommodations within. In a broadly biographical chapter Marcus assesses the considerable influence of Carlyle on Engels during his stay in Britain through a series of parallel passages which reveal similar conceptual concerns and responses. And in his first core chapter he favourably compares the creative achievement of Engels's response to Manchester with that of Mill, Dickens, and Ruskin. In the second, he shows that while Engels's presentation of the working class is 'disinterested', he vilifies the middle class. Marcus attributes this to an ambivalence about the working class illustrated by Engels's approval of the miners' transcendence of their situation in a non-violent strike. At this stage Engels's communism is not unlike Arnold's culture in its transcendence of conflict, class, and interest. Marcus's method, and treatment of Engels as 'representative Victorian' as well as one of the new revolutionary breed, is rewarding and should, despite its apparent otherness, be considered part of the mainstream of literary criticism as well as Victorian studies.

Hugh McLeod's focus in *Class and Religion in the Late Victorian City*[17] on London between 1880 and 1914 allows him to study both the Victorian religious pattern and its fading away. His primary interests include

---

[15] *The Victorian Country Child*, by Pamela Horn. pp. xvi+244. Kineton: The Roundwood P. £6.00.

[16] *Engels, Manchester and the Working Class*, by Steven Marcus. pp. xiv+271. Weidenfeld & Nicolson. £5.25.

[17] *Class and Religion in the Late Victorian City*, by Hugh McLeod. pp. xii+360. Croom Helm. £6.95.

the religious attitudes prevailing at each social level, and the degree to which different religious allegiance integrated the individual into or separated him from his environment. Among McLeod's principal sources of information are autobiography and fiction, and Gissing, A. Morrison, A. Trollope, Mrs H. Ward, H. G. Wells, and Mark Rutherford come within the scope of this study. This book should prove useful to students of Victorian literature as much for its class delineations as for its discussion of the relation of religion specifically to class: sections on the middle-class Sunday, the 'solid' middle class, and the 'Unconscious Broad Churchmen' figure in the chapter on 'The Suburbs'.

Katharine Moore's *Victorian Wives*[18] is informed and of some interest but its informal organization —a series of vignettes on various wives—and the absence of footnotes and bibliography result in a work inappropriate for both scholars and students, as well as the reader who, his interest aroused, is given no guidance of where to go from here. The breakneck speed required by this broad survey permits little serious discourse, and an uncharacteristic pause to compare Isobel Archer and Gwendolen Harleth as reflexions of American and English attitudes towards women is notably fruitful and interesting. This author herself expresses and reflects the informed indignation of contemporary feminism concerning the history of the status of women, and her selection of wives and facts is designed as a glimpse of the developments, issues, and conditions in the period. Thus the lives of the three Patmore 'angels', Jane Carlyle, Caroline Norton, Frances Trollope, Margaret Oli-

phant, Mary Benson, and Louisa Macdonald merit inclusion; a short, general, and in the main highly simplified discussion of fictive wives precedes a final chapter on the American scene. This suffers from the same weaknesses as the bulk of the book, but the comparison of the two cultures and the unfamiliarity of most British readers with the lives of Harriet Beecher Stowe, Abba Alcott, and Hannah Pearsall Smith make it more welcome. The diaries and letters concerning the role of women and the nature of the family in Victorian Britain testify to the existence of a plethora of material on this subject which, presented and documented properly, would put author and publisher into the debt of students of Victorian studies.

In her book on dress reformers of the nineteenth century[19] Stella Mary Newton focuses on the connexion between feminism, health, aestheticism, and fashion reform from 1850 to 1917. Relying heavily on periodicals, newspapers, literature, and art of the day, this book provides a useful perspective on familiar sources and aids in understanding the iconography of nineteenth-century dress—its moral and social significance. Specifically works by Charles Reade, W. S. Gilbert, Mary A. Ward, J. S. Mill, Mrs Oliphant, G. Meredith, Charlotte Yonge, and William Morris are 'read' in this light. Chapters with illustrations on Bloomers, Pre-Raphaelite clothing, the Grecian fillets of the 1860s (which replaced the crinoline), dress of 'good sense and moderation', the sheath 'medievalism' of 'aesthetic' dress of the early 80s, Dr Jaeger's 'bifurcated garment'—both sanitary and woollen, and the International Health Exhibition of 1884, reform in men's clothing, and Socialist Gowns

[18] *Victorian Wives*, by Katharine Moore. pp. xxviii+208. Allison & Busby. £3.25.

[19] *Health, Art and Reason*, by Stella Mary Newton. pp. xii+192. John Murray. £3.95.

guide the reader through the developments of the period. Over the century the author notes a change, from a reformed dress worn as a mission to the unenlightened to a dress worn as a badge which proclaimed the taste of the wearer, which reflects the attempt to eradicate the pressure of fashion on dress.

The reprinting of *Thomas J. Wise in the Original Cloth* (1939, 1947)[20] by Wilfred Partington, a former editor of the *Bookman's Journal*, is welcome. Partington's biography remains standard, eminently readable, and fascinating. Even John Carter (one of the original revealers of Wise's forgeries) who stuffily complained in 1959 that Partington's book was 'rather vulgarly written', acknowledged at the same time that he 'has amassed a great deal of information, much of it based on original research'.

The Victorian Working Class[21] consists of selections from newspaper correspondents' letters to the *Morning Chronicle* between 1849 and 1851; they constitute part of a survey on 'Labour and the Poor', which provided both a general coverage of regions and large towns and detailed examinations of types of occupational communities. Wainwright and Razzell each contribute an introduction, Wainwright focusing on social change and economic transformation, and Razzell on the structure of different types of working class community. The material itself is organized by region, and gives the reader a vivid sense of day-to-day life all over the country. Mayhew was the London correspondent for the *Morning Chronicle*, and this survey of the Victorian working class supplements his later study on the London poor.

In *Hell and the Victorians*[22] Geoffrey Rowell traces developments in theological attitudes and interpretations of hell and the future life from Hartley and the Unitarians through Coleridge, Maurice, the Tractarians, the High Churchman, and the converts to conditionalism. By 1880 the doctrine of hell faced charges of moral indefensibility and inconsistency with ideas of progress and humanitarianism, and the growth of the doctrine of the 'intermediate state' throughout the period indicates a similar departure from Calvinist eschatology. Rowell packs in both history and theology, and if narrowness, brevity, and superficiality often result from this dual interest and the survey method, the reader of the literature of the period may make and find for himself the connexions between doctrine or attitude and the literary expression of punishment, death, despair, hope, and evil. More positively, Rowell's absorption in the theological literature permits him to consider some works and debates unknown to the common reader.

Nineteenth-Century Literary Perspectives,[23] a *Festschrift* for the late Lionel Stevenson, consists of eighteen original articles on Romantic and Victorian poetry, criticism, and fiction, and an introductory biographical essay on Stevenson which includes a bibliography of his publications. Four essays on Romantic literature— U. C. Knoepflmacher on Chapter 15 of the *Biographia Literaria*, John

[20] *Thomas J. Wise in the Original Cloth*, by Wilfred Partington with an appendix by G. B. Shaw. pp. 372. Folkestone and London: Dawsons. £6.50.

[21] *The Victorian Working Class*, ed. by P. E. Razzell and R. W. Wainwright. pp. xii+338. London and Portland: Cass. 1973. £6.50.

[22] *Hell and the Victorians*, by Geoffrey Rowell. pp. xii+242. Oxford: Clarendon P. £4.85.

[23] *Nineteenth-Century Literary Perspectives*, ed. by Clyde de L. Ryals, with J. Clubbe and B. F. Fisher IV. pp. xxiv+294. Durham, N.C.: Duke U.P. $11.75.

Clubbe on Byron's 1816 poems and *Manfred*, Martin J. Svaglic on Shelley and *King Lear*, and Keats's *Lamia* as dramatic illusion by Richard Harter Fogle—will not be considered here. Two articles concern Tennyson. A. Dwight Culler shows that Richard Chenevix Trench's remark to Tennyson that 'we cannot live in art' was made to Tennyson among the Apostles in May or June 1830 before Tennyson's first volume of poetry was published; it referred to Trench, himself somewhat aesthetic, rather than to Tennyson. Thus 'The Palace of Art' is addressed to the Apostles, all England and all Europe; it is not a poem of merely personal guilt. In an essay of comparison between Tennyson's 'The Voyage' (1865) and Baudelaire's 'Le Voyage' (1861), G. Robert Stange explores the contradictions and complexity of Tennyson's use of voyage imagery. Baudelaire's poem contrasts with Tennyson's in its ability to make poetry out of one's ambivalences, and its use of certain poetic conventions unavailable to Tennyson.

Two essays on Browning, 'The Structural Logic of *The Ring and the Book*' and '"Prince Hohenstiel-Schwangau": Browning's "Ghostly Dialogue"' make interesting claims: Boyd Litzinger treats the Roman murder story as a nineteenth-century literary epic, and Clyde de L. Ryals contends that the inconsistencies in 'Prince Hohenstiel-Schwangau' are the character's, and that the poem reflects Browning's increasing awareness of the limitations of the dramatic monologue; in his quest for objectivity Browning has combined the internal monologue with the dramatic monologue, and 'the Prince is speaking solely to himself'.

In a major piece, David J. De Laura provides a context for Arnold's 'Shakespeare' by exploring the range of attitudes held by Arnold's contemporaries and his Romantic predecessors, particularly the attempt by Coleridge, Hazlitt, and Carlyle to define a paradoxical Shakespearian mode of impersonal subjectivity; beside sources, this article specifies a range of allowable interpretation. W. M. Rossetti's poem, 'Mrs. Holmes Grey', emerges as a key poem of the Pre-Raphaelite movement and an alternative to the assumptions often made about Pre-Raphaelitism in an article by William E. Fredeman. While the poem's lack of purely pictorial elements makes it unusual among Pre-Raphaelite poems, its external and psychological detail, and the intensity of its surface realism parallel the principal techniques of the earliest paintings by the Brotherhood.

In the same *Festschrift* Charles Richard Sanders reports on the ups and downs of the long relationship of the Carlyles and Thackeray from the novelist's early and favourable review of *The French Revolution* in *The Times* to Carlyle's mixed responses to Thackeray and his works long after 1863. The absence of any chauvinism —national, class, time, or youth—in Dickens is noted by Edgar Johnson, and Carl Woodring explores Dickens's ways of handling unseen spiritual growth in 'Change in *Chuzzlewit*', in which Dickens is shown to use both gradual change and the sudden regenerative moment. A second suggestive article on Dickens in this collection is Jerome Beatty's on *Little Dorrit*; he seeks to replace prison as the central organizing metaphor with one which accounts for the brighter passages in the novel. *Little Dorrit* explores one arc of the cosmography of Dickens's overall vision of life as divinely created: 'the moral necessity of seeing the temporality of this world as organically cyclical and benevolent'. Richard D. Altick believes the ubiquity in *Our Mutual Friend* of the social implications of education to be topical. One connexion between the dust mounds and the river, illiterate Boffin and illiterate Gaffer Hexam, results from Dickens's interpretation of the Victorian concern with popular education and literacy, the physical reflexion of which was printed paper. In an interesting interpretation, Altick draws attention to the importance of reading—the ability, the act, in this novel.

Two essays on George Eliot, both on *Middlemarch*, by Gordon Haight ('Poor Mr Casaubon') and C. L. Cline ('Qualifications of the Medical Practitioners of *Middlemarch*'), address themselves to questions raised previously. Haight takes up the discussion in the *TLS* of Casaubon's model and impotency, noting that Casaubon's impotency has more to do with his sickness than his age; if George Eliot did have a model for the pedant, it was Dr Brabant whose attentions at 62 to George Eliot in his own home resulted in her ejection by his wife and sister. Cline sets Lydgate in the context of the medical profession and other practitioners; he emerges, from his Paris training, not only in advance of Middlemarch practice but of London as well. In the last essay of the *Festschrift*, *The Ordeal of Richard Feverel* is viewed by Benjamin Franklin Fisher as sensation or Gothic fiction in a minor key, a perspective which takes account of its 'supernatural or melodramatic elements' and which reflects Meredith's interest in sales and recognition.

The Crisis of Imperialism, 1865–1915 by Richard Shannon[24] is part of the Paladin History of England which as a series aims to bring recent developments in history and historiography to the general reader. Shannon uses the considerable space to good purpose, providing alternatives of interpretation gracefully and in detail, and subtle and fresh readings of his own, though his political history seems rather better than his cultural analysis. Students of the literature of the period will find Shannon's overt emphasis on interpretative problems and the meaning of history particularly of interest since so many of the authors of the day were themselves engaged in similar formulations. That the Eyre controversy marks 'the opening of a fault-line in the structure of intellectual Liberalism' provides an interesting perspective with which to view the conflict of Mill with Kingsley, Carlyle, and Ruskin. Short biographies of major figures, light annotation, a basic bibliography, and a detailed index supplement the text. Shannon's history is responsible, useful and academic without being either highly specialized or vulgarly popular.

The fifth Walter Neurath Memorial Lecture by Sir John Summerson[25] on the London building world of the 1860s together with over fifty illustrations of buildings of the decade focus on the contracting builders (responsible for public buildings and churches, commercial and domestic buildings in the city and central area generally), and estate developers, sectors of the biggest industry in London about which little is known. The office-holding architects of this decade (which was the height of the mid-Victorian hatred of official architecture) are also surveyed. By excluding consideration of London buildings of Butterfield, Street, Philip Webb, and

[24] *The Crisis of Imperialism. 1865–1915,* by Richard Shannon. pp. 512. Hart-Davis, MacGibbon. £5.95.

[25] *The London Building World of the Eighteen-Sixties,* by John Summerson. pp. 60. Thames & Hudson. £2.25.

other celebrities, Sir John can consider the 'adequate heroes' of the day-to-day building, the quality of which the illustrations testify.

Periodicals of the Nineties[26] is a checklist of literary periodicals published in the U.K. at longer than fortnightly intervals compiled by J. R. Tye. One hundred and thirty-eight entries, which include alleged circulation as well as publisher, price, printer, editor, and location, comprise the first part of the Checklist and three subsequent lists by Publisher, Printer, and Editor follow. This format reveals that W. R. Nicoll was editing *The Bookman* and *The Woman at Home* simultaneously for six years, that *Tinsley's Magazine* became *The Novel Review* in 1892, and that *The Anti-Philistine* and *Womanhood* enjoyed only brief lives.

In *The Industrial Muse*[27] Martha Vicinus examines British working class literature through its major forms at their best in the nineteenth century—street ballads and broadsides, propaganda, Chartist fiction and poetry, poetry imitative of major writers, dialect and music hall—in order to show its strength and variety. In the first chapter on broadsides, the foundation for a more diverse and sophisticated literature, their nature, publishers, authors, and vendors are described, and their reflection of working class needs and aspirations assessed, along with their stimulation of literacy in the transition from an oral to a written culture. Samples of working-class compositions pervade the discussion throughout but the last section on Broadsides of the weavers is particularly rich in this respect. Propaganda is treated through a

consideration of the literature of the coal miners' union, 1825–1845; it reflects the gradual replacement of the 'straight-forward' broadsides by educational and literary works as does the Chartist's establishment of fiction as a working class artistic medium. In both of these chapters Ms Vicinus discusses the literature as part of a coherent social history, and the texts derive power and interest from their context, and the context specificity from the texts. Thus a miner's political 'catechism' and 'prayer' which in isolation might appear crude or Machiavellian take on urgency and authority in the context of the miner's struggle against exploitation by owner, church, and chapel. The other chapters reveal a similar richness of specificity and breadth which forcibly reminds the reader of the anomalous category of working class literature that high culture has created. Labouring under the same problem that a book on middle class literature of the nineteenth century would have, *The Industrial Muse* is properly selective and representative. But it is necessarily concentrated and allusive. The chapters that follow prove rich, suggestive, and informative, the one on Northern dialect literature (1860–1885) outstanding in its testimony to an affirmation of working class values, and a large audience at penny readings, of almanacs, and journals. A full bibliography and notes, and an Appendix of some of the poetry, indicate the potential of the subject, and provide an invaluable guide to diverse sources. The literature and spirit evident in this book bear on the conceptualization of John Barton, Stephen Blackpool, and Felix Holt among others.

In *VS* John Angus Campbell argues that Darwin's continuing response to nature rather than the decline of his interest in art should be taken as a

---

[26] *Periodicals of the Nineties*, by J. R. Tye. pp. 36. Oxford: Bibliographical Society. (Occasional Publication No. 9). £1.00.

[27] *The Industrial Muse*, by Martha Vicinus. pp. x+357. Croom Helm. £6.95.

fair measure of his affective health. The extent of agreement between Marx's views of the history of human society (*Das Kapital*, 1867) and Darwin's history of organic Nature (*The Origin of Species*, 1859) is shown by Ralph Colp in *JHI*. While acknowledging the 'epoch-making' quality of Darwin's theory, in the main Marx contrasts the two, and objects vehemently to the application of Darwin to social problems. From two letters of Darwin to Marx in 1873 and 1880 Colp speculates on the implied differences and agreement between the two thinkers.

William Baker identifies twenty-seven hitherto unattributed articles in the *Penny Cyclopaedia* (1833–46) as early work of George Henry Lewes; they are particularly rich in commentary on eighteenth-century authors.

In a discussion of the androgyne in nineteenth-century literature and art (*CL*), Bram Dijkstra argues that the concept was a 'counter-offensive among artists against the economic motivation behind . . . sexual stereotypes of bourgeois industrial society' and 'a more natural alternative to the universe of absolute opposites which provided a system of dominance and submission': the ideas of Otto Weininger, *Pamela* and *Clarissa*, and Ingres's 'Jupiter and Thetis' illustrate and sanction the bourgeois sexual stereotype, while Lewis's *The Monk* and Charles Nodier's story *Inez de las Sierras* (1837) both portray male violence as the result of the enforced separation of the male from the female principle, of aggression from passive humanism.

A review of new work on the history of social movements (*VS*) provides John F. C. Harrison with an opportunity for a useful analysis and assessment of subject areas (crowd history, millenarianism, class defini-

tion, the history of cultures), methodology, and tone.

A. J. Heesom (*DUJ*) attempts to rescue the third Lord Londonderry (1778–1854) from over-simple charges of villainy preferred by Dickens and others with relation to his rôle in the coal trade. Londonderry's guilt arose from 'a lack of sensitivity to the growing humanitarianism of his own day', not from malice or greed.

In *JHI* Fred Kaplan follows the star of Mesmerism from its first appearance in Paris in Mesmer's book (1779) to its career in Britain during the nineteenth century. Since Mesmer and his followers believed that they had discovered *the* truth, responses to it on spiritual and metaphysical as well as on scientific grounds are understandable; in the midst of its seventy-five-year life James Braid invented the word 'hypnosis' in 1843, thus anticipating the transfer of emphasis from an external fluid or force of magnetism to an imaginative force within the ordinary workings of the mind.

Robert O'Kell reports on *The Victorian Counter-Culture*, an interdisciplinary conference held at the University of South Florida in 1974 (*VS*). Papers given included Steven Marcus on the ways in which certain nineteenth-century artists discussed or omitted the sexual dimension in their work, Michael Woolf on the 'lesser breeds without the law'—the poor, the workers, the Irish, Hillis Miller on religious doubt, Boniface Obichere on Anti-Imperialism, Noel Annan on the cult of homosexuality in the English upper classes, and Gertrude Himmelfarb on 'Two Nations or Five Classes?'

In a particularly interesting glimpse of social history in *VS*, Christopher Kent focuses on the anomalous Whittington Club (1847–1873), a product of early Victorian social reformers who hoped to establish on the co-operative principle a congenial club for women and lower middle-class clerks and shop assistants as well as gentlemen. Founded by Douglas Jerrold and a committee, the Whittington included many literary figures, and Bohemian and middle-class radicals among its patrons and members. The club's interest in self-improvement in accordance with middle-class values was reflected in its range of classes—in languages, music and elocution, its lectures, and its discussions, all as an alternative to Chartist proletarianism.

Donald J. Olsen's piece on 'Victorian London' (*VS*) hovers uncomfortably between scholarship and travelogue. He sets out to account for and justify 'the structure of Victorian London, physical and social which remains the structure of . . . the 1970's'. In their efforts to preserve privacy for the individual and his family, the Victorians provided London with a functional, moral, and social order as contrasted with the visual and spatial order of Haussmann's Paris. The omnibus (ca 1830) and the tube (1860s) permitted strict social segregation which reflects increasing specialization in other areas—doctors, nurses, industry, and architecture. Suburbs of villas and terraces of small working-class dwellings proliferate. 'What the Victorians desired was privacy for the middle classes, publicity for the working classes, and segregation for both.' But the discussion of Victorian London is sandwiched between some rather stale touristic generalizations about present day London which betray glib and all-too-fashionable elitist social values.

Robert Patten edits a double number of *PULC* which is devoted to 'George Cruikshank: A Revaluation'. It contains ten articles, all of an inspiringly high quality including two on Dickens which will not be reviewed here. The wide range of subjects, the quality of the articles and some seventy plates make this number a desirable volume in both personal and public libraries. E. D. H. Johnson reports on the George Cruikshank Collection at Princeton. In 'The Tradition of Comic Illustration from Hogarth to Cruikshank' Ronald Paulson explores what we mean by 'illustration', 'comic illustration' vs. the moral or satiric tradition of graphic art, and the possible relationships between illustration and text. Anthony Burton stresses Cruikshank's success in matching the style and mood of the novelists whose books he illustrates, but notes that the special qualities of Cruikshank's work may also owe something to the method of monthly publication. In arguing that 'humanity and the vigorous play of a large, free fertile imagination' are characteristic of Cruikshank's work, John Harvey takes issue with Jane Cohen's claim that in his later years he came more and more to identify with Fagin. His 'nervous line' of sharp perception of life in the metropolis is not governed by a hunger for the bizarre, but by a generous humour, a sense of natural relatedness of people and things, and 'an inexhaustible imaginative humanity'. Louis James examines the three eras in which Cruikshank contributes to the form graphic art takes—the Regency, the era of Reform Bill agitation, and the mid-Victorian period—by considering a polemical work from each era (The Political Showman—At Home (1821); The GIN Shop (1829), The Bottle (1847)), and suggesting the respective graphic conventions within which Cruikshank worked, and which he made his own. *Mr. Lambkin*, Cruikshank's first experiment in independent narrative, is seen by David Kunzle as an index to the adaptation of the art of caricature to new conditions and to the evolution of new alternatives. Michael Steig adopts a 'psychodynamic approach' in his essay; Cruikshank's grotesque style is discussed in terms of how it simultaneously arouses and manages or defends against anxiety. In '"At it Again": Aspects of Cruikshank's Later Work' William Feaver shows that the works from the artist's temperance period resolve many of his earlier concerns, and that he survived on the strength of his guiding passions.

Jill H. Pellew uses the relation of the Home Office to the Explosives Act of 1875 (*VS*) to assess the increasing amount of governmental control in the nineteenth century which amounted to a revolution in government.

Michael Rose, in his review of a number of recent publications on late Victorian and early twentieth-century history (*VS*), suggests that a strong case exists for seeing the period from the late eighteen-seventies to 1915 as discrete, and as a pivot between the two centuries.

From the biography of Mary Carpenter (1807–77), an unmarried female social reformer, Harriet Warm Schupf attempts to discuss single women and social reform in mid-nineteenth-century England (*VS*). Instrumental in helping establish ragged, industrial, and borstal schools, Mary Carpenter opened up the broader field of social endeavour to women while remaining reluctant to support the Women's Rights movement. The individual biography is moderately interesting but even the author concludes that Mary Carpenter's life is barely representative: 'an attack on some very real problems derived directly from the compulsion to satisfy strong personal needs, the solutions gaining strength because they fit on both a national and individual level'. The focus on Mary Carpenter's status of unmarried female seems inappropriate. What Harriet Schupf sees as 'the obvious question', why so few women philanthropists achieved positions of prominence, remains unanswered except insofar as 'few others were fortunate to find so suitable a fit'.

In '"Captain Swing" Explained' (*N&Q*) Sheila Smith finds the metaphor for the name of the mythical character who burned ricks and farm machinery in the eighteen-thirties and forties. In a letter of 1840 sent to Dickens (published in *VS*, 1974), John Overs describes the group action of haymakers with scythes who when the leader cries '"swing!" . . . in go the fearful instruments *altogether* levelling every obstacle in swaths before them', in connexion with the indignation of working men at their reduction in wages.

Alan Thomas contributes a highly interesting review article with illustrations on the revival of Victorian photography to *VS* in which he suggests that the camera both encouraged *le bourgeoisisme* of Western Europe, and expressed social attitudes in its literal recording of things as in, for example, the sparsity of photographs which reveal a social mix before 1890.

John Unrau discusses antecedents to the ethical approach to architecture of Pugin and Ruskin (*N&Q*) in articles by John Carter in *The Gentleman's Magazine* (1802) and a lecture of T. Kerrich in 1809.

In his long review article of Dyos and Wolff's *The Victorian City* (*YW* LIV, 306) in *VS*, Alexander Welsh suggests that the thirty-eight essays stress the complexity and variety of Victorian experience rather than 'loose large causes and easy tendencies of historical change'. The article may serve to hearten and tempt the reader to try to read this formidable and expensive book which ranges far beyond the rubric 'city' into poetry, visual art, and the novel.

A considerable number of articles this year concern publishing, the history of periodicals in particular. Maurianne Adams offers a vigorous engaging discussion of the uses of nineteenth-century periodical material in the course of a review of Armstrong's *Victorian Scrutinies* in *VPN*. In *Library* Alan Bell reports on the 1852 entries in the *Journal* of Sir Frederic Madden, Keeper of Manuscripts in the British Museum from 1837 to 1866, and considers both the desirability and problems of publication of the entire *Journal*. A charge of forgery for a series of woodcuts appearing in *A new Biblia pauperum* (1877) is examined by John Buchanan Brown (*Library*) and another forgery figures in *PBSA* where James T. Cox speculates on a new date for the Wiseian forgery of Tennyson's 'trial' issue of *Beckett* (1879). His suggestion of 1893 or before, rather than 1901, has more general significance because until now only one of the Tennyson forgeries predated 1896.

The editorial history of the London *Morning Advertiser* is illuminated in notes on Dr John Sheridan, contributor, leader writer, and editor (1831–45) and the editorship of N. de la Fleurie (1876–77) by Basil L. Crapster in *VPN*. In connexion with this article, also in *VPN*, Anne Lohrli distinguishes between Robert Soutar, journalist (d. 1866) and his son Robert Soutar, playwright, doctor, and stage manager (1827–1908).

Two singular presses merit attention in *Library*. John Dreyfus considers Emery Walker's part in the design of type for the Kelmscott and Dove presses in light of newly examined documents. And William E. Fredeman describes Emily Faithfull (1835–95), founder of the Victoria Press (1860–81), its formation, nature, and productions. Implementing the social theories of the leaders of the women's movement, the press employed female compositors. While *The Victoria Regia* (1862) and some other few works are adjudged splendid examples of the capabilities of the women compositors, the ordinary output of the press was plain and pedestrian. Fredeman provides two Appendices, a 'Chronology of Emily Faithfull and the Victoria Press' and 'A Tentative Short-Title Listing of Victoria Press Publications'.

Linda Burnell Jones calls attention to James Grant's account of Magazine Day in *Travels in the Town* (1839) as a colourful description of a nineteenth-century publishing practice whereby publishers of periodicals supplied them monthly to wholesalers in Paternoster Row who in turn sold them to the booksellers—publishers, bookseller, and wholesaler alike thereby benefiting (*VPN*).

In a piece which focuses on 'the relationship between editorial opinion and financial control, internal arrangements and the audience' in the *Brighton Patriot* (1835–39), Thomas M. Kemnitz considers the origins of editorial policy in early Victorian newspapers (*VPN*). Ranking financial controllers, editor, readers in descending order, he advises scholars to determine individual arrangements of publication rather than to accept titles (of editor, printer, etc.) to understand editorial responsibility. H. W. McCready presents material from the Prothero Papers on the nature of the editorship of the *Quarterly Review* in 1898 and its financial plight in 1919 (*VPN*). In the same journal Peter Morgan uses concepts of Roland Barthes to emphasize the linguistic context of nineteenth-century periodical articles. Comparing newly discovered volumes of John Stuart Mill's annotated *Examiner* articles with the MacMinn edition of the bibliography of Mill's published writings, Ann P. and John M. Robson attribute two articles not in MacMinn and give some examples of corrected readings (*VPN*).

The history of the Acton circle and the scholarly weekly, the *Chronicle* (1867–68), founded by Liberal Catholics as a rival of the *Athenaeum* in literary review and the *Saturday Review* in politics, presented by Guy Ryan in *VPN*, is of general as well as specific interest. Reasons for the cessation of the paper seem to involve the paper's support of too many unpopular causes, among them uniquely Gladstonian liberalism, social reform in England and wholesale reform in Ireland, and Liberal Catholic attacks on the Holy See *and* the English hierarchy. But as the *Chronicle* emerged from the ashes of the *Home and Foreign Review* so the Acton circle went on to found the *North British Review*.

In *VPN* Robert H. Tener explores the editorial career of R. H. Hutton with a first instalment on his connexion (1851–55) with the Unitarian weekly, *The Inquirer*, which Tener shows to be more extensive than realized, Hutton having published there over 200 articles. In his second instalment Tener describes Hutton's connexion with the *Prospective Review*, on which he served an editorial apprenticeship (1853–55), and the *National Review* which he founded and edited (1855–1862), with an eye to confirming the list of attributed writings in Tener's bibliography.

A small collection of correspondence (1891–1901) between Dr James Murray, editor of *NED*, Vols. A–K, and Dr Fitzgerald Hall, the Oriental

scholar and collector of quotations, provides Kathleen Wales (*N&Q*) with valuable insight into the development of the *Dictionary*, and both understanding of the importance of Hall's contributions and of the effect that editing *NED* had on Murray himself.

3. VICTORIAN VERSE AND DRAMA
(a) *Poetry*

In *Victorian Poetry*[28] N. P. Messenger and J. R. Watson have created a useful anthology of the work between 1850 and 1890. Barring Tennyson, Browning, Arnold, and Hopkins, the editors include reasonably lengthy selections from the regional poetry of William Barnes, R. S. Hawker, and Charles Tennyson Turner, from Clough, Patmore, Meredith, the two Rossettis, Morris, and Swinburne, and Smith's 'Glasgow', Thomson's 'The City of Dreadful Night', and Henley's 'In Hospital' in full. Headnotes for each poet, annotation, and numbered lines should make *Victorian Poetry* welcome to students and lecturers.

James Sambrook seeks to define Pre-Raphaelitism through a collection of essays[29] balanced between history and criticism by and about its practitioners; apart from the lack of illustrations in a book with a considerable claim to them, he succeeds. Articles by Ruskin, Pater, the Rossettis, Hunt and others (some here accessible for the first time since original publication) are succeeded by post-war criticism by Stephen Spender, Humphry House, G. Hough, Heath-Stubbs, J. H. Buckley, and Robert L. Peters. Only one

[28] *Victorian Poetry. 'The City of Dreadful Night' and Other Poems*, ed. by N. P. Messenger and J. R. Watson. pp. xxii+242. Totowa: Rowman & Littlefield (Everyman's University Library). £3.50 and £1.75.
[29] *Pre-Raphaelitism: A Collection of Critical Essays*, ed. by James Sambrook. pp. 277. Chicago and London: U. of Chicago P. £6.75.

of the modern essays is new—John Dixon Hunt's intricate exploration of the enshrining of the moment in Pre-Raphaelite poetry and painting via D. G. Rossetti's and Walter Pater's appreciations of Giorgione's *Le Concert Champêtre*. Three of the twentieth-century pieces treat Rossetti, one Swinburne, and the other six thematic aspects of Pre-Raphaelitism such as its aesthetic, the Aesthetic withdrawal, literary painters, and the fear of art. Sambrook's introduction provides an informed intellectual history of Pre-Raphaelitism, although he is quick to call a 'movement' what he elsewhere refers to as a 'loosely-knit company' and properly places among other closely related ideas. *Pre-Raphaelitism* offers a good introduction to the subject with an adequate bibliography; more experienced students may value it for some of its source material, Hunt's essay, and its index; a paperback edition would be welcome. Lionel Stevenson's *The Pre-Raphaelite Poets* (Norton) was not available for review, nor was G. Pickering's *Creative Malady* (Allen & Unwin).

Several articles treat that equally amorphous movement, Aestheticism. In *ELT* Karl Beckson regards the Religion of Art as the most 'comprehensive and revealing mythology of the Aesthetic Movement'. The discussion which follows of the transformation of art into religion, the artist as martyr, art as ritual, the poet as priest, includes comments on Blake, Keats, Yeats, Lionel Johnson, Ernest Dowson, Pater, and Wilde, as well as Ronald Firbank, Joyce and Fr Rolfe. At the heart of the Religion of Art is the commitment to the Platonic world of eternal Beauty rather than to the Heraclitean world of perpetual flux. Aiming at better assessment of poetry of the 'nineties, James G. Nelson (*ELT*) explores some poems by John

Gray, Ernest Dowson, and Lionel Johnson in light of the concept of 'coming to life' through an encounter with beauty described by, above all, Walter Pater. Whereas in Keats's poetry the encounter with beauty leads beyond feeling to waking thought, in John Gray and Dowson the encounter avoids a return to reality, and values the moment for its own sake. Poetry of Lionel Johnson reflects another Paterian concept, that of impassioned contemplation. Ruth Z. Temple notes the rampant mislabelling of the terms 'Pre-Raphaelitism', 'Aestheticism', 'Decadence', and 'Fin de Siecle' (*ELT*), and regards it as a 'scandal in literary history'. She discusses the misapprehensions concerning each of the labels, and concludes by offering her own definitions and an alternative historical model.

The concept of the Victorian poet as outcast is the subject of Lawrence J. Starzyk in *TSLL*. He traces the failed attempt of early Victorian poetic theory to reject Romantic isolation in favour of a poetry more inclusive of society, and its reluctant admission of isolation and an antisocial posture redolent of Romantic theory's antipathy for the external world. Poetic theory from a wide range of critics including Bentham, Clough, Selkirk, Mill, Carlyle, Macaulay, Hazlitt, Hallam, Pater, and Arnold, attests to the self-conscious artist, isolated from society and fragmented within himself. Because the artist never is, but is always becoming 'one must conclude that for Victorian critics art was an impossibility'; for Starzyk the critics transformed this liability into an asset —in the poet's nature 'all faculties are operative and harmonized in the poetic art', and 'the sum of the parts working in unison is greater than the whole considered as an aggregate of independent powers' (i.e. as in the masses)—the asset being what Arnold calls 'Imaginative Reason' by which the artist transcends himself to find an unconscious self. The author dubs this dilemma of the early Victorian theorist, this 'dedication to resolute social action, undermined by intense sensitivity which resulted ultimately in the withdrawal into the self', 'Hamletism'.

In *Genre* Arline Golden describes the revival of the amatory sonnet sequence between 1850 and 1900 which includes E. B. Browning's *Sonnets from the Portuguese*, Meredith's *Modern Love*, and Rossetti's *House of Life*. She regards 1850 as a late start, arguing that had it not been for Wordsworth's successful revival of the weighty Miltonic sonnet, 'the renascence of the amatory sonnet might have occurred in 1810'. In a discussion of Victorian sonnet theory, Golden notes three common qualities: interest in artifice, epigrammatic or gnomic quality, and paradoxically, sincerity. Some poets, such as J. A. Symonds, 'exploited the confusion between true emotion and sonnet convention' to write highly personal or sexual sequences.

Patricia Gallivan gives a full and interesting account of the papers read at the Second Annual Conference of the Victorian Studies Association of Western Canada, including several on Victorian poetry in *VS*.

In *N&Q* Kenneth Allott recovers a quatrain improvised by Matthew Arnold in late 1873 or early '74 for an album that a well-known eccentric clergyman, Mr Haweis, created on the birth of his only daughter. In light of Mr Haweis's subsequent life, Arnold's verse appears satirical. A solid and wide-ranging article in *RES* by Dennis Douglas notes the affinity of Matthew Arnold's conclusion to 'The Scholar Gipsy' with a professional historian's approach. Arnold arrived at the historical notions in the image of the Greek and Tyrian traders by approaching material gleaned from ancient and modern classical historians critically, as Niebuhr and Mommsen advised. In connexion with the disputed logic of the conclusion, Douglas suggests that the scholar-gipsy and Tyrian trader not be identified with each other, but that they should be regarded as complementary, together expressive of accusations against the spirit of the age—its hedonism and its intellectual uncertainty. Douglas observes that though before 'The Scholar-Gipsy' Arnold sanctions the pleasure-loving of the Greeks, after it, in *Culture and Anarchy*, the aesthetic impulse was modified and emerged as 'sweetness and light'. For Arnold the age now demanded synthesis rather than antagonistic confrontations.

George Monteiro makes an addendum to A. K. Davis's checklist of *Matthew Arnold Letters* in *PBSA* concerning the publication of a letter in *The Critic* in 1884. Donald Pady reports in *N&Q* on the discovery of a third edition, revised and enlarged (1889) of *Poems of the Plains* (1888) by the American poet and editor Thomas Brower Peacock; it is registered for copyright with the Stationers' Hall, London, rather than with the Library of Congress as the first two editions were, and as it contains photographs of three letters from Matthew Arnold to the Kansas poet, it reveals a 'previously undiscovered literary relationship'. The dates of the letters, 1882, 1884, and 1887, show that Arnold encouraged Peacock's poetic ambition for at least five years before *Poems of the Plains* appeared. Peacock's 'Sonnet to Matthew Arnold' in that volume and the correspondence perhaps attest to a greater American appreciation for Arnold's works than has hitherto been acknowledged.

In *Criticism* Mark Siegchrist joins the debate on the function of the concluding emblem in Arnold's 'Tristram and Iseult' by exploring the rôle of Vivian: 'Vivian . . . does not represent the experience of either Iseult, but instead embodies the unnaturally powerful force of passion that precipitates the whole tragedy of the poem'. Siegchrist convincingly shows how passion in the character of Vivian not only offers no escape from madness or slavery but combines the worst elements of each— 'frantic routine, mad slavishness'. Vivian embodies a paradoxical fusion of theme and image, 'the unnaturalness of the green world'.

R. H. Super replies to P. G. Scott and Scott responds (*N&Q*) concerning Super's choice of the 1883 'New York' edition of Matthew Arnold's prose as a copy-text for the current Michigan edition. Super takes issue with Scott's alleged preoccupation with the degree of authorial revision, and argues that *who* corrects errors is unimportant, but that it is clear from Arnold's diary that he did see the proofs of the New York edition. Scott uses Super's other defence, that the number and extent of departures from the later London text is very small, for his own purposes when he contends that the 1883 N.Y. edition has produced 'no authoritative new readings', and he regards authorial revision as justification of Super's choice of such a late copy text. Scott places this problem in the context of other recent editions of Victorian texts, and the whole exchange raises important questions of bibliographical theory of interest to all readers of twentieth-century editions.

In *ELN* Robert Tener contends that Richard Holt Hutton's earliest review of Arnold in *The Inquirer* (1853) antedates by almost twenty years the date suggested by Carl Dawson in the Poetry volume of the Arnold *Critical Heritage*. The attribution is made through comparison of parallel passages in the review and in Hutton's signed work and correspondence, and through the identification of favourite allusions and quotations in the review.

Michael Timko explores the implications of Arnold's 'interested' belittling of Tennyson (*TSLL*), particularly his rejection of Tennyson's English idyls based on distaste for poetic use of contemporary life and disagreement with or misunderstanding of Tennyson's narrative technique. For Arnold, Tennyson was English and Philistine, rather than European and a man of culture (as shown by his popularity), and an aesthete. Arnold's ungenerous juxtaposition of 'Michael' with 'Dora' indicates to Timko the main quarrel between the two as that between ancient and modern. Tennyson's attempt to adapt the form and content of an ancient genre, that of the domestic idyl of Theocritus, to new conditions is resisted by Arnold whose critical methods, derived from classical notions, did not allow for the familiar or the eclectic rather than the grand style.

R. H. Super's most recent volume of the Michigan Arnold, *Philistinism in England and America*, Vincent Tollers's *Bibliography* (Penn. State U.P.), and S. Coulling's *Matthew Arnold and His Critics* (Ohio U.P.) were not available for inspection.

C. W. Hatfield's definitive edition of Emily Brönte's *Complete Poems* has been reprinted.[30]

Peter N. Heydon and Philip Kelley edit a volume of thirty-nine letters from E. B. Browning to Mrs David

[30] *The Complete Poems of Emily Jane Bronte*, ed. by C. W. Hatfield. pp. xvi (unnumbered)+262. New York: Columbia U.P. £4.50.

Ogilvy,[31] a neighbour and friend from the Anglo-Florentine community, and a fellow poet. The letters are full, lively, and vivid, and provide insight into the Browning family life, as well as offering us a view of Elizabeth in the round as poet, part of the literary community, politically committed, mother (much of this), wife, and friend. The editing is graceful and unpretentious, each letter being prefaced by a short headnote; the letters are supplemented by five appendices concerning the Ogilvies, illustrations, and two recollections of EBB by Mrs Ogilvy. *The Barretts at Hope End*,[32] the 1831–32 diary of EBB at the age of 25, presents an account of society and the squirearchy in Malvern, which may interest readers of nineteenth-century fiction as well as poetry. The diary reveals its author at a time of crisis and change—an eldest child, denied even the simplest explanation of the family's situation and collapsing finances by an adored but cruelly self-sufficient and possessive father; and an almost adolescent woman, fusing an intellectual mentor and an emotional outlet into a first love. But whereas the light annotation of EBB's letters to Mrs Ogilvy is to be welcomed as appropriate to their familiarity, the cuts in this diary, already expurgated by EBB's brother George—cuts of 'visits and talk about acquaintances' and details of Greek and Latin authors and theological discussions—seem unnecessary and undesirable in terms of social history and as evidence of the growth of a poet. However, an extensive introduction, a detailed *Who's Who*, and a few notes gloss the

remaining material adequately. Two autobiographical essays by Elizabeth Barrett, 'My Own Character' (1818) published for the first time and 'Glimpses Into My Own Life and Literary Character' (1820) with a text slightly different from Henry Buxton Forman's in 1916, are edited by William Peterson (*BIS*), and in the same journal Ronald Hudson publishes and comments on eight letters (1855–1859) from EBB to her younger brother Alfred which are mainly of biographical interest.

William S. Peterson has compiled an eminently useful annotated bibliography (1951–1970) on the Brownings.[33] It is designed to fill the gap between Broughton, Northup, and Pearsall's *Robert Browning, 1830–1950*, and the first annual Browning bibliography for 1971 published in the 1973 volume of *Browning Institute Studies*. Peterson has excluded most ephemera and 'attempted to present a sample of the Brownings' extraordinarily strong impact upon many types of readers'. Lists of reviews are appended to the primary works and the Index includes works by Browning as well as authors. The Annual annotated bibliography of work on Robert and Elizabeth Browning (for 1972) is compiled by William S. Peterson in *BIS*.

Robert Browning, a collection of critical essays edited by Isobel Armstrong,[34] places Browning's poems in appropriate intellectual frameworks. Each volume in the series includes a 'Reader's Guide', and P. J. Keating contributes a graceful annotated bibliography which highlights the contours and issues of Browning

[31] *Elizabeth Barrett Browning's Letters to Mrs David Ogilvy, 1849–1861*, ed. by Peter N. Heydon and Philip Kelley. pp. xxxv+220. John Murray. £3.75.

[32] *The Barretts at Hope End*, ed. by Elizabeth Berridge. pp. xiii+276. John Murray. £3.75.

[33] *Robert and Elizabeth Browning*, by William Peterson. pp. xiii+209. New York: The Browning Institute. $25 or $18.75 to members of the Browning Institute.

[34] *Robert Browning*, ed. by Isobel Armstrong. pp. xxvi+365. G. Bell & Sons (Writers and their Background). £6.20.

scholarship and sends the reader, interested, to the criticism. From the topic 'Sources and Resources in Browning's Early Reading' John Woolford pulls a truly suggestive article on the habits of thought, the post-Romantic strategies, that Browning developed in his early reading which Woolford reconstructs through *Parleyings* and an analysis of Browning's library. Woolford argues that through his reading the youthful Browning came to regard satire and history as modes of imitation, but that the objective poet's imitation is occasionally subordinated by the subjective poet who, as Romantic, had already been discarded. Morse Peckham's piece on Browning and Romanticism concerns itself with determining the Romantic context of 'Pauline', the poem which established Browning's use of the dramatic monologue as an exercise in self-definition by its speaker. The Romantic redemptive pattern in the poem involves both justified fear of risk-taking and insight that requires it. The Pope in Book X in *the Ring and the Book* is Roger Sharrock's vehicle for considering 'Browning and History'. Browning, the expatriate rather than the exile, preserves both the immediacy of the moment of insight and documentation of consciousness in time, the tension sometimes succumbing to an apocalyptic solution. Browning's philosophical alignment against Utilitarianism rather than pro-Intuitionist in the post-1850 poems is the subject of Philip Drew. In *The Ring and the Book* the Pope reflects Browning's intuitionist sympathies while Utilitarianism serves as an index of Guido's character. Trevor Lloyd describes a curve of political development in Browning from Nonconformist to Shelleyan to Benthamite Liberalism, in connexion with *Sordello*, the plays, 'Prince Hohen-

stiel Schwangau', and *Parleyings*. He notes that Browning's political interests are not of primary concern though they figure importantly in several poems of second rank; Browning as an anti-popular intellectual is himself part of a second-rank group in the Victorian Liberal party. Barbara Melchiori, writing on Browning in Italy, also attests to his limited interest in (Italian) politics as seen in his few poems on nineteenth-century Italy, and stresses that while Browning is attached to the Italian landscape his Italy is mainly that of the past, of the Nonconformist Britisher moving in English circles, and from books. Leonée Ormond shows that bookishness also predominates in Browning's responses to art in contrast to Rossetti's. The greatness of 'Andrea del Sarto' and 'Fra Lippo Lippi' does not derive from his profound feeling for art to which his response is characteristically idiosyncratic and personal. These poems can be seen as part of a popular Victorian genre, illustrating lives of the old masters; his poems on art tend to be 'historical, literal, and factual'. While providing an interesting background of nineteenth-century music history as a context for Browning's poems, Penelope Gay's piece on Browning and music illustrates the danger of such an approach in that the poems figure insufficiently. She argues that Browning, well-educated musically, respecting technique and deriving a sense of power from its manipulation, responds to it in an early (rather than largely emotionally in the late) Romantic way. Michael Mason discusses one facet of 'Browning and the Dramatic Monologue'. Arguing that Browning's work becomes increasingly undramatic after 1844, and that Browning then tends to appear as author rather than speaker, he submits that the reason Browning wrote short dramatic poems earlier was that he was a playwright. Mason examines Browning's and his contemporaries' ideas about the stage, 'Porphyria', and Browning's increasing emphasis on self-display rather than self-expression in the dramatic monologue. Browning's sense of a strong naturalistic purpose in the earliest monologues gives way to current assumptions about dramatic writing, and narrative circumstance proliferates. In an essay thoroughly engaged with the poetry, 'Browning and the Victorian Poetry of Sexual Love', Isobel Armstrong relates Browning's Romantic poetry and his avoidance of the pure woman in his poems before the late sixties, with the degrees of sexuality in poems of Patmore, Meredith, Tennyson, and Clough. Only when Browning returns to England after the death of his wife does he become a Victorian poet, and begin to examine the sexual myths of his society, as in *Fifine* (1872). Browning grew as a poet because he could explore his most entrenched beliefs.

Thomas Blackburn's study of Browning[35] originally published in 1967 (*YW* XLVIII 294) appears in a new edition which makes no adjustments to Browning editions or criticism of the past eight years. But the engaged, wide-ranging unacademic readings of Blackburn, a poet himself, are a welcome antidote to some of the more relentless Browning scholarship.

J. R. Watson's *Casebook*[36] on Browning refers to the 1842, 1845, and 1855 collections, and coming as it does after three major critical anthologies on Browning and a Critical Heritage volume, its useful-ness depends on range and originality of selection. While there is some overlapping, Watson offers good and otherwise inaccessible material in Patricia Ball's 'Browning's Godot' and two parodies by C. S. Calverley and J. K. Stephen, sound mainstream criticism (Altick, Raymond, King, Hillis Miller, Langbaum), as well as portions of Vasari, a handy list of Browning's 1842–55 poems in their original collections, spirited suggestions for further reading, and a thoughtful introduction.

Robert Brainard Pearsall's *Robert Browning*[37] provides an introductory overview of Browning's life and works. Its character and limitations are determined by Professor Pearsall's attempt 'to say something useful or interesting about every book and poem that Browning published'. Though it contains a helpful selective bibliography and notes and is never unintelligent, it seems too detailed and textual for those unfamiliar with the poetry, and too superficial for those who know it well.

In *Very Sure of God*[38] E. Le Roy Lawson scrutinizes Browning's 'God-language' to determine his definition of God, and the extent of his orthodoxy and development, and in these respects he does not come to any new conclusions; rather the strength of the book lies in the framework of modern theological concepts of Kierkegaard, William James, Tillich, and Buber in which he convincingly places Browning's beliefs. Browning's affinities with the existentialist's stress on choice, freedom, the empirical, and the individual, resulting in a non-doctrinal, historical, personal, individual, and active faith, is set against

---

[35] *Robert Browning*, by Thomas Blackburn. pp. 210. Woburn P. £2.75.

[36] *Browning: 'Men and Women' and Other Poems*, ed. by J. R. Watson. Macmillan. £1.20 and £2.95.

[37] *Robert Browning*, by Robert Brainard Pearsall. pp. 193. New York: T. Wayne (TEAS 168). $6.95.

[38] *Very Sure of God*, by E. LeRoy Lawson pp. xiii+168. Nashville: Vanderbilt U.P. $8.95.

his more scientific experimentation in poems of 1841 to 1869. Lawson's major chapter on these poems in which their religious language is closely analysed concludes that what appears to be a thorough survey of orthodox religion and of secular thought and endeavour is Browning's rationale for his own theism; likewise an examination of the use of God by these speakers shows that the various definitions preserve their self-justifying ends. Faith is a matter of behaviour rather than of statement, and personal authority the main source of the leap from fact to faith. While Lawson succeeds in showing Browning's religious beliefs to be neither merely idiosyncratic nor 'Victorian', he does seem inexplicably unaware of Philip Drew's considerable work on the religious aspect of Browning's work in *The Poetry of Browning: A Critical Introduction* (1970).

David George publishes with commentary four new Browning letters of 1888–9 to the Rev James Graham (*SBC*) who was preparing a paper to deliver to the Browning Society. Some obscurities are elucidated. Through examination of another Browning letter to Rev Walter Wilkinson on *The Poetical Works* of 1863 (*N&Q*), Nathanial Hart corroborates the case made by Michael Hancher (*BN*, 1971) regarding Browning's atypical revision and correction of sheets while still in the press. He also shows that the 1865 'Fourth Edition' contains revisions; it is not a mere reprint of the 1863 edition as the Broughton, Northup, and Pearsall *Bibliography* suggests. A letter of 1871 from Browning to Mary Baring is printed by William H. Scheuerle in *SBC*; it accompanied the poet's gift to the lady of a rare reprint of a secondary source of *The Ring and the Book*.

BIS reprints the 1913 Catalogue of Browning 'Memorials' of Bertram Dobell, one of the most energetic buyers at the 1913 Sotheby sale at which Pen Browning's belongings were dispersed. The special value of the Catalogue lies in its notes which supplement the vague descriptions and large lots of another Sotheby catalogue, *The Browning Collections*.

The Bible provides the context for a discussion of 'The Ongoing Testament of Browning's "Saul"' in *UTQ* by Elizabeth Bieman who contends that the poem reflects both Browning's maturing consciousness and 'the developing consciousness of the writers of the whole Bible'. She explores the connexions between Saul, Paul, and David, types of king and other types—father, son, prophet, poet, and the effect of the variety on the reader. Victor Neustadt, in an article on 'Saul' in the context of the age (*JEGP*), describes the poem as visionary, rather than as a failed dramatic monologue. It is the poet-prophet's address to his contemporaries as well as autobiographical, and its symbolic and allegorical meaning makes it part of the religious controversies of the day. Neustadt contends that Browning successfully softens the didacticism of the poem and reinforces the intellectual aim by a series of identifications which involve the reader in the poem. In 'Saul' Browning attempts to re-establish a sense of the Real Presence —in a Protestant context.

In 'How to Read a Poem: Browning's *Childe Roland*' (*GR*) Harold Bloom provides a model of his 'antithetical criticism' whereby an analysis of misprision or revisionism, of 'poetic influence', precedes his discussion of sources or literary tradition. He argues that interpretation of the poem is mocked by the poem itself, since 'Roland's monologue is his sublime and grotesque exercise of the will-to-power over the interpretation of his own text', his every interpretation a powerful misreading. Yet Roland is able to accept destruction in the knowledge that his ordeal has provided us with a powerful text.

Michael A. Burr argues (*VP*) that the long note by Browning in the first-edition copy of *Pauline* read by John Stuart Mill has been mistakenly interpreted. It is not addressed to Forster, nor is it Browning's veiled admission of the poem's confessional nature; rather it was written in the same spirit and at the same time as the replies to Mill—it is a self-critical comment by Browning in his own copy of *Pauline*.

Anne Carpenter contributes a note to *SBC* on Browning's personal experience and the dating of 'Mr. Sludge, "The Medium"', while sixty-three watercolours and aquatints with words which relate to the poem, by Browning or his son, are George Connes's subject in *EA*. These and other 'Browningiana' were given to Joseph Milsand, the poet's friend, and the man who first introduced his work to the readers of the *Revue des Deux-Mondes*.

Claudette K. Columbus discusses the various masks and masked meanings in *Fifine at the Fair* (*SBC*). The nameless narrator is not one of many Don Juans, but contains them all—'the ingredients are not polymorphous but chaotic'; 'beyond what untrustworthily appears, nothing is'. Fifine 'destroys relevance makes crooked correspondence, tears out the heart of metaphor and of analogy'. This rather breathless article, like the author's version of the poem, provides local insights rather than understanding of the whole.

In *SBC* Ashby Bland Crowder considers Browning's case for the Elder Man in *The Inn Album* as part of the poet's inclination partially to exonerate the indefensible. In his reading of *The Inn Album* as a record of 1875 the same author identifies topical allusions which might be missed or misinterpreted (*BIS*). In 'Form and Sense in Browning's *The Inn Album*' Charlotte C. Watkins shows that the poem exemplifies Browning's most characteristic methods by extending into a continuous narrative the techniques of the dramatic monologues and *The Ring and the Book*, including the Perseus and Andromeda mythic underlay. The title of the poem used as a Wagnerian motif, is 'referable to both the poem's dramatic action and its pattern of figured meanings' (*BIS*).

Of the three articles on *The Ring and the Book* this year, two concern Guido. In *VP* Dalton H. Gross argues that Guido's last words, far from implying conversion, deny the reality of the moral law which condemns him. Guido's materialism leads him ironically to regard his own failure and Pompilia's testimony as the result of a miracle, and to half-expect a similar interference on his own behalf. James F. Loucks writes a vigorous, detailed rejoinder and corrective (*SBC*) to Robert Langbaum's recent 'Is Guido Saved?' (*YW* LIII. 325) in which he argues that the question of whether Guido is saved remains open; the prevalence of good (Caponsacchi) even in the dustheap is at the centre of the poem, rather than salvation in general and Guido's in particular, as Langbaum assumes.

In a piece on the poem's making of meaning (*PQ*) Claudette K. Columbus emphasizes the openness of the genre, the speculation it invites and points to the variety of interpretations that it has elicited. Through the use of mask Browning dramatizes the process of judgement by which mankind form ideas which parade as 'conclusions'; aspects of the poem—Pompilia, Mask of Place, Time as Masque, and Word as Masque—are considered in this light. The variety of the elaboration on the St George myth in the poem serves to show 'how the images we use in thinking about a person or thing alter the person or thing'.

'Cleon' is viewed from a Teilhardian perspective in *VP* by Wilfred L. Guerin who find the poem's optimism particularly interesting as a twentieth-century reader whose orientation includes a concept of future evolution towards an ultimate. Guerin reviews the critical commentary on the poem as a context for his own, introduces the applicable ideas of Teilhard, and uses them as a basis for analysis of Cleon who fails to acknowledge Incarnation and to follow consistently his scientific and philosophical speculations.

Virginia M. Hyde contends that the structure as well as the argument of Browning's 'A Death in the Desert' is addressed to the Higher Bible Critics of his time. The poem is a 'replica of a contestable early manuscript' and as such it is probably the first dramatic monologue featuring an institution voice. Brief comparisons of this poem with some of Browning's other religious poetry is illuminating. In the Critical Forum in *EIC* Roma King, an editor of the Ohio Browning, protests against Pettigrew's judgement that the edition is 'more harmful than useful'.

The detrimental association of Browning by critics and the public with the Spasmodics in the 1840s and 1850s is linked with the new conservatism in the criticism of poetry in the fifties (typified by Aytoun's burlesque of the Spasmodics in 1854 and Arnold's 1853 'Preface') by David J. De Laura in *SBC*. In a review of recent work on Browning and Tennyson in *Encounter* Lawrence Lerner makes an exemplary diversion on 'Count Gismond', 'Victorian attitudes', and innocence of women.

James F. Loucks argues (*SBC*) that Browning may well have obtained the knowledge of Catholic miracle evident in 'Bishop Blougram's Apology' from both Newman's *Lectures on the Present Position of Catholics in England* and that worldly *Fraserian* 'Father Prout', author of an irreverent poem, 'The Bottle of St Januarius' (here reprinted) and frequent visitor at the Casa Guidi in late 1848. In another note (*SBC*) Loucks suggests that the German philologist and eminent scholar of Greek, Philip Charles Buttmann (1764–1829), was among the models for Browning's Grammarian. The same critic offers a source and interpretation for 'The Soliloquy of the Spanish Cloister' (*VP*) in '"Hy Zy Hine" and Peter of Adano'. In Richard Wear's contribution (*VP*) to the discussion of the meaning of 'Hy, Zy, Hine', Brother Lawrence is put forward as the speaker of this line. In *SBC* Loucks takes issue with De Vane who reads the 'Epilogue' to *Asolando* as about the poet's own mistakes in love. Rather the 'Epilogue' is addressed to a bereaved lover and the poem is a 'piece of instruction' to the bereaved. Another correction of De Vane is made by Marilyn S. Sirugo who suggests that Abt Vogler's orchestration is moderately sized not small (*SBC*). In the same periodical Loucks supports Philip Drew's identification of Alfred Domett rather than Keats as the addressee of Browning's 'Popularity' by the publication of a forgotten Browning letter.

Clinton Machann notes in *PBSA* that a leaflet of 'Helen's Tower' by Browning in the Wrenn Collection in Texas hitherto presumed to be an 1830 offprint from a larger pamphlet, is a page torn from its 1892 edition, and as such 'a previously unreported mode of misrepresentation' by T. J. Wise who sold the pamphlet to Wrenn in 1908.

In *BIS* Julia Markus finds numerous examples in 'Andrea del Sarto' of theories of painting of William Page, Browning's American neighbour in Rome in 1853/54. Biographical parallels between Andrea and Page suggest that the historicism of the poem disguises a contemporary situation, the deteriorating relationship between Page and his wife. Markus ventures to date the poem Spring 1854, the time Browning sat for his portrait by Page. Sarah and William Page are among the live models gathered by Browning for *Men and Women*. Michael L. Ross documents the indebtedness of Henry James to Browning's 'Pictor Ignotus' and 'Andrea del Sarto' in 'The Madonna of the Future'. Theobold's career is an ironically reversed counterpart to Andrea's (*BIS*).

With the recent appearance of Browning's own copy of the sermons of John Harrison, John Maynard (*N&Q*) reveals how the poet in his essay on Chatterton came to identify Harrison as the source for the *Sermon* attributed by Chatterton to the fictitious poet Rowley. This confirms Professor Donald Smalley's attribution of the essay to Browning in 1948.

In 'Pippa's Garden' (*SBC*) Ramona Merchant details the botanical and horticultural imagery of *Pippa Passes* which she links, through the imagery, with *The Ring and the Book*. A hitherto unknown paragraph from the *Atlantic Monthly* (1882) in which Horace Scudder anonymously confessed to his rôle in Browning's legitimizing of *Pauline* in 1868 is reproduced by George Monteiro in *SBC*.

From an examination of three Browning poems, 'The Lost Leader', 'The Patriot', and 'Why I am a Liberal', Maurice O'Sullivan concludes that Browning never accepted the conservative tendencies of Pyrrhonistic scepticism nor did he ever resolve his belief in reform with his cynicism about its practicality. In 'Family Relationships at Saint Praxed's' (*VP*) Laurence Perrine takes issue with Virgil F. Grillo's recent suggestion (*YW* LIV. 328) that Anselm is Gandolf's son, not the Bishop's. In *Expl* Heide Ziegler comments on lines 76–79, 98–100 of 'The Bishop Orders his Tomb at Saint Praxed's Church'. The late Latin of Ulpian serves Gandolf's need and not the Bishop's because 'our friend', Gandolf himself, once even used the Vulgate Latin form *elucescebat*; this interpretation contrasts with that of Frank J. Chiarenza (*Expl*, 1961) who argues that 'our friend' is the master craftsman. In 'Browning Rearranges Browning' (*SBC*) Lawrence Poston III examines the thematic significance of the new sequence and grouping which Browning devised for the 1863 and 1868 editions of his poetry; he concludes with an analysis of the 1868 *Men and Women* as thematically the most tightly unified section but not formally.

Francine Gombery Russo provides a detailed interpretation of a poem neglected by critics of Browning, 'James Lee's Wife' which is treated as a study in neurotic love (*VP*). An epigram by Browning which ridicules Swinburne is unearthed from the papers of Violet Hunt, reprinted, and discussed by Robert Secor in *SBC*. And the manner in which Browning concentrates the various implications of the floral imagery in the name of Clara de Millefleurs of *Red Cotton Night-Cap Country* is Mark Siegchrist's subject in *ELN*. By providing her with a name rich in negative implications, Browning hints at her treachery. The same author reads the same poem in *VP* as one in which Browning records the process of creating his dramatic monologue; it is an example of the method free from the ambiguities of dramatic personification, and the speaker is the poet himself.

Arguing that the flaws of Fra Lippo Lippi are pernicious rather than simply endearing, David Sonstroem in *TSLL* detects hitherto unnoted tensions between sympathy and moral judgement in the monologue. While forced in places, this reading of the poem is worth consideration. Charles Flint Thomas (*SBC*) draws a parallel between Browning's contrast of the asceticism of St Jerome in Lippi's painting with the sensuality of Lippi himself with the similar spirit-flesh dichotomy of Correggio's St Jerome and Bishop Blougram.

Lastly William Whitla rescues 'Four More Fugitives by Robert Browning' (*N&Q*): some lines to Miss Unger, an autograph seeking American (1850); a quatrain on Correggio (before 1861); some stanzas to Ignaz Moschelles (1887); and a quatrain of the same year for the Jubilee window in St Margaret's Church Westminster. The stanzas to Moschelles purport to be a translation from some lines by Karl Klingemann, but Browning's satiric line differs notably from Klingemann's eulogies; they also anticipate the last two stanzas of the 'Epilogue' of *Asolando*. Together the 'fugitives' illustrate the poet's 'virtuosity in versification', his witty inventions, his skill in translation, and his limitations as a writer of occasional verse. The same author (*SBC*) writes three notes on Browning's sources—for 'The Dance of Death' in *Manfred*; for the 'Prologue' to *Fifine* in Blake's *The Gates of Paradise*; and for the 'Epilogue' to

Fifine called 'The Householder' in Poe's 'The Raven'.

Hilda Spear collects the English poems[39] of Charles Stuart Calverley (1831–1884), one of the Cambridge parodists, in an attractive, scholarly, and reasonably priced edition which includes three unpublished poems as well as the 1862 and 1872 volumes. Calverley does for the later Victorians what Praed did for the earlier in that he mocks and depicts most one sector of society, the upper middle class. But the editor argues that the critical parodies—of Tennyson, Wordsworth, Browning, Jean Ingelow—are best, and the annotations unfailingly help us to interpret and enjoy the wit of these unalloyedly comic observations.

The second edition of Clough's poems,[40] edited by F. L. Mulhauser (one of the editors of the 1951 edition) benefits from the recently accessible correspondence and journals of the poet; thus the notes are fuller and the chronology of the poems has been reappraised. Mulhauser uses the edition of 1862 (Boston) as copy text where possible, and the same principles of establishing the text elsewhere as in the 1951 edition. The new edition includes over thirty new poems—all of Clough's juvenilia, the Oxford Prize Poems, and as many of the translations as space allows; it is virtually complete, lacking only poems whose manuscripts are 'so vexed as to be indecipherable or so unfinished as not really to make a poem'. Patrick Greig Scott's edition of Clough's *Amours de Voyage* (Queensland U.P.) was not available for inspection. In *RES* R. S. McGrane

[39] *The English Poems of Charles Stuart Calverley*, ed. by Hilda D. Spear. pp. 120. Leicester U.P. £2.50.

[40] *The Poems of Arthur Hugh Clough*, ed. by F. L. Mulhauser, translations ed. by Jane Turner. pp. xxx+822. Oxford: Clarendon P. (Oxford English Texts) Second Edition. £14.00.

identifies two quotations from Keble's *The Christian Year* in Clough's unsuccessful entry for the 1839 Newdigate English verse prize at Oxford, 'Salsette and Elephanta'. These quotations reflect a more general debt of Clough's poem to *The Christian Year* which McGrane illuminates by establishing a revised earlier date for the poem; from early 1838 Clough was reading and copying out Keble's poetry as an antidote to the dangers of 'theoretic thoughts', and McGrane shows that Clough may well have been working on his entry in October–December, 1838.

An unpublished poem in a letter of 1848 to Clough by J. A. Froude which demonstrates his early interest in writing poetry and provides background for *The Nemesis of Faith* (1849) appears with commentary by Frederick L. Mulhauser in *ELN*. The poem, like the novel, expresses Froude's anguish, but it includes the consolation of faith which the novel lacks.

In *SSF* Keith Cushman identifies the quintessence of Dowsonism in 'The Dying of Francis Donne', the author's only significant prose work, which is 'both artistically austere and rich in felt experience'. The story shows aestheticism as a direct response to breakdown in the culture at large, and aesthetic detachment as a long dying.

In a new selection of Hardy's poems (less than a third of the *Collected Poems*),[41] T. M. R. Creighton arranges them thematically and only secondarily chronologically. In appendices such as Prefaces to the individual volumes, and selected bon mots by Hardy on poetry and the arts, notes which include critical observations on the thematic categories and

lexical annotation, an index to Poem Titles where alone the date and volume of publication are offered, and in the introduction, the central concern is the editor's principles of selection. Creighton's categories and their sequence, 'Nature and Man', 'Love', 'The Past and the Present', 'Poems Dramatic and Personative', 'Ballads and Narrative Poems' *do* serve the poems well, particularly for a new reader who cannot yet readily make connexions between them as they appear in the *Collected Poems*; to that extent it is a selection worth making and publishing; but however undiscernible Hardy's own principles of selections are, it is that order and oeuvre we must ultimately reckon with as mature readers.

Paul Zietlow, in *Moments of Vision*,[42] also attempts to provide alternative categories for Hardy's grouping of the poems, and like Creighton, he considers one of Hardy's volumes as a group, and the rest of the poems by type. Zietlow's is descriptive rather than evaluative criticism, his only thesis being that Hardy turned to poetry from the novel in order to expand possibilities of involvement and self-revelation and at the same time increase his invulnerability. Unlike the novelist, the poet is not committed to a sustained interpretation of life but to accurate recording of moments of experience. Moving from objective to subjective types, Zietlow discusses the variety of voices, poems of irony, ballads and narratives, philosophical fantasies, poems of the past, love poems (which Zietlow compares with *In Memoriam*), and moments of vision—brief lyrical responses to concrete situations which appeal to the human desire for meaning within a

---

[41] *Poems of Thomas Hardy. A New Selection*, ed. by T. M. R. Creighton. pp. xvi+368. Macmillan. £3.50 and £1.75.

[42] *Moments of Vision*, by Paul Zietlow. pp. xii+263. Cambridge, Mass.: Harvard U.P. £4.75.

context of meaninglessness. The inclusiveness of Zietlow's treatment permits him to consider all aspects of 'the variety of form, tone and idea' of Hardy's shorter verse, 'its boldness of style, and dramatic conception', 'its artistic cunning and complexity'. Zietlow makes a respectable attempt to see the poems steadily and whole. Paul C. Doherty and E. Dennis Taylor make a contribution to the ongoing discussion of neutral tone in Hardy's verse with a note on syntax (*VP*). Since in *The Dynasts* Napoleon is neither the villain of an epic or the protagonist of a drama but both, Frank Giordano in *THY* studies Napoleon's character through close textual analysis of the passages involving him as well as through the generic affinities of the poem. In this context he compares *The Dynasts* with *Paradise Lost* to determine if and how Hardy's depiction of Napoleon was influenced by Milton's presentation of Satan's degradation.

Bert G. Hornback detects a pervasive irony in those many unsuccessful poems of Hardy in which he masks his compassion—through irony in subject, theme, manner, tone, and language. Harshness, linguistic objectivity, and formality of diction enable him to avoid communication. For this critic subjectivity characterizes Hardy's successful poems: with the exception of 'The Convergence of the Twain' the idea poems are unfelt or rhetorical and generally pessimistic rather than meliorist like Hardy himself. 'Ozymandias' is identified as a source of Hardy's 'The Children and Sir Nameless' by Vern B. Lentz and Douglas D. Short (*VP*): in both the image of a statue symbolizing immortality is juxtaposed with an image of passing time. Hardy's modifications of Shelley's treatment of the theme and tone provide a paradigm of the transition from the Romantic to the modern temperament. William J. Morgan convincingly treats the 1912–13 poems as a 'carefully ordered whole', and examines the patterns of time and the poet's use of the elegiac tradition in *PMLA*. The tension characteristic of the elegy, between artifice and feeling, is fully exploited; the form of the sequence is a 'significant reshaping of the traditional elegy, and a . . . formulation of the logic of grief in a godless universe'.

Edward H. Cohen reprints a 'lost' caricature of Robert Louis Stevenson, 'Ballade R.L.S.' (1882) by William Henley in which the later Henley–Stevenson rift may be foreseen (*PBSA*). Cohen unearths two poems of more moment, 'A Love by the Sea' (1872) and 'A Thanksgiving' (1875) by Henley written in hospital (*HLQ*) which anticipate 'Invictus', first published in 1888. This find gives weight to the commonly accepted date of drafting (1875); moreover the conflation of these two poems in 'Invictus' reveals a meaningful context for its defiance of pessimism—it is a culmination of Henley's experience and poetry of the hospital.

The Folio Society publishes an extremely handsome volume of Hopkins's poetry[43] based on the revised Fourth Edition (OUP, 1970), and selected and annotated by Norman H. Mackenzie, one of the editors of that definitive edition. The clarity of the Introduction and of the notes should aid new readers of Hopkins. The same author publishes a sample of the Hopkins various readings and commentary on 'Spelt from Sibyl's Leaves' from his edition of the Oxford English Texts, with the idea of eliciting commentary from Hopkins scholars (*Malahat Review*). In an enlightening analysis of grace

[43] *Poems by Gerard Manley Hopkins*, sel. and ed. by Norman H. Mackenzie. pp. 164. London: The Folio Society. £3.50 and $9.50.

and time as latent structures in some sonnets by Hopkins (*TSLL*), Kent Beyette reveals the underthought that shows the "psychology" of the imagery' and the way Hopkins resolves his spiritual conflicts artistically. Beyette contrasts Hopkins's concepts of grace and time with Pater's sense in the 'Conclusion' of the continuous flux of feelings as forces which results in the artistic rather than the religious life.

In *GR* Jerome Bump finds ways in which Hopkins in his poetry anticipated environmental scientists' interest in ecology. His 'unified vision of God, man, and nature' and his creation of new words, rhythms, and metaphor are both part of a plea for the preservation of the earth. In a wide-ranging article, the author compares Hopkins's concept of nature with that of some of his contemporaries. In an astute piece in *ELH* the same critic proposes the convention of the Hebraic sublime as an appropriate context in which to read Hopkins's 'The Wreck of the Deutschland'. The precedents for heightened emotion of the literary tradition of the sublime embrace Hopkins's intensity as normal. In this context the poem can be seen as a transition from 'an ideal of limited proportioned beauty' to that of 'the irregular, the infinitely great'. Bump's lively and sound discussion of the poem includes a section on the rôle of the ocean storm in the tradition of the sublime in eighteenth- and nineteenth-century English literature. And in *VP* Bump links specific weaknesses and strengths of Hopkins's early poems with his efforts respectively to free his work from the influence of Keats's dreamy subjectivity and to absorb Keats's 'mastery of objective correlatives and evocative natural detail'.

Marie Cornelia tellingly explores the Biblical context for the key images of 'Carrion Comfort' in an effort to show that this poem works atypically for Hopkins through 'reverberation' (*Renascence*). In Bertrand F. Richard's search for meaning in the same poem (*Renascence*) his close analysis of word, phrase, sentence, division, and whole reveals that 'true conversion is impossible without the realization that the final adversary is God and that the painful struggle is but the progression from things physical to things spiritual'.

J. B. Ebbatson highlights remarkable similarities of imagery in the works of Hopkins and Richard Jefferies (*English*). Dates seem to rule out borrowing, and 'analagous temperaments . . . have attained a similar vision of the natural world'. Particularly notable are echoes of 'The Windhover' and 'Pied Beauty' in Jefferies's prose works. A hitherto undetected debt of Hopkins in 'The Blessed Virgin compared to the Air we Breathe' (1883) to Ruskin's series of lectures *The Queen of the Air* (1869) is discussed by Judith Fox in *VP*. The focus of C. X. Ringrose's 'F. R. Leavis and Yvor Winters on G. M. Hopkins' (*ES*) is the two twentieth-century critics, but students of Hopkins's poetry and critical reception will find the article interesting. In *Expl* Bernard Richards interprets Hopkins's second sonnet 'To Oxford' in confutation of a 'perverse reading' by Alison G. Sulloway in *Gerard Manley Hopkins and the Victorian Temper* (*YW* 53.327–8).

The metrical patterning of 'The Windhover' is analysed by Charles T. Scott (*Lang & S*) as illustrative of the contention that a 'wrong literary conclusion could have been avoided if proper attention had been given to linguistic stylistic detail'. Scott challenges the usefulness of Hopkins's concept of 'sprung rhythm' (by regarding it as a 'performance direction' rather than a metrical pattern) as well as the claim that Hopkins reintroduced the Old English alliterative system in 'The Windhover'; he shows that a revised theory of iambic meter 'correctly accounts for the metrical patterning of the poem': 'Hopkins appears to have consciously capitalized on characteristics of the two historical systems and to have constructed a poem with the appearance of one of the systems but with the structure of the other'. In 'Hopkinsharvest' (*VP*) Alfred Thomas demonstrates that the problem of evil is basic to both 'The Loss of the Eurydice' and 'The Wreck of the Deutschland' since the word 'messes' in the former poem introduces the image of evil as part of the divine harvest in the latter poem. Malcolm H. Villarubia shows that the grammar of the overthought of the 'terrible sonnets' reveals an interaction of the Ignation affective and elective wills which produces a subtle psychic anguish (*Renascence*).

Graham and Jennifer Speake (74 Duns Tew, Oxford) edit the new annual *Housman Society Journal*. The contents of the first volume include articles by an array of Housman scholars, F. W. Bateson on 'The Composition of *A Shropshire Lad*' lxiii, A. S. F. Gow on 'Housman at Trinity', N. Marlow on the prose style, and a review by John Sparrow. A bibliographical piece 'Writing about A. E. Housman: 1962–72' by B. F. Fisher IV treats short-length studies of the poet, while L. P. Wilkinson's address to the Classical Society on 'A. E. Housman, Scholar and Poet' among other things contrasts the poet's readings of classical texts with those in current editions. The depth and scholarship of this first *HSJ* are promising.

M. Enamul Karim publishes 'Exchange', an uncollected early poem by Rudyard Kipling (*VP*). Twenty whimsical letters (1892–1904) from Kipling to Mary Mapes Dodge, editor of *St. Nicholas*, an American children's magazine in which Kipling first published stories from what came to be *The Jungle Books*, appear for the first time in *PULC* in an article by Catherine Morris Wright.

John Hazard Wildman describes Bulwer Lytton's epic poem *King Arthur* (1848) and its Preface (1870), in *VP*, and in *HLB* thirty-seven unpublished letters (1867–73) from Mary Elizabeth Braddon, one-time actress, popular novelist, and author of *Lady Audley's Secret* (1862), to Bulwer Lytton, and two from him to her are edited and introduced by Robert Lee Woolf. The letters are full and record many of their author's reactions to Bulwer's poetry and drama, as well as her reactions to reviews of her own work.

In *MP* Philip Wilson defines 'affective coherence' as a principle of 'abated action' in *Modern Love* and some Victorian novels. The poem centres 'on the development of the husband's emotional states . . . while he relates . . . events'; it is neither tragic nor comic but has affinities to both. 'Shifts in point of view and tense make us follow the narrator's movement by means of the act of reconstructing his story, towards the new and permanent resolution of his internal instability at the time of narration'. Through a close analysis of the sequence of the sonnets, Wilson shows that while the structure of *Modern Love* relates it to forms of prose fiction, the techniques relate it to the dramatic monologue and the lyric. Meredith may be part of a transition between narrative where external comic fulfilment is delayed by an internal state (as in Jane Austen) and the narrative of James in which significant action is largely internal.

Although the narrator's internal state is unstable in *Modern Love*, this is modified and the form made fully effective by abating the ending with the external event of the wife's suicide 'which fulfills our anxieties about the degree of happiness proof of innocence will bring the narrator'. Abated action may be a principle of coherence of many Victorian novels—if each element of the novel contributes 'conceptual and emotional activity within the mind of the reader, it is not necessary that each . . . contribute to the development of other[s] . . . in the work itself'.

In a major and original study, *The Pastoral Vision of William Morris*,[44] Blue Calhoun shows how continuity, not bifurcation, characterizes the development of William Morris from aesthete to politician, what E. P. Thompson called 'Romantic to Revolutionary'. Rejecting the conventional reading of *The Earthly Paradise* as a poem of despair or escape, Ms Calhoun argues that the infamous idleness of the Apology is partially ironic but primarily a 'positive aesthetic activity with social significance' best understood as part of a pastoral response—impersonal and valuing realism—to an alien Victorian ethic of energy and heroic activity. In three introductory chapters, elements of the poem are richly set in context of the rhetoric of contemporary response to industrialization, the quest and the mood of energy in relation to 'The Defence of Guenevere', and the garden and the pastoral. The complete Prologue, eventually discarded, is the occasion for a discussion of the uses of the past in the poem, and a focus on the presence of the narrator, the 'single most important element in the poem'. This narrator Blue Calhoun shows to be critical of the folly of the Wanderers, and thus part of a pastoral mode which is not escapist, which acknowledges and accepts in a double vision the country and the city. The organization of the poem reflects the proportions of pastoral and the seasonal *mythoi*, echoing the cyclical round of history, and each of the volumes of the poem is considered in detail in this light. If Morris is ultimately rejecting the epic, the heroic, and the Romantic of 'The Defence of Guenevere' in *The Earthly Paradise* he is also moving towards the 'radical innocence' of the Arcadian utopia in *News from Nowhere*. Blue Calhoun's book merits the attention of all students of Victorian poetry.

In *The Stained Glass of William Morris and his Circle*[45] A. Charles Sewter and Yale have produced a beautiful book, with reproductions of high quality and interest. Since this is the first monograph of a nineteenth-century stained-glass artist, the author's methodology is noteworthy, and the format of the work, the notes, glossary, bibliography and General Index make it suitable for reference and reading. Four scholarly chapters on Morris's firm (1861–1940) are supplemented by sections on 'The Victorian Revival of the Art of Stained Glass' and 'Designers of Stained Glass for the Morris Firm'. The modern way in which Morris handled non-modern subjects and this treatment of medievalism in general in his art illuminates such problems and techniques in Pre-Raphaelite poetry; moreover the close collaboration between client or patron and the artist/craftsman contributes to our

[44] *The Pastoral Vision of William Morris. The Earthly Paradise*, by Blue Calhoun. pp. viii+263. Athens, Ga.: U. of Georgia P. $11.

[45] *The Stained Glass of William Morris and His Circle*, by A. Charles Sewter. Vol. I. pp. xiv+120, and 665 illustrations. New Haven and London: Yale U.P. $50.

understanding of Morris's socialism. A financial crisis of Morris in the late 1860's is unearthed by John Le Bourgeois (*DUJ*) in a series of letters from Warrington Taylor, Morris's friend and business manager, to Philip Webb. Dianne F. Sadoff (*VP*) reads Morris's 'Rapunzel' as a primarily Romantic dialectic of consciousness and imagination rather than the Victorian's quest for manhood detected by Robert Stallman. Using Norman O. Brown's concept of Metamorphoses, Ms Sadoff discusses the many transformations in the poem which combine to make it a 'Romantic version of fairy-tale transformation'.

Ian Fletcher introduces and annotates the poems of Victor Plarr (1863–1929)[46] who survives as Pound's 'Monsieur Verog', as a memorialist of Ernest Dowson, and part of the Rhymers' Club. Fletcher includes a full selection from Plarr's work in the nineties, and *The Tragedy of Asgard* as well as uncollected poems and some from manuscript. The brief introduction is biographical in the main; and the editor is perhaps not forthcoming enough in what he readily dubs an '*editio minor* of a minor poet'. The poems both reflect on and reflect other poetry of the period, and if Plarr's work is worth making accessible it merits fuller critical attention.

In *VP* D. M. R. Bentley publishes and discusses an 1848 version of Rossetti's 'My Sister's Sleep' which antedates the text in *The Germ* (1850). Comparison of the two versions and of the iconography of Rossetti's paintings with the imagery of the poem shows the extent to which spiritual issues interested Rossetti at this time. In the course of a review article on 'Rossetti as Painter' (*Mosaic*),

Ralph Berry considers whether Rossetti was a painter or a poet in the context of 'the notorious Victorian addiction to combinations of verbal and visual', and observes that worldliness and calculation are more central to his art than commonly supposed. Elizabeth G. Gitter's comparison of Rossetti's translations of early Italian lyrics in *The Early Italian Poets* (1861) with the originals shows how by change of emphasis they are transformed into Victorian poems. Another instance of transformation in Rossetti's poetry is noted by Robert Keene. Begun in 1847 as 'On Mary's Portrait Which I Painted Six Years Ago', revised in 1869 after Elizabeth Siddal's death and during his fear of losing Jane Morris, and again in 1870, 'The Portrait', an imaginative youthful love poem with a muted sense of loss, is transformed into one darker and more melancholy (*ELN*).

Philip McM. Pittman tries to establish Rossetti and the PRB as 'the initial successful phase of Romanticism in the English pictorial arts' (*N&Q*). Through updating Rossetti's first knowledge of Blake's annotations to Joshua Reynold's *Discourse* to 1862–63, the author claims that Rossetti found in them 'a positive programme in art confirming his own deepest, though as yet unspoken, convictions'. In *VP* the same critic briefly discusses sexuality in Rossetti's poetry in terms of the recurring imagery of Lilith and Eve, damnation and salvation, Body's Beauty and Soul's. As in 'Eden Bower' Lilith's sexuality leads only to destruction and death. In a comparison damaging to Rossetti, Pittman contends that Rossetti does with Lilith just what Milton does with the combined figures of Eve and Satan', and that the story of the fall in *Paradise Lost* is an analogue to 'Eden Bower'.

---

[46] *The Collected Poems of Victor Plarr*, ed. by Ian Fletcher. pp. xviii + 172. Eric and Joan Stevens. £4.50.

A piece in *VS* which illuminates Rossetti's poetry and painting in a genuine but general way is Helene E. Roberts's analysis of the nature of his dream worlds. Using Freudian categories of the day dream and the unconscious dream, she views the early paintings, characterized by an active fanciful world which involves both the poet and the viewer in its personal and literary narrative, under the first category, and the later ones, with their more passive unconscious world, under the second. The author's discussion of aspects and iconography of Rossetti's women is recommended to all those obsessed with the *femme fatale*.

Philip Henderson's full and scholarly biography of Swinburne[47] is studded with information, opinions of other critics, and quotations from friends of the poet as well as from the letters, but these often obscure rather than reveal both Swinburne and his biographer. Moreover, frequent rhetorical passages and a certain coyness mar this judicious if unexciting biography. Comment on the poetry and prose is confined to their autobiographical content but Mr Henderson does make a fairly convincing argument in defence of Watts–Dunton's motives and rôle in connexion with Swinburne's later life; he corrects Gosse's version of the move to Putney while noting that Rossetti and not Swinburne had been 'the master fact' in Watts's life. Apart from this Philip Henderson adds little to our knowledge of the life of the poet as depicted in Jean Overton Fuller's recent biography (*YW* XLIX, 281).

In *A Year's Letters* F. J. Sypher[48]

presents the first unexpurgated edition based on the original MSS. of Swinburne's first attempt at serious prose. The scholarly apparatus of textual notes, of selected variants, and explanatory notes compels the editor's full attention, but the critical aspect of the introduction is less than inspired and careful; he devotes much attention to what he narrowly dubs the 'autobiographical' element of the novel and to Swinburne's insistence on a pseudonym without offering any forceful explanation. This apart, the edition is handsome and scholarly, and should now supersede previous editions. Sypher also contributes a piece on Swinburne to *VP* in which he shows that 'A Forsaken Garden' is modelled on Thomas Campbell's 'Lines Written on Visiting a Scene in Argyleshire'.

In *N&Q* J. C. Maxwell reveals a possible borrowing from *The Newcomes* in Swinburne's 'Dolores'. Terry L. Meyers provides four short Swinburne letters (*N&Q*) which eluded Lang, two of them being published here for the first time. From the diary and letters of W. M. Rossetti, Roger Peattie describes the part played by Rossetti in ensuring that Watts–Dunton honour Swinburne's prohibition for his own funeral of the Church of England burial service. This provides an interesting background to the two letters of Watts–Dunton to Isabel Swinburne of April 14 so often quoted. Also in *N&Q* George Monteiro corrects an error of T. J. Wise in his Bibliography of Swinburne: the poem 'The Brothers' appeared in the U.S. Dec. 19, 1889, three days before its publication in Britain.

For Ross C. Murfin in *VP*, *Erectheus* (1876) exemplifies the 'controlled poetry of ideas' of Swinburne's middle period, and as Swinburne's 'greatest work' it should be set beside

[47] *Swinburne. The Portrait of a Poet*, by Philip Henderson. pp. ix+305. Routledge. £4.95.

[48] *A Year's Letters*, by A. C. Swinburne, ed. by Francis Jacques Sypher. pp. xxxviii+196. New York: New York U.P. $10.

'Atalanta in Calydon', the fervent work of the younger poet. The later poem is a 'symbol of that moment of psychic stasis followed by revolutionary choice' when chaos and fear reign. William J. Reeves traces the source of the phrase 'Triton of the Minnows' (by which Swinburne dismissed Arnold in a letter) to Byron's dismissal of pedestrian poets in *Beppo*. Since Arnold had called Swinburne a pseudo-Shelley and elevated Byron above Shelley, Swinburne satirized him in the language of his preferred poet (*AN&Q*).

In *The Tennysons. Background to Genius*[49] Sir Charles Tennyson and Hope Dyson present a series of essays on the history of the Somersby Tennysons from their beginnings at Holderness and Grimsby in the eighteenth century, through the family of Tennyson's paternal grandparents, portraits of his father in early manhood and middle age, of Hallam, of Tennyson's siblings and their uncles and aunts. The focus on the family rather than the poet allows an enriching multiplicity of perspectives and fully justifies this addition to the numerous and more conventional biographical studies of Tennyson.

In the course of the third of the Occasional Papers of The Tennyson Society,[50] on the career and downfall of Dr Gully whose water cure at Malvern Tennyson took in 1847, Elizabeth Jenkins offers evidence concerning the date of 'The splendour falls' and Tennyson's contacts with mesmerism, psychic phenomena, and spiritualism.

Mary Moorman discourses on the nineteenth-century ancestors of her parents, the Oxford Arnolds and Wards and the Cambridge Macaulays and Trevelyans in 'Poets and Historians',[51] the third annual Tennyson Society lecture. She notes ironically that for all Arnold's impatience with Tennyson's lack of intellect, Arnold never mentions 'In Memoriam' in his letters. Arnold emerges as less optimistic than Tennyson, contending that good may not emerge from evil.

Sir Charles Tennyson's subject for a pamphlet of the Tennyson Society[52] is the poet's connexions with Somersby and its environs which he left after twenty-eight years in 1837, while in another pamphlet[53] he and Hope Dyson focus on Tennyson's relationship (1882–92) with Sir Henry Parkes, the Australian statesman.

In *VP* Joshua Adler reveals the centrality and irony of biblical associations in Tennyson's late and successful poem, 'Rizpah'. Yet another possible source for 'Ulysses' is mooted in *TRB* by Thomas P. Adler, Samuel Daniel's 'Ulysses and the Syren' (1605). In contrast with similarities of diction and theme is Ulysses's character in the two poems. In '"Ulysses" and "Tithonus": Tunnel-Vision and Idle Tears' (*VP*), Arthur D. Ward fruitfully considers the two poems as a pair, and reveals 'a more ironic and dramatic interaction' between them than has yet been acknowledged. David F. Goslee, in a study of the character and structure in *The Princess* (*SEL*), attempts to create a methodology which will

[49] *The Tennysons. Background to Genius*, by Charles Tennyson and Hope Dyson. pp. 220. Macmillan. £4.95.

[50] *Tennyson and Dr. Gully*, by Elizabeth Jenkins. pp. 20. Lincoln: Tennyson Society. (Occasional Papers: No. 3). 90p.

[51] *Poets and Historians: a Family Inheritance*, by Mary Moorman. pp. 16. Lincoln: Tennyson Society. (Occasional Papers: No. 1). n.p.

[52] *Alfred Tennyson and Somersby*, by Charles Tennyson. pp. 16. Lincoln: Tennyson Society. n.p.

[53] *Tennyson, Lincolnshire, and Australia*, by Charles Tennyson and Hope Dyson. pp. 18. Lincoln: Tennyson Society. (Occasional Papers: No. 2). 35p.

account for the split between Tennyson's sensibility and technique in the poem, the virago at the centre with 'its delicate Chinese box construction'. Through a variety of formal patterns—the fortified palace, evolutionary nature, history, visual art—Ida breaks out of the fairy-tale world; she is *then* trapped by the forms, and only when she and the Prince internationalize these forms do they manage to break through the form of the poem itself by reversing its basis of reality and fiction.

In *YES* James Sait connects the prince's 'weird seizures' added to the fourth edition of *The Princess* with Tennyson's knowledge of Mesmerism and his belief in its curative powers, obtained respectively by 1845 and 1854 'during which time he wrote, published, and revised *The Princess*'. Not only is catalepsy, the scientific term Tennyson uses in the poem to describe the seizures, used in the period to describe the mesmeric state but the extended descriptions of the state in the poem resemble passages in Harriet Martineau's *Letters on Mesmerism* (1845). The mesmeric seizures indicate both the Prince's 'will-deficient situation' (the predominance of will lying with the Mesmerist rather than with the patient) and the course of his cure. Sait also publishes two letters of 1831 from Edward Tennyson, the poet's brother, to William Brookfield, an Apostle, in *TRB*: they reveal a melancholy poem which brings to mind 'Tears Idle Tears' and how a friendly editor could brutalize the work of an unknown poet.

A new Tennyson letter of 1879 to Robert Adams showing the Poet Laureate's interest in the Empire appears with commentary by Philip Collins in *TRB*. In a short note in the same journal Winston Collins draws attention to another possible source for the war and peace theme in *Maud*, Franklin Lushington's peace pamphlet called *Points of War I-IV*. If the Lushington poem is not a source of themes, it does show that the view of peace and war in *Maud* is not simply personal or idiosyncratic. Jonathan Wordsworth who contributes a controversial 'post-Freudian' piece on *Maud* to *EIC* has no time for the war resolution; he contends that the poem itself is neurotic, and that 'the writer's unconscious at important moments dominates the poetry' in a way that the writer would presumably have wished to prevent. The subject of the poem emerges from Wordsworth's selective reading as sexual guilt and remorse. The pitfalls of his argument are evident in his summary: 'From being an odd, muddled, experimental work, with no satisfactory narrative thread, and no single element or theme of sufficient importance to constitute a centre, it becomes meaningful, consistent—if one dare say so, well constructed.'

Jonas Spatz views *Maud* as evidence that Tennyson's poetry should be read as a precursor to twentieth-century poetry rather than 'as Romantic gone bad' (*TSLL*). In a reading which tries to account for and not dismiss Part III, the war solution, Spatz suggests that the narrator's love for Maud becomes the most efficient means of committing murder without guilt. Maud's martial song provides the link between honour and duty between love and war. Like Jonathan Wordsworth, Spatz feels that Tennyson was unaware of the full significance of the narrator's transformation: the 'hero's perverse health' in Part III is 'the prototype of man's "adjustment" in a basically bestial and aggressive society'. For the narrator morality is the freedom to act, no matter how immorally, and impotence and passivity are criminal.

Through a study of mythic and archetypal patterns of life-death-rebirth Douglas C. Fricke reveals qualities in 'Enoch Arden' which moved Tennyson to regard it as 'a very perfect thing' (*TRB*). Reynold Harris demonstrates how imagery of cultivation and weeding establishes the moral norm against which the imagery of wildness, rife unweeded growth, canker decay, and flower symbolism is martialled in connexion with Guinevere and Lancelot's betrayal of Arthur in *The Idylls* (*TRB*). Tennyson's fear of the story of the Holy Grail is shown by David Staines to be the primary cause of the ten-year gap between the first and subsequent *Idylls* (*MLR*). By rejecting Galahad as the centre, and 'by making Percivale the poem's focus, he makes the failed quest the poem's centre . . . the entire story . . . is seen through the human eyes of the failing Percivale'. Because Tennyson could not accept the Grail as a symbol of divine grace, he used the quest to portray 'human responses to the spiritual world'. Prose drafts of 'the Holy Grail', 'The Passing of Arthur', 'Gareth and Lynette', and 'Balin and Balan' are presented by Staines in *HLB*. Offering insight into the poet's method of composition, they reveal the central ideas of each idyll, show a closer dependence on source material than in their final poetic form, and reveal Tennyson experimenting with different approaches to the stories. They are a bridge between his reworking of Malory and his final poetic rendering.

A comparison by Celia Morris of Tennyson's Lancelot and Percivale in 'The Holy Grail' with Malory's *Le Morte d'Arthur* (*Mosaic*) shows not only the erosion of Christian belief in the nineteenth century, but also the resulting spiritual crisis. Because in the *Idylls* sin remains without salvation, their world is one of cultural and personal despair. Tennyson's unwillingness to forego the Christian model of human nature and experience in his poem though unable to assent to it reflects the Victorian dilemma. Roger Sale comments vehemently on the *Idylls* in the course of a review article in *HR*.

Tennyson's use of the dramatic monologue as a form of uncertain perspective and a technique of irony in 'Oenone' is explored by James Kincaid in *PQ*. Unlike Langbaum he takes judgement to be an essential response to the form, and the demands for judgement and sympathy create the ironic rhetoric. Kerry McSweeney contributes a full and leisurely review essay on the state of Tennyson criticism to *PLL*.

That affirmation of the will (rather than of truth or belief) moves the speaker in *In Memoriam* through a series of flawed imaginings to a higher quality of imagination in the conclusion is Harry Puckett's contention in *VP*. The poet ordinarily uses the subjunctive to put forward vivid possibilities which he rejects by affirmation. Puckett shows not only the world of loss or decay cancelled, but religious credos to succumb to the affirmation which follows. For Puckett the interest of *In Memoriam* is how the poem and the poet's mind work, not Tennyson's beliefs. Rather, the poem 'frequently invites the reader to regard it as flawed, without providing specific or explicit answers to the inquiry thus instigated'. This reading provides a noteworthy alternative to those of Bradley, Gransden, Eliot, and Buckley. Tennyson, like Keats, Pound, and Stevens, sees 'the aesthetic process . . . as a way of transcending our inability to know and the difficulties of belief'.

In another interesting article in *VP* John D. Rosenberg explores the 'hyper-real' quality of Tennyson's mythical landscapes that symbolize states of human consciousness, and reflect the simultaneous presence of the keenest observation and a double awareness of faith and doubt. Transitional moments when an object or feeling tends towards its opposite attract Tennyson. This critic's *The Fall of Camelot* (Belknap P.) has not been available for inspection.

P. G. Scott treats John Addington Symonds as a type of the reaction of younger literary men against Tennyson after 1870 (*TRB*). To this end he brings together published and unpublished material about Symonds and Tennyson, prints some of Symonds's unpublished letters, and hazards an explanation for the reaction. Characterized by increasingly critical views from 1868 privately, unswerving sychophancy to the poet and his family, and mixed reviews of the poems publicly, Symonds's reaction is ambivalent and complex. But Scott believes that it derives from family and social experience not aesthetic judgement.

In *VP* W. David Shaw distinguishes the late elegies from the poet's more usual ceremonial richness. He detects in 'Crossing the Bar' and 'To the Marquis of Dufferin' a clarity of outline and austere style and thought that signify Tennyson's return to the barrenness of *In Memoriam*. Early and late varieties of the plain style are explored through comparison of drafts for 'To the Marquis of Dufferin'.

In a note on Tennyson's 'Mablethorpe', C. Ricks and Sir Charles Tennyson bring forward evidence only recently available from the Trinity College Tennyson MSS. concerning the date (1833 rather than 1837) and versions of the poem which consists of two stanzas in MSS. rather than the one published in 1850 in the *Manchester Athenaeum Album*. The authors also discuss the possible

sources of a superior version of the first stanza which Hallam Lord Tennyson published in *Tennyson. A Memoir* (*TRB*). An informative lecture on James Spedding (1808–81), Apostle, Bacon scholar, literary critic, and close friend of Tennyson by Sir Charles Tennyson appears in *TRB*.

Emily Lady Tennyson emerges from her letters[54] as an able, intelligent, warm, and supportive person, and in them she provides many insights into the daily life of her family and her role as Tennyson's companion, adviser, and secretary. Her correspondents include Edward Lear, Thomas Woolner, and James Spedding, and forty letters to her husband are published here as well. The 382 letters, from 1844 to her death in 1896, have been selected, and in some cases cut, but annotation is generous, the editing intelligent. Hoge has also usefully provided narrative links between letters by using quotations and information from Lady Tennyson's unpublished redaction of her Journal. Altogether the volume reads well, and particularly in the absence of a full-scale edition of her husband's letters, is a welcome contribution to Tennyson studies.

In an editorial in the *Journal of the Francis Thompson Society* G. Krishnamurti announces that the Society and the *Journal* have extended their activity to the whole period contemporaneous with Francis Thompson. Reflecting this policy the 1974 double-number comprises four articles, two on Thompson, Carol Miller on Crashaw and the poet and Michael Cope on Thompson's influence, and two on more general themes, John Adlard's note on 'Colour Research of the Poets of the Nineties' and Ian Fletcher's on

---

[54] *The Letters of Emily Lady Tennyson*, ed. by James I. Hoge. pp. xviii+404. University Park and London: Penn. State U.P. £7.25.

'Neo-Jacobitism in the 1890s'. Of these, the last—in which Fletcher treats the literary manifestations of Jacobitism—is of both substance and originality.

Both of the articles on James Thomson concern 'The City of Dreadful Night'. Peter C. Noel-Bentley (*VP*) shows how the genealogy of the synthesizing image of Durer's *Melancholia I* in the poem reflects Thomson's development over a period of sixteen years from orthodox Calvinist to despairing atheist. In an interesting piece of literary detection in the same journal Michael R. Steele points to a rationalist history of the world, *The Martyrdom of Man* by Winwood Reade, as a likely source for Thomson's poem which echoes its pessimism and imagery.

(b) *Drama*

Kathleen Barker's pamphlet[55] on 'Entertainment in the Nineties' in Bristol catalogues a range and quality of live theatrical entertainment that few if any provincial cities enjoy today. Drama (including productions of Shakespeare, and of contemporaries such as Pinero, Shaw, and Wilde, pantomime, and music hall), opera, circuses, Myrioramas, minstrel shows, and film competed for patronage, and the author notes that every actor manager of note brought his company to Bristol in the nineties. Students of the literature and culture of the period will find this account of the leisure activity of Bristolians informative. Seven chapters in the same author's exemplary history of *The Theatre Royal Bristol—1766–1966*[56] pertain to the Victorian period. Details of pro-

ductions, architecture, and refurbishing, finance, the star system, rowdyism and audience behaviour, and the variety of the fare (which included the 'Man fly' and 'the Infant Power') provide a vivid sense of day-to-day life of the theatre as well as a longer view. Since Jenny Lind, Charles Kean, Madame Vestris, W. C. Macready, Henry Irving, and the Terry sisters appeared at the Theatre Royal during this period, *its* history is a significant part of theatrical history, to which the policies and personalities of Sarah M'Cready, James Henry Chute, and Andrew Melville, the principal Victorian managers depicted here, also contribute.

Michael R. Booth continues his impressive campaign for the revival of interest in drama of the last century in a selection of nine popular plays.[57] Representatives of four genres—melodrama, drama, comedy, and farce—include *A Factory Lad* (1832) which pre-dates the novel's treatment of industrial themes, *Box and Cox*, *Engaged* by W. S. Gilbert, *The Magistrate* by Pinero, and Henry Arthur Jones's *Mrs. Dane's Defence*. Cumulatively, the plays and the excellent introduction effectively initiate the reader into the variety and wealth of the drama of the period.

D. F. Cheshire confines his history of music hall[58] to the period before 1923. He views the genre not as a unique form of entertainment as Mander and Mitchenson do above, but as 'the organisation of long-established kinds of performance and performer for financial gain, by parties other than the performers'. The method of this history is a sequence

[55] *Entertainment in the Nineties*, by Kathleen Barker. pp. 20. Bristol: The Historical Association. 1973. 30p.

[56] *The Theatre Royal Bristol. 1766–1966*, by Kathleen Barker. pp. xii+278. London: Society for Theatre Research. £5.00 and $12.50.

[57] '*The Magistrate*' and Other Nineteenth-Century Plays, ed. by Michael R. Booth. pp. xxi+464. Oxford U.P. £1.60.

[58] *Music Hall in Britain*, ed. by D. F. Cheshire. pp. 112. Newton Abbott: David and Charles. £3.75.

of documents arranged thematically and linked by short expository passages by the author; the documents begin with Chaucer and are drawn from more diverse sources than Mander and Mitchenson tend to use. Material of much interest and point is presented here, and with the illustrations make a book of value which, however, sacrifices elan to a disengaged methodology. In addition to chapters on the rise and decline of Victorian Music Hall, Cheshire treats the Stars, the audience and atmosphere, the law and finance of the undertakings. This work complements Mander and Mitchenson, and the enthusiast may want to read and own both.

Raymond Mander and Joe Mitchenson have revised and updated their able and spirited account of *British Music Hall*[59] from its beginning in the late eighteenth-century Catch and Glee Clubs to twentieth-century variety. The copy is light but sound and devotes attention to the changing architecture of the halls and patterns of the bill rather than to individual artists. They receive visual attention however, and the graphics and photography in this book are exceptional. Appendices list artists of Royal performances from 1912 to 1973, and authentic recordings of music hall artists.

Students of the revival of interest in nineteenth-century drama and its history are indebted to Leicester U.P. for its reprint of Henry Morley's *Journal of a London Playgoer (1851–66)*.[60] Culled from his dramatic criticism for the *Examiner*, the *Journal* provides evidence concerning just the

years often seen as the nadir of a century wholly deficient in quality drama, and as Michael Booth argues in an informative and discerning introduction, Morley attests to the many developments and changes in a period of dramatic range and quality. The profoundly middle-class taste and morality reflected in Morley's dramatic criticism, coupled with his faith in the stage and his admiration for good acting, mean that his criticism is like Arnold's—both historically informative and speculative, with frequent appeals to the audience to educate themselves in order to provide criteria conducive to the improvement of the life of the theatre. Among reviews of great events in nineteenth-century theatre is a description of Dickens producing and acting in a private performance of *The Lighthouse* by Wilkie Collins.

Clifford John Williams, himself an actor, has written a theatrical biography[61] of Madame Vestris, one of the principal actress/managers and innovators of her time. The details of her career, family and development are assiduously martialled; moreover the book's production and layout are unusually fine, and the number, variety, and quality of the illustrations add greatly to the pleasure the book affords. However, while the author expresses impatience with the merely written word, this is no justification for his consistently inelegant prose ('The Anderson business was all part of the bankruptcy mess').

Kathleen Barker traces the early career (1857–64) of the actress, Madge Robertson, the future Dame Madge Kendall as a product of 'the most perfect of training schools', the Bristol and Bath Stock Company of

[59] *British Music Hall*, by Raymond Mander and Joe Mitchenson. pp. 243. London: Gentry Books. Revised Edition £6.25.

[60] *The Journal of a London Playgoer*, by Henry Morley, introd. by Michael R. Booth. pp. (26)+320. The Victorian Library. Leicester U.P. £5.00.

[61] *Madame Vestris—A Theatrical Biography*, by Clifford John Williams. pp. xiv+240. Sidgwick & Jackson. 1973. £7.50 and £2.95.

the eighteen-fifties and sixties which also trained the Terry sisters (*NCTR*).

The revival of Vanbrugh's *The Relapse* in 1870 by John Hollingshead, manager of the Gaiety, at a time notable for its neglect of Restoration comedy, is fully described by Barry N. Olshen in *NCTR*. Hollingshead tailored the play to his leading actor, Alfred Wigan, and eliminated the scenes and characters relating to the relapse, thus removing most of the indecent and immoral but also much of the intrigue; the new version, entitled *The Man of Quality*, emerges as a farce. The same managers bowdlerized *Love for Love* (1871) which retained little Congreve and proved a failure.

The establishment and quality of Burlesque in New York is the subject of David L. Rinear's piece on William Mitchell's first season (1839/40) at the Olympic (*NCTR*).

Sybil Rosenfeld concentrates on Beerbohm Tree's introduction of Ibsen, Maeterlinck, and Brieux in his Monday night productions between 1892 and 1909 (*NCTR*). Although Tree often selected plays as a vehicle for his own acting, made extensive cuts, and chose easy plays, for special performance matinees and Mondays, he did give audiences the opportunity to see these works of the avant-garde.

Stephen C. Shultz views William Poel as a 'modernist' rather than antiquarian by considering two previously disregarded contemporary influences on Poel's reforms—Samuel Brandram, an English elocutionist who inspired the formulation of Poel's Shakespeare Reading Society, and the Comedie Française who helped Poel formulate his concepts of 'tunes' and 'key words' in his verse reading theory (*NCTR*).

In *VP* John Bush Jones contends that Gilbert based Archibald Grosvenor of *Patience* not on the combination of William Morris and Coventry Patmore, as first suggested, but on the attitude of prudery, 'employing characters of contemporary personages only insofar as they might help to dramatize it and particularize the satire directed against it'. Grosvenor, whom Jones shows to quote Bowdler, is thus anchored to middle-class taste, morality, and is unaesthetic all along. Through Grosvenor, Gilbert broadens the base of his satire from aestheticism to more general problems of prudery in poetry.

Alexander Leggatt, tracing the development of Pinero's work from the early farces to the later social drama, stresses its continuity rather than its bifurcation (*MD*); the vision of life he acquired in the farces created problems of tone in the social dramas which eventually led to original drama far more interesting than *The Second Mrs Tanqueray*. In both farce and social drama the classic Pinero situation is threatened respectability, but whereas farce is ideal for this theme, the focus on things, props, and costume jars in more serious dramatic contexts such as *The Second Mrs Tanqueray*. In the better and later serious pieces, *Iris* and *Mid-Channel*, it contributes to their power and distinction: the assumptions are those of farce, but farce *sans* laughter, and the happy ending, *sans* the controlling dignity. In *N&Q* J. P. Wearing argues that the missing First Act entitled 'The Ferret' of Pinero's *The Money Spinner* must have been added after, not before, the two-act London production. Insofar as the themes of this play foreshadow *The Second Mrs Tanqueray*, the missing act which intensifies Millicent Boycott's unusual social background is of interest. Wearing's edition of Pinero's *Collected Letters* (U. of Minn. P.) has not been available for inspection.

Christopher Nassar's book, *Into the Demon Universe*,[62] aims to establish Oscar Wilde as a major author and as a decadent, but Wilde emerges here as major only insofar as he is a decadent. Thus the early plays and poems prior to 1886 are rejected as part of 'the old Wilde—the boyish, carefree plagiarizer who suddenly disappeared from the scene late in 1886, yielding to the sin-conscious homosexual'. The sequence and content of the fairy tales, *Dorian Gray*, the plays, *De Profundis*, and 'The Ballad of Reading Gaol' are explored solely in terms of Wilde's increasing and ultimately fatal involvement with evil, the identity of this aspect of the work with autobiography being assumed throughout, while Wilde's literary criticism is ignored. The plays, particularly *Salome*, and 'The Ballad of Reading Gaol' are treated at length, and at times perceptively. But overstatement, schematism, simplicities pervade the thought and text, the basis of which is perhaps revealed in the purism implicit in Nassar's suggestion that Salome is 'entirely evil'. The book has some real merit, but Wilde's work requires a wider and deeper net than decadence and autobiography provide.

In *DR* Averil Gardner examines the direct utterance in 'The Ballad of Reading Gaol' as a new and successful departure for Wilde's poetry; prison not only provided him with a subject of suffering in others, but also an ability to respond to these sufferings. Arguing that this directness is hard-won, Gardner discusses evidence of artistic detachment in the poem, including possible echoes of Housman, Coleridge, and Hood.

In *VS* Kevin H. F. O'Brien publishes a reconstruction from newspaper reports for 'The House Beautiful', which Oscar Wilde used as his second lecture when he toured North America in 1882, and an introduction in which the editor sets out his editorial practices and principles. David Parker views *The Importance of Being Earnest* in three contexts: as Oscar Wilde's 'great farce', as drama of the absurd, and in light of existentialist theories of identity (*MLQ*). Actuality is deliberately distorted, and most of the characters behave as if that vision is 'all but universal'. As in Restoration drama, selfishness in Wilde's play becomes symbolic of freedom and a virtue. Wilde exploits the concern of farce with human identity, directing it to the concern with 'Nothingness', which he shares with his French contemporaries. 'Each character . . . is a sort of vacuum that attains . . . identity only through an effort of the creative imagination.' Truth dwindles into insignificance, and lying brings success.

4. NINETEENTH-CENTURY PROSE FICTION

(a) *General*

Though J. H. Buckley's *Season of Youth*[1] is a critical and historical survey of the Bildungsroman, he has also taken a number of novels separately, amongst them *Copperfield*, *Great Expectations*, *Richard Feverel*, *Harry Richmond*, *The Mill on the Floss*, *The Way of All Flesh*, *Marius*, and *Jude*. The writing is just, clear, and informed. In particular, Professor Buckley displays his tact when he touches upon the inevitable autobiographical connexions that play against the conventions of the genre. Hardy's need 'to objectify what he wishes to conceal, yet feels bound to

---

[62] *Into the Demon Universe*, by Christopher S. Nassar. pp. xiii+191. New Haven and London: Yale U.P. £4.00.

[1] *Season of Youth: the Bildungsroman from Dickens to Golding*, by Jerome Hamilton Buckley. Cambridge, Mass.: Harvard U.P. pp. xiii+336. £6.60.

express' is typical. There is also an account of poetic predecessors, *Wilhelm Meister* (*the* prototype), and *The Red and the Black* (important for an 'increase in autobiographical self-consciousness and the sharpening of focus on the motivation of the hero'). We end with contemporary examples in which the hero's alienation is 'virtually—and in his own estimate, virtuously—complete'.

James Simmons's work on the Victorian historical novel[2] has been noticed already (*YW* 52.329). He is most helpful when tracing the changes in early historical fiction and the competition between novelists and revisionist historians. (There were even attempts made to rehabilitate the buccaneer Henry Morgan and his 'associates'!) But a review article by Robert Lee Wolff (*TLS*, 13 Dec.) rightly draws attention to the specifically *Victorian* relevance of historical novels by major writers like Newman, Thackeray, or Pater. Not all 'hearthstone narratives' were quiet and domestic. Ioan Williams's useful book on *The Realist Novel in England*[3] straddles the boundary between fiction and non-fiction, for 'the development of literary form is inextricably related to the development of sensibility or culture'. As well as the studies of half a dozen major novelists, there are pertinent accounts of F. D. Maurice, Julius Hare, John Sterling, Thomas Carlyle, and two minor writers—Harriet Martineau and E. B. Lytton—chosen for the importance of their theorizing about organic integrity in the novel. With such a large scope Williams decided to be rigorously selective, which leads to

some odd asides about Mrs Gaskell's *North and South* or, more seriously perhaps, to a neglect of the basis for Marilyn Butler's recent claims (*YW* 53.341) on behalf of Maria Edgeworth's innovations. Nevertheless, there is a clear, definite analysis of the way in which novels came to embody 'the principles and proportions implicit in experience itself', by a natural emergence from typically Romantic ideas to a discovery of organic coherence in the social and moral sphere.

There are several articles of a general kind. J. Hillis Miller's 'Narrative and History' (*ELH*) uses Henry James's essay on Trollope (1888) to stress how fiction so seriously pretends to be history with a proper 'logic' — shaped, unified, directed, emergent, true. But he then cites *Middlemarch* as a prime example of a 'history' that demythologizes itself, generating form out of unlikeness and difference. In an article[4] dealing with parallels between the Russian and English novel, Ian Milner finds marked similarities between the presentation of Dorothea Brook and that of Turgenev's Elena in *On the Eve*. 'Sentimentality spoils any real development of the critique of the evils of industrialism', writes T. B. Tomlinson in 'Love and Politics in the Early-Victorian Novel' (*CR*); even George Eliot's intelligence succumbed to love-idealization in *Felix Holt*. N. N. Feltes shows, in 'Community and the Limits of Liability in Two Mid-Victorian Novels' (*VS*), that the individual and historical significances of 'liability' allow us to study novels like *The Mill on the Floss*, *Little Dorrit*, and *The Way We Live*

---

[2] *The Novelist as Historian: Essays on the Victorian Historical Novel*, by James C. Simmons. The Hague, Paris: Mouton, 1973. pp. 66. Paperback, 15 Dutch Guilders.

[3] *The Realist Novel in England: a Study in Development*, by Ioan Williams. Macmillan. pp. xv+221. £7.00.

[4] Ian Milner, 'Artistic Idealization and Social Context in Nineteenth-Century Literature, mainly English', offprint from *Acta Universitatis Carolinae—Slavica Pragensia XV*, 1973. In Czech.

Now in a way that illuminates both text and context. Kathleen E. Morgan's 'The Ethos of Work in Nineteenth-Century Literature' (*English*) begins of course with Carlyle; she then surveys a number of authors, especially the social-problem novelists, George Eliot, and Hardy. J. R. Dinwiddy surveys 'Elections in Victorian Fiction' (*VNL*).

Peter Mudford's chronological survey[5] of British–Indian relations from Akbar to Curzon deals with a number of works that are the concern of this chapter. Macaulay's famous 'Minute' of 1835 recommending English as the official language of India is, with careful qualification, seen as the hamartia after which 'even the idea' of mutual understanding passed away. Works by W. D. Arnold, W. B. Hockley, W. H. Kaye, *et al.* are treated in a relatively summary way, but Mudford ends with an extended comparison: Kipling against R. Tagore, 'a measure of the great gulf which still separated the Eastern and Western worlds, as they moved from the "wonderful century" into the darker waters of the twentieth'. Last year I missed *Der englische roman in 19 Jahrhundert: Interpretationem*, ed. by Paul Goetsch *et al.* (Berlin: E. Schmidt, 1973).

Patricia Beer's *Reader, I Married Him*[6] sets out 'to show how women and their situation were depicted' in novels by Jane Austen, Charlotte Brontë, Elizabeth Gaskell, and George Eliot, but even this restricted topic is lightly, discursively, and somewhat variably handled. With

relatively simple cases this critic is often acute and helpful, as when she writes on young women and education in Elizabeth Gaskell's work, but with Jane Austen and perhaps George Eliot she seems sadly adrift at times. Even if the kind of historical approach found in Lloyd W. Brown's *NCF* article last year (*YW* 54.342) was not intended, the discovery and demonstration of something like 'active muddle-headedness' in Jane Austen's treatment of, say, Darcy are hardly convincing. On a related topic, though with much more detail and documentation, Vineta Colby investigates domestic realism in the English Novel,[7] or 'gossip etherialized, family talk generalised'. She agrees with Ioan Williams that the Victorian novel 'cultivated sentimentality, sensibility, idealism, and spirituality', and is not therefore realistic in the hard sense. In particular, a number of minor novelists of the first half of the nineteenth century—Mrs C. Gore, Maria Edgeworth, Charlotte Elizabeth, Charlotte Yonge, Harriet Martineau, *et al.*—are carefully studied as significant anticipators of the great Victorian novelists to come. Fashionable, educational, religious, and community novels all turned to 'a serious treatment of basic questions'. Ruth Yeazell urges us to remember that novels especially suffer from reductive readings; her 'Fictional Heroines and Feminist Critics' (*Novel*) warns that art and life are too easily conflated.

In Forces and Themes in Ulster Fiction,[8] John Wilson Foster trawls through the works of William Carleton to discover a number of chief

---

[5] *Birds of a Different Plumage: a Study of British–Indian Relations from Akbar to Curzon*, by Peter Mudford. Collins. pp. 314. £4.95.

[6] *Reader, I Married Him: a Study of the Women Characters of Jane Austen, Charlotte Brontë, Elizabeth Gaskell and George Eliot*, by Patricia Beer. Macmillan. pp. ix+213. £4.95.

[7] *Yesterday's Woman: Domestic Realism in the English Novel*, by Vineta Colby. Princeton U.P. pp. vii+269. $12.50, £6.50.

[8] *Forces and Themes in Ulster Fiction*, by John Wilson Foster. Gill & Macmillan. pp. xi+299. £4.95.

motifs and styles of twentieth-century Ulster fiction set close to the land. The section is admittedly brief and unliterary, though a single lengthy footnote provides a compact series of suggestions for 'a redirected critique of Carleton'. John R. Reed surveys 'The Public Schools in Victorian Literature' (*NCF*), concluding from a number of examples that they were criticized because they conflicted with the ideal of childish innocence; later, they were seen as the nurseries of heroism. Carol Polsgrove writes in a summary way on 'They Made It Pay: British Short-Fiction Writers, 1820–1840' (*SSF*).

(b) *Individual Novelists*

Robin Mayhead's *Walter Scott*[9] is part of a series intended to introduce authors in a direct way, avoiding 'background study' and promulgating the critical 'methods associated with Cambridge'. Mayhead is certainly very selective: a chapter each to *Waverley* and *The Heart of Midlothian*, two more to six novels, and a final chapter to 'The Poems'—in effect to the practical criticism of 'a few, a very few, pieces of rather special distinction'. There is no doubt that a beginner will be encouraged to discriminate, challenged by Mayhead's constant assertions and proof of value but even within its own terms this study lacks an overall view. It ends with a review Mayhead wrote of Ioan Williams's *Scott on Novelists and Fiction* and some miscellaneous remarks. Twenty-four of the papers given at Edinburgh's Scott conference in 1971 are now published.[10]

[9] *Walter Scott*, by Robin Mayhead. Cambridge U.P. (Introductory Critical Studies), 1973. pp. x+132. £2.30, $7.50.
[10] *Scott Bicentenary Essays: Selected Papers read at the Sir Walter Scott Bicentenary Conference*, ed. by Alan Bell. Edinburgh and London: Scottish Academic Press, 1973. pp. x+344. £3.75.

Not all are on Scott: Wendy Craik writes on Susan Ferrier, John MacQueen on 'John Galt and the Analysis of Social History', and Donald A. Low on 'Periodicals in the Age of Scott'. Others usefully examine Scott's relations with Turner, and with Delacroix, his 'Foreign Contacts', impact on Hungarian literature, knowledge of Italian writings, Old Norse literature, etc. Another group are bibliographical. When gathered with the more straightforward papers on biographical and literary matters—by authors like William Beattie, Edgar Johnson, David Daiches, Francis R. Hart, W. E. K. Anderson, N. T. Phillipson, David Craig, Robert C. Gordon, and Robin Mayhead—they make a remarkably diverse collection.

N&Q contains 'The Year of Scott's Birth: a Question Reconsidered' by Ian C. Gordon at some length, but without definite conclusion. Scott's 'eighteenth-century tastes and rationale' were as important as Romantic influences when he wrote the first historical novel, according to H. G. Hahn in 'Historiographic and Literary: the Fusion of Two Eighteenth-Century Modes in Scott's *Waverley*' (*HSL*). Lawrence J. Clipper writes on 'Edward Waverley's Night Journey' (*SAQ*), using the terminology of myth criticism. P. D. Garside, in '*A Legend of Montrose* and the History of War' (*YES*), carefully argues that Scott uses Dalgetty to examine military professionalism in a more complex assessment of the tone and quality of different societies. Scott has more insight into historical process than Lukacs allowed, Seamus Cooney maintains in his straightforward 'Scott and Progress: the Tragedy of *The Highland Widow*' (*SSF*). Marilyn Georgas puts forward 'A New Source for Hogg's *Justified Sinner*: Greville's *Life of Sidney*' (*NCF*).

Criticism of fiction 'must partake of the three considerations of form as meaning, spatial secondary illusion, and the leitmotif', writes Joseph A. Kestner. His short study[11] of six Jane Austen themes (improvement, intimacy, concealment, imagination, silence, and shyness) is somewhat marred by his failure to use recent Austen criticism. Susan Sontag's *Against Interpretation* is cited; Alistair Duckworth's *The Improvement of the Estate* (*YW* 52.332) is not. The beginning and end contain more interesting ideas, but too much is simply and schematically treated.

Amongst articles are Nicholas A. Joukovsky's 'Another Unnoted Contemporary Review of Jane Austen' (*NCF*), a summary of *Pride and Prejudice*, J. C. Maxwell's analysis of the connexion between 'Jane Austen and [Maria Edgeworth's] *Belinda*' (*N&Q*), and Freimut Friebe's 'Von Marianne Dashwood zu Anne Elliot: Empfindsame Motive bei Jane Austen' (*Anglia*, 1973). In 'The Socialization of Catherine Morland' (*ELH*) Avrom Fleishman addresses himself in detail to the phases and modes of the heroine's socialization. She does not just turn from romance to realism but strengthens her powers of discrimination and appreciates more cultural possibilities. Jane Austen thus achieves 'a complex comic vision of the perceptual illusions involved in all human enterprises'. In 'Surface and Subsurface in Jane Austen's Novels' (*ArielE*), Juliet McMaster shows how strong emotion is presented by indirection, especially in the later novels where, as so often in Charlotte Brontë, a heroine looks on whilst the hero courts an unworthy rival. In

'*Mansfield Park*: Three Problems' (*NCF*), Joel C. Weinsheimer tries to clarify the sources of ambiguity that defeat our critical view of the novel: the absolute antithesis between Fanny and Mary, the sometimes contradictory standards of evil, and Mansfield Park itself as a problematic ideal. 'Fanny and Mrs. Norris: Poor Relations in *Mansfield Park*' (*DR*) are compared by Carol Ames, who maintains it is ironic that Jane Austen does not show how Edmund Bertram exercises power over dependents. 'Jane Austen's Fools' (*SEL*) by John Lauber, is a straightforward survey of the variety of game springing up before us.

That Caroline Norton was the author of six volumes of poetry, three novels, and two novellas is less well known than the fact that her husband cited the Prime Minister in an 1836 criminal conversation suit. Her fascinating but previously inaccessible letters to Lord Melbourne between 1831 and 1844 are now edited by James O. Hoge and Clarke Olney.[12] There is a helpful introduction and the letters are annotated, but there is one oddity: Hoge indicates the omission of a 'few words or sentences' that he has 'judged so awkward or confusing as to hinder the reader'. The next item is treated in a more usual manner, in that deleted passages are restored and errors corrected. William St Clair's edition of Edward Trelawny's *Adventures* (1831)[13] is based upon the recently discovered manuscript. Also, in his introduction and notes St Clair disentangles the 'curious mixture of

[11] *Jane Austen: Spatial Structure of Thematic Variations*, by Joseph A. Kestner. Salzburg: Institut für englische Sprache und Literatur. (Salzburg Studies in English Literature). pp. viii+145. Paperback £4.80.

[12] *The Letters of Caroline Norton to Lord Melbourne*, ed. by James O. Hoge and Clarke Olney. Ohio State U.P. pp. xvii+182. $10.75.
[13] *Adventures of a Younger Son*, by Edward John Trelawny. Ed. by William St Clair. O.U.P. pp. xxiv+477. £5.50. (Oxford English Novels).

fact and fiction', concluding that after the first dozen or so chapters on the author's boyhood and service in the Navy the work is largely fantasy. In 'Things as They Might Be: Things as They Are: Notes on the Novels of William Godwin' (*DR*), George Woodcock emphasizes the paradoxical lack of utopian elements in the novels from *Caleb Williams* (1793) to *Cloudesley* (1830) and *Deloraine* (1833). Godwin's imagination, like that of H. G. Wells, co-existed uneasily with his reason.

Håkan Kjellin's *Talkative Banquets*[13a] is a strongly systematic analysis of Peacock's plot structures, narrative, dramatic dialogue, etc. He devotes some attention to possible models, though he concludes that while most of the elements can be traced back to antiquity, the various syntheses are uniquely Peacockian. Kjellin finds a basic 'pattern of contrasts between the past and the present, cultural decline and progress' and also 'a development in his novels from debate and satire in which there is still some connexion with the real world' to a more autonomous comedy. In an appendix he prints a complete version of *A Dialogue on Friendship after Marriage*, discovered by him amongst the Broughton Papers in the British Museum.

Was Thackeray the archetypal careless artist? At his best, J. A. Sutherland suggests in *Thackeray at Work*,[14] 'narrative problems are worked out in a spirit which, though mercurial, is anything but slapdash'. This short book is perhaps the best kind of defence, in that the devil's advocate (Trollope in this case) is

given full licence, but we still feel inclined to accept the basic contention that the problems caused by Thackeray's working methods forced him to prodigies of invention and control. Sutherland shows him as scholarly in many ways, yet relying on his creative virtuosity to an even greater extent than Dickens. Edgar F. Harden's close study of 'The Challenges of Serialization: Parts 4, 5, and 6 of *The Newcomes*' (*NCF*) arrives at the same conclusion: 'Thackeray found the restraints of the serial form not only confining but stimulating to his imagination' (though one notices Harden's footnote criticizing the detail of Sutherland's argument in *MLQ* for 1971).

In 'The Pygmalion Motif in *The Newcomes*' (*NCF*), R. D. McMaster competently outlines 'the perpetual tension between the ordering imagination and the resisting raw material of life' and demonstrates Thackeray's magnificent allusiveness. This fictional monster, even James admitted, was more than just baggy. Frederick C. Cabot distinguishes between 'The Two Voices in Thackeray's *Catherine*' (*NCF*), those of a parodist and of a didacticist. The result is a failure, but does not lack certain qualities. N. John Hall prints and annotates 'An Unpublished Trollope Manuscript on a Proposed History of World Literature' (*NCF*). Katherine Carolan indicates 'Dickensian Echoes in a Thackeray Christmas Book' (*SSF*), *Dr. Birch and His Young Friends*. In *N&Q* Horst E. Meyer gives a correct text of 'Thackeray's Letter to Baron Tauchnitz' and J. A. Sutherland restores a passage cut from 'Thackeray's Election Speeches at Oxford'. David Leon Higdon brings out the significance of Thackeray's use of the emblem tradition in 'Pipkins and Kettles in *Vanity Fair*' (*VNL*).

[13a] *Talkative Banquets: A Study in the Peacockian Novels of Talk*, by Håkan Kjellin. Stockholm University Studies in History of Literature 14. Stockholm: Almqvist & Wiksell. pp. 147. Paperback.
[14] *Thackeray at Work*, by J. A. Sutherland. Athlone P. pp. ix + 165. £4.00.

Unfortunately Virgil Grillo's critique of *Sketches by Boz*[15] could not profit from J. Hillis Miller's remarkable analysis (*YW* 52.326), but this detailed, extensive account may be of more use to students. Grillo maintains that the *Sketches* anticipate later work in an important sense. The stories are superciliously and negatively told while the sketches are far more genial and affirmative. Here is an ambivalence that Dickens never truly resolves but learns to accommodate. Grillo in fact devotes nearly half of his space to showing this 'continuity of process' in later works: the varying levels of 'mimetic density' in *Nickleby*, for instance, or the conflict between action and rhetorical thrust in *Chuzzlewit*. There is much truth in all this, but it can often seem a solemn and difficult way of putting what is obvious enough.

Fundamental scholarship continues apace. Anne Lohrli has compiled a splendid reference book[16] for the nine years during which Charles Dickens drove a remarkable team of contributors into providing a twopenny miscellany of 'Instruction and Entertainment' for the mid-Victorian family audience. Her introduction describes its style and contents, its contributors, its bibliography, and the Office Book kept by W. H. Wills. This Book helps her to produce an elaborate table of contents, which identifies authors, payments, etc. But the heart of Miss Lohrli's compilation is the alphabetical list of contributors and their contributions, a scholarly and detailed account containing a wealth of discovered facts and correction of errors. The Pilgrim Edition of Dickens's letters, not available for review here (but see *TLS* 6 Dec.), has now reached Volume 3;[17] similarly, the Clarendon *Dombey and Son*[18] (rev. K. J. Fielding, *DUJ*, June 1975) has appeared. E. W. F. Tomlin prints 'Newly discovered Dickens Letters' (*TLS* 22 Feb.), to a French writer called Ernest Legouvé, and a summary of part of the plot of *Copperfield*.

Though in late 1843 Dickens intended to write 'an arm-chair view of Italy', he also found there 'a deepening awareness that the causes of crime and misery were legacies of ingrained historical and economic injustices'. This is pointed out in David Paroissien's preface to Dickens's *Pictures From Italy*.[19] He also teases out the stages in its genesis and Dickens's methods of composition, based upon those of the travel-book writer, Captain Basil Hall, using personal letters rather than a journal.

The Dickensian contains a number of valuable articles: on individual novels (Michael Slater, Richard P. Fulkerson, and Laurence Senelick all write about *Oliver Twist*); on Dickens's popularity by Philip Collins, on his father by Angus Easson, and on rote-learning by Susan Shatto; and several on John Forster by James A. Davies, K. J. Fielding, Anthony

[15] *Charles Dickens' 'Sketches by Boz': End in the Beginning'*, by Virgil Grillo. Boulder, Colorado: The Colorado Associated U.P. pp. xv+240. $11.00.

[16] *'Household Words': a Weekly Journal 1850–1859 Conducted by Charles Dickens—Table of Contents, List of Contributors and Their Contributions based on the 'Household Words' Office Book*, compiled by Anne Lohrli. U. of Toronto P., 1973. pp. x+534. $50. £23.85. (Books Canada Ltd.).

[17] *The Letters of Charles Dickens*, Vol. 3 (1842–43), ed. by Madeline House, Graham Storey, and Kathleen Tillotson. O.U.P. pp. 692. £13.00.

[18] *Charles Dickens: Dombey and Son*, ed. by Alan Horsman. Oxford: Clarendon Press. pp. lx+871. £12.00.

[19] *Pictures From Italy*, by Charles Dickens. Intro. and notes by David Paroissien. André Deutsch, 1973. pp. 270. £2.95. Illustrated.

Burton, and Alec W. Brice. Also, Malcolm Andrews covers some unusual items in 'A Survey of Periodical Literature' for 1973, and there is a review of a book I missed last year: *Studies in the Later Dickens*, edited by J-C. Amalric (Montpellier: U. Paul Valéry, 1973). It is worth noting, too, that *The Dickensian* is now published as a complete set on microfiche, with an analytical index.[20] *EA*, 1975, briefly reviews Koichi Miyazaki, *The Inner Structure of Charles Dickens's Later Novels* (Tokyo: Sanseido Publishing Co.).

Other Dickens articles are mostly on individual novels, though a few are general or comparative. Valerie Purton makes a positive case for 'Dickens and "Cheap Melodrama"' (*EA*). She sees it as a necessary formula for the 'black poetic truth' of his deeper vision. John R. Wilson writes on 'Dickens and Christian Mystery' (*SAQ*), seeing *Oliver Twist* as the precursor of the dark novels and a general movement towards the psychological rather than the transcendental. A sense of loss, anxiety without definite limits, disjunctions of identity, repellent attractions, palsy of the will—all these themes connect the writings of 'De Quincey and Dickens' (*VS*) for Christopher Herbert. Both, he thinks, are 'among the most precocious early analysts of the modern condition'. Ian Milner writes on 'Dickens's Style: A Textual Parallel in *Dombey and Son* and *Daniel Deronda*' (*Philologica Pragensia*). In 'The Influence of Fielding on *Barnaby Rudge*' (*AUMLA*, 1973), Roger Robinson corrects Dickens scholars who have assumed with Dickens that Sir John Fielding was active during the Gordon riots. He goes on to claim

that *Barnaby Rudge* shows a deeper understanding rather than an outgrowing of the eighteenth-century novel and suggests a number of parallels.

How do fairy-tale motifs function in Dickens? Richard Hannaford begins his study of 'Fairy-tale Fantasy in *Nicholas Nickleby*' (*Criticism*) by distinguishing allied popular forms; he then examines the effects on narrative pattern, the contrast with the urban wasteland, unresolved tensions, and final transformation. Branwen B. Pratt, 'Sympathy for the Devil: a Dissenting View of Quilp' (*HSL*) is welcome for its reminder that 'consistency is seldom the hobgoblin of Dickens's mind', though her demonstration of his ambivalence towards his splendid creation, the difficulties found in attempting to disavow evil and the untrammelled id, and the eventually liberating power of his vitality is briefly shown to be less new than she thinks, by Michael Steig in a later number. Richard Hannaford writes briefly on 'Irony and Sentimentality: Conflicting Modes in *Martin Chuzzlewit*' (*VNL*). Jerry C. Beasley's 'The Role of Tom Pinch in *Martin Chuzzlewit*' (*ArielE*) takes issue with Barbara Hardy's claim that Tom Pinch has 'practically nothing to do'; he supplies 'a kind of moral barometer of loving selflessness' in a climate of greed and hypocrisy and an example of moral development. Felicity Hughes believes that 'Narrative Complexity in *David Copperfield*' (*ELH*) involves more disquieting forces than we think, since Dickens does not share his narrator's traditional world view. The treatment of Murdstone, Steerforth, and Heep is indebted to Dickens's interest in hypnotism ('magnetism') and appears to cast doubt upon the freedom of the human will.

---

[20] *The Dickensian*, 1905–1974; with cumulative analytical index by Frank T. Dunn, preface by Michael Slater. Harvester P. £195.00+£25.00.

In *Bleak House*, Grahame Smith maintains in his new short study,[21] 'chance and the inter-connections of fate represent something in the objective nature of the fictional *and* the social world'. The web of various relationships is so well shown by this critic that one does not in the least object to hearing about character in the section 'Point of View', structural matters in 'Characterization', setting in 'Structure', and drama in 'Language'! This is a valuable contribution to a somewhat variable series for students. D. W. Jefferson writes with enthusiasm on 'The Artistry of *Bleak House*' (*E&S*), lucidly showing the reasons for his claim that Dickens's achievement is both impressive and original. Dianne F. Sadoff writes on 'Change and Changelessness in *Bleak House*' for *VNL*, finding 'moral irresolution, regression, and the desire for changeless stability', and Stanley Tick contributes '*Hard Times*, Page One: An Analysis'.

Avrom Fleishman's 'Master and Servant in *Little Dorrit*' (*SEL*) first draws upon Hegel's *Phenomenology* in an attempt to discover *the* unifying theme, a key to aesthetic mythologies. It is, not unexpectedly, dialectical: loving servitude is conquest and transcendence of such relationships, at least in intention. But Arthur Clennam, seen in Lucien Goldmann's terms, is the degraded quester who makes an end of chains. Akira Takeuchi writes on 'The Structure of *Little Dorrit*' for *Studies in Foreign Languages and Literatures* (Osaka University, College of General Education, 1973). He stresses the contribution to unity made by the prison metaphor and the antithetic role played by Little Dorrit, but finds its

foundation in Arthur Clennam's 'pilgrimage of soul'.

A. L. French writes on the ambiguities of 'Beating and Cringing: *Great Expectations*' (*EC*). He draws out the subdued *Hamlet* parallels that show the 'recurrent human situations' of a sensitive being, dominated and determined by early upbringing and traumatic experience, yet able to escape. He also argues that certain characters are both unregenerate and inexplicable, 'naterally wicious'. 'The Fictional Crux and the Double Structure of *Great Expectations*' (*SAQ*), by Peter Wolfe, is often illuminating—apart from the seemingly obligatory references to modern literature that pop up occasionally. *Anglia* has Christian W. Thomsen's 'Das Groteske in Charles Dickens' *Great Expectations*'.

'The Movement of History in *Our Mutual Friend*' (*PMLA*) is lucidly analysed by William J. Palmer; starting with a sense of the deadness of past forms, characters attempt to discover and assert their individual existence in a hopeful future. Angus Wilson, in his introduction to the Penguin *Edwin Drood*,[22] de-emphasizes plot, except in relation to Edwin's murder or Jasper's guilt and this in relation to earlier novels. He suggests in particular 'a continuing, perhaps even a final disillusionment with childlikeness, with wonder and fancy as adequate positive forces'. Dark fancy is only countered by responsible middle class individuals, though the old radical Dickens still survives in the imperialist and muscular Christian. This edition also prints the 'Sapsea Fragment' and Dickens's Notes and Number Plans.

[21] *Charles Dickens: 'Bleak House'*, by Grahame Smith. Edward Arnold (Studies in English Literature 54). pp. 64. £1.70. Paperback 85p.

[22] *The Mystery of Edwin Drood*, by Charles Dickens. Ed. by Arthur J. Cox, intro. by Angus Wilson. Penguin. pp. 314. 40p. Paperback.

Sheila M. Smith prints an extended and valuable critique of Carlyle's *Chartism* in 'John Overs to Charles Dickens: a Working-Man's Letter and its Implications' (*VS*). She also examines the relationship between Overs and Dickens, finding the latter authoritarian and paternalistic despite his aid and sympathy. Another item of Dickens interest is a double issue of the *Princeton University Library Chronicle*[23] (rev. Peter Conrad, *TLS* 26 July), which forms a most attractively illustrated revaluation of the work of George Cruikshank. Several articles give accounts of the artist and his works or place them within the tradition of comic illustration. Also, Louis James takes the historical approach in his 'An Artist in Time: George Cruikshank in Three Eras' (Regency, transitional, and earnest Victorian). Michael Steig's 'George Cruikshank and the Grotesque: a Psychodynamic Approach' is carefully and modestly written, but the 'particular variety of critical language' he develops to cope with the way in which 'art simultaneously arouses and defends against anxiety' seems unnecessary when read after John Harvey's sensitively analytic article, 'George Cruikshank: a Master of the Poetic Use of Line'. Three articles must interest students of literature: Anthony Burton's 'Cruikshank as an Illustrator of Fiction', Harry Stone's 'Dickens, Cruikshank, and Fair Tales', and Richard A. Vogler's 'Cruikshank and Dickens: a Reassessment of the Role of the Artist and the Author'. This last heroically assaults the received version of the artist's claims to have been vitally concerned in the creation of *Oliver Twist* and *Sketches by Boz*—for Stone, 'distortions and delusions'. Vogler does not deny an element of exaggeration in the artist's claims, but at least will force later commentators to more precise statement and assertion.

Wilkie Collins is fortunate to have Norman Page as editor of the Critical Heritage selection[24] of reviews, letters, etc. (rev. J. I. M. Stewart, *TLS*, 6 Sept.). Page fastens quickly on such questions as 'Under what circumstances can a third-rate literary genre accommodate a first-rate work?' Nor does he ignore the fact that even a severe culling will not produce 'a body of consistently first-class criticism'. His balanced and pertinent introduction is an excellent analysis of the problems involved and a good survey of Collins's reputation. Ian V. K. Ousby writes briefly on 'Wilkie Collins's *The Moonstone* and the Constance Kent Case' (*N&Q*).

David R. Johnston-Jones provides a brief life and study of the works of Robert Surtees.[25] It is a simple, appreciative approach: characterization, style, humour, construction, attitude and influence. R. W. Stewart's list of writings by and about Disraeli[26] is full of information. It seems a pity from our point of view that criticism of Disraeli's fiction by F. R. Leavis, Raymond Williams and Arnold Kettle has been excluded by his plan and I would have willingly dispensed with some of the 'notes' in

[23] *George Cruikshank: a Revaluation*, ed. by Robert L. Patten. Princeton University Library. pp. xvi+258. $10.00.

[24] *Wilkie Collins: the Critical Heritage*, ed. by Norman Page. Routledge & Kegan Paul. pp. xvi+288. £6.00.

[25] '*The Deathless Train*': the Life and Work of Robert Smith Surtees, by David R. Johnston-Jones. Salzburg: Institut für Englische Sprache und Literatur. (Salzburg Studies in English Literature). pp. iv+183. Paperback £4.60.

[26] *Benjamin Disraeli: A List of Writings by Him, and Writings About Him, with Notes*, by R. W. Stewart. Scarecrow Author Bibliographies, No. 7. Metuchen, N.J.: Scarecrow P., 1972. pp. xxxvii+240.

favour of more bibliographical detail. A series of thirty-seven letters that give 'a detailed picture of the Victorian best-seller industry' are printed by Robert Lee Wolff, in 'Devoted Disciple: the Letters of Mary Elizabeth Braddon to Sir Edward Bulwer-Lytton, 1862–1873' (*HLB*).

There is more than usual on the Brontës this year. Winifred Gérin adds two good booklets[27] to the Writers and Their Work series. The attention given to the juvenilia, early poems, and novelettes is especially valuable, though her enthusiasm can lead to over-simple views of the relationship with later work. An excellent Critical Heritage volume on the Brontës[28] is edited and introduced by Miriam Allott, who has sought to represent as many critical opinions as possible, though a Swinburne (on Charlotte) receives severer pruning than a Leslie Stephen. The range and intelligence of Victorian criticism is amply shown. Even the early reviewers, Professor Allot shows, were more discerning than is usually thought. A modern critic, F. A. C. Wilson, employs the concept of the androgyne in 'The Primrose Wreath: the Heroes of the Brontë Novels' (*NCF*). *BST* contains Margaret Drabble's address on 'The Writer as Recluse: the Theme of Solitude in the Works of the Brontës', previously unpublished letters by Charlotte, a note on Harriet Martineau's unpublished novel, *Oliver Weld*, and other items, perhaps the most interesting of which is 'An American Defence of *Wuthering Heights*—1848', printed in full by Albert J. von Frank.

Following Hazel T. Martin's *Petticoat Rebels* (New York 1968), a study of the novels of social protest of George Eliot, Elizabeth Gaskell, and Charlotte Brontë, comes Harriet Björk's *The Language of Truth*.[29] This is a Lund doctoral thesis that concentrates upon Charlotte Brontë's 'concern with the woman question', her transformation of the literary tradition in response to the urgent claims of changing times, and her desire to be 'a moralist and social critic of a higher prophetic order'. As one might expect of a thesis, there is a careful study of Brontë criticism, the letters, conduct books, other novels that reflect the debate about emancipation, etc. as well as a meticulous analysis of education, employment, love, and marriage in Charlotte Brontë's works. Charles Burkhart's *Charlotte Brontë: a Psychosexual Study of Her Novels*[29a] is more straightforward than its title suggests. Though in his first chapter he takes up such topics as sexual energy, symbolic release, the Victorian superego, and daydream into myth, his survey of the four novels is often squarely based on the more ordinary work of literary critics and historians. (He provides a relatively long, annotated Bibliography). Fundamentally, however, he maintains that Charlotte's works cannot be separated from her life and that, while in *Jane Eyre* she gave rein to exuberant fantasy, in *Villette* she 'faces out the truth', to discover the universal in self-transcendence.

'More True than Real: Jane Eyre's

---

[27] *The Brontës: I. The Formative Years; II. The Creative Work*, by Winifred Gérin, ed. by Ian Scott-Kilvert. Writers and Their Work, Nos 232, 236. Longman for The British Council, 1973, 1974. pp. 68, 68. Paperback 20p each.

[28] *The Brontës: the Critical Heritage*, ed. by Miriam Allott. Routledge & Kegan Paul. pp. xx+475. £7.50.

[29] *The Language of Truth: Charlotte Brontë, the Woman Question, and the Novel*, by Harriet Björk. Lund: C. W. K. Gleerup. (Lund Studies in English 47). pp. 152. Paperback.

[29a] *Charlotte Brontë: a Psychosexual Study of Her Novels*, by Charles Burkhart. Victor Gollancz, 1973. pp. 159. £2.80.

"Mysterious Summons"' (*NCF*) is Ruth Bernard Yeazell's main proposition, because she believes that the plot primarily mirrors the inner drama of Jane's psyche, where passion must exist with integrity. She finds love because of her need for freedom.

Janet M. Barclay provides an annotated check list of Emily Brontë criticism[30] this century. H. Rauth looks at the great number of dramatizations and film versions of *Wuthering Heights*[31] beginning with an early silent film (1919), an opera by Frederick Delius, a Metro-Goldwyn-Meyer hit (1939), and continuing with a whole spate of operas, radio and television adaptations, establishing *Wuthering Heights* as the second most 'popular' work by the Brontës after *Jane Eyre*. Frau Rauth looks at the merits and demerits of the various attempts by the media to adapt the novel [H.C.C.].

C. P. Sanger's classical essay on the time-scheme of *Wuthering Heights* is often cited. Now appears an essay by A. Stuart Daley, on 'The Moons and Almanacs of *Wuthering Heights*' (*HLQ*), that deploys lunation data to suggest that the historical calendar the novel appears to observe is inadequate. The data do, however, correlate with season activities in other years, especially 1826 and 1827. These are 'Gondal years', and Daley suggests that almanacs of them, piously preserved by Emily, gave as rigorous a control of the time-scheme as topography did of place. (*Cf.* J. F. Goodridge's sketch in *Emily Brontë: Wuthering Heights*,' 1964). H. P. Sucksmith seems to have missed

Q. D. Leavis's 'Fresh Approach' to *Wuthering Heights* (*YW* 50.319–20). His 'The Theme of *Wuthering Heights* Reconsidered' (*DR*) involves a similar effort to relate the work to its Victorian context and assess its universal quality, which Sucksmith sees in the tragedy of 'Civilization and its Discontents', Emily Brontë's theme as well as Freud's. In 'The Ethos of *Wuthering Heights*' (*DR*) Buford Scrivner, Jr. directs his attention to the 'ethical mistake' Catherine makes in marrying Linton and the balance that must be found between the self and society. Charlotte Brontë's *Shirley*[32] is now available in a new edition by Andrew and Judith Hook.

Eckhart G. Franz's 'Heidelberg und Heppenheim in Erzählungen und Briefen der englischen Schriftstellerin Elizabeth Gaskell (1810–1865)' (*Archiv für hessische Geschichte und Altertumskunde*, n.s. 32) is a wide-ranging survey of Anglo-German literary relations in the nineteenth century. It focuses on some of Mrs Gaskell's minor works but takes some account of other English authors of the period. Dr Franz has also written on '*Six Weeks at Heppenheim*: der Gasthof zum Halben Mond als Schauplatz einer englischen Novelle' for *1200 Jahre Mark Heppenheim* (Heppenheim, 1973). 'Elizabeth Gaskell and Nathaniel Hawthorne' (*The Nathaniel Hawthorne Journal*, 1973) is a meticulous account by Anne Henry Ehrenpreis of the ways in which their personal lives touched each other. It is also a good analysis of the curious, unexpected connexions between their writings.

Once again (*cf.* *YW* 52.340) George Eliot's response to the march of the Victorian scientific mind is brought into focus. K. M. Newton's 'George Eliot, George Henry Lewes, and

---

[30] *Emily Brontë Criticism 1900–1968: an Annotated Check List*, by Janet M. Barclay. New York Public Library & Readex Books. pp. 76. Paperback $5.50.

[31] Heidemarie Rauth, *Emily Brontë's Roman 'Wuthering Heights' als Quelle für Bühnen—und Filmversionen*. Universität Innsbruck. pp. 96. n.p.

[32] *Shirley*, by Charlotte Brontë. Ed. by Andrew and Judith Hook. Penguin. pp. 622.

Darwinism' stresses that both she and Lewes agreed that 'in relation to Nature, man is animal'—as long as it was recognized that 'in relation to Culture, he is social'. Newton works out the implications, particularly the treatment of egoism, in *Felix Holt* and other novels. Beginning with a distinction between nature and culture, Elizabeth Ermarth analyses 'Incarnations: George Eliot's Conception of "Undeviating Law"' (*NCF*). Within culture, moral laws are the sum of particulars not reducible to any kind of collective essence (*cf.* L. Feuerbach). Similarly, Spencer's idea of progress is more relevant than a simple teleology: it is geometrically moving towards greater multiplicity. Samuel J. Rogal elucidates attitudes towards hymnody and psalmnody in 'Hymns in George Eliot's Fiction' (*NCF*). She held a middle ground in the transition from psalter to hymnal.

William J. Sullivan examines 'Music and Musical Allusion in *The Mill on the Floss*' (*Criticism*), believing this to be as important as biographical, educational or evolutionary elements. Though Book 6 provides the greatest number of significant references to songs, operas, etc., Sullivan stresses the 'inherent logic which guides George Eliot to use the same matrix of musical language and metaphor' throughout Maggie's development, in its ascetic and emotional phases. Not only Elizabeth Gaskell responded to Hawthorne, it would seem. Jonathan R. Quick examines '*Silas Marner* as Romance: the Example of Hawthorne' (*NCF*). Though George Eliot's contemporaries—J. M. Ludlow and Leslie Stephen are cited—deplored the morbidities of the American imagination, she at least in this novel achieved a success outside 'the more sober and dismaying

realm of realism'. Elizabeth Ermarth's 'Maggie Tulliver's Long Suicide' (*SEL*) is a feminist study: Maggie 'has learned to collaborate in her own defeat', we are told.

Hugh Witemeyer's 'George Eliot, Naumann and the Nazarenes' (*VS*) establishes (with illustrations) the art-history background of *Middlemarch* and describes George Eliot's evaluation of Nazarene painting. In 'The Concept of "Crisis" in *Middlemarch*' (*NCF*), Eugene Hollahan quotes George Eliot's claim that crisis reactions are both revelatory and prophetic. He examines a number of crises, especially what he considers the main crisis, when Ladislaw and Dorothea vow to wed. Once again George Eliot's *intentions* are praised. Ladislaw shows how to combine visionary and practical, however much readers reject his artistic realization. Similarly, '*Deronda* challenges our conceptions of what a novel ought to be', writes Brian Swann in 'George Eliot's Ecumenical Jew, or, The Novel as Outdoor Temple' (*Novel*). It is, simply, a place 'where human beings meet' and, more grandiloquently, greatly designed, homiletic, 'a dream of reconciliation and moral uplift'. William J. Sullivan produces valuable background information about 'The Allusion to Jenny Lind in *Daniel Deronda*' (*NCF*). Neither Lewes nor George Eliot, who had reviewed Henry Chorley's *Modern German Music* in 1854, thought much of Jenny Lind.

Just before he began *The Last Chronicle of Barset* in January 1866, Trollope wrote some 'character' essays of clergymen for the *Pall Mall Gazette*. These are now well introduced by Ruth apRoberts,[33] who

[33] *Clergymen of the Church of England*, by Anthony Trollope. Intro. Ruth apRoberts. Leicester U.P. pp. 130. £3. (The Victorian Library).

stresses their cultural significance and connexion with Matthew Arnold's views. (She suggests positive influence at work in *The Way We Live Now*, 1873.) In an appendix she reprints 'The Zulu in London', Trollope's satirical account of an Evangelical meeting in Exeter Hall. This is associated with Trollope's last piece, 'The Clergyman Who Subscribes for Colenso', which is termed 'Trollope's own modest statement against literalism'.

George Levine's article, 'Can You Forgive Him? Trollope's *Can You Forgive Her?* and the Myth of Realism' (*VS*), is an illuminating analysis and evaluation, based on the idea that realism in English fiction taps forces it cannot control. Though successful in some aspects, this novel cannot sustain its challenge to 'the compromised pragmatism of a contingent, greedy, and complacent world'. Juliet McMaster valiantly tackles the same difficult novel in her '"The Meaning of Words and the Nature of Things": Trollope's *Can You Forgive Her?*' (*SEL*). She stresses the centrality of Alice Vavasor, a character 'whose dilemma is echoed and amplified in the rest of the novel', where Trollope's major concern is the gap between a language and reality. William A. West's 'The Anonymous Trollope' (*ArielE*) examines two unfamiliar novels, *Nina Balatka* and *Linda Tressel*, set in Prague and Munich respectively. Not only are the settings unusual, but both novels are gloomy, powerful studies of fanaticism and anguish. Trollope's experiment with 'a second identity' helped him migrate from Barsetshire to the wider, more troubled world of his later fiction. 'Woman is compelled by her very nature to occupy the roles allotted her by mid-Victorian convention', is a brief summary of 'Trollope on "the Genus Girl"' (*NCF*), writes David

Aitken. Not that, he goes on to say, they are mere dolls; they may be submissive to men, but they are also richly passionate. The liveliest of all are 'vividly, wilfully, and peculiarly themselves.'

Last year I welcomed the increasing number of good comparative studies. Sven-Johan Spånberg's Uppsala doctoral dissertation on *The Ordeal of Richard Feverel*[34] and European traditions of realism is a clear and vigorous effort of the same kind. He refers of course to Meredith's debt to native traditions but after an analysis of the simple parodic relationship with *Sir Charles Grandison*, turns to the more creative stimulus of *Emile*, *Wilhelm Meister*, *Illusions perdues*, and the novels of Stendhal in particular, because of their technical originality and 'during fusion of a distinctive type of dry ironic realism with tragedy'. Ultimately, Spånberg thinks, Meredith's testing of received ideas and attitudes is an examination of life as well as of literature, investigation into 'manners *and* morals'. Spånberg refers to a book I missed: Monica Mannheimer, *The Generations in Meredith's Novels* (Gothenburg Studies in English 23, Stockholm 1972). Michael Collie's bibliography of George Meredith[35] is in five sections: novels and short stories, other prose, poems, collected editions, and translations. He gives a good deal of attention to the evolution of the final texts, the relationships between manuscripts, the circumstances of publication, etc. The collected editions begun in 1885 and

[34] '*The Ordeal of Richard Feverel*' and the *Traditions of Realism*, by Sven-Johan Spånberg. Uppsala. Acta Universitatis Upsaliensis: Studia Anglistica Upsaliensia 20. (Stockholm: Almqvist & Wiksell), pp. 110. Paperback.

[35] *George Meredith: a Bibliography*, by Michael Collie. Dawsons: U. of Toronto P. pp. ix+292. £13.00.

in 1895 are important, since it was for these that Meredith undertook his revision. In particular, 'no prose work escaped the second revision' and only *Celt and Saxon* appeared thereafter. In *N&Q* Norman Page prints 'An Unpublished Meredith Letter' and John R. DeBruyn explains the occasion of a Meredith letter in 'The Tragedy of Wycliffe Taylor'. In *EA* Serge Cottereau writes on 'Repression, Censure et Justification de George Meredith'. He draws mostly upon the later novels to define the various types of conflicts and defence reactions.

Klaus Reichert's approach to Lewis Carroll[36] is twofold: it is psycho-analytical in the chapter on Carroll's 'dream technique' which looks at the genesis of Carroll's 'nonsense', and it is linguistic in the chapters on syntax and semantics in 'Evidence' and 'Jabberwocky' and on 'The Hunting of the Snark'. Reichert describes Carroll's work in terms of a reaction against the 'fears and repressions, the identity problems, and problems of communication, in the Victorian era' [H.C.C.]. Another unusual item is 'The Mythic Appeal of *Lorna Doone*' (*NCF*), by Max Keith Sutton. Blackmore's style, he tells us, was admired by both Hardy and Hopkins, though Sutton's main concern in this article is with the narrative of a struggle, shaped like a seasonal myth of death and renewal.

The Autobiography and Letters of Mrs. Oliphant[37] can now be placed beside the brilliant *Miss Marjoribanks* (see *YW* 50.320), the work of a novelist of genuine wit and originality, still underestimated but in Mrs Leavis's opinion far from dwarfed by more famous contemporaries. The Carlingford novels, for instance, 'can rival Trollope's Barchester series in several respects and contain material much more valuable as sociology and social criticism than anything in his'. This is a most valuable addition to Leicester's Victorian Library. No more representative 'woman of letters' could have been found; she drove as hard and as variously as Charles Dickens himself. She deserves more attention. It always seems a pity literary criticism should be so conglutinant, though lovers of Hardy will again rejoice this year in the number of studies devoted to him.

Penelope Vigar's study of the novels[38] can be recommended to students who recoil from the more subtle or esoteric efforts of recent criticism. She is primarily concerned with technique, maintaining a generally just, plain argument with fair demonstration from the text and apt use of critics, though the 'architectural' are too smartly sent packing. She proposes a painterly Hardy, able to achieve the selective and memorable intensities of Impressionism but also affected by the more tedious representational methods of the Pre-Raphaelites. Her approach is based firmly on Hardy's own statements about his art (so well analysed by Morton Zabel in the famous 1940 *Southern Review*): 'essentially only another way of looking at things, not necessarily a deep interpretation of them'. Out go the 'philosophic' critics as well! Ian Gregor's *The Great Web*[39] deals with a more limited selection, the six main novels in fact,

[36] *Lewis Carroll*, by Klaus Reichert. München: Carl Hanser Verlag. pp. 216. n.p.

[37] *Autobiography and Letters of Mrs. Margaret Oliphant*, ed. by Mrs Harry Coghill, intro. by Q. D. Leavis. Leicester U.P. (The Victorian Library). pp. 35+xv+464. £5.20.

[38] *The Novels of Thomas Hardy: Illusion and Reality*, by Penelope Vigar. Athlone Press. pp. ix+226. £4.50.

[39] *The Great Web: the Form of Hardy's Major Fiction*, by Ian Gregor. Faber & Faber. pp. 236. £3.95.

but has a similar stress upon questions of form. Compared with Vigar's, his prose is more muscular and professional, his interests extending to the nature and significance of the criticism he is undertaking. The theoretical basis for his valuable stress upon dynamic reading was laid down by Walter J. Ong in 1958; indeed, Gregor's style reminds one of some modern American critics: 'Story, or more precisely plot, is mimetic of Hardy's metaphysic'; 'the continual dialectic of feeling that is operative between the narrator and his narrative.' The six main novels are read as a sequence leading to the 'desperate victory' of *Jude*, but by then Wessex was imaginatively dead to Hardy; the web of his fiction was drawn to its extremity. (Even *Far From the Madding Crowd* had its precarious aspects.) Webs of criticism, too, when stretched to their furthest extent can sometimes collapse to a few coarse strands—the often simple lines of the earlier criticism Gregor is at pains to refine. Apart from this, his writing conveys how authentically he has responded to works that allow sensitive comparisons with Hardy's novels, to T. S. Eliot's 'Marina' or to *Troilus and Cressida*, for instance. Oddly, there is not much reference to Hardy's poetry in this study. The stress falls on the movement towards a divided modern consciousness and to the prose form in which Hardy attempted to embody conflicting energies.

Two other books this year remind us of Hardy's Janus-faced and 'idiosyncratic mode of regard'. James Gibson edits for publication *Thomas Hardy and History*,[40] left incomplete by the late R. J. White. This begins with a sensible, undemanding account of Hardy's life and temperament and

then concentrates on *The Trumpet Major* and *The Dynasts*; it ends with a brief comparison of Hardy and Tolstoy. White emphasizes that Hardy used histories but was not a professional historian. His personal outlook and responses were fired by 'oral tradition, accessible scenery, and existing relics'. F. B. Pinion gathers a number of papers[41] on Hardy and the Modern World by himself, J. O. Bailey, F. R. Southerington, Jean R. Brooks, Lord David Cecil, *et al.* There is a distinct emphasis upon Hardy's 'philosophy'. Most original and useful are C. J. P. Beatty's study of *Far from the Madding Crowd* from an architectural point of view, Harold Orel's 'Hardy, War, and the Years of *Pax Britannica*' (which suggests that Hardy 'changed his mind on a matter of deep concern to his art'), James Gibson on 'The Poetic Text', and Robert Gittings's section from his new biography.

There are a few general articles on Hardy. Douglas Wertheimer gives 'Some Hardy Notes on Dorset Words and Customs' (*N&Q*). Norman Page refuses to dismiss Hardy's fifty short stories as mere pot-boilers. In 'Hardy's Short Stories: a Reconsideration' (*SSF*) he concentrates on the romantic or supernatural tales and the later realistic stories of modern life. His account of the revisions of *On the Western Circuit* is of particular interest. David W. Jarrett, in 'Hardy and Hawthorne as Modern Romancers' (*NCF*), claims that both drew nineteenth-century phenomena into the world of the romance (*cf.* p. 430 above). But his comparison of *A Laodicean* with

---

[40] *Thomas Hardy and History*, by R. J. White. Macmillan. pp. vii + 152. £4.95.

[41] *Thomas Hardy and the Modern World: Papers presented at the 1973 Summer School*, ed. by F. B. Pinion. Dorchester: The Thomas Hardy Society. pp. ix + 161. Paperback £2.50, $6.95 from The Secretary, The Vicarage, Haselbury Plucknett, Crewberre, Somerset, TA18 7PB.

The House of the Seven Gables indicates that Hardy, anxious to remain a novelist, reduces Hawthorne's mysterious subtleties. Luther S. Luedtke elaborates the connexions between 'Sherwood Anderson, Thomas Hardy and "Tandy"' (*MFS*). Howard O. Brogan's 'Early Experience and Scientific Determinism in Twain and Hardy' (*Mosaic*) is a brief, somewhat spasmodic attempt to decide why two men of such opposite temperaments should display certain similarities. Two articles in *VNL* elucidate Hardy's attitudes to criticism and to publication: Norman Page, 'Hardy, Mrs. Oliphant, and *Jude*'; Audrey C. Peterson, '"A Good Hand at a Serial": Thomas Hardy and the Art of Fiction'.

In 'Far From the Madding Crowd and The Woodlanders: Hardy's Grotesque Pastorals' (*ELT*), Charles E. May suggests that Hardy's idiosyncratic view of life is 'anti-pastoral' and that the actual endings of these two novels are not the true ones. His vision was distorted by the tradition in which he attempted to write. In *MFS*, Mary M. Saunders writes a note on 'The Significance of the Man-Trap in *The Woodlanders*'. Lewis B. Horne discusses 'Hardy's Little Father Time' (*SAQ*) as a transitional figure between hope and despair, and in 'A Note on the Teasing Narrator in *Jude*' (*ELT*) John Sutherland examines deliberately oblique references; he sees them as a way in which Hardy distanced the apparently autobiographical material.

Michael Collie examines 'Gissing's Revision of *New Grub Street*' (*YES*) for translation into French, especially where it significantly affects our response to the Reardon episodes. But though Collie thinks the revisions were an improvement, Gissing still failed to write a genuinely psychological novel. A number of other Gissing items have not been available for review: Gillian Tindall's *The Born Exile* (Temple Smith, 1973), an edition of *Thyrza* by Jacob Korg, and *The Nether World* by John Goode (both Harvester P.).

In 'Madge and Clara Hopgood: William Hale White's Spinozan Sisters' (*VS*), Linda K. Hughes carefully elucidates the influence of Spinoza as a practical moralist. Madge finally achieves the ability to bring intellect to bear upon impulse, while Clara reaches the very highest form of Spinozan virtue. She also analyses the later sister pairs in Forster and Lawrence. In 'William Hale White ("Mark Rutherford"), and Samuel Bamford' (*N&Q*), V. D. Cunningham quotes parallel passages to show how extensively White had drawn on the latter's *Passages in the Life of a Radical* for *The Revolution in Tanner's Lane*.

'Law is the distinguishing characteristic,' claims James Harrison in his useful analysis of 'Kipling's Jungle Eden' (*Mosaic*), though consensus is more important than content and law must always be kept young by the opposition of anarchic life-forces. In the complex lives of men we still find this 'Edenic balance', as we see in *Kim*: paradise can be found in a fallen world. D. C. R. A. Goonetilleke writes on 'Colonial Neuroses: Kipling and Forster' (*ArielE*). He examines the nightmarish experience depicted in Kipling's early tales. The best of these, 'The Strange Ride of Morrowbie Jukes', achieves both psychological and social depth, though it lacks the kind of philosophical dimension found in Forster's *Passage to India*. Two books on Kipling have been overlooked. One, by Rudolph Sühnel, *Kontemplation und Aktion: Orient und Okzident im Werk von Rudyard Kipling* (Heidelberg: Carl Winter, Universitätsverlag,

1972), is briefly noted in *EA*, 1975. The other, by Vasant A. Shahane, *Rudyard Kipling: Activist and Artist* (Carbondale: Southern Illinois U.P., 1973) was reviewed in *NCF*.

Wilde's *The Picture of Dorian Gray*[42] appears in the Oxford English Novels series edited by Isobel Murray, an authority on the different versions of the text (*cf. YW* 53.355). Her critical introduction, which draws attention to an unknown source (*Ashes of the Future*, by Edward Heron-Allen), is succinct and valuable. Newspaper reports allow Kevin H. F. O'Brien to present '*The House Beautiful*: a Reconstruction of Wilde's American Lecture' (*VS*).

Keith Cushman praises highly a short story of 1896 in 'The Quintessence of Dowsonism: *The Dying of Francis Donne* (*SSF*). He sees it as remarkable both in itself and as a comment on Ernest Dowson's own aesthetic detachment, which offered 'no real escape from the despair of living'. Finally, one must note a facsimile reprint of the 1923 edition of Henry Danielson's bibliography of Arthur Machen.[43]

5. SELECTED PROSE WRITERS
(a) *General*
Robert Bernard Martin's succinct study of comic theory[44] first surveys the philosophic background in Hobbes, Shaftesbury, Kant *et al.* and then probes into the Victorian critical debates, sometimes waged in odd places like *The Phrenological Journal*, that illuminate the broad pattern of

change from Dickensian humour to Wildean wit and paradox. He rather austerely sticks to theory—though Thackeray's glib association of charity and humour forces him to ask what has become of Becky and Lord Steyne. The 'hack theorists' are examined to provide the context and the materials for Professor Martin's analysis of greater theorists: Sydney Smith, Leigh Hunt, George Eliot, Leslie Stephen, and George Meredith especially.

Alan W. Bellringer and C. B. Jones briefly but competently introduce a selection of texts that illustrate 'the ideas by which the Victorians interpreted their society'. *The Victorian Sages*[45] ranges from T. B. Macaulay on Southey's *Colloquies* to extracts from J. S. Mill's *Autobiography*, H. Spencer's *Social Statics*, Ruskin's *Sesame*, etc. Such a compilation has obvious teaching uses and will prove its worth fully if it sends students to the complete texts. Otherwise, the Paper-bags of *Sartor* stand as an awful warning in the first section of this anthology!

Geoffrey Faber's 1936 revision of his character study of the Oxford Movement,[46] focused on J. H. Newman, is now reissued. *Truth to Life: the Art of Biography in the 19th Century*, by A. O. J. Cockshut (Collins; New York: Harcourt) was not made available for review. It includes Arnold, Carlyle, Macaulay, and Newman. Perhaps only marginal to the main concerns of this section but none the less of considerable interest are articles on J. S. Mill,

[42] *The Picture of Dorian Gray*, by Oscar Wilde. Ed. by Isobel Murray. O.U.P. pp. xxxiv+249. £3.00. (Oxford English Novels).

[43] *Arthur Machen: a Bibliography*, by Henry Danielson. With notes by Arthur Machen and intro. by Henry Savage. Ann Arbor, Michigan: Plutarch Press, 1971.

[44] *The Triumph of Wit: a Study of Victorian Comic Theory*, by Robert Bernard Martin. Oxford: Clarendon Press. pp. xiii+105. £3.50.

[45] *The Victorian Sages: An Anthology of Prose*, ed. by Alan W. Bellringer and C. B. Jones. Dent. Totowa, N.J.: Rowman & Littlefield. pp. xvii+241. £3.25. Paperback £1.75.

[46] *Oxford Apostles: a Character Study of the Oxford Movement*, by Geoffrey Faber. Faber & Faber. pp. xxiii+467. Paperback £1.90.

R. H. Hutton, and G. H. Lewes in *VPN*.

(b) *Individual Authors*

Gerald Duff edits thirty-three un-published letters of William Cobbett[47] in the University of Illinois Library. They are, as might have been expected, remarkably diverse and pungent. Duane Schneider provides 'Corrections and Notes' (*N&Q*) to Lamb's *Letters*, edited by E. V. Lucas. Thomas Pinney brings out the first two volumes (1807–February 1831; March 1831–December 1833) of a major scholarly edition, *The Letters of Macaulay*.[48] The volumes are triumphs of compact, clear presenta-tion in print. The text of the letters themselves is slightly adapted to make them accord more with modern practice; it is also extensively anno-tated. In his introduction Pinney out-lines previous publications of the letters, the sources and scope of this edition, and editorial procedures. He also discusses Macaulay and his correspondents and succinctly evalu-ates the nature and worth of the letters as the 'record of the personal-ity of a great Victorian' who 'touched Victorian life at an extraordinary number of points': at Clapham and Cambridge, on circuit, in India, as a contributor to the *Edinburgh Review*, and so on. These two volumes are lightly indexed but a full index is promised for the end of the work.

Robert Ready's 'Hazlitt: In and Out of "Gusto"' (*SEL*) is revisionary. 'Interest', he thinks, is a more reliable term, less involved with painting or the pictorial, evoking his doctrine of the sympathetic imagination and an 'intense conception of things'. 'Gusto' is a product.

John Clubbe introduces and anno-tates his own translation of the neglected but good German bio-graphy of Carlyle by Friedrich Althaus (1866) and Carlyle's un-published 'Reminiscence of Adam and Archibald Skirving'.[49] The Althaus biography is particularly important in that it is printed from Carlyle's own copy, which contains often extensive and usually valuable notes: 'when he writes "Ach Gott!" in the margin opposite Althaus's account of the "deeds of heroism" perpetrated by the North in the American Civil War, those two words say more than would a paragraph.' Clubbe also has some useful com-ments on Carlyle in a review of M. H. Abrams's *Natural Super-naturalism* (*Mosaic*). Philip Rosen-berg, *The Seventh Hero: Thomas Carlyle and the Theory of Radical Activism* (Harvard U.P.) was not made available for review.

In *N&Q* Ian Campbell prints an early German article (with transla-tion) of 'Carlyle in the 1830s' and Wolfgang Franke gives 'Another Derivation of "Teufelsdröckh"', quoting from Luther's works. Gillian Workman's 'Carlyle and the Governor Eyre Controversy: an Account with some New Material' (*VS*) is too modestly titled. A number of manuscript letters are published for the first time and, in addition, a definite reinterpretation is pro-pounded: Carlyle's involvement was not racist but a result of his views on the condition of England and the virtues of work, action, and social order. In 'Carlyle and Ruskin: the

---

[47] *Letters of William Cobbett*, ed. by Gerald Duff. Salzburg: U. of Salzburg (Salzburg Studies in English Literature). pp. vii + 101. Paperback £4.80.

[48] *The Letters of Thomas Babington Macaulay*, ed. by Thomas Pinney. Cambridge U.P. pp. xlii + 330; viii + 383. £10.50 each volume.

[49] *Two Reminiscences of Thomas Carlyle, Now First Published*, ed. by John Clubbe. Durham, N.C.: Duke U.P. pp. xiv + 145. $6.75.

Private Side of the Public Coin' (*VNL*), Eloise K. Goreau argues that we should view Carlyle's 'influence' with some scepticism.

Two articles tackle the manifold problems of *Sartor*. In 'Adam-Kadmon, Nifl, Muspel, and the Biblical Symbolism of *Sartor Resartus*' (*ELH*), Joseph Sigman examines Carlyle's reinterpretations in considerable detail. An early passage is seen as one of the keys to the symbolism; primordial man can be seen as a giant tree, and so can both individuals and the life of mankind in history, amongst the dualities of the dying world of phenomena. In 'Carlyle's "British Reader" and the Structure of *Sartor Resartus*' (*TSLL*), Jerry Allen Dibble states that the book instructs the reader how to move from Understanding to Reason (in its post-Kantian sense), a final synthesis of all ways of knowing. The reader is the protagonist, led to discover a 'Paradise within'. With this approach, Dibble suggests, the final chapters prove to be less anticlimactic than they at first seem.

There are some interesting minor items to report. The 1936 biography of De Quincey by E. Sackville West[50] has now been reissued as the most readable and literary of the full-scale lives; John E. Jordan's notes and bibliography brings matters up-to-date. It would be difficult to find a more pleasantly produced or readable book than the *Autobiographies* of Charles Darwin and T. H. Huxley.[51] There are notes and illustrations, and Gavin de Beer's efficient

introduction gives us necessary explanations of the intellectual bearings. In particular, he draws attention to the crucial fact that Darwin had hit upon his main ideas *before* reading Malthus on population, which cannot be deduced from the Darwin autobiography. In 'Nature, Religion and Emotional Response: a Reconsideration of Darwin's Affective Decline' (*VS*), John Angus Campbell reassesses the standard accounts by studying three relatively neglected questions: the way in which his language manifests feeling, his consistent appreciation of nature if not art, and the 'poetic' aspects of his whole imaginative enterprise. Another welcome title in the Oxford series, Edmund Gosse's *Father and Son*,[52] is introduced by James Hepburn, who lays stress upon its 'perspective' rather than its 'truth' about the march of mind into the twentieth century. The Edmund Gosse, he suggests, 'who thought he escaped to freedom escaped into a smaller life'. Quantum mutatus ab illo Hectore . . .

Eugene R. August argues in 'Mill as Sage: the Essay on Bentham' (*PMLA*) that Mill was far more than a mere rhetorician: a 'sense of disappointed expectation is the central revelation about Bentham that Mill as sage imaginatively conveys'. August considers the evolution as well as the artistry of the essay. Donald F. Winslow prints 'Francis W. Newman's Assessment of John Sterling: Two Letters' (*ELN*).

Volumes 25 and 26 of the *Letters and Diaries of John Henry Newman* appear this year.[53] The expected

---

[50] *A Flame in Sunlight: the Life and Work of Thomas De Quincey*, by Edward Sackville West. New ed. with preface and notes by John E. Jordan. The Bodley Head. pp. xviii+362. £4.00.

[51] *Autobiographies*, by Charles Darwin and Thomas Henry Huxley. Ed. with intro. by Gavin de Beer. O.U.P. pp. xxvi+123. £3.30. (Oxford English Memoirs and Travels).

[52] *Father and Son: a Study of Two Temperaments*, by Edmund Gosse. Ed. with intro. by James Hepburn. O.U.P. pp. xxviii+192. £4.95. (Oxford English Memoirs and Travels.)

[53] *The Letters and Diaries of John Henry Newman*, ed. by C. S. Dessain and T. Gornall. Vol. 25 (The Vatican Council, Jan. 1870–

'Apology for Newman' (*EC*), brief but adequate, is provided by I. T. Ker. (See *YW* 54.360). J. Gibert's 'Histoire de la Publication de l'*Apologia* dans ses Éditions Successives' (*EA*) is based on the idea that we must know the genesis of the work. Gibert surveys the problems, describes the translations and major editions. In 'Some Strategies of Religious Autobiography' (*Renascence*) Dennis Taylor compares the *Apologia* with *Grace Abounding* and Thomas Merton's *The Seven Storey Mountain*.

The Complete Prose Works of Matthew Arnold is almost complete. Volume 10,[54] which contains a number of items of American interest —the three lectures he gave on his tour in 1883–4 and two related essays —and Arnold's version of the Book of Isaiah, with his notes. There are also some minor items, which include Arnold's last statements on Christian doctrine. As usual, this volume is most helpfully annotated (though the argument about copy-text for 'The Michigan Edition of Matthew Arnold' continues in *N&Q*, with contributions from Professor Super, P. G. Scott, and J. C. Maxwell). The essay 'Literature and Science', we are told, was given twenty-nine times in America and is 'perhaps his finest statement' on the value of liberal education.

In 'Death and Champagnole: a Contribution to the Reading of *The Seven Lamps of Architecture*' (*UTQ*), Pierre Fontaney defends both the functional and theoretical aspects of one of Ruskin's purple passages. Richard J. Dellamora writes on 'The Revaluation of "Christian" Art: Ruskin's Appreciation of Fra Angelico 1845–60' (*UTQ*). It is a story of decline. John Hayman's interesting 'Ruskin and the Art of System-making' (*YES*) is an attempt to find the basis of Ruskin's thought and cast of mind in a 'counter-system' where the 'mean' is in opposition to ironically kindred polarities, though Hayman thinks he wrote with most assurance about the particular case and dismissed his dialectic when he needed it most, in later years. Two volumes of an edition of the Ruskin family letters[55] have not been available for review here. They are reviewed in *VS* by Robert Preyer, who writes that the letters are 'of great interest but of little intellectual substance'. He praises the editorial work of Van Akin Burd.

Germain d'Hangest enthusiastically examines 'La Place de Walter Pater dans le Mouvement Esthétique' (*EA*). Pater's role was decisive in that he made aestheticism the direct remedy for disenchantment and secular pessimism. The language of form, especially, is revelatory of a unique, autonomous being, which his disciples at worst made decadent and suicidal. So we must look to the 1890 essay on Prosper Mérimée and the essay on Style for a critique of excess and a revised humanism. Lawrence F. Schuetz defends Pater's ethical concerns and motives in 'The Suppressed "Conclusion" to *The Renaissance* and Pater's Modern Image' (*ELT*). John Y. LeBourgeois suggests further inquiry into the fact that the 'Financial Crisis of William Morris' (*DUJ*) coincided with a marriage crisis. Finally, John Adlard writes on 'The Failure of Francis Kilvert' for *MQR*.

[54] *Philistinism in England and America*, by Matthew Arnold. Ed. by R. H. Super. Ann Arbor: U. of Michigan P. pp. viii+614. $15.00.

Dec. 1871); Vol. 26 (Aftermaths, Jan. 1872– Dec. 1873). Oxford U.P. pp. 496, 437.

[55] *The Ruskin Family Letters: the Correspondence of John James Ruskin, His Wife, and Their Son, John, 1801–1843*, ed. by Van Akin Burd. Ithaca, N.Y. and London: Cornell U.P., 1973, 2 vols. pp. lviii+792. $35.00, £16.65.

XIV

The Twentieth Century

J. BRATTON and R. CAVE
SUSAN PAINTER and JAMES REDMOND

The chapter has the following sections: 1. The Novel, by Jacqueline Bratton and Richard Cave; 2. Verse, by Susan Painter; 3. Drama, by James Redmond.

1. THE NOVEL

The reluctance of some publishing houses to forward copies for review has meant that we have been prevented from making a study as comprehensive as we would wish. The material which has been available to us has shown a sudden burst of interest in the work of Arnold Bennett; and Conrad and Joyce continue to be popular subjects for study. Following considerable attention last year, studies of D. H. Lawrence and Virginia Woolf have been less prominent. In the general field, there have been three notable contributions to our knowledge of Bloomsbury and its achievements, and a fine study of the fiction of Northern Irish writers.

(a) General Studies

Contemporary Novelists,[1] Volume Two of the series *Contemporary Writers of the English Language*, is a most welcome addition to the few comprehensive reference guides to modern authors. Over six hundred living writers are listed. The entries contain biographical and bibliographical material, details about the location of manuscript collections and a short critical analysis of each author's work. An interesting innovation is the listing of critical studies that the novelists themselves consider important views of their fiction, together with, in many instances, comments by the novelists on their own work. The essays by a panel of English and American critics vary in quality, as is inevitable with a venture of this kind: some are content with offering only an account of the narrative incidents and tone of a particular novel; others, miracles of compression, manage to convey a real sense of a writer's development, major preoccupations and unique style and technique. As a document recording creative and critical assumptions, prejudices, problems, and values prevailing at the present time, this bibliography with its special features will be invaluable for the literary historians of the future.

Professor Buckley's valuable study[2] of the Bildungsroman in English develops from a definition of the type and an account of its origins and characteristic features to a detailed study of nine major examples ranging from Dickens to Joyce. The final chapter examines more recent attempts by Maugham, May Sinclair,

---

[1] *Contemporary Novelists*, ed. by James Vinson. London: St. James Press; New York: St. Martin's Press, 1973. pp. xvii + 1442.

[2] *Season of Youth: the Bildungsroman from Dickens to Golding*, by Jerome Hamilton Buckley. Cambridge, Massachusetts: Harvard U.P. pp. x+336. £6.00.

Dorothy Richardson, L. P. Hartley, John Wain, Golding, and, rather incongruously, Virginia Woolf with *Jacob's Room*. Wherever possible, biographical facts about the authors are used to illuminate the analysis of the novels. Generally this is more convincing where the background information relates to intellectual rather than emotional or psychological factors. Quoting Jesse Chambers and Frieda Lawrence extensively in his support, Buckley criticizes *Sons and Lovers*, for example, as over-schematic and marred by a burden of apology for Lawrence's own life; but this is to trust, not the tale, but the commentators without questioning whether their viewpoints are at all biased. The best of the chapters on twentieth-century authors are those devoted to Joyce's *Portrait of the Artist* and Wells's *Tono Bungay*, where there is some discriminating analysis of the contrast between Wells's sensitive portrayal of Ponderevo's intuitions and his crude examination of his amorous affairs, and a good account of how Wells establishes the personality of George's Uncle Teddy through the descriptions of his various homes. Golding's concern in *Free Fall* for the restraints imposed on the imagination of the artist by modern doctrinaire philosophies is also given masterly treatment. In *The Protean Self*[3] Alan Kennedy considers the relation of contemporary writers to the Modern period (1900–1925) and seeks, by the use of the concepts of sociology, especially those dealing with rôle-play, to assess the intentions and achievements of post-Modern novelists in their use of dramatic action. He asserts that 'the aim of this critical consideration of analytic terminology

is to open an avenue to understanding the recurrence in recent fiction of the question of rôle-playing, self-dramatization, masks'. He considers the work of a very wide range of twentieth-century writers, in particular attempting to place Muriel Spark as of central importance, perceiving in her use of paradox and the union of opposites a powerful response to the question of action, a 'central and recurring post-Modern concern' which is also explored in the work of Isherwood, John Fowles, Graham Greene and Joyce Cary. Also in the area of contemporary writing, three articles in *MFS*, by Myron Greenman, Robert S. Ryf, and Stanley Fogel, discuss the theory and practice of the modern experimental novel.

The Reverent Discipline[4] is, as George A. Panichas affirms in his preface, an attempt by a man whose sympathies are those of a Christian Humanist to restore reverence as 'the highest of human feelings' to the discipline of literary criticism. His attitude to literature he sees as akin to that of D. H. Lawrence, for whom 'any good book is a divine service'. Many of the essays fall outside the scope of this review, though they afford an unusual and challenging approach to modern European culture, in the way they establish a tradition and a critical method quite distinct from Eliot's or Leavis's. The approach does offer many fresh insights into a group of modern novelists: Forster and Lawrence's works are examined to illustrate a thesis about their views on education; *Women in Love* is compared with *The Waste Land* to show how both are similar experiences of the apocalyptic convergence of the historical

---

[3] *The Protean Self: Dramatic Action in Contemporary Fiction*, by Alan Kennedy. Macmillan. pp. 304+xi. £5.95.

[4] *The Reverent Discipline*, by George A. Panichas. Tennessee U.P. pp. xiii+462. $16.95.

consciousness and the personal consciousness as each artist lives through the negation and recovery of his religious vision; Lawrence's vision of evil is compared with Dostoevsky's and his concept of tragedy defined through an analysis of his references to Greek life, philosophy, and myth; a sensitive appreciation of Leonard Woolf's *Downhill All The Way* highlights Woolf's interest in the psychology of authorship to explain the remarkable dignity and compassion of his treatment of Virginia. *Six Modern British Novelists*[5] does not attempt the unity of Professor Panichas's study. It is the first of a projected series of volumes that will reprint particularly successful essays from the *Columbia Essays on Modern Writers*. After an introduction, too brief for its aims, in which George Stade attempts to define 'modernism' in fiction, there are the following studies: John Wain on Bennett; David Lodge on Waugh; Grover Smith on Ford Madox Ford; Robert S. Ryf on Conrad; Carl Woodring on Virginia Woolf, and Harry T. Moore on Forster. Each begins with a short biography and then attempts a succinct chronological survey of the chosen author's work. The scope of the essays never really extends beyond the introductory, and the collection does not explore the theme of modernism in any depth except by implication, since the essays as originally composed were not seen as contributing to a discussion of this kind. It is an expensive volume to direct at the student market since it is in no way comprehensive either as a literary history or as a debate on fictional theory.

John Wilson Foster's admirable study of Ulster Fiction[6] is a complex and challenging work since it contrives to be not only a literary critical study of novels by Ulster authors but also an historical account of life in the province. The closeness of fiction to life, of authorial techniques to common attitudes is here quite unique: most of the inhabitants of Ulster share a habit of mind whereby daily psychological stress is transformed into allegory and myth. The living reality of a cultural tradition drawing its strength from the very topography of the land and from the experience of the common man is seen as an organic continuity from the time of Carleton to the present day. To know the novels written there now—and one might say the same of the poetry—is to know the social and psychic quality of life in Ulster with a rare profundity. After a prologue on Carleton, Foster examines the work principally of twentieth-century writers: Bullock, MacGill, Friel, Kiely, Boyle, Reid, Brian Moore, Anthony West, St. John Ervine, and Joyce Cary. Though he devotes most of the book to close analysis of individual novels, Foster indirectly evolves a lucid debate on the nature and necessity of culture. This proved one of the most exciting books for review this year.

Herbert Kenny's history of literary Dublin[7] attempts to trace the continuing impact the city has had on the development of Irish literature from 1592 and the establishing of Trinity College to the present day. The oral tradition in which so much of this literature is based is examined and particular attention is drawn to the strong talent among Irish writers for

---

[5] *Six Modern British Novelists*, ed. with an introduction by George Stade. New York and London: Columbia U.P. pp. xv+294. £5.50.

[6] *Forces and Themes in Ulster Fiction*, by John Wilson Foster. Gill & Macmillan. pp. 299. £4.95.

[7] *Literary Dublin*, by Herbert A. Kenny. New York: Taplinger. Dublin: Gill & Macmillan. pp. 336. £6.

satire. For the most part, Kenny rehearses well-known material, trusting his sources rather too implicitly and taking scant account of the personal bias that is the special challenge confronting the historian of matters Irish. The book has undoubted charm as one man's personal view of the subject, but that is both a strength and a weakness. The closer one comes to the present day, the less organization of the material is attempted which, with the conversational style, creates an effect of frenetic garrulousness. The aim to include everyone, poet, novelist, dramatist, and conversationalist alike, means that the terse summaries of some writers' achievements are unfortunately banal: Edna O'Brien's novels, we are told, 'are strongly oriented towards sex'. One is left wondering to whom the book is directed: scholars in the field will find little that is new here beyond the insight that the book gives us into Kenny's own personality; the ordinary reader will require more detail than is offered to be adequately enlightened about past history and will be bewildered by the whirlwind treatment of the current literary scene.

The Australian Experience[8] is a collection of critical essays which deal with Australian novels, defined broadly as novels 'which have taken as their subjects aspects of human life as they can be observed in their Australian manifestations', and therefore including, as well as critical consideration of works by native and resident Australians such as Browne, Furphy, and Patrick White, an essay on Frederic Manning's Her Privates We by J. M. Douglas Pringle and an Australian view of D. H. Lawrence's Kangeroo by A. D. Hope. The stirring

title of Seduction and Betrayal, Women and Literature[9] covers a rather disappointing collection of disparate essays on women writers and female characters in fiction of the nineteenth and twentieth centuries, beginning with the old subject of the Bronte household and passing on eventually to a rather puzzled view of Bloomsbury and Virginia Woolf.

There are two books this year which deal chiefly with the Bloomsbury experience. David Gadd's portrait of Bloomsbury[10] is notable for stressing the affection, the shared interests and values which held the group together rather than the web of tensions and envy that has been the subject of several recent accounts of the group. Mr Gadd makes no claims for original scholarship in his book; it is, he admits, to be viewed as an attempt to summarize the recent findings of others and to relate these to the large body of biographical and critical works which is currently available. 'It is . . . a reconnaissance, identifying landmarks and indicating possible routes for more comprehensive surveys.' It is aimed frankly at the general reader, but the result is neither patronizing nor naïve. Since the author's concern is with what Bloomsbury as a whole has contributed to the culture of our century, he achieves a critical detachment that frees him from the need to champion particular individuals at the expense of the rest of the group which seems to be the special danger confronting any historian in this field. The detachment is balanced, however, by an infectious delight in the people he is describing: Bloomsbury cultivated individualism and the individuals here

[8] The Australian Experience, ed. by W. S. Ramson. Australian National U.P. pp. xiii + 344. $A9.95.

[9] Seduction and Betrayal: Women and Literature, by Elizabeth Hardwick, Weidenfeld & Nicolson. pp. 208+xi. £3.95.

[10] The Loving Friends. A Portrait of Bloomsbury, by David Gadd. Hogarth Press. pp. xiv + 209. £3.

are each evoked with considerable brio and wit.

A less impartial view is to be found in the second volume of Lady Ottoline Morrell's memoirs[11], 'which dates from her arrival at Garsington and is a record of her relationships with the friends who visited her there during and after the Great War: Lawrence and Frieda, Strachey and Carrington, Aldous and Maria Huxley, Middleton Murry and Katherine Mansfield, Leonard and Virginia Woolf. Something of the special atmosphere which Lady Ottoline created about herself is communicated, which affords interesting contrasts with the literary caricatures of life at Garsington which have found expression in *Women in Love* and *Crome Yellow*. It is Huxley who receives the most extensive treatment: Lady Ottoline develops a portrait of him as a passionless onlooker on life and gives valuable information about Maria's influence on the composition of the novels, while his own defence of *Crome Yellow* to his hostess affords penetrating insights into his fictional aims and methods. However, the most fascinating aspect of the work is the view it gives us of Lady Ottoline herself. The tone and style are self-conscious to a degree that makes one suspect her attempts at disingenuousness (especially regarding her attitude to Lawrence). What steadily emerges is a portrait of a woman with immense reserves of sympathy, capable of profound insights into other people, and able honestly to revise her opinions of them in the light of personal experience after careful reflexion, but a woman tragically incapable of putting her insights to direct practical use in her day-to-day dealings with her author-friends. It was less a failure of tact than a want of courage to trust her own intuitions; that she has often been abused one cannot deny, but she could often have forestalled some of her own heartache. Gathorne-Hardy's introduction attempts rightly to protect her memory against the malicious rumours promoted by her Bloomsbury acquaintances and revived by their biographers; and in a long appendix, he defines her relationship with Bertrand Russell, making extensive use of a manuscript account written by Lady Ottoline herself.

The second volume of Gerald Brenan's autobiography[12] dates from his decision to settle in Spain. A wide range of literary figures crosses his canvas: Strachey, Hemingway, Dylan Thomas, Desmond MacCarthy, Bertrand Russell, Roger Fry, Arthur Waley, and Leonard and Virginia Woolf. Undoubtedly the most vivid and informative pages are devoted to a ruthlessly honest analysis of his love for Carrington (for all his ardour he found her chatter tedious and her body boyish and unloveable), and of his marriage with Gamel Woolsey. Both relationships have been well documented already, the one in Carrington's letters and diaries and Holroyd's biography of Strachey, the other in Alyse Gregory's journals and Llewelyn Powys's latters. Though we are covering familiar ground, there is freshness and excitement, indeed a Jamesian kind of fascination, in tracing a new point of view and gauging its success in creating a pattern of plausible interpretation around known fact. In many ways Brenan's is the most difficult rôle to justify in both triangular relationships, difficult to avoid an air of raffishness or a tone of special-pleading. But the style,

---

[11] *Ottoline at Garsington: Memoirs of Lady Ottoline Morrell 1915–1918*, ed. with an introduction by Robert Gathorne-Hardy. Faber & Faber. pp. 304. £4.95.

[12] *Personal Record: 1920–1972*, by Gerald Brenan. Jonathan Cape. pp. 381. £6.

candid, unemotional, largely factual in its exposition, is wholly convincing; only with the more colourful personalities in his life—Gamel, Strachey, his eccentric great-aunt, or Thomas—are there bolder flourishes.

The remaining books of a general nature may perhaps be said to fall into special categories within that grouping: they deal with popular fiction, and with children's books. Rachel Anderson's *The Purple Heart Throbs*[13] is a spirited and often comic examination of romance writing from Charlotte M. Yonge to the present day. Within a generally chronological survey certain recurring themes and settings—deserts, for example, and hospitals—are isolated for consideration, and many interesting ideas emerge, though without the force of an organized thesis, and without the solid backing of reference to other criticism of popular literature. The author's enjoyment of the books she writes about, however, goes a long way to make up for these defects. Arthur Marshall's *Girls Will Be Girls*[14] makes no pretence to unity either, beyond the unmistakable, ironic, critical voice of the writer. It is in fact a collection of his delightful reviews. Many of his *New Statesman* skirmishes with the writers of school stories for girls are included, and also reprinted are pieces about a great variety of books, including autobiography, popular history, romantic novels, and Marshall's own reminiscences of his school days. Also concerned with books for children is *The Collector's Book of Boys' Stories*,[15] which, as its title suggests,

is primarily a reference and background work for book collectors. In a field, however, which has little purely critical writing, it provides useful bibliographical and biographical notes on books written for boys in the Victorian and early twentieth-century periods. The school story, science fiction, and the adventure tale are pursued into the 1930s, and there is a final section tracing the nineteenth-century traditions of writing for boys beyond the Second World War.

The last book of this group, *Clubland Heroes* by Richard Usborne,[16] deals with material which might be said to combine the appeal of the romance with that of the boys' adventure story: it explains itself in its subtitle, 'a nostalgic study of some recurrent characters in the romantic fiction of Dornford Yates, John Buchan and Sapper'. This is a new edition of a 1953 publication. It is said to be 'thoroughly revised', and includes a new introduction by the author, which adds some further reflexions about sources, and notes some of the new critical work in the field, but makes no alteration of the affectionate and all-forgiving attitude of the writer to his material; an attitude which was remarkable in 1953, and seems likely to try the patience of the critical new reader. One other special category of critical writing must be mentioned: Julian Symons has a regular column in *New Rev* in which he discusses crime fiction, including Robert Littell's *The Defection of A. J. Lewinter*, Len Deighton's *Spy Story*, John Le Carré, and the cult of Raymond Chandler.

(b) *Authors*

Kingsley Amis is the subject of a profile by Clive James in *New Rev*

[13] *The Purple Heart Throbs*, by Rachel Anderson. Hodder & Stoughton. pp. 286. £2.95.

[14] *Girls Will Be Girls*, by Arthur Marshall. Hamish Hamilton. pp. 180+x. £2.95.

[15] *The Collector's Book of Boys' Stories*, by Eric Quayle. Studio Vista. 1973. pp. 160. £4.95.

[16] *Clubland Heroes*, by Richard Usborne. Barrie & Jenkins. pp. 186. £3.25.

which focuses upon the processes and problems of composition. In *Encounter* Jonathan Raban appends a short description of *Ending Up*, in which he finds Amis's pessimism overwhelmed by the force of his good humour, to his longer consideration of Anthony Burgess's two latest novels. In *MFS*, R. Rabinovitz explores the question of the relationship between style and obscurity in Beckett's early fiction. Jennie Skerl examines in *ConL* the use Samuel Beckett makes of Fritz Mauthner's 'critique of language' in *Watt* and argues that the influence of Wittgenstein and of logical positivism is less important in that novel. In *JNT* Brian Wicker examines how, as we study the course of Beckett's development, 'we are privileged to see what happens when the sanity and poise not only of the fictional world, but of the narrator himself is lost'. He sees the death of the god-narrator as closely linked to Beckett's terror of a world in which 'there is no more nature'. Allan Rodway uses Alvarez's book on Beckett as the starting point in an article in *Encounter* for some observations intended to deflate excessive regard for Beckett's progressive paring-down of literary content and form, which he regards as a symbolist trap, destructive of art.

To write a biography of Arnold Bennett would seem a massive and daunting prospect, fraught with difficulties: he is after all his own best commentator in the numerous Journals, and he led (except for the war years) a rather uneventful life. All the tennis-parties, the preoccupation with good food, even the financial dealings over his publications, hardly merit the epithet 'dramatic'. The quintessential living happened in the hours of composition, and that is a kind of life that is immensely difficult to convey as exciting to anyone who is not an author. This is the task Margaret Drabble[17] set herself, and she has succeeded. She has of course some considerable advantages: she comes, as she admits, from the same kind of background, and she has had a life-long enthusiasm for Bennett's work. With her interest as a novelist herself in the formative influences that background has on development, and her sympathy for Bennett's craftsman-like dedication to his writing, she has triumphed over all the problems and produced a biography that reads curiously like the kind of novel Bennett might have written if he had decided to write the life of a man like himself. The greatest service Miss Drabble pays her subject lies in her incidental comments on her quotations from his work, that call attention to the precise observations and the imaginative engagement, to the masterly control of prose, to all the novelistic qualities that Bennett's adverse critics have tended to ignore. In her introduction, Miss Drabble describes Bennett as the least boring of people because he had a profound sense of life as 'full of possibility'. This is not a conventional view of Bennett in critical circles; but it is one that Miss Drabble effectively substantiates.

Andrew Mylett has collected together and edited all of Bennett's 'Books and Persons' articles for the *Evening Standard* written between 1926 and 1931.[18] They reveal Bennett as a critic of considerable stature, even when one has taken into account the eye-catching style that he frequently adopted in his journalism. He was confident that his was 'a

[17] *Arnold Bennett. A Biography*, by Margaret Drabble. Weidenfeld & Nicolson. pp. xii+397. £4.95.
[18] *Arnold Bennett: The 'Evening Standard' Years*, ed. with an introduction by Andrew Mylett. Chatto & Windus. pp. xxviii+481. £6.50.

period of quite unusually good authorship, a period which will compare well with any previous period'. While his reservations are expressed with some fierceness (though more frequently about writers of the past than his contemporaries) his encouragement of new writing was kindly and considerate: Graham Greene, Evelyn Waugh, Henry Williamson, Richard Hughes, and Ivy Compton-Burnett all met with his approval. The range of writers and subjects reviewed is impressive. Since he gained such popularity through his column in the *Standard*, the collection is an invaluable guide to taste in the period: it is notable to find him vindicating the novels of Lawrence, Huxley, Joyce, and Faulkner, for example, or writing passionately about the superiority of Russian fiction to English and French, for a readership that would not for the most part consider itself intellectual. John Lucas, in his book about Bennett,[19] is passionate and, though often very personal, largely convincing in his claim for the serious reconsideration of Bennett's best novels, and in his exposition of their excellencies. He considers Bennett's writing chronologically, pointing out the influence of the realist tradition and showing the sources of both successes and failures in the novels. In *Encounter* P. N. Firbank reviews Margaret Drabble's *Arnold Bennett*, and describes his own sense of the novelist's personality and attitudes in his work.

G. T. Davenport suggests how central the civilization of the Irish big house was as a source of inspiration for Elizabeth Bowen in *SHR*.

Geoffrey Aggeler participates in Anthony Burgess's game with words and Will by pointing out to us in

N&Q a prophetic acrostic which occurs in the third chapter of *Nothing Like the Sun*; he contributes a longer discussion of one of Burgess's themes, the opposition of Pelagian liberals and Augustinian conservatives, to *ES*. William Fitzpatrick, writing in *WVUPP* on 'Black Marketeers and Manichees: Anthony Burgess's Cold War Novels', has the more ambitious intention of placing Burgess's novels in relation to his contemporaries and in a scale of critical evaluation; he discusses them in terms of their concentration upon fundamental issues of good and evil. Jonathan Raban is also concerned with placing Burgess in his discussion in *Encounter* of *The Clockwork Testament* and *Napoleon Symphony*. He begins with the question 'Is he, in fact, really a novelist at all?' and concludes that he is 'a crippled great novelist'.

The greatly acclaimed first part of Hilary Spurling's biography of Ivy Compton Burnett[20] appeared this year, and was greeted (for instance by P. N. Firbank in *Encounter*) with the praise it deserves. Exhaustive biographical and literary research is presented to the fascinated reader with unfailing clarity and sympathy. It is obvious from the novels themselves that the early years of Ivy Compton-Burnett's life, and in particular her life with her family, were crucial in the creation of the world of her fiction; and Hilary Spurling has made that period available to us in a wealth of detail. To the analysis of the author's early life and her character is added a critical discussion of *Dolores* which promises well for the next volume of the biography, which is bound to include more critical material. Marlene R. Hansen explores the Victorian

---

[19] *Arnold Bennett: A Study of His Fiction*, by John Lucas. Methuen. pp. 235. £4.60.

[20] *Ivy When Young: The Early Life of Ivy Compton Burnett 1884–1919*, by Hilary Spurling. Gollancz. pp. 319. £3.80.

character of the settings of Ivy Compton Burnett's novels in *ES*, incidentally substantiating our impresson that they are set in the author's childhood.

In 'Speaking out of both sides of *The Horse's Mouth*' in *ConL*, Alvin J. Seltzer reviews criticism of Joyce Cary's work, and sees the conflict of views he finds there as indicating Cary's own ambivalence. He argues that such an ambivalence, demanding both order and freedom, is a legitimate moral stance, though it is one which has puzzled critics. By way of marking his centenary, R. C. Churchill offers some reflections upon G. K. Chesterton's life in *ContempR*.

This year John Murray and Jonathan Cape issued five volumes in the *Sherlock Holmes Collected Edition*.[21] The format is stylish and nicely period; and the introductions include some interesting brief contributions to the critical consideration of the Holmes saga. Eric Ambler confines himself largely to personal reminiscence about the consequences of first reading the Holmes stories. C. P. Snow argues convincingly that the stories are Doyle's masterpieces, because in them his remarkable romantic imagination was tied down (as it was not in his historical novels, by commitment to the concrete facts of the London he saw about him. Kingsley Amis praises the stories' virtues of pace and economy, and the

subtle narrative uses of the Holmes/Watson relationship, an aspect of their success which Julian Symons analyses more fully, and Angus Wilson also includes in his sketch of the development of the Holmes figure as time passed.

Three full-length studies of Conrad have appeared this year. In *The Modern Imagination*,[22] C. B. Cox examines Conrad's preoccupation with suicide and exile to illustrate his thesis that Conrad's finest fiction is that which courageously faces up to modern man's constant and impossible dilemma of choice between disillusionment and commitment. Cox sees all Conrad's innovations of form in the novels as motivated by his determination to oppose the nihilism that afflicts the modern mind and even to quest for a meaning throughout an apparently meaningless universe. A pattern recurs in the major fictions of a romantic hero whose self-confidence is undermined less by the traditional temptations of the flesh than by an overwhelming imaginative response to the absurd universe he inhabits and against which he must struggle to create an order of personal values, the values of trust, of care for the suffering and afflicted, of honest service. Conrad's own heroism is seen in his enduring faith in art as a means of recording honestly man's determination to resist the attractions of despair. In contrast with Professor Cox's study, David Thorburn[23] argues that it is Conrad's imaginative roots in English Romanticism and his reliance on Romantic modes of story-telling that account for his stoical concern for human sharing in opposition to modern tendencies towards

[21] *The Adventures of Sherlock Holmes*, by Arthur Conan Doyle, intro. by Eric Ambler. pp. 317. £2.95; *The Casebook of Sherlock Holmes*, by Arthur Conan Doyle, intro. by C. P. Snow. pp. 261. £2.50; *The Memoirs of Sherlock Holmes*, by Arthur Conan Doyle, intro. by Kingsley Amis. pp. 266. £2.50; *The Return of Sherlock Holmes*, by Arthur Conan Doyle, intro. by Angus Wilson. pp. 344. £2.95; and *His Last Bow*, by Arthur Conan Doyle, intro. by Julian Symons. pp. 212. £2.50.

[22] *Joseph Conrad: The Modern Imagination*, by C. B. Cox. Dent. pp. vii+191. £3.75.
[23] *Conrad's Romanticism*, by David Thorburn. New Haven and London: Yale U.P. pp. xvi+201. £4.50.

alienation and nausea with life. To substantiate his thesis, Professor Thorburn begins his study with a close analysis of the autobiographical books and *Romance*, the fruit of Conrad's collaboration with Madox Ford. He then uses this material as a context in which to show how the major works avoid qualities that are characteristic of a debased fin-de-siècle Romanticism, qualities which he describes as a simplistic primitivism and bogus melodrama. The most interesting passages in the book occur where Thorburn makes comparisons between Conrad and Wordsworth, especially concerning their use of narrators and styles of narration.

Professor Saveson has continued his research into the subject of morality in Conrad's fiction which he began with his fine study, *The Making of a Moralist* in 1972, by focusing now on the novels written after *Lord Jim*. The study[24] begins with an introduction defining the special qualities of Conrad's fiction in this period and the factors making for the steady displacement of topical subjects by more abstract and philosophical themes, which evolved out of the author's growing preoccupation with Nietzschean thought. Conrad's stance in relation to Nietzsche is then defined through comparisons and contrasts with Ford, Wells, and Galsworthy. In the second part of the study, Saveson uses this material as a context for a new interpretation of *Under Western Eyes*, *Chance*, and *Victory*. The last of these chapters is the most challenging, where Saveson argues that the novel is a fictional equivalent of Nietzsche's polemic against the ascetic ideal and that on these terms it must be judged as Conrad's finest achievement, even

though there are unresolved tensions in *Victory* between the claims of realism and those of allegory. A short postcript examines Conrad's use of classical mythology in this novel.

Everyman Paperbacks have reissued five volumes of Conrad's novels and stories with introductions by C. B. Cox and Norman Sherry.[25] Cox, writing of *Youth, Heart of Darkness*, and *The End of the Tether*, sees the tales as revealing the conflict in Conrad's personality between the exhilarated energetic mariner and the moody, despairing artist. *Heart of Darkness* is in his view a masterpiece because it confronts beneath the surface realism the dark realities of the psyche and achieves the status of myth. The remaining volumes are all edited by Professor Sherry. *The Nigger of the 'Narcissus'* is shown by him to be carefully contrived by Conrad to present a 'microcosmographical picture of human society' and a symbolic interpretation of man's insignificance against the perspective of the universe. *Typhoon* is judged to be a lesser work because its concern is exclusively with character rather than with the rigorous inquiry into the metaphysical and social condition of man that is the mark of Conrad's greatest fiction. In writing of *Nostromo*, Sherry develops this judgement further, concluding that this novel is a panoramic vision of the limited security that is possible for any man. He outlines too the influences on

[24] *Conrad, The Later Moralist*, by John Saveson. Amsterdam: Rodopi N.V. pp. 129.

[25] *Youth, Heart of Darkness and The End of the Tether*, by Joseph Conrad, ed. with an introduction by C. B. Cox. Dent. pp. xxii + 343. £0.75. *The Nigger of the 'Narcissus', Typhoon, Falk and other stories*, by Joseph Conrad, ed. by Norman Sherry. Dent. pp. xvii + 296. £0.60. *Nostromo*, by Joseph Conrad, ed. by Norman Sherry. Dent. pp. xi + 581. £0.75. *The Secret Agent*, by Joseph Conrad, ed. by Norman Sherry. Dent. pp. xxix + 333. £0.50. *Lord Jim*, by Joseph Conrad, ed. by Norman Sherry. Dent. pp. xxii + 327. £0.50.

the work and some of the principal sources for background material; traces parallels with other stories by Conrad in order to define the unique treatment that certain character-types and situations receive in this novel; and shows how the method of the novel and its preoccupation with time creates the central ironic view of history as a cycle constantly being formed and reformed by men 'whose actions, though at the time apparently significant, are formed by the past . . . and which are constantly working for the erosion of what is being achieved'. *The Secret Agent* is interpreted by Sherry as a black comedy of a grim city-world that is not as safe as it prides itself with being but is a living hell. The special tone of this novel, he argues, is the result of Conrad's perfecting of a brilliant form of caricature to depict his view of a world devoid of sympathetic imagination, an Inferno, whose inhabitants horrify the reader for their lack of awareness of their fellow-sufferers' pain. With *Lord Jim*, Sherry again examines the theme of time and its relation to the structure of the novel, to show how, though it partakes of the nature of an inquiry, there can be no logical steps towards an inevitable and precise conclusion. He offers an extensive analysis of Jim's character as a man of typically English ideals who is destroyed by his own imagination for disaster. The edition is completed with a set of notes on the sources for the novel and an account of Conrad's methods during its composition.

Several perceptive short studies relating to Conrad appear in *SSF*. Diana Culbertson contributes a note on *The Informer* as 'Conrad's little joke'; D. M. Martin offers a note on 'the paradox of perspectivism' in *The Lagoon* and also examines in a second essay the final scene with the Intended in *Heart of Darkness* to show how crucial it is to any interpretation of the story. (The same incident is the subject of an essay by B. R. Stark in *TSLL*.) D. M. Walsh writes on the way that Genesis is central to our understanding of *Typhoon* and J. H. Weston argues that *Youth* marks a significant turning-point in Conrad's development in its ironic assumption that 'no view of life is final because any view is the projected image of a particular self'. This idea of the 'open-endedness' of Conrad's fiction is explored by Norman Sherry in *E&S*: 'There is, because of the method', he argues, 'a sense of men doing what they have to do and of there being little point in moral judgement afterwards'. Theo Steimann in *ES* interprets *The Nigger of the 'Narcissus'* as a perverting of the fictional and moral patterns of Melville's *Billy Budd*; while in *N&Q*, C. Wegelin writes on some points of resemblance between Conrad and Faulkner. W. R. Martin in *ESA* defines why he believes *Under Western Eyes* to be written in the Russian manner. The novel shows how 'Western security and political virtues are precarious and perhaps . . . even doubtful advantages'. In *TSLL*, E. Hollahan analyzes the themes of silence and of sound in *Victory* to elucidate the force and meaning of the novel. *Conradiana* was not available for detailed review.

In a long article in *TSLL* Thomas C. Moser prints, with commentary and explanation, sections from the diary of Olive Garnett for the years 1890–1906. The extracts he uses include all the substantive references to Conrad and James in the diary, as well as much material about Ford Madox Ford and his early writing career.

The latest addition to the Abinger E. M. Forster is *Aspects of the*

Novel.[26] In his introduction, Oliver Stallybrass describes the circumstances of Forster's receiving and accepting the invitation to give the Clark Lectures in 1927; he quotes extensively from Forster's letters at this time to show how he set about preparing the series of talks and gives first-hand responses of two academics, George Rylands and F. R. Leavis, who attended their delivery. He concludes with an account of the response of Forster's contemporaries to the publication of the lectures as a book and comments on the strengths and limitations of Forster's methods of criticism. The volume includes a valuable number of appendices giving extracts from Forster's Commonplace Book at this time showing how the ideas for certain lectures or critical stances took shape; Forster's review from the *Daily News* in 1919 of Clayton Hamilton's *Materials and Methods of Fiction* and the relevant passages from Hamilton's book for comparison with Forster's viewpoint; and the text of the BBC talk for the Eastern Service entitled *The Art of Fiction*. There are also textual notes and an annotated index.

Two short studies of *Maurice* have appeared in journals this year: Joyce Hotchkiss in *JNT* shows how Forster's concern in the novel to explore conflicting modes of coping with life is paralleled by tensions within his narrative style between what she terms his 'plain' and his 'elevated' styles of expression; and in *SSF*, J. S. Malek sees the tale 'Albergo Empedocle' as a precursor of *Maurice*. J. T. Boulton writes about an unpublished paper entitled 'Three Generations' which Forster gave at University College, Nottingham in

1939, in *N&Q*; Evelynne Hanquart describes her findings on reading the manuscripts of *The Longest Journey* in *RES*; and in *LMag*, Jeffrey Meyers analyzes the significance of the paintings referred to in the Italian novels.

A. A. De Vitis and William J. Palmer discuss the influence of Hardy upon John Fowles, and in particular the debt of *The French Lieutenant's Woman* to *A Pair of Blue Eyes*, in *ConL*. In *AWR*, Jacqueline Banerjee discusses Galsworthy's development as a novelist, observing a decline in power and truth in his writing as he gave up the 'dangerous experiment' of writing about human passions and fell back upon 'pickling' a section of society for the contemplation of his readers.

J. S. Ryan writes in *ES* about Golding's first three published works and their literary antecedants: he briefly reviews the connexions between *The Lord of the Flies* and *Coral Island*; and between *The Inheritors* and H. G. Wells's rationalist ideas about Neandertal man expressed in his *Outline of History* and the short story *The Grisly Folk*, before concentrating upon his contention that *Pincher Martin* is based upon *Pincher Martin O.D.* by 'Taffrail', Commander Taprell Dorling, D.S.O.

In *Renascence*, D. Heyward Brock and James M. Welsh defend the right of *The Power and the Glory* to the fullest consideration as art, rather than dismissal as propaganda, and Michael Routh discusses *The Comedians* as a book which parodies the genres of farce and comedy, as other novels by Graham Greene parody melodramas and thrillers, for a serious purpose. A. F. Cassis explores Graham Greene's use of the dream as a literary device in his novels, tracing its development as the

[26] *The Abinger Edition of E. M. Forster*, ed. by Oliver Stallybrass. Edward Arnold. Volume 12: *Aspects of the Novel and Related Writings.* pp. xvii + 169. £5.25.

novelist's interest in the activity of the unconscious grew, in *L&P*.

The starting point from Anne Mulkeen's discussion of L. P. Hartley's novels[27] is the intention of exposing, beneath their reproduction of a limited and vanishing social experience, the 'myth' which their concern with 'The point of intersection of the timeless/With time . . .' shapes. The best novels are seen as combining realistic and symbolic genres, in an attempt to find literary expression for a sense of the cosmic which underlies the commonplace. In the course of the discussion, romances concerning the lives of middle class heroes and heroines are shown to be symbolic equivalents for the character and problems of the twentieth century, and in particular for its peculiar spiritual crisis.

Peter Thomas has chosen to concentrate in his study of Richard Hughes[28] on the ways in which Hughes's four novels have explored that 'confused area where instinct or "need" may so easily be rationalized into "principle"'. Thomas shows how Hughes delights in inverting the conventions of familiar forms and in opposing his 'Darwinian' view of Nature to the sentimental pieties and class assumptions of a muddled bourgeois society, in his early work. He argues that Hughes's development reveals a shedding of 'absurdist' beliefs in favour of a more mystical, even Christian viewpoint. Hughes's strength, he concludes, derives from his ability to shun current fashion yet find the true contemporary pulse. Most of this short study is devoted to the novels and stories, but there is an interesting discussion of the place of Hughes's poetry and drama in his development and some useful documenting of Hughes's reviews of the work of some of his contemporaries. Richard Poole contributes a discussion of irony and ironic methods in *High Wind in Jamaica* in *AWR*.

Sybille Bedford continues her masterly account of the life of Aldous Huxley in a second volume[29] which traces the years in which he quested for a state of self-transcendence after the death of his first wife, Maria. The first volume made one very conscious of the distinctions between Huxley the novelist and Huxley the private man, kind, warm, and compassionate. In these later years, as the writing became more preoccupied with the urgent need to find ways whereby twentieth-century man might redeem himself from his tragic, self-destructive impulses, the public man, the writer, the philosopher, the teacher, took on increasingly the warmer qualities of the man formerly known only by his family and closest friends. As with Volume One, the strength of Sybille Bedford's account lies in her refusal to impose any explanation or simplifying analysis on the facts. Unobtrusively she provides a context of information in which Huxley can reveal himself to the reader, through the lavish use of carefully selected quotation from his writings; crises in his life such as his reaction to Maria's death are presented through the accounts of several witnesses so that a sequence of perspectives is offered which allows the reader to reach intuitively after the truth. This discretion on Miss Bedford's part has the effect of creating frank, intimate involvement

[27] *Wild Thyme, Winter Lightning: the Symbolic Novels of L. P. Hartley*, by Anne Mulkeen. Hamish Hamilton. pp. xiv+193. £3.00.

[28] *Richard Hughes*, by Peter Thomas. U. of Wales P. pp. 103. £0.75.

[29] *Aldous Huxley, A Biography. Volume 2: 1939–1963*, by Sybille Bedford. Chatto & Windus. pp. xii+378. £4.50.

with the personality of the subject of a kind one normally experiences only with the best of autobiographies. Pierre Vitoux in *MLR* writes on the intellectual sympathy existing between Lawrence and Huxley and estimates the ways in which Lawrence decidedly influenced Huxley's development as a thinker and as a novelist. In 'Cancer in Utopia' (*DR*), Jerome Meckier defines the positive and negative elements in Huxley's *Island*.

Pamela Hansford Johnson's new book, *Important to Me*,[30] is not an autobiography, and does not tell us very much about the novelist, but it contains essays inspired by some of her personal experiences, and her recent thought. One episode recounted is her acquaintance with Ivy Compton-Burnett.

Professors Hart and Hayman have edited a valuable collection of essays on *Ulysses*,[31] in which eighteen scholars confront one of the eighteen chapters of the novel to examine the style, structure, and strategy of these divisions and to show the relationship of form and action to character development and dramatic conflict. The result places a refreshing emphasis on the naturalistic levels of the novel which are often overlooked in preference for more esoteric symbolic readings. All the contributors agree too on the affirmative quality of Joyce's vision in his concern with communion and renewal; many pass through a study of Joyce's technical experiments to find that while he 'bypasses the familiar conventions of nineteenth-century fiction' he none the less 'shows us another way

in which the novelist's passion for omniscience can be achieved without violating our sense of individual and local reality'. The book is really the first to approach Joyce's masterpiece from the standpoint of recent theorizing about the art of the novel and of narrative. In view of the nature of its composition, the collection is surprisingly uniform in its conclusions and even in quality; to single out particular chapters for special mention would be an unkindness in such a context, but the editors must be praised for following their original idea through to such a worthwhile volume.

Edward Quinn has devised an unusual anthology[32] from Joyce's works by attempting to capture through his photographs much of the mood and spirit of Joyce's descriptions of Dublin. This kind of presentation can easily degenerate into yet another pictorial biography but the illustrations here reveal how firmly Joyce's imaginative portraits of life in the city were rooted in a precise awareness of the actual, for all their verbal brilliance. The anthology allows one to appreciate at once the clarity of Joyce's observations and the uniqueness of his perception and so enhance one's understanding of his artistry.

Professor Ellmann's fine exposition of the total plan of *Ulysses*[33] reviewed in 1972 is now available in paperback.

A. E. McGuiness in *SSF* applies recent phenomenological theories concerning the relation of consciousness to environment to a study of *Dubliners*. J. H. Maddox analyzes

---

[30] *Important To Me: Personalia*, by Pamela Hansford Johnson. Macmillan. pp. 254. £3.95.

[31] *James Joyce's 'Ulysses': Critical Essays*, ed. by Clive Hart and David Hayman. Berkeley, Los Angeles, and London; California U.P. pp. xiv+433. $15.00.

[32] *James Joyce's Dublin* (with selected writings from Joyce's works), by Edward Quinn. Secker & Warburg. pp. 134 with 13 colour and 112 black and white photographs. £5.00.

[33] *Ulysses on the Liffey*, by Richard Ellmann. 1972. Revised paperback edition, 1974. Faber. pp. xviii+210. £1.50.

the device of distancing in the 'Eumaeus' chapter of *Ulysses* to show how it begins to reveal 'the eternal quality of Bloom's odyssey'. M. Lane contributes a 'synecdochic reading' of the 'wandering rocks' episode in *Ulysses* to *WHR*. Three essays on different aspects of experiment in this novel grace the Autumn number of *MFS*: P. Herring analyzes Joyce's experiments with landscape, the 'pornotopography' of *Ulysses*, as he calls it; Richard Pearce the experiments with the grotesque; and K. E. Moore Joyce's play with symbols in parts of the 'Ithaca' chapter. In the winter issue, Grace Eckley writes on Shem and Shaun in *Finnegans Wake*. In *ConL*, Philip Raisor assesses the importance of Joyce's reading of Naturalist writers on his theories and practice; and in *RLV*, G. Melchiori compares Eliot's 'metaphysical evasion' of history with Joyce's acceptance of it as the 'condition humaine', which brought him not to 'obsession but salvation, not nightmare but vision'.

In the first issue of *JJQ* 1973–4, Robert Scholes examines the author's theory of epiphanies in 'In Search of James Joyce'; J. V. D. Card argues that 'contradicting' is the best word to describe Molly as she appears in the last section of *Ulysses*; R. Billings and D. Zochert describe the critical controversy between Roscoe and Hecht in the *Daily News* and the *Chicago Tribune* over the *Ulysses* instalments that had appeared in *The Little Review*. J. MacNicholas explores *Exiles* and defends his view that it is anti-cathartic since the play itself argues for a state of doubt; and R. M. Scotto compares Pater's *Marius* with *A Portrait of the Artist*. The second issue opens with an account by N. Silverstein of the 4th International Joyce Symposium in June 1973; Richard Kain edits an interview he held with Carola Giedion-Welcker and Maria Jolas. W. P. Fitzpatrick offers a lengthy Jungian interpretation of *Ulysses* and its mythic patterns; and David Evans a study of Stephen's developing theory of literary kinds in relation to Croce's *Aesthetic*. There is too a supplemental checklist of Joyce publications for 1971. The Spring number contains recorded interviews with Benedict Kiely and Conor Cruise O'Brien; a critical study of O'Brien by the editor and new poems by Seamus Heaney inspired by *The Bog People*, subsequently published in *North*. J. C. Mays contributes a monograph on Brian O'Nolan's fiction and J. B. Lyons some timely animadversions on 'paralysis' as the central symbol of 'The Sisters'. John Garvin elucidates some allusions in *Finnegans Wake* and R. J. Finneran edits with an introduction some correspondence between Joyce and James Stephens. The fourth number is devoted entirely to articles on *Finnegans Wake*: Sean Kelly contributes a lampoon; Leo Knuth interprets the novel as distinctly a 'product of the Twenties'; David Hayman draws attention to the elements of farce, clowns, and clowning; M. C. Norris examines questions about the novel's structure from the standpoint of its use of the device of repetition; R. van Phul isolates passages which illuminate lyrics in *Chamber Music*. William Dohmen shows how Ondt is a satirical portrait of Wyndham Lewis, while M. Putz defines the relationship of the reader to the novel and E. McLuhan its rhetorical structures. Each issue continues to include short notes and reviews of recent Joyce criticism. The *Wake Newslitter* continues in publication.

After Robert Lucas's rather disappointing biography of Frieda Lawrence, reviewed last year, it is cheering to study Martin Green's double biography of Frieda and her sister Else.[34] Not only does this evoke the real forcefulness of Frieda's personality with conviction, but it also shows how close the two sisters were to most of the major figures who have affected the development of European culture today. The study is much more than a biography, since to read about the sisters is to discover much of the intellectual history of this century. Its value for the student of Lawrence is less for what it tells of Frieda's life (that after all has been well documented elsewhere in the biographies of her husband), but for what it reveals of the intellectual climate to which she introduced him after their elopement in 1912. The extent to which she helped to mould Lawrence into the great novelist he became can now be more easily assessed.

The Spring issue of *DHLR* contains a review-account by C. E. Baron of the Nottingham Festival's Lawrence exhibition in 1972 by way of preface to fifty illustrations from the catalogue, many of which relate particularly to *Sons and Lovers* or to the growth of his taste in art in his early Nottingham years. T. H. Adamowski defends Lawrence against charges of cant in examining the theme of 'otherness' in *The Rainbow*. T. Toyokuni contributes a short note on 'The Man Who Loved Islands'; Keith Cushman writes on John E. Baker and his Lawrence collection; and there is a checklist of criticism and scholarship for the year 1973. Daniel J. Schneider opens the summer issue with a study of the development of ever more complex patterns of symbolism in the fiction to define the

[34] *The von Richthofen Sisters: The Triumphant and the Tragic Modes of Love*, by Martin Green. Weidenfeld & Nicolson. pp. xiv + 396. £6.00.

health or sickness of the soul. W. J. Keith offers an account of the relationship between Lawrence and Rolf Gardiner, and Jeffrey Meyers a stimulating analysis of how Fra Angelico's painting of *The Last Judgement* recurs as a symbol throughout *The Rainbow* and helps to unify the novel's complex structure. Bryan Reddick examines the questions of point of view and narrative tone in *Women in Love* in relation to what he calls Lawrence's portrayal of interpsychic space. David Cavitch relates the themes explored in the poem 'Fish' to the novels and D. I. Janik analyzes *Twilight in Italy*. The issue concludes with a profile by Keith Cushman of John Martin and his Lawrence collection, and Charles Ross reviews Pritchard's *D. H. Lawrence: Body of Darkness* and Frank Kermode's recent study of the novelist in the Modern Masters Series in an article entitled 'Art and Metaphysic'. The Fall issue has an account by Helen Corke about the composition of *The Trespasser*; George Zytaruk edits Dorothy Brett's letters to Koteliansky; and Emile Delavenay and W. J. Keith have an 'exchange' on the subject of whether or not Rolf Gardiner can be described as a 'Neo-Nazi'. Homer O. Brown offers a discussion of the theme of the passionate struggle into conscious being of the characters in *The Rainbow*; Charles Rossman reviews three new studies on Lawrence by Kenneth Inniss, Keith Aldritt, and Stephen Miko; and Giles Mirchell three others by Calvin Bedient, John Paterson, and Richard Swigg. Finally R. M. Beirne transcribes Lawrence's night-letter sent to the publisher, Selzer, on censorship and obscenity, which Harry T. Moore failed to include in his edition of the *Collected Letters*.

Evelyn J. Hinz writes in *DR* of the

significance that Canada held in Lawrence's imagination as 'the place where liberated beings may go to live their liberated lives'. Both *The White Peacock* and *Lady Chatterley's Lover* see Canada as the 'new world' of infinite possibilities. Sibyl Jacobson discusses *Women in Love*, under the title 'The Paradox of Fulfilment', in *JNT*. T. Fritz perceives some interesting relationships between 'The Rocking Horse Winner' and *The Golden Bough* in a note in *SSF*. *RMS* features two articles on Lawrence: J. T. Boulton edits and introduces a previously uncollected essay on the novelist by W. H. Roberts entitled 'Study of a Free Spirit in Literature' which was first published with Lawrence's knowledge in the *Millgate Monthly* of May 1928. Later in this issue, Eleanor Green examines the influence of Nietzsche's political ideas on Lawrence's conceptions of Utopia. John Doheny reviews *John Thomas and Lady Jane* and compares it with *Lady Chatterley's Lover* in *WCR*, while in *WHR*, R. M. Burrell presents a new interpretation of *Sons and Lovers* arguing that 'in this assumption of innate individuality, manifest in *Sons and Lovers* and in the Hardy study, Lawrence is using—perhaps unconsciously—Schopenhauer's condition of modern tragedy'. In *UTQ*, T. H. Adamovski compares and contrasts attitudes to the relationship between character and consciousness in the ideas of Lawrence, Reich, and Sartre. In 'The Greatness in *Sons and Lovers*' (*MP*), J. A. Taylor shows 'how aware Lawrence himself was . . . of the cost of abandoning a mode which he himself considered essentially novelistic, and in which he knew his natural genius lay'. David Kleinbad argues that Laing's concept of ontological insecurity can illuminate our understanding of the characterization of *The Rainbow* and *Women*

in Love*, especially of Will Brangwen. In 'Lyrical Elements in D. H. Lawrence's *The Rainbow*' in *RLV*, V. Raddatz shows how careful Lawrence was 'not to violate the feelings he wanted to express or the language he wanted to use for that purpose'. In *MR*, Janice Harris challenges Kate Millet's attack on Lawrence in *Sexual Politics*; while Lawrence's struggles with Christianity are the subject of an essay in *DR* by C. J. Terry.

ContempR prints a previously unpublished letter from T. E. Lawrence to Herbert Louis Samuel, recently rediscovered by his son Edwin Samuel. James Gindin in *ConL* revalues the work of Rosamund Lehmann, arguing that her strength lies less in her books about childhood than those 'adult' novels which explore her own version of her time and place. Her evocation through suggestive descriptions of life in the Thirties and Forties will, in Gindin's view, be the source of her enduring appeal. In *JNT*, Nancy Joyner analyzes *The Golden Notebook* in relation to *To the Lighthouse* to point out specific debts Doris Lessing owes to Virginia Woolf while carefully discriminating between the aesthetic and philosophical principles of the two writers. Alice Bradley Markow analyzes Lessing's work in *Crit* in terms of a recurring theme: the etiology of feminine 'failure'. Dennis Porter is concerned in *MLQ* with a similar idea: he discusses *The Golden Notebook*'s use of the form of the novel to explore the failure of the modern, detached critical consciousness to come to terms with external realities.

There have been a number of books about C. S. Lewis this year. Three are primarily biographical. The most authoritative, but still, the writers stress, *a* biography rather than *the* biography, is by Roger Lancelyn Green and Walter Hooper.[35] It concentrates largely upon Lewis's adult years, in order to avoid too much overlap with *Surprised by Joy*. Literary criticism is not attempted, nor indeed is any critical analysis of the events recounted, which forms a readable if perhaps rather reverent account of the author's life and his spiritual history. *The Secret Country of C. S. Lewis*[36] is a life apparently intended for the young reader, and therefore spends much more time upon Lewis's youth. Anne Arnott tends to handle the material from *Surprised by Joy* with rather a self-conscious eye upon her audience using, for instance, the names Chartres and Wyvern for no particularly good reason, and generally stepping gingerly round Lewis's own accounts of the miseries of his school days. The biographical element of *C. S. Lewis: Images of his World*[37] is confined to brief introductory notes, which draw upon some previously unpublished letters, to preface a series of photographs of people, places, and scenes associated (sometimes a little remotely) with Lewis's life. One bibliographical volume has appeared, *C. S. Lewis: An Annotated Checklist of Writings about Him and His Works*,[38] which lists and describes secondary material for the study of Lewis published up to June 1972. The divisions of the material are clear, and the scope wide, including

sections on, for example, books about George Macdonald, and 'society and education', which mention Lewis. The long section VI lists and often quotes from reviews of Lewis's works. *Bright Shadow of Reality*[39] is the only full-scale critical work to have appeared. It is said on the jacket to be 'theological literary criticism'. The subject of the study is C. S. Lewis's 'theory of *Sehnsucht*, or the "dialectic of desire"', which the author seeks to define, in his own words and in terms of Lewis's critical usage. He distinguishes *sehnsucht* from romanticism and mysticism, with both of which it has common ground, and broadens the concept from that of simple nostalgia to cover all the experiences which arise from the sense of alienation and longing for reunion. He proceeds to examine Lewis's early life and work, moving towards the definition of this all-embracing idea, and sees his later work as a triumphant embodiment of it. In an interesting article in *MFS*, Kathryn Hume discusses C. S. Lewis's trilogy in terms of structure and organization, each book being considered as a romance or an extension of the romance and the three together as an interlocking structure which can also be regarded as having a romance pattern as well as allegorical and mythical design. *The C. S. Lewis Bulletin* continues to appear but was not available for comment.

Professor Bradbrook has the good fortune to be Malcolm Lowry's exact contemporary and to have known both the region of the Wirral in which he was brought up and Cambridge in the Thirties, where they both read English. This makes her an eminently suitable biographer of his

[35] *C. S. Lewis: A Biography*, by Roger Lancelyn Green and Walter Hooper. Collins. pp. 320. £3,50.

[36] *The Secret Country of C. S. Lewis*, by Anne Arnott. Hodder & Stoughton. pp. 127. £1.60.

[37] *C. S. Lewis: Images of his World*, by Douglas Gilbert and Clyde S. Kilby. Hodder & Stoughton (1973). pp. 192. £4.50.

[38] *C. S. Lewis: An Annotated Checklist of Writings about Him and His Works*, by Joe R. Christopher and Joan K. Ostling. Kent State U.P. pp. xiv+393. $15.00.

[39] *Bright Shadow of Reality: C. S. Lewis and the Feeling Intellect*, by Corbin Scott Carnell. Michigan: William B. Eerdmans. pp. 180. $2.95.

early years but the fascination of her study[40] is that she is not content with this accomplishment but develops on from this a critical interpretation of the work showing the precise relevance of these backgrounds to Lowry's achievement as an artist. His strange and idiosyncratic life and his private obsessions she sees as the consequences of the difficult choice he felt compelled to make between 'perfection of the life or of the work'. With consummate subtlety she explores that most difficult of critical fields—the relation between autobiography and fiction—to achieve, for all the seeming brevity of her study, a remarkably comprehensive exposition of the novels, that elucidates much of the imagery, range of reference, climate of opinion, and background that can confuse a reader embarking on a first study of Lowry's work, while leaving ample room in which an individual experience of the novels can flourish. This fine book concludes with a summary of Lowry's letter to Jonathan Cape defending *Under the Volcano* and the texts of two early stories, 'A Rainy Night' and 'Satan in a Barrel', that were first published in the Leys School magazine, *The Fortnightly*. In *MFS*, Richard K. Cross compares the symbolism and the unfinished structures of *Under the Volcano* and *Moby Dick*.

A detailed obituary by P. Gueguen of Compton Mackenzie appears in the summer issue of *EA* in the form of a short critical biography, a bibliography of his principal works, and some personal notes by Anne Louis-David. Katherine Mansfield's methods of characterizing the Boss in 'The Fly' form the subject of a note

by P. M. Michot in *SSF*, while in *TCL*, Philip Waldron examines her *Journal*. In *N&Q* Waldron also writes about a poem of Katherine Mansfield's which Murry transcribed inaccurately for the *Collected Poems*.

The Pattern of Maugham[41] does not claim to be a biography, or confine itself to critical study, asserting, with some justice, that Maugham himself deliberately discouraged a full biography by the destruction of source-materials, but that critical assessment of his works cannot ignore aspects of his life. In particular, consideration of the facts of the life and the work together is demanded to disperse the critical disapproval of Maugham's contemporaries, who were suspicious of his material success and the polished, and perhaps shallow, professionalism which supported it. Mr Curtis confronts this problem. His analysis is not perhaps sufficiently searching to convince us that he has entirely solved it, but he does succeed in establishing a valuable new perspective, showing the tension between art and professional success as a fruitful one in Maugham's work. This is a valuable survey of all the many aspects of Maugham's activity. John Whitheed suggests in *N&Q* that the term 'whodunit' was taken from Somerset Maugham's short story 'The Creative Impulse', published in *Harper*'s in 1926.

Iris Murdoch[42] by Frank Baldanza is an account of the novels determinedly simple in vocabulary and structure, progressing through 'the background' treated under headings such as 'IV. Characters' and 'VI. Thematic Content' to serial description of each novel from *Under the Net* to *A*

---

[40] *Malcolm Lowry: His Art and Early Life —a Study in Transformation*, by Muriel Bradbrook. Cambridge U.P. pp. xiii+170. £2.50.

[41] *The Pattern of Maugham: A Critical Portrait*, by Anthony Curtis. Hamish Hamilton. pp. ix+278. £3.50.

[42] *Iris Murdoch*, by Frank Baldanza. New York: Twayne. pp. 187. $6.95.

Fairly Honourable Defeat, concluding with a return to the initial categorization in terms of 'crystalline' structures and 'transcendental realism.'

Two contributions to *SSF* this year analyze tales by Flannery O'Connor: D. R. Mayer sees 'A Temple of the Holy Ghost' as an apologia for the Imagination; and J. R. Millichap argues that 'The Comforts of Home' offers a Calvinistic view of man constrained by his human heritage. A. A. Hampton offers a study of the visual and aural effects in Liam O'Flaherty's stories to *ES*.

A volume on George Orwell has been added to the Twentieth Century Views series.[43] It begins with a penetrating essay by the editor on the peculiar nature of the study which the works of Orwell demand of the critic, which is partly determined by the fact that most of his books, and particularly *Animal Farm* and *1984*, were themselves political acts, and became the centres of political controversy. The essays here selected from the various periods and phases of Orwell criticism are therefore interesting, and were often controversial, for their own sakes as well as for their assessment of Orwell's work. They include, for example, essays by Lionel Trilling and Isaac Deutscher which are two of the earliest responses to the political controversy. So that perspective and some sense of the reality of Orwell's own work are possible for the reader, the essays are so arranged that they deal with Orwell's development chronologically, and do not allow the late books and their ideas to cast a distorting backward shadow. Illuminating contrasts of attitude and interpretation can be found throughout the collection which also includes essays by Terry Eagleton, Richard

Hoggart, E. P. Thompson, John Wain, and Conor Cruise O'Brien.

Orwell and the Left, by Alex Zwerdling,[44] is one of the broad, biographical / socio-political / literary studies of the author which Raymond Williams's essay suggested was essential. It is an examination of Orwell's political development and significance, which begins with the thesis that Orwell was an internal critic of socialism, in himself a kind of loyal opposition within the left, in the Thirties. Where others rejected the prevalent Marxist demand for relevance in art and therefore turned away from the left, or submitted to the writing of propaganda until they realized that the revolution which would free them from such a demand was not in fact at hand, Orwell, as a serious and permanently committed socialist, fought against the debasement of art as well as its divorce from political purpose. From this proposition, Zwerdling goes on to examine Orwell's claim to serious consideration as a socialist thinker in his own right, capable of bearing a significant part in conflicts which shaped socialism, and to consider the impact of his developing political ideas upon his writing including his novels. In *CritQ*, Donald Crompton contributes an interesting discussion of Orwell's early novels and biographical writings, tracing their disturbing interrelation and the transformation of fact into fiction which is not confined · to the avowedly fictional works. In *Encounter*, Eric Homberger briefly considers the most recent criticism of Orwell, particularly Alan Sandison's *The Last Man in Europe*, with a warning that writers are apt to reform Orwell in their own image.

John Batchelor has written[45] a cool

[43] *George Orwell: A Collection of Critical Essays*, ed. by Raymond Williams. New Jersey: Prentice Hall. pp. vii + 182. $2.45.

[44] *Orwell and the Left*, by Alex Zwerdling. Yale U.P. pp. xii + 215. £5.00.

[45] *Mervyn Peake: A Biographical and*

and formal account of Mervyn Peake's literary works, treating them serially and making full use of such manuscripts as are available, which he prefaces with a sketch of the formative elements of Peake's life and the circumstances of his writing. *A World Away* has clearly, for Mr Batchelor, pre-empted any exploration of or dwelling upon the strains and tragedies of his subject's life. He provides clear, factual information for the student of the novels and stories before moving on to his descriptive and critical study, which is also remarkable for its analytical detachment.

There is a note to the effect that the University of California, Berkeley, has acquired a collection of Somerville and Ross first editions in *Bancroftiana*. In *ELT*, Shirley Rose writes on Dorothy Richardson's preoccupations with time and its effects on the individual consciousness in its quest for knowledge of the self. Margot Peters and Agate Newaule Krouse briefly consider the detective fiction of Dorothy Sayers in *SWR*, alongside that of Margery Allingham and Agatha Christie, finding in all three women a sexist antifeminism.

Duckworth's have reissued the *Collected Stories* of Osbert Sitwell[46] with a perceptive introduction by Francis King, which defines the nature of Sitwell's satire and wit, comments on the professionalism and the diversity of his art, his craftsmanlike dedication of writing, and, a surprising but just insight this, the extent of his knowledge and sympathy for just the kind of people, lower-middle-class, humdrum, and

unintellectual, from which one might have expected his upbringing to have kept him distant.

Peter Kemp begins his study of Muriel Spark's novels[47] by defining her aesthetic of fiction in relation to the work of the three writers that she claims have most influenced her: Newman, Beerbohm, and Proust. He goes on to challenge the orthodox view of her work as elegant jokes by examining the disturbing qualities that underlie all her wit and powers to entertain: the astringency of her moral discriminations; her concern with self-scrutiny as man's only guard against the dangers of sloth; her unwillingness to find simple answers to the predicaments she explores. She does not resolve an issue, he remarks perceptively, with a decisive 'therefore' but invariably qualifies it with a more challenging 'nevertheless'. This is the source of her special kind of irony. Kemp then examines the novels in chronological order to show how her particular style of 'rich austerity' has steadily grown.

To celebrate Frank Swinnerton's ninetieth birthday this year, Hutchinson have reissued eight of his most popular novels: *Death of a Highbrow, Rosalind Passes, September, The Two Wives, The Bright Lights, On the Shady Side, Elizabeth,* and *Nor All Thy Tears*. Themes which recur in the novels—the special tensions of a friendship between fellow-writers or artists; the life of Fleet Street; the successful author in decline as death approaches—and his rich enjoyment of social comedy—help to explain the enduring appeal and value of his critical work, *The Georgian Literary Scene,* which Hutchinson are now offering in their Radius paperback

---

Critical Exploration, by John Batchelor. Duckworth. pp. 176. £3.95.

[46] *Collected Stories*, by Osbert Sitwell, with an introduction by Francis King. Duckworth. pp. xxiv + 541. £6.50.

[47] *Muriel Spark*, by Peter Kemp. Paul Elek. pp. 167. £3.50.

series.[48] Swinnerton's personal knowledge of the publishing world and his acquaintance with most of the authors about whom he is writing give this a freshness and vitality lacking in most current literary histories of the period, however carefully they may be researched.

The second instalment of Geoffrey Trease's autobiography, following *A Whiff of Burnt Boats*, and beginning at the outbreak of the Second World War, when his first adult novel *Such Divinity* had just appeared, has now been published.[49] Covering his life until he became a grandfather, and giving the impression that he has no more to say about himself, it is a pleasant book about a very English sort of life, modestly and entertainingly told, and providing some personal background to a novelist who has been one of the most successful and prolific of writers for children.

In the summer issue of *EA*, J.-L. Chevalier edits a brief correspondence between Henry Treece and Denton Welch about the embarrassing narcissism and amoral erotics of the latter's fiction. There has been less Tolkein material available for comment this year. In *Haythrop Journal*, William Dowie demonstrates that *The Lord of the Rings* is a deeply religious work because it plunges into the 'sacrality of the natural'.

In *To the War with Waugh*,[50] John St John describes his friendship with Waugh whom he first met on joining the Royal Marines; much of their shared experience at this time found its way into *Put Out More Flags* and the *Sword of Honour* trilogy. It was during this period of basic training and of the attack on Dakar that Waugh encountered the individuals who inspired some of his richest characterizations. The book is largely a memoir of course and not literary criticism, but some judicious quotations from the novels which are given alongside the actual events allow one to infer much about Waugh's artistry. The book is illustrated with a quantity of witty line-drawings by Peter MacKarell and there is an introduction by Christopher Hollis, who argues that Mr St. John 'does not quite sufficiently draw the distinction between his [Waugh's] earlier mood of enthusiasm and the later cynicism about the British cause', when the price of safety meant the betrayal of what he deemed all civilized values. Jeffrey M. Heath has written two articles on Evelyn Waugh: in *ArielE*, he considers *Men at Arms* and *The Ordeal of Gilbert Pinfold*, showing the theological and psychological links between the characteristic motifs of Waugh's fiction; and in *ES* he describes and comments upon the manuscript of *Decline and Fall*. In *English*, B. W. Wilson examines the metaphor of the chivalrous crusader which Waugh uses in *Sword of Honour*, showing how it reflects facets of historical allusion, literary parody, and wry social comment.

Denton Welch by Robert Phillips[51] has a claim to be the first full-length study of his works, and follows the usual pattern of TEAS publications: a biography of the writer (in this case, of course, an unhappy story of a brief life), followed by a carefully basic account of each of his writings, described and analyzed according to themes, influences, and symbolic structure.

[48] *The Georgian Literary Scene: 1910–1935*, by Frank Swinnerton. Radius Books. Hutchinson. pp. x+405. £1.25.

[49] *Laughter at the Door, A Continued Autobiography*, by Geoffrey Trease. Macmillan. pp. 186. £3.50.

[50] *To the War with Waugh*, by John St John. Leo Cooper. pp. x+56. £1.95.

[51] *Denton Welch*, by Robert Phillips. New York: Twayne. pp. 189. $7.95.

This year saw the publication of Gordon Ray's fascinating account of the relationship of H. G. Wells and Rebecca West,[52] based on the more than eight hundred letters from Wells to West which survive from the ten-year period of their love affair. This was probably the most significant relationship of Wells's life, and obviously also of major importance for Rebecca West; it began in 1912, when Wells was at the height of his career and Rebecca West, as a young journalist at the outset of her writing life, reviewed his novel, *Marriage*, for the *Freewoman*. Their relationship is traced in this book with sensitivity and care, and it provides great insight into both personalities, and their interaction. Stephen J. Ingle writing in *QQ* examines the literary forms Wells used and their relation to his social/political objectives, showing that socialism 'stimulated and gave thematic cohesion to his best novels', but then, unfortunately for his art and his later reputation, led him to devote himself to educational and political tract writing. An interesting sidelight is shed upon this critical judgement by H. E. L. Mellersh, who in *ContempR* records his short personal contact with H. G. Wells in 1932 and his much more prolonged and formative contact with his works, affirming that for himself and his generation Wells's greatest significance lay precisely in his rôle as teacher, through his non-fiction as well as his novels.

John Crane has written a painstaking explication,[53] book by book, of all T. H. White's published works, with a brief biographical introduction and a bibliography of White's writing and the surprisingly meagre critical work about him.

In *Renascence*, J. J. Boies seeks to separate Charles Williams as thinker and writer from the identification with C. S. Lewis and J. R. R. Tolkein to which he is usually subject by exploring his 'startling existential view of life' as expressed in his last two novels.

Only two articles on Virginia Woolf were available for review: in *RLV*, J. D. Garant defends the essay 'The Mark on the Wall' against Forster's charge that it is 'inspired breathlessness'; and in *DR*, R. Rubenstein offers a study of the composition of Virginia Woolf's review-article, 'Tchekhov on Pope'.

2. VERSE

There are several excellent general studies this year. Geoffrey Thurley's *The Ironic Harvest*[1] is a study of twentieth-century English poetry distinguished by the author's deep knowledge of a very large number of poems, and by his commitment to the importance of his subject. A masterly first chapter evaluates what Thurley calls 'the intellectualist position'—established in Cambridge and developed by the American New Critics —a position of great influence but limited by its excessive emphasis on a specific range of intellectualism, demanded in 'Richard's "irony", Eliot's "wit", Empson's "ambiguity" and Leavis's "intelligence"'. The poets analyzed and appreciated in this stimulating and rewarding book include Empson, Auden, Spender, David Gascoyne, Dylan Thomas, Roy Fuller, Philip Larkin, Peter Porter, Ted Hughes, and Lee Harwood.

---

[52] *H. G. Wells and Rebecca West*, by Gordon N. Ray. Macmillan. pp. xxvi+215. £2.95.

[53] *T. H. White*, by J. K. Crane. New York: Twayne. pp. 202. $7.50.

[1] *The Ironic Harvest: English Poetry in the Twentieth Century*, by Geoffrey Thurley. Edward Arnold. pp. vii+215. £4.95.

Edwin Morgan's *Essays*[2] range over a wide area of poetry and were written between 1952 and 1973, but there is one dominant theme: 'Our poetry needs greater humanity; but it must be the humanity of man within his whole environment'. Morgan's passionate concern for poetry is the concern of a poet as well as critic and teacher, and by 'whole environment' he means both the international cultural context and the actuality of the modern physical world. Poets are blamed for writing as if they were ignorant of the great poets of other times and other nations: cultural parochialism is seen as a blight. But they are also blamed—as Yeats, and Eliot, and Pound are blamed—if they reveal a lack of interest in ordinary reality or common lives. There is no space here to suggest the variety of subjects in these twenty-seven essays, or adequately to indicate the seriousness or subtlety of the critical analysis and argument, but the volume can be recommended to any reader whose attention has been drawn to these pages, for it has much of crucial importance to say about Scottish, English, European, and American poetry.

A selection of Clive James's literary essays[3] is published by Faber. In the Foreword the tone is established: 'At several points within I make the large claim that literary journalism is the substance of criticism, not the shadow.' The first essay of the volume deals with the 'permanent literary value' of Edmund Wilson's critical output. Wilson's success at publishing first in magazines what was later to become the material for books makes him 'the ideal of the metropolitan critic, who understood from the beginning that the intelligence of the metropolis is in a certain relation to the intelligence of the academy, and went on understanding this even when the intelligence of the academy ceased to understand its relation to the intelligence of the metropolis'. This admiration is contrasted by the cool approach to Leavis. The two critics can usefully be juxtaposed to illustrate James's argument: Wilson is the immediate 'metropolitan critic'; Leavis spends decades thinking up his lectures, which are then published as essays. It is in the spirit of the former that James writes. He is always lucid and intelligent, whether he is writing on approaches to Women's Lib, fellow literary journalists, or the aftermath of the *Oz* trial. It is especially interesting to find a section on poetry: essays by poets on their near contemporaries form a rewarding part of 'metropolitan criticism'. The British poets included in James's commentaries are Keith Douglas, Roy Fuller, Seamus Heaney, Sidney Keyes, George MacBeth, and Peter Porter. The Alvarez of *The Savage God* is reviewed, and there are also essays on American poets, G. B. Shaw, Ford Madox Ford, and the Lawrence of the travel books.

Cyrena N. Pondrom's *The Road From Paris*[4] brings together an important collection of essays, extracts from essays, and letters which together were responsible for the impact of French literary ideas on English poetry between 1900 and 1920. In the long introduction to this excellent volume, the French influence is divided into phases, and the seminal importance of the poetry reviewer Frank S. Flint is made clear. Flint's published essays on French

[2] *Essays*, by Edwin Morgan. Cheadle: Carcanet New Press. pp. vii+299. £3.25.

[3] *The Metropolitan Critic*, by Clive James. Faber. pp. 267. £3.95.

[4] *The Road From Paris: French Influence on English Poetry, 1900–1920*, by Cyrena N. Pondrom. C.U.P. pp. ix+334. £6.95. $19.50.

literature date from 1908; he 'was aware of the significance of Apollinaire, Paul Claudel, Charles Péguy, Jean Cocteau, and Paul Eluard before Pound was'. Four of Flint's major essays, as well as a representative amount of his correspondence with French poets, are reproduced in this volume. One essay by Flint is assessed as 'The First Major Survey of the French Avant Garde' and occupies almost sixty pages of the text. The volume includes essays by John Middleton Murry, T. E. Hulme, Tristan Derème, Ezra Pound, Richard Aldington, Rémy de Gourmont, Nicolas Beauduin, Aldous Huxley, and André Lhote. Scholarly introductions to each essay contribute a general cohesiveness to the collection.

Herbert A. Kenny's *Literary Dublin*[5] relates the history of Dublin to its literature in a broad survey which spans several centuries. Kenny describes his volume as being light-hearted 'because it removes as much emphasis as possible from the violence and tragedy, the bitterness and the bloodshed, the political crimes and international cruelties that have marked Dublin's history from its beginnings'. He thus sets out to analyze neither Dublin's history nor Dublin's literature. This is an anecdotal and superficial gloss over many authors. Twentieth-century writers mentioned include Beckett, Austin Clarke, Patrick Kavanagh, Thomas Kinsella, and Yeats.

M. K. Sen's *Fresh Grounds in English Literature*[6] has essays on Eliot, Shaw, Yeats, and Joyce. Sen aims to look at the moderns in a new light. He tackles such subjects as the Americanism of Eliot, Eliot's use of

Shakespeare, Eliot's obscurity, 'A Psychoanalytical Interpretation of *The Waste Land*', Eliot and the Tarot, an explication of 'The Lake Isle of Innisfree', and Joyce the poet.

Elizabeth Fennings's *Reaching into Silence: A Study of Eight Twentieth-Century Visionaries* (New York: Barnes & Noble), has been unobtainable for review, as has Anthony Thwaite's pamphlet, *Poetry Today: 1960–1973* (published by Longman for the British Council).

The Poetry of Richard Aldington: A Critical Evaluation and an Anthology of Uncollected Poems (Penn. State U.P.) has not been available for notice. Norman T. Gates writes on 'Richard Aldington's "Personal Notes on Poetry"' (*TQ*). Volume 27 in the series Poetic Drama and Poetic Theory, Salzburg Studies,[7] prints papers from a symposium held in Salzburg University English Department. James Hogg's paper is 'James Elroy Flecker: Some Sources for a Study of His Poetry', Sieglinde Pichler's 'Tradition *und* Experiment' offers a consideration of Edith Sitwell's poetic theory, William B. Wahl surveys 'The Poetic Theories of Ronald Duncan', Adolf Wimmer relates John Arden to the English ballad tradition, and Waltraud Mitgutsch writes on Thom Gunn as remaining essentially 'ein Dichter des apollinischen Prinzips'.

A. S. T. Fisher examines the technique of and the influences on 'Auden's Juvenilia' (*N&Q*). In 'Auden, Hopkins, and the Poetry of Reticence' (*TCL*), Wendell Stacy Johnson brings out, in a comparison between Auden and Hopkins, Auden's reluctance to reveal other than the

[5] *Literary Dublin: A History*, by Herbert A. Kenny. Taplinger Publishing and Gill & Macmillan. pp. 336. £6.00.
[6] *Fresh Grounds in English Literature*, by M. K. Sen. New Delhi: Chand & Co. pp. viii+174. Rs.25.

[7] *On Poets and Poetry: A Symposium from the Department of English at the University of Salzburg*, ed. by James Hogg. Poetic Drama and Poetic Theory Series, vol. 27. pp. ii+199. £4.80. $12.50. DM40.AS280.

public man. In 'Poetry Nonetheless: Early Auden' (*ContempR*) G. C. Millard analyzes 'Consider this and in our time'. Hermann Peschmann has a tribute in *English*, 'W. H. Auden (1907–1973)'; he claims the need for a variorum edition or a new *Collected Poems*. Samuel Rees writes an appreciation of Auden for *AWR*. Monroe K. Spears has an article in *SR*, 'In Memoriam W. H. Auden'; he comments on 'the specifically Christian aspect of his work'. Golo Mann has a memoir in *Encounter*. In George Watson's letter to *Encounter*, 'Auden and Violence', he expands on his article of December 1973, 'Were the Intellectuals Duped?'

John Press's pamphlet for the *WTW* series[8] traces John Betjeman's life, prose, and poetry. Betjeman's aesthetic and spiritual values are assessed in an analysis of the essays on architecture. Betjeman the poet is compared with Tennyson; his parodies and allusions are discussed and finally his poetic development is considered. His achievement has limitations: 'Betjeman does not, for all his variety and his keenness of social observation, give us a powerful and comprehensive vision of society, or a sustained argument about the nature of man.' However these limitations, 'this fidelity to his temperament and to his experience, this refusal to pretend, give his poems a rare grace and authenticity'.

J. E. Morpurgo writes on 'Edmund Blunden: Poet of Community' (*ContempR*). Robert B. Pearsall's *Rupert Brooke: The Man and the Poet* (Amsterdam: Rodopi) has not been available for review. In 'Art and Experience: An Approach to Basil Bunting's Ideal of Poetry and the Poet' (*DUJ*), Anthony Suter examines the ambiguity of Bunting's atti-

tude to his means of expression. He concludes that, for Bunting, 'Poetry more than the mere reflection of experience, more than simply the exercise of technique, is a way of being.'

Austin Clarke's *Collected Poems* edited by Liam Miller (Dolmen and O.U.P.) has not been available for review. A long review article by Martin Dodsworth, 'To Forge the Irish Conscience', appears in *TLS* (December 13). *IUR* publishes an Austin Clarke special issue containing biographical and bibliographical material, essays on the plays and poetry, and the entire text of Clarke's 'The Visitation: A Play'. This valuable source for Clarke scholars includes contributions by Maurice Harmon, Brendan Kennelly, Robert Welch, Roger McHugh, Tina Hunt Mahony, Vivian Mercier, Robert Garratt, Martin Dodsworth, Thomas Kinsella, and Gerard Lyne.

Bhupendra Nath Seal writes on 'The Modernity of de la Mare's Poetry' (*Bulletin of the Dept. of English, Calcutta University*). De la Mare is 'typically a modern who sees the restlessness of modern life'. De la Mare is briefly related to Yeats, Eliot, Hardy, Lawrence, Chesterton, Dorothy Wellesley, Hopkins, George Barker, Spender, and MacNeice.

Desmond Graham's *Keith Douglas, 1920–1944: A Biography* (published by O.U.P.) has been unavailable for review, as have Mowbray Allan's *T. S. Eliot's Impersonal Theory of Poetry* (published by Bucknell U.P., 1973) and Anne C. Bolgan's *What the Thunder Really said: A Retrospective Essay on the Making of 'The Waste Land'* (published by McGill—Queens U.P., 1973). Nevill Coghill's edition of *The Cocktail Party*[9] provides

---

[8] *John Betjeman*, by John Press. Longman for the British Council. pp. 54. £0.20.

[9] *T. S. Eliot's 'The Cocktail Party'*, ed. with notes and commentary by Nevill Coghill. Faber. pp. 304. £2.95. Paper £1.20.

detailed notes, helpful extracts from Eliot's private correspondence, and an essay on structure and meaning. Coghill is sympathetic to Eliot's desire that the play should not be 'explained' beforehand, so that the essay comes after the text instead of as introductory material. The annotation is both literary and theatrical, so providing a very well-balanced and valuable commentary. T. S. Matthews's *Great Tom: Notes towards the definition of T. S. Eliot*[10] is self-styled 'a biography of sorts'. Any biography would go against Eliot's wishes that his private life should remain private. This biography also goes against Valerie Eliot's wishes and is sanctioned only by its New York publishers. The result is that we are offered a gossipy and inaccurate piece of journalism. Question marks are the most consistent form of punctuation and often the questions raised show a degree of insensitivity unforgivable in an unofficial biography. Although a bibliography and an index indicate scholarly intentions, this volume is far from scholarly in approach.

'*The Waste Land' in Different Voices*[11] brings together twelve essays originally given as lectures on the occasion of the fiftieth anniversary of *The Waste Land*. The approaches of the contributors vary considerably and each essayist is, in his own way, illuminating and interesting. John Dixon Hunt's '"Broken images": T. S. Eliot and Modern Painting' helpfully includes reproductions of the paintings under discussion. A. C. Charity's 'T. S. Eliot: The Dantean Recognitions' appends verses, and

translations, from the *Inferno*. Donald Davie writes on Eliot from the poet's point of view. A. D. Moody edits this excellent volume, to which he also contributes a paper. He writes of *The Waste Land* that 'proof of its vitality is its outliving the established ways of reading it'. This collection serves to indicate that vitality. The contributors include B. Rajan, D. W. Harding, Richard Drain, J. S. Cunningham, Nicole Ward, Bernard Harris, Denis Donoghue, and Kathleen Nott.

The revised edition of B. C. Southam's *A Student's Guide to the Selected Poems of T. S. Eliot*[12] provides systematic notes to the volume of *Selected Poems*. Southam does not aim to provide interpretation; he offers a background to the poems in a very practical way, commenting that 'Our real understanding of the poetry, and of the poet, begins where these notes end.' The type of information provided is factual: sources of quotations are specified, translation of foreign phrases are made, and allusions are tracked down. This is a helpful introductory reference work which, in this revised edition, takes into account *The Waste Land* manuscript.

Thomas R. Rees's *The Technique of T. S. Eliot: A Study of the Orchestration of Meaning in Eliot's Poetry* (The Hague and Paris: Mouton) has not been available for notice. The same applies to Linda W. Wagner's *T. S. Eliot: A Collection of Criticism* (New York: McGraw-Hill).

The T. S. Eliot Newsletter was founded in 1974. This 'International Survey of Eliot Scholarship' will appear twice a year. It encompasses all aspects of Eliot studies, including contributions on such related figures

---

[10] *Great Tom: Notes towards the definition of T. S. Eliot*, by T. S. Matthews. Weidenfeld & Nicolson. pp. xix+219. £3.50.

[11] *'The Waste Land' in Different Voices*, ed. by A. D. Moody. Edward Arnold. pp. xi+237. £4.95.

[12] *A Student's Guide to the Selected Poems of T. S. Eliot*, by B. C. Southam. Faber. pp. 138. Paper £0.50.

as Joyce, Yeats, Pound, and Wyndham Lewis. D. E. S. Maxwell and Shyamal Bagchee edit *TSEN* from York University, Toronto. Bibliographical material, notes, essays, review articles, and information on works in progress are included.

In a letter to the Editor (*PMLA*) Allen Austin replies to Ronald Schuchard's article, 'Eliot and Hulme in 1916: Toward a Revaluation of Eliot's Critical and Spiritual Development' [*YW* 54:391]. Austin maintains that Eliot 'did not formulate his religious philosophy until the middle or late 'twenties, for which he is not primarily indebted to Hulme, who was much more interested in politics than religion'. Schuchard responds that Austin has misinterpreted the term 'religious', which is used in Schuchard's thesis to indicate a broad philosophical position rather than to mean belief in Christianity. Schuchard's article was the first step towards a new statement in Eliot criticism; he is well aware that his is a 'heterodox position'. In *RES*, Schuchard writes on 'T. S. Eliot as an Extension Lecturer, 1916–1919'. He publishes the syllabuses of Eliot's University Extension courses for Oxford and London. These provide very interesting material. In 1919 to 1920 Eliot wrote essays related to his lectures, and after 1920, he continued to pursue his lecture topics. Schuchard points out that Eliot's courses on modern literature indicate continuity between Eliot and the Victorians that has hitherto been impossible to confirm.

There are six papers on Eliot in *ArQ*. In 'Eliot's "Burial of the Dead": A Note on the Morphology of Culture', John Brooks Barry re-examines Eliot's view of history. F. Peter Dzwonkoski, Jr., argues that 'the movement of "The Hollow Men" may be seen as the negation, the polar opposite, of the movement both of *The Divine Comedy* as a whole and of Eliot's own "Ash-Wednesday"'. In 'Landscape as Symbol in T. S. Eliot's "Ash-Wednesday"', Nancy D. Hargrove discusses Eliot's symbolic use of personal and traditional natural settings. James F. Knapp examines 'Eliot's "Prufrock" and the Form of Modern Poetry'. He analyzes Eliot's views on poetic tradition and creation and shows how 'Prufrock has come to represent the beginning of radical changes in modern poetry'. Marion Montgomery analyzes *The Waste Land*; the poem pinpoints 'the necessity of a self-love corrected'. Audrey T. Rogers writes on 'The Mythic Perspective of Eliot's "The Dry Salvages"'. She examines the structural pattern of myth in the poem, a pattern which is a recurrent feature of all *Four Quartets*: 'All of the Quartets focus on the theme of alienation and the necessity to find a route back to meaningful activity.'

In *PLL*, John Bugge considers 'Rhyme as Onomatopoeia in "The Dry Salvages"'. In the second section 'Eliot uses onomatopoeia in an extraordinary way, both to reinforce the sense of emotional depression that accompanies the idea of endless flux and, at the same time, to point toward the act of divine intervention into temporal affairs from which all human hope springs'. In 'Thematic Consistency in the work of T. S. Eliot' (*RLV* 1973) Paul Deane finds that 'There is no sudden conversion in his work; rather there is a subtle and gradually revealed intention to make available to readers the path of religious progress—the journey of the Magi—from emptiness and futility through doubt and indecisiveness to certainty and its attendant problems.' Deane points out some of the images, ideas, and statements which are repeated in the whole canon. These references 'reveal the religious idea underlying all his work: life without faith, without the knowledge of the real life of the soul, is a wasteland'.

Marjorie Donker finds conscious literary connexions between 'The Waste Land and the Aeneid' (PMLA) such as assume the centrality of Virgil in Eliot's poem. Also in PMLA, James Torrens writes on 'Charles Maurras and Eliot's "New Life"'. Maurras was an influence on Eliot in the late 1920's; in particular, his work on Dante inspired Eliot's own essay on Dante, which he dedicated to Maurras. Maurras's aesthetics gradually cease to exercise their influence on Eliot as '"the system of Dante's organization of sensibility" gradually works upon him'. In 'Dante and Eliot' (CritQ) Graham Hough demonstrates why Eliot enriches his poetic implication with direct quotation, translation, and adaptation of Dante. For Eliot, 'Dante is the supreme imagination of Christendom, and his work the great central expression of the Christian system'. The validity of both art and philosophy is central to Dante; Eliot wished that his own poetry could have such validity. Barbara Everett contributes two intricately argued papers to CritQ. In both she counteracts firm critical approaches to Eliot and looks at fictional sources for his poems. 'Burnt Norton' is linked with 'The Turn of The Screw' and A Tale of Two Cities. 'Prufrock' is linked with a story by Turgenev, The Diary of a Nobody, and The History of Mr. Polly. In these two essays, she illustrates this statement: 'It is often said that Prufrock is in hell and that the soliloquist of "Burnt Norton" goes to heaven, but the fact is that they visit much the same place and go by much the same route.' There are two articles in AL. Lyndall Gordon writes on 'The Waste Land Manuscript'. After Eliot had

shown the poem to Pound, the radical changes it underwent meant that Eliot could not, in The Waste Land, 'give the religious ordeal back to his generation'; Eliot 'was forced to rewrite his saint's life in more explicit terms in "Ash Wednesday" and Four Quartets'. Marion Perret's 'Eliot, the Naked Lady and the Missing Link' traces an allusion in The Waste Land to John Day's The Parliament of Bees. Peter L. Hays writes on 'Commerce in The Waste Land' (ELN). 'Commerce' is present in several meanings in the poem, acting as a linking theme. In a letter to the Editor (TLS, May 24) John Worthen tentatively locates an allusion in The Waste Land. A reference to a German patriotic poem leads him to clarify Eliot's allusions to Marie Larisch. Eva Hesse replies on June 21. She has investigated the relationship between Marie Larisch and The Waste Land in her recently published volume on the poem. Roger Kojecký's 'Eliot the European' (SELit) examines Eliot's social and political position in relation to Europe. Constantinos A. Patrides writes on 'The Renascence of the Renaissance: T. S. Eliot and the Pattern of Time' (MQR 1973). In The Waste Land there are two time-schemes: the concept of eternity is experienced by the reader and that of linear progression is experienced by the protagonist. Eliot has the Christian attitude to time in Four Quartets, the attitude which reached its climax in the Renaissance. Eliot sees time as a continual present rather than as divided into past, present, and future; the relationship between time and eternity remains mysterious. In 'Modernism and the Nonsense Style' (ConL) James Rother traces Eliot's debt to Lewis Carroll, Edward Lear, and the Nonsense tradition. In 'Mapping The Waste Land' (ES) Kristian Smidt discusses some of the most interesting essays of the past three years which have been written in the light of the publication of the manuscripts. P. G. Mudford writes on 'T. S. Eliot's plays and the tradition of "High Comedy"' (*CritQ*). This lucid essay offers a definition of 'High Comedy' as 'that kind of comedy in which the humorous revelation of individual folly, through behaviour and situation, raises social and moral issues which are themselves often seen in the perspective of some further metaphysical belief'. 'High Comedy' has become uncomfortable in our time because of scepticism towards metaphysical belief, and because there are no longer absolute social morals to which an audience can relate. Shakespeare, Molière, and Mozart are used to illustrate the dramatic tradition, and Pope, Byron, and Dickens are cited as examples of the non-dramatic tradition of 'High Comedy'. While Shaw tries to introduce an individualistic scale of values, Eliot works within the tradition by adapting 'the discarded image of a religious world to create, through his verse, a theatre of enlightenment'. *The Family Reunion, The Cocktail Party, The Confidential Clerk,* and *The Elder Statesman* are analyzed. In *N&Q* Christopher Clausen finds 'A Source For Thomas Becket's Temptation in *Murder in the Cathedral*': Edwin Arnold's 'The Light of Asia'. John P. Cutts offers 'Evidence for Ambivalence of Motives in *Murder in the Cathedral* (*CompD*) suggesting that Eliot's selection of historical and liturgical materials leads to the portrayal of Becket as a character 'of ambiguous motives' who plays a series of contradictory roles and whose motives are 'thoroughly ambivalent'. Patrick A. McCarthy writes on 'Eliot's *Murder in the Cathedral*' (*Expl*). In 'Eliot's *The Cocktail Party*: Comic Perspective

as Salvation' (*MD*) Gary T. Davenport finds the play persuasive as a demonstration that comedy, since it requires a degree of detachment from oneself, brings 'salvation from the prison of self'.

Roma Gill's *William Empson: The Man and His Work* (published by RKP) has not been available for review. Contributors to this collection include M. C. Bradbrook, George Fraser, Rintaro Fukuhara, Graham Hough, L. C. Knights, Karl Miller, Kathleen Raine, I. A. Richards, Christopher Ricks, Janet A. Smith, and John Wain. Veronica Forrest-Thomson's interesting analysis, 'Rational Artifice: Some Remarks on the Poetry of William Empson' (*YES*) examines, with reference to Empson's own poetic technique, his 'dislike for poetic techniques that seem to establish a discontinuity between poetry and other kinds of language'. She concludes that 'his devaluation—for all the close reading involved in his critical work—of purely formal qualities makes it impossible for him to recognize the true value of poetic conventions and that these do not necessarily work in conjunction with verbal meaning'.

William Walsh provides a discussion of the career, poetry, and prose of D. J. Enright.[13] He demonstrates both the exceptional critical range of this 'poet of humanism' and the intelligence of the four novels. This is an interesting and informative introduction.

In 'Christopher Fry's *Curtmantle*: The Form of Unity' (*MD*) J. Woodfield sees the play as culminating some of Fry's main themes and techniques and achieving new degrees of clarity, economy, and flexibility. In 'What Happens in *Venus Observed*' (*The Literary Criterion*, Bombay)

[13] *D. J. Enright: Poet of Humanism*, by William Walsh. C.U.P. pp. 107. £2.20.

T. Ghatak argues that 'Fry's play makes us aware that human destiny is determined by countless, varied factors working in multifarious combinations'. The Duke and Rosabel observe Venus from different angles 'and yet they do converge on a point'.

In *Focus*, Alan M. Cohn examines the libretto for Peggy Glanville-Hicks's opera, *Nausicaa*; based on Graves's *Homer's Daughter*, the identity of the librettist remains uncertain. Graves probably assisted Glanville-Hicks in the libretto's composition. A. S. G. Edwards and J. Pinsent make 'Additions to F. Higginson's *Bibliography of Robert Graves*' (*PBSA*). Nicholas Lyons has an article in *DUJ*: 'Satiric Technique in *The Spiritual Quixote*: Some Comments'. David Ormerod interprets 'Graves' "Apple Island"' (*Expl*) in the light of *The White Goddess*. Myron Simon's 'The Georgian Infancy of Robert Graves' (*Focus*) examines Graves's adherence to the poetic principles of Edward Marsh and his Georgian group of poets.

John Wilson Foster writes on 'The Poetry of Seamus Heaney' (*CritQ*). He argues that, should Heaney 'widen his themes, break into new modes, and learn to trust his feeling', he 'might well become the best Irish poet since Yeats'. Heaney's strengths are 'single-mindedness of purpose, a fertile continuity of theme, high competence in execution, a growing unmistakability of voice'. This commentary takes into account the three volumes *Death of a Naturalist*, *Door into the Dark*, and *Wintering Out*. In *IUR* (1973) Sean Lucy has a paper on Seamus Deane, Seamus Heaney, and John Montague.

Volume 22 of the Salzburg series Poetic Drama and Poetic Theory[14]

has two studies of Ted Hughes: Waltraud Mitgutsch, in her *Zur Lyrik von Ted Hughes* offers a long, detailed account of his verse, considering his relationship with the tradition of English lyrical verse, the rôle played by violence in his work, and his treatment of nature and animals; James Hogg's 'Ted Hughes and the Drama' is a short essay on his *Oedipus* and *Orghast* relying on second-hand reactions to them in performance. In *CP*, J. Brooks Bouson offers 'A Reading of Ted Hughes's *Crow*'. In *SELit* Naoki Okubo writes 'On Ted Hughes's "Animal" Poems'. Lawrence R. Ries discusses 'Hughes' "The Hawk in the Rain"' (*Expl*).

In *CritQ*, Atholl C. C. Murray studies *In Parenthesis*. He finds the work to be on one level 'an account of a certain period of the Great War; but, at another and deeper level, it is about a mode of vision—it is a first essay in perspective'. David Jones is seeking to show that meaning and ultimate truth can still be discerned for man in the worst situations. Jones emphasizes the continuity of history and uses religious vocabulary to denote the order behind horrific experience.

In *IUR* (1973) John Nemo provides 'A Bibliography of Writings by and about Patrick Kavanagh'. In '"The Enobling Ritual": Irish Poetry in the Seventies' (*Shenandoah*) Dillon Johnston writes on the intentions and commitments of Thomas Kinsella, John Montague, Richard Murphy, Seamus Heaney, Derek Mahon, Seamus Deane, Richard Ryan, and Paul Muldoon.

Lolette Kuby's *An Uncommon Poet for the Common Man: A Study of*

---

[14] *Zur Lyrik von Ted Hughes: Eine Interpretation Nach Leitmotiven*, by Waltraud Mitgutsch. *Ted Hughes and the Drama*, by James Hogg. Poetic Drama and Poetic Theory Series, vol. 22. Salzburg Studies in English Literature. pp. xiii+282. £4.80. $12.50. DM40. AS280.

Philip Larkin's Poetry (The Hague: Mouton) has been unavailable for notice. The *High Windows* volume (Faber) is appreciated in a long and critically detailed article by Clive James (*Encounter*). Margaret Blum offers an analysis of 'Larkin's "Dry-Point"' (*Expl*). Dan Jacobsen has a long profile on Larkin (*New Review*). He includes interesting biographical information and an assessment of the poems, with particular reference to *High Windows*. *New Review* also has a comment on the editing of Larkin's poems in the editorial section. James Naremore's 'Philip Larkin's "Lost World"' (*ConL*) offers a reading of the poems, and in particular of *The North Ship*, which suggests that, because Larkin yearns for a 'lost world', 'the way things ought to be', so the bitterness of many of the poems is intensified.

In *DHLR* John B. Vickery suggests that Lawrence's poetry is motivated by 'a delicately balanced sense of the realities of matter and the potentialities of myth'. In *N&Q* Philip Waldron notes 'A Katherine Mansfield Poem Printed Incomplete'; this poem is 'Voices of the Air'. In *TCL* Waldron writes on 'Katherine Mansfield's *Journal*'. Christopher Wiseman writes on 'Edwin Muir's Last Poems' (*UWR*). George P. Lilley's *A Bibliography of John Middleton Murry*[15] meticulously lists all of his traceable writings from the undergraduate poems published in a Brasenose magazine in 1911 through almost 1,700 pieces in the following 46 years. In *AWR* Jeremy Hooker's 'The Accessible Song: A Study of John Ormond's Recent Poetry' analyzes the collection *Definition of a Waterfall* to show that 'Ormond has emerged as a major poet'.

Jon Stallworthy's *Wilfred Owen*[16] is a first-rate critical biography which expresses the author's dual powers as scholar and poet. The facts are effectively assembled and marshalled; the appreciation of the verse is sensitive and sympathetic. This volume is offered as a portrait of the *artist*, and is meant to supplement Harold Owen's *Journey from Obscurity*, which is a portrait of Wilfred Owen as elder brother, and the poet's *Collected Letters*, which build up a portrait of himself in relation to his mother. This biography, together with the forthcoming *Complete Poems of Wilfred Owen* which Jon Stallworthy is preparing, will always be essential for any student of twentieth-century poetry. This volume will serve as a model for literary biography. In *New Review* a section of the biography is published as 'Owen and Sassoon: The Craiglockhart Episode'. In 1917, Owen was under observation in Craiglockhart War Hospital in Edinburgh. During his stay of several months he became editor of the hospital journal, lectured to the Edinburgh Field Club, and met Sassoon. The poems written in this period are analyzed in relation to the association between Owen and Sassoon. Stallworthy's pamphlet, *Poets of the First World War* (O.U.P. for the Imperial War Museum) has not been available for review. A detailed article by Jennifer Breen in *N&Q* examines 'The Dating and Sources of Wilfred Owen's "Miners"'. In *ELT* Jennifer Breen writes on 'Wilfred Owen: "Greater Love" and Late Romanticism'. 'Greater Love' is a parody of Swinburne's 'Before the Mirror'. By his use of parody, Owen 'repudiates the values not only of late Romantic love poetry, but also

---

[15] *A Bibliography of John Middleton Murry*, by George P. Lilley. Folkestone: William Dawson & Sons. pp. 226. £10.

[16] *Wilfred Owen: A Biography*, by Jon Stallworthy. O.U.P. and Chatto & Windus. pp. xiv+333. £6.75.

of the culture it represents'. In 'Fragment: Cramped in that Funnelled Hole', Owen parodies Tennyson's 'The Charge of the Light Brigade'. These two examples of parody demonstrate Owen's overall transcendence of the conventions of late Romantic poetry, once he had seen that 'the conventional language of Romantic poetry could not express the truth about men sent to fight in a mechanised war'. Jennifer Breen also has a note in *TLS* (18 January) on the date of composition of 'Wilfred Owen's "Exposure"'. Dominic Hibberd writes on 'Images of Darkness in the Poems of Wilfred Owen' (*DUJ*). In 'Sassoon on Owen' (*TLS*, 31 May) Dennis Welland gives an account of Siegfried Sassoon's discussions and notes on Wilfred Owen, seeing both poets as men divided. 'Drawn imaginatively to the Romantic aesthetic of an earlier age, they were compelled by circumstance to a quite different creative effort: the faithful and exact rendering of a reality particularly hideous'. James F. McIlroy's *Wilfred Owen's Poetry: A Study Guide* (Heinemann) has not been available for review.

In 'A Golden Labyrinth: Edith Sitwell and the Theme of Time' (*Renascence*) John Ower offers a detailed examination of *The Sleeping Beauty*, *Elegy on Dead Fashion*, and 'Metamorphosis': 'The vision of the individual's entrapment in the natural cycles which is developed in *The Sleeping Beauty* is, in *Elegy on Dead Fashion*, placed within the context of the historical degeneration of the race. However, as in Dante's *Inferno*, the centre of the labyrinth joins with a divine 'circumference', which encompasses the poet's difficulties in a redemptive transference. In "Metamorphosis" Dame Edith writes fully with that "outer ring" in a tempered visionary ecstasy'. In *BB* John W.

Ehrstine and Douglas D. Rich have a paper, 'Edith Sitwell: A Critical Bibliography 1951–1973'. Andrew K. Weatherhead's *Stephen Spender and the Thirties* (Bucknell U.P.) has not been available for review.

Richard J. Finneran edits James Stephens's letters.[17] The correspondence spans the years from 1907 to 1946, the correspondents including AE, Austin Clarke, Padraic Colum, John Drinkwater, Oliver St. John Gogarty, Lady Gregory, Joseph Hone, Harold Monro, O'Casey, Shaw, and Yeats. There are two appendixes: one discusses the date of Stephens's birth, and the second is an updated list of his published work, including over 130 items not cited in other bibliographical sources.

Walford Davies edits a good representative selection of Dylan Thomas's poems.[18] He prefaces the edition with an interesting introduction and offers full notes on each poem. He has aimed to date each poem, to suggest for comparison another poem by Thomas or by a different poet, to describe the poem's theme, and to annotate points of difficulty. The poems are helpfully arranged in chronological order. A complex essay on semantics by Joseph M. Barone (*Poetics*) rigorously subjects to analysis 'Light Breaks Where No Sun Shines' in order to clarify the concepts of 'metaphor' and 'semantic deviance'. In *Expl* Barbara T. Gates writes on the relation between *A Midsummer Night's Dream* and 'Thomas' "In My Craft or Sullen Art"'. Brian John writes on 'Dylan Thomas's "Over Sir John's Hill"' (*AWR*). He examines allusions to, and parallels with,

[17] *Letters of James Stephens*, ed. by Richard J. Finneran. Macmillan. pp. xxiv + 481. £10.00.
[18] *Dylan Thomas: Selected Poems*, ed. by Walford Davies. J. M. Dent. pp. vii + 136. Paper £1.

nursery rhyme, Blake, Keats, the Bible, Donne, *Macbeth*, and Wordsworth. Such allusions 'place the elegy in its proper context . . . as a moving celebration of Thomas's awareness of the inevitable tragedy implicit in a world vacillating between the poles of life and death, creation and destruction; of his compassion for the suffering souls of all things; and the weighing of that suffering in the hope and expectation of an eternal mercy and salvation, not of any orthodox kind but epitomized in the renewal of life itself.'

In 'Aspects of Energy in the Poetry of Dylan Thomas and Sylvia Plath' (*CritQ*) D. F. McKay borrows Pound's statement, 'Great literature is simply language charged with meaning to the utmost possible degree'. A poem need not act as 'the vehicle or corroborator of meaning' but as 'a conductor of energy, serving to deliver it as a wire conducts electricity. In terms of Pound's statement, we let the stress fall more heavily upon the word "charged"'. McKay then proceeds comparatively, arguing that 'the techniques generating energy in Thomas' poetry can all be traced back to the primal force, sometimes abstractly construed as time, as it is resisted, accepted or converted by man. The power present in Sylvia Plath's late poetry brooks no such domestication at man's hand; it suggests the sudden violence of wilderness rather than the inexorable passage of seasons across a pastoral landscape.' Christopher Page's 'Dylan and the Scissormen' (*AWR*) analyzes the prose and poems to find the recurrent image of scissors, scissormen, and tailors. Derived from *Struwwelpeter*, these related images 'symbolise the inevitable cruelty of the great natural processes of life and death'. Diana Sautter's 'Dylan Thomas and Archetypal Domination' (*AI*) looks at

archetypal patterns in 'In the beginning was the three-pointed star', 'From love's first fever to her plague', 'Love in the Asylum', 'On the Marriage of a Virgin', 'Out of the sighs a little comes', 'The Conversation of Prayer', and 'Over Sir John's Hill'.

Helen Thomas's pamphlet, *Edward Thomas: A Talk* (Tragara P.) has not been available for review. In *CritQ* Maire A. Quinn examines 'The Personal Past in the Poetry of Thomas Hardy and Edward Thomas'. Thomas's uncertainty of the value of recording the past is representative of the modern outlook.

Marilyn G. Rose's *Katherine Tynan* (Bucknell U.P.) has not been available for review, nor has Roland Mathias's *Vernon Watkins* (U. of Wales P. for the Welsh Arts Council). Ruth Pryor writes on Vernon Watkins in *AWR*. Watkins's use of *terza rima*, and his numerous references to Dante leaves the reader with the sense of Dante's influence 'in single moments of illumination'.

Phases of the Moon by Marilyn Busteed, Richard Tiffany, and Dorothy Wergin,[19] makes evident Yeats's influence on modern astrology. The authors extend *A Vision* by dividing the Great Wheel according to the signs of the zodiac; they proceed to delineate the twenty-eight phases one by one. The subtitle claims for this book the position of 'A Guide' and the writers explain that 'Twentieth-century astrology is moving away from mere prediction of events towards self-knowledge and psychological self-help. Whether as counsellors or students, confused individuals can reintegrate themselves along new

---

[19] *Phases of the Moon: A Guide to Evolving Human Nature*, by Marilyn Busteed, Richard Tiffany, and Dorothy Wergin. Berkeley: Shambhala. Distributed in U.S.A. by Random House, in the Commonwealth and Europe by Routledge & Kegan Paul. pp. 233. £3.75. Paper £1.50.

lines by understanding their own cyclic time patterns.' Here is *A Vision* transformed from private mythology to public astrology, and Yeats scholars may be tempted to question the validity of the whole exercise. However, this is a book for astrologers and not necessarily for Yeats scholars.

George Mills Harper's interesting volume[20] investigates Yeats's thirty-two year commitment to The Second Order of the Golden Dawn. In 1900 and 1901 Yeats was struggling to overcome dissension in the Order. The crisis provoked from Yeats a large amount of correspondence, an essay on 'Is the Order . . . to remain a Magical Order?' as well as several other statements of his philosophical position. This material is helpfully appended to Harper's discussion. It is suggested that Yeats's 'membership in the Order represented a symbolic search for membership in the ideal order of the universe'. *A Vision* 'was in effect an outgrowth of his visionary meditation on the mystical philosophy of the Golden Dawn'. *The Shadowy Waters*, *The Speckled Bird*, and the essays on 'Magic', on Shelley, and on Morris, are discussed in relation to the period of Yeats's most intense involvement with the Order.

Colin Meir's *The Ballads and Songs of W. B. Yeats*[21] traces Yeats's early ambition to create a popular national literature, his turning away in the 1890's from popular balladry in an attempt to create an esoteric Irish literature and his subsequent return to the popular tradition. After 1900, Yeats increasingly drew on the work of Douglas Hyde and other Gaelic translators with regard to his use of dialectal patterns.

C. J. Rawson brings together Peter Ure's uncollected essays and lectures on *Yeats and Anglo-Irish Literature*.[22] Frank Kermode's personal memoir of Ure prefaces this valuable collection : of fifteen essays. The essays are presented in three groups: those on the poems, those on the plays, and those on Yeats's contemporaries. The last and smallest section covers Conrad, George Moore, and Shaw. The essays on the poems and plays take as their topics both general subjects (for example, 'The Plays' and 'The Integrity of Yeats') and also close analyses (of 'The Statues', of 'Demon and Beast', and of the Supernatural Songs). One general subject, 'W. B. Yeats and the musical instruments', captures attention with its directness: 'I have been counting the musical instruments in Yeats', and develops into a shrewd discussion of Yeats's preoccupation with 'the socially cohesive power of music'. The late essay, 'W. B. Yeats and the Shakespearian Moment' traces, in a scholarly and lively manner, Yeats's attitude towards Shakespeare: 'Yeats uses Shakespeare as a stick with which to beat the naturalists in his long campaign against the naturalistic theatre.' This collection is characterized by lucid observation and careful scholarship.

Reg Skene's volume[23] takes as its thesis that the five Cuchulain plays must be grouped together as a play-cycle for there to emerge full understanding. In the first half of the book Skene relates the plays to Yeats generally: to biography, to theatrical theory, to the system, to the Celtic

[20] *Yeats's Golden Dawn*, by George Mills Harper. Macmillan. pp. 322. £7.00.
[21] *The Ballads and Songs of W. B. Yeats: The Anglo-Irish Heritage in Subject and Style*, by Colin Meir. Macmillan. pp. viii+141. £4.95.
[22] *Yeats and Anglo-Irish Literature: Critical Essays by Peter Ure*, ed. by C. J. Rawson. Liverpool U.P. pp. xvi+292. £5.00.
[23] *The Cuchulain Plays of W. B. Yeats: A Study*, by Reg Skene. Macmillan. pp. xiii+278. £5.95.

revival, and to Yeats's attempt to found an Irish Mystical Order. The five plays are then analyzed in turn to demonstrate how the cycle holds its own as a coherent statement. The plays are studied as effective both theatrically and poetically. Skene's ideas on production have been tested in experience and, as a result, his assessment is well-balanced and informative.

Several volumes on Yeats have not been available for review. These include Adelyn Dougherty's *A Study of Rhythmic Structure in the Verse of William Butler Yeats* (The Hague: Mouton 1973), George M. Harper's pamphlet for the Dolmen Press '*Go Back To Where You Belong*': *Yeats's Return from Exile* (1973), Daniel A. Harris's *Yeats: Coole Park and Ballylee* (John Hopkins U.P.), and Gayatri C. Spivak's *Myself I Must Remake: The Life and Poetry of W. B. Yeats* (New York: Crowell).

In *SR*, James Lovic Allen's 'From Puzzle to Paradox: New Light on Yeats's Late Career' argues that Yeats's late career can be interpreted in the light of *A Vision*: 'Yeats believed—literally and wholeheartedly—in the system of religion which he developed for himself and in many of the occult and Neoplatonic bases upon which it rested.' In *TCL*, Allen has a second paper on Yeats, 'Unity of Archetype, Myth and Religious Imagery in the Work of Yeats'. The central concept in Yeats's work is 'the union of man and God, the human and the divine, the natural and the supernatural'. Yeats's motifs suggest 'his controlling theme, the yearned-for union of man with God'. In 'Crazy Jane and "Byzantium"' (*E&S*) Nicholas Brooke argues that 'in both these there is a trafficking between body and soul'. In 'Religion and Literature' (*SR*) Cleanth Brooks writes on Yeats as being representa-

tive of those poets who, no matter how weak or dead their Christian faith, have found it necessary to use Christian rite and dogma as a basis of symbolic reference; analyses of 'The Mother of God', 'Wisdom', and 'A Prayer for My Son' lead to the argument that poetry needs religion, 'even nonreligious poetry needs it; even poetry subversive of religion needs it'. In *Daedalus* Joan S. Carberg writes on *A Vision*, finding that many of its ideas are relevant to the 1970's. Visvaneth Chatterjee offers 'A Reading of Yeats's Byzantine Poems' (*Bulletin of the Dept. of English, Calcutta University*). The poems 'have a greater degree of universality than is generally recognised'; the reader need not go to *A Vision* to recognize that both poems share a theme, that of the dichotomy of man's physical and spiritual natures. Taketosh Furomoto finds a quotation from 'W. B. Yeats's Missing Review' of Katherine Tynan's work (*TLS*, letter to the Editor, January 4). Susan R. Gorsky has a paper in *MD*: 'A Ritual Drama: Yeats's Plays for Dancers'.

Stuart Hirschberg writes on 'Why Yeats Saw Himself as a "Daimonic Man" of Phase 17: A Complementary View' (*ELN*). Perhaps Yeats placed himself in this phase because of his horoscope. In *Expl*, Hirschberg writes on 'Yeats' "The Phases of the Moon", 118–123'; the poem is clarified by reference to 'Per Amica Silentia Lunae'. K. P. S. Jochum has a paper in *Anglia*, 'W. B. Yeats: A Survey of Book Publications 1966–1972'. He covers the Yeatsian texts, the translations, the bibliographies, the concordances, and the biographies published in this six-year period, as well as the introductions to Yeats, the collections of essays on Yeats, the books on specific phases of Yeats's work, the books on influences, those on specific themes, those on the poetry in general, those on special problems of the poetry, those on the plays, and those on the *Autobiographies*. He has nevertheless listed only 'a selection of the material actually produced'. In his excellent survey, Jochum demonstrates the unabated flow of Yeats criticism and also the new areas of Yeats scholarship that have been opened up in recent years. In *SoQ*, Wallace G. Kay looks at 'the concern with the relationship between image, imagining, and perceived reality' in Yeats's 'Among School Children' and Antonioni's *Blowup*. In the poem, as in the film, we are offered the statement that 'images and imaginings occur; they are a part of our lives, they affect how we live and in fact often *determine* what we do and how we do it'. Nandini P. Kuehn has an item in *Expl*: Yeats' "The Indian to His Love"'. In *N&Q* George Monteiro finds 'An Unrecorded Review by Yeats'; this review is on William Carleton. In *ELN* (1973) Edward O'Shea analyzes 'Yeats as Editor: Dorothy Wellesley's *Selections*'. Laurence Perrine's 'Yeats' "Three Things"' (*Expl* 1973) seeks to correct a misreading of that poem by John Unterecker and Morton Irving Seiden. Perrine also offers an interpretation of 'Yeats' "On a Political Prisoner", 19–24' (*Expl*). E. San Juan Jr., writes on 'Yeats's "Sailing to Byzantium" and the limits of Modern Literary Criticism' (*RLV*, 1972). In 'From Divided to Shared Love in the Art of Yeats' (*Renascence*) Alan Spiegel analyzes *John Sherman, The Player Queen, The Only Jealousy of Emer*, 'The Three Bushes', and 'Stories of Michael Robartes and his friends'. The tripartite love relationship is 'a crucial symbol in Yeats' art, life, historical theory, and metaphysic'. Richard Studing has a note on 'Sailing to Byzantium' in *RS*.

Yeats has left ambiguous his referent for 'That' in 'That is no country for old men'; he has deliberately done so in order to include in his statement the country he leaves as well as Byzantium. D. C. Sutton finds 'A Yeats Borrowing From Mangan' (*N&Q*); this is in 'Crazy Jane Talks with the Bishop'. In 'Countercomponents in Yeats's *At the Hawk's Well*' (*MD*) Kathleen M. Vogt considers his rejection of rhetoric in the play and the success with which he projected 'moods, sensations, single states of being' in this, his 'most experimental play'. In *AI* Richard P. Wheeler writes a psychoanalytical account of 'The Second Coming'. He argues that the poem 'builds upon a deeply repressed fantasy of omnipotent, destructive rage, called into service to master an experience of intolerable, infantile helplessness'. This fantasy underlies and enforces the poem's meaning as historical myth. Our collaboration in the fantasy 'enables the poem to impart a sense of power'. Robert W. Witt's contribution to *T. S. Eliot Newsl.* is on 'Yeats, Plato, and the Editor'.

Leonard Clark's edition of *Andrew Young: Complete Poems* (Secker & Warburg) has not been available for review, but a full review is to be found in *TLS* (April 12). John Buxton has a note on Young in a letter to the Editor, *TLS* (May 24).

3. DRAMA

A welcome return is the annual bibliography of international drama published in *MD*. The list is divided into national sections and it is useful to have work on modern British drama recorded in the context of the scholarship and criticism of world drama. A new bibliography *Theatre, Drama and Speech Index* is to be published three times each year by the Theatre, Drama and Speech

Information Centre, 1 Erin Court, Pleasant Hill, California 94523; more than 60 journals are analyzed, drama in performance being covered as well as criticism of drama as literature.

In *Drama and Theatre* Russell Vandenbrouke's 'The London Theatre, 1973–1974' is mainly an appreciation of the Royal Shakespeare Company's productions at Stratford and the Aldwych. In each of the four numbers of *Drama* J. W. Lambert, Eric Shorter, and Randall Craig review metropolitan and provincial productions, giving equal weight to 'experimental' theatre, while the most valuable evaluation of the major London productions is again provided in John Weightman's regular contributions to *Encounter*.

Theatre Quarterly continues to supply information and good critical sense over a wide range of dramatic activity in Britain, Europe, and America. David Mayer surveys the past hundred years in his 'The Sexuality of Pantomime'. Tom Stoppard's 'Ambush for the Audience' is largely concerned with his own plays and with his reactions to politically motivated drama. Peter Hall's 'Directing Pinter' gives a detailed account of a long theatrical collaboration, offering many interesting insights into the plays and their first productions. *ThQ* has overcome the initial financial difficulties facing the establishment of any independent journal and is to be congratulated on maintaining its high standards. *ThR* and *ThS*, established now for many years, also continue to publish articles of interest in the field of twentieth-century British drama and theatre in the general context of world theatre. In 'Commitment and Character Portrayal in the British Politico—Poetic Drama of the 1930's' (*ETJ*) Mirko Jurak writes on the plays of Auden and Isherwood, Spender, and MacNeice; in the same journal

Gillette Elvgren has an account of 'Documentary theatre at Stoke-on-Trent'. In the new Canadian journal *Modernist Studies: Literature and Culture 1920–1940*, Geoffrey Bullough's 'An English Repertory Theatre Between the Wars' reminisces about the repertory theatre in Sheffield.

Arden: A Study of His Plays[1] is in the generally excellent Eyre Methuen series Modern Theatre Profiles. Albert Hunt surveys the plays of John Arden and Margaretta D'Arcy, both those written for the established commercial theatre, which was always a deeply problematic host, and those written for various forms of 'alternative theatre'. The book is informative, and very sympathetic to one of the English theatre's most sensitive and least appreciated talents, and although the arguments are not pursued with much critical rigour the book is to be welcomed for its enthusiasm and warmth. In '*Ein irisches Vermächtnis*' (*ZAA*) Günther Klotz writes briefly on *The Ballygombeen Bequest*.

Ruby Cohn's *Back to Beckett*[2] offers an appreciative analysis of all of his work, read in the light of her personal acquaintance with him and of her detailed knowledge of his biography. In rejecting various approaches which set out to place Beckett's creative work in relation to philosophic traditions or in relation to his own critical writing, Ruby Cohn looks with loving attention at the literary works in turn, responding not to the ideas, or the technique, but to 'the experience itself'. In avoiding the emotional distance and detachment of 'scholarship', Professor Cohn has also surrendered the scholarly advantages of an index and precise

[1] *Arden: A Study of His Plays*, by Albert Hunt. Eyre Methuen. pp. 176. £2.95.

[2] *Back to Beckett*, by Ruby Cohn. Princeton U.P. pp. xx+274. $12.50.

reference; for the reader those advantages would have been especially welcome in a study which makes use of Beckett's unpublished work. Jean-Jacques Mayoux offers a clear survey of Beckett's work within the very restricted format imposed by the series.[3] Beckett's genius is indicated in his literary evolution, an evolution from literature, in which his sombre demand that absolute truth must prevail over aesthetic requirements led him to repress 'his great gifts of wit, verbal invention and brilliant narrative, his buffoonery, his mixture of aggressive satire and sensitive, poetic perceptiveness'. In 'There's a Hole in Your Beckett: The Inflation of Minimalism' (*Encounter*) Allan Rodway compares Beckett with Mann and Joyce, retaining throughout an ironical, unsympathetic tone which can be demonstrated by this conclusion: 'The basic flaw, the hole in your Beckett, seems to be this: for all their façade of modernism his plays are medieval in their assumption that the end of life is the whole of life, that if there is no purpose or reason beyond life there cannot be any purposes or reasons within it—false conclusions both of them'. Rodway argues that 'the current boom in Beckett, like all booms, seems to be inseparably linked with inflation'; the less Beckett creates, the more we admire him; the practical purposes of his work are to indicate 'a way of death-in-life for the aged, the imprisoned or the bed-ridden' and to show 'the spirit of non-resistance needed to pass the time with fewer and fewer resources'.

In 'Noah, *Not I*, and Beckett's "Incomprehensibly Sublime"' (*CompD*) Enoch Brater considers the various effects of Biblical reference in

the plays—elaborate in *Endgame*, present in *Happy Days*, elusive in *Not I*: in *TCL* the same critic offers 'The "I" in Beckett's *Not I*', useful for its report of the exchange between Beckett and Jessica Tandy, when she was preparing to perform *Not I*, and in *College Literature* 'Beckett, Ionesco and the Tradition of Tragi-comedy'. In 'Narrative Salvation in *Waiting for Godot*' (*MD*) Louisa Jones considers the effects of story-telling in the play, with special reference to the four gospels. In '*Waiting for Godot*' (*Expl*) Beverley Ormerod offers an interpretation of the tree as 'a secular symbol of enduring despair'.

The Sting and the Twinkle[4] brings together more than fifty short pieces on Sean O'Casey, some recounting conversations in immediate detail, some reminiscing from greater distance. The volume is very welcome since it includes several reports not easily available, and it will be a source of information and great pleasure for O'Casey's admirers. Naturally, the effect is not to change the picture we already have of O'Casey, but to add many more detailed lines to the portrait. One example of O'Casey defining his own art against contrary dramatic tastes comes in a conversation with Beverley Nichols where he refuses to tolerate *The Vortex* or to believe that the 'artificiality' of the characters is not Coward's own obtuseness. O'Casey argued that his English contemporaries should have been portraying not the superficialities of middle-class drawing rooms, but the extraordinary wealth of 'common life' in London. He was full of excitement about the characters he had listened to at Speakers' Corner in Hyde Park;

[3] *Samuel Beckett*, by Jean-Jacques Mayoux Writers and Their Work. Longmans for the British Council. pp. 48. £0.20.

[4] *The Sting and the Twinkle: Conversations with Sean O'Casey*, ed. by E. H. Mikhail and John O'Riordan. Macmillan. pp. xii+184. £4.95.

religious, political, and dietetic eccentrics caught up in their own fierce earnestness and the crowd's raucous contempt. 'What are your dramatists doing to neglect Hyde Park?' O'Casey demanded, smacking his fist on a café table, 'There's a tragedy, there's a comedy.' In *MD* William A. Armstrong defends 'The Integrity of *Juno and the Paycock*' arguing that it is a genuine tragedy, and Ronald G. Rollins in 'From Ritual to Romance in *Within the Gates* and *Cock-a-Doodle-Dandy*' discusses O'Casey's handling of mythic elements. In *Theoria* Ronald Ayling indicates the 'Ritual Patterns in Sean O'Casey's *Within the Gates*', and in *IUR* (1973) the same writer has a piece on O'Casey's relationship with the Abbey. A new journal, the *Sean O'Casey Review*, is to be reported, although it has not been available for inspection; nor has Thomas Kilroy's *Sean O'Casey: A Collection of Critical Essays*, which is in Prentice-Hall's Twentieth-Century Views series.

In *Notes on Contemporary Literature* Michael Haltresht briefly indicates some signs of 'Sadomasochism in John Osborne's "A Letter to My Fellow Countrymen"'.

In 'Pinero: *The Money-Spinner*' (*N&Q*) J. P. Wearing considers that play as a forerunner of *The Second Mrs. Tanqueray*, and records the confusion surrounding the two-act and three-act versions of the play. J. P. Wearing's edition of *The Collected Letters of Arthur Pinero* (U. of Minneapolis P.) has not been available.

The December number of *MD* is devoted to essays on Harold Pinter: Eric Salmon, Lorraine Hall Burghardt, Charles A. Carpenter, Mary Jane Miller, Austin E. Quigley, Anita R. Osherow, Vera M. Jiji, Enoch Brater, Rüdiger Imhof, Thomas P.

Adler, Alan Hughes, and Francis Gillen contribute papers which range over Pinter's work for stage and radio. In 'Past, Present and Pinter' (*E&S*) Nigel Alexander analyzes *The Birthday Party, The Caretaker*, and *The Homecoming*, defining Pinter's characteristic mode as 'an art which eliminates the future'.

John and Anthea Lahr in their casebook on *The Homecoming*[5] usefully bring together fourteen essays and interviews which approach the play from contrasting points of view. There are interpretations by Martin Esslin, Irving Wardle, Margaret Croyden, John Russell Taylor, Steven M. L. Aronson, Rolf Fjelde, Bernard F. Dukore, Augusta Walker, and John Lahr. Especially interesting are the interviews with Peter Hall, who directed the play for the Royal Shakespeare Company, with John Bury, who designed the set, and with John Normington and Paul Rogers, who played Sam and Max.

In 'Dialogue and Character Splitting in Harold Pinter' (*NS*) Ruth Milberg takes *Landscape* and *Silence* as being typical of Pinter's dramatic form rather than a departure from it, since they make clear what the earlier plays often disguised—that Pinter is preoccupied with dialogue between two figures who represent man and woman, or masculine and feminine. In 'From Pooter to Pinter' (*CritQ*) Roger B. Henkle argues that Pinter is for much of the time offering a variation of the type of domestic comedy employed by George and Weedon Grossmith in *The Diary of a Nobody*; where the Grossmiths used the context of ordinary human activity to relieve the sense of anxiety, Pinter suppresses the kind of laughter which assuages *Angst*. In *Notes on*

---

[5] *A Casebook on Harold Pinter's 'The Homecoming'*, ed. by John Lahr and Anthea Lahr. Davis-Poynter. pp. xix+199. £2.50.

Contemporary Literature Stuart Hirschberg offers 'Pinter's Caricature of *Howards End* in *The Homecoming*', Bernard F. Dukore has a short piece on *The Collection* in *ETJ*, in *QJS* Leonard Powlick offers 'A Phenomenological Approach to Harold Pinter's *A Slight Ache*', and in *LWU* Hans-Wilhelm Schwarze's 'Orientierungslosigkeit und Betroffensein' considers the game-playing elements in *The Birthday Party*.

In 'Anthony and Peter Shaffer's Plays' (*AI*) Jules Glenn analyzes *Equus, White Lies, The White Liars*, and *The Public Eye* and speculates about how the characteristics of twins might influence their creative writing.

In *The Marriage of Contraries: Bernard Shaw's Middle Plays*[6] J. L. Wisenthal analyses *Man and Superman, Major Barbara, John Bull's Other Island, The Doctor's Dilemma, Pygmalion, Misalliance, Heartbreak House, Saint Joan*, and *Back to Methuselah*, seeing a recurring theme of opposing qualities being brought into balance. The thesis is not very convincing, except when it is self-evident, but it provides a general framework for the analytical discussion, which is well-informed and carried out with intelligence and perception. In 'George Bernard Shaw phonéticien' (*EA*) H. Appia is mainly concerned with Shaw's preoccupation with English accents, spelling, and phonetic script, with special reference to *Pygmalion*. In 'Language is Not Enough' (*MSE*), John J. Dolis writes on *St Joan*. In *TLS* (18 January) James Redmond writes on 'A Misattributed Speech in *Man and Superman*', arguing the case for a critical edition of Shaw's plays rather than the simple reprints offered even in the

[6] *The Marriage of Contraries: Bernard Shaw's Middle Plays*, by J. L. Wisenthal. Harvard U.P. pp. 259. $10.00.

new 'standard edition' recently published by Bodley Head.

It would not be appropriate to notice the individual items in the four journals devoted to criticism of Shaw's work, the reprinting of fugitive pieces, and the recounting of anecdotes about Shaw and his confrères: *The Shaw Review, The Shavian, The Independent Shavian*, and *GBS* (Rissho University, Tokyo) will be known to interested students.

There are three essays on Shaw in *MD*. In '*Widowers' Houses*: A Question of Genre' Bernard F. Dukore writes on the play as an example of the modern drama which 'delights, disturbingly'. In 'Sex, Socialism and the Collectivist Poet' Michael J. Sidnell touches on the subjects in his title and on ambivalence and detachment, with special reference to *Misalliance*. In 'The Natural History of *Major Barbara*' Kurt Tetzeli von Rosador defends that play from the critics who see it as 'unresolved paradox'.

In 'The Zealots of Zurich' (*TLS*, 12 July) Richard Ellmann offers a long, appreciative review of Tom Stoppard's *Travesties*, and in *The New Review* Ronald Hayman's 'profile' of Stoppard is especially interesting for Stoppard's discussion of his own work and that of Beckett.

In 'The Vision of J. M. Synge' (*ELT*) Bernard Laurie Edwards offers a general appreciation of *The Playboy of the Western World*, and Donald Gutierrez in 'Coming of Age in Mayo' (*HSL*) sees the same play as a 'rite of passage'. *The Shadow of the Glen* is analyzed by Paul N. Robinson in his 'The Peasant Play as Allegory' (*CEA*), and Nicholas Grene appreciates that play's subtlety and depth in his 'Repetition and Allusion' (*MD*). In 'Stoicism, Asceticism, and Ecstasy: Synge's *Deirdre of the Sorrows*' (*MD*), Brenda Murphy argues that Synge's achievement was to bring those three contrasting qualities together in a play which is complex but beautifully balanced. C. S. Faulk considers 'John Millington Synge and the Rebirth of Comedy' (*SHR*), Albert J. Solomon offers 'The Bird Girls of Ireland' (*CLQ*), and in *TN* Ann Saddlemyer has a short note 'On Editing Synge's Letters'—the volume of *Letters to Molly* will be followed by an edition of his letters to Lady Gregory and to W. B. Yeats. Andrew Carpenter's edition of *My Uncle John: Edward Stephens's Life of J. M. Synge* (O.U.P.) has not been available for review, and nor has Paul M. Levitt's *J. M. Synge: A Bibliography of Published Criticism* (Barnes & Noble).

John M. Ditsky's 'All Irish Here' (*DR*) looks at various portrayals of Irish characters in plays by Synge, O'Neill, Arthur Miller, and Pinter. Harold Ferrar's *Denis Johnston's Irish Theatre* (Dolmen) has not been available, nor has Arthur E. McGuinness's *George Fitzmaurice* (Bucknell U.P.), or Colin Smythe's edition of Lady Gregory's autobiography *Seventy Years* (Smythe).

Three volumes in Basil Blackwell's series Drama and Theatre Studies are very welcome. Arnold P. Hinchliffe's *British Theatre 1950–70*[7] begins with a brief chapter on European dramatists who have influenced our theatre (deciding that Brecht has had more effect than either Beckett or Ionesco), and proceeds to discuss the main playwrights, as well as many minor playwrights and theatrical occurrences, with grace and insight. Micheál ÓhAodha's *Theatre in Ireland*[8] begins with the opening of Dublin's first theatre in 1637, but is mainly concerned with twentieth-century dramatists. O'Casey and Synge are discussed at length, with brief remarks on a host of playwrights, directors, and actors; this is an amiable account from a man very familiar with the Dublin theatrical scene. Sybil Rosenfeld's *A Short History of Scene Design in Great Britain*[9] covers the enormous range of British theatre from the middle ages to the present day, but the narrative is lively and the material has been expertly selected and presented, so that scene design in the theatre is regularly aligned with developments in the visual arts, throughout the five main 'periods' discussed.

In *Play, Drama and Thought*[10] Richard Courtney offers a general account of 'the intellectual background to drama in education'. The ideas of philosophers, literary theorists, psychologists, anthropologists, sociologists from Plato to Piaget are summarized briefly for students of drama in colleges of education. In *The Theatre Crafts Book of Costume*[11] C. Ray Smith brings together twenty-two illustrated articles by and interviews with distinguished costume designers; there is a great deal of practical information and insight into the intricacies of designing for a wide range of plays in various kinds of theatrical settings. An interesting new journal, *Empirical Research in Theatre* (Bowling Green State U.), offers itself as 'a focal point for the collection and distribution of systematically processed information about theatre';

[7] *British Theatre 1950–70*, by Arnold P. Hinchliffe. Oxford: Basil Blackwell. pp. 205. £3.50.

[8] *Theatre in Ireland*, by Micheál ÓhAodha. Oxford: Basil Blackwell. pp. xiv + 160. £3.50.

[9] *A Short History of Scene Design in Great Britain*, by Sybil Rosenfeld. Oxford: Basil Blackwell. pp. xviii + 214. £5.25. Paper £2.50.

[10] *Play, Drama and Thought*, by Richard Courtney. Cassell. pp. xvii + 302. £3.25. Paper £1.95.

[11] *The Theatre Crafts Book of Costume*, ed. and introd. by C. Ray Smith. White Lion Publishers. pp. 224. £2.25.

the main emphasis will apparently be on sociological and psychological studies.

Walter Sorrell's *The Other Face: the Mask in the Arts*,[12] which is imaginatively and generously illustrated, explores the complex rôle played by masks in painting, sculpture, and dance as well as in such twentieth-century dramatists as Eliot, Yeats, Schnitzler, Ionesco, Brecht, Kokoschka, Cocteau, Pirandello, O'Neill, Genet, and Pinter.

J. C. Trewin's anthology[13] brings together more than sixty pieces dating from the seventeenth century, with the twentieth century especially well represented. Shaw, Agate, Synge, Ivor Brown, Ben Travers, Robert Speaight, Charles Morgan, Peter Bull, T. C. Worseley, and the editor himself supply passages of interest and amusement; this 'bedside book' has been put together with expert knowledge and careful discrimination.

[12] *The Other Face: the Mask in the Arts*, by Walter Sorell. Thames & Hudson. pp. 240. £6.00.

[13] *Theatre Bedside Book*, ed. and introd. by J. C. Trewin. David & Charles. pp. 352. £5.50.

XV

American Literature to 1900

DAVID JARRETT and MARY JARRETT

The chapter is divided as follows:
1. General; 2. Poetry; 3. Prose;
4. Drama.

Bibliographies of current articles are published quarterly in *AL* and annually in the summer supplement of *AQ*. Now revised in its fourth edition is the companion bibliography volume to the Macmillan *Literary History of the United States.*[1]

1. GENERAL (Works dealing with historical background to literature)

Frederick W. Turner III, in his introduction to *The Portable North American Indian Reader*,[2] claims that Americans have turned from the 'moral fad' of the Black to that of the American Indian, because they realize that concern about the Black must logically lead to action in the nature of massive socio-economic reform. Yet Turner stresses the moral and political necessity for understanding the Indian too: the 'moral fad' may have value. But it should not be allowed to result in the replacement of one stereotype of the Indian by another, however complimentary, since this equally refuses to acknowledge the Indian as a human being. He refers intriguingly to the Iroquois,

who, while they developed a form of government that inspired the admiration and emulation of America's founding fathers, and a theory of psychoanalysis that anticipated many of the major discoveries of Freud, at the same time waged cruel and barbarous war on their neighbours.

Turner, in order to avoid a stereotyped picture, divides his *Reader* into four sections: 'Myths and Tales' and 'Poetry and Oratory' from the Indians, and 'Culture Contact' and 'Image and Anti-Image' from whites and Indians together. 'Culture Contact' includes Mary Rowlandson's account of her capture by the Indians, a work examined by David L. Minter in 'By Dens of Lions: Notes on Stylization in Early Puritan Captivity Narratives' (*AL*, 1973). 'Image and Anti-Image' includes excerpts from, for example, the poems of Philip Freneau, Melville's *The Confidence-Man*, and Thomas Berger's *Little Big Man*. Each reader will undoubtedly query some omission—such as the elegaic ending of Fenimore Cooper's *The Last of the Mohicans*, but this is an excellent and original collection. Also available this year is John Bierhorst's *Four Masterworks of American Indian Literature*,[3] for which he has provided commentaries and some of the translations. The 'masterworks' are 'Quetzalcoatl', an Aztec hero myth, 'The Ritual of Condolence', an

[1] *Literary History of the United States: Bibliography*, ed. Robert E. Spiller, Willard Thorp, Thomas H. Johnson, Henry Seidel Canby, Richard M. Ludwig, William M. Gibson. New York: Macmillan. London: Collier Macmillan. pp. xxxviii+1466. $25.

[2] *The Portable North American Indian Reader*, ed. by Frederick W. Turner III. New York: Viking P. pp. xi+628. £1.65.

[3] *Four Masterworks of American Indian Literature*, ed. by John Bierhorst. New York: Farrar, Straus & Giroux. pp. xxiv+371; 10 illustrations.

Iroquois ceremonial, 'Cuceb', a Maya prophecy, and 'The Night Chant', a Navajo ceremonial. The illustrations include four maps, with both aboriginal and modern names, of Mexico, Iroquoia, Yucatan, and the Navajo country.

Far wider-ranging are Jerome Rothenberg's anthology of traditional American Indian poetry, *Shaking the Pumpkin*,[4] and *Literature of the American Indian*,[5] an anthology edited by Thomas E. Sanders and Walter W. Peek, both of American Indian descent and both aggressively political in their attitude to their material.

A social document, but with obvious literary relevance, is *Salem Possessed*[6] by Paul Boyer and Stephen Nissenbaum. This book seeks to interpret further the original material edited by the same pair and published in 1972: *Salem-Village Witchcraft: A Documentary Record of Local Conflict in Colonial New England*. It gives the facts of the witchcraft panic in 'Prologue: What Happened in 1692', and then explores the history of Salem Village up to 1692, making a close study of the backgrounds of the people involved.

Richard Beale Davis, in his *Literature and Society in Early Virginia 1608–1840*,[7] points out that 'Even in the seventeenth century when New England was hanging its witches, Virginians were common-sense rationalists who refrained from executing anyone for the alleged practice of the black arts, though their laws and the ignorance and bigotry of certain colonists caused them to bring a few persons to trial.' These trials are described in his chapter 'The Devil in Virginia in the Seventeenth Century'; other chapters deal with translation from the classics, oratory, history, poetry, fiction, letter-writing, and law. Most of these chapters are previously published essays. Davis remarks that he has 'picked up here and there evidences of a many-sided colonial Virginia mind', and his presentation of his material makes it seem more scattered and disjointed than it really is: he treats each piece of research separately in a square-bracketed introduction at the head of the chapter, and makes little effort to connect items together. Of these items, the most important for the student of literature are the argument for a Virginia novel almost a full generation before John P. Kennedy's *Swallow Barn* (1832), the argument for Arthur Blackamore's *Luck at Last or The Happy Unfortunate* (1723) as a genuine forerunner of *Pamela*, and the argument for the verse of the southern pulpit orator Samuel Davies as the 'rhymed representation' of the Great Awakening.

The Great Awakening and its relation to slavery, together with the relation of Benjamin Franklin to Puritanism, is discussed in the section on 'The Life of the Mind in Colonial America' in John C. Miller's social history, *This New Man, The American*.[8] Less helpful from a literary point of view, but worth consulting, is Melvin B. Endy's

[4] *Shaking the Pumpkin: Traditional Poetry of the Indian North Americas*, ed. by Jerome Rothenberg. New York: Doubleday, 1972. pp. xxvi+475.

[5] *Literature of the American Indian*, ed. by Thomas E. Sanders and Walter W. Peek. Collier-Macmillan, 1973. pp. xviii+534.

[6] *Salem Possessed: The Social Origins of Witchcraft*, by Paul Boyer and Stephen Nissenbaum. Cambridge, Mass., and London: Harvard U.P. pp. xxi+231.

[7] *Literature and Society in Early Virginia 1608–1840*, by Richard Beale Davis. Baton Rouge: Louisiana State U.P., 1973. pp. xxiv+332.

[8] *This New Man, The American: The Beginnings of the American People*, by John C. Miller. New York and London: McGraw-Hill. pp. xii+719.

William Penn and Early Quakerism.[9] An extremely important literary critical collection is *The American Puritan Imagination,*[10] important even though all the essays in the volume, except Bercovitch's own introductory essay, have appeared before, between 1957 and 1972. They cover both poetry and prose, and are divided into three groups. The first group, 'Approaches, themes and genres', is written by Norman S. Grabo, Larzer Ziff, David Minter, and Cecelia Tichi. The second group, which is the most useful, and most clearly benefits from the context of the other essays, is called 'Four major figures'. It comprises an essay by Jesper Rosenmeier on William Bradford, whose 'vision of history' has also been shrewdly discussed by Robert Daly (*AL*, 1973); an essay on Anne Bradstreet by Robert D. Richardson, Jr., who gives a very good account of 'Contemplations'; an essay on Edward Taylor by Karl Keller, who argues convincingly for the importance to Taylor of the process of meditation rather than the completed poem; and an essay on Cotton Mather by David Levin. In the last group, 'Continuities', Daniel B. Shea, Jr., writes on Jonathan Edwards, John F. Lynen on Benjamin Franklin, and Ursula Brumm on Christ and Adam as figures in American literature, moving as she does so into the twentieth century, and paying especial attention to Faulkner.

Fawn M. Brodie explains the subtitle of her biography of Thomas Jefferson[11] in her remark that 'This is a book about Jefferson and the life of the heart'. It includes an account of Jefferson's liaison with the slave girl Sally Hemings, on which W. Edward Farrison writes (*CLAJ*, 1973) in connexion with William Wells Brown's *Clotel; Or, The President's Daughter: A Narrative of Slave Life in the United States* (1853). The most useful chapter of the biography is that which deals with Jefferson's *Notes on the State of Virginia* (1784–85).

2. POETRY

Jefferson knew Phillis Wheatley's poetry, but held her talent in contempt. 'Religion indeed has produced a Phyllis Whately,' he wrote, 'but it could not produce a poet.' M. A. Richmond, in *Bid the Vassal Soar: Interpretive Essays on the Life and Poetry of Phillis Wheatley (ca. 1753–1784) and George Moses Horton (ca. 1797–1883),*[12] admits that neither poet had a major gift, and hence the interest of the study becomes biographical and sociological as much as literary. Similarly, R. Roderick Palmer in an article (*CLAJ*) on Jupiter Hammon, a slave poet born about 1712 in New York, sees his work only as 'a quaint prelude' to black poetry a century later. The title of Richmond's book is taken from a poem by George Moses Horton. Unlike Phillis Wheatley, who was born in Africa and brought up as a 'house nigger' in urban New England, Horton was born and brought up as a 'field nigger' in rural North Carolina. Part of his poetic repertoire consisted of love lyrics to southern belles, which he wrote to order for white university students.

[9] *William Penn and Early Quakerism*, by Melvin B. Endy, Jr. Princeton, N.J.: Princeton U.P., 1973. pp. viii+410.

[10] *The American Puritan Imagination: Essays in Revaluation*, ed. by Sacvan Bercovitch. C.U.P. pp. viii+265. £4.50.

[11] *Thomas Jefferson: An Intimate History*, by Fawn M. Brodie. Eyre Methuen. pp. 591; 25 illustrations.

[12] *Bid the Vassal Soar: Interpretive Essays on the Life and Poetry of Phillis Wheatley (ca. 1753–1784) and George Moses Horton (ca. 1797–1883)*, by M. A. Richmond. Washington, D.C.: Howard U.P. pp. xiii+216.

Joan R. Sherman's *Invisible Poets*[13] contains a section on Horton, and a bibliography for Phillis Wheatley; she claims that at least a hundred and thirty black men and women published poetry in America during the nineteenth century, and of these she has selected twenty-six for individual study. *Invisible Poets* is far more critical and analytical than *Bid the Vassal Soar*, but it is very cramped by the limitations of this scheme. The individual sections are very short and, owing to a basic lack of information, cannot really develop.

No more than for the black poets are extravagant claims made for John Trumbull by Victor E. Gimmestad[14] or for Ellery Channing by Robert N. Hudspeth.[15] Gimmestad, indeed, comments a little severely on the poor taste of a youthful 'Epithalamion', and freely admits that Trumbull, 'the wittiest of the "Hartford Wits"', is a minor poet whose only remaining works of general interest are 'The Progress of Dulness' and 'M 'Fingal'. He makes the modest claim that Trumbull could have been (although he was not) the first major American literary critic. Robert N. Hudspeth wonders, even more modestly, whether Thoreau's poet friend Ellery Channing was really the failure he has always been supposed. He certainly appears to have been an exasperating person, pestering in 1846, for example, his friends, relatives, and even slight acquaintances, 'former schoolmates, and anyone he thought sympathetic to poor poets', for money to go abroad as part of his poetic

education, and then returning after only sixteen days in Rome. Hudspeth's account contains an excellent analysis of 'New England and the Pastoral Ideal'.

The Historic Whitman,[16] as Joseph Jay Rubin explains, takes Whitman from 'the Long Island beginnings to July 1855, the month in which he published the first edition of the *Leaves of Grass*—and buried his father'. It includes a fascinating and comprehensive account of Whitman's newspaper work. In addition, Whitman's weekly *Letters from a Travelling Bachelor*, previously uncollected, are here reprinted from the *New York Sunday Dispatch*, October 1849 to January 1850.

A valuable companion volume is Floyd Stovall's *The Foreground of 'Leaves of Grass'*.[17] Its title is taken from Emerson's famous congratulatory letter of 1855: 'I greet you at the beginning of a great career, which yet must have had a long foreground somewhere, for such a start.' Stovall reveals in his Preface that he had originally meant to write a detailed critical study of the poems themselves, and had assembled ten thousand index cards for the purpose. 'Thus the years went by until the cards were yellow and my hair white with age', says Stovall, but when he finally retired and had time to write the study he found that he had completely lost his desire 'to instruct other people in the true meaning of *Leaves of Grass*'. His book, accordingly, makes no direct connexions between Whitman's life and the poems, but it does offer a wealth of material on Whitman's family, his journalism, his politics, his reading of popular

[13] *Invisible Poets: Afro-Americans of the Nineteenth Century*, by Joan R. Sherman. Urbana, Chicago and London: U. of Illinois P. pp. ix+270.

[14] *John Trumbull*, by Victor E. Gimmestad. (TUSAS) New York: Twayne. pp. 183.

[15] *Ellery Channing*, by Robert N. Hudspeth. (TUSAS) New York: Twayne, 1973. pp. 182.

[16] *The Historic Whitman*, by Joseph Jay Rubin. University Park and London: Pennsylvania State U.P. pp. xv+406.

[17] *The Foreground of 'Leaves of Grass'*, by Floyd Stovall. Charlottesville: U.P. of Virginia. pp. x+ 320.

literature, his theatre-going, and his intellectual background generally. The chapters on 'Early Reading: Popular Literature' and 'British Poets' are particularly illuminating.

Bert Hitchcock, in 'Walt Whitman: the Pedagogue as Poet' (*WWR*) reminds us that Whitman's school-mastering between the ages of seventeen and twenty-two helped him to mould his teacher persona as poet. P. Z. Rosenthal discusses 'The Language of Measurement in Whitman's Early Writing' (*WWR*, 1973) and '"Dilation" in Whitman's Early Writing' (*WWR*), and Arthur Wrobel writes on the influence of major phrenological ideas (*PMLA*) on Whitman's work. Leland Krauth examines his use of 'The Comradeship Theme' (*WWR*) and Carl Nelson offers a little-needed rejection of the view that Whitman lacks form (*WWR*). James E. Mulqueen treats 'Song of Myself' as 'Whitman's Hymn to Eros' (*WWR*), in direct opposition to the view of John B. Mason, in 'Walt Whitman's Catalogues: Rhetorical Means for Two Journeys in "Song of Myself"' (*AL*, 1973), that sensuality was something Whitman needed to move away from in his poetic journey. Affinities with other writers are variously suggested: with Jules Michelet by Arthur Geffen (*AL*, 1973), with Jacob Boehme by Monica R. Tisiker (*WWR*), with Hugo by Charles M. Lombard (*WWR*, 1973), and with Rimbaud by David J. Wells (*WWR*, 1973).

Whitman's affinity with Wallace Stevens is suggested in a full-length study by Diane Wood Middlebrook.[18] The analogies are not always very convincing, but there is a good discussion of the possible influence of 'Crossing Brooklyn Ferry' on Stevens's 'The Bouquet'. Middlebrook postulates the relevance to Stevens of Whitman 'as an achieved myth-maker and as the American continuator of the Romantic tradition', and in her last and best chapter, 'Whitman and Stevens: Nature in the Form of a Man', she analyzes the difference between the myths which Whitman and Stevens evolved.

The major literary event in the area covered by this chapter is Richard B. Sewall's brilliant and meticulous biography of Emily Dickinson.[19] It profits from all previous biographical works on Emily Dickinson, but will inevitably supersede them. Sewall treats the first volume as background, and uses it to investigate the relevant culture of the Puritan New England into which Emily Dickinson was born, the Dickinson ancestry, the family environment, and the personalities and personal histories of those who knew her. The second volume opens with Emily Dickinson's birth, and yet the reader already knows her through the eyes of her family, friends, and acquaintances. The poetry is quoted extensively, and viewed with a keen critical intelligence throughout, and the life is described both seriously and with wit. Sewall convincingly contradicts the notion of the austerity of Emily Dickinson's background, and leaves the reader with the impression that his biography is the nearest we can expect to get to this elusive and enigmatic personality.

Although Sewall carefully examines the mystery of the 'Master Letters', his reading of Emily Dickinson's life tends to support the contention of David Porter in 'The Crucial Experience in Emily Dickinson's Poetry'

---

[18] *Walt Whitman and Wallace Stevens*, by Diane Wood Middlebrook. Ithaca and London: Cornell U.P. pp. 238.

[19] *The Life of Emily Dickinson*, by Richard B. Sewall, in two volumes. New York: Farrar, Straus & Giroux. pp. xxvii+821; 93 illustrations.

(*ESQ*) that 'the elementary experience has little to do with inaccessible lovers. The crucial affair for her, rather, is living after things happen.' An interesting light is thrown on this conclusion by Francis J. Molson's explanation of 'Emily Dickinson's Rejection of the Heavenly Father' (*NEQ*): her conviction that God had treacherously refused to fulfil her expectations of success in friendship and love.

Vivian R. Pollak, in 'Emily Dickinson's Valentines' (*AQ*) sets two of Emily Dickinson's surviving youthful poems in the context of the popularity of the valentine as a subliterary genre in the first part of the nineteenth century. Laurence Perrine, in 'Dickinson's "The Robin is the One"' (*Expl*), examines very briefly the organizing principle of progression in the poem, and suggests that Emily Dickinson made a slip in transcribing it. Roland Hagenbüchle addresses himself to a fascinating problem in 'Precision and Indeterminacy in the Poetry of Emily Dickinson' (*ESQ*), but his perception that 'The poet experiences the effects of things, but nature itself remains an enigma' is barricaded behind an impenetrable mass of diagrams and critical terminology.

In 1862, near the beginning of her long correspondence with Thomas Wentworth Higginson, Emily Dickinson wrote, 'When I state myself, as the Representative of the Verse—it does not mean—me—but a supposed person.' John Emerson Todd takes this as the starting point for his short study of *Emily Dickinson's Use of the Persona*;[20] he draws attention to the fact that almost one hundred and fifty of the poems begin with the word 'I'. Todd's divisions of the personae into 'The "Little Girl" Persona', 'The

"Lover-Wife-Queen" Persona', 'Personae in Death and Eternity', and 'Personae Involving Psychology and the Divided Personality' occasionally overlap and otherwise prove recalcitrant, and his style is sometimes bizarrely colloquial in a manner reminiscent of Emily Dickinson herself: 'The persona reaches eternity ahead of schedule'. He remains satisfactorily close to the texts throughout his discussion, as does Inder Nath Kher in *The Landscape of Absence*.[21] Kher's chief concern is to examine the imagery and symbolism of the poems to get a comprehensive view of Emily Dickinson's creative mind, but, like Todd, he looks carefully at his selected poems one by one. Todd sometimes descends to rather obvious explications, which Kher does not, but Kher is ultimately a little vague. He proposes Emily Dickinson as a mythopoeic, ontological, tragic, and existential poet, and compares her very briefly with, for example, Blake, Coleridge, and Wordsworth.

3. PROSE

As in the field of poetry, there is still considerable interest in literary attitudes to the Black American. Richard Slotkin gives a chronological checklist of 'Narratives of Negro Crime in New England, 1675–1800' (*AQ*, 1973) and treats the execution sermon in particular as contributing to a stereotyped myth of the Negro. Dorothy M. Broderick examines this stereotyped myth as it emerged for child consumption between 1827 and 1967 in her *Image of the Black in Children's Fiction*,[22] and finds that the

[20] *Emily Dickinson's Use of the Persona*, by John Emerson Todd. The Hague and Paris: Mouton, 1973. pp. xvi+95.

[21] *The Landscape of Absence: Emily Dickinson's Poetry*, by Inder Nath Kher. New Haven and London: Yale U.P. pp. xi+354. £9.90.

[22] *Image of the Black in Children's Fiction*, by Dorothy M. Broderick. New York and London: R. R. Bowker, 1973. pp. viii+219; 10 illustrations.

literature she surveys is on the whole condescending and patronizing in its attitude rather than aggressively racist. She makes the more general point that children's literature habitually lags behind acceptable social attitudes, and carefully stresses the fact that her study is one written by a white for other whites in an effort to prevent a repetition of past mistakes.

Another very ethnically conscious critic is Sylvia Lyons Render. In her long biographical and analytical introduction to *The Short Fiction of Charles W. Chesnutt*[23] she emphasizes Chesnutt's refusal to pass for a white man, as he could easily have done. At the same time, she makes a serious attempt to assess the literary merit of the stories. William L. Andrews, indeed, in 'The Significance of Charles W. Chesnutt's "Conjure Stories"' (*SLJ*), shows that Chesnutt's initial fame was achieved without reference to his black descent or to the racial issues of the time. Andrews describes the objective balance kept by Chesnutt between the obligations of the artist and the demands of popular local colour realism; Merrill Maguire Skaggs, in *The Folk of Southern Fiction*,[24] deals with the local colour fiction which sprang up between the late eighteen-sixties and the turn of the century. He also discusses southwestern humour, for which Charles E. Davis and Martha B. Hudson offer a checklist of criticism in *MissQ*, and, in his introductory chapter, the use of the Negro narrator, which is also examined in the work of Joel Chandler Harris by Louis D. Rubin, Jr., in 'Uncle Remus

and the Ubiquitous Rabbit' (*SoR*). William Bedford Clark discusses a different kind of ignorant narrator in the Harris story 'Where's Duncan?' in 'The Serpent of Lust in the Southern Garden' (*SoR*).

Richard Hildreth's novel with black hero-narrator, *The Slave or Memoirs of Archy Moore* (1836), despite receiving a chapter of commentary in Jean Fagan Yellin's *The Intricate Knot*,[25] is still being rescued from oblivion. Nicholas Canaday, Jr., writes on it in the context of other early antislavery novels (*CLAJ*, 1973) and Evan Brandstadter in 'Uncle Tom and Archy Moore: The Antislavery Novel as Ideological Symbol' (*AQ*) makes illuminating connexions between Hildreth and Harriet Beecher Stowe, whose *Dred* (1856) is discussed in Theodore R. Hovet's 'Christian Revolution: Harriet Beecher Stowe's Response to Slavery and the Civil War' (*NEQ*). Frederick Trautmann writes on 'Harriet Beecher Stowe's Public Readings in New England' (*NEQ*).

James A. Sappenfield writes on Benjamin Franklin's literary apprenticeship as a journalist. He claims Franklin as the first and the most celebrated of all America's journalist-authors, and takes his title, *A Sweet Instruction*,[26] from a line from *Poor Richard*: 'In every Rill a sweet Instruction flows.' This study is mainly historical and biographical, but Sappenfield writes interestingly on the image of Franklin in American literature. He claims, for example, that Twain, bitterly attacking Frank-

[23] *The Short Fiction of Charles W. Chesnutt*, ed. by Sylvia Lyons Render. Washington, D.C.: Howard U.P. pp. 422.
[24] *The Folk of Southern Fiction*, by Merrill Maguire Skaggs. Athens: U. of Georgia P., 1972. pp. xiii+280.

[25] *The Intricate Knot: Black Figures in American Literature, 1776–1863*, by Jean Fagan Yellin. New York U.P., 1972. pp. ix+260.
[26] *A Sweet Instruction: Franklin's Journalism as a Literary Apprenticeship*, by James A. Sappenfield. Carbondale and Edwardsville: Southern Illinois U.P.; London and Amsterdam: Feffer & Simons, 1973. pp. xiv+230.

lin in a 'Memoir' of 1870, is typical of commentators on Franklin in that he appears to have read only the *Autobiography* and 'The Way to Wealth'; yet Sappenfield's own section on the *Autobiography* is easily the best part of the book.

The Diary of Elihu Hubbard Smith (1771–1798)[27] is a little unrevealing. As the editor, James E. Cronin, remarks: 'Few men today would note in their diaries that they had dined with a president of the United States and fail to add even a word of comment.' Far more valuable than the diary proper is Smith's account, unique in its fullness and vividness of detail, of his childhood in late eighteenth-century New England. These 'Notes from Recollections of My Life from My Birth till the Age of Eleven', compiled in 1797, have a pleasingly terse style. Smith records of his five-year-old self that '"peace of Conscience", an expression in the Catechism, was supposed by me, at the time, to mean a "piece of Hung Beef boiled".' He comments succinctly, 'Such is efficacy of fatiguing the recollection and harassing the mind of infants with Creeds & Catechisms.'

Elihu Hubbard Smith's literary interests included the editing of Charles Brockden Brown, whose *Wieland* is considered as 'The Americanization of Faust' by Joseph A. Soldati (*ESQ*), and whose *Ormond* receives critical attention in 'Ormond: Seduction in a New Key' (*AL*, 1973) by Sydney J. Krause and in 'Brown's *Ormond*: The Fruits of Improvization' (*AQ*) by Paul C. Rodgers, Jr., who shrewdly examines Brown's art in relation to his rapid, free-wheeling mode of writing, but who concludes

only that Brown 'could always think of something more to say'.

Two books on Washington Irving edited by Andrew B. Myers examine Irving's art in relation to the contemporary background of politics, racial tensions, religion, and society generally. *The Worlds of Washington Irving*,[28] richly illustrated, is the less academic of the two. *The Knickerbocker Tradition: Washington Irving's New York*[29] comprises six essays: 'The Popularization of Politics in Irving's New York' by Michael D'Innocenzo, 'New York Society: High and Low' by James F. Richardson, 'Religion and Politics in Knickerbocker Times' by Joseph L. Blau, 'Political Satire in Knickerbocker's *History*' by Michael L. Black, 'Sunnyside: From Saltbox to Snuggery to Shrine' by Andrew B. Myers, and 'New York: A City of Constant Change and Accommodation' by Jacob Judd. Each essay is competent, but Michael L. Black's, showing how Irving used his sources, is the most valuable for the literary critic.

William L. Vance writes on Fenimore Cooper's *The Prairie* in *PMLA*, concluding that Cooper makes various differing distinctions between man and animals, and that Natty Bumppo himself is a 'rare example of fully human life achieved at the most primitive remove from mere animality'.

A short study of Josh Billings (1818–1885)[30] gives a clear and straightforward account of his life and work, and places him usefully in the

[27] *The Diary of Elihu Hubbard Smith (1771–1798)*, ed. by James E. Cronin. Philadelphia: American Philosophical Society, 1973. pp. xiii+481.

[28] *The Worlds of Washington Irving 1783–1859*, ed. by Andrew B. Myers. Tarrytown, N.Y.: Sleepy Hollow Restorations. pp. ix+134; 109 illustrations. $8.95.

[29] *The Knickerbocker Tradition: Washington Irving's New York*, ed. by Andrew B. Myers. Tarrytown, N.Y.: Sleepy Hollow Restorations. pp. vi+153; 7 illustrations. $8.

[30] *Josh Billings (Henry Wheeler Shaw)*, by David B. Kesterson. (TUSAS) New York: Twayne, 1973. pp. 157.

context of other phonetic-spelling humourists.

Paul C. Wermuth writes in the same series on Bayard Taylor.[31] He identifies Taylor as 'The Writer in nineteenth-century America', a literary figure of very great popularity during his lifetime (1825–1878), and one of the best embodiments of the 'Genteel Tradition'. Wermuth, who makes particularly harsh judgements on Taylor's fiction, diagnoses his artistic failure as arising from his own aspirations to the 'genteel' and his willingness to conform in the interests of literary success. Wermuth admits, however, that this is not a complete explanation: '. . . the question of Bayard Taylor still nags at the mind'.

Ralph Waldo Emerson: Portrait of a Balanced Soul[32] is another in Edward Wagenknecht's inexorable list of biographies. It treats the man, not his work, but as Wagenknecht says rather dolefully, 'This book is concerned with the character and personality of Ralph Waldo Emerson rather than with either his ideas or his writings as literature, but it has not always been possible to differentiate clearly between the various elements.'

Erik Ingvar Thurin, in *The Universal Autobiography of Ralph Waldo Emerson*,[33] reminds the reader of Emerson's dictum that all literature is 'plainly the work of one all-seeing, all-hearing gentleman', and that moreover 'no man can write anything' who does not feel that he is that gentleman; in Emerson's own terms his life must have a 'universal validity'. But, despite, for example, a

valiant attempt to assemble coherently Emerson's views on womanhood, Thurin makes dull work of it.

Worthwhile articles on Emerson include Thomas A. Tenney on 'Emerson and *The Encyclopaedia Americana*' (*ESQ*, 1973), Charles W. Mignon on 'Emerson to Chapman: Four Letters about Publishing' (*ESQ*, 1973), Carl M. Lindner on 'Newtonianism in Emerson's *Nature*' (*ESQ*), and Brian M. Barbour on 'Emerson's "Poetic" Prose' (*MLQ*). David Sowd writes on 'Peter Kaufmann's Correspondence with Emerson' (*ESQ*), pondering as he does so whether Peter Kaufmann has written the longest letter in existence. Sheldon W. Liebman examines 'The Origins of Emerson's Early Poetics: His Reading in the Scottish Common Sense Critics' (*AL*, 1973) but, although he cites Hugh Blair, Archibald Alison, and Thomas Campbell as influences, says that 'the specific nature of the Scottish influence on Emerson's poetics must be deferred to a subsequent essay'. Jeffrey Steinbrink, in 'Novels of Circumstance and Novels of Character' (*ESQ*), sets out to show that Emerson did not dismiss fiction 'in a simple, sweeping gesture', but concedes that he was certainly an extremely unsympathetic fiction-reader. Emerson was particularly withering about Jane Austen, but more difficult to understand is his failure to appreciate Hawthorne.

Taylor Stoehr's 'Transcendentalist Attitudes Toward Communitism and Individualism' (*ESQ*), concerned mainly with Emerson, Bronson Alcott, Charles Lane, Thoreau, and the experiments at Brook Farm and Fruitlands, provides incidentally some excellent background for the study of Hawthorne. Bronson Alcott, not only Emerson's 'highest genius of the time', but also his 'tedious archangel', reappears in Joel Myerson's article

[31] *Bayard Taylor*, by Paul C. Wermuth. (TUSAS) New York: Twayne. pp. 199.
[32] *Ralph Waldo Emerson: Portrait of a Balanced Soul*, by Edward Wagenknecht. New York: O.U.P. pp. 307.
[33] *The Universal Autobiography of Ralph Waldo Emerson*, by Erik Ingvar Thurin. Lund: Gleerup. pp. 288.

'Bronson Alcott's "Scripture for 1840"' (*ESQ*). Alcott's 'Scripture' was his journal and Myerson claims that 'The journal selections . . . not only present new information about the Transcendentalists, but also show Alcott changing from a disappointed city-dweller to a contented husband-man, all leading towards the Fruit-lands experiment in 1843.' Myerson introduces another transcendentalist in '"A True and High Minded Person": Transcendentalist Sarah Clarke' (*SWR*), and John J. Duffy edits the letters of another in *Coleridge's American Disciples: The Selected Correspondence of James Marsh*.[34] James Marsh (1794–1842) was a professor of philosophy, President of the University of Vermont from 1826 to 1833, and leader of the Vermont branch of the Transcendental Movement. Duffy concludes: 'That Marsh has a place of import-ance in American intellectual history is thus glaringly apparent.' The letters to and from Marsh run from 1819 to 1842, and Duffy claims that they help to illuminate the tension between the heritage of the Puritan mind and the sensibility formed by the Romantic revolution. But the letters, besides being annoyingly set out, with the footnotes almost invariably over the page, are not really very illuminating, far less so than Duffy's introduction. It is interesting to learn, for instance, that Marsh reorganized the curri-culum of the University of Vermont on the basis of Coleridge's distinction between Reason and Understanding. Nor does Marsh emerge as a very attractive personality. At his best he is endearingly priggish, as in his letter to his brother Leonard from New York in 1822: 'The city is in many respects vastly superior to Boston and the interest much more various. But I soon become tired of seeing the out-side of things however splendid they may be and would rather have an hour's conversation with a man of intelligence than see all the mag-nificence of Broadway.'

James McIntosh's *Thoreau as Romantic Naturalist: His Shifting Stance toward Nature*[35] calls attention to the dialectic set up by Thoreau's desire for involvement in nature con-fronted by his feelings of isolation from it. McIntosh treats as especially important Thoreau's affinities with Wordsworth and Goethe, and pro-vides his own translations for the latter. He uses quotation from Thoreau well, and although his comments on the works, especially *The Maine Woods* and *Walden*, are sometimes rather obvious, he writes extremely well on Thoreau's 'Last Nature Essays': 'Walking', 'Wild Apples', 'The Succession of Forest Trees', and 'Autumnal Tints'. This is a clear and unpretentious study.

William L. Howarth in his pains-taking collection of *The Literary Manuscripts of Henry David Thoreau*[36] offers a first-class aid to Thoreau scholars, together with an absorbing introduction about the history of the manuscripts. Articles worth noticing on Thoreau are Gordon V. Bou-dreau's 'H. D. Thoreau, William Gilpin, and the Metaphysical Ground of the Picturesque' (*AL*, 1973), William J. Scheick's 'The House of Nature in Thoreau's *A Week*' (*ESQ*), Mario L. D'Avanzo's 'Fortitude and Nature in Thoreau's *Cape Cod*' (*ESQ*), Barbara Harrell Carson's

---

[34] *Coleridge's American Disciples: The Selected Correspondence of James Marsh*, ed. by John J. Duffy. Amherst: U. of Massa-chusetts P., 1973. pp. xv+272.

[35] *Thoreau as Romantic Naturalist: His Shifting Stance toward Nature*, by James McIntosh. Ithaca and London: Cornell U.P. pp. 310; 3 illustrations.

[36] *The Literary Manuscripts of Henry David Thoreau*, by William L. Howarth. Columbus: Ohio State U.P. pp. 408.

'An Orphic Hymn in *Walden*' (*ESQ*), and Kenneth W. Rhoads's 'Thoreau: The Ear and the Music' (*AL*).

A good basic survey of the Transcendentalist Movement's literary art and criticism is Lawrence Buell's *Literary Transcendentalism: Style and Vision in the American Renaissance*.[37] Buell gives an informative 'general profile' of the Transcendentalists in his introduction. He writes well on 'Ellery Channing: The Major Phase of a Minor Poet', and on the similarities between Jones Very and Whitman in 'Transcendental Egotism in Very and Whitman', but his preoccupation in this study is to attempt to contribute to a better understanding of the relationship between style and vision in all nonfictional literature.

Even better is *American Transcendentalism, 1830–1860*[38] by Paul F. Boller, Jr. It is always difficult to organize material in a critical work of this nature, but Boller makes convincing divisions into 'Religious Radicalism', 'Intuitional Philosophy', 'Transcendental Idealism', 'Social Reform', 'Cosmic Optimism', and 'Transience and Permanence'. The book remains essentially introductory, but it is clear and coherent, and makes a superb use of quotation and anecdote.

Kevin Starr proposes as his topic *Americans and the California Dream 1850–1915*,[39] but in fact his first chapter is his best, on 'Prophetic Patterns 1786–1850', in which he treats R. H. Dana's *Two Years Before the Mast* (1840) as the 'first best-

selling book about California'. Starr also writes well on Gold Rush literature, and the way 'Bret Harte gave California charm' through his use of human comedy and sentiment. But much of his book hovers on the uneasy borderline between sociology and literature.

Similarly, many of the articles on Poe hover on the borderline between biography and criticism. Examples of this are Karl E. Oelke's 'Poe at West Point—A Revaluation' (*Poe Studies*, 1973) and Benjamin Lease's 'John Neal and Edgar Allan Poe' (*Poe Studies*), on Poe's 'mentor' who gave him what he called 'the first jog in my literary career'. Emilio De Grazia and Burton R. Pollin write on 'Poe's Devoted Democrat, George Lippard' (*Poe Studies*, 1973) and 'More on Lippard and Poe' (*Poe Studies*) respectively, and Burton R. Pollin also gives an account in *TSLL* of 'Poe, Freeman Hunt, and Four Unrecorded Reviews of Poe's Works'. John Ostrom offers a 'Fourth Supplement to *The Letters of Poe*' (*AL*), supplementing the 1948 Gordian Press *Letters of Edgar Allan Poe* and previous articles in *AL* of 1952 and 1957, and giving a poignant picture of Poe soliciting a job from James K. Paulding: 'Could I obtain the most unimportant Clerkship in your gift— *any thing, by sea or land*—to relieve me from the miserable life of literary drudgery to which I now, with a breaking heart, submit, and for which neither my temper nor my abilities have fitted me, I would never again repine at any dispensation of God'. Poe is also shown soliciting articles for the *Southern Literary Messenger*, and Bernard Rosenthal, in 'Poe, Slavery, and the *Southern Literary Messenger*: A Reexamination' (*Poe Studies*), confirms that the 'Paulding Review', a review of two books on slavery (which Rosenthal points out

---

[37] *Literary Transcendentalism: Style and Vision in the American Renaissance*, by Lawrence Buell. Ithaca and London: Cornell U.P., 1973. pp. viii+336.

[38] *American Transcendentalism, 1830–1860: An Intellectual Inquiry*, by Paul F. Boller, Jr. New York: G. P. Putnam's Sons. pp. xxiii+227.

[39] *Americans and the California Dream 1850–1915*, by Kevin Starr. New York: O.U.P., 1973. pp. xv+494; 30 illustrations.

is more accurately the 'Paulding-Drayton Review'), has been correctly ascribed to Poe.

Pasquale Jannaccone's 'The Aesthetics of Edgar Poe' (*Poe Studies*), first published in Italy in 1895 when Jannaccone was twenty-three, is diffuse but interesting historically as an example of Poe scholarship. Two contemporary critics suggest the influence of Dickens on Poe: Benjamin Franklin Fisher's 'Dickens and Poe: Pickwick and "Ligeia"' (*Poe Studies*, 1973) proposes a relationship between Poe's story and the 'madman's manuscript' of the eleventh chapter of *Pickwick Papers*, and Laurence Senelick in 'Charles Dickens and "The Tell-Tale Heart"' (*Poe Studies*, 1973) debates whether Poe drew on *Master Humphrey's Clock*. Roberta Reeder uses the terms of Jungian psychology in '"The Black Cat" as a Study in Repression' (*Poe Studies*), and Allan Smith treats the same story, with 'Berenice' and 'Rue Morgue', in 'The Psychological Context of Three Tales by Poe' (*JAmS*, 1973). Wendy Stallard Flory writes well on 'Usher's Fear and the Flaw in Poe's Theories of the Metamorphosis of the Senses' (*Poe Studies*). Paul John Eakin (*AL*, 1973) discusses Poe's preoccupation with final knowledge and concludes that Poe is most compelling when 'we linger upon the very verge'. He rejects the view that *Arthur Gordon Pym* is existential or absurdist, claiming, 'The equivocation . . . of the double ending of *Pym* does not cast the existence of meaning in doubt but rather man's capacity to apprehend it.' Kathleen Sands argues for 'The Mythic Initiation of Arthur Gordon Pym' (*Poe Studies*): 'If Pym is viewed as the initiate whose journeys are in fact a dramatic and symbolic search for unity in the diversity of the world, the two narratives of Arthur Gordon Pym fuse and form a

logical progression in the formation of the mythic hero.' Robert L. Carringer writes of the 'Circumscription of Space and Form of Poe's *Arthur Gordon Pym*' (*PMLA*) in relation to the isolation of Poe's characters in their limited prospects and interests and their withdrawal into self.

Arne Axelsson writes on the isolation of Hawthorne's characters in his book *The Links in the Chain*.[40] Despite his claim to originality in showing that 'the isolation-interdependence theme is intimately connected with other major themes which have been discovered in Hawthorne's works', his work is not useful in offering any fresh critical insights, but in giving, rather, an extremely clear and comprehensive survey of previous Hawthorne criticism on this topic. Axelsson conscientiously gives credit wherever it is due, but in doing so inevitably undercuts his own claims as innovator. He follows Hawthorne's own advice to 'look through the whole range of his fictitious characters', but, again, although his comments are sensible and just, there are no new perceptions here.

John J. McDonald in '"The Old Manse" and Its Mosses: The Inception and Development of *Mosses from an Old Manse*' (*TSLL*) writes of the way in which Hawthorne distanced himself from his material. He describes the difficulties Hawthorne experienced in writing *Mosses*, partly because of his financial situation and partly because 'The Old Manse' itself eluded him for so long; he concludes that in writing *Mosses* 'Hawthorne moved toward a new way of dealing with reality.' Having abandoned historical material, which automatically distanced him from his

[40] *The Links in the Chain: Isolation and Interdependence in Nathaniel Hawthorne's Fictional Characters*, by Arne Axelsson. Uppsala: Universitetsbiblioteket. pp. 190.

immediate experience, Hawthorne substituted material which was, on the whole, contemporary, achieving distance from this by what he himself called an 'impersonal' style.

Denis Brown examines 'My Kinsman, Major Molineux' and 'Young Goodman Brown' in terms of existential psychoanalysis (*CRevAS*, 1973); Charles Swann, in 'Hawthorne: History versus Romance' (*JAmS*, 1973) reacts against established critical views and deprecates the emphasis given to Romance, myth, and archetype in the consideration of the American novel, insisting on the reading of *The Scarlet Letter* as a political novel; Otis B. Wheeler argues in 'Love Among the Ruins: Hawthorne's Surrogate Religion' (*SoR*) for Hawthorne's view that, in life and art, love 'is a sacred mystery having redemptive force for a fallen world'. Unfortunately for Wheeler's argument, these words arise from his quotation of Hester's 'What we did had a consecration of its own', which is misleading, since Hawthorne is certainly not suggesting here any new dispensation through adultery. Wheeler does offer, however, a sound discussion of Hawthorne's 'ambivalence about feminine nature and love', citing, for example, his 'jocular and irreverent' realistic treatment in the anti-romantic 'Mrs. Bullfrog', and pointing out that Hawthorne's portrayals of triumphant redemption seem either insipid, perverse, and confused, or equivocal, whereas his portraits of failure are far more powerful and interesting.

Daniel B. Banes has a useful note on 'Two Reviews of *The Scarlet Letter* in *Holden's Dollar Magazine*' (*AL*, 1973). One review is summarized, not quoted, but the other is quoted in full: it expresses approval on both moral and artistic grounds, but considers the Custom House introduction, although good in itself, an encumbrance on the novel. The Custom House introduction surely deserves a full consideration in the context of Mary Allan's claim in 'Smiles and Laughter in Hawthorne' (*PQ*, 1973) that Hawthorne's work evokes little humorous response of the benign or the grotesque kind.

Daniel R. Barnes suggests a connexion between 'Orestes Brownson and Hawthorne's Holgrave' (*AL*, 1973): that Holgrave may be a satirical portrait of Brownson, the reformer of the eighteen-forties who turned Roman Catholic. If so, says Barnes, it would help to explain the otherwise puzzling and rather comic 'conversion' of Holgrave at the end of *The House of the Seven Gables*. Taylor Stoehr writes on 'Physiognomy and Phrenology in Hawthorne' (*HLQ*) and shows that although in 1836, as editor of the *American Magazine of Useful and Entertaining Knowledge*, Hawthorne expressed doubts about these pseudo-sciences, not only may his use of physiognomical symbolism be observed in his earliest tales—for example, 'Alice Doane's Appeal', 'Roger Malvin's Burial', and 'My Kinsman, Major Molineux'—but that Hawthorne's favourite plot is 'the reading of character in the face, the risks taken by the artist who exercises his skill in character-reading, and the various "magical" and "supernatural" phenomena, especially prophecies and curses, that might be associated with such feats.' All these themes are elaborated most fully in *Seven Gables*, which Stoehr proceeds to examine in detail.

Wayne T. Caldwell discusses 'Clothing Imagery' in *Seven Gables* (*ESQ*, 1973), suggesting the relevance of Hawthorne's grounding in the allegorical 'emblem' tradition. Donald G. Darnell relates this tradition to Hawthorne's fictional technique, learned from Spenser and Bunyan, in '"Doctrine by Ensample": The Emblem and *The Marble Faun*' (*TSLL*, 1973). Various other articles deal with literary influences or parallels: Clifford C. Huffman uses Spenser's Legend of Temperance in Book II of *The Faerie Queene* as an analogy with 'History in Hawthorne's "Custom House"' (*ClioW*, 1973); Jane Chambers uses the same Legend to illuminate 'The Birthmark' (*ESQ*); John O. Rees, Jr., shows how Shakespeare's *Antony and Cleopatra, The Tempest*, and *As You Like It* contribute to *The Blithedale Romance* (*ESQ*, 1973); Hazel M. Koskenlinna discusses 'Setting, Image, and Symbol in Scott and Hawthorne' (*ESQ*, 1973). David B. Kesterson and Richard H. Fogle suggest Dantean parallels (*ESQ* 1973) and Coleridgean parallels (*ESQ*, 1973) respectively in *The Marble Faun*. Dennis Berthold in 'Hawthorne, Ruskin, and the Gothic Revival: Transcendent Gothic in *The Marble Faun*' (*ESQ*) thinks it likely that Hawthorne knew Ruskin's *Seven Lamps of Architecture* and *Stones of Venice*. Berthold traces Hawthorne's typical American and Protestant initial distrust of Gothic style, and his enthusiastic acceptance of it when he saw the cathedrals of Europe. Berthold then discusses the symbolic function of the Gothic style in chs. 32–35 of *The Marble Faun*, and notes the *Tanglewood Tales* preface in which organic Gothic is used as a symbol of Hawthorne's art. But he does not apply the concept of Gothic to Hawthorne's romances as a whole: for example to *Seven Gables*, with its Gothic conventions, and its 'purified Gothic' made part of nature.

David Jarrett, in 'Hawthorne and Hardy as Modern Romancers' (*NCF*) demonstrates how *Seven Gables* influenced Hardy's *A Laodicean*,

and Richard Poirier[41] writes of the debt of James in *The Ambassadors* to *The Blithedale Romance*, although he finds the former the superior work. Poirier calls his article 'From Visionary to Voyeur' because he sees Miles Coverdale as Emersonian man debased to voyeuristic dandy. But it could equally be called 'From Voyeur to Visionary', since it moves from Coverdale's narcissism to Strether's triumph of the artistic imagination which 'is finally responsible not for what it receives from reality but for the reality it creates'. The article becomes lopsided in its sympathies for James, and, for example, expresses surprise that Hawthorne should be connected with the development of the concept of art as an activity rather than a product—whereas Hawthorne is always writing about the activity of the artist.

The character of Coverdale is also considered by Kent Bales in 'The Allegory and the Radical Romantic Ethic of *The Blithedale Romance*' (*AL*). The opening of his article is not very helpful, but Bales goes on to propound the notion that when Coverdale confronts Hollingsworth and Priscilla he is allegorically confronting himself, or aspects of himself, so that the question 'What retribution is there here?' is addressed as much to himself as to Hollingsworth. The answer to his question is that convention in the person of Priscilla is in control; because Coverdale too loves conventional Priscilla he has become an idler, and, argues Bales, 'To love convention is to love repression, and to love repression is—for the neurotic—to love oneself. What better image of that truth than "frosty bachelor" Miles Coverdale frozen before his mirror?' Carl Dennis, on

[41] In *Der Amerikanische Roman im 19. und 20. Jahrhundert*, ed. by Edgar Lohner. Berlin: Erich Schmidt Verlag.

the other hand, in '*The Blithedale Romance* and the Problem of Self-Integration' (*TSLL*, 1973), decides that no character in the novel solves this problem, but in the process very much underrates the selfishness of Coverdale.

Terence Martin's 'Hawthorne's Public Decade and the Values of Home' (*AL*) tells how Hawthorne in England extended his sense of 'home-feeling' and how he praised London after his 'divided and swirling feelings about Rome'. Martin goes on to claim that 'the human element, so crucial to his life and art, is made possible only by scarceness or sparseness', and that since Hawthorne deliberately courted 'thin' settings, he worked under a handicap in *The Marble Faun* and failed to finish *The Ancestral Footstep* and *Dr. Grimshawe's Secret*. Claudia D. Johnson, in 'Hawthorne and Nineteenth-Century Perfectionism' (*AL*, 1973) suggests the influence of perfectionist thought on Hawthorne, particularly that of Thomas C. Upham, who was on the faculty at Bowdoin College while Hawthorne was a student there.

The Myth of America by Viola Sachs[42] and *The Three Masks of American Tragedy* by Dan Vogel[43] both treat Hawthorne and Melville; both go on to consider Faulkner, and both are fundamentally unoriginal. As Daniel Aaron's preface admits, 'Dr. Viola Sachs is not the first scholar to point out the disparities between the American dream and reality or to measure the "pollution" in Eden.' Nevertheless she goes at the task with undaunted energy. The virtues of the study are its clarity and its

very close engagement with the texts, but Sachs is never afraid to state the obvious. She writes, for example, of *The Scarlet Letter*, '. . . It thus becomes clear that the rose, the letter A and Pearl belong to the same symbolic cluster', a point which Hawthorne himself obligingly makes clear. The Melville chapter deals with *Moby-Dick*, with the aid of elaborate word-unravelling and an ingenious but unconvincing word-diagram. The Bibliographical Notes for both Hawthorne and Melville are useful. Dan Vogel's three masks of American tragedy are the masks of Oedipus, Christ, and Satan, which may be worn, according to him, by 'grandiose figures and schnooks'. In the section on 'The Mask of Christ' Vogel considers *The Scarlet Letter* in the context of his perception that 'The primal tragic myth for Hawthorne is the catastrophe of Adam'. He concedes that R. W. B. Lewis in *The American Adam* (1955) and Roy R. Male in *Hawthorne's Tragic Vision* (1957) make 'parallel assertion', but continues to make a claim for originality. He similarly develops Hyatt Waggoner's comparison of the dying Dimmesdale with Christ on the cross in a tone that argues a fresh perception. But Vogel comes up with little that is new: his view of Billy Budd as a Christ-figure breaks no fresh ground, nor his reading of *Moby-Dick* in 'The Mask of Satan'.

Another book on Melville which includes a discussion of Hawthorne, among others, is Susan Kuhlmann's selective survey of the figure of confidence man as he appears in nineteenth-century American fiction.[44] She opens her preface: 'This study is

[42] *The Myth of America: Essays in the Structures of the Literary Imagination*, by Viola Sachs. The Hague: Mouton, 1973. pp. 162. $8.25. See *YW* 54. 452.

[43] *The Three Masks of American Tragedy*, by Dan Vogel. Baton Rouge: Louisiana State U.P. pp. xiv+180.

[44] *Knave, Fool, and Genius: The Confidence Man as He Appears in Nineteenth-Century American Fiction*, by Susan Kuhlmann. Chapel Hill: U. of North Carolina P., 1973. pp. x+142.

the result of a longstanding affection for Melville coupled with hesitation in accepting the rôle of a "Melville-ist"'. She argues that, when a critic specializes in the work of any one writer, that critic will almost inevitably deal in terms of a 'reconstituted reality', or the real world of that writer. Without any hostility towards this kind of scholarship, Kuhlmann opts herself for the scholarship of 'reconstituted fiction': in the present instance, this means that she builds on the fictional creations of the confidence man in other writers, both earlier and later than Melville, before concluding with her examination of Melville's achievement. Paradoxically, however, the discussions which lead up to her appraisal of Melville are more valuable than this appraisal itself. Kuhlmann discusses Johnson Jones Hooper's *Some Adventures of Captain Simon Suggs* (1850), making some useful connexions with Fenimore Cooper's Natty Bumppo and with the work of Bret Harte and Mark Twain, and W. D. Howells's *The Undiscovered Country* (1880). She writes perhaps most interestingly on the confidence man in Hawthorne and James, a figure she takes to include Westervelt in *The Blithedale Romance*, and Mme. Merle and Kate Croy in *The Portrait of a Lady* and *The Wings of the Dove*. Martha A. Woodmansee, writing, in *Der Amerikanische Roman im 19. und 20. Jahrhundert*, on the way that the 'discrepancy between a society's apparent harmony and the actual reality' is dramatized in *The Confidence-Man*, speaks of the work as having received 'comparatively little attention.' Yet this now appears to be changing: Elizabeth Keyser, for example, argues for the positive moral aspect of the character of the Cosmopolitan (*TSLL*, 1973), and Helen P. Trimpi examines 'Harlequin-

Confidence-Man: The Satirical Tradition of Commedia dell' Arte and Pantomime in Melville's *The Confidence-Man*' (*TSLL*).

In '*White-Jacket*: Melville and the Man-of-War Microcosm' (*AQ*, 1973) Priscilla Allen, after offering some general observations on sea-narratives, demonstrates the way in which the Neversink stands for America, and the male world of the frigate for the autocratic structure of government, seen as ugly, harsh, and ruthless.

Joseph L. Basile's 'The Meridians of Melville's Wicked World' (*SDR*, 1973) sees *Moby-Dick* as being, after all, a 'wicked book' in that it is a study of human depravity. Jerome M. Loving (*NEQ*) claims that Hawthorne's influence on the development of *Moby-Dick* from a comparatively simple sea narrative into a 'complex allegory which rages against the inequities of the universe' was not as great as has generally been supposed. Loving argues in particular against Hawthorne's part in shaping 'the damnable soul of Ahab', for which Melville had already undergone a literary apprenticeship of pessimism in *Mardi*, *Redburn*, and *White-Jacket*. Henry L. Golemba in 'The Shape of *Moby-Dick*' (*SNNTS*, 1973) offers a close structural analysis of the novel in terms of Ahab's and Ishmael's contrapuntal perceptions of the universe.

Tyrus Hillway shows that 'Melville's Education in Science' (*TSLL*) meant, in part, that he became increasingly knowledgeable and discriminating in his treatment of scientific authorities during his preparation of *Moby-Dick*; John T. Irwin's assertions of the symbolic importance of hieroglyphics in the American Renaissance (*AQ*) also apply most aptly to Melville's composition of *Moby-Dick*. Irwin claims that when in 1822 Jean François Champollion deciphered the Egyptian hieroglyphic writing from the Rosetta stone, an event mentioned by Emerson, Poe, Thoreau, and Melville, it 'transformed what had been a symbol of the divine and the mysterious into something human and conventional'. The effect of this was to transform metaphysical or epistemological questions in the work of a writer like Melville into linguistic questions: 'not questions of what really is, nor how do we know what really is, but rather how in our knowable model of the world does our language create what really is.' Robert J. Schwendinger writes more prosaically on 'The Language of the Sea: Relationships Between the Language of Herman Melville and Sea Shanties of the 19th Century' (*SFQ*, 1973) pointing out similarities in tone, symbols, figurative language, and subject matter.

Joseph Flibbert writes in *Melville and the Art of Burlesque*,[45] 'The mode of burlesque came easily to Melville. It was natural to one who recognized an "infirmity of jocularity" in himself. The essential design of its appearance in his works is reflected in an observation he recorded in his journal as he arrived in England in 1849: "This time tomorrow I shall be on land, & press English earth after the lapse of ten years—*then* a sailor, *now* H.M. author of 'Peedee' 'Hullabaloo' & 'Pog-Dog'."' It is this inveterate habit of mockery, and self-mockery, that Flibbert investigates. This is not a fully comprehensive Melville study, but Flibbert examines the following uses of burlesque in Melville's work: to undercut certain values of a primitive culture in *Typee* and *Omoo*; to evaluate his travels, the profession of literary criticism, his reading, the advice of his friends and relatives,

and the viability of contemporary forms and conventions of literary expression in *Mardi*; to question the effectiveness of traditional modes of perception in *Moby-Dick*; to examine the problems of authorship in *Pierre*; and to criticize the codes, postures, and ideals of mid-nineteenth century America in *Israel Potter* and the *Confidence-Man*. The best sections are on the general popular background of literary burlesque, on the literary burlesque of *Mardi*, and on the influence of the popularity of Phineas T. Barnum on *Moby-Dick*.

Christopher W. Sten in 'Bartleby the Transcendentalist: Melville's Dead Letter to Emerson' (*MLQ*) sees Bartleby, in his rejections and denials, as a parody of Emerson's transcendentalist, and the lawyer-narrator the materialist as defined in Emerson's 'The Transcendentalist'. Like Marvin Fisher in '"Bartleby", Melville's Circumscribed Scrivener' (*SoR*), Sten concludes that the narrator begins as a materialist and becomes more of an idealist, so that there is some optimism in an otherwise bleak tale. Fisher stresses the importance of the descriptive 'A Story of Wall-Street' which was part of the original title for the two-part serialization in *Putnam's Monthly* of 1853, in that the Wall Street setting is 'expressionistic', suggesting the whole social order which walls people in and makes automatons of them. Fisher does not believe that the religious imagery in the story makes Bartleby's death a liberation, but does believe that by the end the narrator, at first walled in by Wall Street standards, has changed and that his awareness has been expanded.

Two articles on *Billy Budd* stress the rôle of the narrator. Robert T. Eberwein's 'The Impure Fiction of *Billy Budd*' (*SNNTS*) concentrates on the concluding ballad 'Billy in the

[45] *Melville and the Art of Burlesque*, by Joseph Flibbert. Amsterdam: Rodopi. pp. 163.

Darbies', building here on two previous articles by Ray B. West (*HudR*, 1952) and Paul Brodtkorb (*PMLA*, 1967). Eberwein declares that 'the poem embodies the meaning implicit in the narrator's activity, and, indeed, in all genuine art. To recognize the function of the poem is, finally, to see the narrator's tone not as one of ironic disdain or contempt, but as one indicative of humility as he submits to the artistic process.' Robert Merrill, writing on 'The Narrative Voice in *Billy Budd*' (*MLQ*, 1973), rejects an 'ironist' reading, emphasizing that the narrator is at pains to show Billy as more child-like than Christ-like, and to present Vere to us in the best possible light. But Irene Friedman, in 'Melville's Billy Budd: "A Sort of Upright Barbarian"' (*CRevAS*, 1973), firmly accepts an 'ironist' reading, with Vere as victim, no less than Billy, of the laws whose destructive power Vere perpetuates.

The Melville *Critical Heritage*[46] is, as is usual with this series, a very useful volume. The time span is from 1846, the year of *Typee*, to 1892, the year after Melville's death, and the range is from the 1850 'Hawthorne and His Mosses' by Melville himself to obscure unsigned reviews. The earlier reviews give a valuable impression of the literary culture of the time. George Washington Peck, for example, complains in the *American Review*, July 1847: 'The manliness of our light literature is curdling into licentiousness on the one hand and imbecility on the other; witness such books as *Omoo*, and the namby-pamby Tennysonian poetry we have of late so much of.' The latest articles, written just after Melville's death, are a striking reminder of how thoroughly he had been forgotten. This collection

makes an admirable companion for Hugh W. Hetherington's *Melville's Reviewers: British and American 1846–1891* (1961), a book which quotes no review in full, but which moves through Melville's works summarizing critical opinion.

Melville and Twain, with the journalist John Ross Browne, are treated together in Franklin Walker's *Irreverent Pilgrims*;[47] the purpose of the book is to show how reaction to the Holy Land sheds light on personality and on the nature of the creative process in each. Walker gives a much fuller biographical introduction for John Ross Browne than for Melville or Twain, since he realizes that Browne is not a household name, and he is at pains to point out the similarities between his life and Melville's and Twain's. In the event, the account of Browne's 1851 Christmas in Bethlehem is one of the most vivid touches in the book. However, for the literary critic the most illuminating section is undoubtedly Walker's discussion of the expurgations from Twain's *The Innocents Abroad*.

Hawthorne, Melville, and Twain, with Emerson and Thoreau, Whitman, and Edward Bellamy, feature in the more worthwhile passages of *The Idea of Fraternity in America* by Wilson Carey McWilliams.[48] McWilliams rather engagingly admits in his preface that his book is 'pretentious' and 'intolerably long'; its main flaw is that his definition of 'fraternity' is too loose to hold the book together, so that it remains an assortment of diffuse and random insights.

Two more books which similarly

[47] *Irreverent Pilgrims: Melville, Browne, and Mark Twain in the Holy Land*, by Franklin Walker. Seattle and London: U. of Washington P. pp. xii+234.

[48] *The Idea of Fraternity in America*, by Wilson Carey McWilliams. Berkeley, Los Angeles, and London: U. of California P., 1973. pp. xiv+695.

[46] *Melville: The Critical Heritage*, ed. by Watson G. Branch. London and Boston: Routledge & Kegan Paul. pp. xix+444.

cover a wide range of authors, Harry B. Henderson III's *Versions of the Past*[49] and David Ketterer's *New Worlds for Old*,[50] each give a particularly fine account of Twain's *A Connecticut Yankee*. The basis of Harry B. Henderson III's examination of historical art is his assessment of the function of two alternative frameworks in the works he discusses. One is the 'progressive' framework, which sees the nature of man as eternally constant and history as consisting of measurable change on an absolute scale. The other is the 'holist' framework, which takes a relativist view of man and sees historical change as incapable of measurement except in terms of the specific period under consideration. Henderson opens with a discussion of the great American historians of the nineteenth century: Bancroft, Prescott, Motley, Parkman, and Adams. Apart from his excellent discussion of Twain's views of history in *A Connecticut Yankee*, Henderson also offers very good critiques of Cooper's *The Last of the Mohicans*, and of Hawthorne's 'The Gentle Boy', 'Roger Malvin's Burial', and 'My Kinsman, Major Molineux'. He is, however, less helpful on *The Scarlet Letter*, and his chapter on Melville is less convincing and comparatively perfunctory in argument. There are further chapters on Bellamy, Cable, James, Adams, and Crane, and on twentieth-century writers.

Ketterer's achievement is far more uneven than Henderson's, probably because his book is, to a certain extent, an amalgamation of previously published articles. His best piece, for

instance, the chapter on Twain's use of imagery called 'Epoch-Eclipse and Apocalypse: Special "Effects" in *A Connecticut Yankee*', appeared under the same glib title in *PMLA*, 1973. His material in Part One, which gives its title to the whole book, is excellent: he is very convincing on the essential connexions between the 'apocalyptic imagination' and American literature, but this also has appeared before in a self-contained form, and therefore it is not surprising that the book as a whole does not live up to the promise of what appears to be its introduction. There are, however, two good, previously unpublished chapters worth noting: 'The Transformed World of Charles Brockden Brown's *Wieland*' and 'Edgar Allan Poe and the Visionary Tradition of Science Fiction'. Ketterer does cast his net very wide, dealing with much very recent popular literature, but he does not invariably apply standards of literary merit, and he does not include what would have been an exceedingly useful bibliography.

The essays which make up Kenneth S. Lynn's *Visions of America*[51] have all previously appeared, between 1957 and 1971. They include '*Walden*', '*Uncle Tom's Cabin*', '*Huckleberry Finn*', 'Howells in the Nineties', and 'Violence in American Literature and Folklore'. The last essay makes a good, though brief, connexion between Melville's 'Benito Cereno' and Twain's *Pudd'nhead Wilson*, but states inaccurately that the babies exchanged in their cradles in *Pudd'nhead Wilson* had the same white father. '*Huckleberry Finn*' is in part a discussion of the images of captivity which haunted Twain's imagination.

[49] *Versions of the Past: The Historical Imagination in American Fiction*, by Harry B. Henderson III. New York: O.U.P. pp. xviii + 344.

[50] *New Worlds for Old: The Apocalyptic Imagination, Science Fiction, and American Literature*, by David Ketterer. Bloomington and London: Indiana U.P. pp. xii + 347.

[51] *Visions of America: Eleven Literary Historical Essays*, by Kenneth S. Lynn. Westport, Conn., and London: Greenwood Press, 1973. pp. xv + 205.

Harold Beaver treats *Huckleberry Finn* as a fugitive slave narrative in 'Run, Nigger, Run' (*JAmS*); Georg Meri-Akri Gaston on 'The Function of Tom Sawyer in *Huckleberry Finn*' (*MissQ*) asserts that 'Twain meant to suggest a pervading pessimism by stressing the ubiquitous nature of Tom's sinister spirit'; James D. Wilson in '*Adventures of Huckleberry Finn*: From Abstraction to Humanity' (*SoR*) takes us through all the codes of behaviour encountered by Huck, and shows that all are inadequate 'to meet the demands of his intuitive moral nature'. All these articles are competent, but hardly strikingly original. Rather more interesting are, strangely, the more technical and biographical insights offered in articles like Norton D. Kinghorn's 'E. W. Kemble's Misplaced Modifier: A Note on the Illustrations for *Huckleberry Finn*' (*MTJ*, 1973) or Beverly R. David's much fuller 'The Pictorial *Huck Finn*: Mark Twain and his Illustrator, E. W. Kemble' (*AQ*). David shows how 'Mark Twain's "ideas" on the usefulness of the illustrations reduced the impact of the major elements of the novel. Because one of his main concerns was the manipulation and control of a mass audience, illustration became a tool that converted the cruelty and sexuality of the story into a series of humorous boyish adventures.'

Ernest J. Moyne gives (*AL*, 1973) an amusing account of 'Mark Twain and Baroness Alexandra Gripenberg', the Finnish baroness whom Twain met in Hartford, Connecticut, in 1888, and whom he later disturbed by a 'plagiarism'. Twain's attitude to the baroness appears to have been very genial. Conversely, the relationship described, also very amusingly, in Mark K. Wilson's 'Mr. Clemens and Madame Blanc: Mark Twain's

First French Critic' (*AL*) is an addition to the list of explanations for Twain's hostility toward the French. Twain was annoyed by Marie-Thérèse Blanc's translation of 'The Jumping Frog' (*Revue des Deux Mondes*, 1872), which he satirically retranslated, but annoyed even more, Wilson suggests, by the condescending attitude of the long article she wrote about him.

Tom H. Towers in '"Hateful Reality": The Failure of the Territory in *Roughing It*' (*WAL*) argues for disillusion, rather than growth or initiation, as the prevailing pattern of the work, while Herman Nibbelink's 'Mark Twain and the Mormons' (*MTJ*) shows how *Roughing It* gives a hackneyed subject a new twist through unconventional irony.

Joan Baum writes in 'Mark Twain on the Congo' (*MTJ*) on the reissue of *King Leopold's Soliloquy*, and L. W. Denton gives an unsurprising summary of 'Mark Twain on Patriotism, Treason, and War' (*MTJ*). Stanley Brodwin discusses 'Blackness and the Adamic Myth in Mark Twain's *Pudd'nhead Wilson*' (*TSLL*, 1973) and 'Mark Twain's Masks of Satan: The Final Phase' (*AL*, 1973). The latter article is a study of the black satirical phase of the eighteen-nineties and early nineteen-hundreds, during which Twain was preoccupied with the figure of Satan. Brodwin identifies four masks: Satan as father of lies, as the sympathetic commentator on the tragedy of man's fall, as the mischievous, sarcastic questioner of God, and as the force of spiritual though amoral 'innocence' charged with divine-seeming creative power.

Hamlin Hill writes of Twain's 'final phase' in his *Mark Twain: God's Fool*,[52] the title for which is taken from one of Twain's letters to

---

[52] *Mark Twain: God's Fool*, by Hamlin Hill. New York and London: Harper & Row, 1973. pp. xxviii + 308; 18 illustrations.

Howells: 'Ah, well, I am a great & sublime fool. But then I am God's fool, & all His works must be contemplated with respect.' Hill points out that since Albert Bigelow Paine produced his official biography of Twain in 1912, in which he presented his firsthand account of the years 1900–1910, this last decade of Twain's life has remained substantially unexamined, although Paine 'was the victim of a fastidious Victorian sense of propriety'. Hill's detailed and powerful account of these years does therefore shed new light on the ageing Twain. The family tensions, and Twain's quarrel with his secretary Isabel Lyon, with his cruel unfounded accusations of her, make melancholy but compulsive reading.

Justin Kaplan's *Mark Twain and His World*[53] draws on much of the same material as his definitive *Mr. Clemens and Mark Twain* (1966), but it goes back to the beginnings of the life rather than starting at the age of thirty. It is colloquially but extremely well written, and the illustrations, including photographs, paintings, and sketches of people and places, do add considerably to our knowledge of and feeling for Mark Twain and his world. This is an important and very enjoyable book.

The essays in *Mark Twain: A Collection of Criticism*[54] are all reprinted, with the exception of Dean Morgan Schmitter's 'Introduction: Mark Twain and the Pleasures of Pessimism'. Part I of the collection consists of 'Biography and General Criticism', Part II of 'Criticism of the Major Works': *The Innocents Abroad,*

Tom Sawyer, Huckleberry Finn, A Connecticut Yankee, Pudd'nhead Wilson, and 'The Mysterious Stranger'. It has a very useful annotated bibliography.

Another collection of reprinted essays, *Seven Novelists in the American Naturalist Tradition,*[55] contains an unpretentious, unambitious account of Stephen Crane's life and work by Jean Cazemajou. Thomas A. Sancton in 'Looking Inward: Edward Bellamy's Spiritual Crisis' (*AQ*, 1973) concentrates on Bellamy's inner conflicts, expressed in his journals and culminating in the Nationalist ideals of *Looking Backward*. Sancton claims that the importance of the Nationalist movement for Bellamy was that it 'brought his fantasies to life. He now had a glorious cause to lose himself in, his own "moral equivalent of war"'. Russell Roth in 'Ambrose Bierce's "Detestable Creature"' (*WAL*) writes mainly about the story 'Killed at Resaca' from *In the Midst of Life*, in the context of Bierce's misogyny, his hatred of his hymn-singing mother, and his identification of women with poisonous snakes.

Robert F. Marler adopts Northrop Frye's distinctions between the tale and the short story in his discussion of the flood of magazine tales in the eighteen-fifties (*AL*). A critical survey of *The American Short Story* by Arthur Voss[56] is useful as a bibliography and for its basic historical material, but it is only marginally critical, and the judgements made are naïve in the extreme.

This section ends on an ethnic note. Rose Basile Green's *The Italian-*

[53] *Mark Twain and His World*, by Justin Kaplan. New York: Simon & Schuster. pp. 224; 110 illustrations, including 31 colour plates.

[54] *Mark Twain: A Collection of Criticism*, ed. by Dean Morgan Schmitter. New York: McGraw-Hill Paperbacks. pp. vi + 154. $2.45

[55] *Seven Novelists in the American Naturalist Tradition: An Introduction*, ed. by Charles Child Walcutt. Minneapolis: U. of Minnesota P. pp. 331.

[56] *The American Short Story: A Critical Survey*, by Arthur Voss. U. of Oklahoma P., 1973. pp. xi + 399. $7.95. See *YW* 54. 443.

American Novel: A Document of the Interaction of Two Cultures[57] is a formidable piece of work. As Mario Pei says in his foreword: 'We have until now lacked a comprehensive study, historical, descriptive and bibliographic, of this particular current of American literature which, while it consists of isolated and separate works of uneven value, nevertheless sums up, in its entirety, the Italian experience in America'. Many of the novels, indeed, seem to be of very little literary value, as far as one may deduce this from the fact that Paul Gallico is given serious attention. Green clearly realizes that the reader will have no knowledge of the works she discusses, and she invariably offers a summary of the plot in her account of each novel. Her bibliography is immensely useful, probably unique, and yet her book inspires one with no enthusiasm for reading any of the fiction she describes.

4. DRAMA

As one might anticipate, this is an exceedingly brief section.

Garff B. Wilson's *Three Hundred Years of American Drama and Theatre*,[58] intended, as he says, for 'the general reader and the beginning student', is a good guide to the social and historical background, but has no critical pretensions. Wilson deals, in his rather cosy and gushing style, not only with plays and playwriting, but with acting, stagecraft, theatre architecture, and management. Incidentally, his reference to the luxury of modern theatre-going may not strike

a responsive chord in the English reader.

Kent G. Gallagher writes on 'The Tragedies of George Henry Boker: The Measure of American Romantic Drama' (*ESQ*), but comes to the modest conclusion that 'Viewed in relation to similar works by Hugo, Schiller, Ibsen (the saga-dramas), or Shakespeare, none of Boker's tragedies, not even *Francesca*, manifests comparable complexity of thought and characterization or excellence of dramatic poesy. More important, the tastes of his time demanded an elevated and romantically refulgent stage diction which sounds overly figurative and too highly emotional to the modern ear.' Billy J. Harbin discusses 'Hodgkinson and his Rivals at the Park: The Business of Early Romantic Theatre in America' (*ESQ*). John Hodgkinson, who suffered in his time harsh critical comment, not least about his portliness, from the pens of Washington Irving and others, was the leading actor of William Dunlap's Old American Company, which moved to the Park Street Theatre, New York, after a number of financially unstable seasons elsewhere. Harbin records that 'During this nine-months engagement at the Park Theatre (October 20, 1800–June 11, 1801) Hodgkinson, besides performing some forty familiar parts, created a total of twenty-three new rôles, nine of which were in sentimental drama, seven in eighteenth-century comedy, four in tragedy, and three in pantomime.' William R. Reardon, in 'The American Drama and Theatre in the Nineteenth Century: A Retreat from Meaning' (*ESQ*), postulates two cultural factors for the poverty of nineteenth-century drama: 'The first is the economic problems for theatre resulting from organizational changes and growth in nineteenth-century America. The second is the less than

---

[57] *The Italian–American Novel: A Document of the Interaction of Two Cultures*, by Rose Basile Green. Rutherford, N.J.: Fairleigh Dickinson U.P. pp. 415.

[58] *Three Hundred Years of American Drama and Theatre: From 'Ye Bear and Ye Cubb' to 'Hair'*, by Garff B. Wilson. Englewood Cliffs, N.J.: Prentice-Hall, 1973. pp. viii + 536; 97 illustrations.

felicitous nature of national topics as content for the drama, as exemplified by the popularity of the Barbary Wars.'

Daniel F. Havens seeks in *The Columbian Muse of Comedy*[59] to fill a 'critical gap', pointing out how little scholarly attention of a critical nature is given to drama before 1850. However, Havens does concede that this drama owes at least some of its value to the fact that it paved the way for subsequent, superior work, and, like Rose Basile Green on the Italian–American novel, he gives conscientious plot summaries. He covers American drama from Royall Tyler's *The Contrast* (1787) to Anna Cora

[59] *The Columbian Muse of Comedy: The Development of a Native Tradition in Early American Social Comedy, 1787–1845*, by Daniel F. Havens. Carbondale and Edwardsville: Southern Illinois U.P.; London and Amsterdam: Feffer and Simons, 1973. pp. vii + 181.

Mowatt's *Fashion* (1845). He discusses 'Nine Minor Comedies', 1789–1834, by Samuel Low, J. Robinson, John Murdock, Lazarus Beach, A. B. Lindsley, Mordecai M. Noah, Samuel Woodworth, and Cornelius A. Logan, and 'Three Significant Comedies': William Dunlap's *The Father* (1789), James Nelson Barker's *Tears and Smiles* (1808), and Robert Montgomery Bird's *The City Looking Glass* (1828), which last Havens compares favourably with Webster. He writes, too, of such actors as George Handel Hill ('Yankee' Hill). Havens repeats in connection with Hill the anecdote which Hank Morgan gloomily condemns in *A Connecticut Yankee*: 'That anecdote never saw the day that it was worth the telling; and yet I had sat under the telling of it hundreds and thousands and millions and billions of times, and cried and cursed all the way through.'

XVI

American Literature: The Twentieth Century

PETE MESSENT and MARK LEAF

The chapter is divided as follows:
1. General; 2. Poetry; 3. The Novel;
4. Drama. Parts 1 and 3 are by Pete
Messent, Parts 2 and 4 by Mark Leaf.

Bibliographies of current articles in
American Literature are published
quarterly in *American Literature*, and
annually in the Summer Supplement
of *American Quarterly*.

1. GENERAL

In his original 1968 preface to
*Sixteen Modern American Authors:
A survey of research and criticism*,[1]
reprinted in this revised edition of the
work, Jackson R. Bryer pointed to the
avalanche of critical material on
modern American writers appearing
at that time. Faced with this quantitative increase, the original 'survey'
attempted to separate the permanently valuable scholarly comment
from the chaff, in its presentation of
selected bibliographical material on a
limited number of significant
twentieth-century American writers.

Since that time, of course, the
avalanche has continued to grow both
in size and in speed of descent, thus
the need for this revised edition.
Each contributor has written a
Supplement section updating his
original essay, Milton J. Friedman
taking the Hemingway section for
his late colleague, Frederick J. Hoff-

man. Of major importance, a bibliographical essay on William Carlos
Williams by Linda Wagner, reprinted
from the inaugural issue of *Resources
for American Literary Study*, appears
in the survey for the first time.

This is a useful collection, both for
the beginning student and for the
more advanced teacher-critic. However, even though the original selection of authors for the first edition
of this work was through a ballot of
teachers and students in the field of
American literature, it does seem
strange to see an essay on the work of
Willa Cather while John Dos Passos
remains ignored. Also the survey
already looks somewhat out of date:
there are very few references indeed
to 1973 critical material.

Appearing similarly in a new and
revised edition this year, is the
Literary History of the United States,[2]
edited by Robert E. Spiller and others.
A final section has been added to this
work, entitled 'Mid-Century and
After'. This section includes the
following chapters: 'The New Con-
sciousness' and 'Fiction', both by
Ihab Hassan; 'Poetry' by Daniel
Hoffman; and 'Drama' by Gerald
Weales. Stanley Williams's chapter
on Emily Dickinson and Sidney
Lanier has been rewritten by William
M. Gibson, and the original chapter

[1] *Sixteen Modern American Authors: A
survey of research and criticism*, ed. by Jackson R. Bryer. Revised edition. Durham,
North Carolina: Duke U.P. pp. xx+673.
$10.00.

[2] *Literary History of the United States*
ed. by Robert E. Spiller and others. Fourth
edition, revised. New York: Macmillan.
pp. xxvi+1556. $25.

by Willard Thorp and Robert E. Spiller entitled 'The End of an Era' has had material added by Ihab Hassan and Daniel Hoffman. The selected bibliography has also been brought up to date.

In *The End of Intelligent Writing: Literary Politics in America*,[3] Richard Kostelanetz argues most interestingly that 'a panoply of growing forces forecast the likely end of "intelligent writing" or "literature" as we have known those traditions'. The channels of communication between intelligent writer and inte lligent reader are Kostelanetz's main concern in this book. Good literature, he claims, is being written but much of it is being effectively stifled by a literary establishment which, in its ability to determine both what is published and what is promoted and recognized, has near total control over the American reading public, a control that is by no means for the best.

The book begins with a general consideration of literary politics in America, an examination in detail of 'literary power' and how it is exercised. This, as Kostelanetz points out, constitutes a radical activity since the print media has previously considered this kind of discussion forbidden territory. This may well have accounted for the author's major difficulties in finding a publisher for this volume. He quotes Orwell, who faced similar difficulties in getting *Animal Farm* published: 'Veiled censorship . . . operates in books and periodicals. . . . Anyone who challenges the prevailing orthodoxy finds himself silenced with surprising effectiveness.' Fortunately both *Animal Farm*, of course, and this book eventually found publishers.

Why is it, Kostelanetz enquires,

that the reputations of certain 'leading' writers, Allen Tate and Robert Creeley, for example, should seem so much larger than their ostensible achievements? Why have Philip Roth and John Updike become literary household words while Walter N. Miller Jr. and Paule Marshall remain neglected? He answers that a writer's place in America ultimately reflects 'literary politicking', that the opinion makers are completely entwined in the literary-political process. This study becomes then an examination into the ways in which literary art and literary life in America reflect the demands of professional business. In his analysis, Kostelanetz exposes the principal deceit of literary politics as the establishment of a system of taste based upon nonaesthetic criteria.

In the first part of this book the author consequently shows just how the literary industry can be held primarily responsible for the 'imminent death of intelligent writing' in America, the villains (for this is a polemic) lying within the publishing system, in the shapes of restrictive policies and deleterious attitudes. In the second part, Kostelanetz examines the present state of the literary arts in America: new literary periodicals, alternative presses, the young writers of North America, and the 'New Poetries'. He then puts forth hypotheses as to what is to be done to help this 'intelligent writing' to continue to appear in an American cultural context, for, 'If writers fail to act now they will discover sometime soon that even the opportunity for action is gone . . . were the institutions of literature rejuvenated, and the editorial-industrial complex ignored, and literary power diffused, then perhaps the traditions of intelligent writing would continue to evolve.'

[3] *The End of Intelligent Writing: Literary Politics in America*, by Richard Kostelanetz. New York: Sheed and Ward. pp. xviii+480. $12.95.

In 'Some Random Thoughts on Contemporary Writing' (*TCL*) Theodore Solotaroff fails to recognize the problems Kostelanetz raises. He affirms his own belief in the abundance of literary talent appearing in America today by pointing to the quality and quantity of material appearing in *The American Review*. He examines the general atmosphere of critical thought which provides the basis for the exercise of creative power in America and finds a new libertarian democratic critical consciousness in operation, providing a concerted opposition to specific political evils and a series of imaginative alternatives to the 'system' itself.

Another work of lesser importance than Kostelanetz's and concerning itself with just one branch of his literary politics is Philip Nobile's *Intellectual Skywriting: Literary Politics and The New York Review of Books*.[4] Merle Miller comments on this work: 'Since Mr Nobile can write, the whole thing reads like the best detective story', a detective story however in which one of the chief witnesses gives but grudging assistance at his cross-examination. For early in his study, Mr Nobile spends much time and obvious energy examining the personal and political lives of *The New York Review*'s editorial staff as relevant to editorial policy-making, though one remains uncertain quite how relevant to this concern is Robert Lowell's separation from advisory editor Elizabeth Hardwick. Nobile then finally admits that he has been unable to discover the ideological whereabouts of, or in fact much at all about co-editor Robert Silvers, who appears in fact to be the king-pin of the whole opera-

tion. Exit our detective hero, stage right.

The book, however, is an often interesting though frequently infuriating study of the shifts in both literary and, more particularly, political emphasis of *The New York Review of Books*, lauded by the author as 'the premier literary-intellectual journal in the English speaking world'. The book is infuriating in Mr Nobile's love of gossip, also his New Journalistic approach, which, if it can be called witty at times, can only be seen as glib and unintelligent at others. I quote his comparative view of 'Barbara Epstein as Anne Frank . . . there is a seeming vulnerability about this delicate, girlish woman who sits deep in her office behind the sign "I must soon quit the scene. Benjamin Franklin to George Washington, March 5, 1780" that allows the identification'. The author obviously has not done his proof reading very carefully, either: *Slaughterhouse V* published in 1952?

Mr Nobile is over-interested in personality. The New York intellectuals are divided into 'families' pursuing various feuds, and it is the personal animosities raised that seem to interest the author to as great an extent as the ideological nature of the arguments. His discussion of the *Review*'s move away from literary criticism towards radical politics, that famous 'Molotov cocktail cover', and the magazine's political realignments since that time, are however of real interest, and the book has a definite point in its favour with the many reproductions of David Levine's illustrations. Although the author does criticize the *Review*, this work is, in the main, celebratory; there is never any doubt exactly where Nobile's sympathies lie.

The pre-war literary periodical is the subject of 'Forgotten Pages:

[4] *Intellectual Skywriting: Literary Politics and The New York Review of Books*, by Philip Nobile. New York: Charterhouse. pp. vii+312. $7.95.

Black Literary Magazines in the 1920s' (*JAmS*), by Abby Ann Arthur Johnson and Ronald M. Johnson. The authors point out the significance of such small magazines as *Stylus*, *Fire*, and *Black Opals* to show that the Negro Renaissance of the decade was not just circumscribed within the boundaries of Harlem.

With *Granville Hicks in the New Masses*,[5] edited by Jack Allan Robbins, we shift from one American minority group to another, and from one decade to the next. In International Publishers' 1970 anthology of selected writings of the *New Masses*, not one essay or book review written by Granville Hicks appears. This perhaps suggests a certain selective historicism, on the part of the editors of this volume at least, in that a critic who had been active in the Communist Party but who subsequently left, loses all claim to inclusion in their compilation of the writings of the era.

In fact, Hicks was the most influential writer on the staff of *New Masses* between 1933 and 1939, and became its literary editor when the journal was converted from a monthly to a weekly. His writings for the magazine, collected here for the first time, show the first sustained effort at the development of a Marxist interpretation of literature in America. Hicks himself had previously refused to allow the collection of these writings, since not only did they no longer reflect his views on literature but also, as journalism, he considered them to lack enduring literary merit. Though the latter may be true as evidenced in some of the material displayed here, nevertheless Hicks's attempts to fashion a Marxist critique of litera-

ture are of real importance in the history of American criticism.

As one of the most widely read and influential literary critics of the 1930s it is pleasing, both from an historical and a literary point of view to see Hicks's writings reissued in one collection. The book is divided into ten sections which move through Hicks's interest in the state of American criticism and of the novel itself to his essays written in 1938 in answer to problems raised by his book, *I Like America*, his classic statement of the Communist position in the popular front period, the first and last of Hicks's books that the Party endeavoured to promote seriously—a book in which Hicks toed absolutely the Party line.

In *The Uneasy Chair: A Biography of Bernard De Voto*,[6] Wallace Stegner discusses the life of the editor and critical scholar who was editing the *Saturday Review of Literature* (1936–8) and working on *Harper's Magazine* while Hicks was with the *New Masses*. Stegner here gives an objective account of his friend and contemporary, one who shared the same Western heritage and same shift in career emphasis from novelist to historian as the author. This is an authoritative and obviously carefully researched volume in which Stegner succeeds in his recreation of 'Benny De Voto as he was—flawed, brilliant, provocative, outrageous . . . often wrong, often spectacularly right . . . a force in his time'. This is a lively and thorough biography of one of the few all round American men of letters of the twentieth century.

Concerned with the more general field of American letters and culture are Suzanne Ellery Greene's *Books For Pleasure: Popular Fiction, 1914–*

[5] *Granville Hicks in the New Masses*, ed. by Jack Alan Robbins. Port Washington, New York, and London: Kennikat Press. pp. xviii+437. $17.50.

[6] *The Uneasy Chair: A Biography of Bernard De Voto*, by Wallace Stegner. New York: Doubleday. pp. xi+464. $12.50.

45^7 and John Hohenberg's *The Pulitzer Prizes: A History of the Awards in Books, Drama, Music and Journalism, Based on the Private Files over Six Decades.*[8] The former consists of an examination of the best selling novels that appeared in the United States from 1914–45. Popular fiction, Suzanne Greene claims, has been neglected as a mode for the study of attitudes and values, yet from this one source it is possible to obtain a comprehensive reflection of the thoughts and the beliefs of a whole society. The best sellers which are examined in this book provide an index, in a whole range of areas, of social and moral change in America from the beginning of the First to the end of the Second World War.

Although John Hohenberg, who wrote *The Pulitzer Prizes*, has been secretary to the Advisory Board on the Pulitzer Prizes for twenty years, he does not write an 'authorized history' only interested in the glorification of the award. Instead, he records both the achievements and mistakes of the administration in the past. He discusses the history of the Pulitzer Prize from 1902 to the present day, suggesting the various rôles the Prize has played in American cultural life. Hohenberg ranges wide in his material. He discusses President Butler of Columbia University and his amendment of Pulitzer's specifications for the novel prize, from being an award 'for the American novel published during the year which shall best present the whole atmosphere of American life' to that 'novel . . . which shall best present the *wholesome*

[7] *Books For Pleasure: Popular Fiction, 1914–1945*, by Suzanne Ellery Greene. Ohio: Bowling Green U. Popular P. pp. 200. $9.95.
[8] *The Pulitzer Prizes: A History of the Awards in Books, Drama, Music and Journalism, Based on the Private Files over Six Decades*, by John Hohenberg. New York and London: Columbia U.P. pp. 434. $14.95.

atmosphere of American life', the difference between a Theodore Dreiser and a Booth Tarkington. Then he gradually comes up to date, to the presentation of the 1970 Prize for International Reporting to Seymour M. Hersh for his article on the My Lai massacre in Vietnam. There is a full list of the prizes awarded, as appendix, where the overall conservative nature of the Board's choice becomes most evident.

Were there a Pulitzer prize for literary criticism, one would expect to see the names of Cleanth Brooks, Philip Rahv, and Edmund Wilson among the prizewinners. In 'Cleanth Brooks, Critic of Critics' (*SoR*) René Wellek makes a plea for Cleanth Brooks as an historian of criticism, a critic of critics, and suggests that his comments on criticism have not received the attention they deserve. William Barrett writes an obituary for Philip Rahv in 'The Truants: *Partisan Review* in the 40s' (*Commentary*) in which he discusses the political animal in Rahv: he suggests that Rahv's Liberal Marxism of the 1940s reflected the flaw of a generation. His political stance was one which failed to come to terms with American reality, a stance which kept its purity by means of total dissociation from what it saw as the 'wicked deeds of American capitalism'. George H. Douglas in 'Edmund Wilson: The Critic as Artist' (*TQ*) comments on what he calls 'the genius of (Wilson's) historical imagination'. He examines the ways in which Wilson differed from F. O. Matthiessen, the way in which he attempted to understand and analyze literature as part of an ongoing personal and historical process.

This highly personalized critical imagination is in evidence in Edmund Wilson's last collection of literary criticism, *The Devils and Canon*

Barham: Ten Essays on Poets, Novelists and Monsters.[9] Wilson, justly called by the *Times Literary Supplement*, 'one of the greatest men of letters of our century', died in June 1972. All the essays found here have been previously published and there is little overall coherence to the collection, nor does there pretend to be: this is plainly a gathering together of Wilson's final critical writings, produced during the last four or five years of his life.

The 'Poets' of the book's subtitle are T. S. Eliot and Ezra Pound. Wilson discusses Pound's 'operation' on the early draft of *The Waste Land* and points out how Pound and Eliot between them managed in the final version of the poem to concentrate an intensity of image and feeling which is not to be found in its early versions. The 'Novelists' are the English amateur, Maurice Baring, and two neglected American writers, Henry Blake Fuller and Harold Frederic. There is also a brief but important essay on Hemingway entitled 'An Effort at Self-Revelation' in which he suggests the importance of *Islands in the Stream* and its relation in the Hemingway canon to *The Sun Also Rises*: the thematic similarity of compelling tension conveyed, 'of men on the edge of going to pieces, who are just hanging on by their teeth and just managing to retain their sanity'.

As to the 'Monsters', Wilson discusses the violent, eerie, nightmare world of the *Ingoldsby Legends* and their creator Canon Barham. 'The Monsters of Bomarzo' is his travelogue on the monster statutes of the Orsini Park. Also contained in this collection is Wilson's vigorous polemical essay on the editing of modern editions of American authors, 'The Fruits of the MLA', where he criticizes the Modern Language Association's policies in their reprinting of the American classics, where the massive commentaries and listings of textual variants tend to reveal more about the pedantries and hermeticism of the modern critic than about the work of art itself. As Leon Edel writes in the Foreword to this collection, 'Each essay of Edmund Wilson's is a voyage into literary history, biography, criticism, society: and a demonstration to the prolix and the half-hearted that writing is a stern discipline.'

Another series of essays, this time on eight modern American writers, including Edmund Wilson himself, is *Private Dealings: Modern American Writers in Search of Integrity*,[10] by David J. Burrows, Lewis M. Dabney, Milne Holton, and Grosvenor E. Powell. The major theme of this collection is the quality of inner direction, an aggressive commitment, on the part of the writers discussed, to the absolute integrity of their private and autonomous judgements in a twentieth-century society in which any kind of personal integrity is found to be increasingly difficult. At times this interconnecting theme leads to a misdirection in the focus of the essays themselves. For example, in 'Allie and Phoebe. Death and Love in J. D. Salinger's *The Catcher in the Rye*', David Burrows rather forces an optimistic reading of the novel when claiming that Phoebe's love creates for Holden a bridge to the environment from which he has been running.

[9] *The Devils and Canon Barham: Ten Essays on Poets, Novelists and Monsters*, by Edmund Wilson. Macmillan, 1973. pp. xiv + 219. $4.50.

[10] *Private Dealings: Modern American Writers in Search of Integrity*, by David J. Burrows, Lewis M. Dabney, Milne Holton and Grosvenor E. Powell. Maryland: New Perspectives. pp. 145. $9.50.

The essays discuss a selection of novels (*The Catcher in the Rye*, Malamud's *A New Life*, and Ellison's *Invisible Man*); the poetry of Robert Frost, Robert Lowell, William Carlos Williams, and Wallace Stevens; and the criticism of Edmund Wilson. One might question the authors' rather random choice of subject matter here. If their general theme is to be a confidence that true artistic value is still to be found in integrated and personal vision which exists amid the tensions of modern society, for what reasons is a novel like *The Old Man and the Sea* not mentioned, while *The Catcher in the Rye* and *Invisible Man* are closely analyzed? It would have been useful if some more detailed statement of selection procedure had been made; also if an index had been provided. One wonders too if Edmund Wilson is the *one* twentieth-century American essayist who 'repeatedly manifests a commitment to the absolute integrity of his private and autonomous judgements'?

H. L. Mencken, for example, surely belongs in this category. Fred. C. Hobson, Jr. examines the 'curious relationship' between Mencken and the American South in *Serpent in Eden: H. L. Mencken and the South*.[11] He focuses his attention on Mencken's rôle in Southern literary and intellectual life in the 1920s, Mencken as 'truth-telling serpent in a self-deluded Eden . . . the forbidden fruit he offered was a knowledge of the South's inadequacies'. Hobson charts Mencken's influence on the region from his scathing essay of 1920, 'The Sahara of the Bozart', to the publication in 1930 of the Fugitives' *I'll Take My Stand*, in many ways a reply to

Mencken on the issue of tradition versus modernism that he had raised.

Hobson traces in this volume Mencken's 'crusade', commencing after the publication of 'The Sahara of the Bozart' and the fierce reactions to it, to bring about a literary and intellectual rebirth in a South entrapped, as he saw it, within a bankrupt tradition. He shows the hostility Mencken—this 'scurrilous, South-hating icoclast' (*sic*) as one opponent described him—aroused and, more important, the way in which Mencken played a seminal rôle in the revival of Southern letters in this period. Shocking young Southern writers—W. J. Cash is a conspicuous example—into an awareness of the literary and intellectual poverty of the postbellum South, Mencken became 'the leader of the forces of liberation, the symbol of a new spirit that could transform the South and purge it of its myths and prejudices'. Hobson examines the effects of Mencken's writings on the South throughout the 1920s with particular final reference to the changing attitude of the Fugitives towards his criticism, showing in conclusion how in Mencken's questioning of longheld Southern assumptions 'lay the roots . . . of the Southern Renaissance'.

Mencken's writings, together with those of Henry Adams, William James, Randolph Bourne, Van Wyck Brooks, Kenneth Burke, and Reinhold Niebuhr, are discussed in *Makers of American Thought: An Introduction to Seven American Writers*,[12] edited by Ralph Ross. The seven essays appearing here were first published separately in the series of *University of Minnesota Pamphlets on American Writers*, and are

[11] *Serpent in Eden: H. L. Mencken and the South*, by Fred C. Hobson, Jr. Chapel Hill: U. of North Carolina P. pp. xv+242. $8.95.

[12] *Makers of American Thought: An Introduction to Seven American Writers*, ed. by Ralph Ross. Minneapolis: U. of Minnesota P. pp. 301. $10.50.

collected together here to give an overall view of some of the important shapers of American thought since the Civil War. Those essays on Henry Adams and William James which begin this useful volume suggest some of the continuing tensions in thinking within this American context. Adams, 'world weary, cynical, Europeanized', looked backwards for his ideal towards medieval France; James, 'the ideal type of intellectual pioneer', was concerned with the future, believed in 'the strenuous life', and was insistent on the necessity for man to think empirically in his relation to his existence in a world very much of the present. The differences between these two, so Ross claims, are guideposts in American thought, reflected in the concerns of those of their successors examined here. Though, therefore, it is very obvious that these essays are meant to be read separately, some unity is given to the collection by the very nature of the writers' concerns. No real reason is given why only these American thinkers merit inclusion in this volume; nevertheless, given the lack of critical material of this type, the appearance of this collection is to be welcomed.

Tongues of Fallen Angels[13] by Selden Rodman consists of 'conversations' with Jorge Luis Borges, Robert Frost, Ernest Hemingway, Pablo Neruda, Stanley Kunitz, Gabriel García Márquez, Octavio Paz, Norman Mailer, Allen Ginsberg, Vinícius de Moraes, João Cabral de Melo Neto, and Derek Walcott. The title of the book refers to the innocence of vision that the author feels must be recaptured on the poet's tongue, no matter how 'crippling or bestial' life's experiences may be. The selection procedure for this volume

appears somehat random, consisting of geographical opportunity and 'the pleasure principle': 'I loved the different ways these men wrote, and found their personalities sympathetic.' The author's 'notions of significance and excellence' happily were also involved.

In these informal and unrehearsed conversations Selden Rodman appears in almost as important a rôle as those he interviews: '"I'm a hungry schizophrenic" I said (to Mailer), "let's eat!"' His critical comment is not to be trusted. 'Hemingway's genius, like Lord Byron's was essentially comic; but unlike Byron, Hemingway, though he died at sixty two rather than thirty six, never lived to write his "Don Juan"'. This comic genius is claimed on the basis of 'Ernst von Hemingstein's Journal'—an exercise in wit dreamed up evidently by Hemingway with Rodman's promptings—a journal which includes such gems as '*Tuesday*—Drunk with Joyce in the literal rather than the figurative sense', and '*Monday*—Pound turned up here. He is immensely popular because of some broadcasting he has been doing, in Greece I believe'. However, these interviews are certainly conducted in a lively manner and, as in his conversation with Mailer, of value in understanding a writer and his philosophy of life.

Stephen Butterfield, in *Black Autobiography in America*,[14] uses both historical and literary critical techniques to trace the growth and progress of the Black autobiography in America from the slave narratives of the abolitionist era to the revolutionary works of the 1960s and 1970s. He divides his material into three sections which correspond roughly to

[13] *Tongues of Fallen Angels*, by Selden Rodman. New York: New Directions. pp. 271. $12.

[14] *Black Autobiography in America*, by Stephen Butterfield. Amherst: U. of Massachusetts P. pp. 303. $15.

stages in the black political and cultural expression; the first on the slave narrative period from about 1835 to 1895, ending with a chapter on Frederick Douglas whose literary career spanned over half the century in which he lived. The second section concerns what Butterfield calls 'The Period of Search', search for a unified self, a social rôle, and a voice, and extends from about 1901 to 1961. Again his final chapter here on Richard Wright sums up many of the themes in the black writing of the era as a whole, a time when alienation, not only from white Americans but from other blacks too, is evidenced within the autobiographical frame. The final and the longest part of the book is entitled 'The Period of Rebirth (Since 1961)' and consists of a discussion of the new time of reawakened political commitment, and the trend away from the consciously 'literary' towards a more colloquial style on the part of the black writer. The autobiographical works of Baldwin, Ida Wells, Anne Moody, Maya Angelou, Malcolm X, Eldridge Cleaver, Bobby Seale, H. Rap Brown, George Jackson, Julius Lester, and Claude McKay come under consideration here.

Discussing those two worlds in which the genre of autobiography lives, the worlds of history and of literature, of objective fact and of subjective awareness, Butterfield shows how many characteristic black modes of thought, feeling, and expression, run through all three periods virtually unchanged. He argues that Black writers were forced to discover their identities while resisting the false images imposed on them by white society. He demonstrates that the tension between the Black writers' emergent identities and their stereotyped public images gives their work an 'incandescent power'

seldom found in comparable narratives by white authors.

Arthur P. Davis writes a general study of the development of Black writing during the first six decades of this century in *From the Dark Tower: Afro-American Writers 1900 to 1960*.[15] Designed as a supplementary text for courses in Negro-American literature or Black Studies, the work is divided into two long sections, 'The New Negro Renaissance (1900–1940)', and 'In the Mainstream (1940–1960)'. Mr Davis has attempted to give a comprehensive view of the major black literary figures of the period proposing the loose general thesis that Negro literature, though dealing with a unique experience in American life and thought largely excluded from white critical commentary and anthologies, is nevertheless American literature, and as such becomes one with the 'mainstream' of national writing. This presumably is why he stops his examination at 1960; so that he does not have to deal with a movement with whose aims he cannot agree.

A concern with the actual teaching of Ethnic Studies, in particular Black Studies, is also the subject matter of a series of three related articles in *College English*. Blyden Jackson in 'A Survey Course in Negro Literature' advocates a division of black literary materials, when being taught in a survey course, into six periods from Lucy Terry and her 1746 poem 'Bars Flight' to the present. Not only, he says, would this provide a study of Black literature as an integrated literary tradition, it would also provide a course in the humanities for those who believe in 'the parliament of man'. Frederick C. Stern in 'Black

[15] *From the Dark Tower: Afro-American Writers 1900–1960*, by Arthur P. Davis. Washington D.C.: Howard U.P. pp. xiv + 306. $10.95.

Lit., White Crit.' discusses the relationship of the white critic to the work of the black artist and critic in the United States. He examines existing discussion on this subject, then proceeds to claim that the white critic has, in fact, an important rôle to play in this field providing he accepts certain limitations and conditions in order to function appropriately. Finally, Rose Mary Prosen's article '"Ethnic Literature"—of Whom and for Whom; Digressions of a Neo-American Teacher' discusses the importance of Ethnic literature in an American teaching context.

2. POETRY

M. L. Rosenthal[16] investigates the relationship between poetry and the common life. He defines common life in a variety of forms: ordinary reality, historical reality, ordinary consciousness, subjective feeling, and the extraordinary commonplaces of love and death. By quotation and exegesis he shows the way in which these commonplaces are the very stuff of some kinds of poetry, and how poetry sheds epiphanic light on the quotidian. Veronica Forrest Thompson, in an essay on 'Dada, Unrealism and Contemporary Poetry' (*TCS*), glancingly explicates fragments from Ashbery and O'Hara to demonstrate the formal and syntactic 'meaning' which in non-naturalistic works replaces verbal (semantic?) reality. Not so much unconvincing, as not designed to convince, but rather to replace poetic by critical metaphor, her treatment is suggestive in parts.

William Slaughter's 'Eating Poetry' (*ChiR*) is less bizarre than its title suggests. Starting from Eliot's remark that in seeking to go beyond the

visual and auditory imagination, 'one must look into the cerebral cortex, the nervous system, the digestive tracts', Slaughter identifies the gustatory imagination, drawing our attention to a striking poem by Mark Strand, and bringing together references to Eve Merriam, Peter Michelson, and Allen Ginsberg. He relates Robert Penn Warren's parable of eating poetry in 'Pure and Impure Poetry' to the idea of the 'assimilation' of artistic experience in the work of Fritz Perls and the exponents of Gestalt therapy. To describe our reception of poetry as visual or auditory is no less metaphoric than to call it gustatory. This essay at least forces the critic to ask whether the eating metaphor is not a more adequate and nourishing one. Juxtaposed pertinently is a review of Peter Michelson *The Eater* (*ChiR*), by David S. Lenfest, which points to Michelson's metaphoric association between taste, in the artistic sense, and appetite.

Perhaps not all that irrelevant either are two articles by R. P. Dickey (*SewR*) and Marion Montgomery (*SR*). Dickey attacks what he calls 'The New Genteel Tradition in American Poetry' in a manifesto which divides contemporary poets into what he calls 'good guys' who are bad, and 'good/bad guys' who are good. The list of those anathematized includes Ginsberg, Bly, Snyder, and Creeley; the admired group brackets Leonard Cohen and James Dickey with Robert Lowell and Allen Tate. While one can concede that the distinction relies on something, it is pretty tenuous, and certainly seems inadequate for such intemperate judgements. But manifestos have a habit of provoking sceptical reactions. Marion Montgomery initiates us slightly into the mysteries of theoretical physics in 'Eliot and the Particle Physicists: the Merging of Two Cul-

---

[16] *Poetry and The Common Life*, by M. L. Rosenthal. New York: Oxford U.P. pp. x + 148. $6.95.

tures' (*SR*) to make ingeniously the apparently simple point that both physicists and poets have recourse to mythic hypotheses as a means of grounding their ordering methods. More pseudo-analytics from Richard Kostelanetz.[17] His investigative account of cultural 'fixing' by the literary-financial establishment adduces crushing evidence. His presentation of the American poetic avant-garde provokes variously disappointment, disbelief, and disgust. The clogging of the literary circulation Kostelanetz describes may not, it seems, be reversed in time to save from gangrene the genuine new poetics presented for our inspection in his chapter entitled 'The New Poetries'. In another chapter he lists, in five three-columned pages, the names of relatively unknown young poets, as a reproach to academic critics. Committed too, but, as one would expect, in a different way, is James F. Mersman's discussion of poets and poetry against the Vietnam War.[18] But it is much more than a political book. Mersman's analysis of the changing nature of war poetry, through this century is clearly written and neatly illustrated. It provides him with a suitable basis for a lively, and deftly selective, examination of four poets, Ginsberg, Levertov, Bly, and Duncan. He sees these four as exhibiting a range of response and revulsion, related most obviously by a common stridency, as in varying degrees they see the war in Vietnam as an extension of a war within the socio-psychic society. The book tails off with a catalogue of 'Other Poems and Poets',

and a summary coda, in both of which a certain naïve assertiveness, which has scarcely been more than an occasional 'nag' in the interesting central chapters, becomes irritating.

The collection of essays on *Modern Black Poets*,[19] edited by Donald B. Gibson was among items missed last year. The inclusion of two essays among a batch of generally rather undistinguished offerings, many of which are reprinted, prompts belated reference. Lee A. Jacobus's 'Imamu Amiri Baraka: The Quest for Moral Order' and Richard K. Barksdale's 'Humanistic Protest in Recent Black Poetry' both point to a constructive search by young black poets for 'a new order, a new wholeness'. Jacobus's essay offers a number of suggestions about Baraka's relationship to, and participation in, a wider poetic consciousness, while Barksdale shows that among the writing of don l lee, Sonia Sanchez, and Nikki Giovanni there is a passionate humane interest that transcends 'Black Poetry' protest. This volume includes a solid and useful bibliography of twentieth-century black poetry and criticism, listing 260 items. Five essays by Darwin T. Turner, Robert A. Lee, George E. Kent, and Catherine H. Copeland, in a special Harlem Renaissance number of *CLAJ*, place the work of Martha A. Cobb, Paul Laurence Dunbar, Claude McKay, Countee Cullen, and Langston Hughes in the context of black writing in America and elsewhere. In an earlier number *CLAJ* includes two articles on Jean Toomer. Mabel M. Dillard in 'Jean Toomer—The Veil Replaced', discusses Toomer's ideas on the formation of a new race in two poems,

[17] *The End of Intelligent Writing: Literary Politics in America*, by Richard Kostelanetz. New York: Sheed & Ward Inc. pp. xviii + 480. $12.95.
[18] *Out of the Vietnam Vortex: A Study of Poets and Poetry against the War*, by James F. Mersman. Kansas. pp. xii + 277. $10.50.

[19] *Modern Black Poets: A Collection of Critical Essays*, ed. by Donald B. Gibson Englewood Cliffs, N.J., Prentice Hall Inc. (Spectrum Books). pp. viii + 181. $1.95 (paperback).

'Brown River Smile' and 'Blue Meridian'. On the evidence produced, Toomer's verse is clearly interesting as a vehicle for his theories about a multi-racial America, less valuable for intrinsic quality. In 'The Mid Kingdom of Crane's "Black Tambourine" and Toomer's "Cane"', Victor A. Kramer draws parallels between Hart Crane and Toomer, showing that, whether or not Toomer knew Crane's poem, both works were preoccupied with 'the fact that Black Culture must span a gap between past and present'.

Mowbray Allan[20] examines the relationship between T. S. Eliot's philosophical studies and his central preoccupation with perception-and-reality, in his theoretical critical writing. The unpretentious tone and the very thorough specific use of examples, together with detailed reference, combine to produce a book which is more valuable than its *seeming* unoriginality might have suggested. Professor Mowbray patiently illuminates a number of issues and aspects to which pedagogues and critics of Eliot have often merely directed a cursory flash. Among articles on Eliot is Marion Perrett's ingenious, but not overly so, examination of the parallel myths of Actaeon and Diana and Tiresias and Athene, in 'Eliot, The Naked Lady, and The Missing Link' (*AL*). She shows how Eliot's footnoting of Day's *The Parliament of Bees* directs us to versions of the two stories, and points, through a contrast in the responses of the two embarrassed goddesses, to a possible transition from justice (seen as horrific in 'The Waste Land') to mercy.

In a precise, selective treatment of Wallace Stevens's goal and achievement,[21] Lucy Beckett persuades us amply of the influence of Santayana on both Stevens and Eliot, at Harvard. She stresses the centrality of Stevens's search for an embracing formula to describe the relationships between reality, imagination, and belief, which informs his major, but not final, theoretic statement in 'Notes Towards a Supreme Fiction'. In following the philosopher in Stevens through the major phases of his recircling intellectual and spiritual quest, she tends inevitably to ignore somewhat the dandy poet, and rather disappoints us of judgements of the poetry itself. Her analyses are learned and sensitive, but she does not quite succeed in avoiding the pitfall that lurks for all who seek to interpret and paraphrase the meaning of a poet who so finely qualifies his statements precisely to avoid the danger that the words to express and embody the human drive towards good-feeling, charity, love, and peace have been vulgarized in our culture by a pre-empting religious usage. The problem is brought into focus by Adelaide Kirby Morris[22] who argues that, as the Supreme Fiction overthrew the Supreme Being, it assumed many of the accoutrements of traditional religion. Stevens inherited from a grandfather of whom he was acutely aware an ineradicable allegiance to the forms and symbols of the fundamental faith of his Zeller forbears, which provided him with a language of reference, and a parabolic mode of expression, in his search for a substitute 'religion' to replace a Christianity no longer credible. Miss Kirby examines in detail Stevens's critique of the 'deaf-mute' church and shows that he was

[20] *T. S. Eliot's Impersonal Theory of Poetry*, by Mowbray Allan. Lewisburg: Bucknell U.P. pp. 189. $10.00.

[21] *Wallace Stevens*, by Lucy Beckett. Cambridge U.P. pp. 222. $10.95. £3.50.

[22] *Wallace Stevens: Imagination and Faith*, by Adelaide Kirby Morris. Princeton, N.J.: Princeton U.P. pp. xi+205. $9.50. £5.10.

seeking to construct a mystical system that would replace Christian theology, which no longer, as it had for his Lutheran ancestors, fused the human and divine. God becomes equivalent to the Imagination, the Holy Ghost to the Imagination inhering in man, Christ to the Imagination Incarnate. The moral dimension of Stevens's religion offers rewards for the acceptance of what is, while the function of the imagination is to reveal and celebrate the real. Stevens's apperception of transfiguration is non-Christian, but closely parallel to Christianity because its expression is derived from Christian belief and theology. The Supreme Fiction constructs a world which fully replaces, and provides rewards as rich as those provided by, the world of his ancestors. Somewhat in the same vein, Wendell Stacey Hopkins's 'Auden, Hopkins, and the Poetry of Reticence' (*TCL*), traces in Auden's work both the persisting influence of G. M. Hopkins, and a conscious desire to dissociate his own verse from what he saw as a too direct and explicit expression of erotic or devotional feeling in the older poet. G. M. Hopkins's voice is audible, it is claimed, in Auden's late verse, as well as in the earlier, where it is occasionally parodied. Herman Peschmann's 'W. H. Auden (1907–1973)' (*English*) is a conventional brief summary of Auden's career, ending with a plea for a variorum Auden, with which most would concur.

The Frost celebrations continue. Reginald L. Cook's presentation[23] of taped conversations, and recollections of meetings with Frost over forty years provide more grist for the Ph.D. mills. His own interpretations are sensitive and persuasive, and confirm, as much from critical analysis of the poems as from the utterances of the poet, the generally accepted view of Frost as both a 'personality' and an impersonal representative of an undying strain of intuitive humanism, which transcends the occasional folksy, merely aphoristic, aspects of his poetic statement. The book is a successful blend of criticism and biography which enlightens, and will rank with the more important assessments of Frost which the author acknowledges. In an essay entitled 'Robert Frost: An Equilibrist's Field of Vision' (*MassR*) Cook insists that Frost's notorious ambiguousness is not an evasion, nor a sceptical tension, but an equilibrium of opposites, such that at no time is the poem (or the world) resolved. Rather both rely on dynamic relationships to exist at all. Rather elaborately argued, with a range of reference from Niels Bohr to Euripides, the thesis is true enough, one suspects. Frost's ambiguity is something of a chestnut. But in a neatly concluded essay, 'Poetic Ambiguity in Frost' (*WHR*), which begins ponderously, V. Y. Kantak points to a clue to its source, to be found in God's explanation of his behaviour in 'A Masque of Reason'. Frost, whose inexplicitness has variously been seen as a kind of classicism or just plain evasiveness, works to produce a 'noumenal' effect which reacts against his preference for a 'Lucretian' materialism. Kantak sees this as a recognition derived from Emerson, that there is a necessary hiatus between the nature of reality and our capacity to understand it in conceptual terms Human questions about the world are only to be answered by formulations into which human — and cosmic — irrationality and ambivalence have entered. On a more or less parallel track, Floyd C. Watkins (*SAQ*) looks for evidence of religious belief in Frost's poetry and

[23] *Robert Frost: A Living Voice*, by Reginald L. Cook. Amherst: U. of Mass. pp. xi + 331. $12.50.

prose; in an essay entitled 'Going and Coming Back: Robert Frost's Religious Poetry', he comes rather simply to the not very revolutionary conclusion that the quality of the poetry varies inversely with the depth of conventional religious feeling expressed. Elaine Barry's *Robert Frost*[24] is rather disappointing, even given the modest constraints of the series for which it is written. She offers biography followed by the customary selective reference to, and exegesis of, longer and shorter poems, commenting on the main aspects of Frost's 'philosophy' and his characteristic motifs. In scope, if not at all in critical enlightenment, this book complements Miss Barry's *Robert Frost on Writing* (*YW* LIV:431).

Charles E. Burgess, in an elegant, carefully documented essay, 'Masters and Some Mentors' (*PLL*), illuminates both the background of, and the very direct influences on, the *Spoon River Anthology*. He refers to a number of people in the intellectual communities of Petersburg and Lewiston, notably to William H. Hendon, biographer of Lincoln, Margaret Gilman, George Davidson, poet and friend of the young Masters, to show that the latter was drawing quite heavily on his reminiscences of their ideas, voices, and personalities, when he constructed the mythical community of Spoon River.

For one reader at least, Scott Donaldson's biography of Winfield Townley Scott[25] provoked and sustained interest in a poet of whom he was previously unaware, and merits inclusion, having escaped mention when it was first published in 1972. The copious detail never overwhelms

the sprightly narrative, and invites us to examine those poems we ignored in the anthologies, between the verses of Scott's illustrious contemporaries.

Two books from Twayne appeared this year. Richard McDougall writes at times as though he were addressing a Freshman class, and his book on Delmore Schwartz[26] tends to repetitiousness. He sketches the main creative concerns of a writer whose more important contribution, as Philip Rahv saw, was to criticism and reviewing. Nevertheless the book does remind us of a Jewish–American experience and protest that was nearer, both politically and socially, to that of contemporary black ethnic writing than to the Jewish fictions of the last twenty years. J. M. Linebarger's study of John Berryman[27] is instructive as to meanings and modes, less so when he discusses form. The reader understands better from having read this book what the poems, especially the Dream Songs, which are treated in bright detail, are saying, but is likely to be disappointed when he comes to the discussion of Berryman's style, which is treated rather scantly, with the sort of objectivity that suggests a critic unwilling to commit himself. In 'John Berryman: Sorrows and Passions of His Majesty the Ego' (*Poetry Nation*) Jonathan Galassi describes Berryman's literary career as 'a continuous search for a viable style'. He points to Berryman's use of personae as a mask for self-scrutiny, which becomes obsessive later, as he gives up Freudian 'changes and disguises'. Reviewing Berryman's later work, which he characterizes as predominantly an insistent passionate

[24] *Robert Frost*, by Elaine Barry. New York: Frederick Ungar. (Modern Literature Monograph Series). pp. xi+145. $6.00.

[25] *Poet in America: Winfield Townley Scott*, by Scott Donaldson. Austin & London: U. of Texas P. (1972). pp. xiii+400. $12.50.

[26] *Delmore Schwartz*, by Richard McDougall. New York: Twayne (TUSAS). pp. 156. $7.50.

[27] *John Berryman*, by John Linebarger. New York: Twayne (TUSAS). pp. 176. $6.50.

dwelling on autobiographical concerns, he concludes that it demands so much 'involvement between reader and artist that a great deal of its impact and effectiveness lies beyond the normal bounds of poetic art'. A third Twayne volume, from 1972, Morgan Gibson's *Kenneth Rexroth*,[28] although the 'beat' enthusiasm of the Rexroth devotee is never far away, is written densely. Its critical assertions are concentrated and complex at their best, and the book provides an interesting introduction, not only to Rexroth himself, but to the San Francisco Renaissance and other mid-50s phenomena associated with the Beats.

Roethke uses dynamic imagery within comparatively static traditional stanzas. Richard Allen Blessing's examination[29] is convincing on this point. The quotations from Roethke's unpublished papers, the quoted opinions of others, and the not too striking 'explications' provide a decrescendo of additional interest. In 'Roethke, Water Father' (*AL*), Anthony Libby examines influences, imitations, and borrowings, which connect Robert Bly and Sylvia Plath with the older poet. Roethke provides a more 'vegetal' source for subsequent developments in American poetry than the 'abstract' Eliot. The connexions Libby discovers are more profound than imitation, no less real for being almost indefinable. Roethke's Jungian vision, not completely developed in his poetry, is carried forward, and taken further by Bly and Plath. John Romero (*Commentary*) discusses Sylvia Plath's poetry alongside her novel, provocatively alleging, that the 'collation of

her suicide and her poetry' by some critics, unfeeling and irresponsible as it is, has created a myth of her martyrdom, which prevents our seeing in her poetry an artistic failure 'rooted in a failure to apprehend the self in others'.

The interaction of history and literature receives treatment in James J. Wilhelm's 'The Dragon and the Duel: A Defense of Pound's Canto 88' (*TCL*). In a lucid, detailed commentary, Wilhelm compares the Canto with its source in Thomas Hart Benton's *Thirty Years View*, and defends conservative repugnance in Pound, Benton, and the Jacksonians over the national banks' 'private control' of public money against the liberal attack on Pound by Ron Baer in an article in *AL* (Vol. 42). The argument is expanded tentatively in two directions: towards a definition of the relationship between poetic and historic truth, coming to the Emersonian conclusion 'that the true guide to history lies in the heart' and towards a condemnation in passing of the Federal Reserve System and Wall Street finance.

In a brief revaluatory essay, 'The Poetry of James Agee: The Art of Recovery' (*SR*), Donald E. Stanford reminds us that Agee published in 1934 a book of poems, *Permit Me My Voyage*, which critics have usually referred to as pastiche, since they in large measure consist of exercises in traditional poetic styles and modes. Stanford would have us see them as 'recovery' in subject matter as well as form, in particular the subjects of love and religious faith in a sixteenth-century spirit.

A number of articles in *SR* marked the death of John Crowe Ransom. Allen Tate in 'Reflections on the Death of John Crowe Ransom' writes of him with sober dedication, as a pupil of a revered master.

[28] *Kenneth Rexroth*, by Morgan Gibson. New York: Twayne (TUSAS). pp. 156. $6.50.

[29] *Theodore Roethke's Dynamic Vision*, by Richard Allen Blessing. Bloomington and London: Indiana U.P. pp. x+240. £4.40.

Thomas Daniel Young contributes a memoir of Ransom's time at Oxford, and its influence on his ideas, in 'Mostly Nurtured From England'. In 'The Wary Fugitive: John Crowe Ransom', Louis D. Rubin Jr. describes Ransom among his Fugitive colleagues, and demonstrates from a selection of examples, the tough intellectual commitment of Ransom's poetry and criticism, while George Core's 'Mr Ransom and the House of Poetry' considers extensively the strengths and weaknesses of his theory and, briefly, its application to his critical practice.

Southern Agrarianism and the Fugitives receive additional attention with the publication this year in a tabulated, indexed, and annotated volume of letters between Allen Tate and Donald Davidson.[30] Other Fugitive items are a listing of the writing of Fugitive poets, to 1929 for their contributions to anthologies and periodicals, but to 1972 for books of poetry and criticism.[31] The latter contains a prefatory article by Louis D. Rubin Jr., entitled 'Fugitives as Agrarians: The Impulse behind *I'll Take My Stand*' which illustrates its theme in a characteristically Southern, anecdotal fashion. An interesting review of the former, 'A Friendship of Poets: The Statesman and the Poet' (*GR*), by Charles Edward Eaton, points out that, in general, Davidson is for expansive poetry, Tate for intensive. What they seem to have in common is an obsessive interest in the subject of poetry, but their dissimilar temperaments meant that they had little else. Davidson sees Tate as a

poet of aesthetic dissertation. The letters show them drifting inevitably apart in the post-war phase of their epistolary relationship. In fact Tate's poems do expand into more general significances, while Davidson's are firmly tied to the Old South. Davidson remains nostalgically in Nashville, while Tate moves outward and into the world. Eaton describes Davidson as 'the Field Marshall of the Fugitive Movement'—he was the elder by six years—and Tate as a 'foot-soldier slogging his way to ultimate victory'.

Julia A. Bartholomay has read Howard Nemerov's poetry and prose with intelligence, and with a dedication so intense that one comes to recognize, as one reads *The Shield of Perseus: The Vision and Imagination of Howard Nemerov*,[32] how valuable a certain agnosticism can be in literary criticism. The centrality of the image of the mirror in Nemerov's work, and his preoccupation with the nature of the imaginative process, was worth insisting on, and she explicates his text in thorough detail, but her encomious language and occasional over-insistence are a barrier. Raymond Smith illustrates, in 'Nemerov and Nature: The Stillness in Moving Things' (*SR*), by exegesis of a number of poems, that the work of Nemerov, who is to be compared with Stevens or Frost, and contrasted—in this respect—with Dickey, reveals a dichotomy between the view of Man as contemplator, and Nature as contemplated. Nemerov does not celebrate Nature, but exercises reason upon it, not absorbing it as myth, but pondering its emblematic significances. Smith relates what he calls, a little oddly, 'this alienation from Nature' seen as

[30] *The Literary Correspondence of Donald Davidson and Allen Tate*, ed. by John Tyree Fain and Thomas Daniel Young. Athens, Georgia: U. of Georgia. pp. lxx+442. $15.00.

[31] *A Catalogue of the Fugitive Poets, with an Essay by Louis D. Rubin Jr.* (*Focus* 3), by J. Howard Woolmer. Andes, N.Y.: J. Howard Woolmer (1972). pp. 53. $3.00.

[32] *The Shield of Perseus: The Vision and Imagination of Howard Nemerov*, by Julia A. Bartholomay. Gainsville, Fla.: U. of Florida. pp. 168. $6.00.

continuous and permanent, even though 'running down', to Nemerov's pessimism at the finiteness of the human mind.

Frances C. Ferguson in 'Randall Jarrell and the Flotations of Voice' (*GR*), examines the mode of Jarrell's critical essay, 'Stories', to introduce a sensitive argument about his use of unlocated voice in the poems. 'The voice of some crucial Jarrell poems ["The Death of the Ball Turret Gunner", "Jerome", "Cinderella", "Eight Air Force"] has abandoned the perception of self as an individual entity.' Moralism, which requires a more specific identification of a character which persists long enough to permit of being judged, 'seems an inappropriate response to voices which are not seen as individual selves', so that 'moral judgements have become inexplicable'. Such unlocated voices in Jarrell's poems tend to disappear, and merge into a generalized 'fictional temporal infinitude'.

George Monteiro's 'Dylan in the Sixties' (*SAQ*) looks back over Bob Dylan's career in the 1960s to identify a development, from the traditional folk-artist to apocalyptic poet, by way of protest and rock-and-roll. In spite of the unusual use of adventitious material, the argument is serious and plausible.

Alan Williamson's *Pity the Monsters*[33] offers a close reading of a number of Robert Lowell's key poems as well as more general reference. His selective thesis deals with the nature of Lowell's political response, between commitment and criticism, radical and conservative, to the events of his poetic lifetime. His writings are prophetic rather than either states-manlike or revolutionary. Williamson's alert and sensitive assessment vibrates continually on the sexual, mystical, and religious wavelengths of Lowell's pervasive allusions to private and public politics. He acknowledges apologetically his exclusion of the more private, confessional, realistic elements in Lowell's oeuvre, but in his concentration on the 'politics' of his subject, in the very widest sense, he ignores very little in practice. The most important consequence of the bias of his treatment is that he comes to see 'Memories of West Street and Lepke' as the pivotal poem, and to move the centre of greatest interest away from *Life Studies* to *Near The Ocean* and the more recent work. J. F. Crick's volume[34] in Oliver and Boyd's *Modern Writers* series is more crammed, less emphatically directed to a particular view of Lowell. In the small compass of an introductory guide, he deals compressedly—perhaps too much so for the audience he might anticipate—with the major critical and biographical issues. The effect is of a bigger book scaled down to fit a format which can scarcely contain it. He gives essentially a chapter to each major collection, his chapter headings offer a quintessential comment, and each chapter provides a provocation to, and a substantial base for, further study. A full bibliography of critical works is thoughtfully provided. Jonathan Raban[35] offers a selection of Lowell's poems, representing the poet's own choice from the range of his work. There is some emphasis on the more recent volumes, *Notebook* and *The Dolphin*. Rabin's introduction gets close to the techniques of the

---

[33] *Pity the Monsters: The Political Vision of Robert Lowell*, by Alan Williamson. New Haven and London: Yale U.P. pp. xi+221. $10.00.

[34] *Robert Lowell*, by J. F. Crick, Edinburgh: Oliver & Boyd. pp. 166. £1.25.

[35] *Robert Lowell's Poems: A Selection*, ed. by Jonathan Raban. London: Faber & Faber. pp. 192. £1.10 (paper).

poems, and recognizes amply the wider relevance of the confessional subject matter. Acknowledging Hugh B. Staples's study of Lowell as his main source for the explication of the earlier poems, he gives us twenty-seven pages of notes which go well beyond factual glossing.

Frankly admitting that their publication is narcissistic, Robert Creeley prints the texts of ten interviews he gave between 1961 and 1971.[36] The interviewers ask the usual questions, and Creeley mines away, as poets do on these occasions, at prosaic enough answers. The editor's rôle seems to have been slight. The interest of the volume lies undoubtedly in its typicality.

Joan St. C. Crane has compiled a descriptive catalogue[37] of Frost materials in the Clifton Waller Barrett Library of the University of Virginia. With the poet's collaboration, Barrett, a philanthropical fanatic, as it would seem, collected Frostiana diligently over thirty-five years, for presentation to the University. The collection was obviously a work of devotion and a similar devoted care has been applied to the catalogue, which lists and describes books, pamphlets, first appearances of prose, manuscripts, and letters, while Frost's famous Christmas cards receive equally meticulous treatment. In an introduction, doyen Bowers himself praises the volume, which he sees as the commendable beginning of an industry. Other tools for the scholar appeared

this year. With surprising speed comes Ernest C. Stefanik Jr.'s bibliography of John Berryman[38] in the Pittsburgh series, as impeccable and thoughtfully arranged as volumes in this series always are. Scarecrow Press have inaugurated an annual bibliography[39] of American verse in periodicals, by a volume dealing with 1971. The authors checked 158 periodicals, and have listed entries under authors, with an index of poems by title.

3. THE NOVEL

Two genres, historical fiction and science fiction, often mistakenly considered unworthy of critical attention, receive some well merited appreciation this year. Harry B. Henderson III examines the historical fiction of major American writers in *Versions of the Past: The Historical Imagination in American Fiction*,[40] analyzing the genre from a literary, social, and historical viewpoint. He discusses the novels of many of the major American writers, treating *Satanstoe, The Scarlet Letter, Billy Budd, A Connecticut Yankee in King Arthur's Court, The Red Badge of Courage*, and *Absalom, Absalom!* as belonging in significant respects within the same literary category.

Mr Henderson does not only examine those novels set in the unexperienced past, that world existing before the birth of the author concerned. He also analyzes novels of contemporary history, of social changes that place a specifically

[36] *Robert Creeley, Contexts of Poetry: Interviews 1961–1971*, ed. by Donald Allen. Bolinas: Four Seasons Foundation. pp. 214. $3.00.

[37] *Robert Frost: A Descriptive Catalogue of Books and Manuscripts in the Clifton Waller Barrett Library, University of Virginia*, compiled by Joan St. C. Crane. Charlottesville: U. of Virginia P. (Published for the Associates of the University Library). pp. xxv + 280. $17.50.

[38] *John Berryman: A Descriptive Bibliography*, by Ernest C. Stefanik, Jr. U. of Pittsburg P. (Pittsburg Series in Bibliography). pp. xxix + 285. $22.00.

[39] *Index of American Periodical Verse 1971*, by Sander W. Zulauf and Irwin H. Weiser. Metuchen, N.J.: Scarecrow P. pp. xxxiii + 467. $13.50.

[40] *Versions of the Past: The Historical Imagination in American Fiction*, by Harry B. Henderson III. New York: Oxford U.P. pp. xiii + 344. $12.50.

historical perspective on events lived through by the author. Thus such works as *U.S.A., Invisible Man, V.,* and *The Armies of the Night* are discussed, with particular reference to their emphasis on a history which is evolving through the present and which is to shape the future.

Somewhat narrow definitions are imposed by the author in the course of this study of the historical imagination. He establishes two categories, the 'progressive' and the 'holist', into which the various works discussed can be sorted. The 'progressive' assumes a linear development in history, history as 'measurable change on an absolute scale'; whereas the 'holist' frame, 'a relativistic view of time-bound man' assumes 'historical change is not measurable except *in terms of the period under consideration*'. This leads to a rather awkward movement throughout the text between these two structures, and to a failure to pursue the full implications of the work studied: for example, Mr Henderson's treatment of *A Connecticut Yankee* as a 'progressive historical novel *par excellence*' surely misses much of the novel's relativistic subtlety.

Unfortunately the author died before completing this work and his chapter on the post-1945 novel, 'Liberal Conscience and Apocalyptic Parody' remains unfinished, more a series of short jottings than a detailed critical study, and as far as it goes, hardly very original. Nevertheless, this is an interesting work which, through close textual analysis, succeeds in creating some appreciation of the self-awareness and complexity of the historical imagination of the American writer.

David Ketterer's concern is with the future rather than the past in *New Worlds for Old: The Apocalyptic Imagination, Science Fiction, and American Literature.*[41] Science fiction, so Mr Ketterer rightly believes, has been artificially divorced from the critical mainstream for too long. He approaches examples of the genre in a rigorously analytical manner, to show science fiction is a viable area of literary study. As he points out, though the genre derives from the same source as Hawthorne's 'romance', its position of significance in the American literary experience has on the whole been ignored. David Ketterer, in this study, remedies at least some of this large gap in scholarship.

He believes that science fiction relates most closely to 'accepted literature' in its 'apocalyptic' aspect. The interesting and critically rewarding way in which he develops this relationship is by setting 'classic' non-science-fictional exemplars of the apocalyptic imagination against a science fiction work with a parallel theme to exemplify just how closely related is the latter material to the work taken from the literary mainstream. Among others, he rewardingly pairs the chapter on 'Edgar Allen Poe and the Visionary Tradition of Science Fiction' with the best chapter in this study, 'The Left Hand of Darkness: Ursula K. Le Guin's Archetypal "Winter Journey"'; and 'Melville's *The Confidence-Man* and the Fiction of Science' with 'Vonnegut's Spiral Siren Call: From Dresden's Lunar Vistas to Tralfamadore'.

This last chapter title suggests a major objection to Ketterer's work. Though this is certainly an intelligent book and effectively opens up the science fiction field to serious study, he is over concerned with shaping his science fiction to fit his thesis. When

[41] *New Worlds for Old: The Apocalyptic Imagination, Science Fiction, and American Literature,* by David Ketterer. Indiana U.P. pp. xii+347. $10.95.

only very brief mention is made of Samuel Delany, how can there be justification for an entire chapter on Vonnegut? This is a highly selective study of science fiction material. The word 'apocalyptic', examined in the first chapter, reveals the author's central concern, and Mr Ketterer's attraction to chaos becomes evident in his failure to examine the other sides of his subject, that type of science fiction, for example, he terms 'fantastic literature'. In pursuing his thesis, he ignores this continuing strand of the genre which remains highly optimistic, this utopian side which must be studied in any complete examination of the subject. However, Mr Ketterer's is a well-written and interesting study of a type of literature far too often critically skirted. Ketterer is an obvious leader of that movement on which Lloyd Biggle Jr. comments in 'Science Fiction goes to College: Groves and Morasses of Academe' (*RQ*): that new academic respectability of science fiction, which represents a turning-away from self-perpetuating traditionalism in literary criticism.

Alfred Kazin, however, works within largely traditional critical boundaries in his *Bright Book of Life: American Novelists and Storytellers from Hemingway to Mailer.*[42] Though some of the chapters in this book were delivered in early draft as the Ewing Lectures at the University of California, Los Angeles, in 1969, and though sketches for some sections of the book have previously appeared in article form, this volume was apparently conceived as, and remains, an integrated account of post-1939 American fiction. This fiction, as Kazin views it, reflects and embodies

[42] *Bright Book of Life: American Novelists and Storytellers from Hemingway to Mailer,* by Alfred Kazin. Boston: Little, Brown. 1973. pp. 334. $8.95.

more variously and truthfully than any other form of written art, the nature of the American experience.

Kazin believes that the novel has retained all its energy in the present era. He leads us from the later Hemingway and the way in which he orders and shapes a threatening and potentially chaotic reality through literature itself, to Bellow and his capacity, and his protagonists', 'for taking hold, for getting there, for being on top of the desperate situation'. Alfred Kazin has taken the modern novel in all its various forms, from Salinger to Burroughs, from McCullers to Gass, in order to give his reader an overall view both of life and literature in the modern age. He continues to celebrate the novel as 'bright book of life' marked by an 'openness to life, to life in any direction and in any volume'; marked by the quality of a literary imagination which has retained its sense of inexhaustible delight in its power to order the random elements of our world right up to the present moment.

This celebration is the major unifying strand of this collection in which Kazin tries to contain the whole of modern American literature. This hints at a flaw in the book. The level of Kazin's thoughtful and patient critical statement is consistently high, but in his attempt to discuss thirty authors in just over 300 pages he takes on too much. *Why Are We in Vietnam?* surely deserves more than a brief page of comment; *The Crying of Lot 49* more than three paragraphs. It is also strange to see Kazin mentioning many essentially minor authors and making no reference to Hawkes and little to John Barth. This is an interesting and comprehensively stimulating survey of mid-twentieth century material which tends to remain just that, a survey and little else, because of its attempt to cover too much material in too little space.

John O. Stark takes a very different view of the contemporary novel to that of Kazin in *The Literature of Exhaustion: Borges, Nabokov and Barth*.[43] He suggests that although the combination of Nabokov, Borges, and Barth seems at first glance 'bizarre', in fact they can be grouped as members of a significant twentieth-century literary movement, practising 'the Literature of Exhaustion'. Barth's essay of this title, applied in the course of this study to the three examined authors, provides Stark with his starting point. The main concern of Barth's essay is in suggesting that some twentieth-century writers use as their major theme for new works of literature the agonizing hypothesis that literature is finished. Barth is saying two things here. First, literature itself is almost totally worn out (a suggestion Kazin would entirely reject). From there he goes on to say that this hypothesis can be employed to produce further works of fiction, and to imply paradoxically that the imagination can create endless and inexhaustible possibilities by actually writing about the present exhausted state of literature itself. This provides the central thesis of this study.

Stark first studies Borges's work to show how he can be placed firmly in this 'Literature of Exhaustion' camp, and suggests that the fact that he can so easily be labelled suggests certain 'limitations in his work that make him less than a truly major writer'. Barth's fictional output is then examined, particularly *The Sot-Weed Factor* and *Lost in the Funhouse*, to show that he too fits the label fairly

completely. Stark finally concentrates his attentions on Nabokov's *Lolita, Pale Fire*, and *Ada*, as belonging to this same literary tradition, but goes on to show that many of Nabokov's distinguishing characteristics fall outside this limiting bracket. This wider fictional range, he suggests, indicates that Nabokov has done more important work than the other two writers: that he can be seen as 'a truly major writer'.

John Barth is again one of the centres of attention in *The New Fiction: Interviews with Innovative American Writers*,[44] edited by Joe David Bellamy, though in this book more figures share the stage with him. For besides an interview with Barth, interviews with Joyce Carol Oates, William H. Gass, Donald Barthelme, Ronald Sukenick, Tom Wolfe, John Hawkes, Susan Sontag, Ishmael Reed, Jerzy Kosinski, John Gardner, and Kurt Vonnegut Jr., also appear. These interviews, seven of which have been published previously in periodicals, are carried out by a panel of seven interviewers. Joe Bellamy, the editor, sets forth the scope of the book in his introduction: to examine, through conversation with these authors, the startling change of literary climate in modern America. He points out the transformations of sensibility and language, the great variety of formal and technical explorations and sophistication of a fiction, until recently 'the most arrière garde' of contemporary art forms, which is now catching up with the artistic process of the age.

New fiction is based on totally revised assumptions about the nature and purpose of art, and in the interviews presented here the change in

[43] *The Literature of Exhaustion: Borges, Nabokov and Barth*, by John O. Stark. Durham, N. Carolina: Duke U.P. pp. 196. $7.95.

[44] *The New Fiction: Interviews with Innovative American Writers*, ed. by Joe David Bellamy. U. of Illinois P. pp. xv+210. $7.95.

fictional forms and themes which has occurred in the last decade is examined, as a means of assessing those transformations of sensibility, language, and formal and technical device, which mark the novel in the present era. The writers interviewed are those who seem to this editor most involved in effecting significant change, whose artistic theorizations, innovations, and critical formulations, seem most provocative and influential.

Bellamy admits this is merely a representative grouping of writers presented here, rather than a complete spectrum of new fictionalists. He rightly claims, however, that rigorously intelligent and closely edited interviews of this kind can prove to be valuable and unique literary artifacts, and has provided overall coherence to the collection through the asking of a number of central questions of the 'what fictional modes now appear moribund?' and the 'what is the relation between art and reality?' variety, which recur throughout. By unifying his material in this manner, this editor has successfully gathered together a body of interesting and intelligent commentary about the state of current fiction.

This subject, the state of current fiction, is also the concern of the following four articles in the *MFS* special number on 'Some Experimental Modes'. In this issue Myron Greenman in 'Understanding New Fiction' suggests that it is erroneous to speak of new fiction as a departure from the mimetic tradition. He claims that new fiction is the first literary movement towards a total refusal to define reality, and therefore towards a redefinition of literature's purpose. New fiction acts as an index to the recognition of literature as subjective act: a mimesis of subjective internalized reality. Robert S. Ryf discusses recent changes which have taken place

in the fictional concept of character in 'Character and Imagination in the Experimental Novel'. Taking Nabokov and Mailer as his main examples he shows the stress they place on the nature and workings of the novelist's own imagination and consequently the different, but more basic, rôle that 'character' has come to play in their work.

In '"And all the Little Trytopies": Notes on Language Theory in the Contemporary Experimental Novel', Stanley Fogel explains how a number of contemporary novelists whom he calls 'writers of metafiction' are showing an interest in the strange relationship between the provinces of words and things. Their interest is in language not as a conveyor of information but as a construct in its own right. Charles Russell is also concerned with attitudes towards language in 'The Vault of Language: Self Reflective Artifice in Contemporary American Fiction'. He sees language as silence in disguise. Metaphor, asserting meaning, is 'a bridge over an abyss'. Pynchon, Barth, Nabokov, Kosinski, and Brautigan, are shown to recognize their vision, or creation, of meaning through language as purely an artifice.

Frederick Busch in 'The Friction of Fiction: A *Ulysses* Omnirandum' (*ChiR*) suggests the influence of Joyce's great work on many contemporary American writers especially in regard to its reflections on language and design. Edward Marcotte's 'Intersticed Prose' (*ChiR*) is a discussion, presented in intersticed form, of that new prose to be found in the works of Coover, Barthelme, and Gass among others. Marcotte explains how fixations on the historical model, the fact/fiction dichotomy, viewpoint, direction, motivation, and character, are all being abandoned in the new fiction to a degree perhaps never before attempted. In 'Don Quixote and Selected Progeny: Or, the Journey-man as Outsider' (*SoR*), Louis D. Rubin Jr. points out the relevance of Don Quixote, 'a man escaping from a version of reality that is not to his liking and going forth, as an outsider in society, in search of another version that perhaps can be', not only to Hemingway and Faulkner but also to Barth and the 1960s school of fabulation.

Seven Novelists in the American Naturalist Tradition: An Introduction,[45] edited by Charles Child Walcutt, is made up of a collection of material from the *University of Minnesota Pamphlets on American Writers* series, with an introductory history of the naturalist tradition in North America provided by the editor. The essays included in this volume, and their authors, are 'Stephen Crane' by Jean Cazemajou, 'Frank Norris' and 'Theodore Dreiser' by W. M. Frohock, 'Jack London' by Charles Walcutt, 'Sherwood Anderson' by Brom Weber, 'John Steinbeck' by James Gray, and 'James T. Farrell' by Edgar M. Branch.

Charles Walcutt is concerned with showing in his introduction how 'naturalism' has been used as a blanket term to cover writers who actually differ widely in both stress and tone: the 'vehement parodic impressionism' of Crane differs as widely from London's 'bristling ideas and brutal action' as from Anderson's delicate analysis of the hidden life. Walcutt describes the implications of naturalism as applicable to the writers treated here who all 'have a new concept of physical-social-political-moral process . . . all protest

. . . against convention and hypocrisy . . . are seeking new forms of dealing with a world that has forever departed from the . . . certainties of orthodox tradition. They carry us into the affirmation and the despair of the twentieth century'. These essays constitute a coming to terms with the naturalist philosophy as expressed in literature. They show naturalism as a continuing American literary tradition and not just as a turn of the century phenomenon.

The collection, however, suffers from its transition from pamphlet form. The *Minnesota Pamphlets* serve as general introductions to American writers and their concentration on biographical detail and presentation of authorial career in full mean that there is really little overall coherence to the book, which is more loosely organized than even its title suggests. It is also surprising to see Sherwood Anderson discussed here, while Dos Passos is ignored.

In 'Thirties Fiction: A View from the '70s' (*TCL*) Walter Allen says that at the time of publication Dos Passos's *U.S.A.* was thought 'the most ambitious work of fiction by any writers in English during the 1930s'. He can point out its failings now that he is no longer influenced by the 'blinkered' political and social climate of the times, and can see the rise of the Jewish novel and of Southern writing as of clearer importance. William Bedford Clark, in 'The Serpent of Lust in the Southern Garden' (*SoR*), examines the writing of the American South as a whole, from fugitive slave narratives, through Tate and Faulkner, to Ernest J. Gaines, to show the important rôle the theme of miscegenation has played in Southern writing for over a century. He shows how the basic miscegenation myth extends to take in most themes of any importance in

[45] *Seven Novelists in the American Naturalist Tradition: An Introduction*, ed. by Charles Child Walcutt. U. of Minneapolis P. pp. 331. $10.50.

Southern literature, and one theme, that of 'identity', of more than regional interest.

Denis Donoghue takes Allen Tate as one of his examples in 'The American Style of Failure' (*SR*). He suggests that conditions of failure exist in the American writer's 'bones'. Donoghue takes Trilling, James, and Henry Adams, as well as Tate, as representative of his thesis that American literature's achievement is a stylistic one, an achievement which thrives upon the conditions of defeat. Three successes, at least in catching the attention of their public, are considered in Robert F. Lucid's 'Three Public Performances: Fitzgerald, Hemingway, Mailer' (*ASch*). The author suggests that these writers caught the public eye because of their personal presence, combined with their cultural rôle: that of artist as supreme individualist supposedly independent from any institutional pressure. Mailer differs from his two predecessors, Lucid claims, in his deliberate attempt to awaken his audience to the fact and function of this illusion in their lives.

In *Black Fiction*,[46] Roger Rosenblatt suggests that his subject matter should be regarded not from the traditional linear point of view of historical progression, but from a distinctive thematic angle. There have, he claims, been discernible and continuing patterns in black fiction since 1890, all contained within the major structural and thematic motif of the circle: reality as cyclical nightmare from which escape appears impossible. He examines *Native Son*, *Go Tell it on the Mountain*, and *Cane*, to illuminate these cyclical patterns; quite unsatisfactorily in the case of *Native Son*, where he loses direction with his overly religious

[46] *Black Fiction*, by Roger Rosenblatt. Harvard U.P. pp. 211. £4.25.

interpretation, and of *Cane*, where by stressing the idea of 'repetition of loss', he virtually ignores the prophetic note which is straining throughout much of the book to transcend this repetitive plaint.

Rosenblatt claims black experience, as depicted in black fiction, to be unique and, I think, totally misinterprets Wright's statement, 'The Negro is America's metaphor', to mean that 'whatever spirit of decency and courage may have originally inspired the founding of the nation, having since been perverted, now resides, if incubatively, in the black man who has borne the brunt of that perversion'. I would question Rosenblatt's argument that the black writer is writing from a metaphysical stance which is completely distinct from that of the white writer, and also question his suggestion that Ellison's Invisible Man's statement, 'Who knows but that, on the lower frequencies, I speak for you', applies only to one particular societal stratum.

Black Fiction, though, contains much interesting material. The author discusses a wide and unusual selection of twentieth-century black literature, examining the failure of religion, love, education, or primitivism, to provide an escape from the Negro's cycle of despair. He discusses black humorous writing and its importance, and depicts that indictment of white American values portrayed in black literature. His final argument is that an understanding of oppression and its forces can only lead to submission or to total retreat from reality on the part of the black protagonist. His arguments here are convincing, though his selection of material does raise questions. The black arts movement of the 1960s is, for instance, virtually ignored, and in his thematic insistence throughout, Rosenblatt is content not to evaluate in terms of literary merit. Nevertheless, the study presents an original and often intelligent approach to its subject.

Rose Basile Green studies the literature of another minority group in *The Italian–American Novel: A Document of the Interaction of Two Cultures*.[47] She divides her material into three sections, 'Autobiographical Accounts of the early Italian Immigrants', 'The Emergence of the Italian–American Novel', and 'Contemporary Italian–American Novelists'. The author discusses the dual pattern that appears to evolve in the Italian–American writing she examines. First she traces a fictional development through five stages before this writing can be identified with the national literature. Second, within each stage of this dominant developmental pattern she reveals a minor design of conflict, isolation, and assimilation, which underlies each phase of the integration experience. Miss Green examines novels of both sociological and aesthetic value and discusses them in the context of this suggested framework, illustrating the process of each of these patterns in the development of an Italian–American fiction which shows two cultures at point of interaction.

Finally, the author presents the Italian–American novel as a positive contribution to American civilization. The final result of cultural interaction she considers to be not only a realistic depiction of one section of American life, but also a distinctive fictional interpretation of this life. In this Italian–American novel, the individual is shown as possessing the moral power to triumph in his struggle against a hostile environment, a positive attitude towards the material of American life which the author celebrates as counteracting a great deal of modern fiction which has presented this life as antagonistic to the demands of the spirit, 'materialistic in purpose' and 'nihilistic in achievement'. Miss Green terminates her study by claiming that both the characteristic 'constructive humanistic optimism' of the American novelist of Italian ancestry, and the quality of his work, admit him to the American literary mainstream.

In *The Expatriate Perspective: American Novelists and the Idea of America*,[48] Harold T. McCarthy returns, thematically at least, to the continent of Europe in an examination of the American novelist abroad. Proceeding chronologically, from Fenimore Cooper to James Baldwin, he shows how some of America's most important writers, through their lives as expatriates, both came to terms with themselves and with their American culture afresh, and communicated these discoveries in their subsequently written novels. This work becomes both a critical study of certain individual American writers and an analysis of American civilization itself as McCarthy leads his reader through a somewhat random sample of novelists. He commences with discussion of Cooper, Melville and Hawthorne in his section entitled 'The Romantic Realists', seeing these three writers as 'great romancers (who) . . . in their criticism of America distinguish themselves by their realism'. In the second part of the book, 'The American Jacobins', he studies James and Twain, whose work he suggests demonstrates the consequences, both tragic and comic, of enclosing the American spirit in

[47] *The Italian–American Novel: A Document of the Interaction of Two Cultures*, by Rose Basile Green. Fairleigh Dickinson U.P. pp. 415. $18.

[48] *The Expatriate Perspective: American Novelists and the Idea of America*, by Harold T. McCarthy. Fairleigh Dickinson U.P. pp. 244. $11.50.

European forms. In his rather narrow approach here McCarthy does James's subtleties less than justice.

In the third section of the book, 'The Neo-Transcendentalists', Hemingway, Cummings, and Henry Miller come under the author's scrutiny. It seems surprising that McCarthy should approach expatriate life and literature in the post-World War I era without mentioning Fitzgerald and only referring to Gertrude Stein twice. McCarthy uses the term 'neo-transcendentalism' after discussing the rebirth on the part of the individual protagonist, as revealed in the novels of all three writers discussed here, and the consequent final feeling in their work of a new belonging as part of 'an infinite, eternal Being'. The logic of the author's connexions are apparent here, but his description of Hemingway as 'neo-transcendentalist' indicates his desire to force the novelist's work into his critical pigeon-hole. The final section of the book is entitled 'Native Sons' and Richard Wright and James Baldwin are its subjects, black writers who only through expatriation could free themselves 'of the omnipresent, insidious, coercive myth of the "American Negro"', recover their individual humanity, and accept their racial heritage in what McCarthy calls 'a true perspective'.

In the introduction to his book, *Irony in the Mind's Life: Essays on Novels by James Agee, Elizabeth Bowen, and George Eliot*,[49] the child psychiatrist Robert Coles explains his rebellion against those classifications and categorizations into which people are so often pigeonholed by those in his profession. He tells of his turning

[49] *Irony in the Mind's Life: Essays on Novels by James Agee, Elizabeth Bowen, and George Eliot*, by Robert Coles. U.P. of Virginia. pp. 210. $9.75.

to the novel to learn 'a more intricate, a more subtle kind of psychology', and in this study examines a number of philosophers and novelists who have asked 'the broadest questions about man's nature' to suggest those subtleties of thought and complexities of feeling their writings contain and which a rigid scientific categorization of humanity so often denies.

A first printing of the 1973 Page-Barbour Lectures at the University of Virginia, this book has as its major theme what Coles calls 'the persistence of irony'. He examines the emergence of this concern in the writings of Christian thinkers, such as St Augustine, and of philosophers, Pascal and Kierkegaard among others, then turns his attention to the novels *A Death in the Family, The Death of the Heart*, and *Middlemarch*. He studies these novels, at first glance a rather peculiar grouping, to show, within the context of personal development from childhood to maturity, these 'ironies' or 'psychological tensions' inherent in our mental life, 'in the various faiths we uphold', and in 'the political and social and psychological ideas we have had handed down to us'.

Also concerned in examining handed down psychological ideas and, in addition, in questioning the validity of these ideas are the feminist writers of today. Jane Larkin Crain examines and attacks the work of these writers, analyzing recent novels by Anne Roiphe, Alix Kates Shulman and Erica Jong in 'Feminist Fiction' (*Commentary*). She suggests these novels are too steeped in ideology to allow for 'the human complexity of good fiction', that the vision of sex in the novels is demeaning and reductive, and that their protagonists are presented as dependent 'emotional cripples and children' rather than as genuine women's lib. heroines, autonomous and self-determining. Erica Jong herself, however, in 'Writing a First Novel' (*TCL*), though obviously concerned with her rôle both as woman and as writer, claims that the 'feminist novel' is just one of those 'meaningless reviewers' categories' like 'first novel'.

Ellen Killoh's article, 'Patriarchal Women: A Study of Three Novels by Janet Lewis' (*SoR*) inspects Janet Lewis's fiction in the light of this modern general revaluation of women writers. This fiction treats the particular authority exercised by women in patriarchal societies and Ms. Killoh suggests that this type of domestic specialization which could be rationalized under a feudal order can no longer provide the scope necessary for strong, visionary, women to act as preservers of culture and tradition. The problems of the historical novelist generally is one of the subjects discussed in 'A Conversation with Janet Lewis' (*SoR*) by Roger Hofheins and Dan Tooker. The experience of black women in America as reflected in fiction, with reference to particular novels by George Wylie Henderson and Chester Himes is the concern of Patricia Kane and Doris Y. Wilkinson's 'Survival Strategies: Black Women in *Ollie Miss* and *Cotton Comes to Harlem*' (*Crit*). The rôle of 'Women in the Novels of Anne Petry' (*Crit*) is discussed by Thelma J. Shinn to show that this black novelist's first concern is for the 'acceptance and realization of individual possibilities', both black and white, male and female, in a world in which overwhelming social pressures restrict the chance of personal development.

Henry James Letters, Volume I: 1843–1875[50] is the first volume of the long awaited edition of James's letters

[50] *Henry James Letters, Volume I: 1843–1875*, ed. by Leon Edel. Macmillan. pp. xxxvi + 493. £10.00.

edited by one of the foremost Jamesian scholars, Leon Edel. James's own words stand as prefacing quote to the collection, 'The best letters seem to me the most delightful of all written things—and those that are not the best the most negligible. If a correspondence has not the real charm I wouldn't have it published even privately; if it has, on the other hand, I would give it the glory of the greatest literature.' These letters, written before the author's thirty-third year, only eleven of which have been published previously, though showing some signs of 'the real charm' cannot as a whole lay any claim to membership of James's 'greatest literature' category. Nevertheless this is an important collection which is thoroughly worthy of publication, from any point of view other than the Jamesian extreme.

As these letters progress, so the gradual maturity of James's style and mind becomes evident. In fact, from the early letters his concern with style is evident with his seventeen-year-old satire of romanticism, his depiction of ''Enry James de Jeames . . . born of a race who counted their ancestors far back into the dim ages of chivalry'.

A reading of this selective edition of the letters reveals the extent of James's movements between America and Europe and his growing 'sense of delight' with the latter continent, his obvious early interest in the art of fiction, his brief single mention of the American civil war, 'awful . . . I mean for wives &c.', and his realization of the 'dreadful pass' at which American literature had arrived. A light humour plays continually as the young James prepares himself for his career as novelist and comes to grips personally with what was to be the subject matter of much of his early fiction. Paris haunts his imagination, and he admires France as a whole for her 'felicity of *manner* . . . completeness of form'; he feels 'disgustingly naturalized' in London; acquires what he calls the '*Italian feeling*'; and becomes, in overall terms, totally conscious of 'the aesthetic presence of the past': all these things are of obvious importance in regard to the fictional concerns of his entire career, and also provide a full chart of the personal development of the Jamesian sensitivity.

Of course there's a mass of material of purely biographical interest, much of which indeed becomes over repetitive at times, particularly his continual preoccupation with his close family relations, social gossip, and his recurring constipation problem. But so many of the letters reveal information of real critical interest. The anti-Catholicism of *The American* is in evidence here: James describes the Pope as a 'flaccid old woman waving his ridiculous finger over the prostrate multitude'. Also there are many examples of James as art critic, that early profession which again was to have so great an impact on his fiction. Most important of all, perhaps, is the continued comment on just *how* it is 'a complex fate being an American', James's feeling that 'salvation' is to be found in Europe, and his obvious concern with the craft of writing: his refusal to write for the multitude, his horror of writing 'thin', and his belief in the need to find a correct balance in his fiction between 'brain' and 'form'.

The whole series of letters relives James's reasons for preferring to live in Europe, with the sense of discovery and excitement reflected in them. It is nevertheless obvious that the bulk of the collection reveals Henry James the apprentice writer at work, and further volumes of the letters are likely to be of even greater interest.

This volume closes appropriately with James's 1875 decision to move permanently to Europe, and the joyous nature of this decision is obvious in his final celebratory outburst on his return once more to that continent: 'I take possession of the old world—I inhale it—I appropriate it!' Two small criticisms are to be made of this volume, however. For a book of this price, there are really far too many misprints to be found; also, though Edel's editorship is for the most part efficient, more explanatory notes are necessary at times. Edel also briefly introduces this year *The Bodley Head Henry James: Volume Eleven: 'Daisy Miller', 'The Turn of the Screw'*,[51] those two of James's stories which are universally popular, both of which reveal the author's 'fascination with the mind and manners of the young female adult'.

Henry James's close personal relationship with his brother William is very evident in the *Letters*. In *Henry James and Pragmatistic Thought: A Study in the Relationship between the Philosophy of William James and the Literary Art of Henry James*,[52] Richard A. Hocks concentrates more on their professional relationship. The central key on which the thesis of this work turns is Henry James's grasp and understanding of William James's philosophy. The book studies a subject which has long been skirted and which this author holds to be of central importance to a proper understanding of Henry James and his work: the impact of William's

[51] *The Bodley Head Henry James: Volume Eleven: 'Daisy Miller' and 'The Turn of the Screw'*. The Bodley Head. pp. 198. £2.25.

[52] *Henry James and Pragmatistic Thought: A Study in the Relationship between the Philosophy of William James and the Literary Art of Henry James*, by Richard A. Hocks. U. of North Carolina P. pp. xii + 258. $9.95.

philosophical thought on Henry as novelist. Richard Hocks's thesis is that in the latter's mature work, 'William James' pragmatistic thought is literally *actualized* as the literary art and idiom of his brother Henry James'.

Hocks examines William James's pragmatism and radical empiricism and discusses their consequences both in ethical and religious terms. He then proceeds to show how Henry's style and content can be seen as full embodiment of this thought. While William is effectively concerned with 'naming and defining', Henry is concerned with portrayal and dramatization: as Hocks pithily expresses it, 'the relationship that obtains between William and Henry James might perhaps be imaged as that between "vitamin C" and the orange'.

In his intelligent study, the author divides his material into three sections. In the first, 'William and Henry James: The Nature of the Relationship', he concerns himself with the brothers' attitudes towards each other's work, and in particular with Henry's literary use of William's concern with 'ambulatory' relations. In the second part, 'The Brothers "Confluent", "Conjoined", "Concatenated": A Letter to Henry Adams', an explication is offered of the well-known letter of March 1914 from James to Adams. The text of this letter is used as the basis of an extended exploration into the Jamesian mode of thinking, as demonstration of the William–Henry relationship, 'the total identity of William's thought with Henry's idiom', and also to suggest something of what Hocks calls 'the inner life of the nineteenth century'. Finally in 'Pragmatistic Thought and the Art of Fiction: Ambulation into Polarity', the author extends his examination into the field of the novels and short stories themselves

with particular emphasis on *The Spoils of Poynton*, *The Ambassadors*, 'The Real Thing', and 'The Beast in the Jungle'.

Harry T. Moore's concern is with the outer, rather than the inner, life of the nineteenth, and early twentieth, century in *Henry James and his world*,[53] a biographical sketch of James, a portrayal of that world in which he lived, and a brief description of his fictional achievement. And when I say brief, I mean brief: Moore gives three pages only to *The Ambassadors*, seemingly treating the novel merely as a response and gradual surrender on the part of Strether to the attraction of Paris. This suggests that Moore is not particularly interested in a critical approach to James's work here: he is more concerned, as the book's title suggests, with an all round presentation of the author's world. Relying heavily on photographs, engravings, cartoons, drawings, and paintings, he recreates a picture of the Europe and America of James's lifetime, and suggests James's social and literary rôle in these surroundings.

The book relies heavily on its visual material. For the most part these illustrations are of genuine interest, though occasionally the impression is given of an attempt to use some kind of pictorial matter whatever the excuse. Thus, when the text relates how James usually 'avoided the winters at Rye by staying in London at the Reform Club, one of several he belonged to', we are given a half-page photograph of a corner, empty bar tables, chairs, and ornate decorated ceiling, of a room in the Athenaeum Club, with caption below reading 'one of James's headquarters in London', Again, there's a photograph of Burgess Noakes, James's

[53] *Henry James and his world*, by Harry T. Moore. Thames & Hudson. pp. 128. £2.25.

valet and butler at Lamb House who, the text irrelevantly relates, was 'eventually to become bantamweight champion of Sussex'. The continued emphasis on the visual throughout the work is suggested by the detailed list of illustrations at the end of the book, when at the start there is no introduction, preface, or even list of contents.

Gordon Pirie's *Henry James*[54] offers a general critical introduction to James's work. The book concentrates on a study of five novels in particular, *The Europeans*, *Washington Square*, *The Portrait of a Lady*, *The Bostonians* and *What Maisie Knew*, to provide a lucid approach to James for the intelligent first time reader of his fiction: thus the concentration on James's early works which offer the easiest pathway into the Jamesian world. One of these works, *The Bostonians*, is also the subject of two articles this year. Howard D. Pearce, in 'Witchcraft Imagery and Allusion in James' Bostonians' (*SSNTS*), suggests that the characters of this novel are engaged in ambiguous magical rites, that the richness of the work derives in great measure from implications of the supernatural, especially witchcraft. In 'The Psychology of Characterization: James's Portraits of Verena Tarrant and Olive Chancellor' (*SSNTS*), Lee Ann Johnson examines James's methods of depicting Verena and Olive to reveal his successes and failures in meeting the needs of his first realistic novel. The author asserts that while James's portrayal of Verena miscarries, his rendering of Olive, the true heroine of the novel, provides one of his earliest and most successful psychological portraits.

Manfred Mackenzie, in 'A Theory of Henry James's Psychology' (*YR*), suggests that as a psychological

novelist James is preoccupied with the emotion of shame. He examines 'The Jolly Corner' as illustration of his theory that the 'shock' of self-exposure and its consequences consistently provide a working axis in James's fiction. Daniel J. Schneider examines the idea of freedom and the images of entrapment in 'The Theme of Freedom in James's *The Tragic Muse*' (*ConnR*). In 'Unintentional Fallacy: Critics and *The Golden Bowl*' (*MLQ*), Mildred E. Hartsock shows how critics have tended to misread this novel, which concerns 'the human mandate to mature through a full consciousness and the human responsibility to solve common and difficult marital problems in a civilized way'. Lydia Rivlin Gabbay studies Ford Madox Ford's relationship with Henry James and the effect that relationship might have had on *The Good Soldier* in 'The Four Square Coterie: A Comparison of Ford Madox Ford and Henry James' (*SSNTS*). She suggests that Ford's novel can be read as a vehicle to expose the absurdity of Jamesian values.

A picture of the American world from the turn of the century to 1943 is presented in *Letters of George Ade*, edited by Terence Tobin.[55] This humourist's reactions to the details of his own career and his observations about people and events form an amalgam of autobiography and popular history, as he corresponds with many of the important of his time, Theodore Roosevelt, William Howard Taft, and Hamlin Garland, as well as with business acquaintances, friends, and ordinary citizens, of his own state of Indiana. Though a humourist by profession, Ade was remarkably serious in much of his letter writing. His friendships, more-

[54] *Henry James*, by Gordon Pirie. Evans Brothers. pp. 152. £2.50.

[55] *Letters of George Ade*, ed. by Terence Tobin. Purdue U.P. 1973. pp. xi+251. $9.75.

over, were so diversified that his correspondence forms 'a patchwork of popular history, literature, politics, and entertainment', and provides an unusual angle into varied aspects of American cultural life of the twentieth century. The letters are arranged in chronological order and annotated with explanatory material and with sources. Photographs, sketches, and other illustrations evoking the man and his times are interspersed with the text.

Adam J. Sorkin views Booth Tarkington's work in relation to the life of his times in '"She Doesn't Last, Apparently": A Reconsideration of Booth Tarkington's *Alice Adams*' (*AL*). He examines this novel in the light of the inherent seriousness of its social realism as Tarkington aims to 'fix the configuration of his contemporary America in terms of its meaningful social and historical dimensions'.

Philosophy, rather than social history, provides the content of Theodore Dreiser's *Notes on Life*, edited by Marguerite Tjader and John J. McAleer.[56] Selected writings are presented here, the results of Dreiser's 'philosophical' research during the last forty years of his life. In the foreword to this work, Marguerite Tjader relates how a young scholar, Sydney Horovitz, intrigued with Dreiser's *Notes*, undertook to sort the relevant papers at the University of Pennsylvania into two categories: the main, creative writing, and secondary material: 'he started to compress the work into an outline of his own; however, he took ill and could not finish the task.' Given the nature of the task, the quantity and content of the material involved, this fact is not really surprising. These short essays, notes, and jottings of the order of 'Does the fear of Death prove that Life is worthwhile?', are collected here to suggest Dreiser's scientific and philosophical quest for Meaning. Dreiser certainly has his banal moments while engaged on this quest: 'Laughter is above all a corrective. Being intended to humiliate, it must make a painful impression on the person against whom it is directed', and 'Unless a thing is written down it is forgotten. Mountains are remembered because they stick around', being exemplars.

This collection will be of undoubted value to committed Dreiser scholars, if not to the more casual reader. The discontinuous nature of the manuscript means that there's not a great deal of coherency to the volume as a whole. And though the author's fascination with life's processes is in evidence throughout the book, his style militates against that 'lyricism' to which Tjader attempts to draw the reader's attention. Dreiser's thoughts on the Universe, Man, Chance, Memory, and Free Will, as well as his celebration of his 'Creator', are presented here, thoughts which are of interest as addenda to Dreiser's novels and as regards our understanding of the man himself, rather than as any kind of coherent and formal philosophy in its own right.

In *Theodore Dreiser: His Thought and Social Criticism*,[57] indeed, R. N. Mookerjee examines the 'philosophy', as mostly revealed in the non-fictional writings of the last twenty years of Dreiser's life, to suggest that although there is some overall consistence to this thought, Dreiser certainly proves his ignorance of philosophy as a whole, and also has a tendency to get

[56] *Notes on Life*, by Theodore Dreiser, ed. by Marguerite Tjader and John J. McAleer. U. of Alabama P. pp. xiv+346. $14.50.

[57] *Theodore Dreiser: His Thought and Social Criticism*, by R. N. Mookerjee. Delhi: National Publishing House. pp. xi+259. 45 Re.

trapped between statements which are finally irreconcilable.

Mookerjee is basically uninterested in analyzing Dreiser's fiction: his philosophical development is, throughout, the major concern. Mookerjee charts Dreiser's journey towards both Communist Party and 'Creator' to show that there is no real lack of philosophical consistency in such a move. He also charts the rôle of the author's 'naturalism' on such a journey, contending that Dreiser's denunciation of injustice, his compassion, and his concern with the supernatural constantly qualified his supposed cold determinism.

Much the same argument is used in James Lundquist's *Theodore Dreiser*,[58] but with a more direct literary application. Lundquist initially examines how many of Dreiser's peculiarities as well as his strengths can be understood in terms of the era in which he came to maturity. He focuses on the influence of post-Darwinian evolutionary thinking and of the Progressive movement on Dreiser; also on those sentimental influences which affected both the writer and his song-writing brother, Paul Dresser.

Lundquist insists, however, that education and environment do not wholly explain Dreiser's fiction. Like Mookerjee, he insists that the naturalistic element in this fiction, the result of Dreiser's mechanistic philosophy, is less vital in accounting for his importance than his 'compassion' which 'dominates in his novels'. Lundquist also shows how Dreiser develops a particularly American concept of classic tragedy, drawing, as Fitzgerald did, on the delusions of the Horatio Alger ethic. He discusses all Dreiser's major fiction, with

particular reference to *An American Tragedy* (where incidentally, he wrongly names the girl with whom Clyde finally falls in love as 'Sondra Finch'). He also examines Dreiser's philosophy and politics, to bridge the same gap as Mookerjee, that between the author's professed pessimistic acceptance of a deterministic life view and his later involvement in social and political reform. In 'The Survivors: Into the Twentieth Century' (*TCL*), Ellen Moers calls Dreiser one of the few American writers to come successfully 'across that trench we call the turn of the century'. She suggests that Dreiser's intellectual explorations were in fact of a more difficult nature than those of any writer of his time, as he searched for the answers to those questions which were to dominate his art as a novelist, questions arising from the relationship between mind and will, between individual and act.

In *Charmed Circle: Gertrude Stein & Company*,[59] James R. Mellow attempts, as he states modestly in his Afterword, not a definitive biography of Gertrude Stein, but a study of 'her life, her life-style, and the ways in which both informed her writing'. The result is a long, meticulously documented book whose main virtue is also, in essence, its chief fault. Mr Mellow impresses by his thoroughness, his patience in collecting and collating the details of Miss Stein's life, and his obvious interest in Stein herself as writer and with regard to her influence on those who came into contact with her, both in the literary and the artistic world. Unfortunately, he seems to work on the premise that eclecticism guarantees success, and it is his failure to sift the facts, to select that which is important and that

---

[58] *Theodore Dreiser*, by James Lundquist. New York: Frederick Ungar. pp. ix+150. $6.

[59] *Charmed Circle: Gertrude Stein & Company*, by James R. Mellow. Phaedon Press. pp. 528. £3.95.

which is not, to omit the frankly tedious, as well as his often facile and over-whimsical style, that constitute the main failing of his book.

However, within his mass of information, there are certainly fascinating and rewarding passages. Mr Mellow is especially interesting on Stein's early years in Paris, when he deals in depth with her growing coterie. The people and paintings she collected during these years are intrinsically interesting, as is the interaction between the two, and Mellow is particularly good on the personal and artistic relationship between Gertrude Stein and Picasso. Indeed, one wishes that he could have concentrated more on the interaction between Cubism and Stein's writing, and the influence she exerted upon, and received from, the Modernist movement.

The most intimate member of Gertrude Stein's charmed circle was, of course, Alice B. Toklas. The relationship between Toklas and Gertrude Stein lies at the heart of *Staying on Alone: Letters of Alice B. Toklas*,[60] edited by Edward Burns. Alice B. Toklas 'took on' letter-writing after Gertrude Stein's death in 1946, referring to it as 'my work'. In this selection, Edward Burns has chosen only from those letters written during the last twenty years of Miss Toklas's life, after Stein's death, for which period the widest selection of letters were available. Letters included are of biographical, literary, and artistic significance, and contain some shrewd comment on several of the major artists, musicians, and writers of the twentieth century.

After a somewhat inept introduction, in which a description of Toklas's final lonely years, sans Gertrude,

[60] *Staying on Alone: Letters of Alice B. Toklas*, ed. by Edward Burns. New York: Liveright. 1973. pp. xxii+426. $11.95.

is concluded with the words, 'There had to be a heaven. How else could they be reunited?', and the initial sentimentality of approach (Gertrude as 'Baby Woojums'), the letters themselves do become genuinely interesting. Gertrude Stein's shadow falls continually on Toklas's day to day Paris life—'Gertrude's memory is all my life', she writes—and many of the letters are concerned with the sending of Stein's manuscripts and letters to the Yale Library and with making arrangements to bring the still unpublished works into print. The passages in which Toklas refers to Gertrude Stein's lawyer and those monetary arrangements to be made, by and through him, in order to publish these writings, read like a Nabokovian literary joke. In her will, Stein declared herself a citizen of the United States, 'legally domiciled in Baltimore, Maryland, but residing at 5 rue Christine, Paris'. Her will was probated in Maryland, where her affairs were handled by a Mr Edgar Allan Poe, of the firm of Bartlett, Poe and Claggett. As Toklas comments, 'is it possible?'

Alice B. Toklas's obvious concern for literature is evident throughout the collection in references which are interesting, if eccentric: 'I think this generation is finished—it really ended with Fitzgerald . . . However good Faulkner may be he isnt (*sic*) virile—and as for poor Hem and Steinbeck . . . the least said the better for one's digestion.' It's Gertrude Stein's literature, though, in which she's especially interested. For it's Toklas's feelings of responsibility to Gertrude as writer and artist, and to Gertrude as friend, which become evident in this collection. The advancement of Stein's literary fame, the attempts to preserve her picture collection, and her own feuds with Gertrude's eventual heirs over these pictures, make up a large part of these witty and gossipy letters. One fault, however, of this volume is in the editing: there are many small errata, particularly in the foreign language references; and there is constant evidence of bad editing especially in the use of notes: for example, the first reference to the lawyer Poe appears on page twenty-seven, yet no information is offered about him till page fifty-five. Carelessness of this kind is evident throughout.

Gilbert A. Harrison edits and introduces *Gertrude Stein's America*,[61] excerpts from the author's writings about America and Americans, which has been republished this year to mark the centennial of Stein's birthdate. David D. Cooper examines Gertrude Stein's mode of writing in *Tender Buttons* in 'Gertrude Stein's "Magnificent Asparagus": Horizontal Vision and Unmeaning in "Tender Buttons"' (*MFS*). Stein's perception here, her 'horizontal vision' is, he claims, nothing more than a recognition of chaos and the necessary 'unmeaningfulness' of life.

Hensley C. Woodbridge has made extensive additions to *Jack London: A Bibliography*,[62] an enlarged edition of the volume compiled by John London, George H. Tweney, and Woodbridge himself, first published in 1966. This comprehensive bibliography will be of service to all Jack London scholars regardless of language or country. More bibliographical material appears in *James Jones: A Checklist*,[63] compiled by John R.

Hopkins, a checklist which coincides with the interest in Jones recently stimulated on his return to the United States after a decade of self-imposed exile in France. This list provides complete bibliographical descriptions of Jones's works, which are treated chronologically under the sectional headings of 'Books', 'First Book Appearances', 'Stories', 'Articles', 'Interviews' and 'Published Letters'. Whether such a checklist, at such a price, is necessary is another question. A full bibliography will no doubt eventually appear rendering this work useless. The information here, about an author who is not of major literary stature, would be just as useful and much cheaper published in journal form. The volume is, however, well presented and commences with an interesting previously unpublished interview with Jones.

Walter B. Rideout, the editor of *Sherwood Anderson: A Collection of Critical Essays*,[64] brings together a range of critical opinion on Sherwood Anderson according to the chronology of events in Anderson's literary career rather than to publication date of the essays themselves. Generally, the essays are arranged so as to move from a discussion of the author's individual works to a consideration of his achievement as a whole. The essays on the individual books include the following: 'Emerging Greatness (Review of *Windy McPherson's Son*)' by Waldo Frank, '*Winesburg, Ohio*: Art and Isolation' by Edwin Fussell, 'The Artist as Prophet' by Rex Burbank, where *Many Marriages*, *Dark Laughter*, and *A Story Teller's Story* are discussed, and 'The Short Stories' by Irving Howe. In the final essays—'Sherwood

[61] *Gertrude Stein's America*, ed. by Gilbert A. Harrison. New York: Liveright. pp. 103. $5.95.

[62] *Jack London: A Bibliography*, comp. by Hensley C. Woodbridge, John London, and George H. Tweney. New York: Kraus Reprint. 1973. pp. 554. $28.

[63] *James Jones: A Checklist*, comp. by John R. Hopkins. Detroit: Gale Research. pp. viii+67. $12.50.

[64] *Sherwood Anderson: A Collection of Critical Essays*, ed. by Walter B. Rideout. New Jersey: Prentice-Hall. pp. ix+177. $6.95.

Anderson' by Lionel Trilling, 'Introduction to *Letters of Sherwood Anderson*' by Howard Mumford Jones, 'Sherwood Anderson: American Mythopoeist' by Benjamin T. Spencer, and 'Sherwood Anderson: An Appreciation' by William Faulkner—Anderson's position in twentieth-century American literature is assessed. These assessments vary considerably. Trilling questions Anderson's use of language, his antirationalism, and his excessive emotionalism, and suggests that his themes are primarily adolescent in their appeal. Benjamin Spencer, on the other hand, sees Anderson as belonging to the American Transcendentalist tradition, and as proceeding from the local to the universal, from the individual to the archetype, in his attempt, like Whitman, to catch 'the essence of things', in a committed, mythopoeic approach to American experience. In 1966, Susan Sontag dismissed *Winesburg, Ohio* as 'bad to the point of being laughable'. Though Rideout's collection is too highly conservative in its nature, only one of the essays selected having been first published within the last ten years, it does provide a useful point of departure for the re-evaluation of a writer who has been too quickly dismissed for too long.

Indeed, Frank Baldanza has not got much time for Anderson in 'Northern Gothic' (*SoR*), a comparison of Sherwood Anderson and James Purdy as essentially mid-Western writers using 'Northern Gothic' materials. Baldanza claims Purdy's work is of greater complexity, his ideas are tougher, than Anderson's. The whole metaphysical context of Purdy's microcosm is given, the author claims, in the 'Sermon' from *Children Is All*. Baldanza continues his study of Purdy in 'The Paradoxes of Patronage in Purdy' (*AL*), where

he examines those patron-protégé tensions which underlie so much of Purdy's work.

A highly unusual evaluation of Henry Miller's work is offered in *Henry Miller: His World of Urania* by Sydney Omarr,[65] which is reprinted this year. Omarr, an astrologer himself, examining both writings and biographical data, suggests the rôle that astrology plays in Miller's life and art. Miller himself has written a long foreword to this study of a previously unexplored dimension in Miller's world. Omarr gives a full list of the astrological references in the author's writings.

Steven Marcus brings us down to earth again with 'Dashiell Hammett and the Continental Op' (*PR*). He gives a brief biography of Hammett, then discusses the ways in which he raised the crime story 'to the status of literature'. He examines the 'literary, social and moral opacities, instabilities, and contradictions' which mark Hammett's best work: that, so Marcus claims, done in the 1920s and early 1930s.

If Hammett's crime stories must be considered from the viewpoint of their literary merit so, according to Charles S. Holmes, the editor of *Thurber: A Collection of Critical Essays*,[66] must James Thurber's humorous short stories. Holmes asserts in the introduction to this volume that Scott Fitzgerald's 'creative gifts were surely no greater than Thurber's', and proceeds from this statement to claim that Thurber's work deserves the same systematic and detailed study that Fitzgerald's has received. This suggests the tone of excessive

[65] *Henry Miller: His World of Urania*, by Sydney Omarr. Village Press. pp. 112. 65p. (paperback).
[66] *Thurber: A Collection of Critical Essays*, ed. by Charles S. Holmes. New Jersey: Prentice-Hall. pp. xi+180. $6.95.

flattery which marks this collection. Thurber is certainly a major comic writer, but one perhaps should ask why he never moved beyond the very short *New Yorker* story and the humorous autobiographical sketch, a question never put here. It is time that Thurber was given critical examination as the original and important interpreter of modern life that Holmes suggests he is, but in fact there is disappointingly little close critical analysis of Thurber's work here. The editor, in his introductory essay, correctly identifies Thurber's major themes; points to Peter de Vries's essay, 'James Thurber: The Comic Prufrock', which identifies the author's imagination as 'Symbolist'; shows the variety of Thurber's personae—reporter, social historian, memoirist, social critic, satirist, and biographer; and suggests that Thurber's drawings stand in the 'long tradition of Western symbolic art and the comic branch of it which stems from Edward Lear'. Few of these areas, however, are given adequate study within the essays themselves.

Many of the articles in this collection are valuable. Norris Yates examines Thurber's inconsistent humorous mixture of despair and of militancy (with its concomitant of hope) in 'James Thurber's Little Man and Liberal Citizen'. De Vries's previously mentioned article is penetrating and revealing. Robert H. Elias interestingly places Thurber in a temporal and humanistic perspective in 'James Thurber: The Primitive, the Innocent, and the Individual', and Jesse Bier sets *Fables for Our Time* (1940) against *Further Fables for Our Time* (1956) to show Thurber's complete later misanthropy. But for the most part the volume's material is undistinguished, and much of the blame must be placed on the editor.

He, in rather egocentric manner, commences the collection of writings with John Seelye's 'From Columbus to New York', a review of Holmes's own book on Thurber, *The Clocks of Columbus*, a tactic which leads to the repetition of material from the editor's own introduction. Furthermore Holmes has consistently included material of ridiculously short length: two and a half pages of Dorothy Parker, followed by two of Auden, then by two and a half of Robert Coates, with little continuity between.

Some of the longer articles are really too weak for inclusion, and there's a certain feeling of scratching for material throughout the collection. Statements such as '*Is Sex Necessary*? is very funny, on the lines of the ordinary funny book' from David Garnett's 'Thurber through British Eyes' hardly inspire critical confidence, nor does John Mortimer's remark that his unease with Thurber is due to the fact that while the author's 'little man . . . bruised by life' is appealing, 'the trouble is . . . he goes not at all with cocktails at the Algonquin'! There are too many short, formless, and weak snippets in this volume, and when there are good essays they are often too heavily cut. Holmes's aims in editing this book are to be admired, the results though are unfortunate. Carl M. Lindner reinforces Holmes's portrayal of Thurber as belonging in the American literary mainstream in 'Thurber's Walter Mitty—The Underground American Hero' (*GaR*), where he discusses that conflict between the individual and society in 'The Secret Life of Walter Mitty'.

Ellen Glasgow's concern is with a very different type of society than Mitty's urban pressured one. For the subject matter in her Queensborough Trilogy is the Virginian aristocracy. C. Hugh Holman examines the nature of this concern in 'April in Queensborough: Ellen Glasgow's Comedy of Manners' (SR). The Queensborough novels, he claims, reveal Glasgow's success in that difficult and rare genre, the American comedy of manners, as she treats Virginian life and manners with knowing affection, yet submits them to the gently corrosive irony of 'a great comic wit'.

In 'Looking-Glass Reflections: Satirical Elements in Ship of Fools' (SR), Jon Spence opposes that adverse criticism which sees Katherine Anne Porter's view of man as pessimistic and misanthropic, by his reading of the novel which emphasizes its satiric nature.

In his monograph, John Dos Passos,[67] George J. Becker approaches Dos Passos as artist-observer of the twentieth-century. His preparation for his rôle as writer, Becker suggests, was his undergoing of four 'rites of passage': major spiritual and mental initiations which determined both his view of the world and the nature of his art. The four initiations undergone were: his coming to grips with a form of life in the United States from which he was alienated due to birth and upbringing; World War One, which smashed his conventional beliefs and expectations; his facing of the Russian communist experience; and his coming to terms with the literary experimentations of twentieth-century America.

Becker details these various initiations and shows how they affected his work. Novels such as Three Soldiers, U.S.A., and The Adventures of a Young Man reflect, he shows, both the realities of twentieth-century life, and Dos Passos's own education into that way of life, in their portrayal of the continual clash of youthful hopes and expectations with a brute reality. This duality, this tension between the individual and the social, so Becker claims, sets the author's work apart. Individually, Dos Passos's novels must be read as chronicles of the times; in their totality they chart an individual's response to those times. Becker also examines Dos Passos's own changing political response to his America, particularly his break with Communism, which was so deeply to affect his life and work, that retreat from radicalism which is reflected in his less powerful and, perhaps surprisingly, less objective later novels.

In his introduction to Dos Passos: A Collection of Critical Essays,[68] the editor, Andrew Hook, disagrees with Becker's thesis that, in the 'Camera Eye' sections of U.S.A., the individual subjective sensibility relates to the larger socio-political and artistic world of the novel as a whole. This subjective consciousness, Hook claims, remains formally isolated. The 'Camera Eye' allows this individual sensibility fictional survival, but it is an ineffectual kind of existence, totally cut off from the collective encompassing reality. This, Hook suggests, results in the undoubted failure of the later fiction: with U.S.A. the 'gap between public and private experience' becomes 'unbridgeable'.

However, Hook's purpose in editing this collection of essays is to help to re-establish Dos Passos in his proper place as one of the major American writers of the 1920s and 1930s. In this volume, such critics as Edmund Wilson, Sartre, Leavis, Trilling, and Kazin, examine Dos Passos as creative artist with major social and cultural significance, rather than

[67] John Dos Passos, by George J. Becker. New York: Frederick Ungar. pp. ix+133. $7.

[68] Dos Passos: A Collection of Critical Essays, ed. by Andrew Hook. New Jersey: Prentice-Hall. pp. vi+186. $6.95.

as that political spokesman for left or right, in which rôle he has far too often been cast.

In his introduction, the editor suggests some of the reasons for Dos Passos's recent critical neglect: the tendency, based on incorrect assumptions, to classify the author exclusively with the 'naturalist' school of writers; the quality of the formal structures of Dos Passos's work, which do not conform with the canons of art established by Henry James; and the unpopularity of literary radicalism in critical circles from the late 1940s right through to the sixties. As Hook points out, there are signs that Dos Passos is now taking his rightful place in the American literary heritage: signs which include the two books written about him this year, and also John P. Diggins's article 'Visions of Chaos and Visions of Order: Dos Passos as Historian' (*AL*). Diggins analyzes the changes in the author's vision of historical reality, his own American past, and human character, as he moved from writing novels to writing history. He examines Dos Passos's use of history, both in the fiction and in the more traditional structure of historical narrative, and the theoretical and interdisciplinary problems a historian faces in analyzing this work.

The lives and times of the Scott Fitzgeralds have been well documented before now. However, in *The Romantic Egoists: Scott and Zelda Fitzgerald*,[69] edited by Matthew J. Bruccoli, Scottie Fitzgerald Smith, and Joan P. Kerr, we are presented with what Fitzgerald's daughter insists is Scott and Zelda's '*own* story of their lives, rather than someone else's interpretation of them'. The

[69] *The Romantic Egoists: Scott and Zelda Fitzgerald*, ed. by Matthew J. Bruccoli, Scottie Fitzgerald Smith, and Joan P. Kerr. New York: Charles Scribner's. pp. 246. $25.

editors present us with written and pictorial record of the Fitzgeralds by Fitzgerald, using the author's meticulous personal career record—his own scrapbooks, photograph albums, and excerpts from his *Ledger*—as well as photostatted material from the newspapers and magazines of the time. In his *Ledger*, Fitzgerald summarized each year of his life from approximately 1920 to 1937, noting the memorable events of each month and giving a capsule comment on the year's meaning for him. The comment for the year of 1929 for example, runs 'The Crash! Zelda and America' and gives some indication of the way in which personal and social history were always intermingled for Fitzgerald himself. Indeed the importance of this relationship, both for Fitzgerald and his contemporaries, becomes very evident in an examination of this collection of material.

This volume is a 'pictorial autobiography'. Photographs, letters, contemporary articles, pictures (including Zelda's paintings, some reproduced in colour), selections from Fitzgerald's writings and from Zelda's *Save Me the Waltz*, and illustrations, combine to give a documentary picture of an author, a marriage, and a generation. In the final section of this interesting social and biographical record, 'Restoration: Fitzgerald's Posthumous Vindication', Matthew Bruccoli points out how 'the Fitzgerald revival' since his death is unequalled in American literature, and reviews the gradual establishing of Fitzgerald's permanent reputation.

This permanent reputation is marked by the examination now of any and all Fitzgerald material by scholars. In 'The Unpublished Stories: Fitzgerald in His Final Stage' (*TCL*), Ruth Prigozy offers synopses of a number of unpublished Fitzgerald stories: stories illustrating the technical problems plaguing him throughout his career, and stories reflecting his own emotional difficulties in the years following his physical collapse. Most important, these stories throw light on Fitzgerald's developing style in the last years of his life, and give a record of the way in which he finally unlocked new creative energies to be revealed in *The Last Tycoon*. Kermit W. Moyer also examines Fitzgerald's work done during this period in 'Fitzgerald's Two Unfinished Novels: The Count and the Tycoon in Spenglerian Perspective' (*ConL*), showing *Philippe, Count of Darkness* to be, in some respects, thematic forerunner of *The Last Tycoon*. In 'F. Scott Fitzgerald and the Quest to the Ice Palace' (*CEA*), Edwin Moses shows the inability of Stahr, Diver, and Gatsby to see the reality behind those glittering surfaces which confront them, as the theme of the mistaken quest takes on major importance in Fitzgerald's fiction.

After the Good Gay Times: Asheville—Summer of '35, A Season with F. Scott Fitzgerald,[70] is yet another Fitzgerald memoir, this one by Tony Buttita who ran the Intimate Bookshop in the George Vanderbilt Hotel in Asheville, and with whom Fitzgerald became friendly during the summer of 1935. This was the summer Fitzgerald stayed in Asheville (of Thomas Wolfe fame), the summer of the year of Fitzgerald's physical and emotional bankruptcy, the 'wasted summer' which directly preceded his 'Crack-Up' essays.

Buttita, a writer himself and editor of a little magazine, *Contempo*, from 1931 to 1933 in Chapel Hill, saw Fitzgerald frequently in the book-

[70] *After the Good Gay Times: Asheville—Summer of '35, A Season with F. Scott Fitzgerald*, by Tony Buttita. New York: Viking P. pp. xii+173. $7.95.

shop he ran, and the book he writes here is a record of what actually happened that summer. He records Fitzgerald's affair with the married woman, 'Rosemary'; his association with 'Lottie', the Asheville prostitute; his alcoholism and the attempts to cure it; and his worry about Zelda, who was being treated for schizophrenia in a Baltimore clinic. This book complements Laura Guthrie Hearne's previous article about this period in Fitzgerald's life, 'A Summer with F. Scott Fitzgerald', and also gives background information on literary and social life in the North Carolina of the 1930s. Fitzgerald's comments are given, often as reported direct conversation, on Hemingway, Mencken, Spengler, and Marx, the last two 'the only modern thinkers who had any meaning today, he [Fitzgerald] declared. Marx had helped to form his own class-consciousness and influenced some of his best writing.'

This is a well written book which helps to keep the wheels of the Fitzgerald industry moving, and which has little more value than the purely biographical. One must remain sceptical, though, about Buttita's original claim, that having jotted notes down at the time on the fly leaves of about sixty books, notes comprising a kind of log of Fitzgerald's life during this period, now 'in spite of the years that have passed, I had no difficulty reproducing his monologues from notes I had scribbled in the books. As a reporter I rarely had taken more than a few lead words; they enabled me to quote dialogue and conversations verbatim in stories and interviews'. The relationship between Fitzgerald and Buttita finally ended, if the latter's memory and notes are to be trusted, in disagreement on the civil rights issue. Fitzgerald seems to have rigidified, at this stage of his life and on this topic at least, into a Tom Buchanan; Lottie reports Fitzgerald's attitudes to Buttita: 'he said our race was superior and we shouldn't weaken it by mixing'.

Joseph Blotner quotes a somewhat similar statement which Sherwood Anderson claims the young Faulkner made, in his vast biography, *Faulkner*.[71] Anderson reports the twenty-seven year old's contention 'that the cross between the white man and the Negro woman always resulted, after the first crossing, in sterility'. This remark, in fact, as Blotner suggests, sounds like a bit of Southern tall tale telling on the part of Faulkner, with Anderson as willing Northern victim. Faulkner's early fictional attitudes to the black race were, however, very unsophisticated, and Blotner traces Faulkner's growing understanding of the complexities of black-white relations in the American South as this book proceeds.

Blotner's biography tends towards over-reverence, but nevertheless fills a long empty gap in Faulkner scholarship. In his introduction, the author claims that 'I hope this study will provide some critical insights as well as biographical'. From this point of view he fails. His 'insights' are somewhat simplistic, and he often tends merely to limit himself to description of plot with brief digressionary comment such as that offered on *The Sound and the Fury*: 'Early in Benjy's section, Luster . . . revealed that today . . . was Benjy's thirty-third birthday and that there would be a small cake [bought by Dilsey] to celebrate it. Thus [Faulkner] opened out for himself further possibilities in the use of Christian symbolism for ironic commentary on the Compsons'. His critical commentary never moves far beyond this low and essentially unoriginal level.

However, it is as biography that Blotner's work is important. Readable, though hardly bursting with vitality, Blotner has brought together in this book a massive amount of information about Faulkner's life and work, some of which had been previously available from various scattered sources, much of which has been painstakingly collected here by Mr Blotner for the first time, presented here in systematic and detailed fashion in easily followed chronological order. Little has been considered too unimportant for inclusion. Blotner ranges from a description of Faulkner's 'light, pleasant tenor' rendition of 'The Ballad of Captain Kidd' while an R.A.F. cadet in Canada, to the actual story of Faulkner's writing of *As I Lay Dying* in that power station on that night-shift. Though one might object to Blotner's somewhat peculiar presentation of footnotes, there remains no doubt that this is a book of very real value to the Faulkner scholar. The facts of Faulkner's life are revealed for the first time in a coherent, full, and well ordered fashion, and the critic and general reader are presented with a biography which will not be quickly superseded.

In *William Faulkner: The Abstract and the Actual*,[72] Panthea Reid Broughton charts the map of Faulkner's fiction rather than the map of his life. In fact this cartographical metaphor suggests the nature of her concern. For she compares Faulkner's fiction to a map in the way that it provides a means of ordering and explaining a particularly hazardous landscape, the complexity of exper-

[71] *Faulkner*, by Joseph Blotner. New York: Random House. 2 vols. Vol. 1, pp. xv+909+127 notes. Vol. 2, pp. ix+933+269 notes+index. $25.

[72] *William Faulkner: The Abstract and the Actual*, by Panthea Reid Broughton. Louisiana State U.P. pp. xviii+222. $7.95.

ience itself. Like a map, Panthea Broughton contends, fiction is 'utilitarian and teleological', though in an ultimate rather than an immediate sense, with 'general and existential ends' rather than immediate and specific. Rejecting a New Critical approach, the author attempts to reconnect the forms of literature with its human context, to show how Faulkner's fiction is ultimately useful in its ability to allow the reader to both discover and understand life, to see his way towards a fuller and more comprehensive mode of existence.

Miss Broughton examines Faulkner's fiction to show that the study of abstraction plays a central part in his work. Extensively quoting philosophers, Bergson especially, she shows that this study is finally based on Faulkner's acceptance that abstractions can enhance, rather than diminish, experience. In the first part of this book, Miss Broughton studies the relationship between 'Abstraction and Aesthetics', the way in which Faulkner's use of abstraction relates to his 'abstract, baroque, grandiose' style. In the second section, 'Abstraction and Inauthenticity', she examines one of Faulkner's major themes, the misuse of abstractions by so many of his characters and the results of such a misuse. In the final section, 'Abstraction and Authenticity', the author presents Faulkner's specific examples of achieved 'authenticity', those few characters who manage to encounter a chaotic world and surmount it, whose abstract values are actualized in the fiction itself. Miss Broughton presents a convincing argument, while readily admitting and showing that the ideas behind Faulkner's works are 'too diverse, too multidimensional to be reduced to any simplistic formulas'.

Lewis M. Dabney concentrates on a single dimension of these works in *The Indians of Yoknapatawpha: A Study in Literature and History*.[73] Dabney examines the rôle of those Indians who provide the basis for Faulkner's Yoknapatawpha novels, who constituted Faulkner's 'usable past', and whose vanishing history and folk culture form the subject matter of six Faulkner stories which he analyzes in detail in this volume.

Faulkner, so the author claims, is the 'one major author since pre-Civil War time to make substantial use of the Indians'. He shows how Faulkner rejects conventional attitudes to the Indian, presenting him neither as natural nobleman nor as brute, rather as individual possessing unmistakeably Faulknerian complexity of character. Dabney presents a clear picture of the Mississippi Indian tribes, though the correlation between them and their fictional counterparts remains, perhaps deliberately, slightly muddy. More important is the author's concentration, thematically and artistically, on those Indian stories written by Faulkner: 'Lo!', 'A Courtship', 'A Justice', 'Red Leaves', 'The Old People', and 'The Bear'. These are analyzed in order to show both the position of the Indian in the Yoknapatawpha saga, and in relation to the rest of Faulkner's work, the way in which these tales offer perspective on Faulkner's examination of a later American scene. E. Volpe's useful book on Faulkner, *A Reader's Guide to William Faulkner*,[74] has recently been reprinted for the ninth time. The number of reprintings suggests how valuable a critical introduction to the author's work this book is.

[73] *The Indians of Yoknapatawpha: A Study in Literature and History*, by Lewis M. Dabney. Louisiana State U.P. pp. 163. $6.95.
[74] *A Reader's Guide to William Faulkner*, by E. Volpe. New York: Farrar, Straus & Giroux. 1973. pp. 427. $3.95 (paperback).

In 'Collapse of Dynasty: The Thematic Centre of *Absalom, Absalom!*' (*PMLA*), Ralph Behrens suggests that *Absalom, Absalom!* achieves mythic significance and universality through Faulkner's deliberate use of parallels between Sutpen's attempt to found a dynasty in the Old South and the attempts of the ancient Hebrew rulers to establish their kingdoms. John Middleton examines Shreve's rôle in the same novel in 'Shreve McCannon and Sutpen's Legacy' (*SoR*) and propounds the thesis that in Shreve, who is moved to participate in the Sutpen legend, the legend loses its bitterness. Because he is a stranger to Yoknapatawpha County he is able to realize that eventually racial distinctions would fade out, leaving only a bond of common humanity, which must and can be accepted. Shreve's rôle is also the concern of Terrence Doody in 'Shreve McCannon and the confessions of *Absalom, Absalom!*' (*SSNTS*). He sees the 'remarkable participation' of Shreve as the culmination of the novel's confessional design. In his imaginative participation, in giving Charles Bon's story central importance, Shreve becomes a model for the reader, renewing the novel's enterprise, confirming the difficulty of the search for freedom and love, and extending the community of the novel. Mary Anne Wilson discusses the Bergsonian concept of time used by both Faulkner and Robert Penn Warren in 'Search for an Eternal Present: *Absalom, Absalom!* and *All the King's Men*' (*ConnR*).

Richard P. Adams suggests in 'At Long Last, *Flags in the Dust*' (*SoR*), that there is no convincing reason to assume that the Random House edition of this text is not corrupt. He calls *Flags in the Dust* a significant failure, as Faulkner tried to put Yoknapatawpha County all into one book, rather than the six or more his subject matter needed for its proper growth. Violet M. Howarth translates André Malraux's short 'Preface to William Faulkner's *Sanctuary*' (*SoR*), where Malraux claims that, in the book, Greek tragedy intrudes into the detective novel. In a more general article on 'The Survival of the Gothic Response' (*SSNTS*), James M. Keech writes about the Gothic novel in the twentieth century, with particular reference to *Sanctuary* and *Absalom, Absalom!* suggesting the use of this form in presenting a present day fearfully incomprehensible world, and the sense of impotence felt by the individual within it. Joseph F. Trimmer examines the rôle of Faulkner's favourite character, V. K. Ratliff, in the Snopes trilogy, in 'V. K. Ratliff: A Portrait of the Artist in Motion' (*MFS*). Ratliff's main contribution to the trilogy is not heroic action, but aesthetic creation, claims Trimmer. Ratliff is a legend maker: the legend of Snopesism his creation. Glenn O. Carey analyzes Faulkner's attitudes to the age of mechanization in 'William Faulkner on the Automobile as Socio-Sexual Symbol' (*CEA*). Mrs Maud Falkner's conversations, and attitudes towards her son's work, are the subject matter of James Dahl's 'A Faulkner Reminiscence: Conversations with Mrs Maud Falkner' (*JML*).

Hemingway In Our Time,[75] edited by Richard Astro and Jackson J. Benson, is the published record of the papers delivered at a conference devoted to a study of the work of Ernest Hemingway at Oregon State University in 1973. The title of the book suggests its content: the essays

[75] *Hemingway In Our Time*, ed. by Richard Astro and Jackson J. Benson. Oregon State U.P. pp. vii+214. $8.

included focus on the novelist's literary reputation, on his late and posthumous works, and on his influence on contemporary fiction. Philip Young, the noted Hemingway scholar, opens the collection with 'Posthumous Hemingway, and Nicholas Adams'. Defending his edition of *The Nick Adams Stories* from the criticism it received on publication, and assessing the impact of the four books published posthumously in any consideration of Hemingway's stature, Young, at the same time, announces his withdrawal from the Hemingway 'field'. He also criticizes the 'publish/perish' situation in America where, as soon as a writer is recognized as major, the wheels of the publishing industry start turning and articles such as 'When Hemingway's Mother Comes to Call' and 'Nick Adams, Prince of Abissinia' (*sic*), start appearing. Is Fitzgerald's mother still alive?

Other essays in this collection include Richard Lehan's examination of Hemingway's reputation, 'Hemingway among the Moderns', and John Clark Pratt's 'A Sometimes Great Notion: Ernest Hemingway's Roman Catholicism'. Taking as his starting point Hemingway's baptism 'just in case they were right', after his wounding in Italy, and his marriage to the staunch Catholic, Pauline Pfeiffer, Pratt examines the author's references to Roman Catholicism and his ambivalent attitudes to it throughout his career. This collection as a whole is divided into five parts: 'The Posthumous Works', 'The Neglected and Unpopular Reconsidered', 'Reconsideration by Parallel', 'Philosophy and Theme in Retrospect', and 'Reputation'. No index is provided.

Of the twenty-two essays included in *Ernest Hemingway: Five Decades of Criticism*,[76] edited by Linda

Wagner, only six have appeared in any of the other anthologies of criticism on the author's work. Fifteen of these essays have been published since the author's death, eight within the last five years. This collection tends to ignore much of the posthumous work on which *Hemingway In Our Time* initially focuses, since the editor here considers, perhaps too rigidly, 'that any work not finished by Hemingway the craftsman is truly not finished, and therefore not worthy of being judged beside the acknowledged masterpieces'.

This, though, is a much more comprehensive set of essays than that edited by Astro and Benson. Section One of the book, 'The Development of the Writer', contains information about Hemingway's own writing practices, his judgement as a literary critic, and his admiration for other writers. Harold Hurvitz's study of 'Hemingway's Tutor, Ezra Pound' particularly illuminates Hemingway's professional relationship with, and indebtedness to, the founder of Imagism. Part Two, 'The Work, Studies of the Work as a Whole', contains five essays, each of which surveys Hemingway's writings from a different thematic perspective.

Section Three, 'The Work, Studies of Method and Language' includes five examinations of Hemingway's much discussed style. Paul Goodman examines this style in terms of its 'sweetness'; Julian Smith in terms of its 'omissive' nature. Richard Bridgman concentrates rather on Hemingway's use of the 'vernacular', examines 'in our time' as a deliberately conceived set of stylistic exercises, and analyzes the influence of Pound and Gertrude Stein on the author. The final section of this book, 'The Work,

---

[76] *Ernest Hemingway: Five Decades of Criticism*, ed. by Linda Wagner. Michigan State U.P. pp. 328. $10.

Studies of Individual Novels', is composed of essays treating each major novel or story collection separately. The range of critics included in the collection is impressive, including Robert Penn Warren, Frederick I. Carpenter, and Carlos Baker as well as others new to the Hemingway field. All in all, this is a well conceived, intelligently edited, and useful volume.

Hemingway in Spain,[77] by José Luis Castillo-Puche, first published in 1968, has now been translated into English from the original Spanish by Helen R. Lane. Castillo-Puche analyzes Hemingway's attitudes towards Spain as revealed in his fiction, and discusses his own personal relationship with Hemingway after the latter's return to Spain, after a period of self-imposed exile, in 1954. The author, a Spanish novelist of whom Hemingway himself thought highly, writes, not a critical and scrupulously detailed biography, but what he calls 'a deeply felt, passionate, intuitive, personal book that . . . would serve as a reminder to Spain that Hemingway was the most outstanding observer of our country in modern years'. At the same time, he does discuss critically Hemingway's obsession with bullfighting and the moral code, important to Hemingway as man and writer, which emerged from this concern.

Bullfighting is also one of the subjects spotlighted in *The Enduring Hemingway: An Anthology of a Lifetime in Literature*,[78] where Charles Scribner Jr., who edits and introduces the volume, presents a selection of Hemingway's work representative of the author's literary career. The book

[77] *Hemingway in Spain*, by José Luis Castillo-Puche. Translated from the Spanish by Helen R. Lane. New York: Doubleday. pp. xv+388. $10.95.
[78] *The Enduring Hemingway: An Anthology of a Lifetime in Literature*, ed. by Charles Scribner Jr. New York: Charles Scribner's. pp. xxix+864. $14.95.

is divided into six sections which centre around the beginnings of Hemingway's literary career, World War One, bullfighting, big game hunting, the Spanish Civil War and the importance of the sea in his work. Each of these sections includes both fiction and non-fiction related to its particular theme—though Scribner's description of 'A Natural History of the Dead', or as he retitles it, 'The Natural History of the Dead', as 'sardonic essay' seems surprising. After a somewhat crass introduction written in terms of the relation between Hemingway's life and writing, with comments of the 'it is interesting to note that no character in [*The Sun Also Rises*] corresponds to Hadley Hemingway' type, *A Farewell to Arms, In Our Time* and *The Old Man and the Sea* are reprinted in their entirety. I always feel, though, that it is of little service to a novelist's literary reputation to give a mere smattering of chapters from his major novels, as is done here in the case both of *The Sun Also Rises* and *For Whom the Bell Tolls*.

In 'The Education of Ernest Hemingway' (*JAmS*), George Monteiro discusses the links between *In Our Time* and *The Education of Henry Adams*. He also suggests Adams's influence on Hemingway and on the post-war literary generation as a whole. Robert Merrill, in his examination of 'Tragic Form in *A Farewell to Arms*' (*AL*), suggests that Hemingway in this novel has written a tragedy which departs from the Aristotelian formula. *A Farewell to Arms*, he claims, is a new form of tragedy in which the hero acts, not mistakenly, but supremely well, and suffers a doom which is not directly caused by his actions at all. J. F. Kobler examines Hemingway's criticism of romantic love in *A Farewell to Arms* in 'Let's Run Catherine

Barkley up the Flag Pole and See Who Salutes' (*CEA*).

In 'Hemingway via Joyce' (*SoR*), James Schroeter discusses the radical construction of *The Green Hills of Africa*. He suggests that if this book were read in the way one reads Joyce, it would be recognized as the source for *The Old Man and the Sea*, which is little more than a rewriting and conventionalization of a more eccentric and brilliant original. Schroeter claims *The Green Hills of Africa* is one of Hemingway's great works, 'the pivotal book in understanding Hemingway as writer and as man'.

Douglas Fowler's aim in *Reading Nabokov*[79] is to isolate in Nabokov's fiction what he calls 'constants' or recurrent thematic and technical characteristics, and to this end he restricts his argument to *Bend Sinister*, *Pale Fire*, *Pnin*, *Lolita*, and *Ada*, as well as some short fiction and the poem 'The Ballad of Longwood Gun'. The recurrent concerns he discovers are fairly predictable. Firstly, he discusses the 'favourite', the character with whom Nabokov himself sympathizes, and who appears in the fiction as actual creator of that fiction. Fowler is often unhappy about the development of this character at the expense of plot or narrative interest, and as a result *Pale Fire* and *Ada* are judged inferior to *Lolita* and *Pnin* in their blending of 'voice and activity' or character and plot.

The second constant Fowler finds is an obsession with time and mortality, a refusal to accept the passing of time and the inevitability of death by Nabokov's major protagonists, and clearly this is crucial in determining the tension between dream and reality in so much of the fiction. This is related, too, to what Fowler sees as

another—perhaps more surprising— constant, a clear moral schema. The novels, he argues, are pure moral constructions, where Good and Evil are absolutely differentiated, and this leads him to call them fairy-tales. Fowler does not, however, make it sufficiently clear that these absolute moral schemes are intimately related to the *characters'* way of seeing the world, rather than Nabokov's, and this points, I think, to a weakness in Fowler's reading. He often seems quite prepared to take Nabokov's characters as spokesmen for the author himself, even to the point of creating the hyphenated figure of Van-Nabokov in discussion of *Ada*.

This is precisely the sort of confusion which Bobbie Ann Mason is arguing against in *Nabokov's Garden: A Guide to Ada*,[80] a useful and enthusiastic analysis of this novel. In this book, she manages to combine a willingness to follow up all of Nabokov's clues, which means taking seriously the intellectual games involved, with a presentation of an overall view of the fictional techniques involved in the novel. This allows her to argue forcefully that Van and Nabokov are quite separate, and that we must see the whole invention of the world of Anti-Terra as Van's. The self-indulgence involved in the creation of this world, then, is also Van's rather than Nabokov's, and we are meant to see this flight from reality as a result of guilt about incest and the suicide of Lucette. The images of gardens and nature, which are Mason's main concern, are examined to show that Van's images of perfection are in fact frozen. The 'natural' imagery is therefore ironic in effect, since the Paradise created is based on unnaturalness—incest and

[79] *Reading Nabokov*, by Douglas Fowler. Cornell U.P. pp. 224. $9.75.

[80] *Nabokov's Garden: A Guide to Ada*, by Bobbie Ann Mason. Ann Arbor: Ardis. pp. 196. $8.95.

the implied stopping or warping of time on Anti-Terra. The book is helpful, then, not only in giving the necessary information about Lepidoptera and orchids to allow us to understand Nabokov's allusions, but in relating even the most recondite material to Nabokov's artistic concerns.

Nabokov's Dark Cinema,[81] by Alfred Appel Jr., is a book that is difficult to categorize. Basically, it is an extensive survey of the ways in which Nabokov's fiction utilizes images and materials, as well as actual techniques, from film. Appel's approach, however, is leisurely, his organization seemingly almost random, and the book is full of interesting detail about the cinema which is barely relevant to Nabokov or his work: the first chapter, in fact, scarcely mentions Nabokov at all.

Appel sees Nabokov's attitude to the material of popular culture as 'firmly moral and humanistic', which involves his using the simplifications and vulgarities of popular films and cartoons in an ironic context. The best and fullest treatment of this idea is the chapter on *Lolita*, 'Tristram in Movielove'. *Lolita* is the only book dealt with separately in Appel's study, although many details from *Laughter in the Dark*, *Camera Obscura*, and *Ada*, are all commented on interestingly elsewhere. There is a chapter based on Nabokov's relation to early screen comedy, and one on the 'film noir' of the 1940s and 1950s, plus an interesting section on the making of Kubrick's film version of *Lolita*.

The book's copious illustrations reflect the oblique nature of much of the text, in that the film stills often have the most tenuous connexion with

any of Nabokov's actual fictional material. For example, Appel offers five stills involving venetian blinds to illustrate one short passage from *Lolita*. The name of Vivian Darkbloom in the Acknowledgments as well as the oblique, often whimsical, approach may raise doubts about this book's seriousness. However, fascinating insights are offered, throughout this volume, both into Nabokov and into film.

James Joyce suggests in 'Lolita in Humberland' (*SSNTS*) that the most pointed allusions in *Lolita* are to *Alice's Adventures in Wonderland* and *Through the Looking Glass*, not to Appel's movieland. Lolita, he suggests, is the Alice in Humbert's wonderland (Humberland), the nymphet of his imagination. Joyce also points out Carroll's and Nabokov's common delight in the manipulation of language. He claims that both thematically and structurally the allusions to Carroll's novels have important consequences for a proper understanding of *Lolita*.

Howard Levant discusses John Steinbeck's longer fictions from the point of view of 'structural adequacy' in *The Novels of John Steinbeck: A Critical Study*.[82] Claiming that Steinbeck's work has too often been viewed 'piecemeal', even when the intention has been for a rounded view, Levant compares the individual success or failures of the fictions against those 'constructionist' criteria which he formulates in a precise manner at the start of the book.

Levant believes that 'Steinbeck has an abundance of every gift and craft the novelist can have—except an intelligent and coherent sense of what structure is and can do'. It is this structural inadequacy which accounts

[81] *Nabokov's Dark Cinema*, by Alfred Appel Jr. New York: Oxford U.P. pp. 324. $14.95.

[82] *The Novels of John Steinbeck: A Critical Study*, by Howard Levant. U. of Missouri P. pp. xxii+304. $12.50.

for much of the weakness of the post-1940 fiction, *East of Eden* for example. Steinbeck's successes, on the other hand, are to be found in novels like *The Grapes of Wrath* and *In Dubious Battle* when the author has managed to fuse the structure of the novel harmoniously with the greatest possible variety of materials.

The major problem for Steinbeck as writer, Levant claims, was exactly this fusing of structure and fictional materials. He examines Steinbeck's fiction from beginning to end, showing how from the start of his fictional career Steinbeck made use of two distinct kinds of novelistic structures —'panoramic' and 'dramatic'—to order his materials. He reached his peak, as an artist, Levant suggests, when he managed to combine these two structures, with most evident success in *In Dubious Battle*. Steinbeck's parallel search for harmony between structure and materials justifies the welter of technical devices and the widely differing fictional materials he uses, and explains his move towards a very loose narrative method in his later novels. Levant here examines the adequacy of the author's blueprints to the embodiment of his vision, and an introduction by Warren French puts this book into the context of previously published Steinbeck criticism.

Warren French also wrote the foreword to *A Study Guide to Steinbeck: A Handbook to his Major Work*,[83] edited by Tetsumaro Hayashi. A product of the Steinbeck Society, this book is very much designed as a teaching aid, its specified purpose 'to enlighten students on Steinbeck's major works, to stimulate interest and curiosity and to encourage independent study and research'. Despite containing essays by Peter Lisca and Warren French among others, the editor and authors involved in this production never raise their critical sights very high. The book obviously aims to provide a very basic introduction indeed to Steinbeck's world. Mark Spilka in 'Of George and Lennie and Curley's Wife: Sweet Violence in Steinbeck's Eden' (*MFS*), speaks of Steinbeck's power as lying in his 'ability to bring into ordinary scenes of social conflict the psychological forcefulness of infantile reactions'. Spilka examines the themes of violence and sex in *Of Mice and Men*, relating the latter to Steinbeck's treatment of Cathy Ames in *East of Eden*.

The tone of the foreword to *Black Like It Is/Was: Erskine Caldwell's Treatment of Racial Themes*[84] by William A. Sutton suggests the intent of the whole. 'The malevolent acts that Caldwell depicts reveal', so Sutton suggests, 'the depths to which one race stooped to make themselves superior'. He then continues in a more hysterical voice, 'The dogs have not been called off and millions of black Americans are still locked in symbolic, economic and psychological chains'. In this foreword Caldwell gets little attention. It is the present state of the black movement in America that is Sutton's subject: that conservative, affluent, minority wedge of blacks who have 'made it'; the mass of blacks 'clamouring about' without unity and direction 'destined to remain in their ghettos and black like it is, will be black like it was'. This is an overtly propagandist book then: 'why do we wait for people to explode before we stop to listen to

[83] *A Study Guide to Steinbeck: A Handbook to his Major Work*, ed. by Tetsumaro Hayashi. New Jersey: Scarecrow P. pp. xvi + 316. $10. £7.

[84] *Black Like It Is/Was: Erskine Caldwell's Treatment of Racial Themes*, by William A. Sutton. New Jersey: Scarecrow P. pp. xiii + 164. $6. £4.20.

what they are saying?' his foreword rather despairingly ends.

Sutton's intention in examining Caldwell's work is to show how oppression of the black race operated in Caldwell's Georgia. The longest chapter by far in the book is entitled 'The Manipulation of Blacks'. In it we are given a long list of these manipulations as evidenced in Caldwell's work. Sutton trudges his way steadily through the kind of jobs blacks do in Caldwell's fiction, black status in Caldwell's Georgian society, punishments for black misdemeanours revealed there, black poverty, and white Southern violence and bigotry evidenced in his work, and the exploitations of the black consumer exposed there by Caldwell. The chapter entitled 'The Character of Blacks' is another list showing how black feelings and character are expressed in Caldwell's fiction. There are a number of addenda to the book: Caldwell's own 1926 article, 'The Georgia Cracker', and three other reprinted articles on Caldwell and *God's Little Acre*. Despite the indictment of white America's treatment of the black man which this book presents, Sutton still feels able to add a patriotic touch: America is finally better than Russia for, he brightly asserts, 'a writer as outspoken and individualistic as Erskine . . . would not last five minutes under either a Fascist or a Communist regime'!

Paul N. Siegal examines lawyer Max's speech in 'The Conclusion of Richard Wright's *Native Son*' (*PMLA*), to suggest that this is not just a Communist Party line oration whose propaganda is poorly related to the rest of the novel. Bigger Thomas finds Meaning in a hatred of the oppressor, Siegal suggests, and there's a final active belief on his part in a genuine unity in a common struggle between blacks and activist whites (like Jan) to build through revolution a better form of society. There is a special number this year of the *College Language Association Journal* on the work of Richard Wright, James Baldwin, and Ralph Ellison. In '"The Kingdom of the Beast": The Landscape of *Native Son*', which appears here, Robert Felgar examines Wright's use of bestial imagery throughout the novel, a form of imagery which obviously correlates to the white man's view of the black man's world. Don B. Graham suggests in '*Lawd Today* and the Example of *The Waste Land*' that Wright's novel gets its principle of coherence from Eliot's poem. Embedded in the novel, he shows, are images, motifs, and symbols adapted from the poem. In 'The Death of Richard Wright's American Dream: "The Man Who Lived Underground"', Mildred W. Everette claims that the complete pessimism of Wright's long short story reveals the extinction of belief in that 'American Dream' still apparent in *Black Boy*. Jean-François Gounard discusses the effect of self-exile on the development of Richard Wright as author and as individual in 'Richard Wright as a Black American Writer in Exile'. He says that though Wright's works grew in maturity while an expatriate, his most powerful writing remained what he did while in close contact with that racial problem he knew best.

There are three essays on Ralph Ellison in this same *CLAJ* special number. In '*Invisible Man* as History', Russell G. Fischer examines Ellison's novel as literary interpretation of the history of the Negro American during the first forty years of the twentieth century. Charles W. Scruggs calls attention to a classical analogue to Ellison's 'so-called underground man' in his 'Ralph Ellison's Use of *The Aeneid* in *Invisible Man*', to suggest that the underground experience *has* proven fruitful to the novel's protagonist. Louis D. Mitchell celebrates the same fruitfulness in 'Invisibility— Permanent or Resurrective'. Taking issue with Edward Margolies's interpretation of *Invisible Man*, he claims Ellison's philosophy of 'possibility' to be an artistic triumph due to Ellison's continual play in this novel on the western resurrective theme. Marjorie Pryse discusses the extent, in 'Ralph Ellison's Heroid Fugitive' (*AL*), to which the reader becomes the protagonist in *Invisible Man*, to what extent he shares the narrator's invisibility.

Ralph Ellison: A Collection of Critical Essays,[85] edited by the novelist John Hersey, brings together in one volume much of the best writing on Ellison's work. The essays include Tony Tanner's 'The Music of Invisibility', Robert Bone's 'Ralph Ellison and the Uses of the Imagination', and Larry Neal's 'Ellison's Zoot Suit', among others. The collection, of necessity, concentrates on *Invisible Man*: the novel as 'profoundly comic work' (Earl H. Rovit: 'Ralph Ellison and the American Comic Tradition'); as a 'quest for identity that describes America in the twentieth century' (William J. Schafer: 'Ralph Ellison and the Birth of the Anti-Hero'); and as 'seminal for subsequent American fiction' (Tanner). The book opens, though, with an interesting interview with Ellison, conducted by the editor. Here Ellison speaks, among other things, of the importance to him of his musical education, his literary influences, the use of anger as a motivating force for a novelist, and his own use of

what he calls 'the *Negro* American Experience' as fictional material.

Another of this useful *Twentieth Century Views* series, *James Baldwin: A Collection of Critical Essays*,[86] edited by Keneth Kinnamon, has been published this year. I have never understood why none of the volumes in this series has an index: surely a necessity for any work of this kind. Kinnamon himself places Baldwin's work in a general perspective. He points to the quest for Love, both in terms of personal emotional security, and as an agent of racial reconciliation and national survival, as one of Baldwin's most recurrent themes. He suggests, however, that by 1972 and *No Name in the Street*, given the Black Panther activity of the previous years, the social utility of Love had for Baldwin become of dubious value; violence was rather to be seen as the arbiter of history, as suggested by the end of *Tell Me How Long the Train's Been Gone*. Kichung Kim gives this same theme a slightly different emphasis in 'Wright, The Protest Novel, and Baldwin's Faith' (*CLAJ*). Baldwin, Kim suggests, reacted so strongly to *Native Son*, since Bigger Thomas's rôle in the novel was anathema to his own ideal vision of the black man in America, potentially free and fulfilled. Kim identifies Baldwin's own later loss of faith in America, however, with Martin Luther King's assassination, and he too points to *No Name in the Street* as revealing this change of vision.

Some of the problems concerning Baldwin's work, problems arousing diverse critical comment, are examined in Kinnamon's edition of collected essays. Was Baldwin so influenced by white literature and social values that he became totally out of

[85] *Ralph Ellison: A Collection of Critical Essays*, ed. by John Hersey. New Jersey: Prentice-Hall. pp. viii+180. $6.95.

[86] *James Baldwin: A Collection of Critical Essays*, ed. by Keneth Kinnamon. New Jersey: Prentice-Hall. pp. xii+169. $6.95.

touch with the real facts of black life in America, particularly during his 'integration through love' period? Is he a better essayist than novelist? Is he an 'accomplished prose stylist' or one whose style is rather marked by 'pseudo-poetic floridity and reliance on clichés'? These are some of the critical questions discussed in this volume in essays including Benjamin DeMott's 'James Baldwin on the Sixties: Acts and Revelations', F. W. Dupee's 'James Baldwin and the "Man"', and Eldridge Cleaver's 'Notes on a Native Son' which extends the Baldwin–Wright controversy into the 1960s. It is unfortunate, though, that Kinnamon has chosen to reprint here that very weak chapter on Baldwin from Robert A. Bone's *The Negro Novel in America*.

In 'The Dilemma of Love in "Go Tell It on the Mountain" and "Giovanni's Room"' (*CLAJ*), George E. Bell suggests the final optimistic quality of these works. Love, he claims, is shown in Baldwin's first two novels to be possible if one is willing to live existentially, to abandon the puritan mythology of man's corruption and to live freely, unashamedly, and unselfishly as a trusting and committed person.

In 'Ernest J. Gaines: Change, Growth, and History' (*SoR*), Jerry H. Bryant suggests that Gaines's fiction combines moral commitment and aesthetic distance in a way which characterizes the 'classic' American writer. He examines *Catherine Carmier*, *Of Love and Dust*, *Bloodline*, and Gaines's most important novel, *The Autobiography of Miss Jane Pittman*, to show the author's treatment of the themes of black fiction with humanity, humour, and breadth of vision. Gaines himself discusses *The Autobiography of Miss Jane Pittman* as 'a folk autobiography' in 'A Conversation with Ernest Gaines'

(*SoR*) by Ruth Laney. He also talks about his attitudes towards the whole subject of 'black writing', and about his own Louisiana background and its importance to his fiction.

Neil Schmitz points to a new direction taken in Afro-American literature in 'Neo-HooDoo: The Experimental Fiction of Ishmael Reed' (*TCL*). Reed's concern, Schmitz suggests, is in radically severing his destiny as a writer from the fate of his white contemporaries. With his 'Neo-HooDoo' approach to fiction, he is moving along the same metafictive angle of Barthelme and Pynchon, but in a much more thoroughly optimistic manner.

Robert Penn Warren discusses modern fiction generally in 'Robert Penn Warren: An Interview' (*JAmS*) by Marshall Walker. Among other subjects, he also talks about the fugitives and his novels *All the King's Men* and *At Heaven's Gate*. James H. Justus considers this last novel as an important foreshadowing of *All the King's Men* in 'On the Politics of the Self-Created: *At Heaven's Gate*' (*SR*). Justus suggests that the novel concerns a world in which Agrarian values—the integration of personality, a sense of mutual responsibility, and a harmony between man and nature—are conspicuously absent. As a result, the world of *At Heaven's Gate* is one in which the self has to attempt its entire recreation, a recreation process which is often finally self-destructive in spiritual terms. Flo Witte discusses the theme of self-definition, in 'Adam's Rebirth in Robert Penn Warren's *Wilderness*' (*SoQ*), as connecting this rather atypical novel to Penn Warren's other novels. She examines Adam Rosenzweig's symbolic rebirth in the book, as his pretences are stripped and he comes to a discovery of his 'real self'. Lawrence D. Stewart's *Paul Bowles:*

The Illumination of North Africa[87] is the first book-length critical study to appear on Bowles's life and work. Stewart asserts that it is Bowles's fictional exploration of North Africa which will give the author his lasting reputation, and so focuses on this (undoubtedly major) aspect of the author's work as critical centre of his study. In his first chapter Stewart examines Bowles's early career as a writer, with particular reference to the influence of Gertrude Stein on his personal and literary development. He shows the way in which Bowles's expatriation to an extent paralleled Stein's, and also states the eventual importance North Africa as fictional locale was to have for Bowles: 'In North Africa's golden light, clear air, and alien culture, he and his fictive heroes work through their visions and impose upon the world a reality which otherwise, in a geographical America, could not be. Those constructs reflect not merely the American in exile but the twentieth-century American dilemma.'

Stewart examines, then, Bowles's existentialist themes. He shows how these arise out of the positioning of characters, products of a Western urban society in decay, within the context of an alien African culture, and analyzes his 'African' novels and short stories, in order of publication, in the course of this book. Unfortunately, there's too great a tendency throughout, on Stewart's part to concentrate on biographical detail and on the process of literary composition rather than on close and analytical textual criticism. However, he has rescued Bowles from relative obscurity and provided a base on which others can build.

Sandy Cohen commences his cele-bration of Malamud in *Bernard Malamud and the Trial by Love*[88] with the extravagant statement that '*The Assistant* may very well be the best novel written in America since World War II'. His study focuses on the way in which Malamud 'blends myth and reality into viable fiction', a fiction which reflects a contemporary American society and its problems. Cohen examines Malamud's central theme, that of self-transcendence from a myth-dominated existence, a process which is the ideal controlling much of the development of character in the novels. This self-transcendence is shown to be a painful process in Malamud, and is normally connected to some kind of 'elaborate and ritualistic trial by love', a trial normally related in the author's work to 'the seasonal cycles and their various attending myths'. This 'trial by love' forces Malamud's protagonists into intense self-scrutiny where past mistakes are recognized as well as the need for concern for others. In pursuing this straightforward thesis, Cohen has a tendency to force his material into a somewhat rigid pattern. Also, more alarmingly, though vitally concerned with ideas of 'myth' and 'ritual', Cohen allows these terms to remain noticeably loosely defined throughout his study.

Cohen discusses Malamud's American Jewish heritage, with especial reference to the use and importance of suffering in his fiction, and suggests that the 'new life' attained by Malamud's protagonists through suffering is 'life' on a spiritual rather than a physical level. Cohen traces the careers of these protagonists—examining Malamud's five novels and the Fidelman stories in detail—to show the 'transcending' process in action

---

[87] *Paul Bowles: The Illumination of North Africa*, by Lawrence D. Stewart. Southern Illinois U.P. pp. xvi+175. $6.95.

[88] *Bernard Malamud and the Trial by Love*, by Sandy Cohen. Amsterdam: Rodopi N.V. pp. 132. Fl. 18.

and the implications of this process. The author also shows how Malamud presents the unstable nature of American society, and develops within this context his protagonists' quest for 'full maturation', a quest, so Cohen claims, 'unfortunately . . . conspicuously rare in twentieth-century American literature'.

John Horne Burns: An Appreciative Biography[89] by John Mitzel is the first work to appear on the life and writings of Burns since his death in 1953 at the age of thirty-six. Burns's distaste for American life is obviously shared by his biographer who reveals in his rather telegraphic style, 'Civilization is the least concern of plutocracy. Don't I know it! I have to live here . . . Conditioned to be satisfied with puffed-up hype and capitalist clichés. One is never graduated from High School in America'. This style annoys after a short time by its presumption: 'Burns was graduated from Harvard in 1937. He goes to work as a schoolmaster. Faith begins to wane. About time'.

One of Mitzel's major concerns is obviously Burns's homosexuality. I wonder, by the way, what Henry James would think of being placed within Mitzel's defining bracket of the 'Gay Sensibility'. Mitzel also offers Burns as a model of one whose excellence and antisocial attitudes led to his 'elimination' from a perverted egalitarian America. Mitzel has rescued Burns from obscurity and this is important, but he seems more concerned in writing a defence of Burns's homosexual life and fictional themes, and an attack on American civilization generally, than with any comprehensive attempt at a biographical and critical study. For example, when he comes to discuss Burns's important

first novel, Mitzel claims 'I haven't much to say about *The Gallery* actually'.

Mitzel's appreciative biography of Burns is at least coherent in terms of its form: the same cannot be said about another book by the same author, this time written in conjunction with Steven Abbott, called *Myra & Gore*[90]—an essay, or series of comments, or notes, about Gore Vidal's *Myra Breckinridge*, very loosely examined in terms of its relation to American culture and life in the 1940s and 1960s. A sample of the text should tell enough: 'Why not put Myra in a Broderick Crawford wide-brim hat, huge Stewart Granger lapels, and have her star in the 1954 AIP classic: I WAS A MALE LESBIAN FOR THE FBI'. More interesting, if perhaps again over concerned with the subject of homosexuality, is the interview with Gore Vidal concluding the book.

The Apostate Angel: A Critical Study of Gore Vidal[91] by Bernard F. Dick, provides a more analytical discussion of Vidal's work. Vidal, so Dick claims, is pre-eminently a 'classicist' so far as his fiction is concerned. Traditional, often intricate but rarely innovative, his plot centred novels look more to the past than to the present. Even *Myra Breckinridge*, Dick claims, 'had more in common with the Age of Petronius than it did with the Age of Aquarius'.

The author's approach to Vidal is, for the most part, by means of a chronologically ordered study of the novels, except for his eighth chapter, 'The Political Animal', which covers

[89] *John Horne Burns: An Appreciative Biography*, by John Mitzel. Massachusetts: Manifest Destiny. pp. 135. $2 (paperback).

[90] *Myra & Gore*, by John Mitzel and Steven Abbott. Massachusetts: Manifest Destiny. pp. 90. $2 (paperback).

[91] *The Apostate Angel: A Critical Study of Gore Vidal*, by Bernard F. Dick. New York: Random House. pp. 203. $6.95.

Vidal's political involvement between 1960, when he ran for Congress, and 1972 when he wrote *An Evening with Richard Nixon and . . .* Dick gives Vidal the title 'man of letters' and shows his ability to switch from one literary form to another and to cut across genres with total ease. Vidal's essays which 'have made classical rhetoric palatable to a non-classical age' are not treated separately in this study, but are integrated with a discussion of the novels. Dick's final judgement on the novels is that, though Vidal will always be known as a popular novelist, this is a term which should not necessarily be used disparagingly: 'he has perfected his own brand of fiction—the literary novel with echoes from Crane, Melville, Twain, Cooper, the eighteenth-century *Bildungsroman*, futuristic fiction, the *Satyricon*, *Nausea*, The New Novel, and even the films of the forties now studied on the campus as "documents of the age"'.

Sarah B. Cohen examines Saul Bellow's particular brand of fiction in *Saul Bellow's Enigmatic Laughter*.[92] Miss Cohen takes Bellow's statement —'Obliged to choose between complaint and comedy, I choose comedy, as more energetic, wiser and manlier' —and proceeds from it to analyze his use of the comic element in his work, that element with which Bellow continually retaliates when faced with the possibility of despair. Cohen examines what she calls Bellow's 'comedy of character . . . of language . . . [and] of ideas' as well as his fictional use of 'militant irony', the whimsically fantastic, and the burlesque. She indicates, meanwhile, Bellow's debt to the comic traditions of Russian, Jewish, and American culture.

Sarah Cohen explores the function of Bellow's comedy from *Dangling Man* to *Mr. Sammler's Planet*, showing how there has been a progressively more sophisticated and versatile use of the comic made in each of his novels. This development is traced by her as approximately paralleling the advancing maturity of Bellow's heroes and the increasing novelty of his fictional forms.

That comic element most emphasized by Bellow, so Cohen reveals, is 'comedy of character'. This is that comedy which realistically and amply exposes 'the damaged nature of man'. Ridiculing deeply subjective self-concern and stubborn adherence to insufficient 'versions of reality' Bellow treats those who show no awareness of the nature of their flaws unsympathetically; but those protagonists like Henderson aware of their failings and struggling to make internal repair, he treats with highly sympathetic laughter. Though Bellow acknowledges man as incorrigible, 'doing always the same stunts, repeating the same disgraces', he nevertheless always believes in mankind's possibilities, in human worth. In a world where evil would appear to be the norm, Bellow develops a comic vision in order to 'interrupt, resist, reinterpret, and transcend adversity'.

M. Gilbert Porter also examines Bellow's celebration of human possibility despite the continuing presence of highly adverse conditions, but from a very different critical stance, in *Whence the Power? The Artistry and Humanity of Saul Bellow*.[93] For Porter's reading of Bellow's fiction is based on New Critical assumptions, and draws heavily from analytical work in that tradition. Through close analysis of the interaction of themes and forms in Bellow's fiction, Porter

[92] *Saul Bellow's Enigmatic Laughter*, by Sarah B. Cohen. U. of Illinois P. pp. 242. $8.95.

[93] *Whence the Power? The Artistry and Humanity of Saul Bellow*, by M. Gilbert Porter. U. of Missouri P. pp. ix+209. $10.

examines Bellow's artistry, and his 'neo-transcendentalist' affirmation of humanity, to answer his own question: 'whence the power?'

Porter gives a close reading and explication of all Bellow's novels. He shows evidence of his obvious critical concerns when he follows W. J. Handy's equation of the fictional scene with the poetic image and Joseph Frank's concept of 'spatial form' in the novel, to examine the scenes in *Seize the Day* as nearly as possible as poetic images, and to relate each of these scenes to the organic central metaphor in the novel, the image of a drowning man. Having approached each of Bellow's novels separately, searching out the qualities of unity in structure and texture that each possesses, and analyzing and demonstrating the techniques employed in the single scenes which make up the complex fabric of the whole, Porter, in his final chapter examines the author's fiction as totality. Here he offers a brief statement about Bellow's vision of man as reflected in the experiences of his protagonists. He shows that despite the power of 'dread' in Bellow's world, dread of the possibility of the manipulation of man in an indifferent cosmos, the writer always finally celebrates man as possessor of free will with the capacity for heroism.

Bellow himself discusses in 'Starting Out in Chicago' (*ASch*), what it was in the 1930s that drew an adolescent in Chicago to writing and to books. He compares that era with this, attacking that 'Great Noise' which opposes the symbolic discipline of poetry in America today. Daniel Fuchs suggests Bellow's movement in a direction opposite to the present fictional mainstream in 'Saul Bellow and the Modern Tradition' (*ConL*). He stresses the need for community on the part of the Bellow protagonist and an almost confessional technique on Bellow's part which goes against the 'nihilism, immoralism, and . . . aesthetic tradition' of what Fuchs calls 'the modern tradition'. Douglass Bolling in his discussion of the 'Intellectual and Aesthetic Dimensions of Mr Sammler's Planet' (*JNT*), argues for the 'excellence' of this, Bellow's latest novel.

In *Kurt Vonnegut, Jr.: A Descriptive Bibliography and Annotated Secondary Checklist*,[94] Jerome Klinkowitz, who seems to hold a virtual monopoly in the Vonnegut critical field, and Asa B. Pierratt Jr., bring together the material appearing both by, and about, Vonnegut from 1950 to the end of 1973. The bibliography lists all Vonnegut's works, including his contributions as a student to the *Cornell Sun*. One of the latter articles is entitled 'Gloomy Wednesday—or Why We Wish We Were an an (*sic*) Independent': thirty-two years later he finally worked his way back to *Blue Monday*.

Full descriptions of both American and British editions of Vonnegut's books are supplied here as well as many foreign language editions. The volume is divided into separate sections, which include material on the author's books, short fiction, poetry, drama, and essays. A brief description of critical material which has appeared on Vonnegut's work is included in a useful section of the book entitled 'Annotated Secondary Checklist of Criticism on Kurt Vonnegut, Jr.' In this respect, this collection differs, to its advantage, from the earlier mentioned *James Jones: A Checklist*.

[94] *Kurt Vonnegut, Jr.: A Descriptive Bibliography and Annotated Secondary Checklist*, by Asa B. Pierratt Jr. and Jerome Klinkowitz. Connecticut: Archon Books. pp. xix + 138. $10.

Edward Grossman, in 'Vonnegut & His Audience' (*Commentary*) discusses the author's work from *Player Piano* to *Wampeters, Foma, & Granfalloons* in order to ask why Vonnegut is so popular in America. The affinity of his work to comic books and movies, his anti-scientific and morally relativist messages, and the modern necessity, as Vonnegut claims, to become 'an enemy of truth and a fanatic for harmless balderdash' in the face of an oppressive reality, provide some of the answers. In 'Breakfast of Champions: The Direction of Kurt Vonnegut's Fiction' (*JAmS*) Peter B. Messent suggests that both thematically and formally Vonnegut's latest novel must be accounted a failure.

In *Kerouac: A Biography*,[95] Anne Charters writes up the results of what Allen Ginsberg claims in his (very) brief foreword to be 'her vast tactful scholarship . . . [applied] to the understanding of [Kerouac's] musical sound as American lonely Prose Trumpeter of drunken Buddha Sacred Heart'. These words forewarn of a certain lack of objectivity reflected at times in the biography itself as Anne Charters herself mirrors, in her style, Kerouac's own romantic image of himself: 'he didn't last long as a seaman. As he admitted himself, he was incapable of acting like an ordinary man, never cracking a smile unless it was a superior one, and all because he had an angel of loneliness riding on his shoulder.' The author consistently takes Kerouac just as seriously as he took himself. She reports Kerouac's image of himself, having completed *On The Road*, *Doctor Sax*, and *Maggie Cassidy*, as Melville, 'worn out and exhausted' after *Moby Dick* and *Pierre*, with no

critical rider. She also compares Kerouac consistently to Thoreau, at one stage calling him 'a drop out in the great American tradition of Thoreau, Mark Twain, and Daniel Boone'!

Anne Charters, however, certainly demythifies Kerouac's public image as 'King of the Beats'. For Kerouac was a man obviously totally emotionally tied to his mother, always, for example, writing to her for his bus fare home when he ran out of money on his various travels. The longest distance in fact the writer of *On The Road* ever hitchhiked was from Chicago to Denver. His best books were centred round characters who were fictional representations of his friends and people other than himself, with Neal Cassady particularly playing the rôle of alter ego. Charters gives us glimpses of Kerouac's hard drinking, on one occasion 'to bury his depression after his cat's death', and shows that, politically, he was hardly a radical; totally unsympathetic to Ken Kesey and his psychedelic bus, 'Kerouac was sure [LSD] had been introduced into America by the Russians as a plot to weaken the country'.

Though Anne Charters gives us much information about Kerouac's theory of 'Spontaneous Prose', her critical comment on his writing is on the whole weak, of the 'no book has ever caught the feel of . . . the mindless joyousness of "joyriding" like *On The Road*' variety. She is, however, obviously more concerned with biographical detail, and her picture of Kerouac himself and his literary acquaintances and friends—among them Burroughs, Cassady, Ginsberg, and Snyder—is of real interest in any consideration of post-war cultural activity.

George Dardess is more interested in the work than the man in 'The

[95] *Kerouac: A Biography*, by Anne Charters. San Francisco: Straight Arrow Books. 1973. pp. 419. $7.95.

Delicate Dynamics of Friendship: A Reconsideration of Kerouac's *On The Road*' (*AL*). Examining *On The Road* in the light of its formidable complexity of structure, he suggests that 'Kerouac may legitimately be, even on the basis of *On The Road,* a great American author—an author the equal of Mailer himself'.

In *Down Mailer's Way*,[96] Robert Solotaroff examines Mailer's own status as a writer in close detail. Mailer's fundamental purpose, Solotaroff accurately affirms, has remained constant throughout his career, 'to drive to the centre of the American psyche and report what he finds there'. Solotaroff examines Mailer in his rôle as American literary 'moralist-prophet'. He also traces the way in which Mailer's continuing fascination with growth, with the possibility of self-development, has led him in his work through a variety of philosophical, moral, political, religious, and literary influences.

Solotaroff's major thesis is that Mailer's fiction has never quite lived up to its enormous promise. He examines Mailer's style, themes, and influences, through analysis of both fiction and non-fiction, to show a basic confusion of direction in the author's work as a whole. Mailer himself, Solotaroff suggests, remains on Rojack's parapet wanting to jump both ways at once: in *An American Dream* balancing between a realistic and a non-realistic form, in *The Naked and The Dead* between Hearn and his Marxist liberal principles, and Croft, 'prototype of the hipster', with his authoritarianism and his personal courage. The final example of this confusion of purpose is, according to Solotaroff, the division in Mailer's

energies between fiction and non fiction.

Solotaroff also claims that Mailer's obsession with the idea of personal growth—and his consequent need to present extreme characters in extreme situations—has been to some extent unfortunate in that it has led to a basic failure of modesty, both towards experience and towards his own fiction, on his part. He suggests that Mailer's twenty year obsession 'with the workings of his mind' has tended to preclude that imaginative effort without which major fiction, of which Mailer is still capable, cannot be written.

Laura Adams, the editor of *Will the Real Norman Mailer Please Stand Up*,[97] presents a collection of essays, mostly previously published, which attempts to cover the whole spectrum of activity with which Mailer has been involved since 1948. The volume includes, therefore, after an initial introduction and series of three 'overviews' on Mailer, sections on Mailer as philosopher-metaphysician, Mailer as belonging to a specifically American tradition, as contemporary novelist, as poet, playwright, filmmaker, journalist, male chauvinist, and as 'performer'.

Laura Adams points out in her introduction that Mailer's bewildering mixture of rôles can be seen as part and parcel of his attempt to alter 'the consciousness of our time', to rescue man's consciousness from controlling totalitarian systems, so that once more, as in Renaissance and frontier American times, that human potential for vitality and creativity, for that 'growth' of which Solotaroff talks, may be explored. Mailer, through his continued experimentation with styles and forms, is attempt-

[96] *Down Mailer's Way,* by Robert Solotaroff. U. of Illinois P. pp. x+289. $10.

[97] *Will the Real Norman Mailer Please Stand Up,* ed. by Laura Adams. New York: Kennikat Press. pp. 274. $9.95. £7.00.

ing to discover the most effective means to this end. The concentration here on the whole range of Mailer activity, though praiseworthy in intent, does mean that the collection tends to survey rather briefly every area of the Mailer achievement, ultimately lacking really detailed analysis of any of the material with which it concerns itself.

In 'The Malign Deity of *The Naked and the Dead*' (*TCL*), Paul N. Siegel examines Croft's and Cumming's mutual belief within this novel that life is to be controlled by man, that there is a pattern to life which can be grasped. In fact, Siegel points out, the real pattern revealed by the novel is of a universe ruled over by a supernatural power, cruelly indifferent to man's needs. In 'Myth and Animism in *Why Are We in Vietnam?*' (*TCL*), Rubin Rabinovitz shows how Mailer's animism brings his story closer to primitive myth and provides a metaphor for psychological forces. He also examines the novel to show the purposeful nature of Mailer's use here of both violence and obscenity.

Robert Merrill examines Mailer as journalist in 'Norman Mailer's Early Nonfiction: The Art of Self Revelation' (*WHR*). He studies Mailer's early nonfictional innovations and shows the gradual emergence of Mailer's 'personal' approach to non-fiction, an approach seen in 'Ten Thousand Words a Minute', that 1962 'minor masterpiece' which anticipates the achievement of *The Armies of the Night*. In 'Of Adams and Aquarius' (*AL*), Gordon O. Taylor discusses the evolutionary link between the author-protagonists of *The Education of Henry Adams* and *A Fire on the Moon*.

In *William Styron*,[98] Melvin J.

[98] *William Styron*, by Melvin J. Friedman. Ohio: Bowling Green Popular P. pp. viii + 72. $2.50 (paperback).

Friedman examines the work of this author to illuminate a sensibility 'with broad and far-ranging sympathies', and to suggest his versatility as a novelist. Friedman also places Styron's work in an international context and asserts his belief that 'he is the least parochial of contemporary American writers'. This short study is comprised of four chapters, chapter one, 'An Overview', in which Friedman gives a general introduction to Styron's work, suggesting his concern in proving that the novel still remains a plausible art form. In the second chapter, 'William Styron and the *Nouveau Roman*', Styron's relation to the French avant-garde novel of the 1950s and 1960s is examined, with particular reference to *Lie Down in Darkness* and *Set This House on Fire*.

In the third chapter, 'Politics, "A Vile Racist Imagination", and William Styron', Friedman analyzes the political consciousness at work in Styron's novels. He gives special attention to *The Confessions of Nat Turner* and the controversy it aroused, completely dismissing Ernest Kaiser's 'vile racist imagination' charge. Finally Friedman, in 'William Styron Now', gives an account of Styron's work in progress, and examines his biting and satirical 1973 first play *In the Clap Shack*.

In 'Tragedy and Melodrama in *The Confessions of Nat Turner*' (*TCL*), David Eggenschwiler suggests that melodrama is the major subject as well as the major genre of the novel, a melodrama which is qualified by the novel's ironic structure. He claims Nat's final leap of faith is a leap beyond both tragedy and melodrama. There's an interesting discussion of *The Confessions of Nat Turner* and *Lie Down in Darkness*, as well as the novel Styron is working on at the present time, in 'An Interview with William Styron' (*SoR*), by Ben Forkner and Gilbert Schricke.

John Romano examines John Hawkes's latest novel, *Death, Sleep & the Traveller*, in 'Our Best Known Neglected Novelist' (*Commentary*). He suggests Hawkes's recent movement towards that self-conscious artificiality and obliquity now fashionable has led in his case to a loss of literary power and conviction. He also claims that in general the overall quality of Hawkes's vision as a novelist is not so impressive as the polish, density, virtuosity, and verbal power, of the fictional parts.

Preston M. Browning Jr., in his *Flannery O'Connor*,[99] examines another writer often put in the same 'grotesque' category as Hawkes. Browning here analyzes closely the nature of her art in its entirety. He explores the implications of her situation as 'Catholic novelist in the Protestant South', a South where she felt herself 'both native and alien'. Browning also points out the centrality of a certain yoking of opposites in Flannery O'Connor's work, producing a tension which gives her 'extraordinary creative power and unique vision'. He shows how that concern for crime and violence which seems to be a hallmark of modern Southern literature is balanced, on O'Connor's part, with that 'attraction for the Holy' which springs from her essentially religious temperament.

Browning's main thesis, then, is that Flannery O'Connor's work may be seen as an attempt to recover this idea of 'the Holy' in an age in which both the meaning and reality of this concept have been obscured. Her protagonists, in trying to recover this 'idea', to recover also that 'depth' and sense of 'being' which has been lost by contemporary man, often become involved in a journey through what Browning calls the 'radically profane', embracing evil so as to rediscover good, pursuing the demonic in order finally to arrive at 'the Holy'. The other side of this coin is shown to be O'Connor's satirization of that American world of the 1950s, that world of unbelief in which her protagonists' quest occurs. It is in the tension between these two worlds, so Browning claims, that Flannery O'Connor's artistic and moral vision functions at its best. From this point of departure Browning examines her work, with separate chapters on *Wise Blood, A Good Man Is Hard to Find, The Violent Bear It Away*, and *Everything That Rises Must Converge*.

In 'Flannery O'Connor's Rage of Vision' (*AL*), Claire Katz discusses the way in which O'Connor's characters find their attempt to live autonomously impossible and discover the need for absolute submission to Christ's power. Violence—a violence which is aimed in rage at the limits imposed on us in a closed universe—leads, Claire Katz shows, to the possibility in O'Connor's fiction of the moment of grace.

All moments of religious grace have disappeared for good in John Barth's fictional universe. *John Barth: The Comic Sublimity of Paradox*,[100] by Jac Tharpe, is the first full length book to appear on Barth, and not before time. Tharpe examines the author's novels to show how, as a group, 'they comprise a history of philosophy'. He shows how the problem of right conduct is a major theme of Barth's first three novels, mentioning how, in these novels, Barth presents roughly five concepts

[99] *Flannery O'Connor*, by Preston M. Browning, Jr. Southern Illinois U.P. pp. x + 143. $6.95.

[100] *John Barth: The Comic Sublimity of Paradox*, by Jac Tharpe. Southern Illinois U.P. pp. ix + 133. $6.95.

of human actuality, each of which provides a metaphysic that ignores details in providing a view of the whole. Despite his fusion of the two major subjects of right conduct and knowledge in *Giles Goat-Boy*, Barth is still coming, as Tharpe shows, to Todd Andrews's conclusion that 'nothing has intrinsic value', a conclusion which remains constant throughout his fiction. Aware then of the ironies resulting from this realization, Barth's 'genius', so Tharpe claims, lies in his ability to dramatize humorously the paradoxes of the universe.

'Ultimately', Tharpe asserts, 'Barth says nothing—positively'. He shows how Barth makes language operate 'analogously to the metaphysics of relativity that he perceives in the universe'. If it is impossible to describe reality accurately, then, Barth concludes, let what language creates be the reality: 'The only reality described . . . is what comes through that method—the edifice that exists is whatever edifice the language constructs. Thus it is possible for poetry to write history. And that idea is a metaphysics—perhaps also a truth'. In this way Barth re-invents the world, creating, so Tharpe finally claims, 'a world of fiction, not a fictional world'.

Jac Tharpe continues his obvious celebration of John Barth's artistic vision in his article, 'The Intellectual Scene Since World War II: Notes on Cultural History' (*SoQ*). Here he claims Barth's fiction to be the best produced in the post-war period: in a period where most American writers are, as Tharpe claims, lost in diversity without a view of any whole, Barth has been 'nearly able' to systematize pragmatism and existentialism and use it as a myth. The total commitment Tharpe gives to Barth is perhaps best suggested in his dismissive obser-

vations on other writers: *Catch 22* is cast aside as 'of dubious value': Mailer is disposed of in a sentence, 'the greatest innocent of them all, Norman Mailer, has properly turned to reporting'.

In 'John Barth's "Glossolalia"' (*CL*), Clayton Koelb examines the 'Glossolalia' in *Lost in the Funhouse* from the point of view of the traditional distinction between verse and prose: the difference being meter. Barth's 'Glossolalia' is metrical in a perfectly uuambiguous way, yet still remains a piece of prose.

Modern Fiction Studies offers a John Updike Special Number this year. Robert McCoy examines 'John Updike's Literary Apprenticeship on the Harvard Lampoon' to show the way this apprenticeship helped to sharpen 'his wit, his artist's descriptive eye, and his sense of the essential ambiguity of life'. Joseph Waldmeir, in 'It's the Going that's Important, Not the Getting There' illustrates the way in which Updike lays down the lines of that feud between the pragmatic and the transcendental in *Rabbit, Run* which was to provide the heart of the conflict in all his future work. In 'The Centaur's Myth, History and Narrative', John B. Vickery examines the nature, function, and motive, of the mythic element in that novel.

Paula and Nick Backscheider chart, in 'Updike's *Couples*: Squeak in the Night', Piet's search for happiness, and his progression from one false God to another to his final construction of a faith from within, in a situation where all around him is corrupted and empty. Alan T. McKenzie emphasizes the painstaking care of Updike's craftsmanship in the same novel in 'A Craftsman's Intimate Satisfactions: The Parlor Games in *Couples*'. He examines the use of two of these games—'Impressions' and

'Wonderful'—to show Updike's careful construction and precision of detail here.

In 'Rabbit Redux: Time/Order/God', Wayne Falke focuses on Updike's exploitation of topical materials, and his simultaneous creation of a work of art. Falke also analyzes the way in which Rabbit matures within the novel. Robert Alton Regan examines 'Updike's Symbol of the Center' as it appears throughout his fiction. Robert S. Gingher suggests in 'Has John Updike Anything to Say?' that in his work, style and content harmonize in a way which places Updike 'squarely within the first rank of contemporary authors'. A useful selected checklist of criticism of John Updike, by Arlin J. Meyer, with Michael A. Olivas, is also contained in this Updike Special Number. John Updike offers a statement of his own reasons for writing in 'Why Write?' (*SoRA*).

John N. McDaniel introduces his study of *The Fiction of Philip Roth*[101] by defending his position as Protestant in writing about an author whose Jewishness has always been of central critical concern. McDaniel suggests that though the 'Jewish question' in Roth's fiction is a legitimate area of enquiry, it is not the only area, and indeed 'leaves unexplored the larger questions of Roth's fictional world—its characters, themes and values'. These are the concerns which McDaniel studies here. He examines Roth's artistic stance as revealed both by his fiction and by his own critical comments, observations which, he claims, 'provide an often ignored or misunderstood context for assessing the scope of his fiction and the direction it has taken'.

McDaniel commences his study by

[101] *The Fiction of Philip Roth*, by John N. McDaniel. New Jersey: Haddonfield House. pp. vii + 243. $10.

analyzing one of Roth's first published stories, 'The Contest for Aaron Gold', and setting it against one of his latest: '"I Always Wanted You to Admire My Fasting"; Or, Looking at Kafka'. In this way, he is able to suggest Roth's essential themes and hero types, and also to reveal the slight changes which have taken place in his artistic technique, especially 'his movement into the fantastic, his increasing reliance on autobiographical materials for his fiction, and his growing willingness . . . to be both subversive and perverse in his attack on traditional social values'. In this introductory chapter McDaniel also discusses the question of Roth's position as a Jewish writer: the conclusion he reaches is that his fiction is broadly humanistic rather than specifically Jewish.

McDaniel then proceeds chronologically to examine both Roth's novels and his short stories, comparing his protagonists with those of Bellow and Malamud as he goes. Finally, in the chapter entitled 'Distinctive Features of Roth's Artistic Vision', he assesses Roth's development and achievement as a writer of fiction. Having pointed out the author's significant movement from the presentation of an activist hero as protagonist to that of a victim-hero, and the implications of this fact, McDaniel then comes to the following tentative conclusion: that Roth may best be viewed 'as a writer whose artistic intentions are "moral", whose artistic method is "realistic" and whose central artistic concern is with man in society'.

Charles M. Israel, in 'The Fractured Hero of Roth's *Goodbye, Columbus*' (*Crit*), suggests that the major theme of the novel is neither ethnic nor social. The main interest of the novel, he argues, is in Neil's quest to find 'the coordinated soul'. Its major theme is what Neil fails to learn: he is 'the first of Roth's fractured heroes'. In '*The Great American Novel* and "The Great American Joke"' (*Crit*), Bernard F. Codgers Jr. again moves away from Roth's ethnic background, to suggest his fictional use of the techniques of the nineteenth-century American humourists. Mark Schechner examines *My Life as a Man* in 'Philip Roth' (*PR*), showing how Roth appears to return to a mode of writing he had used early in his fictional career in this book, which Schechner claims engages his talent fully at 'its most frantic, most ironic, and most subtle'.

Finally, mention should be made of two editions of *Critique* published this year. One of these editions carries a series of four articles on Richard Brautigan, as well as 'Richard Brautigan: A Working Checklist', a compilation of primary and secondary material on Brautigan. The other contains five articles on Thomas Pynchon, three of them on his latest major work, *Gravity's Rainbow*. Both of these compilations will prove useful to those working in the field of post-war American literature.

4. DRAMA

If one puts down Malcolm Goldstein's *The Political Stage: American Drama and Theater of the Great Depression*[102] with a certain relief, it is with the conviction too that it will have to be taken up again. For it is a book written with the kind of tension which demands and deserves great concentration on the part of the reader. The organization of the book, as the author seems to admit—is somewhat unsatisfactory. He divides the Depression years at 1935, which

---

[102] *The Political Stage: Drama and Theater of the Great Depression*, by Malcolm Goldstein. New York: O.U.P. pp. x+482. $13.95.

he sees as a political and social watershed, marked by the anti-fascist alignment of the liberals and the Left, and by the promise of some of the New Deal measures. After a prefatory discussion of the New Playwrights and other Twenties groups, we get five chapters on the major theatre companies and movements, both on and off Broadway, to 1935, and then in six chapters the development away from the earlier and more crudely realistic phase, in the years from 1935 to 1942. The final chapter glances at the experiences of some of the personalities of the Thirties theatre during the McCarthy era. Thematically this makes good sense, but is a little confusing for the reader, especially as each chapter, after the first in each section, backtracks, in order to pick up the story of its particular subject at the beginning of the phase. Professor Goldstein avoids simplistic effect, but at some expense. His account of the work of the various groups of playwrights, actors, and directors includes a very comprehensive reference to plays and performances, as well as to the financial structure of the industry, with brief comments, artistic, political, and personal, which provide a great deal of incidental information, as they create for the reader a moving sense of the excitements and disappointments of this hectic period for the American stage. The sheer number of references, and the brevity of the comments and allusions, tantalize, and even frustrate, but they illuminate too, and provide a stimulating whole, a book for the student of the theatre and for a wider readership with an interest in the intellectual life of the Depression years. The fairly copious notes incorporate bibliographical guidance, though not systematically. There is a notable lack of a chronological table of plays and performances, which would provide a useful map for the less well versed reader. Jay Williams's *Stage Left*[103] is something of a hybrid. It contains personal, occasionally nostalgic, 'showbiz' recollections with a reasonably sympathetic treatment of the various movements in the theatre between the wars. Compared with Goldstein's book it is light, but it does convey through tone and anecdote, something of the subjective feel of the period. It seems, at times, a little too collected and easy-paced, in spite of its rather stagey insistence in the first chapter, that it has an I-was-there authenticity. Goldstein seems more excited and exciting. Both books contain photographic illustrations, but rather few. In contrast to Goldstein's scholarly, critical, analytic approach, and Williams's retrospective synthesis, is John Weisman's *Guerilla Theatre*[104] dedicated to Daniel and Luis Valdez, and in memory of George and Jonathan Jackson. Weisman describes the interwar political theatre as safety-valve escapism, created by the white bourgeoisie, preoccupied with dogma and fund-raising. There was a noticeable lack of emphasis, relatively speaking, on the nature of the audience, and on the interaction of playwrights, directors, and actors with the proletarian society which was their subject-matter, in the rather academic-engagé treatment by Goldstein and Williams. Weisman insists on what the other two merely recognized, the tendency to elitism on the one hand and to institutionalism on the other, in the radical theatre of the Twenties and Thirties. If the partnership between Jewish minority political

drive and Highbrow liberalism can be said to have marked that theatre, the Guerilla theatre of the late Sixties and the early Seventies is Black, Red, and Brown theatre, according to Weisman—inevitably street theatre, since its audiences are too poor, or otherwise disinclined, to enter commercial theatres—addressing its target audiences directly by a combination of the realistic and symbolic, which seems at first sight very close to the techniques of agit-prop, but which differs from it by a pragmatic, less doctrinal demand for more specific direct action, with its springs in the immediate response to *local* tyranny or suffering. Only at a secondary level is this protest to be identified with White Left radicalism. Weisman is inclined to exaggerate differences to show that the despised, because compromised, theatre of that earlier discontent was too tainted by liberalism to provide lessons for the present agonized protest. The book contains a number of short dramatic ephemera, dealing with Chicano, Negro, Indian, and Women's protest, and against the corporations and White Bureaucracy, from such sources as El Teatro Campesino, The Bodacious Buggerilla, The San Francisco Mime Troupe, The Street Players' Union, City Street Theatre, etc., and interleaved commentary in the form of letters from 'j' to 'Nancy', or short manifestos. It is a committed work, and possesses the virtues and shortcomings of such things. Most interesting, perhaps are the short plays themselves, which demonstrate that, while the subject of protest drama has shifted somewhat, is more focused on minority issues, audience orientated, and less *apparatchik*, its form is not altogether different from that of Living Newspaper or agit-prop performances of forty years before. Stephen Mamber examines the origins, in documentary

---

[103] *Stage Left*, by Jay Williams. New York: Charles Scribner's Sons. pp. 278. $8.95.

[104] *Guerilla Theater: Scenarios for Revolution*, by John Weisman. New York: Anchor P. (Anchor Books edition). pp. 201. $3.50.

and neo-realism, of cinema verité,[105] which seems to bear the same relationship to 'serious' scripted cinema that Naturalism, at the turn of the century, bore to serious realistic fiction. The author examines the work of a number of 'fringe' film-makers, who have attempted to depict objectively, which is not the same as unanalytically situations of crisis in real life, in such a way as to bring home to us, shorn of sentimentality, avoiding stock-response, the responses of individuals in their several ways under acute pressure. The apparently uncommenting presentation implied by the term 'verité' scarcely conceals, of course, a profound political intent.

Something of the dedication and excitement which lies behind Weisman's book can be discovered in a number of articles in *Drama Review*'s eighteenth volume. As usual, contemporary theatre is in a crisis of definition. Francois Kourilsky in 'Dada and the Circus: Peter Schumann's Bread and Puppet Theatre' gives an adulatory account of some of the work of this playwright, showing a similarity between the principles underlying the formal relationships exhibited by the performances of the New Dance Group in Germany in the Fifties and Schumann's current work in indoor and street theatre. Both had, and have, affinities with Dada and Circus, in that conventional aesthetic relationships between theme, actors, audience, and stage properties are transcended in drama as a communal act. Theodore Shank, in 'Political Theatre and Popular Entertainment' discusses the San Francisco Mime Troupe's parodic use of melodrama and *commedia dell' arte* plays and situations to provide them with a frame

for political satire. The reversion to older non-realistic forms frees them from association with an establishment, political and theatrical, which they abhor, and permits them to focus the force of a naive audience response on to contemporary political targets. Paul Ryder Ryan discusses The Living Theatre's agit-prop production, 'The Money Tower', alongside the play's scenario, describing its genesis. He draws attention to the social significance of Living Theatre, under Julian Beck and Judith Malina, its communal structure, and to a new phase of The Living Theatre Collective's ideological attack on the establishment, not through confrontation, but through a subtler persuasive address to its agents, the police and the military. He quotes Beck as saying, 'At the moment the police arrive at the pits or a steel mill, and workers say "Don't shoot", and the police don't, that will be the play'.

Joseph Chaikin, in an interview (*TQ*), discusses his Other Theatre. 'Implicit in [Other Theatre's writers' and performers'] early work was the belief that the primary function of the actor in the theatre was not the presenting of a playwright's work . . . performers should share equally with member playwrights the act of creation.' The characteristic of Open Theatre is 'the tight correspondence between performer and rôle', which renders it 'unlikely that works can be effectively presented without the original performer-creators'. The development towards the Open Theatre's major works, *Terminal*, *The Mutation Show*, and *Nighttrack*, came through the improvisations, transformations, songs, and plays or scenarios for action. Formed in 1963, under Chaikin's direction, the Open Theatre was disbanded in 1973. Chaikin indicates that the company decided to disband rather than

[105] *Cinema Verité in America: Studies in Uncontrolled Documentary*, by Stephen Mamber. Cambridge, Mass., and London: M.I.T. Press. pp. 288. £5.00.

become institutionalized. The very personal range of referents in the interview does not make its significant points entirely clear, but, as an oblique summary, it can perhaps be said that the theatrical doctrine on which the Open Theatre was originally based, with its roots in Julian Beck's Living Theatre, and with its affinities with The People Show, discussed by Victoria N. Kirby (*DR*), which saw theatrical performances as continuously changing and transforming, was likely to weaken and become dissipated with public success, so that Chaikin's decision to stop when he was reaching the crest of a wave of critical approval, was inevitable, given the aims and theories of the founders and practitioners. For the principles of Open Theatre were hostile to such institutions as first-nights, drama critics, to the renting of commercial theatres, and to the employment of unionized labour. More interviews can be read by those with an appetite for such things (*DR*). Four drama critics and four directors are interviewed, by Judith Searle and Bill Eddy, respectively, and encouraged to express their views on, or attitudes to, the criticism of drama. In the same volume, Abiodan Jeyifous discusses 'Black Critics of the Theatre', and fashionably 'libbish' are Margaret Lamb's 'Feminist Criticism' and Charlotte Rea's 'Women for Women', dealing with Women's Theatre. All this is heady stuff. However, another essay, by Michael Kirby 'On Literary Theatre', provides a coherent gloss. His summing up is rather cool alongside the partipris tone of the various accounts, scripts, scenarios, performances, and occurrences, but it has a place in the continuing discussion.

To return to more conventional items, James Milton Highsmith, in '*The Personal Equation*: Eugene

O'Neill's Abandoned Play' (*SHR*), usefully summarizes the plot, to claim that while this early play is understandably immature, it exhibits promise of technical developments to come, and presages a number of what were to become important themes in O'Neill's work. The play was written between 1914 and 1917, and exists in an undated typescript in the Houghton Library at Harvard, which reveals clearly O'Neill's drastic pruning and rewriting. Jack Richardson entitles his essay 'O'Neill Reconsidered' (*Commentary*). He is reconsidering, it seems, the reasons for O'Neill's sudden transformation as a playwright in the later plays, but is content to fail to discover anything new. Stephen R. Greco's search for enlightenment in 'High Hopes: Eugene O'Neill and Alcohol' (*YFS*) amounts to a breathtakingly simple assertion of a connexion between O'Neill's heavy drinking and the inferiority of plays written before 1933, and contrasts the success of the later plays of his 'dry' period. He is convincing only if we agree that *Mourning Becomes Electra* is 'tedious' and that *The Iceman Cometh* is 'predominantly naturalistic'.

'Strangers in a Room: *A Delicate Balance* Revisited', by E. G. Bierhaus Jr., is a neat, clear essay, which occasionally drives an argument over the edge of tendentiousness. He points to and explicates a number of Albee's allusive devices, his naming of characters, the permutation of their rôles, and the parable of the cat, seeking to show that *A Delicate Balance* (*MD*) is about political relationships rather than friendship and responsibilities. Robert H. Tener argues in 'Amiri Baraka's *The Toilet*' (*MD*), that Baraka is dramatizing the limitations imposed on black boys by the stereotypes of white culture, which render them incapable of responding completely to the changes in their sexual and social nature, attendant upon the crisis of puberty. He does not clearly demonstrate that the effect he clearly establishes in Baraka's play is necessarily restricted to *black* boys, and that it does not affect the culturally unsupported, regardless of colour. The result of his argument is to limit, as it points up, this theme of the play.

If evidence were needed of the persistence of traditional dramatic modes, in spite of the waves of radical upsurge in the contemporary American theatre, three highbrow plays by Philip Freund, described as 'off-Broadway'[106] provide it. It is clear that Freund and Weisman or Chaikin inhabit such different worlds that to bridge the gap between them seems inconceivable. Even Freund's 'Ballad Opera, *Miss Lucy in Town*, based on Fielding (and which reads at times like a parody of Greek tragedy in translation), described in the blurb as a romp, but manifesting detachment, irony, and pastiche, shows just how far off-Broadway, the ambience of Theatre Guild and its unconventional successors, has shifted towards orthodoxy.

As a research tool, Scarecrow Press have issued a supplement to the *Index of Plays in Periodicals* it published in 1971, and which included items through 1969. The new volume[107] lists 2,334 plays, and continues the indexing of plays from 1969 to 1971 in those periodicals covered in the 1971 listing, and includes plays published throughout the century to 1971 in a new list of periodicals. Not all the entries relate to American drama, and a number of items are in languages other than English, but the inclusion of a large number of American items earns a mention of this useful book here. Jennifer McCabe Atkinson's bibliography of Eugene O'Neill[108] brings up to date the 1931 bibliography by Sanborn and Clark. Miss Atkinson confines herself to published material, and includes separate publications of plays, and volumes of several plays. There are sections containing contributions to books and pamphlets, first appearances of O'Neill items in newspapers and periodicals, blurbs, catalogues, and anthologized plays. The author modestly explains that this book is only a beginning. It will provide a solid base for all those labours to come, not least because of its thoroughness within the scrupulous limits it observes.

[106] *More Off-Broadway Plays*, by Philip Freund. London: W. H. Allen. pp. 261. £2.85.

[107] *Index to Plays in Periodicals: Supplement*, by Dean H. Keller. Metuchen, N.J.: The Scarecrow Press Inc. pp. x+263. $8.50.

[108] *Eugene O'Neill: A Descriptive Bibliography*, by Jennifer McCabe Atkinson, University of Pittsburgh Press (Pittsburgh Series in Bibliography), pp. xxiii+410. $27.50.

Index I. Critics

Index II. Authors and Subjects Treated